ANNUAL REVIEW OF PSYCHOLOGY

EDITORIAL COMMITTEE (1990)

ANNUAL REVIEW OF PSYCHOLOGY

VOLUME 41, 1990

MARK R. ROSENZWEIG, *Editor*
University of California, Berkeley

LYMAN W. PORTER, *Editor*
University of California, Irvine

ANNUAL REVIEWS INC.   4139 EL CAMINO WAY   P.O. BOX 10139   PALO ALTO, CALIFORNIA 94303-0897

BF
30
 ANNUAL REVIEWS INC.
Palo Alto, California, USA .A56

International Standard Serial Number: 0066–4308
International Standard Book Number: 0–8243–0241-9
Library of Congress Catalog Card Number: 50-13143

Annual Review and publication titles are registered trademarks of Annual Reviews
Inc.

∞ The paper used in this publication meets the minimum requirements of American National Standard for Information Sciences—Permanence of Paper for Printed
Library Materials, ANSI Z39.48-1984.

Annual Reviews Inc. and the Editors of its publications assume no responsibility
for the statements expressed by the contributors to this *Review*.

Typesetting by Kachina Typesetting Inc., Tempe, Arizona; John Olson, President
Typesetting Coordinator, Janis Hoffman

PRINTED AND BOUND IN THE UNITED STATES OF AMERICA

PREFACE

The Master Plan

What are the processes involved in planning a volume of the *Annual Review of Psychology* such as the present one? Over the 27 different Annual Revew series there is a wide variety of practices, with those of the *Annual Review of Psychology* being toward the more tightly organized end of the spectrum. The Editorial Committee members, whose names appear opposite the title page, meet once a year in the spring, usually with one or two guests from institutions located close to that year's meeting site. Each year the Committee chooses the main chapter topics to be considered at the next year's meeting, so that the Committee members may be thinking about them during the year. Most of the topics come from the Master Plan in which main areas of psychological research are listed, along with the recommended frequency of reviews for each topic: Some topics are scheduled to be reviewed each year, some every other year, and some still less often. We published the Master Plan occasionally in the past, but it now changes too often to be of use outside the Committee. Also, the Committee often decides to include special chapters about subjects not in the Master Plan in order to accommodate new and timely subjects. One such Timely Topic chapter appears in the present volume: "Moral rules: their content and acquisition" by John M. Darley and Thomas R. Shultz. Although the Master Plan is no longer published in each volume, readers can gain a good idea of the distribution and frequency of topics by perusing the Cumulative Index of Chapter Titles for Volumes 35-41 on pages 731–35 of this volume.

At each meeting, the Committee draws up a list of prospective authors for each Master Plan topic. These are outstanding experts who are known to write well and who are believed to carry out the commitments they undertake. The quality of the *Annual Review of Psychology* rests on the choice of authors. They have the difficult task of selecting the most important trends and advances in each field and writing about them clearly and succinctly. Authors are free to choose a specific topic within the assigned area.

The schedule of production of the volume does not permit extensive editing in most cases, although occasionally chapters must be returned with requests for substantial reductions in length when an author gets carried away with the progress in a field and drafts a monograph instead of a selective review.

Readers are indebted to our authors, who carry out their demanding task extraordinarily well.

CHAPTER LENGTH   Because many authors feel restricted by the page allotments assigned to them, we would like to ask readers this question: Would you prefer to see somewhat longer and correspondingly fewer chapters per volume, realizing that most topics would therefore appear in the series somewhat less frequently?

UPDATING THE MASTER PLAN   At our meeting in spring, 1990, we intend to devote an additional day to review and revision of the Master Plan. We invite readers who would like to make suggestions or propose topics to communicate with us or with other members of the Committee, preferably by mid-April, 1990.

Changes in the Editorial Committee

Members of the Editorial Committee usually serve five-year terms. We regret to announce the end of the term of Janet T. Spence, who has served with great distinction, drawing upon her wide experience and incisive knowledge of psychological research and research psychologists.

Mark R. Rosenzweig
Lyman W. Porter

Annual Review of Psychology
Volume 41 (1990)

CONTENTS

viii   CONTENTS   (*Continued*)

RELATED ARTICLES OF INTEREST TO PSYCHOLOGISTS

From the *Annual Review of Anthropology,* Volume 18

Psychoanalytic Anthropology, R. A. Paul

From the *Annual Review of Medicine,* Volume 41

Central Nervous System Effects of Human Immunodeficiency Virus, Type 1, T. P. Bridge and L. Ingraham

Serotonin-Specific Drugs for Anxiety and Depressive Disorders, D. S. Charney, J. H. Krystal, P. L. Delgado, and G. R. Heninger

Neurochemical and Psychopharmacologic Aspects of Aggressive Behavior, B. S. Eichelman

From the *Annual Review of Neuroscience,* Volume 12

Emerging Principles Governing the Operation of Neural Networks, P. A. Getting

Integrating with Neurons, D. A. Robinson

Short-Term Synaptic Plasticity, R. S. Zucker

Startle, Categorical Response, and Attention in Acoustic Behavior of Insects, R. R. Hoy

Learning Arm Kinematics and Dynamics, C. G. Atkeson

Involvement of Hormonal and Neuromodulatory Systems in the Regulation of Memory Storage, J. L. McGaugh

From the *Annual Review of Pharmacology and Toxicology,* Volume 30

Interactions Between the Brain and the Immune System, R. Ader, D. Felton, and N. Cohen

Muscarinic Receptor Subtypes, E. C. Hulme, N. J. M. Birdsall, and N. J. Buckley

Subtypes of Receptors for Serotonin, A. Frazer, S. Maayani, and B. B. Wolfe

Molecular Characterization of Opioid Receptors, H. H. Loh and A. P. Smith

From the *Annual Review of Public Health,* Volume 11

Measurement of Health Status for the 1990s, D. L. Patrick and M. Bergner

Health Promotion as a Health Strategy in the 1990s, L. W. Green

From the *Annual Review of Sociology,* Volume 15

Some Reflections on the Golden Age of Interdisciplinary Social Psychology, W. H. Sewell

Structural Change in Corporate Organization, N. Fligstein and K. Dauber

The Social Psychology of Self-Efficacy, V. Gecas

Analysis of Events in the Study of Collective Action, S. Olzak

The Sociology of Emotions, P. A. Thoits

Herbert A Simon

Annu. Rev. Psychol. 1990. 41:1–19

INVARIANTS OF HUMAN BEHAVIOR[1]

Herbert A. Simon*

Department of Psychology, Carnegie-Mellon University, Pittsburgh, Pennsylvania 15213

CONTENTS

The fundamental goal of science is to find invariants, such as conservation of mass and energy and the speed of light in physics. In much of science the invariants are neither as general nor as "invariant" as these classical laws. For instance, the isotopes of the elements have atomic weights that are *nearly*

---

[1]The US Government has the right to retain a nonexclusive, royalty-free license in and to any copyright covering this paper.

*This is the eleventh in a series of prefatory chapters written by eminent senior psychologists.

integral multiples of the weight of hydrogen. *Some* inheritable traits of plants and animals observe the classical 1–2–1 ratio of Mendel. The number of familiar information chunks that can be held in short-term memory is *approximately* seven. It takes about 30 seconds to memorize an unpronouncable three-consonant nonsense syllable, but only *about* nine seconds to memorize a three-letter word.

Much biological knowledge is extremely specific, for biology rests on the diversity of millions of species of plants and animals, and most of its invariants apply only to single species. Because of inter-species molecular differences, even the important general laws (e.g. the laws of photosynthesis) vary in detail from one species to another (and sometimes among different individuals in a single species). Only at the most abstract and qualitative level can one find many general strict invariants in biology.

Moreover, some of the most important invariants in science are not quantitative at all, but are what Allen Newell and I (1976) have called "laws of qualitative structure." For example, the germ theory of disease, surely one of Pasteur's major contributions to biology, says only something like: "If you observe pathology, look for a microorganism—it might be causing the symptoms." Similarly, modern molecular genetics stems from the approximately correct generalization that inheritance of traits is governed by the arrangement of long helical sequences of the four DNA nucleotides.

Finally, in biological (including human) realms, systems change adaptively over time. Simple change is not the problem, for Newton showed how we can write invariant laws as differential equations that describe the eternal movements of the heavens. But with adaptative change, which is as much governed by a system's environment as by its internal constitution, it becomes more difficult to identify true invariants. As a result, evolutionary biology has a rather different flavor from physics, chemistry, or even molecular biology.

In establishing aspirations for psychology it is useful to keep all of these models of science in mind. Psychology does not much resemble classical mechanics, nor should it aim to do so. Its laws are, and will be, limited in range and generality and will be mainly qualitative. Its invariants are and will be of the kinds that are appropriate to adaptive systems. Its success must be measured not by how closely it resembles physics but by how well it describes and explains human behavior.

On another occasion (Simon 1979a) I have considered the form a science must take in order to explain the behavior of an adaptive, hence of an artificial, system. By "artificial" I mean a system that is what it is only because it has responded to the shaping forces of an environment to which it must adapt in order to survive. Adaptation may be quite unconscious and unintended, as in Darwinian evolution, or it may contain large components of conscious intention, as in much human learning and problem solving.

Taking the artificiality of human behavior as my central theme, I should like to consider its implications for psychology. Moreover, since *Homo sapiens* shares some important psychological invariants with certain nonbiological systems—the computers—I shall want to make frequent reference to them also. One could even say that my account will cover the topic of human and computer psychology.

PHYSICAL SYMBOL SYSTEMS

An important law of qualitative structure underlies the information processing paradigm in psychology. The Physical Symbol System Hypothesis (Newell & Simon 1976) *states that a system will be capable of intelligent behavior if and only if it is a physical symbol system.* A physical symbol system is a system capable of inputting, outputting, storing, and modifying symbol structures, and of carrying out some of these actions in response to the symbols themselves. "Symbols" are any kinds of patterns on which these operations can be performed, where some of the patterns denote actions (that is, serve as commands or instructions).

We are all familiar with the physical symbol systems called computers. Computers store symbols in the form of electro-magnetic patterns of some kind (quite different kinds in different computers); some of these patterns serve to instruct the computer what to do next (the stored program), while others contain numerical or nonnumerical information.

Information processing psychology claims that intelligence is achievable by physical symbol systems and only such systems. From that claim follow two empirically testable hypotheses: 1. that computers can be programmed to think, and 2. that the human brain is (at least) a physical symbol system. These hypotheses are tested by programming computers to perform the same tasks that we use to judge how well people are thinking, and then by showing that the processes used by the computer programs are the same as those used by people performing these tasks. In making the comparison we use thinking-aloud protocols, records of eye movements, reaction times, and many other kinds of data as evidence.

The physical symbol system hypothesis has been tested so extensively over the past 30 years that it can now be regarded as fully established, although over less than the whole gamut of activities that are called "thinking." For starters in reviewing the evidence, I would recommend Newell & Simon (1972), Simon (1979a, b, 1989a), and Anderson (1983). Readers can continue the survey with numerous references they will find in those sources. The exact boundaries of our present knowledge need not concern us: The territory in which the hypothesis has been confirmed is broad, encompassing many of the kinds of activities that define human professional and scholarly work.

Some skeptics continue to regard thinking as something to be explained at some unknown future date. Their imperviousness to the empirical evidence, which shows that the main processes of thinking have already been accounted for quite specifically, perhaps stems from the reluctance of human beings to view themselves as "mere machines." Even some biologists who have long since rejected vitalism where bodily functions are concerned remain vitalists when it comes to the mind.

It is still incorrectly thought by some that contemporary information processing psychology leaves unexplained such "holistic" phenomena—treasured by humanistic, existentialist, Marxist, and Gestalt psychologists—as intuition, insight, understanding, and creativity. A brief guide to the literature that deals with these phenomena in terms of the physical symbol system hypothesis will be found in Simon (1986). I will say no more about these matters in this paper, but will simply use the present rather than the future tense in describing the psychology of thinking.

What is the unfinished business? There is plenty of it, but I will mention just two important research targets that remain. First, each kind of task to which the human mind addresses itself may be regarded as defining a different "species" of thought. A certain number of these species have already been described in greater or lesser detail (e.g. solving puzzles like the Tower of Hanoi or Missionaries and Cannibals, playing chess like a master or a novice, making medical diagnoses, solving problems in elementary physics and mathematics, making certain kinds of scientific discoveries, learning language, using diagrams to solve problems, and understanding problem instructions). But since many other species of thought remain undescribed, a vast work of taxonomy and empirical exploration lies ahead. We should avoid thinking of this work as "mere" taxonomy, for it will unearth multitudes of interesting and important phenomena and extend our repertory of explanatory laws and invariants accordingly.

Second, in stark contrast to our complete understanding of the physical underpinnings of the operation of computers, we have only the vaguest knowledge today of how the symbol processing capabilities of the human brain are realized physiologically. Information processing psychology explains the software of thinking, but says only a little about its "hardware" (or "wetware"?). Information processing psychology and neural science are still miles apart, with only slight indications of how a bridge will be built between them—as it certainly will.

This situation is not without precedent. Organismic and cell biology made extensive progress long before biochemistry could explain their structures and processes. Nineteenth-century chemistry achieved substantial understanding of the reactions among molecules long before physics supplied any picture of atomic structure that could account for the observed chemical regularities.

Science suspended from skyhooks is not new, nor is it limited to particular disciplines. Contemporary physics provides a prime example of skyhook science in its continual movement downward to ever more fundamental and "elementary" particles, its greatest uncertainties lying always at the foundations.

The separation of information processing from neural science presents an important challenge to research, and a second great direction for exploration in psychology. What arrangement of neurons or neuronal circuits corresponds to a symbol? What is the physiological basis for the magical number seven? By what mechanism does the presence of a symbol in short-term memory initiate or guide a mental action? The agenda, containing these and many other items, provides work for both neural scientists and information processing psychologists, for the bridge will have to be built out from both banks before it can link in the middle.

ADAPTIVITY

Let me now put aside biological questions and return to human adaptivity and its implications for the laws of psychology. A look at computer adaptivity may cast some light on the human kind. A computer, it is said, can only do what it is programmed to do (which may be quite different from what the programmer *intended* it to do). Generally, it is not instructed to do specific things at all (e.g. to solve a particular linear programming problem), but to adapt its behavior to the requirements of a given task chosen from a whole population of tasks (e.g. to solve *any* linear programming problem lying within given size limits). Then its behavior in response to each task is adapted to the requirements of the task, and it behaves differently, in appropriate ways, with each task it is given. In short, it is an adaptive system.

The adaptiveness of computers leads to a question that is the converse of the one raised above. Can a computer be programmed to do *anything*? Of course not. Upper limits are set by the famous theorems of Gödel, which prove that every symbol processing system must be, in a certain fundamental sense, incomplete. It is a truth of mathematics and logic that any program (including those stored in human heads) must be unable to solve certain problems.

Computational Limits on Adaptivity

Far more important than the Gödel limits are the limits imposed by the speed and organization of a system's computations and sizes of its memories. It is easy to pose problems that are far too large, require far too much computation, to be solved by present or prospective computers. Playing a perfect game of chess by using the game-theoretic minimaxing algorithm is one such infeasible computation, for it calls for the examination of more chess positions than there are molecules in the universe. If the game of chess, limited to its 64 squares and six kind of pieces, is beyond exact computation, then we may expect the same of almost any real-world problem, including almost any problem of everyday life.

From this simple fact, we derive one of the most important laws of qualitative structure applying to physical symbol systems, computers and the human brain included: *Because of the limits on their computing speeds and power, intelligent systems must use approximate methods to handle most tasks. Their rationality is bounded.*

Reasoning Under the Optimality Principle

Historically, human adaptiveness (that is to say, rationality) has preoccupied economists even more than psychologists. Modern mainstream economic theory bravely assumes that people make their decisions in such a way as to maximize their utility (Simon 1979a). Accepting this assumption enables economics to predict a great deal of behavior (correctly or incorrectly) without ever making empirical studies of human actors.

If we wish to know what form gelatin will take when it solidifies, we do not study the gelatin; we study the shape of the mold in which we are going to pour it. In the same way, the economist who wishes to predict behavior studies the environment in which the behavior takes place, for the rational economic actor will behave in whatever way is appropriate to maximize utility in that environment. Hence (assuming the utility function to be given in advance), this maximizing behavior is purely a function of the environment, and quite independent of the actor.

The same strategy can be used to construct a psychology of thinking. If we wish to know how an intelligent person will behave in the face of a particular problem, we can investigate the requirements of the problem. Intelligence consists precisely in responding to these requirements. This strategy has, in fact, been pursued occasionally in psychology; the theories of perception of J. J. Gibson (1966) and John Marr (1982) exemplify it, as do some of the recent rational models of my colleague John R. Anderson (1989).

Why don't we, then, close up the laboratory, frequently a place of vexing labors and unwelcome surprises, and build a psychology of intelligence by rational analysis, as the economists have done? The answer, already suggested, lies in the law that I have called the Principle of Bounded Rationality (Simon 1989b). Since we can rarely solve our problems exactly, the optimizing strategy suggested by rational analysis is seldom available. We must find techniques for solving our problems approximately, and we arrive at different solutions depending on what approximations we hit upon. Hence, to describe, predict and explain the behavior of a system of bounded rationality, we must both construct a theory of the system's processes and describe the environments to which it is adapting.

Computational Feasibility: Bounded Rationality

Human rational behavior (and the rational behavior of all physical symbol systems) is shaped by a scissors whose two blades are the structure of task environments and the computational capabilities of the actor.

The study of cognitive psychology is the study of computational capabilities in the face of diverse tasks. It is not a trivial detail but a fundamental limit upon computation that human short-term memory can hold only a half dozen chunks, that an act of recognition takes nearly a second, and that the simplest human reactions are measured in tens and hundreds of milliseconds rather than microseconds or picoseconds. These basic physiological constants determine what kinds of computations are feasible in a given kind of task situation and how rapidly they can be carried out (Newell & Simon 1972; Simon 1979a). They are among the most important invariants that cognitive psychology has discovered, accounting for many phenomena observed in thinking and learning.

Noting that computational limits must be a central preoccupation of cognitive psychology does not exhaust the complications of the subject. We have also to take into account that thinking capacities are a function of skill and knowledge, stored neural structures in the brain. The expert can reach solutions that are unattainable by the novice, using computations and knowledge that are simply not available to the latter.

A lightning calculator carries out elementary symbolic processes no more rapidly than a person with ordinary skills in arithmetic; empirical studies reveal little or no difference in the speeds of their basic processes. Superiority in computation derives almost entirely from superior knowledge of arithmetic facts (e.g. knowledge of the multiplication table up to relatively large numbers, or of the table of squares, or of prime factors), combined with a superior repertory of computational strategies that save steps and conserve short-term and long-term memory capacity. In Chi et al (1988) the reader will find recent papers on expert performance in a variety of tasks, including memory and computational feats.

A major way to relax the limits of bounded rationality is to store in long-term memory knowledge and strategies that reduce the computational requirements of tasks. This would seem to add new plausibility to the argument for studying the requirements of the task rather than the properties of the actor. But the argument still fails. In tasks of any complexity, knowledge and strategies do not allow the expert to find an optimal solution, but only to find approximations that are far better than those available to "native" (or naive) intelligence. A knowledge of the calculus allows its possessor to solve many problems that could not be solved without it, but the domain of differential equations that cannot be exactly integrated in closed form vastly exceeds the domain of those that can be.

Rationality Without Optimization

The wide-ranging attempts since the Second World War to apply the optimizing tools of operations research (linear programming, integer and dynamic programming, queuing theory, and so on) to the decision problems of management have underlined the computational complexity of real-world problems, even relatively well-structured problems that are easily quantified. Using queuing theory, an optimum production schedule can be found for a factory that manufactures one or two products, using one or two different pieces of equipment. Adding even one more product or piece of equipment puts the problem beyond computational bounds for the fastest supercomputer. (An optimal class schedule for a university lies even further beyond the limits of practical computation.)

Yet factories (and universities) are scheduled every day. We are forced to conclude that methods other than optimization are used—methods that respect the limits of human and computer rationality. Perhaps the feasible methods are specific to each specific situation, in which case it is hard to see what cognitive psychology should say about them.

On the other hand, it is possible that some common properties, deriving from human bounded rationality, are shared by the approximating procedures people use in many kinds of complex situations. If so, it is the task of cognitive psychology to characterize these procedures, to show how they are acquired, and to account for their compatibility with the known computational limitations of the human brain.

MECHANISMS FOR RATIONALITY

Let me illustrate some of the mechanisms used by human bounded rationality to cope with real-life complexity. I will give just three examples from a much larger number that could be cited: processes used in problem solving by recognition, processes of heuristic search, and processes for inducing sequential patterns.

Recognition Processes

We now know that experts make extensive use of recognition processes, based on stored knowledge, to handle their everyday tasks. This recognition capability, based (by rough estimate) on 50,000 or more stored cues and associated knowledge, allows them to solve many problems "intuitively"— that is, in a few seconds, and without conscious analysis. Recognizing key cues allows experts to retrieve directly from memory information for dealing with the situations that the cues identify. Recognition processes have been shown to play a major role, perhaps *the* major role, in such diverse tasks as grandmaster chessplaying, medical diagnosis, and reading. Introductions to the evidence will be found in de Groot (1978), Simon (1979a) and Chi et al (1988).

Computer simulation models like EPAM (Feigenbaum & Simon 1984) provide explanatory mechanisms for recognition-based expertise, including a learning mechanism for acquiring the stored chunks on which it is based. Alternative models are being developed in the form of parallel, connectionist systems (EPAM is a basically serial system). The theoretical explanations and computer models assume processing speeds that are well within the known human physiological limits, and EPAM, as least, predicts a wide range of the phenomena that have been reported in the verbal learning literature (including the times reported by Ebbinghaus for the learning of nonsense syllables). We can regard intuition as a phenomenon that has been rather thoroughly explained: It is achieved through acts of recognition.

Heuristic Search

What about problems whose solutions are not provided by immediate recognition, but which require analysis? Here also, a number of the principal processes have been identified and simulated. Collectively, they are usually called heuristic (or selective) search. When a great space of possibilities is to be explored (and humans commonly balk at searching spaces when the possibilities number even in the hundreds), search becomes very selective. It is then guided by various rules of thumb, or heuristics, some of which are specific to particular tasks, but some of which are more general (Newell & Simon 1972).

If the task domain is highly structured, the task-specific heuristics may be very powerful, drawing upon the structural information to guide search directly to the goal. For instance, most of us apply a systematic algorithm when we must solve a linear equation in algebra. We don't try out different possible solutions, but employ systematic steps that take us directly to the correct value of the unknown.

If the task domain has little structure or the structure is unknown to us, we apply so-called "weak methods," which experience has shown to be useful in many domains, but which may still require us to search a good deal. One weak method is *satisficing*—using experience to construct an expectation of how good a solution we might reasonably achieve, and halting search as soon as a solution is reached that meets the expectation.

Picking the first satisfactory alternative solves the problem of making a choice whenever (*a*) an enormous, or even potentially infinite, number of alternatives are to be compared and (*b*) the problem has so little known structure that all alternatives would have to be examined in order to determine which is optimal. Satisficing also solves the common problem of making choices when alternatives are incommensurable, either because (*a*) they have numerous dimensions of value that cannot be compared, (*b*) they have uncertain outcomes that may be more or less favorable or unfavorable, or (*c*) they affect the values of more than one person. Then a satisficing choice can still be made as soon as an alternative is found that (*a*) is satisfactory along all dimensions of value, (*b*) has satisfactory outcomes for all resolutions of the uncertainty, or (*c*) is satisfactory for all parties concerned, respectively.

Another weak mothod is *means-ends analysis*—noting differences between the current situation and the desired goal situation, and retrieving from memory operators that, experience has taught us, remove differences of these kinds.

A small collection of heuristics, of which satisficing and means-ends analysis are important examples, have been observed as central features of behavior in a wide range of problem-solving behaviors where recognition capabilities or systematic algorithms were not available for reaching solutions without search. The prevalence of heuristic search is a basic law of qualitative structure for human problem solving.

Beginning with the General Problem Solver (GPS) in about 1958, a sizeable number of computer programs have been built to simulate heuristic search in various task domains. With their help, a rather detailed account has been given of human heuristic search, particularly in relatively well-structured domains that call upon only limited amounts of domain-specific knowledge (Newell & Simon 1972). With these programs as foundation, other investigations have built processes that can create problem representations for simple situations, using natural language inputs to supply information about the problem and task domain.

Serial Pattern Recognition

Ability to find patterns in sequences of numbers, letters, or geometric figures is an important component of human intelligence (Simon & Kotovsky 1963; Kotovsky & Simon 1973). The Thurstone Letter Series Completion Test and the Ravens tests are examples of tasks aimed at measuring this component. Laboratory studies of these tasks and computer simulations show that successful human performance depends on a few basic pattern-recognizing and pattern-organizing capabilities. In extrapolating sequential patterns, for example, subjects notice when identical symbols recur, or when there are subsequences of symbols that are successive items in a familiar list or "alphabet."

When subsequences repeat in a sequence, subjects can notice this fact and treat the repetitive subsequences as unitary components in a higher-level pattern. Thus, recursive or hierarchical patterns can be detected and extrapolated. These capabilities can be shown to be adequate for detecting pattern in complex pieces of music, and their sufficiency has been demonstrated by simulation programs capable of carrying out nontrivial musical analysis (Simon & Sumner 1968).

Procedural Rationality

Problem solving by recognition, by heuristic search, and by pattern recognition and extrapolation are examples of rational adaptation to complex task environments that take appropriate account of computational limitations—of bounded rationality. They are not optimizing techniques, but methods for arriving at satisfactory solutions with modest amounts of computation. They do not exhaust, but they typify, what we have been learning about human cognition, and they go a long way toward explaining how an organism with rather modest computational capabilities can adapt to a world that is very complex indeed.

The study of human behavior in the face of difficult tasks shows why we need a theory of processes (procedural rationality) as well as a theory of the requirements of the task (substantive rationality). A theory based only on task requirements could not tell us how behavior depends on knowledge of relevant cues or strategies. It could not explain why we satisfice instead of optimizing, or how we solve most everyday problems by recognizing cues that evoke their solutions. It could not give us a grasp of the range of strategies that may be available for handling a particular task, or the differences between expert and novice performance on the task. All these phenomena become understandable as we explore, by laboratory experiments and computer simulations, actual human behavior in a variety of task environments.

THINKING AND REASONING

If we go back, say, to Woodworth's *Experimental Psychology* (1938), we find that accounts of the human "higher mental functions" flow along two quite different channels, representing different intellectual ties to the adjacent disciplines. Woodworth devotes two chapters to complex cognitive tasks: one to problem solving, the other to reasoning (but titled "Thinking"). Woodworth's own comment (1938, p. 746) is "Two chapters will not be too many for the large topic of thinking, and we may make the division according to the historical sources of two streams of experimentation, which do indeed merge in the more recent work. One stream arose in the study of animal behavior and went on to human problem solving; the other started with human thinking of the more verbal sort." In particular, research on problem solving had its origins in the disputes about trial-and-error versus insightful learning. Research on reasoning derived from attention to theories of language and logic as models of thought processes.

The problem-solving model, or metaphor, has generally been preferred by Gestalt psychologists, with their common belief that insightful thinking is nonverbal in nature, and by researchers in artificial intelligence, who have from the beginning described thinking as heuristic search. The reasoning model, or metaphor, has generally been preferred by linguists with an interest in cognitive science and by philosophers who stray into this domain. They describe thought processes in terms of propositions and logical manipulations of propositions.

A study of mutual citations would show that communication between these two streams of inquiry has been poor. This reveals itself also in the different programming languages the two groups adopt when they simulate thinking processes. The programming languages associated with heuristic search are list-processing languages like LISP and production-system languages like OPS5. The programming languages associated with reasoning are logic languages (languages adapted to theorem proving in the predicate calculus) like PROLOG.

The division is further reinforced by disagreement about the respective roles in thinking of sentences (or the propositions they denote) and imagery of one or another kind. The reasoning metaphor views goals as described by sentences, derived from other sentences by processes similar to the processes of logic. The problem-solving metaphor views goals as achieved by sequences of moves through a problem space. (The very phrase "problem space" suggests the importance that is attached to a visual or spatial metaphor.)

When the reasoning metaphor is used, information is expressed mainly in declarative sentences. A small number of rules of inference (like the rule of syllogism in formal logic) are used to derive new sentences from old. The research tasks most commonly employed to study human reasoning are tasks of concept formation or tasks of judging the validity or invalidity of formal syllogisms, the presumption being that human thinking consists in drawing valid inferences from given premises or data.

When the problem-solving metaphor is used, information is expressed in schemas, which may resemble interrelated sets of sentences or may resemble diagrams or pictures of the problem situation. The problem situation is modified by applying "move operators," which are processes that change a situation into a new one. Nowadays, the move operators usually take the form of productions—condition-action pairs, $C \rightarrow A$. Whenever the information in short-term memory matches the conditions of a production, the actions of the production are executed. The execution of a sequence of productions accomplishes a search through the problem space, moving from one situation to another until a situation satisfying the goal requirements is reached.

All of these differences can be seen by comparing the corresponding two chapters, mentioned above, of Woodworth (1938), and chapters 8 and 10 of Anderson (1985).

Determining to what extent human thinking fits the problem-solving metaphor and to what extent it fits the reasoning metaphor stands high on the agenda of cognitive psychology today. Of course, the answer may be "both of the above," the processes of thought varying with the task domain and with learned or innate differences among the thinkers. It is perhaps of interest that Johnson-Laird, one of the leaders among those who emphasize the ties between cognition and linguistics, has recently begun to describe thinking in terms of "mental models," an approach that lies much closer to the heuristic search paradigm than to the reasoning paradigm (Johnson-Laird 1983). But I would hesitate to predict what this particular defection from the linguistic camp portends for the future.

COGNITIVE ARCHITECTURE

The whole congeries of mechanisms of human rationality must somehow be organized in the human brain to work together in a coordinated fashion. Today, a good deal of effort of theorists in psychology is devoted to specifying the architectures that achieve this coordination. In this context, "architecture" refers to description of the cognitive system at an abstract, usually symbolic, level, and has little to say about the underlying biology of neurons.

Early information-processing architectures of cognition (e.g. Broadbent 1958) emphasized memory "boxes" and their interconnections. Today, architectures specify organizations of processes as well as storage. Among the proposals that enter prominently into current discussion are Anderson's (1983) Act*, Newell's (1989) SOAR (both symbolic), and the connectionist system of McClelland & Rumelhart (1986).

Confining our discussion to symbolic architectures, while there are significant differences among them, none of them are incompatible with the recognition, heuristic search, and pattern-induction mechanisms described in the last section. *For many purposes, it is sufficient to think of the "whole cognitive man" as comprised of the following components:*

- *Memories:* A short-term memory of limited capacity (working memory), an associative long-term memory, an EPAM discrimination net to index the long-term memory, and smaller short-term memories associated with various sensory and motor modalities.
- *Sensory processors* to extract features from stimuli.
- *Interpreters of motor signals.*
- *EPAM: A discrimination net* for sensory features that learns new discriminations and "chunks" familiar stimuli patterns.
- *GPS: A problem solver* that employs heuristic search, and that can be used by the learning subsystem.

- *A Pattern induction system* that searches for regular patterns in stimuli.
- *Systems for encoding natural language* input and producing natural language output.
- *Systems for encoding to and from image-like representations.*
- *An adaptive production system,* capable of creating new processes on the basis of information gained through instruction, through examining worked-out examples, and by solving problems.

This may appear to be a lot of baggage, but all of the processing systems listed are implementable as production systems that can be stored in the associative long-term memory. Moreover, examples of all of these components have been simulated with computer programs, and their mutual compatibility tested to some degree. For example, the UNDERSTAND system (Hayes & Simon 1974) can encode natural language descriptions of puzzles into internal representations that are suitable problem spaces for GPS. The ISAAC system (Novak 1976) can encode natural language statements of physics problems into internal images, and use these images to produce algebraic equations, which it then solves.

From this we may conclude that, while many issues about architecture are fluid at the present time, the knowledge we gain about architectures is unlikely to invalidate, or require major revision of, the knowledge we have already gained about component mechanisms like EPAM or GPS, or about their roles in cognition.

LINKAGES TO OTHER PARTS OF PSYCHOLOGY

Contemporary information-processing psychology holds forth significant possibilities for a greater unification among domains of psychology that are now quite separate. It may be possible to forge stronger links of cognitive psychology with the study of child development, with research on individual differences, with psycholinguistics, and with social psychology.

There is already vigorous research in cognitive developmental psychology that makes use of many of the constructs discussed here. Computational linguistics and psycholinguistics also have proceeded along parallel—and sometimes even intersecting—lines. Some researchers on individual differences [the names of Hunt (1975) and Sternberg (1977) come immediately to mind] work within an information-processing framework. The linkages to social psychology are somewhat more tenuous, but are beginning to form, as we shall see. Without attempting a systematic review, I would like to offer comments on several of these topics—in particular, individual differences, social psychology, and psycholinguistics.

Individual Differences

Traditionally, the study of individual differences has employed psychometric methods of research. It has been motivated by interest in the nature/nurture controversy as well as by more practical concerns of predicting and explaining school and job performance. L. L. Thurstone's *Vectors of the Mind* (1935), which characterized each individual by a vector of weights for individual traits and predicted individual performance on specific tasks from the correlations between these weights and the importance of the corresponding traits for the tasks, provides a template (or perhaps a caricature) for this view of individual differences.

Thinking-aloud protocols, by providing rich information about the behavior of individual subjects, have focused attention on the large differences in these behaviors (Ericsson & Simon 1984). While protocol analysis has proved much more receptive to the study of individual differences than experimental designs that take averages over sets of subjects, it has been incorporated only incompletely into the current literature on individual differences. For example, Carroll's (1988) chapter on "Individual Differences in Cognitive Functioning," in the new *Stevens' Handbook of Experimental Psychology,* Volume 2, makes almost no reference to the new methods or the research on expert-novice differences produced by them.

Attending to the processes that subjects use in performing complex tasks has enabled us to characterize the differences between expert and novice performance in many task domains. In all of these domains, differences in knowledge (which must include learned skills as well as factual knowledge) prove to be a dominant source of differences in performance (Chi et al 1988).

Of course, this finding should not be taken to deny the existence of "innate" differences, but rather to account for their relative (quantitative) insignificance in explaining differences in skilled adult performance. No one would argue that any randomly selected person could be trained to play world-class tennis; but one could argue, on the basis of the evidence now available, that most normal human beings could become reasonably good players with sufficient training and practice, and that none could become excellent players without extensive training and practice.

Knowledge includes knowledge of strategies. A good deal of the research on expert-novice differences has been aimed at understanding the strategies that experts acquire and apply, how these strategies can be learned, and to what extent they are transferable from one task domain to another. Hence, in the contemporary paradigms, the study of individual differences is closely tied to the study of learning and transfer of training. These ties, in turn, introduce a strong taxonomic aspect into the study of individual differences, making clear that a great many task domains will have to be analyzed before we can generalize safely about human skills.

The new connections between skills and processes affect not only our understanding of complex performances, but also our interpretations of the simple processes that underlie them. We are aware today of the centrality of short-term memory limits to performance on many, if not most, cognitive tasks, and we have long used George Miller's seven chunks to characterize those limits.

But a chunk is not an innate measure of storage capacity. A chunk is any stimulus that has become familiar, hence recognizable, through experience. Hence, the capacity of short-term memory is itself determined by learning, and can grow to vast size as individual acts of recognition access larger and richer stores of information in long-term memory. Two EPAM systems possessing the same basic structure can differ greatly in measured STM capacity simply because one has a more elaborate differentiation net and associated store of schemas than the other.

Social Psychology

Just as individual differences find a natural place in information processing psychology, so do social phenomena. To the extent that cognitive peformance rests on skill and knowledge, it is a social, rather than a purely individual, phenomenon. Language skills and skills in social interaction can be approached within the same theoretical framework as knowledge and skills for dealing with the physical environment.

The recent work of Voss et al (1983) illustrates how cognitive and social psychology can mutually reinforce each other. He has studied how people who have different professional backgrounds and information approach the same problem-solving situation. When asked to write an essay on agricultural reform in the USSR, subjects who are experts in agronomy address themselves to entirely different variables and strategies than subjects who are experts on Russian political affairs. And both of these groups of subjects respond quite differently from novices. When we study expert behavior, we cannot help studying the structure of professional disciplines in our society.

Cognitive psychology still has an important task of studying the domain-independent components of cognitive performance. But since the performance depends heavily on socially structured and socially acquired knowledge, it must pay constant attention to the social environment of cognition. Many of the invariants we see in behavior are social invariants. And since they are social invariants, many are invariant only over a particular society or a particular era, or even over a particular social or professional group within a society. Social variables must be introduced to set the boundaries of our generalizations.

CONCLUSION

Let me summarize briefly this account of the invariants of human behavior as they are disclosed by contemporary cognitive psychology. The problem of identifying invariants is complicated by the fact that people are adaptive systems, whose behavior is highly flexible. The invariants must be sought in the mechanisms that allow them to solve problems and learn: the mechanisms of intelligence.

The Physical Symbol System Hypothesis, strongly supported by empirical evidence, asserts that a system will be capable of intelligent behavior if and only if it is a physical symbol system: if it can input, output, store, and manipulate symbols. The hypothesis, and consequently information-processing psychology, describes intelligence at a symbolic, "software," level, saying little about brain physiology. That fact need not impede our progress, nor has it, toward understanding at this symbolic level how a physical symbol system like the brain achieves intelligent behavior.

Because of the limits on their computing speeds and power, intelligent systems must use approximate methods. Optimality is beyond their capabilities; their rationality is bounded. To explain the behavior of a system of bounded rationality we must describe the system's processes and also the environments to which it is adapting. Human short-term memory can hold only a half dozen chunks, an act of recognition takes nearly a second, and the simplest human reactions are measured in tens and hundreds of milliseconds, rather than microseconds, nanoseconds, or picoseconds. These limits are among the most important invariants of intelligence.

A major strategy for achieving intelligent adaptation with bounded rationality is to store knowledge and search heuristics in a richly indexed long-term memory in order to reduce the computational requirements of problems. Experts use recognition processes, based on this stored, indexed knowledge, to handle their everyday tasks. When recognition does not suffice, because a great space of possibilities must be explored, they resort to highly selective search, guided by rich stores of heuristics.

When intelligence explores unfamiliar domains, it falls back on "weak methods," which are independent of domain knowledge. People satisfice— look for good-enough solutions—instead of hopelessly searching for the best. They use means-ends analysis to reduce progressively their distance from the desired goal. Paying attention to symmetries and orderly sequences, they seek patterns in their environments that they can exploit for prediction. Problem solving by recognition, by heuristic search, and by pattern recognition are adaptive techniques that are compatible with bounded rationality.

Several cognitive architectures have been proposed to account for the processes just described, but these architectures represent relatively modest variations on a basic pattern that is widely accepted today. This basic pattern involves some sensory processors that provide input into short-term and long-term memory, a recognition process that discriminates the features detected by the senses, a problem solver that employs heuristic search, a pattern induction system, systems for handling natural language, systems for handling image-like representations, and learning mechanisms that permit new processes and data structures to be constructed and stored in memory.

The picture I have drawn of cognitive psychology and the invariants of intelligence holds forth the promise of linking several parts of psychology that now mostly go their separate ways. Developmental psychology has already been strongly influenced by the cognitive revolution. The approach to intelligence and individual differences is beginning to be modified in an information-processing direction. But we are just beginning to see that, because of the strong dependence of intelligence on stored knowledge, cognitive and social psychology must be brought much closer together than they have been in the recent past. When we have made these new connections solid, the challenge will remain of bringing affect and emotion more centrally into the picture.

ACKNOWLEDGMENTS

This research was supported by the Personnel and Training Programs, Psychological Sciences Division, Office of Naval Research, under Contract No. N00014-86-K-0768; and by the Defense Advanced Research Projects Agency, Department of Defense, ARPA order 3597, monitored by the Air Force Avionics Laboratory under contract F33615-81-K-1539.

Literature Cited

Anderson, J. R. 1983. *The Architecture of Complexity.* Cambridge MA: Harvard Univ. Press

Anderson, J. R. 1985. *Cognitive Psychology and Its Implications.* New York: Freeman

Anderson, J. R. 1989. The place of cognitive architectures in a rational analysis. *22nd Annu. Symp. Cognit., Dept. Psychol.,* Carnegie-Mellon Univ.

Broadbent, D. E. 1958. *Perception and Communication.* New York: Pergamon

Carroll, J. B. 1988. Individual differences in cognitive functioning. In *Stevens' Handbook of Experimental Psychology,* ed. R. C. Atkinson, et al, Vol. 2:813–62. New York: Wiley. 2nd ed.

Chi, M. T. H., Glaser, R., Farr, M., eds. 1988. *The Nature of Expertise.* Hillsdale, NJ: Erlbaum

De Groot, A. 1978. *Chance and Choice in Chess.* The Hague: Mouton. 2nd ed.

Ericsson, K. A., Simon, H. A. 1984. *Protocol Analysis.* Cambridge, MA: MIT Press

Feigenbaum, E. A., Simon, H. A. 1984. EPAM-like models of recognition and learning. *Cogn. Sci.* 8:305–36

Gibson, J. J. 1966. *The Senses Considered as Perceptual Systems.* Boston: Houghton Mifflin

Hayes, J. R., Simon, H. A. 1974. Understanding written problem instructions. In *Knowledge and Cognition,* ed. L. W. Gregg, pp. 167–200. Hillsdale, NJ: Erlbaum

Hunt, E. B., Mansman, M. 1975. Cognitive theory applied to individual differences. In *Handbook of Learning and Cognitive Processes,* ed. W. K. Estes, Vol. 1. Hillsdale, NJ: Erlbaum

Johnson-Laird, P. N. 1983. *Mental Models.* Cambridge, MA: Harvard Univ.

Kotovsky, K., Simon, H. A. 1973. Empirical tests of a theory of human acquisition of concepts for sequential patterns. *Cogn. Psychol.* 4:399–424

Marr, D. 1982. *Vision.* San Francisco: Freeman

McClelland, J. L., Rumelhart, D. E. 1986. *Parallel Distributed Processing,* Vol. 2. Cambridge, MA: MIT Press

Newell, A. 1989. *Unified Theories of Cognition.* The William James Lectures. Cambridge, MA: Harvard Univ. Press. Forthcoming

Newell, A., Simon, H. A. 1972. *Human Problem Solving.* Englewood Cliffs, NJ: Prentice-Hall

Newell, A., Simon, H. A. 1976. Computer

science as empirical inquiry: symbols and search. *Commun. ACM* 19:111–26

Novak, G. S. Jr. 1976. *Computer understanding of physics problems stated in natural language.* Tech. Rep. No. NL-30. Austin, TX: Dept. Comput. Sci., Univ. Texas

Simon, H. A. 1979a. *The Sciences of the Artificial.* Cambridge, MA: MIT Press. 2nd ed.

Simon, H. A. 1979b. *Models of Thought,* Vol. 1. New Haven: Yale Univ. Press

Simon, H. A. 1986. The information processing explanation of Gestalt phenomena. *Comput. Hum. Behav.* 2:241–55

Simon, H. A. 1989a. Models of Thought, Vol. 2, New Haven: Yale Univ Press

Simon, H. A. 1989b. Cognitive architectures and rational analysis: comments. *21st Annu. Symp Cognit.,* Dept. Psychol., Carnegie-Mellon Univ.

Simon, H. A., Kotovsky, K. 1963. Human acquisition of concepts for serial patterns. *Psychol. Rev.* 70:534–46

Simon, H. A., Sumner, R. K. 1968. Pattern in music. In *Formal Representation of Human Judgment,* ed. B. Kleinmuntz. New York: Wiley

Sternberg, R. J. 1977. *Intelligence, Information Processing, and Analogical Reasoning.* Hillsdale, NJ: Erlbaum

Thurstone, L. L. 1935. *Vectors of the Mind.* Chicago: Univ. Chicago Press

Voss, J. F., Greene, T. R., Post, T. A., Penner, B. C. 1983. Problem solving skill in the social sciences. In *The Psychology of Learning and Motivation,* ed. G. H. Bower, Vol. 17. New York: Academic

Woodworth, R. S. 1938. *Experimental Psychology.* New York: Holt

Annu. Rev. Psychol. 1990. 41:21–54

PSYCHOTHERAPY FOR CHILDREN AND ADOLESCENTS

Alan E. Kazdin

Department of Psychiatry, University of Pittsburgh School of Medicine, Pittsburgh, Pennsylvania 15213

CONTENTS

INTRODUCTION

The effectiveness of psychotherapy is a topic of keen interest in clinical psychology. Evaluations of treatment have often served as the battleground for alternative conceptual views about the nature of personality and clinical

0066-4308/90/0201-0021$02.00

dysfunction. Psychotherapeutic techniques, considered to represent different theoretical approaches, are often pitted against each other in seemingly crucial tests. Although the value of such comparisons, their yield in knowledge, and their utility in testing theoretical positions can be challenged, the interest they pique is great (e.g. Heimberg & Becker 1984; Kazdin 1986a; Stiles et al 1986).

Interest in the effectiveness of psychotherapy has also increased among legislators, policymakers, and consumers of treatment (DeLeon et al 1983). Attention has focused on whether psychotherapy should be covered under health-care financing programs, and, if so, which techniques and for what clinical problems and clients. Awareness of the social and economic impact of mental illness has heightened concern about the costs and benefits of treatment.

Such interest derives from the significance of the clinical and social problems therapy is designed to address. The scope of mental health problems among children and adolescents is great. Between 12% and 15% of children suffer emotional disturbance (e.g. Gould et al 1980; President's Commission on Mental Health 1978; Tuma 1989). Approximately 2–4% of children suffer severe disorders (including psychoses) and 8–10% evince other disturbances that require treatment. Thus a conservative assumption that 12% of the children are in need of treatment translates to almost 8 million children in the United States (see US Congress, OTA, 1986). The rates of childhood dysfunction vary as a function of several factors including age, sex, type of disorder, ethnic background, and geographical region, to mention a few. Thus, summary percentages obscure the complexity of the problem. Nevertheless, by most counts several million youths in the United States alone suffer psychological impairment and could profit from effective treatment.

Although interest in the effectiveness of psychotherapy is great, there remain central ambiguities that render evaluation difficult. Psychotherapy is difficult to define with great precision. Any definition is necessarily general, since individual, group, family, insight-oriented, behavioral, and cognitive therapies must be accommodated. Here let us define psychotherapy to include interventions designed to decrease distress, psychological symptoms, and maladaptive behavior or to improve adaptive and prosocial functioning through the use of interpersonal interaction, counseling, or activities following a specific treatment plan (see Garfield 1980; Walrond-Skinner 1986). In the case of adults, the usual model of treatment entails the interaction between one person (the patient or client) who has sought help for a particular problem and another person (the therapist) who provides conditions to alleviate the first person's distress. Some aspects of this model apply to child psychotherapy. However, children rarely seek treatment for themselves. In addition, diverse persons (e.g. parents, teachers, peers) other than a professional therapist may play central roles in administering interventions to children. The model of therapy and how and to whom it is applied may vary widely in child treatment. For children as well as adults, therapy is designed to improve adjustment and functioning and to reduce maladaptive behaviors and various psychological and often physical complaints. These ends are sought primarily through interventions that rely on various interpersonal sources of influence such as learning, persuasion, discussion, and similar processes.[1] Treatment focuses on some facet of how clients feel (affect), think (cognition), and act (behavior).

The notion of "effectiveness" is also ambiguous. The effects of treatment can be measured in several ways, including the reduction of symptoms, improvements in adjustment at home or in the community, increases in self-reported happiness, evaluations by relatives and friends, and improvements in physical well-being. Which of these or other alternatives should define effectiveness? One might look for concurrent changes in several measures, but improvements in one measure or set of measures are not always associated with improvements on others. Thus, whether treatment is considered to be effective may depend on the specific measure one examines. How much change on a measure indicates "effective" treatment? Symptoms and adjustment are matters of degree. If the client's depression or fears decrease a little by the end of treatment should that therapy be regarded as effective or successful? There are no widely agreed upon answers to such questions.

Notwithstanding the ambiguities, major advances have been made in the evaluation of psychotherapy. In the treatment of adults, many studies have been completed. Reviews (e.g. Garfield & Bergin 1986), indeed reviews of reviews (e.g. Brown 1987), have attested to the capacity of various forms of treatment to produce change. Research on the effectiveness of therapies for children and adolescents has lagged greatly behind research with adults (see Hoghughi 1988; Johnson et al 1986; Kazdin 1988). Nevertheless, in recent years considerable progress has been made in evaluating treatments for children and adolescents. The present chapter examines progress in treatment including an evaluation of the effects of treatment, exemplary individual studies, and programs of research. In addition, the chapter highlights current

[1]Excluded from the definition are interventions that focus on biological and biomedical methods such as medication, diet, megavitamins, and psychosurgery. Although such interventions are often directed toward improved psychological functioning (e.g. medication to control hyperactivity, exercise to reduce depression), many of the methods, theoretical rationales, and clinical-research issues differ from those that emerge in the evaluation of psychotherapy. Also excluded are interventions directed toward educational objectives. Thus, various significant and useful tutorial and counseling procedures intended solely to enhance achievement and academic performance of children and adolescents are excluded here. Here our definition is restricted to focus on the current status of psychotherapy techniques.

deficiencies in the evaluation of treatments, special issues to improve the yield from outcome studies, and methodological features that warrant increased attention.

EFFECTIVENESS OF PSYCHOTHERAPY

The number of psychotherapy techniques currently in use and the number of disorders to which they are applied have not been as well documented or traced over time for children as they have been for adults.[2] Although it is difficult to identify the precise number of techniques currently in use for children and adolescents, a search of key resource material yields a conservative estimate of over 230 alternative psychosocial treatments (see Kazdin 1988). Needless to say, most of these treatments have never been subjected to controlled outcome studies, but studies of several treatments have been completed and reviews have periodically evaluated their yield.

Historical Overview: A Review of the Reviews

The review by Eysenck (1952) is invariably a starting point in contemporary evaluations of psychotherapy. Eysenck's review of psychotherapy with adults suggested that under traditional forms of psychotherapy improvement rates were no better than those occurring from "spontaneous remission" (i.e. without formal treatment). Eysenck's review stimulated a remarkable number of rebuttals, critiques, and rereviews; and the effects continue to be evident in contemporary writings (e.g. see Garfield & Bergin 1986; Smith et al. 1980).

In the child literature, parallel reviews have not been as provocative in stimulating thought or treatment research. The reviews begin with Levitt (1957), who evaluated 18 studies of child psychotherapy that focused on youths whose problems could be classified generally as neuroses. The therapeutic approaches included a mixture of counseling, guidance, and psychoanalytic and other treatments that were not invariably well specified in the original reports. Levitt combined the studies for his analyses and concluded that the rates of improvement among children who received psychotherapy were approximately 67% and 78% at posttreatment and follow-up, respectively. Children who did not receive treatment improved at about the same rate (73%). Thus Levitt concluded that the efficacy of traditional forms of psychotherapy for children had not been demonstrated.

The clarity of this general conclusion masked a number of problems. To begin with, the "children" encompassed by the studies were diverse in both age (preschool to 21 years old) and clinical dysfunction. Second, baseline or

[2]The term *children* is used generically in the present chapter to refer to children and adolescents. When age and development are discussed, separate age ranges or terms are used.

improvement rates of nontreated youths were derived in part from children who terminated treatment early. Youths who fail to complete treatment may differ systematically from youths who complete treatment and hence might not adequately reflect the base rate of improvement without treatment. Third, improvement rates were based on evaluation of children by the therapists at the end of treatment. Therapist ratings alone, especially by current methodological standards, are an inadequate measure of outcome.

Levitt's review generated rebuttals and reevaluations of the data (Eisenberg & Gruenberg 1961; Heinicke & Goldman 1960; Hood-Williams 1960). Cogent points were raised that not only challenged Levitt's conclusions, but also drew attention to methodological issues in designing outcome studies such as the need to consider diagnoses of children and family factors as moderators of treatment and to use multiple measures to examine treatment outcome. Essentially, the rebuttals conveyed that the original method of analysis, the criteria used, and the research reviewed by Levitt did not permit clear conclusions about the effectiveness of treatment.

Levitt's (1963) subsequent review evaluated 22 additional studies and addressed a number of criticisms, such as consideration of different diagnoses. The conclusions essentially remained the same. Summing across diagnostic groups, Levitt's analyses showed improvements in treated youths to be approximately 65% and slightly below the rate of children who did not receive treatment (73%). Rebuttals and reevaluations of these later reviews continued (Barrett et al 1978; Heinicke & Strassmann 1975).

Over the period covered, the need for greater specificity in evaluating treatment became apparent. One sign of this was the initial effort to distinguish different diagnostic groups in which the outcomes of treatment and so-called spontaneous remission rates differed. For example, Levitt (1963) noted that improvement rates were greater for neurotic than for delinquent or psychotic cases. However, the number of dimensions upon which treatment effects are considered to depend and the level of specificity have continued to expand. Currently, analyses of psychotherapy effects suggest that outcomes may depend on multiple characteristics of treatments, patients, therapists, and measures (e.g. Casey & Berman 1985; Smith et al 1980; Weisz et al 1987).

General Comments

From the standpoint of evaluating the effectiveness of alternative forms of treatment, reviews of early research in the field have been wanting. Major issues were repeatedly raised in these reviews noting the paucity of studies, methodological shortcomings, and the neglect of variables that are likely to influence treatment outcome. Thus, even using the criteria invoked at the time to evaluate research, difficulties were identified that precluded clear verdicts on treatment. Perhaps of even greater importance, in the ensuing years the criteria for evaluating treatment outcome in individual patients (e.g. Lambert et al 1983) and for conducting outcome research more generally (e.g. Kazdin 1986b) have changed. Early reviews did not focus on the level of specificity now considered essential. Contemporary research focuses on the impact of specific interventions as applied to better-specified problems and examines influences (e.g. child age, cognitive development) that may moderate (interact with) treatment effects.

Contemporary Evaluations

Given the changing standards for conducting and evaluating outcome research, the value of reworking previous reviews and their constituent studies is questionable. Progress has been made in the range of outcome studies now available and the different types of evaluations that sift through their findings. Two types of literature reviews can be cited to reflect current evaluations, namely, meta-analyses of child treatment and narrowly focused qualitative reviews.

META-ANALYSES   A major development in the last 15 years is the emergence of meta-analysis. The method is an alternative to traditional narrative and qualitative evaluation (i.e. a review of the literature) where an author synthesizes multiple studies and derives conclusions about treatments and their effectiveness. Meta-analysis refers to a set of quantitative procedures that can be used to evaluate multiple studies. Results from different studies are quantified to permit their combination and comparison. One can compute *effect size*, which provides a common metric across a variety of investigations. Effect size is calculated as the difference between means of an experimental (treatment) and control (no-treatment) group, divided by the standard deviation of the control group (or of the pooled sample of both groups). Effect size constitutes the dependent measure for the meta-analysis and is used as a summary statistic to examine the impact of other variables. Individual characteristics of the investigations (e.g. age of the subjects, type of treatment, duration of treatment) and their interactions become the independent variables (see Glass et al 1981).

Numerous meta-analyses of the adult psychotherapy literature have appeared (see Brown 1987), beginning with the seminal work of Smith & Glass (1977; Smith et al 1980). In the 1980 study, the more comprehensive of the two, 475 controlled-treatment outcome studies were evaluated. An effect size was calculated separately for each dependent measure in each study, yielding a total of 1760 different effect sizes. Two of the more general conclusions drawn by Smith & Glass were that alternative psychotherapies produce greater therapeutic change than no-treatment control conditions; and that different treatments, based on alternative models or approaches (e.g. psychodynamic, behavioral), tend to be equally effective. The conclusions are neither revolutionary nor particularly strong, but the study's method seemed heir to less bias than the usual narrative review.

Few meta-analyses of child therapies have been reported. The original work of Smith & Glass included studies with children, but separate effects of child vs adult psychotherapy were not evaluated. Smith & Glass subjected approximately 90 studies of children or adolescents to meta-analysis almost half of which were unpublished dissertations or theses. Thus a significant portion of this relatively small literature was not easily available for review.

Casey & Berman (1985) completed a meta-analysis of the child psychotherapy literature. The review included 75 studies published between 1952 and 1983 in which some form of psychotherapy with children was compared with a control group or another treatment. Studies were included with children (ages 3–15) across a wide range of clinical problems. Selected treatment techniques were excluded (drug therapy, peer counseling, family therapy), while several traditional therapies (e.g. psychodynamic, client-centered) and behavioral approaches (e.g. behavior therapy, cognitive-behavioral treatments) were included.

The typical treatment outcome study was conducted with slightly over 40 youths, most of whom were boys near the age of 9, slightly behind in their grade level, who received 9–10 weeks of therapy. Most studies (72%) included as their clients school children who had not sought treatment or who had been recruited from the community. Clinic samples from outpatient or inpatient facilities were used in a small percentage (24%) of studies. Although clinical problems were not always described in sufficient detail in the original studies, the largest segment of dysfunction encompassed was aggressive and withdrawn behavior (40% of the studies), followed by hyperactive or impulsive behavior (12%) and phobias (12%). Finally, most studies (56%) included some form of behavior therapy (e.g. desensitization, modeling); client-centered therapy and psychodynamic therapy were included in a small percentage of the studies (29% and 9%, respectively).

Summing across different therapies to reach general conclusions, Casey & Berman (1985) reported a significant effect size due to treatment when compared to control conditions. An effect size of .71 was obtained across all techniques. This number is based on standard deviation units and indicates that the average outcome of child psychotherapy was slightly more than two thirds of a standard deviation better than that of untreated control children. Stated another way, the average child who is treated is better off at the end of therapy than 76% of the children who did not receive treatment. Therapy is clearly effective on the average in improving children.

Behavioral therapies, as a general class of procedures, led to greater effect sizes than nonbehavioral therapies. However, the differences appeared to be associated with the use of different types of outcome measures and clinical problems in studies of behavioral and nonbehavioral techniques. When the latter effects were controlled, the outcomes of behavioral techniques were no longer significantly different from those of nonbehavioral techniques. Effect size did not vary significantly for alternative techniques (e.g. play vs nonplay therapy; individual vs group therapy; child- vs parent-focused treatment) or for characteristics of the therapist (e.g. experience, education, sex). However, effect sizes did vary as a function of child characteristics. In general, treatments were less effective with problems of social adjustment (aggressive or withdrawn behavior) than with other problems (hyperactivity, phobias, somatic complaints). Studies with a greater proportion of boys yielded smaller effect sizes.

A second meta-analysis of child and adolescent therapy was completed by Weisz et al (1987), who examined over 100 controlled studies that encompassed youths ages 4–18. Relatively few of these (29.6%) overlapped with the studies reviewed by Casey & Berman (1985). The results were similar in many ways. Weisz et al found that the mean effect size across different treatments, clinical problems, and patient samples was .79. Effect sizes tended to be greater for behavioral than for nonbehavioral techniques and for children (ages 4–12) than for adolescents (ages 13–18). No differences in effect sizes were found in the outcomes between boys and girls, recruited samples and cases referred for treatment (analogue and clinic samples), or types of dysfunction (externalizing and internalizing problems). Effect sizes were similar at posttreatment and follow-up (mean = 5–6 months after treatment) which suggests that the effects of treatment were durable. Although level of training of the therapist did not lead to overall differences in effect size, training interacted with age of the children treated. Specifically, professional therapists tended to be equally effective with children and adolescents. In contrast, graduate students and paraprofessionals (e.g. parents, teachers) were more effective with younger than with older clients.

From these meta-analyses, several conclusions are noteworthy. First, psychotherapy appears to be more effective than no treatment. Second, the magnitude of these effects closely parallels those obtained with adults. Third, treatment differences, when evident, tend to favor behavioral rather than nonbehavioral techniques. Both analyses revealed that studies of behavioral and cognitively based techniques greatly outnumber studies of more traditional and more frequently practiced forms of treatment, such as client-centered, psychodynamic, and family therapies. Thus, the meta-analyses have been helpful in highlighting priority areas of research.

The use of meta-analysis upon the adult psychotherapy literature has been controversial (see Garfield 1983; Michelson 1985; Prioleau et al 1983). Major points of contention are the hazards of combining studies that differ greatly in methodology, the reliance on few studies for variables of interest, the meaningfulness of conclusions regarding broad categories (e.g. behavioral therapies), and the methods of combining measures to generate effect sizes. In addition, considerable judgment is needed in selecting measures and identifying effect sizes within a given study, and these can materially affect the conclusions (Matt 1989). Nevertheless, the meta-analysis provides an additional method of evaluation. The ground rules for inclusion or exclusion of studies in a meta-analysis, including how the different studies are evaluated and weighted, are made explicit. Although this feature does not by any means remove the role of judgment at several critical points in the analysis, meta-analyses have permitted new types of evaluations regarding treatment effectiveness.

FOCUSED NARRATIVE REVIEWS   A problem with early reviews in the field, and even with more contemporary reviews and meta-analyses, is their attempt to reach summary conclusions across a large number of treatment techniques. The question such reviews address follows in the tradition of the global question, "Does psychotherapy work?" No doubt the effectiveness of treatment for children depends on a number of conditions, including the specific version of treatment as applied to particular problems and patients and as evaluated in relation to specific outcome measures.

In recognition of the greater need for specificity, several focused literature reviews (primarily narrative) have concentrated on individual treatment techniques or "families" of conceptually or procedurally related techniques. Thus, there are now separate reviews of individual, group, family, behavior, and traditional psychotherapies (e.g. Hazelrigg et al 1987; Hobbs & Lahey 1983; Kovacs & Paulauskas 1986; Meador & Ollendick 1984; Tuma & Sobotka 1983). Reviews that are limited to specific techniques can identify potentially unique substantive and methodological issues that emerge. Even so, the individual categories (e.g. verbal psychotherapy or family therapy) are often broad, and the constituent techniques might encompass diverse clinical problems.

Clinically, the major concern is not what the effects are of a particular treatment across diverse problem areas, but rather what the effective options are for a specific type of dysfunction. In recognition of this priority, separate reviews have focused on the effects of treatment for specific problems such as hyperactivity, anxiety and phobias, depression, oppositional behavior, and conduct disorder (e.g. Gard & Berry 1986; Kazdin 1985; Reynolds 1985).

Finally, a number of sources evaluate several specific techniques by individual areas of child dysfunctions (Bornstein & Kazdin 1985; Morris & Kratochwill 1983). In these sources, the complexity of reviewing the evidence is conveyed because multiple techniques have been applied to individual problem areas. The efficacy of each treatment is examined in relation to these problem areas.

Although reviews focused on individual treatment techniques, clinical dysfunctions, or techniques-by-dysfunction represent a desirable move toward greater specificity in examining the evidence, such an approach has an obvious inherent limitation. Because a relatively small number of controlled-outcome studies are available to begin with, finer subdivisions do not necessarily yield more informative conclusions.

CRITICAL DIRECTIONS AND PROGRESS

Given ambiguities in defining effectiveness, variations among techniques, clinical problems, and the quality of the evidence, the question of whether psychotherapy works has plagued the field. Researchers' primary reaction has been to reject as much too general the question, "Does therapy work?" and to replace it with "*What* treatment, by *whom*, is most effective for *this* individual with *that* specific problem, under *which* set of circumstances" (Paul 1967:11). At this more molecular level of analysis, several critical areas can be identified that at once convey exemplars of research and needed directions.

Large-Scale Evaluations of Treatment

Large-scale studies represent an important development in child psychotherapy research. Scale affects the kinds of questions that can be addressed. Studies with sufficiently large samples not only provide sensitive (statistically powerful) tests of treatment but also enable evaluation of factors other than treatment technique. Two large-scale investigations illustrate exemplary features in the types of questions addressed and in alternative approaches to treatment evaluation.

SCHOOL-BASED TREATMENTS OF NEUROTIC AND ANTISOCIAL BEHAVIOR   Kolvin et al (1981) conducted a study in England between 1972 and 1979 to evaluate different interventions for maladjusted children. The objective was to examine the impact of different school-based treatments, on different types of clinical problems, with children at different stages of development and dysfunction. Two types of child dysfunction were investigated—*neurotic* and *conduct disorders*. Neurotic disorder was defined broadly to include internalizing problems (e.g. neuroses, depression, anxiety); conduct disorder was defined to include externalizing problems (e.g. disruptive behavior, bullying, delinquency). Because of the potential significance of developmental stage on the nature of child dysfunction and response to treatment, two different age levels were selected. Children ages 7–8 and

11–12 years old were included and referred to, respectively, as juniors and seniors.

Screening of 4300 children was undertaken to identify the final group of children (slightly fewer than 600) who showed maladjustment problems at school and were at risk for psychiatric impairment (juniors) or who already evinced psychiatric disturbance (seniors). Multiple measures involving parent, teacher, peer, and clinician evaluations were used to conduct screening and to evaluate treatment outcome. Major characteristics of the study are highlighted in Table 1.

Once identified, children were assigned randomly to one of four conditions. The conditions varied slightly for younger and older children (see Table 1), but for each age level there was a no-treatment control group. *Parent-counseling plus teacher-consultation* consisted of social work consultation with parents and teachers in an effort to coordinate school and home activities, casework with the family, and support for the teacher. *Nurture work* consisted of providing enrichment activities for the children, close interaction with the child, and behavioral shaping for individual child goals. *Group therapy* was based on client-centered principles and practices and

Table 1 Characteristics of the outcome study conducted by Kolvin et al (1981)

Domain	Major Characteristics
Sample	ages 7–8 (juniors) or 11–12 (seniors)
Sample size	60–90 youths per group (N = 574)
Screening	multi-stage screening to identify dysfunctional youths
Setting	regular public schools
Treatments (juniors)	parent-counseling/teacher consultation
	group (play) therapy
	no-treatment
Treatments (seniors)	parent-counseling/teacher consultation
	group (nondirective, discussion) therapy
	behavior modification
	no-treatment
Treatment sessions	number and duration varied for each treatment.
Sources of data	parent, teacher, peer, self, and clinician ratings
Assessment domain	adjustment, psychopathology, cognitive, and social functioning
Major outcome measures	Rutter teacher and parent scales, parent interview to assess neurotic, antisocial, and psychosomatic behavior; Junior Eysenck Personality Inventory; Devereax Elementary School Behavior Rating Scale; measures of vocabulary, intelligence, and reading ability; sociometric data
Assessment periods	pretreatment, posttreatment, follow-up (18 months after treatment ended)
Training of therapists	special programs for trainers involving formal and informal instruction and supervision, varying as needed by condition.

consisted of play group therapy (for younger children) or discussion (more traditional) group therapy for older children. In each case, the focus was on the expression of feelings, acceptance of the child, warmth, and the therapeutic relationship. The *behavior modification* program (for seniors only) consisted of classroom reinforcement systems relying on social and token reinforcement to improve deportment and classroom performance. The treatments involved different models of care delivery and different personnel (e.g. social workers, teachers, teacher aides). The treatments were carefully developed, structured, and implemented. Training of staff provided formal and informal supervision and discussion, along with reading and background information on the principles and practices underlying treatment.

The effects of treatment are not easily summarized given the large number of outcome measures and different sources of information. In general, for the younger children, play group therapy and nurture work led to significantly greater changes than for no-treatment controls and for children in the parent-teacher condition. For the other children, group therapy and behavior modification led to significantly greater changes than occurred in controls or in children under the parent-teacher condition. Among the different treatments, children with neurotic disorders (as defined earlier) responded better than children with conduct disorders; girls responded better to treatments than did boys. There were no consistent interactions between the type of treatment and type of child disorder or between treatment and child gender.

This study offers a number of excellent features. The use of multiple measures for screening, a comparison of separate treatments with a randomly comprised no-treatment control group, the assessment of multiple domains of functioning (maladjustment, cognitive functioning, social relations with peers), and the evaluation of follow-up make this study truly outstanding. Also, in both adult and child therapy literatures, studies rarely include a sufficient number of subjects to provide a statistically powerful test of treatments (see Kazdin & Bass 1989). The sample size in each group here (60–90) is almost without peer.

Few studies have attempted to examine the effects of different treatments on alternative problems with children of different ages. Kolvin et al (1981) addressed treatment at the level of complexity that avoids highly diluted and diffuse conclusions. The focus on different treatments and clinical problems in children of different ages within a single study may serve as an excellent basis for drawing conclusions about treatment. Qualitative or quantitative literature reviews that attempt to piece together conclusions with inadequately designed studies as a data base are unlikely to do as well.

COMMUNITY-BASED TREATMENT FOR ANTISOCIAL YOUTH   Feldman et al (1983) conducted a community-based treatment project for antisocial youths.

Treatment was integrated in a resource already available within the community, specifically with the activities of the Jewish Community Centers Association in St. Louis, Missouri. The study included youths (ages 8–17) who were referred for antisocial behavior (referred youths) or who normally attended the regular activities programs and were not identified as showing problem behavior (nonreferred youths). The project began with approximately 700 youths; this number declined to approximately 450 by the end of treatment.

The design of the study was complex because of the interest in evaluating the separate and combined effects of different influences on outcome (see Table 2). The study evaluated the effects of three types of treatment, two levels of therapist experience, and three different ways to compose the groups. The three treatments were *traditional group social work* (focus on group processes, social organization, and norms within the group), *behavior modification* (use of reinforcement contingencies, focus on prosocial behavior), and *minimal treatment* (no explicit application of a structured treatment plan; spontaneous interactions among group members). Activity groups within the center were formed and assigned to one of these three interventions. The groups were led by trainers, some of whom were *experienced* (graduate students of social work with previous experience) and others who were *inexperienced* (undergraduate students). Finally, the groups were comprised in three ways: Either all members were youths *referred* for antisocial behavior, all members were *nonreferred* ("normal") youths, or members were a mixture of *referred and nonreferred* youths.

The main objective was to evaluate changes in antisocial behavior of referred youths over the course of the intervention. Measures were obtained from parents, referral agents, the youths, and group leaders as well as through direct observations of the groups. The intervention was conducted over a period of a year in which the youths attended sessions and engaged in a broad range of activities (e.g. sports, arts and crafts, fund raising, discussions). The specific treatments were superimposed on the usual activity structure of the community facility. Treatment sessions ranged from 8–29 sessions (mean = 22.2 sessions), each lasting about 2–3 hours.

The results indicated that treatment, trainer experience, and group composition affected at least some of the measures. Youths showed greater reductions in antisocial behavior with experienced than with inexperienced leaders. Antisocial youths in groups that included nonreferred children showed greater improvements than similar youths in groups comprised only of antisocial youths. Treatments were differentially effective; behavior modification led to greater reductions in antisocial behavior than did traditional group treatment. Traditional treatment reduced antisocial behavior relative to the minimal contact group. However, treatment technique accounted for only a small amount of variance in predicting outcome.

Table 2   Characteristics of the outcome study conducted by Feldman et al (1983)

Domain	Major Characteristics
Sample	referred for antisocial behavior (ages 8–17, M = 11.2)
Sample size	N = 452 participants, N = 54 at follow-up
Screening	severity of antisocial behavior on checklists completed by referral agent and parent.
Setting	Jewish Community Center
Treatments	traditional group social work
	behavior modification
	minimal treatment (no explicit or structured plan)
Treatment sessions	range from 8–29 session (m = 22.2 sessions) 2–3 hours each
Sources of data	referral agency, parents, children, therapists
Assessment domain	antisocial, prosocial, nonsocial behavior
Major outcome measures	checklist questions designed to measure prosocial, antisocial, and nonsocial behavior completed by professionals at referral agencies, parents, therapists, and youths; direct observations of youths in the groups designed to measure prosocial, antisocial, and nonsocial behavior; therapist and observer completed measures of group norms, child and peer relations; aggression scale completed by youths
Therapists	experienced (social work graduate students) vs inexperienced (undergraduates)
Training of therapists	in-service training; prior course work and practical training for "experienced" therapists.

Overall, antisocial youths benefited from the program, especially those who received the most favorable intervention condition (i.e. behavior modification with an experienced leader in a group of referred and nonreferred peers). For a small subsample (n = 54), follow-up data were available one year later. Follow-up data revealed slight (nonsignificant) increases in antisocial behavior from posttreatment levels based on information from parents and referral agents. However, the size of the follow-up sample precluded evaluation of the effects of treatment, trainer experience, and group composition.

GENERAL COMMENTS   The two studies illustrate the evaluation of multiple treatments, the reliance upon multiple measures and perspectives to examine outcome, and the sampling of different "types" of youths to examine the differential responsiveness of clients to treatment. Both studies focus on the interaction of treatment outcome with other variables (e.g. clinical problem, child age, referral status). This level of specificity is what is needed in outcome research, a fact widely recognized but rarely translated into action. The results of these studies could be included in a meta-analysis of treatment, but such an analysis would fail to represent their rich findings.[3] The analysis of each study on its own provides a clearer statement of the effects of the constituent treatments along with the requisite qualifications based on design issues.

Programs of Research

Even more than individual studies, programs of research convey the advances in and promise of current treatments for children. Typically, programs are systematic and consecutive studies by an individual investigative team exploring a particular treatment technique. For present purposes, it is useful to extend the definition of programmatic research to include the accumulation of findings among separate researchers who have explored a particular treatment approach. Research programs, in this broader sense, systematically study particular clinical problems and develop treatments. The programs highlighted here are both illustrative and exemplary.

PARENT MANAGEMENT TRAINING   Parent management training (PMT) is designed to alter the pattern of interchanges between parent and child so that prosocial behavior is directly reinforced and supported within the family. Although PMT has been applied to a variety of childhood problems, its most frequent application has focused on aggressive and oppositional behavior. Several different parenting behaviors are developed, such as establishing the rules for the child to follow, providing positive reinforcement for appropriate behavior, delivering mild forms of punishment to suppress behavior, and negotiating compromises. PMT is based on the general view that aggressive child behavior is inadvertently developed and sustained in the home by maladaptive parent-child interactions. In fact, research has shown that parents of aggressive youths engage in several practices that promote aggressive behavior and suppress prosocial behavior. These practices include directly reinforcing deviant behavior, frequently using commands and harsh punishment, and failing to attend to appropriate behavior (Patterson 1982). Through such behaviors, parents systematically, albeit unwittingly, shape coercive behavior on the part of the child.

PMT has been evaluated in a large number of outcome studies with behavior problem children varying in age and degree of severity of dysfunction (see Kazdin 1985; Moreland et al 1982). The work of Patterson and his colleagues, spanning more than two decades, exemplifies the programmatic outcome research on parent training with antisocial youths. Over 200 families have been seen that include primarily aggressive children (ages 3–12) referred for outpatient treatment (see Patterson 1982). Several controlled studies have

---

[3]It is interesting that the two studies highlighted here were not included in the meta-analyses of child treatments reviewed earlier (Casey & Berman 1985; Weisz et al 1987).

demonstrated marked improvements in child behavior over the course of treatment. Moreover, these changes surpass those achieved with variations of family-based psychotherapy, attention-placebo (discussion), and no-treatment conditions (Patterson et al 1982; Walter & Gilmore 1973; Wiltz & Patterson 1974). Spanning different programs of research, the effects of treatment have also been shown to bring the problematic behaviors of treated children within normative levels of nonreferred peers who are functioning adequately (Eyberg & Johnson 1974; Patterson 1974; Wells et al 1980). Follow-up assessment has shown that the gains are often maintained one year after treatment (e.g. Fleischman & Szykula 1981). The continued benefits of treatment have been evident up to 4–10 years later (Baum & Forehand 1981; Forehand & Long, 1988).

Several features of PMT make it one of the more promising treatments for aggressive behavior. First, the treatment has been effective with children varying in severity of clinical dysfunction. Changes at home and at school can bring deviant behavior of treated children within the range of children functioning normally. Second, the benefits of treatment often extend beyond the target child to siblings and parents. Behaviors of siblings of the referred child often improve, and symptoms of the parent, particularly maternal depression, decrease following PMT (see Kazdin 1985). Third, along with treatment outcome investigations, basic research has been conducted on family interaction patterns and influences outside of the home that affect treatment outcome. This research has enhanced our understanding of the emergence of antisocial behavior (see Patterson 1986). Fourth, treatment manuals and training materials are available for parents and professional therapists (see Ollendick & Cerny 1981 for a list). Thus PMT can be readily investigated as well as disseminated for clinical application.

Several limitations of PMT can be identified as well. First, some families characterized by social disadvantage, marital discord, high levels of stress, poor social support systems, and psychopathology do not respond to treatment. Explicit procedures may need to be included in treatment to address family and parent issues that influence the parent-child interactions in the home. Second, PMT makes several demands on the parents: They must master educational materials that convey social learning principles, systematically observe deviant child behavior, implement specific behavior change procedures at home, attend weekly sessions, and respond to frequent telephone contacts by the therapist. For some families, the demands may be too great to continue in treatment. Third, for many children PMT is simply not a viable option because no parent is available, willing, and capable of following through with treatment.

Overall, PMT illustrates excellent progress in the development and evaluation of treatment. The treatment has emerged through several controlled studies that have addressed questions about the effectiveness of treatment relative to alternative control conditions and other forms of treatment, the persons for whom treatment is effective, and the components of treatment that contribute to change. In addition, the research exemplifies the interplay of basic research, in this case on family processes, and areas that serve as the focus of treatment (Patterson 1986).

COGNITIVE PROBLEM-SOLVING SKILLS TRAINING   Problem-solving skills training (PSST) focuses on the child's cognitive processes that underlie maladaptive behavior. Impulsive cognitive style, deficits in taking the perspective of others, and misattribution of the intentions of others are some of the processes that have been studied in relation to deviant child behavior. The relationship between cognitive processes and behavioral adjustment has been evaluated in programmatic studies by Spivack & Shure (1982; Spivack et al 1976). These investigators have identified several cognitive processes that underlie social behavior (e.g. generating alternative solutions, means-ends thinking) and have shown that the ability to engage in these problem-solving steps is related to behavioral adjustment in the classroom.

Spivack & Shure have developed and evaluated their interpersonal cognitive problem-solving skills program for several years and with a variety of child and adult populations (e.g. Spivack et al 1976; Spivack & Shure 1982). Many variations of problem-solving skills training for children and adolescents have emerged from other research programs as well (e.g. Camp & Bash 1985; Kendall & Braswell 1985). The variations share many characteristics, such as focusing on how the child approaches situations; teaching the use of a step-by-step approach to solving problems; using structured tasks involving games, academic activities, and stories; applying skills to real-life situations; and modeling, practice, and role-playing with the therapist.

A number of researchers have conducted programmatic series of studies showing the efficacy of PSST (see Kendall & Braswell 1985; Spivack & Shure 1982). Research has established the efficacy of alternative treatment variations. Many studies, perhaps especially those completed in the late 1970s and early 1980s, have evaluated the impact of training on cognitive processes and laboratory-task performance, rather than deviant child behavior and adjustment at home and at school (see Kazdin 1987). More recent studies of impulsive, aggressive, and antisocial children and adolescents have shown that cognitively based treatment can significantly change behavior at home, at school, and in the community and that these gains are evident up to one year later (Arbuthnot & Gordon 1986; Kazdin et al 1987; Kendall & Braswell 1982; Lochman et al 1984).

At present, several features make PSST one of the more promising psychosocial approaches to disruptive behavior of children. First, PSST draws on theory and research in developmental psychology. Theory and research on the emergence and maturation of cognitive processes and the relationship of these processes to adjustment provide an important foundation for generating and testing treatment techniques (see Shirk 1988). Second, developmental differences can be considered in designing effective treatments based on basic research. For example, processes highly significant at one age (e.g. means-ends thinking in adolescents) may be less critical at other ages (early childhood) (Spivack et al 1976). Treatment can be varied according to data on developmental differences. Finally, a major feature of PSST for purposes of both clinical application and research is that variations of the approach are available in manual form (e.g. Camp & Bash 1985; Kendall & Braswell 1985; Spivack et al 1976) which can promote further research on the efficacy of treatment.

There are clear limitations to the application of PSST as well. Although research to date has generally adopted the view that children with problems of adjustment, broadly conceived, have cognitive deficits, there has been little attempt to relate specific cognitive deficits to particular types of clinical dysfunction. Existing studies show that various forms of PSST can produce relatively consistent changes on a variety of measures that reflect cognitive style, thought processes, perception, aspects of intelligence, and academic performance. Further efforts to alter specific clinical problems on measures of dysfunction at home, at school, or in the community are needed. Nevertheless, major advances have been achieved in developing variations of PSST for application to child dysfunctions.

GENERAL COMMENTS   Parent management training and problem-solving skills training illustrate programs of research that are exemplary in the child treatment research. While many questions about the effectiveness and limits of such specific treatments remain, these programs suggest that developing effective treatments requires an interplay of studies on the nature of the processes underlying the clinical problem and treatment outcome.

In passing, the specific techniques used to illustrate programmatic research on child treatments warrant comment. The bulk of clinical practice is devoted to relationship, insight-oriented, play, and family therapies (see Gould et al 1980; Koocher & Pedulla 1977; Tuma & Pratt 1982), but these were not used to illustrate the significance of programmatic lines of work. The generic and eclectic forms of individual, group, and family therapy commonly used in clinical practice are infrequently the object of programmatic research or indeed of individual outcome studies (see Casey & Berman 1985; Hazelrigg et al 1987; Weisz et al 1987). The programs of research outlined above convey the type of systematic evaluation from which these other treatments would profit.

PRIORITY AREAS FOR RESEARCH

Considerable progress has been made in establishing the efficacy of treatments. The progress has resulted from direct tests of treatment as well as from increased understanding of childhood and adolescent dysfunction. Current evidence, as well as emerging information regarding the nature of child and adolescent dysfunction, indicate several priorities for research.

Clinical Focus

EVALUATIONS OF CLINIC SAMPLES   Research has infrequently evaluated treatments among clinical samples of children or adolescents in settings where treatment usually is conducted. For example, in their meta-analysis of the child psychotherapy literature, Casey & Berman (1985) found that 72% of the studies were conducted with school children not seeking treatment or community volunteers rather than clinic populations. There remains a need to evaluate treatments with persons to whom they are applied.

Research with clinic samples in settings where treatment is ordinarily provided is needed not only to test the generality of findings obtained in highly controlled settings, but also to better elucidate treatment. In clinical settings, the type and range of dysfunctions among children and their families are likely to be greater than evident in school volunteer samples. Developing treatments to meet the needs of clinical samples is likely to generate new hypotheses and procedures that may address clinical exigencies more fully and effectively. From clinical research, hypotheses can be generated that will fuel the conceptual basis of treatment as well (Maher 1988).

COMORBIDITY   Studies often identify children with a well-specified clinical problem either through standard diagnostic criteria or cutoff scores on dimensional scales. Such selection procedures have been encouraged to focus on homogeneous groups of patients. Increasingly evident is the finding that children may meet criteria for more than one disorder, a phenomenon referred to as comorbidity. For example, epidemiological studies have found that among children and adolescents who meet criteria for one psychiatric diagnosis, approximately half also meet criteria for at least one other disorder as well (e.g. Anderson et al 1987; Bird et al 1988). Many disorders are known to coexist, including conduct disorder and attention deficit hyperactivity disorder; depression and anxiety; and autism and mental retardation, to mention a few. These specific associations and comorbidity in general have important implications for selecting, administering, and evaluating treatment.

Treatment is usually provided for the most salient dysfunction (principal diagnosis). Perhaps treatment modalities need to be combined more routinely or planned in such a way as to consider multiple forms of dysfunction. Thus, single treatments (e.g. parent management training) for a problem (e.g. conduct disorder) may be incomplete for children who evince other disorders as well (e.g. depression, hyperactivity, anxiety).

Comorbidity may also have implications for evaluating treatments. The effectiveness of a given treatment may well depend upon the other (nontarget) dysfunctions within a sample. At the very least, the diversity of other dysfunctions may lead to wide variation of treatment effects among children receiving a given intervention. The large within-group variability of youth due to diversity in comorbid diagnoses may make treatment effects more difficult to demonstrate. Further work is needed to assess the multiple conditions that children may exhibit, even within a sample of children who meet criteria for a particular disorder, and to evaluate the effectiveness of treatment on comorbid conditions that are not directly focused upon. In addition, it may be useful to determine whether or not comorbidity predicts or otherwise moderates treatment outcome.

FOCUS ON UNDERSERVED AND AT-RISK POPULATIONS   As a population in general, children are underserved. Apparently, most children in need of mental health services do not receive them. Estimates suggest that only 20–30% of children with clinically significant dysfunction actually receive treatment (Knitzer 1982; Tuma 1989). Children with severer dysfunctions are slightly less likely to receive treatment than those with less serious dysfunctions (Sowder 1975). Thus, there remains a great need to identify and deliver effective treatments.

Although children and adolescents in general may not be sufficiently served, there remain populations that warrant special attention because they may have special needs, are poorly served by existing resources, suffer social disadvantage, and/or are at risk for psychopathology given the dysfunction of their parents (e.g. depression, alcohol abuse), untoward living conditions (e.g. homeless children), and parent child-rearing practices (e.g. abuse or neglect). Special populations represent high priority areas because they are underserved in clinical research and practice.

The treatment of ethnic and racial minorities illustrates special populations that warrant increased attention. The type and percentage of dysfunctions, environmental and familial conditions associated with impairment, and likelihood of seeking and obtaining treatment vary among racial and ethnic groups (e.g. Berlin 1986; Canino et al 1986; Sue & Sue 1987), yet ethnic and racial issues are infrequently considered in treatment and service delivery and infrequently evaluated in relation to treatment outcome. There are notable exceptions.

For example, Costantino et al (1986) developed treatment for Puerto Rican children (ages 5–11) based on presenting folktales *(cuentos)* designed to convey thoughts, feelings, values, and behaviors representative of Puerto Rican culture. Similarly, in a program for young Cuban drug abusers, Szapocznik et al (1978) developed treatment consistent with the expressed values of the culture. Specifically, treatment emphasized the influence of the hierarchical structure and network of the family, a problem-solving approach to crises, and a present rather than historical orientation to problems.

Further work is needed to develop or adapt interventions for populations with special needs. The task is great because it is unclear to what extent alternative interventions can be widely applied across types of dysfunctions, ages, and various ethnic and other groups. Ideally, treatment investigations can identify procedures effective in altering specific types of dysfunctions (e.g. depression, anxiety, antisocial behavior) for a specific target population. Extensions to various groups may then involve adaptation to make the procedures relevant and culturally acceptable, without a sacrifice in efficacy.

Alternative Treatment Techniques

ATTENTION TO UNDERSTUDIED TECHNIQUES   Most outcome research has focused on behavioral and cognitively based techniques for children and adolescents—not the interventions relied upon most heavily in clinical practice. Occasional exceptions can be noted and serve as examples that may foster similar research.

Efforts to evaluate psychoanalytic treatment reflect a positive move toward developing the empirical base of insight-oriented treatments for children. For example, Heinicke & Ramsey-Klee (1986) evaluated psychoanalytic treatment for children (7–10 years old) referred for learning disturbances and academic deficiencies. In separate groups the frequency of the treatment sessions (1 vs 4 per week) was varied. Both versions of treatment led to gains in reading and in measures related to adaptation, self-esteem, and capacity for relationships. At a one-year follow-up assessment, greater gains were evident for the treatment with more frequent sessions.

As another example, Moran & Fonagy (1987a,b) have examined psychoanalytic attempts to help children and adolescents control their diabetes. The treatment program is based on the view that disturbances of psychosexual development and/or object relations are expressed indirectly in behaviors that impair control of blood glucose concentrations. In single-case and group comparison studies, intensive psychoanalytic treatment that focuses on individually pertinent themes improved control of diabetes.

These are significant efforts to establish the empirical basis of treatment forms more traditional than those usually examined in contemporary outcome studies. The specific examples are particularly noteworthy because they attempt to operationalize conceptually complex treatments.

COMBINED TREATMENT MODALITIES   Although the research agenda with existing therapeutic techniques is quite significant, there are reasons to lobby for research that combines alternative procedures and hence focuses on new variations. To begin with, many individual techniques, even if demonstrated to produce change, may not be optimally effective in ameliorating the child's dysfunction. The limits of effectiveness of an individual technique may be especially evident for problems that are manifest in diverse domains of functioning, such as behavior problems at home and at school, academic performance, and peer relations. Combinations of treatment may add to the benefits of individual treatments by capturing a broader set of domains. Second, many children meet criteria for multiple disorders (comorbidity). Depending on the specific diagnoses, combinations of treatment may be essential.

Attention-deficit hyperactivity disorder is a prime candidate for a combined-treatment approach. Alternative medications (e.g. methylphenidate) reduce excessive activity and improve classroom deportment among youths with the disorder. However, the effects are considered short lived and insufficient against the full range of dysfunctions (Hunt et al 1987). Additional interventions, particularly those based on cognitive behavioral approaches or behavior modification, can address academic skills, cognitive processes (e.g. problem solving), and interpersonal behavior, which are less clearly improved with medication. The viable treatment combinations may be based on the domains of dysfunction that the problem entails. For example, family based treatment, individual therapy for the child, and school-based intervention might be useful and complementary (e.g. Satterfield et al 1979).

As a general approach, treatments might be viewed in a modular fashion. Interventions and their combinations might be selected from a larger treatment armamentarium based on the domains of dysfunction and other factors (e.g. age, developmental level) that must be addressed (Kazdin 1988). As yet, the specific effects and limits of generality of individual treatments are not well understood. Consequently, selection of one technique to compensate for the limits of another has to be based on rational grounds and clinical experience rather than empirical data.

The focus of combined treatments is important because it shifts the emphasis of the field from contrasting individual treatments to building effective treatment packages. However, this approach has disadvantages as well. The primary disadvantage is that at the end of an investigation one might not know which component in the package was critical to change. Nevertheless, evaluating combined treatments emphasizes the initial priority of establishing maximally effective treatment. Additional research can isolate critical mechanisms once such a treatment has been demonstrated.

Outcome Evaluation

REDUCING SYMPTOMS AND INCREASING PROSOCIAL FUNCTIONING The impetus for seeking treatment is usually the presence of symptoms, or maladaptive, disturbing, or disruptive behaviors. Naturally, the effects of treatment are measured by the extent to which the problems identified at the outset of treatment are reduced. Prosocial functioning of the child is rarely assessed at pretreatment or used as a basis to examine outcome. Prosocial functioning refers to the presence of positive adaptive behaviors and experiences such as participation in activities, social interaction, and making friends. With children and adolescents, adjustment may depend heavily on the positive adaptive behaviors or skills, given the significance of the peer group and prosocial experiences outside the home.

Reducing symptoms can be assumed to improve functioning, but the absence of symptoms does not assure the presence of prosocial behaviors. The overlap of symptom reduction and positive prosocial functioning appears to be modest. For example, in one treatment study, child symptoms (encompassing a wide array of dysfunctions) and prosocial behavior were evaluated by parents on a standardized parent rating scale (Kazdin et al 1989). The correlation between symptom severity and prosocial behavior was low ($r = -.31$), indicating relatively little (9.6%) shared variance. Over the course of treatment, change in symptoms did not correlate highly with changes in prosocial behavior ($r = -.17$). Similar results were evident when teacher evaluations of symptoms and prosocial functioning were evaluated. These results suggest the expected negative relation between symptoms and prosocial behavior, but the magnitude of the correlations indicates that symptoms and prosocial functioning are relatively independent.

Prosocial functioning may be an important indicator for treatment evaluation in several ways. Treatments that appear equally effective in reducing symptoms may vary in the extent to which they promote and develop prosocial behaviors. In addition, for children whose symptom reduction is similar, the prognosis for long-term adjustment may vary as a function of prosocial behaviors evident at treatment outcome. For these reasons, prosocial behavior warrants further attention in the evaluation of treatment outcome.

CLINICAL AND STATISTICAL SIGNIFICANCE Evaluations of treatment typically focus on statistically significant differences in outcome measures. It is also important to examine the extent to which treatment has produced an effect that is of practical significance and that makes a difference in the client's life—i.e. is clinically significant. Several measures of clinical significance have been proposed: the extent to which treatment returns clients to

normative levels of functioning, the degree to which improvement is perceptible to significant others in the client's everyday life, whether the magnitude of
change exceeds a particular cutoff (as expressed in standard deviation units),
and the elimination of the presenting problem (see Jacobson 1988; Kazdin
1977; Yeaton & Sechrest 1981). As yet no uniformly adopted procedure or
measurement strategy has been adopted to assess clinical significance.

Relatively few psychotherapy studies, whether with child or adult populations, incorporate measures designed to evaluate the clinical significance
of change. Those that do frequently measure the extent to which treated
patients are returned to normative levels of functioning. To invoke this
criterion, a comparison is made between treated patients and peers who are
functioning well or without problems in everyday life. Prior to treatment, the
patients presumably depart considerably from their well-functioning peers in
the area identified for treatment (e.g. anxiety, social withdrawal, aggression).
At the end of treatment, clinically important changes are evident if the patient
sample is indistinguishable from, or well within the range of, the sample of
well-functioning peers.

There remain many issues and ambiguities surrounding the assessment and
evaluation of clinical significance of change including the absence of agreed
upon criteria, the obstacles in identifying the appropriate reference (normative) groups, and defining realistic or achievable outcomes for various clinical
populations. For the child psychotherapy literature, it may be premature to
examine the clinical significance of change, since relatively few studies have
even begun to examine the statistical significance of changes in controlled
trials. However, the paucity of outcomes studies and the costs of their
execution increase the need to design individual studies in such a way that
their yield is maximized.

CRITICAL METHODOLOGICAL ISSUES

Although methodological issues in psychotherapy research are raised primarily in the context of adult treatment, topics such as selection of outcome
measures, utilization of alternative control conditions, means of addressing
attrition, and others are relevant to evaluation of child treatment as well.
Several methodological issues are particularly critical in outcome research for
childhood and adolescent disorders and have marked impact on conclusions
about treatment effectiveness.

Identification of Clinical Dysfunction

In most treatment studies, children are referred to informally as "emotionally
disturbed," "conduct problems," "impulsive," or "socially withdrawn."

Although such terms imply that the children suffer impairment, the severity, duration, and scope of dysfunction are rarely specified. Among the untoward consequences that result from using general and nonstandardized terms, two are salient. First, the terms foster the selection of heterogeneous cases within a given study. The variability within groups that emanates from diverse types and severity of dysfunction may decrease the likelihood of detecting treatment differences among alternative conditions; variability may mask subject × treatment interactions. Second, without an agreed upon method of referring to children, it is difficult to accumulate information about a particular clinical problem in a consistent fashion across studies.

The field would be greatly advanced by adoption of a standard way of specifying clinical problems. The use of standard diagnostic criteria [e.g. *Diagnostic and Statistical Manual of Mental Disorders* (American Psychiatric Association 1987)] and other assessment devices (e.g. Child Behavior Checklist, Revised Behavior Problem Checklist) is obviously helpful in this regard. Nevertheless, agreement among researchers to use a single diagnostic approach or specific assessment devices is unlikely. Also, "standard" diagnostic criteria periodically change and may not reflect firm ground for a long-term investment. In the absence of standard criteria, it is reasonable to demand careful documentation and operationalization of criteria for case selection. Also, clarification of the scope and severity of dysfunction relevant to nonreferred (nonclinic or "normal") age mates would greatly aid the identification of effective treatments.

Treatment Integrity

Interpretation of outcome studies depends on the integrity of treatment—i.e. that treatment was carried out as intended (Yeaton & Sechrest 1981). If treatment is not conducted correctly, the outcome effects are extremely difficult to evaluate. A pattern of no difference between two or more treatments might result from a failure to implement one or both of the treatments faithfully, or from large variation in how individual treatments are carried out. Even when two treatments differ significantly, it is important to rule out the possibility that the differences are due to variations of the integrity with which each was conducted.

The ambiguities introduced by the breakdown of treatment integrity can be illustrated by the previously discussed study that compared behavior modification, traditional group social work, and minimal treatment for antisocial children (8–17 years old) (Feldman et al 1983). In general, the type of treatment had little impact on therapeutic outcome, particularly in relation to other factors in the design, such as therapist experience and method of comprising groups. However, checks on how the conditions were executed revealed a breakdown in treatment integrity. For example, observations of treatment sessions revealed that approximately 35% of the therapists (group leaders) did not implement the behavior modification procedures appropriately; only 25% of the leaders in the social work treatment condition carried out the intervention appropriately; finally, approximately 44% of the minimal-treatment leaders carried out systematic interventions even though none was supposed to. It is difficult to draw conclusions about the relative impact of alternative treatments if the treatments have not been fairly tested. There might have been marked differences in outcome and substantially different conclusions if the treatments had been conducted as intended.

Further attention to treatment integrity is essential in outcome research. The difficulty of conducting treatment studies places increased pressure on obtaining maximally clear answers, even (if not especially) when no differences are evident between treatments in a given study. The absence of clear data on treatment integrity risks the possibility that large bodies of research and years of outcome studies can be dismissed as not providing fair and clear tests of alternative treatments (see Sechrest et al 1979).

Timing of Follow-up Assessment

Treatment outcome is invariably evaluated by administering measures immediately after treatment (posttreatment); occasionally assessment is conducted later at a point ranging from weeks to years (follow-up). Follow-up assessment is usually regarded as important for addressing the question of whether gains evident at posttreatment are maintained, but a more rudimentary efficacy issue is also involved. Conclusions about the treatment or relative effectiveness of alternative treatments may vary greatly depending on when assessments are conducted.

For example, in the school-based treatment study by Kolvin et al (1981), highlighted previously, two of the interventions (group therapy, behavior modification) provided to maladjusted children showed different effects depending on when assessment was completed. Immediately after treatment, relatively few improvements were evident for these treatments in relation to neuroticism, antisocial behavior, and total symptom scores. These areas improved markedly over the course of follow-up (approximately 18 months after treatment ended) and altered the conclusions about the impact of treatment. Several other studies involving child and adult samples point to the significance of the timing of outcome assessments (e.g. for reviews see Kazdin 1988; Wright et al 1976). In such studies, conclusions about the effectiveness of a given treatment relative to a control condition or another treatment differed at posttreatment and follow-up. Thus, the treatment that appeared more or most effective at posttreatment did not retain this status at follow-up.

Not all studies find this difference (see Nicholson & Berman 1983; Weisz et al 1987). However, it is clear that conclusions about a given treatment in any particular study may well depend on when the assessment is conducted. Of course, the number of follow-up occasions cannot be indefinite, but follow-up assessment, often viewed as a luxury, is central to the evaluation. Given the marked changes often associated with maturation, the case for follow-up assessment may be particularly strong in evaluating treatments for children and adolescents. Treatments that appear effective or differentially effective in the short run may not surpass the impact of developmental changes.

Power to Detect Group Differences

A critical research issue is the extent to which an experiment can detect differences between groups when differences exist. This notion, of course, denotes the *power of the test,* which can be estimated quantitatively.[4] Although power is an issue in all research, it raises special issues for treatment studies. For many studies, the goal may be to compare treatment with a no-treatment or waiting-list control condition. In research with children, a comparison of treatment versus no treatment needs to be considered more cautiously. Depending on the age of the children and the specific dysfunction, marked improvements may occur with no formal treatment. If improvements are likely without treatment, the difficulty in identifying differences between groups may be great.

Considerations related to the power of the investigation become especially salient when outcome studies evaluate two or more active treatments. When both interventions are expected to produce change, the investigation must be sufficiently powerful to detect what might prove to be relatively small differences. A recent evaluation of comparative outcome research studies has indicated that effect sizes when two treatments are compared tend to be in the small-to-medium range (see Kazdin & Bass 1989).[5] To achieve a power of .80, most studies would need to include 35–230 subjects per group or condition. This range is larger than the usual sample size (median=12 subjects per group) in treatment outcome studies. Thus, the frequently noted conclusion that treatments are not differentially effective might well be related to the weak power of the evaluations used.

The importance of considering power in advance of designing an investigation has been discussed frequently, and helpful guidelines are available (e.g. Cohen 1988). The use of such guidelines requires estimation of the likely differences (effect size) among treatment and control conditions. Investigators

---

[4]Power refers to the probability of rejecting the null hypothesis when it is false. Stated differently, power is the likelihood of finding differences between treatments tested when their outcomes truly differ. The power of a test (1-beta) is a function of sample size (n), the significance level (alpha), and the differences between the conditions compared (effect size).

seem to be reluctant to guess the likely effect size in advance. They often choose sample sizes based on other considerations, such as precedent, even though the option of providing more informed estimates of the requisite sample size is available. Approximations of the likely effect sizes between alternative treatments or treatment and control conditions can be obtained from meta-analyses of psychotherapy (e.g. Casey & Berman 1985; Weisz et al 1987). Once effect size is estimated, guidelines for sample sizes are easily obtained.

Of course the power of a test goes beyond considerations of effect size to include sample size and the significance level. Because effect size depends on within-group variability of the observations, any facet of the experiment that can reduce this variability can augment power. Attention to methodological issues such as treatment integrity and selection of a homogeneous set of subjects can increase the precision of the test by reducing extraneous variability.

CURRENT STATUS

The Effectiveness of Therapy

A number of well-designed individual studies, programs of research, and large-scale evaluations show treatment is more effective than no treatment for a variety of problems of children and adolescents. Perhaps the significance of this rather general statement can only be appreciated in historical context. Whether treatment for children and adolescents is more effective than changes due to maturation and other influences associated with the passage of time has long been debated. Against this backdrop, firm evidence from controlled studies of treatment is significant. Nevertheless, one would like to reach more specific conclusions. For whom is treatment effective, for what clinical problems, with what interventions, and under what conditions? Such questions cannot yet be answered because the seeds for carefully conducted and informative research have been planted only recently and the methodological and theoretical soil has suffered years of drought. Tentative conclusions have been drawn from large-scale reviews (e.g. behavioral techniques tend to be more effective than nonbehavioral techniques; treatments tend to be more effective for children than for adolescents), but these more specific results are hazardous and easily debated. More carefully designed studies and more

---

[5]Cohen (1988) has provided guidelines for small, medium and large effect size as .2, .5, and .8, respectively. Effect size is determined by:

$$\frac{m_1 - m_2}{S}$$

where m_1 and m_2 refer to two group means and S is a standard deviation.

elaborate evaluations and definitions of treatment outcome are needed to reach the level of specificity required to guide clinical work.

Obstacles to Research

Important progress has been made, and the field seems poised to make advances in addressing the more specific questions; but it is also critical to acknowledge many obstacles to progress. In developmental psychopathology many basic issues that serve as the foundation for treatment research are far from resolution. (Kazdin 1989). Questions regarding the classification and course of various disorders and the methods of assessing dysfunction types are fundamental to treatment evaluation because they involve patient selection, treatment focus, and outcome evaluation. Although advances in these areas are ongoing, treatment evaluation must proceed without the benefit of clear, agreed upon selection or outcome criteria, and often without well-validated measures of effectiveness.

Although treatment research is invariably complex, the investigation of children and adolescents raises special issues. Developmental considerations (e.g. many problem behaviors, such as destructiveness, lying, and fears, wax and wane over the course of development and then typically disappear) make the discrimination of some problematic behaviors from normal development difficult. Also, the fact that children rarely refer themselves for treatment and may not consider themselves in need of treatment once referred poses obstacles regarding treatment delivery and evaluation. No less significant than these obstacles is the wide range of problems that children and adolescents bring to treatment. As adults do, children present many identifiable disorders (e.g. depression, anxiety); but many other types of problems emerge as well. Children are often victims, as in cases of abuse and neglect. Sometimes children react adversely to life events (e.g. divorce, death) that occur at critical periods of developmental vulnerability. These obstacles raise fundamental questions about the most useful focus of diagnosis, assessment, and treatment.

The evaluation of treatment in outcome studies is inherently difficult. The difficulty stems from the amount of time it may take to develop, implement, and evaluate treatment. Critical areas of delay include recruitment of a sufficient number of patients, retention of these in treatment, and assessment after treatment and at some point in the future (e.g. one year follow-up). The long period such an evaluation requires has implications for individual investigators as well for the field as a whole. It is unlikely that an investigator will be able to conduct a number of studies on a given technique or that the field will enjoy the benefits of multiple replications. The costly and slow process precludes rapid accretion of a body of knowledge on a given treatment.

Because individual studies are not easily repeated and because multiple techniques, clinical problems, and patients groups are in need of research, there is a special premium on the design of individual studies. Critical methodological features such as careful specification of patient dysfunction, assessment of multiple domains of functioning, evaluation of treatment integrity, evaluations of clinical significance of change, and follow-up are essential to maximize the yield from individual investigations.

CONCLUSIONS

In the three decades since early reviews began to appear, major advances have been made in child and adolescent therapy. The number of studies, the quality of the evidence, and the range of techniques have all increased remarkably. Evidence shows that many types of intervention alleviate suffering in children and their families, but many questions remain about the persons to whom and the dysfunctions to which treatment can effectively be applied.

Treatment research is essential given the serious needs of children and adolescents. However, advances depend upon accretion of knowledge in many areas that elaborate how the psychosocial and biological determinants of adaptive and maladaptive behavior converge and evolve over development. In addition, many of the tools for evaluating treatments, such as assessment instruments for particular sorts of dysfunctions and criteria for evaluating change, have evolved to improve the quality of studies that can be completed.

The present chapter has focused on child and adolescent psychotherapy and the current status of treatment outcome research. It is important to place this work in a larger context. The burden of mental illness, psychological impairment, and maladjustment of children and adolescents is great. Psychotherapy serves as one class of intervention. Other efforts are also relevant. Specific types of treatment facilities (psychiatric hospitals, residential treatment settings, and educational settings) as well as alternative interventions (medications, foster care placement, and family assistance programs) are directed toward many of the same ends as psychotherapy. Interventions directed toward prevention of disorders of childhood and adolescence are critical to the overall effort as well.

Psychotherapy is one facet of the overall effort to controvert dysfunctions and to improve adjustment of children and adolescents. Its advances have been, at the very least, respectable. However, in the larger scheme, the effort toward which psychotherapy is directed is in dire need of further work. Not only must effective treatments be identified, but services must be extended to the majority of children and adolescents in need of care but not seen.

ACKNOWLEDGMENTS

Completion of this paper was facilitated by a Research Scientist Development Award (MH00353) from the National Institute of Mental Health and a grant on the evaluation of treatments for children and adolescents from The Robert Wood Johnson Foundation.

Literature Cited

American Psychiatric Association. 1987. *Diagnostic and Statistical Manual of Mental Disorders—Revised.* Washington, DC: Am. Psychiatr. Assoc.

Anderson, J. C., Williams, S., McGee, R., Silva, P. A. 1987. The prevalence of DSM III disorders in pre-adolescent children: prevalence in a large sample from the general population. *Arch. Gen. Psychiatry* 44:69–76

Arbuthnot, J., Gordon, D. A. 1986. Behavioral and cognitive effects of a moral reasoning development intervention for high-risk behavior-disordered adolescents. *J. Consult. Clin. Psychol.* 54:208–16

Barrett, C. L., Hampe, I. E., Miller, L. C. 1978. Research on child psychotherapy. In *Handbook of Psychotherapy and Behavior Change: An Empirical Analysis*, ed. S. L. Garfield, A. E. Bergin, pp. 411–35. New York: Wiley & Sons. 2nd ed.

Baum, C. G., Forehand, R. 1981. Long-term follow-up assessment of parent training by use of multiple outcome measures. *Behav. Ther.* 12:643–52

Berlin, I. N. 1986. Psychopathology and its antecedents among American Indian adolescents. *Adv. Clin. Child Psychol.* 9:125–52

Bird, H. R., Canino, G., Rubio-Stipec, M., Gould, M. S., Ribera, J., Sesman, M., et al. 1988. Estimates of the prevalence of childhood maladjustment in a community survey of Puerto Rico: the use of combined measures. *Arch. Gen. Psychiatry* 45:1120–26

Bornstein, P. H., Kazdin, A. E., eds. 1985. *Handbook of Clinical Behavior Therapy with Children.* Homewood, IL: Dorsey

Brown, J. 1987. A review of meta-analyses conducted on psychotherapy outcome research. *Clin. Psychol. Rev.* 7:1–23

Camp, B. W., Bash, M. A. S. 1985. *Think Aloud: Increasing Social and Cognitive Skills—A Problem Solving Program for Children.* Champaign, IL: Research Press

Canino, I. A., Gould, M. S., Prupis, S., Shaffer, D. 1986. A comparison of symptoms and diagnoses of Hispanic and black children in an outpatient mental health clinic.

J. Am. Acad. Child Psychiatry 25:254–59

Casey, R. J., Berman, J. S. 1985. The outcome of psychotherapy with children. *Psychol. Bull.* 98:388–400

Cohen, J. 1988. *Statistical Power Analysis for the Behavioral Sciences.* New York: Academic 2nd ed.

Costantino, G., Malgady, R. G., Rogler, L. H. 1986. Cuento therapy: a culturally sensitive modality for Puerto Rican children. *J. Consult. Clin. Psychol.* 54:639–45

DeLeon, P. H., VandenBos, G. R., Cummings, N. A. 1983. Psychotherapy—Is it safe, effective, and appropriate? *Am. Psychol.* 38:907–11

Eisenberg, L., Gruenberg, E. M. 1961. The current status of secondary prevention in child psychiatry. *Am. J. Orthopsychiatry* 31:355–67

Eyberg, S. M., Johnson, S. M. 1974. Multiple assessment of behavior modification with families: effects on contingency contracting and order of treated problems. *J. Consult. Clin. Psychol.* 42:594–606

Eysenck, H. J. 1952. The effects of psychotherapy: an evaluation. *J. Consult. Psychol.* 16:319–24

Feldman, R. A., Caplinger, T. E., Wodarski, J. S. 1983. *The St. Louis Conundrum: The Effective Treatment of Antisocial Youths.* Englewood Cliffs, NJ: Prentice-Hall

Fleischman, M. J., Szykula, S. A. 1981. A community setting replication of a social learning treatment for aggressive children. *Behav. Ther.* 12:115–22

Forehand, R., Long, N. 1988. Outpatient treatment of the acting out child: procedures, long-term follow-up data, and clinical problems. *Adv. Behav. Res. Ther.* 10:129–77

Gard, G. C., Berry, K. K. 1986. Oppositional children: taming tyrants. *J. Clin. Child Psychol.* 15:148–58

Garfield, S. L. 1980. *Psychotherapy: An Eclectic Approach.* New York: Wiley & Sons

Garfield, S. L. 1983. Effectiveness of psychotherapy: the perennial controversy. *Prof. Psychol.* 14:35–43

Garfield, S. L., Bergin, A. E., eds. 1986. *Handbook of Psychotherapy and Behavior Change: An Empirical Analysis*. New York: Wiley & Sons. 3rd. ed.

Glass, G. V., McGaw, B., Smith, M. L. 1981. *Meta-analysis in Social Research*. Beverly Hills, CA: Sage

Gould, M. S., Wunsch-Hitzig, R., Dohrenwend, B. P. 1980. Formulation of hypotheses about the prevalence, treatment, and prognostic significance of psychiatric disorders in children in the United States. In *Mental Illness in the United States: Epidemiological Estimates*, ed. B. P. Dohrenwend, B. S. Dohrenwend, M. S. Gould, B. Link, R. Neugebauer, R. Wunsch-Hitzig, pp. 9–44. New York: Praeger

Hazelrigg, M. D., Cooper, H. M., Borduin, C. M. 1987. Evaluating the effectiveness of family therapies: an integrative review and analysis. *Psychol. Bull.* 101:428–42

Heimberg, R. G., Becker, R. E. 1984. Comparative outcome research. In *Issues in Psychotherapy Research*, ed. M. Hersen, L. Michelson, A. S. Bellack, pp. 251–83. New York: Plenum

Heinicke, C. M., Goldman, A. 1960. Research on psychotherapy with children: a review and suggestions for further study. *Am. J. Orthopsychiatry* 30:483–94

Heinicke, C. M., Ramsey-Klee, D. M. 1986. Outcome of child psychotherapy as a function of frequency of session. *J. Am. Acad. Child Psychiatry* 25:247–53

Heinicke, C. M., Strassmann, L. H. 1975. Toward more effective research on child psychotherapy. *J. Am. Acad. Child Psychiatry* 14:561–88

Hobbs, S. A., Lahey, B. B. 1983. Behavioral treatment, In *Handbook of Child Psychopathology*, ed. T. H. Ollendick, M. Hersen, pp. 427–60. New York: Plenum

Hoghughi, M. 1988. *Treating Problem Children: Issues, Methods and Practice*. Newbury Park, CA: Sage

Hood-Williams, J. 1960. The results of psychotherapy with children: a reevaluation. *J. Consult. Psychol.* 24:84–88

Hunt, R. D., Brunstetter, R. W., Silver, L. B. 1987. Attention deficit disorder: clinical evaluation and treatment. In *Basic Handbook of Child Psychiatry*, ed. J. D. Noshpitz, 5:483–94. New York: Basic Books

Jacobson, N. S., ed. 1988. Special issue: defining clinically significant change. *Behav. Assess.* 10: whole issue

Johnson, J. H., Rasbury, W. C., Siegel, L. J. 1986. *Approaches to Child Treatment: Introduction to Theory, Research, and Practice*. New York: Pergamon

Kazdin, A. E. 1977. Assessing the clinical or applied importance of behavior change through social validation. *Behav. Mod.* 1:427–52

Kazdin, A. E. 1985. *Treatment of Antisocial Behavior in Children and Adolescents*. Homewood, IL: Dorsey Press

Kazdin, A. E. 1986a. Comparative outcome studies of psychotherapy: methodological issues and strategies. *J. Consult. Clin. Psychol.* 54:95–105

Kazdin, A. E. 1986b. The evaluation of psychotherapy: research design and methodology. See Garfield & Bergin 1986, pp. 23–68

Kazdin, A. E. 1987. Treatment of antisocial behavior in children: current status and future directions. *Psychol. Bull.* 102:187–203

Kazdin, A. E. 1988. *Child Psychotherapy: Developing and Identifying Effective Treatments*. New York: Pergamon

Kazdin, A. E. 1989. Developmental psychopathology: current research, issues, and directions. *Am. Psychol.* 44:180–87

Kazdin, A. E., Bass, D. 1989. Power to detect differences between alternative treatments in comparative psychotherapy outcome research. *J. Consult. Clin. Psychol.* 57:138–47

Kazdin, A. E., Bass, D., Siegel, T., Thomas, C. 1989. Cognitive-behavioral treatment and relationship therapy in the treatment of children referred for antisocial behavior. *J. Consult. Clin. Psychol.* In press

Kazdin, A. E., Esveldt-Dawson, K., French, N. H., Unis, A. S. 1987. Problem-solving skills training and relationship therapy in the treatment of antisocial child behavior. *J. Consult. Clin. Psychol.* 55:76–85

Kendall, P. C., Braswell, L. 1982. Cognitive-behavioral self-control therapy for children: a components analysis. *J. Consult. Clin. Psychol.* 50:672–89

Kendall, P. C., Braswell, L. 1985. *Cognitive-Behavioral Therapy for Impulsive Children*. New York: Guilford

Knitzer, J. 1982. *Unclaimed Children: The Failure of Public Responsibility to Children and Adolescents in Need of Mental Health Services*. Washington, DC: Children's Defense Fund

Kolvin, I., Garside, R. F., Nicol, A. R., MacMillan, A., Wolstenholme, F., Leitch, I. M. 1981. *Help Starts Here: The Maladjusted Child in the Ordinary School*. London: Tavistock

Koocher, G. P., Pedulla, B. M. 1977. Current practices in child psychotherapy. *Prof. Psychol.* 8:275–87

Kovacs, M., Paulauskas, S. 1986. The traditional psychotherapies. In *Psychopathological Disorders of Childhood*, ed. H. C. Quay, J. S. Werry, pp. 496–522. New York: Wiley & Sons. 3rd ed.

Lambert, M. J., Christensen, E. R., DeJulio,

S. S., eds. 1983. *The Assessment of Psychotherapy Outcome.* New York: Wiley & Sons

Levitt, E. E. 1957. The results of psychotherapy with children: an evaluation. *J. Consult. Psychol.* 21:189–96

Levitt, E. E. 1963. Psychotherapy with children: a further evaluation. *Behav. Res. Ther.* 60:326–29

Lochman, J. E., Burch, P. R., Curry, J. F., Lampron, L. B. 1984. Treatment and generalization effects of cognitive-behavioral and goal-setting interventions with aggressive boys. *J. Consult. Clin. Psychol.* 52:915–16

Maher, A. R. 1988. Discovery-oriented psychotherapy research: rationale, aims, and methods. *Am. Psychol.* 43:694–702

Matt, G. E. 1989. Decision rules for selecting effect sizes in meta-analysis: a review and reanalysis of psychotherapy outcome studies. *Psychol. Bull.* 105:106–15

Meador, A. E., Ollendick, T. H. 1984. Cognitive behavior therapy with children: an evaluation of its efficacy and clinical utility. *Child Fam. Behav. Ther.* 6:25–44

Michelson, L. 1985. Editorial: introduction and commentary. *Clin. Psychol. Rev.* 5:1–2

Moran, G. S., Fonagy, P. 1987a. Psychoanalysis and diabetic control: a single-case study. *Br. J. Med. Psychol.* 60:57–72

Moran, G. S., Fonagy, P. 1987b. *Insight and symptomatic improvement.* Paper presented at the Workshop on Psychotherapy Outcome Research with Children, Natl. Inst. Mental Health, Bethesda, MD

Moreland, J. R., Schwebel, A. I., Beck, S., Wells, R. 1982. Parents as therapists: a review of the behavior therapy parent training literature—1975 to 1981. *Behav. Modif.* 6:250–76

Morris, R. J., Kratochwill, T. R., eds. 1983. *The Practice of Child Therapy.* New York: Pergamon

Nicholson, R. A., Berman, J. S. 1983. Is follow-up necessary in evaluating psychotherapy? *Psychol. Bull.* 93:555–65

Ollendick, T. H., Cerny, J. A. 1981. *Clinical Behavior Therapy with Children.* New York: Plenum

Patterson, G. R. 1974. Interventions for boys with conduct problems: multiple settings, treatments, and criteria. *J. Consult Clin. Psychol.* 42:471–81

Patterson, G. R. 1982. *Coercive Family Process.* Eugene, OR: Castalia

Patterson, G. R. 1986. Performance models for antisocial boys. *Am. Psychol.* 41:432–44

Patterson, G. R., Chamberlain, P., Reid, J. B. 1982. A comparative evaluation of a parent-training program. *Behav. Ther.* 13:638–50

Paul, G. L. 1967. Outcome research in psychotherapy. *J. Consult. Psychol.* 31:109–18

President's Commission on Mental Health Task Panel Reports, Vols. I–II. 1978. Washington, DC: USGPO

Prioleau, L., Murdock, M., Brody, N. 1983. An analysis of psychotherapy versus placebo studies. *Behav. Brain Sci.* 6:275–310

Reynolds, W. M. 1985. Depression in childhood and adolescence: diagnosis, assessment, intervention strategies, and research. In *Advances in School Psychology,* ed. T. R. Kratochwill, 4:133–89. Hillsdale, NJ: Erlbaum

Satterfield, J. H., Cantwell, D. P., Satterfield, B. T. 1979. Multimodality treatment: a one-year follow-up of 84 hyperactive boys. *Arch. Gen. Psychiatry* 36:965–74

Sechrest, L., White, S. O., Brown, E. D. 1979. *The Rehabilitation of Criminal Offenders: Problems and Prospects.* Washington, DC: Natl. Acad. Sci.

Shirk, S. R., ed. 1988. *Cognitive Development and Child Psychotherapy.* New York: Plenum

Smith, M. L., Glass, G. V. 1977. Meta-analysis of psychotherapy outcome studies. *Am. Psychol.* 32:752–60

Smith, M. L., Glass, G. V., Miller, T. I. 1980. *The Benefits of Psychotherapy.* Baltimore, MD: Johns Hopkins Univ. Press

Sowder, B. J. 1975. *Assessment of Child Mental Health Needs,* Vols. I–VIII. McLean, VA: General Res. Corp.

Spivack, G., Platt, J. J., Shure, M. B. 1976. *The Problem-Solving Approach to Adjustment.* San Francisco: Jossey-Bass

Spivack, G., Shure, M. B. 1982. The cognition of social adjustment: interpersonal cognitive problem solving thinking. *Adv. Clin. Child Psychol.* 5:323–72

Stiles, W. B., Shapiro, D. A., Elliott, R. 1986. Are all psychotherapies equivalent? *Am. Psychol.* 41:165–80

Sue, D., Sue, S. 1987. Cultural factors in the clinical assessment of Asian Americans. *J. Consult. Clin. Psychol.* 55:479–87

Szapocznik, J., Scopetta, M. A., King, O. E. 1978. Theory and practice in matching treatments to the special characteristics and problems of Cuban immigrants. *J. Commun. Psychol.* 6:112–22

Tuma, J. M. 1989. Mental health services for children: the state of the art. *Am. Psychol.* 44:188–99

Tuma, J. M., Pratt, J. M. 1982. Clinical child psychology practice and training: a survey. *J. Clin. Child Psychol.* 11:27–34

Tuma, J. M., Sobotka, K. R. 1983. Traditional therapies with children. In *Handbook of Child Psychopathology,* ed. T. H. Ollendick, M. Hersen, pp. 391–426. New York: Plenum

United States Congress, Office of Technology Assessment. 1986. *Children's Mental Health: Problems and Services—A Background Paper*. Washington, DC: USGPO

Walrond-Skinner, S. 1986. *Dictionary of Psychotherapy*. London: Routledge & Kegan Paul

Walter, H. I., Gilmore, S. K. 1973. Placebo versus social learning effects in parent training procedures designed to alter the behavior of aggressive boys. *Behav. Ther.* 4:361–77

Weisz, J. R., Weiss, B., Alicke, M. D., Klotz, M. L. 1987. Effectiveness of psychotherapy with children and adolescents: Meta-analytic findings for clinicians. *J. Consult. Clin. Psychol.* 55:542–49

Wells, K. C., Forehand, R., Griest, D. L. 1980. Generality of treatment effects from treated to untreated behaviors resulting from a parent training program. *J. Clin. Child Psychol.* 9:217–19

Wiltz, N. A., Patterson, G. R. 1974. An evaluation of parent training procedures designed to alter inappropriate aggressive behavior of boys. *Behav. Ther.* 5:215–21

Wright, D. M., Moelis, I., Pollack, L. J. 1976. The outcome of individual child psychotherapy: increments at follow-up. *J. Child Psychol. Psychiatry* 17:275–85

Yeaton, W. H., Sechrest, L. 1981. Critical dimensions in the choice and maintenance of successful treatments: strength, integrity, and effectiveness. *J. Consult. Clin. Psychol.* 49:156–67

Annu. Rev. Psychol. 1990. 41:55–80

HEMISPHERIC ASYMMETRY

Joseph B. Hellige

Department of Psychology, University of Southern California, Los Angeles, California 90089-1061

CONTENTS

INTRODUCTION

The left and right cerebral hemispheres of humans differ in their information processing abilities and propensities. While hemispheric asymmetries have been known to exist for centuries, the upsurge of interest in them during the last 25 years can be traced to the pioneering work with commissurotomy (i.e. split-brain) patients reported by Roger Sperry, Michael Gazzaniga, and their

55

0066-4308/90/0201-0055$02.00

colleagues (e.g. Gazzaniga 1985; Sperry et al 1969). The vivid demonstrations of hemispheric asymmetry provided by this research captured the imagination of both scientists and the lay public. As a result, we have witnessed a nearly geometric increase in the number of published articles dealing with aspects of hemispheric asymmetry. With the increase in research has come the realization that aspects of hemispheric asymmetry have implications for a variety of topics in psychology and related disciplines. The new status conveyed by this realization is acknowledged by the inclusion of a chapter on hemispheric asymmetry in the present series.

Here I selectively review and evaluate the current status of research on the information processing differences between the left and right cerebral hemispheres. I emphasize research published within the last decade or so; the references given provide excellent entry points into research reported before that time. I cite theoretical developments that illustrate the relevance of hemispheric asymmetry for broad topics in psychology, and note the most promising directions for future research.

HEMISPHERIC ASYMMETRIES IN HUMANS

Behavioral Asymmetries

Information processing differences between the left and right hemispheres of humans have been studied using a variety of populations and research techniques. I begin by reviewing these techniques, citing sources that discuss the methodological issues involved in each case to make inferences about hemispheric asymmetry.

The oldest strategy for learning about hemispheric asymmetry is the observation of patients with brain injury restricted to one hemisphere or the other. With appropriate care, one can make inferences about the functional significance of a region of the cortex by observing what functions are impaired when that region is damaged (see chapters by Hellige, by Caramazza & Martin, and by Meier & Thompson in Hellige 1983). Indeed, it was the noting of relationships between injury to particular regions of the left hemisphere and specific language disorders that led Broca (1861) and Wernicke (1874) to postulate the importance of the temporoparietal area of the left hemisphere for language.

Very dramatic demonstrations of hemispheric asymmetry have come from the study of patients whose hemispheres have been surgically disconnected for the treatment of severe epilepsy (the so-called split-brain patients). By using appropriate techniques of stimulus presentation and response measurement it is possible in these patients to observe the functioning of each hemisphere in isolation, what Zaidel (in Hellige 1983) calls the "positive competence" of each hemisphere. Care must be taken when generalizing from these patients to neurologically normal individuals (e.g. Bradshaw & Nettleton 1983; Gazzaniga 1985; Hellige 1983; Whitaker & Ojemann 1977).

In addition, a variety of techniques have enabled investigation of hemispheric asymmetry in neurologically normal individuals. In fact, the availability of such techniques led to the proliferation of research on hemispheric asymmetry. One strategy is to present stimuli so that they reach only one hemisphere directly and then measure performance as a function of which hemisphere is stimulated. Of course, in the normal brain information can be passed from one hemisphere to the other, and this can create problems of interpretation (see Bryden 1982; Bradshaw & Nettleton 1983; Hellige 1983); but with appropriate caution these techniques are useful. In the auditory modality the typical strategy is to present two different stimuli simultaneously, one to each ear. With such dichotic presentation there is evidence that the stimulus presented to one ear projects primarily or exclusively to the contralateral cerebral hemisphere. When appropriate care is taken in the design of such studies, ear differences reflect hemispheric asymmetry (e.g. Bryden 1982; Hellige 1983; Hugdahl 1988). Another strategy is to project visual stimuli briefly to the left or right of an observer's fixation point. In the human visual system, stimuli from each visual field project exclusively to the contralateral cerebral hemisphere. Consequently, in appropriately designed studies visual half-field differences are influenced by hemispheric asymmetry. [For discussion of the use of visual half-field techniques in the study of hemispheric asymmetry, see the special issue of *Brain and Cognition* (1986, *Vol. 5, No. 2*), Bryden (1982), and Beaumont (1982).] Tactile identification studies take advantage of the fact that tactile information presented to one hand is presented primarily or exclusively to the contralateral cerebral hemisphere (e.g. O'Boyle et al 1987).

An additional strategy used to study hemispheric asymmetry in neurologically normal individuals measures responses generated by one hemisphere or the other and examines response asymmetry as a function of the cognitive activity being undertaken. Such studies have involved motor responses of the fingers and other limbs (e.g. see the chapter by Kinsbourne & Hiscock in Hellige 1983; Friedman et al 1988), eye and head turning (e.g. Ehrlichman & Weinberger 1978), electrophysiological measures taken at the scalp (e.g. see the chapter by Gevins in Hellige 1983 and the chapter by Molfese in Kitterle 1989), and measures of regional cerebral blood flow (e.g. see the chapters by Wood in Hellige 1983 and in Kitterle 1989; and the chapter by Risberg in Ottoson 1987).

I will now consider those asymmetries (of the many suggested) that have been most well-established by converging evidence from a number of the techniques described above. The findings described are characteristic of right-handed individuals. Non-right-handers are considered in a later section.

The most well-established asymmetry is left-hemisphere dominance in the production of speech. From clinical neurological data it is estimated that the production of speech is limited to the left hemisphere in 95% or so of right-handers (e.g. see the chapter by Segalowitz & Bryden in Segalowitz 1983). This asymmetry in the production of speech is corroborated in studies with split-brain patients (see Gazzaniga 1985). There is also converging evidence from both patient populations and neurologically normal individuals that the left-hemisphere is dominant in many aspects of language perception and verbal processing of stimulus material (for reviews see Bradshaw & Nettleton 1981, 1983; Bryden 1982; Hellige 1983; Springer & Deutsch 1985). However, unlike speech production (which the right hemisphere may not be able to accomplish at all), the left-hemispheric superiority in the recognition of verbally processed stimuli is more a matter of degree. This does not necessarily mean that the two hemispheres use the same mode of processing to recognize verbal stimuli. In fact, the two hemispheres often process stimuli in qualitatively different ways, with the mode of processing favored by one hemisphere sometimes being superior to the mode of processing favored by the other (e.g. Bradshaw & Nettleton 1983; Levy et al 1983; chapters by Hellige in Ottoson 1987, and in Kitterle 1989).

Although no one has yet discovered an instance of right-hemisphere dominance that is as complete as left-hemisphere dominance for speech production, converging evidence now suggests that the right hemisphere is superior to the left for certain aspects of visuospatial and manipulospatial processing, discussed below (e.g. Bryden 1982; Bradshaw & Nettleton 1981, 1983; Kosslyn 1987; the chapter by Meier & Thompson in Hellige 1983). It has been argued also that the right hemisphere is superior to the left in the recognition of faces (for review see de Schonen & Mathivet 1989), but this is not uniformly true and may have more to do with right-hemisphere superiority in visuospatial processing than with face recognition per se (e.g. Sergent 1987a). The right hemisphere is also superior to the left for the production and perception of emotion; this seems to be true over and above any right-hemisphere superiority for manipulo- and visuospatial processing (e.g. Bryden 1982; Bradshaw & Nettleton 1983; Bowers et al 1985). Given that unilateral neglect is far more frequent after right-hemisphere injury than after left-hemisphere injury (e.g. Heilman & Valenstein 1985), it appears that the right-hemisphere is also more involved than the left in the distribution of attention across space (e.g. Kosslyn 1987).

The Nature of Hemispheric Asymmetry

It is tempting to postulate a fundamental hemispheric dichotomy that defines information processing differences between the two hemispheres. Implicit in the search for such a fundamental dichotomy is the assumption that the information processing functions of one cerebral hemisphere are all similar at some level (e.g. Stillings et al 1987). So far no fundamental dichotomy has been found and there is reason to doubt that one exists.

One of the first fundamental dichotomies suggested was between verbal (left) and nonverbal (right) capacities. When it became clear that the verbal/ nonverbal nature of the stimulus was not the fundamental factor, it was suggested that the critical characteristic was whether or not the stimuli were *processed* in a verbal manner. While it was clearly a step in the right direction to emphasize processing differences rather than stimulus differences, the verbal/nonverbal dichotomy was rejected as the number of counterexamples grew (e.g. left-hemisphere superiority for certain nonverbal tasks; for examples and a discussion of these points see Allen 1983, Bryden 1982; Bradshaw & Nettleton 1981, 1983;). Several dichotomies were suggested in its place. The most widely accepted idea was that the left hemisphere is specialized for "analytic" processing, the right for "holistic" processing. Perhaps the strongest case for an analytic/holistic dichotomy has been made by Bradshaw & Nettleton (1981, 1983). In fact, this hypothesis has such intuitive appeal that it is still frequently presented as capturing the fundamental difference between the hemispheres (e.g. Anderson 1985; Stillings et al 1987).

However, the analytic/holistic dichotomy was immediately called into question (e.g. see the commentary that accompanies Bradshaw & Nettleton 1981). The primary problem is that the analytic/holistic distinction has not been operationalized sufficiently to make empirical tests possible: Researchers often disagree about whether a task requires analytic or holistic processing. Given the variety of tasks that evidence hemispheric asymmetries, it may be impossible to collapse the results into any single well-defined dichotomy.

Instead of expecting a single information processing dimension to account for all hemispheric asymmetries, we can test for such a dimension empirically. One strategy is to have the same individuals perform a variety of tasks (chosen because they are known to produce reliable and valid hemispheric asymmetries) and then to determine whether laterality on one task is related to laterality on the others. For example, suppose that each of two tasks, A and B, produces a left-hemisphere superiority in 80 of 100 individuals tested. For the sake of simplicity, assume that individuals who do not show a left-hemisphere superiority show a right-hemisphere superiority. By testing the same 100 individuals on both tasks, we can look at the number of individuals who fall into each cell of a 2 × 2 table defined by whether the individual showed a left-hemisphere or a right-hemisphere advantage for each task. Suppose we obtain the following results: left-hemisphere advantage for both tasks, 64 subjects; right-hemisphere advantage for both tasks, 4 subjects; left-hemisphere advantage for Task A and right-hemisphere advantage for Task B,

16 subjects; right-hemisphere advantage for Task A and left-hemisphere advantage for Task B, 16 subjects. Given this pattern of results, is it likely that the overall left-hemisphere advantage for the two tasks occurs because both tasks tap into one side of the same fundamental dichotomy?

At first glance this seems reasonable because both tasks produce the same laterality effect. However, if both tasks produce a left-hemisphere advantage for the same reason, then individuals who show a left-hemisphere advantage for Task A will be more likely to show a left-hemisphere advantage for Task B than will individuals who show a right-hemisphere advantage for Task A. That is, hemispheric differences for the two tasks should be correlated positively; but in the example given, the probability that the two tasks produce an advantage for the same hemisphere (either both left or both right) is exactly the value predicted by assuming that laterality for one task is completely independent of laterality for the other. Thus it is unlikely that the left-hemisphere advantages for the two tasks are produced by a single underlying dichotomy. Of course, it is possible to test for this type of independence using other measures, such as correlation coefficients between laterality indexes that preserve both the magnitude and direction of asymmetry. Such techniques as factor analysis and principal components analysis are likewise useful.

Despite the potential value of multi-task studies, only a few such reports have reached the literature. Most of these show weak or no relationships between asymmetries for two tasks (e.g. Dagenbach 1986; Hellige et al 1988a; see Bryden 1982 for similar logic applied to whether left- and right-hemisphere superiorities are complementary or independent). Thus it appears unlikely on empirical grounds that a single dichotomous information processing dimension underlies all hemispheric asymmetries.

A Computational Approach to Hemispheric Asymmetry

Even relatively simple tasks require the coordination of a number of information processing subsystems or modules (e.g. Anderson 1985; Stillings et al 1987). The hemisphere that is dominant for one subsystem may not be dominant for all others involved in the task (e.g. Allen 1983). For example, in a memory-scanning task with letters I (Hellige 1980) found a left visual field/right hemisphere advantage for encoding a visually presented probe letter but a right visual field/left hemisphere advantage for memory comparison. As a result, the hemispheric advantage that emerged depended on the relative difficulty of stimulus encoding (manipulated by perceptually degrading the probe stimulus on some trials) and memory comparison (manipulated by varying memory set size from 2 to 5 letters).

The fact that hemispheric asymmetry can vary from subsystem to subsystem within a task suggests that such asymmetry is best studied in terms of relevant subsystems. It is particularly worthwhile to consider subsystems or modules postulated by contemporary computational models of perception, cognition, and action. The existence of certain asymmetries can have important implications for the refinement of computational models, as discussed in a subsequent section of this chapter. The remainder of this section reviews three promising illustrations of this approach.

The quality of stimulus input is important for determining hemispheric asymmetry in visual information processing. For many tasks that use visual stimuli, reducing perceptual quality by utilizing masking stimuli, blurring, and so forth interferes with performance more when stimuli are projected to the left than when they are projected to the right hemisphere. The resistance of the right hemisphere to perceptual degradation may be related to the superiority of that hemisphere for processing a variety of visuospatial relationships (for entry points into the relevant literature see Hardyck's chapter in Hellige 1983; Kitterle's chapter in Kitterle 1989; Sergent 1983; Sergent 1987a,b; Sergent & Hellige 1986).

As pointed out by Sergent (1983, 1987a,b; see also Sergent & Hellige 1986), the nature of stimulus input is an extremely important variable in determining how the brain will process information. Incoming visual information is broken down into discrete neural signals that represent intensity variations over spatial intervals of different sizes, so that each point in the visual field is multiply encoded by size-tuned filters (i.e. spatial frequency channels) corresponding to overlapping receptive fields (e.g. De Valois & De Valois 1980; see also Marr 1982). In view of this, Sergent (1983, 1987a,b) has hypothesized that, at some level of processing beyond the sensory cortex, the left and right hemispheres are biased toward efficient use of higher and lower visual spatial frequencies, respectively. The effects of reducing stimulus perceptibility can be explained by this spatial frequency hypothesis if it is assumed that manipulations used to reduce perceptibility result in the selective removal of higher spatial frequency information.

The advantage of the spatial frequency hypothesis over previous dichotomies is that it is, in principle, more amenable to operational definition and rigorous empirical test. In the time since the hypothesis was formulated, a number of experiments have demonstrated the importance of spatial frequency contents for determining visual hemispheric asymmetry, although the picture is not as simple as it might have been. Under many conditions selective removal of higher ranges of spatial frequency impairs left- relative to right-hemispheric performance, as predicted. However, there is growing evidence that the range of spatial frequency information *required* to perform an experimental task is as important as the range of spatial frequencies *contained* in the stimuli, with some complex interactions emerging when both things are varied (e.g. Christman 1987, 1990; Sergent 1987b; Sergent & Hellige 1986). Among the important questions to consider in future research is whether the two hemispheres are predisposed to utilize different ranges of absolute frequency or to utilize the relatively high versus relatively low ranges contained in a particular stimulus, whether the hemispheres have different response biases to high versus low spatial frequencies, and whether input characteristics are as important for highly linguistic tasks as for nonlinguistic tasks (in addition to the references already noted, see Chiarello et al 1986, the chapter by Hardyck in Kitterle 1989, and Peterzell et al 1989). It is also important to consider both the role of spatial phase in models of pattern recognition and recent demonstrations of right-hemisphere superiority for the discrimination of spatial phase (e.g. Fiorentini & Berardi 1984).

A second example of the computational approach is illustrated by Kosslyn (1987), who hypothesized that the human brain computes two different kinds of spatial-relation representations. One type of representation is used to assign a spatial relation to a category (e.g. "outside of" or "above") whereas the other preserves location information using a metric coordinate system in which distances are specified effectively. Kosslyn argues that the left hemisphere makes better use of the categorization processing subsystem whereas the right hemisphere makes better use of the distance processing subsystem. He bases these predictions on several intriguing assumptions about different "seeding" of the left and right hemispheres for the control of speech output and search control, respectively, and a "snowball" mechanism that biases the lateralization of specific processing subsystems to one side or the other. The predictions have received empirical support (Hellige & Michimata 1989; Kosslyn 1987; Kosslyn et al 1989a), and the theory has led to an interesting computer simulation of hemispheric asymmetry (e.g. Kosslyn et al 1989b).

Another example of the computational approach deals with hemispheric asymmetry in certain aspects of visual imagery. The traditional view has been that the right hemisphere is superior for visual imagery, largely because of its association with visuospatial perceptual processing. In recent years, computational models have decomposed visual imagery into several subsystems or modules (e.g. Kosslyn 1987), and hemispheric asymmetry need not be identical for all of them. In fact, the left hemisphere may be superior to the right for the generation of visual images, and it has even been suggested that the right hemisphere is typically unable to generate visual images (see Farah 1984; Kosslyn et al 1985). However, this conclusion has generated controversy, and the issue demands additional investigation (e.g. Sergent 1989). In any case, the more modular approach of contemporary computational models has provided a much-needed analytic focus to research on hemispheric asymmetry concerning imagery.

Biological Asymmetries

Until recently it was thought that the cerebral hemispheres in humans were roughly symmetrical in terms of anatomy and other biological characteristics. However, contemporary interest in the information processing differences between the hemispheres and an increasing sophistication in the study of biological variables have led to the discovery of a number of potentially important biological asymmetries. Because the temporoparietal areas of the left hemisphere are known to be important for language, it is not surprising that a number of anatomical and cytoarchitectonic left-right differences have been found in those regions. In addition, a number of pharmacological asymmetries have been discovered. Thorough reviews of these findings are provided by Geschwind & Galaburda (1984, 1987), by Tucker & Williamson (1984; see also the chapter by Tucker in Ottoson 1987), and by Witelson & Kigar (see their chapter in Ottoson 1987). It is interesting that some biological asymmetries found in the brains of adults are also present in those of the human fetus and of ancestral hominids (see Geschwind & Galaburda 1987, for an extensive review). This may ultimately help us to understand the ontogenetic and phylogenetic origins of cerebral laterality, especially as we come to understand the relationships between biological and behavioral asymmetry.

The relationships between specific biological asymmetries and specific asymmetries of information processing are not now understood. Among other things, it will be important in the future to obtain both biological and behavioral measures from the same individuals (cf the chapter by Witelson & Kigar in Ottoson 1987).

ASYMMETRIES IN NONHUMANS

Until recently, systematic left/right asymmetries in the brains of nonhumans were considered rare, unimportant, and unrelated to hemispheric asymmetry in humans. In part, these attitudes derived from a research emphasis on hemispheric asymmetry involving language, a cognitive skill presumably not possessed by other species. Consequently, there were few systematic attempts during the first 60 years of this century to document asymmetries in nonhumans. However, the increased interest in functional hemispheric asymmetry in humans and the discovery that such asymmetries were not restricted to language raised interesting questions about whether functionally important left/right asymmetries were unique to humans and led to a search for animal models of brain asymmetry. The resulting literature documents the ubiquity of behavioral and biological asymmetries in nonhumans. Excellent entry points into this literature are provided by Geschwind & Galaburda (1987) and Glick (1985).

Behavioral Asymmetries

The most obvious behavioral asymmetry in humans is the right-handedness of approximately 90% of the population. Such a large population bias is atypical among species. However, MacNeilage et al (1987) have recently reexamined the data on nonhuman primate handedness and suggested that there are, in fact, population biases when hand preferences for specific types of activity are considered. For example, they suggest that the left hand is favored for reaching whereas the right hand is favored for manipulation. As the commentary that accompanies the MacNeilage et al article indicates, this suggestion about population biases and the possible relationship to human handedness is controversial.

In many species, however, individuals show a strong and consistent side preference (left- and right-sided preferences occurring with approximately equal frequency in the population). For example, individual rats prefer to circle toward one side or the other, and individual mice exhibit a reliable paw preference, with the direction and magnitude varying across the individual members of a species (e.g. the chapter by Collins and the chapter by Glick & Shapiro in Glick 1985). In a very interesting set of experiments, Collins and his colleagues (see the chapter by Collins in Glick 1985) have discovered that it is generally not possible to breed for the direction of paw preference in mice but it is possible to breed for the strength or degree of paw preference. This indicates a dissociation between the genetic control of degree of lateralization and the largely nongenetic control of the direction of lateralization, raising interesting questions about the control of laterality in humans.

After handedness, the most well-established behavioral asymmetry in humans is left-hemisphere dominance for the production and perception of speech. For this reason, it is interesting that possible analogs of this asymmetry occur in other species. In what is probably the most often cited asymmetry of this sort, Nottebohm provides evidence of left-sided brain dominance in the production of vocalizations in certain songbirds (e.g. 1970, 1979; see also the chapter by Arnold & Bottjer in Glick 1985). Asymmetry for the perception of species-relevant vocalizations has also been demonstrated for at least one primate species. Peterson et al (1978) reported that the Japanese macaque discriminates between two forms of its "coo" vocalizations better when the stimuli are presented to its right ear than when the stimuli are presented to its left ear. A similar right-ear advantage for the recognition of speech is found in humans and is known to be related to left-hemisphere superiority in speech recognition (for reviews see Bryden 1982; Bradshaw & Nettleton 1983; Hugdahl 1988). The hypothesis that the left hemisphere of Japanese macaques plays a dominant role in the discrimination of coo vocalizations is also supported by the finding that unilateral ablation of the left superior temporal gyrus (including auditory cortex and corresponding to left-hemisphere language areas in humans) impairs this discrimination, whereas a corresponding lesion in the right hemisphere does not (Heffner & Heffner 1984; for evidence of hemispheric asymmetry involving speech sounds in dogs see Adams et al 1987).

As noted above, the human right hemisphere may be dominant in certain aspects of visuospatial processing and in the production and perception of emotion. At least some of these processes appear to be lateralized in other species as well. For example, in chicks the two sides of the brain are differentially involved in visual discrimination learning, auditory habituation, attack behavior, and copulatory behavior (e.g. Rogers 1986; see also the chapter by Arnold & Bottjer in Glick 1985). In addition, Denenberg and his colleagues (e.g. Denenberg 1981; the chapter by Denenberg & Yutzey in Glick 1985) have reported right-sided brain dominance in certain rat species for various spatial functions and affective behaviors. This right-sided dominance was more pronounced for males than for females and more pronounced in animals that were handled while young than in animals that were not. Hamilton & Vermeire (1988, and in Kitterle 1989) have found in split-brain monkeys a left-hemisphere advantage for distinguishing between tilted lines and a right-hemisphere advantage for discriminating faces. Interestingly, these two laterality effects were distributed independently.

Biological Asymmetries

A number of anatomical, cytoarchitectonic, and biochemical asymmetries have been discovered in the brains of many nonhuman species. In some cases, these seem related to behavioral asymmetries in those species, and in some cases the biological asymmetries in nonhumans are similar to corresponding biological asymmetries in humans. For reviews and recent examples of this work see Geschwind & Galaburda (1984, 1987), Glick (1985), McShane et al (1988), and Stewart & Kolb (1988).

In great apes as well as humans the Sylvian fissure is longer and straighter on the left side than on the right for most individuals (for review see Geschwind & Galaburda 1987). This anatomical asymmetry is of interest because in humans the left Sylvian fissure helps to define the so-called language areas of the left hemisphere. Kolb et al (1982) found that the right hemisphere was larger than the left in rat, mouse, rabbit, and cat. More recent work with the rat suggests that this asymmetry is related to the presence of testosterone in the perinatal period (e.g. Stewart & Kolb 1988). In addition, Glick and his colleagues (e.g. the chapter by Glick & Shapiro in Glick 1985; the chapter by Glick et al in Ottoson 1987) have demonstrated that the direction of a number of biochemical asymmetries in rats is related to the preferred direction of rotation. Specifically, the levels of dopamine in the left and right striata differed by approximately 15%, with the side containing more dopamine contralateral to the individual rat's side preference. The left and right hemispheres of humans also differ in dopamine content and in the content of other neurotransmitters (see Tucker & Williamson 1984).

Implications

The ubiquity of behavioral and biological asymmetries in nonhumans indicates that brain asymmetry is neither unique to humans nor completely dependent on the development of language. Furthermore, the discovery of so many animal models of brain asymmetry has provided several additional ways of converging on important questions about the genetic transmission of asymmetry, the phylogenetic and ontogenetic development of asymmetry, hormonal effects on asymmetry, and so forth.

IMPLICATIONS FOR MODELS OF COGNITION

The discovery that different processing subsystems have different neurological substrata lends support to computational models of cognition in which such subsystems are treated as separable and independent. Consequently interest is now growing in what has come to be called "cognitive neuropsychology" (e.g. Ellis & Young 1988).

Above I reviewed several examples of a computational approach to the study of hemispheric asymmetry. In each, a processing distinction that had been proposed independently of data on hemispheric asymmetry was used to generate predictions about what sorts of tasks would produce left- or right-hemisphere superiority. In each case, the fact that different hemispheric advantages were shown for specific processing subsystems supports the conceptual usefulness of decomposing processing into those specific subsystems. For example, the fact that the spatial frequency content of visual stimuli influences the pattern of hemispheric asymmetry confirms the importance of the spatial frequency dimension for visual perception (e.g. Sergent & Hellige 1986). The fact that there is a left-hemisphere advantage for assigning spatial relations to a category but a right-hemisphere advantage for judging distances provides evidence for two separate types of spatial-relation representations (e.g. Kosslyn 1987). To the extent that the left hemisphere is superior in the "generation" of visual images but not in other processing of visual imagery, there is evidence of a distinction between an image generation subsystem and other visual imagery subsystems (e.g. Farah 1984; Kosslyn et al 1985). Similar logic has used hemispheric superiorities to verify subsystems involved in part/whole organization (e.g. Robertson & Delis 1986).

Recent research at the interface between neuropsychology and psycholinguistics has helped to refine our view of hemispheric differences involving language. It has also provided evidence about the separability of syntactic, semantic, and pragmatic aspects of language. As noted by Berndt et al in Segalowitz (1983), early characterizations of different language disorders were based on grossly defined language tasks. For example, damage to an area of the left hemisphere anterior to the fissure of Rolando (Broca's area) was thought to impair the ability to produce fluent speech whereas damage to an area posterior to the fissure of Rolando (Wernicke's area) impaired the ability to comprehend speech. Recent work by Caramazza, Zurif and their colleagues has reevaluated this distinction in view of contemporary developments in linguistics and psycholinguistics (e.g. Berndt et al in Segalowitz 1983; the chapter by Caramazza & Martin in Hellige 1983). These investigations generally conclude that patients with damage to Broca's area are deficient in using *syntactic* information in both the production and comprehension of language. In contrast, patients with damage to Wernicke's area are deficient in using *semantic* information in both the production and comprehension of language.

For some time it was believed that the right hemisphere played little or no role in either the production or comprehension of language. However, the right hemisphere has been shown to be superior to the left in the production and perception of affective intonation (e.g. Bryden 1982). In addition, recent studies by Gardner and his colleagues (e.g. Gardner et al 1983) indicate that damage to certain areas of the right hemisphere produces an impairment in the processing of complex linguistic materials that require the use of context and the integration of material across sentences and larger units of language (i.e. a deficiency in the use of what have been called *pragmatic* cues to language). The fact that syntax processing, the processing of semantics, and pragmatics processing depend on different neurological substrata is consistent with computational models that treat them as separable subsystems.

Research with split-brain patients has also helped us distinguish different processing subsystems-e.g. the various subsystems involved in the use of visual imagery (e.g. Kosslyn et al 1985). In addition, research with these patients provides data on the kinds of information that can and cannot be transferred from one hemisphere to the other, either subcortically or via whatever connecting fibers have been spared. That some types of information, but not others, can be transferred further indicates the separability of different processing subsystems. For example, Holtzman et al (1981) tested two split-brain patients and found that information about spatial location could be transferred from one hemisphere to the other if that information was used to focus visual attention on a cued location. However, information about the same spatial locations could not be transferred from one hemisphere to the other if subjects were required to identify spatial location. These results clearly indicate two dissociable subsystems for processing visual space, one subserving the control of visual attention and the other subserving the identification of spatial location. This distinction has not typically been made explicit in computational models of visual information processing, but these results indicate that it should be.

Further implications of hemispheric asymmetry for models of cognition concern attention. Recent research indicates that two tasks performed simultaneously interfere with each other more if they require the processing resources of the same cerebral hemisphere than if the processing load can be distributed more evenly across the two hemispheres. Studies with neurologically normal individuals have examined the effects of concurrent activities known to require processing primarily in one hemisphere. Such hemisphere-specific concurrent activities influence visual half-field asymmetry, ear differences in dichotic listening, and motor activity known to be controlled by one hemisphere or the other (for reviews and examples see Friedman et al 1982, 1988; Hellige et al 1979; Hellige & Wong 1983; Herdman & Friedman 1985; the chapter by Kinsbourne & Hiscock in Hellige 1983; Moscovitch & Klein 1980).

These reports of hemisphere-specific interference must be incorporated into theories of attention; they seem to fit better within some contemporary conceptualizations than within others. Hemisphere-specific interference is particularly difficult to account for in terms of a single pool of completely undifferentiated attentional resources for which all resource-demanding processes must compete. Thus it has been suggested that the two hemispheres operate as somewhat separate subprocessors, each with a processing capacity partially independent of the other's (e.g. Hellige et al 1979; Moscovitch & Klein 1980). This point of view has been carried to its logical extreme by Friedman & Polson (e.g. Friedman et al 1982, 1988; Herdman & Friedman 1985), who interpret these effects as evidence for a multiple-resource model of attention such as described by Navon & Gopher (1979). They assert that each hemisphere has processing resources completely independent of the other's and that within a hemisphere the processing resources are completely undifferentiated (but see Friedman et al 1988).

An alternative model has been proposed by Kinsbourne and his colleagues and stems from a view of the brain as a network of parallel distributed processing (e.g. Goldman-Rakic 1988; Kinsbourne 1982; the chapter by Kinsbourne & Hiscock in Hellige 1983). According to their principle of "functional cerebral distance," two tasks will interfere with each other to the extent that they require incompatible neural processes. Such tasks are considered functionally close to each other in terms of the neural areas involved in performance of the tasks. With few exceptions, functional cerebral distance is proposed to be shorter within a hemisphere than between hemispheres and, in this way, hemisphere-specific interference is predicted.

I cannot specify here how models of attention should be changed by the phenomenon of hemisphere-specific interference. In fact, research needs to sharpen the various models so that their differences can lead to critical experiments. Learning more about aspects of hemispheric asymmetry will be a useful part of that research.

INTERHEMISPHERIC INTERACTION

How do the two hemispheres, with their different processing abilities and propensities, interact to form an integrated processing system? As we look around the world, hear sounds, and touch objects, most information is presented to both hemispheres; it is frequently the case that both hemispheres can generate some appropriate behavioral response. Furthermore, electrophysiological studies and studies of regional metabolism indicate that both hemispheres are activated for virtually all tasks, albeit not always equally (e.g. the chapters by Gevins and by Wood in Hellige, 1983; the chapters by Molfese and by Wood in Kitterle 1989; the chapter by Risberg in Ottoson 1987).

Here I consider some of the behavioral techniques used to study interhemispheric interaction and some of the interaction types that have been identified. I emphasize the cooperation of the two hemispheres on tasks that involve subsystems for which different hemispheres are specialized, compare within- versus between-hemisphere presentation of information, and discuss the concept of metacontrol for tasks that the hemispheres are predisposed to handle in qualitatively different ways.

Cooperative Collaboration

For many tasks, different hemispheres are dominant for different task-relevant subprocesses (e.g. Allen 1983; Hellige 1980). It is likely that when such a task is performed under conditions where both hemispheres have access to stimulus information the two hemispheres coordinate their activity, each taking the lead in performing those subprocesses that it handles best. For example, the left hemisphere is superior to the right in handling syntactic and semantic aspects of language whereas the right seems more involved in handling pragmatic aspects of languages. In the normal course of events each aspect of language is likely handled primarily by the hemisphere dominant for it. Such cooperation demands that the hemispheres share various types of information, making it important to study exactly what types of information can and cannot be transferred from one hemisphere to the other (e.g. Berardi & Fiorentini 1987; Berardi et al 1987; Gazzaniga 1985; Holtzman et al 1981; Moscovitch 1986).

We have also seen that two logically unrelated concurrent tasks may interfere with each other more when they require resources from the same hemisphere. This raises the possibility that even single tasks may be performed most efficiently when their different information processing components are distributed between the hemispheres. Green (1984) reported several choice reaction-time tasks in which responses were faster when the hemisphere that received the stimulus was different from the hemisphere that was required to program the response than when a single hemisphere received the stimulus and programmed the response. Thus one evolutionary advantage of functional hemispheric asymmetry may be the reduction of maladaptive interaction among simultaneous processes and among processing subsystems involved in a single task.

Cross-Hemispheric Integration

What are the consequences of requiring the two hemispheres to share information in order to perform a task? Consider a task that requires neurologically normal individuals to indicate whether two visually presented letters are the same or different. When both letters are presented to the same visual field (hemisphere) the task does not require any collaboration between the hemispheres. However, when one letter is presented to each visual field (hemisphere) some collaboration is required in order to answer correctly. As a result, comparison of within-hemisphere and between-hemisphere conditions can shed light on the cross-hemispheric integration of information.

Given that some tasks are performed better when the processing load is distributed across both hemispheres, one might expect better performance in the between-hemisphere than in the within-hemisphere condition, and just such a between-hemisphere advantage is often obtained when the two stimuli to be compared are presented simultaneously (e.g. Davis & Schmit 1971). However, when the two stimuli are presented successively, better performance in the within-hemisphere condition has typically been observed (e.g. Banich 1985; Dimond et al 1972; the chapter by Hellige in Ottoson 1987). This suggests that in some cases it is better to place the entire processing load on one hemisphere than to demand cross-hemispheric integration.

Refinements have been introduced into within- and between-hemisphere comparisons in an attempt to understand exactly what information is passed from one hemisphere to the other (for review and examples see Banich 1985; the chapter by Hellige in Ottoson 1987; Liederman et al 1985, 1986). It appears that the specific information passed depends on a variety of task conditions that include the type of stimulus material, simultaneous versus successive presentation of stimuli, and level of practice. In general, the advantage of spreading the processing load across both hemispheres (i.e. the between-hemisphere condition) becomes greater when the information processing task becomes more difficult (cf the chapter by Hellige in Ottoson 1987). When the task is sufficiently simple, the cost associated with cross-hemispheric integration is greater than the benefit associated with the spread of perceptual processing across both hemispheres.

Metacontrol

In a series of studies with split-brain patients, Levy & Trevarthen (1976) distinguished between hemispheric ability (i.e. how well each hemisphere can perform a particular task) and hemispheric dominance (i.e. the degree to which each hemisphere assumes control of processing and behavior). They discovered that the ability differences between the hemispheres are not the sole determinants of hemispheric dominance. That is, the hemisphere that assumed control for a task was not always the hemisphere with greater ability to perform the task. They refer to the neural mechanism that determines which hemisphere will attempt to control cognitive operations as *metacontrol*.

The concept of metacontrol is particularly important in considering information processing in the intact brain. For many tasks, both hemispheres have some competence but go about the processing in qualitatively different ways (for examples see Hellige 1980, 1983; Levy & Trevarthen 1976; Levy et al 1983). (Note that this is somewhat different from the cases in which each hemisphere is superior for different task-relevant subprocesses). For such tasks it is important to understand what happens when the same stimulus information is presented to both hemispheres. Metacontrol enables the intact brain to assign tasks according to the mode of processing favored by each hemisphere.

Only recently has an experimental paradigm been devised to test the metacontrol concept in neurologically normal individuals (e.g. the chapter by Hellige in Ottoson 1987). We begin by choosing a task for which both hemispheres have some competence and for which there is evidence that the two hemispheres use qualitatively different modes of processing. We can then examine the qualitative nature of processing when the same stimulus information is presented to both hemispheres (bihemispheric trials). When the mode of processing on these trials is identical to the mode of processing favored by one hemisphere, that hemisphere's preferred mode of processing evidently dominates when there is a choice.

In several recent visual half-field studies using this logic, the mode of processing on bihemispheric trials has been identical to that of one hemisphere but not the other (e.g. the chapters by Hellige in Ottoson 1987, and in Kitterle 1989; Hellige et al 1988b, 1989; Hellige & Michimata 1989). Furthermore, the mode of processing characteristic of bihemispheric trials was not always the mode of processing utilized by the hemisphere with greater ability. For example, we have reported a case in which the mode of processing was identical on right-hemisphere and bihemispheric trials, even though the verbal task produced a left-hemisphere advantage (Hellige 1989). Further research is needed to elucidate the metacontrol of hemispheric preference.

Studies of hemispheric interaction may have more general implications. Cognitive neuropsychologists currently seek to account for the emergence of unified information processing from a brain consisting of a variety of processing subsystems. The left and right hemispheres can be characterized as two very general subsystems with different processing propensities and biases. Continued investigation of hemispheric interaction and metacontrol may thus

provide important clues about the emergence of unified information processing.

INDIVIDUAL DIFFERENCES

Individuals can differ widely in aspects of hemispheric asymmetry. Here I
consider some dimensions along which individuals have been shown to differ.
I briefly review the relationship of such subject variables as handedness, sex,
and psychopathology to individual differences in hemispheric asymmetry.
The section ends with a consideration of whether individual differences in
patterns of hemispheric asymmetry are related to differences in human intellectual performance.

Dimensions of Individual Difference

It is useful to distinguish several logically orthogonal dimensions along which
individuals appear to differ. I consider four such dimensions. For a more
detailed discussion of these see O'Boyle & Hellige (1989).

Individuals can differ in the *degree of hemispheric asymmetry*. For example, two individuals may both show left-hemisphere superiority in certain
aspects of verbal processing, with the hemispheric asymmetry being larger for
one individual than for the other. Two individuals can also show equal
degrees of hemispheric asymmetry but differ in the *direction of hemispheric
asymmetry;* for example, one may show a left-hemisphere superiority, the
other shows an equally large right-hemisphere superiority for the same processing task. Since the two cerebral hemispheres can be at different levels of
activation or arousal, it has been hypothesized that individuals may differ with
respect to their habitual or characteristic pattern of *arousal asymmetry* (e.g.
the chapter by Levine et al and the chapter by Levy & Heller in Ottoson 1987;
Levy et al 1983). Furthermore, individuals can differ in asymmetric arousal
even when they show exactly the same magnitude and direction of hemispheric asymmetry for a particular task (e.g. Levy et al 1983).

The final dimension of individual difference to be considered here is what
has been called *complimentarity of function* (e.g. Bryden 1982; Hamilton &
Vermeire 1988; O'Boyle & Hellige 1989). At the population level each
cerebral hemisphere is dominant for specific tasks or subprocesses. Consider
that Task A typically reveals a left-hemisphere advantage, Task B a right-
hemisphere advantage. Subjects who show opposite hemispheric asymmetries for Tasks A and B are said to exhibit complimentary lateralization for
the tasks. Another group of subjects may show the same direction of hemispheric asymmetry for both tasks. This dimension of individual difference
is important because there may be disadvantages to having subsystems
that are typically lateralized to opposite hemispheres uncharacteristically

"crowded" into one hemisphere (e.g. Geschwind & Galaburda 1987; O'Boyle & Hellige 1989).

Subject Variables and Individual Differences

There has been a great deal of interest in examining the relationship between subject variables and individual differences in aspects of hemispheric asymmetry, with particular attention given to differences in the degree and magnitude of asymmetry. Here I consider the current status of research on hemispheric differences related to handedness, sex, and psychopathology. The section ends with a brief discussion of the development of hemispheric asymmetry. Keep in mind that the findings described earlier in this chapter apply generally to right-handed male adults with no left-handed relatives.

HANDEDNESS   Left-handers are more variable than right-handers in both the degree and the direction of hemispheric asymmetry. For example, approximately 62% of left-handers are left-hemisphere dominant for speech (contrasted with 95% for right-handers) and approximately 19% of left-handers are right-hemisphere dominant for speech (contrasted with 5% for right-handers), the remainder of left-handers showing bilateral representation of speech (e.g. the chapter by Segalowitz & Bryden in Segalowitz 1983). This pattern of increased variability for left-handers is characteristic of other tasks as well (for reviews see Bryden 1982; Bradshaw & Nettleton 1983). Several of the biological asymmetries considered above are also more variable for left-handers than for right-handers (see Geschwind & Galaburda 1987). Furthermore, the corpus callosum is approximately 11% larger in left-handers and ambidextrous individuals than in right-handers, suggesting the possibility of more efficient interhemispheric communication (e.g. the chapter by Witelson in Ottoson 1987). The greater variability among left-handers has led to the search for additional variables that might indicate which left-handers show the pattern of hemispheric asymmetry characteristic of right-handers and which do not. Among the variables examined are hand posture used for writing (for reviews see Weber & Bradshaw 1981; Levy 1982) and presence of left-handedness in the close relatives of an individual (e.g. O'Boyle & Hoff 1987). Neither of these variables has proved to be a uniformly good indicator of the hemispheric asymmetry of cognitive processes in left-handers, although there is some evidence of reduced left-hemisphere dominance for verbal processes in both left- and right-handers who have a left-handed parent (e.g. Kee et al 1983; McKeever et al 1983). In future studies it will be interesting to determine whether left- and right-handers differ in arousal asymmetry and complimentarity of function.

SEX   In view of the fact that fetal hormones influence biological and behavioral asymmetry in so many nonhuman species (e.g. Geschwind & Behan
1982; Geschwind & Galaburda 1984, 1987; McShane et al 1988; Stewart &
Kolb 1988), it would not be surprising to find that male and female patterns of
hemispheric asymmetry differ for humans. In fact, various possibilities have
been suggested, the most frequent being that females show less hemispheric
asymmetry than males. However, recent reviews indicate that the support for
this hypothesis is equivocal, at best, especially in studies that use neurologically normal individuals (e.g. Bryden 1982; Bradshaw & Nettleton 1983;
Springer & Deutsch 1985). Evidence favoring the hypothesis seems restricted
to verbal tasks, and even here the differences may have more to do with
sex-related differences in preferred strategy than with hard-wired differences
in hemispheric asymmetry. Consequently, if there are sex differences in
hemispheric asymmetry in humans they are neither obvious nor consistent
across all lateralized subsystems.

PSYCHOPATHOLOGY   Emotional reactions to unilateral brain damage differ
depending on the hemisphere involved. Catastrophic reactions are more
common in patients with left-hemisphere lesions whereas indifference reactions are more common in patients with right-hemisphere lesions (for reviews
see the chapter by Gianotti and the chapter by Tucker in Ottoson 1987; Tucker
& Williamson 1984). These results and others favor the hypothesis that the
right hemisphere plays a dominant role in the production and perception of
emotion (e.g. Bowers et al 1985; Bryden 1982; Bradshaw & Nettleton 1983;
the chapter by Gianotti in Ottoson 1987). Certain psychopathologies may also
be related to abnormalities of hemispheric asymmetry and arousal. For example, Flor-Henry (1969; see also Gruzelier & Flor-Henry 1979 and Posner et
al 1988) has suggested a link between schizophrenia and left-hemisphere
dysfunction; poor right-hemisphere performance has been reported during
episodes of depression in psychiatric patients (for examples see Tucker &
Williamson 1984). Because some of the hypotheses advanced concern relative arousal levels of the two hemispheres (see Levy et al 1983), future studies
might usefully include measures that separate individual differences in arousal
asymmetry from individual differences in the degree and direction of functional asymmetry.

DEVELOPMENT OF HEMISPHERIC ASYMMETRY   Thoughtful entry points
into the massive literature dealing with the development of hemispheric
asymmetry are provided by Best (1985), de Schonen & Mathivet (1989),
Geschwind & Galaburda (1987), and Witelson (1987).
    Any developmental theory of hemispheric asymmetry must account for the
fact that certain aspects of hemispheric asymmetry for processing language

stimuli are present from birth. Furthermore, it now appears that at birth the right hemisphere is more mature than the left (e.g. Geschwind & Galaburda 1987). When this is combined with the fact that a neonate's sensorimotor system provides the brain with degraded sensorimotor information, interesting developmental possibilities emerge (for discussion see de Schonen & Mathivet 1989 and the commentary that follows it). For example, a right-hemisphere bias toward lower ranges or visuospatial frequency in adults may be related to the fact that at birth the more mature right hemisphere is influenced by incoming visual information that (in neonates) lacks higher ranges of spatial frequency (see de Schonen & Mathivet 1989).

Human Intellectual Performance and Hemisphericity

Are individual differences in hemispheric asymmetry related to differences in cognitive ability and style? (For a fuller review and evaluation see O'Boyle & Hellige 1989). It should be noted at the outset that if relationships between hemispheric asymmetries and cognitive abilities exist, they are likely to be subtle and complex. They may not account for much of the normal variation in cognitive ability. Therefore, I focus on suggested relationships between hemispheric asymmetry and cognitive performance outside of the "normal" range. Specifically, I consider intellectual precocity and dyslexia.

INTELLECTUAL PRECOCITY   Guided by the work of Geschwind & Behan (1982), Benbow and her colleagues (e.g. Benbow 1986) have found a link between intellectual precocity, left-handedness, sex, and behaviorally measured patterns of hemispheric asymmetry. The theoretical idea that has guided this work is that there is greater right-hemisphere involvement in intellectually (especially mathematically) precocious children than in intellectually normal children, with the greater right-hemisphere involvement traced to higher fetal testosterone levels (which may increase right- relative to left-hemisphere development; see Geschwind & Galaburda 1987). This complex hypothesis has not yet received adequate experimental investigation, but it is interesting that a group of intellectually precocious children has recently been suggested to have greater right- relative to left-hemisphere arousal compared to a control group (Benbow et al cited in O'Boyle & Hellige 1989).

DYSLEXIA   Certain forms of dyslexia may be related to abnormal patterns of hemispheric asymmetry (for various contemporary hypotheses see Best 1985; O'Boyle & Hellige 1989; the chapter by Pirozzolo et al in Hellige 1983). Experimental investigation of the various hypotheses has proven difficult because "dyslexia" is probably a collection of disorders of reading rather than a single disorder with a single neurological cause. At the present time, no simple relationship has been discovered between hemispheric asymmetry and dyslexia, but two leads seem especially promising. One is that there is a relationship between some forms of dyslexia and dysfunction of the language areas of the left hemisphere. For example, Galaburda and his coworkers (see Geschwind & Galaburda 1987) have reported abnormal cytoarchitecture of temporal language areas of the left hemisphere in dyslexics. In addition, recent behavioral studies suggest that both dyslexics and normals rely primarily on the left hemisphere for processing printed material, but the left-hemisphere performance of dyslexics is impaired (e.g. the chapter by Moscovitch in Ottoson 1987; Levy 1985; see also O'Boyle & Hellige 1989). A second hypothesis that merits further investigation is that at least a subgroup of dyslexics have normal lateralization of cognitive functions but have a great deal of difficulty with interhemispheric communication (for discussion see the chapter by Gladstone & Best in Best 1985; O'Boyle & Hellige 1989).

HEMISPHERICITY   If individuals have preferred cognitive styles or preferred modes of cognitive processing determined by reliance on the activity of one hemisphere or the other, they are said to exhibit "hemisphericity." Popularized accounts have gone so far as to claim that this hemisphericity can be measured readily and used to classify individuals as "right-brained" or "left-brained." These same accounts frequently present training programs that might be addressed to one hemisphere or the other or that attempt to overcome hemisphericity by training "whole-brain thinking" (for discussion of several examples see Druckman & Swets 1988).

Although the concept of hemisphericity has a certain simplistic elegance and intuitive appeal, there is no scientific foundation for the idea that individuals rely on only one hemisphere for thinking. Several neuroscientists have suggested that the concept of hemisphericity be viewed with skepticism or abandoned altogether (e.g. Beaumont et al 1984; Druckman & Swets 1988; Kinsbourne 1982). This is not to deny that individuals differ in their preferred modes of cognitive processing. They clearly do. Some of the training programs proposed may even do a reasonable job of encouraging a worthwhile diversity of thought. However, there is no evidence that this is accomplished by expanding the neural space used for thinking.

CONCLUDING COMMENTS

Twenty-five years ago hemispheric asymmetry was little more than an interesting curiosity to most psychologists. Today it is clear that various aspects of hemispheric asymmetry have had implications for a number of important topics in contemporary psychology. Consequently, the phenomenon continues to generate interest, leading to a rapidly expanding database. In this chapter I have tried to illustrate the utility of incorporating certain hemispheric asymmetries into models of perception, cognition, and action. The best of such models serve as a useful guide for thinking about the neurological substrata of processing modules. At the same time, the best research on hemispheric asymmetry can help refine such models by suggesting which modular distinctions are most plausible and by showing how different processing subsystems can interact. It is exciting to anticipate the discoveries that will be made possible by the many animal models and by continued refinement of techniques for studying individual differences in hemispheric asymmetry. We can all look forward to the next *Annual Review* chapter on this topic.

ACKNOWLEDGEMENTS

Preparation of this manuscript was supported in part by Grant BNS-8608893 from the National Science Foundation. I am grateful to Steve Christman and Fred Kitterle for helpful comments on an earlier draft of this chapter.

Literature Cited

Adams, C. L., Molfese, D. L., Betz, J. C. 1987. Electrophysiological correlates of categorical speech perception for voicing contrasts in dogs. *Dev. Neuropsychol.* 3:175–89

Allen, M. 1983. Models of hemispheric specialization. *Psychol. Bull.* 93:73–104

Anderson, J. R. 1985. *Cognitive Psychology and Its Implications*. New York: Freeman

Banich, M. T. 1985. The nature and time course of interhemispheric communication. PhD thesis. Univ. Chicago

Beaumont, J. G., ed. 1982. *Divided Visual Field Studies of Cerebral Organisation*. New York: Academic

Beaumont, J. G., Young, A. W., McManus, I. C. 1984. *Cognit. Neuropsychol.* 1:191–212

Benbow, C. P. 1986. Physiological correlates of extreme intellectual precocity. *Neuropsychologia* 24:719–25

Berardi, N., Bisti, S., Maffei, L. 1987. The transfer of visual information across the corpus callosum: spatial and temporal properties in the cat. *J. Physiol.* 384:619–32

Berardi, N., Fiorentini, A. 1987. Interhemispheric transfer of visual information in humans: spatial characteristics. *J. Physiol.* 384:633–47

Best, C. T., ed. 1985. *Hemispheric Function and Collaboration in the Child*. New York: Academic

Bowers, D., Bauer, R. M., Coslett, H. B., Heilman, K. M. 1985. Processing of face by patients with unilateral hemisphere lesions. I. Dissociations between judgements of facial affect and facial identity. *Brain Cognit.* 4:258–72

Bradshaw, J. L., Nettleton, N. C. 1981. The nature of hemispheric specialization in man. *Behav. Brain Sci.* 4:51–63

Bradshaw, J. L., Nettleton, N. C. 1983. *Human Cerebral Asymmetry*. Englewood Cliffs, NJ: Prentice-Hall

Broca, P. (1861) 1950. Remarques sur le siège da la faculté du language articulé, suive d'une observation d'aphémie. Transl. J. Kann. *J. Speech Hear. Disord.* 15:16–20

Bryden, M. P. 1982. *Laterality: Functional Asymmetry in the Intact Brain*. New York: Academic

Chiarello, C., Senehi, J., Soulier, M. 1986. Viewing conditions and hemisphere asymmetry for the lexical decision. *Neuropsychologia* 24:521–30

Christman, S. 1987. Effects of perceptual quality on hemispheric asymmetries in visible persistence. *Percept. Psychophys.* 41: 367–74

Christman, S. 1990. Perceptual characteristics in visual laterality research. *Brain Cognit.* In press

Dagenbach, D. 1986. Subject variable effects in correlations between auditory and visual language processing asymmetries. *Brain Lang.* 28:169–77

Davis, R., Schmit, V. 1971. Timing the transfer of information between the hemispheres in man. *Acta Psychol.* 35:335–46

Denenberg, V. H. 1981. Hemispheric laterality in animals and the effects of early experience. *Behav. Brain Sci.* 4:1–49 de Schonen, S., Mathivet, E. 1989. First come, first served: a scenario about the development of hemispheric specialization in face recognition during infancy. *Eur. Bull. Cognit. Psychol.* 9:3–44

De Valois, R. L., De Valois, K. K. 1980. Spatial vision. *Annu. Rev. Psychol.* 31: 117–53

Dimond, S. J., Gibson, A. R., Gazzaniga, M. S. 1972. Cross field and within field integration of visual information. *Neuropsychologia* 10:379–81

Druckman, D., Swets, J. A., eds. 1988. *Enhancing Human Performance: Issues, Theories, and Techniques.* Washington: Natl. Acad. Press

Ehrlichman, H., Weinberger, A. 1978. Lateral eye movements and hemispheric asymmetry: a critical review. *Psychol. Bull.* 85: 1080–101

Ellis, A. W., Young, A. W. 1988. *Human Cognitive Neuropsychology.* Hillsdale, NJ: Erlbaum

Farah, M. J. 1984. The neurological basis of mental imagery. *Cognition* 18:245–72

Fiorentini, A., Berardi, N. 1984. Right-hemisphere superiority in the discrimination of spatial phase. *Perception* 13:695–708

Flor-Henry, P. 1969. Psychosis and temporal lobe epilepsy: a controlled investigation. *Epilepsia* 10:363–95

Friedman, A., Polson, M. C., Dafoe, C. G. 1988. Dividing attention between the hands and the head: performance trade-offs between rapid finger tapping and verbal memory. *J. Exp. Psychol.: Hum. Percept. Perform.* 14:60–68

Friedman, A., Polson, M. C., Dafoe, C. G., Gaskill, S. 1982. Dividing attention within and between hemispheres: testing a multiple resources approach to limited-capacity information processing. *J. Exp. Psychol.: Hum. Percept. Perform.* 8:625–50

Gardner, H., Brownell, H. H., Wapner, W., Michelow, D. 1983. Missing the point: the role of the right hemisphere in the processing of complex linguistic materials. In *Cognitive Processing in the Right Hemisphere*, ed. E. Perecman, pp. 169-92. New York: Academic

Gazzaniga, M. S. 1985. *The Social Brain: Discovering the Networks of the Mind.* New York: Basis Books

Geschwind, N., Behan, P. 1982. Left-handedness: association with immune disease, migraine, and developmental learning disorder. *Proc. Natl. Acad. Sci. USA* 79: 5097–5100

Geschwind, N., Galaburda, A. M., eds. 1984. *Cerebral Dominance: The Biological Foundations.* Cambridge: Harvard Univ. Press

Geschwind, N., Galaburda, A. M. 1987.

Cerebral Lateralization: Biological Mechanism, Associations, and Pathology. Cambridge: MIT Press

Glick, S. D., ed. 1985. *Cerbral Lateralization in Nonhuman Species.* New York: Academic

Goldman-Rakic, P. S. 1988. Topography of cognition: parallel distributed networks in primate association cortex. *Annu. Rev. Neurosci.* 11:137–56

Green, J. 1984. Effects of intrahemispheric interference on reaction times to lateral stimuli. *J. Exp. Psychol.: Hum. Percept. Perform.* 10:292–306

Gruzelier, J. H., Flor-Henry, P., eds. 1979. *Hemisphere Asymmetries of Function in Psychopathology.* Amsterdam: Elsevier/ North Holland Biomedical Press

Hamilton, C. R., Vermeire, B. A. 1988. Complementary hemispheric specialization in monkeys. *Science* 242:1991–94

Heffner, H. E., Heffner, R. S. 1984. Temporal lobe lesions and perception of species-specific vocalizations by macaques. *Science* 226:75–76

Heilman, K. M., Valenstein, E. 1985. *Clinical Neuropsychology.* New York: Oxford Univ. Press

Hellige, J. B. 1980. Effects of perceptual quality and visual field of probe stimulus presentation on memory search for letters. *J. Exp. Psychol.: Hum. Percept. Perform.* 6:639–51

Hellige, J. B., ed. 1983. *Cerebral Hemisphere Asymmetry: Method, Theory, and Application.* New York: Praeger

Hellige, J. B., Bloch, M. I., Taylor, A. K. 1988a. Multi-task investigation of individual differences in hemispheric asymmetry. *J. Exp. Psychol.: Hum. Percept. Perform.* 14:176–87

Hellige, J. B., Cox, P. J., Litvac, L. 1979. Information processing in the cerebral hemispheres: selective hemispheric activation and capacity limitations. *J. Exp. Psychol.: Gen.* 108:251–79

Hellige, J. B., Johnson, J. E., Michimata, C. 1988b. Processing from LVF, RVF and BILATERAL presentations: metacontrol and interhemispheric interaction. *Brain Cognit.* 7:39–53

Hellige, J. B., Michimata, C. 1989. Categorization versus distance: hemispheric differences for processing spatial information. *Mem. Cognit.* In press

Hellige, J. B., Taylor, A. K., Eng, T. L. 1989. Interhemispheric interaction when both hemispheres have access to the same stimulus information. *J. Exp. Psychol.: Hum. Percept. Perform.* 15: In press

Hellige, J. B., Wong, T. M. 1983. Hemisphere-specific interference in dichotic listening: task variables and individual differences. *J. Exp. Psychol.: Gen.* 122:218–39

Herdman, C. M., Friedman, A. 1985. Multiple resources in divided attention: a cross-modal test of the independence of hemispheric resources. *J. Exp. Psychol.: Hum. Percept. Perform.* 11:40–49

Holtzman, J. D., Sidtis, J. J., Volpe, B. T., Wilson, D. H., Gazzaniga, M. S. 1981. Dissociation of spatial information for stimulus localization and the control of attention. *Brain* 104:861–72

Hugdahl, K., ed. 1988. *Handbook of Dichotic Listening: Theory, Methods and Research.* New York: Wiley

Kee, D. W., Hellige, J. B., Bathurst, K. 1983. Lateralized interference of repetitive finger tapping: Influence of family handedness, cognitive load, and verbal production. *Neuropsychologia,* 21:617-25

Kinsbourne, M. 1982. Hemispheric specialization and the growth of human understanding. *Am. Psychol.* 37:411–20

Kitterle, F. 1989. *Cerebral Laterality: Theory and Research.* Hillsdale, NJ: Erlbaum

Kolb, B., Sutherland, R. J., Nonneman, A. J., Whishaw, I. Q. 1982. Asymmetry in the cerebral hemispheres of the rat, mouse, rabbit, and cat: the right hemisphere is larger. *Exp. Neurol.* 78:348–59

Kosslyn, S. M. 1987. Seeing and imagining in the cerebral hemispheres: a computational approach. *Psychol. Rev.* 94:148–75

Kosslyn, S. M., Holtzman, J. D., Farah, M. J., Gazzaniga, M. S. 1985. A computational analysis of mental image generation: evidence from functional dissociations in split-brain patients. *J. Exp. Psychol.: Gen.* 114:311–41

Kosslyn, S. M., Koenig, O., Barrett, A., Cave, C. B., Tang, J., Garieli, J. D. E. 1989a. Evidence for two types of spatial representations: hemispheric specialization for categorical and coordinate relations. *J. Exp. Psychol.: Hum. Percept. Perform.* 15:In press

Kosslyn, S. M., Sokolov, M. A., Chen, J. C. 1989b. The lateralization of BRIAN: a computational theory and model of visual hemispheric specialization. In *Complex Information Processing Comes of Age,* ed. D. Klahr, K. Kotovsky, Hillsdale, NJ: Erlbaum

Levy, J. 1982. Handwriting posture and cerebral organization: How are they related? *Psychol. Bull.* 91:589–608

Levy, J. 1985. *Language laterality and reading.* Presented at Annu. Meet. Am. Educ. Res. Assoc., Chicago

Levy, J., Heller, W., Banich, M. T., Burton, L. A. 1983. Are variations among right-handed individuals in perceptual asymmetries caused by characteristic arousal differences between hemispheres? *J. Exp. Psychol.: Hum. Percept. Perform.* 9:329–59

Levy, J., Trevarthen, C. 1976. Metacontrol of hemispheric function in split-brain patients. *J. Exp. Psychol.: Hum. Percept. Perform.* 2:299–312

Liederman, J., Merola, J., Hoffman, C. 1986. Longitudinal data indicate that hemispheric independence increases during early adolescence. *Dev. Neuropsychol.* 2:183–201

Liederman, J., Merola, J., Martinez, S. 1985. Interhemispheric collaboration in response to simultaneous bilateral input. *Neuropsychologia* 23:673–84

MacNeilage, P. F., Studdert-Kennedy, M. G., Lindblom, B. 1987. Primate handedness reconsidered. *Behav. Brain Sci.* 10:247–303

Marr, D. 1982. *Vision.* San Francisco: Freeman

McKeever, W. F., Seitz, K. S., Hoff, A. L., Marino, M. F., Diehl, J. A. 1983. Interacting sex and familial sinistrality characteristics influence both language lateralization and spatial ability in right-handers. *Neuropsychologia* 21:661–68

McShane, S., Glaser, L., Greer, E. R., Houtz, J., Tong, M. F., Diamond, M. C. 1988. Cortical asymmetry—a preliminary study: neurons—glia, female—male. *Exp. Neurol.* 99:353–61

Moscovitch, M. 1986. Afferent and efferent models of visual perceptual asymmetries: theoretical and empirical implications. *Neuropsychologia* 24:91–114

Moscovitch, M., Klein, D. 1980. Material-specific perceptual interference for visual words and faces: implications for models of capacity limitations, attention and laterality. *J. Exp. Psychol.: Hum. Percept. Perform.* 6:590–604

Navon, D., Gopher, D. 1979. On the economy of the human information-processing system. *Psychol. Rev.* 86:214–55

Nottebohm, F. 1970. Ontogeny of birdsong. *Science* 167:950–56

Nottebohm F. 1979. Origins and mechanisms in the establishment of cerebral dominance. In *Handbook of Behavioral Neurobiology,* ed. M. Gazzaniga, 2:295–348. New York: Plenum

O'Boyle, M. W., Hellige, J. B. 1989. Cerebral hemisphere asymmetry and individual differences in cognition. *Learn. Individ. Differ.* 1:7–35

O'Boyle, M. W., Hoff, E. J. 1987. Gender and handedness differences in mirror tracing random forms. *Neuropsychologia* 25:977–82

O'Boyle, M. W., van Wyhe-Lawler, F., Miller, D. A. 1987. Recognition of letters traced in the right and left palms: evidence for a process-oriented tactile asymmetry. *Brain Cognit.* 6:474–94

Ottoson, D., ed. 1987. *Duality and Unity of the Brain.* London: Macmillan

Peterson, M. R., Beecher, M. D., Zoloth, S. R., Moody, D. B., Stebbins, W. C. 1978. Neural lateralization of species-specific vocalizations by Japanese macaques (*Macaca fuscata*). *Science* 202:324–27

Peterzell, D. H., Harvey, L. O., Hardyck, C. D. 1989. Spatial frequencies and the cerebral hemispheres: contrast sensitivity, visible persistence, and letter classification. *Percept. Psychophys.* 43:In press

Posner, M. I., Early, T. S., Reiman, E., Pardo, P. J., Dhawan, M. 1988. Asymmetries in hemispheric control of attention in schizophrenia. *Arch. Gen. Psychiatry* 45: 814–21

Robertson, L. C., Delis, D. C. 1986. "Part-whole" processing in unilateral brain-damaged patients: dysfunction of hierarchical organization. *Neuropsychologia* 24: 363–70

Rogers, L. J. 1986. Lateralization of learning in chicks. 16:147–89

Segalowitz, S. J., ed. 1983. *Language Functions and Brain Organization.* New York: Academic

Sergent, J. 1983. The role in the input in visual hemispheric asymmetries. *Pscyhol. Bull.* 93:481–512

Sergent, J. 1987a. Information processing and laterality effects for object and face perception. In *Visual Object Processing: A Cognitive Neuropsychological Approach*, ed., G. W. Humphreys, M. J. Riddoch. Hillsdale, NJ: Erlbaum

Sergent, J. 1987b. Failures to confirm the spatial frequency hypothesis: fatal blow or healthy complication? *Can. J. Psychol.* 41:412–28

Sergent, J. 1989. Image generation and processing of generated images in the cerebral hemispheres. *J. Exp. Psychol.: Hum. Percept. Perform.* 15:170–78

Sergent, J., Hellige, J. B. 1986. Role of input factors in visual field asymmetries. *Brain Cognit.* 5:174–99

Sperry, R. W., Gazzaniga, M. S., Bogen, J. E. 1969. Interhemispheric relationships: the neocortical commissures, syndromes of hemispheric disconnection. In *Handbook of Clinical Neurology*, Vol. 4: *Disorders of Speech, Perception, and Symbolic Behavior*, ed. P. J. Vinken, G. W. Bruyn, pp. 145–53. Amsterdam: Elsevier/North Holland Biomedical Press

Springer, S. P., Deutsch, G. 1985. *Left Brain, Right Brain.* San Francisco: Freeman. 2nd ed.

Stewart, J., Kolb, B. 1988. The effects of neonatal gonadectomy and prenatal stress on cortical thickness and asymmetry in rats. *Behav. Neural. Biol.* 49:344–60

Stillings, N. A., Feinstein, M. H., Garfield, J. L., Rissland, E. L., Rosenbaum, D. A., Weisler, S. E., Baker-Ward, L. 1987. *Cognitive Science: An Introduction.* Cambridge: MIT Press

Tucker, D. M., Williamson, P. A. 1984. Asymmetric neural control systems in human self-regulation. *Psychol. Rev.* 91:185–215

Weber, A. M., Bradshaw, J. L. 1981. Levy and Reid's model in relation to writing hand/posture: an evaluation. *Psychol. Bull.* 90:74–88

Wernicke, C. 1874. The symptom of complex aphasia. Translated and republished in *Disorders of the Nervous System*, ed. A. Church. New York: Appleton-Century-Crofts

Whitaker, H. A., Ojemann, G. A. 1977. Lateralization of higher cortical functions: a critique. *Ann. NY Acad. Sci.* 299:459–73

Witelson, S. F. 1987. Neurobiological aspects of language in children. *Child Dev.* 52:653–88

Annu. Rev. Psychol. 1990. 41:81–108

MECHANISMS OF SEASONAL CYCLES OF BEHAVIOR

Randy J. Nelson

Departments of Psychology and Population Dynamics, The Johns Hopkins University, Baltimore, Maryland 21218

Lori L. Badura and Bruce D. Goldman

Department of Physiology and Neurobiology, University of Connecticut, Storrs, Connecticut 06268

CONTENTS

ULTIMATE AND PROXIMATE FACTORS UNDERLYING SEASONALITY

Many animals and plants are exposed to seasonal fluctuations in the deterioration and renewal of their environments. Organisms frequently restrict energetically expensive activities to a specific time of the year. Animals migrate or reduce activity when food availability is low; reproduction, preparation for migration, and other energy demanding activities have evolved to coincide with abundant local food resources or other environmental conditions that promote survival. Precise timing of behavior is, therefore, a critical feature of

81

individual reproductive success and subsequent fitness. Animals have evolved to fill temporal as well as spatial niches.

In some cases, physiological and behavioral changes may occur in direct response to environmental fluctuations that have an obvious and immediate adaptive function. For example, a decrease in the amount of available food or water can lead to reproductive inhibition (Bronson 1988; Nelson 1987). These types of environmental factors have been termed the "ultimate factors" underlying seasonality (Baker 1938). Many animals need to forecast the optimal time to breed so that spermatogenesis, nest construction, or any other time-consuming preparation for reproduction will be complete at the start of the breeding season. Therefore, seasonally breeding animals frequently detect and respond to environmental cues that accurately signal, well in advance, the arrival or departure of seasons favoring reproductive success. The cues used to predict environmental change may or may not have direct survival value. These are referred to as "proximate factors" (Baker 1938). The most notable example of a proximate factor is day length, a cue that can serve as a precise reference for the time of year. Under some circumstances proximate and ultimate factors are identical (Negus & Berger 1987). For example, some individuals may not begin breeding until food cues are detected (Bronson 1988).

Seasonal changes in behavior are observed even among tropical animals where the annual cycle of changing day length is not as evident as it is at higher latitudes. Despite relatively constant photoperiodic and temperature conditions, seasonal food availability is common for many tropical species. In East Africa, the irregular timing of the onset of rain, or some coincident factor, induces the red-billed quelea *(Quelea quelea)* to breed (Disney et al 1959); consequently, the onset of breeding in East African quelea is erratic from year to year (Murton & Westwood 1978). In West Africa, where the onset of the rainy season is more consistent each year, the quelea display a predictable breeding season (Ward 1965). In contrast, several species of oceanic sea birds, inhabiting equatorial waters, experience virtually no seasonal variation in food supplies or other environmental factors. Reproductive activities and moult impose large, conflicting energetic demands for these birds and are separated in time. However, in their stable environment, breeding and moult may occur at any time of the year, and the frequency of the cycle between these two energetic demands is limited only by the physiological capability of the birds. The frequency of the breeding and moult cycle varies among tropical birds; for example, breeding recurs every eight months for the bridled tern *(Sterna anaethetus)* (Diamond 1976), every nine months for the brown pelican *(Pelecanus occidentalis;* lat. 0°, long. 90° W; Harris 1969) and Audubon's shearwater *(Puffinus lherminieri;* Snow 1965), and every ten months for the swallow-tailed gull *(Creagrus fucatus)* in the

Galapagos Islands (Snow & Snow 1967). Thus, mating behavior in some tropical birds is distributed throughout the year. With the exception of these and other animals living in very stable environments, seasonal changes in behavior are common.

This review addresses the physiological mechanisms underlying the detection of and response to environmental factors. Most research in this area has focused on the role of photoperiod (the duration of the light period in the 24-hr cycle, also called day length) in providing temporal information. Presumably, with only two bits of data, length of day and direction of change in the photoperiod, an animal could tell precisely the time of year and might then use this information to anticipate subsequent seasonal environmental changes. Here we review the seasonal regulation of steroid-dependent and steroid-independent behaviors, using reproduction as a model, and explore the physiological bases underlying photoperiodism and endogenous circannual rhythms. We discuss the seasonal regulation of a variety of nonreproductive behaviors and examine the possibility of seasonal fluctuations in human behavior and physiology, with particular reference to the phenomenology and putative mechanisms of Seasonal Affective Disorder.

NEUROENDOCRINE MECHANISMS UNDERLYING SEASONALITY

There is an extensive literature on the mechanisms regulating seasonal cycles in reproduction. The principles of seasonality derived from this literature will serve as a basis for the examination of the sparser information base directly related to seasonal changes in behavior. The mechanisms that regulate seasonal reproductive changes may be classified under two categories: 1. One set of mechanisms is directly responsible for regulating changes in the reproductive system. For example, changes in the rate or pattern of pituitary hormone secretion are important for "driving" changes in reproductive activity. We refer to these as "activational" mechanisms because they generally involve activational effects of hormones (Beach 1975). 2. A second set of neuroendocrine mechanisms is directly responsible for *timing* the seasonal rhythms and ensuring that they are synchronized to the annual geophysical cycles. In mammals, the pineal gland and its hormone, melatonin, are involved in mediating the effects of day length on the timing of a wide variety of seasonal changes in physiology and behavior (Goldman & Elliott 1988; Goldman 1983).

Activational Mechanisms

REPRODUCTION   In mammals, seasonal changes in reproductive activity are generally associated with changes in pituitary gonadotropin secretion. For example, Syrian hamsters *(Mesocricetus auratus)* are long-day breeders and exhibit decreased circulating concentrations of luteinizing hormone (LH) and follicle stimulating hormone (FSH) following exposure to simulated winter day lengths (Tamarkin et al 1976). In ewes, animals that breed when day lengths are short, exposure to short days leads to increased LH secretion, manifested as an increase in the frequency of pulsatile LH release (Karsch et al 1984). Such changes in pituitary gonadotropin secretion lead to changes in gonadal growth and gonadal steroid hormone secretion (Berndston & Desjardins 1974). Although there is little direct evidence bearing on seasonal changes in the secretion of hypothalamic releasing and inhibiting hormones, it is presumed that changes in gonadotropin secretion are mainly the result of alterations in the hypothalamic-pituitary axis (Karsch et al 1984). Thus, the current concept is that extrinsic factors that mediate seasonal changes in reproductive activity do so primarily via actions on the hypothalamic-pituitary axis that secondarily alter gonadal activity.

STEROID-DEPENDENT REGULATION OF REPRODUCTION   During periods of reproductive activity, one of the important mechanisms regulating the pituitary secretion of FSH and LH is the gonadal hormone feedback system. In males, testicular androgens, especially testosterone, are capable of acting on the hypothalamic-pituitary axis to inhibit the secretion of both gonadotropins. In effect, this feedback system helps to maintain appropriate levels of gonadotropin—i.e. the gonadotropins stimulate the biosynthesis and secretion of testicular androgens and the negative feedback effect of the androgens prevents "over-secretion" of the gonadotropins. In females, a similar negative feedback system utilizes estrogens and progestins to hold FSH and LH concentrations in check. This system is especially important for regulating the number of ovarian follicles that mature during each ovulatory cycle. As follicles become more mature, they produce increased amounts of steroid hormones, resulting in decreased levels of gonadotropins and a cessation of recruitment of new follicles (Bast & Greenwald 1977; Bex & Goldman 1975). In both sexes, gonadal peptide hormones, called inhibin or folliculostatin, also serve to inhibit the secretion of gonadotropins, particularly FSH (Steinberger & Ward 1988).

   One of the mechanisms employed to inhibit the secretion of pituitary LH and FSH during seasonal periods of reproductive quiescence is an increased sensitivity of the hypothalamic-pituitary axis to the negative feedback effects of gonadal steroid hormones (Tamarkin et al 1976; Turek et al 1975; Ellis & Turek 1980b). In males, low concentrations of testosterone are more effective in inhibiting post-castration increases in pituitary gonadotropin secretion in hamsters (Tamarkin et al 1976; Turek & Campbell 1979) and rams (Pelletier & Ortavant 1975) when the animals are exposed to nonstimulatory photoperiods. A return to the lower level of sensitivity is then able to return the animal to a state of reproductive activity via increased pituitary hormone secretion. A similar phenomenon has been implicated in puberty, where a prepubertal decrease in sensitivity to steroid negative feedback leads to increased secretion of LH and FSH and activation of the reproductive system (Ramirez & McCann 1963; McCann & Ramirez 1964). The effects of photoperiod on seasonal changes in sensitivity to steroid feedback are mediated by the pineal hormone, melatonin. Thus, in male hamsters exposed experimentally to long days, exogenous melatonin induces an increase in the sensitivity of the hypothalamic-pituitary axis to the negative feedback effects of testosterone (Sisk & Turek 1982).

STEROID-INDEPENDENT REGULATION OF REPRODUCTION   In addition to changes in the sensitivity of the gonadotropin secretion system to gonadal steroid hormones, a steroid-independent mechanism has also been implicated in the regulation of seasonal changes in the rate of gonadotropin secretion. Castrated male snowshoe hares display seasonal variation in gonadotropin levels despite the absence of negative feedback from gonadal steroids (Davis & Meyer 1973). Likewise, castration of male Syrian hamsters results in elevated blood levels of LH and FSH in both long and short days, but the post-castration gonadotropin levels are higher in animals housed under a long photoperiod than in short-day hamsters (Ellis & Turek 1980a). A steroid-independent effect of photoperiod on gonadotropin secretion is particularly evident in female Syrian hamsters. In long days, female hamsters exhibit an approximately 8–10-fold increase in baseline serum LH titers following ovariectomy, and LH levels can be returned to baseline by administration of estrogen (Yellon et al 1989). After several weeks of exposure to short days, female hamsters become anovulatory and serum LH concentrations are very low during most of the 24-hr cycle; however, the anovulatory females show daily surges of LH during the afternoon (Seegal & Goldman 1975). This pattern of LH secretion continues following ovariectomy (Bridges & Goldman 1975) or after combined ovariectomy and adrenalectomy (Bittman & Goldman 1979). That is, removal of the sources of steroid hormones does not result in any detectable increase in the baseline serum LH concentration in short-day female hamsters, and daily surges of LH are still apparent in the steroid-deprived animals. These observations suggest that, in female Syrian hamsters, the effect of short day lengths on LH secretion is mediated primarily via a steroid-independent mechanism. Seasonal variations in circulating and pituitary concentrations of gonadotropins have also been observed after ovariectomy in pony mares (Garcia & Ginther 1976), ground squirrels (Zucker & Licht 1983), and snowshoe hares (Davis & Meyer 1973).

RELATIONSHIP OF BEHAVIOR TO REPRODUCTIVE STATE   A wide variety of behaviors vary with changes in reproductive state. Some of these, most notably mating behaviors, bear an obvious direct relationship to reproduction. In most vertebrates, mating occurs at about the same time as peak gamete production. Since gametogenesis is a steroid-dependent process in all vertebrates, the evolution of steroid hormone regulation of mating behavior likely occurred as a means to provide temporal coordination between gamete maturation and mating. Other behaviors, such as territorial behavior and migration, are less directly related to reproduction but are frequently associated in an adaptive way with the reproductive process. It is probably because of the close temporal association between gonadal activity and behaviors that are directly or indirectly associated with reproduction that many behaviors are largely regulated by the gonadal steroid hormones. As one would anticipate, the regulation of behavior by reproductive hormones is most evident for those behaviors most closely associated with reproduction—i.e. mating behaviors.

It has been thoroughly documented for many species that the seasonal changes in the display of mating behaviors are regulated primarily by seasonal changes in the amounts of circulating gonadal steroid hormones. In addition, seasonal fluctuations in behavioral *sensitivity* to steroid hormones have also been observed. In castrated male golden hamsters, copulatory behavior can be restored by administration of exogenous testosterone; however, larger doses of the steroid are required to elicit behavior in animals exposed to a short photoperiod (Campbell et al 1978; Morin & Zucker 1978). The various components of masculine sexual responsiveness—i.e. chemosensory behaviors, mounting, intromission, and ejaculation—are not equally affected by exposure to short days (Miernicki et al 1988). These behavioral effects of short-day exposure in male hamsters are prevented by pinealectomy (Miernicki et al 1988). In female hamsters estrogen is less effective for activating lordosis during exposure to short days (Badura et al 1987). Unlike the case for males, this decrease in behavioral sensitivity to estrogen is not altered either by pinealectomy or by melatonin administration (Badura & Nunez 1989). It is possible that photoperiod influences female sexual behavior through a direct neural route. Neural input from the retina to the suprachiasmatic nuclei (SCN) of the hypothalamus is probably required for pineal-dependent responses to changes in day length. However, there are also direct retinal projections to the basal forebrain and to hypothalamic regions outside the SCN (Pickard & Silverman 1981; Youngstrom et al 1987) that concentrate ovarian steroids (Fraile et al 1987; Morrell & Pfaff, 1978) and may have a role in female sexual behavior.

DISSOCIATED REPRODUCTIVE PATTERNS AND STEROID-INDEPENDENT MATING BEHAVIOR   There are some notable exceptions to the usual association between reproductive hormones and sexual behavior (Crews 1984).

Some vertebrates exhibit a so-called "dissociated" reproductive pattern, whereby the production of gametes and mating do not occur during the same phase of the annual cycle. In the red-sided garter snake *(Thamnophis sirtalis parietalis)*, for example, sperm are produced during the summer and are stored in the male reproductive tract through the 8–9-month period of winter torpor. Experiments involving castration and treatment with androgens have revealed that the level of androgens present during the mating phase has no influence on the presence or intensity of mating behavior (Crews 1984). Rather, mating behavior, which persists for about three weeks, seems to occur only in snakes that have experienced a period of torpor. The pineal gland may be involved in determining when mating will occur, since removal of the pineal gland prior to entry into winter torpor prevents the display of mating behavior that normally occurs immediately after emergence from hibernation (Nelson et al 1987; Crews et al 1988). A seasonal timing mechanism is probably involved in determining the time for mating in this species, and this mechanism may be partially or entirely independent of gonadal hormones. Clearly, for a species that has evolved a dissociated reproductive pattern, it is appropriate for reproductive behavior to be liberated from the influence of sex hormones, and an alternative mechanism evidently ensures that mating occurs at the proper time. Dissociated reproductive patterns are also known in mammals, particularly in several species of bats where sperm are stored in the male reproductive tract during winter hibernation (Wimsatt 1969; Gustafson 1979). The role of hormones in sexual behavior has not been definitively examined in these mammalian species.

White-crowned sparrows *(Zonotrichia leucophrys)*, while not displaying a dissociated reproductive pattern, exhibit an unusual pattern of hormonal regulation of seasonal changes in masculine sexual behavior and territorial defense. In this species, territorial behavior appears to be more strongly influenced by androgens than is sexual behavior. Sexually inexperienced, castrated male sparrows display vigorous sexual behavior when exposed to a long photoperiod, but sexual behavior is markedly decreased in short days. Sparrows exposed to short days do not show increased mounting behavior during treatment with androgens (Moore & Kranz 1983). However, aggressive behavior of male sparrows can be stimulated by androgen treatment. The adaptive significance of this pattern of response to androgens may result from the mating strategies of white-crowned sparrows. Male sparrows are monogamous, but they do not participate in the incubation of the eggs or feeding of the nestlings. Rather, they may seek extra-pair copulations while their mates are performing these tasks. The independence of male sex behavior from androgens might permit extended mating behavior while the dependence of aggressive behavior on androgens may help to coordinate mate-guarding behavior with the seeking of extra-pair copulations (Moore 1984).

AGONISTIC BEHAVIOR   Perhaps the most general case for seasonal regulation of a behavior by gonadal hormones is that represented by the lizard, *Sceloporus jarrovi*, where a single behavior is largely regulated by testicular androgens during the breeding season but is expressed independently of testicular hormones during another phase of the annual cycle. *S. jarrovi* begins to exhibit territorial behavior, expressed as male-male aggression, during the midsummer phase that precedes mating. At this time, castration does not result in a decrease in the level of male-male aggressiveness (Moore & Marler 1987). During the subsequent reproductive phase, the level of territorial behavior increases; this increase can be prevented by castration and reinstated by exogenous androgens. Castrated, mating-phase lizards do not stop showing territorial behavior altogether; rather, aggressiveness declines to a level similar to that exhibited during the earlier, premating phase (Moore 1987). Yet a third condition occurs in this species subsequent to the mating phase when territorial behavior is completely absent and the animals aggregate, tolerating close proximity and even physical contact by members of the same sex. It seems that testicular hormones act only to regulate the *intensity* of territorial behavior in *S. jarrovi* and that other, as yet unknown, mechanisms determine the overall annual pattern of territoriality.

There are many reports of seasonal changes in agonistic and territorial behavior among birds and mammals. For example, male starlings *(Sturnus vulgaris)* form rigorously defended territories during the breeding season (Feare 1984). Their territorial behavior is correlated with high circulating levels of androgens. At the end of the breeding season, blood androgen levels diminish and territorial behaviors stop. The reduction in agonistic behavior allows the formation of so-called "winter feeding flocks." These flocks appear to confer advantages vis-à-vis predator avoidance and foraging success (Feare 1984).

Birds that migrate must compete with resident animals for food and shelter. In some situations, the resident birds are in reproductive condition and highly territorial. Although first reported as anomalous behavior, territorial systems have recently been described in wintering migrants and may be common among neotropical migrant passerines (Greenberg 1986). These nonresident birds are not in reproductive condition and their gonads are not producing steroids. The physiological mechanisms underlying territoriality or short-term site defense in nonresident migrants have not been studied.

Small rodents also display seasonal changes in territorial behavior. Microtine rodents (lemmings and voles), and probably most rodent species in temperate and boreal regions, form winter aggregations. Animals huddling together presumably benefit by reducing energetic requirements in the winter. During the summer, two patterns of social behavior are observed among these group-huddling rodents: isolated and territorial, or socially interactive. Winter nest sharing appears common among these rodents, and energy and moisture conservation are likely important driving forces in the evolution of this behavior (Madison 1984). The communal huddling and nest sharing groups are composed of mixed sexes and species. Presumably, the lack of circulating androgens permits the social tolerance necessary for this pattern of behavior to appear. However, this proposition requires testing. If reduced blood androgen levels are necessary to allow close social contact, individuals that maintain their reproductive systems during the winter may forfeit the energy savings inherent in communal huddling (Nelson 1987)—i.e. animals that maintain high levels of circulating androgens throughout the winter may be too aggressive to tolerate close proximity to others and thereby lose energetic benefits (West & Dublin 1984).

Since the physiological costs of maintaining the reproductive system of males during the winter are minimal, the question of why male rodents have evolved to undergo seasonal collapse and regrowth of the reproductive apparatus may require a behavioral answer. Androgen-dependent behaviors (i.e. mating and territorial behaviors) obviously reduce foraging opportunities. Perhaps the energy costs incurred by individuals too aggressive to huddle reduce their fitness more than the reproductive benefits of successful matings during the winter would increase it.

Red deer *(Cervus elaphus)* also undergo seasonal changes in behavior and morphology (Lincoln et al 1972). The males normally live in bachelor groups except during the fall. A great deal of aggression is observed among the males during the autumn. These animals develop antlers throughout the summer and fall and use them during the battles for females. The antlers are cast in late winter and the animals are in "velvet horn" during spring and early summer. Each male attempts to control a group of females (hinds) in order to have exclusive mating rights when the hinds come into estrus. Territorial, aggressive, and reproductive behaviors are mediated by testosterone.

Stags that were castrated during the early winter promptly cast their antlers and acquired velvet horns. The castrated stags also plummeted in social rank. In spring, the gonad-intact males were also in velvet horn and the castrated animals regained their prior social position. Testosterone was implanted in four intact males, and two of these showed increased aggression during the winter and spring. These stags also climbed in social rank because they retained hard horn antlers. Despite the elevated levels of testosterone, the hormone-treated males exhibited mating behavior only at the appropriate time of year—i.e. late fall and early winter. These results suggest an annual cycle of androgen-sensitivity of brain areas that regulate rutting behavior. Stags that were castrated during the early winter were given testosterone implants in the early summer, and that increased their position in the dominance hierarchy *before* their antlers began to grow. Thus, testosterone promoted behavioral changes prior to changes in morphology. Consequently, the seasonal cycle of testicular function and subsequent androgen secretion affects social behavior directly via its effects on the central nervous system and indirectly by acting on morphology.

In wood rats *(Neotoma fuscipes)* seasonal changes in aggressive behavior are apparently independent of testicular hormones. The level of inter-male aggression increases during the breeding season in this species, but this seasonal increase in aggression is also observed in males that have been castrated postpubertally. The independence of aggression from androgen has been rationalized as follows: The greatest threat to reproductive success from conspecific males comes during the breeding season, but the greatest need for nest defense comes later in the year after the young have been weaned and begin seeking nests of their own (Caldwell et al 1984).

DAILY ACTIVITY PATTERNS   Field observations of several species of microtine rodents (e.g. *Microtus agrestis, M. oeconomus, M. montanus, Clethrionomys gapperi,* and *C. glareolus*) have indicated a seasonal shift in activity patterns (Ostermann 1956; Erkinaro 1961; Herman 1977; Rowsemitt 1986). The animals tend to be nocturnal during the summer and diurnal during the winter. The adaptive function of the seasonal shift in daily activity patterns may involve energetic savings (Rowsemitt 1986). By constraining most locomotor activity to the daylight hours during the winter, the animal avoids the coldest part of the day; likewise, bouts of activity during summer nights allow the animal to avoid thermal stress or dehydration (Rowsemitt 1986).

Testosterone appears to mediate the seasonal shift in activity patterns in *M. montanus* (Rowsemitt 1986). Adult male voles were either castrated or left intact and maintained in long (LD 16:8) or short (LD 8:16) days. Testosterone replacement therapy was given to some castrated animals via subcutaneously implanted Silastic capsules. Castrated montane voles increased diurnal and decreased nocturnal wheel-running activity as compared to intact animals. Voles implanted with testosterone increased nocturnal activity relative to voles implanted with empty capsules. There was a great deal of individual variation among the experimental animals; however, it appears that photoperiod primarily mediates the dramatic seasonal shift in activity patterns by affecting androgen production (Rowsemitt 1986). Other environmental cues such as temperature and food quality and quantity may also affect activity patterns. Although many subtle effects of steroids on the timing of activity have been reported in other rodents species (Morin et al 1977; Ellis & Turek 1983; Morin & Cummings 1981), it has been difficult to assess the functional significance of these effects.

BRAIN SIZE AND LEARNING   Seasonal changes in brain weight have been reported for several species of rodents and shrews (e.g. *C. glareolus, C. rutilus, M. oeconomus, M. gregalis, Sorex auraneus,* and *S. minutus*) (Bielak & Pucek 1960; Pucek 1965; Yaskin 1984). Brains are heavier in summer-captured than in winter-captured animals (Yaskin 1984). The adaptive function of the seasonal variation in brain weight may also involve energetic savings (Yaskin 1984). Although the brain comprises only 2–3% of the body mass of rodents and insectivores, it uses about 20% of the energy expended by the animal. Minor reductions in brain mass could result in substantial energy savings.

A significant part of the seasonal change in brain weight could be attributed to differences in water content (Yaskin 1984); however, several parts of the brain, specifically the neocortex and the basal portion of the brain (i.e. the corpus striatum) show cytoarchitectural changes in rodents and shrews. Relative weight of the forebrain declines during the winter; relative weight of the hippocampus increases from winter to summer; and the relative weights of the olfactory bulbs, myelencephalon, and cerebellum increase during the winter (Yaskin 1984). A sex difference in brain weight is observed among bank voles *(C. glareolus)* only during the winter months; male brains are heavier than female brains at this time. The absolute and relative weight of the hippocampus is significantly higher in males throughout the year, but the difference is most pronounced during the winter (Yaskin 1984). Meadow voles *(M. pennsylvanicus)* also show seasonal changes in brain weight. Photoperiod appears to organize the seasonal fluctuation in brain weight in meadow voles (Dark et al 1987); short-day males have smaller brains with less DNA than long-day animals.

Despite the evidence for seasonal changes in brain weight in rodents, there has been relatively little research investigating seasonal changes in learning among mammalian species. This may reflect the influence of studies on laboratory rats, relatively seasonal animals. A few studies have addressed seasonal changes in learning and memory in fishes, reptiles, and birds. Among reptiles, the seasonal torpor appears to interfere with learning during the winter; in many of these studies, it is not clear whether learning or memory function is depressed because of cold exposure or quiescent animals simply cannot make appropriate responses.

Goldfish exhibit a seasonal change in learning ability, with maximal learning occurring during January–March, prior to spawning. Poor learning was observed during the summer after the spawning season (Shashoua 1973). Seasonal changes in learning to swim with a tethered float (Shashoua 1973), conditioned avoidance responding (Agranoff & Davis 1968), and maze learning (Shashoua 1973) have been reported. Increased learning capacity in late winter coincides with gonadal recrudescence and high blood levels of steroidal hormones. Suggestive data indicate that photoperiod may regulate the seasonal cycle of learning ability in goldfish (Shashoua 1973).

In canaries, direct evidence links photoperiod, testicular function, and learning capacity. The testes grow and produce testosterone and singing behavior increases in males during the spring. Females do not really sing, but rather make simple "calls" (Gurney & Konishi 1980). The male canary song repertoire and specific brain nuclei—namely the hyperstriatum ventrale, pars caudale or higher vocal center (HVC), and robustus archistriatalis (RA)—increase during the long days of spring (Nottebohm 1980). In the autumn, the testes regress, singing frequency decreases, the repertoire is reduced, and the volumes of the HVC and RA decrease. Treatment with testosterone in the autumn mimics spring-like changes in behavior and brain morphology. Each spring, every individual male must reestablish his repertoire and perhaps expand it. The increase in frequency of singing and the addition of new songs to the repertoire in the spring are accompanied by the increased size of the HVC over that of the prior year. During the winter, the birds do not hear songs; consequently, there must be a representation of old songs somewhere in the brain.

Individual male canaries differ in the size of their song repertoires. Canaries with small HVC and RA always have small repertoires; animals with large HVC and RA may or may not have large repertoires (Nottebohm 1989). An analogy has been drawn between the size of brain nuclei in canaries and the number of bookshelves in a library (Nottebohm 1989). This brain space hypothesis suggests that a library must have substantial shelf space if it is to hold many books; however, these shelves may not always be filled. Data indicate that learning new songs can directly increase the size of the HVC (Nottebohm 1989). As far as we can determine, few other vertebrate systems have been investigated for seasonal changes in learning ability.

MATERNAL BEHAVIOR AND LITTER SEX RATIOS   Seasonal fluctuations in the capacity to exhibit maternal behavior have not been examined in detail because it has been widely assumed that seasonally induced reproductive quiescence precludes the display of this behavior during part of the year. However, some environmental factors affect maternal responses. Several avian species adjust clutch size in response to changes in food availability (Lack 1954). Syrian hamsters (Huck et al 1986) and house mice (Marstellar & Lynch 1987) display increased cannibalism toward their young during periods of food restriction. The opportunity to hoard food reduces, but does not abolish, cannibalism in hamsters (Miceli & Malsbury 1982). It is interesting that food restriction during development can affect second-generation offspring; litter survival and growth rate are reduced in hamsters born to a dam that had been food restricted during development. In addition, the sex ratios of litters born to food-restricted female hamsters are skewed in favor of females (Huck et al 1986). It is unclear whether this bias towards female offspring in food-restricted hamsters reflects a gestational event or an active culling of males via postpartum cannibalism. Montane voles display a similar sex ratio bias toward female offspring when the dam is given 6-methoxyben-zoxazolinone (6-MBOA) (Berger et al 1987), a plant derivative present in young seedlings at a time coincident with the onset of the breeding season in this species. Ingestion of 6-MBOA appears to induce the birth of more females during the early portions of the breeding season.

The mechanisms of seasonal changes in maternal behavior may involve photoperiodic changes that modulate behavior through the endocrine system. Increased prolactin levels during pregnancy are required for the induction of the full maternal behavior repertoire in rats (Loundes & Bridges 1986). In hamsters, decreased prolactin levels following administration of ergocornine or bromocriptine have been related to decreased maternal aggression toward male intruders, increased aggression toward pups, disruption of retrieval behavior, and an increased incidence of maternal cannibalism of the pups (Wise & Pryor 1977; M. M. McCarthy, G. H. Curran, H. I. Siegal, personal communication). In hamsters and several other species, seasonal changes in circulating prolactin concentrations are largely under photoperiodic control (Goldman et al 1981; Martinet et al 1982; Smale et al 1988; Worthy et al 1985; Blank & Desjardins 1985). It is not known whether day length would also influence prolactin secretion during pregnancy or lactation. However, it has been reported that while pinealectomized hamsters maintained under natural photoperiod were able to bear litters during the winter, the dams displayed a high degree of cannibalism (Reiter 1973/1974). It is possible that the females in this study failed to secrete sufficient prolactin to support maternal behavior, since pinealectomy only partially prevents the effects of short-day exposure on prolactin cell activity in female hamsters (Blask et al 1986).

MORTALITY   The brown marsupial mouse *(Antechinus stuartii)* is one of several species of Dasyuridae, the Australian group of carnivorous and insectivorous marsupials. The life-history strategies of these mice include several unusual features. The breeding season is highly synchronized and is completed in approximately two weeks (Wood 1970). The breeding season is followed, in the field, by the death of all reproductive males (Woolley 1966; Wood 1970) and, in laboratory studies, by mortality or reproductive senescence (Woolley 1966). Copulation is very prolonged, usually lasting for more than five hours and often twelve hours (Marlow 1961). Postmortem examination of males in the laboratory has suggested that death results from hyperactivity of the adrenal glands (Wood 1970). Apparently, reproduction is so stressful that it kills the males. Subsequent breeding in the field involves young of the previous year and one-year-old females. The possibility exists that the mortality of male brown marsupial mice may be seasonal but not directly related to reproductive behavior. A similar adrenal mechanism was hypothesized to induce mortality of postspawning salmon; the stress of migration to natal streams was believed to stimulate the oversecretion of adrenal steroids, resulting in death. However, salmon also died immediately after spawning in captive fish that did not participate in the strenuous upstream migration (Robertson & Wexler 1959). Thus in salmon, too, the programmed death that follows the act of reproduction may involve the actions of adrenal steroids.

Timing Mechanisms

EXOGENOUS AND ENDOGENOUS FACTORS   Studies of seasonal rhythms in reproductive physiology have revealed a variety of mechanisms used for timing seasonal changes in reproduction. Appropriate timing of reproductive activities enables the various stages of the process to occur when environmental conditions are most favorable. Photoperiodism—the ability to use day-length cues to time a variety of physiological and behavioral changes—has been the most widely studied of these mechanisms. For purposes of this discussion, photoperiodic mammals may be divided into two categories: those that exhibit circannual cycles that are "entrained" or synchronized by photoperiodic cues, and those that fail to exhibit endogenous circannual cycles. Deer exhibit circannual rhythms of reproductive activity that persist even when the animals are maintained under a constant day length. Changes in the day length are able to influence reproductive activity in deer, and natural photoperiodic changes are presumably largely responsible for establishing the seasonal pattern of reproduction (Goss & Rosen 1973; Goss 1980, 1984; Plotka et al 1984). Sheep may also exhibit circannual cycles of reproductive activity in the absence of environmental cues, and these rhythms are clearly responsive to photoperiod under natural environmental conditions (Karsch et al 1984).

Many mammals fail to exhibit endogenous cycles when housed under a fixed day length. For example, a variety of relatively short-lived rodent species remain reproductively active so long as they are maintained in long photoperiod. While these species require photoperiodic changes for the continuance of seasonal cycles, they all display a prominent element of endogenous seasonal timing. Thus, in each of these species, a "spontaneous" activation of the reproductive system occurs after several months of exposure to short days. It is thought that this event is triggered by an endogenous timing mechanism that allows the animals to prepare for the environmental changes that will take place in the spring (Reiter 1970; Elliott & Goldman 1981).

MECHANISMS OF HIBERNATION AND ENDOGENOUS SEASONAL TIME KEEPING   Perhaps the most striking example of the operation of an endogenous timing device in photoperiodic species is observed in several species of hibernating mammals. Most hibernators undergo gonadal regression before entering hibernation. Yet, when these animals emerge from their hibernacula in early spring they are approaching full breeding condition. Since the process of spermatogenesis requires several weeks in mammals, it would appear that reproductive activation in males must begin before emergence from hibernation. Laboratory studies have shown that pituitary gonadotropin secretion and testicular growth begin during the last few weeks of hibernation in Turkish hamsters *(Mesocricetus brandti)*. Hibernation is terminated when testosterone levels exceed a threshold; this mechanism may serve to coordinate emergence from hibernation with testicular recrudescence (Hall & Goldman 1980; Hall et al 1982). The timing of testicular recrudescence in Turkish hamsters is probably accomplished by the same type of seasonal timer that operates in other photoperiodic rodents. Male Turkish hamsters that are exposed to short days in a warm environment cannot hibernate; yet, these animals exhibit a cycle of testicular regression and subsequent recrudescence very similar in timing to that seen in hibernating males (Darrow et al 1987). A similar mechanism for temporal coordination of the seasons of hibernation and reproduction appears to exist in European hamsters *(Cricetus cricetus)* (Darrow et al 1988) and hedgehogs *(Erinacus europaeus)* (Saboureau 1986). An endogenous timing mechanism that anticipates spring conditions may be particularly useful for hibernators, since these animals are not exposed to photoperiod cues during the winter and are relatively buffered from changes in ambient temperature in their hibernacula.

Males that have just undergone testicular recrudescence may produce more androgens and gonadotropins than animals that have been continuously maintained in long day lengths (Berndtson & Desjardins 1974). This "overshoot" of endocrine activity may have functional behavioral consequences. Long-term castrated rodents require higher levels of androgen to maintain mating behavior as compared to recently castrated or intact animals (DaMassa et al 1977). Brain centers that control reproductive behavior may require sensitization by androgen exposure after prolonged gonadal quiescence in order to respond appropriately (Morin & Zucker 1978).

Virtually no information is available regarding the mechanism for *endogenous* seasonal timekeeping. Attempts have been made to disrupt circannual rhythmicity by lesioning brain regions thought to be involved. Lesions of the paraventricular nuclei (PVN) fail to disrupt circannual cycles of body mass fluctuation in ground squirrels *(Spermophilus lateralis)* (Dark & Zucker 1985), while lesions of the SCN disrupt circannual rhythmicity in some individuals. However, most of the squirrels continue to display circannual rhythms following destruction of the SCN despite the fact that *circadian* rhythms are absent in these animals (Dark et al 1985). This observation and others in both ground squirrels and birds suggest that circannual rhythms and circadian rhythms may not be regulated by the same neural substrate (Gwinner 1986).

PHOTOPERIODISM   A good deal has been learned about the neuroendocrine basis for photoperiodism in mammals, especially over the past three decades. In virtually all species of mammals that have been carefully examined, pinealectomy severely interferes with most photoperiodic responses (Goldman 1983). This was first demonstrated in Syrian hamsters, where removal of the pineal gland prevented the inhibition of reproductive activity that typically occurs in this species following exposure to day lengths of less than 12.5 hr (Hoffman & Reiter 1965). This observation led to the common belief that the pineal gland exerts an inhibitory effect on the reproductive system (Reiter 1970). However, pinealectomy does not result in the maintenance of reproductive activity in all species. Indeed, in Turkish and European hamsters pinealectomy frequently *induces* testicular regression (Carter et al 1982; Masson-Pevet et al 1987). That the effects of pinealectomy in these two species are opposite to those in Syrian hamsters is of particular interest because 1. all three hamster species are long-day breeders and 2. Turkish and Syrian hamsters are closely related species.

The seemingly disparate results following pinealectomy in various long-day breeding mammals may be explained in part by the results of further research on the neuroendocrine mechanisms of photoperiodism. The pineal hormone melatonin has been shown to mediate pineal effects on photoperiodic responses in a wide variety of mammals (Goldman 1983). Pineal melatonin synthesis and secretion are rhythmic, peak levels of melatonin being secreted during the night. The rhythm in pineal melatonin is largely regulated by one or more circadian oscillators, probably in the SCN (Goldman & Darrow 1983; Darrow & Goldman 1986). In almost all mammals that have been examined, including species generally considered to be reproductively nonresponsive to changes in day length (e.g. the laboratory rat), the duration of the nocturnal peak of melatonin increases as the photoperiod decreases (Karsch et al 1984; Illnerova et al 1986; Darrow & Goldman 1986). In Siberian hamsters and sheep, daily infusions of melatonin have been administered to pinealectomized animals and reproductive responses have been measured. In both species, responses characteristic for animals exposed to long day lengths (i.e. stimulation of reproduction for hamsters, inhibition for sheep) are elicited by daily melatonin infusions of short duration. Melatonin infusions of longer duration result in short-day-type responses (Carter & Goldman 1983a,b; Bittman & Karsch 1984). In Siberian hamsters *(Phodopus sungorus),* nonreproductive parameters—i.e. body mass, carcass lipid content, enzymatic activities of fat pads—are also differentially affected by long- as compared to short-duration infusions of melatonin (Bartness & Goldman 1988a,b). The time of day at which the infusions of melatonin were given did not appear to be critical in either sheep or hamsters (Carter & Goldman 1983a; Bartness & Goldman 1988a; Wayne et al 1988). Based upon these data, it has been proposed that the duration of the nocturnal elevation of pineal melatonin secretion is inversely related to day length—or directly related to the length of the dark phase—and that changes in the duration of the elevated phase of the daily melatonin rhythm convey a photoperiodic message to a variety of physiological systems (Goldman 1983; Goldman & Elliott 1988). Recent data in Syrian hamsters and white-footed mice *(Peromyscus leucopus)* suggest that these species may respond to changes in the duration of the phase of elevated melatonin in a manner similar to that reported for Siberian hamsters and sheep (Dowell & Lynch 1987; M. Hastings, personal communication).

PHOTOPERIODIC HISTORY   Recent evidence indicates that photoperiodic responses in mammals are not based solely on absolute day length; animals may respond differently to a given photoperiod depending on whether day lengths are increasing or decreasing. This phenomenon has been reported in two types of situations: prenatal transfer of photoperiodic information by mothers, and prior effects of photoperiod on adult rodents. In Siberian hamsters and montane voles, photoperiodic information is transmitted from the mother to her fetuses. In both species, postnatal testicular development in an LD 14:10 photoperiod is rapid if gestation occurs in a day length of 14 hr or less. However, if the photoperiod of gestation is longer than 14 hr, then postnatal testicular maturation occurs slowly in 14 hr photoperiods (Horton 1984; Stetson et al 1986). Cross-fostering experiments reveal that a photoperiodic message is transmitted from the mother to her fetuses prior to birth (Horton 1985; Elliott & Goldman 1989). In the Siberian hamster, the maternal pineal gland is involved in this phenomenon (Elliott & Goldman 1989), and melatonin appears to be instrumental in the transmission of photoperiodic information (Weaver & Reppert 1986; Weaver et al 1987).

Reproductive responses of adult Siberian hamsters and sheep to photoperiod cues are also influenced by prior photoperiodic history. Testicular regression occurs when hamsters are transferred from LD 16:8 to LD 14:10; however, LD 14:10 appears to be stimulatory to testis growth when animals are transferred from a shorter day length (i.e. LD 8:16) that had resulted in testicular regression (Hoffman et al 1986). In ewes, the progressively decreasing natural day lengths experienced during fall and winter appear to be important determinants for the duration of the breeding season. Ewes subjected to a single-step decrease in photoperiod from LD 16:8 to LD 8:16 or from LD 16:8 to LD 12:12 show increased LH secretion for a period of 50–60 days. However, when the day length was decreased in two stages, the period of elevated LH levels lasted almost twice as long (Malpaux et al 1988). The ability of mammals to modify their responses to photoperiod in conjunction with photoperiodic history would appear to provide them with an added measure of precision in using day length as a predictive cue. Thus, in the examples cited above, increasing day lengths favor responses that are characteristic of spring and summer, while decreasing day lengths favor autumn or winter responses. In all likelihood, photoperiodic influences on behavioral parameters also have a component related to photoperiodic history.

HUMAN SEASONALITY

Population Data

Seasonal rhythms in the rates of human conception, mortality, and suicide have been reported (Aschoff 1981). In each case, it is generally necessary to sample a large population to obtain statistically significant data since the fluctuations from season to season are relatively small. Thus, these rhythms are quantitatively different from most of those discussed for other animals. Since the human data are derived from populations exposed to both natural and artificial environmental changes, it is impossible to know the underlying causes of these rhythms.

It is of interest to consider the absence of major seasonal fluctuations in human reproductive activity in relation to the selective forces that presumably led to the evolution of reproductive seasonality in other species. Human reproduction is characterized by a relatively long gestation period and an extremely prolonged period of intensive parental care. These energy-demanding processes cannot be compressed into one portion of the year, as is typical for most seasonal species; rather, these processes require several years. There may thus be little selective advantage to beginning this lengthy process at any particular time of year. Future research into human seasonality might benefit from asking how seasonality may contribute to human fitness.

Endogenous circannual cycles have not been reported in humans. Collecting such data would be problematic, since the studies necessary to test for the presence of circannual rhythms would require the isolation of individuals under constant environmental conditions for periods of more than one year.

Seasonal Affective Disorder

SYMPTOMS   Despite the lack of evidence for endogenous rhythms in humans, many reports demonstrate seasonal cycles in human behavior (Poikolainen 1982; Mathers & Harris 1983; Becker 1981; Ehrenkranz 1983; Gjessing 1983). One such seasonal rhythm that has received much attention is winter depression, or Seasonal Affective Disorder (SAD). SAD is characterized by depressed affect, lethargy, loss of libido, hypersomnia, excessive weight gain, carbohydrate cravings, anxiety, and inability to concentrate or focus attention during the late autumn or winter (Rosenthal et al 1988). In the northern hemisphere, symptoms usually begin between October and December and undergo remission during March. These symptoms do not merely reflect the "holiday blues," for individuals suffering from SAD in the southern hemisphere display symptoms six months out of phase with inhabitants of the northern hemisphere (Terman 1988). With the onset of summer, SAD patients regain their energy and become active and elated, often to the point of hypomania or mania. The atypical features of depression, hyperphagia, carbohydrate cravings, and hypersomnia set SAD apart from nonseasonal depression; SAD patients are frequently diagnosed as experiencing "Bipolar II" depression or "Atypical Bipolar Disorder," particularly if hypermania or mania is present (DSM-III). Recently, several forms of therapy have been used for patients with SAD. Phase advance of the sleep cycle may alleviate depression under some conditions (Wehr et al 1979). Attention has been directed to the use of light in the treatment of SAD. Patients are usually exposed to bright light for a few hours in the morning or evening, and signs of remission are often apparent within a few days (Rosenthal et al 1988).

Improperly set circadian rhythms may be involved in patients suffering from SAD (Lewy et al 1985, 1988). It was suggested that changing the onset of sleep time would reset biological clocks, ameliorating the depression (reviewed in Lewy et al 1988). In one study, a depressed patient was phase-advanced in the sleep-wake cycle by six hours. Her depression was temporarily ameliorated (Wehr et al 1979). Four of seven other patients who underwent spontaneous remission from depression simultaneously phase-advanced their times of awakening (Wehr et al 1979). Lithium, tricyclic antidepressants, and estrogen affect symptoms in depressive illnesses, and these substances also affect endogenous timekeeping mechanisms (Wehr et al 1979). The efficacy of pharmacological and sleep-wake cycle manipulation in ameliorating depression suggested that treatments may affect common mechanisms.

More recently, bright lights have been used in place of sleep-wake therapy in the treatment of SAD. Phototherapy induces rapid recovery rates, perhaps also by affecting timekeeping mechanisms to phase-advance biological rhythms (Lewy et al 1988). It has been suggested that light possesses two antidepressant effects. Light treatment in the morning may ameliorate depression by realignment of inappropriately phased circadian rhythms, and light may serve as a general "energizer" of mood that may be attributable wholly or in part to a placebo effect (Lewy et al 1988).

POSSIBLE MECHANISMS   Serotonin may be involved in the symptoms of SAD (Skwerer et al 1988; Wurtman & Wurtman 1989). Tryptophan, an amino acid circulating in the blood at low levels, is converted to serotonin in the brain, specifically in the raphe nuclei (Cooper et al 1986). Diet affects this conversion process since carbohydrates stimulate pancreatic beta cells to secrete insulin that in turn facilitates the uptake of sugars and nontryptophan amino acids into peripheral cells. This results in a relatively high ratio of tryptophan to other amino acids in the blood, and since tryptophan is competing with the other amino acids for access to central nervous tissue, carbohydrate ingestion results in more tryptophan crossing the blood-brain barrier and higher production of serotonin (Wurtman & Wurtman 1989). Serotonin levels feed back to regulate the intake of carbohydrates. It is possible that patients suffering from SAD may have cyclic disruptions in their serotonin-carbohydrate regulating mechanisms (Wurtman & Wurtman 1989). Serotonin is involved in normal sleep onset, and faulty serotonin regulation may also contribute to the hypersomnia reported in SAD patients. If it is true that symptoms of SAD result from faulty serotonin metabolism, then pharmacological interventions that elevate serotonin levels should reduce the severity of some SAD symptoms. Administration of the serotonin agonist delta-fenfluramine to patients with SAD reduces carbohydrate intake and the associated body mass gain (Wurtman et al 1985). Delta-fenfluramine also reduces the depression associated with SAD (Wurtman et al 1985).

Serotonin is converted in a two-step process to melatonin in the pineal gland. Melatonin levels are higher at night than during the daytime in both nocturnal and diurnal animals (Goldman 1983). In humans, as with other mammals, phase shifting the light-dark cycle results in a comparable shift in the timing of the daily nighttime peak of melatonin secretion (Lewy et al 1988). In a variety of mammals, including humans, the nocturnal synthesis and secretion of pineal melatonin can be rapidly inhibited by exposure to brief periods of light at night (Lewy et al 1980; Hoffman et al 1981; Illnerova & Vanecek 1984). Thus light has two actions in humans, as it does in other mammals: light can entrain, or synchronize, the melatonin rhythms; and light can acutely suppress daily melatonin secretion. Either or both of these effects may be involved in the therapeutic effects of bright light exposure in the treatment of SAD (Lewy et al 1988; Wurtman & Wurtman 1989).

Illumination levels outdoors at temperate latitudes range between 12,000 and 100,000 lux (Benoit 1964; Wurtman 1975), while levels of artificial illumination indoors typically vary from 200 to 500 lux. The human visual system exhibits rapid adaptation to changing intensities of illumination. Consequently, the light levels encountered outdoors may not be visually perceived as orders of magnitude more intense than indoor illumination levels. Physiologically, however, humans respond quite differently to the higher levels of illumination provided by exposure to sunlight. For example, exposure to 1500 lux or greater is necessary for the acute inhibition of human melatonin secretion (Lewy et al 1980). The requirement for high intensity illumination to suppress nighttime melatonin secretion in humans contrasts with the results from several other mammalian species, where very low light intensities are capable of preventing pineal biosynthetic and secretory activity (Brainard et al 1983). In this context, it is intriguing that normal indoor levels of artificial illumination are insufficient to relieve the symptoms of SAD; much brighter light must be used for effective treatment.

The depressive symptoms of SAD cause much human suffering. However, it must be emphasized that depression, however salient to the patient, physician, and family members, is only one of several foci of the seasonal disorder. Other phenomena associated with the syndrome are increased food intake, body mass, lethargy, and sleep-bout length. A random sample of New York City residents indicated seasonal changes in all of these symptoms associated with SAD (Terman 1988). However, the annual cycle of weight gain, mood change, and sleep-bout increase are less pronounced in the general population than in the SAD sample. It has been suggested that these changes have evolved to provide for seasonal energy savings. Thus, milder forms of depression may be part of an adaptive constellation of traits. In conjunction with this hypothesis, one might view SAD as an exaggerated form of this strategy.

It may be difficult to develop animal models for this disorder. Clinicians focus on the affective aspects of SAD, and seasonally breeding animals may be an inappropriate model for seasonal depression in humans (Zucker 1988). There have also been attempts to use—inappropriately—other seasonal phenomena, hibernation for example, as model systems in which to study the mechanisms of SAD (Mrosovsky 1988). However, even among rodents, there are many adaptive strategies for coping with seasonal environmental changes; some animals lose body mass in the autumn to reduce food requirements, while others increase autumnal body mass in order to have endogenous energy stores (Nelson 1987). It may be prudent to discover the nature and number of human seasonal cycles before animal models are developed.

While bright light therapy may relieve the symptoms of SAD via a mechanism that involves phase-shifting circadian rhythms (Lewy et al 1988), an alternative hypothesis is that supplementary light may act through a photoperiodic mechanism to alter a seasonal response (Kripke 1981). This idea is consistent with the seasonal nature of SAD, particularly the occurrence of the depression phase in the winter, when day lengths are shortest. It is of interest to consider this hypothesis in conjuction with what is known of photoperiodic responses and seasonality in other mammals: 1. In mammals, most overt responses to an abrupt change in day length require periods of several weeks (Goldman 1983). This contrasts with the rapid ameliorative effect of bright light exposure in SAD patients. However, there are a few exceptions to the long time requirement for overt responses to photoperiod change; for example, immature Siberian hamsters exhibit changes in the rate of testis growth within five days after being shifted from long to short days (Carter & Goldman 1983a). 2. Several long-lived mammalian species exhibit endogenous circannual rhythmicity, and in some of these animals photoperiod is an important synchronizer. Artificial manipulation of photoperiod may be used to entrain circannual rhythms or to induce animals to display more than one complete cycle in a year (Gwinner 1986). However, it is not possible to keep animals in one phase of the cycle indefinitely by manipulation of the photoperiod. Thus, if SAD is related to human circannual rhythmicity, one might expect light therapy merely to rephase rather than eliminate or reduce the amount of annual depression.

Clearly, there are major gaps in our knowledge since we have virtually no data that bear directly on whether or not humans are either photoperiodic or circannual. Nevertheless, the growing body of data in seasonal mammals may be useful in pointing the way to obtaining such information for humans.

CONCLUSIONS

Most seasonal changes in behavior reflect strategies to manage an annual energy budget. Consequently, migration, foraging, nest construction, hibernation, and reproduction should be expected to vary on an annual basis. Reproduction is expensive; breeding activities must be appropriately timed to maximize their success. Reproductive steroids are necessary in the production of vertebrate gametes; during the course of evolution, these steroids have been co-opted to mediate reproductive behaviors in most species (Crews 1974). It appears that other behaviors involved in energetic savings have also co-opted the gonadal steroids in adaptive ways. For example, the onset of testicular androgen production in the spring terminates hibernation and stimulates subsequent mating behavior in Turkish hamsters (Hall & Goldman 1980). An enormous variety of behaviors vary on a seasonal basis in direct response to annual changes in reproductive function.

The physiological mechanisms underlying seasonal reproduction are often involved in other seasonal behaviors. In most cases, however, only the phenomenology has been described. For instance, androgens appear to mediate seasonal changes in learning and memory capability in goldfish and canaries (Nottebohm 1989; Shashoua 1973). It is not known if these seasonal changes in performance reflect annual changes in perception, central processing, output systems, or some combination of these factors.

An understanding of the seasonality of behavior is important to behavioral scientists for two reasons. First, an awareness of the annual variation in many behaviors may minimize any unintended influences of seasonality upon experimental results. Care should be exercised in obtaining experimental animals, in using appropriate lighting conditions, and in the timing of data collection. Second, seasonal changes in phenomena of interest to psychologists have been documented. Reliable seasonal differences in learning and memory, perception, communication, developmental rates, social behavior, parental behavior, and mating behavior have been reported for many species. Few data are available addressing the mechanisms underlying these seasonal changes in behavior. The mechanisms underlying seasonal phenomena not linked to reproduction have essentially not been investigated.

Seasonal cycles in human behavior have been reported, but little is known about the mechanisms underlying these rhythms. We lack basic information about human seasonality. For example, it is not known whether humans are photoperiodic or possess endogenous annual cycles. Seasonal differences in developmental rates, learning, or perceptual abilities have not been well studied. Studies on nonhuman mammals should be useful in obtaining information about the function and mechanisms of seasonal cycles of behavior.

ACKNOWLEDGMENTS

The preparation of this review was supported in part by grant HD 22201 (RJN); BRS grant SO7 RR 07041 awarded by the Biomedical Research Support Grant Program, Division of Research Resources, NIH (RJN); and grant HD 15913 (BDG).

Literature Cited

Agranoff, B. W., Davis, R. E. 1968. The use of fishes in studies of memory formation. In *The Central Nervous System and Fish Behavior*, ed. D. Ingle. pp. 193–202. Chicago: Univ. Chicago Press

Aschoff, J. 1981. Annual rhythms in man. In *Handbook of Behavioral Neurobiology*, ed. J. Aschoff, 4:475–90. New York: Plenum

Badura, L. L., Yant, W. R., Nunez, A. A. 1987. Photoperiodic modulation of steroid-induced lordosis in golden hamsters. *Physiol. Behav.* 40:551–54

Badura, L. L., Nunez, A. A. 1989. Photoperiodic modulation of sexual and aggressive behavior in female golden hamsters *(Mesocricetus auratus):* Role of the pineal gland. *Horm. Behav.* 23:27–42

Baker, J. R. 1938. The evolution of breeding seasons. In *Evolution*, ed. J. DeBeer, pp. 161–77. Oxford: Clarendon Press

Bartness, T. J., Goldman, B. D. 1988a. Peak duration of serum melatonin and short-day responses in adult Siberian hamsters. *Am. J. Physiol.* 255:R812–22

Bartness, T. J., Goldman, B. D. 1988b. Effects of melatonin on long-day responses in short-day housed adult Siberian hamsters. *Am. J. Physiol.* 255:R823–30

Bast, J. D., Greenwald, G. S. 1977. Acute and chronic elevation in serum levels of FSH after unilateral ovariectomy in the cyclic hamster. *Endocrinology* 100:955–66

Beach, F. A. 1975. Behavioral endocrinology: an emerging discipline. *Am. Sci.* 63:178–87

Becker, S. 1981. Seasonality of fertility in Matlab, Bangladesh. *J. Biosoc. Sci.* 13:97–105

Benoit, J. 1964. The role of the eyes and of the hypothalamus in the photostimulation of gonads in the duck. *Ann. NY Acad. Sci.* 117:204–17

Berger, P. J., Negus, N. C., Rowsemitt, C. N. 1987. Effect of 6-methoxybenzoazolinone on sex ratio and breeding performance in *Microtus montanus. Biol. Reprod.* 36:255–60

Berndtson, W. E., Desjardins, C. 1974. Circulating LH and FSH levels and testicular function in hamsters during light deprivation and subsequent photoperiodic stimulation. *Endocrinology* 95:195–205

Bex, F. J., Goldman, B. D. 1975. Serum gonadotropins and follicular development in the Syrian hamster. *Endocrinology* 96:928–33

Bielak, T., Pucek, Z. 1960. Season changes in the brain weight of the common shrew (*Sorez araneus araneus Linnaeus*, 1758). *Acta Theriol.* 3:297–300

Bittman, E. L., Goldman, B. D. 1979. Serum levels of gonadotrophins in hamsters exposed to short photoperiods: effects of adrenalectomy and ovariectomy. *J. Endocrinol.* 83:113–18

Bittman, E. L., Karsch, F. J. 1984. Nightly duration of pineal melatonin secretion determines the reproductive response to inhibitory day length in the ewe. *Biol. Reprod.* 30:585–93

Blank, J. L., Desjardins, C. 1985. Photic cues induce multiple neuroendocrine adjustments in testicular function. *Am. J. Physiol.* 238:R181–89

Blask, D. E., Leadem, C. A., Orstead, M., Larsen, B. R. 1986. Prolactin cell activity in female and male Syrian hamsters: an apparent sexually dimorphic response to light deprivation and pinealectomy. *Neuroendocrinology* 42:15–20

Brainard, G. C., Richardson, B. A., King, T. S., Matthews, S. A., Reiter, R. J. 1983. The suppression of pineal melatonin content and N-acetyltransferase activity by different light irradiances in the Syrian hamster: a dose-response relationship. *Endocrinology* 113:293–96

Bridges, R. S., Goldman, B. D. 1975. Diurnal rhythms in gonadotropins and progesterone in lactating and photoperiod induced acyclic hamsters. *Biol. Reprod.* 13:617–22

Bronson, F. H. 1988. Seasonal regulation of reproduction in mammals. In *Physiology of Reproduction*, ed. E. Knobil, J. D. Neill, pp. 1831–72. New York: Raven

Caldwell, G. S., Glickman, S. E., Smith, E. R. 1984. Seasonal aggression is independent of seasonal testosterone in wood rats. *Proc. Natl. Acad. Sci. (USA)* 81:5255–57

Campbell, C. S., Finkelstein, J. S., Turek, F. W. 1978. The interaction of photoperiod and testosterone on the development of copulatory behavior in male hamsters. *Physiol. Behav.* 21:409–15

Carter, D. S., Goldman, B. D. 1983a. Antigonadal effects of timed melatonin infusion in pinealectomized male Djungarian hamsters (*Phodopus sungorus sungorus*): Duration is the critical parameter. *Endocrinology* 113:1261–67

Carter, D. S., Goldman, B. D. 1983b. Pro-

gonadal role of the pineal in the Djungarian hamster (*Phodopus sungorus sungorus*): mediation by melatonin. *Endocrinology* 113:1268–73

Carter, D. S., Hall, V. D., Tamarkin, L., Goldman, B. D. 1982. Pineal is required for testicular maintenance in the Turkish hamster (*Mesocricetus brandti*). *Endocrinology* 111:863–71

Cooper, J. R., Bloom, F. E., Roth, R. H. 1986. *The Biochemical Basis of Neuropharmacology*. New York: Oxford Univ. Press. 400 pp.

Crews, D. 1984. Gamete production, sex hormone secretion, and mating behavior uncoupled. *Horm. Behav.* 18:22–28

Crews, D., Hingorani, V., Nelson, R. J. 1988. Role of the pineal gland in the control of annual reproductive behavioral and physiological cycles in the red-sided garter snake (*Thamnophis sirtalis parietalis*). *J. Biol. Rhythms* 3:293–302

DaMassa, D. A., Davidson, J. M., Smith, E. R. 1977. The relationship between circulating testosterone levels and male sexual behavior in rats. *Horm. Behav.* 8:275–80

Dark, J., Dark, K. A., Zucker, I. 1987. Long day lengths increase brain weight and DNA content in the meadow vole, *Microtus pennsylvanicus*. *Brain Res.* 409:302–7

Dark, J., Pickard, G. E., Zucker, I. 1985. Persistence of circannual rhythms in ground squirrels with lesions of the suprachiasmatic nuclei. *Brain Res.* 332:201–7

Dark, J., Zucker, I. 1985. Circannual rhythms of ground squirrels: role of the hypothalamic paraventricular nucleus. *J. Biol. Rhythms* 1:17–23

Darrow, J. M., Yogev, L., Goldman, B. D. 1987. Patterns of reproductive hormone secretion in hibernating Turkish hamsters. *Am. J. Physiol.* 253:R329–36

Darrow, J. M., Duncan, M. J., Bartke, A., Bona-Gallo, A., Goldman, B. D. 1988. Influence of photoperiod and gonadal steroids on hibernation in the European hamster. *J. Comp. Physiol. A* 163:339–48

Darrow, J. M., Goldman, B. D. 1986. Circadian regulation of pineal melatonin and reproduction in the Djungarian hamster. *J. Biol. Rhythms* 1:39–53

Davis, G. J., Meyer, R. K. 1973. Seasonal variation in LH and FSH of bilaterally castrated snowshoe hares. *Gen. Comp. Endocrinol.* 20:61–68

Day, C. S. D., Galef, B. D. 1977. Pup cannibalism: one aspect of maternal behavior in golden hamsters. *J. Comp. Physiol. Psychol.* 91:1179–89

Diamond, A. W. 1976. Subannual breeding and moult cycles in the bridled tern *Sterna anaethetus* in the Sewchelles. *Ibis* 114:395–98

Disney, H. J., Lofts, B., Murton, A. J. 1959. Duration of the regeneration period of the internal reproductive rhythm in a xerophilous equatorial bird, *Quelea quelea*. *Nature* 184:1659–60

Dowell, S. F., Lynch, G. R. 1987. Duration of the melatonin pulse in the hypothalamus controls testicular function in pinealectomized mice *(Peromyscus leucopus)*. *Biol. Reprod.* 36:1095–1101

Ehrenkranz, J. R. L. 1983. Seasonal breeding in humans: birth records of the Labrador Eskimo. *Fertil. Steril.* 40:485–89

Elliott, J. A., Goldman, B. D. 1989. Seasonal reproduction: photoperiodism and biological clocks. In *Neuroendocrinology of Reproduction*, ed. N. T. Adler, pp. 377–423. New York: Plenum

Ellis, G. B., Turek, F. W. 1980a. Photoperiodic regulation of serum luteinizing hormone and follicle-stimulating hormone in castrated and castrated-adrenalectomized male hamsters. *Endocrinology* 106:1338–44

Ellis, G. B., Turek, F. W. 1980b. Photoperiod-induced change in responsiveness of the hypothalamic-pituitary axis to exogenous 5-alpha-dihydrotestosterone and 17B-estradiol in castrated male hamsters. *Neuroendocrinology* 31:205–9

Ellis, G. B., Turek, F. W. 1983. Testosterone and photoperiod interact to regulate locomotor activity in male hamsters. *Horm. Behav.* 17:66–75

Erkinaro, E. 1961. The seasonal change of the activity of *Microtus agrestis*. *Oikos* 12:157–63

Feare, C. 1984. *The Starling*. New York: Oxford Univ. Press. 315 pp.

Fraile, I. G., Pfaff, D. W., McEwen, B. S. 1987. Progestin receptors with and without estrogen induction in male and female hamster brain. *Neuroendocrinology* 45:487–91

Garcia, M. C., Ginther, O. J. 1976. Effects of ovariectomy and season on plasma luteinizing hormone in mares. *Endocrinology* 98:958–62

Gjessing, L. R. 1983. Periodicity in "schizophrenia". *Adv. Biol. Psychiatr.* 11:95–113

Goldman, B. D. 1983. The physiology of melatonin in mammals. In *Pineal Research Reviews*, ed. R. J. Reiter, pp. 145–82. New York: Alan R. Liss

Goldman, B. D., Darrow, J. M. 1983. The pineal gland and mammalian photoperiodism. *Neuroendocrinology* 37:386–96

Goldman, B. D., Elliott, J. A. 1988. Photoperiodism and seasonality in hamsters: role of the pineal gland. In *Processing of Environmental Information in Vertebrates*, ed. M. H. Stetson, pp. 203–18. New York: Springer-Verlag

Goldman, B. D., Matt, K. S., Roychoudhury, P., Stetson, M. H. 1981. Prolactin release in golden hamsters: photoperiod and gonadal influences. *Biol. Reprod.* 24:287–92

Goss, R. J. 1980. Photoperiodic control of antler cycles in deer. *J. Exp. Zool.* 211: 101–5

Goss, R. J. 1984. Photoperiodic control of antler cycles in deer. VI. Circannual rhythms on altered day lengths. *J. Exp. Zool.* 230:265–71

Goss, R. J., Rosen, J. K. 1973. The effects of latitude and photoperiod on the growth of antlers. *J. Reprod. Fertil. (Suppl.)* 19:111–18

Greenberg, R. 1986. Competition in migrant birds in the nonbreeding season. In *Current Ornithology*, ed. R. J. Johnson, pp. 281–307. New York: Plenum

Gurney, M. E., Konishi, M. 1980. Hormone-induced sexual differentiation of brain and behavior in zebra finches. *Science* 208: 1380–83

Gustafson, A. W. 1979. Male reproductive patterns in bats. *J. Reprod. Fertil.* 56:317–31

Gwinner, E. 1986. *Circannual Rhythms*. Berlin: Springer-Verlag. 154 pp.

Hall, V. D., Bartke, A., Goldman, B. D. 1982. Role of the testes in regulating the duration of hibernation in the Turkish hamster *(Mesocricetus brandti)*. *Biol. Reprod.* 27:802–10

Hall, V., Goldman, B. D. 1980. Effects of gonadal steroid hormones on hibernation in the Turkish hamster *(Mesocricetus brandti)*. *J. Comp. Physiol.* 135:107–14

Harris, M. P. 1969. Breeding seasons of seabirds in the Galapagos Islands. *J. Zool.* 159:145–65

Herman, T. B. 1977. Activity patterns and movements of subarctic voles. *Oikos* 29: 434–44

Hoffman, R. A., Reiter, R. J. 1965. Pineal gland: influence on gonads of male hamsters. *Science* 148:1609–15

Hoffmann, K., Illnerova, H., Vanecek, J. 1981. Effect of photoperiod and of one minute light at night-time on the pineal rhythm on N-acetyltransferase activity in the Djungarian hamster, *Phodopus sungorus*. *Biol. Reprod.* 24:551–56

Hoffmann, K., Illnerova, H., Vanecek, J. 1986. Change in duration of the nighttime melatonin peak may be a signal driving photoperiodic responses in the Djungarian hamster *(Phodopus sungorus)*. *Neurosci. Lett.* 67:68–72

Horton, T. 1985. Cross-fostering of voles demonstrates in utero effect of photoperiod. *Biol. Reprod.* 33:934–39

Horton, T. H. 1984. Growth and maturation in *Microtus montanus:* effects of photoperiods before and after weaning. *Can. J. Zool.* 62:1741–46

Huck, U. W., Labov, J. B., Lisk, R. D. 1986. Food restricting young hamsters *(Mesocricetus auratus)* alters sex ratio and growth of subsequent offspring. *Biol. Reprod.* 36:592–98

Illnerova, H., Hoffmann, K., Vanecek, J. 1986. Adjustments of the rat pineal N-acetyltransferase rhythm to change from long to short photoperiod depends on the direction of the extension of the dark period. *Brain Res.* 362:403–8

Illnerova, H., Vanecke, J. 1984. Circadian rhythm in inducibility of rat pineal N-acetyltransferase after brief light pulses at night: control by a morning oscillator. *J. Comp. Physiol. A* 154:739–44

Karsch, F. J., Bittman, E. L., Foster, D. L., Goodman, R. L., Legan, S. J., Robinson, J. E. 1984. Neuroendocrine basis of seasonal reproduction. *Rec. Prog. Horm. Res.* 40:185–232

Kripke, D. F. 1981. Photoperiodic mechanisms for depression and its treatment. In *Biological Psychiatry,* ed. C. Perris, G. Struwe, B. Jansson, pp. 1249–52. Amsterdam: Elsevier

Lack, D. 1954. *The Natural Regulation of Animal Numbers.* Oxford: Clarendon

Lewy, A. J., Sack, R. L., Singer, C. M. 1985. Melatonin, light and chronobiological disorders. In *Photoperiodism, Melatonin and the Pineal: Ciba Foundation Symposium 117,* ed. D. Evered, S. Clark. pp. 231–52. London: Pitman

Lewy, A. J., Sack, R. L., Singer, C. M., White, D. M., Hoban, T. M. 1988. Winter depression and the phase-shift hypothesis for bright light's therapeutic effects: history, theory, and experimental evidence. *J. Biol. Rhythms* 3:121–34

Lewy, A. J., Wehr, T. A., Goodwin, F. K., Newsome, D. A., Markey, S. P. 1980. Light suppresses melatonin secretion in humans. *Science* 210:1267–69

Lincoln, G. A., Guinness, F., Short, R. V. 1972. The way in which testosterone controls the social and sexual behavior of the red deer stag *(Cervus elphaus). Horm. Behav.* 3:375–96

Loundes, D. D., Bridges, R. S. 1986. Length of prolactin priming differentially affects maternal behavior in female rats. *Biol. Reprod.* 34:495–501

Madison, D. M. 1984. Group nesting and its ecological and evolutionary significance in overwintering microtine rodents. *Carnegie Mus. Nat. Hist. Spec. Publ.* 10:267–74

Malpaux, B., Robinson, J. E., Brown, M. B., Karsch, F. J. 1988. Importance of changing photoperiod and melatonin secretory patterns in determining the length of the breeding season in the Suffolk ewe. *J. Reprod. Fertil.* 83:461–70

Marlow, B. J. 1961. Reproductive behaviour of the marsupial mouse, *Antechinus flavipes* (Waterhouse) and the development of the pouch young. *Austr. J. Zool.* 9:203–18

Marstellar, F. A., Lynch, C. B. 1987. Reproductive responses to variation in temperature and food supply by house mice: II. Lactation. *Biol. Reprod.* 37:844–50

Martinet, L., Ravault, J. P., Meunier, M. 1982. Seasonal variations in mink *(Mustela vison):* plasma prolactin measured by heterologous radioimmunoassay. *Gen. Comp. Endocrinol.* 48:71–75

Masson-Pevet, M., Pevet, P., Vivien-Roels, B. 1987. Pinealectomy and constant release of melatonin or 5-methoxytryptamine induce testicular atrophy in the European hamster *(Cricetus cricetus,* L.). *J. Pineal Res.* 4:79–88

Mathers, C. D., Harris, R. S. 1983. Seasonal distribution of births in Australia. *Int. J. Epidemiol.* 12:326–31

McCann, S. M., Ramirez, V. D. 1964. The neuroendocrine regulation of hypophyseal luteinizing hormone secretion. *Rec. Prog. Horm. Res.* 20:131–70

Miceli, M. O., Malsbury, C. W. 1982. Availability of a food hoard facilitates maternal behaviour in virgin female hamsters. *Physiol. Behav.* 28:855–56

Miernicki, M., Pospichal, M., Karg, J., Powers, J. B. 1988. Photoperiodic effects on male sexual behavior. Abstract presented at *Conf. Reprod. Behav.,* Omaha, p. 64

Moore, M. C. 1984. Changes in territorial defense produced by changes in circulating levels of testosterone: a possible hormonal basis for mate-guarding behavior in white-crowned sparrows. *Behavior* 88:215–26

Moore, M. C. 1987. Castration affects territorial and sexual behavior of free-living male lizards, *Sceloporus jarrovi. Anim. Behav.* 35:1193–99

Moore, M. C., Kranz, R. 1983. Evidence for androgen independence of male mounting behavior in white-crowned sparrows *(Zonotrichia leucophrys gambelli). Horm. Behav.* 17:414–23

Moore, M. C., Marler, C. A. 1987. Effects of testosterone manipulations on nonbreeding season territorial aggression in free-living male lizards, *Sceloporus jarrovi. Gen. Comp. Endocrinol.* 65:225–32

Morin, L. P., Cummings, L. A. 1981. Effect of surgical or photoperiodic castration, testosterone replacement or pinealectomy on male hamster running rhythmicity. *Physiol. Behav.* 26:825–38

Morin, L. P., Fitzgerald, K. M., Zucker, I. 1977. Estradiol shortens the period of hamster circadian rhythms. *Science* 196:305–7

Morin, L. P., Zucker, I. 1978. Photoperiodic regulation of copulatory behavior in the male hamster. *J. Endocrinol.* 77:249–58

Morrell, J. I., Pfaff, D. W. 1978. A neuroendocrine approach to brain function: localization of sex-steroid concentrating cells in vertebrate brains. *Am. Zool.* 18:447–60

Mrosovsky, N. 1988. Seasonal affective disorder, hibernation, and annual cycles in animals: chipmunks in the sky. *J. Biol. Rhythms* 3:189–208

Murton, R. K., Westwood, N. J. 1978. *Avian Breeding Cycles.* New York: Oxford Univ. Press. 594 pp.

Negus, N. C., Berger, P. J. 1987. Mammalian reproductive physiology. In *Current Mammalogy*, ed. H. H. Genoways, pp. 149–73. New York: Plenum

Nelson, R. J. 1987. Photoperiod-nonresponsive morphs: a possible variable in microtine population-density fluctuations. *Am. Nat.* 130:350–69

Nelson, R. J., Mason, R. T., Krohmer, R. W., Crews, D. 1987. Pinealectomy blocks vernal courtship behavior in red-sided garter snakes. *Physiol. Behav.* 39:231–33

Nottebohm, F. 1980. Brain pathways for vocal learning in birds: a review of the first 10 years. In *Progress in Psychobiology and Physiological Psychology*, ed. J. M. Sprague, A. N. Epstein, 9:85–124. New York: Academic

Nottebohm, F. 1989. From bird song to neurogenesis. *Sci. Am.* 260:74–79

Ostermann, K. 1956. Zur Aktivität heimischer Muriden und Gliriden. *Zool. Jahrb. Abt. Allg. Zool. Physiol. Tiere* 66:355–75

Pelletier, J., Ortavant, R. 1975. Photoperiodic control of LH release in the ram. *Acta Endocrinol.* 78:442–50

Pickard, G. E., Silverman, A. J. 1981. Direct retinal projections to the hypothalamus, piriform cortex and accessory optic nuclei in the golden hamster as demonstrated by a sensitive anterograde horseradish peroxidase technique. *J. Comp. Neurol.* 196:155–72

Plotka, E. D., Seal, U. S., Letellier, M. A., Verme, L. J., Ozoga, J. J. 1984. Early effects of pinealectomy on LH and testosterone secretion in white-tailed deer. *J. Endocrinol.*

Poikolainen, K. 1982. Seasonality of alcohol-related hospital admissions has implications for prevention. *Drug Alcohol Dep.* 10:65–69

Pucek, M. 1965. Water contents and seasonal changes of the brain weight in shrews. *Acta Theriol.* 10:353–67

Ramirez, V. D., McCann, S. M. 1963. Comparisons of the regulation of luteinizing hormone (LH) secretion in immature and adult rats. *Endocrinology* 72:452–64

Reiter, R. J. 1970. Endocrine rhythms associated with pineal gland function. In *Biological Rhythms and Endocrine Function*, ed. L. W. Hedlund, J. M. Franz, A. D. Kenny, pp. 43–78. New York: Plenum

Reiter, R. J. 1973/1974. Influence of pinealectomy on the breeding capability of hamsters maintained under natural photoperiod and temperature conditions. *Neuroendocrinology* 13:366–70

Reiter, R. J. 1989. The pineal and its indole products: basic aspects and clinical applications. In *The Brain as an Endocrine Organ*, ed. M. P. Cohen, P. P. Foley, pp. 96–149. Vienna: Springer

Robertson, O. H., Wexler, B. C. 1959. Hyperplasia of the adrenal cortical tissue in Pacific salmon *(Genus Oncorhynchus)* and rainbow trout *(Salmo gairdnerii)* accompanying sexual maturation and spawning. *Endocrinology* 65:225–38

Rosenthal, N. E., Sack, D. A., Skwerer, R. G., Jacobsen, F. M., Wehr, T. A. 1988. Phototherapy for seasonal affective disorder. *J. Biol. Rhythms* 3:101–20

Rowsemitt, C. N. 1986. Seasonal variations in activity rhythms of male voles: mediation by gonadal hormones. *Physiol. Behav.* 37:797–803

Saboureau, M. 1986. Hibernation in the hedgehog: influence of external and internal factors. In *Living in the Cold: Physiological and Biochemical Adaptations*, ed. H. C. Heller, X. J. Musacchia, L. C. H. Wang, pp. 253–63. New York: Elsevier

Seegal, R. F., Goldman, B. D. 1975. Effects of photoperiod on cyclicity and serum gonadotropins in the Syrian hamster. *Biol. Reprod.* 12:223–31

Shashoua, V. E. 1973. Seasonal changes in the learning and activity patterns of goldfish. *Science* 181:572–74

Sisk, C. L., Turek, F. W. 1982. Daily melatonin injections mimic the short day-induced increase in negative feedback effects of testosterone on gonadotropin secretion in hamsters. *Biol. Reprod.* 27:602–8

Skwerer, R. G., Jacobsen, F. M., Duncan, C. C., Kelly, K. A., Sack, D. A., Tamarkin, L., et al. 1988. Neurobiology of seasonal affective disorder and phototherapy. *J. Biol. Rhythms* 3:135–54

Smale, L., Nelson, R. J., Zucker, I. 1988. Daylength influences pelage and plasma prolactin concentrations but not reproduction in the prairie vole, *Microtus ochrogaster. J. Reprod. Fertil.* 83:99–106

Snow, D. W. 1965. The breeding of Audubon's shearwater *(Puffinus herminieri)* in the Galapagos. *Auk* 82:591–97

Snow, D. W., Snow, B. K. 1967. The breeding cycle of the swallow-tailed gull *Creagrus furcatus. Ibis* 109:14–24

Steinberger, A., Ward, D. N. 1988. Inhibin. In *The Physiology of Reproduction*, ed. E. Knobil, J. D. Neill, pp. 567–83. New York: Raven

Stetson, M. H., Elliott, J. A., Goldman, B. D. 1986. Maternal transfer of photoperiodic information influences the photoperiodic response of prepubertal Djungarian hamsters *(Phodopus sungorus sungorus)*. *Biol. Reprod.* 34:664–69

Tamarkin, L., Hutchison, J. S., Goldman, B. D. 1976. Regulation of serum gonadotropins by photoperiod and testicular hormone in the Syrian hamster. *Endocrinology* 99:1528–33

Terman, M. 1988. On the question of mechanism in phototherapy for seasonal affective disorder: considerations for clinical efficacy and epidemiology. *J. Biol. Rhythms* 3:155–72

Turek, F. W., Campbell, C. S. 1979. Photoperiodic regulation of neuroendocrine-gonadal activity. *Biol. Reprod.* 20:32–50

Turek, F. W., Elliott, J. A., Alvis, J. D., Menaker, M. 1975. The interaction of castration and photoperiod in the regulation of hypophyseal and serum gonadotropin levels in male golden hamsters. *Endocrinology* 96:854–60

Ward, P. 1965. Seasonal changes in the sex ratio of *Quelea quelea*. *Ibis* 107:397–99

Wayne, N. L., Malpaux, B., Karsch, F. J. 1988. How does melatonin code for day length in the ewe: duration of nocturnal melatonin release or coincidence of melatonin with a light-entrained sensitive period. *Biol. Reprod.* 39:66–75

Weaver, D. R., Keohan, J. T., Reppert, S. M. 1987. Definition of a prenatal sensitive period of maternal-fetal communication of day length. *Am. J. Physiol.* 253:E701–4

Weaver, D. R., Reppert, S. M. 1986. Maternal melatonin communicates daylength to the fetus in Djungarian hamsters. *Endocrinology* 119:2861–63

Wehr, T. A., Wirz-Justice, A., Goodwin, F. K., Duncan, W., Gillin, J. C. 1979. Phase advance of the circadian sleep-wake cycle as an antidepressant. *Science* 206:710–13

West, S. D., Dublin, H. T. 1984. Behavioral strategies of small mammals under winter conditions: solitary or social? *Carnegie Mus. Nat. Hist. Spec. Publ.* 10:293–300

Wimsatt, W. A. 1969. Some interrelations of reproduction and hibernation in mammals. *Symp. Soc. Exp. Biol.* 23:511–49

Wise, D. A., Pryor, T. L. 1977. Effects of ergocornine and prolactin on aggression in the postpartum golden hamster. *Horm. Behav.* 8:30–39

Wood, D. H. 1970. An ecological study of *Antechinus stuartii* (Marsupialia) in a south east Queensland rain forest. *Austr. J. Zool.* 18:185–207

Wooley, P. 1966. Reproduction in *Antechinus* spp. and other dasyurid marsupials. *Symp. Zool. Soc. London* 15:281–94

Worthy, K., Haresign, W., Dodson, S., McLeod, B. J., Foxcroft, G. R., Haynes, N. B. 1985. Evidence that the onset of the breeding season in the ewe may be independent of decreasing plasma prolactin concentrations. *J. Reprod. Fertil.* 75:237–46

Wurtman, J. J., Wurtman, R. J., Mark, S., Tsay, R., Gilbert, W., Growdon, J. 1985. D-Fenfluramine selectively suppresses carbohydrate snacking by obese subjects. *Int. J. Eating Dis.* 4:89–99

Wurtman, R. J. 1975. The effects of light on man and other animals. *Annu. Rev. Physiol.* 37:467–83

Wurtman, R. J., Wurtman, J. J. 1989. Carbohydrates and depression. *Sci. Am.* 262:68–75

Yaskin, V. A. 1984. Seasonal changes in brain morphology in small mammals. *Carnegie Mus. Nat. Hist. Spec. Publ.* 10:183–92

Yellon, S. M., Hutchison, J. S., Goldman, B. D. 1989. Sexual differentiation of the steroid feedback mechanism regulating follicle-stimulating hormone secretion in the Syrian hamster. *Biol. Reprod.* In press

Youngstrom, T. G., Weiss, M. L., Nunez, A. A. 1987. A retinal projection to the paraventricular nuclei of the hypothalamus in the Syrian hamster *(Mesocricetus auratus)*. *Brain Res. Bull.* 19:747–50

Zucker, I. 1988. Seasonal affective disorders: animal models *non fingo*. *J. Biol. Rhythms* 3:209–23

Zucker, I., Licht, P. 1983. Circannual and seasonal variations in plasma luteinizing hormone levels of ovariectomized ground squirrels *(Spermophilus lateralis)*. *Biol. Reprod.* 28:178–85

Annu. Rev. Psychol. 1990. 41:109–39

HUMAN LEARNING AND MEMORY: CONNECTIONS AND DISSOCIATIONS

Douglas L. Hintzman

Department of Psychology, University of Oregon, Eugene, Oregon 97403

CONTENTS

> It is only in the context of a particular process model that inferences can be meaningfully drawn from the experimental data.
>
> Tulving & Bower 1974, pp. 296–97

> It could well be held that the standard of precision in theoretical statements in the experimental journals is now markedly lower than it was at the height of the Hullian movement 40–50 years ago.
>
> Broadbent 1987, pp. 169–70

INTRODUCTION

This review is concerned with two major trends in recent work on human learning and memory: theoretical efforts toward the development of formal models, and empirical work comparing different memory tasks. The models

0066-4308/90/0201-0109$02.00

can be loosely labeled "connectionist," and the experiments "dissociationist." I also attempt to connect (or associate) the two topics, as my page allotment allows.

To many psychologists, the fanfare surrounding connectionism (a.k.a. PDP modeling, or neural networks) may seem extreme: Meetings and journals are devoted entirely to the topic. Schneider (1987) declares connectionism a "paradigm shift" for psychology. A physicist calls neural networks "one of the great intellectual adventures for the end of the twentieth century" (Phillips 1988:404). A Defense Department official compares the significance of neural networks to that of nuclear weapons, and calls for research expenditures of $400 million. "Neural network enthusiasts in attendance responded with cheers" (*MacWeek,* Aug. 8, 1988:32). Any day now, some clinician will announce a program of connection therapy, promising to get clients out of local minima by adjusting their weight space. Faced with a force beyond their control, many cognitive researchers are wondering privately whether it will be easier to take tensor calculus or early retirement—but even those who are not contemplating this choice should have a basic idea of what connectionist models are about. One of my goals in this chapter is to give an overview of similarities and differences among current models formulated in the connectionist framework, as broadly conceived. I confine the discussion primarily to models that have been applied to empirical data (to spare readers nightmares of Boltzmann machines).

Dissociationism has not had the publicity that connectionism has, but nonetheless has been enormously influential. For over a century, progress in the study of human memory has been marked by a proliferation of tasks. The most recent infusion includes measures of perception and performance that, prior to 1980, would not have been considered memory tasks at all. Inevitably, comparative work on similarities and differences among tasks has become a priority in the field. This trend has been fueled by fascinating data from amnesics, and by renewed interest in conscious awareness. The term "dissociation," borrowed from the neuropsychology and hypnosis literatures, is now routinely used by memory researchers to spice up the bland finding that two different tasks give different results. As I will argue, some of the dissociation research suffers from a lack of theoretical rigor and could benefit from the modeling approach. A point in favor of the models discussed in the next section is that most can be applied to several memory tasks. Later in the chapter, I discuss model-based insights into certain dissociation results.

CONNECTIONS

Formal (i.e. mathematical or computational) theories have a number of advantages that psychologists often overlook. They force the theorist to be explicit, so that assumptions are publicly accessible and the reliability of derivations can be confirmed (Smolensky 1988). A further argument for formal models in psychology is that synthesis is easier than analysis (Braitenberg 1985; Phillips 1988). The common strategy of trying to reason backward from behavior to underlying processes (analysis) has drawbacks that become painfully apparent to those who work with simulation models (synthesis). To have one's hunches about how a simple combination of processes will behave repeatedly dashed by one's own computer program is a humbling experience that no experimental psychologist should miss. Surprises are especially likely when the model has properties that are inherently difficult to understand, such as variability, parallelism, and nonlinearity—all, undoubtedly, properties of the brain. Simulation models also have a flexibility and transparency that endow them with great heuristic value. A simple working system that displays some properties of human memory may suggest other properties that no one ever thought of testing for, may offer novel explanations for known phenomena, and may provide insight into which modifications the next generation of models should include.

In this section, I introduce readers to some current developments in models of memory. The emphasis is on models that invite comparison by being constructed of common components: primitive features, nodes having activation values, and links (possibly having weights or strengths). These models might best be identified as feature-based, or content-addressable, but they also fit under the connectionist rubric. A number of interesting models have been left out. One deserving specific mention is the SAM model, which has demonstrated its generality by being applied, in slightly different versions, to free and cued recall (Raaijmakers & Shiffrin 1980), recognition memory (Gillund & Shiffrin 1984), and transfer and forgetting in paired associates (Mensink & Raaijmakers 1988). Although SAM has many similarities to the models to be discussed, direct comparison would require that it be cast in the connectionist framework. Such an exercise might be illuminating, but I do not undertake it here.

Models Without Hidden Units

COMPOSITE VECTOR MODEL   The notion of a composite memory trace may be the most difficult for newcomers to connectionism to understand. A simple vector model will illustrate the principle (see Figure 1a). Suppose each stimulus is a subset of eight features, and can be represented by an ordered vector of $+1$s and -1s, indicating presence or absence of the feature associated with each position (e.g. $+1,+1,+1,+1,-1,-1,-1,-1$). If we have a set of such vectors that are orthogonal to each other (i.e. uncorrelated), then we can add them one at a time to a memory vector. A simple measure of the degree to which two vectors match is the Pearson r. As more and more vectors are added to the memory vector, it declines in how well it matches the first one that was stored. Since the square of the correlation coefficient represents the proportion of variance in the memory vector due to each stored item, r^2 declines as $1/N$ (1.00, .50, .33, .25, etc), where N is the number of vectors stored. For a new vector from the orthogonal set that was not stored, r^2 is always 0.

The limit to the number of orthogonal vectors that can be stored in such a memory can be raised by increasing the number of features. Moreover, by relaxing the requirement of strict orthogonality, one can have a model in which the correlation of a vector with the composite memory is only an imperfect guide to whether it is old or new. Such imperfect discrimination is assumed by applications of signal detection theory to recognition memory. Indeed, vector models of item recognition similar to this one have been proposed by Anderson (1973) and Murdock (1989). The vector model depicted in Figure 1a suffers from a serious problem, however: it lacks information about associations among features, so it cannot be used for recall.

MATRIX MODELS   Figure 1b shows a single-layered network of four feature nodes and their associations. The network can serve as a composite memory if, whenever a four-feature vector is presented, positive and negative adjustments are made to strengths (weights) of the links so as to indicate which pairs of features did and did not co-occur. Here, we accumulate information about feature pairs, instead of single features, so we represent the weights in the cells of an n × n matrix, where n is the number of features. Each node in the left-hand diagram has both a row (input) and a column (output) in the matrix. In this case, one has the option of leaving the diagonal cells empty, and typically, the weights entered above the diagonal mirror those below. Matrixes representing different stimuli are added into a composite memory, as vectors were in the previous model. Probing the matrix with an input vector produces an output vector. This memory acts as an autoassociator, in that the different features of a stimulus are all interlinked. Thus if a fragment of a previously stored stimulus is presented as input, cooperative action among the redundant associations will tend to reconstruct the whole. Recognition memory can be done in an autoassociator by using the input vector to get an output vector, and then determining how well the input and output vectors match.

A simple modification of the autoassociator is the associator shown in Figure 1c. In this case, rows and columns of the corresponding matrix represent different features, because the input and output nodes are in different layers. After weight matrixes from several pairs of vectors have been summed, the composite matrix can be probed with one of the original input vectors to reproduce its associated pattern on the output nodes.

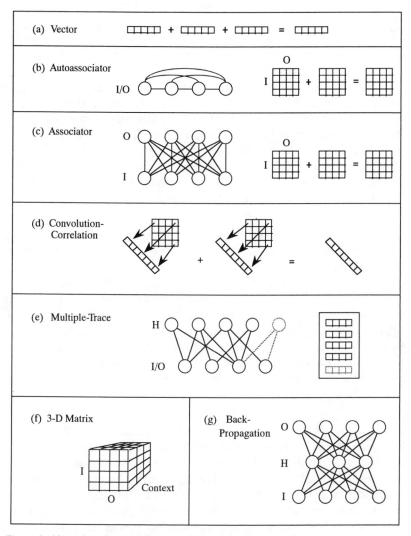

Figure 1   Network and matrix diagrams of the models discussed in the text.

In either the autoassociator or the associator, if weights are simply added according to the presence or absence of feature combinations (the Hebb rule), perfect performance is possible only if orthogonal vectors were used. This is a serious constraint, but it can be overcome by using an adaptive learning algorithm such as the delta rule. An input vector is presented, and the difference between the output and the target output is used to proportionally adjust the weights. Learning pairs of nonorthogonal (similar) vectors requires adjusting the weights so that they come as close as possible to simultaneously satisfying the constraints of all the pairs. The delta-rule algorithm can find a least-mean-squares solution to the entire set of input-output pairs, provided the entire set is presented for learning many times in an iterative fashion and the proportion by which weights are adjusted on each iteration is very small. Delta-rule models were applied with some success to the representation of prototypes and exemplars by McClelland & Rumelhart (1985), and to categorization by Gluck & Bower (1988). Interesting though these efforts are, they model only asymptotic performance, and not learning. Asymptotic performance is reached only after very many iterations through the entire set of items. A point I return to later is that this kind of learning schedule is unrealistic, either in natural settings or in standard cognitive tasks, but it may be required in order for the delta rule to work.

NONLINEARITY   The simplest networks are linear—that is, the output of any node is a simple weighted sum of its inputs. Linear systems are mathematically tractable but limited in their behavior. Various kinds of nonlinearity can be introduced—output can be truncated at $+1$ and -1, set to zero unless a threshold is exceeded, or set to $+1$ when input is positive and -1 when it is negative (see Rumelhart & McClelland 1986a). Nonlinearity can give an autoassociator the ability to take messy or distorted input and "relax" into a state representing one of the vectors that was learned. The first output vector is fed back to the network as input, producing a second output vector, and so on, until the network reaches a steady state determined jointly by the original input and the weights on all the links.

3-D MATRIX   A 3-dimensional elaboration of the basic matrix model has been proposed by Humphreys et al (1989). The matrix stores feature-triplets (i.e. trinary associations), which allows context vectors to modulate associations between input and output nodes (Figure 1f). Context can be used to restrict retrieval to a particular setting such as a particular experimental room, but its use is optional. Thus, the episodic tasks of recognition memory and cued recall when context is cued become the generic memory tasks of familiarity judgment and free association when it is not. Humphreys et al (1989) show how this interesting model might explain performance in a variety of episodic and generic memory tasks, but provide no simulations or quantitative fits. The basic idea of the model is that connections can modulate other connections. This potentially powerful idea (called "sigma pi units" by Rumelhart & McClelland 1986a) has so far had surprisingly little application.

CONVOLUTION-CORRELATION   Related to both the vector model and the basic matrix model are the convolution-correlation models called TODAM

(Murdock 1982) and CHARM (Eich 1982). Convolution is a mathematical operation for combining two vectors. One can obtain the convolution of two n-element vectors by multiplying them to form an n $\times$ n matrix (Figure 1d), and then summing diagonally to get a vector with $2n-1$ cells (to save computing time, sometimes only the middle n cells are used). Retrieval is done by correlation—an operation related to the familiar r, but in this case producing a vector. Correlating the composite vector and the original input vector produces the original output vector with added noise. Several input-output pairs can be learned by adding each of their convolutions in a single composite vector. Eich (1982) shows how one such model simulates phenomena of paired-associate learning, and Murdock (1987) shows how serial-order learning can be modeled by associative chaining. To handle recognition memory in TODAM, single items are simply added to the composite vector nonassociatively, as in the vector model described earlier. Alternatively, one can compute a convolution for each item, using its autoassociation matrix (Eich 1985)—an approach that also allows reconstruction of a whole stimulus from a part.

Like matrix models, convolution-correlation models can be made to learn adaptively, so that nonorthogonal vectors can be learned. A disadvantage of convolution-correlation models is that they are inherently noisier than matrix models (Pike 1984; Murdock 1985). Also, because the systems are linear, they cannot relax into a better interpretation of noisy output. Thus, to explain how recall can succeed, it has been necessary to assume a separate memory, extraneous to the model itself, which takes noisy output and turns it into an acceptable experimental response.

Models with Hidden Units

The models described so far suffer from a serious drawback: They cannot learn a set of input-output mappings unless all mappings are linearly independent. Concretely, what this means is that similar inputs must produce similar outputs. Thus, for example, the models are not capable of configuring, which requires responding differently to a compound stimulus (e.g. bell + light) than to either of its components (bell alone or light alone). This is known in the connectionist literature as the exclusive-or problem, and a general solution requires a layer of nodes that serve for neither input nor output, and hence are called "hidden units."

MULTIPLE TRACES   The network shown in Figure 1e—with one layer of nodes for both input and output and a layer of hidden units—represents the multiple-trace model MINERVA 2 (Hintzman 1986; 1988). This model differs in an important way from the ones described so far, in that representation is local, rather than distributed. That is, each hidden unit represents a conjunction of features corresponding to a separate experience—an episodic trace. Although the input-output layer is of fixed size, every new experience adds a new node to the hidden layer. The memory can also be viewed as a collection of vectors—one for each hidden unit. Instead of being combined in a composite vector, as in the first model described here, the vectors are stored in memory individually. This is so even if several are identical. Due either to imperfect learning or to forgetting, an encoded vector may be a fragmented copy of the original input. At retrieval, an input vector is matched in parallel with all stored vectors, and the resulting activation level of each vector is passed down to its features. The output vector is the sum of these individual, activation-weighted vectors.

This model escapes being just a less efficient version of the vector model by using nonlinearity. In particular, the activation of each hidden unit is a positively accelerated function of its match to the input vector, limiting the number of units that will respond significantly to any input, and thereby reducing noise. In this model, each trace can be viewed as an n-way association, in which features are interassociated by virtue of existing in the same vector. Information in the input vector will tend to be completed, in the output vector, in a way that reflects co-occurrence of features among events that were stored. To encode a pair, features of both members are listed in a single vector. Like a nonlinear autoassociator, this model can relax into an interpretation of the input that is most consistent with the stored information. Nonlinearity and the hidden layer also give it the ability to do configuring (exclusive or). The model has been applied primarily to category learning (Hintzman 1986) and to memory for frequency (Hintzman 1988). Recognition memory is treated as a special case of memory for frequency, where frequencies of 0 must be discriminated from those greater than 0.

BACK-PROPAGATION   The back-propagation model has an input layer, a hidden layer, and an output layer (Figure 1g). Unlike the hidden layer of the multiple-trace model, this one is a distributed representation, and the number of units is fixed. Activation of the hidden units is nonlinear (a smooth approximation to a threshold function). As in the matrix models, learning is done by adjusting weights on links. Learning is accomplished by the generalized delta rule, in which differences between the actual output and the target output are used to adjust weights on the final set of links, and are also propagated back to compute differences at the hidden layer. These differences are used in turn to adjust weights on the initial set of links (Rumelhart et al 1986a). This scheme can be used with any number of hidden layers.

The back propagation model can do configuring and can even learn the parity problem—an elaboration of configuring in which there is one response when the number of $+1$s in the input vector is odd and another response when it is even. Given enough hidden units to do the job, such a network can learn virtually any mapping of input vectors onto output vectors. This power is the basic reason that connectionist networks are of so much interest in artificial intelligence and neural modeling. Massaro (1988) has argued that this power is a drawback in a psychological theory, because a model that can fit anything predicts nothing. This criticism, however, misses an important point: The back-propogation model may be able to fit any input-output mapping asymptotically, but it is highly constrained—and therefore testable—in the way asymptotic performance is reached.

Indeed, attempts to apply back-propagation models to human learning have uncovered serious problems. As was mentioned earlier, using the delta rule as a least-mean-squares algorithm requires many iterations through the entire set of items to be learned, making tiny weight adjustments on each cycle. What happens when different items are learned sequentially, as in virtually all human memory tasks? McClosky & Cohen (1989) trained a 3-layer model to criterion on one list of pairs, and then on a second list. The second list interfered "catastrophically" with retention of the first. They tried various alterations in learning assumptions, including freezing a subset of the weights after list 1 had been learned, but nothing worked. Catastrophic failure occurred even when list 1 continued to be trained after list 2 was introduced. Ratcliff (1990) applied a version of the back-propagation model to recognition memory. Repeating a list had sometimes bizarre effects: Discrimination between old and new items typically declined, or—depending on parameters—was a nonmonotonic function of trials. Like McClosky & Cohen (1989), Ratcliff found drastic interference whenever any new learning intervened between study and test; again, obvious modifications of the model did not help. In one attempt, two new hidden units were introduced for each new item learned, and only connections to and from the new nodes were changed. This seems to make the system similar to the multiple-trace model, described above. But when all hidden units were allowed to participate in a test on a just-trained vector, recognition matching was poor. By analogy, people who have been highly trained to perform a task by cooperating in pairs may interfere with each other and fumble the job badly when required to do it in a larger-sized group.

These problems may be inherent in adaptive, distributed memories. If a network has been finely tuned to give a particular input-output mapping, and then weights are adjusted to learn something new, the old learning is largely lost. Unlike the retroactive interference found with human subjects, this interference is massive and occurs whether the new items are similar to the old ones or not. It now seems likely that the apparent success of Rumelhart & McClelland's (1986b) model of children's acquisition of past-tenses of irregular verbs—first learning them (e.g. ran), then regularizing them (e.g. to runned), and then gradually relearning them—was a manifestation of catastrophic failure, induced by an unnatural and abrupt change in the vocabulary the model was given to learn.

ADAPTIVE RESONANCE   Adaptive networks' difficulties with sequential learning were foreseen by Grossberg (1987). His adaptive resonance theory (ART) is more complex than others reviewed here but uses an input-output layer and a hidden layer similar to those shown in Figure 1e. As in the multiple-trace model, representation at the hidden layer is local, rather than distributed. The system is nonlinear, and relaxes into an interpretation of the input that is consistent with a single hidden unit that suppresses the others via lateral inhibition. "Resonance" is a measure of how well the input and the interpretation match. ART has two kinds of learning. In one, the hidden unit that resonates most to the input is tuned, to accommodate any discrepancies from what was previously learned. In the other, a new hidden unit is set up and adjusted to represent the new input. A threshold parameter determines which kind of learning will occur: If resonance is above this value, minor tuning is all that is done; if it is below the value, indicating a substantially new type of stimulus, a new hidden unit is recruited and learned. This mechanism allows new learning to go on while old learning is preserved, but does not build new capacity when what already exists will do the job. For some applications of ART to topics in human learning and memory, see Grossberg & Stone (1986).

Comment on Models

If the measure of a good model is that it be informative in failure as well as in success, then the models reviewed here qualify. The difficulty with sequential learning encountered by the back-propagation model—and more generally by the delta rule—is surprising in light of all the favorable attention these ideas have received. It is perhaps less surprising when one considers that the model was not originally developed with laboratory tasks in mind. Back-propagation is just one learning algorithm, and the multilayered, distributed system is just one architecture, of many that need to be explored. Cognitive psychology could benefit from a kind of metatheory of connectionism that sketches out the universe of possible models and allows the properties of new systems to be anticipated from the particular combinations of assumptions made. We may be approaching this state now with regard to some assumptions, but our understanding of these systems is still crude.

Despite limitations of the present models, they have given us new insights into the possible causes of behavior in several learning and memory tasks. One appeal of feature-based models, as a group, is that they offer a natural account of similarity effects. These models tend to classify stimuli based on family resemblance—indeed, even the simplest vector model will store a prototype. In paired-associate learning, they predict effects of similarity both within and between lists; and in recognition memory they predict false positives to lures that resemble targets and easy rejection of those that do not. Many seemingly different phenomena in a variety of tasks may turn out simply to reflect the tendency to respond to similar stimuli in a similar way. An example is the intuitively puzzling test-pair similarity effect: Following study of a recognition list containing items A and B, forced-choice recognition is more accurate between similar test pairs like A-A' than between dissimilar pairs like A-B'. This result, which is due to a combination of similarity and variability, emerges from the multiple-trace model with no special assumptions (Hintzman 1988), and for the same reasons should be predicted by some of the other models summarized above.

Signal-detection theory has been applied to recognition memory for more than 30 years, and its usefulness for this purpose has been repeatedly confirmed (e.g. Snodgrass & Corwin 1988). Because they explain the origins of the old- and new-item familiarity distributions, models of the type discussed above mesh nicely with the signal-detection model. Recognition is based on a principle of "global matching," involving all the contents of memory, rather than on a search of memory for a single memory trace (cf Gillund & Shiffrin 1984). The familiarity distribution for new items (and much of the variability in that for old items) thus reflects the cumulative effect of slight matches of the test item with traces of many items that were in the list. One implication, which has been confirmed many times, is that recognition performance should decline with increasing length of the study list.

Recognition memory raises challenges to these global matching models, despite their success. One problem is to explain in a principled way how criteria (e.g. that for the decision old vs new) are placed on the familiarity scale. Another problem is to explain the mirror effect (Glanzer & Adams 1985). The most familiar example of this effect is that low-frequency words are responded to correctly more often than high-frequency words—whether the words in question are old or new. More generally, the pattern of hit rates across various categories of items (when they are old) is mirrored in the pattern of correct rejection rates (when they are new). This turns out to be a difficult phenomenon for global matching models to explain. A model may manage to juggle means, variances, criterion settings, etc well enough to account for effects of word frequency (e.g. Gillund & Shiffrin 1984; Grossberg & Stone 1986; Hintzman 1988) but not be applicable to mirror effects due to concreteness, meaningfulness, or pictures-vs-words. A new approach to understanding the mirror effect may be required (e.g. Glanzer & Adams 1990).

Broadbent (1987), McClelland (1988), and Rumelhart et al (1986b) present examples of models suggesting new explanations for old phenomena. Here is another: Short-term priming (e.g. faster lexical decision on TIGER when it is preceded by LION) has traditionally been explained as resulting from spreading activation in an associative network—indeed, in the absence of alternative theories, this hypothesis has routinely been accepted as fact. Ratcliff & McKoon (1988), however, saw that priming could be predicted by certain memory models, by assuming that the prime and target combine to form a compound cue that matches something previously stored (e.g. a trace of the pair, LION-TIGER). This compound-cue model differs from the spreading-activation one in the degree to which the current stimulus exercises direct control. The compound-cue model predicts that replacing the prime by a neutral stimulus (e.g. interpolating TREE between LION and TIGER) should abruptly cancel priming—a result reported by Ratcliff & McKoon (1988, Exp. 2). However, it does not predict mediated priming (e.g. from LION to STRIPES), as the spreading-activation hypothesis does. Mediated priming has been reported by Balota & Lorch (1986) and McNamara & Altarriba (1988).

DISSOCIATIONS

The degree of current interest in comparisons among memory tasks is indicated by several recently published reviews (Johnson & Hasher 1987; Richardson-Klavehn & Bjork 1988; Schacter 1987). These efforts—especially the mammoth chapter by Richardson-Klavehn and Bjork—free me to use this section to address the general issue of what a dissociation between two tasks means. These days, the word *dissociation* is used indiscriminately to describe almost any interaction—a practice that blurs important distinctions. Accordingly, I discuss dissociations under three main headings: task dissociations, dissociations of consciousness, and amnesic dissociations.

Task Dissociations

Task dissociations drew attention in the context of hypotheses about distinct memory systems. The basic notion was spelled out by Tulving (1983:73), who argued that when a manipulated variable has an effect on one task and not on another, or opposite effects on two tasks, this could be taken as evidence for separate systems. The argument runs into immediate problems. First, process models can easily predict dissociations between tasks performed by the same memory system (e.g. Anderson & Reder 1988; Humphreys et al 1989). Second, unless the hypothesis of separate systems is fleshed out with more detail, there is no way of knowing specifically which dissociations count in its favor and which do not. Sherry & Schacter (1987) argued that the inference of separate systems should be reserved for cases where the two tasks make use of different information and different acquisition, retention, and retrieval rules. They further proposed that separate systems will evolve when two mutually incompatible functions must be served. From a pretheoretical standpoint this is not a useful approach either, because the decision for separate systems requires a prior understanding of the representations and rules, and whether two functions are mutually incompatible is likely to depend on the mechanism(s) available to carry them out.

The basic question concerning task dissociations is this: What conclusion can be drawn from the fact that a variable has different effects on the performance of two different tasks? At the lowest level, this raises concerns about scaling. Interactions can occur simply due to nonlinearities in the measures used, such as ceiling and floor effects. Such considerations led Dunn & Kirsner (1988) to propose that only a "reversed association" could be trusted as proof of different processes. This type of dissociation is best revealed by a scatter diagram, with Task-1 performance plotted on one axis and Task-2 on the other, using one data point for each condition of the experiment. If all such points fall on a monotonic function (i.e. the two tasks rank conditions in the same way), then the data can be explained by a single underlying process. Only a reliably nonmonotonic function compels the conclusion that different processes operate in the two tasks.

The reversed-association diagnostic seems on the surface to be a theory-free method for discovering where different memory systems underlie different tasks, but this is an illusion. Except in trivial cases, it is hard to see how one can have two tasks without at least one difference in underlying processes (a point that Dunn & Kirsner concede). This being the case, the method can only prove or fail to prove something that even the most superficial process theory would assume to be true. If different tasks involve different processes, and different processes make dissociations possible, then dissociations (even reversed associations) are to be expected whenever two tasks are compared. Kolers & Roediger (1984) made precisely this point: task dissociations are "the natural state of affairs; it is the characteristics of tasks—and relations among their underlying procedures—that need explaining" (p. 439). Explanation in this sense demands a theory of memory that predicts effects of the manipulated variables on performance of each task. Crude distinctions between "systems" are seldom sufficient for this purpose. Further, once a sufficiently elaborate process model is in hand, it is not clear that the notion of a system is any longer of much use. Once the model has been spelled out, it makes little difference whether its components are called systems, modules, processes, or something else; the explanatory burden is carried by the nature of the proposed mechanisms and their interactions, not by what they are called. Thus, the significance of an experimental outcome rests on its theoretical interpretation, not on whether it counts as a dissociation or not.

COMPATIBILITY   Many dissociations among memory tasks seem amenable to a theoretical approach stressing relationships between encoding and retrieval tasks. The basic idea was inherent in the Gestaltists' assumptions that memory traces are copies of perceptual experiences, and that similarity is one determinant of whether a new experience will contact a particular trace. To these notions, modern cognitive psychology adds the idea of mental transformations and abstract codes. The effectiveness of retrieval can then be seen as reflecting the relationship between the operations used at retrieval and those used during encoding. This basic notion has been expressed in several tongue-twisting ways, including "the encoding specificity principle," "transfer-appropriate processing," and "encoding-retrieval interactions." To promote easy communication, I refer to the principle and its manifestations with a single word: compatibility.

The human memory literature is full of compatibility effects. I choose an example from Jacoby (1983) because it will figure in later discussion. Two of Jacoby's encoding conditions were: (*a*) a *generate* condition, in which subjects had to give antonyms to word cues (e.g. hot–????)—a task so constrained that nearly all subjects gave the target answer (COLD); and (*b*) a *read* condition, in which subjects read targets aloud in the absence of a cue (e.g. xxx–COLD). The two retrieval conditions were recognition memory (old vs new) and tachistoscopic identification—a task known to show long-term priming. The result was a crossover interaction. Recognition memory gained much more from generating than from reading, while identification showed the opposite outcome.

To account for these results, Jacoby (1983) appealed to the notions of data-driven and conceptually driven processing. To generate the word, subjects must deal with it conceptually, and to read it they deal with it visually. Likewise for the two retrieval tasks, recognition memory is heavily conceptual and identification primarily visual. Transfer is best when encoding and retrieval tasks involve the same type of processing. Note that this explanatory framework need not refer to different memory systems; qualitative differences between memory traces could exist even within the same system. Note also that it is broadly consistent with the class of models discussed earlier. An encoding task that uses one subset of features should transfer differentially to retrieval tasks using the same or a different subset of features.

Roediger and his students have extended Jacoby's analysis (e.g. Roediger & Blaxton 1987; Roediger et al 1989). They demonstrate that manipulation of visual features of the encoding task (e.g. by using different typographies) affects retrieval tasks thought to be data-driven, while manipulation of conceptual features (e.g. repeating meaning via synonyms) affects tasks identified as conceptually driven. They interpret their evidence as suggesting a continuum, rather than the dichotomy that the labels suggest. For example, free recall is thought to be more conceptually driven than recognition memory, in which perceptual factors play a small but significant role.

GENERATION EFFECTS   A survey of recent publications on human memory suggests that our journals have been invaded by a literature virus, appropriately called the generation effect (i.e. words that subjects generate are better remembered than words they read). Unlike its more benign cousin, the self-reference effect, which may be a simple effect of clustering (Klein & Kihlstrom 1986), the generation-effect virus replicates and mutates at an astonishing rate. There is no room to survey the relevant literature here; suffice it to say that, depending on what article you read, you may conclude either that the generation effect does or does not depend on: (*a*) whether the encoding manipulation is within or between lists, (*b*) whether learning is intentional or incidental, and (*c*) whether the materials are nonwords, high-frequency words, or low-frequency words. Further, these factors are likely to interact with the type of retention test (recognition, free recall, or spelling bias of homophones). It appears there is not one generation effect but many. McDaniel et al (1988) and other authors have begun to argue that effects of generation may be understood within a compatibility framework. If this is right, then future progress will require a principled theoretical and empirical analysis of how subjects perform specific generation and nongeneration tasks, and of how they perform specific retrieval tasks. Note that if generation effects are manifestations of compatibility, then it should be possible to find retrieval tasks for which the generation effect is reversed—that is, reading a word should yield better performance than generating the word. As I described earlier, this is precisely what Jacoby (1983) found.

CORRELATIONS   Dunn & Kirsner's (1988) scheme, in which a scatter diagram shows the relationship between Task 1 and Task 2, can be generalized to a situation with only one manipulated condition. One way to do this is by using subjects, instead of conditions, to define data points. Underwood et al (1978) used this approach in a study involving 33 memory measures and 200 subjects. A factor analysis showed that various versions of each retrieval task (e.g. free recall, paired associates) clustered together. In other words, subjects were ordered differently by the different retrieval tasks (i.e. the tasks dissociated) as would be expected if different processes are involved in different tasks. Another way to generalize the Dunn & Kirsner method to a single-condition study is to use items to define the data points. Rubin (1985) applied this "unit analysis" approach to understanding relations between encoding tasks and between retrieval tasks. He argued that a difference in average performance following two encoding tasks (e.g. semantic vs phonemic coding) could simply reflect more vs less of the same thing. To establish a qualitative difference in processes, one must demonstrate that the tasks give rise to different orderings of the items. Rubin's unit-analysis approach has not been given the attention it deserves.

STOCHASTIC RELATIONS   Suppose that subjects study a set of items and then are tested twice on each, in two different retrieval tasks. Each subject-item combination can be categorized with regard to success or failure on Task 1 and Task 2, and a contingency table can summarize the relationship between performances on the two tasks. The study of such stochastic relations between retrieval tasks has played an important role in attempts to determine empirically how many memory systems there are. In this work a special status is usually accorded to "finding independence" (an inappropriately affirmative way of describing failure to reject the null hypothesis).

This method has been criticized for likely carry-over effects from one task to the other (Shimamura 1985), and for its susceptibility to Simpson's paradox (Hintzman 1980). In Simpson's paradox, two contingency tables showing independence might show a positive or negative relation when collapsed into a single table; or two contingency tables showing a positive relationship could show independence or even a negative contingency when collapsed into one. In general, the pattern shown by a summary table is not a reliable guide to the patterns within the tables that have been summed. The paradox arises when each component table represents a different level of some third variable that is correlated with both Task 1 and Task 2. If the two correlations have the same sign, a positive bias is induced in the summary table; if they have opposite signs, a negative bias is induced. The net effect depends on the strengths and directions of all the variables involved.

Despite these objections to contingency analyses in task comparisons, many articles in the current literature report their use (e.g. Gardiner 1988; Hayman & Tulving 1989). Nearly always, the central question is whether independence was found. If so, this is often taken as evidence that different systems underlie performance in Task 1 and Task 2. In an unusually explicit example of the reasoning, Witherspoon & Moscovitch (1989) argue that "statistical independence should not occur between two . . . tests of memory . . . that are presumed to be mediated by the same system," and that "at least a small, but reliably dependent, relationship should always be found" (p.23). Surprisingly, articles advocating the method seem never to derive either independence or dependence from theoretical postulates—as though the significance of the finding were so obvious as to render any such exercise superfluous. As I show next, work with formal models shows that even the intuitively obvious may be wrong.

MODELS, INTUITION, AND INDEPENDENCE   I discuss here two applications of formal models to stochastic relations between tasks. The first example concerns exemplar models of classification learning, which assume that people categorize test stimuli based on their similarity to traces of past exemplars. Several articles have claimed that this approach to classification learning implies a substantial positive relationship between classification and recognition memory—a prediction not born out by experimental results. For example, Metcalfe & Fisher (1986) performed a contingency analysis of the relationship between classification and recognition memory, and failed to find a significant deviation from independence. Nosofsky (1988) criticized articles making this claim for their "failure to specify and test an explicit decision rule by which exemplar models are used to make recognition judgments" (p. 700). He went on to apply an exemplar model to both the classification task and the recognition memory task, showing that the requirements of the two tasks— discriminating members of one category from those of another vs discriminating old items from new ones—are typically orthogonal. Of most relevance here, Nosofsky (1988) showed that the exemplar model is consistent with the Metcalfe & Fisher (1986) result. Thus, tasks based on what Nosofsky calls a "common representational substrate" can display stochastic independence if they use different decision rules.

The second example concerns the relationship between cued recall and recognition, as studied in the "recognition failure" paradigm. Here, subjects study pairs of cue words and target words, are later tested for recognition of the targets, and still later tested for recall of the targets from the cues. Contingency analyses typically show a small, positive relationship between the two attempts to remember the same target words (e.g. Flexser & Tulving 1978). Because the multiple-trace model can do both recognition and cued recall, Hintzman (1987) simulated the stochastic relationship between the two tasks. Both tasks used the same memory traces, and a random encoding process ensured that these traces varied in how complete they were. Nevertheless, the first simulation yielded data that were indistinguishable from independence. Aware that the independence could be due to Simpson's paradox, Hintzman (1987) hypothesized that a third variable was correlated in opposite directions with performance on the two tasks, and identified similarity as a likely candidate. (A target that is unusually similar to other list items benefits in recognition, but suffers in cued recall.) Experiments with the model confirmed the hypothesis: Increasing variation in trace similarity yielded a negative contingency, while decreasing it produced a positive one; increasing variation in trace completeness yielded a positive contingency, while decreasing it produced a negative one. Essential to the present argument is the point that it was possible to get independence, or even a negative relationship, even though the same memory system mediated performance on the two tasks.

If stochastic independence can be derived from single-system models, why does it seem so compelling as evidence for separate systems? One possibility is that our research is often guided by implicit, intuitive theories that intrude, unrecognized, into our thinking about laboratory research. Our intuitive theory of memory may assume that traces differ in retrievability because they vary in strength. This might explain the persuasive power of independence, in the following way: If two tasks use the same set of memory traces, and retrievability is solely a function of relative strength, then the traces should be ranked the same by both tasks. An imperfect correlation between the two rankings could indicate task-specific factors superimposed on the single factor of strength. But two *orthogonal* sets of rankings (the reasoning goes) can only mean one thing: two different sets of strengths, thus two sets of traces—i.e. two systems. Note that this explicit version of the alleged intuitive model explains the special significance assigned to stochastic independence (see the earlier quotation from Witherspoon & Moscovitch 1989).

However useful the implicit-strength theory is in everyday life, in the laboratory it may be out of place. We experimenters use carefully selected, uniform stimuli, presented for equal durations and repeated the same number of times. We add primacy and recency buffers to the ends of lists, and exhort subjects to process each item in a specified way. All this may not eliminate strength differences, but it should minimize them. One could almost define the perfect experiment as one in which traces do not vary in strength. In this situation, the intuitive theory does not apply. If variation in strength is low, then task-specific factors will determine Task 1 and Task 2 rankings almost completely, and stochastic independence (or near independence) is a possibility whether the tasks tap two different sets of traces or just one. Report titles such as "Stochastic independence between two implicit memory tasks" should cause no surprise.

Dissociations of Consciousness

Unconscious retrieval and unconscious learning are examined separately here. I do not discuss reversible dissociations in which memories retrievable in one state are not accessible in another, as appears in extreme form in patients with multiple-personality disorder. For an interesting attempt to study memory in such a patient, see Nissen et al (1988).

UNCONSCIOUS RETRIEVAL   I have suggested that an intuitive memory theory sometimes influences our research and that one assumption of the theory is that differences in retrieval reflect differences in strength. Both Hayes & Broadbent (1988) and Jacoby et al (1989a) have suggested another assumption of this theory: that we must consciously remember a past experience if it is to influence present behavior. There is an obvious reason why this assumption should be intuitively compelling, and this may account for memory researchers' apparent bias against evidence that retrieval can be unconscious. Mainstream memory research virtually ignored memory-without-awareness for nearly 100 years, despite claims by such prominent figures as

Ebbinghaus, Helmholtz, and Freud (cf Schacter 1987). Perceptual learning and skill learning have long research traditions, but they have never fit comfortably in the mainstream of work on human learning and memory, which has been preoccupied with conscious memory for experiences. Against this background, the recent surge of interest in unconscious memory is significant.

The terms *explicit memory* and *implicit memory* have been proposed for memory with and without awareness, respectively. The common use of these terms as category labels for tasks, however, confuses matters. Tasks that have been given either label can be performed either with or without awareness (Richardson-Klavehn & Bjork 1988); and as I argued above, there is nothing particularly remarkable in finding dissociations between tasks. Accordingly, in agreement with Johnson & Hasher, I use the term *direct* when task instructions refer somehow to a past event that affects performance, and *indirect* when they do not (Johnson & Hasher 1987). I follow Jacoby (1989b) in referring to *conscious* and *unconscious* memory—the latter denoting a "dissociation" as the term was traditionally understood.

As noted by Roediger et al (1989), many indirect memory tasks can be seen as primarily data-driven (e.g. lexical decision, picture naming, identifying briefly flashed words, and completing word fragments). However, some indirect tasks are conceptually driven (e.g. word association and category judgments), which shows that the data-vs-conceptual and direct-vs-indirect distinctions are not the same. Further, unconscious memory can be conceptual—as in cases of cryptomnesia, which can appear as unconscious plagiarism—and experimental instructions give no guarantee that subjects perform an indirect task without consciousness of a particular past event.

Because task instructions cannot preclude conscious retrieval, some additional means of ruling out consciousness is needed. The usual method is to wait until the experiment's end and then ask subjects about their awareness. There are serious drawbacks to this technique. Subjects may forget being aware of a memory, the questioning may not be thorough enough, or the subject's and investigator's verbal descriptions may not match up well. Another technique involves the direct manipulation of consciousness. In posthypnotic amnesia, subjects produce a fact acquired under hypnosis but dissociate content from context by attributing it to an incorrect source. This form of amnesia is reversible, however. Evidence implicates a disruption of normal retrieval strategies (Evans 1988), so posthypnotic amnesia may be a special case. In postsurgery interviews, patients can reliably respond to suggestions made under anesthesia (e.g. by tugging the left ear when given a signal), despite irreversible amnesia for the suggestion. The same has been reported for suggestions made during sleep (see Bennett 1988). The use of sleeping, anesthetized, or otherwise immobile subjects has obvious disadvantages for research, including severe restrictions on the nature of the encoding task.

A third way to rule out conscious retrieval, advocated by Jacoby et al (1989b), is to place the two in opposition—that is, arrange things so that subjects will respond in one way to a conscious memory and in another way to an unconscious one. The basic idea is that a memory's unconscious influence can be resisted or discounted only if one becomes aware of the memory. The same memory representation may be used unconsciously, as a *tool* to accomplish a task (e.g. to aid perception), or consciously, as an *object* of subjective reflection. Its use as a tool is essentially automatic, while its use as an object requires a separate, optional act. For example, showing a word too briefly for conscious perception just prior to its exposure on a recognition-memory test induces subjects to call it "old," whether or not it is from the target list; but showing it for a time that allows conscious perception may have the opposite effect (Jacoby & Whitehouse 1989). The argument is that recognition memory is an attributional process: In the first case, the boost in "perceptual fluency" induced by exposure is attributed to the word's appearance on the target list; while in the second case it is attributed, correctly, to the exposure immediately preceding the test. Note that this attribution hypothesis can be maintained without the "preceptual fluency" notion, which might be rejected on other grounds (e.g. Watkins & Gibson 1988).

Jacoby et al (1989b, Exp. 3) investigated another way of preventing the optional attribution process. Subjects were first given a list of names identified as nonfamous people. They then made judgments of fame for these preexposed nonfamous names, in a longer list of famous and nonfamous names, under conditions of divided or undivided attention. Under divided attention, subjects tended to accept the preexposed names as famous, presumably because the simultaneous task allowed automatic retrieval but prevented the act of assigning a name to the preexposed, nonfamous list. Speed-accuracy trade-off techniques could also be used to test the hypothesis that attribution is a secondary, optional process (cf Dosher 1984; Gronlund & Ratcliff 1989). One implication of the attribution hypothesis is that subjects' attributions will depend on their own intuitive theory of mental processes. Cognitive and perceptual illusions will occur when that theory is wrong. Jacoby et al (1988) first exposed subjects to sentences, and later played both old and new sentences over a noisy background, asking subjects to judge the loudness of the noise. Judged loudness was substantially lower for old sentences than for new ones—i.e. subjects attributed differences in ease of comprehension not to memory, but to the noise.

Two points are worth making about the Jacoby et al (1988) demonstration. First, this kind of indirect memory was recognized a century ago by Helmholtz, who wrote:

> . . . reminiscences of previous experiences act in conjunction with present sensations to produce a perceptual image . . . without our being conscious of how much of it is due to memory and how much to present perception (Helmholtz 1962:12).

> We are not in the habit of observing our sensations accurately, except as they are useful in enabling us to recognize external objects (Helmholtz 1962:6).

Second, the inability of subjects to accurately parse the sources of an experience into sensation and memory is generally consistent with those connectionist networks that relax into an interpretation of the input. Relaxation is a joint function of present inputs and past experience, as reflected in the weights.

Viewing recognition judgments as attributions raises the question of what cues subjects use to make attributions when retrieval is conscious. A memory may be attributed to an incorrect class of events (e.g. one extraneous to the memory task itself) even when it is consciously remembered. In a systematic extension of the reality-monitoring framework, Johnson (1988) has described an experimental phenomenological approach to such issues. Purely phenomenological considerations, however, suggest that a simple dichotomy between conscious and unconscious memory may be too crude (see Brewer & Pani 1983).

UNCONSCIOUS LEARNING   The notion that learning can occur unconsciously has always been controversial. Some forms of conditioning are probably unconscious, and there are reports that patients under general anesthesia sometimes encode and later recall personally relevant remarks by operating-room personnel (Bennett 1988). Highly skilled acts can be performed without awareness, but the generally accepted view is that acquisition begins with conscious, declarative representation of the goal and steps to be performed, and that with practice this representation is transformed into—or supplemented by—one that supports execution with few attentional demands (e.g. Anderson 1987; Logan 1988). However, there is now growing evidence that skills can be acquired without going through a conscious, declarative stage.

In a study by Lewicki et al (1987), the location of a target digit in a visual display was related by a complex rule to the pattern of locations over six previous trials. After about 1500 trials on each pattern, scanning times for predictable target positions were shorter than those for unpredictable ones. Because subjects were unable to articulate the rules, Lewicki et al (1987) suggested that they had been learned subconsciously; however, the difference in scanning times might be explained by knowledge only moderately correlated with the experimenters' rules. In this case, the complexity of the contingencies and emergence of the performance difference only after several hours of practice speaks as strongly for subconscious learning as the subjects' retrospective reports.

Hayes & Broadbent (1988) compared skill learning under two conditions: In one, feedback was related to the present response; in the other it was related to the response on the previous trial. Learning occurred in both conditions, but the former differed from the latter in several ways: Learning and reversal were faster, retrospective reports could be used effectively to simulate performance of the task, and reversal learning was inhibited by divided attention. The two conditions were said to illustrate two forms of learning: a conscious one that encodes only attentively selected contingencies, and an unconscious one in which all contingencies are stored. Willingham et al (1989) studied conscious and unconscious learning using a serial reaction time task in which subjects respond on each trial to one of four lights by pressing the corresponding key. When the lights come on in a repeating 10-trial sequence, speeds gradually improve. Some of the subjects who show such clear evidence of learning are unable to describe the sequence better than would be expected by chance. Moreover, these subjects show no savings when transferred to a task in which they must overtly predict the next light. Like Hayes & Broadbent (1988), Willingham et al (1989) argue for two forms of learning. Unlike the Hayes & Broadbent (1988) task, however, learning in the sequential reaction time task appears to be prevented by divided attention (Nissen & Bullemer 1987).

Amnesia

The ideal data base on amnesia would consist of data from thousands of patients having no other disorders, and having precisely dated lesions of known location and extent, and would include many reliable measures spanning all types of knowledge and skills, acquired at known times ranging from the recent to the distant past. Reality falls near the opposite pole of each dimension of this description, but because of basic advances in neuroscience, new animal models of human amnesia, and the concerted efforts of a few laboratories able to locate and test amnesic patients, progress is being made. For summaries of this work, see the book by Squire (1987) and the chapter by Shimamura (1989).

What makes certain amnesic patients interesting is not just that their memory problems coexist with intact cognitive functions (e.g. normal IQ), but that there is also a dissociation among memory functions themselves. Some memory abilities may be virtually intact even when others are severely impaired. One pattern—common enough to be called the "amnesic syndrome"—has been related to damage in either the medial temporal lobe structures (primarily the hippocampus), or the mediodorsal nucleus of the thalamus (Squire 1987). Patients with hippocampal damage include the much-studied H. M., and the recent case of R. B., which implicates hippocampal cell layer CA1 (Zola-Morgan et al 1986). So far there is no good evidence from amnesics that hippocampal and thalamic lesions have different behavioral affects. Interestingly, transient amnesias like those due to electroconvulsive shock and head trauma resemble the amnesic syndrome in many ways, although the structures that are involved are unknown.

The amnesics most widely available for study are alcoholic Korsakoff patients, who typically have thalamic lesions, but may also suffer damage to other areas such as the frontal lobes. Patients who have only frontal lobe damage, although essentially normal in recognition and cued recall, show deficits in recency discrimination, source amnesia, metamemory, and strategic aspects of free recall. It has been suggested that Korsakoff patients may show disproportional deficits in these functions because effects of frontal lobe atrophy are superimposed on the basic amnesic syndrome (Janowsky et al 1989). The difficulty in dating onset of the lesion is another factor making Korsakoff patients less desirable subjects for memory research (but see Butters & Cermak 1986).

Basal forebrain damage can cause a memory disorder that is qualitatively different from the amnesic syndrome, although it has yet to be studied systematically. The patients have been described as able to recognize components of a previous experience—such as a doctor's face, name, or voice—but not to integrate them. Reported memories are described as wild fabrications that combine components from diverse experiences from both before and after the lesion. For example, personal experiences may be combined with things that were read or seen on television, including current news events (Damasio et al 1985).

In the amnesic syndrome itself, patients can consciously remember new information for several seconds. Their short-term memory is often said to be normal (but typically is slightly impaired). Unless constantly rehearsed, new declarative information is quickly lost. This learning disability—or anterograde amnesia—is accompanied by retrograde amnesia, for facts learned and events witnessed prior to the lesion. The retrograde amnesia may extend back for a year, or for as long as two or more decades; but access to the oldest memories is least impaired and is typically normal. Similarly, in transient amnesias (e.g. due to shock therapy), the oldest memories are typically the least affected. Memories tend to return in chronological order, and the residual retrograde amnesia that never recovers may be as brief as a minute or less. Recent interest in the amnesic syndrome has centered on the ability of even profoundly amnesic patients to display some kinds of new learning, apparently without deficit. This has been shown using a number of indirect memory tasks. I discuss three classes of indirect tasks here: long-term priming, skill learning, and conditioning.

Long-term (repetition) priming is analogous to the short-term priming discussed earlier but lasts longer than a second or two. For example, prior exposure may affect the speed of naming a word, bias the spelling of a homophone, enhance the probability of giving a completion to a word stem, or increase the expressed preference for a picture. According to Shimamura (1986) such priming effects last less than two hours in amnesics. They may last longer in normals (e.g. Hashtroudi et al 1988; Mitchell & Brown 1988, Sloman et al 1988). A central question is whether priming in amnesics reflects the establishment of new traces, or some kind of temporary sensitization of preexisting ones. Using a word-completion task modified to reveal associative effects in priming, Graf & Schacter (1985) claimed to have shown new associative learning in amnesics, but a reanalysis (Schacter & Graf 1986) suggested that only their less amnesic subjects learned (see also Shimamura & Squire 1989).

Other evidence that long-term priming in amnesics may not be confined to preexisting representations was reported by Johnson et al (1985). Korsakoff patients and controls heard previously unfamiliar melodies and then gave either preference or recognition ratings for the tunes. Preference was affected by repetition—but only slightly—for both groups. If there was any difference, amnesics were affected more than the controls. Recognition memory was also affected by repetition for both groups, although the amnesics did much worse than the controls. Thus, while the Korsakoff patients clearly showed associative learning, they did so on both tests. Further, it is possible that the superior recognition memory of normals may have led them to discount the effect of earlier exposures when doing the preference test (see the discussion of this phenomenon, above). Preference effects for controls might have exceeded that for the amnesics if such discounting strategies had been ruled out. The hypothesis that long-term priming in the amnesic syndrome is confined to sensitization of information acquired prior to the amnesic period may yet turn out to be right.

Amnesics can learn some motor and perceptual skills, such as mirror drawing and reading inverted text, although they typically fail to recall having ever performed the task. Such skills resemble priming, in that they can be elicited without direct instructions to use memory; but they differ from priming in that they are longer lasting, and new associative learning is clearly involved. Nissen et al (1989) found that amnesics were able to learn and retain a repeating pattern in the serial reaction time task (described earlier), although none were able to report the sequence. The same researchers trained Korsakoff amnesics and controls on a tactual maze that had entrances to cul-de-sacs blocked. Although the amnesics became faster initially, their performance differed from that of controls in several respects, and—unlike controls—they were unable to learn the maze when the blocks were removed. Nissen et al (1989) suggest that amnesics are deficient on any task in which the subject must generate the response independently of environmental constraints. This view seems contrary to reports that H. M. had mastered the Tower of Hanoi problem, but appears consistent with the failure of other amnesics to learn the problem and with the more recent claim that even H. M. cannot do the Tower of Hanoi—or even improve at it—without prompting (see discussion by Shimamura 1989).

Considering all the attention given to devising new tasks to test different kinds of learning in amnesics, there has been surprisingly little research on conditioning in these subjects. Apparently, amnesics can be classically conditioned (Weiskrantz & Warrington 1979), but the literature is silent on more cognitive aspects of conditioning, such as blocking and configuring effects. Configuring could be particularly interesting, because according to Wickelgren's (1979) theory it depends on the hippocampus. (And in connectionist networks it requires hidden units, as was indicated earlier.)

What accounts for the pattern of impaired and intact abilities in amnesics? If amnesics indeed cannot show new associative learning in priming, or learn cognitive skills like the Tower of Hanoi, then priming may be nothing more than the temporary sensitization of preexisting representations, and the associative skill learning that remains intact may be of an evolutionarily primitive S-R kind (cf Wickelgren 1979). We need more evidence on these questions to decide.

A central mystery in amnesia concerns what functions the hippocampus serves. Apparently it is not necessary for forming new representations (short-term memory). But without it, new cognitive representations either cannot be consciously retrieved, cannot be learned in a way that allows conscious retrieval, or cannot be learned at all. A new memory requires support from the hippocampus for some time after encoding but eventually becomes independent of it. Long-term priming and new "noncognitive" learning may occur without the hippocampus. Why does hippocampal damage produce both anterograde and retrograde amnesia, and why is its involvement time-limited in the latter case? A theory of Teyler (1986) holds that memories are in neocortex, and gives the hippocampus an "indexing" role. This theory fails to explain why retrieval eventually becomes independent of the hippocampus. To Squire (1987), the hippocampus maintains new cognitive learning (in the cortex) and supports its retrieval while consolidation gradually takes place. Wickelgren's (1979) theory accounts for the hippocampus's time-limited role but does not explain why behaviorally significant consolidation would still be going on 20–30 years after learning (Squire et al 1989). There is some indication that memory problems in older normal subjects resemble those of amnesics in the pattern of tasks that are relatively affected and spared (e.g. Light & Singh 1987). This is consistent with the view that, in normal aging, hippocampal function is impaired.

Comment on Dissociations

The evidence from task-comparison research appears too complex for a single explanation. Research on amnesia provides evidence for memory-related functions with anatomically distinct locations. Whether these are crucial functions in the operation of a single memory system, or should be characterized as separate memory sytems in themselves, is a question that may not be answerable outside the context of a particular theory. Research on awareness and memory suggests that some kinds of learning and retrieval are available to consciousness while other kinds are not. Whether this is a fundamental distinction or just a matter of degree is again a theoretical question. Evidence suggests that the forms of memory that are intact in the amnesic syndrome may be those that are unconscious in normal subjects (i.e. "implicit" or "nondeclarative" memories), although this correspondence may not be complete.

Task dissociations across experimental conditions could reflect different systems, but the most-studied ones appear to be better understood as compatibility effects. Such data provide evidence for separate systems only to the extent that they are predicted by a theory specifying the nature of the systems and their interaction, and are not easily explained in other ways. Even if the compatibility approach is on the right track, however, serious theoretical work needs to be done. To explain the obtained tasks interactions in detail will require close attention to the processes engaged by each encoding task and each retrieval task, and to the way in which transfer occurs. Computer modeling is the obvious way to attack this complex problem, but existing models such as those reviewed here do not deal with encoding tasks like generating or reading, and so are obviously not up to the job.

CONCLUDING REMARKS

Throughout this review I stressed the need for explicit theory, and the unreliability of intuitive reasoning in drawing conclusions from experimental results. I have emphasized mathematical and computational models, because they force the theorist to be explicit, and because formal systems can be used as an aid to human reasoning, which can be notoriously unreliable by itself. Connectionist models of the type discussed here have the advantage of assuming "brain-style computation" (McClelland 1988), although our definition of what that means will certainly change. One hope is that such models will eventually serve as a reductionist bridge between the neurobiological evidence, on one hand, and behavioral evidence, on the other. Given the current state of our knowledge, such a goal may seem to be science fiction; but explicit comparisons are already being made between circuitry of the hippocampus and specific connectionist networks (e.g. McNaughton & Morris 1987). Such ambitious efforts will require cooperation by experts in neuroscience, modeling, and the psychology of memory, in order to succeed.

The biggest obstacle to the development of more adequate models may be the complexity of the system we are trying to understand. One reason to prefer simple model systems is that they can help one to discover general principles; but such simple systems—if they exist in the brain—must each serve to perform only part of a cognitive task. Brain imaging suggests that even simple tasks are carried out cooperatively by several brain regions (Posner et al 1988)—each, presumably, one module of a larger system. Modular connectionist systems can be powerful (e.g. Grossberg & Stone 1986; Schneider & Detweiler 1987), but their complexity makes them inherently more difficult to test and to learn from than single-module networks are (Shepard 1988; den Uyl 1988). Evidence from neuropsychology patients suggests some anatomical separation of modules that perform different memory functions, and further refinement of this knowledge should come from advances in brain imaging techniques. Clues to modular structure may also come from studies of conscious awareness. Finally, processes can sometimes be temporarily "lesioned" in normal subjects by occupying them with a secondary task, as has been done so effectively in the study of working memory (e.g. Baddeley 1986). If the currently popular task-comparison methodology is to be used effectively, however, it should be guided by theories that make explicit predictions across the appropriate tasks.

ACKNOWLEDGMENT

Preparation of this review was supported by National Science Foundation Grant BNS-87-11218. I thank Morton Gernsbacher, Hill Goldsmith, Jeri Janowsky, Gail McKoon, Roger Ratliff, and Don Tucker for commenting on earlier drafts.

Literature Cited

Anderson, J. A. 1973. A theory for the recognition of items from short memorized lists. *Psychol. Rev.* 80:417–38

Anderson, J. R. 1987. Skill acquisition: compilation of weak-method problems solutions. *Psychol. Rev.* 94:192–210

Anderson, J. R., Reder, L. M. 1988. Effects of number of facts studied on recognition versus sensibility judgments. *J. Exp. Psychol. Learn. Mem. Cogn.* 13:355–67

Baddeley, A. 1986. Working Memory. Oxford: Clarendon

Balota, D. A., Lorch, R. F. 1986. Depth of automatic spreading activation: mediated priming effects in pronunciation but not in lexical decisions. *J. Exp. Psychol.: Learn. Mem. Cogn.* 12:336–45

Bennett, H. L. 1988. Perception and memory for events during adequate general anesthesia for surgical operations. In *Hypnosis and Memory*, ed. H. M. Pettinati, pp. 193–231. New York: Guilford

Braitenberg, V. 1985. *Vehicles: Experiments in Synthetic Psychology*. Cambridge: MA: MIT Press

Brewer, W. F., Pani, J. R. 1983. The structure of human memory. *Psychol. Learn. Motiv.* 17:1–38

Broadbent, D. 1987. Simple models for experimental situations. In *Modelling Cognition*, ed. P. Morris, pp. 169–85. London: Wiley

Butters, N., Cermak, L. S. 1986. A case study of the forgetting of autobiographical knowledge: implications for the study of retrograde amnesia. *Autobiographical Memory*, ed. D. C. Rubin, pp. 253–72. Cambridge Univ. Press

Damasio, A. R., Graff-Radford, N. R., Eslinger, P. J., Damasio, H., Kassell, N. 1985. Amnesia following basal forebrain lesions. *Arch. Neurol.* 42:263–71

den Uyl, M. J. 1988. The essential opacity of modular systems: why even connectionism cannot give complete formal accounts of cognition. *Behav. Brain Sci.* 11:52

Dosher, B. A. 1984. Discriminating preexperimental (semantic) from learned (episodic) associations: a speed-accuracy study. *Cognit. Psychol.* 16:519–55

Dunn, J. C., Kirsner, K. 1988. Discovering functionally independent mental processes: the principle of reversed association. *Psychol. Rev.* 95:21–101

Eich, J. M. 1982. A composite holographic associative recall model. *Psychol. Rev.* 89:627–61

Eich, J. M. 1985. Levels of processing, encoding specificity, elaboration, and CHARM. *Psychol. Rev.* 92:1–38

Evans, F. J. 1988. Posthypnotic amnesia: dissociation of content and context. In *Hypnosis and Memory*, ed. H. M. Pettinati, pp. 157–92. New York: Guilford Press

Flexser, A. J., Tulving, E. 1978. Retrieval independence in recognition and recall. *Psychol. Rev.* 85:153–71

Gardiner, J. M. 1988. Recognition failures and free-recall failures: implications for the relation between recall and recognition. *Mem. Cogn.* 16:446–51

Gillund, G., Shiffrin, R. M. 1984. A retrieval model for both recognition and recall. *Psychol. Rev.* 91:1–67

Glanzer, M., Adams, J. K. 1985. The mirror effect in recognition memory. *Mem. Cogn.* 13:8–20

Glanzer, M., Adams, J. K. 1990. The mirror effect in recognition memory: data and theory. *J. Exp. Psychol.: Learn. Mem. Cogn.* 16: In press

Gluck, M. A., Bower, G. H. 1988. Evaluating an adaptive network model of human learning. *J. Mem. Lang.* 27:166–95

Graf, P., Schacter, D. L. 1985. Implicit and explicit memory for new associations in normal and amnesic subjects. *J. Exp. Psychol.: Learn. Mem. Cogn.* 1:501–18

Gronlund, S. D., Ratcliff, R. 1989. The time-course of item and associative information: implications for global memory models. *J. Exp. Psychol.: Learn. Mem. Cogn.* 15:846–58

Grossberg, S. 1987. Competitive learning: from interactive activation to adaptive resonance. *Cognit. Sci.* 11:23–63

Grossberg, S., Stone, G. 1986. Neural dynamics of word recognition and recall: attentional priming, learning, and resonance. *Psychol. Rev.* 93:46–74

Hashtroudi, S., Ferguson, S. A., Rappold, V. A., Chrosniak, L. D. 1988. Data-driven and conceptually driven processes in partial-word identification and recognition. *J. Exp. Psychol.: Learn. Mem. Cogn.* 14:749–57

Hayes, N. A., Broadbent, D. E. 1988. Two modes of learning for interactive tasks. *Cognition* 28:249–76

Hayman, C. A. G., Tulving, E. 1989. Contingent dissociation between recognition and fragment completion: the method of triangulation. *J. Exp. Psychol.: Learn. Mem. Cogn.* 15:228–40

Helholtz, H. von. 1962. *Helmholtz's Physiological Optics.* Ed. & Transl. J. P. C. Southall. New York: Dover (Orig. publ. 1910)

Hintzman, D. L. 1980. Simpson's paradox and the analysis of memory retrieval. *Psychol. Rev.* 87:398–410

Hintzman, D. L. 1986. "Schema abstraction" in a multiple-trace memory model. *Psychol. Rev.* 93:411–28

Hintzman, D. L. 1987. Recognition and recall in MINERVA 2: analysis of the "recognition failure" paradigm. In *Modelling Cognition*, ed. P. E. Morris, pp. 215–29. London: Wiley

Hintzman, D. L. 1988. Judgments of frequency and recognition memory in a multiple-trace memory model. *Psychol. Rev.* 95: 528–51

Humphreys, M. S., Bain, J. D., Pike, R. 1989. Different ways to cue a coherent memory system: a theory for episodic, semantic, and procedural tasks. *Psychol. Rev.* 96:208–33

Jacoby, L. L. 1983. Remembering the data: analyzing interactive processes in reading. *J. Verbal Learn. Verbal Behav.* 22:485–508

Jacoby, L. L., Allan, L. G., Collins, J. C., Larwill, L. K. 1988. Memory influences subjective experience: noise judgments. *J. Exp. Psychol.: Learn. Mem. Cogn.* 14:240–47

Jacoby, L. L., Kelley, C., Brown, J., Jasechko, J. 1989a. Becoming famous overnight: limits on the ability to avoid unconscious influences of the past. *J. Pers. Soc. Psychol.: Gen.* In press

Jacoby, L. L., Whitehouse, K. 1989. An illusion of memory: false recognition influenced by unconscious perception. *J. Exp. Psychol.: Gen.* 118:126–35

Jacoby, L. L., Woloshyn, V., Kelley, C. 1989b. Becoming famous without being recognized: unconscious influences of memory produced by dividing attention. *J. Exp. Psychol.: Gen.* 118:115–25

Janowsky, J. S., Shimamura, A. P., Kritchevsky, M., Squire, L. R. 1989. Cognitive impairment following frontal lobe damage and its relevance to human amnesia. *Behav. Neurosci.* In press

Johnson, M. K. 1988. Reality monitoring: an experimental phenomenological approach. *J. Exp. Psychol.: Gen.* 117:390–94

Johnson, M. K., Hasher, L. 1987. Human learning and memory. *Annu. Rev. Psychol.* 38:631–68

Johnson, M. K., Kim, J. K., Risse, G. 1985. Do alcoholic Korsakoff's syndrome patients acquire affective reactions? *J. Exp. Psychol.: Learn. Mem. Cogn.* 11:22–36

Klein, S. B., Khilstrom, J. F. 1986. Elaboration, organization, and the self-reference effect in memory. *J. Exp. Psychol.: Gen.* 115:26–38

Kolers, P. A., Roediger, H. L. 1984. Procedures of mind. *J. Verbal Learn. Verbal Behav.* 23:425–49

Lewicki, P., Czyzewska, M., Hoffman, H. 1987. Unconscious acquisition of complex procedural knowledge. *J. Exp. Psychol.: Learn. Mem. Cogn.* 13:523–30

Light, L. L., Singh, A. 1987. Implicit and explicit memory in young and older adults. *J. Exp. Psychol.: Learn. Mem. Cogn.* 13:531–41

Logan, G. D. 1988. Toward an instance theory of automatization. *Psychol. Rev.* 95:492–527

MacWeek. 1988. Aug. 8, pp. 2, 32

Massaro, D. W. 1988. Some criticisms of connectionist models of human performance. *J. Mem. Lang.* 27:213–34

McClelland, J. L., Rumelhart, D. E. 1985. Distributed memory and the representation of general and specific information. *J. Exp. Psychol.: Gen.* 114:159–88

McClelland, J. L. 1988. Connectionist models and psychological evidence. *J. Mem. Lang.* 27:107–23

McClosky, M., Cohen, N. J. 1989. Catastrophic interference in connectionist networks: the sequential learning problem. *Psychol. Learn. Motiv.* 23: In press

McDaniel, M. A., Waddill, P. J., Einstein, G. O. 1988. A contextual account of the generation effect: a three-factor theory. *J. Mem. Lang.* 27:521–36

McNamara, T. P., Altarriba, J. 1988. Depth of spreading activation revisited: Semantic

mediated priming occurs in lexical decisions. *J. Mem. Lang.* 27:545–59

McNaughton, B. L., Morris, R. G. M. 1987. Hippocampal synaptic enhancement and information storage within a distributed memory system. *Trends Neurosci.* 10:408–15

Mensink, G. J., Raaijmakers, J. G. W. 1988. A model of interference and forgetting. *Psychol. Rev.* 95:434–55

Metcalfe, J., Fisher, R. P. 1986. The relation between recognition memory and classification learning. *J. Exp. Psychol.: Learn. Mem. Cogn.* 14:164–73

Mitchell, D. B., Brown, A. S. 1988. Persistent repetition priming in picture naming and its dissociation from recognition memory. *J. Exp. Psychol.: Learn. Mem. Cogn.* 14:213–32

Murdock, B. B. 1982. A theory for the storage and retrieval of item and associative information. *Psychol. Rev.* 89:609–26

Murdock, B. B. 1985. Convolution and matrix systems: a reply to Pike. *Psychol. Rev.* 92:130–32

Murdock, B. B. 1987. Serial-order effects in a distributed-memory model. In *Memory and Learning: The Ebbinghaus Centennial Conference*, ed. D. S. Gorfein, R. R. Hoffman, pp. 227–310. Hillsdale, NJ: Erlbaum

Murdock, B. B. 1989. Learning in a distributed memory model. In *Current Issues in Cognitive Processes: The Tulane Symposium of Cognition*, ed. C. Izawa. Hillsdale, NJ: Erlbaum

Nissen, M. J., Bullemer, P. 1987. Attentional requirements of learning: evidence from performance measures. *Cognit. Psychol.* 19:1–32

Nissen, M. J., Ross, J. L., Willingham, D. B., Mackenzie, T. B., Schacter, D. L. 1988. Memory and awareness in a patient with multiple personality disorder. *Brain Cogn.* 8:117–34

Nissen, M. J., Willingham, D., Hartman, M. 1989. Explicit and implicit remembering: When is learning preserved in amnesia? *Neuropsychologia.* 27:341–52

Nosofsky, R. M. 1988. Exemplar-based accounts of relations between classification, recognition, and typicality. *J. Exp. Psychol.: Learn. Mem. Cogn.* 14:700–8

Phillips, W. A. 1988. Brainy minds. *Q. J. Exp. Psychol.* 40A:389–405

Pike, R. 1984. Comparison of convolution and matrix distributed memory systems. *Psychol. Rev.* 91:281–94

Posner, M. I., Petersen, S. E., Fox, P. T., Raichle, M. E. 1988. Localization of cognitive operations in the human brain. *Science* 240:1627–31

Raiijmakers, J. G. W., Shiffrin, R. M. 1980. SAM: a theory of probabilistic search of associative memory. *Psychol. Learn. Motiv.* 14:207–62

Ratcliff, R., McKoon, G. 1988. A retrieval theory of priming in memory. *Psychol. Rev.* 95:385–408

Ratcliff, R. 1990. Connectionist models of recognition memory: Constraints imposed by learning and forgetting functions. *Psychol. Rev.* In press

Richardson-Klavehn, A., Bjork, R. A. 1988. Measures of memory. *Annu. Rev. Psychol.* 39:475–543

Roediger, H. L. III, Blaxton, T. A. 1987. Retrieval modes produce dissociations in memory for surface information. In *Memory and Learning: The Ebbinghaus Centennial Conference*, ed. D. S. Gorfein, R. R. Hoffman, pp. 349–79. Hillsdale, NJ: Erlbaum

Roediger, H. L. III, Weldon, M. S., Challis, B. H. 1989. Explaining dissociations between implicit and explicit measures of retention: a processing account. In *Varieties of Memory and Consciousness: Essays in Honour of Endel Tulving*, ed. H. L. Roediger III, F. I. M. Craik. Hillsdale, NJ: Erlbaum. In press

Rubin, D. C. 1985. Memorability as a measure of processing: a unit analysis of prose and list learning. *J. Exp. Psychol.: Gen.* 114:213–38

Rumelhart, D. E., Hinton, G. E., Williams, R. J. 1986a. Learning internal representations by error propagation. See Rumelhart & McClelland 1986a, pp. 318–62

Rumelhart, D. E., McClelland, J. L. 1986a. *Parallel Distributed Processing, Vol. 1.* Cambridge, MA: MIT Press

Rumelhart, D. E., McClelland, J. L. 1986b. On learning the past tenses of English verbs. In *Parallel Distributed Processing*, ed. J. L. McClelland, D. E. Rumelhart, 2: 216–71. Cambridge: MA: MIT Press

Rumelhart, D. E., Smolensky, P., McClelland, J. L. Hinton, G. E. 1986b. Schemata and sequential thought processes in PDP models. In *Parallel Distributed Processing*, ed. J. L. McClelland, D. E. Rumelhart, 2:7–57. Cambridge, MA: MIT Press

Schacter, D. L. 1987. Implicit memory: history and current status. *J. Exp. Psychol.: Learn. Mem. Cogn.* 13:501–18

Schacter, D. L., Graf, P. 1986. Preserved learning in amnesic patients: perspectives from research on direct priming. *J. Clin. Exp. Neuropsychol.* 6:727–43

Schneider, W. 1987. Connectionism: Is it a paradigm shift for psychology? *Behav. Res. Methods Instrum. Comput.* 19:73–83

Schneider, W., Detweiler, M. 1987. A connectionist/control architecture for working memory. *Psychol. Learn. Motiv.* 21:54–119

Shepard, R. N. 1988. How fully should con-

nectionism be activated? Two sources of excitation and one of inhibition. *Behav. Brain Sci.* 11:52

Sherry, D. F., Schacter, D. L. 1987. The evolution of multiple memory systems. *Psychol. Rev.* 94:439–54

Shimamura, A. P. 1985. Problems with the finding of stochastic independence as evidence for muliple memory systems. *Bull. Psychon. Soc.* 23:506–8

Shimamura, A. P. 1986. Priming effects in amnesia: evidence for a dissociable memory function. *Q. J. Exp. Psychol.* 38A:619–44

Shimamura, A. P. 1989. Disorders of memory: the cognitive science perspective. In *Handbook of Neuropsychology*, ed. F. Boller, J. Grafman. Amsterdam: Elsevier

Shimamura, A. P., Squire, L. R. 1989. Impaired priming of new associations in amnesia. *J. Exp. Psychol. Learn. Mem. Cogn.* In press

Sloman, S. A., Hayman, C. A. G., Ohtun, N., Law, J., Tulving, E. 1988. Forgetting in primed fragment completion. *J. Exp. Psychol.: Learn. Mem. Cogn.* 14:223–39

Smolensky, P. 1988. On the proper treatment of connectionism. *Behav. Brain Sci.* 11:1–74

Snodgrass, J. G., Corwin, J. 1988. Pragmatics of measuring recognition memory: application to dementia and amnesia. *J. Exp. Psychol.: Gen.* 117:34–50

Squire, L. R. 1987. *Memory and Brain.* New York: Oxford Univ. Press

Squire, L. R., Haist, F., Shimamura, A. P. 1989. The neurology of memory: quantitative assessment of retrograde amnesia in two groups of amnesic patients. *J. Neurosci.* In press

Teyler, T. J. 1986. Memory: electrophysiological analogs. In *Learning and Memory: A Biological View*, ed. J. L. Martinez Jr., R. P. Kesner, pp. 237–65. New York: Academic

Tulving, E. 1983. Elements of Episodic Memory. New York: Oxford Univ. Press

Tulving, E., Bower, G. H. 1974. The logic of memory representations. *Psychol. Learn. Motiv.* 8:265–302

Underwood, B. J., Boruch, R. F., Malmi, R. A. 1978. Composition of episodic memory. *J. Exp. Psychol.: Gen.* 107:393–419

Watkins, M. J., Gibson, J. M. 1988. On the relation between perceptual priming and recognition memory. *J. Exp. Psychol.: Learn. Mem. Cogn.* 14:477–83

Weiskrantz, L., Warrington, E. K. 1979. Conditioning in amnesic patients. *Neuropsychologia* 17:187–94

Wickelgren, W. A. 1979. Chunking and consolidation: a theoretical synthesis of semantic networks, configuring in conditioning,

S-R versus cognitive learning, normal forgetting, the amnesic syndrome, and the hippocampal arousal system. *Psychol. Rev.* 86:44–60

Willingham, D. B., Nissen, M. J., Bullemer, P. 1990. On the development of procedural knowledge. *J. Exp. Psychol.: Learn Mem. Cogn.* In press

Witherspoon, D., Moscovitch, M. 1989.

Stochastic independence between two implicit memory tasks. *J. Exp. Psychol.: Learn. Mem. Cogn.* 15:22–30

Zola-Morgan, S., Squire, L. R., Amaral, D. G. 1986. Human amnesia and the medial temporal region: enduring memory impairment following a bilateral lesion limited to field CA1 of the hippocampus. *J. Neurosci.* 6:2950–67

Annu. Rev. Psychol. 1990. 41:141–68

SOCIAL AND COMMUNITY INTERVENTION

Kenneth Heller

Department of Psychology, Indiana University, Bloomington, Indiana 47405

CONTENTS

INTRODUCTION

This chapter covers the field of social and community intervention for the period 1986–1988. Recent *Annual Review* chapters present summaries of social factors in psychopathology (Kessler et al 1985) and psychosocial preventive intervention (Gesten & Jason 1987; Iscoe & Harris 1984). This review examines social factors at a more macro-environmental level, suggesting that social and community interventionists need to pay greater attention to ongoing community structures (Heller 1989) and normal social-role functioning (Heller et al 1990b).

Social and community intervention as a substantive interest of psycholo-

0066-4308/90/0201-0141$02.00

gists arose in the 1960s as part of the social reform spirit of that era (Walsh 1987). The psychologists who assembled at Swampscott, Massachusetts, in May of 1965 for a conference on the "Education of Psychologists for Community Mental Health" saw an opportunity to develop a "new agenda for psychology" (Kelly 1987) that would end the discipline's longstanding isolation from societal events. Participants were frustrated by the dominant individual-centered therapeutic model of mental health service delivery, and were groping for conceptual models that would increase psychology's social relevance (Walsh 1987). Environmental theories were not new in the mental health fields (Caplan 1969; Levine & Levine 1970), but in the first half of this century they were eclipsed by intriguing intrapsychic theories that seemed to promise a more direct route to unravelling the complexities of human motivation. In contrast, Kurt Lewin and his disciples, who founded the Society of the Psychological Study of Social Issues (Division 9 of APA), and the founders of the Division of Community Psychology (Division 27 of APA) were among those who strove to return a sense of balance to psychological theory by reemphasizing the social and environmental determinants of behavior (Klein 1987). Since that time, even though the political climate of the country has become increasingly conservative with each passing decade, the influence of community psychology ideology on general psychological theory has not diminished. If anything, community psychology themes that highlight the importance of social and environmental factors in behavior, and the necessity of conceptualizing intervention from a proactive and preventive stance, have become "mainstream." Within psychology, ecological points of view emphasizing setting and context determinants of behavior and person-environment interactions can be found in areas such as social, developmental, environmental and community psychology (Altman & Wandersman 1987; Heller et al 1984; Holahan & Wandersman 1987), as well as in the related fields of social ecology, public health (Berkman 1984; Kasl 1984), environmental design (Lindheim & Syme 1983), sociology (House et al 1988; Katz 1981; Keys 1987; Summers 1986), political science and public interest law (Levine et al 1987).

Throughout this chapter, I focus on what has been learned about social and community change since the 1960s. The field has moved beyond its initial unbridled optimism and unsubstantiated rhetoric to solid accomplishment in theory construction (McMillan & Chavis 1986: Perkins et al 1988) and well-controlled demonstration projects (Price et al 1988). However, social change is more easily recommended than accomplished, because social problems are woven into the fabric of society and reflect longstanding political and economic policies. True community change requires public consensus, resolve, and dedication of resources that are difficult to achieve even in the best of times. Public commitment to redress social inequity ebbs and flows over time, and in the past decade the national emphasis has been so focused on self-fulfillment and the pursuit of the "good life" that many citizens have been blinded to the fate of less fortunate others (Conger 1988). Thus any review of accomplishments must be tempered both by a realistic counteremphasis on impediments to social change and by a full explication of the complex processes by which theory and research become part of a community action agenda.

In the sections that follow, I highlight molar environmental variables linked to disorder and its prevention. Stressing the importance of including molar social events in psychological theories, I first briefly review epidemiological evidence linking environmental variables to both mortality and morbidity. Interventions to strengthen social resources can occur at a number of levels (community, organizational, interpersonal, and individual), but psychological theories, and ensuing interventions, rarely go beyond individual and interpersonal levels. The result is a limited understanding of the operation of the social forces that impinge upon behavior.

In describing recent work in social intervention, I pay particular attention to limiting conditions. I do so in the spirit of sharpening our knowledge and dispelling "uniformity myths" (Kiesler 1966) that encourage wholesale adoption of social programs wihout sufficient thought to the setting contexts and constraints within which they operate. Complex interactions of setting factors and program elements often make it difficult to generalize from one setting to the next. What is often called for is a clear understanding of the role of context variables in determining the outcomes attained before widespread adoption is attempted.

THE NATURE OF THE LINK BETWEEN ENVIRONMENTAL STRESSORS AND DISORDER

In a review of the studies linking socioeconomic status (SES) with mortality and morbidity, Syme & Berkman (1976) concluded that the vast body of evidence has consistently shown that the lower social classes have higher mortality, morbidity, and disability rates across a wide array of illnesses. We still do not know what accounts for this general susceptibility. While there is an abundance of evidence that social and environmental conditions influence mortality, morbidity, and psychological well-being, the processes by which these effects occur and the most potent ingredients among various stressors and resources are still largely unknown. The mortality-rate gap between the social classes has not diminished over the centuries despite the fact that mortality rates have generally declined as improvements have been made in environmental quality and medical care. Syme & Berkman (1976) urge a focus on factors that affect general susceptibility to disease, such as hazardous and toxic environmental conditions, greater life stress, fewer environmental resources, and poorer coping.

This general formulation is also reflected in the common operating assumption of prevention-oriented psychologists that the incidence of psychological disorder should be viewed as a direct function of environmental stressors and an inverse function of environmental resources. So, for example, Albee (1982) presented a general equation: Incidence of psychological disorder = (organic factors + stress)/(coping skills + self-esteem +support groups). This equation represents an interactionist view of the factors leading to disorder in that organic factors, coping skills, and self-esteem represent personal attributes, while stress and social support are environmental characteristics. In this, and in similar models (S. Cohen 1988), facets of social support and various learned coping behaviors are said to moderate the effects of environmental stress.

While accepting the general theoretical overview described above, Elias (1987) suggests an important macro-level reformulation. The Albee model is criticized for being person-centered and not sensitive to either situational differences or a developmental perspective. Elias proposes that: Likelihood of disorder in a population = (stressors & risk factors in the environment)/ (socialization practices + social support resources + opportunities for connectedness). While the Elias reformulation does not consider individual vulnerability, it has greater heuristic value because of its focus on more modifiable environmental stressors and resources. For example, socialization practices can be improved by parenting courses or by supportive and educational outreach projects to first-time parents (Olds 1988). Support resources can be increased by structural changes in society that counter isolation and loneliness, and by the development of mutual help organizations (Levine 1988). Similarly, opportunites for social connectedness can be increased by community and neighborhood participation that provide citizens with some semblance of control over their own destinies. A good share of this chapter will be devoted to promising programs that attempt to achieve these goals and to the dilemmas and difficulties that are likely to be encountered in community change programs.

While there is some continuing debate over the relative importance of constitutional and environmental variables, in most quarters the controversy appears to be settled. The protagonists recognize that both constitutional and environmental conditions influence behavior and the incidence of disorder (Dohrenwend et al 1987). The best evidence for the potency of environmental conditions as risk factors for mortality and morbidity comes from prospective studies that control for individual-level behaviors. For example, in a study of residents of Alameda County, California, first contacted in 1965 and followed up in 1974, Haan et al (1987) found an increased risk for mortality from all causes associated with SES, after a multivariate adjustment for a number of baseline covariates, such as health status, race, income, employment, access to medical care, smoking, alcohol consumption, physical activity, relative weight, sleep pattern, social isolation, marital status, depression, and personal uncertainty. Thus, factors associated with poverty-area residence appear to be associated with mortality independent of other correlated individual-level risk factors.

When psychologists refer to environmental stressors, they usually mean life events that are subjectively cited as "stressful," such as death of a spouse or a chronic illness (L. Cohen 1988). Less well studied and more difficult to determine are the pathways by which more molar environmental events (e.g. economic policies, unemployment, urbanization, and housing patterns) influence health and psychological well-being. While there is evidence that economic downturns, particularly unemployment, influence the development of psychological symptoms (Dooley et al 1987; Kessler et al 1987), the link is probably indirect, mediated by such factors as loss of support and esteem. The operation of such factors can be vividly illustrated in the problem of homelessness in America. The increase in homelessness reflects a complex interplay among factors that include national economic policies designed to shift tax funds away from public support programs (e.g. subsidized, low-income housing) and a shift in the labor market toward automation of older, labor-intensive industries (Dooley et al 1987; Shinn 1990). The result is a demoralized population of homeless people experiencing isolation, loss of contact with home and community, and draining of energies by the daily struggle for survival (Rivlin 1987).

Here I do not present a detailed review of social epidemiological risk factors. However, there is now clear evidence to support the assumption of prevention psychologists that environmental stressors and resources influence the onset of disorder. The question now is how environmental resources are best strengthened and deleterious environmental conditions modified. I discuss these issues first at the community and organizational levels, then at the interpersonal level, and finally at the level of individual coping behaviors.

Mobilizing Community-Level Resources

Any analysis of community change should first attend to the multifaceted nature of communities (Heller 1989; McKeown et al 1987). We belong to multiple communities defined by the places in which we live and work, by the institutions and organizations to which we belong, and by the activities we share with others. The village is a community, but so is the neighborhood; membership in a religious, racial, or political group; or membership in a professional organization. The term *community* is used in at least two generally recognized ways: As a locality, a community is a territory or geographic area—a neighborhood, town, or city. As a relational concept a community is defined by the qualities of human interaction and social ties that draw people together (Gusfield 1975; Hunter & Riger 1986; McMillan & Chavis 1986). This second meaning of the term emphasizes networks of individuals who interact within formal organizations and institutions, and as members of informal groups. What brings people together is not only propinquity, but common interests around which social relationships develop (Heller 1989).

Bernard (1973) claims that "people no longer really live their lives in neighborhoods" (p. 183), so the nonlocality-based nature of social ties produces a major problem in organizing political constituencies. This is particularly true in neighborhoods in which neighbors interact infrequently and have little in common. Because a number of neighborhoods, particularly more affluent ones, are set up to maximize privacy and minimize interaction among neighbors (Merry 1987), the minimum ingredients for effective organization may be absent. While neighborhood-based organizations are most likely to form when there is an external threat [e.g. a crime wave or an unfavorable zoning change (Unger & Wandersman 1985)], fewer than half of neighborhood-based organizations survive more than one year (Prestby & Wandersman 1985).

What are the conditions under which community members are apt to come together for concerted action? McMillan & Chavis (1986) propose that a sense of community develops among group members who have a common history, share common experiences, and develop emotional closeness, and whose group membership conveys a recognition of common identity and destiny. But there are limiting conditions that impede concerted action. One important factor is the normativeness of precipitating events. Local groups are more likely to work together to resolve problems that are normative and that affect the entire population of an area. However, nonnormative events, those that are unexpected or that affect only a small number of individuals (e.g. accidental injury or death, cancer, widowhood at an early age, being fired from a job, etc) are more difficult to cope with and are less likely to be associated with effective indigenous support. Network members have little experience with nonnormative events, and there are fewer institutionalized coping resources available (Levine 1988; Schulz & Rau 1985). Furthermore, it is hard to organize a broadly based coalition of support for events that affect only a small segment of the population.

These points can be illustrated by two case studies of towns facing toxic chemical contamination of their homes and water supplies (Edelstein & Wandersman 1987; Stone & Levine 1985). When residents organized to combat the environmental threat, it was difficult for them to obtain support from friends and family members who lived elsewhere. Those not directly involved found it hard to identify with the aroused residents and to comprehend fully their sense of impotence and rage.

Additional factors that influence the likelihood of citizens' organizing to take collective action are the level of skill and resources required for effective action, and whether group action increases or decreases the perceived threat. Group action is more probable when citizens see concrete steps that can be taken, when resources are available to complete action, and when solutions are within the capabilities and skills of ordinary people. Thus, citizens are more likely to organize for self-help projects (Jason et al 1988) but are less likely to be able to offer meaningful support to cancer or AIDS patients (Albino & Tedesco 1987; Taylor et al 1988)—individuals with threatening conditions unlikely to be ameliorated through concrete action.

A number of factors increase the chances that viable neighborhood organizations will be developed and maintained (Prestby & Wandersman 1985; Unger & Wandersman 1985). The greatest amount of neighboring occurs when there is similarity among residents, when there are young children in the neighborhood, and when there is at least a moderate level of residential tenure. However, high levels of neighboring do not guarantee participation in formal neighborhood organizations. As a matter of fact, close, dense networks of old friends can be an impediment to community organization (Unger & Wandersman 1985), since members of long-standing friendship cliques are often unaccustomed to obtaining satisfaction outside of their predefined friendship circle. Once formed, neighborhood organizations that survive have been found to be those that maintain a task focus, have formal organizational structures and active roles for members, use more democratic decision-making procedures, and have members with links to organizations outside the neighborhood capable of contributing additional resources (Wandersman & Florin 1990).

It is misleading to expect that neighborhood or community development organizations are appropriate for dealing with all types of citizen needs. They are more easily activated for projects that have a community-wide focus, such as a threatened water or sewer system, or a crisis in the schools. It is more difficult to get community-wide action for projects of primary interest only to a particular subgroup (Porter et al 1982).

In retrospect, one of the mistakes of the community mental health movement was its lack of specificity with regard to the level of community involvement that would be required for the community treatment of mental patients. For example, Hunter & Riger (1986) claim that community was an inadequately understood and nebulous concept for the framers of the community mental health legislation. Similarly, Naparstek et al (1982) argue that the rhetoric of community mental health expected too much of ordinary citizens.

While organized neighborhoods might successfully accomplish a number of social change initiatives such as improving their social and economic climate, thereby reducing the environmental precipitants to disorder, citizens may lack the skill or training to integrate chronic mental patients into their midst.

The appeal of mutual-aid and self-help groups is that they bring people together with common concerns that may not resonate with majority community sentiments. At the same time, they provide a welcome opportunity for participants to experience empathic understanding, mutual support, and assistance while learning effective coping strategies (Levine 1988; Maton 1988). The mutual assistance ideology has a wide variety of potential applications. It can be used as a basis for political action (e.g. women's consciousness raising groups) or as an alternative community for those shunned by the majority (e.g. lesbians and gay men) (D'Augelli 1989; D'Augelli & Hart 1987; Levine & Perkins 1987). Support and self-help groups have been found useful in the treatment of those with unique medical conditions (Gottlieb 1987b) and as a primary mode of treatment for chronic mental patients (Rappaport et al 1985; Salem et al 1988).

Organizational Resources

The study of organizations has a rich history in psychology, but little of that literature has influenced research on social and community change. One reason may be the tendency to focus on organizational effectiveness and productivity rather than on the capacity of organizational structures and processes to enhance the quality of life (Keys & Frank 1987). This state of affairs is slowly changing because of a growing awareness that "individuals cannot be understood apart from their actions and interactions in the various organizational/community settings in which they belong" (Keys & Frank 1987: 242). After all, formal and informal organizations represent many of the "mediating structures" (Berger & Neuhaus 1977) that stand between the individual and the larger institutions of society.

While there are a wide variety of organizational environments that impinge on individuals, work and school settings probably account for the largest number of daily interpersonal interactions. Children spend as much time at school as they do at home, and as they grow older, school friends take on increasing importance as sources of social support (Cauce & Srebnik 1989). Similarly, for adults, work associates are as much a part of everyday life as are family members (Klein & D'Aunno 1986; Price 1985).

Serious attempts to improve the work environment must recognize the existence of a number of limiting conditions. Many workers are employed in large, impersonal, bureaucratic organizations, performing tasks that are neither satisfying nor fulfilling (Levin 1983). In a number of business firms, division of labor into simple tasks has been adopted as a major device to limit labor costs and boost production, despite the growing evidence that worker initiative and participation are directly related to productivity (Akabas 1987; Klein & D'Aunno 1986). Furthermore, since approximately 80% of jobs in the United States are in the private sector, attempts to intervene to improve the quality of the work environment are not likely to succeed unless they lead to greater profits.

Even with these constraints, a number of possible initiatives are worthy of policy consideration (Klein & D'Aunno 1986; Levin 1983). Workers can press to have their pension funds invested in firms with worker-oriented policies. Since most pension funds are large, competition for them should be substantial, so it might not be too difficult to require that investment strategy balance a firm's performance and investment return with worker-oriented practices. Other initiatives that can improve job availability and worker participation might include encouraging the growth of small businesses, gain-sharing plans in which employees receive a share of company profits, worker-owned and managed firms, and incentives for community development corporations whose goals are to diversify the job base and to increase the stability of local economies. In contrast to these environmentally oriented suggestions, a focus on deficits of individual workers, as in the currently popular job training programs, is less likely to be successful except in reasonably vigorous economies that can absorb trainees into already established production positions (Levin 1983).

Schools are equally important social organizations, since that is where children spend most of their waking hours. Sarason & Klaber (1985) contend that schools, as social institutions, have changed in major ways over the decades in response to political and social events. Some of these pressures have involved responses to court-ordered desegregation, the advent of Public Law 94-142 concerning instructional planning for handicapped students, the rise of teachers' unions, and the widespread adoption of preschool education. The dilemma is that while schools are being pushed by external forces to change, there also are intractable aspects of school functioning that tend to mute attempts at innovation. So, while programs might be developed that have an impact upon the lives of individual students, schools and the nature of the learning enterprise are much more difficult to change. For example, Sarason & Klaber (1985) note that the assumption that education takes place best inside encapsulated classrooms in encapsulated schools is rarely questioned.

There is research specifying the type of classroom environment that is likely to enhance children's learning and friendship formation. In some of the original work with the Classroom Environment Scale, Moos and his associates demonstrated a number of relationships between social environment dimensions and student outcomes (Moos 1979). Classes that emphasized relationship dimensions reported higher levels of student satisfaction and friendliness, while an atmosphere high on task orientation, order, and organization was associated with higher levels of student achievement. Toro et al (1985) extended this research to the elementary school grades and demonstrated that classrooms perceived as high on order, organization, and affiliation were likely to be those that encouraged sociability and liking among children. Classrooms rated by teachers as having a firm and structured atmosphere were those in which teachers reported fewer instances of acting-out problems. A similar finding was reported by Figueira-McDonough (1986), who compared two high schools in the same community with comparable student bodies. The school with more predictable supervision had stronger friendship bonds among students and fewer incidents of minor delinquency. Since these are correlational studies, they are subject to the alternative explanation that friendlier, more achievement-oriented students see their classrooms as more affiliative and organized. Nevertheless, they provide descriptive data that can suggest the direction of future intervention.

Implementing effective classroom interventions is clearly a more difficult task than is the study of the ecology of existing classrooms. Hawkins & Lam (1987) tested a teacher training program that involved proactive classroom management techniques, interactive teaching, and cooperative learning. The study was conducted in a large school system involving 33 teachers and over a thousand children, with teachers assigned randomly to intervention or control conditions. After one year, there were modest results. There were fewer suspensions and expulsions from intervention classrooms, but no significant differences between experimental and control classes on student attitudes toward school, prosocial friendship formation, or minor delinquency. Leitenberg (1987) believes that it is unreasonable to expect that teacher training programs can be major vehicles for large-scale school change. Teaching is an undervalued and underpaid profession, and without a change in national priorities, the best teachers may not be recruited or retained. National rates of teacher turnover are such that 40% of teachers leave the profession within seven years.

An example of a program that successfully modified aspects of the school environment was conducted by Felner and his associates (Felner et al 1982; Felner & Adan 1988) who attempted to decrease the complexity of the school setting and to increase its supportiveness. Homeroom teachers expanded their roles to include counseling activities with the youngsters, and outreach and linking functions to their families. At the same time, the daily life of the student was restructured to establish a stable peer support system by assigning all project students to the same classes for their primary academic subjects. The findings of the research indicated that, compared to matched control group youngsters, project students reported greater clarity of expectations and higher levels of teacher support. Project participants also showed better school attendance, reported more stable self-concepts, and had higher grade-point averages at the end of the year.

Designers of social and behavioral programs to be imbedded in school and work environments are, of necessity, learning to work within the constraints of setting "regularities" (Sarason 1982). Their working axiom is that effective projects are those whose critical elements are integrated into the structure of the setting (Elias 1987). For example, Price & Lorion (1989) argue that effective prevention programming entails a process of organizational reinvention in which the core features of a program are adapted to local circumstances. A key factor in adoption is organizational readiness, which can be assessed by noting several features, including the support and/or demands impinging from the environment; the awareness and acceptance of the problem by the host organization; the attitudes, motivation, and practices of organizational staff; and the resources and organizational structures available to support the innovation. There are examples of preschool programs that have met these conditions and have demonstrated long-term benefits (Berrueta-Clement et al 1987; Johnson 1988). These tend to be programs that pay attention to family and school contexts by being culturally sensitive, by involving parents, and by having a dedicated staff and sufficient resources (Schorr 1988).

Do local adaptation and modification of empirically established programs dilute or compromise their integrity and effectiveness? In studying the effectiveness of disseminated educational and criminal justice programs, Blakey et al (1987) found that program fidelity was important for effectiveness but that local additions also enhanced effectiveness. As long as core program elements were present in undistorted form, local adaptation augmented core elements with additional local variants that enhanced effectiveness.

Interpersonal Resources

There is now a fair amount of evidence from prospective studies indicating that social support serves as a protective factor, enhancing physical health and psychological well-being (Gottlieb 1987a; House et al 1988). For example, social isolation has been found to be related to all-cause mortality (Berkman & Syme 1979; Blazer 1982), pregnancy complications (Boyce et al 1986), increased risk for depressive symptoms (Kaplan et al 1987), heart disease incidence in men (Seeman & Syme 1987), and cancer incidence and mortality in women (Reynolds & Kaplan 1986). However, the social support *intervention* literature is much less consistent. Evidence that naturally occurring support is effective does not mean that the same can be expected of artificially induced support (Rook & Dooley 1985); and it is not clear when, and under what conditions, intentionally provided support can overcome prior support deficiencies. The most basic problem is that the exact mechanisms by which supportive ties produce health-protective benefits are still largely unknown. Support programs seem to be applied indiscriminately to populations "at risk," without much thought about whether the treatment provided in any way meets the specific needs of targeted individuals. The result is the kind of ambiguity that marked early outcome research in psychotherapy. Both positive and negative findings are reported without a clear idea of the factors responsible for the observed effects. The question, "Is social support effective?" is as unanswerable as the earlier question, "Is psychotherapy effective?". Underspecified and indiscriminately applied intervention programs do not tend to generate meaningful information (Heller et al 1990b).

One way to think about support interventions is to recognize the social context within which support occurs. Supportive relationships are imbedded in social rules and structures that define the parameters within which these relationships occur (House et al 1988). So, support interventions are most useful when they restore or enhance normal role functioning, and when they reinforce rather than bypass existing social structures (Heller et al 1990b). Thus, a more focused view of social support seems to be required, one that pays attention to support needs and to the manner of support expression as they vary by gender across the life cycle. This implies, for example, that a program providing opportunities to learn new job skills (Caplan et al 1989) is likely to be viewed as more "supportive" by unemployed men than is a support group that exclusively focuses on the ventilation of feelings. Most men do not typically interact with one another on the basis of shared emotional disclosure (Gottlieb 1987b; Heller et al 1990b). On the other hand, concrete steps that help men return to useful social roles (employment) are likely to be highly valued.

Support interventions may be most useful for the isolated and lonely, for those undergoing difficult role transitions, and for those experiencing non-normative events. In each of these cases, support that reinforces competent role functioning is likely to be a useful adjunct to coping (Thoits 1986) but may not be readily available from indigenous network members. Research by Olds (1988) provides an example of a project that reinforced normative role behavior during a stressful life transition. In this case, the target population comprised low-SES, pregnant teenagers about to have their first children. The support intervention strategy involved home visits by a public health nurse who provided parent and health information to familiarize the teenagers with the caregiver role. An attempt also was made to strengthen informal support. The teenagers were asked to name others whom they could "count on" for help. These friends and relatives were encouraged by intervention staff to offer the teenagers support for maintaining health behaviors, such as quitting smoking and reducing weight. Links to the health and human service agencies in the community also were strengthened. Results indicated that program mothers were more likely than controls to give birth to heavier infants who were seen less frequently in hospital emergency rooms. Also, program mothers reported greater interest in their pregnancies by their babies' fathers; they were more likely to be accompanied to the hospital by a support person; and they were less likely to be involved in instances of child abuse and neglect. Nurse-visited mothers also tended to return to school and to gainful employment, and to have fewer subsequent pregnancies (Olds et al 1986a,b, 1988).

Support groups may be of value to persons experiencing nonnormative life events because of the difficulty such individuals might have in obtaining focused support from indigenous network members. Support received by cancer patients can be used as an example. On the one hand, some studies show that cancer patients do not report deficiencies in support from friends and family (Taylor et al 1986). Yet there also are claims that significant others have some conflict in knowing how to interact with such patients, vacillating between the belief that they must present a cheerful and optimistic facade and their feelings of vulnerability and helplessness in the face of an intractable illness (Wortman & Lehman 1985). In a study that experimentally varied a cancer patient's self-presentation, Silver et al (1990) found that presentations that emphasized discomfort with the illness and poor coping resulted in less attractive ratings by others, greater discomfort, and less willingness to engage in future interactions. When the patient showed more positive coping attempts, she received more positive ratings and produced significantly less interpersonal discomfort. Thus, it would appear that the very individuals needing greatest support, poor copers, are the least likely to receive sympathy and support from others.

Support from similar others could potentially overcome this problem since they should show greater understanding and less intense feelings of vulnerability. Indeed, cancer patients who regularly attend cancer support groups generally report high levels of satisfaction (Taylor et al 1986), less mood disturbance, fewer phobic reactions, and more adaptive coping (Spiegel et al 1981). What is intriguing is the possibility that the beneficial effects of support-group participation may be due to the protective "illusion" of well-being that such groups foster (Taylor & Brown 1988). Taylor et al (1988) report that in a survey of cancer support-group members who were asked to contrast themselves with other members, 93% described themselves as less ill, and 96% believed that they were coping as well or better than other group members. There are several possible explanations for this curious finding. Individuals may interpret their own openness about problems in the group setting as a sign of strength, since they are aware of their own positive coping attempts. They may see their own willingness to disclose as a positive act of sharing. These positive attitudes may be less apparent when others disclose, and the airing of problems by others may be seen as more of an indication of weakness. It is also possible that the norms of support groups that emphasize acceptance and respect provide a level of positive feedback that leads individuals to believe that they are coping more positively than they actually are. These comments are meant to emphasize how little we really know about the processes by which support groups produce their effects.

The effects of support groups are probably more specific and focused than is usually acknowledged. Consider the findings of Hinrichsen et al (1985) that scoliosis support groups were more beneficial for adults with severe conditions who had undergone onerous medical treatment than for adolescent patients or their parents. Adult patients have lived with their condition for quite some time and may have adjusted their expectations in ways that are more accepting of their medical condition. Adolescents and their parents may have found contact with other patients to be more disturbing, destroying the illusion of normalcy and the hope of overcoming the disability. Another example of the need to think of support in more specific terms can be illustrated by work on the effects of social support on smoking cessation (Cohen et al 1988). In two longitudinal prospective studies, Mermelstein et al (1986) found that partner support was related to initial smoking cessation and short-term abstinence, but that the presence of smokers in the individual's social network was a more significant factor in relapse and long-term abstinence. Furthermore, buddy systems, a popular mode of smoking cessation, did not seem particularly effective (Cohen et al 1988). This may be because salient cues from others may discourage adherence by both buddies. It also was difficult to get men to comply with recommended buddy phone calls, which may indicate that men, in particular, may have difficulty in both bonding to a buddy and providing support for abstinence.

In summary, while the most effective ingredients of social support are still unknown, my impression is that support should be viewed as only one component of a multi-pronged program, rather than as a free-standing intervention. Other components might include those that contribute to the achievement of role competence, such as learning new skills, or being given the opportunity to display already learned behaviors. Support occurs naturally as individuals engage in shared activities, are socially useful, provide for others, and demonstrate mastery of stressful life transitions. These reciprocal characteristics of normal social relationships are the elements that should be captured in support programs (Heller et al 1990b).

Strengthening Individual Skills and Competencies

It has been suggested that the field of community psychology involves a basic conceptual paradox. The term *community* implies macro-level analyses of groups, organizations, and interorganizational relations, yet psychology primarily focuses on the individual (Keys & Frank 1987; Shinn 1990). The individualistic bias of psychology is further reinforced by the notion of individual responsibility, which has always has been a cherished and pervasive value in American society (Seidman & Rappaport 1986). So, it should come as no surprise that in the last decade, federal grant support for prevention has emphasized individual- rather than social-level interventions, and that the bulk of the prevention literature concerns efforts to help individuals develop the skills to overcome environmental stressors, rather than dealing with deleterious social conditions directly (Price et al 1988).

Advocates of individually oriented prevention programs are implicitly accepting the assumptions that, regardless of how social and psychological programs originate, individuals are responsible for problem solutions, and that they can be trained to deal more effectively with impinging negative events. It is reasonable to ask under what conditions these assumptions are likely to be correct.

The research on acquisition of social problem-solving skill is based on models independently developed by D'Zurilla & Goldfried (1971) and Spivack & Shure (1974, 1985). The now familiar approach involves teaching the components of problem solving in a series of steps that includes problem recognition and definition, the generation of alternative solutions, selecting the best alternative, and noting its degree of success so that self-correction becomes possible. Variations of this basic strategy have been used as approaches to prevention in a variety of contexts, with the expectation that the enhancement of problem-solving skills will positively influence adjustment by reducing the negative effects of environmental stress. The evidence is fairly clear that appropriate social problem-solving skills can be learned by a variety of individuals. What is less clear is whether these skills transfer to problem situations in everyday life, and whether general adjustment is improved when individuals practice problem-solving skills. Positive evidence comes from studies such as the one by Elias et al (1986), who found that one year of interpersonal problem-solving training in elementary school led to a reduction in the rated severity of stressors children experience in the transition to middle school. However, Weissberg & Allen (1986) report that the results of social problem-solving training programs generally have been inconsistent. It appears that better results are obtained when training is started early, in the preschool years (Shure & Spivack 1988), when programs are of adequate duration, and when program content is matched to the sociodemographic and ethnic characteristics of the trainees (Gilchrist et al 1987; Schinke et al 1988). In some programs, peer leaders tend to produce more consistently positive results than do adult teachers (Botvin & Tortu 1988), emphasizing the importance of the social milieu in which skill-acquisition programs are imbedded.

The proponents of social problem-solving approaches to prevention believe that a generalized problem-solving strategy can be learned that will be applicable across a wide variety of problem situations. Learning sets do have a powerful influence on behavior, and individuals can "learn how to learn." But as with any other learned behavior, whether learning sets are utilized depends upon a number of factors—e.g. the similarity between training and generalization situations, the motivation and prior experience of the learner, and the potency of other competing responses (Heller et al 1984). Learning sets are least likely to generalize when there is an unmotivated learner who does not see the relevance of what is being taught, and who has strong prior interfering habits that come into play almost automatically in real-life eliciting situations.

It can be argued that learning is most effective when it occurs in situation-specific contexts. And, indeed, social problem-solving approaches have been applied to a variety of adolescent and adult problem situations with a fair degree of success. They have been an important component of antismoking campaigns (Jason et al 1987a), programs to prevent substance abuse (Botvin & Tortu 1988; Schinke & Gilchrist 1985), heart disease prevention programs (Meyer et al 1980), programs to prevent teenage pregnancy (Gilchrist & Schinke 1983; Winett et al 1989), programs to prevent alcohol abuse (Ferrence 1984; Milgram & Nathan 1986), programs for children of divorce (Pedro-Carrol et al 1986), and programs to lower the incidence of teen suicide (Davis et al 1988).

There is a growing consensus that social competency skill training programs are not sufficient for dealing with strong adverse cultural norms, or with socioeconomic conditions that maintain undesirable behavior (Caldwell et al 1988; Maccoby & Altman 1988; O'Donnell et al 1988). For example, in the context of AIDS prevention, Mays & Cochran (1988) argue that it is difficult for low-income ethnic women to say no to unsafe sex when "sex is money and unsafe sex is often more money" (p. 952). For some low-income women, sex is their only source of employment; for others, sex may be their only means of obtaining some proprietary rights in a relationship; and for still others, sex may be their only means of obtaining tangible or emotional support. If women lack power in intimate relationships, or are culturally excluded from the decision to use contraceptives, teaching them skills to say no to unsafe sex is beside the point, because they will never be in a position to use those skills. Macro-level changes in cultural attitudes and expectancies toward sexual relationships seem to be more important prevention targets.

UNRESOLVED ISSUES

Appropriate Methodologies for Community Research

A major unresolved issue for community research concerns the consequences of a mismatch between the level at which phenomena are conceptualized and the level at which they are typically measured (Shinn 1990). Community research deals with macro-level concepts whose effects are usually measured not at that level but at the level of individual perceptions and behaviors. Data collected only at the individual level can, at times, lead to erroneous conclusions when dealing with cross-level phenomena. For example, the precipitants of homelessness in cities can be studied by noting unemployment rates and policies concerning federal subsidies for the construction and maintenance of low-income housing. However, if causative factors are investigated only at the individual level, one can be overimpressed by measures of personal vulnerability (e.g. family disruption and lack of support, poor social and job skills, and chronic patterns of maladjustment).

Finding appropriate measures for community-level phenomena poses a number of difficulties. One major problem is the small sample size from which observations are usually made in macro-level analyses. For example, a study of the effectiveness of a school intervention administered to 100 students in one school is essentially a case study with an N of 1 at the group level (Cowen 1978; Shinn 1990). Larger-scale evaluations across a number of organizational units increase generalizability but are likely to be rare. Furthermore, local variants of national programs often differ significantly (Cook & Shadish 1986), so that aggregating across units can produce difficult-to-interpret results.

A second problem stems from the common practice in psychology of using perceptions aggregated across individuals as measures of characteristics of settings (Moos 1973, 1975). One sometimes forgets that such data involve subjective perceptions that tell us much about the beliefs and expectations of setting inhabitants as they do about the settings themselves. An intervention may not only change how a setting operates, but also the expectations of those within the setting. So while settings and environments may be changing, they may not be changing as fast as participant expectations. In this instance, an intervention might be producing positive changes but would be viewed in a negative light if evaluated only on the basis of aggregated perceptions (Shinn 1990).

There are no simple solutions to these dilemmas, but they do remind us of some important caveats about community research. Straightforward experimental designs and traditional methodologies appropriate for individual-level variables are likely to be insufficient to capture the transactional complexity of multi-level phenomena. Campbell (1987), for example, recommends that prevention centers employ a historian-enthnographer to document the manner in which setting contexts influence the effectiveness of experimental interventions. Campbell argues for greater attention to "local molar validity" ("Did this complex treatment package make a difference in this unique application at this particular place and time?"), not only because the treatment package itself may be a hodgepodge of active and inert elements, but also because complex interactions of setting factors and treatment variables make it difficult to generalize from one setting to another. According to Campbell, the starting place in intervention research should be the demonstration of effects in specific, well-described settings before generalization to other settings is attempted. Even then, generalization should occur first with populations and settings closest in overall similarity to the original intervention. Implied in these comments is the recognition that true experimental studies, while extremely useful in eliminating some plausible rival hypotheses, are not sufficient to describe adequately the limiting conditions within which interventions are apt to be successful.

Consider the wise tips that are generated when the designers of successful programs are asked to reflect upon the key ingredients and limitations of their programs (Munoz et al 1979; Price et al 1988), or the insights that can be obtained from detailed case studies (Bond & Keys 1988; Gruber & Trickett 1987), or from historical analyses (Felton & Shinn 1981; Heller et al 1990a; Levine 1981; Price & Smith 1983). An example of the importance of careful historical analysis can be seen in a paper by B. L. Levine (1986) that attempts to counter the widespread concerns over the inevitability of the "tragedy of the commons" (Hardin 1968). The commons metaphor is taken to represent the damage to the common good that occurs when individuals in the aggregate act in self-serving ways. Contrary to the expectation of environmental deterioration, Levine demonstrates that medieval commons villages were successful in maintaining communal land for centuries through a set of agreed-upon regulatory procedures arrived at through participatory democracy. However, with a change from subsistence farming to larger-scale commercial farming, enclosure of land became a way of increasing profits for individual "capital farmers." Only the least desirable land was left in the commons system. Levine concludes that the deterioration of the commons was a result of enclosure, not greedy overgrazing, and that the "tragedy of the commons" is preventable when common interests strengthen a "sense of community," and when social structures are in place to protect the common good.

We are coming to recognize that community research strategies involve a number of decisional trade-offs that are constantly being made by community researchers (Shadish 1990). Interventions are more easily implemented if they are consistent with community beliefs and structures; but paradoxically, the more an intervention fits in, the more minor it is likely to be and the less likely it is to be different enough to produce a significant change. Similarly, there is a trade-off between basic and applied research in terms of program importance and immediate usefulness. Focusing on applied research and local instrumental use increases immediate utility but restricts the breadth of phenomena studied. Focusing on issues of broader conceptual interest (the strategy usually taken in basic research) may address more important problems but may also produce results of less immediate consequence. Thus, the merits of community research cannot be judged by the exclusive use of methodological criteria. Community research involves a series of value trade-offs that are made in the conduct of the research and by those concerned with research utility and usefulness (Shadish 1990a).

The Gap Between Empowerment Values and Culturally Sensitive Research and Action Programs

A number of commentators have noted the mismatch between community psychology's theoretical perspectives, which emphasize molar social change and empowerment of disenfranchised groups, and day-to-day research and practice that rarely reach these ideal values (Elias et al 1984; Novaco & Monahan 1980; Snowden 1987; Shadish 1990b). Theoretical perspectives are presented in terms of overarching values that are not tied to concrete action plans, so there is often little translation to practical applications (Mulvey 1988). In part, this problem derives from the lack of a firm base in practice, from which applied theories normally are constructed. Some classic community psychology studies represent theoretical reflections upon attempts to produce social change (Graziano 1969; Gruber & Trickett 1987; Reppucci & Saunders 1974; Sarason et al 1966), but, in the main, theories in community psychology are less well grounded. They are more likely to represent attempts to grapple with issues associated with how psychological phenomena are best conceptualized (e.g. ecological models and systems analyses), sprinkled with a healthy mixture of skepticism and social conscience.

The gap between the field's most prominent value, the empowerment of disenfranchised groups, and its programmatic accomplishments can be seen in the paucity of research on cultural diversity and ethnicity. The critiques of traditional psychology that were so prominent in the origins of community psychology emphasized the needs of lower socioeconomic classes and ethnic minority groups, but for years these topics were neglected by community psychology as well. That situation has been slowly changing, and content analyses of community psychology journals now reveal greater attention to ethnicity and cultural diversity (Loo et al 1988). Still, a problem remains because most community psychologists do not have a clear enough understanding of the cultural mores of disenfranchised groups to enable them to mount culturally sensitive programs.

Some informative exceptions are worth noting. Maultsby (1982) presents a well-reasoned historical analysis of the poor treatment Blacks received from the mental health establishment, mostly due to stereotyped racial attitudes adopted by White professionals from their cultural milieu. Trimble & Hayes (1984) describe an informal, non-office-based approach to counseling in American Indian communities. Boyd (1982) details some cultural considerations that are important in working with Black families, and Tucker

(1982) provides a similar account of important issues in the treatment of sexual disorders in Black couples. But these examples represent insightful approaches to clinical treatment and are not community programs. While culturally sensitive individual-level prevention programs have been developed (Gilchrist et al 1987; Schinke et al 1988; Johnson & Walker 1987), there is still a paucity of such programs at the community level. In part, this lack is associated with two major gaps in many community psychology training programs—inadequate training in community intervention, and insufficient attention to the manner in which ethnic and cultural considerations influence psychological theory and practice. It must also be recognized that, given the conservative nature of American society and the apparent widespread lack of concern for social and economic inequity (Serrano-Garcia 1984), such programs are liable to have difficulty finding consistent, long-term popular support.

Levels of Community Intervention: National vs Local Involvement

In an insightful critique, Shadish (1990b) argues that community researchers seem content with convenient, easy-to-control demonstration projects that conform with their own social values. In contrast to the field of program evaluation, where the focus is more likely to be on large-scale programs that have relevance to state and federal social policies, community researchers are described as tending to "think small," experimenting with local innovations that, while giving a sense of what is possible, generally ignore factors that lead to widespread adoption of social innovation. The adoption of innovation in the real world requires dealing with the harsh realities of competing social values, unclear political agendas, and restricted budgets.

The defenders of community research at the local level argue that small, local projects are more likely to generate focused, interpretable results than are large-scale programs whose implementation is as varied as the settings in which they are placed. Furthermore, national programs that do not develop local constituencies have little staying power. What is needed is a strengthened local focus with increased local participation and citizen-researcher collaboration (Chavis et al 1983; Maccoby & Altman 1988; Shinn 1987). However, a number of factors operate against local involvement and control of community projects, and it is still unclear how successful local projects can achieve widespread adoption if their very success depends on manageable size, personal contact, and citizen commitment.

Many sociological observers have noted that modern local communities have diminished power and political influence, with decisions and resources flowing downward from the federal level (Davidson 1979; Nisbet 1973).

Local communities often find themselves dealing with fractionated constituencies competing for scarce resources. It can be argued that community researchers might do better to bypass local involvement, concentrating instead on influencing policy at the national level.

Reasons to return to strengthening local involvement in community intervention projects come from the lessons learned from past federal involvement in human services. Programs sustained by federal funding alone are extremely vulnerable to shifting political priorities (Heller et al 1984). The fate of community intervention should not be dependent on the political atmosphere in the nation's capital, when that climate is likely to change every four or eight years. To be sure, federal funding can facilitate community work, but the lessons of the recent past are that federal dollars alone are insufficient to produce lasting community change. Few localities are ready to assume financial responsibility for programs they view as imposed upon them. Those programs that did survive the phase-out of federal funding in the 1970s were those that had taken seriously the need to establish local constituencies (Heller et al 1984).

One way to help local programs develop national influence is regionalization of community building (Heller 1989; Heller et al 1990a). We are now seeing federated national associations built from local groups, as citizens in both cities and suburbs are finding that coalitions of groups with similar interests provide the leverage to address their concerns (Berkowitz 1987; Hunter 1979; Street & Davidson 1978). Groups like MADD (Mothers Against Drunk Driving) and the Gray Panthers are examples of successful local groups that have developed national constituencies and influence through regional coalition building.

In the past, state and local governments were reluctant to fund human service research, so the federal initiatives of the 1960s and 1970s were welcomed, and national programs seemed to be a way of overcoming local intransigence. With federal policies in the 1980s moving away from investment in community programs, already established federal programs without a local base became extremely vulnerable. So, in contrast to more university-based research, community research is not under the researcher's exclusive control. Community research requires a supportive constituency willing to devote energy and resources to overcome social inertia and competing claims on the public's interest. Support can come from public or private funding sources or from indigenous coalitions of like-minded citizens acting outside official governmental channels. But regardless of its source of support, community research requires more than an investigator's psychological expertise and good intentions. Lasting community change initiated by research efforts ultimately depends upon consistent group effort and the will to overcome social problems.

CONCLUSION

This chapter reviews recent accomplishments in community intervention, while keeping in focus the conceptual limitations and practical impediments community programs typically encounter. The field has clearly moved beyond simple calls for social betterment to a more realistic sense of what can be accomplished through prevention programs focused on specific stressful events. However, most prevention studies concern efforts to help individuals develop the skills to overcome environmental stressors; they do not deal with deleterious social conditions directly. Measured against community psychology's idealistic goals, the lack of a substantive body of literature concerned with community change indicates an unfulfilled promise, 25 years after Swampscott.

Part of the difficulty is our inability to move beyond the constraints of our professional traditions. Psychologists see individuals as independent units who can be subjected to carefully defined experimental control. However, communities are composed of interdependent individuals, whose structural and relational interdependence is at the heart of community psychology's field of inquiry. We study the reciprocal transactions between individuals and their social surroundings in ways that can frustrate the search for simple causal relationships. We still lack agreed-upon methodologies for studying community change; and with meager conceptual templates, our attempts to understand the processes of community change remain at a rudimentary level. At this point, descriptive and analytical studies of the conditions that facilitate community change would be extremely helpful. Despite the pressures for quick solutions to social problems, we might gain more, in the long run, if ethnography preceded and helped inform attempts at social intervention.

Although the last decade marked a retreat from social concerns, demographic pressures are fueling a renewed interest in quality-of-life issues, and concerted citizen efforts to improve the common good may once again be part of a social agenda. Community research and scholarship can be used by coalitions of citizens interested in community change. Our job is to learn how to collaborate with such groups if we expect our work to be socially useful.

ACKNOWLEDGMENTS

Special thanks go to colleagues and students who offered comments on a draft version of this chapter. They include: Arnold Goldstein, John Hogg, Richard Jenkins, Richard Price, Ann Steffen, Mark Thompson, Petri Trueba, and Irene Vlachos-Weber. Preparation of the chapter was facilitated by Grant R01 MH41457 from the National Institute of Mental Health.

Literature Cited

Akabas, S. H. 1987. Mighty oaks: the potential of prevention in the workplace. In *Prevention Planning in the Workplace*, ed. J. Hermalin, J. A. Morrell, pp. 191–226. Newbury Park, CA: Sage

Albee, G. W. 1982. Preventing psychopathology and promoting human potential. *Am. Psychol.* 37:1043–50

Albino, J. E., Tedesco, L. A. 1987. Public health and community wellness. See Jason et al 1987b, pp. 207–39

Altman, I., Wandersman, A., eds. 1987. *Neighborhood and Community Environments*. New York: Plenum

Berger, P. L., Neuhaus, R. J. 1977. *To Empower People: The Role of Mediating Structures in Public Policy*. Washington, DC: Enterprise Inst. Public Policy Res.

Berkman, L. F. 1984. Assessing the physical health effects of social networks and social support. *Annu. Rev. Public Health* 5:413–32

Berkman, L. F., Syme, S. L. 1979. Social networks, host resistance, and mortality: a nine-year follow-up study of Alameda County residents. *Am. J. Epidemiol.* 109:186–204

Berkowitz, B. 1987. *Local Heroes*. Lexington, MA: Heath

Bernard, J. 1973. *The Sociology of Community*. Glenview, IL: Scott, Foresman & Co.

Berrueta-Clement, J. R., Schweinhart, L. J., Barnett, W. S., Weikart, D. P. 1987. The effects of early educational intervention on crime and delinquency in adolescence and early adulthood. See Burchard & Burchard 1987, pp. 220–40

Blakey, C. H., Mayer, J. P., Gottschalk, R. G., Schmitt, N., Davidson, W. S., et al. 1987. The fidelity-adaptation debate: implications for the implementation of public sector social programs. *Am. J. Community Psychol.* 15:253–68

Blazer, D. G. 1982. Social support and mortality in an elderly community population. *Am. J. Epidemiol.* 115:684–94

Bond, M. A., Keys, C. B. 1988. *Empowerment, diversity and collaboration: dilemmas when multiple constituencies join community boards*. Presented at Annu. Meet. Am. Psychol. Assoc., Atlanta

Botvin, G. J., Tortu, S. 1988. Preventing adolescent substance abuse through life skills training. See Price et al 1988, pp. 98–110

Boyce, W. T., Schaefer, C., Harrison, H. R., Haffner, W. H. J., Lewis, M., et al. 1986. Social and cultural factors in pregnancy complications among Navajo women. *Am. J. Epidemiol.* 124:242–53

Boyd, N. 1982. Family therapy with Black families. In *Minority Mental Health*, ed. E. E. Jones, S. J. Korchin, pp. 227–49. New York: Praeger

Burchard, J. D., Burchard, S. N., eds. 1987. *Prevention of Delinquent Behavior*. Newbury Park, CA: Sage

Caldwell, R. A., Bogat, G. A., Davidson, W. S. 1988. The assessment of child abuse potential and the prevention of child abuse and neglect. *Am. J. Community Psychol.* 16:609–24

Campbell, D. T. 1987. Guidelines for monitoring the scientific competence of Preventive Intervention Research Centers. *Knowl.: Creation, Diffusion, Util.* 8:389–430

Caplan, R. B. 1969. *Psychiatry and the Community in Nineteenth Century America: The Recurring Concern with the Environment in the Prevention and Treatment of Mental Illness*. New York: Basic Books

Caplan, R. D., Vinokur, A. D., Price, R. H., van Ryn, M. 1989. Job seeking, reemployment, and mental health: a randomized field experiment in coping with job loss. *J. Appl. Psychol.* In press

Cauce, A. M., Srebnik, D. S. 1989. Peer networks and social support: a focus for preventive efforts with youth. In *Primary Prevention and Promotion in the Schools, Primary Prevention of Psychopathology*, Vol. 12, ed. L. Bond, B. Compas. Newbury Park, CA: Sage. In press

Chavis, D. M., Stucky, P. E., Wandersman, A. 1983. Returning basic research to the community: a relationship between scientist and citizen. *Am. Psychol.* 38:424–34

Cohen, L. H. 1988. *Life Events and Psychological Functioning: Theoretical and Methodological Issues*. Newbury Park, CA: Sage

Cohen, S. 1988. Psychosocial models of the role of social support in the etiology of physical disease. *Health Psychol.* 7:269–97

Cohen, S., Lichtenstein, E., Mermelstein, R., Kingsolver, K., Baer, J., et al. 1988. Social support interventions for smoking cessation. See Gottlieb 1988, pp. 211–40

Conger, J. J. 1988. Hostages to fortune: youth, values, and the public interest. *Am. Psychol.* 43:291–300

Cook, T. D., Shadish, W. R. Jr. 1986. Program evaluation: the worldly science. *Annu. Rev. Psychol.* 37:193–232

Cowen, E. L. 1978. Some problems in community program evaluation research. *J. Consult. Clin. Psychol.* 46:792–805

D'Augelli, A. R. 1989. The development of a helping community for lesbians and gay men: a case study in community psychology. *J. Community Psychol.* 17:18–29

D'Augelli, A. R., Hart, M. M. 1987. Gay women, men, and families in rural settings: toward the development of helping communities. *Am. J. Community Psychol.* 15: 79–93

Davidson, J. L. 1979. *Political Partnerships: Neighborhood Residents and Their Council Members.* Beverly Hills: Sage

Davis, J. M., Sandoval, J., Wilson, M. P. 1988. Strategies for the primary prevention of adolescent suicide. *Sch. Psychol. Rev.* 17:559–69

Dohrenwend, B. P., Levav, I., Shrout, P. E., Link, B. G., Skodol, A. E., et al. 1987. Life stress and psychopathology: progress on research begun with Barbara Snell Dohrenwend. *Am. J. Community Psychol.* 15:677–715

Dooley, D., Catalano, R., Serxner, S. 1987. Economic development and community mental health. See Jason et al 1987b, pp. 91–115

D'Zurilla, T. J., Goldfried, M. R. 1971. Problem solving and behavior modification. *J. Abnorm. Psychol.* 78:107–26

Edelstein, B. A., Michelson, L., eds. 1986. *Handbook of Prevention.* New York: Plenum

Edelstein, M. R., Wandersman, A. 1987. Community dynamics in coping with toxic contaminants. See Altman & Wandersman 1987, pp. 69–112

Elias, M. J. 1987. Establishing enduring prevention programs: advancing the legacy of Swampscott. *Am. J. Community Psychol.* 15:539–53

Elias, M. J., Dalton, J. H., Franco, R., Howe, G. W. 1984. Academic and nonacademic community psychologists: an analysis of divergence in settings, roles and values. *Am. J. Community Psychol.* 12:281–302

Elias, M. J., Gara, M., Ubriaco, M., Rothbaum, P. A., Clabby, J. F., et al. 1986. Impact of a preventive social problem solving intervention on children's coping with middle-school stressors. *Am. J. Community Psychol.* 14:259–75

Felner, R. D., Adan, A. M. 1988. The School Transitional Environment Project: an ecological intervention and evaluation. See Price et al 1988, pp. 111–22

Felner, R. D., Ginter, M., Primavera, J. 1982. Primary prevention during school transitions: social support and environmental structure. *Am. J. Community Psychol.* 10:277–90

Felton, B. J., Shinn, M. 1981. Ideology and practice of deinstitutionalization. *J. Soc. Issues* 37:158–72

Ferrence, R. G. 1984. Prevention of alcohol problems in women. In *Alcohol Problems in Women: Antecedents, Consequences and*

Intervention, ed. S. C. Wilsnack, L. J., Beckman, pp. 413–42. New York: Guilford

Figueira-McDonough, J. 1986. School context, gender, and delinquency. *J. Youth Adolesc.* 15:79–98

Gesten, E. L., Jason, L. A. 1987. Social and community intervention. *Annu. Rev. Psychol.* 38:427–60

Gilchrist, L. D., Schinke, S. P. 1983. Coping with contraception-cognitive and behavioral methods with adolescents. *Cogn. Theor. Res.* 7:379–88

Gilchrist, L. D., Schinke, S. P., Trimble, J. E., Cvetkovich, G. T. 1987. Skill enhancement to prevent substance abuse among American Indian adolescents. *Int. J. Addict.* 22:869–79

Gottlieb, B. H. 1987a. Using social support to protect and promote health. *J. Primary Prev.* 8:49–70

Gottlieb, B. H. 1987b. Marshalling social support for medical patients and their families. *Can. Psychol.* 28:201–17

Gottlieb, B. H., ed. 1988. *Marshaling Social Support: Formats, Processes and Effects.* Newbury Park, CA: Sage

Graziano, A. M. 1969. Clinical innovation and the mental health power structure: a social case history. *Am. Psychol.* 24:10–18

Gruber, J., Trickett, E. J. 1987. Can we empower others? The paradox of empowerment in the governing of an alternative public school. *Am. J. Community Psychol.* 15:353–71

Gusfield, J. R. 1975. *The Community: A Critical Response.* New York: Harper Colophon

Haan, M., Kaplan, G. A., Camacho, T. 1987. Poverty and health: prospective evidence from the Alameda County study. *Am. J. Epidemiol.* 125:989–98

Hardin, G. 1968. The tragedy of the commons. *Science* 162:1243–48

Hawkins, J. D., Lam, T. 1987. Teacher practices, social development, and delinquency. See Burchard & Burchard 1987, pp. 241–74

Heller, K. 1989. The return to community. *Am. J. Community Psychol.* 17:1–15

Heller, K., Jenkins, R. A., Steffen, A. M., Swindle, R. W. 1990a. Prospects for a viable community mental health system: reconciling ideology, professional traditions, and political reality. See Rappaport & Seidman 1990. In press

Heller, K., Price, R. H., Hogg, J. R. 1990b. The role of social support in community and clinical intervention. See Sarason et al 1990. In press

Heller, K., Price, R. H., Reinharz, S., Riger, S., Wandersman, A. 1984. *Psychology and Community Change: Challenges of the Future.* Homewood, IL: Dorsey, 2nd ed.

Hinrichsen, G. A., Revenson, T. A., Shinn,

M. 1985. Does self-help help? An empirical investigation of scoliosis peer support groups. *J. Soc. Issues* 41:65–87

Holahan, C. J., Wandersman, A. 1987. The community psychology perspective in environmental psychology. In *Handbook of Environmental Psychology*, ed. D. Stokols, I. Altman, 1:827–61. New York: Wiley

House, J. S., Umberson, D., Landis, K. R. 1988. Structures and processes of social support. *Annu. Rev. Soc.* 14:293–318

Hunter, A. 1979. The urban neighborhood: its analytical and social contexts. *Urban Affairs Q.* 14:267–88

Hunter, A., Riger, S. 1986. The meaning of community in community mental health. *J. Community Psychol.* 14:55–71

Iscoe, I., Harris, L. C. 1984. Social and community intervention. *Annu. Rev. Psychol.* 35:333–60

Jason, L. A., Gruder, C. L., Martino, S., Flay, B. R., Warnecke, R., et al. 1987a. Work site group meetings and the effectiveness of a televised smoking cessation intervention. *Am. J. Community Psychol.* 15:57–72

Jason, L. A., Hess, R. E., Felner, R. D., Moritsugu, J. N., ed. 1987b. *Prevention: Toward a Multidisciplinary Approach.* New York: Haworth

Jason, L. A., Tabon, D., Tait, E., Iacono, G., Goodman, D., et al. 1988. The emergence of the Inner-City Self-Help Center. *J. Community Psychol.* 16:287–95

Johnson, D. L. 1988. Primary prevention of behavior problems in young children: the Houston Parent-Child Development Center. See Price et al 1988, pp. 44–52

Johnson, D. L., Walker, T. 1987. Primary prevention of behavior problems in Mexican-American children. *Am. J. Community Psychol.* 15:375–85

Kaplan, G. A., Roberts, R. E., Camacho, T. C., Coyne, J. C. 1987. Psychosocial predictors of depression: prospective evidence from the Human Population Laboratory studies. *Am. J. Epidemiol.* 125:206–20

Kasl, S. V. 1984. Stress and health. *Annu. Rev. Public Health* 5:319–41

Katz, A. H. 1981. Self-help and mutual aid: an emerging social movement? *Annu. Rev. Soc.* 7:129–55

Kelly, J. G. 1987. Some reflections on the Swampscott Conference. *Am. J. Community Psychol.* 15:515–17

Kessler, R. C., House, J. S., Turner, J. B. 1987. Unemployment and health in a community sample. *J. Health Soc. Behav.* 28:51–59

Kessler, R. C., Price, R. H., Wortman, C. B. 1985. Social factors in psychopathology: stress, social support and coping processes. *Annu. Rev. Psychol.* 36:531–72

Keys, C. B. 1987. Synergy, prevention and the Chicago School of Sociology. See Jason et al 1987b, pp. 11–34

Keys, C. B., Frank, S. 1987. Community psychology and the study of organizations: a reciprocal relationship. *Am. J. Community Psychol.* 15:239–51

Kiesler, D. J. 1966. Some myths of psychotherapy research and the search for a paradigm. *Psychol. Bull.* 65:110–36

Klein, D. C. 1987. The context and times at Swampscott: My/story. *Am. J. Community Psychol.* 15:531–38

Klein, K. J., D'Aunno, T. A. 1986. Psychological sense of community in the workplace. *J. Community Psychol.* 14:365–77

Leitenberg, H. 1987. Primary prevention of delinquency. See Burchard & Burchard 1987, pp. 312–30

Levin, H. M. 1983. The workplace: employment and business interventions. In *Handbook of Social Intervention*, ed. E. Seidman, pp. 499–521. Beverly Hills: Sage

Levine, B. L. 1986. The tragedy of the commons and the comedy of community: the commons in history. *J. Community Psychol.* 14:81–99

Levine, M. 1981. *The History and Politics of Community Mental Health.* New York: Oxford Univ.

Levine, M. 1988. An analysis of mutual assistance. *Am. J. Community Psychol.* 16:167–83

Levine, M., Ewing, C. P., Levine, D. I. 1987. The use of law for prevention in the public interest. See Jason et al 1987b, pp. 241–77

Levine, M., Levine, A. 1970. *A Social History of Helping Services: Clinic, Court, School and Community.* New York: Appleton-Century-Crofts

Levine, M., Perkins, D. V. 1987. *Principles of Community Psychology: Perspectives and Applications.* New York: Oxford Univ.

Lindheim, R., Syme, S. L. 1983. Environments, people and health. *Annu. Rev. Public Health* 4:335–59

Loo, C., Fong, K. T., Iwamasa, G. 1988. Ethnicity and cultural diversity: an analysis of work published in community psychology journals, 1965–1985. *J. Community Psychol.* 16:332–49

Maccoby, N., Altman, D. G. 1988. Disease prevention in communities: the Stanford Heart Disease Prevention Program. See Price et al 1988, pp. 165–74

Maton, K. I. 1988. Social support, organizational characteristics, psychological well-being, and group appraisal in three self-help group populations. *Am. J. Community Psychol.* 16:53–77

Maultsby, M. C. 1982. A historical view of

blacks' distrust of psychiatry. See Turner & Jones 1982, pp. 39–55

Mays, V. M., Cochran, S. D. 1988. Issues in the perception of AIDS risk and risk reduction activities by Black and Hispanic/Latina women. *Am. Psychol.* 43:949–57

McKeown, C. T., Rubinstein, R. A., Kelly, J. G. 1987. Anthropology, the meaning of community and prevention. See Jason et al 1987b, pp. 35–64

McMillan, D. W., Chavis, D. M. 1986. Sense of community: a definition and theory. *J. Community Psychol.* 14:6–23

Mermelstein, R., Cohen, S., Lichtenstein, E., Baer, J. S., Kamarck, T. 1986. Social support and smoking cessation and maintenance. *J. Consult. Clin. Psychol.* 54:447–53

Merry, S. E. 1987. Crowding, conflict and neighborhood regulation. See Altman & Wandersman 1987, pp. 35–68

Meyer, A. J., Nash, J. D., McAlister, A. L., Maccoby, N., Farquhar, J. W. 1980. Skills training in a cardiovascular health education campaign. *J. Consult. Clin. Psychol.* 48:129–42

Milgram, G. G., Nathan, P. E. 1986. Efforts to prevent alcohol abuse. See Edelstein & Michelson 1986, pp. 243–62

Moos, R. H. 1973. Conceptualizations of human environments. *Am. Psychol.* 28:652–65

Moos, R. H. 1975. *Evaluating Correctional and Community Settings.* New York: Wiley

Moos, R. H. 1979. *Evaluating Educational Environments.* San Francisco: Jossey-Bass

Mulvey, A. 1988. Community psychology and feminism: tensions and commonalities. *J. Community Psychol.* 16:70–83

Munoz, R. F., Snowden, L. R., Kelly, J. G. 1979. *Social and Psychological Research in Community Settings.* San Francisco: Jossey-Bass

Naparstek, A. J., Biegel, D. E., Spiro, H. R. 1982. *Neighborhood Networks for Humane Mental Health Care.* New York: Plenum

Nisbet, R. A. 1973. Moral values and community. In *Perspectives on the American Community,* ed. R. L. Warren, pp. 85–93. Chicago: Rand McNally

Novaco, R. W., Monahan, J. 1980. Research in community psychology: an analysis of work published in the first six years of the American Journal of Community Psychology. *Am. J. Community Psychol.* 8:131–45

O'Donnell, C. R., Manos, M. J., Chesney-Lind, M. 1988. Diversion and neighborhood delinquency programs in open settings: a social network interpretation. In *Behavioral Approaches to Crime and Delinquency,* ed. E. K. Morris, C. J. Braukmann, pp. 251–69. New York: Plenum

Olds, D. L. 1988. The prenatal/early infancy project. See Price et al 1988, pp. 3–17

Olds, D. L., Henderson, C. R., Chamberlin, R., Tatelbaum, R. 1986a. Preventing child abuse and neglect: a randomized trial of nurse home visitation. *Pediatrics* 78:65–78

Olds, D. L., Henderson, C. R., Tatelbaum, R., Chamberlin, R. 1986b. Improving the delivery of prenatal care and outcomes of pregnancy: a randomized trial of nurse home visitation. *Pediatrics* 77:16–28

Olds, D. L., Henderson, C. R., Tatelbaum, R., Chamberlin, R. 1988. Improving the life-course development of socially disadvantaged mothers: a randomized trial of nurse home visitation. *Am. J. Public Health.* 78:1436–45

Pedro-Carrol, J. L., Cowen, E. L., Hightower, A. D., Guare, J. C. 1986. Preventive intervention with latency-aged children of divorce: a replication study. *Am. J. Community Psychol.* 14:277–90

Perkins, D. V., Burns, T. F., Perry, J. C., Nielsen, K. P. 1988. Behavior setting theory and community psychology: an analysis and critique. *J. Community Psychol.* 16:355–72

Porter, R. A., Peters, J. A., Heady, H. R. 1982. Using community development for prevention in Appalachia. *Soc. Work* 27:302–7

Prestby, J. E., Wandersman, A. 1985. An empirical exploration of a framework of organizational viability: maintaining block organizations. *J. Appl. Behav. Sci.* 21:287–305

Price, R. H. 1985. Work and community. *Am. J. Community Psychol.* 13:1–12

Price, R. H., Cowen, E. L., Lorion, R. P., Ramos-McKay, J. 1988. *Fourteen Ounces of Prevention: A Casebook for Practitioners.* Washington, DC: APA

Price, R. H., Lorion, R. P. 1988. Prevention programming as organizational reinvention: from research to implementation. In *Prevention of Mental Disorders, Alcohol, and Drug Use in Children and Adolescents,* ed. D. Schaffer, I. Phillips, N. B. Enzer. Rockville, MD: Office of Substance Abuse Prevention, and American Academy of Children and Adolescents

Price, R. H., Smith, S. S. 1983. Two decades of reform in the mental health system (1963–1983). In *Handbook of Social Intervention,* ed. E. Seidman, pp. 408–37. Beverly Hills: Sage

Rappaport, J., Seidman, E., eds. 1990. *Handbook of Community Psychology.* New York: Plenum. In press

Rappaport, J., Seidman, E., Toro, P. A., McFadden, L. S., Reischl, T. M., et al.

1985. Collaborative research with a mutual help organization. *Soc. Policy* 15:12–24

Reppucci, N. D., Saunders, J. T. 1974. Social psychology of behavior modification: problems of implementation in natural settings. *Am. Psychol.* 29:649–60

Reynolds, P., Kaplan, G. A. 1986. Social connections and cancer: a prospective study of Alameda County residents. Presented at Annu. Meet. Society of Behav. Med., San Francisco

Rivlin, L. G. 1987. The neighborhood, personal identity and group affiliations. See Altman & Wandersman 1987, pp. 1–34

Rook, K., Dooley, D. 1985. Applying social support research: theoretical problems and future directions. *J. Soc. Issues* 41:5–28

Salem, D. A., Seidman, E., Rappaport, J. 1988. Community treatment of the mentally ill: the promise of mutual help organizations. *Soc. Work.* 33:403–8

Sarason, I. G., Sarason, B. R., Pierce, G. R., eds. 1990. *Social Support: An Interactional View. Issues in Social Support Research.* New York: Wiley. In press

Sarason, S. B. 1982. *The Culture of the School and the Problem of Change.* Boston: Allyn & Bacon. 2nd ed.

Sarason, S. B., Klaber, M. 1985. The school as a social situation. *Annu. Rev. Psychol.* 36:115–40

Sarason, S. B., Levine, M., Goldenberg, I. I., Cherlin, D. L., Bennett, E. M. 1966. *Psychology in Community Settings: Clinical, Educational, Vocational, Social Aspects.* New York: Wiley

Schinke, S. P., Gilchrist, L. D. 1985. Preventing substance abuse with children and adolescents. *J. Consult. Clin. Psychol.* 53: 596–602

Schinke, S. P., Orlandi, M. A., Botuin, G. J., Gilchrist, L. D., Trimble, J. E., et al. 1988. Preventing substance abuse among American-Indian adolescents: a bicultural competence skills approach. *J. Counsel. Psychol.* 35:87–90

Schorr, L. B. 1988. *Within Our Reach: Breaking the Cycle of Disadvantage.* New York: Anchor

Schulz, R., Rau, M. T. 1985. Social support through the life course. In *Social Support and Health,* ed. S. Cohen, S. L. Syme, pp. 129–49. Orlando. FL: Academic

Seidman, E., Rappaport, J. 1986. *Redefining Social Problems.* New York: Plenum

Seeman, T. E., Syme, S. L. 1987. Social networks and coronary artery disease: a comparison of the structure and function of social relations as predictors of disease. *Psychosom. Med.* 49:341–54

Serrano-Garcia, I. 1984. The illusion of empowerment: community development within a colonial context. *Prev. Hum. Serv.* 3:173–200

Shadish, W. R. 1990a. *Criteria for excellence in community research.* See Tolan et al 1990. In press

Shadish, W. R. 1990b. What can we learn about problems in community research by comparing it to program evaluation? See Tolan et al 1990. In press

Shinn, M. 1987. Expanding community psychology's domain. *Am. J. Community Psychol.* 15:555–74

Shinn, M. 1990. Mixing and matching: Levels of conceptualization, measurement and statistical analysis in community research. See Tolan et al 1990. In press

Shure, M. B., Spivack, G. 1988. Interpersonal cognitive problem solving. See Price et al 1988, pp. 69–82

Silver, R. C., Wortman, C. B., Crofton, C. 1989. The role of coping in support provision: the self-presentational dilemma of victims of life crises. See Sarason et al 1990. In press

Snowden, L. R. 1987. The peculiar success of community psychology: service delivery to ethnic minorities and the poor. *Am. J. Community Psychol.* 15:575–86

Spiegel, D., Bloom, J. R., Yalom, I. 1981. Group support for patients with metastatic cancer: a randomized prospective outcome study. *Arch. Gen. Psychiatr.* 38:527–33

Spivack, G., Shure, M. B. 1974. *Social Adjustment of Young Children.* San Francisco: Jossey-Bass

Spivack, G., Shure, M. B. 1985. ICPS and beyond: centripetal and centrifugal forces. *Am. J. Community Psychol.* 13:226–43

Stone, R. A., Levine, A. G. 1985. Reactions to collective stress: correlates of active citizen participation at Love Canal. *Prev. Hum. Serv.* 4:153–77

Street, D., Davidson, J. L. 1978. Community and politics in city and suburb. In *Handbook of Contemporary Urban Life,* ed. D. Street, pp. 468–93. San Francisco: Jossey-Bass

Summers, G. F. 1986. Rural community development. *Annu. Rev. Soc.* 12:347–71

Syme, S. L., Berkman, L. F. 1976. Social class, susceptibility and sickness. *Am. J. Epidemiol.* 104:1–8

Taylor, S. E., Brown, J. D. 1988. Illusion and well-being: a social psychological perspective on mental health. *Psychol. Bull.* 103: 193–210

Taylor, S. E., Falke, R. L., Mazel, R. M., Hilsberg, B. L. 1988. Sources of satisfaction and dissatisfaction among members of cancer support groups. See Gottlieb 1988, pp. 187–208

Taylor, S. E., Falke, R. L., Shoptaw, S. J., Lichtman, R. R. 1986. Social support, support groups, and the cancer patient. *J. Consult. Clin. Psychol.* 54:608–15

Thoits, P. A. 1986. Social support as coping assistance. *J. Consult. Clin. Psychol.* 54: 416–23

Tolan, P. H., Keys, C., Chertok, F., Jason, L., eds. 1990. *Researching Community Psychology: Integrating Theories and Methods.* Washington, DC: Am. Psychol. Assoc. In press

Toro, P. A., Cowen, E. L., Gesten, E. L., Weissberg, R. P., Rapkin, B. D., et al. 1985. Social environmental predictors of children's adjustment in elementary school classrooms. *Am. J. Community Psychol.* 13:353–64

Trimble, J. E., Hayes, S. A. 1984. Mental health intervention in the psychosocial context of American Indian communities. In *Ecological Approaches to Clinical and Community Psychology,* ed. W. A. O'Connor, B. Lubin, pp. 293–321. New York: Wiley

Tucker, C. M. 1982. Sexual disorders. See Turner & Jones 1982, pp. 249–78

Turner, S. M., Jones, R. T. 1982. *Behavior Modification in Black Populations: Psychosocial Issues and Empirical Findings.* New York: Plenum

Unger, D. G., Wandersman, A. 1985. The importance of neighbors: the social, cognitive and affective components of neighboring. *Am. J. Community Psychol.* 13:139–69

Walsh, R. T. 1987. A social historical note on the formal emergence of community psychology. *Am. J. Community Psychol.* 15: 523–29

Wandersman, A., Florin, P. 1990. Citizen participation. See Rappaport & Seidman 1990. In press

Weissberg, R. P., Allen, J. P. 1986. Promoting children's social skills and adaptive interpersonal behavior. See Edelstein & Michelson 1986, pp. 153–75

Winett, R. A., King, A. C., Altman, D. G. 1989. *Health Psychology and Public health: An Integrative Approach.* New York: Pergamon

Wortman, C. B., Lehman, D. R. 1985. Reactions to victims of life crises: support attempts that fail. In *Social Support: Theory, Research and Applications,* ed. I. G. Sarason, B. R. Sarason, pp. 463–89. Dordrecht, The Netherlands: Martinus Nijhoff

Annu. Rev. Psychol. 1990. 41:169–211

ANIMAL MEMORY AND LEARNING

Norman E. Spear, James S. Miller, and Joyce A. Jagielo

Center for Developmental Psychobiology, State University of New York at Binghamton, Binghamton, New York 13901

CONTENTS

INTRODUCTION

The present chapter emphasizes the expression of learning apart from its acquisition. Unexpected variability in expression has become a major issue

169

0066-4308/90/0201-0169$02.00

for many considerations of learning, memory, and cognition, including those concerned with interactions between cognition and memory in humans (Isaacson & Spear 1982; Johnson & Hasher 1987; Richardson-Klavehn & Bjork 1988) and those involving basic conditioning in animals (Holland 1984; Rescorla & Holland 1982; Spear 1984a). Control over experiential history, greater variation in the content of memory, and avoidance of linguistic complications provide only part of the reason to study this topic with animals.

We emphasize two parts of the expression problem: How does the expression of learning depend on previous and subsequent events, particularly those associated with the test for retention, and how do phenomena of learning depend on the mode or circumstances of their expression? Among the major considerations in the first case are forgetting and retention and in the second are stimulus selection and the influence of traditional variables on learning.

Expression and Memory

During the past 20 years the *Annual Review of Psychology* has included several chapters bearing on animal learning, but these have rarely considered expression. Most have been concerned either with motivation ("basic" in some cases, "derived" or "acquired" in others) or with the "physiological basis" of learning. A few have dealt with ethological studies of animal learning and another few with more general issues of animal cognition. The term "memory" has appeared in the title of only those chapters dealing with "physiological bases"; and only in the context of foraging behavior has memory been focused upon as a process that might be considered separately from learning, although given a secondary role (Kamil & Roitblat 1985). These chapters collectively confirm the tendency during the previous 50 years to ignore factors that control the expression of what an animal has learned apart from motivational determinants (Spear 1978). Only the chapter by Rescorla & Holland (1982) has dealt seriously with this "expression problem," and even in this case only one of its aspects was covered, albeit with extraordinary insight.

It is not difficult to generate explanations for the historical avoidance of issues of expression in the field of animal learning. There has long been a disposition in our field to treat learning as inseparable from the response used to measure it. The S-R orientation of Thorndike sponsored this distortion. The influence of logical positivism and of behaviorism maintained it. The first American review of Pavlov's work, which deemed such research too difficult to be applied in animals other than dogs, slighted the possibility that the learned relationship between an acoustical or visual signal and food is expressible in a wide variety of behaviors (Boakes 1984). Logical positivism helped blur the distinction between experiments, which necessarily measure a particular response to a particular stimulus, and theoretical interpretations of what is learned. Consequent acceptance of a theoretical, associative (excitatory) strength that mapped directly onto whatever was measured also contributed to a disregard for how learning was expressed. And although the issue of learning vs performance (expression) had significant theoretical implications for persons such as Tolman, too often the issue was trivialized empirically with examples such as the satiated rat that would not exhibit an appetitively trained behavior, and taken as important only for methodological purposes. That issues of far greater importance are involved is emphasized in this chapter by using "expression" rather than "performance," although technically either would do in most cases.

Finally, beyond the historical reasons why scientists have ignored issues of retention and forgetting (Spear 1978), there has persisted the dominant perspective that the critical processes responsible for variance in behavioral plasticity take place during the learning episode (encoding, attention, association) rather than at the time of expression (retrieval, performance). Despite the obvious significance of acquisition processes, however, empirical evidence from increasingly thorough measurement of behavior is forcing upon us now the alternative view that most of the variance in learning and memory is determined by mode of expression and post-acquisition events.

Contemporary Basic Conditioning

By focusing on animal memory (expression) we unavoidably consider contemporary issues in animal learning and celebrate the recent discoveries that enable this focus. The facts have forced a change in the conceptualization of basic conditioning compatible with the general view that what is learned is not immutable reflexes but, rather, representations of events and relationships— memories—that are subject to substantial variance in their expression. Rescorla (1988) provides an incisive reminder of these conceptual changes, what Pavlovian conditioning is and what it accomplishes. Such conditioning is "the learning that results from exposure to relations among events in the environment" and as such provides "a primary means by which the organism represents the structure of its world" (Rescorla 1988:152).

If this is not the way you and your students treat conditioning, you are not alone. Rescorla cites clear misconceptions about conditioning that leaders in other areas of psychology have conveyed in textbooks. In contrast with the situation of 20–30 years ago, the study of conditioning now proceeds quite apart from philosophical issues and does not pretend to provide a basis for a general theory of behavior. The contributions of this area are instead relatively concrete: a detailed analysis of a sample learning process that provides a simple model for studying the modification of behavior through experience; information of value to related fields such as neuroscience and cognitive science; and solutions to practical problems of health, such as experiential control of the immune system, tolerance to drugs, and psychotherapies based upon behavior modification.

Experimental evidence correcting prevalent misconceptions was described by Rescorla (1988; also see e.g. Flaherty 1985). Involved are these issues of continued significance for the present chapter: 1. Contiguity between elements, typically a conditioned stimulus (CS) and an unconditioned stimulus (US), is neither sufficient nor necessary for conditioning an association between them. Contiguity is not sufficient because individual experience with either the CS or US can weaken or eliminate the conditioning otherwise observed from their contiguous pairing (Rescorla 1968; Kamin 1969; Lubow 1973); and it is not necessary because conditioned inhibition occurs in circumstances when the CS is predictably unpaired with the US (R. Miller & Spear 1985) and because excitatory conditioning can occur despite a substantial interval between the CS and US (Revusky 1971; Kaplan & Hearst 1982). 2. Conditioning is not a consequence of "stimulus substitution" of a conditioned response (CR) for an unconditioned response (UR) that is inevitably elicited by a US. The CR differs from the UR and depends on factors apart from the US. For instance, with footshock as the US, conditioning is expressed by suppression to a tone that predicted the US but by active hiding of a prod that had predicted it (Pinel et al 1980). Conditioning to food as a US can be expressed by crouching and swaying if predicted by a tone or by rearing if predicted by a light (Holland 1977). 3. Conditioning is not necessarily a slow process. Even in the simplest or most immature animals conditioning can take place almost immediately, depending on factors such as the preexperimental relationship between the CS and US, circumstances of stimulus selection, and CS-US contingency (Carew & Sahley 1986; Spear & Rudy 1990). 4. Conditioning does not usually involve a single association, and the associations need not be linear. Conditioning instead yields a number of associations even when the nominal procedures include only a single CS and US, and the associations formed can be hierarchical rather than linear or serial. Despite minor exceptions—e.g. conditioning in some circumstances is notably, and predictably, slow (Bouton & Schwartzentruber 1989) and contiguity remains a powerful force that sometimes seems sufficient (Matzel et al 1988b)—these points represent an accurate view of animal learning and memory today.

Orientation for Animal Memory and Learning

In this chapter four areas of animal learning and memory are sampled for their relevance to issues of expression. The first includes conventional topics of Pavlovian conditioning that have arisen in the development of basic principles and theory. Serious problems occur in this development when it is established that an animal actually had learned despite the appearance that it had not.

Unexpected learning has been revealed by selected response measures or circumstances at the time of acquisition and also, perhaps to a larger extent, by treatment subsequent to acquisition. The most widespread instance of the latter is found in studies that focus on retention and forgetting. These behaviors are defined operationally ("retention" is the extent to which prior learning influences current behavior, and "forgetting" occurs to the extent that this influence is less than observed immediately after learning), and are intrinsically linked to the expression issue. As the second area, therefore, we provide a limited sample of recent studies on retention and forgetting after short intervals. The third section considers treatments that alleviate forgetting induced by special amnestic treatments or by the more common instances of explicit associative interference or a relatively lengthy retention interval. Finally, a few recent discoveries about the ontogeny of learning and memory are reviewed to illustrate how this area has advanced by attention to aspects of the expression issue.

BASIC CONDITIONING AND EXPRESSION

Multiple Measures of Learning

Conclusions about the impact of certain variables on conditioning depend on the specific behavioral assessment chosen as the index of learning. Different phenomena are subject to observation, for example, during concurrent recording of specific somatic and autonomic responses in the course of conditioning (for a review, see Schneiderman 1972). Such studies indicate that: (a) conditioning and discrimination learning emerged earlier in training when indexed by changes in heart rate than when the nictitating membrane response was used as the measure of learning; (b) heart rate diminished over the course of the conditioning session, whereas the nictitating membrane response did not; and (c) suppression of ongoing behavior (pressing a lever) occurred prior to, and sometimes in the absence of, conditioned changes in heart rate. Schneiderman (1972) cites numerous other examples in which these (and other) measures are differentially sensitive to a variety of variables that have seemed fundamental to rate of conditioning, such as the interstimulus interval and US intensity. Subsequent experiments also have indicated that autonomic and somatic measures may be differentially susceptible to sources of forgetting (Springer 1975). Thus conclusions about learning and memory should be viewed skeptically when based on a single measure of conditioning.

The importance of this caution is illustrated nicely in recent consideration of the ontogeny of learning. Campbell and his colleagues have noted differences in the ages of the emergence of conditioning expressed through the autonomic and somatic systems. Somatic conditioning may *precede* autonomic conditioning ontogenetically to a substantial degree (Campbell & Ampuero

1985). This finding is unchanged whether the CS involves olfactory, auditory, or visual processing. It suggests sharp limits on the notion that somatic conditioning is mediated by autonomic conditioning. This suggestion has yet to be confirmed with experiments that directly compare these two indexes of learning within a single experiment or within the same animals, but there seems little doubt that this innovative series will have considerable impact in the study of cognitive development and of learning and memory in general.

Despite evidence favoring the use of multiple behavioral indexes to assess conditioning (Rescorla & Holland 1982; Rescorla 1980; Wasserman 1981), and the general agreement that a given "target response" merely constitutes one possible index of whether learning has occurred, the failure to observe a change in behavior following a conditioning regimen is more often than not treated as evidence that the subject has not acquired the CS-US association. It is perhaps no coincidence that the major theories of conditioning have dealt with the acquisition rather than the expression of learning (e.g. Pearce & Hall 1980; Rescorla & Wagner 1972). There is, however, increasing evidence that many phenomena previously considered as failures to learn are more appropriately viewed as failures to express learned associations in behavior.

BACKWARD CONDITIONING   A particularly persuasive recommendation for the use of multiple measures of conditioning is provided by Tait & Saladin (1986). Rabbits were first trained to drink from a spout in a conditioning chamber. Following this adaptation phase, the subjects received *backward* pairings of paraorbital shock US and a tone CS using the nictitating membrane conditioning procedure. Conditioning was measured in terms of lick suppression in the presence of the CS and in terms of how rapidly forward excitatory conditioning of the nictitating membrane response could be established to the "backward" CS (retardation test). The results indicated that the backward CS functioned as an excitatory stimulus in suppressing drinking below control levels during the lick suppression test, but as an inhibitory stimulus during the retardation test in that the percentage of nictitating membrane responses elicited by the previously backward paired CS fell significantly below control levels. This concurrent development of excitation and inhibition following a common training regimen (also see Matzel et al 1988b) emphasizes that how learning is measured can determine both the magnitude and type of conditioning observed.

AFFECTIVE CONDITIONING   Even in the simplest of circumstances, conclusions about conditioning can depend on how it is measured. A single conditioning trial was given to preweanling (16-day-old) rats with the following procedures: in the CS+ ONLY condition subjects were placed in a black compartment (CS+) for 20 sec and administered a mild footshock; two other groups were treated similarly except that immediately prior to (CS−/CS+) or following (CS+/CS−) conditioning they were exposed to a white chamber (CS−) for 20 sec with no footshock administered. A conditioned aversion for entering the black compartment rather than the white was substantial only in the CS−/CS+ condition, weak or nonexistent in the CS+/CS− condition and clearly absent in the CS+ ONLY condition (Kucharski et al 1985; J. Miller & Spear 1989). In later experiments these effects were analyzed in part by reexposing the rats to the CS+ or CS− after conditioning and measuring their freezing responses (J. Miller et al 1989a). This index indicated that although the effect of CS order was still present in the form of significantly stronger conditioning in the CS−/CS+ group, an aversion to the chamber in which footshock was administered was evident in all three (CS+ ONLY, CS+/CS−, and CS−/CS+) treatment conditions. In other words, the same results as before (Kucharski et al 1985; J. Miller & Spear 1989) were found when the same response measure was used, but new conditioning was revealed in some circumstances when a different measure was used.

Behavior Systems

Analysis of how conditioning is expressed is not a new concern. Based on his work with salivary conditioning in dogs, Zener (1937) believed that by restricting observation to an isolated component of behavior, as suggested by the view that the CS merely comes to substitute for the US, a number of behavioral changes resulting from the pairing of the CS and US would be ignored. He believed that instead, when the limitations of the physiological and psychological barriers provided by the training situation were removed, then *"salivation reveals itself as a dependent component within a complex, widespread, organized, goal-directed behavioral act which varies adaptively with changes in the experimental situation"* (Zener 1937: 402). Observations such as these provide the foundation for the behavior-systems view of conditioning, summarized most clearly by Timberlake and his colleagues (Timberlake 1983; Timberlake & Lucas 1989). The behavior systems approach suggests that the animal brings to the conditioning situation a number of evolutionarily determined, species-specific behavior systems related to a particular function or need of the organism such as reproduction or feeding.

The behavior-systems view considers conditioning and learning to have the role of modifying an already functioning system. For example, within the feeding system subjects may engage in a sequence of behaviors appropriate to the expectancy of the food US. When environmental events such as the CS indicate that the probability of the US has increased, subjects might initially engage in a generalized search mode, followed by a more focused search, ultimately concluding in the handling and rejection or ingestion of food. If a long delay occurs between CS onset and US onset, more generalized search behavior should be elicited shortly following CS onset, with eventual replacement by goal-directed behaviors later in the interstimulus interval, as the probability of US occurrence increases. Timberlake et al (1982) found that rats directed little behavior toward a rolling ball bearing followed by food when the food was presented shortly after the ball bearing entered the chamber, and instead moved quickly to the food tray. With a longer delay between the ball bearing and food, the rat was more likely to contact the bearing with behaviors in the predatory subsystem that would be expected to be activated by a small moving object. These include digging the ball bearing out of the entrance hole, seizing it in the mouth and paws, carrying it to a corner of the apparatus, and alternately chewing, releasing, and retrieving it (Timberlake & Lucas 1989). Another example is the begging and sign-pointing components of food procuring in dogs in response to a CS paired with food (Jenkins et al 1978).

Such observations indicate that the CS serves as a signal for the availability of food rather than as a substitute for food. Expression may depend on the point in the behavioral sequence at which the behavior system is brought under stimulus control and on how effectively conditioning procedures simulate the circumstances of species-specific adaptations. Holland (1984) has discussed such experiments, in conjunction with several especially incisive tests of his own, to indicate that the nature of the experimental context may interact with species-typical behavior to determine the conditioned response.

Pavlovian Paradigms as Tools for Unmasking Latent Learning

SECOND ORDER CONDITIONING   To establish second-order conditioning, a CS that has been paired with a US (CS_1) is subsequently paired with a second stimulus (CS_2). Second-order conditioning is revealed if the animal responds to CS_2 as if it had been paired with the US. Of importance here is the use of second-order conditioning to reveal learning in response to CS_1 that is not expressed in conventional tests of first-order conditioning. An example has been reported using the autoshaping preparation in pigeons. When a tone was paired with food there was no evidence of learning in the form of elicited keypecking in the presence of the tone, but substantial keypecking was observed to a keylight that was paired with the tone in a second-order conditioning preparation (Rescorla 1980). This indicates that otherwise undetected learning may be revealed with second-order conditioning procedures.

SENSORY PRECONDITIONING   Undetected associations also may be expressed in behavior through the sensory preconditioning paradigm. Sensory preconditioning is like second-order conditioning, except that it is in the initial phase, rather than the second phase, that subjects receive pairings of two relatively neutral stimuli (CS_2-CS_1). Subsequently, one of these stimuli is paired with a US (CS_1-US) and the alternative (CS_2) is tested for conditioned responding. This procedure was used to test the sufficiency of contiguity between the CS and US for development of an association between them (Matzel et al 1988b). Empirical and theoretical developments (e.g. Egger & N. Miller 1962; Rescorla & Wagner 1972) have led to the common view that contiguity between stimuli is not sufficient for learning to occur, and that instead, the CS must provide the subject with information regarding the occurrence of the upcoming US. This predictive relationship between the CS and US is satisfied by a forward CS-US pairing, but not by a backward (US-CS) or simultaneous pairing of the stimuli, whereas temporal contiguity between the CS and US is satisfied by all three arrangements of the stimuli. To differentiate these accounts of conditioning, Matzel et al (1988b) presented subjects with pairings of clicks followed by a tone. The tone was then presented prior to (forward pairing), following (backward pairing), or simultaneously with the footshock US. When subjects were tested with the tone, only the subjects in the forward-pairing condition expressed a CR. However, when tested with the click stimulus, which had been paired with the tone, subjects in all three conditions expressed a condition response. These data suggest that mere contiguity between the CS and US *was* sufficient to promote an association between the two stimuli. The data illustrate the usefulness of the sensory preconditioning paradigm in differentiating failures in acquisition from the failure to express what has been learned.

Postconditioning Manipulations Resulting in the Expression of Learned Associations

FEATURE POSITIVE EFFECT   An interesting example of undetected (latent) learning revealed by postconditioning treatment is provided in terms of discrimination learning. Learning a discrimination between two displays differentiated by a distinguishing feature depends on whether the feature appears on the reinforced (S+) or nonreinforced (S−) trials. In one of the original experiments, pigeons were presented with a dot on a keylight on feature trials, or with the keylight alone on nonfeature trials. The discrimination was learned readily when the distinctive feature (dot) appeared on S+ trials (the feature-positive or FP condition), but only after extensive training, if at all, when the feature appeared on S− trials (the feature-negative or FN condition). This superiority of FP performance relative to FN performance has been referred to as the feature-positive effect or FPE (Jenkins & Sainsbury 1969). The FPE has since been demonstrated with a variety of tasks, across a wide range of species (see Hearst 1978, 1984 for reviews). Given the apparent similarity between the FN task and the Pavlovian conditioned inhibition paradigm (AX−, X+), in which the A stimulus has been shown to acquire inhibitory properties (R. Miller & Spear 1985), this pervasive inability of FN subjects to inhibit responding on S− (feature) trials, and thus to solve the discrimination, has seemed especially puzzling.

An experiment by McCoy et al (1984) provided evidence that failure to express latent learning might underly the difficulty pigeons have with FN discriminations. Pigeons were presented simultaneously with a 400 Hz tone and a red keylight on feature trials and the red keylight alone on nonfeature trials. The tone therefore served as the feature and the keylight as the common stimulus, and as usual the FP discrimination was learned much more effectively than the FN case. Half of the birds in the FN condition (tone and light nonreinforced, light reinforced) were then given a test for generalization to different frequencies of tone stimulus. This indicated surprising learning about the feature in the form of an inhibitory gradient with the minimum amount of responding to the original tone feature. The remaining FN birds were given a summation test with three types of nonreinforced presentations: the tone-light combination, the light alone, and the tone followed by the light. The majority of responding was to the light alone (S+ during training) with significantly less to the light + tone combination (S− during training) and less still when the tone preceded the light. This indicates better discrimination during this extinction phase than during the original training phase, and suggests that the subjects had in fact learned the feature-negative discrimination but did not express it under the original training conditions.

Hearst (1987) has provided other evidence for an expression-based explanation of the FPE. Pigeons given FP training discriminated more effectively than those given FN training—the expected effect. During subsequent extinction the latter birds surprisingly exhibited an immediate and dramatic improvement in FN discrimination (see J. Miller et al 1988 for a similar finding in 1- and 4-day-old chicks). These results suggest that the FPE may result, in part, from the failure of FN subjects to express what they have learned in behavior, rather than from an inability of subjects to acquire the FN task. However, the withdrawal of reinforcement may also enhance the expression of a FP discrimination if extinction begins prior to the achievement of asymptotic discrimination performance (Hearst 1987; J. Miller et al 1988). In light of measurement constraints such as ceiling effects due to asymptotic performance following the removal of reinforcement, it is unclear whether FN discrimination increases more than FP performance during extinction. Given that it is the difference between FP and FN performance that defines the FPE, only an unambiguous measure of this difference will reveal the extent to which this effect is due to factors of expression rather than acquisition.

OVERSHADOWING   Extinction procedures also have revealed latent learning in investigations of Pavlovian conditioning with compound stimuli. When a two-element compound stimulus AB is paired with a US, conditioned responding to the less salient element (say, B) is weaker than if it alone had been paired with the US (Kamin 1969). Such "overshadowing" of B by A has been interpreted in terms of the failure of the overshadowed element to be attended to or associated with the US (Mackintosh 1975; Rescorla & Wagner 1972). Yet recent evidence identifies overshadowing as largely due to post-acquisition processes. Nonreinforced presentations of the overshadowing stimulus following conditioning of a compound CS result in a facilitated conditioned response to the overshadowed stimulus. The strength of this conditioning can be comparable to that otherwise observed for the over-shadowing stimulus. This extinction-induced recovery from overshadowing has been reported with either general activity (Kaufman & Bolles 1981) or suppression of drinking (Matzel et al 1985) as the index of conditioning.

Recovery from overshadowing also has been observed after a long retention interval (Kraemer et al 1988). Rats were given pairings of either a gustatory CS alone or an odor-taste compound with LiCl. A test for an aversion to the taste alone was given either 1 or 21 days following conditioning. Over-shadowing was clearly indicated 1 day after conditioning. Subjects con-ditioned with the taste alone expressed stronger aversions to it than subjects conditioned with the odor-taste compound. After a 21-day retention interval, however, no overshadowing was evident despite maintenance of strong taste aversions. There was, in fact, an increase in the magnitude of the previously overshadowed taste aversion expressed by subjects in the compound CS condition. At least part of the overshadowing effect is based on neither attentional nor associative effects during acquisition; it seems instead due to a failure to retrieve and/or express learned associations in behavior.

LATENT INHIBITION   Finally, apparent impairment of conditioning by CS preexposure ("latent inhibition"; Lubow 1973) also has been alleviated by introducing a long retention interval between conditioning and testing (Kraemer & Roberts 1984), indicating that this effect, too, is at least partly due to a failure in expression rather than acquisition.

Associations Revealed by Prior Cuing

OVERSHADOWING   Experiments in which subjects are presented with some feature of the training episode following conditioning and just prior to testing (prior cuing) have provided further evidence that a wide variety of Pavlovian conditioning phenomena once thought to represent acquisition failures might be more appropriately viewed as failures of expression. Kasprow et al (1982) conditioned rats with a light-tone compound using parameters that produced reliable overshadowing of the light by the tone. Subjects given exposure to the overshadowed stimulus (the light) outside of the conditioning context during the retention interval showed an increase in conditioned responding (attenuation of overshadowing) when subsequently tested with the light.

BLOCKING   Similar results have been obtained in terms of "blocking," in which pairings of CS_1 and the US (CS_1-US) are followed by conditioning of CS_1 in compound with a second CS (CS_1CS_2-US), and little or no conditioning to CS_2 is observed (Kamin 1969). Like overshadowing, blocking has been viewed by contemporary learning theories (e.g. Mackintosh 1975; Pearce & Hall 1980; Rescorla & Wagner 1972) as an acquisition failure. More recent evidence indicates, however, that if subjects are reexposed to either the blocked stimulus, the US, or apparatus cues between the compound conditioning trials and testing, significant attenuation of blocking is observed (Balaz et al 1982; Schachtman et al 1983).

OTHER EXAMPLES   Similar treatments preceding tests for conditioning have also been effective in reinstatement of a taste-LiCl association following extinction of conditioned taste aversion (Schachtman et al 1985), in reinstatement of conditioned suppression to lights or tones after extinction (Bouton 1990; Bouton & Bolles 1979; Rescorla & Heth 1975), in attenuation of latent inhibition (Kasprow et al 1984), and in the unmasking of conditioned inhibition that was obscured by a within-compound association between the inhibitor and the excitor with which it was presented (Williams et al 1986). The suggestion is that these effects (extinction, latent inhibition, failure of conditioned inhibition) do not indicate permanent effects on associative strength and are instead acting on memory retrieval and expression.

Summary and Implications for Theory

Prototypic stimulus selection phenomena seem to be controlled by factors surrounding the expression of associations, in some cases apparently more than by those at acquisition. It would be dangerous to underestimate the significance of this observation. One of several unfortunate consequences could be misdirection of studies of the physiological basis of learning and memory. A recent example involves "blocking," in which prior learning of an association between stimulus A and a US precludes or limits the conditioning of stimulus X that results from pairing compound AX with the US. Blocking is important because it has seemed to illustrate so clearly that contiguity of a CS and US (in this case, of X and the US) is not sufficient for conditioning.

One of the most systematic and thoroughly evolved models of the physiological basis of conditioning is that of Thompson (e.g. 1986). As Thompson (1989) has noted, "it seems almost obligatory for a model to predict blocking in order to be taken seriously . . ." (p. 257). All of the well-known theories of conditioning do account for blocking—*in terms of processes that act during acquisition*. Thompson's physiologically based account of blocking does so as well, in the same terms, perhaps unfortunately.

Thompson's model as well as other major theories of conditioning that emphasize acquisition (e.g. Hawkins & Kandel 1984; Pearce & Hall 1980; Rescorla & Wagner 1972) would appear to need revision if stimulus selection phenomena such as overshadowing, blocking and latent inhibition, as well as other conditioning effects, turn out to be completely or even primarily due to variation in expression (R. Miller & Grahame 1990; Spear 1981). Caution is wise until we determine how many specific instances of these effects are in fact due to expression and how much of each effect can be traced to variation in expression. It is difficult to imagine a more significant issue than this for evaluation of conditioning theories.

ANIMAL MEMORY: FORGETTING AND RETENTION

Delayed Matching-to-Sample

Delayed matching-to-sample (also referred to as delayed conditional discrimination or delayed matching) has become a popular method for assessing short-term retention among several species (Blough 1959; D'Amato 1973; Herman & Gordon 1974; Wallace et al 1980). The procedure for delayed matching begins by presenting a sample (e.g. a color, pattern, tone, or object) that is terminated after a fixed duration or upon a response by the animal. A retention (or delay) interval follows, and ends with presentation of the sample and an alternative comparison stimulus (test stimuli). If the animal chooses the comparison that matches the sample, a reinforcer (usually food) is presented, but otherwise the trial terminates and the intertrial interval begins. A particularly useful variation on this task is "symbolic matching" in which the actual sample does not appear at the test and, instead, a learned associate of the sample is to be chosen over the comparison stimulus at the test. Another variation of analytical value is the serial probe recognition task. Animals are presented with a "list" of samples (3, 6, 10, and 20 are common). Following a delay, the animal must indicate whether a "probe" item was a member of the previous list. This is typically done by requiring the animal to respond "same" or "different," or by having the subject choose between a member of the list and a nonmember.

A number of factors are known to affect the expression of accurate delayed matching. The question is, which factors reflect effects on memory per se, and which are attributable to more general performance effects?

RETENTION-INTERVAL LENGTH   Length of the retention interval has repeatedly been shown to affect retention. With increasing delays, decreasing test performance is observed. The rate of this forgetting depends not only on the species tested (Beritoff 1971) but also on the amount of practice given. Variation in the limits of rate of forgetting limits is considerable, depending on associative interference, differential in outcome associated with test alternatives (Linwick et al 1988; Overmier 1988), and other factors, some of which are matters of expression. For example, Wilkie & Spetch (1981) found that when required to complete a fixed number of responses to the comparison key, pigeons pecked more slowly following an incorrect choice than after a correct choice. The rate measure was, then, a more sensitive assessor of memory than actual choice.

How the delay is incorporated into the task greatly influences the likelihood of memory expression, sometimes independently of the delay's absolute effect. Berryman et al (1963) reported that naive birds failed to acquire delayed matching if a variety of delays were presented from the beginning (i.e. delayed matching not preceded by simultaneous matching). In a particularly incisive study that seems to address the same general effect, Honig (1987) used one sample stimulus to predict the occurrence of either a 1- or 5-sec delay, and a second sample to predict either a 5- or 10-sec delay. He found (in a within-subjects design) that performance at the 5-sec delay depended on the sample used to cue it. With the sample that signalled the short delays (1 or 5 sec), performance at the 5-sec delay was superior to that seen at the 5-sec delay when the long-delay (5- or 10-sec) cue was used. Performance curves and retention functions (which were essentially flat) indicated that the birds "averaged" the delays associated with each cue. Honig suggests that these striking results may be due to a memory contrast effect, which he relates to behavioral contrast (Reynolds 1961). White & Bunnell-McKenzie (1985) reported results consistent with Honig's ideas.

Jagielo & Zentall (1986) provided a motivational rather than an attentional explanation for the effects of variable-length retention intervals. They found that when long delays were made predictable by cuing (whether or not the long delays were presented in the context of short delays), the pigeon's latency to initiate the retention interval increased as the predicted delay increased, whereas latency to initiate predictable short delays did not differ from those for unpredictable long or short delays. In terms of discrimination of the sample from the comparison stimulus, however, birds given predictable, unpredictable or all-long delays did not differ. The authors suggest that predictable long delays may adversely affect motivation owing to their association with long delay of reinforcement (also see D'Amato 1973), or owing to the anticipated increased difficulty in retention of sample information associated with the long delay. As Jagielo & Zentall suggest, the finding that predictable long delays increase sample response latencies without differentially affecting selection of the sample relative to the alternative is similar to reports that altering drive changes absolute running speed but not discrimination in terms of relative speed (Hillman et al 1953; Spence 1958) and is consistent with the notion that motivation and learning or memory are independent (Hull 1943).

MacDonald & Grant (1987) convincingly rule out interpretation of these effects in terms of differential attention to the sample, by demonstrating that the effect of cuing is unchanged if the predictive cue is presented only after termination of the sample. Other of their results suggest that the predictive cue does not operate by differentially affecting postsample processing (rehearsal). The authors suggest that Wasserman et al's (1982) rejection of the idea that cued long delays affect performance by signalling a long delay of reinforcement may have been premature. MacDonald & Grant cite Mazur's (1986) evidence that delayed reinforcement in a delayed matching task is not of the same value as a delayed reinforcer for which the animal just waits (the basis of Wasserman et al's equation). That predictable long delays can signal a long delay of reinforcement and affect motivation levels accordingly seems to provide the best account for these effects of predictable length of delay.

DIRECTED FORGETTING   Presentation of cues to "remember" or "forget" a previously presented sample can importantly affect delayed matching of that sample. Poorer performance on "forget"-cued than on "remember"-cued probe trials has been found in monkeys (Roberts et al 1984), rats (Grant 1982), and pigeons (Grant 1981; Stonebraker & Rilling 1981). This effect typically is attributed to reduced postsample processing when given the "forget" cue. More rapid forgetting is found for the birds cued to forget, and this cue is more effective (greater drop in performance) the earlier during the delay that it occurs (Grant 1981).

An important insight into this effect and into short-term retention generally was provided by Roberts et al (1984), who noted that all experiments showing the directed forgetting effect have involved a limited number of alternative samples (usually two). Roberts et al found, moreover, that directed forgetting was exhibited in monkeys only when just two alternative samples were used. When repetition of samples within a session was precluded by using a large number of alternative samples, cues to forget or remember made no difference, and all samples were relatively well remembered.

Roberts et al (1984) suggest that the alternatives to be compared during a test serve as retrieval cues for the sample. When many different samples are used, the test stimuli cue the retrieval of a relatively unique memory from its inactive state (in long-term memory) and permit a fairly straightforward response decision. When only two sample stimuli are used, so that these same stimuli also are the only alternatives at the test, memories for each sample will be retrieved and the animal must determine which of the two samples was last presented. Roberts et al suggest that to combat the difficulty in having retrieved two conflicting memories, the animal can "rehearse" during the retention interval and maintain an active representation of information derived from the sample (Rilling et al 1984 and Spear 1978 offer compatible analyses). Conditions that attenuate the directed forgetting effect (e.g. Kendrick et al 1981) can be argued to have done so by aiding the animal's ability to maintain information about the sample in an active state throughout the retention interval.

PROACTIVE INTERFERENCE   Studies that assess proactive interference examine the effect on delayed matching of stimuli or events that occur prior to the sample. Retroactive interference is assessed by examining the effect of events that occur between the sample and the retention test.

The size of the pool of samples used during repeated testing of a particular animal has a tremendous effect on delayed matching (Mishkin & Delacour 1975; Wright et al 1986). The inferior performance observed when only a few alternative stimuli are used is attributable to the build-up of proactive interference within the session. Use of only a few stimuli has resulted in rather severe overestimations of forgetting. The number of potential samples is finite, however, so use of even a relatively large sample pool can not prevent the build-up of proactive interference across sessions when subjects are trained and tested for a prolonged period (Jitsumori et al 1988).

It has often been reported that delayed matching is better when longer intertrial intervals are used (e.g. Maki et al 1977; Roberts 1980). The poor performance with short intertrial intervals has commonly been attributed to interference from events of the previous trial. Data from several sources indicate that elements of the previous trial (n-1) do, in fact, interfere with performance on the current trial (n). Three different procedures (Edhouse & White 1988; Roberts 1980; Roitblat & Scopatz 1983) have indicated that the test stimulus selected on trial n-1, whether or not it was reinforced, most interferes with performance on trial n. [Interference from other sources such as the sample on trial n-1 (Edhouse & White 1988) and position (right/left) of the test stimulus pecked on trial n-1 (Roberts 1980) have occasionally been reported.] With all three procedures, interference from the preceding comparison choice was not, however, affected by length of the intertrial interval. The explanation for poor matching performance with short intertrial intervals therefore must lie elsewhere.

Edhouse & White (1988) also report that the test stimulus pecked on trial n-1 (but not length of intertrial interval) interacts with length of the retention interval on trial n. The effects of intertrial interval length and of previous sample pecked therefore seem to involve different processes. Edhouse & White suggest that the latter affects rate of forgetting on trial n (consistent with conventional effects of proactive interference on retention) while the effect of intertrial interval is on general performance.

That lengthening the intertrial interval does not serve to "erase" memories of the previous trial is complemented by the failure of contextual illumination during the intertrial interval (which speeds up forgetting in other circumstances, see below) to improve performance on trials preceded by a short intertrial interval. In fact, relative to a dark intertrial interval, illumination impairs performance at all delays in a similar manner (Edhouse & White 1988; Santi 1984). Apparently the effect of length of the intertrial interval is not determined by the amount of forgetting that does, or does not, occur during that interval.

Santi (1984) found a direct linear relationship between matching accuracy and the ratio between log intertrial interval and delay (replicating Roberts & Kraemer 1982) only when the intertrial interval was dark. Illumination during the intertrial interval destroyed this effect. Santi suggests the interesting hypothesis that "the beneficial effects of trial spacing may be dependent upon similar background stimulus conditions existing during the intertrial interval and the presentation of trial events" (p. 163).

RETROACTIVE INTERFERENCE   Illumination of the chamber (context) has striking effects on delayed matching. For both monkeys (Etkin 1972) and pigeons (Jagielo & Zentall 1986) performance is better when the entire trial is dark or dimly lit than when illuminated. To determine whether illumination affects memory processing apart from acquisition strength, illumination during the retention interval has been varied. D'Amato & O'Neill (1971) and Salmon & D'Amato (1981) report that a dark retention interval within an otherwise illuminated trial markedly improved delayed matching by monkeys. Maki et al (1977) and Grant & Roberts (1976) report that illumination during the retention interval disrupted performance in pigeons, and that, for a given retention interval, the brighter the illumination the poorer was retention.

Retroactive interference from illumination has been attributed to the change in illumination conditions between training and test phases (Cook 1980; Tranberg & Rilling 1980). These studies found that interpolation of dark during the retention interval for animals trained with illumination during the retention interval also resulted in poor retention. However, change per se cannot account completely for studies that report inferior performance with illumination among monkeys or pigeons given extensive experience with both dark (or dim) and illuminated trials (e.g. Etkin 1972; Jagielo & Zentall 1986).

Reconciling effects of illumination   Grant (1988) seems to have resolved these apparent discrepancies in how illumination change and the point of its interpolation affect retention. Grant found that if illumination during the retention interval was terminated after subjects had been trained with an illuminated interval, a decrease in performance was observed. The deficit, however, was demonstrably smaller than when illumination was interpolated for subjects that had been trained with a dark retention interval, and it disappeared with further experience. Yet the illumination-induced disruption among pigeons that had been trained with a dark interval did not disappear. Apparently any change in illumination may temporarily disrupt performance (verifying the results of Cook 1980, and Tranberg & Rilling 1980), but with more extensive testing illumination per se seems to yield a more persistent retention deficit.

Grant (1988) also resolved the effect of point of interpolation of illumination (or darkness). Darkness or illumination was interpolated either during the first or last 2 sec of a 5-sec delay. Only minimal, transitory and nondifferential disruption occurred with darkness, but illumination had dramatic effects at both points. With illumination immediately prior to the test comparison presentation, the retention deficit was quite large but was attenuated with experience. Illumination at the beginning rather than the end of the retention interval resulted in an initially smaller but still substantial retention decrement which, however, was not attenuated with further experience. The initially larger deficit seen with illumination at the end of the retention interval is in agreement with Roberts & Grant (1978). The novel finding that the deficit from illuminating the end of the interval was attenuated with further experience while that from illuminating the beginning of the interval was not led Grant (1988) to propose a two-process theory, stating that illumination affects both rehearsal and choice responding.

NATURE OF MEMORY PROCESSING IN DELAYED MATCHING   How do animals bridge the delay between sample presentation and retention test? Since the earliest delayed matching studies (Hunter 1913) experimenters have been alert to the possibility that sample-specific mediating behaviors, whether required by the task, or self-generated by the subject, might improve delayed matching (e.g. Blough 1959; Zentall et al 1978). The sample might serve as a cue for a chain of behaviors during the retention interval that ends in a particular comparison response. While the use of covert mediating behaviors can never be ruled out, overt mediating behaviors do not commonly occur when not required by the task, and when they do occur explanations other than response chaining have seemed more plausible (Kendrick & Rilling 1984). The following are some alternative explanations of how expression of an acquired memory is accomplished despite a delay.

Early proposals   D'Amato's (1973) temporal discrimination hypothesis states that at the time of test stimuli presentation, the subject scans back in its memory to determine which sample was last presented, and makes its response based on this discrimination. Anything that would help the subject discriminate the most recently presented sample from either a previously presented sample or test stimulus should therefore aid performance. Effects of intertrial interval, size of sample pool, and retention interval are generally consistent with this view, and it remains a viable theory. No similar consistency with such general determinants of delayed matching is held by Roberts & Grant's (1976) trace/decay model of memory. Basically, in this model, presentation of the sample stimulus sets up a memory trace that fades with time and determines test performance. Although originally influential, the facts have required that this model be revised.

A different approach by another leader in this field, Honig (1978), has incorporated a distinction between working and reference memory. "Reference memory" processes events of the task that are unvarying—e.g. that an illuminated key should be pecked to initiate a trial. Working memory processes events specific to a particular trial that will allow correct behavior at the retention test. Working memory operates only during the delay and is reset between trials. Honig & Thompson (1982) regard working memory as loosely equivalent to short-term memory, and reference memory as loosely equivalent to long-term memory. Within the working/reference memory model, there has been growing interest in the precise nature of the process and the representation in working memory. In terms of process, this is basically asking the original question of how animals bridge the retention interval.

Retrospection and prospection in memory   Both temporal discrimination and trace/decay theories have assumed that at the time of the test, animals look back in their memories ("retrospection") to determine what the sample was. The possibility also exists that animals bridge the retention interval by "prospection"—anticipating the correct response at the time the sample is presented and maintaining it until testing.

The issue of "prospective memory" arises most obviously in the case of symbolic delayed matching. Santi & Roberts (1985) found striking evidence of prospection in the pigeon. Using red, green, circle, triangle, horizontal-line, and vertical-line samples, subjects were trained with either three samples mapped onto each test stimulus (red and green), or one sample (red or green) mapped onto three test stimuli. Retrospective processing by pigeons would predict that the one-sample-to-three comparisons group should perform at least as well as, if not better than, the three-samples-to-one-comparison group (since the three-samples-to-one-comparison group would have to distinguish among three associated samples, if they were retrospecting). Santi & Roberts found that for all trial types, the latter group had superior delayed matching, indicating prospection. An interesting factor, differential outcome, was manipulated within the same study. Differential outcome has been shown to have a powerful effect on delayed matching, and it is thought to be effective by allowing the animal to bridge the retention interval by anticipation of the reinforcement outcome selectively associated with a particular sample and comparison set (e.g. Honig et al 1984; Peterson & Trapold 1980). If the pigeons were indeed prospecting, then the incorporation of a differential outcome should allow the birds with three test stimuli corresponding to each sample to show improved performance by changing the number of *outcomes* associated with each sample from three to one. Santi & Roberts found just that. In fact, for the trials using only color stimuli (the only trials identical across groups) the differential outcome led to equivalent performance in the two groups. This would seem to provide strong support for prospective processing.

The distinction between retrospection and prospection during delayed matching requires a few qualifications at this point. First, there is little or no conclusive evidence that the process of memory is at all different in these two cases (a recent exception may be Linwick et al 1988). The distinction refers in practice to the alternative dispositions to encode the sample in terms of its physical attributes or in terms of its associate—the symbolic equivalent that will appear at the retention test. The distinction is more in what is remembered than in how remembering occurs. Perhaps it might someday be shown that variables of importance to memory affect retention differently when retrospection and prospection are used; if so, it might then be useful to consider these as two types of memory. This by no means precludes interest in this distinction, however, as illustrated by some interesting tests to determine when prospection and when retrospection might occur. Urcuioli & Zentall (1986) suggest, for instance, that something like memorability, in terms of the type or number of stimuli involved, might determine whether animals choose to encode the sample in terms of its physical qualities (retrospection) or in terms of the alternatives to be presented at the test (prospection).

Conclusions   The memory process used by animals for delayed matching may well depend on details of the task. An important factor appears to be the number of sample stimuli that have been experienced by the animals in a particular context. As Roberts et al (1984) suggest, if the animal is required, or has been required, to remember one of a number of possible samples, the test stimuli may be used to cue retrieval of the correct sample memory from its inactive state. In order to counteract associative interference when only a few stimuli are used, animals can develop instead a strategy of maintaining actively a representation of the sample information (prospectively or retrospectively) during the retention interval. This maintenance may be similar to Honig's (1978) definition of working memory, although it is not clear that anything other than maintenance of an active memory ("rehearsal") need be hypothesized. It is probable that animals primarily anticipate outcome (prospect), and that studies reporting retrospection may actually be reflecting issues such as sample discriminability or memorability.

Spatial Memory

Olton & Samuelson (1976) popularized the use of the radial arm maze for investigation of animal spatial memory. It has generated a vast body of literature that is more varied but less systematic than that for the nonspatial delayed matching task reported above. The maze has been used widely in drug and lesion studies, which are beyond the scope of this paper.

The maze consists of a central platform with arms (alleys) extending out from the platform. Typically, the end of each arm is baited, and correct performance requires that the animal collect each reinforcer without reentering an arm from which the reinforcer has already been obtained. Rats quickly acquire and maintain high levels of performance when one trial a day is run (e.g. Olton & Collison 1979).

Most often, an open 8-arm radial maze is used. An open maze is preferred because it has been demonstrated repeatedly that rats predominantly employ extramaze cues (the relationship of maze arms to walls, windows, furniture, etc) to solve the task (Mazmanian & Roberts 1983; Olton & Collison 1979; Suzuki et al 1980), although sufficiently salient intramaze cues (arm inserts that provide differential tactile and visual information) can produce performance equivalent to that found with salient extramaze cues (Kraemer et al 1983). Intramaze cues such as odor trails and scent of the reinforcer do not seem to play a major role in guiding behavior (Olton & Collison 1979; Olton & Samuelson 1976). When extramaze cues are inadequate, as is typical in enclosed mazes, rats often solve the maze by adopting a response strategy such as always entering the adjacent arm (e.g. Suzuki et al 1980). This strategy is usually considered to reflect something other than spatial memory, and conditions that encourage this type of responding are typically avoided. Response chaining does not necessarily indicate a lack of spatial encoding. For example, Dale (1986) reports that rats that chain their responses will pause after the selection of the final (eighth) arm, indicating task completion.

When multiple trials are given relatively close together, spatial, like nonspatial, memory is susceptible to proactive interference from preceding trials (Roberts & Dale 1981; Hoffman & Maki 1986). It is interesting that in a free choice procedure, massed trials resulted in the development of chained responding, apparently in an effort to alleviate the effects of proactive interference (Roberts & Dale 1981). Subsequently Roberts & Dale used forced choices for the first half of the trial, a procedure that would make response chaining a poor strategy. They did not find significant prevention of proactive interference when trials were spaced 60, 120, or 240 sec apart, or when the intertrial interval was spent outside of the maze. Maki et al (1980; cited in

Roberts & Dale 1981), however, found that a 4-hr intertrial interval does prevent proactive interference.

Insertion of a retention interval midway through the trial (in an 8-arm maze, between the fourth and fifth choices) can disrupt performance, but well-practiced animals can perform above chance with a 4-hr retention interval (Beatty & Shavalia 1980). Surprisingly, spatial memory appears very resistant to many forms of retroactive interference (see Maki et al 1986 for a review). Roberts (1981) observed retroactive interference when similarity between an interpolated maze trial and the completion of the original maze trial was high (same room, same maze, same arms) or when a sufficient number of maze runs (in this case 3) in different rooms on different mazes was interpolated.

It is fairly clear that good open-maze performance, in the absence of a response chain, depends on a permanent representation of the maze and its relationship to extramaze cues. Roberts & Dale (1981) suggest that this permanent representation is activated (from long-term storage) for a trial, and temporal markers placed on the entered arms. Ability to discriminate which arms have been entered on a trial would depend on the ease with which the temporal discriminations could be made. This is compatible with D'Amato's (1973) temporal discrimination hypothesis.

The fact that rats perform so well on a task that requires them to avoid returning to a place of reinforcement (in opposition to traditional theories of reinforcement) might be best explained in terms of adaptive foraging behavior. Briefly, it would be to the animal's benefit not to return immediately to a location from which food had been depleted. Indeed, studies examining the depletion vs nondepletion of reward in spatial memory tasks indicate that nondepletion of reward increases the rat's likelihood of returning to the reinforced location (e.g. Gaffan et al 1983). Recently, an increasing number of studies investigating foraging effects (e.g. Batson et al 1986; Ilersich et al 1988; Yoerg & Kamil 1982) indicate that such an analogy may provide extremely useful insight into the subject's behavior. Typically, pigeons run on mazes comparable to the radial arm do not perform well (Bond et al 1981; but see Roberts & Van Veldhuizen 1985). A sensitivity to foraging issues, however, allowed Spetch & Edwards (1986) to design tasks that allow pigeons to demonstrate good spatial memory. Shettleworth (1989) provides a thoughtful commentary on foraging behavior in laboratory animals.

It seems fairly clear that spatial memory can withstand greater retention intervals, and is more resistant to specific sources of interference, than nonspatial memory. Perhaps this is due only to differences in degree of learning or distribution of practice that accompany the task differences. This may be due, also, at least in part, to the relationship between spatial memory and natural foraging. Ease of retrieval for each type of memory, however, is quite strongly influenced by the context in which the animal is asked to retrieve it. The closer the test context is to training conditions and the more unique the context is for specific memories, the better the retrieval.

ENVIRONMENTAL CONTROL OF EXPRESSION: PRIOR CUING AND ALLEVIATION OF FORGETTING

Many investigators of animal learning have been led to employ language and concepts associated with animal memory (cf Honig & James 1971) by the observation that associations apparently lost from or never established in an animal's behavior repertoire become expressed in special circumstances. These circumstances have been referred to as "reactivation treatments" or "reminders," but our preference is to apply the more neutral term of either "prior cuing" or, if given simultaneously with testing, cuing with contemporary context (Spear 1976). Once treatments were established that could make forgotten learning expressable—could make the memory of the conditioning episode active (Lewis 1969; Spear 1978)—analytic variables could be applied concurrent with these treatments to modify the memory in the absence of the conditioned behavior. It is difficult to consider such experiments without reference to memory, either as a representation or a process. A sample of this research will illustrate further the profound variability in the expression of learning that can occur despite equivalent acquisition.

Alleviation of Forgetting

Amnesic effects induced experimentally by a variety of gross insults to the brain can be reduced substantially by environmental or pharmacological events prior to testing (e.g. Lewis 1969). Similar events, typically some component of the learning episode, can alleviate forgetting from more common sources such as a retention interval (between conditioning and test) or associative interference (Spear 1973). Such alleviation of forgetting by a prior cuing treatment (also termed "direct reactivation," "reminder," etc) is quite independent of any new learning that prior cuing might induce. This is illustrated, for example, by experiments showing that a prior cuing treatment can alleviate forgetting even if that same treatment has extinction consequences that weaken expression in other circumstances (e.g. Gordon 1981).

There is striking generality in this means of alleviating forgetting. It has been observed in the rat after a variety of sources of forgetting, including long retention intervals (Deweer et al 1980), short intervals (e.g. Gordon & Feldman 1978), and a wide variety of amnestic agents (Lewis 1969; Riccio & Richardson 1984; Spear 1978). It has been observed with pigeons in terms of generalization of appetitively reinforced instrumental pecking of colors (Moye & Thomas 1982; Thomas 1981), with infant rats in terms of active avoidance (Spear & Smith 1978) or Pavlovian conditioning (Spear & Parsons 1976; Haroutunian & Riccio 1979), and in adult rats in terms of passive avoidance (Mactutus et al 1980) or Pavlovian conditioning (Spear & Parsons 1976). It has been observed in terms of memory for complex maze behavior (Deweer et al 1980), simple discrimination behavior (Hamberg & Spear 1978) and taste aversion (Smotherman 1985). A wide range of prior cuing treatments has alleviated forgetting, including not only presentation of the CS, US, or context alone, but also combinations of these with neuropeptides (e.g. ACTH) and context (Mactutus et al 1980) or neuropeptides alone (e.g. enkephalin—Rigter 1978).

That forgetting can be alleviated by pretest administration of drugs having identifiable effects on specific neurotransmitters, particularly the amines, has been well established by the thorough studies of Quartermain and his colleagues. Following any of several varieties of learning, forgetting by rats or mice due to specific brain insult by amnestic treatment or to a long retention interval has been alleviated in these studies by pretest administration of a variety of drugs. The effective drugs typically have been those acting on catecholaminergic activity; in some cases modulation of cholinergic or serotonergic transmission has been similarly effective (Quartermain 1983; Quartermain et al 1988). Alleviation of forgetting has been analyzed in a similar manner by Sara and her colleagues (e.g. Sara & Deweer 1982).

CONDITIONS FOR ALLEVIATING FORGETTING   Principles to determine the effectiveness of prior cuing have not been established. Prior cuing does not always alleviate forgetting, even in circumstances in which the cuing treatment seems quite reasonable (Palfai et al 1983). The "richness" of the prior cuing treatment seems to be an important factor. For instance, even when a neuropeptide such as adrenocorticotrophic hormone (ACTH) is not itself effective it can alleviate forgetting if some aspect of the training apparatus is presented along with the ACTH (Mactutus et al 1980), and the duration and number of pretest cues seem generally to be important determinants of the alleviation of forgetting (Deweer & Sara 1985). Multiple pretest cues are not merely additive in their effect; Deweer (1986) found that simple forgetting was alleviated by prior cuing with training context but not with the training reinforcer, although the prior cuing effect with both was more effective than that with context alone. Similarly, although prior cuing with the reinforcer plus the motivational state of training alleviated forgetting of a discrimination (maze) memory following brain damage, presentation of the motivational state alone did not (LeVere et al 1984). Prior cuing generally is most effective if it immediately precedes testing (for an important exception see Rovee-Collier 1989). Simple forgetting of the cuing occurs thereafter (Spear et al 1980; Riccio & Richardson 1984).

Alleviation of forgetting is occasionally reported in the absence of an explicit prior cuing treatment. In some cases apparent "spontaneous" recovery occurs, presumably the consequence of a cuing event that was not under experimental control. Although the simple time-dependent, uncued recovery from amnestic agents such as electroconvulsive shock has not been observed in all circumstances, the effect remains a viable, albeit little understood phenomenon (Day & Han 1982; Spear 1978).

A thorough search for features that determine alleviation of forgetting through prior cuing has been conducted by Riccio and his colleagues (for reviews see Riccio & Spear 1990; Richardson & Riccio 1990). Riccio's work has been guided by two basic notions: 1. Expression of the target memory depends on the circumstances of testing being sufficiently similar to those of original learning; and 2. An important memory attribute encoded as a part of the original learning episode is the amnestic treatment itself. Fundamental to these studies is Riccio's observation that hypothermia prior to testing alleviates forgetting induced by preceding or following conditioning with hypothermia (Hinderliter et al 1975).

PRIOR CUING AND STATE DEPENDENT RETENTION   Interpretation of prior cuing by Riccio and his colleagues is related to drug-induced state-dependent retention—retention promoted by reinstatement of the internal state present during training (Overton 1982). Endogenous substances such as neuropeptides might similarly affect retention. If so, the animal's "natural" neurochemical constitution, peripheral or central, would be expected to promote retention most effectively if it corresponds at the test to the animal's neurochemical constitution during original learning. In memory for aversive conditioning, the action of the ACTH regularly released by the normal stressed animal has been taken by some as a potential mediator for such endogenously induced state-dependent retention (Klein 1972; Spear 1971). There is good support for this specific function of ACTH as well as for the notion that endogenous hormones/neuropeptides can influence retention in several ways (Riccio & Concannon 1981; Richardson & Riccio 1990; Spear 1978). Even when a neuropeptide such as ACTH acts primarily after the conditioning episode, a state-dependent interpretation remains viable (Izquierdo 1989; Izquierdo & Dias 1983).

The consequences of an amnestic agent can be alleviated by pretest administration of ACTH or one of its fragments (Rigter et al 1974), implying the incorporation of ACTH as an attribute of the memory for the conditioning episode. Further tests by Richardson, Riccio, and their colleagues established that exogenous ACTH given prior to testing alleviated the response-suppressing consequences of extinction (Richardson et al 1984; Ahlers et al 1986). Their interpretation was that the animal's memory representing acquisition, which had included an ACTH attribute, was made manifest in behavior by the occurrence of endogenous ACTH at the test. If correct, animals administered dexamethasone (which suppresses ACTH release) during acquisition should excrete relatively little ACTH and so should not incorporate ACTH as an attribute of their memory for acquisition. In these circumstances, therefore, pretest ACTH should not promote the expression of acquisition behavior following extinction. This prediction was confirmed despite a substantial alleviation of extinction effects among animals given only pretest ACTH and no dexamethasone during acquisition (Ahlers & Richardson 1985; also see Santucci et al 1987 for confirmation with a different test).

WHY IS ALLEVIATION OF FORGETTING INTERESTING?   It is not especially exciting to observe over and over again that most instances of forgetting reflect difficulty in retrieval and expression rather than a permanent loss of the memory from storage. What makes it interesting to us is that it provides a means for operating on a memory independently of the animal's overt behavior, which may be taken as operating on cognition.

With a direct reactivation treatment such as prior cuing, a particular memory is implicitly made active and its characteristics potentially susceptible to alteration by new treatments (Spear 1973, 1976; Gordon 1983). Such modification of an unexpressed memory may be said to be possible when the memory is "implicitly reactivated" and provides an experimental paradigm to study dynamic changes in memory with experience. It also allows comparison of two kinds of active memories—new memories that were recently acquired, and old memories that were previously acquired but recently reactivated.

IMPLICIT REACTIVATION   Although amnestic or hypermnestic treatments do not ordinarily alter the characteristics of a memory if they occur long after its acquisition, they do if a treatment known to induce direct reactivation immediately precedes the treatment. For instance, inhibition of protein synthesis does not ordinarily affect retention if it occurs 3 hr after training; but if immediately preceded by reexposure to the apparatus or a similar context, the animal is rendered amnesic despite the 3-hr interval (Quartermain 1982). Similarly, "analeptic" drugs such as strychnine do not ordinarily enhance retention if given long after learning, but such enhancement does occur in such a case if the strychnine is immediately preceded by a reactivation treatment (Gordon & Spear 1973).

Characteristics of the rat's memory for recent Pavlovian conditioning were compared with those of a similar memory inferred to have been reactivated by a prior cuing treatment following hypothermia-induced amnesia (Mactutus et al 1982). The results indicated that: (a) whereas new (recently acquired) memories were affected only by deep hypothermia, old (reactivated) memories were disrupted by either mild or deep hypothermia; (b) amnesia, which typically grows over time following the amnestic agent, appeared sooner for the old memory; and (c) an amnestic treatment given a relatively long time after either initial acquisition (new) or reactivation (old) was more likely to yield amnesia for the latter case (old, reactivated memory). Tests of forgetting at different intervals following acquisition of a new memory or reactivation of an old one have indicated, however, that an old, reactivated memory may be more resistant to simple forgetting than a recently acquired memory (Spear et al 1980). The distinguishing characteristics of these two memory states therefore remain uncertain (for a review, see Riccio & Richardson 1984).

Perhaps the most creative use of the prior cuing paradigms has been by Rovee-Collier and her colleagues in tests of positively reinforced instrumental learning and memory in human infants under normal circumstances (i.e., no amnestic treatments). Human infants share with animals a lack of verbal facility, and the Rovee-Collier studies provide a good model for similar experiments with other animals. The following discoveries of Rovee-Collier et al are notable for our purposes: Previously undetected capabilities for long-term retention in the two- and three-month old infant are revealed by a prior cuing treatment; a previously acquired memory made active by a prior cuing treatment has many characteristics in common with a recently acquired memory, but there are some subtle differences; contextual features of original learning play an important role in the expression of the acquired behavior; and prior cuing procedures establish that preverbal human infants organize external events into categories and provide a means to study the nature of this category formation (e.g. Rovee-Collier & Hayne 1987; Rovee-Collier 1989).

REACTIVATION AND CONTEXTUAL INFLUENCES ON CONDITIONING   Prior cuing with portions of the conditioning context can alleviate the consequences of extinction treatment (nonreinforced CS presentations) as well as forgetting. A widely cited study of recovered expression of conditioning following extinction is that of Rescorla & Heth (1975); they found that prior cuing with the US alleviated the effect of extinction on a CS (see Delameter & LoLordo 1990, for a summary of similar revaluation effects). This was interpreted as reinstatement of the value of the US, with the assumption that the US value had been decreased during extinction. That the US value actually does decrease during extinction is unlikely, however; if two CSs are separately conditioned to the same US, one of these CSs can be extinguished without affecting response to the other (Bouton 1990). Together with other evidence (e.g. Richards & Sargent 1983) this suggests that the animal's representation of the US is not changed during extinction. The context of CS presentation seems to be critical, although simple summation of the associative strengths of CS and context with the US apparently cannot account for this reactivation effect either. Animals given a low degree of conditioning to a CS show no further increase in response to that CS following interpolated US-only presentation in the same context (Bouton 1984). Yet the greater the extinction of the CS, the greater the reactivation effect from presenting a US alone (Bouton & King 1986).

A promising alternative approach is that extinction yields competition between two stored associations, one between the CS and US and the other between the CS and no notable event, in a manner analogous to paradigms established years ago to study associative interference in human memory (e.g. Postman & Underwood 1973; Underwood 1949) and other instances of animal memory (Spear 1967, 1971). Bouton's (1990) view of various phenomena of Pavlovian conditioning in terms of associative interference is an approach that potentially can deal with problems of expression.

It is in this respect that Bouton (1990) discusses the alleviation of extinction effects. He emphasizes the "renewal effect," which occurs when animals conditioned to a CS in context A and extinguished in context B, show conditioning in context A but not in context B. Context A can be a particular chamber, a drug, or some external, punctate event such as a tone. The effect is a special case of state-dependent retention that is perhaps most closely linked historically to Asratian's (1965) "switching" paradigms with Pavlovian conditioning. The effect is in some ways quite general, occurring over a variety of types of conditioning and context, and for discrimination reversal or counterconditioning as well as for extinction (e.g. Spear 1971). Bouton (1990) dismisses with good evidence interpretations that depend on direct context-US associations or configural conditioning. This renewal or switching effect is more likely a consequence of control by context over the CS-US association and functions the way occasion setters do. Evidence that discrete occasion setters can block the contextual control observed with the renewal effect implies that the context and the occasion setter can serve a common function (Bouton 1990).

Bouton (1990) confirms that each of three theoretically significant transfer effects in conditioning—latent inhibition, Hall-Pierce negative transfer (decreased associability of a CS due to pairing with any US; Hall & Pierce 1979), and learned irrelevance—can be weakened substantially by a change in context between stages 1 and 2. Furthermore, following acquisition and extinction, rate of reacquisition depends on the contextual similarity among the three stages: reacquisition is slow if its context resembles that of extinction but rapid if it resembles that of acquisition (Bouton & Schwartzentruber 1989).

Summary and Conclusions

The alleviation of forgetting by cuing prior to or concurrent with the retention test has been observed in a striking variety of circumstances and forms of learning. Forgetting attributable to environmental, pharmacological, or surgical sources has been reduced by diverse pharmacological or environmental treatments. The effects are so robust and widespread that any strong conclusions about permanent loss of specific learning have become suspect. A great deal remains to be learned about the necessary and sufficient conditions for the alleviation of forgetting, despite the availability of techniques for effecting it. An analytical advantage of these techniques is to enable studies of memory modification in the absence of overt expression of the original memory. Contextual control over relatively complex phenomena of conditioning has supported a view of context as a discriminative stimulus for a conditional discrimination or as an occasion setter rather than an event functionally equivalent to the CS, an advance of value for understanding the influence of context on expression.

ANIMAL MEMORY AND LEARNING DURING ONTOGENY

The developing animal provides in many ways a prototypic case for consideration of issues of expression. This is clearest in the case of altricial mammals, born with a central nervous system that still must undergo a great deal of development. Such animals (primarily rats) are the focus of this section.

Among infants a limited response repertoire is likely to mask significant learning. Sensory limitations and experiential deficits in the developing animal yield an age-specific encoding of the environment that might limit expression of early learning when that encoding changes later. Finally, a disposition for rapid forgetting despite the obvious significance of early experience encourages the notion that appropriate allowance for expression might unlock a vast store of learning that is otherwise not manifest.

A good deal of progress has been achieved recently in identifying changes in learning and memory that take place during ontogeny. This has been made possible in part by methodological advances permitting the experimental separation of the effects of age from those of nonassociative variation such as motivation or perception (e.g. Campbell 1967) and by technological innovation in the measurement of learning during infancy (for a recent review see Spear & Rudy 1990). Infants differ considerably from adults not only in quantitative aspects of learning but also in phenomena that have been considered basic to the understanding of animal learning. The former is important because the differences are unlike those conventionally supposed—despite clear instances of slower learning by infants than adults (Rudy et al 1984), the opposite relationship frequently has emerged (Spear & Molina 1987). The latter is important because many phenomena of learning that form the data base for contemporary models and theories are either not observed or are observed in different form when tested in developing rather than adult animals.

Identifying the Ontogenesis of Learning

What is the earliest age at which learning occurs and what is the earliest age at which learning of any particular event or response occurs? Over the past 20–30 years increasing sensitivity to issues of expression have led to progressive "corrections" of the youngest age at which learning can be accomplished in animals. Examples here are taken from observations of instrumental learning.

Simple passive avoidance can illustrate how accommodation for age-specific expression has altered estimates of the age at which learning can occur. Conventional passive avoidance learning requires that the animal withhold movement from one distinctive compartment to another to avoid an annoying footshock. Preweanling rats (younger than postnatal day 21) have a difficult time learning this type of passive avoidance. Relative to older animals the apparent deficiency of 15–18 day old rats in learning passive avoidance was observed to be greater than that in learning active avoidance (Feigley & Spear 1970; Riccio et al 1968). This supported the notion that infants are especially ineffective in learning to withhold behaviors. Rats younger than 15 days seemed unlikely or even unable to learn passive avoidance. The source of this "learning deficit" was later found to be as much in expression as in the animal's age. If required to withhold responding in all directions – to not touch any wall – rats as young as 10 days postnatal learned passive avoidance (Stehouwer & Campbell 1980). And if age-related movement deficiencies were reduced by a gentle breeze in the direction of the shocked location (neonates move with the breeze), rats only 2–3 hr old learned passive avoidance (Myslivecek & Hassmannova 1983).

Estimates of the onset of capability for instrumental learning of other kinds have similarly decreased as technology has improved to accommodate the limitations of infant animals, which were largely (but not exclusively) those of expression. For instance the age at which rats could learn to escape or avoid actively was decreased by 30–40% by removing the directional requirement (Misanin et al 1974; Spear & Smith 1978). Modification of the ambient odor for training resulted in a similar decrease in the age at which the infant rat could learn a discrimination for instrumental escape from footshock. With conventional procedures the infant rat seemed unable to learn a position discrimination until 10–11 days of age (Misanin et al 1974), but in the context of the odor of the pups' home nest this learning was facilitated and occurred as early as 7 days postnatal (Misanin & Hinderliter 1989; Smith & Spear 1981a).

The learning of simple instrumental behavior to obtain food or warmth is possible only a few hours after birth, if the responses required allow the neonate to express the learning at this age. Johanson & Hall (1979) found that within 24 hr of birth the rat could not only learn to push with its body a piece of cotton in order to obtain an infusion of milk, it could learn to do so preferentially when one odorized cotton piece resulted in milk but another did not. Guenaire et al (1982) found that neonatal rats would learn to raise their head in order to receive a warm burst of air. Pfister & Alberts (1987) refined this procedure so that only a slight head movement was needed to trigger the receipt of warm air, and found that rat pups learned this task quite readily within a few hours after birth.

Age-related differences observed in Pavlovian conditioning may similarly be governed by factors of expression. Hoffmann & Spear (1988) reported that 5-day-old rats are more likely than 15-day-olds (and apparently, adults) to acquire an aversion to sucrose solution paired with footshock, as expressed by decreased ingestion. This relationship is the opposite of that observed for aversion induced by pairing LiCl with a specific taste (Rudy et al 1984), understandable perhaps in terms of an interaction between the type of US and how the aversion is to be expressed. Hoffmann (1989) compared rats of different ages in terms of several alternative measures of conditioned taste aversion induced with any of three USs: footshock, LiCl, or an oral infusion of a bitter taste (citric acid). Degree of learning in terms of sucrose ingestion was held constant. The 15-day-olds given LiCl as the US behaved like adults in displaying conditioned orofacial and associated responses similar to those exhibited to unpalatable taste. Also as with adults these responses were not seen after conditioning with either of the other USs. In contrast, 5-day-old rats responded to sucrose in the same way regardless of the US with which it had been paired previously (see Pelchat et al 1983 for a similar study with adults).

Stimulus Selection

In contrast to older animals, infants generally exhibit: a greater likelihood for potentiation and a lesser likelihood for overshadowing (e.g. Kucharski & Spear 1985; Hinderliter & Misanin 1988; Kraemer et al 1988); an enhanced disposition to process redundant contextual events (Solheim et al 1980); a greater tendency functionally to equate events that are processed by different sensory modalities (Kraemer et al 1989; Spear & Molina 1987); and greater benefit during Pavlovian conditioning from information that may act to limit stimulus selection (Spear et al 1989). Given the examples cited elsewhere in the present chapter to indicate that stimulus selection phenomena seem in large part to reflect peculiarities of expression, it seems reasonable to expect that age-related differences in stimulus selection as well as those observed in other learning or memory tests may in part reflect nontrivial differences in expression rather than in potential for acquisition.

Ontogeny of Access to an Olfactory Memory

Kucharski & Hall (1987) made a discovery of special relevance to the expression issue. It is known that the left and right sides of the olfactory bulb are not connected neurally during the first postnatal week. This connection, mediated by the anterior commissure, becomes functional later, by the latter portion of the second postnatal week. Hall, Kucharski and their colleagues developed a soft rubber plug that could be inserted into a single naris of the six day old rat to prevent detection of odors on that side of the nostrum. With the left naris blocked, conditioning of an odor preference by odor-milk pairings was evident only in response to olfactory stimulation of the contralateral side of the olfactory bulb linked directly to the right naris, whereas tests with only the left naris yielded no evidence of conditioning, and vice versa (Kucharski et al 1986).

Kucharski & Hall (1987) asked how the memory of such one-sided conditioning at 6 days of age would be expressed later at 12 days of age. At this point neural communication between the left and right sides of the olfactory bulb is in effect. Conditioning of a single side of the olfactory bulb on day 6 was expressed through the contralateral side on day 12 (although it had not been on day 6). If, however, the retention test on day 12 was preceded by surgical sectioning of the anterior commissure, a memory acquired on one side was not evident when only the opposite naris was exposed. In other words, it was as if the memory remained stored on a single side of the olfactory bulb after day 6, but could be accessed by the other side when anatomical development provided neural communications. This may provide a model for understanding the fate of memories in general that are acquired prior to full development of the brain.

Infantile Retention and Forgetting: Infantile Amnesia

Forgetting during infancy is especially rapid and extends later in life to drastic forgetting of the events of infancy; these effects collectively have been termed "infantile amnesia" (Campbell & Spear 1972). Although important generally for the theme of expression, our consideration of infantile amnesia is limited here to short-term retention.

Forgetting over intervals of a few seconds or minutes is more rapid earlier in development. This conclusion is important because it addresses theories of infantile amnesia that attribute the drastic forgetting of infancy to neural development between learning in infancy and testing in adulthood. If we assume that brain growth during a period of a few seconds or minutes is insufficient to promote memory loss, the infantile deficiency in short term retention limits the significance of such growth in infantile amnesia.

Four procedures have confirmed the infantile deficiency in short term retention. 1. With trace conditioning, infants are retarded in acquisition more than older animals the longer the interval between the offset of the CS and onset of the US, whether the conditioning involves the olfactory (Rudy & Cheatle 1979), gustatory (Gregg et al 1978; Steinert et al 1979), auditory, or visual sensory systems (Moye & Rudy 1985). 2. With minimal conditioning procedures involving the olfactory or visual systems—a single pairing of the CS and US—retention by younger infants declines more rapidly than by adults over the next several minutes (J. Miller & Spear 1989; J. Miller et al 1989b). 3. In some circumstances a single pairing of US and CS is insufficient for conditioning unless preceded by a "CS−," another value of the same stimulus dimension used for the CS+ but not paired with the US. The extent to which the CS+ is conditioned when an interval elapses between the CS− and CS+ provides an index of forgetting of the CS−. For both visual and olfactory conditioning, forgetting of the CS− assessed in this way has been found to be more rapid earlier in development (Kucharski et al 1985; J. Miller & Spear 1989; J. Miller et al 1989b). 4. After rats 21–38 days old had learned that reinforcement (escape) of swimming to a particular location was always followed by nonreinforcement at a particular location but reinforcement at an alternative location, length of the interval between the first and second responses was varied (Castro et al 1987). Correct responding was maintained by 21-day-old pups with a 30-sec but not a 60-sec interval, by 28 day olds with a 60-sec but not a 180-sec interval, and by 38-day-old rats with all intervals including 180 sec. The simple but important point is, each test indicates that rate of forgetting after very short intervals is more rapid the younger the animal. This complements the substantial evidence for the same ontogenetic differences in forgetting over long intervals (Campbell & Spear 1972).

There has been no clear resolution of whether the rapid forgetting of learning that occurs early in development is due to processes that operate only at that time or reflects instead a special susceptibility to the same processes responsible for forgetting in adulthood (Spear 1979). Evidence tends to favor the latter alternative. Whereas animals have been shown to be more susceptible than adults to common causes of forgetting such as retroactive and proactive interference (eg. Smith & Spear 1981b), there are as yet no convincing experiments comparing infants and adults to indicate that infantile amnesia can be alleviated or increased.

Summary and Conclusions

Despite the immature neurophysiology and neuroanatomy of the rat at birth, learning and memory are evident in a variety of forms from that moment on (and before). Technological developments have permitted increasingly clearer measurement of learning and memory early in life. Age-related limitations on the acquisition of certain associations have been observed together with differences in what is learned, how events are encoded and the influence of redundant or irrelevant events during conditioning. Infants and adults learn different things and in different amounts, although there are no clear indications as yet that the process of learning differs.

The profound susceptibility of infantile learning to forgetting focuses attention on ontogenetic determinants of the expression of learning. Learning that takes place during infancy is readily forgotten over short as well as long intervals, which limits the general applicability of brain growth during the retention interval as an explanatory factor. Factors of encoding or expression that are peculiarly infantile provide an alternative basis for explaining infantile amnesia.

CONCLUDING COMMENTS

The progress and increasing breadth in the study of animal memory and learning are as much staggering as impressive when viewed over an 8–10 year period. The increasing complexity of the information processing studied in animals has been accompanied by a corresponding increase in the sophistication of theories and continued elegance of experimental design. The breadth achieved is in terms of the issues tested, not the kinds of animals tested, leading to an increased depth of understanding of learning and memory within a few species. The consequent gain in precision of analysis may be accompanied by some cost in generalizability (although this review has not attempted to represent the breadth of species actually tested for learning and memory).

A frighteningly large number of significant issues, theories, and experiments could not be included in this chapter. It was necessary to bypass the continuing, and increasingly important, issue of whether the "memory process" that we study is unitary or consists of a variety of separate systems; a particularly incisive summary has been accomplished by Holland (1989). Also excluded were the increasingly sophisticated models and theories of basic conditioning and learning derived from animal research (e.g. Kehoe 1988; Klein & Mowrer 1989a,b) and the advances in topics of aversive conditioning that are critical to issues and treatment in clinical psychology and yet testable experimentally only with animals (Archer & Nillson 1989; Denny 1990).

Among the fundamental issues of animal learning that have been advanced in recent years but omitted from the present review are revised conceptualizations, based on increasingly sophisticated research, of reinforcement (Collier 1982, 1986; Collier & Rovee-Collier 1983) and expectancy (Overmier 1988), and the understanding of some important issues of long-term retention and forgetting (Hendersen 1985; Kraemer 1984). Analytical advances in the neurophysiological determinants of animal memory and learning have been especially notable in the work of McGaugh and of Gold (e.g. Gold 1989; McGaugh 1983, 1989; McGaugh & Gold 1976), but this work, too, could not be covered. And the increasing use of research on animal memory and learning to provide solutions for practical problems of behavior of significance to general society is an especially notable omission (Domjan 1987).

For the general purpose of understanding behavioral plasticity, the vast importance of expression factors does not imply that the consequences of treatments to induce learning and memory are hopelessly variable. Quite the opposite may be inferred from the evidence. What we have witnessed over the past 10–20 years is development of a technology to reveal influences of conditioning treatments that otherwise seem absent. Given the success of this technology, it is as if relationships among reasonably salient events presented to a reasonably alert animal will inevitably be learned. In this respect it is because acquisition seems so invariant that understanding behavioral plasticity requires an understanding of expression.

ACKNOWLEDGMENTS

Preparation of this report was supported in part by Grant 1 RO1 MH35219 from the National Institute of Mental Health and Grant 5 RO1 AA06634 from the National Institute of Alcohol Abuse and Alcoholism. The authors are grateful for the excellent secretarial and linguistic assistance provided by Teri Tanenhaus. Several experts in the field read an earlier draft and provided incalculable improvement in it by incisive insights and suggestions; they cannot, however, be held accountable for any shortcomings of the chapter. They are Mark Bouton, Charles F. Flaherty, William C. Gordon, Peter Holland, J. Bruce Overmier, David C. Riccio, Rick Richardson, and William A. Roberts. The authors are extremely grateful for their generous help.

A more extensive version of this chapter may be obtained from N. E. Spear, Center for Developmental Psychobiology, SUNY, Binghamton, New York 13901.

Literature Cited

Ahlers, S. T., Richardson, R. 1985. Administration of dexamethasone prior to training blocks ACTH-induced recovery of an extinguished avoidance response. *Behav. Neurosci.* 99:760–64

Ahlers, S. T., Richardson, R., West, C., Riccio, D. C. 1986. Short- and long-term effects of ACTH administration on recovery of an extinguished avoidance response. *Soc. Neurosci. Abstr.* 12:1158

Archer, T., Nilsson, L. G. 1989. *Aversion, Avoidance, and Anxiety: Perspectives on Aversively Motivated Behavior.* Hillsdale, NJ: Erlbaum

Asratian, E. A. 1965. *Compensatory Adaptations, Reflex Activity and the Brain.* Oxford: Pergamon

Balaz, M. A., Gustin, P., Cachiero, H., Miller, R. R. 1982. Blocking as a retrieval failure: reactivation of associations to a blocked stimulus. *Q. J. Exp. Psychol.* 34B: 99–113

Batson, J. D., Best, M. R., Phillips, D. L., Patel, H., Gilleland, K. R. 1986. Foraging on the radial-arm maze: effects of altering the reward at a target location. *Anim. Learn. Behav.* 14:241–48

Beatty, W. W., Shavalia, D. A. 1980. Rat spatial memory: resistance to retroactive interference at long retention intervals. *Anim. Learn. Behav.* 8:550–52

Beritoff, J. S. 1971. *Vertbrate Memory: Characteristics and Origin.* New York: Plenum

Berryman, R., Cumming, W. W., Nevin, J. A. 1963. Acquisition of delayed matching in the pigeon. *J. Exp. Anal. Behav.* 6:101–7

Blough, D. S. 1959. Delayed matching in the pigeon. *J. Exp. Anal. Behav.* 2:151–60

Boakes, R. 1984. *From Darwin to Behaviorism.* Cambridge: Cambridge Univ. Press

Bond, A. B., Cook, R. G., Lamb, M. R. 1981. Spatial memory and the performance of rats and pigeons in the radial-arm maze. *Anim. Learn. Behav.* 9:575–80

Bouton, M. E. 1984. Differential control by context in the inflation and reinstatement paradigms. *J. Exp. Psychol: Anim. Behav. Proc.* 10:56–74

Bouton, M. E. 1990. Context and retrieval in extinction and in other examples of interference in simple associative learning. In *Current Topics in Animal Learning: Brain, Emotion, and Cognition*, ed. L. W. Dachowski, C. F. Flaherty. Hillsdale, NJ: Erlbaum

Bouton, M. E., Bolles, R. C. 1979. Role of conditioned contextual stimuli in reinstatement of extinguished fear. *J. Exp. Psychol.: Anim. Behav. Proc.* 5:368–78

Bouton, M. E., King, D. A. 1986. Effect of context on performance to conditioned stimuli with mixed histories of reinforcement and nonreinforcement. *J. Exp. Psychol.: Anim. Behav. Proc.* 12:1–12

Bouton, M. E., Schwartzentruber, D. 1989. Slow reacquisition following extinction: context, encoding and retrieval mechanisms. *J. Exp. Psychol.: Anim. Behav. Proc.* 15:43–52

Campbell, B. A. 1967. Developmental studies of learning and motivation in infraprimate mammals. In *Early Behavior: Comparative and Developmental Approaches*, ed. H. W. Stevenson, E. H. Hess, H. L. Rheingold, pp. 43–72. New York: Wiley

Campbell, B. A., Ampuero, M. X. 1985. Dissociation of autonomic and behavioral components of conditioned fear during development in the rat. *Behav. Neurosci.* 99:1089–1102

Campbell, B. A., Spear, N. E. 1972. Ontogeny of memory. *Psychol. Rev.* 79: 215–36

Carew, T. J., Sahley, C. L. 1986. Invertebrate learning and memory: from behavior to molecules. *Annu. Rev. Neurosci.* 9:435–87

Castro, C. A., Paylor, R., Rudy, J. W. 1987. A developmental analysis of the learning and short-term memory processes mediating performance in conditional spatial discrimination problems. *Psychobiology* 15: 308–16

Collier, G. H. 1982. Determinants of choice. In *Nebraska Symposium on Motivation*, ed. D. J. Burnstein, pp. 69–127. Lincoln: Univ. Nebraska Press

Collier, G. H. 1986. The dialogue between the house economist and the resident physiologist. *Nutr. Behav.* 3:9–26

Collier, G. H., Rovee-Collier, C. K. 1983. An ecological perspective of reinforcement and motivation. In *Handbook of Behavioral Neurobiology*, ed. E. Satinoff, P. Teitelbaum, 6:427–41. New York: Plenum

Cook, R. G. 1980. Retroactive interference in pigeon short-term memory by a reduction in ambient illumination. *J. Exp. Psychol.: Anim. Behav. Proc.* 6:326–38

Dale, R. H. I. 1986. Spatial and temporal response patterns on the eight-arm radial maze. *Physiol. Behav.* 36:787–90

D'Amato, M. R. 1973. Delayed matching and short-term memory in monkeys. In *The Psychology of Learning and Motivation: Advances in Research and Theory*, ed. G. H. Bower, 7:227–69. New York: Academic

D'Amato, M. R., O'Neill, W. 1971. Effect of delay-interval illumination on matching behavior in the capuchin monkey. *J. Exp. Anal. Behav.* 15:327–33

Day, H. D., Han, Y. K. 1982. Time-dependent recovery from electroconvulsive shock-induced amnesia. *Physiol. Behav.* 29:387–91

Delameter, A., LoLordo, V. 1990. Event revaluation procedures and associative structures. In *Current Topics in Animal Learning: Brain, Emotion and Cognition*, ed. L. Dachowski, C. Flaherty. Hillsdale, NJ: Erlbaum

Denny, M. R. 1990. *Aversive Events and Behavior.* Hillsdale, NJ: Erlbaum

Deweer, B. 1986. Pretest cuing after forgetting of a food-motivated maze task in rats: synergistic action of context in reinforcement. *Anim. Learn. Behav.* 14:249–56

Deweer, B., Sara, S. J. 1985. Alleviation of forgetting by pretest contextual cuing in rats. *Ann. NY Acad. Sci.* 444:507–9

Deweer, B., Sara, S. J., Hars, B. 1980. Contextual cues and memory retrieval in rats: alleviation of forgetting by a pretest exposure to background stimuli. *Anim. Learn. Behav.* 8:265–72

Domjan, M. 1987. Animal learning comes of age. *Am. Psychol.* 42:556–64

Edhouse, W. V., White, K. G. 1988. Sources

of proactive interference in animal memory. *J. Exp. Psychol.: Anim. Behav. Proc.* 14: 56–70

Egger, M. D., Miller, N. E. 1962. Secondary reinforcement in rats as a function of information value and reliability of the stimulus. *J. Exp. Psychol.* 64:97–104

Etkin, M. W. 1972. Light produced interference in a delayed matching task with capuchin monkeys. *Learn. Motiv.* 3:313–24

Feigley, D. A., Spear, N. E. 1970. Effect of age and punishment condition on long-term retention by the rat of active- and passive-avoidance learning. *J. Comp. Physiol. Psychol.* 73:515–26

Flaherty, C. F. 1985. *Animal Learning and Cognition.* New York: Knopf

Gaffan, E. A., Hansel, M. C., Smith, L. E. 1983. Does reward depletion influence spatial memory performance? *Learn. Motiv.* 14:58–74

Gold, P. E. 1989. Neurobiological features common to memory modulation by many treatments. *Anim. Learn. Behav.* 17:94–100

Gordon, W. C. 1977. Susceptibility of a reactivated memory to the effects of strychnine: a time-dependent phenomenon. *Physiol. Behav.* 18:95–99

Gordon, W. C. 1981. Mechanisms of cue-induced retention enhancement. In *Information Processing in Animals: Memory Mechanisms,* ed. N. E. Spear, R. R. Miller. Hillsdale, NJ: Erlbaum

Gordon, W. C. 1983. The malleability of memory in animals. In *Animal Cognition and Behavior,* ed. R. L. Mellgren. New York: North Holland

Gordon, W. C., Feldman, D. T. 1978. Reactivation-induced interference in a short-term retention paradigm. *Learn. Motiv.* 9:164–17

Gordon, W. C., Spear, N. E. 1973. The effects of strychnine on recently acquired and reactivated passive avoidance memories. *Physiol. Behav.* 10:1071–75

Grant, D. S. 1981. Stimulus control of information processing in pigeon short-term memory. *Learn. Motiv.* 12:19–39

Grant, D. S. 1982. Stimulus control of information processing in rat short-term memory. *J. Exp. Psychol: Anim. Behav. Proc.* 8:154–64

Grant, D. S. 1988. Sources of visual interference in delayed matching-to-sample with pigeons. *J. Exp. Psychol.: Anim. Behav. Proc.* 14:368–75

Grant, D. S., Roberts, W. A. 1976. Sources of retroactive inhibition in pigeon short-term memory. *J. Exp. Psychol: Anim. Behav. Proc.* 2:1–16

Gregg, B., Kittrell, E. M. W., Domjan, M., Amsel, A. 1978. Ingestional aversion learning in preweanling rats. *J. Comp. Physiol. Psychol.* 92:785–95

Guenaire, C., Costa, J. C., Delacour, J. 1982. Conditionnement operant avec renforcement thermique chez le rat nouveau-né. *Physiol. Behav.* 29:419–24

Hall, G., Pearce, J. M. 1979. Latent inhibition of a CS during CS-US pairings. *J. Exp. Psychol.: Anim. Behav. Proc.* 5:31–42

Hamberg, J. M., Spear, N. E. 1978. Alleviation of forgetting of discrimination learning. *Learn. Motiv.* 9:466–76

Haroutunian, V., Riccio, D. C. 1979. Drug-induced "arousal" and the effectiveness of CS exposure in the reinstatement of memory. *Behav. Neural Biol.* 26:115–20

Hawkins, R. D., Kandel, E. R. 1984. Is there a cell-biological alphabet for simple forms of learning? *Psychol. Rev.* 91:375–91

Hearst, E. 1978. Stimulus relationships and feature selection in learning and behavior. In *Cognitive Processes in Animal Behavior,* ed. S. H. Hulse, H. Fowler, W. K. Honig, pp. 51–88. Hillsdale, NJ: Erlbaum

Hearst, E. 1984. Absence as information: some implications for learning, performance, and representational processes. In *Animal Cognition,* ed. H. L. Roitblat, T. G. Bever, H. S. Terrace, pp. 311–32. Hillsdale, NJ: Erlbaum

Hearst, E. 1987. Extinction reveals stimulus control: latent learning of feature-negative discriminations in pigeons. *J. Exp. Psychol.: Anim. Behav. Proc.* 13:52–64

Hendersen, R. E. 1985. Fearful memories: the motivational significance of forgetting. In *Affect, Conditioning and Cognition: Essays on the Determinants of Behavior,* ed. F. R. Brush, J. B. Overmier, pp. 43–53. Hillsdale, NJ: Erlbaum

Herman, L. M., Gordon, J. A. 1974. Auditory delayed matching in the bottlenose dolphin. *J. Exp. Anal. Behav.* 21:19–26

Hillman, B., Hunter, W. S., Kimble, G. A. 1953. The effect of drive level on the maze performance of the white rat. *J. Comp. Physiol. Psychol.* 46:87–89

Hinderliter, C. F., Webster, T., Riccio, D. D. 1975. Amnesia induced by hypothermia as a function of treatment test interval and recooling in rats. *Anim. Learn. Behav.* 3:257–21

Hinderliter, C. F., Misanin, J. R. 1988. Weanling and senescent rats process simultaneously presented odor and taste differently than young adults. *Behav. Neural. Biol.* 49:112–17

Hoffman, N., Maki, W. S. 1986. Two sources of proactive interference in spatial working memory: multiple effects of repeated trials on radial maze performance by rats. *Anim. Learn. Behav.* 14:65–72

Hoffmann, H. 1989. *Taste aversion conditioning in preweanling rats: examination of cue-consequence specificity in comparison* among gustatory aversions established by different reinforcers. PhD thesis. State Univ. New York, Binghamton

Hoffmann, H., Spear, N. E. 1988. Ontogenetic differences in conditioning of an aversion to a gustatory CS with peripheral US. *Behav. Neural. Biol.* 50:16–23

Holland, P. C. 1977. Conditioned stimulus as a determinant of the form of the Pavlovian-conditioned response. *J. Exp. Psychol.: Anim. Behav. Proc.* 3:77–104

Holland, P. C. 1984. Origins of behavior in Pavlovian conditioning. In *The Psychology of Learning and Motivation*, ed. G. Bower, 18:129–74. New York: Academic

Holland, P. C. 1989. Forms of memory in Pavlovian conditioning. In *Brain Organization and Memory: Cells, Systems and Circuits*, ed. J. L. McGaugh, N. M. Weinberger, G. Lynch. New York: Oxford Univ. Press

Honig, W. K. 1978. Studies of working memory in the pigeon. In *Cognitive Processes in Animal Behavior*, ed. S. H. Hulse, H. Fowler, W. K. Honig, pp. 211–48., Hillsdale, NJ: Erlbaum Assoc.

Honig, W. K. 1987. Memory interval distribution effects in pigeons. *Anim. Learn. Behav.* 15:6–14

Honig, W. K., James, P. H. R. 1971. *Animal Memory*. New York: Academic

Honig, W. K., Matheson, W. R., Dodd, P. W. D. 1984. Outcome expectancies as mediators for discriminative responding. *Can. J. Psychol.* 38:196–217

Honig, W. K., Thompson, R. K. R. 1982. Retrospective and prospective processing in animal working memory. *Psychol. Learn. Motiv.: Adv. Res. Theory* 16:239–83

Hull, C. L. 1943. *Principles of Behavior*. New York: Appleton-Century

Hunter, W. S. 1913. The delayed reaction in animals and children. *Behav. Monogr.* 2, No. 6

Ilersich, T. J., Mazmanian, D. S., Roberts, W. A. 1988. Foraging for covered and uncovered food on a radial maze. *Anim. Learn. Behav.* 16:388–94

Isaacson, R. L., Spear, N. E., eds. 1982. *The Expression of Knowledge*. New York: Plenum

Izquierdo, I. 1989. Different forms of post-training memory processing. *Behav. Neural Biol.* 51:171–202

Izquierdo, I., Dias, R. D. 1983. Memory as a state-dependent phenomenon: role of ACTH and epinephrine. *Behav. Neural. Biol.* 38:144–50

Jagielo, J. A., Zentall, T. R. 1986. Predictable long-delay matching-to-sample trials result in long-latency sample responding by pigeons. *Learn. Motiv.* 17:269–86

Jenkins, H. M., Barrera, F. J., Ireland, C., Woodside, B. 1978. Signal-centered action patterns of dogs in appetitive classical conditioning. *Learn. Motiv.* 9:272–96

Jenkins, H. M., Sainsbury, R. S. 1969. The development of stimulus control through differential reinforcement. In *Fundamental Issues in Associative Learning*, ed. N. J. Mackintosh, W. K. Honig, pp. 123–61. Halifax: Dalhousie Univ. Press

Jitsumori, M., Wright, A. A., Cook, R. G. 1988. Long-term proactive interference and novelty enhancement effects in monkey list memory. *J. Exp. Psychol.: Anim. Behav. Proc.* 14:146–54

Johanson, I. B., Hall, W. G. 1979. Appetitive learning in 1-day old rat pups. *Science* 205:419–21

Johanson, I. B., Hall, W. G., Palefone, J. M. 1984. Appetitive conditioning in neonatal rats: conditioned ingestive responding to stimuli compared with oral infusions of milk. *Dev. Psychobiol.* 17:357–81

Johnson, M. K., Hasher, L. 1987. Human learning and memory, *Annu. Rev. Psychol.* 38:631–68

Kamil, A. C., Roitblat, H. L. 1985. The ecology of foraging behavior: implications for animal learning and memory. *Annu. Rev. Psychol.* 36:141–70

Kamin, L. J. 1969. Predictability, surprise, attention, and conditioning. In *Punishment and Aversive Behavior*, ed. B. A. Campbell, R. M. Church, pp. 279–96. New York: Appleton-Century-Crofts

Kaplan, P. S., Hearst, E. 1982. Bridging temporal gaps between CS and US in autoshaping: insertion of other stimuli before, during and after CS. *J. Exp. Psychol.: Anim. Behav. Proc.* 8:187–203

Kasprow, W. J., Cachiero, H., Balaz, M. A., Miller, R. R. 1982. Reminder-induced recovery of associations to an overshadowed stimulus. *Learn. Motiv.* 13:155–66

Kasprow, W. J., Catterson, D., Schachtman, T. R., Miller, R. R. 1984. Attenuation of latent inhibition by postacquisition reminder. *Q. J. Exp. Psychol.* 36B:53–63

Kaufman, M. A., Bolles, R. C. 1981. A nonassociative aspect of overshadowing. *Bull. Psychonom. Soc.* 18:318–20

Kehoe, E. J. 1988. A layered network model of associative learning: learning to learn and configuration. *Psychol. Rev.* 95:411–33

Kendrick, D. F., Rilling, M. 1984. The role of interpolated stimuli in the retroactive interference of pigeon short-term memory. *Anim. Learn. Behav.* 12:391–401

Kendrick, D. F., Rilling, M., Stonebraker, T. B. 1981. Stimulus control of delayed matching in pigeons: directed forgetting. *J. Exp. Anal. Behav.* 36:241–51

Klein, S. B. 1972. Adrenal pituitary influence in reactivation of avoidance memory in the rat after intermediate intervals. *J. Comp. Physiol. Psychol.* 79:341–59

Klein, S. B., Mowrer, R. R. 1989a. *Contemporary Learning Theories*, Vol. 1: *Pavlovian Conditioning and the Status of Tradition.* Hillsdale, NJ: Erlbaum

Klein, S. B., Mowrer, R. R. 1989b. *Contemporary Learning Theories. Vol. 2: Instrumental Conditioning Theory and the Impact of Biological Constraints on Learning.* Hillsdale, NJ: Erlbaum

Kraemer, P. J. 1984. Forgetting of visual discriminations by pigeons. *J. Exp. Psychol.: Anim. Behav. Proc.* 10:530–42

Kraemer, P. J., Gilbert, M. E., Innis, N. K. 1983. The influence of cue type and configuration upon radial-maze performance in the rat. *Anim. Learn. Behav.* 11:373–80

Kraemer, P. J., Kraemer, E. L., Smoller, D. E., Spear, N. E. 1989. Enhancement of flavor aversion in weanling but not adult rats by prior conditioning to an odor. *Psychobiology* 17:34–42

Kraemer, P. J., Lariviere, N. A., Spear, N. E. 1988. Expression of a taste aversion conditioned with an odor-taste compound: overshadowing is relatively weak in weanlings and decreases over a retention interval in adults. *Anim. Learn. Behav.* 16:164–68

Kraemer, P. J., Roberts, W. A. 1984. The influence of flavor preexposure and test interval on conditioned taste aversion in the rat. *Learn. Motiv.* 15:259–78

Kucharski, D., Hall, W. G. 1987. New routes to early memories. *Science* 238: 786–88

Kucharski, D., Johanson, I. B., Hall, W. G. 1986. Unilateral olfactory conditioning in 6-day old rat pups. *Behav. Neural Biol.* 46:472–90

Kucharski, D., Richter, N. G., Spear, N. E. 1985. Conditioned aversion is promoted by memory of CS−. *Anim. Learn. Behav.* 13:143–51

Kucharski, D., Spear, N. E. 1985. Potentiation and overshadowing in preweanling and adult rats. *J. Exp. Psychol.: Anim. Behav. Proc.* II:15–34

LeVere, T. E., LeVere, N. D., Chappell, E. T., Hankey, P. 1984. Recovery of function after brain damage: on withdrawals from the memory bank. *Physiol. Psychol.* 12:275–79

Lewis, D. J. 1969. Sources of experimental amnesia. *Psychol. Rev.* 76:461–72

Linwick, D., Overmier, J. B., Peterson, G. B., Mertens, M. 1988. Interaction of memories and expectancies as mediators of choice behavior. *Am. J. Psychol.* 101:313–34

Lubow, R. E. 1973. Latent inhibition. *Psychol. Bull.* 79:398–407

MacDonald, S. E., Grant, D. S. 1987. Effects of signaling retention interval length on delayed matching-to-sample in pigeons. *J.*

Exp. Psychol.: Anim. Behav. Proc. 13:116–25

Mackintosh, N. J. 1975. A theory of attention: variations in the associability of stimuli with reinforcement. *Psychol. Rev.* 82:276–98

Mactutus, C. F., Ferek, J. M., George, C. A., Riccio, D. C. 1982. Hypothermia-induced amnesia for newly acquired and old reactivated memory: commonalities and distinctions. *Physiol. Psychol.* 10:79–95

Mactutus, C. F., Smith, R. L., Riccio, D. C. 1980. Extending the duration of ACTH-induced memory reactivation in an amnestic paradigm. *Physiol. Behav.* 24:541–46

Maki, W. S. 1985. Differential effects of electroconvulsive shock on concurrent spatial memories: "Old" memories are impaired while "new" memories are spared. *Behav. Neural Biol.* 43:162–77

Maki, W. S., Beatty, W., Berg, B., Lunn, R. 1980. *Spatial memory in rats: temporal release from proactive interference.* Presented at the Psychonom. Soc. Meet., St. Louis

Maki, W. S., Hoffman, N., Fritsche, B. 1986. Release from proactive interference by experimental amnesia: Electroconvulsive shock improves radial-arm maze performance in rats. *Behav. Neural Biol.* 45:300–18

Maki, W. S., Moe, J. C., Bierley, C. M. 1977. Short-term memory for stimuli, responses and reinforcers. *J. Exp. Psychol.: Anim. Behav. Proc.* 3:156–77

Matzel, L. D., Gladstein, L., Miller, R. R. 1988a. Conditioned excitation and conditioned inhibition are not mutually exclusive. *Learn. Motiv.* 19:99–121

Matzel, L. D., Held, F. P., Miller, R. R. 1988b. Information and expression of simultaneous and backward associations: implications for contiguity theory. *Learn. Motiv.* 19:317–44

Matzel, L. D., Schachtman, T. R., Miller, R. R. 1985. Recovery of an overshadowed association achieved by extinction of the overshadowing stimulus. *Learn. Motiv.* 16: 398–412

Mazmanian, D. S., Roberts, W. A. 1983. Spatial memory in rats under restricted viewing conditions. *Learn. Motiv.* 14:123–39

Mazur, J. E. 1986. Fixed and variable ratios and delays: further tests of an equivalence rule. *J. Exp. Psychol: Anim. Behav. Proc.* 12:116–24

McCoy, D. F., Serwatka, J. H., Miller, J. S., Kelly, K. S. 1984. *Inhibitory control in feature-negative discrimination learning.* Presented at 55th Annu. Meet. Eastern Psychol. Assoc., Baltimore, MD

McGaugh, J. L. 1983. Hormonal influences on memory. *Annu. Rev. Psychol.* 34:297–323

McGaugh, J. L. 1989. Involvement of hormonal and neuromodulatory systems in the regulation of memory storage. *Annu. Rev. Neurosci.* 12:255–87

McGaugh, J. L., Gold, P. E. 1976. Hormonal modulation of memory. In *Psychoendocrinology*, ed. R. B. Brush, S. Levine. New York: Academic

Miller, J. S., Jagielo, J. A., Gisquet-Verrier, P., Spear, N. E. 1989a. Backward excitatory conditioning can determine the role of the CS- in aversion learning. *Learn. Motiv.* 20:115–29

Miller, J. S., Jagielo, J. A., Spear, N. E. 1989b. Age-related differences in short-term retention of the separable elements of a conditioned odor aversion. *J. Exp. Psychol.: Anim. Behav. Proc.* In press

Miller, J. S., McDougall, S. A., Zolman, J. F. 1988. The ontogeny of the feature-positive effect in young chicks. *Anim. Learn. Behav.* 16:195–99

Miller, J. S., Spear, N. E. 1989. Ontogenetic differences in the short-term retention of Pavlovian conditioning. *Dev. Psychobiol.* 22:277–87

Miller, R. R., Grahame, N. J. 1990. Expression of learning. In *Current Topics in Animal Learning: Brain, Emotion and Cognition*, ed. C. F. Flaherty, L. W. Dachowski. Hillsdale, NJ: Erlbaum

Miller, R. R., Spear, N. E. 1985. *Information Processing in Animals: Conditioned Inhibition*. Hillsdale, NJ: Erlbaum

Misanin, J. R., Chubb, L. D., Quinn, S. A., Schweikert, G. E. 1974. An apparatus and procedure for effective instrumental learning of neonatal and infant rats. *Bull. Psychon. Soc.* 4:171–73

Misanin, J. R., Hinderliter, D. V. 1989. The role of home cage environmental stimuli in the facilitation of shock-motivated spatial discrimination learning in rat pups. *Dev. Psychobiol.* 129:140

Mishkin, M., Delacour, J. 1975. An analysis of short-term visual memory in the monkey. *J. Exp. Psychol.: Amin. Behav. Proc.* 1: 326–34

Moye, T. B., Rudy, J. S. 1985. Ontogenesis of learning. VI. Learned and unlearned responses to visual stimulation in the infanthood rat. *Dev. Psychobiol.* 18:395–409

Moye, T. B., Thomas, D. R. 1982. Effects of memory reactivation treatments on post-discrimination generalization performance in pigeons. *Anim. Learn. Behav.* 10:159–66

Myslivecek, J., Hassmannova, J. 1983. The development of inhibitory learning and memory in hooded and albino rats. *Behav. Brain Res.* 8:151–66

Olton, D. S., Collison, C. 1979. Intramaze cues and "odor trails" fail to direct choice behavior on an elevated maze. *Anim. Learn. Behav.* 7:221–23

Olton, D. S., Samuelson, R. J. 1976. Remembrance of places passed: spatial memory in rats. *J. Exp. Psychol.: Anim. Behav. Proc.* 2:97–116

Overmier, J. B. 1988. *Expectations: from animal laboratory to the clinic.* Presidential Address. Presented at Midwest. Psychol. Assoc. Meet., Chicago

Overton, D. A. 1982. Memory retrieval failures produced by changes in drug state. In *The Expression of Knowledge*, ed. R. L. Isaacson, N. E. Spear, pp. 113–40. New York: Plenum

Palfai, T. L., Wichlinski, L., Brown, O. 1983. The effect of reserpine, syrosingopine and guanethidine on the retention of discriminated escape reversal: Peripherally administered catecholamines cannot reverse the reserpine amnesia in this situation. *Behav. Neural Biol.* 38:120–26

Pearce, J. M., Hall, G. 1980. A model for Pavlovian learning: variations in the effectiveness of conditioned but not of unconditioned stimuli. *Psychol. Rev.* 6:532–52

Pelchat, M. L., Grill, H. J., Rozin, P., Jacobs, J. 1983. Quality of acquired responses to taste by *Rattus norvegus* depends on type of associative discomfort. *J. Comp. Psychol.* 97:140–53

Peterson, G. B., Trapold, M. A. 1980. Effects of altering outcome expectancies on pigeons' delayed conditional discrimination performance. *Learn. Motiv.* 11:267–88

Pfister, J., Alberts, J. 1987. *Rat pups' responses to cold and hot: preferences, regulation and learning.* Presented at Meet Int. Soc. Dev. Psychobiol., Toronto, Canada

Pinel, J. P. J., Treit, D., Wilkie, D. M. 1980. Stimulus control of defensive burying in the rat. *Learn. Motiv.* 11:150–63

Postman, L., Underwood, B. J. 1973. Critical issues in interference theory. *Mem. Cogn.* 1:19–40

Quartermain, D. 1982. Catecholamine involvement in memory retrieval processes. In *Changing Concepts of the Nervous System*, ed. A. Morrison, P. Strick, pp. 667–79. New York: Academic

Quartermain, D. 1983. The role of catecholamines in memory processing. In *The Physiological Basis of Memory*, ed. J. A. Deutsch, pp. 387–423. New York: Academic

Quartermain, D., Judge, M. E., Leo, P. 1988. Attenuation of forgetting by pharmacological stimulation of aminergic neurotransmitter systems. *Pharmacol. Biochem. Behav.* 30:77–81

Rescorla, R. A. 1968. Probability of shock in the presence and absence of CS in fear conditioning. *J. Comp. Physiol. Psychol.* 66:1–5

Rescorla, R. A. 1980. *Second-Order Conditioning.* Hillsdale, NJ: Erlbaum

Rescorla, R. A. 1988. Pavlovian conditioning: It's not what you think it is. *Am. Psychol.* 43:151–60

Rescorla, R. A., Heth, C. D. 1975. Reinstatement of fear to an extinguished conditioned stimulus. *J. Exp. Psychol.: Anim. Behav. Proc.* 1:88–96

Rescorla, R. A., Holland, P. C. 1982. Behavioral studies of associative learning in animals. *Annu. Rev. Psychol.* 33:265–308

Rescorla, R. A., Wagner, A. R. 1972. A theory of Pavlovian conditioning: variations in the effectiveness of reinforcement and nonreinforcement. In *Classical Conditioning II: Current Research and Theory,* ed. A. H. Black, W. F. Prokasy, pp. 64–99. New York: Appleton-Century-Crofts

Revusky, S. 1971. The role of interference in association over a delay. In *Animal Memory,* ed. W. K. Honig, P. H. R. James, pp. 155–214. New York: Academic

Reynolds, G. S. 1961. An analysis of interactions in a multiple schedule. *J. Exp. Anal. Behav.* 4:107–17

Riccio, D. C., Concannon, J. T. 1981. ACTH and the reminder phenomena. In *Endogenous Peptides and Learning and Memory Processes,* ed. J. L. Martinez, R. A. Jenson, R. B. Messing, H. Rigter, J. L. McGaugh, pp. 117–42. New York: Academic

Riccio, D. C., Richardson, R. 1984. The status of memory following experimentally induced amnesias: gone but not forgotten. *Physiol. Psychol.* 12:59–72

Riccio, D. C., Richardson, R., Ebner, D. L. 1984. Memory retrieval deficits based upon altered contextual cues: a paradox. *Psychol. Bull.* 96:152–65

Riccio, D. C., Rorbaugh, M., Hodges, L. A. 1968. Developmental changes in passive avoidance learning in the rat. *Dev. Psychobiol.* 1:108–11

Riccio, D. C., Spear, N. E. 1990. Changes in memory for aversively motivated learning. In *Aversive Events and Behavior,* ed. M. R. Denny. Hillsdale, NJ: Erlbaum

Richards, R. W., Sargent, D. M. 1983. The order of presentation of conditioned stimuli during extinction. *Anim. Learn. Behav.* 11: 229–36

Richardson, R., Riccio, D. C. 1990. Memory processes, ACTH, and extinction phenomena. In *Current Topics in Animal Learning: Brain, Emotion, and Cognition,* ed. L. Dachowski, C. F. Flaherty. Hillsdale, NJ: Erlbaum. In press

Richardson, R., Riccio, D. C., Devine, L. 1984. ACTH-induced recovery of extinguished avoidance responding. *Physiol. Psychol.* 12:184–92

Richardson-Klavehn, A., Bjork, R. A. 1988. Measures of memory. *Annu. Rev. Psychol.* 39:475–544

Rigter, H. 1978. Attenuation of amnesia in rats by systematically administered enkephalins. *Science* 200:83–85

Rigter, H., van Riezen, H., deWeid, D. 1974. The effects of ACTH- and vasopressin-analogs on CO_2-induced retrograde amnesia in rats. *Physiol. Behav.* 13:381–88

Rilling, M., Kendrick, D. F., Stonebraker, T. B. 1984. Directed forgetting in context. *Psychol. Learn. Motiv. Adv. Res. Theory* 18:175–98

Roberts, W. A. 1980. Distribution of trials and intertrial retention in delayed matching to sample with pigeons. *J. Exp. Psychol.: Anim. Behav. Proc.* 6:217–37

Roberts, W. A. 1981. Retroactive inhibition in rat spatial memory. *Anim. Learn. Behav.* 9:566–74

Roberts, W. A., Dale, R. H. I. 1981. Remembrance of places lasts: proactive inhibition and patterns of choice in rat spatial memory. *Learn. Motiv.* 12:261–81

Roberts, W. A., Grant, D. S. 1976. Studies of short-term memory in the pigeon using the delayed matching-to-sample procedure. In *Processes of Animal Memory,* ed. D. L. Medin, W. A. Roberts, R. T. Davis, pp. 79–112. Hillsdale, NJ: Erlbaum

Roberts, W. A., Grant, D. S. 1978. An analysis of light-induced retroactive inhibition in pigeon short-term memory. *J. Exp. Psychol.: Anim. Behav. Proc.* 4:219–36

Roberts, W. A., Kraemer, P. J. 1982. Some observations of the effects of intertrial interval and delay on delayed matching to sample in pigeons. *J. Exp. Psychol.: Anim. Behav. Proc.* 8:342–53

Roberts, W. A., Mazmanian, D. S., Kraemer, P. J. 1984. Directed forgetting in monkeys. *Anim. Learn. Behav.* 12:29–40

Roberts, W. A., Van Veldhuizen, N. 1985. Spatial memory in pigeons on the radial maze. *J. Exp. Psychol.: Anim. Behav. Proc.* 11:241–60

Roitblat, H. L., Scopatz, R. A. 1983. Sequential effects in pigeon delayed matching-to-sample performance. *J. Exp. Psychol.: Anim. Behav. Proc.* 9:202–21

Rovee-Collier, C. 1989. The "memory system" of prelinguistic infants. In *The Development and Neural Bases of Higher Cognitive Functions,* ed. A. Diamond. New York: Oxford. In press

Rovee-Collier, C., Hayne, H. 1987. Reactivation of infant memory: implications for cognitive development. *Adv. Child Dev. Behav.* 20:185–238

Rudy, J. W., Cheatle, M. D. 1979. Ontogeny of associative learning: acquisition of odor aversions by neonatal rats. In *Ontogeny of*

Learning and Memory, ed. N. E. Spear, B. A. Campbell, pp. 157–88. Hillsdale, NJ: Erlbaum

Rudy, J. W., Vogt, M. B., Hyson, R. L. 1984. A developmental analysis of the rat's learned reaction to gustatory and auditory stimulation in Comparative Perspectives on the Development of Memory, ed. R. Kail, N. E. Spear, pp. 181–208. Hillsdale, NJ: Erlbaum

Salmon, D. P., D'Amato, M. R. 1981. Note on delay-interval illumination effects on retention in monkeys (Cebus apella). J. Exp. Anal. Behav. 36:381–85

Santi, A. 1984. The trial spacing effect in delayed matching-to-sample by pigeons is dependent upon the illumination condition during the intertrial interval. Can. J. Psychol. 38:154–65

Santi, A., Roberts, W. A. 1985. Prospective representation: the effects of varied mapping of sample stimuli to comparison stimuli and differential trial outcomes on pigeons' working memory. Anim. Learn. Behav. 13: 103–8

Santucci, A., Schroeder, H., Riccio, D. C. 1987. Suppression of ACTH release blocks memory recovery from hypothermia-induced retrograde amnesia in rats. Presented Meet. Eastern Psychol. Assoc., Arlington, VA

Sara, S. J., Deweer, B. 1982. Memory retrieval enhanced by amphetamine after a long retention interval. Behav. Neural Biol. 36:146–60

Schachtman, T. R., Brown, A. M., Miller, R. R. 1985. Reinstatement-induced recovery of a taste-LiCl association following extinction. Anim. Learn. Behav. 13:223–27

Schachtman, T. R., Gee, J. L., Kasprow, W. J., Miller, R. R. 1983. Reminder-induced recovery from blocking as a function of the number of compound trials. Learn. Motiv. 14:154–64

Schneiderman, N. 1972. Response system divergencies in aversive classical conditioning. In Classical Conditioning II: Current Research and Theory, ed. A. H. Black, W. F. Prokasy, pp. 341–76. New York: Appleton-Century-Crofts

Shettleworth, S. J. 1989. Animals foraging in the lab: problems and promises. J. Exp. Psychol.: Anim. Behav. Proc. 15:81–87

Smith, G. J., Spear, N. E. 1981a. Home environmental stimuli facilitate learning of shock escape spatial discrimination in rats 7–11 days of age. Behav. Neural. Biol. 31: 360–65

Smith, G. J., Spear, N. E. 1981b. Role of proactive interference in infantile forgetting. Anim. Learn. Behav. 9:371–80

Smotherman, W. P. 1985. Glucocorticoid and other hormonal substrates of conditioned taste aversions. Ann. NY Acad. Sci. 443: 126–44

Solheim, G. S., Hensler, J. G., Spear, N. E. 1980. Age-dependent contextual effects on short-term active avoidance retention in rats. Behav. Neural Biol. 30:250–59

Spear, N. E. 1967. Retention of reinforcer magnitude. Psychol. Rev. 74:216–34

Spear, N. E. 1971. Forgetting as retrieval failure. In Animal Memory, ed. W. K. Honig, P. H. R. James, pp. 45–109. New York: Academic

Spear, N. E. 1973. Retrieval of memory in animals. Psychol. Rev. 80:163–94

Spear, N. E. 1976. Retrieval of memories. In Handbook of Learning and Cognitive Processes, Attention and Memory, ed. W. K. Estes, 4:17–90. Hillsdale, NJ: Erlbaum

Spear, N. E. 1978. The Processing of Memories: Forgetting and Retention. Hillsdale, NJ: Erlbaum

Spear, N. E. 1979. Memory storage factors in infantile amnesia. Psychol. Learn. Motiv. 13:91–154

Spear, N. E. 1981. Extending the domain of memory retrieval. In Information Processing in Animals: Memory Mechanisms, ed. N. E. Spear, R. R. Miller, pp. 341–78. Hillsdale, NJ: Erlbaum

Spear, N. E. 1984a. Behaviors that indicate memory. Can. J. Psychol. 38 (Spec. Ed.):348–67

Spear, N. E. 1984b. Ecologically determined dispositions control the ontogeny of learning and memory. In Comparative Perspectives on the Development of Memory, ed. R. Kail, N. E. Spear, pp. 325–58. Hillsdale, NJ: Erlbaum

Spear, N. E., Hamberg, J. M., Bryan, R. G. 1980. Effect of retention interval on recently acquired or recently reactivated memories. Learn. Motiv. 11:456–75

Spear, N. E., Molina, J. C. 1987. The role of sensory modality in the ontogeny of stimulus selection. In Perinatal Development: A Psychobiological Perspective, ed. N. Krasnegor, E. M. Blass, M. A. Hofer, W. P. Smotherman, pp. 83–110. Orlando: Academic

Spear, N. E., Parsons, P. 1976. Alleviation of forgetting by reactivation treatment: a preliminary analysis of the ontogeny of memory processing. In Processes in Animal Memory, ed. D. Medin, W. Roberts, R. Davis, pp. 135–66. Hillsdale, NJ: Erlbaum

Spear, N. E., Rudy, J. W. 1990. Tests of learning and memory in the developing rat. In Developmental Psychobiology: Current Methodological and Conceptual Issues, ed. H. N. Shair, G. A. Barr, M. A. Hofer. New York: Oxford Univ. Press

Spear, N. E., Smith, G. J. 1978. Alleviation

of forgetting in neonatal rats. *Dev. Psychobiol.* 11:513–30

Spear, N. E., Kucharski, D., Miller, J. 1989. The CS− effect in simple conditioning and stimulus selection during development. *Anim. Learn Behav.* 17:70–82

Spence, K. W. 1958. Behavior theory and selective learning. In *Nebraska Symposium on Motivation,* ed. M. R. Jones, pp. 73–107. Lincoln: Univ. Nebraska Press

Spetch, M. L., Edwards, C. A. 1986. Spatial memory in pigeons *(Columbia livia)* in an open-field feeding environment. *J. Comp. Physiol. Psychol.* 100:266–78

Springer, A. D. 1975. Vulnerability of skeletal and autonomic manifestation of memory in the rat to electroconvulsive shock. *J. Comp. Physiol. Psychol.* 88: 890–903

Stehouwer, D. J., Campbell, B. A. 1980. Ontogeny of passive avoidance: role of task demands in development of species-typical behaviors. *Dev. Psychobiol.* 14:385–98

Steinert, P. A., Infurna, R. N., Jardula, M. F., Spear, N. E. 1979. Effects of CS concentration on long delay taste aversion learning in preweanling and adult rats. *Behav. Neural Biol.* 8:10–16

Stonebraker, T. B., Rilling, M. 1981. Control of delayed matching-to-sample performance using directed forgetting techniques. *Anim. Learn. Behav.* 9:196–20

Suzuki, S., Augerinos, G., Black, A. H. 1980. Stimulus control of spatial behavior on the eight-arm maze in rats. *Learn. Motiv.* 11:1–18

Tait, R. W., Saladin, M. E. 1986. Concurrent development of excitatory and inhibitory associations during backward conditioning. *Anim. Learn. Behav.* 14:133–37

Thomas, D. R. 1981. Studies of long-term memory in the pigeon. In *Information Processing in Animals: Memory Mechanisms,* ed. N. E. Spear, R. R. Miller, pp. 257–90. Hillsdale, NJ: Erlbaum

Thompson, R. F. 1986. The neurobiology of learning and memory. *Science* 233:941–47

Thompson, R. F. 1989. The essential memory trace circuit and the essential reinforcement system for a basic form of associative learning. See Archer & Nilsson 1989, pp. 251–64

Timberlake, W. 1983. The functional organization of appetitive behavior: behavior systems and learning. In *Advances in the Analysis of Behavior:* Vol. 3. *Biological Factors in Learning,* ed. M. D. Zeiler, P. Harzem, pp. 177–221. Chichester, England: Wiley

Timberlake, W., Lucas, G. A. 1989. Behavior systems and learning: from misbehavior to general principles. In *Contemporary Learning Theories: Instrumental Conditioning Theory and the Impact of Biological Constraints on Learning,* ed. S. B. Klein, R. R. Mower. Hillsdale, NJ: Erlbaum. In press

Timberlake, W., Wahl, G., King, D. 1982. Stimulus and response contingencies in the misbehavior of rats. *J. Exp. Psychol.: Anim. Behav. Proc.* 8:62–85

Tranberg, D. K., Rilling, M. 1980. Delay-interval illumination changes interfere with pigeon short-term memory. *J. Exp. Anal. Behav.* 33:39–49

Underwood, B. J. 1949. *Experimental Psychology: An Introduction.* New York: Appleton Century Crofts

Urcuioli, P. J., Zentall, T. R. 1986. Retrospective coding in pigeons' delayed matching-to-sample. *J. Exp. Psychol.: Anim. Behav. Proc.* 12:69–77

Wallace, J., Steinert, P. A., Scobie, S. R., Spear, N. E. 1980. Stimulus modality and short-term memory in rats. *Anim. Learn. Behav.* 8:10–16

Wasserman, E. A. 1981. Response evocation in autoshaping: contributions of cognitive and comparative-evolutionary analyses to an understanding of directed action. In *Autoshaping and Conditioning Theory,* ed. C. M. Locurto, H. S. Terrace, J. Gibbon, pp. 21–54. New York: Academic

Wasserman, E. A., Grosch, J., Nevin, J. A. 1982. Effects of signaled retention intervals on pigeon short-term memory. *Anim. Learn. Behav.* 10:330–38

White, K. G., Bunnell-McKenzie, J. 1985. Potentiation of delayed matching with variable delays. *Anim. Learn. Behav.* 13:397–402

Wilkie, D. M., Spetch, M. L. 1981. Pigeons' delayed matching-to-sample errors are not always due to forgetting. *Behav. Anal. Lett.* 1:317–23

Williams, D. A., Travis, G. M., Overmier, J. B. 1986. Within-compound associations modulate the relative effectiveness of differential and Pavlovian conditioned inhibition procedures. *J. Exp. Psychol.: Anim. Behav. Proc.* 12:351–62

Wright, A. A., Urcuioli, P. J., Sands, S. F. 1986. Proactive interference in animal memory. In *Theories of Animal Memory,* ed. D. F. Kendrick, M. E. Rilling, M. R. Denny, pp. 101–25. Hillsdale, NJ: Erlbaum

Yoerg, S. I., Kamil, A. C. 1982. Response strategies in the radial arm maze: running around in circles. *Anim. Learn. Behav.* 10:530–34

Zener, K. 1937. The significance of behavior accompanying conditioned salivary secretion for theories of the conditioned response. *Am. J. Psychol.* 50:384–403

Zentall, T. R., Hogan, D. E., Howard, M. M., Moore, B. S. 1978. Delayed matching in the pigeon: effect on performance on sample-specfic observing responses and differential delay behavior. *Learn. Motiv.* 9:202–18.

Annu. Rev. Psychol. 1990. 41:213–41

PSYCHOLOGY IN JAPAN

Jyuji Misumi

Nara University, Japan

Mark F. Peterson

Management Area, Texas Tech University, Lubbock, Texas 79409

CONTENTS

0066-4308/90/0201-0213$02.00

INTRODUCTION

After World War II, Japanese psychological research began to deal with many varied topics, a breadth of interest that eventually led to multiple subdivisions within psychology. In more recent times, many interdisciplinary studies are conducted with related sciences. However, these studies tend to lose their "psychological" character. The subdivision of psychological research and its combination with other fields has raised such questions as "What is psychology?" and "What is the foundation of modern psychology?" Soon after World War II, Taturo Yatabe (1956), in his *Introduction to Psychology,* divided the results of modern psychology into "Mental Morphology," "Mental Physiology," and "Mental Ecology."

Misumi (1985) also proposed a general system for classifying experimental social psychology, group dynamics, and especially leadership behavior research. His paradigm includes "General Behavioral Morphology" (GBM), "Specific Behavioral Morphology" (SBM), "General Behavioral Dynamics" (GBD), and "Specific Behavioral Dynamics (SBD). While GBD includes a large number of general psychological studies dealing with perception and learning, SBD includes experimental psychological research conducted in different fields of applied psychology. The results of behavioral dynamics research have provided the grounds for redefining and refining concepts such as "mind," which originally was only used in its commonsense meaning in early GBM theory. Refinements in such basic concepts as "mind" led to the redefinition of concepts within the SBM fields that emphasize basically individual, environmental, and developmental differences. As developments in these four research areas influence each other, there is a need for balanced, coordinated progress.

The methodology of psychological research has been strongly influenced by modern cognitive psychology. It has largely revised the old S-R paradigm by treating the independent variable (Stimulus S) not as a purely nonbehavioral variable, but instead as a quasi-nonbehavioral independent variable (Quasi-Stimulus S'). This change in emphasis led Markus & Zajonc (1985) to propose the O-S-O-R paradigm and Misumi (1988) his O-S'-O-R paradigm. According to the latter, S' is a stimulus interpreted and modified by the organism, rather than S, which directly influences the R (Response) under the control of O (Organism).

J. B. Watson, the father of the S-R paradigm, was a graduate student at the University of Chicago when G. H. Mead (1934) proposed his behaviorism, paving the way for modern Symbolic Interactionism. The ideas that initiated the O-S'-O-R paradigm come rather close to the ideas of Mead and his disciples. It is to be hoped that in the 21st century we will witness a return to the source of this early 20th-century behaviorism.

Topics and Reviewers

Psychology in Japan has previously been reviewed by Tanaka (1966), Tanaka & England (1972), and Omura (1988). Consequently, the present chapter focuses on the period from 1970 until now, reviewing 11 main areas in psychology. The following list identifies these research areas and the scholars who have summarized the areas for the present review: Perception: Hiroto Katori & Takeo Watanabe, University of Tokyo; cognition and understanding: Giyoo Hatano, Dokkyo University (Tokyo); memory: Takao Umemoto, Konan Women's University; the Item Response Theory (IRT) model: Sukeyori Siba, University of Tokyo; developmental psychology: Nobumoto Tajima, Tokyo University of Foreign Studies; animal psychology: Naosuke Itoigawa, Osaka University; social psychology: Yoshiaki Nagata, Gakushuin University (Tokyo); prosocial behavior: Seisoh Sukemune, Hiroshima University; leadership research: Mark F. Peterson, Texas Tech University (Lubbock); educational psychology: Akimichi Omura, University of Tokyo; clinical psychology: Takao Murase, University of Tokyo; comparative cultural research: Chikio Hayashi, University of the Air (Tokyo) and Tatzuzo Suzuki, The Institute of Statistical Mathematics (Tokyo).

Associations and Journals

Several academic associations have contributed to the present status of psychology in Japan. Except as noted below, the journals published by these associations are in Japanese. The first psychological laboratory was established at Tokyo University in 1903. An academic journal, *Psychological Research* has been regularly published by that laboratory since then. Since 1954, an English version of this journal, *Japanese Psychological Research* has been published. Another journal, *Psychological Monographs,* devotes each issue to a different subject. The Japanese Psychological Association, which includes basic psychology and applied psychology, is the largest psychological association in Japan, with 4450 members.

Founded in 1931, the Japanese Applied Psychology Association publishes a journal in Japanese, *Research in Applied Psychology,* and a handbook, the *Industrial Psychology Handbook.*

The Japanese Society for Animal Psychology was established in 1933. It has published 38 volumes of the *Annual of Animal Psychology* and now has 500 members.

The Japanese Group Dynamics Association, founded in 1949, has 610 members. Its 36th annual meeting was held in October 1988. It publishes a quarterly journal, the *Journal of Experimental Social Psychology*. It also publishes edited works such as *Group Dynamics in Japan* (Misumi 1973).

The next-oldest association is the Japanese Educational Psychology Association, which was founded in 1952 and has 3627 members. It publishes a quarterly journal, *Educational Psychological Research,* and the *Educational Psychology Annual Report*. The Psychologia Society was founded in 1957. One of its major goals has been to promote psychological research exchanges between Japan and other countries. Accordingly, it publishes the English language journal *Psychologia*. This journal and the English edition of *Japanese Psychological Research* provide the best basis for information exchange between Japanese and non-Japanese psychology researchers.

Founded in 1960, the Japanese Social Psychology Association now has 868 members. Its first annual publication, *Annals of Social Psychology,* which began publication at the Association's foundation, was interrupted after its 21st issue and replaced by a quarterly journal, *Social Psychological Research*. The Association also publishes a short periodical pamphlet, *Social Psychology in Japan*.

The Japanese Criminal Psychology Association was founded in 1963. It numbers 793 members. Its main publications are a quarterly journal, *Criminal Psychology Research* (in Japanese), and occassional reports such as *Research Project on Recent Crimes and Delinquency in Japan* (in Japanese), and the *Catalogue of Publications in Criminal Psychology in Japan*.

The Japanese Association of Education for the Handicapped was founded in 1963. Since 1964 it has published a journal, *Research in Education for the Handicapped*. The founding of the Japanese Clinical Psychology Association goes back to 1964; it now has 2900 members. The most recent issue of its publication, *Clinical Psychology Research,* is Volume 18 (1989). A second clinical psychology association, the Japanese Association of Clinical Psychology is a newly founded association with 2980 members.

The Organizational Science Association's beginning goes back to 1959. It publishes a journal under the title of *Organizational Science*.

The Japanese Psychonomic Society is a relatively new association. It was established in 1981. The latest issue of its publication, *The Japanese Journal of Psychonomic Science,* is Volume 6. The society has 450 members.

One of the newest associations is the Industrial and Organizational Psychology Association, founded in 1985.

SENSATION AND PERCEPTION

The study of sensation and perception in Japan is relatively advanced compared to other specialties. In 1981, the Japanese Psychonomic Society was founded to develop and promote basic psychological research including the study of sensation and perception. Some studies have been published in internationally established journals. Many others have been published in Japanese journals such as the *Japanese Journal of Psychonomic Science*, the *Japanese Journal of Psychology*, and *Japanese Psychological Research*. Since many of the articles published in the former two journals are written in Japanese, they may not be well known to foreign researchers in spite of their quality.

The studies may be roughly divided into five fields.

Brightness, Color, and Form: Various aspects of brightness have been closely examined by using psychophysical methods (e.g. Mitsuboshi 1986). Some studies of color have been conducted using psychophysical methods and measurements (e.g. Ayama & Ikeda 1986). The affective aspects of color (Nakagawa et al 1984) have been examined. Visual illusions have been actively examined in Japan for a long time. Recent examples are studies of geometrical illusions by Imai (1984) and of illusory contours by Sato (1983) and Watanabe & Oyama (1989). Nozawa (1982) has reviewed form perception from a field theory perspective.

Spatial Vision: The relation of depth perception to depth cues such as vergence movements (Inui et al 1984) and binocular disparity (Binguishi 1983) have been closely examined. Models of visual space have been built or improved beginning from Luneberg's Non-Euclidean model (e.g. Higashiyama 1984).

Motion Perception: Traditional phenomenological studies have been conducted (e.g. Sumi 1984) and physiological studies have been done (e.g. Funakawa & Aiba 1987). Recently, some researchers have used computational models (e.g. Ishiguchi 1988). Nakatani has built a model of motion perception (1988) in terms of correlation.

Auditory Perception: Auditory "tau effects" of temporal intervals on pitch and speech have been systematically investigated (Shigeno 1986). Otherwise, a wide range of studies have been conducted on topics such as auditory masking (e.g. Miyazaki & Sasaki 1981), speech perception (e.g. Nakajima 1981), the perception of temporal intervals (Nakajima et al 1988), and loudness (Namba et al 1978).

Development of Perception: The mechanism of perceptual development has been clarified by observing the development process of the early blind who regained sight after an operation (Umezu et al 1987), by examining the effect of optical transposition created by up-down or left-right reversed goggles (e.g. Amemiya 1983; Makino 1984), and by exploring infant vision (Katori 1984; Shimojo & Held 1987).

Visual Information Processing: Studies to analyze the structure of a pattern have been conducted by Imai (1977) and Ichikawa (1985). Various other phenomena have been examined, such as mental rotation (Sekiyama 1987; Suzuki & Nakata 1988), same-different tasks (Watanabe 1988), and visual masking (Kikuchi 1981).

COGNITION AND UNDERSTANDING

Cognitive studies are becoming more and more popular in Japan. The Japanese Cognitive Science Society has about 800 members, a little less than half of whom are psychologists. A number of these psychologists have published papers in American and European journals, some of which have been cited often. However, their worldwide contribution is still very limited.

One promising direction for enhancing their contributions is to study those cognitive practices that are not readily accessible to Westerners, those that are unique to or especially salient in the Japanese culture. Another will be to propose ideas and perspectives that most Western psychologists have not yet recognized because of their shared cultural, methodological, and theoretical biases.

Cognitive Practices Specific to the Japanese Culture

Studies in reading and writing using Japan's very distinctive orthography, which uses kanji (Chinese characters) and kana (syllabaries) in combination, have been informative. Experimental studies (for reviews see Goryo 1987; Kaiho & Nomura 1983) have found that kanji-transcribed words take longer to pronounce than kana-transcribed words. However, kanji words are semantically more transparent than kana words. These results suggest that the processes through which phonetic codes and meanings are retrieved from strings of characters vary between orthographies and different types of written scripts. Clinical studies showing selective impairments of kanji or kana among dyslexic and alexic patients strongly suggest that kanji and kana words are not only processed differently, but also are organized differently in the brain (Yamadori 1986). To establish a universal taxonomy of patients with lexical disorders, these Japanese studies must be taken into account.

Another good example of a uniquely Japanese cultural practice is mathematical calculation based on *soroban* (abacus). Hatano and his associates (Hatano 1988) have suggested that experts in abacus operation use a "mental abacus" for calculation to increase speed. Hishitani (1987), using an improved method for comparing forward and backward reproductions of series of digits, and Hatta & Ikeda (1985) and Ikeda & Hatta (1986), by examining hemispheric dominance in calculation, offered strong support for the acquisition of the mental abacus through experience. Together, these studies have shown that there are multiple ways of doing mental calculations and becoming skillful at them.

Japanese Perspectives on Understanding

Several Japanese psychologists (e.g. Sayeki 1978) have conceptualized understanding based on an anthropomorphic epistemology. Anthropomorphism here means personifying a nonhuman object and/or projecting a "self" onto the object, so that the knowledge about a human/self can be transferred by analogy to the object.

A prediction from this anthropomorphism is that one can readily solve a problem without necessarily using logical reasoning. Instead, one can place an imaginary "self" in the problem situation. This prediction has been confirmed by Sayeki (1980) for Wason's four-card problems (though contradicted by Koyazu et al 1984), by Tsukano (1985) for missing addend problems, and by Ueno et al (1986) for number conservation tasks.

Another prediction is that personification or animism is adaptive. It tends to induce educated guesses. Even adults rely on it as a heuristic or fall-back strategy. Studies of everyday biology (as against scientific) (Inagaki 1989) and personifying physics (Ueno 1987) have lent support.

Anthropomorphic epistemology assumes that one's understanding is facilitated through dialogue. Interacting with others requires people to coordinate different perspectives. Inagaki (1982) and Miyake (1986) have presented strong cases for this assumption.

MEMORY

The development of memory psychology in Japan has always shown trends similar to those of world psychology. After some substantial, original studies in the fields of verbal learning in the 1950s and 1960s (Umemoto 1959, 1974), memory research in Japan has turned to information theory models, and then to cognitive theories like those in other countries. Short-term memory (STM) was one of the most popular topics in memory psychology during the 1970s. A symposium entitled "Mechanisms of short-term memory" organized by Murdock and Umemoto, with participation by Tulving, Sperling, Murdock, and Anokhin as speakers, and Kintsch and Norman as discussants, held at the 20th International Congress of Psychology in 1972, had a strong impact on memory psychologists in Japan. The *Japanese Psychological*

Review published a special issue (1976, Vol. 19, No. 1) on STM with eight papers on coding, rehearsal, organization, retrieval, the role of image, relationships to information theory, and the development of STM, written by young psychologists. Other topics, such as levels of processing, encoding specificity, priming, sensory memory, working memory, sentence memory, and semantic memory, gradually gained the interest of researchers.

Three influential books on memory have been published since 1980 during the surge of cognitive psychology. One is a book entitled *Memory* (1982), edited by Koyazu. It contains nine chapters covering sensory memory, short-term memory, long-term memory, working memory, memory representation (including structure and image), nonverbal memory (visual, auditory, tactile, and olfactory memory), control of memory information, memory dynamics, and mathematical models. These chapters are well written, with many evaluative comments about current studies. The second book is entitled *Memory and Knowledge* (1985), edited also by Koyazu. It consists of an introductory chapter by Koyazu, and nine chapters covering such topics as memory, cognition, attention, retrieval, comprehension, schema, and simulations. In the introductory chapter, Koyazu interpreted memory from an evolutionary point of view, and tried to integrate neuropsychological findings with representational ones. The third book, entitled *Episodic Memory* (1988), edited by Ohta, consists of 10 chapters on episodic memory, coding, organization and schema, retrieval, interference and facilitation, image, context, working memory, meta-memory, and memory and consciousness. Priming effects are discussed in Chapter 5 and in the last chapter. The former focuses on long-range priming as found by Kolers (1976), and the latter focuses on short-range priming as studied by Posner (1975).

In these books on memory, citations from Japanese studies are not frequent. The primary contributions from Japanese researchers are studies using kanji and kana. For example, kanji usually have two different pronunciation systems: *kun*, the Japanese pronunciation, and *on*, the Chinese system. There is a formal order for writing kanji. The complex properties of kanji allow an experimenter to manipulate variables that could not be studied by researchers in other countries. The *Information Processing Psychology of Kanji* by Kaiho & Nomura (1983) has contributed indirectly to the development of memory psychology in Japan. Many interesting findings in kanji memory are noted.

ITEM RESPONSE THEORY (IRT) RESEARCH

Samejima (1962) presented a model of IRT to evaluate the scalability of items. She also described the basic idea of the Graded Response Model (Samejima 1969). For over 10 years after that paper, no substantial IRT research was reported in Japan except for a study conducted by Shiba (1969).

He analyzed the relationship between test structures described using IRT models and the amount of information per subject transmitted by test scores.

Most IRT studies in Japan have appeared in the last decade. Shiba (1978) applied IRT to evaluate the unidimensionality of about 400 items comprising a vocabulary test. This scale is used to measure a broad range of language ability from the level of preschool children to that of adults (Samejima 1980). The scale has been extended further in order to measure language ability in early childhood (Shiba et al 1984) and in infants (Takei & Ogino 1983). These extended scales measure language ability indirectly by using mothers' answers to questions about their children's verbal and cognitive behaviors. Item parameter estimates for each question using the IRT model indicated that the discriminating power of each question was impressively high.

Several papers have been published concerning test equating procedures. Haebara (1980) formulated a general procedure for equating logistic ability scales. The procedure uses a loss function and an optimization process. He showed the advantage of a weighted least squares method in applications to achievement and intelligence scales. Noguchi (1986) proposed methods for equating scales by using ability estimates or response patterns of "anchor examinees" who completed more than two alternate test forms. Toyoda (1986), considering the sampling distribution of the maximum likelihood estimates of ability of anchor examinees, proposed an equating method using information functions. The advantage of his method in reducing the error of estimate was shown by a simulation study. Hattori (1985, 1986) proposed methods for equating several Rasch scales by means of the weighted least squares technique. Some advantages of his methods were reported.

Shiba et al (1978) studied the effect of a stratified adaptive test. They prepared booklets in which items were ordered by difficulty level into strata. An empirical study showed that the test is highly efficient for measuring a wide range of ability. A short version of this stratified adaptive test, used as a pretest to measure the language ability of overseas Japanese pupils, worked very well (Shiba et al 1979). A computer-assisted adaptive test showed higher efficiency than a conventional paper-pencil test (Shibayama et al 1987).

Other interesting directions in Japanese IRT research include: a procedure to estimate the parameters in the logistic model as a full realization of the general Baysian hierarchical method (Shigemasu & Fujimori 1985) and an adaptive questionnaire for measuring the language ability of children (Taira et al 1987).

DEVELOPMENTAL PSYCHOLOGY

One of the fundamental issues in developmental psychology is how social processes are related to psychological processes (e.g. Wertsch 1985a,b). In fact, human cognitive activity has been considered to be both embedded and constituted within sociocultural activities. Most developmental psychologists seem to agree that the analysis of social factors will play an important role in attempts to explain the emergence of individual psychological phenomena. In spite of that notion, we have often failed to comprehend the interaction of psychological processes with social factors. This failure is evident both in cognitive socialization studies relating individual differences in cognitive development to environmental factors (Azuma et al 1981) and in cross-cultural research investigating the effects of socioeconomic status, urbanization, and schooling on Piagetian cognitive development (Hatano et al 1980). The reason for this failure seems to lie mainly in methodological problems (Tajima & Usui 1980). It is difficult for us to deal with both individual and social factors together using traditional research methods. Besides, it is difficult to obtain the process-oriented information that really represents the dynamics of development.

Microgenetic View

When we need process-oriented data, the direct interaction process between a subject and his/her environment should be our main focus. Such an analytic base is needed to maintain the ecological validity of cognitive activity in the individual. The "microgenetic method" employing a single subject design seems to be very useful for understanding the dynamics of cognitive development (Tajima 1988). This method refers to the gradual course of skill/knowledge acquisition during the social interaction session. It is used to show how a psychological process develops in an individual over a relatively short period. Interactional exchanges either in the real world or in experimental situations are recorded on video or audio tape, then transcribed into a protocol. The protocol is analyzed in full detail by coding it into categories that represent the dynamic characteristics of social interaction.

Several studies based on the microgenetic view (Tajima 1984, 1986, 1987; Uemura & Tajima 1987a,b; 1988) describe how a young child processes information given by his/her mother in a cooperative problem-solving situation. In these social interactions, the problems were as follows: 1. What kind of information (knowledge) is acquired by a child; 2. how is that new knowledge learned by a child; and 3. what kind of role does the mother take in such cooperative work?

The analyses of mother-child social interaction suggested four conclusions. 1. The child positively processes task-related information without his/her mother's guidance at the beginning of this situation ("self-initiated learning"). 2. The mother's role in interaction is to clarify the goal required by the task, to help her child find the way to attain that goal independently at first, and then to evaluate and refine her child's performance ("other-dependent learning"). 3. These kinds of mother's behaviors gradually decrease as her child acquires skill/knowledge. 4. The child finally becomes independent in problem-solving, understanding the proper goal for the task and obtaining the means to assess and correct his/her own performance ("self-dependent learning"). The analysis shows that even in this adult-child interaction, a child's spontaneous participation and joint cooperation with an adult are necessary for achieving deeper understanding and also for child development.

Future Research

Research based on the microgenetic view suggests that child development should be viewed as a changing process mutually regulated between the child and his/her environment. The results appear to be much richer than those obtained by traditional methods. However, the problems of data validity and reliability need to be overcome. The results must be compared with other kinds of data from different demographic/cultural situations (Azuma 1986), or from different sociohistorical settings (Kojima 1986a,b).

ANIMAL PSYCHOLOGY

A universal subject of controversy among animal psychologists is whether the chief goal of animal psychology should be to contribute to human psychology, or whether its purpose should be to understand animals themselves. This debate is active among Japanese animal psychologists. Research aims and subject species do not differ substantially between animal psychology in Japan and that in other countries. One distinctive aspect of Japanese animal psychology is the long-term study of particular species of animals by psychologists interested more in clarifying species-specific characteristics than in using animals as substitutes for humans. These psychologists would postpone comparisons of animals with humans until a further stage of research. This attitude is typical of many psychologists who have been studying the native species of Japan, such as Japanese monkeys *(Macaca fuscata)*. The present review deals only with studies of Japanese monkeys in their natural habitat in order to emphasize the importance of long-term studies in animal psychology.

Studies of Japanese monkeys in their natural habitat were begun in the mid-1950s by zoologists from Kyoto University. They identified individual members of groups by feeding them in a section of the group's home range where the monkeys could be observed closely. Animal psychologists also began to study Japanese monkeys in their natural habitat in the late 1950s using practically the same method of observation, but with different aims from those of zoologists. The psychologists focused their research on the development of social behavior by individual group members with respect to the historical development of a group's social organization. In addition to natural observation, the psychologists conducted experimental studies of captive monkeys. The experiments were designed to clarify factors influencing the development of individual social behavior and the maintenance of group social organization.

A free-ranging group of Japanese monkeys has been observed since 1958 at Katsuyama in Okayama prefecture by psychologists from Osaka University. The group members have been individually identified and their life histories have been documented (Itoigawa 1988). The most significant event in the history of the group was a fission of the group that occurred in 1973. The group's fission occurred primarily through social conflict between mating partners of the alpha male of the group and the alpha male's kin females, including his mother, grandmother, and other relatives. The alpha male's grandmother was killed by his mating partners, and several monkeys were severely injured by fighting during the approximately one-year period of the group's fission. The group's fission, however, had adaptive significance for the species. The intense antagonism between the mating partners of the alpha male and his kin females helped split the original group into two reproductive units. The split functioned to avoid incest among kin members of the group. The challenge by the low-ranking mating partners of the alpha male toward the alpha male's high-ranking kin females had been created through multi-generational effects of mothers' influence upon their offspring's acquisition of social behavior.

The development of social behavior by maturing group members in relation to the social organization of their group has been studied for many years by Japanese primatologists and animal psychologists. Recently, data have been collected about infants' development of social relationships with both their mothers and other group members (Nakamichi 1989), and on immature members' co-feeding relationships with other group members (Imakawa 1988). These studies indicate the importance of follow-up studies on individual members during historical changes in their group. Perhaps a framework for comparison between animals and humans eventually can be built on the basis of these studies.

SOCIAL PSYCHOLOGY

The present review of social psychology in Japan covers the 10-year period since an English language review edited by Misumi (1978). During the last 10 years, the number of social psychologists in colleges and universities has increased enormously, as has the number of students studying social psychology. Research activities by Japanese social psychologists have covered a wide range of phenomena and theoretical problems. Because of space limitations, however, only themes that have appeared in featured articles in the two primary social psychology journals, in another major psychology journal, and in another journal related to social psychology are listed in Table 1.

The basic trend in social psychology can be summed up as follows: A heavy emphasis is placed on cognitive studies relevant to interpersonal relations and studies of social issues relevant to daily life and to Japanese traditional cultural characteristics are prevalent.

While these feature articles reflect the interests of Japanese researchers, they also reveal the considerable influence of research trends in the United States and elsewhere. For example, Takata (1987) reported an experiment concerning the function of social comparisons in forming self-evaluations. Contrary to earlier results by Schwartz & Smith (1967) Takata found that self-deprecatory tendencies became salient when subjects were asked to compare their abilities with those of other people. Such tendencies may be distinctively characteristic of Japanese people's self-presentation. As this example shows, even where foreign work is used as a starting point, new directions have been developed by Japanese researchers.

PROSOCIAL BEHAVIOR

The large amount of research on "prosocial behavior" indicates that this phenomenon is one of the main recent emphases in psychological research throughout the world. In the last 10 years (Hirai & Hamazaki 1985; Kikuchi 1984) the same tendency is apparent in Japan. Bullying in schools is one of the topics over which much ink has recently been spilt (Sukemune et al 1983). The gravity and increase of this phenomenon in Japan are such that it must be viewed not simply as an education-related problem, but rather as a general societal problem.

Research on prosocial behavior covers a large number of topics, such as sharing behavior (Kawashima, 1980a,b, 1982; Okajima 1984), helping behavior (Matsui 1981; Harada 1985; Harada & Araragi 1981), comforting behavior, and assistance behavior. To investigate these different subjects, different research methods (interview, questionnaire, observation, laboratory experiment, etc) are used. The most important issues discussed are factors that determine prosocial behavior, such as personality, gender, social skills, courage, and other personal factors, and situational factors, such as others' presence or absence. To study the effect of both personal and situational factors on sharing behavior, Hamazaki (1985), for instance, conducted the following experiment. Based on the score obtained in the Empathy Test, he divided subjects (children) into a High Empathy Group and a Low Empathy Group. Regardless of others' presence or absence, sharing behavior was more

Table 1 Recent trends in Japanese social psychology represented by special issues of major journals

Year	Theme of special issue	Editor of special issue	Topics or key words in featured articles
1978	Methodological problems[a]	Kuroda, M. et al	subject matters of social psychology; practical and theoretical subjects; data analysis
1979	Social psychology of relations[a]	Sato, T.	gift-giving in Japan; family; neighborhood relations & population density
	Cross-cultural psychology[b]	Takuma, T. & Hoshino, A.	cross-national differences in cognitive socialization processes
1980	Social psychology of continuity and change[a]	Akuto, H.	political attitudes; consumer behavior; national character; fashion
	Cognition[b]	Sayeki, Y.	questioning behavior of Japanese students; cognitive dissonance
1981	Family disorganization[a]	Seki, T.	violence in the family; family therapy
1982	Social psychology of "public" vs. "private"[a]	Inoue, T.	"public" & "private" attitudes; manner of self-presentation; Japanese style of the relation between individual and collectivity
	Attribution & attitude formation[b]	Mizuhara, T.	self-attribution processes; achievement motivation and attribution
1983	Social psychology of disaster[a]	Misumi, J.	a case study in an airplane fire; earthquake prediction and the "panic potential"
	Interpersonal behavior[c]	Ohashi, M.	informational social influence by a similar or dissimilar other; structure of implicit personality theory; effects of self-esteem on causal attribution
1984	Consumer behavior[a]	Akuto, H.	motivation research; international comparison of advertising expression
	Attributional processes[c]	Furuhata, K.	perceptions of crowding; effects of interpersonal attraction on causal attributions of partner's behavior; inference processes in attributions of others' behavior
1985	Group processes and cognition[c]	Hirota, K.	assumed similarity in the perception of the likable other's attitude; the relationship between leadership behavior and supervisor's perceived personality; dimensions of cognition of social situations
1986	Interpersonal communication[c]	Nagata, Y.	person description as a communicative act; relations between self-disclosure and perceived similarity; qualitative analysis of conversation; linguistic styles of requests
	Human behavior in extreme situations[d]	Murai, K.	extreme situations; reactions of criminals in confinement; receptive promotion to death for dying people

Table 1   *(Continued)*

Year	Theme of special issue	Editor of special issue	Topics or key words in featured articles
1987	Self perception[c]	Hashimoto, H.	the identity of "Japanese American"; dimensions of causal attribution for helping and non-helping behavior; self-deprecative tendencies in self-evaluation; self-schemata; persever-ance of personality impressions
	Man & robot[d]		body figure, robotization and humani-zation; post-humanization; post in-dustrial society, tradition in Japan; information systems in an aging society
1988	The group and its environ-ment[c]	Hachiya, Y.	managerial behavior; job characteris-tics; SIMSOC; effects of leadership behavior on follower's coping be-havior when an emergency occurs
	Psychological problems of children returned from overseas[d]	Nomura, A.	the psychological reorganization pro-cesses of overseas experience after returning to Japan; impact of returning children from overseas upon existing Japanese educational system

[a] Special issue of *The Japanese Annals of Social Psychology*
[b] Special issue of *Japanese Psychological Review*
[c] Special issue of *The Japanese Journal of Experimental Social Psychology*
[d] Special issue of *Research in Social Psychology*

frequent among High Empathy Group than among Low Empathy Group members. However, in the Low Empathy Group, sharing behavior was more frequent in the condition of others' presence. These results suggest that the children's sharing behavior was motivated by both low empathy and others' presence.

Sukemune et al (1981) conducted a laboratory experiment to investigate preschool children's helping behavior. Based on a 2 × 2 factorial design, they introduced two conditions, a Modeling Condition (Helpful Model and Neutral Model), and a Motivational Cost Condition (High Motivational Cost and Low Motivational Cost). The results indicated that helping behavior was more frequent in the Helpful Model/Low Motivational conditions than in the other three conditions. These findings show that, in the case of preschool children, a Modeling Effect can be observed only when the Motivational Cost is low. Thus, there is an interaction between Modeling and Motivational Cost, such that a Modeling Effect is also likely to be influenced by the Children's Motivational Cost level.

As another representative study concerning prosocial behavior, we can cite Munekata & Ninomiya's (1985) study on preschool children's prosocial moral judgment. The results of this study confirm the findings and the classification by Eisenberg (1982) in the United States.

The above three representative studies indicate that research on prosocial behavior should take into account both personal and situational factors.

JAPANESE LEADERSHIP RESEARCH

Several English reviews describe leadership research by Japanese scholars (Misumi & Peterson 1985, 1987; Smith 1984). A considerable amount of work by Japanese scholars has taken constructs developed in the United States, translated questionnaires from English, and replicated or extended the work in Japan (e.g. Lincoln & Kalleberg 1985; Matsui & Ohtsuka 1978; Wakabayashi & Graen 1984). In many instances, the Japanese scholars have provided qualitative accounts or modifications needed to adapt US methods to the Japanese situation.

One Japanese leadership research program has developed in Japan while maintaining conceptual links with major Western social psychological research programs. This research program, the "Performance-Maintenance (PM) Theory of Leadership," has been developed through a series of several dozen laboratory and field studies spanning the history of Japan's post-war development (Misumi 1985).

A PM Study of Senior Managers

A recent survey study of senior managers provides an example of the conceptual and methodological approach taken in the research program. As in prior PM field studies, the leadership constructs are theoretically linked to the "performance" (P) function of leadership in contributing to a group's (or in this case an organization's) production of things that can be exchanged with other parties, and to the "maintenance" (M) function of preserving sufficient internal (or organizational) integrity and stability that goods or services can be produced (Cartwright & Zander 1960). The application of PM ideas to a particular domain of study is then based on a review of prior classical and recent, largely Western, research. In the case of senior management leadership, Bass's (1985) idea of "transformational leadership," Selznick's (1957) idea of leadership in setting and pursuing new goals, and Parsons' (1960) "four-part action framework" (adaptation, goal attainment, interpretation, latent pattern maintenance) were anticipated to be particularly relevant to the forms of leadership likely to appear among senior managers.

Consistent with prior PM field research, the theoretical framework is set aside at the point of preparing items. Instead of working deductively from theory, items were prepared based on a series of interviews with company presidents, and were screened for meaningfulness, redundancy, and importance based on a pretest with other senior managers. Having reduced a preliminary survey from 154 to 77 items, the leadership questionnaire and a set of 25 attitude criteria were administered to 312 people in two organizations who described their organization's senior managers. Factor analysis was then used to identify a set of factors, eight in this case, that could be interpreted in terms of the original theoretical constructs.

At the point of identifying and interpreting the eight resulting factors, the inductive-deductive link is reestablished. The validity and utility of clustering the eight factors into four simpler PM types were then evaluated by showing convergence with the attitude criteria. Causal interpretation and interpretation assuming that the leadership measures reflect "true" or "objective" behavior, like that which might be recorded by a movie camera, are resisted. In the case of senior management leadership, the justification to generalize from PM laboratory research (Misumi & Peterson 1985) is argued less strongly than it has been in some other PM field studies. In effect, the senior management setting serves as a "contingency" for the way that leadership is expressed. Senior management leadership in Japan appears to be quite like that in the West, and quite distinct from leadership at lower levels in Japan.

Recent Experimental Research

The most recent innovations in experimental research that has spun-off of earlier PM laboratory studies have some of the characteristics of the most successful recent US leadership paradigms. This recent research takes an event or incident, most often some kind of emergency situation, and compares the effects of very concrete actions by leaders on how followers interpret the situation (e.g. as an occasion for panic, or as a manageable situation) and on how followers behave (Kugihara et al 1980; Misumi & Sako 1982.) Interpretations of the concrete leadership behaviors (e.g. "Follow-Me" and "Follow-Directions" methods of escape; Sugiman & Misumi 1988) in terms of general leadership patterns are treated as secondary issues.

The combination of inductive and deductive work in Japan provided by the PM research program is a largely untapped resource for pursuing research into the culturally specific and transcultural aspects of leadership and social processes.

EDUCATIONAL PSYCHOLOGY

Throughout the 30-year history of the Japanese Association of Educational Psychology, classroom teaching has been a primary concern.

Teacher Effects

Although many researchers believe it is important to study the effects of teachers' teaching styles, personality, and belief systems on student achievement, few studies have been done because of difficulty in getting cooperation from teachers. Fujisaki (1986) emphasized the importance of research on the nature of communication in classrooms. Kishi (1981) observed spoken interactions between teachers and pupils and classified teaching styles into six types: lecture, narrow question, broad question, chairmanship, acceptance, and discussion. The "jigsaw learning method" (a method of small group and cooperative learning) was found effective in learning social studies (Araragi 1983). Student achievement, self-image, and motivation are also influenced by a teacher's beliefs about teaching, a teacher's expectations for students, a teacher's kindness, and friends' positive attitudes (Ishida et al 1986; Kojo et al 1982; Kono 1988; Yoshida & Yamashita 1987).

Reading and Writing

The effects of oral reading and silent reading were studied by Mori (1980) and Tanaka (1983). Tanaka found that self-verbalization (whispering to oneself) facilitated five-year-olds' understanding of causal relations among events in a story. Omura et al (1980) and Ikeda (1981) found that stating conjunctive relations among sentences had different effects on remembering text according to a reader's inference ability. Fitting the number of conjunctive expressions in a text to a student's inference ability may enhance reading comprehension. Taniguchi (1988) confirmed that inserting analogies into a text helped college students construct a macrostructure of the text. The traditional methods for teaching children to write Chinese characters are tracing and copying models. Copying practice was found to be better than tracing for four- and five-year-old children, but combining both methods was found to be better than either alone (Onose 1987, 1988). Studies of story writing and causal sequencing in children's narratives have implications for teaching writing (Akita & Omura 1987; Anzai & Uchida 1981; Moro 1982; Uchida 1982, 1985).

Learning Mathematics, Natural Sciences, and Other Subjects

The teaching and learning of concepts are important topics in this area. Magara & Fushimi (1982) found that nonequilateral triangles and irregular quadrilaterals were more effective examples than were regular shapes to teach the concepts of triangles and quadrilaterals. Acceleration is harder to understand than are distance and speed. "Acceleration" was difficult for second graders, but it could be learned (Yamada & Shiomi 1986; Soga & Shiomi 1987). Cognitive psychologists are interested in research on computation with the abacus. Amaiwa (1987) found that skills of computation with an abacus did not transfer to normal paper-and-pencil computation.

Motivation

Taketsuna (1984) showed the effectiveness of self-evaluation as well as teacher evaluation for kanji (Chinese character) learning. Showing an exception to a rule enhanced students' interest (Magara 1986), and giving symbolic rewards (small prizes) and verbal praise had detrimental effects on intrinsic motivation (Omiya & Matsuda 1987). Research based on causal attribution models about academic achievement showed that student attribution of poor performance to lack of effort was a strong tendency even at lower grades (Higuchi et al 1983; Hayamizu, 1984). Since most students feel their performance is poor (Aikawa et al 1985), more research on perceived control over one's own performance and on expectation and confidence levels will be needed (Higuchi et al 1986; Niwa 1988).

Several research programs have addressed the function of education in relation to Piagetian concepts of development. Magara & Fushimi (1980) used stories to explain the facts and rules about the conservation of weight. They found that dramatizing the stories by having the children play the roles of story characters helped the children form cognitive frameworks into which the facts and rules could be placed. Children in the lower elementary school grades often misjudge that the areas of two shapes are the same if their circumferences are identical. Nishibayashi (1988) found that this error was made because the children overgeneralized from the logic that applies to the conservation of weight and volume. Using a test closely related to Piaget's "three mountain task," Joh (1980) reported that third-graders could learn to draw and read orthographic views (third-angle projections) with the aid of an elaborate training program.

In mathematics, Okada (1987) had second-, third-, and fifth-graders evaluate the correctness of a four-step process for solving arithmetic word problems: 1. understanding the problem, 2. planning, 3. executing a solution strategy, and 4. writing the result. The fifth-graders paid equal attention to the four steps, but the second- and third-graders paid less attention to the final step of writing the result. Many pupils realized that there was something amiss in the way they had carried out the step but could not specify exactly where they had gone wrong.

Studies of foreign language learning, especially English learning, have been important. Murakami (1981) found that putting an oral recitation period for questions and answers in English at the end of a class session was more effective than ending the session by reciting and copying English sentences. High school students seem to use the following methods for learning English: cramming, running exercises quickly when facing a difficult problem, keeping one's own pace, and seeing one's friends as rivals (Uda 1988). Mori & Tagashira (1981) found "the keyword method" proposed by R. C. Atkinson (mnemonics based on phonetic similarity and images) effective in learning Spanish words.

Ichikawa (1988) evaluated the use of computer-aided experimentation for teaching psychology. Most students favored it, but some complained that they could not understand the meaning of each experiment and doubted the utility of the method.

CLINICAL PSYCHOLOGY IN JAPAN

Clinical psychology in modern Japan is a rapidly growing field with about 5000 practitioners. A certification procedure for clinical psychologists is expected to begin soon. Although the field's main trend is still the introjection and digestion of American clinical psychology, some attempts at innovation have been made. Four of the major applications of American clinical psychology are psychological assessment using the Rorschach technique; client-centered and psychoanalytically oriented psychotherapy; behavior therapy; and family therapy.

Journals

The new *Journal of Japanese Clinical Psychology* has been published three times a year since 1983, including a special issue on case study. Besides this journal, *Rorschachiana Japonica* has been published annually for the past 28 years.

The *Journal of Japanese Clinical Psychology* represents the major research trends in clinical psychology. As an example, a recent issue covered the following topics:

Opinion: On the training and certification of clinical psychologists in Japan; *Original Articles:* 1. Personality characteristics of age-related "dementia" Rorschach test findings; 2. patients' appropriate efforts against their symptoms—questions raised against some common beliefs in clinical psychology; *Minor Articles:* 1. An attempt at combined individual-and-group psychotherapy with two borderline adolescents; 2. on the "conjoint sand play therapy," and 3. reexamination of client-centered therapy.

The client-centered or person-centered approach and experiential therapy (including such techniques as focusing, as developed by Gendlin) have been the most popular orientations in Japan. A few years ago the *Journal of Humanistic Psychology* was established.

Hakoniwa or Sand Play Therapy

The introvertive, intuitive, and image-dominant tendency of the Japanese may be syntonic with the Jungian way of thinking. Consequently, a technique called "*Hakoniwa*-therapy," literally "miniature garden therapy," is now widely used (Kawai 1969, 1985). The original idea of this therapy technique came from an assessment tool called "The World Test," designed by Lowenfeld (a pediatrician in England) and C. Buhler (a child and clinical psychologist). This tool was constructed from various miniature objects (e.g. human beings, animals, plants, and man-made objects) that have significance in our lives. It was assumed that the test reveals the inner world of the testee. D. Kalff, a Jungian therapist in Switzerland, modified the World Test and called her method "Sand Play Therapy." The sand in its box-shaped container is almost flat and can be used as a stage for arranging the miniatures. The sand often symbolizes the earth or the unconscious in general, and the box frame symbolizes the boundary of unconscious activity. The client can freely express otherwise inhibited impulses within this relatively safe frame.

When H. Kawai, a representative Jungian in Japan, introduced this technique to Japanese clinicians he named it *hakoniwa* therapy. *Hakoniwa* is a familiar artistic hobby for the Japanese, and this may be one of the reasons why this method has become so popular in a relatively short time. A wealth of theoretical and practical studies on *hakoniwa* therapy has accumulated, especially in the past 10 years, and a journal devoted to this therapy method was recently published. The Japanese association of *hakoniwa* therapy was also started in 1987. Due to its nonverbal quality, *hakoniwa* therapy has proved to be applicable to and effective for the therapy of relatively older children.

Tsubo Imagery Therapy

Tsubo or pot imagery therapy, developed recently by a clinical psychologist named Seiichi Tajima (1987), is another uniquely Japanese technique. The basic idea of this method is that when one imagines pots and puts oneself inside a pot, the imagery functions as a safe barrier to protect one from negative imagery experiences. Compared to other imagery methods this one has proven effective for clients to keep a proper distance from their problems so that inner feelings can be unblocked. This new method has gradually spread among clinicians. This first book on *tsubo* imagery therapy was published in 1987. The method has proven effective not only for such clinical cases as borderline patients, neurotics, and psychosomatics, but also for nonclinical clients.

Naikan Therapy

Naikan or self-introspection is another psychotherapy method that originated from a thoroughly Japanese background (Murase 1989). The method consists of a highly systematic way of examining one's memory regarding interpersonal relationships. The client is asked to examine an attitude he/she took toward a particular person (e.g. mother) from the following three standpoints: recollect concretely what he/she has received from that person (services, financial support, attention, gifts, and the like); ask what he/she has returned to that person (in terms of goods and services), and assess what troubles and worries he/she has caused that person.

Naikan clients engage in these three kinds of mental activities for a week, from very early in the morning until going to bed. The *naikan* interviewer visits him or her approximately every two hours and listens to the client's very brief report about the immediately preceding *naikan* experience. In practice, a number of technical considerations are beautifully combined to operate together as a very effective therapeutic system.

This *naikan* system has proved effective for various kinds of both clinical and subclinical cases such as neurotics, psychosomatics, alcoholics, delinquents, couples in trouble, and the like. Although few rigorous outcome studies have been conducted, several valuable studies have been reported at the annual convention of the Association of *Naikan* Therapy Research during the past 11 years.

Case Study Movement

One feature of modern Japanese clinical psychology is the special emphasis placed on case study. Eleven books of case studies have been published as part of the "Case Study Movement" under the editorship of the Association of Clinical Psychology. There is no doubt that the movement has made a great contribution to the development of competent clinicians. On the other hand, scientific research is still underdeveloped.

COMPARATIVE CULTURAL RESEARCH

There are few methodological approaches to the cross-societal study of social attitudes. Here we introduce a cross-societal study still under way to develop a new methodology for both comparative survey design and statistical data analysis.

Introduction to an Example Study

The objective of our comparative research is the theoretical development and application of a new statistical social survey method for use in comparative studies of attitudinal structures of persons belonging to different cultural spheres (Hayashi & Suzuki 1974, 1975, 1986).

The method opens to comprehension the dynamic nature of similarities and differences in multifaceted thought structures among different subgroups.

The method has three components.

The Cultural Link Method for Comparative Research

The link method provides a means for exploring the similarities and differences in cognitive structures and ways of thinking in different cultures. The major feature of this method is its relative freedom from cultural and linguistic biases, problems inherent in previous work on the assessment of human cognitive structures. Such an unbiased assessment method should ultimately provide a means for combining the unique information made available from three ordinarily separated kinds of research:

a. A *spatial link* inherent in the selection of the subject culture or society. The connections seen in such selection may be considered along the dimensions of social environment, culture, and ethnic characteristics.
b. An *item structure* link inherent in the commonalities and differences in item response patterns within and across different cultures.
c. A *temporal link* inherent in longitudinal analysis.

Thus, the cultural link method combines information from three different areas: the sample, the item content, and stability and change over time. In addition to the cultural link method, we adopt a method of quantification of response patterns that has been developed in Japan since 1956 (i.e. a multi-dimensional analysis of categorical data based on the interrelationships among responses equivalent to the correspondence analysis used in France since 1973; Benzecri 1973, Hayashi 1956). By using link and pattern analysis procedures, the underlying information can be apportioned between the common and specific characteristics of the respondents being compared. By clustering individual subjects' response patterns, the unique characteristics of the opinion structures of the subject cultures as wholes can be more clearly ascertained than has been possible in the past. This will be the first application of this cultural link survey technique in the field of comparative social attitudinal research.

Verification of the Practical Applicability and Validity of the Cultural Link Method in Comparative International Survey Research

To date, the link survey method has been applied in comparative studies of attitudes in the United States and Japan through a series of surveys conducted in Honolulu, Hawaii. Through this work, the validity of the method has been confirmed. However, generalization of the inferences drawn from this application is seriously limited. Universality cannot be claimed based on an application to only two societies. For this reason, it is necessary to extend the application of the method by applying it to cross-sectional and longitudinal data from nations that seem to have undergone significant social and cultural changes. Consequently, surveys in West Germany, France, and Great Britain were completed in 1987 and surveys in the US mainland, Hawaii, and Japan were done in 1988. Data analysis is now under way.

The Construction of a Statistical System for use with Multiplex Parallel Data-Set Analysis (MPDA)

A statistical analysis system for handling multiplex parallel data sets has been designed using a method of successive approximations. Research efficiency may be expected to rise markedly, thus enhancing international research exchanges in the future.

CONCLUSION

The first psychological laboratory was established at the University of Tokyo in 1903. The Japanese Psychological Association (JPA), which includes basic psychology and applied psychology, is the oldest and largest association, with about 4450 members. There are many other associations of equal importance: Japanese Society for Applied Psychology (founded in 1931), Japanese Society for Group Dynamics (1949), Japanese Society for Educational Psychology (1952), Japanese Society of Social Psychology (1960), Japanese Society for Criminal Psychology (1963), Japanese Society of Clinical Psychology (1964), Japanese Society for Psychonomics (1981), and Japanese Society for Industrial and Organizational Psychology (1985).

Before World War II, psychology in Japan was influenced by European psychology, especially by the German Gestalt school. However, after World War II, the important role played by European psychology in Japanese psychology was assumed by American psychology. In spite of the great influence that American psychology has had, and continues to have, on Japanese psychology, we are witnessing a birth of a nativistic trend in psychological research that has led to a number of local or national research projects that seem to be full of promise for the 21st century.

Literature Cited

Aikawa, A., Mishima, K., Matsumoto, T. 1985. Effects of causal attributions on an achievement test of students: an examination of Weiner's causal attribution model of motivation. *Jpn. J. Educ. Psychol.* 33:195–204 (In Japanese)

Akita, K., Omura, A. 1987. The development of causal sequencing in children's narrative production. *Jpn. J. Educ. Psychol.* 35:65–73 (In Japanese)

Amaiwa, S. 1987. Transfer of subtraction procedures from abacus to paper and pencil computation. *Jpn. J. Educ. Psychol.* 35:41–48

Amemiya, T. 1983. Adaptation to a tilted visual field: a long-term experiment. *Jpn. J. Psychonom. Sci.*, 2:27–38

Anzai, Y., Uchida, N. 1981. How do children produce writings? *Jpn. J. Educ. Psychol.* 29:323–32 (In Japanese)

Araragi, C. 1983. The effect of the jigsaw learning method on children's academic performance and learning attitude. *Jpn. J. Educ. Psychol.* 31:102–12 (In Japanese)

Ayama, M., Ikeda, M. 1986. Additivity of yellow chromatic valence. *Vis. Res.* 26:763–69

Azuma, H. 1986. Why study child development in Japan? In *Child Development and Education in Japan*, ed. H. Stevenson, H. Azuma, K. Hakuta, pp. 3–12. New York: Freeman. 316 pp.

Azuma, H., Kashiwagi, K., Hess, R. D. 1981. *Mother's Attitude, Behavior and Child's Cognitive Development: Japan-*

U.S. Cross-national Study. Tokyo: Univ. Tokyo Press. 312 pp. (In Japanese)

Bass, B. M. 1985. *Leadership and Performance Beyond Expectations.* NY: The Free Press

Benzecri, J. P. 1973 (1980 rev.). *Analyse des données,* Tome 1, Tome 2. Paris: Dunod, 424 pp., 466 pp.

Binguishi, K. 1983. Disappearance of stereopsis in the line stereograms. *Jpn. J. Psychol.* 54:314–20

Cartwright, D., Zander, A., eds. 1960. *Group Dynamics: Research and Theory.* New York: Harper and Row. 2nd. ed.

Eisenberg, N. 1982. The development of reasoning regarding prosocial behavior. In *The Development of Prosocial Behavior,* ed. N. Eisenberg. New York: Academic

Fugimori, S. 1985. A new multidimensional item response model. *Human. Rev.* 11:79–89

Fujisaki, H. 1986. Communication in classrooms. *Jpn. J. Educ. Psychol.* 34:359–68 (In Japanese)

Funakawa, M., Aiba, T. S. 1987. Spatial localization of objects on long-range apparent motion. *Jpn. Psychol. Res.* 29:103–11

Goryo, K. 1987. *Recognition of Written Words.* Tokyo: Univ. Tokyo Press. (In Japanese)

Haebara, T. 1980. Equating logistic ability scales by a weighted least squares method. *Jpn. Psychol. Res.* 22:144–49 (In English)

Hamazaki, T. 1985. The effects of empathy and presence of another person on prosocial behavior in preschool children. *Jpn. J. Psychol.* 56:103–6 (In Japanese)

Harada, J. 1985. Bystander intervention: the effect of ambiguity of the helping situation and the interpersonal relationship between bystanders. *Jpn. Psychol. Res.* 27:177–84 (In Japanese)

Harada, J., Araragi, C. 1981. The effect of interpersonal distance and number of potential helpers on helping behavior. *Jpn. J. Exp. Soc. Psychol.* 21:35–39 (In Japanese)

Hatano, G. 1988. Becoming an expert in mental abacus operation: a case of routine expertise. Japanese Cognitive Science Society (ed.) In *Advances in Japanese Cognitive Science,* ed. 1:141–60 (In Japanese with English abstract)

Hatano, G., Inagaki, K. 1987. A theory of motivation for comprehension and its application to mathematics instruction. In *The Monitoring of School Mathematics: Background Papers. Vol. 2. Implications from Psychology; Outcomes from Instruction,* ed. T. A. Romberg, D. M. Stewwart. Madison: Center for Education Research

Hatano, G., Miyake, K., Tajima, N. 1980. Mother behavior in an unstructured situation and child's acquisition of number conservation. *Child Dev.* 51:379–85

Hatta, T., Ikeda, K. 1985. Brain function of abacus experts (1). *Proc. 27th Cong. Jpn. Assoc. Educ. Psychol.,* pp. 20–21 (In Japanese)

Hattori, T. 1985. An equating method considering the various conditions among anchor tests. *Jpn. J. Educ. Psychol.* 33:345–49 (In Japanese)

Hattori, T. 1986. Methods of simultaneous equating for scales with the Rasch model using common-item technique. *Jpn. J. Behav.* 14: 1:39–46 (In Japanese)

Hayamizu, T. 1984. The development of inference process of causal attribution about academic achievements. *Jpn. J. Educ. Psychol.* 32:256–65 (In Japanese)

Hayashi, C. 1956. Theory and example of quantification (II). *Proc. Inst. Statistist. Math.* 4:19–30

Hayashi, C., Suzuki, T. 1974. Quantitative approach to cross-societal research I. *Ann. Inst. Statist. Math.* 26:451–516

Hayashi, C., Suzuki, T. 1975. Quantitative approach to cross-societal research, II. *Ann. Inst. Statist. Math.* 27:1–32

Hayashi, C., Suzuki, T. 1986 *Social Survey and Data Analysis.* Tokyo: Iwanami Shoten. 281 pp.

Higashiyama, A. 1984. Curvature of binocular visual space: a modified method of right triangle. *Vis. Res.* 24:1713–18

Higuchi, K., Kambara, M., Ohtsuka, Y. 1983. An examination of causal attribution model about academic achievement of elementary school children. *Jpn. J. Educ. Psychol.* 31:18–27 (In Japanese)

Higuchi, K., Kambara, M., Ohtsuka, Y. 1986. Relationship between types of causal attributions children make in achievement situations and their goal settings. *Jpn. J. Educ. Psychol.* 34:220–29 (In Japanese)

Hirai, S., Hamazaki, T. 1985. Prosocial behavior. In *Annual Review of Japanese Child Psychology,* ed. K. Harano, et al, pp. 219–46 (In Japanese)

Hishitani, S. 1987. Imagery processing of expert abacus operators. *Seinan-Gakuin Univ. Stud. Childhood Educ.* 14:1–15

Ichikawa, S. 1986. Quantitative and structural factors in the judgment of pattern complexity. *Percept. Psychophys.* 38:101–9

Ichikawa, S. 1988. Psychological experiments by the computer: effects and problems in college education. *Jpn. J. Educ. Psychol.* 36:84–9 (In Japanese)

Ikeda, K. 1981. A developmental study on effects of explicitly stating conjunctive relations and inferential abilities upon organization in multiple free recall of sentences presented in context-disorganized order. *Jpn. J. Educ. Psychol.* 29:207–16 (In Japanese)

Ikeda, K., Hatta, T. 1986. Brain function of abacus experts (2). *Proc. 28th Cong. Jpn. Assoc. Educ. Psychol.,* pp. 876–77 (In Japanese)

Imai, S. 1977. Pattern similarity and cognitive transformations. *Acta Psychol.* 41:433–47

Imai, S. 1984. *Figures inducing geometric illusions.* Tokyo: Saiensu-sha.

Imakawa, S. 1988. Development of co-feeding relationships in immature free-ranging Japanese monkeys (*Macaca fuscata fuscata*). *Primates* 29(4):493–504

Inagaki, K. 1982. Motivation for knowing. In *Handbook of Cognitive Psychology,* ed. G. Hatano, 4:95–132. Learning and development, Tokyo: Univ. Tokyo Press (In Japanese)

Inagaki, K. 1989. Developmental shift in biological inference processes: from similarity-based to category-based attribution. *Human Dev.* 32:79–87

Inui, T., Ohmi, E., Kani, K. 1984. Analyses of small vergence eye-movement in stereopsis with random-dot stereograms. *Jpn. J. Psychonom. Sci.* 3:1–7

Ishida, S., Ito, A., Kajita, M. 1986. Personal teaching theory of elementary and junior high school teachers on mathematics. *Jpn. J. Educ. Psychol.* 34:230–38 (In Japanese)

Ishiguchi, A. 1988. Interpolated elastic structure from the motion of dots. *Percept. Psychophys.* 43:457–64

Itoigawa, N. 1988. Life histories of Japanese monkeys in a free-ranging group. *Proc. IXth Bien. Meet. Int. Soc. Behav. Dev.,* pp. 222–30

Joh, H. 1980. On the formation of actions of projection-construction of the technical drawing and its teaching. *Jpn. J. Educ. Psychol.* 28:219–28 (In Japanese)

Kaiho, H., Nomura, Y. 1983. *Information Processing Psychology of Kanji.* Tokyo: Kyoiku-Shuppan (In Japanese)

Katori, H. 1984. Sensation and perception. In *Experimental Psychology 10 Development II Ontogenesis,* ed. H. Katori, pp. 61–100. Tokyo: Univ. Tokyo Press

Kawai, H., ed. 1969. *HAKONIWA Ryouhou Nyuumon or An Introduction to HAKONIWA Therapy.* Tokyo: Seishinshobo

Kawai, H. 1985. *HAKONIWA Ryouhou Kenkyu 1 & 2 or Studies on HAKONIWA Therapy.* Tokyo: Seishinshobo

Kawashima, K. 1980a. Effects of presence of another person and learning styles on donating behavior in children. *Jpn. J. Psychol.* 50:345–48 (In Japanese)

Kawashima, K. 1980b. The effect of attribution on donating behavior among young children. *Jpn. J. Educ. Psychol.* 28:256–60 (In Japanese)

Kawashima, K. 1982. Effects of characteristics of another person on donating behavior in children. *Jpn J. Psychol.* 53:1–8 (In Japanese)

Kikuchi, A. 1983. Development of prosocial behavior. *Annu. Rep. Educ. Psychol. Jpn.* 23:118–29 (In Japanese)

Kikuchi, A. 1984. *Psychology of Contact and Consideration.* Tokyo: Kawashima (In Japanese)

Kikuchi, T. 1981. Effects of dot density and duration of mask stimulus upon visual backward masking. *Jpn. Psychol. Res.* 23:37–42

Kishi, T. 1981. The analysis of teaching-learning process: patterns of utterance relation. *Jpn. J. Educ. Psychol.* 29:1–9 (In Japanese)

Kohler, P. A. 1976. Reading a year later. *J. Exp. Psychol.: Human Learn. Mem.* 2:554–65

Kojima, H. 1986a. Child rearing concepts as a belief-value system of the society and the individual. In *Child Development and Education in Japan,* ed. H. Stevenson, H. Azuma, K. Hakuta, pp. 39–53. New York: Freeman. 305 pp.

Kojima, H. 1986b. Japanese concepts of child development from the mid-17th to the mid-19th century. *Int. J. Behav. Dev.* 9:315–29

Kojo, K., Amane, T., Aikawa, A. 1982. Teacher expectation, authoritarianism, and attributions of causality for pupils' performances. *Jpn. J. Educ. Psychol.* 30:91–99 (In Japanese)

Kono, Y. 1988. Effects of affiliative cues of teachers on children's task performance. *Jpn. J. Educ. Psychol.* 36:161–65 (In Japanese)

Koyazu, T., ed. 1982. Memory. In *Contemporary Basic Psychology Series,* Vol. 4. Tokyo: Univ. Tokyo Press

Koyazu, T., ed. 1985. Memory and knowledge. *Lectures on Cognitive Psychology,* Vol. 2. Tokyo: Univ. Tokyo Press

Koyazu, T., Ito, M., Matsuda, M. 1984. The effects of thematic materials and viewpoint in the Wason's four card problem. *Jpn. J. Psychonom. Sci.,* 3:21–29 (In Japanese with English abstract)

Kugihara, N., Misumi, J., Sato, S. 1980. Experimental study of escape behavior in a simulated panic situation: 1. *Jpn. J. Exp. Soc. Psychol.* 20:55–67

Lincoln, J. R., Kalleberg, A. L., 1985. Work organization and workforce commitment: a study of plants and employees in the U.S. and Japan. *Am. Soc. Rev.* 50:738–60

Magara, K. 1986. Effects of teaching a rule with exceptions on arousing interest in learners. *Jpn. J. Educ. Psychol.* 34:139–47 (In Japanese)

Magara, K., Fushimi, Y. 1980. The effect of dramatized learning materials on rule learning in pre-school children. *Jpn. J. Educ. Psychol.* 28:212–18 (In Japanese)

Magara, K., Fushimi, Y. 1982. The effect of the different types of the focus instances on learning of figure concepts in children. *Jpn. J. Educ. Psychol.* 30:147–51 (In Japanese)

Makino, T. 1984. Bibliography of Japanese

studies of disarranged vision. In *Sensory Experience, Adaptation and Perception*, ed. L. Spillman, B. R. Wooten, pp. xxv–xxvii. London: Lawrence Erlbaum Assoc.

Markus, H., Zajonc, R. B. 1985. The cognitive perspective in social psychology. In *The Handbook of Social Psychology*, ed. G. Lindzey, E. Aronson 1:137–230. NY: Random House. 3rd ed.

Matsui, Y. 1981. A structural analysis of helping. *Jpn. J. Psychol.* 52:226–32 (In Japanese)

Matsui, T., Ohtsuka, Y. 1978. Within-person expectancy theory predictions of supervisory consideration and structure behavior. *J. Appl. Psychol.* 63:128–31

Mead, G. H. 1934. *Mind, Self and Society* (posthumous, ed. C. M. Moris). Chicago: Univ. Chicago Press

Misumi, J. 1973. *Group Dynamics in Japan: Introduction.* Jpn. Group Dynam. Assoc. pp. 1–5

Misumi, J., ed. 1978. Social psychology in Japan. *Soc. Sci. Info.* 17:629–85

Misumi, J. 1985. *The Behavioral Science of Leadership* (M. F. Peterson, general editor). Ann Arbor, MI: Univ. Michigan Press

Misumi, J. 1989. The science of leadership behavior within a new paradigm for interdisciplinary behavioral research. Proc. XXIV Int. Cong. Psychol. Sydney

Misumi, J., Peterson, M. F. 1985. The performance-maintenance theory of leadership: review of a Japanese research program. *Admin. Sci. Q.* 30:198–223

Misumi, J., Peterson, M. F. 1987. Developing a performance-maintenance (PM) theory of leadership. *Bull. Fac. Hum. Sci., Osaka Univ.* 13:135–70

Misumi, J., Sako, H. 1982. An experimental study of the effect of leadership behavior on followers' behavior of following after the leader in a simulated emergency situation. *Jpn. J. Exp. Soc. Psychol.* 22:49–59

Mitsuboshi, M. 1986. Independence or interaction? The problem forgotten in the study of the Stiles' mechanisms. *Jpn. J. Psychonom. Sci.* 5:15–25

Miyake, N. 1986. Constructive interaction and the iterative process of understanding. *Cogn. Sci.* 10:151–77

Miyazaki, K., Sasaki, T. 1981. Auditory masking patterns in forward-, backward-, and simultaneous-masking situations. *Jpn. J. Psychol.* 52:106–12

Mori, T. 1980. Effects of silent reading and vocal reading upon memory for prose. *Jpn. J. Educ. Psychol.* 28:57–61 (In Japanese)

Mori, T., Tagashira, H. 1981. Acquisition of a Spanish vocabulary by using the mnemonic keyword method. *Jpn. J. Educ. Psychol.* 29:252–55 (In Japanese)

Moro, Y. 1982. Children's text production: an analysis of coherence realization. *Jpn.*

J. Educ. Psychol. 30:29–36 (In Japanese)

Munekata, H., Ninomiya, K. 1985. The development of prosocial moral judgments. *Jpn. J. Educ. Psychol.* 33:157–64 (In Japanese)

Murakami, Y. 1981. A study of an English teaching method: based on a comparative study on the effect of recititation and "questions and answers". 29:30–37 (In Japanese)

Murase, T. 1989. *NAIKAN Ryouhou* or *NAIKAN Therapy.* Tokyo: Nakayama Shoten.

Nakagawa, M., Tomiie, T., Yanase, T. 1984. The construction of a color affective space. *J. Color Sci. Assoc. Jpn.* 8:147–58

Nakajima, S. 1981. Speech perception. In *Experimental Psychology 3 Perception II Cognitive Processes*, ed. S. Torii, pp. 105–15. Tokyo: Univ. Tokyo Press

Nakajima, Y., Nishimura, S., Teranishi, R. 1988. Ratio judgments of empty durations with numeric scales. *Perception* 17:93–118

Nakamichi, M. 1989. Sex differences in social development during the first four years in a free-ranging group of Japanese monkeys (Macaca fuscata). *Animal Behav.* 38:370–81

Nakatani, K. 1988. Early stages of visual process. *ITEJ Tech. Rep.* 9:25–30

Namba, S., Kuwano, S., Kato, T. 1978. An investigation of L_{eq}, L_{10}, and L_{50} in relation to loudness. *J. Acoust. Soc. Jpn.* 34:301–7

Nishibayashi, K. 1988. The origin of misjudgment in area. *Jpn. J. Educ. Psychol.* 36:120–28 (In Japanese)

Niwa, Y. 1988. Effects of expectations on academic achievement in school age children. *Jpn. J. Educ. Psychol.* 36:276–81 (In Japanese)

Noguchi, H. 1986. An equating method for latent trait scale using common subjects' item response patterns. *Jpn. J. Educ. Psychol.* 34:315–23

Nozawa, S. 1982. Temporal and spatial structure in form perception. In *Experimental Psychology 3 Perception II Cognitive Processes*, ed. S. Torii, pp. 151–82. Tokyo: Univ. Tokyo Press

Ohta, N., ed. 1988. *Episodic Memory.* Tokyo: Seishin Shobo

Okada, T. 1987. A developmental study of children's evaluation of problem solving process. *Jpn. J. Educ. Psychol.* 35:49–56 (In Japanese)

Okajima, K. 1984. The effect of attribution on donating behavior of children. *Jpn. J. Educ. Psychol.* 32:10–17 (In Japanese)

Omiya, T., Matsuda, F. 1987. Effects of external reinforcement by teacher on children's intrinsic motivation. *Jpn. J. Educ. Psychol.* 35:1–8 (In Japanese)

Omura, A. 1988. *A Status Report on Psychology in Japan.* UNESCO Reg. Off. Educ. in Asia and the Pacific

Omura, A., Utsuo, T., Higuchi, K. 1980.

Effects of explicitly stating conjunctive relations between sentences upon memory in prose. *Jpn. J. Educ. Psychol.* 28:174–82 (In Japanese)

Onose, M. 1987. The effect of tracing and copying practice on handwriting skills of Japanese letters in preschool and first grade children. *Jpn. J. Educ. Psychol.* 35:9–16 (In Japanese)

Onose, M. 1988. Effect of the combination of tracing and copying practices on handwriting skills of Japanese letters in preschool and first grade children. *Jpn. J. Educ. Psychol.* 36:129–34 (In Japanese)

Parsons, T. 1960. *Structure and Process in Modern Societies.* NY: Free Press.

Posner, M. I., Snyder, C. R. R. 1975. Attention and cognitive control. In *Information Processing and Cognition,* ed. R. L. Folso. Hillsdale, NJ: Erlbaum

Samejima, F. 1962. The study of the distribution of non-verbal reasoning factor in the LIS measurement scale for non-verbal reasoning factor. *Jpn. J. Psychol.* 33(4):183–92

Samejima, F. 1962. Development and application of Lord's theory of test scores. *Bull. Nippon Res. Cent.* 1(1):60–69

Samejima, F. 1969. Estimation of latent ability using a response pattern of graded scores. *Psychometrica* 34(4, 2): Mono. Suppl.

Samejima, F. 1980. Scientific monograph. ONRT M3. Research on the multiple-choice test item in Japan. Tokyo: Dep. Navy Office of Naval Res.

Sato, T. 1983. Depth seen with subjective contours. *Jpn. Psychol. Res.* 25:213–21

Sayeki, Y. 1978. *Knowledge Acquisition and Learning through "Imagination".* Tokyo: Toyo-kan. (In Japanese)

Sayeki, Y. 1980. Understanding by empathy and its information processing analyses. *Proc 44th Jpn. Psychol. Assoc.* 4. (In Japanese)

Schwartz, J. M., Smith, W. P. 1967. Social comparison and the influence of ability differences. *J. Person. Soc. Psychol.* 34:1268–75

Sekiyama, K. 1987. Mental rotation of kinesthetic hand images and modes of stimulus presentation. *Jpn. J. Psychol.* 57:342–49

Selznick, P. 1957. *Leadership in Administration.* NY: Harper & Row

Shiba, S. 1969. Information transmission rate of psychological tests. *Jpn. J. Psychol.* 40(2):68–75, 121–29

Shiba, S. 1978. Construction of a scale for acquisition of word meanings. *Bull. Fac. Educ., Univ. Tokyo* 17:47–58 (In Japanese)

Shiba, S., Noguchi, H., Haebara, T. 1978. A stratified adaptive test of verbal ability. *Jpn. J. Educ. Psychol.* 26, 4:229–38 (In Japanese)

Shiba, S., Noguchi, H., Ohama, K. 1979. The efficiency of preliminary measurement by means of a short form of the stratified adaptive test in measuring verbal ability. *Bull. Fac. Educ., Univ. Tokyo* 19:27–34 (In Japanese)

Shiba, S., Takei, S., Ogino, M. 1984. Construction of a scale for acquisition of word meanings in early childhood. *Bull. Fac. Educ., Univ. Tokyo* 24:47–60 (In Japanese)

Shibayama, T., Noguchi, H., Shiba, S., Kamara, M. 1987. An adaptive testing procedure for measuring verbal ability. *Jpn. J. Educ. Psychol.* 35(4):363–67 (In Japanese)

Shigemasu, K., Fujimori, S. 1985. Joint estimates of parameters in item response model. *Jpn. J. Educ. Psychol.* 32(4):266–75 (In Japanese)

Shigeno, S. 1986. The auditory tau and kappa effects for speech and nonspeech stimuli. *Percept. Psychophys.* 40:9–19

Shimojo, S., Held, R. 1987. Vernier acuity is less than grating acuity in 2- and 3-month-olds. *Vis. Res.* 27:77–86

Smith, P. B. 1984. The effectiveness of Japanese styles of management. A review and critique. *J. Occ. Psychol.* 57:121–36

Soga, S., Shiomi, K. 1987. Understanding and the relationship of speed and acceleration in elementary and secondary school children. *Jpn. J. Educ. Psychol.* 35:122–31 (In Japanese)

Sugiman, T., Misumi, J. 1988. Development of a new evacuation method for emergencies: control of collective behavior by emergent small groups. *J. Appl. Psychol.* 73:3–10

Sukemune, S., Dohno, K., Matsuzaki, M. 1981. Model and motivational cost effects on helping behavior through modeling in preschool children. Report of research project. In *Basic Factors and Learning Modes in Observational Learning by Children,* ed. S. Sukemune, pp. 44–47. Hiroshima: Ministry of Educ., Sci., Cult., Japan

Sukemune, S., Dohno, K., Matsuzaki, M. 1983. *Fostering Children's Empathy and Altruistic Behavior.* Tokyo: Yuhikaku. (In Japanese)

Sumi, S. 1984. Upside-down presentation of the Johansson moving light-spot pattern. *Perception* 13:283–86

Suzuki, K., Nakata, Y. 1988. Does the size of figures affect the rate of mental rotation? *Percept. Psychophys.* 44:76–80

Taira, N., Takei, S., Ogino, M. 1987. Measurement of language comprehension by an adaptive of questionnaire. *Bull. Fac. Educ., Univ. Tokyo* 27:279–92 (In Japanese)

Tajima, N. 1984. How does the child process the information given in social interaction? *Hattatsu (Development)* 5:95–103 (In Japanese)

Tajima, N. 1986. Effects of social interaction on the child's cognitive development. *Tokyo Univ. Forei. Stud. Bull.* 36:209–230 (In Japanese)

Tajima, N. 1987. Child's understanding process in mother-child interaction: a microgenetic view. Presented at Bienn. Meet. Int. Soc. Stud. Behav. Dev., 9th, Tokyo

Tajima, N. 1988. The process of the child's information-processing in mother-child interaction. *Jpn. Psychol. Rev.* 31:158–77 (In Japanese)

Tajima, N., Usui, H. 1980. Cognitive socialization research: review. Ann. Rep. Educ. Psychol. in Japan 19:125–44 (In Japanese)

Tajima, S., ed. 1987. *TSUBO Image Therapy*. Osaka: Sougensha

Takata, T. 1987. Self-deprecative tendencies in self evaluation through social comparison. *Jpn. J. Exp. Soc. Psychol.* 27:27–36

Takei, S., Ogino, M. 1983. Construction of a scale for acquisition of language. *Bull. Fac. Educ., Univ. Tokyo* 23:111–25

Taketsuna, S. 1984. The effects of self-evaluative reactions on kanji learning. *Jpn. J. Educ. Psychol.* 32:315–19 (In Japanese)

Tanaka, S. 1983. Inducing an effective self-verbalization to facilitate the comprehension of a story by preschool children. *Jpn. J. Educ. Psychol.* 31:1–9 (In Japanese)

Tanaka, Y. 1966. Status of Japanese experimental psychology. *Annu. Rev. Psychol.* 17:233–72

Tanaka, Y., England, G. W. 1972. Psychology in Japan. *Annu. Rev. Psychol.* 23:695–732

Taniguchi, A. 1988. Effect of inserted analogies on the retention of a text. *Jpn. J. Educ. Psychol.* 36:282–86 (In Japanese)

Toyoda, H. 1986. An equating method of two latent ability scales by using subjects' estimated scale values and test information. *Jpn. J. Educ. Psychol.* 34:163–67 (In Japanese)

Tsukano, H. 1985. Understanding missing addend word problems. *Proc. 27th Cong. Jpn. Assoc. Educ. Psychol.*, pp. 590–91. (In Japanese)

Uchida, N. 1982. How do young children produce stories? *Jpn. J. Educ. Psychol.* 30:211–22 (In Japanese)

Uchida, N. 1985. Integration and production of causal sequences by preschool children. *Jpn. J. Educ. Psychol.* 33:124–34 (In Japanese)

Uda, H. 1988. Learning styles among high school students: personal theories of English learning. *Jpn. J. Educ. Psychol.* 36:38–44 (In Japanese)

Uemura, K., Tajima, N. 1987a. Effects of social interaction on the child's understanding process in the problem-solving situation. Presented at Bienn. Meet. Int. Soc. Behav. Dev., 9th, Tokyo

Uemura, K., Tajima, N. 1987b. The effect of social interaction on the child's information-processing: comparison of mother-child pair with father-child pair. *Boshi-Kenkyu (Res. Mother-Child Relat.)* 8:1–21 (In Japanese)

Uemura, K., Tajima, N. 1988. Child's information-processing in social interaction: the content analysis. *Boshi-Kenkyu (Res. Mother-Child Relat.)* 9:76–86 (In Japanese)

Ueno, N. 1987. Mental model as theatre. Paper presented at the Third Int. Imagery Conf.

Ueno, N., Tsukano, H., Yokoyama, N. 1986. Preschoolers' concept of number conservation in significant transformation. *Jpn. J. Educ. Psychol.* 34:94–103. (In Japanese with English abstract)

Umemoto, T. 1959. Japanese studies in verbal learning and memory. *Psychologia* 2:1–19

Umemoto, T. 1974. Progress of Japanese studies in verbal learning and memory. *Psychologia* 14:77–82

Umezu, H., Torii, S., Uemura, Y. 1987. Activity of sign system of the early blind in the initial stage after operation. *Jpn. J. Psychonom. Sci.* 6:67–78

Wakabayashi, M., Graen, G. B. 1984. The Japanese career progress study: a 7 year follow-up. *J. Appl. Psychol.* 69:603–14

Watanabe, T. 1988. Effect of irrelevant differences as a function of the relations between relevant and irrelevant dimensions in the same-different task. *J. Exp. Psychol.: Human Percept. Perf.* 14:132–42

Watanabe, T., Oyama, T. 1989. Are illusory contours a cause or consequence of apparent differences in brightness and depth in the Kanizsa square? *Perception* 17:513–21

Wertsch, J. V., ed. 1985a. *Culture, Communication and Cognition: Vygotskian Perspectives*. Cambridge: Cambridge Univ. Press. 358 pp.

Wertsch, J. V. 1985b. *Vygotsky and the Social Formation of Mind*. Cambridge/London: Harvard Univ. Press. 262 pp.

Yamada, E., Shiomi, K. 1986. Differences between adult and child on perception and conjecture of constant velocity and acceleration. *Jpn. J. Educ. Psychol.* 34:239–46 (In Japanese)

Yamadori, A. 1986. Category specific alexia and a neuropsychological model of alexia. In *Linguistics, Psychology, and the Chinese Language*, ed. H. S. R. Kao, R. Hoosain. Hong Kong: Cent. Asian Stud., Univ. Hong Kong

Yatabe, T. 1956. *Introduction to Psychology*. Osaka: Sogensha. 473 pp. (In Japanese)

Yoshida, M., Yamashita, I. 1987. The factors affecting the pupils' learning motivation and their teachers' perceptions. *Jpn. J. Educ. Psychol.* 35:309–17 (In Japanese)

Annu. Rev. Psychol. 1990. 41:243–88

CONSUMER PSYCHOLOGY

Joel B. Cohen

College of Business Administration, University of Florida, Gainesville, Florida 32611

Dipankar Chakravarti

Karl Eller Graduate School of Management, University of Arizona, Tucson, Arizona 85721

CONTENTS

INTRODUCTION

A quadrennial (1985–1988) review of a field can focus intensively on cutting-edge topics, but it can also offer a broader perspective that organizes knowledge and displays both gaps and potential research synergies. Despite length constraints, we try to perform both tasks here. Inevitably, many topics receive only passing attention; our coverage is not all-inclusive.

Three distinct sets of research issues now occupy the field's attention: 1. Research on consumer judgment and choice is largely process-driven, with

0066-4308/90/0201-0243$02.00

attention paid to theoretically relevant task and contextual factors that often serve as real world constraints or mediators. 2. Examinations of consumer responses to marketer-initiated stimuli (e.g. advertising, packaging, price) draw on judgment and choice research, but they focus primarily on variations on the stimulus side. 3. Descriptive research on patterns of consumption behavior (i.e. consumer role enactment and how consumers assess consumption outcomes) provides "grist for the mill" for those interested in building more realistic models and more domain-relevant theory.

There are pervasive differences in how consumer researchers structure problems within these domains. One orientation is essentially perceptual/cognitive. This research stresses how ability, knowledge, memory, and related information-processing differences influence judgment, choice, and responses to marketing stimuli, as well as patterns of behavior and their outcomes. A second orientation focuses on motivational and predispositional factors (e.g. individual differences in values, personality, attitudes, involvement, and affective states) to provide insights into the "why" of consumer behavior and to segment the marketplace. Finally, a socio-environmental orientation takes either an aggregate view of consumer differences (e.g. group membership, ethnic identity) or examines environmental and "life space" factors (e.g. resources, role obligations, time) that enhance or constrain options and responses.

These research domains and orientations intersect in important ways. For example, motivational variables affect both decision-making processes and responses to persuasion. Socio-environmental factors modify wants and influence information search and deliberation. More integrative approaches seem necessary to further our understanding of how consumers cope with complex environments. Here we attempt to link microanalytic research on consumer judgment and choice to research on consumer responses to marketing stimuli. We seek touchpoints with studies of broader consumption behavior, which are often rich in description and have implications for improved problem-definition in microanalytic research.

JUDGMENT AND CHOICE PROCESSES

The field has traditionally emphasized the formal and logical operations involved in consumer decision-making. However, perceptual/cognitive studies of how consumers construct situations and frame problems (e.g. analogical reasoning, categorization, availability) sometimes overlook non-cognitive factors that also help form the perceived reality that influences consumer decisions. For example, motivational explanations (e.g. self-esteem enhancement) may not be invoked when cognitive explanations (e.g. easier retrieval of favorable outcomes) can be made to suffice. Research should address noncognitive personal and social factors that color decisions (e.g. internalized values and personal commitments) or external pressures that constrain the options considered (Etzioni 1988).

Perceptual/Cognitive Approaches

In contrast to an earlier emphasis on search heuristics in stimulus-based choices, researchers with perceptual/cognitive orientations have adopted a contingent-processing perspective on consumer judgment and choice, with increased consideration of knowledge and memory issues (Bettman et al 1990). We review four aspects of this research: attention and encoding, knowledge organization, knowledge operations, and judgment processes.

ATTENTION AND ENCODING   Three ideas have influenced recent research in the area. First, consumers have limited attentional capacity and often acquire knowledge via processes needing minimal effort or conscious control. Second, consumers encode information selectively so that mental representations may not always be veridical records of what was encountered. Finally, search and choice are guided by prior knowledge and are realizations of adaptive and contingent information processing.

Research on automatic processes in consumer choice is sparse. Hoyer (1984) noted that many in-store decisions for common products were made with little cognitive effort. His results suggest that attentional processes, speeded-up by experience, simplify decision-making by helping consumers locate familiar brands and previously chosen alternatives. Park et al (1989) found increased brand switching and unplanned purchasing when consumers shopped under time pressure in unfamiliar stores (i.e. with cues facilitating automatic detection processes removed).

It is now well-established that prior knowledge moderates selective exposure, attention, and interpretation. Johnson & Russo (1984) found that, in a choice task, product familiarity had an inverted U–shaped relation with learning and may have induced subjects to focus selectively on choice-relevant information. Brucks (1985) and Simonson et al (1988) also noted selectivity in information acquisition due to processing contingencies. Novices seem to select information based on expediency whereas experts may use relevance or importance criteria (Alba & Hutchinson 1987). However, if selectivity is motivationally induced, expert-novice differences may be attenuated.

Brucks (1985) found that prior knowledge improved external search efficiency, allowing quicker identification or elimination of inappropriate alternatives. Subjective knowledge (confidence) increased reliance on own evaluations versus other's recommendations. Her findings imply an adaptive process, where current task status determines sequential search. The certainty and valence of brand-attribute beliefs determined information search order in a choice task (Simonson et al 1988). Finally, Biehal & Chakravarti (1986) reported adaptive and contingent search of memory and external information in a mixed (stimulus-based and memory-based) choice.

While prior knowledge, confidence, and memory-control processes guide search and cause selective attention to informational stimuli in choice tasks, the effects do not always replicate in judgment tasks. Here, Johnson & Russo (1984) found familiarity and learning to be monotonically related. This appears to stem from elaboration of new information rather than from selective exposure. Simonson et al (1988) reported that search order effects found in a choice task vanished in a ranking-judgment task.

Subjects with different prior beliefs about the relationship between price and quality were asked to sample products in order to assess the relationship objectively (John et al 1986). Those who believed in a price-quality relationship chose to sample higher-priced products. However, Bettman et al (1986a) found that consumers' covariation judgments for given price-quality data were accurate and unaffected by prior beliefs about price-quality relations. Selective perception and task contingency effects seem less dramatic in judgment tasks when all relevant data are given as opposed to sequentially acquired.

KNOWLEDGE ORGANIZATION   Consumer researchers have begun to investigate the role of associative-memory structures in judgment. Research on cognitive representations of products links perceptual-scaling work to current ideas on category structure. Using retrieval data, Johnson & Fornell (1987) found that the more abstract the alternatives, the better consumer judgments are fit by multidimensional scaling maps versus feature-based additive trees. Though retrieval data are not isomorphic with memory representations, a product's abstractness may influence whether its representation is dimensional or feature based.

Studies show how related facts and concepts in memory may become parts of scripts in which the integrative theme is a predetermined and stereotyped sequence of actions in a consumption domain (Smith & Houston 1985). More general associative structures such as memory schemata help consumers assimilate, integrate, and retrieve information and may trigger affective and evaluative reactions towards stimuli based on schemata-consistency dynamics (Alba & Hutchinson 1987).

Evaluative judgments of products may stem from their category placement, which can depend on category salience and criteria used to determine category membership (Sujan 1985). Cohen & Basu (1987) discuss alternative categorization processes and criteria and present a contingency model of category learning and product identification. For example, when attentional resources are limited, consumers may rely on exemplar-based representations and nonanalytical processing (e.g. overall similarity) rather than attribute-based rules to determine category membership. The level of generality and the graded structure of product categories are related to expertise (Nedungadi & Hutchinson 1985; Alba & Hutchinson 1987). Ad hoc and goal-derived categories (Barsalou 1985) may be especially important in consumers' organization of product information and resulting judgments (see Coupey & Nakamoto 1988; Sujan & Tybout 1988 for empirical work).

KNOWLEDGE OPERATIONS   Although prior knowledge is available in memory, it must be perceived as relevant and be accessible in order to be used in a given judgment or choice. Also, consumers transform knowledge by abstracting and elaborating existing information and generating inferences. Both of these issues have produced significant research.

Retrieval facilitation and inhibition phenomena (e.g. part-list cuing) were demonstrated with consumer stimuli such as brand names (Alba & Chattopadhyay 1985; 1986). Priming (by prior selective attention in judgment and choice tasks) and framing (by varying current task goals) were shown to influence information recall and brand attitudes (Loken & Hoverstad 1985). Retrieval contingencies, moderated by memory accessibility of previously encountered brand-attribute information, had dramatic effects on choices (Biehal & Chakravarti 1986). Also, when opportunity for evaluative analysis is low and memory for semantic detail is poor, consumers may retrieve and use frequency counts of positive and negative attributes possessed by a brand in making judgments (Alba & Marmorstein 1987).

The relative influence of recalled attributes versus prior evaluations in memory-based judgments has received attention. Lichtenstein & Srull (1985) found that mental representations of overall evaluations influenced memory-based judgments independent of the attribute information on which they were based. Initial stimulus-based judgments influenced subsequent memory-based judgments over and above attribute information in memory (Kardes 1986). Selective use of an input in choice was explained by its memory accessibility and diagnosticity relative to other inputs for the task (Feldman & Lynch 1988; Lynch et al 1988). Such accessibility and priming phenomena may affect risk perception and handling (Dowling 1986) and other mental accounting processes (Thaler 1985). Attention and distinctiveness manipulations affect product performance judgments and are correlated with self-reported retrieval of success and failure instances (Folkes 1988b).

Elaboration helps comprehension by establishing coherence between facts, by drawing semantic and logical inferences and interpretations, and by abstracting the essential (often evaluative) meaning of facts. Experts and novices differ in elaborative processing (Alba & Hutchinson 1987). Type of elaboration is strongly related to recall performance, has less impact on recognition, and is dissociated from performance on implicit memory tests (Schachter 1987). These principles have guided consumer researchers in using various elaboration instructions to manipulate locus of attention and nature of encoding (Obermiller 1985). Cognitive responses to messages coded by abstractness of elaboration (thus memorability) explained more variance in attitudes than did traditional valence-based coding schemes, especially after delay. Over time, inferences and judgments that summarize multiple facts or generalize a particular fact come to dominate memory for advertising content unless attention is directed to attribute-based comparisons at exposure (Chattopadhyay & Alba 1988).

Imagery-based elaboration, in which multisensory information finds unitized representation in working memory, is a promising area for consumer information-processing research. MacInnis & Price (1987) discuss the effects of low and high elaboration imagery on memory, incidental learning, and choice. Encoding and retrieval through verbal and visual modes have begun to receive some needed attention (Smith & Houston 1987). However, processing in olfactory and tactile modes (which often capture critical aspects of consumer stimuli) has been little studied.

Inferences elaborate, embellish, or create information from presented facts and prior knowledge. One issue is how consumers handle missing brand-attribute information in judgment or choice tasks (Johnson & Levin 1985; Ford & Smith 1987). While consumers do not always respond to missing information with inferences (Lim et al 1988; C. J. Simmons working paper; but see Kardes 1988), these are more likely if the information is perceived as decision relevant. Whether missing attribute values are inferred (so as to be consistent with a prior overall evaluation) or based on perceived correlation is a function of memory accessibility and the diagnosticity or reliability of each input (A. S. Dick, D. Chakravarti, and G. J. Biehal, working paper). Alba & Hutchinson (1987) identify two other inferential mechanisms. Similarity-based inferences transfer properties between objects purely by salience-driven similarity judgments. In schema-based inferences, products seen as good category instances are attributed the typical, but not the atypical, category features. Both approaches involve the assignment of general default values for unpresented information. Hence, the inferences may not be veridical.

JUDGMENT PROCESSES   Research has shifted from an emphasis on information integration and sophisticated ways of estimating multiattribute weights and scales values (Lynch 1985) to factors affecting the interdependence among perception, task variables, and preference judgments. Meyer (1987; Meyer & Sathi 1985) found that consumers learn multiattribute judgment policies with fairly little feedback but learn faster and more accurately about good versus bad options. Glazer (1984) showed that in multiattribute judgments, subjects' preferences were correlated with perceptions and discrimination ability. In particular, brands at either end of the evaluative continuum had a recognition advantage. These studies define the predictive and descriptive limits of normative, multiattribute judgment models that assume independence of perception and preferences.

Grether & Wilde (1984) experimentally tested models of conjunctive choice, reporting the use of conjunctive cutoffs in decision-making. Klein & Bither (1987) indicated that decision-makers pick cutoffs that maximally discriminate between retained and rejected alternatives in utility terms. Although the reality of conjunctive decisions is debated (J. G. Lynch 1984, working paper), these studies present conditions under which they are plausible. Research also addressed hierarchical choice processes. Hauser's (1986) normative analysis showed that agendas (processing constraints) that change the feature hierarchy (relative to a representational hierarchy) may alter choice, though the empirical effects do not always follow theoretical predictions (Kahn et al 1987).

Brand choices in the same product category involve comparisons on similar attributes, but choices may also involve alternatives from categories as diverse as refrigerators and stereos (Johnson 1984, 1986). Since brands are described on different attributes, consumers may use holistic processing to integrate information across attributes and compare brands. Or, they may represent the brands on abstract attributes and then use attribute comparison processes. Arguing that comparable and noncomparable alternative sets differ in the ready availability of decision criteria versus the need to evolve them, Bettman & Sujan (1987) showed that priming different decision criteria influenced evaluations of noncomparable alternatives for both experts and novices. With comparable alternatives, framing affected only novices. The comparability of alternatives in a set also influences use of categorical or hierarchical processing (Johnson 1988). These findings show that both choice-set structure and choice strategy influence the predictive performance of multiattribute judgment and choice models (see Johnson & Meyer 1984).

Contextual factors and decision framing influence decisions dramatically. For example, even in formally identical problems, the use of base and case information in judgments varies with the numerical values of cues and with each cue's perceived relevance and surface detail variations (Ofir & Lynch 1984). Adding asymmetrically dominated alternatives to choice sets changed choice proportions of target brands (Huber & Puto 1983; Burton & Zinkhan 1987). Yet, not all context effects in judgment tasks are attributable to true changes in psychological perceptions of stimuli. Stimulus meaningfulness and product familiarity moderated "attraction" and "substitution" effects (Ratneshwar et al 1987). Also, in examining the locus of attribute range variation effects, J. G. Lynch, D. Chakravarti, and A. Mitra (working paper) found that both experts and novices showed contrast effects in ratings of unidimensional stimuli, but novices were more susceptible than experts to contextual effects on psychological representations. Thus, contrast effects in experts' ratings often may be attributable to mere changes in "response language" (i.e. how context-invariant judgments are reported on rating scales) as opposed to true changes in mental representations.

Many studies in economics and behavioral decision theory have shown the advantages of Kahneman & Tversky's (1979) prospect theory over traditional subjective expected utility (SEU) theory. In consumer research, Kahn & Sarin (1988) found the SEU theory was unable to explain ambiguity-related behavior. Their subjects' orientations toward ambiguity paralleled the risk aversion patterns predicted by prospect theory. Wiener et al (1986) tested the prospect theory notion that outcomes are evaluated against reference points. They found that insurance purchase propositions framed as losses received lower mean purchase intentions than when they were framed as gains. See also Levin & Johnson (1984), Levin et al (1987), and Diamond (1988).

The prospect theory value function is concave in gains and convex in losses, and the curve is steeper for losses than for gains. Thaler (1985) discusses the implications of these value-function properties for how consumers may code combinations of gains and losses. Though widely discussed, the normative implications (i.e. that gains be segregated and losses integrated) have not been tested empirically. While not a theory of risky choices, Thaler's transaction utility and mental accounting notions deserve empirical attention in consumer research.

Motivational and Predispositional Approaches

Attitudinal approaches have dominated research relating motivational factors to judgment and choice. A more recent genre of research examined how affect, viewed as either an evaluative cognition or as a valenced feeling state, predisposes consumer judgments. Finally, the interplay of motivational and cognitive factors has continued to receive attention.

ATTITUDE AND BEHAVIORAL INTENTIONS MODELS   Multiattribute attitude models continue to be widely applied. The Fishbein & Ajzen (1975) model was adapted to include nonfunctional (e.g. hedonic and value expressive) aspects of choice alternatives (Ahtola 1985). Prakash (1986; see also Gutman 1985) identified terminal and instrumental values associated with population subgroups and linked these to consequences of product use and ownership. Researchers revisited the issue of including representations of past behavior (e.g. habit) in behavioral-intentions models to incorporate continuing effects of contextual factors not fully captured in stated intentions (McQuarrie & Langmeyer 1987). Behavior-intention models were also adapted for situations where pursuing an uncertain outcome or goal (e.g. dieting to lose weight) rather than performing a behavior (eating less) is a policy objective (Warshaw & Droge 1986; Sheppard et al 1988). Perceived consequences of both success and failure for behaviors having uncertain outcomes may often need to be represented in such models. Despite conceptual and operational challenges the Fishbein-Ajzen model has been shown to possess strong predictive value (Sheppard et al 1988).

MOTIVATIONAL FACTORS AND SEARCH   Consumer search is mainly viewed as focused activity in the prepurchase phase of decision-making. Reported time spent and calls to retailers were associated (Beatty & Smith 1987) with the perceived value of shopping for the item, concern about the purchase, time availability, and, sometimes, low knowledge (but not so low as to affect adversely the perceived value of shopping). However, Bloch et al (1986) contend that search is part of a larger information-gathering activity enjoyed both for its own sake and because consumers are intrinsically interested in particular products. Rook's view of the "buying impulse" (Rook & Hoch 1985; Rook 1987) exemplifies unplanned purchasing in its purest form (i.e. not merely an effect of in-store retrieval cues).

INTERACTIONS AMONG COGNITIVE AND AFFECTIVE SYSTEMS   Recent research has incorporated the direct and indirect impact of affect and emotion (marketer-initiated, contextual, and consumer feeling states) on resulting evaluations (attitude judgments) and behavior. That affect and emotion are ongoing parts of the consumer experience (e.g. thinking about buying and using products, shopping itself) is well established (e.g. Holbrook 1986b; Gardner 1985a; Havlena & Holbrook 1986). They may have a significant mediating role in cognitive processes and decision outcomes. Unfortunately, the term "affect" is used to refer both to evaluative judgments (e.g. good-bad, favorable-unfavorable) and to valenced feelings states that can produce evaluatively tagged memory traces. This has caused confusion (see Cohen & Areni 1990).

The debate on the independence of cognitive and affective systems spilled over into consumer research (Zajonc & Marcus 1982; Tsal 1985). Though preconscious "attitudes" may form for selected stimuli and for tasks allowing hemispheric specialization (Janiszewski 1988), the two systems are probably not truly independent (Obermiller 1985; Anand et al 1988). Attention has been focused on mechanisms whereby affect might produce evaluations in the absence of cognitive processes usually implicated in judgment. Noncognitively mediated transfer of affect through classical conditioning became a "hot" topic (Gorn 1982; McSweeney & Bierley 1984; Bierley et al 1985). Stuart et al (1987) found fairly robust evidence for attitude conditioning. However, Allen & Madden (1985) argued that the evidence for affective conditioning is tenuous and that affective responses (especially complex ones) require underlying cognitive activity. Many conceptual and methodological issues in noncognitive versus cognitive mediation of affect transfer remain unresolved (Cohen & Areni 1990). The role of awareness as a contingent factor may be decisive (Kahle et al 1987; Allen & Janiszewski 1989).

Thus far, the key finding on mood effects on decision processes is that mood at both exposure and retrieval can bias recall and affective judgment in a mood-congruent fashion (Gardner 1985a). Positive and negative moods at encoding influenced product evaluations if the latter were formed at that time but not if they were formed later based on retrieved information (Srull 1984). Positive *retrieval* mood influenced evaluations congruently if evaluations were generated from retrieved information, but not if they were previously formed (Srull 1987). Implications for judgment processes have prompted significant interest (Isen 1989). Mood at encoding may influence attention and elaboration of stimuli and may influence problem representation. Retrieval mood may cue affectively similar memory traces, biasing inputs to memory-based judgments. Domain expertise may moderate susceptibility to mood effects (Srull 1987), and positive and negative moods may have asymmetric effects on recall and judgment. Finally, broad decision orientations (e.g. risk aversion and framing) and even participation in specific types of decisions may depend on motivational processes that consciously focus on maintaining dispositional balance (Isen 1989). See also Mitchell (1986b) and Cohen & Areni (1990).

B. J. Calder and C. L. Gruder (1988, working paper) manipulated positive and negative emotional states via hypnotic induction and retrieval of strong emotional experiences. Induced emotional states influenced subjects' selection/use of objective information, biasing attitudes and enhancing recall of items with similar affective content. Although complex relationships were found among specific emotions, the results confirm that emotions can play a key role in consumer decisions (see Holbrook & Batra 1987).

INTERPRETING PRODUCT EXPERIENCE   Attribution theory provides explanations for how consumers develop causal inferences, such as the attribution of causes for product failure (Lichtenstein & Bearden 1986; Folkes 1988a). Wiener & Mowen (1986) noted that endorser incentives lowered source credibility. Similar reasoning about product performance may underlie Marks & Kamins' (1988) findings on sampling-based versus advertising-based product attitudes. Folkes (1984; Folkes et al 1987) found that consumers' attributions for product failure influenced responses such as requesting refunds, product exchange, etc. Curren & Folkes (1987) found that attributional locus (buyer-seller), controllability (volitional or not), and stability (fluctuating or not) affected consumers' desire to complain or compliment a firm. Causal attributions also display self-serving biases and may help preserve self-esteem (Folkes & Kostos 1986).

Socio-Environmental Influences

Environmental (i.e. task and contextual) factors have been studied primarily as part of a contingent-processing approach, as discussed above. In this section we review research on how consumer decisions vary by selected individual and social factors.

AGE DIFFERENCES   John & Cole (1986) and John & Whitney (1986) reviewed the literature on information-processing capabilities of young children, older children, and elderly adults. They concluded that memory limitations handicap both young children and the elderly in complex processing tasks. Young children lack a knowledge base and an understanding of how to use memory strategies, whereas the elderly have difficulty with memory control processes. Older children process information better than younger children and develop more integrated knowledge structures as they obtain more information and experience. Consistent with Piaget's theory, Bahn (1986) found that children's brand perceptions and preferences vary by development stage (preoperational versus concrete-operational) and product category.

FAMILY INFLUENCES   Over a set of similar products, responses to a marital happiness scale were negatively related to reported purchase conflict and positively related to joint involvement in purchase decisions (Kirchler 1988). This 28-day diary study takes a broader view of the resources exchanged and explicitly considers the role of emotional bonds. It demonstrates the value of longitudinal studies of consumer decision-making in understanding how purchase decisions and tradeoffs (i.e. "utility debts") are interwoven into daily life.

Knowledge sharing is important in family decision-making. Davis et al (1986) found that in predicting spousal preferences for new product concepts, both spouses anchored heavily on their own preferences. However, each overestimated the relative influence that spouses would wield on the decision, biasing predictions. Since spousal judgments of relative preference intensity and influence help shape family purchase decisions (Corfman & Lehmann 1987), the findings suggest a level of inefficiency and potential dissonance associated with "co-operative and joint" family decisions (Seymour 1986). For a scale to assess spousal conflict arousal (via joint decision involvement, power, and both interpersonal and product-related motivation) see Seymour & Lessne (1984).

SOCIAL TIES AND INTERPERSONAL INFLUENCE   There has been a concerted effort to understand the relationship between consumers' integration into various kinds of social structures and their degree of reliance on those networks for information and legitimation. Leonard-Barton (1985), for example, examined the role of experts in the diffusion of a technological innovation and concluded that adopters were not more active information-seekers; nonadopters simply acted on different information. Gatignon & Robertson (1985) organized the literature on new product diffusion through the social structure and provided an extensive inventory of propositions to guide further research. Reingen et al (1984; Reingen & Kernan 1986; Brown & Reingen 1987) applied formal network analysis methods to study word-of-mouth referral behavior. The work distinguishes flow of information from flow of influence and highlights the role of weak social ties as an information bridge between different subgroups (within which there are stronger social ties and more potential influence).

Research has also shown that others' recommendations may substitute for or complement one's own knowledge. Such information helps form brand consideration sets and supplements attribute information in brand comparisons (Olshavsky & Rosen 1985, Brucks 1985). Whereas "opinion leaders" may, more often than not, simply be those who are knowledgeable and are sought out for advice, "market mavens" not only have information to share (i.e. they are more "tuned in" to information sources) but they enjoy sharing it across several product categories (Feick & Price 1987; Price et al 1987). A related consumer orientation is generalized "purchasing involvement" (Slama & Tashchian 1985; Slama et al 1988). Initial evidence using a newly developed scale suggests that some groups of consumers tend to be more involved in the purchase process. Possible consistency biases in the self-report methods used in this domain suggest caution regarding self-designated "super consumers."

RESPONSES TO MARKETER-INITIATED STIMULI

The underlying judgment and choice processes reviewed in the previous section provide insight into consumer responses to marketer-initiated stimuli. However, the focus here is on stimulus variations, particularly in advertising, and on research that seeks to explain the nature of the effects.

Perceptual/Cognitive Approaches

The extensive treatment of advertising effects with this orientation can be grouped into: (a) how specific characteristics of ad stimuli affect consumer responses and the mediating effects of elaboration; (b) effects of comparative advertising and interference; and (c) measurement and testing of ad effects, including potential deceptive impact. We also review new research on how branding, pricing, and sales-presentation strategies influence perceptions and related judgments.

MESSAGE FACTORS   Many advertising stimulus factors (e.g. color in print ads, presentation in radio commercials) affect attention, recall, and attitudinal judgments (Sewall & Sarel 1986). Compared to normal-density ads, time-compressed ads captured less attention and evoked fewer cognitive responses to ad claims, such that message quality exerted a small impact and source credibility a larger impact on brand attitudes. Thus, disrupting the opportunity for cognitive elaboration increased ad persuasiveness (Moore et al 1986).

Pictorial ads did better than verbal-only ads on both immediate and delayed recall when processing focused on appearance features of the ads. With semantic processing instructions, verbal-only stimuli did as well on immediate recall but worse on delayed recall (Childers & Houston 1984). Recall was superior when brand name, attributes, and visual components were integrated pictorially but the copy conveyed discrepant information. Thus, elaborative processing may be heightened by discrepant pictures and words. Reducing processing opportunity may inhibit associative linkages in memory and attenuate recall (Houston et al 1987). Keller (1987) found that using visual and verbal elements from an ad to cue retrieval of ad memory traces may also affect brand evaluations. Such cues could enhance the effectiveness of point-of-purchase reminders. Finally, verbal and visual components of ads may induce hemispheric dominance shifts (Rothschild et al 1988).

Kahle & Homer (1985) showed that an endorser's physical attractiveness need not be a peripheral influence on attitudes (Cacioppo & Petty 1985) but may provide information regarding product quality, benefits, or image. When a communication contains strong arguments, each delivered by a separate source, more positive thought and increased persuasion are likely. Renewed attention may be devoted to the arguments not yet heard (Moore & Reardon 1987). Affirmative disclosures and other message-discounting cues may have complex effects on longer-term attitudes if they are processed separately instead of integrated into the message at encoding. With dissociation, retrieval may be limited to the more easily cued and normally pro-message elements (Mazursky & Schul 1988).

Kamins & Assael (1987a) found support for a two-sided refutational ad appeal. By collecting cognitive responses in an improved design (Kamins & Assael 1987b) the authors found support for both inoculation theory (fewer counterarguments given a refutational approach) and attribution theory (fewer source derogations, suggesting high imputed credibility, given a two-sided approach). Reactions to a disconfirming product trial were less negative for subjects receiving either refutational or nonrefutational two-sided advertisements.

Attitudinal judgments do not result directly from attentional improvement and greater information accessibility but also depend on the valence of retrieved information. This idea is central to expectancy-value models and other models of judgment and decision. Kisielius & Sternthal (1986) refer to the judgmental outcome of message comprehension and favorability as the "availability-valence" hypothesis and stress message-elaboration as a key cognitive aspect of this process. They discuss factors that affect both information accessibility and valence of retrieved information; they interpret both earlier studies (Kiselius & Sternthal 1984) and the vividness "controversy" from this perspective.

An inverted-U relationship between ad repetition and attitudes is often asserted. It is based on an initially positive response to uncertainty reduction and an increase in knowledge and message elaboration. Thereafter, boredom, satiation, or counterarguing produce negative responses. These effects should be mediated substantially by factors such as prior knowledge, message complexity, and the overall favorability of the advertising execution. Rethans et al (1986) found learning with repetition, but at three exposures tedium was evident in attitudinal and cognitive response data. Yet, viewers seemed able to separate their attitudes toward seeing the commercial from their attitudes toward the product. After two exposures to equivalently rated simple or complex magazine ads, subjects' liking for the complex ad increased more than for the simple ad (Cox & Cox 1988). However, increased liking for the complex ad did not mediate the increase in liking for the brand found in both ad conditions. Possible subject sensitization within the repeated-measures design hinders interpretation.

The "saturation point" beyond which ad exposure decreases evaluation may result from stimulus characteristics (e.g. emotional tone, information content, and variety) as well as subjects' interest in the product, events, and people portrayed in the ad. Based on Cacioppo & Petty's (1985) cognitive response analysis of message repetition, Batra & Ray (1986b) argue that an attitudinal downturn will occur later when motivation and ability to process information are at lower levels initially. Motivation and ability were not manipulated but were intertwined by selecting products for which brand choice "mattered" and by using knowledgeable subjects (the high motivation/ability condition). Ads with more attribute statements were viewed as providing more opportunity for counterargument, though process measures were absent. Over two sessions, separated by a week, four exposure ads showed a downturn in attitudes and behavioral intentions under high motivation/ability whereas a continual increase occurred under low motivation/ability.

COMPARATIVE CLAIMS AND CONFUSION   Droge & Darmon (1987) examined the effectiveness of comparative and noncomparative ads with product-based and nonproduct-based content. Direct comparative ads were superior only for overall brand positioning. A comparative ad attained better positioning clarity only if it had product-based content. Gorn & Weinberg (1984) found that comparative advertising by a challenger brand enhanced perceived similarity between challenger and leader, regardless of exposure to the leader's ad. Johnson & Horne (1988) found that under both forced and natural exposure conditions and regardless of advertiser intent, comparative ads promoted associations between the compared brands. However, the degree of explicit comparison and the comparison mode may moderate associations, and the effects may vary for experts and novices since they rely on different inferential processes (Sujan & Dekleva 1987).

Some attentional issues of theoretical and public policy interest include interference effects, subliminal advertising (Saegert 1987), and comprehension of affirmative disclosure messages by target groups (Funkhouser 1984). MacKenzie (1986) found that bi-directional effects between viewer attention and ad features moderated the ad's effects on perceived attribute importance. Responses to ad stimuli may be influenced by the extent to which the viewing environment contains distractions (Nelson et al 1985) or competing stimuli (Keller 1987). Burke & Srull (1988) found both retroactive and proactive interference effects on consumers' memory for ads in competitive contexts. Recall was inhibited by ad exposure to other products in a manufacturer's line and to ads for competing brands in the product class, either before or after exposure to target brand ads. Repetition positively affected recall only if there was little or no advertising for similar products.

MEASUREMENT AND TESTING METHODOLOGIES   Information-processing research has contributed new ways of measuring ad effectiveness. These include response latency measures for spokesperson effectiveness (Burroughs & Feinberg 1987), models for print ad recognition readership (Finn 1988), recognition tests tracking viewer attention through a TV commercial sequence (Young & Robinson 1987), and ad recognition tests based on signal detection theory (Singh & Churchill 1986; Tashchian et al 1988). Singh et al (1988) concluded that recognition scores are more discriminating and sensitive measures of ad memory than recall tests. Thorson & Snyder (1984) used a psycholinguistic model to analyze the propositional structure of specific commercial scripts and that of associated protocols generated by viewers in day-after recall or free recall. They used the script measures as regression predictors of viewer performance on a set of recall-related criteria to evaluate how message structure related to message recall.

A number of challenging measurement problems require additional work. One of these involves assessing deceptive effects of ad claims. Grunert & Dedler (1987) addressed the deception potential of particular message components. Burke et al (1988) provided two tests for misleading ads. The first examines increased false beliefs from ad exposure by comparison to a no-ad control. The second tests for reduced false beliefs by comparison to an ad purged of the inaccurate claims. Using computer-constructed ads and a computer-based measurement procedure, they found that inferential expansions of literally true but imprecise, claims and noninformatively qualified (e.g. inconspicuous) expansionary claims increased false brand-attribute beliefs, attitudes, and purchase intentions compared to the controls. Their method has promise, though the use of structured elicitation questions may not be ideal.

A second problem involves developing more diagnostic tests of ad effectiveness including ways to identify patterns of recall and recognition performance that distinguish between ad encoding versus retrieval difficulties. One promising measure focuses on implicit ad memory traces that affect brand belief and attitudes but are undetected in recall or recognition tests (Schachter 1987).

RESPONSES TO BRAND NAMES AND PRICES   Robertson (1987) found that high-imagery brand names had a significant recall advantage relative to low-imagery names. Brand name deception (Reece & Ducoffe 1987) and brand confusion (Loken et al 1986) involve issues common to deceptive advertising. Approaches involving categorization and the resulting clarity of brand concepts have been applied to brand names and brand family decisions (e.g. Park et al 1986). Research examines how categorization influences pioneering brands' competitive advantage (Carpenter & Nakamoto 1989); how consideration sets in memory affect choice (P. Nedungadi 1989, working paper); and how elaboration, inference, and affect generalization may affect brand name extensions (Boush et al 1987; D. A. Aaker and K. L. Keller 1988, working paper; Chakravarti et al 1989).

Theories of framing and contextual effects fueled a resurgence in pricing research. Liefield & Heslop (1985) found that different presentations of reference prices did not alter perception of ordinary prices, but subjects estimated lower ordinary prices in a sale context. Accuracy was unrelated to the recency of a subjective shopping experience. Helgeson & Beatty (1987) examined the impact of deviations from an expected (reference) price on price recall error. Errors were usually in the direction of price expectations, and the effect was stronger and more consistent for less- than for more-involving products. Urbany et al (1988) found that a plausible reference price raised estimates of the regular price and perceived offer value even for more skeptical subjects. With an advertised sale price above the lowest expected price, the exaggerated reference price increased the percentage of subjects who purchased the advertised product without checking other prices. Finally, using Universal Product Code (UPC) scanner panel data, Winer (1986) found that incorporating reference prices in a brand choice model improved predictions relative to models using only observed price.

A second category of pricing research deals with the evaluative aspects of price. Buyukkurt (1986) examined how serially sampled price information and discount structures affected the perceived value of a basket of items. A large number of noticeable discounts led to a higher perceived value than a small number of extreme discounts. Petroshius & Monroe (1987) found that price characteristics of a product line affected consumer evaluations of a model in the line. Lichtenstein et al (1988) found that price consciousness and product involvement (i.e. importance) are inversely related and have opposite implications for several price constructs such as beliefs about price-quality relationships. Greater price acceptability produces a wider latitude of price acceptance as price is linked to quality. Mobley et al (1988) reported that a tensile price claim (e.g. save up to 50%) used together with large advertised price reductions lowered perceived offer value and led to discounting of expected price reductions.

Judgmental processes underlying framing effects have been examined in a study of salesperson expectations (Sujan et al 1986). When salespeople were perceived as typical (i.e. fit a schema), product evaluations were unaffected by product argument quality. More analytical information processing occurs when the salesperson does not conform to expectations. Responses to sales promotion, such as dollar-equivalent discounts, may have different motivational and information-processing implications depending on how they are framed. Also, alternative ways of bundling accessories, service contracts, and warranties may make the risk of product failure differentially salient. Thaler's (1985) notion of segregating multiple gains and integrating multiple losses based on the value function described in prospect theory (Kahneman & Tversky 1979) may be useful for understanding consumer responses in these cases.

Motivational and Predispositional Approaches

We next turn to research on motivational (want/relevance inducing) and attitudinal (goal/benefit oriented, positively/negatively valenced) properties of marketing stimuli and interactions between these and motivational and attitudinal predispositions.

INVOLVEMENT AND MESSAGE FACTORS   Celsi & Olson (1988) exposed subjects having differing levels of intrinsic interest in tennis to ads under baseline situational relevance or with the further inducement of participation in a product lottery. Both involvement sources exerted significant and independent effects on attention to the ads, comprehension effort, and focus/amount of elaboration. Domain knowledge was unrelated to processing effort but raised the number of product-related thoughts and inferences. The authors suggest that involvement be viewed as a motivational state that activates domain knowledge, thereby influencing comprehension.

Viewer involvement may influence spontaneous inferences from advertising. Highly involved viewers were more likely spontaneously to infer omitted conclusions from ads. Their brand attitudes were more favorable and accessible than those of less involved subjects or of subjects exposed to ads with explicit conclusions (Kardes 1988). Thus, increasing effort during message encoding (via distraction, message complexity, or rhetorical questions) should increase attitude accessibility and hence its likelihood of guiding subsequent behavior. However, comprehension may be undermined. Munch & Swasy (1988; Swasy & Munch 1985) examined the effects of rhetorical questions in sales presentations. In high-involvement settings, rhetorical questions reduced message-relevant thinking and lowered argument recall. Recall of strong arguments was attenuated by rhetoricals, but recall of weak arguments was not, perhaps owing to initial attention differences. Finally, Sanbonmatsu & Kardes (1988) found that peripheral cues such as celebrity status led to greater persuasion under high arousal (produced by an exercise task to avoid confounding with message content). Argument strength produced more persuasion under moderate arousal. Thus, arousal may deflect attention from message elaboration so that peripheral cues receive more weight.

ATTITUDE TOWARD THE AD   MacKenzie et al (1986) evaluated four views of how attitude toward the ad (A_{ad}) mediates ad effectiveness: 1. affect transfer—a one-way causal flow from A_{ad} to attitude toward the brand (A_b) due to low involvement, peripheral processing of ad execution elements, classical conditioning, or mood congruency; 2. dual mediation—in addition to affect transfer, increased message acceptance due to a favorable A_{ad}; 3. reciprocal mediation—a two-way flow between A_{ad} and A_b reflecting people's preference for balance in liking; and 4. independent influences—A_{ad} and A_b separately determine purchase intention. Cognitive responses to ads were assigned to ad cognition (e.g. source bolstering, negative ad execution) or brand cognition (e.g. counter or support argument) categories, and A_{ad} and A_b were measured in terms of overall favorable/unfavorable reactions to each. The dual-mediation version of a structural equation model was judged best.

Reactions to ad execution (valenced feelings, image associations, usage experiences) may affect not only A_{ad} but also A_b, even under a brand-processing set (Gardner 1985b). Gardner found an A_{ad} effect on A_b whether people were evaluating linguistic style or the brands advertised. However, A_{ad} assessment is typically fraught with problems. Much depends on the measures used (e.g. A_{ad} measures may pick up nonattribute aspects of the product portrayal) and on task instructions (e.g. subjects may tell researchers what they think of the ads in post-exposure A_b assessment because that's what they think the researcher is evaluating). In another study, unrelated visual components of ads affected both brand and ad attitudes, in a manner consistent with evaluations of the photographs but dissociated from brand-attribute beliefs (Mitchell 1986a). Clearly, ad responses and subsequent attitudes toward the product and the ad are related in a complex fashion, and more work is needed to understand fully the automatic or reasoned "transfer of affect" or evaluation between A_{ad} and A_b.

Stayman & Aaker (1988) tested the proposition that specific feeling responses (warmth, amusement, and irritation) can affect attitudes toward an advertised product apart from A_{ad}. Subjects viewed four programs in a two-week period. Two ads for each feeling type and 4, 8, and 12 exposure levels were used. A_{ad} influenced post-exposure brand attitude beyond prior brand attitude. At lower exposures, for warm and humorous executions, ad-induced feelings directly affected brand attitudes. One limitation is that feelings about and overall liking for the ads were assessed retrospectively, rather than on-line. Also, since their A_{ad} measure mainly addresses evaluative judgments about the ad, other aspects of a person's attitude toward the ad may be reflected directly in the multidimensional product ratings.

ASSESSING AFFECTIVE RESPONSES   Since consumers' effective responses to advertising are undoubtedly more differentiated and subtle than simple directional measures (e.g. happy-sad) can capture, several alternatives have become popular. These include Izard's Differential Emotions Scale (Allen et al 1988) and a variety of factor-analyzed lists of emotional self-descriptors (e.g. Edell & Burke 1987). Although specific dimensions of affective response are of interest in ad research (Gresham & Shimp 1985), measurement should also be tied to theories of emotion; and the discriminatory power and validity of the measures must be given added attention (Aaker et al 1986).

Retrospective response protocols avoid the intrusiveness and reactivity of concurrent protocols. Hill & Mazis (1986) exposed subjects to emotional or factual advertising and coded subsequent written protocols into positive (e.g. feeling good) and negative (e.g. feeling angry) affect categories. Subjects rated each commercial using adjectives developed in a previous factor analysis of TV-commercial responses. Emotional ads produced more affective comments. Although they could not be distinguished from factual ads on evaluative scales, they differed on the execution-related adjectives.

Batra & Ray (1986a) distinguished between affective and cognitive responses to advertising using a 9-category coding scheme of which six were primarily cognitive (e.g. support arguments, execution discounting) and three were affective (surgency/elation, deactivation, and social affection). There was a small, incremental impact of feeling-related responses in predicting attitudes toward the ad. Holbrook & Batra (1987) analyzed judges' ratings of ads on batteries of ad content as well as emotion items. Six dimensions (emotional, threatening, mundane, sexy, cerebral, and personal) were extracted from the ad content items. The emotional response items yielded pleasure, arousal, and dominance dimensions as in previous taxonomies (Russell 1978). Although low interjudge reliabilities signal that emotional responses are not merely stimulus driven, the model's causal flow through A_{ad} was supported. Emotions mediated effects of the somewhat intercorrelated content dimensions.

The importance of task instructions and perceptions on subjects' responses to advertising was demonstrated by Madden et al (1988). Otherwise positive affective responses to a humorous ad were suppressed by an evaluative set, and ad evaluations tended to be unfavorable. Under non-ad-focused viewing, evaluative responses to the humorous and nonhumorous ads did not differ, but subjects reported more favorable affect when subsequently asked how the (humorous) commercial made them feel. Thus, attitudinal (evaluative) responses to ads and reported feeling-state information appear to be separable.

Edell & Burke (1987) distinguished between the way consumers describe an ad and the feelings that the ad generates. Following the Puto & Wells (1984) characterization of ads' being informational or transformational, feelings were hypothesized to be more important (relative to semantic judgments) for ads high in transformation. A large feelings inventory was factor analyzed, resulting in scales described as upbeat, negative, and warm. When combined with three semantic judgment scales (evaluation, activity, gentleness) in a regression, feelings contributed to predictions of A_{ad} and A_b, though results for transformational and informational ads were inconsistent. A second study again demonstrated that the self-rated feelings/reactions to the ad contribute to relevant attitudes and judgments about the ad and brand when these were unfamiliar to subjects. Reliabilities and intercorrelations for the indexes are reported in Burke & Edell (1989). They again found an incremental effect of the "feeling" factors on A_{ad} and A_b and also on brand-attribute evaluations (even after the ads were seen repeatedly and after a four-week delay). The latter seemed to be mediated by the relationship between the feeling indexes and the judgment scales.

While relationships among particular feelings, judgments, and attitudes derived from structural models are interesting, they are based on correlations among response scales whose validity and link to manipulated feeling states deserves study. One may question whether predictive gains come from adding a separate class of variables (i.e. feelings) or simply from a set of somewhat different dimensions of judgment. Verbal protocols, scaled self-reports, and the like may not be adequate measurement systems for affective responses.

They may fail to isolate affect from evaluations/inferences, may fail to tap more immediate and transitory feeling states, and may be insufficiently diagnostic. Physiological measures may have a role to play (e.g. Rothschild et al 1988), but they are difficult to administer and link to specific feeling states. There is some evidence to support the reliability and convergent validity of the "warmth monitor" (Aaker et al 1986), a paper and pencil instrument people respond to by moving down the paper at a constant speed while watching a commercial. Similar instruments may be used to tap other feeling states, although the methodology seems limited to assessing only one dimension at a time.

CONTEXTUAL FACTORS AND AFFECTIVE RESPONSES   Friestad & Thorson (1986) argued that during emotional arousal, a message should leave strong episodic traces that become integrated with product-related semantic memory. This is more likely under higher involvement, personal relevance, and on-line judgment. Their subjects were asked either to watch and evaluate embedded promotional messages for personal relevance (semantic processing) or simply to watch the material carefully (episodic condition). Emotional messages had a higher level of free recall two months later, and episodic instructions provided a weak but consistent advantage. They were also better liked and had a higher perceived influence than "thinking" (objective) appeals. Music and pictures often dominate emotional ads (Mitchell 1986a). Establishing the content equivalence of emotional and neutral messages and using nonreactive task instructions are critical for understanding the underlying processes and are a limitation of much prior research.

Involvement may not imply analytical thought or a reliance on message arguments. Park & Young's (1986) processing-set instructions led high-involvement subjects to focus either on performance attributes or image aspects of a shampoo commercial. Attention to performance attributes was reflected in their greater effect on A_b, but this was reduced to the level of A_{ad} when distracting background music was added. Attention to the emotional appeal and image led to a much stronger contribution of A_{ad} than the performance attributes under both music and no-music conditions. However the overall explanatory power was low. A low product-relevance/distraction (i.e. low-involvement) condition produced comparable effects.

Three mechanisms that may explain the influence of a program-induced mood on reactions to TV commercials are 1. priming of mood-congruent material related to the commercial, 2. affect transfer based on temporal association, and 3. consistency-induced judgments of program-commercial fit (Goldberg & Gorn 1987). Informational and emotional ads were embedded in either happy or sad TV programs. Those viewing the happy programs were happier, evaluated the ads as more effective, and had improved recall of the ads, though there was no program effect on purchase intention. Subjects also felt happier watching the emotional ads, evaluated them as more effective, and indicated a higher intention to purchase. Whether the results apply to products for which informational appeals are anticipated awaits further study. Program valence influenced subjects' felt mood more as they watched the emotional commercials, but commercial- and program-induced moods had no interactive effect on either perceived effectiveness or purchase intentions.

Positive feelings did not facilitate recall for those viewing SuperBowl XX in the winning city (presumably a pleasurable experience) as compared to those in the losing city and a neutral city (Pavelchak et al 1988). The neutral-city viewers recalled more ads, with winners recalling the fewest. While positive feelings did not enhance encoding of the advertising material, emotional intensity/arousal may have inhibited it by narrowing attention to the contextual stimuli responsible for the emotional experience. Also, the program probably competed more for viewers' attention in the winning and (to a lesser extent) the losing city. Presumably, in the neutral city there was less carryover of game-related thoughts when the commercials appeared. If arousal due to contextual factors (e.g. TV programs) is misattributed to embedded advertisements, additional attitudinal effects may occur (Singh & Churchill 1987). On a related note, variations in diurnal rhythms of arousal may be associated with different encoding and retrieval strategies and memory performance (Hornik 1988).

The notion of a relatively independent affect-producing hemisphere may be incorrect. Using a dichotic listening task with music and verbal information delivered to either the more "efficient" or less "efficient" hemisphere (verbal to the right ear and thus the left hemisphere), Anand et al (1988) showed that either hemisphere can generate an affective response, though efficiency plays an important mediating role. "Old" stimuli (more so for those correctly recognized) and correctly identified new stimuli were liked better. The effects may be due to a preference for certainty or for being correct (see Obermiller 1985). If so the effect should disappear for new stimuli that are easier to identify as new. Better-designed studies are needed to consider the role of recognition in evaluative judgment.

Experimental manipulations of mood are also needed to trace its effects in purchase settings. People who reported being in a positive mood after making a retail purchase spent more money, more time, bought more items and had a more favorable image of the store (Sherman & Smith 1987). However, the positive mood may merely reflect a successful shopping trip. Gardner & Siomkos (1986) asked subjects to imagine themselves or others in either a high- or low-image store. Store atmospherics were simulated using written descriptions high in detail and evaluative tone (e.g. dirty, dingy). The descriptions elicited consistent evaluative ratings. Milliman (1986) found that slow background music in a restaurant led customers to stay longer and to consume more alcoholic beverages but not more food.

RESPONSES TO PERSONAL REQUESTS   Both large and small ("even a penny would help") anchor points can affect the rate of favorable response, the donation size, or both (Fraser et al 1988). Using both together may be ineffective because a large anchor can render a minimal request suspect and vice versa. Fern et al (1986) offer a general accessibility explanation for multiple request (i.e. foot-in-the-door and door-in-the-face) outcomes in that the initial request and response provide an accessible overall judgment and cognitive elements supportive of the behavior. However, the equivocal findings from many of these studies makes it desirable to confirm that some type of self-labeling (e.g. "I am a concerned citizen") or attitudinal attribution (e.g. "I put the sign up because I like this cause") and not opposing beliefs (e.g. "I've satisfied my obligation") resulted from the initial request. Since tapping intervening cognitive responses may produce confounds, separate manipulation check studies are warranted.

Socio-Environmental Approaches

Consumer researchers have been interested in response-predisposing consumer characteristics because these may help them to identify market segments and because they have special interests in particular groups or traits. In addition, environmental factors and personal attributes are important to those examining interactions and boundary conditions for more general models.

GENERAL RESPONSE MEDIATORS   Including customer perceptions of substitution-in-use improves market structure definition and the predictive ability of segmentation schemes (Srivastava et al 1984). Responses to price are complex, sometimes positively affecting perceptions and attitudes but often affecting behavioral intentions negatively (Erickson & Johansson 1985). Consumers predisposed to frugality (Pettit et al 1985) may respond to price cues as indicators of expense while other consumers may view them as indicators of quality.

Not surprisingly, consumers respond to shopping area image and to global evaluations of stores for store selection (Golden & Zimmer 1986). Credit card cues (e.g. insignia, replicas of charge cards) increase tipping, willingness to spend money, and both estimated and actual donations to charity (Feinberg 1986). Consumers who are "coupon-prone" (rather than category-specific users) tend to be somewhat upscale, urban, and less brand loyal (Bawa & Shoemaker 1987); they often use coupons to buy higher-priced brands (Levendahl 1988). In some product categories, consumers exhibit temporal variety (Pessemier & Handelsman 1984) by exhibiting preferences for a pattern of dissimilar product experiences. Models of brand loyalty and variety seeking are typically based on individual or household purchase data. Some (e.g. Kahn et al 1986) rely on individual-level brand switching–based indicants of such constructs. Other models help identify substitute and complementary products (Lattin 1987) and use individual-level measures to predict aggregate consumer choice.

Friedman & Churchill (1987) examined how various aspects of social power may be used to enhance physician effectiveness in patient encounters. They found that patients preferred high-referent and low–coercive power behaviors regardless of the riskiness of the situation or degree of patient-physician familiarity. However, the effectiveness of expert and legitimate power behaviors was contingent upon an ongoing relationship between the physician and the patient.

Wright's (1986) notion of consumers' intuitive theories about marketers' persuasive tactics ("schemer schemas") and their development and functioning is worthy of study.

AGE-RELATED RESPONSES TO ADVERTISING   The effects of advertising on children have been studied in relation to the development of attitudes toward products consumed by adults (Gorn & Florsheim 1985). Research indicates that very few 3–4-year-olds and between 20% and 40% of 5-year-olds recognize the persuasive intent of commercials (Macklin 1987). Hoy et al (1986), however report that 3–7-year-olds could distinguish a host-selling (animated) commercial from the program. Interestingly, Fischer (1985) suggests that, compared to 8-year-olds, 5-year-olds may be less persuaded by TV commercials (e.g. for toys) if their attention strays from key aspects of the presentation. The spontaneous retrieval of prior knowledge about ads by 9–10-year-olds may be low. Shown instructional films to develop "cognitive defenses" against misleading ad techniques, 9–10-year-olds were later unable to generate counterarguments during ad exposure unless an immediate cue activated the prior knowledge (Brucks et al 1988).

Cole & Houston (1987) exposed elderly and younger consumers to a series of news and commercial messages presented by TV or transcribed into newspaper format. Encoding deficiencies were noted for the elderly, who consistently performed at a lower level on recognition and recall measures. While misleading pragmatic implications (i.e. those that provide meaning in communication but in which the conclusion is not logically true) are generally hard to discriminate from assertions, older consumers had greater difficulty with such ads. Training reduced susceptibility but caused general skepticism about claims (Gaeth & Heath 1987).

PATTERNS OF CONSUMPTION BEHAVIOR

What consumers, or groups of consumers, do in their "consumer roles" is the essence of consumer research. Such research is important for its own sake as well as to inform research on judgment and choice processes and on marketer-initiated stimuli about key "real world" factors that would make such work more meaningful and complete. At a more macro level, systematic descriptive research—with its focus on substantive issues (e.g. nutrition, health care, energy conservation) and broader consumer welfare and marketplace efficiency concerns—is in short supply. This section highlights research that spans the broad spectrum.

Perceptual/Cognitive Approaches

We first examine information-search studies that draw on economic principles as well as psychological findings. Second, we describe research on the use of information in consumer decisions. Finally, we address the role of performance and other comparative standards in post-consumption judgments.

INFORMATION SEARCH AND USE   Furse et al (1984) developed a clustering-based typology of search strategies among new car buyers. In addition to traditional shopper categories based upon search extent and underlying motivations, two new groups (self-reliant and advisor-assisted shoppers) were identified. Urbany (1986) tested information-search propositions derived from Stigler's work in economics. His results were consistent with a cost-benefit framework, with moderating effects of prior knowledge. Buyers with more certain beliefs about retailers' price images searched less and were less responsive to changes in search costs and benefits than buyers with less-certain beliefs. Allowing for individual and situational differences, cost-benefit frameworks have provided good working models of external search (Blaylock & Smallwood 1987). They also provide the basis for normative models of price-quality patterns in markets as a function of information structure (Tellis & Wernerfelt 1987).

Previous findings on format effects supported recommendations for the design of labels for risk information (Bettman et al 1986b). With regard to nutritional information, Brucks et al (1984) found that only early information-processing stages were affected by the provision of information. However, Russo et al (1987) focused on different information-presentation formats and argued that there may not be sufficient incentive to use nutrition information unless the benefits relative to alternatives (e.g. a typical diet plus a vitamin/mineral supplement) are clear. Further, summary ratings impede selection on individual attributes and must be credible before they are likely to be used.

Levy et al (1985) used "special diet alert" brand-specific shelf markers to deliver nutrition information (e.g. low in sodium, low cholesterol) to shoppers in 20 supermarkets over two years. Sales changes of 4–8% were found, but may, in part, be attributable to other components of the supermarket chain's efforts. Muller's (1985) controlled field experiment demonstrated that brands had to show significant variance in nutrient levels to affect behavior and found that results vary dramatically with consumer perceptions of overall nutrient importance for the product class. These findings suggest that in supermarket settings, motivation to use specific nutrition information may have more impact than presentation-related factors.

INFORMATION FRAMING AND CONTEXTUAL EFFECTS   Levin & Johnson (1984) found that price-quality trade-off judgments for ground-beef purchases were affected by whether price or quality judgments were requested as well as by whether the quality dimension was stated positively (percentage lean) or negatively (percentage fat). Levin & Gaeth (1988) found a similar result, but the framing effect was attenuated when consumers actually tasted the meat. Hoch & Ha (1986) found that advertising framed how consumers encode and retrieve product evidence in quality judgments, especially if the evidence is ambiguous. The effect disappeared with unambiguous evidence. Puto (1987) reported a similar use of reference points for judging and comparing decision alternatives.

Even though framing phenomena may guide consumers' subjective experiences in significant ways, the effects are often limited to cases where consumers are dealing with truly unfamiliar stimuli. Behavioral variations of consequence may not occur if product experience is anchored by strong sensory or use experience (J. G. Lynch, D. Chakravarti, and A. Mitra, working paper). However, framing does trigger memory biases and selective retrieval phenomena that may influence consumers' responses in surveys and in general prediction tasks (Blair & Burton, 1987; Hoch 1988; Feldman & Lynch 1988).

ADAPTING TO INFORMATION LOAD   Consumers' limited information-processing capabilities and the information overload issue attracted more debate (Malhotra 1984; Jacoby 1984). Taking a different perspective, Keller & Staelin (1987) separated information into two components (quality and quantity) and tested the effect of each on job choice decisions. They claimed that decision effectiveness improved with information quality but decreased with quantity. However, concerns about their measures weaken the conclusions (Meyer & Johnson 1989; Keller & Staelin 1989). It is now well-accepted that consumers are adaptive information processors and make decisions contingent upon task status and task goals (Payne et al 1988). Hence, information load variables should probably be viewed as contingencies to which consumers adapt, given specific resource constraints. Research stressing the relation between resource constraints and the adaptive solutions that emerge may be more fruitful.

Hagerty & Aaker (1984) developed an information-search model in which consumers sample information sequentially so as to maximize the expected value of information. Their model reflects adaptive criteria for uncertainty reduction given a choice goal and posits relations among processing cost, perceived interattribute correlation, and perceived attribute importance to information sampled and to brand or attribute search patterns. An information-display-board study supported these propositions. More support for contingent decision making by consumers is available from field studies of housing choice among two-career households (Gronhaug et al 1987).

EVALUATIVE FRAMES OF REFERENCE   The degree to which consumers rely on prechoice expectations to judge postpurchase satisfaction (thus placing emphasis on disconfirmation) or instead use comparative performance norms remains under study (Cadotte et al 1987; Sirgy 1985). Oliver & Winer (1987) review the role of expectations regarding product attribute levels and purchase related outcomes. Oliver & DeSarbo (1988) evaluated the joint impact of expectancy, performance, disconfirmation, perceived equity, and attribution on overall satisfaction. There may be an initial performance effect followed by effects of disconfirmation, with expectations providing an anchor. The authors suggest that responses to such mediators may be individual specific. Tse & Wilton (1988) extended the notion that post-purchase dissatisfaction can result directly from inferior product performance regardless of the level of prior expectations. Their research suggests that alternative comparison standards and criteria (e.g. the level of performance deemed reasonable, ideal performance, and average expected performance for the product class) may affect satisfaction. Inferior performance, when unequivocal, may outweigh uncertain expectations. However, quality assessments may be difficult at the time of purchase, and price and performance expectations are often formed on the basis of information acquired through product trial (Goering 1985).

Motivational and Predispositional Approaches

Motivational and personality constructs have traditional status as stable internal influences on consumer behavior. However, the motivational construct receiving most attention of late has been involvement.

INVOLVEMENT AND AROUSAL   Researchers have sought to identify aspects of a consumer's relationship to a product category or brand that produce a heightened degree of personal importance, self-relevance (e.g. Belk 1988), and involvement. Such enduring involvement may be reflected in opinion leadership and result in word-of-mouth communication (Richins & Bloch 1986), whereas situational involvement, owing to a temporary heightening of product importance, may prompt word-of-mouth communication directly. Segmenting by involvement may capture differential price sensitivity and also improve predictions from multiattribute models. High involvement may lead to the use of a larger set of attributes rather than (under low involvement) a sequential choice structure (Gensch & Javalgi 1987).

Zaichkowsky (1985) has developed a Personal Involvement Inventory (PII) to capture the degree of a product's personal relevance and has claimed adequate reliability and validity. Laurent & Kapferer's (1985) measure of consumers' involvement with a product category combines the separate (but overlapping) dimensions of perceived importance of a product and the consequences of a mispurchase, the likelihood of a mispurchase, hedonic value, and the sign (social identification) value of the product class.

Involvement is fast becoming the "concept of convenience" through which to study product-related motivations as well as arousal and intentional mechanisms important in the processing of advertising information (Costley 1988). The field may be banking too heavily on involvement as an explanatory concept if behavior toward broad categories of products is explained in relation to measured involvement components. Other shopping proclivities (beyond product involvement) that seem worth exploring are differences in price consciousness, interest in generic products (McEnally & Hawes 1984), and variety and novelty seeking (Joachimsthaler & Lastovicka 1984).

INDIVIDUAL DIFFERENCE VARIABLES   The pace has slowed with respect to work on individual difference variables. Childers et al (1985) have developed a Style of Processing scale to examine differences in responses to visual and verbal information. Holbrook (1986a) has assessed individual differences in consumers' aesthetic responses using instruments that appear to have promise in separating visualizing/verbalizing tendencies, intrinsic/extrinsic motivation, and romanticism/classicism. Some preliminary work on differences in decision-making styles has been carried out by Sproles & Kendall (1986).

The popularity of life-style and psychographic work in market segmentation and advertising development remains high and reflects a current commercial emphasis on brand and consumer image. Lastovicka et al (1987) apply life-style segmentation to the problem of young male drinking and driving. Consistency pressures in responding to self-report items continue to be a problem in this domain (Malhotra 1988; McDaniel & Zeithaml 1984). Some reported congruities between self-concept and product preference may only reflect respondents' understanding of how to use the self-related adjectives to indicate products they like, particularly since the hypotheses are often transparent and the measures are administered together.

Individual differences in traits or states remain important variables for both grouping and understanding behaviors. A single predictor of a behavior having multiple determinants cannot be expected to produce large correlations (say an upper bound of 0.50). Since a correlation of 0.40 is equivalent to a contingency table with roughly twice as many hits as misses, even modest correlations may not be trivial (Ahadi & Diener 1989). The current emphasis on reliability in individual-differences research may overstate scale quality. Greater emphasis is needed on validity in measurement as well as the selection of meaningful trait-behavior relationships and, most importantly, multiple predictor approaches. Using a multiple-act criterion to understand the function of a particular trait is also desirable (Lastovicka & Joachimsthaler 1988).

VALUES   Differences in values and their role in product decisions as well as more general patterns of behavior have been explored using the List of Values (LOV) and the Values and Life Style (VALS) combination of attitude statements and demographic items (Kahle 1986; Kahle et al 1986). Published reports suggest only modest success, although applying value differences to more theoretically meaningful behavior patterns (e.g. "materialism") may be useful (Belk 1986).

Socio-Environmental Approaches

Several personal descriptors (gender, age, and ethnicity) and consumer socialization received attention as determinants of marketplace behavior and attitudes. We also review research on consumers' responses to economic conditions and information and to aggregate marketplace performance.

EFFECTS OF GENDER AND SPOUSAL ROLES   In addition to well-established gender-product and gender-brand interactions, gender preferences for achievement themes (males) and empathy/intimacy themes (females) in advertising have been advanced (Prakash & Flores 1985); but the relationship is likely to be far more complex. When sex roles were made salient in two very different ways (Meyers-Levy 1988), males responded more favorably to self-oriented information while females responded more favorably to self-oriented and other-oriented cues (e.g. information on others' judgments and feelings). Sex role activation (by priming introduced after the information but prior to judgment or by strong cues) was essential in order to produce a gender-based effect. Gender schematic subjects (i.e. for whom sex is a particularly salient perceptual cue and organizing heuristic) did not differ from gender aschematic subjects across three experiments (Schmitt et al 1988).

Data from 89 married couples involved in purchasing a home were used to select among measures of sex role orientation and to build a structural model of how this influences family decision-making (Qualls 1987). Sex role orientation helped determine household decision responsibility and role structure but not the system of exchanges that lead to decisions or the dominant member's ability to force certain outcomes. Time constraints, varied responsibilities, and self-selection may explain why working wives (relative to nonworking housewives) have more negative attitudes toward food shopping and are less involved in food preparation (Jackson et al 1985). Consideration of present occupational status together with career orientation differences between working and nonworking wives may better explain role conflict and differences in consumption behavior (Joag et al 1985). In view of changes in both husband and wife roles, the role obligations of both spouses seem important considerations in this context (Zeithaml 1985).

CONSUMER SOCIALIZATION   Moschis (1985; Moschis et al 1986) examined the direct and observational influence of parents on children's attitudes toward the marketplace, products sold, and television viewing as a function of family communication structure and background variables such as SES and racial identification. Socialization style (authoritarian, permissive, neglecting) may be a key mediator and was found to be related to parent-child communication about consumption, the child's consumption autonomy, media habits, etc (Carlson & Grossbart 1988). Consumer socialization is also reflected in the intergenerational influence of mothers on their daughters' brand preferences and grocery-shopping choice rules (Moore-Shay & Lutz 1988) One concern is that advertising to children often adds to parent-child conflict by stimulating repeated purchase requests (Isler et al 1987). The acquisition of consumer skills in areas such as financial management, health, safety, and nutrition (e.g. Dardis 1988) as well as specific shopping skills needed by school children (Reece 1986) have begun to receive attention.

The presence of children at various life-cycle stages affects household consumption patterns (e.g. Douthitt & Fedyk 1988). Changes in consumer attitudes and patterns of consumption (e.g. eating out, entertainment) were observed by Andreasen (1984) as a result of changes in life status (household composition, job changes), possibly owing to stress-related dissatisfaction or to manage one's emotional state. Similarly, important changes occur in behavior as a function of advancing age. Research on these issues seems a natural priority given the attention devoted to the problems of the elderly (Gilly & Zeithaml 1985; Hama & Chan 1988).

ETHNICITY, CULTURAL IDENTIFICATION AND ETHNOCENTRISM   An instrument to assess US consumer "ethnocentrism"—stressing the tendency of consumers to support the domestic economy rather than in-group/out-group psychosocial concerns—was developed and validated against various belief, attitude, and behavioral measures, including predictions for people threatened the most by foreign competition (Shimp & Sharma 1987). The possible role of consumer "patriotism" on purchase intentions for automobiles and televisions was noted by Han (1988). Country-of-origin effects on product evaluation have also been explored (e.g. Johansson et al 1985; Tan & Farley 1987).

Considerable attention had been focused on the product preferences (particularly food) and brand loyalty characteristics of Hispanic consumers (e.g. Reilly & Wallendorf 1987; Deshpande et al 1986; Saegert et al 1985), with some additional work on other groups' food variety preferences (e.g. Hager 1988; Schaninger et al 1985). Methodological problems such as confounding of socioeconomic and regional variables, response biases linking self-reports of ethnic identification and preference for ethnic-oriented behaviors, and variance due to family size and composition often make it difficult to attribute differences to cultural variables. Taking a broader perspective, Hirschman (1985) stresses that the meaning of consumption cannot be found simply in within-individual cognitive and decision-making explanations but is likely to be based in broad cultural and social-identification antecedents.

ECONOMIC ASPECTS OF CONSUMERS' BEHAVIOR   From an initial set of 44 items available to consumers in 25% of supermarkets in 1977, generic labeling has now spread to over 320 categories and is available in 75% of supermarkets (Szymanski & Busch 1987). A meta-analysis revealed quality and price perceptions to have a much stronger association with generic product acceptance than consumer descriptors or shopping behavior; hence understanding the "generic mentality" rather than the "generic personality" seems most productive (see Fugate 1986). Other research on food consumption has examined the effects of retail food price–reporting systems (Faminow & Benson 1985) and the impact of double-digit inflation (McDaniel et al 1986).

Criteria that affect budget priorities and the pattern of durable goods acquisition have been examined by Hauser & Urban (1986) and Mayo & Qualls (1987). Several studies view the household as a technology-user/ adopter, with a particular focus on home computing (e.g. Venkatesh & Vitalari 1987). The household has also been seen as a production unit to examine the value added by in-home employment and durable goods acquisition (Bivens & Volker 1986; Bryant 1988). Studies of consumer characteristics and beliefs related to home ownership (Silver 1988), using home equity to fund current consumption (Chen & Jensen 1985), energy use (e.g. Hutton et al 1986; Sexton & Sexton 1987), purchase of lottery tickets (McConkey & Warren 1987), and participation in financial investments and institutions (e.g.

Mills & Gardner 1986) catalog other important economic aspects of consumer behavior.

Evidence of optimizing behavior is sparse in these studies. In fact, when consumers do seek to obtain a particular level of product quality or a desired set of product attributes at the lowest price available, they often discover inefficient markets (Hjorth-Andersen 1984, 1986; Curry & Faulds 1986; Sproles 1986; Kamakura et al 1988). By one estimate, using price as a guide to quality would produce an inefficient choice with an equal or higher probability in 65% of the product categories studied (Sproles 1986). Gerstner (1985), using data for 145 products from Consumer Union's *Buying Guide*, found a weak overall positive relationship between quality and price. Warranties, on the other hand, seem to be a good predictor of product reliability (Wiener 1985). Mitigating this general market inefficiency is the fact that consumers make use of information such as *Consumer Report's* readers' survey of problems with various cars (Friedman 1987), and brand recommendations from product testing organizations (Olshavsky & Rosen 1985).

CONSUMER SATISFACTION AND COMPLAINT BEHAVIOR   Research continues on factors producing complaint behavior (Singh 1988). Westbrook (1987) examined post-purchase affective responses to product/consumption experiences and their relation to judged satisfaction, seller-directed complaint actions, and word-of-mouth activity. Using field data connected with automobile and CATV ownership, he found independent dimensions of positive and negative affect, with both directly related to the examined postpurchase behaviors. Gilly (1987) confirmed that consumers' perception of how their complaint was handled is important for repurchase behavior.

Ursic (1985) examined factors leading to a decision to seek legal redress and concluded that demographics are less important than perceived effectiveness and access to court. Samuels et al (1986) presented evidence that post-decisional processes often have impact beyond immediate purchases. If rampant quality problems lead to aggressive customer complaints, state and federal legislation is more likely to follow (e.g. automobile "lemon" laws). A complicating factor is that quality levels are often difficult to judge a priori, and the information used to judge quality is often unreliable, misleading, or even deceptive.

THE CONSUMER ENVIRONMENT   A study of grocery store patronage in the UK (Keng & Ehrenberg 1984) reported low store loyalty and little or no segmentation between chains or store groups; over time, consumers spread purchases across brands and stores, in line with market shares. Spiggle & Sewall (1987) characterized retail stores based on an extended evoked-set notion and examined shifts in store patronage as consumers move through various buying-process stages.

Advertising has become an object of evaluation from both commercial and societal standpoints. This includes what consumers like and dislike about advertising themes and execution (e.g. Aaker & Bruzzone 1985) and the media vehicles used to attract consumers (e.g. Barwise & Ehrenberg 1987). Meta-analyses of consumers' and professionals' attitudes toward advertising of professional services over a 10-year span identify differences in beliefs regarding appropriateness, effect on professional image, and potential benefits (Hite & Fraser 1988). Hite & Eck (1987) also compare a limited sampling of consumer and business attitudes toward advertising directed toward children, with consumers holding far less-positive attitudes.

Commercial portrayals of women and minorities in demeaning roles are responded to far more negatively by those for whom the issue is (made) salient (McIntyre et al 1986). Even though stereotypical role portrayals appear to be less frequent today (Wyckham 1987), a content analysis of one limited sample of ads in the United States, Mexico, and Australia indicated that women were less often employed and less often used in voiceovers to convey product information; when women were used they were younger than comparable men and less independent (Gilly 1988). The depth of the problem can be illustrated by a content analysis of personal advertisements in newspapers: Men more frequently sought physical attractiveness and offered financial resources while women did the opposite (Hirschman 1987). Ursic et al (1986), reviewing over 5,000 magazine ads from 1950 to 1980, noted an underrepresentation and a lack of increase in the proportion of people over 60 years of age (most of whom were males appearing in work settings or with expensive products).

Aspects of materialism were a popular focus of content analyses. Friedman (1985) content-analyzed a sample of 31 best-selling novels published between 1946 and 1975 and discovered more than a five-fold increase in the number and variety of brand names despite essentially no change in the use of generic product references. Belk & Pollay (1985) focused on home settings (the most dominant advertising setting) and noted that between 1903 and 1977 magazine ads increased in appeals to luxury, pleasure, and ownership, with a corresponding decrease in practical and functional appeals and product-use themes. However, the considerable fluctuation in products featured and used for background is a possible confound (see Firat 1987). Spiggle (1986) found that both Sunday comic strips and underground "comix" books showed unexpectedly pervasive "materialism" despite differences in such aspects as heroes' and villains' goals. It is unclear whether such materialism was cast in a positive light. It is much easier and more reliable, though not always more meaningful, to code occurrences than nuances of expression (e.g. approval vs disapproval) or interpretation (e.g. exhibiting wealth vs exhibiting taste; Kelly 1987).

There is some evidence (Richins 1987) that possible effects of exposure to mass media (e.g. increasing materialism) are moderated by the perceived realism of the programs, although heavy viewers of TV tend to overestimate the true frequency of portrayed circumstances (e.g. types of crimes, stable families) and seem to have views (e.g. more sexist attitudes) more in keeping with those portrayed (O'Guinn & Faber 1987). Whether watching TV programs or ads produces such attitudes and values or whether people having them are attracted to such programs is a complex issue. The case is made and debated that advertising is a "distorted mirror," reflecting not the reality of the underlying culture but a biased selection of values more readily applied to consumption and products. Such advertising may also reinforce these values and make them more acceptable (Pollay 1986; Lantos 1987; but see Holbrook 1987c and Pollay 1987).

"POSTMODERNISM"   Some researchers have sought to explore consumption on a level "richer and deeper" than that captured by traditional approaches. This has led to a debate on philosophy-of-science issues as well as to helpful expositions of theoretical perspectives and method (Anderson 1986; Belk 1986; Calder & Tybout 1987; Holbrook 1987a,b; Holbrook & O'Shaughnessy 1988; Belk et al 1988; Hudson & Ozanne 1988; Mick 1986; Sherry 1990; Wallendorf & Belk 1989). Attention has been directed to the holism of the humanities (e.g. philosophy, history, literary studies) and the macro-level social sciences as well as descriptive and interpretive methods (e.g. participant observation, depth interviews, projective techniques, archaeological procedures, cinematic analysis).

Three theoretical papers (McCracken 1986; Belk 1988; and Belk et al 1989) have attracted particular attention. McCracken emphasized the fluidity of cultural meaning (characterizing its trajectory as from the culturally constituted world to consumer goods to individual consumers) and illustrated the central role of advertising, the fashion system, and consumption rituals as venues for transmission of cultural meaning. Belk (1988) argued that typical conceptions of possessions are overly restrictive and that consumers use possessions to create and maintain meaning in their lives through their different life-cycle stages. Collections, pets, people, and money are among the wider range of possessions that reflect identity and extend the self in space and time (but see Cohen 1989; Belk 1989). Finally, Belk et al (1989) explore transcendent experiences brought about by consumption—particularly how these experiences may sacralize the profane or ordinary aspects of contemporary society. They discuss how sacralization may occur (e.g. through rituals), how sacredness is maintained, and what processes produce desacralization.

In the area of consumer aesthetics, Holbrook & Grayson (1986) interpreted the film *Out of Africa* from a semiological viewpoint. They assess how the lead character's changing apparel and gradual loss of cultured possessions (furniture, husband) may thematically communicate both her individual maturation from sophisticate to farmer and the general impermanence of life. Hirschman (1988) employed a hybrid interpretive approach based on structuralism and narrative syntactics to explain the consumption ideology in the TV programs "Dallas" and "Dynasty." She argues that the binary opposition between secular and sacred features of consumption activities has pervaded characterizations, plots, and themes in both programs.

Rook (1985) studied the ritual of grooming behavior, using a Thematic Apperception Test to uncover latent psychosocial meanings (e.g. identity projection, intimacy aspirations). Sherry & Camargo (1987) illustrated the subtle but pervasive connotative effects that English loanwords have exerted on Japanese culture and consumption (e.g. *pasokon* for personal computer), a symbol of modernization via the English language. Belk et al (1988) carried out an ethnographic investigation to explore consumption meanings exhibited through buyer-seller behaviors at a swap meet. Dialectical themes (freedom-rules, boundaries-transitions, competition-cooperation, and sacred-profane) emerged as explanations of the behaviors. Wallendorf & Arnould (1988) explored the meanings of favorite possessions in two cultures (US and Niger) and compared types of cherished objects for their meanings and symbolic values. Solomon (1988) drew from categorization theory and research to explain how consumers share product-role symbolizations (e.g. the brand of automobile a banker vs a used car salesman might own).

It is too early to evaluate the contributions of the somewhat heterogeneous approaches that characterize the postmodern view. Recent publications (e.g. Umiker-Sebeok 1987; Hirschman 1989; a special semiotics issue of the *International Journal of Research in Marketing* 1988) offer interesting ideas and may help to guide meaningful research programs. Although appropriate criteria for evaluating research in this tradition are still at issue, it has contributed in-depth descriptions and some richer constructions of consumers' behavior.

Recent research in consumer psychology has moved beyond a replication style that substituted consumption stimuli for their counterparts in traditional psychological paradigms (e.g. brand names in memory-interference studies and product attributes in impression-formation research). This research has forged links between underlying psychological processes and consumer behavior. The challenge for future research is to develop broader and more realistic specifications of the contextual factors that constrain and mediate consumer behavior. We hope that the next review of consumer psychology will report further progress in this direction.

ACKNOWLEDGMENTS

The chapter represents the collaborative efforts of both authors, who contributed equally to the project. The section "postmodernism" is based on David G. Mick's paper, "The Meaning of Consumption: Symbolism and Beyond," which was prepared especially for this chapter and benefitted from the comments of Melanie Wallendorf. Special thanks also go to Charles S. Areni, Stephen J. Holden, Harishankar Krishnan, and Mark Spence for their assistance in assembling reference material and their many helpful comments. Preparation of this chapter was partially supported by the Karl Eller Center for the Study of the Private Market Economy, University of Arizona.

Literature Cited

Aaker, D. A., Bruzzone, D. E. 1985. Causes of irritation in advertising. *J. Mark.* 49:47–57

Aaker, D. A., Stayman, D. M., Hagerty, M. R. 1986. Warmth in advertising: measurement, impact, and sequence effects. *J. Consum. Res.* 12:365–81

Ahadi, S., Diener, E. 1989. Multiple determinants and effect size. *J. Pers. Soc. Psychol.* 56:398–406

Ahtola, O. T. 1985. Hedonic and utilitarian aspects of consumer behavior: an attitudinal perspective. *Adv. Consum. Res.* 12:7–10

Alba, J. W., Chattopadhyay, A. 1985. Effects of context and part-category cues on recall of competing brands. *J. Mark. Res.* 22:340–49

Alba, J. W., Chattopadhyay, A. 1986. Salience effects in brand recall. *J. Mark. Res.* 23:363–69

Alba, J. W., Hutchinson, J. W. 1987. Dimensions of consumer expertise. *J. Consum. Res.* 13:411–54

Alba, J. W., Marmorstein, H. 1987. The effects of frequency knowledge on consumer decision making. *J. Consum. Res.* 14:14–25

Allen, C. T., Janiszewski, C. A. 1989. Assessing the role of contingency awareness in attitudinal conditioning with implications for advertising research. *J. Mark. Res.* 26:30–43

Allen, C. T., Machleit, K. A., Marine, S. S. 1988. On assessing the emotionality of advertising via Izard's differential emotions scale. *Adv. Consum. Res.* 15:226–31

Allen, C. T., Madden, T. J. 1985. A closer look at classical conditioning. *J. Consum. Res.* 12:301–13

Anand, P., Holbrook, M. B., Stephens, D. 1988. The formation of affective judgments: the cognitive-affective model vs. the independence hypothesis. *J. Consum. Res.* 15:386–91

Anderson, P. F. 1986. On method in consumer research: a critical relativist perspective. *J. Consum. Res.* 13:155–73

Andreasen, A. R. 1984. Life status changes and changes in consumer preferences and satisfaction. *J. Consum. Res.* 11:784–94

Bahn, K. D. 1986. How and when do brand perceptions and preferences first form? A cognitive developmental investigation. *J. Consum. Res.* 13:382–93

Barsalou, L. W. 1985. Ideals, central tendency, and frequency of instantiation as determinants of graded structure in categories. *J. Exp. Psychol: Learn. Mem. Cognit.* 11:629–54

Barwise, T. P., Ehrenberg, A. S. C. 1987. The liking and viewing of regular TV series. *J. Consum. Res.* 14:63–70

Batra, R., Ray, M. L. 1986a. Affective responses mediating acceptance of advertising. *J. Consum. Res.* 13:234–49

Batra, R., Ray, M. L. 1986b. Situational effects of advertising repetition: the moderating influence of motivation, ability and opportunity to respond. *J. Consum. Res.* 12:432–45

Bawa, K., Shoemaker, R. W. 1987. The coupon-prone consumer: some findings based on purchase behavior across product classes. *J. Mark.* 51:99–110

Beatty, S. E., Smith, S. M. 1987. External search effort: an investigation across several product categories. *J. Consum. Res.* 14:83–95

Belk, R. W. 1986. Art versus science as ways of generating knowledge about materialism. In *Perspectives on Methodology in Consumer Research*, ed. R. J. Lutz, pp. 3–34. New York: Springer-Verlag

Belk, R. W. 1988. Possessions and the extended-self. *J. Consum. Res.* 15:139–68

Belk, R. W. 1989. Extended self and extending paradigmatic perspective. *J. Consum. Res.* 16:129–32

Belk, R. W., Pollay, R. W. 1985. Images of ourselves: the good life in twentieth century advertising. *J. Consum. Res.* 11:887–97

Belk, R. W., Sherry, J. F. Jr., Wallendorf, M. 1988. A naturalistic inquiry into buyer and seller behavior at a swap meet. *J. Consum. Res.* 14:449–70

Belk, R. W., Wallendorf, M., Sherry, J. F. Jr. 1989. The sacred and the profane in consumer behavior: theodicy on the odyssey. *J. Consum. Res.* 16:1–38

Bettman, J. R., John, D. R., Scott, C. 1986a. Covariation assessment by consumers. *J. Consum. Res.* 13:316–26

Bettman, J. R., Payne, J. W., Staelin, R. 1986b. Cognitive considerations in designing effective labels for presenting risk information. *J. Public Policy Mark.* 5:1–28

Bettman, J. R., Sujan, M. 1987. Effects of framing on evaluation of comparable and noncomparable alternatives by expert and novice consumers. *J. Consum. Res.* 14:141–54

Bettman, J. R., Johnson, E. J., Payne, J. W. 1990. Consumer decision making. In *Handbook of Consumer Theory and Research,* ed. H. H. Kassarjian, T. Robertson. Englewood Cliffs, NJ: Prentice-Hall. In press

Biehal, G., Chakravarti, D. 1986. Consumers' use of memory and external information in choice: macro and micro perspectives. *J. Consum. Res.* 12:382–405

Bierley, C., McSweeney, F. K., Vannieuwkerk, R. 1985. Classical conditioning of preferences for stimuli. *J. Consum. Res.* 12:316–23

Bivens, G. E., Volker, C. B. 1986. A value-added approach to household production: the special case of meal preparation. *J. Consum. Res.* 13:272–79

Blair, E., Burton, S. 1987. Cognitive processes used by survey respondents to answer behavioral frequency questions. *J. Consum. Res.* 14:280–88

Blaylock, J. R., Smallwood, D. M. 1987. Intrahousehold time allocation: the case of grocery shopping. *J. Consum. Affairs* 21:183–201

Bloch, P. H., Sherrell, D. L., Ridgeway, N. M. 1986. Consumer search: an extended framework. *J. Consum. Res.* 13:119–26

Boush, D., Shipp, S., Loken, B., Geneturk, E., Crockett, S., et al. 1987. Affect generalization to similar and dissimilar brand extensions. *Psychol. Mark.* 4:225–37

Brown, J. J., Reingen, P. H. 1987. Social ties and word-of-mouth-referral behavior. *J. Consum. Res.* 14:350–62

Brucks, M. 1985. The effects of product class knowledge on information search behavior. *J. Consum. Res.* 12:1–16

Brucks, M., Armstrong, G. M., Goldberg, M. E. 1988. Children's use of cognitive defenses against television advertising: a

cognitive response approach. *J. Consum. Res.* 14:471–82

Brucks, M., Mitchell, A. A., Staelin, R. 1984. The effect of nutritional information disclosure in advertising: an information processing approach. *J. Public Policy Mark.* 3:1–9

Bryant, W. K. 1988. Durables and wives' employment yet again. 1988. *J. Consum. Res.* 15:37–47

Burke, M. C., Edell, J. A. 1989. The impact of feelings on ad-based affect and cognition. *J. Mark. Res.* 26:69–83

Burke, R. R., DeSarbo, W. S., Oliver, R. L., Robertson, T. S. 1988. Deception by implication: an experimental investigation. *J. Consum. Res.* 14:483–94

Burke, R. R., Srull, T. K. 1988. Competitive interference and consumer memory for advertising. *J. Consum. Res.* 15:55–68

Burroughs, W. J., Feinberg, R. A. 1987. Using response latency to assess spokesperson effectiveness. *J. Consum. Res.* 14:295–99

Burton, S., Zinkhan, G. M. 1987. Changes in consumer choice: further investigation of similarity and attraction effects. *Psychol. Mark.* 4:255–66

Buyukkurt, B. K. 1986. Integration of serially sampled price information modeling and some findings. *J. Consum. Res.* 13:357–73

Cacioppo, J. T., Petty, R. E. 1985. Central and peripheral routes to persuasion: the role of message repetition. In *Psychological Processes and Advertising Effects,* ed. L. F. Alwitt, A. A. Mitchell, pp. 91–111. Hillsdale, NJ: Erlbaum

Cadotte, E. R., Woodruff, R. B., Jenkins, R. L. 1987. Expectations and norms in models of consumer satisfaction. *J. Mark. Res.* 24:305–14

Calder, B. J., Tybout, A. M. 1987. What consumer research is. . . . *J. Consum. Res.* 14:136–40

Carlson, L., Grossbart, S. 1988. Parental style and consumer socialization of children. *J. Consum. Res.* 15:77–94

Carpenter, G. S., Nakamoto, K. 1989. Consumer preference formation and pioneering advantage. *J. Mark. Res.* 26:285–98

Celsi, R. L., Olson, J. C. 1988. The role of involvement in attention and comprehension processes. *J. Consum. Res.* 15:210–24

Chattopadhyay, A., Alba, J. 1988. The situational importance of recall and inference in consumer decision making. *J. Consum. Res.* 15:1–12

Chakravarti, D., MacInnis, D., Nakamoto, K. 1989. Product category perceptions, elaborative processing and brand name extension strategies. *Adv. Consum. Res.* 16:In press

Chen, A., Jensen, H. H. 1985. Home equity use and the life cycle hypothesis. *J. Consum. Affairs* 19:37–56

Childers, T. L., Houston, M. J. 1984. Conditions for a picture—superiority effect on consumer memory. *J. Consum. Res.* 11:643–54

Childers, T. L., Houston, M. J., Heckler, S. E. 1985. Measurement of individual differences in visual versus verbal information processing. *J. Consum. Res.* 12:125–34

Cohen, J. B. 1989. An over-extended self? *J. Consum. Res.* 16:125–28

Cohen, J. B., Areni, C. 1990. Affect and consumer behavior. In *Handbook of Consumer Theory and Research*, ed. H. H. Kassarjian, T. Robertson. Englewood Cliffs, NJ: Prentice-Hall. In press

Cohen, J. B., Basu, K. 1987. Alternative models of categorization: toward a contingent processing framework. *J. Consum. Res.* 13:455–72

Cole, C. A., Houston, M. J. 1987. Encoding and media effects on consumer learning deficiencies in the elderly. *J. Mark. Res.* 24:55–64

Corfman, K. P., Lehmann, D. R. 1987. Models of cooperative group decision-making and relative influence: an experimental investigation of family purchase decisions. *J. Consum. Res.* 14:1–13

Costley, C. L. 1988. Meta analysis of involvement research. *Adv. Consum. Res.* 15:554–63

Coupey, E., Nakamoto, K. 1988. Learning context and the development of product category perceptions. *Adv. Consum. Res.* 15:77–82

Cox, D. S., Cox, A. D. 1988. What does familiarity breed? Complexity as a moderator of repetition effects in advertisement evaluation. *J. Consum. Res.* 15:111–16

Curren, M. T., Folkes, V. S. 1987. Attributional influences on consumers' desires to communicate about products. *Psychol. Mark.* 4:31–45

Curry, D. J., Faulds, D. J. 1986. Indexing product quality: issues, theory and results. *J. Consum. Res.* 13:134–45

Dardis, R. 1988. Risk regulation and consumer welfare. *J. Consum. Affairs* 22:303–18

Davis, H. L., Hoch, S. J., Ragsdale, E. K. 1986. An anchoring and adjustment model of spousal predictions. *J. Consum. Res.* 13:25–37

Deshpande, R., Hoyer, W. D., Donthu, N. 1986. The intensity of ethnic affiliation: a study of the sociology of hispanic consumption. *J. Consum. Res.* 13:214–20

Diamond, W. D. 1988. The effect of probability and consequence levels on the focus of consumer judgments in risky situations. *J. Consum. Res.* 15:280–83

Douthitt, R. A., Fedyk, J. M. 1988. The influence of children on family life cycle spending behavior: theory and applications. *J. Consum. Affairs* 22:220–48

Dowling, G. R. 1986. Perceived risk: the concept and its measurement. *Psychol. Mark.* 3:193–210

Droge, C., Darmon, R. Y. 1987. Associative positioning strategies through comparative advertising: attribute versus overall similarity approaches. *J. Mark. Res.* 24:377–89

Edell, J. A., Burke, M. C. 1987. The power of feelings in understanding advertising effects. *J. Consum. Res.* 14:421–33

Erickson, G. M., Johansson, J. K. 1985. The role of price in multi-attribute product evaluations. *J. Consum. Res.* 12:195–99

Etzioni, A. 1988. Normative-affective factors: toward a new decision-making model. *J. Econ. Psychol.* 9:125–50

Faminow, M. D., Benson, B. L. 1985. spatial economics: implications for food market response to retail price reporting. *J. Consum. Affairs* 19:1–19

Feick, L. F., Price, L. L. 1987. The market maven: a diffuser of marketplace information. *J. Mark.* 51:83–97

Feinberg, R. A. 1986. Credit cards as spending facilitating stimuli: a conditioning interpretation. *J. Consum. Res.* 13:348–56

Feldman, J. M., Lynch, J. G. 1988. Self generated validity and other effects of measurement on belief, attitude, intention and behavior. *J. Appl. Psychol.* 73:421–35

Fern, E. F., Monroe, K. B., Avila, R. A. 1986. Effectiveness of multiple request strategies: a synthesis of research results. *J. Mark. Res.* 23:144–52

Finn, A. 1988. Print ad recognition readership scores: an information processing perspective. *J. Mark. Res.* 25:168–78

Firat, A. F. 1987. Towards a deeper understanding of consumption experiences: the underlying dimensions. *Adv. Consum. Res.* 14:342–46

Fischer, M. A. 1985. A developmental study of preference for advertised toys. *Psychol. Mark.* 2:3–12

Fishbein, M., Ajzen, I. 1975. *Belief, Attitude, Intention and Behavior*. Redding, MA: Addison-Wesley

Folkes, V. S. 1984. Consumer reactions to product failure: an attributional approach. *J. Consum. Res.* 10:398–409

Folkes, V. S. 1988a. Recent attribution research in consumer behavior: a review and new directions. *J. Consum. Res.* 14:548–65

Folkes, V. S. 1988b. The availability heuristic and perceived risk. *J. Consum. Res.* 15:13–23

Folkes, V. S., Koletsky, S., Graham, J. L. 1987. A field study of causal inferences and consumer reaction: the view from the airport. *J. Consum. Res.* 13:534–38

Folkes, V. S., Kotsos, B. 1986. Buyers' and

sellers' explanations for product failure: Who done it? *J. Mark.* 50:74–80

Ford, G. T., Smith, R. A. 1987. Interferential beliefs in consumer evaluations: an assessment of alternative processing strategies. *J. Consum. Res.* 14:363–71

Fraser, C., Hite, R. E., Sauer, P. L. 1988. Increasing contributions in solicitation campaigns: the use of large and small anchor points. *J. Consum. Res.* 15:284–87

Friedman, M. 1985. The changing language of a consumer society: brand name usage in popular American novels in the postwar era. *J. Consum. Res.* 11:927–38

Friedman, M. L. 1987. Survey data on owner-reporter car problems: how useful to prospective purchasers of used cars? *J. Consum. Res.* 14:434–39

Friedman, M. L., Churchill, G. A. 1987. Using consumer perceptions and a contingency approach to improve health care delivery. *J. Consum. Res.* 13:492–510

Friestad, M., Thorson, E. 1986. Emotion-eliciting advertising: effect on long term memory and judgment. *Adv. Consum. Res.* 13:111–15

Fugate, D. L. 1986. The effects of manufacturer disclosure on consumer perceptions of private brand product attributes. *J. Consum. Affairs* 20:118–30

Funkhouser, G. R. 1984. An empirical study of consumers' sensitivity to the wording of affirmative disclosure messages. *J. Public Policy Mark.* 3:26–30

Furse, D. H., Punj, G. N., Stewart, D. W. 1984. A typology of individual search strategies among purchasers of new automobiles. *J. Consum. Res.* 10:417–31

Gaeth, G. J., Heath, T. B. 1987. The cognitive processing of misleading advertising in young and old adults. *J. Consum Res.* 14:43–54

Gardner, M. P. 1985a. Mood states and consumer behavior: a critical review. *J. Consum. Res.* 12:281–300

Gardner, M. P. 1985b. Does attitude toward the ad affect brand attitude under a brand evaluation set? *J. Mark. Res.* 22:192–98

Gardner, M. P., Siomkos, G. J. 1986. Toward a methodology for assessing effects of in-store atmospherics. *Adv. Consum. Res.* 13:27–31

Gatignon, H., Robertson, T. S. 1985. A propositional inventory for new diffusion research. *J. Consum. Res.* 11:849–67

Gensch, D. H., Javalgi, R. G. 1987. The influence of involvement on disaggregate attribute choice models. *J. Consum. Res.* 14:71–82

Gerstner, E. 1985. Do higher prices signal higher quality? *J. Mark. Res.* 22:209–15

Gilly, M. C. 1987. Postcomplaint processes: from organizational response to repurchase

behavior. *J. Consum. Affairs* 21:293–313

Gilly, M. C. 1988. Sex roles in advertising: a comparison of television advertisements in Australia, Mexico and the United States. *J. Mark.* 52:75–85

Gilly, M. C., Zeithaml, V. A. 1985. The elderly consumer and adoption of technologies. *J. Consum. Res.* 12:353–57

Glazer, R. 1984. Multiattribute perceptual bias as revealing of preference structure. *J. Consum. Res.* 12:74–82

Goering, P. A. 1985. Effects of product trial on consumer expectations, demand, and prices. *J. Consum. Res.* 12:74–82

Goldberg, M. E., Gorn, G. J. 1987. Happy and sad TV programs: how they affect reactions to commercials. *J. Consum. Res.* 14:387–403

Golden, L. L., Zimmer, M. R. 1986. Relationships between affect, patronage frequency and amount of money spent with a comment on affect scaling and measurement. *Adv. Consum. Res.* 13:53–57

Gorn, G. J. 1982. The effects of music in advertising on choice behavior: a classical conditioning approach. *J. Mark.* 46:94–101

Gorn, G. J., Florsheim, R. 1985. The effects of commercials for adult products on children. *J. Consum. Res.* 11:962–67

Gorn, G. J., Weinberg, C. B. 1984. The impact of comparative advertising on perception and attitude: some positive findings. *J. Consum. Res.* 11:719–27

Gresham, L. G., Shimp, T. A. 1985. Attitude toward the advertisement and brand attitudes: a classical conditioning perspective. *J. Advert.* 14:10–17

Grether, D., Wilde, L. 1984. An analysis of conjunctive choice: theory and experiments. *J. Consum. Res.* 10:373–85

Gronhaug, K., Kleppe, I. A., Haukedal, W. 1987. Observation of a strategic household purchase decision. *Psychol. Mark.* 4:239–53

Grunert, K. G., Dedler, K. 1987. Misleading advertising: in search of a measurement methodology. *J. Public Policy Mark.* 5:153–59

Gutman, J. 1985. Analyzing consumer orientations toward beverages through means-end chain analysis. *Psychol. Mark.* 1:23–33

Hager, C. J. 1988. Shopping for variety in red meat, poultry, and fish. *Adv. Consum. Res.* 15:19–21

Hagerty, M. R., Aaker, D. A. 1984. A normative model of consumer information processing. *Mark. Sci.* 3:227–46

Hama, M. Y., Chan, W. S. 1988. Food Expenditure and nutrient availability in elderly households. *J. Consum. Affairs* 22:3–19

Han, C. M. 1988. The role of consumer

patriotism in the choice of domestic versus foreign products. *J. Advert. Res.* 28:25–32

Hauser, J. R. 1986. Agendas and consumer choice. *J. Mark. Res.* 23:199–212

Hauser, J. R., Urban, G. L. 1986. The value priority hypotheses for consumer budget plans. *J. Consum. Res.* 12:446–62

Havlena, W. J., Holbrook, M. B. 1986. The varieties of consumption experience: comparing two typologies of emotion in consumer behavior. *J. Consum. Res.* 13:394–404

Helgeson, J. G., Beatty, S. E. 1987. Price expectation and price recall error: an empirical study. *J. Consum. Res.* 14:379–86

Hill, R. P., Mazis, M. B. 1986. Measuring emotional responses to advertising. *Adv. Consum. Res.* 13:164–69

Hirschman, E. C. 1985. Primitive aspects of consumption in modern American society. *J. Consum. Res.* 12:142–54

Hirschman, E. C. 1987. People as products: analysis of a complex marketing exchange. *J. Mark.* 51:98–108

Hirschman, E. C. 1988. The ideology of consumption: a structural-syntactical analysis of "Dallas" and "Dynasty". *J. Consum. Res.* 15:344–59

Hirschman, E. C., ed. 1989. *Interpretive Consumer Research*, Provo, UT: Assoc. Consum. Res.

Hite, R. E., Eck, R. 1987. Advertising to children: attitudes of business vs consumers. *J. Advert. Res.* 27:40–53

Hite, R. E., Fraser, C. 1988. Meta-analyses of attitudes toward advertising of professionals. *J. Mark.* 52:95–105

Hjorth-Andersen, C. 1984. The concept of quality and the efficiency of markets for consumer products. *J. Consum. Res.* 11:708–18

Hjorth-Andersen, C. 1986. More on multidimensional quality: a reply. *J. Consum. Res.* 13:149–54

Hoch, S. J. 1988. Who do we know: predicting the interests and opinions of the American consumer. *J. Consum. Res.* 15:315–24

Hoch, S. J., Ha, Y. W. 1986. Consumer learning: advertising and the ambiguity of product experience. *J. Consum. Res.* 13:221–33

Holbrook, M. B. 1986a. Aims, concepts, and methods for the representation of individual differences in aesthetic responses to design features. *J. Consum. Res.* 13:337–47

Holbrook, M. B. 1986b. Emotion in the consumption experience: toward a new model of the human consumer. In *The Role of Affect in Consumer Behavior*, ed. R. A. Peterson, W. D. Hoyer, W. R. Wilson. Lexington, MA: Heath

Holbrook, M. B. 1987a. O, consumer, how you've changed: some radical reflections on the roots of consumption. In *Philosophical and Radical Thought in Marketing*, ed. A. F. Firat, N. Dholakia, R. P. Bagozzi, pp. 157–77. Lexington, MA: Heath

Holbrook, M. B. 1987b. What is consumer research? *J. Consum. Res.* 14:128–32

Holbrook, M. B. 1987c. Mirror, mirror, on the wall, what's unfair in the reflections of advertising? *J. Mark.* 51:95–103

Holbrook, M. B., Batra, R. 1987. Assessing the role of emotions as mediators of consumer responses to advertising. *J. Consum. Res.* 14:404–20

Holbrook, M. B., Grayson, M. W. 1986. The semiology of cinematic consumption: symbolic consumer behavior in *Out of Africa*. *J. Consum. Res.* 13:374–81

Holbrook, M. B., O'Shaughnessy, J. 1988. On the scientific status of consumer research and the need for an interpretive approach to studying consumption behavior. *J. Consum. Res.* 15:398–402

Hornik, J. 1988. Diurnal variation in consumer response. *J. Consum. Res.* 14:588–91

Houston, M. J., Childers, T. L., Heckler, S. E. 1987. Picture-word consistency and the elaborative processing of advertisements. *J. Mark. Res.* 24:359–70

Hoy, M. G., Young, C. E., Mowen, J. C. 1986. Animated host-selling advertisements: their impact on young children's recognition, attitudes, and behavior. *J. Public Policy Mark.* 5:171–84

Hoyer, W. D. 1984. An examination of consumer decision making for a common repeat purchase product. *J. Consum. Res.* 11:822–29

Huber, J., Puto, C. 1983. Market boundaries and product choice: illustrating attraction and substitution effects. *J. Consum. Res.* 10:31–44

Hudson, L. A., Ozanne, J. L. 1988. Alternative ways of seeking knowledge in consumer research. *J. Consum. Res.* 14:508–21

Hutton, R. B., Mauser, G. A., Filiatrault, P., Ahtola, O. T. 1986. Effects of cost-related feedback on consumer knowledge and consumption behavior: A field experimental approach. *J. Consum. Res.* 13:327–36

Isen, A. M. 1989. Some ways in which affect influences cognitive processes: implications for advertising and consumer behavior. In *Advertising and Consumer Psychology*, ed. A. M. Tybout, P. Cafferata, pp. 91–117. New York: Lexington Books

Isler, L., Popper, E. T., Ward, S. 1987. Children's purchase requests & parental responses: results from a diary study. *J. Advert. Res.* 27:28–39

Jackson, R. W., McDaniel, S. W., Rao, C. P. 1985. Food shopping and preparation: psychographic differences of working wives and housewives. *J. Consum. Res.* 12:110–13

Jacoby, J. 1984. Perspectives on information overload. *J. Consum. Res.* 10:432–35

Janiszewski, C. 1988. Preconscious processing effects: the independence of attitude formation and conscious thought. *J. Consum. Res.* 15:199–209

Joachimsthaler, E., Lastovicka, J. L. 1984. Optimal stimulation level—exploratory behavior models. *J. Consum. Res.* 11:830–35

Joag, S. G., Gentry, J. W., Hupper, J. 1985. Explaining differences in consumption by working and non-working wives. *Adv. Consum. Res.* 12:582–85

Johansson, J. K., Douglas, S. P., Nonaka, I. 1985. Assessing the impact of country of origin on product evaluations: a new methodological perspective. *J. Mark. Res.* 22:388–96

John, D. R., Cole, C. A. 1986. Age differences in information processing: understanding deficits in young and elderly consumers. *J. Consum. Res.* 13:297–315

John, D. R., Scott, C. A., Bettman, J. R. 1986. Sampling data for covariation assessment: the effect of prior beliefs on search patterns. *J. Consum. Res.* 13:38–47

John, D. R., Whitney, J. C. 1986. The development of consumer knowledge in children: a cognitive structure approach. *J. Consum. Res.* 12:406–17

Johnson, E. J., Meyer, R. J. 1984. Compensatory choice models of noncompensatory processes: the effect of varying context. *J. Consum. Res.* 11:528–41

Johnson, E. J., Russo, J. E. 1984. Product familiarity and learning new information. *J. Consum. Res.* 11:542–50

Johnson, M. D. 1984. Consumer choice strategies for comparing noncomparable alternatives. *J. Consum. Res.* 11:741–53

Johnson, M. D. 1986. Modeling choice strategies for noncomparable alternatives. *Mark. Sci.* 5:37–54

Johnson, M. D. 1988. Comparability and hierarchical processing in multialternative choice. *J. Consum. Res.* 15:303–14

Johnson, M. D., Fornell, C. 1987. The nature and methodological implications of the cognitive representation of products. *J. Consum. Res.* 14:214–28

Johnson, M. D., Horne, D. A. 1988. The contrast model of similarity and comparative advertising. *Psychol. Mark.* 5:211–32

Johnson, M. D., Levin, I. P. 1985. More than meets the eye: the effect of missing information on purchase evaluations. *J. Consum. Res.* 12:169–77

Kahle, L. R. 1986. The nine nations of North America and the value basis of geographic segmentation. *J. Mark.* 50:37–47

Kahle, L. R., Beatty, S. E., Homer, P. 1986. Alternative measurement approaches to consumer values: the list of values (LOV) and values and lifestyle (VALS). *J. Consum. Res.* 13:405–9

Kahle, L. R., Beatty, S. E., Kennedy, P. 1987. Comment on classically conditioning human consumers. *Adv. Consum. Res.* 14:411–14

Kahle, L. R., Homer, P. M. 1985. Physical attractiveness of the celebrity endorser: a social adaptation perspective. *J. Consum. Res.* 11:954–61

Kahn, B. E., Kalwani, M. U., Morrison, D. G. 1986. Measuring variety-seeking multi-alternative choice. *J. Mark. Res.* 23:89–100

Kahn, B. E., Moore, W. L., Glazer, R. 1987. Experiments in constrained choice. *J. Consum. Res.* 14:96–113

Kahn, B. E., Sarin, R. K. 1988. Modeling ambiguity in decisions under uncertainty. *J. Consum. Res.* 15:265–72

Kahneman, D., Tversky, A. 1979. Prospect theory: an analysis of decision under risk. *Econometrica* 47:163–91

Kamakura, W. A., Ratchford, B. T., Agrawal, J. 1988. Measuring market efficiency and welfare loss. *J. Consum. Res.* 15:289–302

Kamins, M. A., Assael, H. 1987a. Moderating disconfirmation of expectations through the use of two-sided appeals: a longitudinal approach. *J. Econ. Psychol.* 8:237–53

Kamins, M. A., Assael, H. 1987b. Two-sided versus one-sided appeals: a cognitive perspective on argumentation, source derogation and the effect of disconfirming trial upon belief change. *J. Mark. Res.* 24:29–39

Kardes, F. R. 1986. Effects of initial product judgments on subsequent memory-based judgments. *J. Consum. Res.* 13:1–11

Kardes, F. R. 1988. Spontaneous inference processes in advertising: the effects of conclusion omission and involvement on persuasion. *J. Consum. Res.* 15:225–33

Keller, K. L. 1987. Memory factors in advertising: the effect of advertising retrieval cues on brand evaluations. *J. Consum. Res.* 14:316–33

Keller, K. L., Staelin, R. 1987. Effects of quality and quantity of information on decision effectiveness. *J. Consum. Res.* 14:200–13

Keller, K. L., Staelin, R. 1989. Assessing biases in measuring decision effectiveness and information overload. *J. Consum. Res.* 15:504–9

Kelly, R. F. 1987. Culture as commodity: the marketing of cultural objects and cultural experiences. *Adv. Consum. Res.* 14:347–51

Keng, K. A., Ehrenberg, A. S. C. 1984. Patterns of store choice. *J. Mark. Res.* 21:399–410

Kirchler, E. 1988. Diary reports on daily economic decisions of happy versus unhappy couples. *J. Econ. Psychol.* 9:327–57

Kiselius, J., Sternthal, B. 1984. Detecting and explaining vividness effects in attitudinal judgments. *J. Mark. Res.* 21:54–64

Kiselius, J., Sternthal, B. 1986. Examining the vividness controversy: an availability-valence interpretation. *J. Consum. Res.* 12:418–31

Klein, N. M., Bither, S. W. 1987. An investigation of utility-directed cutoff selection. *J. Consum. Res.* 14:240–56

Lantos, G. P. 1987. Advertising: looking glass or molder of the masses? *J. Public Policy Mark.* 6:104–28

Lastovicka, J. L., Joachimsthaler, E. A. 1988. Improving the detection of personality-behavior relationship in consumer research. *J. Consum. Res.* 14:583–87

Lastovicka, J. L., Murry, J. P. Jr., Joachimsthaler, E. A., Bhalla, G., Scheurich, J. 1987. A lifestyle typology to model young male drinking and driving. *J. Consum. Res.* 14:257–63

Lattin, J. M. 1987. A model of balanced choice behavior. *Mark. Sci.* 6:48–66

Laurent, G., Kapferer, J. N. 1985. Measuring consumer involvement profiles. *J. Mark. Res.* 22:41–53

Leonard-Barton, D. 1985. Experts as negative opinion leaders in the diffusion of a technological innovation. *J. Consum. Res.* 11:914–26

Levendahl, J. W. 1988. Coupon redeemers: Are they better shoppers? *J. Consum. Affairs* 22:264–83

Levin, I. P., Gaeth, G. J. 1988. How consumers are affected by the framing of attribute information before and after consuming the product. *J. Consum. Res.* 15:374–78

Levin, I. P., Johnson, R. D. 1984. Estimating price-quality tradeoffs using comparative judgments. *J. Consum. Res.* 11:593–600

Levin, I. P., Johnson, R. D., Davis, M. L. 1987. How information frame influences risky decisions: between-subjects and within-subject comparisons. *J. Econ. Psychol.* 8:43–54

Levy, A. S., Mathews, O., Stephenson, M., Tenney, J. E., Schucker, R. E. 1985. The impact of a nutrition information program on food purchases. *J. Public Policy Mark.* 4:1–13

Lichtenstein, D. R., Bearden, W. O. 1986. Measurement and structure of Kelley's covariance theory. *J. Consum. Res.* 13:290–96

Lichtenstein, D. R., Bloch, P. H., Black, W. C. 1988. Correlates of price acceptability. *J. Consum. Res.* 15:243–52

Lichtenstein, M., Srull, T. K. 1985. Conceptual and methodological issues in examining the relationship between consumer memory and judgment. *Psychological Processes and Advertising Effects: Theory, Research Application,* ed. L. F. Alwitt, A. A. Mitchell, pp. 113–28. Hillsdale, NJ: Erlbaum

Liefeld, J., Heslop, L. A. 1985. Reference prices and deception in newspaper advertising. *J. Consum. Res.* 11:868–76

Lim, J., Olshavsky, R. W., Kim, J. 1988. The impact of inferences on product evaluations: replication and extension. *J. Mark. Res.* 25:308–17

Loken, B., Hoverstad, R. 1985. Relationships between information recall and subsequent attitudes: some exploratory findings. *J. Consum. Res.* 12:155–68

Loken, B., Ross, I., Hinkel, R. L. 1986. Consumer "confusion" of origin and brand similarity perceptions. *J. Public Policy Mark.* 5:195–203

Lynch, J. G. Jr. 1985. Uniqueness issues in the decompositional modeling of multiattribute overall evaluations: an information integration perspective. *J. Mark. Res.* 22:1–20

Lynch, J. G. Jr., Marmorstein, H., Weigold, M. F. 1988. Choices from sets including remembered brands: use of recalled attributes and prior overall evaluations. *J. Consum. Res.* 15:169–84

MacInnis, D. J., Price, L. L. 1987. The role of imagery in information processing: review and extensions. *J. Consum. Res.* 13:473–91

MacKenzie, S. B. 1986. The role of attention in mediating the effect of advertising on attribute importance. *J. Consum. Res.* 13:174–95

MacKenzie, S. B., Lutz, R. J., Belch, G. E. 1986. The role of attitude toward the ad as a mediator of advertising effectiveness: a test of competing explanations. *J. Mark. Res.* 23:130–43

Macklin, M. C. 1987. Preschoolers' understanding of the informational function of television advertising. *J. Consum. Res.* 14:229–39

Madden, T. J., Allen, C. T., Twibble, J. L. 1988. Attitude toward the ad: an assessment of diverse measurement indices under different processing "sets". *J. Mark. Res.* 25: 242–52

Malhotra, N. K. 1984. Reflections on the information overload paradigm in consumer decision making. *J. Consum. Res.* 10:436–40

Malhotra, N. K. 1988. Self concept and product choice: an integrated perspective. *J. Econ. Psychol.* 9:1–28

Marks, L. J., Kamins, M. A. 1988. The use of product sampling and advertising: effects of sequence of exposure and degree of advertising claim exaggeration on consumers' belief strength, belief confidence, and attitudes. *J. Mark. Res.* 25:266–82

Mayo, M. C., Qualls, W. J. 1987. Household durable goods acquisition behavior: a longitudinal study. *Adv. Consum. Res.* 14:463–67

Mazursky, D., Schul, Y. 1988. The effects of advertisement encoding on the failure to discount information: implications for the sleeper effect. *J. Consum. Res.* 15:24–35

McConkey, C. W., Warren, W. E. 1987. Psychographic and demographic profiles of state lottery ticket purchasers. *J. Consum. Affairs* 21:314–27

McCracken, G. 1986. Culture and consumption: a theoretical account of the structure and movement of the cultural meaning of consumer goods. *J. Consum. Res.* 13:71–84

McDaniel, S. W., Rao, C. P., Jackson, R. W. 1986. Inflation-induced adaptive behavior. *Psychol. Mark.* 3:113–22

McDaniel, S. W., Zeithaml, V. A. 1984. The effect of fear on purhcase intentions. *Psychol. Mark.* 1:73–82

McEnally, M. R., Hawes, J. M. 1984. The market for generic brand grocery products: a review and extension. *J. Mark.* 48:75–83

McIntyre, P., Hosch, H. M., Harris, R. J., Norvell, D. W. 1986. Effects of sex and attitudes toward women on the processing of television commercials. *Psychol. Mark.* 3:181–90

McQuarrie, E. F., Langmeyer, D. 1987. Planned and actual spending among owners of home computers. *J. Econ. Psychol.* 8:141–59

McSweeney, F. K., Bierley, C. 1984. Recent developments in classical conditioning. *J. Consum. Res.* 11:619–31

Meyer, R. J. 1987. The learning of multiattribute judgment policies. *J. Consum. Res.* 14:155–73

Meyer, R. J., Johnson, E. J. 1989. Information overload and the nonrobustness of linear models: a commend on Keller and Staelin. *J. Consum. Res.* 15:498–504

Meyer, R. J., Sathi, A. 1985. A multiattribute model of consumer choice during product learning. *Mark. Sci.* 4:41–61

Meyers-Levy, J. 1988. The influence of sex roles on judgment. *J. Consum. Res.* 14:522–30

Mick, D. G. 1986. Consumer research and semiotics: exploring the morphology of signs, symbols, and significance. *J. Consum. Res.* 13:196–213

Milliman, R. E. 1986. The influence of background music on the behavior of restaurant patrons. *J. Consum. Res.* 13:286–89

Mills, D. L., Gardner, M. J. 1986. Consumer response to adjustable rate mortgages: implications of the evidence from Illinois and Wisconsin. *J. Consum. Affairs* 20:77–105

Mitchell, A. A. 1986a. The effect of verbal and visual components of advertisements on brand attitudes and attitude toward the advertisement. *J. Consum. Res.* 13:12–24

Mitchell, A. A. 1986b. Some issues surrounding research on the effects of "feeling advertisements". *Adv. Consum. Res.* 13:623–28

Mobley, M. F., Bearden, W. O., Teel, J. E. 1988. An investigation of individual responses to tensile price claims. *J. Consum. Res.* 15:273–79

Moore, D. J., Reardon, R. 1987. Source magnification: the role of multiple sources in the processing of advertising appeals. *J. Mark. Res.* 24:412–17

Moore, D. L., Hausknecht, D., Thamodaran, K. 1986. Time compression, response opportunity, and persuasion. *J. Consum. Res.* 13:85–99

Moore-Shay, E. S., Lutz, R. J. 1988. Intergenerational influences in the formation of consumer attitudes and beliefs about the marketplace: mothers and daughters. *Adv. Consum. Res.* 15:461–67

Moschis, G. P. 1985. The role of family communication in consumer socialization of children and adolescents. *J. Consum. Res.* 11:898–913

Moschis, G. P., Prahasto, A. E., Mitchell, L. G. 1986. Family communication influences on the development of consumer behavior: some additional findings. *Adv. Consum. Res.* 13:365–69

Muller, T. E. 1985. Structural information factors which stimulate the use of nutrition information: a field experiment. *J. Mark. Res.* 22:143–57

Munch, J. M., Swasy, J. L. 1988. Rhetorical question, summarization frequency, and argument strength effects on recall. *J. Consum. Res.* 15:69–76

Nedungadi, P., Hutchinson, W. 1985. The prototypicality of brands: relationships with brand awareness, preference and usage. *Adv. Consum. Res.* 12:498–503

Nelson, J. E. N., Calvin, P., Frontczak, N. T. 1985. The distraction hypothesis and radio advertising. *J. Mark.* 49:60–72

Obermiller, C. 1985. Varieties of mere exposure: the effects of processing style and repetition on affective response. *J. Consum. Res.* 12:17–30

Ofir, C., Lynch, J. G. 1984. Context effects on judgment under uncertainty. *J. Consum. Res.* 11:668–79

O'Guinn, T. C., Faber, R. J. 1987. Mass mediated consumer socialization: nonutilitarian and dysfunctional outcomes. *Adv. Consum. Res.* 14:473–77

Oliver, R. L., DeSarbo, W. S. 1988. Response determinants in satisfaction judgments. *J. Consum. Res.* 14:495–507

Oliver, R. L., Winer, R. S. 1987. A

framework for the formation and structure of consumer expectations: review and propositions. *J. Econ. Psychol.* 8:469–99

Olshavsky, R. W., Rosen, D. L. 1985. Use of product-testing organizations' recommendations as a strategy for choice simplification. *J. Consum. Affairs* 19:119–39

Park, C. W., Iyer, E. S., Smith, D. C. 1989. The effects of situational factors on in-store grocery shopping behavior: the role of store environment and time available for shopping. *J. Consum. Res.* 15:422–23

Park, C. W., Jaworski, B. J., MacInnis, D. J. 1986. Strategic brand concept-image management. *J. Mark.* 50:135–45

Park, C. W., Young, S. M. 1986. Consumer response to television commercials: the impact of involvement and background music on brand attitude formation. *J. Mark. Res.* 23:11–24

Pavelchak, M. A., Antil, J. H., Munch, J. M. 1988. The superbowl: an investigation into the relationship among program context, emotional experience, and ad recall. *J. Consum. Res.* 15:360–67

Payne, J. W., Bettman, J. R., Johnson, E. J. 1988. Adaptive strategy selection in decision making. *J. Exp. Psychol.* 14:534–52

Pessemier, E., Handelsman, M. 1984. Temporal variety in consumer behavior. *J. Mark. Res.* 21:435–45

Petroshius, S. M., Monroe, K. B. 1987. Effect of product-line pricing characteristics on product evaluations. *J. Consum. Res.* 13:511–19

Pettit, K. L., Sawa, S. L., Sawa, G. H. 1985. Frugality: a cross-national moderator of the price-quality relationship. *Psychol. Mark.* 2:253–65

Pollay, R. W. 1986. The distorted mirror: reflections on the unintended consequences of advertising. *J. Mark.* 50:18–36

Pollay, R. W. 1987. On the value of reflections on the values in the distorted mirror. *J. Mark.* 51:104–9

Prakash, V. 1986. Segmentation of a women's market based on personal values and the means-end chain model: a framework for advertising strategy. *Adv. Consum. Res.* 13:215–20

Prakash, V., Flores, R. C. 1985. A study of psychological gender differences: applications for advertising format. *Adv. Consum. Res.* 12:231–37

Price, L. L., Feick, L. F., Higie, R. A. 1987. Information sensitive consumers and market information. *J. Consum. Affairs* 21:328–41

Puto, C. P. 1987. The framing of buying decisions. *J. Consum. Res.* 14:301–15

Puto, C. P., Wells, W. D. 1984. Informational and transformational advertising: the differential effects of time. *Adv. Consum. Res.* 11:638–43

Qualls, W. J. 1987. Household decision behavior: the impact of husbands' and wives sex role orientation. *J. Consum. Res.* 14:264–79

Ratneshwar, S., Shocker, A. D., Stewart, D. W. 1987. Toward understanding the attraction effect: the implications of product stimulus meaningfulness and familiarity. *J. Consum. Res.* 13:520–33

Reece, B. B. 1986. Children and shopping: some public policy questions. *J. Public Policy Mark.* 5:185–94

Reece, B. B., Ducoffe, R. H. 1987. Deception in brand names. *J. Public Policy Mark.* 6:93–103

Reilly, M. D., Wallendorf, M. 1987. A comparison of group differences in food consumption using household refuse. *J. Consum. Res.* 14:289–94

Reingen, P. H. 1987. A word-of-mouth network. *Adv. Consum. Res.* 14:213–17

Reingen, P. H., Foster, B. L., Brown, J. J., Seidman, S. B. 1984. Brand congruence in interpersonal relations: a social network analysis. *J. Consum. Res.* 11:771–83

Reingen, P. H., Kernan, G. B. 1986. Analysis of referral networks in marketing: methods and illustrations. *J. Mark. Res.* 23:370–78

Rethans, A. J., Swasy, J. L., Marks, L. J. 1986. Effects of television commercial repetition, receiver knowledge, and commercial length: a test of the two-factor model. *J. Mark. Res.* 23:50–61

Richins, M. L. 1987. Media, materialism and human happiness. *Adv. Consum. Res.* 14:352–55

Richins, M. L., Bloch, P. H. 1986. After the new wears off: the temporal context of product involvement. *J. Consum. Res.* 13:280–85

Robertson, K. R. 1987. Recall and recognition effects of brand name imagery. *Psychol. Mark.* 4:3–15

Rook, D. W. 1985. The ritual dimension of consumer behavior. *J. Consum. Res.* 12:251–64

Rook, D. W. 1987. The buying impulse. *J. Consum. Res.* 14:189–99

Rook, D. W., Hoch, S. J. 1985. Consuming impulses. *Adv. Consum. Res.* 12:23–27

Rothschild, M. L., Hyun, Y. J., Reeves, V., Thorson, E., Goldstein, R. 1988. Hemispherically lateralized EEG as a response to television commercials. *J. Consum. Res.* 15:185–98

Russell, J. A. 1978. Evidence of convergent validity on the dimensions of affect. *J. Pers. Soc. Psychol.* 36:42–68

Russo, J. E., Staelin, R., Nolan, C. A., Russell, G. J., Metcalf, B. L. 1987. Nutrition information in the supermarket. *J. Consum. Res.* 13:48–70

Saegert, J. 1987. Why marketing should quit giving subliminal advertising the benefit of the doubt. *Psychol. Mark.* 4:107–20

Saegert, J., Hoover, R. J., Hilger, M. T. 1985. Characteristics of Mexican-American consumers. *J. Consum. Res.* 12:104–9

Samuels, L. B., Coffinberger, R. L., McCrohan, K. F. 1986. Legislative responses to the plight of new car purchasers: a missed marketing opportunity. *J. Public Policy Mark.* 5:61–71

Sanbonmatsu, D. M., Kardes, F. R. 1988. The effects of physiological arousal on information processing and persuasion. *J. Consum. Res.* 15:379–85

Schachter, D. L. 1987. Implicit memory: history and current status. *J. Exp. Psychol.* 13:501–18

Schaninger, C. M., Bourgeois, J. C., Buss, W. C. 1985. French English Canadian subcultural consumption differences. *J. Mark.* 49:82–92

Schmitt, B. H., LeClerc, F., Dube-Rioux, L. 1988. Sex typing and consumer behavior: a test of gender schema theory. *J. Consum. Res.* 15:122–28

Sewall, M. A., Sarel, D. 1986. Characteristics of radio commercials and their recall effectiveness. *J. Mark.* 50:52–60

Sexton, R. J., Sexton, T. A. 1987. Theoretical and methodological perspectives on consumer responses to electricity information. *J. Consum. Affairs* 21:238–57

Seymour, D. 1986. Forced compliance in family decision-making. *Psychol. Mark.* 3:223–37

Seymour, D., Lessne, G. 1984. Spousal conflict arousal: scale development. *J. Consum. Res.* 11:810–21

Sheppard, B. H., Hartwick, J., Warshaw, P. R. 1988. The theory of reasoned action: a meta-analysis of past research with recommendations for modifications and future research. *J. Consum. Res.* 15:325–43

Sherman, E., Smith, R. B. 1987. Mood states of shoppers and store image: promising interactions and possible behavioral effects. *Adv. Consum. Res.* 14:251–54

Sherry, J. F. Jr. 1990. Postpositivism and cultural perspective. In *Handbook of Consumer Theory and Research*, ed. H. H. Kassarjian, T. Robertson. Englewood Cliffs, NJ: Prentice-Hall

Sherry, J. F. Jr., Camargo, E. G. 1987. May your life be marvelous: English language labelling and the semiotics of Japanese promotion. *J. Consum. Res.* 14:174–88

Shimp, T. A., Sharma, S. 1987. Consumer ethnocentrism: construction and validation of the CETSCALE. *J. Mark. Res.* 24:280–89

Silver, S. D. 1988. Interdependencies in social and economic decision making: a conditional logit model of the joint homeownership-mobility decision. *J. Consum. Res.* 15:234–42

Simonson, I., Huber, J., Payne, J. 1988. The relationship between prior brand knowledge

and information acquisition order. *J. Consum. Res.* 14:566–78

Singh, J. 1988. Consumer complaint intentions and behavior: definitional and taxonomical issues. *J. Mark.* 52:93–107

Singh, S. N., Churchill, G. A. Jr. 1986. Using the theory of signal detection to improve ad recognition testing. *J. Mark. Res.* 23:327–36

Singh, S. N., Churchill, G. A. Jr. 1987. Arousal and advertising effectiveness. *J. Advert.* 16:4–10

Singh, S. N., Rothschild, M. L., Churchill, G. A. Jr. 1988. Recognition versus recall as measures of television commercial forgetting. *J. Mark. Res.* 25:72–80

Sirgy, M. J. 1985. A social cognition model of consumer satisfaction/dissatisfaction. *Psychol. Mark.* 1:27–38

Slama, M. E., Tashchian, A. 1985. Selected socioeconomic and demographic characteristics associated with purchasing involvement. *J. Mark.* 49:72–83

Slama, M. E., Williams, T. G., Tashchian, A. 1988. Compliant, aggressive and detached types differ in generalized purchasing involvement. *Adv. Consum. Res.* 15;158–62

Smith, R. B., Houston, M. J. 1985. A psychometric assessment of measures of scripts in consumer memory. *J. Consum. Res.* 12:214–24

Smith, R. B., Houston, M. J. 1987. The effects of schematic memory on imaginal information processing: an empirical assessment. *Psychol. Mark.* 2:13–29

Solomon, M. R. 1988. Mapping product constellations: a social categorization approach to consumption symbolism. *Psychol. Mark.* 5:233–58

Spiggle, S. B. 1986. Measuring social values: a content analysis of Sunday comics and underground comix. *J. Consum. Res.* 13:100–13

Spiggle, S. B., Sewall, M. A. 1987. A choice sets model of retail selection. *J. Mark.* 51:97–111

Sproles, G. B. 1986. The concept of quality and the efficiency of markets: issues and comments. *J. Consum. Res.* 13:146–48

Sproles, G. B., Kendall, E. L. 1986. A methodology for profiling consumers' decision-making styles. *J. Consum. Affairs* 20:267–79

Srivastava, R. K., Alpert, M. I., Shocker, A. D. 1984. A customer-oriented approach for determining market structures. *J. Mark.* 48:32–45

Srull, T. 1984. The effects of subjective affective states on memory and judgment. *Adv. Consum. Res.* 11:530–33

Srull, T. K. 1987. Memory, mood, and consumer judgment. *Adv. Consum. Res.* 14:404–7

Stayman, D. S., Aaker, D. A. 1988. Are all

the effects of ad-induced feelings mediated by A_ad? *J. Consum. Res.* 15:368–73

Stuart, E. W., Shimp, T. A., Engle, R. W. 1987. Classical conditioning of consumer attitudes: four experiments in an advertising context. *J. Consum. Res.* 14:334–49

Sujan, M. 1985. Consumer knowledge: effects on evaluation strategies mediating consumer judgments. *J. Consum. Res.* 12:31–46

Sujan, M., Bettman, J. R., Sujan, H. 1986. Effects of consumer expectations on information processing in selling encounters. *J. Mark. Res.* 23:346–53

Sujan, M., Dekleva, C. 1987. Product categorization and inference making: some implications for comparative advertising. *J. Consum. Res.* 14:372–78

Sujan, M., Tybout, A. M. 1988. Applications and extension of categorization research in consumer behavior. *Adv. Consum. Res.* 15:50–55

Swasy, J. L., Munch, J. M. 1985. Examining the target of receiver elaborations: rhetorical question effects on source processing and persuasion. *J. Consum. Res.* 11:877–86

Szymanski, D. M., Busch, P. S. 1987. Identifying the generics-prone consumer: a meta-analysis. *J. Mark. Res.* 24:425–31

Tan, C. T., Farley, J. U. 1987. The impact of cultural patterns on cognition and intention in Singapore. *J. Consum. Res.* 13:540–44

Tashchian, A., White, J. D., Pak, S. 1988. Signal detection analysis and advertising recognition: an introduction to measurement and interpretation issues. *J. Mark. Res.* 25:397–405

Tellis, G. J., Wernerfelt, B. 1987. Competitive price and quality under asymmetric information. *Mark. Sci.* 6:240–54

Thaler, R. 1985. Mental accounting and consumer choice. *Mark. Sci.* 4:199–214

Thorson, E., Snyder, R. 1984. Viewer recall of television commercials: prediction from the propositional structure of commercial scripts. *J. Mark. Res.* 21:127–37

Tsal, Y. 1985. On the relationship between cognitive and affective processes: a critique of Zajonc and Markus. *J. Consum. Res.* 12:358–62

Tse, D. K., Wilton, P. C. 1988. Models of consumer satisfaction information: an extension. *J. Mark. Res.* 25:204–12

Umiker-Sebeok, J., ed. 1987. *Marketing Signs: New Directions in the Study of Signs for Sale.* Berlin: Mouton de Gruyter

Urbany, J. E. 1986. An experimental examination of the economics of information. *J. Consum. Res.* 13:257–71

Urbany, J. E., Bearden, W. O., Weilbaker, D. C. 1988. The effect of plausible and exaggerated reference prices on consumer perceptions and price search. *J. Consum. Res.* 15:95–110

Ursic, A. C., Ursic, M. L., Ursic, V. L. 1986. A longitudinal study of the use of the elderly in magazine advertising. *J. Consum. Res.* 13:131–33

Ursic, M. L. 1985. A model of the consumer decision to seek legal redress. *J. Consum. Affairs* 19:20–36

Venkatesh, A., Vitalari, N. 1987. A post-adoption analysis of computing in the home. *J. Econ. Psychol.* 8:161–80

Wallendorf, M., Arnould, E. J. 1988. "My favorite things": a cross-cultural inquiry into object attachment, possessiveness, and social linkage. *J. Consum. Res.* 14:531–47

Wallendorf, M., Belk, R. W. 1989. Assessing trustworthiness in naturalistic consumer research. In *Interpretive Consumer Research,* ed. E. C. Hirschman. Provo, UT: Assoc. Consum. Res.

Warshaw, P. R., Droge, C. 1986. Economic utility versus the attitudinal perspective of consumer choice. *J. Econ. Psychol.* 7:37–60

Westbrook, R. A. 1987. Product/consumption-based affective responses and post-purchase processes. *J. Mark. Res.* 24:258–70

Wiener, J. L. 1985. Are warranties accurate signals of product reliability? *J. Consum. Res.* 12:245–50

Wiener, J. L., Gentry, J. W., Miller, R. K. 1986. The framing of the insurance purchase decision. *Adv. Consum. Res.* 13:251–56

Wiener, J. L., Mowen, J. C. 1986. Source credibility: on the independent effects of trust and expertise. *Adv. Consum. Res.* 13:251–56

Winer, R. S. 1986. A reference price model of brand choice for frequently purchased products. *J. Consum. Res.* 13:250–56

Wright, P. 1986. Schemer schema: consumers' intuitive theories about marketers' influence tactics. *Adv. Consum. Res.* 13:1–3

Wyckham, R. G. 1987. Self-regulation of sex-role stereotyping in advertising: the Canadian experience. *J. Public Policy Mark.* 6:76–92

Young, C. W., Robinson, M. 1987. Guideline: tracking the commercial viewer's wandering attention. *J. Advert. Res.* 27:15–22

Zaichkowsky, J. L. 1985. Measuring the involvement construct. *J. Consum. Res.* 12:341–52

Zajonc, R. B., Markus, H. 1982. Affective and cognitive factors in preferences. *J. Consum. Res.* 9:123–31

Zeithaml, V. A. 1985. The new demographics and marketing fragmentation. *J. Mark.* 49:64–75

Annu. Rev. Psychol. 1990. 41:289–319

PERSONNEL SELECTION

Neal Schmitt

Department of Psychology, Michigan State University, East Lansing, Michigan 48824-1117

Ivan Robertson

Manchester School of Management, University of Manchester, Institute of Science & Technology, P.O. Box 88, Manchester M60 1QD England

---

CONTENTS

0066-4308/90/0201-0289$02.00

INTRODUCTION

With few diversions, the outline of past reviews on personnel selection (Guion & Gibson 1988; Hakel 1986; Zedeck & Cascio 1984) has followed what is traditionally defined as the criterion-related validation model: (*a*) job analysis; (*b*) criterion development and measurement; (*c*) predictor development and measurement; (*d*) evaluation of the relationship between predictor and criterion, or conceptualizations of validity; and (*e*) consideration of the practical utility and social, legal, or organization implications of implementing the selection strategy. Our review follows the same outline.

We attempt to be comprehensive in our review of published research and selective in our review and citation of unpublished manuscripts, dissertations, and journals directed to personnel administrators. We make a special effort to identify contributions by authors outside the United States, particularly those publishing in English. Our objective is to cover the research publications appearing in 1987 and 1988, though we do cite some papers that did not appear in journal form till 1989. One new comprehensive text in personnel selection has appeared (Gatewood & Feild 1987). In Europe, a text on personnel selection (Cook 1988) has been published, and Herriot et al (1989) have compiled a major European handbook on selection and assessment, with contributions from authors in the United Kingdom, The Netherlands, West Germany, and elsewhere in Europe. Selection is usually associated with a decision to hire; but in this paper, we are also concerned with other decisions, such as promotion, classification, or termination. Research on other criteria such as withdrawal behavior (McEvoy & Cascio 1987) and citizenship behavior (Puffer 1987) are also relevant to this chapter, but space considerations preclude a discussion of these topics.

JOB ANALYSIS

Gael's (1988) edited volume on job analysis includes chapters that deal with various practical problems associated with job analyses in organizations [e.g. how to choose a job analysis method(s) that is ideally suited to a particular organizational need].

Research on job analysis has focused on the nature and quality of job analysis ratings. Harvey et al (1988) showed that a simplified version of the Position Analysis Questionnaire (PAQ) yields job dimensions very similar to those of the full-length original version of that instrument. Harvey & Lozada-Larsen (1988) used averaged incumbent PAQ ratings as a standard to show that subjects who did PAQ ratings with a short job description and the description plus job title were not particularly accurate. These "non-experts" were least capable of predicting differences between jobs on individual dimensions. Contrary to at least one earlier study (Smith & Hakel 1979), there was no evidence that job stereotypes invoked by using a job title had any influence on PAQ ratings. In a related study, DeNisi et al (1987) reaffirmed the findings that Does Not Apply (DNA) items in the PAQ inflate interrater reliability and that jobs for which there are large numbers of DNA items may not be appropriate for PAQ analyses. They also found that neither naive nor expert job analysts produced PAQ responses that matched PAQ target profiles well. This suggests either that DeNisi et al's (1987) experts were inaccurate, that the PAQ profiles were inappropriate, or that both lacked objectivity. In these studies, the lack of any standard or criterion against which to judge the accuracy of a particular technique continues to be a problem.

Conley & Sackett (1987) found no differences between high- and low-performing job incumbents in generation of tasks or knowledge, skills, and abilities (KSAs) or in ratings of KSAs and tasks on six different rating scales. Schmitt & Cohen (1989) examined job level, occupation, tenure, sex, and race differences in task ratings of supervisory and administrative tasks. The expected differences in occupation and level were observed, but relatively few sex, race, or tenure (virtually all raters had worked one year or more) differences. These two studies in combination suggest that the often extreme care taken in selecting job experts to provide ratings may not be necessary. Mullins & Kimbrough (1988), however, reported that different groups of patrolperson job incumbents produced significantly different ratings and rankings of job analysis dimensions.

Butler & Harvey (1988) found near-zero convergence between rating profiles of jobs made on overall PAQ dimensions and profiles derived from the ratings of individual PAQ items. This suggests that it may not be possible to reduce the number of tasks or abilities rated by job analysts.

In a policy capturing study, Sanchez & Levine (1989) found task importance ratings were most closely related to task criticality and difficulty of learning a task across incumbents in four different jobs.

The fact that taxonomies of job activities and taxonomies of human abilities and attributes both exist but that there is no taxonomy that satisfactorily links the two has been mentioned frequently during this review period (e.g. Burke & Pearlman 1988; Carter & Biersner 1987; Levine et al 1988) as well as in past reviews of the personnel selection literature (Zedeck & Cascio 1984). As in the original PAQ research (McCormick et al 1972), Carter & Biersner (1987) showed that PAQ-based predictions regarding necessary human attributes were correlated with mean mental abilities as measured by the Armed Forces Vocational Aptitude Battery for 25 Navy jobs. They also extended the earlier PAQ research in showing that physical strength requirements of 26 Navy jobs were related to PAQ-based predictions of job requirements. Continued work on job attribute profiles would help researchers studying individual differences in work performance to communicate more efficiently and to generalize across events more appropriately and frequently. The issues involved in an integration of attribute and job characteristic taxonomies are discussed in detail in Burke & Pearlman (1988).

Job analysis research has tended to become more process oriented as researchers have begun to seek to understand the job analysis information they collect, but most studies have focused on the questionnaire method of data collection, and within that subset of studies, on the PAQ. Job analyses are central to three components of the personnel selection process: determination of relevant job performance criteria, decisions regarding the use and development of measures of required KSAs, and decisions about the way to recruit qualified applicants. Attention to the relative effectiveness of various aspects or methods of job analyses in serving these goals is still relatively rare.

CRITERIA

Personnel selection research and development often require a relevant and psychometrically adequate index of job performance. Most research on criteria has focused on job performance ratings. As was true for the last decade, attempts to understand or improve ratings have focused on either the raters' cognitive processes (see DeNisi & Williams 1988, for a recent review) or the format of the rating scale used by the rater.

Rater Cognitive Processes

Several researchers examined the impact of cognitive categorization on ratings, though the way cognitive categories are measured or manipulated seems to be unique to the particular study. Hogan (1987) found that a disconfirmation of initial expectations regarding ratees' capabilities serves to lower subsequent performance ratings, but she found no support for the hypothesis that disconfirmation enhances attribution to external factors. The results did, however, support the hypothesis that the higher the ratings supervisors give, the more they will attribute performance to internal causes. Mount & Thompson (1987) also defined cognitive categorization as the degree to which the ratee's behavior met the rater's expectations. They found that congruence of expectations produced more accurate (Cronbach 1955) subordinate ratings but that those ratings were more lenient and subject to halo. Similarly, Schoorman (1988) found supervisors' performance ratings were biased downward or upward depending on whether they agreed or disagreed with the initial hiring or promotion of a subordinate, suggesting that individuals escalate their commitment to hiring or promotion decisions.

Cardy et al (1987) found that experience in the conduct of performance appraisals was related to performance rating accuracy. They also found that similarity between raters' a priori notions of the important performance dimensions and the incorporation of those dimensions in the rating instrument were related to performance rating accuracy (i.e. differential accuracy; Cronbach 1955). Experimental familiarization with the rating categories had no effect on rating accuracy (Cardy et al 1987). Krzystofiak et al (1988) also found evidence that raters used "implicit personality factors" in making overall performance judgments, even when the information available to the rater was restricted to behavioral incidents. Jolly et al (1988) used a novel interviewing strategy to show that nurse-managers organized ratee information along several basic value dimensions.

Kozlowski & Kirsch (1987) presented relatively strong evidence that raters' preconceived notions of how performance dimensions covaried influenced their performance ratings for low-job-knowledge raters. For high-job-knowledge raters, the covariation between rated performance dimensions more closely matched the actual covariation. Their study of the systematic distortion hypothesis (Schweder 1982) was an especially complex individual-level analysis. Such analyses may be necessary to evaluate appropriately many of the hypotheses regarding cognitive-processing influences on ratings.

Kozlowski & Kirsch (1987) also reported that perceived covariation between performance dimensions was less than actual covariation. Smither & Reilly (1987) found that raters' ability to discriminate among ratees was better in the presence of high than in the presence of low intercorrelations between performance dimensions. Efforts to improve rater accuracy while simultaneously diminishing what is thought to be rater error have been unsuccessful (Hedge & Kavanagh 1988; Mount & Thompson 1987). These various studies suggest that one or more of these constructs (accuracy, halo, leniency) may be inappropriately conceptualized or measured.

In evaluating the relative impact of rater and ratee characteristics, objective performance, and performance standards on four rater judgments, Huber et al (1987) found that (a) objective performance accounted for the greatest variance; (b) ratee characteristics (job tenure and prior performance) affected ratings directly; and (c) the interaction of rater characteristics and objective performance was a significant predictor of rating variance.

In three studies (Athey & McIntyre 1987; Hedge & Kavanagh 1988; Heneman 1988), researchers tried to train raters in ways that were consistent with cognitive hypotheses so as to help raters to categorize appropriately. Hedge & Kavanagh (1988) found observational-skills training and training on decision-making skills effectively increased accuracy but that rater-error training was more effective in reducing halo and leniency. Heneman (1988) found ratings on trait-oriented scales better than on behaviorally oriented scales; he found no difference in training methods designed to improve rater accuracy. Athey & McIntyre (1987) found positive results (more accuracy, less halo, retention of training information) for a frame-of-reference training that included a description of the work to be evaluated, practice and feedback with ratings, and a behavioral rationale for the expert ratings provided.

Srinivas & Motowidlo (1987) found differences in the dispersion of performance ratings between raters in high- and low-workload conditions, confirming the hypothesis that stress in the form of high workload would affect cognitive processes in performance evaluation. Higher intercorrelations among the ratings of low-workload raters was interpreted as meaning that stressed raters do not discriminate between different dimensions as well as unstressed raters.

Rating Scale Format

In the only study comparing rating scale formats using an index of the scales' sensitivity to actual behavior variance versus context-dependent variance, Doverspike et al (1987) reported that graphic rating scales were superior to both behaviorally anchored rating scales (BARS) and behavioral expectation scales. Several papers (Champion et al 1988; Kinicki & Bannister 1988; Murphy & Constans 1987) presented evidence critical of aspects of the development of BARS, ranging from the fact that actual observation of a particular behavioral anchor would bias ratings inappropriately when the behavior witnessed by the rater was atypical of the ratee's overall performance (Murphy & Constans 1987), to the finding that a shortcut method of developing BARS was comparable to traditionally developed BARS in terms of leniency, halo, discriminant validity, and reliability.

Prien & Hughes (1987) reported that efforts to correct mixed standard scale items and behavior triads resulted in decreased rater inconsistencies in rating triads, though it should be noted that fewer inconsistencies do not necessarily translate to greater interrater or rate-rerate reliability. Deselles & Dobbins (1987) found a change in scoring of mixed standard scales proposed by Saal (1979) was superior to the original Blanz & Ghiselli scheme (1972) in discriminating between ratee performance levels within dimensions. Finally, Bannister et al (1987) presented a leniency scale that they used to control for leniency and halo rating errors.

Heneman et al (1987) provided a substantive review of the rater accuracy literature. They pointed out the continued problem of the observed positive correlation between halo error and accuracy in this body of research and questioned the generalizability of the research, which has most frequently been conducted in the laboratory using videotaped performance. Even given the limitations of this research, Heneman et al (1987) argued that individual differences (i.e. memory, intelligence, self-confidence, and familiarity with the job performance being rated), positive ratee performance, increased opportunity to observe, and specific behavioral-rating-scale formats are associated with increases in rater accuracy.

A central problem in research on cognitive processes in rating, training raters, and investigating scale format effects is the usual absence of a standard against which to evaluate the accuracy of ratings. Usually some aggregated index of expert opinion is used as the actual performance level of target ratees, but there is also the issue of which of the many available indexes of accuracy to use. Sulsky & Balzer (1988) provided an in-depth empirical and theoretical analysis of various measures of accuracy. Anyone contemplating the use of development of "true scores" in research on rating scale formats or rater training should consult this paper first. When using ratings as a criterion against which to evaluate selection procedures, it is not clear that the relatively small effects produced by cognitive processing errors produce any practically significant problems.

Self and Peer Appraisal

In a study of peer appraisals, McEvoy & Buller (1987) reported greater acceptance of peer appraisals than has been true in past studies, especially among relatively short-tenure employees who were satisfied with prior peer ratings and did not believe peer ratings involved a friendship bias. Their subjects were hourly employed personnel in a non-union food-processing plant, whereas most other studies have been done with military samples.

Fox & Dinur (1988) found greater leniency error in self ratings than in peer and superior ratings. Correlations with superior and peer ratings were significant but relatively low, even when subjects were told that there would be an independent assessment of their skills. Telling subjects that their self ratings would be compared with those from other sources had little effect on the relatively low predictive validity of these ratings, contrary to the suggestions by Mabe & West (1982) that such information might improve self-ratings. Campbell & Lee (1988) provide various theoretical reasons (informational, cognitive, and affective) for a discrepancy between self and superior ratings in arguing that future-oriented self ratings be used for developmental purposes only. Fahr et al (1988) reported much better results for self ratings (i.e. better convergence with superior ratings and objectively verifiable data), but supervisors in their study of university faculty had access to the faculty members' self ratings when they made their own. George & Smith (1988) found evidence of inflation of self assessments by seasonal workers in New Zealand. Correlations of self ratings with later performance ratings and tenure were small and negative.

Construct Issues

Several papers have addressed the construct validity of performance criteria. Yammarino et al (1987) used the Dansereau et al (1984) data-analytic approach to specify and assess individual versus work-group effects (leniency and contrast) in self and supervisor ratings. Dickinson (1987) proposed using a combination of analysis-of-variance treatments of multitrait-multimethod matrixes and Cronbach's (1955) accuracy indexes to isolate the influence of rater, ratee, and context factors on the quality of performance ratings. This expansion of the usual multitrait-multimethod design could be useful in designing and analyzing more meaningful and systematic research on performance ratings. Vance et al (1988) provided an example of the use of confirmatory factor analysis as a means of illuminating similarities and differences between multiple measures of job performance.

A meta-analysis (Harris & Schaubroeck 1988) of the relationship between peer and supervisory ratings, self-peer ratings, and self-supervisor ratings indicated that while peer and supervisor ratings were moderately correlated (.62), self ratings were not highly correlated with either peer (.36) or supervisor ratings (.35). Various moderator analyses designed to explain these differences were not particularly helpful in providing support for any explanation.

Sackett et al (1988) extended the traditional distinction between typical and maximum measures of individual differences to the measurement of the job performance of grocery checkout clerks. They reported very low (.36 or less) correlations between typical and maximum performance. The importance of this distinction is obvious; many of our criteria differ on this dimension. Perhaps, more importantly, many of our predictors are likely to be maximum performance measures while our criteria are typical performance indexes. Minimum performance should be influenced primarily by ability differences, whereas typical performances would more likely be the outcome of both ability and motivation differences.

Meyer (1987) argued for the increased use of salary progress or promotional criteria as opposed to ratings of performance. Correlations of predictor scores with the promotional progress measures in two different studies were .40 or higher, while correlations with supervisor ratings were .10. Henry & Hulin (1987) showed that the intercorrelations of performance data for major league baseball players showed what they describe as a superdiagonal pattern in which the highest correlations are observed between data from adjacent time periods and the correlations decrease regularly as a function of the temporal gap between data points. Henry & Hulin argued that this finding was evidence that players' tasks or players' ability or both change even after tasks are overlearned. This lack of stability in performance data, along with some research (e.g. Alvares & Hulin 1972) showing that predictive validities decrease with increases in time between the collection of predictor and criterion data, implies that there are systematic changes in the rank order of individuals in terms of ability and performance; dynamic and changing models of human performance are appropriate. These results have implications for the long-term utility of selection procedures. Furthermore, they are inconsistent with data on the validity for some selection procedures (e.g. Jensen 1980; Mitchel 1975). As we describe in the next section, Schmidt et al (1988a) report data and provide interpretations that differ greatly. More research on the meaning and nature of work-performance measures such as the work referenced in this section is long overdue.

PREDICTORS

While psychologists continue to study the validity and psychometric adequacy of various selection procedures, the major trend in research is oriented toward greater understanding of the constructs being measured. This is particularly evident in the research on interviews, biodata, personality, and assessment centers reviewed in this section.

Assessment Centers

Research on the dimensionality and combination of center ratings—their meaning (Klimoski & Brickner 1987) and validity (Feltham 1988a,b)—continues. Bycio et al's (1987) and Robertson et al's (1987) analyses reconfirmed that the dimensionality of assessment center ratings involves exercise more than ability factors. Russell (1987) provided limited evidence of the viability of a role-congruence explanation of assessment center dimensionality. His article illustrates the difficulty of examining this explanation. Bycio et al (1987) provide two other suggestions about how to increase the ability-related variance in assessment centers: elicit a larger number of ability-related behaviors in the center exercises, and reduce the cognitive demands on the assessors—by decreasing either the observer-to-assessee ratio or the number of rated dimensions.

Walsh et al (1987) reported that women did better than men overall in an assessment center, particularly when women were evaluated by an all-male assessor team. O'Hara & Love (1987) described the innovative use of community members in the development and use of a mini-assessment-center for the evaluation of candidates for a police chief's job in a small community.

Sackett (1987) provided a thoughtful analysis of the use of content validity arguments as defense for the use of assessment centers, and Klimoski & Brickner (1987) explored the credibility of various explanations of why assessment center ratings are valid in a predictive sense. Both papers discuss the practical and research implications of their analyses and should stimulate additional empirical work.

Finally, Gaugler et al's (1987) meta-analysis of 50 assessment center studies included 107 validity coefficients. The corrected average validity was .37, but there remained a reasonably large variability in the validities after correction. Evaluation of a large set of potential moderators indicated some evidence that validities varied systematically as a function of characteristics of the assessees, the assessors, the center itself, and the quality of the validation effort. Equally surprising was the finding that some center practices generally thought to be desirable (e.g. longer assessor training and days of observation) did not seem to affect validity. With a large number of potential moderators and a relatively small number of studies, many of the findings regarding the presence or absence of moderator effects may be spurious.

In summary, although assessment centers provide practically significant predictions of various performance criteria (Gaugler et al 1987), we know little about the constructs responsible for this predictive validity.

Biodata

Five studies on the development and use of biographical data were reported. Aamody & Pierce (1987) showed that traditional item-criterion keying of weighted application blanks was superior to a rare-response method proposed by Telenson et al (1983). Smith & George (1987) concluded that a linear discriminant function was superior to the horizontal percentage method in terms of descriptive power but not in terms of validity. Smith et al (1988) described the validation of a weighted application blank and compared written and computerized methods of using the data to make decisions. Lautenschlager & Schaffer (1987) showed that the life experience components developed from a large biographical inventory (Owens & Schoenfeldt 1979) were stable. Finally, Stone & Stone (1987) found that individuals who did not respond to a question about previous criminal convictions were rated lower on job qualifications and potential success by a group of MBA and executive development students than were individuals who indicated no previous convictions. Further research was recommended on other types of omitted information (medical, sex, drug abuse, etc), the type of job for which application is made, and the job relevance of the missing information.

Drakeley et al (1988) found that validities of scored biodata for prediction of training success were equal to those of four cognitive ability tests and an overall assessment center rating; such validities added incrementally to regression equations that included the test scores and assessment center ratings. Biodata also predicted voluntary turnover at a relatively low level ($r = .24$) whereas no other predictor did.

Mumford & Owens (1987) provided a comprehensive review of the research on biographical data. They called for additional studies in which empirical keying, subgrouping studies, and factorial studies are compared with rational development of biodata measures. Mumford & Owens encourage researchers to pay more attention to content and construct validity in the development of background data measures. Item development should be preceded by a careful definition of the domain of experience and antecedent behavior relevant to the performance of interest.

Interviews

Recent studies continue to generate positive evidence regarding the validity of carefully constructed structured interviews, particularly situational interviews (Arvey et al 1987; Campion et al 1988; Weekley & Gier 1987). Observed validities in all three studies ranged from .34 to .51. Moreover, Maurer & Fay (1988) reported significantly greater interviewer agreement for situational than conventional structured interviews. A whole day of training had no effect on interviewer agreement. Campion et al (1988) reported that their exceptionally well-developed structured situational interview was highly correlated with employment tests of cognitive aptitudes, suggesting that their interview may have included a strong cognitive component. Dreher et al (1988) note that the typical interview validity study, which employs multiple interviewers who very often differ in their mean ratings (leniency or severity), may underestimate the validity of the selection interview. The obvious recommendation is to standardize each interviewer's ratings of job applicants, but the operationalization of this recommendation may be difficult in situations where each interviewer evaluates a small number of applicants.

In a meta-analytic investigation of the validity of employment interviews Wiesner & Cronshaw (1988) found good validity coefficients for structured interviews (uncorrected mean $r = .35$ for structured, individual interviews; mean $r = .63$ after correction for direct restriction of range and criterion unreliability). Unlike previous research, however, their study also found fairly good mean validity coefficients for interviews in general (corrected mean $r = .47$). Even for unstructured, individual interviews the corrected mean validity coefficient was .20; furthermore, all of the variance in observed validity coefficients for unstructured interviews was accounted for after adjusting for statistical artifacts.

Employment interview research also continues on several process issues. Two studies indicate that interviewers do question applicants differently when their initial impressions of the applicant differ. Binning et al (1988) produced strong evidence of a confirmatory bias and sex differences in the use of questions, while Macan & Dipboye (1988) found that persons who were initially evaluated positively were asked more questions that were likely to generate more positive information than were persons whose initial evaluations were negative. Questions put to negatively evaluated candidates were more likely neutral. In both of these studies, the researchers had interviewers self-generate questions. Earlier research, which had failed to find a confirmatory bias, had used a structured checklist of questions (Sackett 1982; MacDonald & Hakel 1985).

Gordon et al (1988) showed that student interviewers who were led to believe that they would be held accountable for their evaluations of job applicants gave more positive hiring recommendations to young applicants than to older applicants. With low accountability, such age effects were absent. The authors suggested that the increased accountability generated greater reliance on easily accessible stereotypes and hence increased the potential for age bias.

In three studies (Graves & Powell 1988; Raza & Carpenter 1987; Wareing & Stockdale 1987), researchers have tried to investigate process issues in actual employment interviews. Applicant demographic characteristics played little or no role in the interviewer decisions in these studies, while interviewers' subjective appraisals of skill and interpersonal attraction accounted for a great deal of interviewer judgment variance. Since subjective qualifications, interpersonal likability or attraction, and interviewer judgments were all collected in the same self-report instrument, their high intercorrelation is not surprising. It will be more difficult to determine why interviewers are attracted to certain applicants. In a study of promotion interview boards in the UK Metropolitan Police, Wareing & Stockdale (1987) reported that post-interview ratings were predicted accurately from pre-interview ratings in 74.7% of the cases, but that post-interview ratings were more extreme than pre-interview ratings. Various possible social and cognitive explanations were offered.

An edited volume on the interview (Eder & Ferris 1989) contains a heuristic model of the interview process that includes the roles various parties (interviewer, applicant, organization, and society) play in determining the conduct and outcomes of interviews. The various theoretical, methodological, and practical perspectives represented in this volume ought to stimulate more interview research, especially on process issues.

Personality

Hough (1988) reported encouraging evidence for the criterion-related validity and incremental validity (over an aptitude test battery) of personality measures for large samples of military recruits when the personality measures were developed and evaluated from a construct-oriented view (that is, the predictor and criterion were logically related). Various response scales were successful in detecting and correcting for examinee distortion. Pulakos et al (1988) also reported higher validities when predictor and criterion were similar in a construct sense. Bernardin (1987) reported the development of a valid ($r = .31$) forced-choice predictor of voluntary turnover among customer service representatives employed by a large newspaper. Comparisons of applicant and incumbent scores suggested the forced-choice scale was resistant to faking, though several other personality measures used in the study were susceptible to faking. Love & O'Hara (1987) reported positive results for the validity of a behavioral assessment of work maturity in the prediction of the performance of individuals in a youth training project. Ash et al (1988) reported on the validity and fairness of tests designed to select urban bus drivers. They argued that their tests measured emotional and temperamental factors associated with successful driving rather than skill or aptitude factors. Finally, Ferris et al (1986) reported a validity of .46 between the 16 PF instrument and the training performance of flight attendants.

Two studies reported data on the factorial nature of existing personality scales. Harris & Sackett (1987) found evidence for four factors in the Personnel Selection Inventory, which purports to identify potentially dishonest job applicants. The factors included ideas or temptations related to theft, actual or expected dishonest activities, ideas about what dishonest activities other people engage in, and impulsivity or unreliability. Eberhardt et al (1988) reported low internal consistency for the subscales of the multiple choice form of the Miner Sentence Completion Blank and no evidence for the a priori factor structure of this test.

In a laboratory study, Paunonen et al (1987) found that judgments about the job suitability of audiotaped interviewees were influenced by judges' perceptions of the interviewees' competence and personality. Candidates were evaluated as suitable for the target job when the perceived job personality fit was high. Personality effects were not observed when competence discrepancies between candidates were large. In a field study using candidates for a bachelor's degree program in a British university, Fletcher (1987) found zero or small correlations between candidate personality (extraversion, neuroticism, self-monitoring, and state anxiety) and interviewer ratings. Candidate neuroticism scores were statistically significantly related to interviewer ratings of verbal expression and emotional stability.

On a discouraging note, Johnson et al (1988) cited the continued use of ipsative scales in personality measures for prediction purposes. Using data from various tests, they reconfirmed the inappropriateness of ipsative measures.

Other Selection Procedures

Two reviews of the literature (Ash et al 1989; McDaniel et al 1988) on training and work experience evaluations in personnel selection have appeared. McDaniel et al (1988) reported very low overall validity (observed $r = .09$) for training and experience inventories but indicated that validities for behavioral consistency approaches were significantly higher (observed $r = .25$). Ash et al (1989) indicate that methods such as the behavioral consistency method show promise as predictive selection procedures. Such methods link the training and experience requirements to job analyses data supporting the need for certain knowledge, skill, and ability requirements and/or the requirement to perform certain tasks. More criterion-related research is needed.

Gordon and his colleagues (Gordon et al 1987; Gordon & Leighty 1988) report two additional studies using a test of visuospatial skills (mental rotation and locating points in space) and verbosequential skills (verbal fluency and memory of serial order). The hypothesis is that the two types of skills are associated respectively with right- and left-brain hemispheric functioning. Visuospatial skills were related to successful completion of flight training among student naval aviators after selection by the Navy's standard screening procedure. In a study of managerial performance, Gordon et al (1987) found verbosequential skills related to job performance when the managerial jobs involved responsibility for a large number of activities and people; visuospatial skills were related to job performance in jobs that involved a great deal of coordination or complexity.

A review and critique of the use of computerized psychological testing are provided by Burke & Normand (1987), and a special issue of *Applied Psychology: An International Review* was devoted to this topic (Eyde 1987). The review by Burke & Normand highlights the need for additional research on the validity of computerized tests and the degree of equivalence between computerized tests and test norms and their written counterparts. In a study of the Minnesota Clerical Test, Silver & Bennett (1987) reported no difference in validity between the traditional paper form of this test and a video-display-terminal version, but mean performance was much higher on the paper-and-pencil form than the computer form. Burke et al (1987) report validities on computer-administered ability tests in the .30s for overall performance on one or more clerical job families. They also found that examinee attitudes toward the computerized testing were generally favorable and predicted by past computer-related experience and numerical ability. Bartram (1987) described the development and validation of an automated system for pilot selection. The system contains a library of tests for psychomotor ability and of information management ability. Validation studies with UK Army Air Corps pilot trainees showed that the system predicted success in training (multiple R = .57). The results of construct validity studies suggested that the new tests were tapping facets of pilot aptitude not measured by traditional psychometric instruments. Clearly, a variety of important issues in computerized testing have received little or no attention (see also Fleishman 1988).

Two areas of personnel selection that have not previously received much attention have been addressed in this review period. Ryan & Sackett (1987) described the results of a survey of 163 persons who do individual assessment. McDaniel (1988) reported that the greater the self-reported use of drugs and the earlier the age at which a drug was used, the greater the probability that a military recruit would subsequently be given an unsuitable discharge.

These selection procedures as well as job-related medical screening (Fleishman 1988) deserve greater attention.

Use of Combinations of Predictors or Test Batteries

In one study focusing on job performance (Colarelli et al 1987), and in another study focusing on training (Mumford et al 1987), researchers have tried to predict performance using a combination of selection procedures and situational measures. Both sets of researchers found important situational and ability determinants of performance. In a study limited by a small sample and lack of cross-validation, Hakstian et al (1987) found items in the cognitive, personality, and administrative-skill domains that predicted ratings of job performance of first-level supervisors in a telephone company.

Schmidt et al (1988a) used data from individuals in four different jobs to show that the validity of a general ability test battery was relatively constant up to at least five years of job experience. Mean differences in job knowledge, performance on work sample tests, and supervisory performance ratings between high- and low-ability groups were virtually constant for workers over this period. Schmidt et al (1988a) recognized and provided some potential explanations for the inconsistency between their results and those both of Henry & Hulin (1987) and of Humphreys and his colleagues (e.g. Humphreys 1968). We agree with Schmidt et al's (1988a) call for additional research, particularly longitudinal rather than cross-sectional research, on job performance and predictor-criterion relationships across time.

Psychometric Issues in Predictor Development

Feldt et al (1987) provided a synthesis of developments in testing the significance of coefficient alpha and differences between alphas calculated from responses of independent samples or under conditions when the same sample is used. They also provide numerical examples of each test.

Additional papers have appeared on the use of item response theory (IRT) in the solution of practical testing problems such as computer adaptive testing (Wainer & Kiely 1987), item bias (McLaughlin & Drasgow 1987), and the appropriateness of examinee's responses (Drasgow & Guertler 1987; Drasgow et al 1987). Thissen & Steinberg (1988) provided examples of the application and interpretation of IRT analyses of personality, aptitude, and cognitive ability tests.

SOCIAL PROCESSES IN PERSONNEL SELECTION: RECRUITMENT AND ATTRACTION

Herriot (1989) argued that applied psychologists have treated social processes as intrusions into the selection process and that social processes are seen as elements that interfere with objectivity, reliability, and validity. He proposed that, rather than being construed as sources of bias in need of standardization and removal, social processes should be used as a basis for conceptualizing and gaining insight into selection procedures. The selection process should be seen as the first stage of a continuing relationship between the organization and the applicant. Herriot also argued that personnel selection researchers have overemphasized the importance of assessment by the organization and thus have failed to provide a coherent theoretical account of the recruitment and selection process as a whole. Increased interest in recruitment appears to represent some evidence of the validity of Herriot's view.

Taylor & Bergmann (1987) attempted to measure applicants' reactions to recruiting practices at five stages: campus interview, post-campus interview, site visit, job offer, and job acceptance. Recruiter demographics and recruitment activities (as reported by the recruiters) and applicants' reports of recruiter empathy were significantly related to applicants' perceptions of company attractiveness and probability of job offer acceptance at the initial recruitment stage, but job attributes rather than recruitment effects were the primary predictors of applicant reactions at the next stages of recruitment. However, Harris & Fink (1987), using pre-post measures of reactions to a campus interview reported that perceptions of job attributes as well as regard for job and company and the likelihood of joining the company were all correlated with applicants' perceptions of the recruiter. The Taylor & Bergmann (1987) study illustrates the difficulty of tracking job applicants over time as their sample size of 910 dwindled to 38 at the fifth and final data-collection point. Taylor & Bergmann make a plea for consideration of a broadened set of dependent variables in recruitment research, including overall company image and applicant adaptation to work in their new organization. This message is also conveyed by Rynes (1989) and Rynes & Boudreau (1986). This research should also now be moving beyond its traditional reliance on applicant perceptions as a source of both dependent and independent variables.

Some studies, going beyond eliciting applicants' reactions to the assessment process, examine the impact of personnel selection procedures on candidates' psychological reactions. In a study of a post-assessment training program, Noe & Schmitt (1986) found that trainees' reactions to the prior skill assessment helped to predict their subsequent satisfaction with training. Noe & Steffy (1987) examined the impact of assessment center evaluations on the subsequent career behavior and job attitudes of participants. The favorability of the evaluation from the assessment center was related to the participants' subsequent exploratory career behavior, information seeking, and experimentation with skills. Robertson & Smith (1989) presented a tentative view of the processes involved in the psychological impact of personnel selection methods on candidates and argued that more research attention should be paid to these issues.

Several conceptual papers or reviews relevant to recruitment research have appeared. Bergmann & Martin (1987) argue from a utility perspective that organizations should develop a coordinated organization-wide recruitment activity as a means of reducing costs. Indeed, Rynes & Boudreau (1986) found that centralization of the recruiting effort was one of the correlates of perceived recruiting strength among vice presidents of human resources in Fortune 1000 companies. Meglino & DeNisi (1987) reviewed the literature on realistic job previews (RJPs) and outlined the conditions under which they appear to reduce turnover. In an examination of the literature on sex effects in recruitment, Powell (1987) distinguished between sex effects (actual differences between men and women) and gender effects (differences in beliefs about men and women). He found no evidence of sex effects and mixed results with respect to gender effects. As most studies were laboratory studies with college students working in hypothetical recruitment situations making decisions about hypothetical applicants, he also indicated the need for more field studies and more studies of applicant as opposed to recruiter perceptions. Baker et al (1988) described the development of a Career Plans Checklist that would be computer-administered and used to assess the vocational guidance needs of military job applicants.

VALIDITY ISSUES

Researchers considering the evidence to collect in support of the use of selection procedures and how to analyze and interpret that evidence have produced important papers in several areas.

Moderator Variable Issues

Stone (1988) provided a comprehensive review of the literature (including conceptual definitions and a historical perspective) on moderator variables. He described various statistical methods used to detect moderator effects and provided a large and useful list of do's and don'ts for the detection and description of moderator variables. Stone's review (1988), as well as papers by Dunlap & Kemery (1987, 1988), Paunonen & Jackson (1988), and Cronbach (1987) should give researchers renewed confidence and guidance with respect to the use of moderated multiple regression in the analysis of moderator effects.

Range Restriction

Gross and his colleagues have examined the implications of the use of the traditional correction of observed validity for restriction of range due to selection. Gross & Fleishman (1987) showed that small departures from linearity produced inappropriate estimates of the unrestricted correlation using the range-restriction correction. Their recommendation is to use the un-corrected correlation as the estimate of true correlation when a nonlinear predictor-criterion relationship is suspected. Gross & McGanney (1987) pro-duced two procedures to estimate the unrestricted correlation between pre-dictor and criterion when some unobservable variable related to the criterion is responsible for selection on the criterion. While both procedures provided accurate estimates of validity in a Monte Carlo effect, Gross & McGanney (1987) gave several reasons why it was not practical to use these procedures at the present time and suggested additional research. Finally, Alexander (1988) refuted the existence of a range-enhancement effect (Schmitt & Schneider 1983). He pointed out that any increases or decreases in measured individual differences that occur as a function of job experience will have no effect on the observed validity in that group.

Validity Generalization

Meta-analysis continues to be applied to various questions in validation research as is evident in this review and others (Schmidt 1988; Hunter & Hirsh 1987). Research and critiques of the methods of meta-analysis and validity generalization (VG) procedure also have appeared frequently in this review period.

Schmidt et al (1988b) and James et al (1988) debated various issues regarding VG models and procedures. Some readers might draw conclusions that estimates of population correlations using the Fisher z transformation yield results trivially different from those using analyses of correlations, that use of percentage rules is not the best way to make decisions about the presence or absence of VG (see also Rasmussen & Loher 1988), and that one should be wary of the power to detect moderator effects in many meta-analytic efforts. Conclusions about other issues such as the logic of hypothesis testing in VG and the appropriateness of different confidence intervals de-serve additional attention. The latter issue was addressed by Millsap (1988), who presented two new methods of constructing credibility intervals around the mean true validity in VG analyses. His procedures estimate the proportion of true validities falling above some point in repeated VG studies. He recommends these two more conservative approaches when a small number (<50) of studies are available. Thomas (1988) critically evaluated the VG computation of true validity variance and concluded that hypotheses about VG and specificity of validity cannot be tested with estimates based on the $S\hat{\rho}$ $= S_r^2 - S_e^2$ formula.

Burke & Raju (1988) provided a very readable review of six different procedures used to estimate the mean and variance of true validity coefficients in validity generalization research. They also described covariance and re-gression-slope models of VG and reviewed various simulation studies designed to assess the accuracy of various VG parameter estimations. They concluded that there was general support for the accuracy of the models and procedures for estimation of mean and variance of validities when the true artifact distributions match the hypothetical distributions typically used in the absence of actual data on these distributions. When these distributions do not match, parameter estimation appears to be seriously affected. Hedges (1988) also described and illustrated a Bayesian model of VG that allows for the intuitively appealing conclusion that validities are both situation-specific and generalizable.

Other Analysis Issues in Validation Research

Papers by Hollenbeck & Whitener (1988) and Hamilton & Dickinson (1987) reexamined the utility of synthetic validity in validation. Silver & Dunlap (1987) and Strube (1988) both reported simulation studies of the aggregation of correlations either as correlations or as transformed Fisher z, and both recommend the latter, particularly when the researchers are aggregating correlations based on small sample sizes and a small number of correlations. Averaging Fisher z transformations may not yield results much different from averaging correlations, but the variance of z may be different, making the transformation more important in tests of significance (James et al 1988).

Raymond & Roberts (1987) compared regression results when various methods to solve missing-data problems were used. Deletion of cases with missing values produced the worst estimates of the actual beta weights and multiple correlation; either of two regression-based methods did significantly better than deletion of missing cases and slightly better than replacement of missing values with the mean. Finally, Maier (1988) cautions practitioners to be wary of collecting performance measures from groups with different standards for criterion performance.

Meaning of Validity

Several papers have appeared in which the notion of validity is examined (Binning & Barrett 1989; Fiske 1987; Guion 1987). An edited book on test validity (Wainer & Braun 1988) included several chapters (see especially chapters by Messick, Cronbach, and Angoff) devoted to conceptual issues regarding validity and validation. Chapters on validity as it applies in various specialized domains such as mental tests, computer-based tests, and the evaluation of handicapped and non-English speaking individuals were also included.

These authors continue to emphasize the value of considering multiple lines of evidence in deciding whether inferences about test scores are appropriate. Various considerations in determining what evidence ought to be collected are discussed by Binning & Barrett (1989), Cronbach (1988), and Messick

(1988a,b). Clearly, these authors are asserting the role that theory ought to play in the validation of psychological measures in general as well as in selection procedures. Finally, Mehrens (1987) discusses issues related to the validity of teacher licensure exams. Licensure exams ought to receive more attention from researchers interested in selection; they certainly play a significant societal role and often dictate the type of labor pool available to any given organization.

UTILITY

Studies continue to address the comparability of various estimates of the standard deviation (SD_y) of an employee's economic value to the organization. Greer & Cascio (1987) found the CREPID (Cascio & Ramos 1986) approach yielded significantly lower estimates of the SD_y of route salespersons in a softdrink bottling company than did global estimates (Schmidt et al 1979) or a cost-accounting estimate. The latter two estimates were nearly equal. One of the problems with the use of the CREPID method is the relatively large amount of data-collection time demanded of organizational members. Edwards et al (1988) found that archival information regarding job analysis dimensions and job performance could be used to obtain SD_y values comparable to those of the original CREPID approach, though both differed greatly from the global judgment-based estimates (Schmidt et al 1979).

Frustration with some aspects of utility estimation has led to calls for investigation of the cognitive process underlying utility judgments and the influence of context factors on utility estimation (Bobko et al 1987; Edwards et al 1988). Raju et al (1989) presented a promising new utility formulation that circumvents the need to compute SD_y. Utility is expressed in terms of the estimated mean value of an individual to an organization (e.g. the value of the total compensation package). Based on the assumption that true job performance is linearly related to true dollar value of an individual to the organization, this model represents a general case of which the CREPID method and the 40% estimate (Hunter & Schmidt 1982) are special cases. Whatever estimate is used, researchers and practitioners need also to be aware of the need to communicate in a credible manner with their nonpsychological colleagues in organizations (Rauschenberger & Schmidt 1987).

Some researchers have begun to attend to the variability in utility estimates and the degree of risk or uncertainty associated with the outcomes of psychological interventions in organizations. In the most thorough of these studies, Rich & Boudreau (1987) found that, compared to three other techniques, a Monte Carlo simulation of the risks associated with various possible circumstances and expected utilities provided a more realistic range of utility values and probabilities associated with these values. The Monte Carlo approach also allowed for the consideration of interactions and nonnormal distributions of the factors affecting reliability. Whether these very sophisticated approaches to decision-making ever become widely used, however, remains doubtful in our view. Cronshaw et al (1987) also examined the uncertainty associated with estimates of the utility of a selection program and showed that most of the variability in utility estimates was associated with estimates of how many people would be selected. Possible variability in the validity of the test, tenure of selectees, and cost of program implementation had relatively little effect on the range of utility. Alexander & Barrick (1987) presented and illustrated a method to compute the standard error and confidence intervals associated with the overall estimate of the utility of an intervention.

Hunter et al (1988) discussed various ways (e.g. contribution to after-tax profit, percentage reduction in unit labor costs, etc) of presenting utility information. Their advice—i.e. that these various definitions of utility as well as various corrections to overall utility (e.g. discounting, variable cost estimates, and changing tax rates) should be used only as the circumstances warrant—seems reasonable and important. Estimates of the utility of selection programs continue to be very large (Burke & Doran 1989). For readers interested in other conceptualizations of the worth of human resources, Steffy & Maurer (1988) presented an integration of ideas from firm-specific human capital theory, human resource accounting, and utility analysis (Cronbach & Gleser 1965).

SOCIETAL, LEGAL, AND ETHICAL ISSUES

In this final section of our review, we describe briefly issues relevant to the use of selection procedures in the society in which they are used. Work reviewed in this section is directed toward goals such as affirmative action hiring of minorities or due process. Analyses of the degree to which these goals and that of predictive efficiency are in conflict are summarized in Schmitt (1989).

McKinney (1987) illustrates the quandary faced by organizational decision-makers who have available evidence of the validity of a selection procedure that produces unequal hiring rates across ethnic subgroups. The solution proposed to maximize both predictive efficiency and affirmative action progress under these circumstances is to select the best-scoring individuals from each racial subgroup in proportions that equal their representation in the applicant pool. The US Employment Service has used scores from the General Aptitude Test Battery in this way for some time, but some legal personnel have regarded this practice as discriminatory because it uses ethnic subgroup as an explicit hiring criterion. A National Academy of Sciences panel has currently studied this practice and published a report reviewing the scientific and societal rationale for this procedure (Hartigan & Wigdor 1989).

The fact that tests may differentially predict the performance of different cultural or ethnic subgroups continues to receive some attention. Zeidner (1987, 1988) found little evidence of differential prediction of academic success between subgroups using cognitive aptitude tests in Israel. Dunbar & Novick (1988) showed that the Armed Services Vocational Aptitude Battery (ASVAB) underpredicted women's performance in training for clerical jobs by one third to one half of a standard deviation unit. Use of educational attainment in combination with ASVAB reduced the underprediction of female scores. Also using ASVAB scores, Houston & Novick (1987) found that regression slopes for blacks were lower than those for whites and that the regression lines crossed above the predictor score cutoff. Hence the criterion performance of blacks was underpredicted at the lower end of the scale and overpredicted at the upper end of the predictor scale when a pooled regression equation was used.

In a study directly relevant to recent attempts to purify tests of items that display subgroup performance differences, Roznowski (1987) constructed subsets of items on which males or females did substantially better than the other gender subgroup. Tests containing these subtests were equally "valid" in the sense that they correlated with a general intelligence measure. She asserts that between-group differences on an item or scale indicate little about the relevance of within-group differences (on the same items or scales) for the measurement of ability. An appropriate test construction strategy, she suggests, is to select item content broadly within the conceptual definition of the trait to be measured.

In an interesting study of the effects of affirmative action goals and minority-majority differences on the decision-making process, Mellers & Hartka (1988) examined judges' priority ratings for hypothetical medical school applicants given information about Medical School Aptitude Test (MCAT) scores, GPAs, and minority status. Affirmative action goals and minority-majority status had no effect on the way information was combined or weighted, but judges simply added a constant to minority applicants' priority rating.

A number of reviews of the legal status of various aspects of personnel selection have appeared. Barrett & Kernan (1987) discussed the legal status of performance appraisal systems in the termination of employees and provided a list of performance appraisal characteristics that have been favorably viewed in court decisions. Cascio et al (1988) reviewed the legal and psychometric bases for setting cutoff scores. Gregory (1988) described a problem that has received little attention—the legal dilemma of employers faced both with tight legal restrictions on pre-hiring investigations (and the use of information acquired through those investigations) and with the threat of large punitive damages if a "negligent" hiring decision results in harm to some customer or employee.

Kleiman & Faley (1988) reviewed Supreme Court decisions regarding the legality of voluntary Affimative Action Plans (AAPs). Overall, the courts favored such plans when they remedied past discrimination, represented "reasonable" action, did not completely exclude members of any group, resulted in hiring qualified minorities, and did not involve preferential layoffs. Kleinman & Faley identified an interesting research issue—namely, the impact of preferential treatment on the attitudes and behavior of employees. In a study relevant to this issue, Heilman et al (1987) found that females who knew they had been selected for a position on the basis of their sex viewed themselves and their job less positively than those selected on the basis of merit.

A meta-analysis of experimental studies of hiring decisions (Olian et al 1988) indicated that effects of applicant gender (men were perceived as more qualified) were minimal compared to the effects of education and experience. Heilman et al's (1988) results are a good example of the complexities of the bias issue. When college students were told that female applicants for extremely male sex-typed jobs were competent, they overvalued female applicants. Outside of these restrictive conditions, female candidates for nontraditional jobs were undervalued. Cleveland et al (1988) also reported nonobvious results in a study of age bias—namely, that older employees were assessed as less capable for employment when they were evaluated with a group of younger persons than when they were included in a group more nearly equal in age.

CONCLUSION

Researchers in personnel selection have recently become much more interested in how and why their procedures work. In the job analysis area, we see research on the individual-difference correlates of task and ability ratings and on how job experts reach conclusions about the importance of tasks. Interest in the construct validity of work performance has increased. Construct issues continue to interest researchers in areas of biodata, interview, and assessment center techniques. The conceptualization of validity and validation continues to evolve. Recruitment researchers are expanding our knowledge of what impact selection procedures have on the persons who take our measures. Even in the utility area, researchers are concerned with how judgments are made and how people react to utility estimates. If this rational, theoretical approach to personnel selection continues to direct our research inquiry, it will produce advances in our understanding of human behavior in organizations as well as more practically useful knowledge.

ACKNOWLEDGMENTS

The authors acknowledge the able assistance of Lisa Wood in compiling and organizing the literature reviewed in this paper. We thank J. Kevin Ford for his comments on an earlier version of this review.

Literature Cited

Aamody, M. G., Pierce, W. L. 1987. Comparison of the rare response and vertical percent methods for scoring the biographical information blank. *Educ. Psychol. Meas.* 47:505–11

Alexander, R. A. 1988. Group homogeneity, range restriction, and range enhancement effects on correlations. *Personnel Psychol.* 41:773–78

Alexander, R. A., Barrick, M. R. 1987. Estimating the standard error of projected dollar gains in utility analysis. *J. Appl. Psychol.* 72:475–79

Alvares, K. M., Hulin, C. L. 1972. Two explanations of temporal decay in the prediction of performance: a literature review and theoretical analysis. *Hum. Factors* 14:295–308

Arvey, R. D., Miller, H. E., Gould, R., Burch, P. 1987. Interview validity for selecting sales clerks. *Personnel Psychol.* 40:1–12

Ash, P., Baehr, M. E., Joy, D. S., Orban, J. A. 1988. *Appl. Psychol.: Int. Rev.* 37:351–62

Ash, R. A., Johnson, J. C., Levine, E. L., McDaniel, M. A. 1989. Job applicant training and work experience evaluation in personnel selection. In *Research in Personnel and Human Resources Management*, ed. K. R. Rowland, G. R. Ferris. Greenwich, CT: JAI Press

Athey, T. R., McIntyre, R. M. 1987. Effect of rater training on rater accuracy: levels-of-processing theory and social facilitation theory perspectives. *J. Appl. Psychol.* 72:567–72

Baker, H. G., Berry, V. M., Kazan, J. B., Diamond, E. E. 1988. Career plans checkup: automated assessment of career maturity. *J. Comput.-Based Instr.* 15:29–32

Bannister, B. D., Kinicki, A. J., DeNisi, A. S., Hom, P. W. 1987. A new method for the statistical control of rating error in performance ratings. *Educ. Psychol. Meas.* 47:583–96

Barrett, G. V., Kernan, M. C. 1987. Performance appraisal and terminations: a review

of court decisions since Brito V. Zia with implications for personnel practice. *Personnel Psychol.* 40:489–503

Bartram, D. 1987. The development of an automated testing system for pilot selection: the micropat project. *Appl. Psychol.: Int. Rev.* 36:279–98

Bergmann, T. J., Martin, G. E. 1987. Optimal large-scale manpower recruitment policies. *Hum. Resour. Plan.* 10:93–101

Bernardin, H. J. 1987. Development and validation of a forced choice scale to measure job-related discomfort among customer service representatives. *Acad. Manage. J.* 30:162–73

Binning, J. F., Barrett, G. V. 1989. Validity of personnel decisions: an examination of the inferential and evidential bases. *J. Appl. Psychol.* 74:478–94

Binning, J. F., Goldstein, M. A., Garcia, M. F., Scatteregia, J. H. 1988. Effects of preinterview impressions on questioning strategies in same- and opposite-sex employment interviews. *J. Appl. Psychol.* 73:30–37

Blanz, F., Ghiselli, E. E. 1972. The mixed standard scale: a new rating system. *Personnel Psychol.* 25:185–99

Bobko, P., Karren, R., Kerkar, S. P. 1987. Systematic research needs for understanding supervisory-based estimates of SDy in utility analysis. *Organ. Behav. Hum. Decis. Process.* 40:69–95

Burke, M. J., Doran, L. I. 1989. A note on the economic utility of generalized validity coefficients. *J. Appl. Psychol.* 73:171–75

Burke, M. J., Normand, J. 1987. Computerized psychological testing: overview and critique. *Prof. Psychol.* 18:42–51

Burke, M. J., Normand, J., Raju, N. S. 1987. Examinee attitudes toward computer-administered ability testing. *Comp. Hum. Behav.* 3:95–107

Burke, M. J., Pearlman, K. 1988. Recruiting, selecting, and matching people with jobs. In *Frontiers in Industrial/Organizational Psychology*, ed. J. P. Campbell, R. J. Campbell, pp. 97–142. San Francisco: Jossey-Bass

Burke, M. J., Raju, N. S. 1988. A review of validity generalization models and procedures. In *Readings in Personnel and Human Resource Management*, ed. R. Schuler, S. A. Youngblood, V. L. Huber, pp. 542–54. St. Paul, MN: West Publishing Co.

Butler, S. K., Harvey, R. J. 1988. A comparison of holistic versus decomposed rating of Position Analysis Questionnaire work dimensions. *Personnel Psychol.* 41:761–72

Bycio, P., Alvares, K. M., Hahn, J. 1987. Situational specificity in assessment center ratings: a confirmatory factor analysis. *J. Appl. Psychol.* 72:463–74

Campbell, D. J., Lee, C. 1988. Self appraisal in performance evaluation: development versus evaluation. *Acad. Manage. Rev.* 13:302–13

Campion, M. A., Pursell, E. D., Brown, B. K. 1988. Structured interviewing: raising the psychometric properties of the employment interview. *Personnel Psychol.* 41:25–42

Cardy, R. L., Bernardin, H. J., Abbott, J. G., Senderak, M. P., Taylor, K. 1987. The effects of individual performance schemata and dimension familiarization on rating accuracy. *J. Occup. Psychol.* 60:197–205

Carter, R. C., Biersner, R. J. 1987. Job requirements derived from the Position Analysis Questionnaire and validated using military aptitude test scores. *J. Occup. Psychol.* 60:311–21

Cascio, W. F., Alexander, R. A., Barrett, G. V. 1988. Setting cutoff scores: legal, psychometric, and professional issues and guidelines. *Personnel Psychol.* 41:1–24

Cascio, W. F., Ramos, R. A. 1986. Development and application of a new method for assessing job performance in behavioral/economic terms. *J. Appl. Psychol.* 71:20–28

Champion, C. H., Green, S. B., Sauser, W. I. 1988. Development and evaluation of short-cut-derived behaviorally anchored rating scales. *Educ. Psychol. Meas.* 48:29–41

Cleveland, J. N., Festa, R. M., Montgomery, L. 1988. Applicant pool composition and job perceptions: impact on decisions regarding an older applicant. *J. Vocat. Behav.* 32:112–25

Colarelli, S. M., Dean, R. A., Konstans, C. 1987. Comparative effects of personal and situational influences on job outcomes of new professionals. *J. Appl. Psychol.* 72:558–66

Conley, P. R., Sackett, P. R. 1987. Effects of using high- versus low-performing job incumbents as sources of job analysis ratings. *J. Appl. Psychol.* 72:434–37

Cook, M. 1988. *Personnel Selection and Productivity*. Chichester, England: Wiley

Cronbach, L. J. 1955. Processes affecting scores on "understanding of others" and "assumed similarity." *Psychol. Bull.* 52:177–93

Cronbach, L. J. 1987. Statistical tests for moderator variables: Flaws in analyses recently proposed. *Psychol. Bull.* 102:414–17

Cronbach, L. J. 1988. Five perspectives on the validity argument. In *Test Validity*, ed. H. Wainer, H. I. Braun, pp. 3–18. Hillsdale, NJ: Erlbaum

Cronbach, L. J., Gleser, G. C. 1965. *Psychological Tests and Personnel Decisions*. Urbana: Univ. Illinois

Cronshaw, S. F., Alexander, R. A., Wiesner, W. H., Barrick, M. R. 1987. Incorporating risk into selection utility: two models for sensitivity analysis and risk simulation. *Organ. Behav. Hum. Decis. Process.* 40:270–86

Dansereau, F., Alutto, J. A., Yammarino, F. J. 1984. *Theory Testing in Organizational Behavior: The Variant Approach*. Englewood Cliffs, NJ: Prentice-Hall

DeNisi, A. S., Cornelius, E. T. III, Blencoe, A. G. 1987. Further investigation of common knowledge effects on job analysis. *J. Appl. Psychol.* 72:262–68

DeNisi, A. S., Williams, K. J. 1988. Cognitive approaches to performance appraisal. In *Research in Personnel and Human Resource Management*, ed. K. R. Rowland, G. R. Ferris, 6:109–56. Greenwich, CT: JAI Press. 328 pp.

Deselles, M. L., Dobbins, G. H. 1987. A comparison of mixed standard scale ratings calculated with Blanz and Ghiselli's and Saal's scoring algorithms. *Educ. Psychol. Meas.* 47:799–806

Dickinson, T. L. 1987. Designs for evaluating the validity and accuracy of performance ratings. *Organ. Behav. Hum. Decis. Process.* 40:1–21

Doverspike, D., Cellar, D. F., Hajek, M. 1987. Relative sensitivity to performance cue effects as a criterion for comparing rating scale formats. *Educ. Psychol. Meas.* 147:1135–39

Drakeley, R. J., Herriot, P., Jones, A. 1988. Biographical data, training success and turnover. *J. Occup. Psychol.* 61:145–52

Drasgow, F., Guertler, E. 1987. A decision-theoretic approach to the use of appropriateness measurement for detecting invalid test and scale scores. *J. Appl. Psychol.* 72:10–18

Drasgow, F., Levine, M. V., McLaughlin, M. E. 1987. Detecting inappropriate test scores with optimal and practical appropriateness indices. *Appl. Psychol. Meas.* 11:59–79

Dreher, G. F., Ash, R. A., Hancock, P. 1988.

The role of the traditional research design in underestimating the validity of the employment interview. *Personnel Psychol.* 41: 315–27

Dunbar, S. B., Novick, M. R. 1988. On predicting success in training for men and women: examples from Marine Corps clerical specialties. *J. Appl. Psychol.* 73:545–50

Dunlap, W. P., Kemery, E. R. 1987. Failure to detect moderating effects: is multicollinearity the problem? *Psychol. Bull.* 102:418–20

Dunlap, W. P., Kemery, E. R. 1988. Effects of predictor intercorrelations and reliabilities on moderated multiple regression. *Organ. Behav. Hum. Decis. Process.* 41: 248–58

Eberhardt, B. J., Yap, C. K., Basuray, M. T. 1988. A psychometric evaluation of the multiple choice version of the Miner Sentence Completion Scale. *Educ. Psychol. Meas.* 48:119–26

Eder, B. W., Ferris, G. R., eds. 1989. *The Employment Interview: Theory, Research, and Practice.* Newbury Park, CA: Sage

Edwards, J. E., Frederick, J. T., Burke, M. J. 1988. Efficacy of modified CREPID SDys on the basis of archival organizational data. *J. Appl. Psychol.* 73:529–35

Eyde, L. D., ed. 1987. Special issue on computerized psychological testing. *Appl. Psychol.: Int. Rev.* 36:223–439

Fahr, J. L., Werbel, J. D., Bedeian, A. G. 1988. An empirical investigation of self-appraisal-based performance evaluation. *Personnel Psychol.* 41:141–56

Feldt, L. S., Woodruff, D. J., Salih, F. A. 1987. Statistical inference for coefficient alpha. *Appl. Psychol. Meas.* 11:93–103

Feltham, R. 1988a. Assessment centre decision-making: judgmental vs. mechanical. *J. Occup. Psychol.* 61:237–41

Feltham, R. 1988b. Validity of a police assessment centre: A 1–19 year follow-up. *J. Occup. Psychol.* 61:129–44

Ferris, G. R., Bergin, T. G., Gilmore, D. C. 1986. Personality and ability predictors of training performance for flight attendants. *Group Organ. Stud.* 11:419–35

Fiske, D. W. 1987. Construct invalidity comes from method effects. *Educ. Psychol. Meas.* 46:285–307

Fleishman, E. A. 1988. Some new frontiers in personnel selection research. *Personnel Psychol.* 41:679–702

Fletcher, C. 1987. Candidate personality as an influence on selection interview assessments. *Appl. Psychol.: Int. Rev.* 36:157–62

Fox, G., Dinur, Y. 1988. Validity of self-assessment: a field evaluation. *Personnel Psychol.* 41:581–92

Gael, S., ed. 1988. *The Job Analysis Handbook for Business, Industry and Government.* New York: Wiley

Gatewood, R. D., Feild, H. S. 1987. *Human Resource Selection.* New York: Dryden

Gaugler, B. B., Rosenthal, D. B., Thornton, G. C., Bentson, C. 1987. Meta-analysis of assessment center validity. *J. Appl. Psychol.* 72:493–511

George, D. I., Smith, M. C. 1988. Self assessment in personnel selection: an investigation using seasonal workers. *Appl. Psychol.: Int. Rev.* 37:337–50

Gordon, H. W., Charns, M. P., Sherman, E. 1987. Management success as a function of performance on specialized cognitive tests. *Hum. Relat.* 40:671–98

Gordon, H. W., Leighty, R. 1988. Importance of specialized cognitive function in the selection of military pilots. *J. Appl. Psychol.* 73:38–45

Gordon, R. A., Rozelle, R. M., Baxter, J. C. 1988. The effect of applicant age, job level, and accountability of the evaluation of job applicants. *Organ. Behav. Hum. Decis. Process.* 41:20–33

Graves, L. M., Powell, G. N. 1988. An investigation of sex discrimination in recruiters' evaluations of actual applicants. *J. Appl. Psychol.* 73:20–29

Greer, O. L., Cascio, W. F. 1987. Is cost accounting the answer? Comparison of two behaviorally based methods for estimating the standard deviation of job performance in dollars with a cost-accounting-based approach. *J. Appl. Psychol.* 72:588–95

Gregory, D. L. 1988. Reducing the risk of negligence in hiring. *Employee Relat. Law J.* 14:31–40

Gross, A. L., Fleishman, L. E. 1987. The correction for restriction of range and nonlinear regressions: an analytic study. *Appl. Psychol. Meas.* 11:211–17

Gross, A. L., McGanney, M. L. 1987. The restriction of range problem and nonignorable selection processes. *J. Appl. Psychol.* 72:604–10

Guion, R. M. 1987. Changing views for personnel selection research. *Personnel Psychol.* 40:199–213

Guion, R. M., Gibson, W. M. 1988. Personnel selection and placement. *Annu. Rev. Psychol.* 39:349–74

Hakel, M. D. 1986. Personnel selection and placement. *Annu. Rev. Psychol.* 37:351–80

Hakstian, A. R., Woolsey, L. K., Schroeder, M. L. 1987. Validity of a large-scale assessment battery in an industrial setting. *Educ. Psychol. Meas.* 47:165–88

Hamilton, J. W., Dickinson, T. L. 1987. Comparison of several procedures for generating J-coefficients. *J. Appl. Psychol.* 72:49–54

Harris, M. M., Fink, L. S. 1987. A field study

of applicant reactions to employment opportunities: Does the recruiter make a difference? *Personnel Psychol.* 40:765–84

Harris, M. M., Sackett, P. R. 1987. A factor analysis and item response theory analysis of an employee honesty test. *J. Bus. Psychol.* 2:122–35

Harris, M. M., Schaubroeck, J. 1988. A meta-analysis of self-supervisor, self-peer, and peer-supervisory ratings. *Personnel Psychol.* 41:43–62

Hartigan, J. A., Wigdor, A. K., eds. 1989. *Fairness in Employment Testing.* Washington, DC: Natl. Acad. Press

Harvey, R. J., Friedman, L., Hakel, M. D., Cornelius, E. T. III. 1988. Dimensionality of the Job Element Inventory, a simplified worker-oriented job analysis questionnaire. *J. Appl. Psychol.* 73:639–46

Harvey, R. J., Lozada-Larsen, S. R. 1988. Influence of amount of job descriptive information on job analysis rating accuracy. *J. Appl. Psychol.* 73:457–61

Hedge, J. W., Kavanagh, M. J. 1988. Improving the accuracy of performance evaluations: comparison of three methods of performance appraiser training. *J. Appl. Psychol.* 73:68–73

Hedges, L. V. 1988. The meta-analysis of test validity studies: some new approaches. In *Test Validity,* ed. H. Wainer, H. I., Braun, pp. 191–212. Hillsdale, NJ: Erlbaum

Heilman, M. E., Martell, R. F., Simon, M. C. 1988. The vagaries of sex bias: conditions regulating the undervaluation, equivaluation, and overvaluation of female job applicants. *Organ. Behav. Hum. Decis. Process.* 41:98–110

Heilman, M. E., Simon, M. D., Repper, D. P. 1987. Intentionally favored, unintentionally harmed? Impact of sex-based preferential selection on self-perceptions and self-evaluations. *J. Appl. Psychol.* 72:62–68

Heneman, R. L. 1988. Traits, behaviors, and rater training: some unexpected results. *Hum. Perform.* 1:85–98

Heneman, R. L., Wexley, K. N., Moore, M. L. 1987. Performance-rating accuracy: a critical review. *J. Bus. Res.* 15:431–48

Henry, R. A., Hulin, C. L. 1987. Stability of skilled performance across time: some generalizations and limitations on utilities. *J. Appl. Psychol.* 72:457–62

Herriot, P. 1989. Selection as a social process. In *Advances in Selection and Assessment,* ed. M. Smith, I. T. Robertson, pp. 171–88. Chichester, England: Wiley

Herriot, P., Drenth, P. J., Dulewicz, V., Jones, A., Robertson, I. T., Roe, R., eds. 1989. *Handbook of Assessment in Organizations.* Chichester, England: Wiley

Hogan, E. A. 1987. Effects of prior expectations on performance ratings: a longitudinal study. *Acad. Manage. J.* 30:354–68

Hollenbeck, J. R., Whitener, E. M. 1988. Criterion-related validation for small sample contexts: an integrated approach to synthetic validity. *J. Appl. Psychol.* 73:536–44

Hough, L. M. 1988. *Development of personality measures to supplement selection decisions.* Presented at Annu. Conf. Int. Cong. Psychol., 24th, Sydney, Australia

Houston, W. M., Novick, M. R. 1987. Race-based differential prediction in Air Force technical training programs. *J. Educ. Meas.* 24:309–20

Huber, V. L., Neale, M. A., Northcraft, G. B. 1987. Judgment by heuristics: effects of ratee and rater characteristics and performance standards on performance-related judgments. *Organ. Behav. Hum. Decis. Process.* 40:149–69

Humphreys, L. G. 1968. The fleeting nature of the prediction of college academic success. *J. Educ. Psychol.* 59:375–80

Hunter, J. E., Hirsh, H. R. 1987. Applications of meta-analysis. In *International Review of Industrial and Organizational Psychology,* ed. C. L. Cooper, I. T. Robertson, pp. 321–58. New York: Wiley

Hunter, J. E., Schmidt, F. L. 1982. Fitting people to jobs: The impact of personnel selection on national productivity. In *Human Performance and Productivity: Human Capacity Assessment,* ed. M. D. Dunnette, E. A. Fleishman, pp. 232–84. Hillsdale, NJ: Erlbaum

Hunter, J. E., Schmidt, F. L., Coggin, T. D. 1988. Problems and pitfalls in using capital budgeting and financial accounting techniques in assessing the utility of personnel programs. *J. Appl. Psychol.* 73:522–28

James, L. R., Demaree, R. G., Mulaik, S. A., Mumford, M. D. 1988. Validity generalization: rejoinder to Schmidt, Hunter, and Raju. *J. Appl. Psychol.* 73:673–78

Jensen, A. R. 1980. *Bias in Mental Testing.* New York: Macmillan

Johnson, C. E., Wood, R., Blinkhorn, S. F. 1988. Spuriosor and spurioser: the use of ipsative personality tests. *J. Occup. Psychol.* 61:153–62

Jolly, J. P., Reynolds, T. J., Slocum, J. W. 1988. Application of the means-end theoretic for understanding the cognitive bases of performance appraisal. *Organ. Behav. Hum. Decis. Process.* 41:153–79

Kinicki, A. J., Bannister, B. D. 1988. A test of the measurement assumptions underlying behaviorally anchored rating scales. *Educ. Psychol. Meas.* 48:17–21

Kleiman, L. S., Faley, R. H. 1988. Voluntary affirmative action and preferential treatment: legal and research implications. *Personnel Psychol.* 41:481–96

Klimoski, R., Brickner, M. 1987. Why do assessment centers work? The puzzle of assessment center validity. *Personnel Psychol.* 40:243–60

Kozlowski, S. W. J., Kirsch, M. P. 1987. The systematic distortion hypothesis, halo, and accuracy: an individual level analysis. *J. Appl. Psychol.* 72:252–61

Krzystofiak, F., Cardy, R., Newman, J. 1988. Implicit personality and performance appraisal effectiveness. *J. Appl. Psychol.* 73:515–21

Lautenschlager, G. J., Schaffer, G. S. 1987. Reexamining the component stability of Owens's biographical questionnaire. *J. Appl. Psychol.* 72:149–52

Levine, E. L., Thomas, J. N., Sistrunk, F. 1988. Selecting a job analysis approach. In *The Job Analysis Handbook for Business, Industry, and Government*, ed. S. Gael, pp. 339–52. New York: Wiley

Love, K. G., O'Hara, K. 1987. Predicting job performance of youth trainees under a job training partnership act program (JTPA): criterion validation on a behavior-based measure of work maturity. *Personnel Psychol.* 40:323–40

Mabe, P. A. III, West, S. G. 1982. Validity of self-evaluation of ability: a review and meta-analysis. *J. Appl. Psychol.* 67:280–96

Macan, T. H., Dipboye, R. L. 1988. The effects of interviewers' initial impressions on information gathering. *Organ. Behav. Hum. Decis. Process.* 41:20–33

MacDonald, T., Hakel, M. D. 1985. Effects of applicant race, sex, suitability, and answers on interviewer's questioning strategy and ratings. *Personnel Psychol.* 38:321–34

Maier, M. H. 1988. On the need for quality control in validation research. *Personnel Psychol.* 41:497–502

Maurer, S. D., Fay, C. 1988. Effect of situational interviews, conventional structured interviews, and training on interview rating agreement: an experimental analysis. *Personnel Psychol.* 41:329–44

McCormick, E. J., Jeanneret, P. R., Mecham, R. C. 1972. A study of job characteristics and job dimensions as based on the Position Analysis Questionnaire (PAQ). *J. Appl. Psychol.* 56:347–68

McDaniel, M. A. 1988. Does pre-employment drug use predict on-the-job suitability? *Personnel Psychol.* 41:717–29

McDaniel, M. A., Schmidt, F. L., Hunter, J. E. 1988. A meta-analysis of the validity of methods for rating training and experience in personnel selection. *Personnel Psychol.* 41:283–314

McEvoy, G. M., Buller, P. F. 1987. User acceptance of peer appraisals in an industrial setting. *Personnel Psychol.* 40:785–97

McEvoy, G. M., Cascio, W. F. 1987. Do good or poor performers leave? A meta-analysis of the relationship between performance and turnover. *Acad. Manage J.* 30:744–62

McKinney, W. R. 1987. Public personnel selection: issues and choice points. *Public Personnel Manage. J.* 16:243–57

McLaughlin, M. E., Drasgow, F. 1987. Lord's chi-square test of item bias with estimated and with known person parameters. *Appl. Psychol. Meas.* 11:161–73

Meglino, B. M., DeNisi, A. S. 1987. Realistic job previews: some thoughts on their more effective use in managing the flow of human resources. *Hum. Resour. Plan.* 10: 157–67

Mehrens, W. A. 1987. Validity issues in teacher licensure tests. *J. Pers. Eval. Educ.* 1:195–229

Mellers, B., Hartka, E. 1988. Fair selection decisions. *J. Exp. Psychol.: Hum. Percept. Perform.* 14:572–81

Messick, S. 1988a. The once and future issues of validity: assessing the meaning and consequences of measurement. In *Test Validity*, ed. H. Wainer, H. I. Braun, pp. 33–46. Hillsdale, NJ: Erlbaum

Messick, S. 1988b. Validity. In *Educational Measurement*, ed. R. L. Linn. New York: Macmillan

Meyer, H. H. 1987. Predicting supervisory ratings versus promotional progress in test validation studies. *J. Appl. Psychol.* 72: 696–97

Millsap, R. E. 1988. Tolerance intervals: alternatives to credibility intervals in validity generalization research. *Appl. Psychol. Meas.* 12:27–32

Mitchel, J. O. 1975. Assessment center validity: a longitudinal study. *J. Appl. Psychol.* 60:573–79

Mount, M. K., Thompson, D. E. 1987. Cognitive categorization and quality of performance ratings. *J. Appl. Psychol.* 72:240–46

Mullins, W. C., Kimbrough, W. W. 1988. Group composition as a determinant of job analysis outcomes. *J. Appl. Psychol.* 73: 657–64

Mumford, M. D., Owens, W. A. 1987. Methodology review: principles, procedures, and findings in the application of background data measures. *Appl. Psychol. Meas.* 11:1–31

Mumford, M. D., Weeks, J. L., Harding, F. D., Fleishman, E. A. 1987. Measuring occupational difficulty: A construct validation against training criteria. *J. Appl. Psychol.* 72:578–87

Murphy, K. R., Constans, J. I. 1987. Behavioral anchors as a source of bias in rating. *J. Appl. Psychol.* 72:573–77

Noe, R. A., Schmitt, N. 1986. The influence of trainee attitudes on training effectiveness: test of a model. *Personnel Psychol.* 39:497–523

Noe, R. A., Steffy, B. D. 1987. The influence of individual characteristics and assessment center evaluation on career exploration behavior and job involvement. *J. Vocat. Behav.* 30:187–202

O'Hara, K., Love, K. G. 1987. Accurate selection of police officials within small municipalities: "*Et tu* assessment center?" *Public Personnel Manage. J.* 16:9–14

Olian, J. D., Schwab, D. P., Haberfeld, Y. 1988. The impact of applicant gender compared to qualifications on hiring recommendations: a meta-analysis of experimental studies. *Organ. Behav. Hum. Decis. Process.* 41:180–95

Owens, W. A., Schoenfeldt, L. F. 1979. Toward a classification of persons. *J. Appl. Psychol.* 64:569–607

Paunonen, S. V., Jackson, D. N. 1988. Type I error rates for moderated multiple regression analysis. *J. Appl. Psychol.* 73:569–73

Paunonen, S. V., Jackson, D. N., Aberman, S. M. 1987. Personnel selection decisions: effects of applicant personality and the letter of reference. *Organ. Behav. Hum. Decis. Process.* 40:96–114

Powell, G. N. 1987. The effects of sex and gender on recruitment. *Acad. Manage. Rev.* 12:731–43

Prien, E. P., Hughes, G. L. 1987. The effect of quality control revisions on mixed standard scale rating errors. *Personnel Psychol.* 40:815–23

Puffer, S. M. 1987. Prosocial behavior, noncompliant behavior, and work performance among commission salespeople. *J. Appl. Psychol.* 72:615–21

Pulakos, E. D., Borman, W. C., Hough, L. M. 1988. Test validation for scientific understanding: two demonstrations of an approach to studying predictor-criterion linkages. *Personnel Psychol.* 41:703–16

Raju, N. S., Burke, M. J., Normand, J. 1989. *A New Model for Utility Analysis. J. Appl. Psychol.* 74:In press

Rasmussen, J. L., Loher, B. T. 1988. Appropriate critical percentages for the Schmidt and Hunter meta-analysis procedure: comparative evaluation of Type I error rate and power. *J. Appl. Psychol.* 73:683–87

Rauschenberger, J. M., Schmidt, F. L. 1987. Measuring the economic impact of human resource programs. *J. Bus. Psychol.* 2:50–59

Raymond, M. R., Roberts, D. M. 1987. A comparison of methods for treating incomplete data in selection research. *Educ. Psychol. Meas.* 47:13–26

Raza, S. M., Carpenter, B. N. 1987. A model

of hiring decisions in real employment interviews. *J. Appl. Psychol.* 72:596–603

Rich, J. R., Boudreau, J. 1987. The effects of variability and risk in selection utility analysis: an empirical comparison. *Personnel Psychol.* 40:55–84

Robertson, I., Gratton, L., Sharpley, D. 1987. The psychometric properties and design of managerial assessment centres: dimensions into exercises won't go. *J. Occup. Psychol.* 60:187–95

Robertson, I. T., Smith, M. 1989. Personnel selection methods. In *Advances in Selection and Assessment,* ed. M. Smith, I. T. Robertson, pp. 89–112. Chichester, England: Wiley

Roznowski, M. 1987. Use of test manifesting sex differences as measures of intelligence: implications for measurement bias. *J. Appl. Psychol.* 72:480–83

Russell, C. J. 1987. Person characteristic versus role congruency explanations for assessment center ratings. *Acad. Manage. J.* 30:817–26

Ryan, A. M., Sackett, P. R. 1987. A survey of individual assessment practices by I/O psychologists. *Personnel Psychol.* 40:455–88

Rynes, S. L. 1989. Recruitment, organizational entry, and early work adjustment. In *Handbook of Industrial and Organizational Psychology,* ed. M. D. Dunnette, Chicago: Rand-McNally. In press

Rynes, S. L., Boudreau, J. 1986. College recruiting in large organizations: practice, evaluation, and research implications. *Personnel Psychol.* 39:729–58

Saal, F. E. 1979. Mixed standard rating scales: a consistent system for numerically coding inconsistent response combinations. *J. Appl. Psychol.* 64:422–28

Sackett, P. R. 1982. The interviewer as hypothesis tester: the effects of impression of applicant on subsequent interviewer behavior. *Personnel Psychol.* 35:789–804

Sackett, P. R. 1987. Assessment centers and content validity: some neglected issues. *Personnel Psychol.* 40:13–25

Sackett, P. R., Zedeck, S., Fogli, L. 1988. Relations between measures of typical and maximum job performance. *J. Appl. Psychol.* 73:482–86

Sanchez, J. I., Levine, E. L. 1989. Capturing rater policies for judging overall task importance. *J. Appl. Psychol.* 74:336–42

Schmidt, F. L. 1988. Validity generalization and the future of criterion-related validity. In *Test Validity,* ed. H. Wainer, H. I. Braun. Hillsdale, NJ: Erlbaum

Schmidt, F. L., Hunter, J. E., McKenzie, R. C., Muldrow, T. W. 1979. Impact of valid selection procedures on workforce productivity. *J. Appl. Psychol.* 64:609–26

Schmidt, F. L., Hunter, J. E., Outerbridge, A. N., Goff, S. 1988a. Joint relation of experience and ability with job performance: test of three hypotheses. *J. Appl. Psychol.* 73: 46–57

Schmidt, F. L., Hunter, J. E., Raju, N. S. 1988b. Validity generalization and situational specificity: a second look at the 75% rule and the Fisher's Z transformation. *J. Appl. Psychol.* 73:665–72

Schmitt, N. 1989. Fairness in employment selection. In *Advances in Personnel Selection and Assessment,* ed. M. Smith, I. Robertson, pp. 133–52. Chichester: Wiley

Schmitt, N., Cohen, S. A. 1989. Internal analyses of task ratings by job incumbents. *J. Appl. Psychol.* 74:96–104

Schmitt, N., Schneider, B. 1983. Current issues in personnel selection. In *Research in Human Resources Management,* ed. K. R. Rowland, G. R. Ferris. Greenwich, CT: JAI Press

Schoorman, F. D. 1988. Escalation bias in performance appraisals: an unintended consequence of supervisor participation in hiring decisions. *J. Appl. Psychol.* 73:58–62

Schweder, R. A. 1982. Fact and artifact in trait perception: the systematic distortion hypothesis. In *Progress in Experimental Personality Research: Normal Personality Processes,* ed. B. A. Maher, W. B. Maher, pp. 65–100. New York: Academic

Silver, E. M., Bennett, C. 1987. Modification of the Minnesota Clerical Test to predict performance on video display terminals. *J. Appl. Psychol.* 73:153–55

Silver, N. C., Dunlap, W. P. 1987. Averaging correlation coefficients: Should Fisher's z transformation be used? *J. Appl. Psychol.* 72:146–48

Smith, J. E., Hakel, M. D. 1979. Convergence among data sources, response bias, and reliability and validity of a structured job analysis questionnaire. *Personnel Psychol.* 32:677–92

Smith, M. C., George, D. I. 1987. Weighted application forms for personnel selection: a comparison of old and new methodologie. *Australian Psychol.* 22:351–75

Smith, M. C., Smith, J. M., George, D. I. 1988. Improving practitioner access through a software design for the weighted application form. *J. Occup. Psychol.* 61:257–64

Smither, J. W., Reilly, R. R. 1987. True intercorrelation among job components, time delay in rating, and rater intelligence as determinants of accuracy in performance ratings. *Organ. Behav. Hum. Decis. Process.* 40:369–91

Srinivas, S., Motowidlo, S. J. 1987. Effects of raters' stress on the dispersion and favorability of performance ratings. *J. Appl. Psychol.* 72:247–51

Steffy, B. D., Maurer, S. D. 1988. Conceptualizing and measuring the economic effectiveness of human resource activities. *Acad. Manage. Rev.* 13:271–86

Stone, D. L., Stone, E. F. 1987. Effects of missing application-blank information on personnel selection decisions: Do privacy protection strategies bias the outcome? *J. Appl. Psychol.* 72:452–56

Stone, E. F. 1988. Moderator variables in research: a review and analysis of conceptual and methodological issues. In *Research in Personnel and Human Resource Management,* ed. K. R. Rowland, G. R. Ferris, 6:191–230. Greenwich, CT: JAI Press. 328 pp.

Strube, M. J. 1988. Averaging correlation on coefficients: influence of heterogeneity and set size. *J. Appl. Psychol.* 73:559–68

Sulsky, L. M., Balzer, W. K. 1988. Meaning and measurement of performance rating accuracy: some methodological and theoretical concerns. *J. Appl. Psychol.* 73:497–506

Taylor, M. S., Bergmann, T. J. 1987. Organizational recruitment activities and applicants' reactions at different stages of the recruitment process. *Personnel Psychol.* 40:261–85

Telenson, P. A., Alexander, R. A., Barrett, G. V. 1983. Scoring the biographical information blank: a comparison of three weighting techniques. *Appl. Psychol. Meas.* 7:73–80

Thissen, D., Steinberg, L. 1988. Data analysis using item response theory. *Psychol. Bull.* 104:385–95

Thomas, H. 1988. What is the interpretation of the validity generalization estimate $S\hat{\rho} = S_r^2 - S_e^2$? *J. Appl. Psychol.* 73:679–82

Vance, R. J., MacCallum, R. C., Coovert, M. D., Hedge, J. W. 1988. Construct validity of multiple job performance using confirmatory factor analysis. *J. Appl. Psychol.* 73:74–80

Wainer, H., Braun, H. I., eds. 1988. *Test Validity.* Hillsdale, NJ: Erlbaum

Wainer, H., Kiely, G. L. 1987. Item clusters and computerized adaptive testing: a case for testlets. *J. Educ. Meas.* 24:185–201

Walsh, J. P., Weinberg, R. M., Fairfield, M. L. 1987. The effects of gender on assessment centre evaluations. *J. Occup. Psychol.* 60:305–9

Wareing, R., Stockdale, J. 1987. Decision making in the promotion interview: an empirical study. *Personnel Rev.* 16:26–32

Weekley, J. A., Gier, J. A. 1987. Reliability and validity of the situational interview for a sales position. *J. Appl. Psychol.* 72:484–87

Wiesner, W. H., Cronshaw, S. F. 1988. A meta-analytic investigation of the impact of interview format and degree of structure on the validity of the employment interview. *J. Occup. Psychol.* 61:275–90

Yammarino, F. J., Dubinsky, A. J., Hartley, S. W. 1987. An approach for assessing individual versus group effects in performance evaluations. *J. Occup. Psychol.* 60: 157–67

Zedeck, S., Cascio, W. F. 1984. Psychological issues in personnel decisions. *Annu. Rev. Psychol.* 35:461–518

Zeidner, M. 1987. Test of the cultural bias hypothesis: some Israeli findings. *J. Appl. Psychol.* 72:38–48

Zeidner, M. 1988. Cultural fairness in aptitude testing revisited: a cross-cultural parallel. *Prof. Psychol.* 19:257–62

Annu. Rev. Psychol. 1990. 41:321–53

REASONING

Lance J. Rips

Department of Psychology, University of Chicago, Chicago, Illinois 60637

CONTENTS

Reasoning infiltrates other forms of thought. Perceiving, for example, includes reasoning if, as is commonly assumed, perceptions result from inductive combination of sensory and memory information. Categorizing includes reasoning in exactly the same way. Comprehending includes reasoning since it involves filling in missing information and predicting new information as we read or listen. Problem-solving, decision-making, learning, and social understanding all obviously include reasoning. In fact, when we conceive of reasoning in this very general way, it seems to encompass almost any process of forming or adjusting beliefs and is nearly synonymous with cognition itself.

0066-4308/90/0201-0321$02.00

By contrast, the psychology of reasoning has been something of a research backwater. Although the topic has been part of experimental psychology since the turn of the century (circa Störring 1908), it has played only a minor role in work on mental processes. A glance at the Standard References on this topic may convince you that research on deductive reasoning is preoccupied with a couple of clever brain-teasers invented by Peter Wason (e.g. Wason & Johnson-Laird 1972) and with the categorical syllogisms invented by Aristotle (but now considered by most logicians little more than a historical curiosity within the much more powerful systems of modern logic). Similarly, most research on inductive reasoning seems to busy itself with the way people learn arbitrary sets of geometric shapes, random dot patterns, or schematic faces. The "long and dull history" of other areas of experimental psychology (Tulving & Madigan 1970) appears lively and eventful by comparison.

This bleak record may be changing, however, under internal pressure for broader, more naturalistic cognitive theories, and external pressures from philosophy, mathematical logic, and artificial intelligence. Experiments with syllogisms and dot patterns still go on, of course, but the game is being played by different rules. Investigators are beginning to propose more general models, and it may therefore be the right time for a reassessment.

OVERVIEW

To see what's at stake, let's consider two opposing pictures of reasoning. It might not be too misleading to call these the *Strict* and *Loose* views.

According to the Strict view, reasoning takes place in discrete steps from one belief (or set of beliefs to another). You begin by believing that Donald Trump is rich, for example, and as a result you then come to believe that someone is rich or that financiers are rich. From this new belief others may follow in a similar way. This stepwise progress is relatively local, in the sense that only a delimited set of old beliefs are effective in triggering the new one. You may need to believe that Trump is a financier to get from *Trump is rich* to *Financiers are rich,* but it doesn't matter for this inference whether you believe that snow is white or that Margaret Mead was naughty. Moreover, not all aspects of the old and new beliefs are important in this process. In any given instance of reasoning, there will be distinguished parts or characteristics of beliefs that are instrumental in the inference; the other parts just go along for the ride. For example, in the step from *Trump is rich* to *Someone is rich,* the expression *someone* is essential, but the predicate *is rich* could be replaced, in both statements, by almost any other. Because of this difference between essential and nonessential parts, we can group these inferences with others of the same kind. For instance, we can regard the inference at hand as one among many that have the form: *c is P; therefore something is P.*

The Loose view of reasoning takes a much more homogeneous approach. Instead of supposing that an inference is a quantal event, the Loose view sees reasoning as a continuous process of updating the confidence or strength of a belief. Increasing your confidence that Trump is rich increases your confidence that someone is rich or that financiers are rich and may also decrease your confidence in yet other beliefs (e.g. that Trump sells pencils on 42nd Street). The Loose view is also homogeneous with respect to which beliefs can affect others and which parts of a belief figure in the updating process. According to this approach, any belief can potentially raise or lower your confidence in any other. Furthermore, there is no special structure within a belief that is crucial in updating. The amount of confidence that flows from *Trump is rich* to *Financiers are rich* depends on all parts of the sentence: Our confidence that Trump is left-handed, for instance, would produce a much smaller increase in our confidence that financiers are left-handed. It is therefore much more difficult within the Loose view than within the Strict view to sort inferences into types on the basis of their parts.

Issues

The contrast between the Strict and Loose views is a stark one that calls attention to some of the main issues in the field. Table 1 summarizes these issues and reviews the stance that Strict and Loose theories take. Although we can find compromises between them, these views are not just straw men, since there are cognitive scientists whose approaches come very close to each. (See McCarthy 1988 for a Strict view and Rumelhart et al 1986 for something resembling a Loose one.) The two extreme positions are simple and internally coherent, in that a stance on one of the issues invites a like stance on the others. Once you've said "yes" to special structure, for example, it's tough to say "no" to abstract specification. In fact, it's easy to put yourself into a frame of mind in which Strict reasoning seems inevitable and Loose reasoning impossible, and equally easy to take the opposite point of view. In what follows, we examine these issues to see the advantages and disadvantages of the Strict and Loose conceptions.

Given two attractive alternatives, it's tempting to find a place for both of them. Perhaps the Strict view describes reasoning of a particular type, whereas the Loose view describes another. Or perhaps each view applies at a distinct level of the cognitive system. In the next section of this chapter, we try to gain some perspective on the issues of Table 1 by examining how appropriate they are to different inference forms and different levels. The remaining sections take up the issues and their surrounding controversies in psychology. The third section deals with the question of whether inference depends on special structure in beliefs—for example, on special constants like SOMETHING or IF or CAUSE or on the special distinction between one- and

Table 1   Strict and Loose approaches to key issues in the psychology of reasoning

Issue	Strict	Loose
Special structure?	yes	no
Abstract specification?	yes	no
Discrete inference steps?	yes	no

multiple-place predicates. The following section then confronts the related problem of the abstractness of the inference process: Do human reasoners possess mechanisms for dealing with abstract classes of problems (e.g. rules or schemata or heuristics devoted to reasoning about causes) or do they deal with each problem on an individual basis? The final section takes up the question of whether inference is a continuous affair.

I hope no one thinks I'm going to resolve any of these issues. The goal of this review isn't to decide whether one view or the other is correct but to clarify what the real problems are. My guess is that at least some of the controversies in this area have been framed in ways that are sure to lead to an impasse, and it may be worthwhile for contestants and spectators to take time to figure out what's worth fighting for.

Ground Rules

Some further warnings are in order about the scope of this discussion. Although there is no neat way to confine the topic, the emphasis will be on psychological research on inference in normal adults. Some of the research on children's reasoning is too important to pass up, but my coverage of the developmental literature will be spotty at best. The same is true of work in adjacent disciplines in cognitive science. Knowledge of relevant parts of philosophy, logic, and Artificial Intelligence (AI) is now essential for doing competent research in this area, but there is no hope of covering this vast terrain in a single chapter. Finally, I've tried to give most attention to research published since 1985 in order to avoid overlap with earlier *Annual Review* articles on thinking (Medin & Smith 1984; Oden 1987). For other reviews of this domain, see Braine & Rumain (1983), Evans (1982), Galotti (1989) and Wason & Johnson-Laird (1972).

TYPES OF REASONING

The usual idea is that reasoning comes in two flavors: deductive and inductive. Deductive reasoning is the sort that takes us from given beliefs to others that necessarily follow from them. Inductive reasoning takes us from given beliefs to others that are supported, but aren't entailed, by the given ones. So it's deductive reasoning that gets us from the belief that Donald Trump is rich to the belief that someone is rich, and it's inductive reasoning that gets us from *Donald Trump is rich* to *All financiers are rich.*

The distinction between inductive and deductive inference is a convenient organizational device for writers of cognition textbooks and of review chapters like this one. Moreover, the distinction fits the intuition that there's something right about both the Strict and Loose views of reasoning—i.e. that the Strict view applies to deductive reasoning and the Loose view to inductive reasoning. On one hand, we can think of deductive reasoning in terms of formal proofs in which a conclusion is derived from a delimited set of premises via abstractly formulated rules. These rules apply in a stepwise fashion in virtue of the logical form of the sentences that comprise the proof. On the other hand, a natural way to think of inductive reasoning is as a process of mutual adjustment to the subjective probability or strengths of beliefs. New evidence triggers an increase or decrease in the strength of related beliefs, where strength is a continuous quantity. Strength revision need not rely on any special form in the beliefs' representation, and the interdependencies between beliefs can change with experience. Strength can also transmit itself over an unpredictable number of beliefs because of the complex network of interdependencies. Thus conceived, deduction corresponds to the Strict view and induction to the Loose view on a point-by-point basis (see Table 1).

But what's the chance that this neat distinction has any psychological validity? Are there really two qualitatively different cognitive processes that answer to deductive and inductive reasoning? The point of departure for this distinction is a philosophical difference in evaluative criteria for formal *arguments,* where an argument in this sense is just a set of sentences (possibly empty), called the *premises,* followed by a final sentence, called the *conclusion.* We can write these arguments in the usual way in vertical lists:

<u>Donald Trump is rich.</u>   1.
Someone is rich.

<u>Donald Trump is rich.</u>   2.
All financiers are rich.

<u>Donald Trump is rich.</u>   3.
Xavier Cugat is bald.

An argument is *deductively valid* if (roughly speaking) the conclusion is true in every state of affairs in which all of the premises are true. An argument is *inductively strong* if it is not deductively valid but if the conclusion is more likely to be true when the premises are (Skyrms 1966). So Argument 1 is deductively valid according to these criteria, and 2 is inductively strong. Argument 3 is neither deductively valid nor inductively strong since the premise provides negligible evidence for the conclusion.[1]

How Many Kinds of Reasoning Are There?

The fact that we can distinguish deductive validity from inductive strength doesn't by itself demonstrate a psychological distinction between the two types of reasoning (Harman 1986). Notice that even in the case of arguments, we don't necessarily have an independently defined set of "deductive arguments," some valid and some invalid, or a set of "inductive arguments," some strong and some weak. The definitions of validity and strength only give us ways of *assessing* arguments within an otherwise undifferentiated set.

So if arguments aren't in themselves deductive or inductive, is there any reason to suppose that there are distinct psychological processes devoted to deductive and inductive reasoning? Perhaps a single process governs the internal transmission of belief—a process that would cause us to believe (or increase our confidence in) the conclusions of both Arguments 1 and 2, given a belief (or increase in confidence) in the premise.

Any theory of reasoning has to resolve the question of how many psychological types of reasoning there are. If you take the position that there is only one relevant process, then your task is to specify the details of this process and to show how it is responsible for the different manifestations of reasoning in solving syllogisms, testing hypotheses, drawing analogies, and so on. Your choice of a unified process is likely to depend on your predispositions about cognitive architecture and belief representation; for example, the process might be a production system (Holland et al 1986; Newell & Simon 1972) or a parallel network (Rumelhart et al 1986). As an alternative to such a unified view, you could cling to the induction/deduction split and try to explicate the differences between them in terms of distinct mental activities. Or you could contend that there are more than two reasoning types—deductive, probabilistic, analogical, causal, and the lot.

Levels of Reasoning

The problem of the number of reasoning types is complicated by the level of analysis. Computers do a kind of reasoning at the circuit level, since their

[1] *Induction* has been used in several different ways in both the psychological and philosophical literature on reasoning (Barker 1965). For some authors, an inductively strong argument must have a conclusion that is more general than any of its premises. Under this definition, however, many reasonable inferences are neither deductively valid nor inductively strong (e.g., all observed canaries have been yellow; therefore, the next canary to be observed will be yellow). For this reason, we stick to the definitions in the text throughout this chapter.

AND and OR gates provide logical control for the operation of components and, ultimately, of the system as a whole. Computer languages also implement a sort of reasoning. For example, the computer language PROLOG—short for *Pro*gramming in *Log*ic—executes programming tasks by proving theorems (Clocksin & Mellish 1981; Sterling & Shapiro 1986). At yet a higher level, a user could write a PROLOG program to carry out a different type of reasoning of its own. For example, I've written a simple PROLOG program (Rips 1989a) to simulate the reasoning of subjects on liar/truth-teller puzzles such as those proposed by Smullyan (1978). Lower-level reasoning puts only modest constraints on reasoning at higher levels in such a system. PROLOG's sleek resolution theorem-proving is a far cry from the more tedious natural-deduction method that I implemented to simulate the data, and both differ from circuit-switching techniques.

By analogy, what we can say about types of human reasoning may depend on the level we are studying. Production systems provide an important case in point, since Holland et al (1986), among others, take them as the basis of induction. These systems are collections of conditional rules of the form: IF $condition_1$ AND $condition_2$ AND . . . AND $condition_k$ THEN $action_1$ AND $action_2$ AND . . . AND $action_n$. That is, when conditions 1–k are jointly satisfied (usually by matching the conditions to the contents of working memory), each of actions 1–n is performed.[2] At the level of the mechanism that applies these rules, the behavior of the system is a series of simple, deductively valid steps from the rules and the conditions to the actions. We could represent these steps by arguments of this form:

IF $condition_1$ AND $condition_2$ AND . . . AND $condition_k$ 4.
   THEN $action_1$ AND $action_2$ AND . . . AND $action_n$.
$Condition_1$ AND $condition_2$ AND . . . AND $condition_k$.
―――――――――――――――――――――――――――
$Action_1$ AND $action_2$ AND . . . AND $action_n$.

This is just an instance of the modus ponens inference schema from formal logic (albeit when a person carries out such a practical inference, the effect is to execute the actions, not merely to assert or believe their description). However, at the next level down, we can think of the rules themselves as corresponding to inferences from the conditions to the actions. At this level, we are concerned with an inference whose argument form is not that of Example 4 but that of Example 5, and which will not in general be deductively valid:

―――――――――――――――

[2]In this chapter, words in all capital letters represent connectives in some underlying system (e.g. classical logic), and their meanings may therefore differ from those of their natural language counterparts.

$$\frac{\text{Condition}_1 \text{ AND condition}_2 \text{ AND } \ldots \text{ AND condition}_k.}{\text{Action}_1 \text{ AND action}_2 \text{ AND } \ldots \text{ AND action}_n.} \qquad 5.$$

For instance, a typical rule in a production system might be *IF something is an animal and flies THEN classify it as a bird*. If we think of this as an argument along the lines of Example 5 (Something is an animal and it flies; therefore, it is a bird), then the argument has some inductive strength but is certainly not deductively valid—after all, there are flying animals that are not birds. But in the form of Example 4 *(IF something is an animal and flies THEN it is a bird; there's something that is an animal and flies; therefore, it is a bird)*, it has the deductive validity of all modus ponens arguments. Whether we should say that a system with rules like this operates deductively or inductively seems to depend on whether we are trying to describe the behavior of the rule-applier or the rule itself.

The situation becomes even more complex if we add assumptions about belief activation to the basic production system. For example, a production system like Anderson's (1983) represents beliefs (or, at least, remembered sentences) as individual units in memory, each possessing a fluctuating level of activation. Activation is passed from one unit to another along prior associative pathways. If we take this level of activation as a measure of confidence in the corresponding belief, then the system provides yet another (Loose) source of inferences. We need to be careful here, however, since it would be incorrect to suppose that *any* change in the representation of a belief is an inference. Migraines, electrical shock, and head injuries may change belief representations, but the change is not an inferential one. Similarly, we could interpret level of activation as simply a matter of the accessibility of a belief rather than a matter of its acceptability. This, in fact, seems closer to Anderson's own interpretation. Whether activating a belief counts as an inference depends on how the rest of the system responds to such shifts.[3]

Without firm knowledge about the overall structure of the cognitive system, it is hard to come to grips with the issues that separate Strict from Loose theories of reasoning. Theorists in the Loose camp, faced with an inference along the lines of Example 1, are likely to construe it as a limiting case of

---

[3]It is also true, of course, that the accessibility of a belief can become the premise of an inference. For example, in Tversky & Kahneman's (1973) availability heuristic, in Brown et al's (1985) accessibility principle, and in Collins's (1978; Gentner & Collins 1981) lack-of-knowledge inference, the accessibility of a belief about an event determines subjects' judgments of the frequency, recency, or existence of the event itself. The present point is that accessibility may produce these judgments via mediating inferences (perhaps of this sort: If an event is relatively inaccessible, then it probably happened infrequently, long ago, or not at all). A change in accessibility needn't itself be an inference.

confidence updating in which belief in the premise confers maximum confidence on belief in the conclusion. Theorists of the Strict persuasion are likely to construe Example 2 as an *enthymeme:* In argument 2, information that people bring to bear in making the inference is left implicit (e.g. the beliefs that (*a*) IF a prototype of a class possesses some property THEN the other members of the class probably also possess it, and (*b*) Trump is a prototype of the class of financiers). When we properly consider this information, the inference falls under the Strict theory (Hayes 1987).

This last dodge on the Strict theorist's part won't quite do as it stands (Osherson et al 1986), but it does begin to indicate that distinctions based on the way arguments are logically evaluated do not foreclose the Strict (or the Loose) positions. In particular, they don't automatically decide the issues listed in Table 1. We must consider each issue from a psychological perspective, in the light of what we know about the cognitive system in general and about the results of specific experiments in this area.

SPECIAL STRUCTURE VS NO SPECIAL STRUCTURE

A central difference between Strict and Loose theories is that, according to the former (but not the latter), reasoning depends on distinguished parts of belief representations. Suppose you think *Trump is rich and Koch is famous.* Your subsequent inference to *Trump is rich* is explainable, from the Strict perspective, on the basis of the fact that the original belief is represented as a complex sentence composed of two atomic sentences (i.e. *Trump is rich, Koch is famous*) linked by the logical constant AND. The cognitive procedure responsible for this inference is differentially sensitive to this structure and would *not* react in the same way if we had started with, for instance, *Trump is rich or Koch is famous* or *Max imagined that both Trump is rich and Koch is famous.* Loose theorists, however, are prone to say that, although this may be the way things work in logic proofs, there's no reason to think it's how humans draw inferences. Either there is no internal representation that conforms to this type of structure or, if there is, it is not a direct causal component in the inference.

This issue is especially salient for theories of the way people deal with deductively valid arguments. This is because proof theory in logic provides us with a paradigm of how operations sensitive to special structure (i.e. logical form) can recognize arguments of this type. No such methods exist for recognizing inductively strong arguments, for reasons discussed below; so the special-structure hypothesis is weaker for the corresponding inferences. Nevertheless, modified forms of the hypothesis are possible in nondeductive contexts and are actually a focus of debate in the area of analogical reasoning.

Is Deduction a Matter of Logical Form?

Inferences like the one about Trump from the premise about Trump and Koch, which correspond to deductively valid arguments, present the best case for special structure. First, subjects almost unanimously judge certain arguments of this type logically correct. For example, subjects generally agree about the correctness of modus ponens arguments, that is, arguments whose form matches Example 6 (e.g. Braine et al 1984; Evans 1977; Marcus & Rips 1979; Markovits 1987, 1988), unless context makes it clear that the argument is elliptical (Byrne 1989).

IF p THEN q.
<u>p.</u>   6.
q.

Braine et al (1984) have also reported perfect or near perfect agreement on the correctness of other arguments of the forms shown in Table 2.

Moreover, subjects' decisions are sometimes impervious to what the arguments happen to be about. No matter which sentences fill in for p and q in Example 6, subjects concur that the argument is logically correct (e.g. Marcus & Rips 1979; Markovits 1988). Indeed, it's not even necessary to have meaningful sentences; subjects will still judge the argument correct when arbitrary letters or numbers replace the variables (Evans 1977). This independence strongly suggests that what subjects are attending to is the structure of the argument: the fact that the first premise is a conditional, the second premise is the antecedent of the conditional, and the conclusion its consequent.

However, subjects' decisions sometimes do seem to depend on more than the logical form of the problem. The question of exactly when this happens, though, is complicated by the fact that what counts as logical form depends on the logic you are dealing with: Logics differ in which aspects of a sentence they formalize as logical constants. In predicate logic, for example, the constants are usually a small set of sentential connectives (e.g. AND, OR, IF . . . THEN, NOT) and one or two quantifiers (FOR ALL, FOR SOME); the rest of the language (e.g. predicates and terms) has no special role to play in determining which arguments are deductively correct. But in modal logics, the stock of logical constants can include sentence modifiers such as IT IS NECESSARY THAT p/IT IS POSSIBLE THAT p (e.g. Hughes & Cresswell 1968), x KNOWS THAT p/x BELIEVES THAT p (e.g. Hintikka, 1962), IT IS OBLIGATORY THAT p/IT IS PERMITTED THAT p (e.g. Føllesdal & Hilpinen 1971; Lewis 1974), IT WILL BE THE CASE THAT p/IT WAS THE CASE THAT p (e.g. Rescher & Urquhart 1971), p CAUSES q (e.g. Lewis 1973), and others.

Table 2 Some arguments producing 97% or greater agreement in Braine et al (1984)

1.	IF p THEN q	5.	IF p OR q THEN r
	p		p
	q		r
2.	p	6.	p OR q
	q		IF p THEN r
	p AND q		IF q THEN r
			r
3.	p AND q	7.	p OR q
	p		IF p THEN r
			IF q THEN s
			r OR s
4.	NOT NOT p	8.	p OR q
	p		NOT p
			q

This point is an important one, and overlooking it has led to some confusion in the literature. For example, Cheng & Holyoak (1985) and Cheng et al (1986) propose that people often reason using "pragmatic reasoning schemas," which are abstract rules that deal with "classes of goals and types of relationships" (Cheng et al 1986:294). These schemas are explicitly contrasted with "syntactic logical rules," which are rules sensitive to logical form. However, the pragmatic schemas that Cheng and her colleagues discuss are all based on relations of permission, obligation, or causality—for example, the fact that the sentence *If action A is to be taken, then precondition B must be satisfied* implies that *If precondition B is not satisfied then Action A must not be taken*. Relationships like these can be expressed in terms of modal operators in the types of logic discussed by Lewis (1974) and others. Thus, the evidence so far adduced for "pragmatic schemas" does not challenge the idea that deduction occurs via "syntactic" or special structure. Indeed, it is remarkable that the very relationships (permission, obligation, and causality) that are supposed to constitute "pragmatic schemas" are ones for which modal logics are already available.

Other findings, though, seem to go beyond what the special-structure hypothesis can explain, even when it is equipped with fancy modal operators. For example, a line of research begun by Janis & Frick (1943) suggests that subjects' preexperimental belief in the conclusion of an argument sometimes influences their judgments of its logical correctness. Recent experiments tend to confirm this "belief-bias" effect, both in tasks where subjects must evaluate complete arguments (Evans et al 1983; Markovits & Nantel 1989; Revlin et al

1980) and in tasks where they must supply a conclusion that follows from stated premises (Markovits & Nantel 1989; Oakhill & Johnson-Laird 1985).[4] For example, Markovits & Nantel found that subjects were more apt to accept Argument 7 than Argument 8 as logically correct, and they were more likely to produce the conclusion in Argument 7 than the conclusion in Argument 8 in response to their respective premises:

All things that have a motor need oil.
Automobiles need oil.   7.
Automobiles have motors.

All things that have a motor need oil.
Opprobines need oil.   8.
Opprobines have motors.

Arguments 7 and 8 differ simply by substitution of the nonsense word *opprobines* for *automobiles*. Thus, the logical structure of these arguments is presumably the same, and a special structure hypothesis based on logical form cannot explain the differences in response.

Evidence for a belief bias, however, does not necessarily contradict the special-structure hypothesis. Subjects' responses in experiments like these have been found to be the product of many mental operations other than reasoning; thus, it is possible that reasoning proceeds by way of special structure and that belief bias affects these other operations. One possible scenario, for example, is that subjects use the believability of the conclusion as a quick check on their answer, much as one might use the overall plausibility of an arithmetic result as a check on the accuracy of a lengthy computation. If the conclusion subjects derive is implausible, they may be more willing to reject the argument as invalid than if they have no pre-conceived idea about it. Similarly, if they can derive no conclusion, but the argument provides a plausible one (as in Example 7) or easily suggests one, they may be more willing to accept the argument, blaming their own reasoning for the inability to figure out how it follows. In other words, the plausibility of the conclusion may act as a kind of filter for the responses subjects allow themselves to give (Oakhill et al 1989).

Another idea along the same lines is that subjects may conflate different standards for goodness of an argument. In most cases of everyday argumenta-

---

[4]Evidence for belief-bias in production is somewhat problematic. Although Oakhill & Johnson-Laird found such an effect, it was limited to cases where the likely conclusion was "definitionally false" (e.g. *Some of the actresses are not women*). Potential conclusions that were empirically false (e.g. *Some of the athletes are not healthy*) yielded no effect or a reversed effect.

tion—for example, debates about political or personal policies—we care not only about the soundness of the reasoning, but also about the truth of our conclusion. Implausible conclusions in these situations suggest that something has gone wrong, although at first we may not know where the trouble lies. In most experiments on belief bias subjects are instructed to assume that the premises are true and to decide what "follows logically" from them. But this instruction may be hard to obey for subjects who have no formal training on validity and provability (as is invariably the case in experiments of this sort). Explanations of this kind go back to Henle (1962), but the present point is not that subjects never make mistakes in reasoning; it's simply that subjects may be using special structure in processing arguments like 7 and 8 and yet produce evidence of belief bias. Since the special-structure hypothesis is a convenient way to account for the universality of inferences like those in Table 2, it is tempting to find other explanations for belief bias and related effects.

Is Analogical Reasoning a Matter of Special Structure?

Goodman's (1955) New Riddle of Induction suggests that the special-structure hypothesis is inapplicable to inductively strong arguments. Let *grue* be the color of an object at time *t* if and only if the object is green and *t* is before the beginning of the year 2000 or the object is blue and *t* is on or after the beginning of 2000. Then arguments 9 and 10 have the same logical form (and indeed have the same high degree of empirical support for their premise):

All emeralds so far observed have been green.	9.
The first emerald to be observed after the beginning of 2000 will be green.	

All emeralds so far observed have been grue.	10.
The first emerald to be observed after the beginning of 2000 will be grue.	

However, Argument 9 is inductively strong whereas Argument 10 is not, since 9 predicts the first emerald of 2000 to be green while 10 predicts it to be blue. Hence, inductive strength can't be entirely a matter of logical form. (For psychological investigations of inferences with concepts like grue, see Sternberg 1982; Tetewsky & Sternberg 1986.) Along much the same lines, Osherson et al (1986) point out the deficiencies of various attempts to reduce the intuitive strength of an inductive argument to the deductive validity of a related argument.

But although inductive strength can't be entirely a matter of logical form, there may nevertheless be a more limited role that special structure can play. For example, most current investigators agree that analogical reasoning depends on the underlying structure of the analogy's two domains. Although people may notice analogs partly on the basis of their superficial properties, the use or interpretation of the analogy is also a function of deeper factors (Holyoak & Koh 1987; Keane 1987; Novick 1988; Reed 1987; Ross 1987). Gentner and her colleagues (1983; Gentner & Clement 1988; Gentner & Toupin 1986) have advanced a strong form of this idea in claiming that the analogy's interpretation depends on the specifically relational structure of the domains. According to this account, an analogy such as *A battery is like a reservoir* turns on two-place or multi-place predicates in the mental representation of reservoirs [e.g. $Store(x,y)$, $Release(x,y)$] that also describe batteries. One-place predicates [e.g. $Damp(x)$] don't play a part in the interpretation. Further, analogies favor those multiple-place predicates that are themselves part of higher-order relations [e.g., $Cause(Release(x,y)$, $Flow(y,z))$]. Gentner argues that interpreting analogies is thus a purely structural matter, depending only on the shape of the mental representations—the *arity* (the presence of relations rather than one-place predicates) and the *order* (the depth or level of nesting) of the predicates—and not on what those predicates denote.

Several researchers (e.g. Holyoak 1985; Kedar-Cabelli 1988) have attacked Gentner's theory on the grounds that the predicates' arity and order provide neither necessary nor sufficient constraints on what's part of an analogy's interpretation. The problem can be illustrated with an example from Gentner & Toupin (1986). These investigators consider a case in which people who have no previous knowledge of atomic structure learn the analogy *The atom is like the solar system*. According to Gentner & Toupin, a systematic representation of the solar system like graph *a* in Figure 1 is more likely to enable correct transfer of the relational structure to a representation of an atom than is a less-systematic representation, like graph *b*.[5] The trouble is that the unsystematic character of Structure 1*b* doesn't depend solely on the arity or order of its relations. To see this, note that we can redraw 1*b* as 1*c* so that its relational structure is now isomorphic with that of 1*a*. All that's required is a switch from a trinary to a binary AND (as is, in fact, more usual in logic). This change surely doesn't alter the unsystematic character of 1*b*: 1*c* is still less systematic than 1*a*. But if that is so, then systematicity and, presumably, analogical transfer, can't be entirely a matter of the arity and order of relations in a representation.

[5]The second figure incorporates a small correction to Gentner & Toupin's drawing. In the original figure corresponding to 1*b*, the arguments of *revolves around* are reversed (D. Gentner, personal communication).

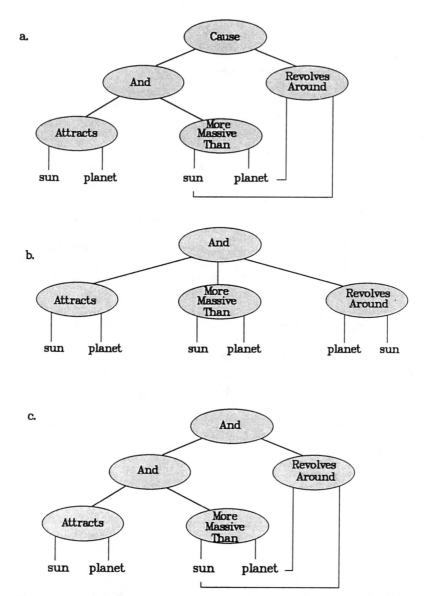

Figure 1   Possible representations of the solar system: (*a*) a systematic representation, (*b*) an unsystematic representation, and (*c*) an unsystematic representation with relational structure equivalent to that of *a*. Graphs *a* and *b* after Gentner & Toupin (1986).

Notice, though, that this example does not challenge the idea that analogical reasoning depends on some type of special structure. It's possible to maintain that what's important for analogical transfer is not only the relations' arity and order, but the type of connective–CAUSE vs AND in the case of Figure 1. In deductive reasoning, an inference's correctness usually turns on differences between connectives; for example, premises of the form *p* CAUSES *q* lend themselves to different conclusions than premises of the form *p AND q*. It wouldn't be surprising if analogical inference is also sensitive to these variations. And as we've discussed in the preceding section, Strict theorists can accept operators like CAUSE without sacrificing the idea of special structure. In later work, Gentner (Gentner & Clement 1988) affirms the need for additional constraints of this sort.

The more interesting question about analogical arguments—like the parallel question about deductive arguments—is whether their intuitive strength depends on more than what we can formalize in terms of special structure. In most of the examples that appear in the literature, analogical reasoning is a straightforward matter because the causal (or other important) relations of the source domain are known in advance, as in the case of Figure 1*a*. But we often draw analogies in situations where the causal relations are obscure or where there are several possible causal scenarios. For instance, we may use the results of an earlier study to make analogous predictions about the outcome of a planned experiment. In this case the causal workings of the first study may be unclear (as they typically are at the start of a research program), and hence we may have trouble deciding which properties of the old study we should project to the new one. We are thus in exactly the same position as we were with respect to the green/grue arguments in Examples 9 and 10. We have to appeal to something other than special causal structure in order to determine which of the possible inter-experiment analogies is the best one.

RULE VS INSTANCE: HOW CONCRETE IS REASONING?

Once we grant the idea that inferencing is sensitive to special structure, then we can look at inferences schematically, as examples of a framework in which special structure is constant and the rest is variable. For example, we can view the transition from *Trump is rich and Koch is famous* to *Trump is rich* as an example of the schema (sometimes called AND Elimination in logic textbooks) which appears as item 3 in Table 2. In this schema, AND is a logical constant and the variables *p* and *q* can be replaced by any sentences whatever. It is then a very short step to the proposal that the cognitive system carries out its inferences by applying schemas like this to mental sentences that instantiate them. If we believe *Trump is rich and Koch is famous*, we can deduce *Trump is rich* by applying an inference rule corresponding to the schematic argument.

This move seems obvious in the case of deductively correct inferences such as this example, but it may also work in the case of inductively strong ones. Even for analogical reasoning—where you might suppose that the train of thought proceeds directly from one concrete analog to the other—it is possible that schemas play a role. We begin with one of the analogs, form a schema by abstracting over its less important elements, and then apply the schema to the second analog in order to complete the analogy (see Gick & Holyoak 1983).

Theorists of the Loose view, of course, turn up their noses at talk of abstract rules and schemas. The Loose way to reason relies solely on concrete instances. They argue that the reasoning problem at hand may be similar enough to traces of earlier ones that we can solve it directly in terms of those prior cases. Another possibility is that we can solve the problem by tinkering with our representation of the problem itself. The idea of reasoning by instance is similar to what goes under the name of *exemplar models* in research on categorization (e.g. Hintzman 1986; Jacoby & Brooks 1984; Medin & Schaffer 1978; Nosofsky 1986). Although exploring categorization would take us too far afield, it's worth noticing that category decisions (e.g. Is this thing an example of a zebra?) pose an inductive problem, since they usually require us to select a category in the absence of definitive information. Exemplar models are therefore proposals about how we perform certain sorts of inductively strong inferences in the absence of abstract rules or schemas, and we can view the debate over abstractness in categorization as continuous with the corresponding debate in reasoning (see Smith 1989 for an elaboration of this point).

Rule vs Instance in Deduction

In the late 1970s and early 1980s, a number of cognitive psychologists proposed accounts of deduction based on systems of inference rules (Braine 1978; Johnson-Laird 1975; Osherson 1974–1976; Rips 1983). The idea was that even people with no formal training in logic have an intuitive sense of what it means for one sentence to follow from another in a deductively valid way. To capture this notion, these theorists assumed that there are mental inference rules, similar to those in the formal Natural Deduction systems often found in introductory logic texts (e.g. Fitch 1952; Suppes 1957). Each rule corresponds to an elementary inference schema, like the ones in Table 2; but by chaining these elementary inferences together, reasoners can create a mental proof or derivation for more complex problems. The inference rules construct the proof by monitoring the contents of working memory, chaining forward from the given information (premises), and chaining backward from the goal (conclusion). Monitoring both the givens and the goal keeps the rules from producing inferences that are blatantly irrelevant to the problem. These models explain reasoning failures on the part of subjects in terms of capacity limits on working memory, retrieval difficulties in applying the rules, and misinterpretations of the problems, among other factors.

These proposals drastically increase the scope of psychological reasoning theories. Instead of merely documenting biases in the way people evaluate Aristotelian syllogisms, these theories give an explanatory account of an unbounded set of possible inference problems (i.e. the theorems that can be produced by combining the inference rules). Of course these are models of *psychological* processes: They attempt to explain not only people's successes in reasoning but also the difficulties they have, as seen in verbal protocols, reactions times, or percentages of correct response (Braine et al 1984; Osherson 1974–1976; Rips 1983, 1989a; Rips & Conrad 1983). The main contribution of these theories, however, is to provide an account of how deductively correct reasoning is possible.

INSTANCE-BASED MODELS AND THE SELECTION TASK   The factor that makes this approach powerful—the abstract rule base—is also the factor that has provoked the most criticism. We've already seen that subjects' performance is sensitive to components that the rules don't capture (subjects' belief in the conclusion, for example). Even bigger effects appear in studies of Wason's (1966) *selection task*. In the typical version of this task, subjects view four cards, each of which is supposed to have a letter on one side and a number on the other. The face-up sides of the cards might display the characters E, K, 4, and 7; the face-down sides are, of course, invisible to the subjects. Subjects are given a rule such as *If there's a vowel on one side, there's an even number on the other,* and they are asked to select all of the cards (and only those cards) that have to be turned over to determine whether the rule is true or false for the four target cards. Performance on this version of the task is usually very poor. The usual finding is that less than 20% of subjects come up with the correct (E and 7) answer (Wason & Johnson-Laird 1972; Evans 1982). Recent evidence shows that neither instruction on material conditionals (Cheng et al 1986) nor graduate training in natural science improves subjects' performance (Griggs & Ransdell 1986; Jackson & Griggs 1988; Lehman et al 1988; Nisbett et al 1987). However, explaining the correct answer to an initial problem like the one above sometimes improves later solutions (Klaczynski et al 1989).

Some analogs of the problem, though, produce massive improvement in selection-task scores. For example, if the rule is phrased in terms of police checking a drinking regulation *(If a person is drinking beer, then the person must be over 19)* and the cards represent a person's age (15, 25) and the beverage he or she is drinking (coca-cola, beer), then performance can run as high as 70% correct (Griggs & Cox 1982; Pollard & Evans 1987). Similarly, Cheng & Holyoak (1985; Cheng et al 1986) report improvement when the problem is phrased in terms of authorities checking rules that emphasize permission or obligation (e.g. *If one is to take action 'A,' then one must first satisfy precondition 'P'*). These reports are replicable, but seem to depend in part on subtle features of the problem statement. For example, Pollard & Evans (1987) report little facilitation when the problem is phrased in terms of secret police checking a regulation about identity cards *(If there is a B on a card, then there is a number over 18 on it)*. In unpublished work, Jackson and Griggs find no facilitation on the same action-precondition rule quoted above if subjects are not told to imagine that they are authorities checking the rule, but are merely told to decide which of the cards they need to turn over in order to find out whether the regulation is being followed.

One way to view these selection-task results is to suppose that successes are due, not to reasoning by abstract rule, but to reasoning by analogy to a remembered instance (Griggs 1983). If we already know that rule violators are underage people and beer drinkers (or know a closely analogous situation), then we can read the correct answer directly from this previous experience. Similarly, a rule phrased in terms of necessary preconditions may remind us of a prior situation in which violators were those who had taken the action and had not satisfied the preconditions. Of course, we must still account for the reminding or analogizing process (see below), but the point is that the answer to the selection problem comes from the analog, not from more abstract information.

Instance-based analogical theories of this sort seem a plausible explanation of content effects in the selection task (although they need to be fleshed out to account for some of the instabilities mentioned earlier). We must be careful, however, in generalizing these theories beyond the limits of the selection task itself. In particular, such theories don't provide any insight into the near universality of the inferences cataloged in Table 2, which rule-based theories were designed to explain. It's absurd to assume, for example, that our confidence in the inference from p *AND* q to p depends on an analogy to a specific instance that we remember, since, as we've already noted, subjects will usually assent to this inference no matter what we substitute for p and q. Analogy to exemplars may supplement abstract rules, especially in situations where it's easier to retrieve a related exemplar than to solve the problem anew. But analogy can't supplant these rules without making a mystery of our ability to recognize inferences about previously unknown subject matter. An exclusive focus on modus ponens, AND elimination, and similar rules may lead to a inflated view of human reasoning; but an exclusive focus on the selection task leads to a seriously restricted one.

INSTANCES IN MENTAL MODELS   If the instances that we use for reasoning are limited to those we have actually encountered, then instance-based theories are far too weak to deal with the deductively correct inferences that people recognize. Hence, one way to make an instance theory more powerful is to have it generate instances for novel situations. This is the line that Johnson-Laird (1983) pursues in proposing that people reason by means of "mental models." A mental model in his sense is a kind of diagrammatic representation of a specific situation. So if we are told, for example, that all of the green blocks are round, we could represent this in an array of the following sort, in which the g's represent individual green blocks and the r's round blocks:

$$g_1 = r_1$$
$$g_2 = r_2$$
$$0r_3$$

11.

The equal sign in this model indicates that the tokens on either side denote the same instance, and the 0 means that the extra round block may or may not exist. If we are also told that none of the big blocks are green, we can add this new information to our array, producing this combined model:

$$b_1$$
$$b_2$$
$$\overline{}$$
$$g_1 = r_1$$
$$g_2 = r_2$$
$$0r_3$$

12.

According to Johnson-Laird's theory, when we try to draw deductively correct conclusions from premises like these, we do so by forming a combined model like the one above and then generating alternative models in which the premises continue to hold but which support different conclusions. For example, the above premises are also consistent with the following two alternatives:

$$b_1 \qquad\qquad\qquad b_1 \quad 0r_4$$
$$b_2 \quad 0r_3 \qquad\qquad b_2 \quad 0r_3$$
$$\overline{} \qquad\qquad\qquad \overline{}$$
$$g_1 = r_1 \qquad\qquad g_1 = r_1$$
$$g_2 = r_2 \qquad\qquad g_2 = r_2$$

13.

Valid conclusions are ones that hold in all models of the premises. For example, the conclusion *Some of the round blocks are not big* is true in all of the alternative models in Examples 12 and 13 and is a valid conclusion. The theory predicts that the more mental models a given set of premises has, the more difficult subjects should find the problem of producing a conclusion.[6] Johnson-Laird & Bara (1984) and Johnson-Laird et al (1986) present evidence supporting this prediction for reasoning with Aristotelian syllogisms by both adults and 9–12 year olds. The theory has met with more mixed results in direct comparisons with the inference-rule approach (Galotti et al 1986). Moreover, encouraging subjects to produce external models with actual tokens does not appear to facilitate reasoning (Lee & Oakhill 1984). See Ford (1985), Macnamara (1986), and Rips (1986) for criticisms of this theory.

Obviously, the mental-model theory presupposes cognitive routines or procedures for translating premises into models, combining models, permuting them to form alternatives, testing the models for consistency with the premises, and reading possible conclusions from them. From our current perspective, what's important about these routines is their abstractness. Although Johnson-Laird (1983) insists that the routines are not logical rules, it is nevertheless the case that they must be general enough to treat any two tokens connected by "=" as the same individual, to treat tokens on the opposite sides of the horizontal line in Examples 12 and 13 as different individuals, and so on. In other words, they must enjoy much the same generality as the rules in predicate calculus with identity, even if they operate in a different mode. This generality is reflected in another fact about mental models: They seem no better off than standard logical rules in accounting for content effects in the selection task.

Where deductively correct arguments are concerned, reasoning theories suffer when they are chained to concrete instances. Remembered instances may serve a useful function for reasoners; indeed, they may provide exactly the same kind of reasonableness check that we discussed earlier in connection with belief bias. They also give a convincing account of facilitation in the selection task. However, they are simply too limited to explain novel inferences about unfamiliar domains, even when supplemented by an analogizing mechanism. There seems nothing analogous about AND Elimination arguments (item 3 in Table 2) when phrased in terms of *gax's* and *riv's* and when phrased in terms of sentences about Trump and Koch, except of course the form of the arguments themselves. This suggests ascent to the level of abstract routines, whether of the inference-rule or model-manipulating variety.

The Abstractness of Induction and Analogy

In the previous section, we considered the possibility that people reason about deductively correct arguments using an analogy to some concrete exemplar.

---

[6]We can recast this prediction in a way that is less theory bound: The greater the number of syllogistic conclusions (i.e. ones of the form *ALL p ARE q, SOME p ARE q, NO p ARE q*, or *SOME p ARE NOT q*) that are consistent with the premises (i.e. do not contradict the premises), the more difficult the syllogism will be. When subjects produce an incorrect conclusion, it is likely to be drawn from this set of consistent ones.

This was supposed to be a way of salvaging the idea—a kind of psychologized nominalism—that deduction can proceed without mental representations of an abstract sort. But of course we can also ask about the abstractness of the analogical process itself. It may seem self-evident that analogical reasoning must proceed in an instance-to-instance manner rather than by way of abstraction and rules, but interestingly the evidence suggests that this is not always true.

ABSTRACT MEDIATORS IN INDUCTION AND ANALOGY   We've already noted that analogy is a type of inductive inference that transfers properties from one domain to another and in which the two domains are at about the same level of specificity. The paradigm of concern here is one in which we know that a property G holds of some instance α and we wish to decide whether it also holds of another instance β. In general, though, properties are not transferable in this way. For one thing, G must be a "projectible" property like green (and unlike grue). For another, we need more information about α and β, since, for example, knowing that one object is green doesn't justify the assumption that an arbitrary second object is also green. Analogies seem justified when we know that both α and β share a further property or set of properties H; in other words, we know that $G(\alpha)$, $H(\alpha)$, and $H(\beta)$, and the inference is of the following form (Davies 1988):

$$\frac{\begin{array}{l} G(\alpha) \\ H(\alpha) \ \& \ H(\beta) \end{array}}{G(\beta)} \qquad \qquad 14.$$

But even these qualifications aren't enough, since not any H will do. The fact that α is a green house$[G(\alpha) \ \& \ H(\alpha)]$ and that β is a house $[H(\beta)]$ doesn't persuade us that β is green $[G(\beta)]$. In order to get a strong inductive inference on the basis of instance properties alone, there must be additional constraints on H.

At this point theorists of the Loose persuasion have a card to play. Suppose that H in Example 14 represents a collection of properties that we know apply to both α and β. Then one possibility is that the strength of Example 14 depends on the similarity between α and β as determined by these properties. (If we like, we could also factor non-overlapping properties into the similarity computation à la Tversky 1977.) The more similar α and β, the stronger the inference should be. Unfortunately, though, this idea still doesn't work very well. Even if α and β are otherwise identical Queen Ann houses on the same block, the inference just doesn't seem very strong that one is green if the other one is; houses aren't the sort of things that pass along their color with their other properties (see Osherson et al 1986 for related criticism).

Inductions of this sort often depend on knowing something about the category or kind that α and β belong to and about the relation of this category to the property, G, that we wish to project. If we know, for example, that H is (the property of being) a particular type of mineral, then we might be more apt to infer that sample β of this mineral is green if sample α is. This means that the raw similarity between instances will not be sufficient to determine inductive strength [unless, of course, category membership is the dominant factor in the similarity computation, as in Shepard (1987) or by way of Tversky's (1977) "diagnosticity principle"]. Another way to say this is that we must have information about the variability (or, better, co-variability) of G across H (Nisbett et al 1983), although this statistical way of putting the matter is silent about why these induction-supporting relations hold in some kind-property pairs (e.g. minerals and colors) but not others (houses and colors). There is now ample evidence that both adults (Rips 1975; Osherson et al 1989) and children (Carey 1985; Gelman 1988; Gelman & Markman 1986) use category information when generalizing a property from one instance to another.

We reach much the same conclusion about the insufficiency of instances from experiments on problem solving by analogy. Many recent theories in this domain assume that transfer occurs, not by direct mapping from one analog to another, but by instantiating an abstract structure that applies to both (e.g. Gentner 1983; Greiner 1988; Holyoak 1985). Thus, even those inductive inferences that seem most conducive to an instance-based model—inferences transferring a property from one instance to another—may sometimes require knowledge of subsuming categories or schemata. Those who hold the Loose view can still take refuge in the idea that people form the relevant abstractions on the fly through parallel computation rather than storing them in a permanent way (e.g. Hintzman 1986; Kahneman & Miller 1986); but the abstractions must be there at some point in order to explain the data.

INDUCTION BY RULE?   Although reasoning about inductively strong arguments may employ higher-level categories or schemata, it is much less obvious that it also uses rules. In the case of deduction, rules suggest themselves when we abstract over information that is not part of the inference's special structure, as in Table 2. But as we have noticed earlier, induction is less dependent on special structure, and as a result, the brief for rules is less compelling. Nevertheless, researchers who have attempted computational theories of induction have used rules to capture important classes of inferences.

For example, Collins & Michalski (1989) suggest a number of rules for plausible inferences. In their notation, $d(a)$ denotes (roughly speaking) the value of attribute d of object a, $SPEC(A)$ the subordinate instances (specializations) of category A, and $SIM(a)$ in $CX(A, D(A))$ instances similar to a in the context of A and attribute D. The sign "$\leftrightarrow$" means that there is a functional dependency between the connected values. In these terms, one of Collins & Michalski's rules is expressed this way:

$$d(a) = r: \gamma_1, \phi, \mu_a \qquad\qquad 15.$$
$$a' = SIM(a) \text{ in } CX(A, D(A)):\sigma, \gamma_2$$
$$D(A) \longleftrightarrow d(A): \alpha, \gamma_3$$
$$\underline{a, a' = SPEC(A): \gamma_4, \gamma_5}$$
$$d(a') = r: \gamma = f(\gamma_1, \phi, \mu_a, \sigma, \gamma_2, \alpha, \gamma_3, \gamma_4, \gamma_5)$$

The parameters at the right of each sentence (after the colon) denote factors that affect the subjective strength of the inference; the strength itself is given by the function shown in the conclusion. As a specific example, we might have:

color(emeralds-before-2000) = green: γ_1, ϕ, μ_a 16.
emeralds-after-2000 = SIM(emeralds-before-2000) in CX(emeralds,
                chemistry(emeralds)): σ, γ_2
chemistry(emeralds) $\longleftrightarrow$ color(emeralds): α, γ_3
emeralds-before-2000, emeralds-after-2000 = $SPEC$(emeralds): γ_4, γ_5

color(emeralds-after-2000) = green: $\gamma = f(\gamma_1, \phi, \mu_a, \sigma, \gamma_2, \alpha, \gamma_3, \gamma_4, \gamma_5)$

In English, if emeralds observed before 2000 are green, if emeralds observed after 2000 are similar to them with respect to their chemical structure, if the chemical structure of emeralds determines their color, and if emeralds before and after 2000 are indeed varieties of emeralds, then the color of emeralds after 2000 will also be green. This inference won't be certain, of course. It will be *nonmonotonic* (McDermott & Doyle 1980) or *defeasible* (Pollock 1987) in that further information may cause us to reject the conclusion or may undercut the relation of the conclusion to the premises. According to Collins & Michalski, the certainty of Example 16 is a positive function of the certainty of the first premise (γ_1), the proportion of emeralds observed before 2000 that are green (ϕ), and the proportion of emerald types that are green (μ_a), among other parameters listed above.

Rules like Example 15 seem reasonable summaries of common inference patterns, but they admit too many unwarranted inferences. For instance, Example 15 not only licenses the conclusion that emeralds observed after 2000 will be green, but also that the same emeralds will be grue. The only change that we need to make is substitution of *grue* for *green* in the first premise and conclusion of Example 16.

Of course, this doesn't mean that a rule-based approach to induction is necessarily wrong. The New Riddle of Induction is a notoriously difficult one. It does suggest, however, that the rules in such an approach will have to specify their predicates more explicitly. We might be able to frame a rule about the probable color of unobserved emeralds, but such a rule may have to include predicates like *green* and *emerald* directly in order to avoid counterexamples such as the one just considered. Specific rules of this sort have been proposed in many cognitive and AI systems for inductive inference (e.g. Cohen 1985; Holland et al 1986). But to achieve any kind of generality, these systems would seem to require an enormously large number of rules. Theorists of the Loose view may see an opportunity here, since they might legitimately question the advantage of proliferating rules in this way.

CONTINUOUS INFERENCE

Let's consider a Looser alternative to the Strict rule-based approach of the previous section. The best known idea along these lines is to suppose that each of our beliefs is associated with some level of confidence, a level that we can represent as a real number between 0 and 1. Suppose, too, that there are relations between beliefs that tell us the confidence we would attach to $Belief_i$ in the event that $Belief_j$ were true. As we learn new facts—for example, that $Belief_j$ is true—we use these relations to readjust the confidence profile over all our beliefs, replacing the old levels with the ones specified in the relations. Thus, we don't have individual rules like Examples 15 or 16 for all of the inductive inferences we make; all we need are prior confidence levels and conditional confidence relations. Under certain idealizations, this story turns into Bayesianism, in which we can interpret the confidence levels as probabilities and the relations as conditional probabilities (e.g. Jeffrey 1983). Experiments by Tversky, Kahneman, and others make it seem likely that these idealizations fail for many situations in which people estimate probabilities (e.g. Tversky & Kahneman 1983) or judge the value of gambles (Kahneman & Tversky 1979). But even if we don't buy the full Bayesian story for human inference, it may be valuable to think in terms of confidence or degrees of belief. The same advantages and disadvantages ought to accrue to other updating schemes, including parallel constraint-satisfaction.

Some Advantages

An inductive inference schema such as Example 15 produces conclusions that don't follow in a strong way from the premises. Even if we ignore green/grue cases, we could presumably find ways to instantiate Example 15 for any pair of objects (or we could chain together several instantiations of Example 15 in order to link the pair). Of course, the schema gives us a way of calculating the strength of the inference, and this strength will presumably turn out to be low for arbitrary objects. But, at first glance, this suggests that what's really doing the work in Example 15 are the parameters (γ_1, ϕ, μ_a, etc), not the form of the schema. Why not acknowledge this explicitly and eliminate rules in favor of conditional adjustments to degrees of belief? It does no harm to list as premises the sentences that caused the adjustment in a given case; however, there may be a large number of ways in which a change in one belief or set of beliefs can affect others. The possibility of capturing all of them by means of explicit rules may be remote. As the number of rules approaches the number of conditional relations between belief pairs, there seems less and less point to a rule-based approach.

Moreover, some of the snags for the Strict approach that we found in previous sections may have natural solutions within a confidence-level framework. Chapman & Chapman (1959) may have been the first to point out that incorrect responses in experiments on deductive reasoning may be the result of probabilistic inferences that would be quite rational in other circumstances. Chapman & Chapman were concerned with the case of Aristotelian syllogisms, but a similar probabilistic analysis has been offered by Haviland (1974) for reasoning with conditional sentences. It's not easy for experts to say which inferences are "logically correct" and which aren't, given the choice of logical vocabulary that we noticed earlier (Harman 1986); so why should we expect our subjects to do any better when we ask them whether a conclusion "logically follows"? Maybe they take the instructions to mean that a conclusion follows if it is based on any reasonably strong argument.

As an example of how the probabilistic approach works, take the case of belief bias. Let's suppose the subjects in these experiments evaluate the stimulus arguments not in terms of deductive soundness but in terms of the extent to which the premises increase confidence in the conclusion. The higher the confidence in the conclusion, given the premises, the better the inference should seem. We can abbreviate this relation as $B(C|P)$, where C is the conclusion and P is the conjunction of the premises. If B were a probability function, this quantity would depend on $B(C)$, since according to Bayes' Theorem $B(C|P) = [B(P|C)\ B(C)]\ /\ B(P)$. That is, the higher the prior probability of the conclusion, the higher the conditional probability of the conclusion, given the premises. Even if B isn't a bona fide probability function, we might at least expect $B(C|P)$ to increase with $B(C)$. But this means that confidence in the conclusion should enhance the perceived goodness of the argument on the above assumptions, and this is exactly what the belief-bias phenomenon amounts to (see also Evans et al 1985).[7]

What about evidence from the selection task? One way to account for the data along the Loose lines we're pursuing is to assimilate the task to more ordinary cases of rule testing. Let's suppose that we're investigating the

---

[7]One possible objection is that people sometimes fail to take base-rates like $B(C)$ into account when making probability judgments (e.g. Kahneman & Tversky 1973). Whether they do or not seems to depend on whether they perceive the base-rate as having some causal influence on the judged outcome (Tversky & Kahneman 1982). However, I am not here advocating the probabilistic account as a serious explanation of belief bias, but instead illustrating how a Loose approach to the issue might proceed.

hypothesis or rule that a certain mineral V always contains a compound of type E. In such a situation, it usually makes more sense to find samples of V and check them for E than to examine non-E compounds to see whether any of them appears in V. This is true even though both procedures could result in disproof of the rule. (Either procedure could in principle turn up a case in which V contained no E compounds.) The reason for this stems from the fact that there are ordinarily many more samples of non-E than V. Thus, if the rule happens to be false, it will take us fewer trials to find a disconfirming (V and non-E) case. Suppose the rule is wrong and let p be the proportion of V and E samples, q the proportion of V and non-E samples, and s the proportion of non-V and non-E samples. Then the probability of finding a disconfirming instance given the selection of a V sample is $q/(p + q)$, whereas the probability of disconfirmation given the selection of a non-E sample is $q/(s + q)$. Since p is usually much lower than s, the first ratio is larger and V sampling is more efficient. A very similar argument can be given in terms of our degree-of-belief function B, and it is in fact identical to Bayesian solutions to the so-called paradox of confirmation (e.g. Horwich 1982, Ch. 3).[8]

If subjects bring to bear their usual hypothesis-testing strategies in the selection task, then we might expect to see the same sorts of preference. When the rule is *If there's a vowel on one side then there's an even number on the other,* they might prefer to test by choosing the vowel rather than the non-even number, on an analogy with choosing the V samples over the non-E

---

[8]We would like to set up our test so that the evidence distinguishes the possibility that the rule is true from the possibility that it is false. In terms of our B function, we would like the confidence that the rule is true given the test to differ as much as possible from our confidence that the rule is false given the same test. Let D be the ratio $B(\text{rule is true} \mid \text{test}) / B(\text{rule is false} \mid \text{test})$. Discriminating tests will evidently be ones in which $D \neq 1$, and test x will be more discriminating than test y if $|D_{\text{test }x} - 1| > |D_{\text{test }y} - 1|$. If B is a probability function, Bayes' Theorem gives us:

$$D = \frac{B(\text{test} \mid \text{rule true})}{B(\text{test} \mid \text{rule false})} \cdot \frac{B(\text{rule true})}{B(\text{rule false})}$$

We can suppose that a priori the rule is no more likely to be true than false; so D will depend on just the first term in the above expression. Now consider the tests of selecting a sample of V versus a sample of non-E, and suppose as before that our confidence of sampling the various types of minerals are $B(V \& E) = p$, $B(V \& \text{non-}E) = q$, and $B(\text{non-}V \& \text{non-}E) = s$ if the rule is false. If we select a sample of V and find non-E or if we select a sample of non-E and find V, then both tests will be equally discriminating (D will be 0 since such a finding is impossible if the rule is true). On the other hand, what if we select a V sample and turn up E? Then $D = 1 / [p/(p + q)]$ $= 1 + (q/p)$. By contrast, if we select a non-E sample and find non-V, then $D = 1/[s/(s + q)] = 1$ $+ (q/s)$. Under the same assumption that $p < s$, the first test is more discriminating than the second; hence we should prefer the V test to the non-E test. Notice that this explanation does not assume that subjects are suffering from a bias to confirm rather than disconfirm the rule in question. Although some subjects do possess a confirmation bias, not all do (Beattie & Baron 1988).

ones in the example above. Of course, this would not explain why many subjects also choose the card with the even number, but perhaps this is a result of subjects' interpreting the rule as a biconditional—(IF Vowel THEN Even) AND (IF Even THEN Vowel)—and applying the same strategy. We might also expect these effects to go away if subjects are more familiar with the priors in the situation described by the rule. For example, given the rule *If a person is drinking beer, then the person must be over 19*, subjects may assume that $p \approx s$ (the proportion of beer-drinkers over 19 is about the same as the proportion of cola-drinkers under 19); so testing beer drinkers and testing under-age patrons are equally reasonable. Again, I am not proposing this account as a full explanation of the selection task (but see Fischhoff & Beyth-Marom 1983 and Klayman & Ha 1987 for theories in this vein). Instead, I am merely trying to indicate the general line that a Loose approach might take in attempting to clean up some of the Strict theory's problems. If Loose theories are successful in dealing with tasks that are supposed to be tapping deductively correct reasoning, that is all to their credit.

Some Disadvantages

As attractive as the Loose view seems, it has some serious deficiencies in accounting for human styles of reasoning. In the first place, the Loose approach is inarticulate. Although it can explain changes in the acceptability of beliefs via updating, it has nothing to say about where these beliefs come from or how new ones are produced. By contrast, rule schemata such as Example 15 do produce new beliefs, since they are derived by instantiation of the schema's variables. Perhaps a proponent of the Loose perspective could account for belief production by invoking processes other than reasoning. For instance, beliefs might be the result of understanding others' speech or writing and then updating them in the usual way to determine confidence levels. But for one thing, the updating process requires not only the belief itself but also the conditional relations to other beliefs; unless these are also transmitted from others, there is no obvious way to get started. For another, new beliefs *do* seem to result from reasoning. Given the belief *Trump is rich and Koch is famous*, we have no trouble at all in generating the belief *Trump is rich*. There seems to be nothing in the Loose approach to explain how we do this.

Inarticulateness is manifest in a second way. Once we've carried out the updating process, what we have is just a new degree of belief for the conclusion. But it's often the case that we need to justify belief in a proposition (or convince others of it) by giving some sort of argumentation. This requires a trace of what led us to the belief in question or, if we've forgotten the original reason, some way of reconstructing one. Strict approaches give us this for free, since the rules generate a derivation of the belief that can stand as an argument for it. We've already seen that similar higher-order structure also seems required to account for analogical reasoning, and the same is true for categorization (Murphy & Medin 1985; Rips 1989b), high-level learning (DeJong 1986; Schank et al 1986), and decision making (Pennington & Hastie 1988). Loose approaches are at a disadvantage here, since they must invoke some additional mechanism to provide a justification or explanation (cf Cohen 1985; Glymour 1980, Ch. 3).

Third, although we may be able to reconstruct the strength of an argument in terms of confidence in the conclusion given the premises, $B(C|P)$, this relation itself stands in need of explication. Identifying inductive strength with conditional confidence is of no help unless we have some theory of conditional confidence to back it up (Osherson et al 1986). One move is to ·take conditional confidence as conditional probability, but this runs into problems in predicting subjects' intuitions about argument strength. For example, compare the strength of the following arguments:

Donald won the first event in the decathlon.   17.

Donald won the decathlon.

Donald won the decathlon.   18.

Donald won the first event in the decathlon.

Argument 18 appears much stronger than 17. However, as Tversky & Kahneman (1980) point out, the prior probabilities P(Donald won the decathlon) $= P$(Donald won the first event in the decathlon) $= 1/N$, where N is the number of contestants. In these circumstances, the conditional probabilities are also equal: P(Donald won the decathlon | Donald won the first event) $= P$(Donald won the first event | Donald won the decathlon). Hence, the conditional probabilities cannot account for the apparent differences in argument strength. Tversky & Kahneman hypothesize that what makes Example 18 stronger is that winning the decathlon is a better indication of the underlying trait (athletic ability) that's responsible for both outcomes. For this reason, the premise of Example 18 provides a better causal explanation of its conclusion than does the premise for the conclusion of Example 17. The inability of probabilistic methods to cope with causal relations yields related problems for classical decision theory (e.g. Gibbard & Harper 1978).

An alternative is to drop probability and to explain conditional confidence in terms of learning from environmental feedback. But learning is itself a complex inductive process and may therefore presuppose an answer to the same questions it is being used to explain. It's also hard to see how learning could by itself account for the differences in strength between arguments like Examples 17 and 18 above, particularly without some sort of high-level causal theory to support it. Perhaps an answer to these problems can be framed in terms of connectionist methods or in terms of rival systems of confidence assignment, but at present it's not clear to me how this can be done.

SUMMARY

Strict theories of reasoning are schoolmarmish in their insistence on rules and structure, but this gives them an advantage when inference is relatively well behaved. In the case of reasoning with deductively valid arguments, Strict theories give a convincing account of the universality of certain inference forms and the productivity of reasoning in comprehension and production. However, Strict views are rather frail, since they have to appeal to nonreasoning processes (memory limitations, comprehension failure, conversational factors) when inferencing breaks down. They seem less suited to inductive and analogical arguments, though they may be helpful in restricted situations where the inference is routine or the domain well understood.

By contrast, Loose theories are inarticulate and nerdy. They dispense with formal rules in favor of continuous functions defined over beliefs, and the inferences they describe are modulations of these functions. In some sense, they are more robust than Strict theories, since they apply not only to inductively strong arguments but also to deductively valid ones as a limiting case. In fact, we have seen that they can provide insight into subjects' responses to purportedly deductive problems that are too unruly for Strict theories to handle. They are also extremely literal-minded in refusing to recognize permanent generalizations. Their only generalities are temporary products of their updating schemes. Because of these features, Loose theories have trouble producing new beliefs, explaining or justifying their own inferences, and keeping straight the difference between correlational and causal evidence.

As I've described them here, Strict and Loose views are postures, not scientific theories. It's hard to see how either point of view could be exclusively true, but equally hard to combine their insights successfully.

ACKNOWLEDGMENTS

NIMH Grant MH39633 supported the preparation of this manuscript. Dedre Gentner, Jeff Schank, and Edward Smith provided invaluable comments on an earlier draft.

Literature Cited

Anderson, J. R. 1983. A spreading activation theory of memory. *J. Verbal Learn. Verbal Behav.* 22:261–95

Barker, S. F. 1965. Must every inference be either deductive or inductive? In *Philosophy in America*, ed. M. Black, pp. 58–73. London: Allen & Unwin

Beattie, J., Baron, J. 1988. Confirmation and matching bias in hypothesis testing. *Q. J. Exp. Psychol.* 40A:269–97

Braine, M. D. S. 1978. On the relation between the natural logic of reasoning and standard logic. *Psychol. Rev.* 85:1–21

Braine, M. D. S., Reiser, B. J., Rumain, B. 1984. Some empirical justification for a theory of natural propositional logic. *Psychol. Learn. Motiv.* 18:313–71

Braine, M. D. S., Rumain, B. 1983. Logical reasoning. In *Handbook of Child Psycholo-*

gy, ed. J. H. Flavell, E. M. Markman, 3:263–340. New York: Wiley

Brown, N. R., Rips, L. J., Shevell, S. K. 1985. Subjective dates of natural events in very long term memory. *Cognit. Psychol.* 17:139–77

Bryne, R. M. J. 1989. Suppressing valid inferences with conditionals. *Cognition* 31: 61–83

Carey, S. 1985. *Conceptual Change in Childhood.* Cambridge, MA: MIT Press

Chapman, L. J., Chapman, J. P. 1959. Atmosphere effect re-examined. *J. Exp. Psychol.* 58:220–26

Cheng, P. W., Holyoak, K. J. 1985. Pragmatic reasoning schemas. *Cognit. Psychol.* 17:391–416

Cheng, P. W., Holyoak, K. J., Nisbett, R. E., Oliver, L. M. 1986. Pragmatic versus syntactic approaches to training deductive reasoning. *Cognit. Psychol.* 18:293–328

Clocksin, W. F., Mellish, C. S. 1981. *Programming in PROLOG.* Berlin: Springer

Cohen, P. R. 1985. *Heuristic Reasoning About Uncertainty: An Artificial Intelligence Approach.* Boston: Pitman

Collins, A. 1978. *Studies of Plausible Reasoning.* Tech. Rep. 3810. Cambridge, MA: Bolt, Beranek & Newman

Collins, A., Michalski, R. 1989. The logic of plausible reasoning: a core theory. *Cognit. Sci.* 13:1–50

Davies, T. R. 1988. Determination, uniformity, and relevance: normative criteria for generalization and reasoning by analogy. In *Analogical Reasoning,* ed. D. H. Helman, pp. 227–50. Dordrecht: Kluwer

DeJong, G. 1986. An approach to learning from observation. In *Machine Learning: An Artificial Intelligence Approach,* ed. R. S. Michalski, J. G. Carbonell, T. M. Mitchell, 2:571–91. Los Altos, CA: Morgan Kaufmann

Evans, J. St. B. T. 1977. Linguistic factors in reasoning. *Q. J. Exp. Psychol.* 29:297–306

Evans, J. St. B. T. 1982. *The Psychology of Deductive Reasoning.* London: Routledge & Kegan Paul

Evans, J. St. B. T., Barston, J., Pollard, P. 1983. On the conflict between logic and belief in syllogistic reasoning. *Mem. Cognit.* 11:295–306

Evans, J. St. B. T., Brooks, P. G., Pollard, P. 1985. Prior beliefs and statistical inference. *Br. J. Psychol.* 76:469–77

Fischhoff, B., Beyth-Marom, R. 1983. Hypothesis evaluation from a Bayesian perspective. *Psychol. Rev.* 90:239–60

Fitch, F. B. 1952. *Symbolic Logic: An Introduction.* New York: Ronald

Føllesdal, D., Hilpinen, R. 1971. Deontic logic: an introduction. In *Deontic Logic: Introductory and Systematic Reading,* ed. R. Hilpinen, pp. 1–35. Dordrecht: Reidel

Ford, M. 1985. Review of *Mental Models* by P. N. Johnson-Laird. *Language* 61:897–903

Galotti, K. M. 1989. Approaches to studying formal and everyday reasoning. *Psychol. Bull.* 105:331–51

Galotti, K. M., Baron, J., Sabini, J. P. 1986. Individual differences in syllogistic reasoning: deduction rules or mental models? *J. Exp. Psychol.: Gen.* 115:16–25

Gelman, S. A. 1988. The development of induction within natural kind and artifact categories. *Cognit. Psychol.* 20:65–95

Gelman, S. A., Markman, E. M. 1986. Categories and induction in young children. *Cognition* 23:183–209

Gentner, D. 1983. Structure-mapping: a theoretical framework for analogy. *Cognit. Sci.* 7:155–70

Gentner, D., Clement, C. 1988. Evidence for relational selectivity in the interpretation of analogy and metaphor. *Psychol. Learn. Motiv.* 22:307–58

Gentner, D., Collins, A. 1981. Studies of inference from lack of knowledge. *Mem. Cognit.* 9:434–43

Gentner, D., Toupin, C. 1986. Systematicity and surface similarity in the development of analogy. *Cognit. Sci.* 10:277–300

Gibbard, A., Harper, W. L. 1978. Counterfactuals and two kinds of expected utility. In *Foundations and Applications of Decision Theory,* ed. C. A. Hooker, J. J. Leach, E. F. McClennen, pp. 125–62. Dordrecht: Reidel

Gick, M., Holyoak, K. J. 1983. Schema induction and analogical transfer. *Cognit. Psychol.* 15:1–38

Glymour, C. 1980. *Theory and Evidence.* Princeton, NJ: Princeton Univ. Press

Greiner, R. 1988. Learning by understanding analogies. *Artif. Intell.* 35:81–125

Griggs, R. A. 1983. The role of problem content in the selection task and THOG problem. In *Thinking and Reasoning: Psychological Approaches,* ed. J. St. B. T. Evans, pp. 16–43. London: Routledge

Griggs, R. A., Cox, J. R. 1982. The elusive thematic-materials effect in Wason's selection task. *Br. J. Psychol.* 73:407–20

Griggs, R. A., Ransdell, S. E. 1986. Scientists and the selection task. *Soc. Stud. Sci.* 16:319–30

Goodman, N. 1955. *Fact, Fiction, and Forecast.* Indianapolis: Bobbs-Merrill

Harman, G. 1986. *Change in View: Principles of Reasoning.* Cambridge, MA: MIT Press

Haviland, S. E. 1974. *Nondeductive strategies in reasoning.* PhD thesis. Stanford Univ.

Hayes, P. J. 1987. A critique of pure treason. *Comp. Intell.* 3:179–85

Henle, M. 1962. On the relation between logic and thinking. *Psychol. Rev.* 69:366–78

Hintikka, J. 1962. *Knowledge and Belief: An Introduction to the Logic of the Two Notions.* Ithaca, NY: Cornell Univ. Press

Hintzman, D. L. 1986. "Schema abstraction" in a multiple trace memory model. *Psychol. Rev.* 93:411–28

Holland, J. H., Holyoak, K. J., Nisbett, R. E., Thagard, P. R. 1986. *Induction: Processes of Inference, Learning, and Discovery.* Cambridge, MA: MIT Press

Holyoak, K. J. 1985. The pragmatics of analogical transfer. *Psychol. Learn. Motiv.* 19:59–87

Holyoak, K. J., Koh, K. 1987. Surface and structural similarity in analogical transfer. *Mem. Cognit.* 15:332–40

Horwich, P. 1982. *Probability and Evidence.* Cambridge: Cambridge Univ. Press

Hughes, G. E., Cresswell, M. J. 1968. *An Introduction to Modal Logic.* London: Methuen

Jackson, S. L., Griggs, R. A. 1988. Education and the selection task. *Bull. Psychon. Soc.* 26:327–30

Jacoby, L. L., Brooks, L. R. 1984. Nonanalytic cognition: memory, perception, and concept learning. *Psychol. Learn. Motiv.* 18:1–47

Janis, I. L., Frick, F. 1943. The relationship between attitudes toward conclusions and errors in judging the logical validity of syllogisms. *J. Exp. Psychol.* 33:73–77

Jeffrey, R. C. 1983. *The Logic of Decision.* Chicago: Univ. Chicago Press. 2nd ed.

Johnson-Laird, P. N. 1975. Models of deduction. In *Reasoning: Representation and Process in Children and Adults,* ed. R. Falmagne, pp. 7–54. Hillsdale, NJ: Erlbaum

Johnson-Laird, P. N. 1983. *Mental Models.* Cambridge, MA: Harvard

Johnson-Laird, P. N., Bara, B. 1984. Syllogistic inference. *Cognition* 16:1–61

Johnson-Laird, P. N., Oakhill, J., Bull, D. 1986. Children's syllogistic reasoning. *Q. J. Exp. Psychol.* 38A:35–58

Kahneman, D., Miller, D. T. 1986. Norm theory: comparing reality to its alternatives. *Psychol. Rev.* 93:136–53

Kahneman, D., Tversky, A. 1973. On the psychology of prediction. *Psychol. Rev.* 80:237–51

Kahneman, D., Tversky, A. 1979. Prospect theory: an analysis of decision under risk. *Econometrica* 47:263–91

Keane, M. 1987. On retrieving analogues when solving problems. *Q. J. Exp. Psychol.* 39A:29–41

Kedar-Cabelli, S. 1988. Analogy—from a unified perspective. In *Analogical Reasoning,* ed. D. H. Helman, pp. 65–103. Dordrecht: Kluwer

Klaczynski, P. A., Gelfand, H., Reese, H. W. 1989. Transfer of conditional reasoning: effects of explanations and initial problem types. *Mem. Cognit.* 17:208–20

Klayman, J., Ha, Y.-W. 1987. Confirmation, disconfirmation, and information in hypothesis testing. *Psychol. Rev.* 94:211–28

Lee, G., Oakhill, J. 1984. The effects of externalization on syllogistic reasoning. *Q. J. Exp. Psychol.* 36A:519–30

Lehman, D. R., Lempert, R. O., Nisbett, R. E. 1988. The effects of graduate training on reasoning: formal discipline and thinking about everyday-life events. *Am. Psychol.* 43:431–42

Lewis, D. 1973. Causation. *J. Philos.* 70:556–67

Lewis, D. 1974. Semantic analyses for dyadic deontic logic. In *Logical Theory and Semantic Analysis,* ed. S. Stenlund, pp. 1–14. Dordrecht: Reidel

Macnamara, J. 1986. *A Border Dispute: The Place of Logic in Psychology.* Cambridge, MA: MIT Press

Marcus, S. L., Rips, L. J. 1979. Conditional reasoning. *J. Verbal Learn. Verbal Behav.* 18:199–224

Markovits, H. 1987. Incorrect conditional reasoning: competence or performance? *Br. J. Psychol.* 76:241–47

Markovits, H. 1988. Conditional reasoning, representation, and empirical evidence on a concrete task. *Q. J. Exp. Psychol.* 40A:483–95

Markovits, H., Nantel, G. 1989. The belief-bias effect in the production and evaluation of logical conclusions. *Mem. Cognit.* 17:11–17

McCarthy, J. 1988. Mathematical logic in artificial intelligence. In *The Artificial Intelligence Debate,* ed. S. R. Graubard, pp. 297–311. Cambridge, MA: MIT Press

McDermott, D. V., Doyle, J. 1980. Nonmonotonic logic I. *Artif. Intell.* 13:41–72

Medin, D. L., Schaffer, M. M. 1978. Context theory of classification learning. *Psychol. Rev.* 85:207–38

Medin, D. L., Smith, E. E. 1984. Concepts and concept formation. *Annu. Rev. Psychol.* 35:113–38

Murphy, G. L., Medin, D. L. 1985. The role of theories in conceptual coherence. *Psychol. Rev.* 92:289–316

Newell, A., Simon, H. 1972. *Human Problem Solving.* Englewood Cliffs, NJ: Prentice-Hall

Nisbett, R. E., Fong, G. T., Lehman, D. R., Cheng, P. W. 1987. Teaching reasoning. *Science* 238:625–31

Nisbett, R. E., Krantz, D. H., Jepson, D., Kunda, Z. 1983. The use of statistical heuristics in everyday inductive reasoning. *Psychol. Rev.* 90:339–63

Nosofsky, R. M. 1986. Attention, similarity, and the identification-categorization relationship. *J. Exp. Psychol.: Gen.* 115:39–57

Novick, L. R. 1988. Analogical transfer, problem similarity, and expertise. *J. Exp. Psychol.: Learn. Mem. Cognit.* 14:510–20

Oakhill, J. V., Johnson-Laird, P. N. 1985. The effects of belief on the spontaneous production of syllogistic conclusions. *Q. J. Exp. Psychol.* 37A:553–69

Oakhill, J. V., Johnson-Laird, P. N., Garnham, A. 1989. Believability and syllogistic reasoning. *Cognition* 31:117–40

Oden, G. C. 1987. Concept, knowledge, and thought. *Annu. Rev. Psychol.* 38:203–27

Osherson, D. N. 1974–1976. *Logical Abilities in Children*, Vols. 2–4. Hillsdale, NJ: Erlbaum

Osherson, D. N., Smith, E. E., Shafir, E. B. 1986. Some origins of belief. *Cognition* 24:197–224

Osherson, D. N., Smith, E. E., Wilkie, O., López, A., Shafir, E. 1989. Category-based induction. *Psychol. Rev.* In press

Pennington, N., Hastie, R. 1988. Explanation-based decision-making: effects of memory structure on judgment. *J. Exp. Psychol.: Learn. Mem. Cognit.* 14:521–33

Pollard, P., Evans, J. St. B. T. 1987. Content and context effects in reasoning. *Am. J. Psychol.* 100:41–60

Pollock, J. L. 1987. Defeasible reasoning. *Cognit. Sci.* 11:481–518

Reed, S. K. 1987. A structure-mapping model for word problems. *J. Exp. Psychol. Learn. Mem. Cognit.* 13:124–39

Rescher, N., Urquhart, A. 1971. *Temporal Logic.* New York: Springer

Revlin, R., Leirer, V., Yopp, H., Yopp, R. 1980. The belief bias effect in formal reasoning: The influence of knowledge on logic. *Mem. Cognit.* 8:584–92

Rips, L. J. 1975. Inductive judgments about natural categories. *J. Verbal Learn. Verbal Behav.* 14:665–81

Rips, L. J. 1983. Cognitive processes in propositional reasoning. *Psychol. Rev.* 90:38–71

Rips, L. J. 1986. Mental muddles. In *Representation of Knowledge and Belief,* ed. M. Brand, R. M. Harnish, pp. 258–86. Tucson: Univ. Arizona Press

Rips, L. J. 1989a. The psychology of knights and knaves. *Cognition* 31:85–116

Rips, L. J. 1989b. Similarity, typicality, and categorization. In *Similarity and Analogical Reasoning,* ed. S. Vosniadou, A. Ortony. Cambridge: Cambridge Univ. Press

Rips, L. J., Conrad, F. G. 1983. Individual differences in deduction. *Cognit. Brain Theory* 6:259–85

Ross, B. H. 1987. This is like that: the use of earlier problems and the separation of similarity effects. *J. Exp. Psychol.: Learn. Mem. Cognit.* 13:629–39

Rumelhart, D. E., Smolensky, P., McClelland, J. L., Hinton, G. E. 1986. Schemata and sequential thought processes in PDP models. In *Parallel Distributed Processing: Explorations in the Microstructure of Cognition,* ed. J. L. McClelland, D. E. Rumelhart, 2:7–57. Cambridge, MA: MIT Press

Schank, R. C., Collins, G. C., Hunter, L. E. 1986. Transcending inductive category formation in learning. *Behav. Brain Sci.* 9:639–86

Shepard, R. N. 1987. Toward a universal law of generalization for psychological science. *Science* 237:1317–23

Skyrms, B. 1966. *Choice and Chance.* Belmont, CA: Dickenson

Smith, E. E. 1989. Concepts and induction. In *Foundations of Cognitive Science,* ed. M. Posner, Cambridge, MA: MIT Press. In press

Smullyan, R. 1978. *What Is the Name of This Book?: The Riddle of Dracula and Other Logical Puzzles.* Englewood Cliffs, NJ: Prentice-Hall

Sterling, L., Shapiro, E. 1986. *The Art of Prolog.* Cambridge, MA: MIT Press

Sternberg, R. J. 1982. Natural, unnatural, and supernatural concepts. *Cognit. Psychol.* 14:451–88

Störring, G. 1908. Experimentelle Untersuchungen über einfache Schlussprozesse. *Arch. Gesamte Psychol.* 11:1–127

Suppes, P. 1957. *Introduction to Logic.* Princeton, NJ: Van Nostrand

Tetewsky, S. J., Sternberg, R. J. 1986. Conceptual and lexical determinants of nonentrenched thinking. *J. Mem. Lang.* 25:202–25

Tulving, E., Madigan, S. A. 1970. Memory and verbal learning. *Annu. Rev. Psychol.* 21:437–84

Tversky, A. 1977. Features of similarity. *Psychol. Rev.* 84:327–52

Tversky, A., Kahneman, D. 1973. Availability: a heuristic for judging frequency and probability. *Cognit. Psychol.* 5:207–32

Tversky, A., Kahneman, D. 1980. Causal schemas in judgments under uncertainty. In *Progress in Social Psychology,* ed. M. Fishbein. Hillsdale, NJ: Erlbaum

Tversky, A., Kahneman, D. 1982. Evidential impact of base rates. In *Judgment under Uncertainty: Heuristics and Biases,* ed. D. Kahneman, P. Slovic, A. Tversky, pp. 153–60. Cambridge: Cambridge Univ. Press

Tversky, A., Kahneman, D. 1983. Extensional versus intuitive reasoning: the conjunction fallacy in probability judgments. *Psychol. Rev.* 90:293–315

Wason, P. C. 1966. Reasoning. In *New Horizons in Psychology,* ed. B. M. Foss, pp. 135–51. Harmondsworth: Penguin

Wason, P. C., Johnson-Laird, P. N. 1972. *Psychology of Reasoning.* Cambridge, MA: Harvard Univ. Press

Annu. Rev. Psychol. 1990. 41:355–86

COUNSELING PSYCHOLOGY: Theory and Research on Interventions

Charles J. Gelso

Department of Psychology, University of Maryland, College Park, Maryland 20742

Ruth E. Fassinger

Department of Counseling and Personnel Services, University of Maryland, College Park, Maryland 20742

CONTENTS

In his 1984 *Annual Review* chapter on counseling psychology, Borgen noted much ferment and controversy in the field (Borgen 1984a). He viewed this stirring and searching as signs of vigorous health. Borgen's views were echoed in the deliberations about counseling psychology research (Gelso et al

355

1988) at the Third National Conference for Counseling Psychology in 1987 (the "Georgia Conference"; Gazda et al 1988).

It appears that all of this stirring, searching, and controversy are beginning to pay off. During the period of our review, exciting developments have enriched counseling psychology. This chapter builds on the two most recent analyses of counseling psychology published in the *Annual Review*. Since Borgen's (1984) chapter reviewed counseling psychology research through 1982, coverage here is for the years 1983 through 1988, with an emphasis on the more recent years. Osipow's (1987) chapter focused on the career area through 1985, and serves as a starting point for the career discussion in this review.

In our selective review, we focus on theory and research directly relevant to counseling psychology *interventions*—their processes and outcomes, diagnosis and assessment as related to interventions, and the training and supervision of the professionals who offer the interventions. Our central concerns in this review are with the counseling psychology scientific literature (theory and empirical research) rather than the literature on ethical and professional issues.[1] Our primary sources were the *Journal of Counseling Psychology (JCP)* and *The Counseling Psychologist (TCP)*, the two main publication outlets in the specialty; selected research from other journals and from scholarly books is incorporated where relevant.

CONTENT DEVELOPMENTS

Counseling Effects and Processes

Probably the largest body of intervention-related literature in counseling psychology pertains to personal-adjustment counseling. Some of this work is done within the framework of established theories or their derivatives. The rest examines counseling without making established theories a central element (although theoretical hypotheses may be tested, and theoretical statements may be the eventual aim). For convenience, the latter kind is termed "counseling interaction" research.

WORK WITHIN ESTABLISHED THEORY   Wampold & White's (1985) cluster analysis of articles appearing in the "Counseling Process and Outcomes"

---

[1]Our review addresses developments only in the scientific/scholarly side of counseling psychology, but the specialty as a whole has been involved in some highly significant professional and political events. Probably the most significant was the Georgia Conference (Gazda et al 1988), held in Atlanta in 1987. This was the first national conference in the field in approximately 25 years, and the many recommendations emanating from it should serve as a sound guide to the specialty in the years ahead.

section of *JCP* suggested that research on the social influence model represented a dominant and recurrent theme. Since the seminal pieces of Strong (1968) and Strong & Matross (1973), counseling research studying extrapolations from the social psychology of interpersonal influence has been produced at a remarkable pace.

During the 1983–1988 period, however, the pace of research on the classical model of social influence in counseling gradually slowed down, perhaps as researchers and editors became more mindful of the issues and problems in this line of research. Thoughtful discussions of these difficulties were presented by Heppner et al (1986) and in an important extended treatise by Heppner & Claiborn (1989), two of the leading researchers in this area. To name but a few of the salient issues, Heppner et al note that most studies have examined only the initial phase of counseling and have been based on extremely brief analogues. Therefore, generalizability to even the earliest stages of real-life counseling is suspect. Also, researchers now seem acutely aware that the role of client factors in the influence process has been seriously underemphasized (Friedlander & Schwartz 1985; Heppner & Claiborn 1989; Heppner et al 1986).

As part of the effort to develop sounder and more clinically relevant theory and research in social influence, some exciting new theoretical statements and research formulations have been offered. For example, Heesacker (1986a,b) studied the Elaboration Likelihood Model of persuasion in a counseling context; and Friedlander and colleagues, using an impression management perspective, developed and offered beginning tests of a theory of strategic self-presentation in counseling (Friedlander & Schwartz 1985; Schwartz et al 1986) and supervision (Ward et al 1985). Both Heesacker's and Friedlander's lines of research place client factors in the center of change processes. Finally, Heppner & Claiborn's (1989) formulations about social influence research in counseling should serve to reorient and guide this area for years to come.

Another recent conceptualization of counseling that views client factors as pivotal is the information-processing approach to personal problem-solving proposed by Heppner & Krauskopf (1987). This formulation actually represents an integration of social and cognitive psychology, counseling theory, and research on problem-solving (e.g. Larson & Heppner 1985; Neal & Heppner 1986; Nezu & Ronan 1988; Phillips et al 1984). Asserting that clients' problem-solving difficulties are rooted in faulty information processing (e.g. encoding, goal-setting), Heppner & Krauskopf propose a detailed assessment and intervention strategy showing much promise.

One line of highly visible work in counseling psychology (Wampold & White 1985) revolves around theory and research on behavioral, cognitive, and cognitive-behavioral interventions. Mahoney & Lyddon (1988) have presented a thoughtful treatise that reflects recent developments in the cognitive approaches, and differentiates rationalist from constructivist views. Deffenbacher (1988c) has edited an entire issue of *TCP* devoted to four approaches to cognitive and behavioral counseling. Empirical efforts have supported the efficacy of a range of cognitive and behavioral (and their amalgamation) treatments for a wide variety of problems and situations—e.g. anger problems (Deffenbacher 1988a; Deffenbacher et al 1987), general anxiety (Cragan & Deffenbacher 1984), test anxiety (Crowley et al 1986; Dendato & Diener 1986), stress (West et al 1984), depression (McNamara & Horan 1986), and Type A behavior patterns (Kelly & Stone 1987; Thurman 1985).

It is an interesting post-Eysenck phenomenon that during this review period virtually all outcome studies of the cognitive and behavioral interventions appearing in *JCP* report positive results. The typical finding is that two behavioral or cognitive interventions each surpasses one or more control groups on various outcomes, whereas the treatments are equivalent to each other. Current research in this area seeks to determine the optimum match between problem situation or client and specific treatment; the challenges of such research are discussed by Deffenbacher (1988b).

Although other theory-based efforts produced less research than those in the social influence and behavioral areas, some significant work has appeared. Within the general psychoanalytic area, Bryant-Tuckett & Silverman (1984) extended Silverman's prolific program and found that certain subliminally presented messages enhance the academic performance of emotionally handicapped students. Robbins & Jolkovski (1987) uncovered interesting interaction effects that may partly account for counselors' countertransference problems with clients. Much of the field research on time-limited therapy presented by Gelso & Johnson (1983) was on counseling with dynamic leanings. Work within the humanistic framework was scant, although Clarke & Greenberg (1986) did continue the fruitful line of research demonstrating the efficacy of the Gestalt two-chair technique.

COUNSELING INTERACTION RESEARCH   Some of the most promising research in counseling psychology is now occurring in what has been traditionally called "counseling process." Not only does this line of work seek to unravel the enormous complexities of the process ("What goes on in counseling?" "What leads to what in the hour?" "How does counseling work?"), but more than ever before it also aims to tie process to outcome ("What within the process leads to change?")

There are now a number of creative and productive research programs under the rubric of counseling process. The leading one in counseling psychology may be represented by the ongoing work of Hill and her colleagues.

One of Hill's central research questions is "What counselor techniques are helpful in counseling?" She and her collaborators have done pioneering research combining quantitative and qualitative methods in the analysis of case study data (Hill et al 1983; O'Farrell et al 1986). Hill's program has also theorized about and empirically examined the constructs of therapist intentions, therapist response modes, client reactions, and their relation to both process and outcome (Hill & O'Grady 1985; Hill et al 1988a,b). Within this same counseling process domain, Martin has postulated (Martin 1984) and then studied (Martin et al 1986; Martin et al 1987) what he calls a cognitive-mediational paradigm. Some of Martin's most significant work (e.g. Martin & Stelmaczonek 1988) has focused on significant events in counseling. His research in this area coincides with that of Elliott (1985), who has uncovered specific "helpful and nonhelpful events" in counseling.

Stiles's program (Dill-Standiford 1988; Stiles & Snow 1984; Stiles et al 1988) has focused on a variable (session impact) construed as midway between the internal process of the session and the outcomes of counseling. The Stiles group has studied session-to-session variability, counselor-client agreement, and theoretical orientation differences in session impact. The Session Evaluation Questionnaire, devised by Stiles and his colleagues (see Stiles & Snow 1984), is used to access such impact, and has become a popular device among process researchers.

Tracey's research program has focused on the constructs of complementarity and symmetry in terms of who controls whom in the counseling interaction. Using both replicated N-of-1 and more conventional group designs, Tracey and his collaborators have found empirical support for a stage theory of counseling that differentiates successful from unsuccessful cases (Tracey 1985, 1987; Tracey & Ray 1984). Other investigators have usefully studied similar constructs regarding the reciprocal impact or the "push and pull" of the counselor-client interaction (Friedlander & Phillips 1984; Heatherington 1988; Heatherington & Allen 1984; Kiesler & Goldston 1988).

While empirical work on counseling process has flourished, research on a previously central topic has nearly come to a standstill. The counseling relationship, and especially counselor-offered relationship conditions, received little attention during this review period, although there is now general agreement that the relationship is highly important (Gelso & Carter 1985; Highlen & Hill 1984). Only a few studies, for example, examined counselor empathy as a central construct (e.g. Barkham & Shapiro 1986; Harman 1986). It appears that earlier ways of studying "relationship conditions" may have reached an inevitable limit, and investigators have not yet devised methods to study the newer theoretical formulations that have been offered about relationship constructs such as the working alliance (see Bordin 1987; Gelso & Carter 1985) and empathy (Barrett-Lennard 1986; Gladstein 1983).

Although tests of the formulations about working alliance, for example, are appearing in several scholarly journals, none have yet appeared in the major counseling psychology outlets. These newer theoretical statements await empirical scrutiny.

The counselor's contribution to the counseling situation may be conceptualized as consisting of relationship factors and technical factors or techniques. Whereas research on relationship factors was distressingly scarce, technique research has continued at a fast pace. Some of Hill's aforementioned work was focused on technique (*response modes,* in her terms). The most vigorous research efforts on a given set of techniques have been on paradoxical interventions, where Dowd and his collaborators have conducted a series of studies (Dowd et al 1988; Kraft et al 1985; Perrin & Dowd 1986) and presented an integrative conceptual piece (Dowd & Milne 1986). Additional research has been offered by Conoley & Garber (1985), Shoham-Salomon & Jancourt (1985), and Westerman et al (1987). Many therapists worry about the presumed "trickiness" of paradox in counseling (e.g. Johnson 1986); and potential clients appear to feel likewise (Perrin & Dowd 1986), although such client perceptions do not necessarily disrupt the counseling experience (Perrin & Dowd 1986). Generally, it has not been established that paradoxical interventions are any more effective than a range of other techniques, yet they may be especially effective with some less cooperative clients (Westerman et al 1987).

Another technique studied frequently during the review period was counselor interpretation. Studies have focused on the effects of interpretation style, content, and discrepancy (e.g. Claiborn & Dowd 1985; Jones & Gelso 1988; Hill et al 1983; O'Farrell et al 1986). More than with any other technique, research during the review period supported the helpfulness of interpretation on a range of measures (cf Hill's research; Elliott 1985; Barkham & Shapiro 1986). Claiborn's (1982) conceptual piece appeared to guide several of the interpretation studies, and Spiegel & Hill's (1989) current guidelines promise to inform the next wave of efforts.

Large classes of variables studied in relation to counseling process and outcome are individual counselor, client, and client-counselor matching variables. During the review period, studies were done on a range of counselor variables too numerous to examine individually—e.g. age, experience, training level, physical appearance, feminist values, conceptual level, gender, and sex-role orientation. Likewise, a range of studies was done on client variables—e.g. introversion, attributional style, problem type, self concept, and locus of control. Although many of these studies are potentially valuable, most needed in the areas of client and counselor variables are programmatic efforts that include extended replications, deriving from and contributing to sound theoretical statements. For example, Tracey et al (1988) compared beginning graduate students, advanced students, and doctoral-level counselors in terms of their responses to a range of client statements. Fascinating results emerged regarding counselor techniques as related to experience—e.g. doctoral counselors apply their skills more flexibly but are less likely to gratify client "demands" than are inexperienced counselors. Such research should be further developed and then used to construct an empirically based theory on the role of experience. Researchers of counselor experience, however, have tended to incorporate an experience factor into their designs almost as an afterthought, and have rarely done more than a study or two on the construct. The result is one of the most confused bodies of research in all of counseling (see Auerbach & Johnson 1977; Parloff et al 1978).

Much of what has been said about counselor and client variables could also be said for counselor-client matching variables, although valuable results have been obtained by Claiborn & Dowd (1985) for matching interpretations with client attributional style, Maurer & Tindall (1983) for nonverbal behavior, and Foon (1986) for locus of control. Neurolinguistic programming, focused on such variables as sensory mode preference and use (e.g. Graunke & Roberts 1985) and predicate matching (e.g. Elich et al 1985; Mercier & Johnson 1984) had shown promise at the beginning of the decade, but after several years of conflicting and confusing results, Sharpley (1984, 1987) reviewed the research and concluded that there was little support for the assumptions of NLP. This research is now clearly on the decline, underscoring the value of thoughtful reviews and the publication of nonsupportive results in guiding empirical efforts. Another review, Atkinson & Schein's (1986) integrative analysis of counselor-client similarity research, should help guide future work in the area of counselor-client matching.

In the remainder of this section, we discuss developments in a few content areas deserving special note. An area of practical importance that received much attention is premature termination, typically addressed within university counseling centers. During the review period, the complexities in this area were abundantly clear (e.g. see the debate over research design and reporting between Saltzman 1984 and Rapaport et al 1985). Some of the most promising findings suggested that satisfaction with intake may be an underlying factor in continuance vs premature termination (Kokotovic & Tracey 1987; McNeill et al 1987). Also, counselors' early recognition of clients' problem definition stood out in two studies as being a key variable in continuance (Epperson et al 1983; Pekarik 1988). Despite ongoing interest in termination, only one study (Marx & Gelso 1987) was done on the actual termination phase (the ending of counseling), suggesting the need for much more work in this area. We have studied the beginning of counseling often and well but have heretofore virtually ignored its ending.

In the 1980s counseling psychology finally discovered the family. This has occurred as counseling practice moved beyond the university counseling center setting. After years of inattention, this topic generated a number of publications. Entire issues of *TCP* were devoted to reviews on dual-career families (Gilbert 1987) and family interventions (Levant 1983). At the empirical level, work was completed on instruments measuring family dynamics (Kunce & Priesmeyer 1985) and post-divorce attachment (Brown & Reimer 1984). Studies have examined sexual enhancement treatments for (Cooper & Stoltenberg 1987) and intimacy and satisfaction of (Tolstedt & Stokes 1983) married couples. Sustained lines of research have begun to explore the impact of the family on the psychological health of college students, including the interrelationships among psychological separation, family structure and dynamics, parental divorce, depression, and college adjustment (Hoffman 1984; Hoffman & Weiss 1987; Lopez 1987; Lopez et al 1986, 1988). Finally, in two seminal studies using sophisticated analytic methods, similarities and divergences among four prominent family therapists treating a single family were presented (Friedlander & Highlen 1984; Friedlander et al 1985). Common themes across apparently diverse approaches were discovered.

Historically, counseling psychology has placed a premium on relatively brief interventions. When treatments were becoming increasingly extended, an interest in time-limited procedures ensued. Early in the review period, Gelso & Johnson (1983) presented their series of process and outcome studies of time-limited counseling. Other studies using a time-limited format (e.g. Hill et al 1983; Tracey & Ray 1984), however, have been primarily interested in counseling process rather than the effects of duration issues themselves on process and outcome. Given the widespread use of time-limited interventions in counseling centers (Magoon 1989), more research is clearly called for on the efficacy and processes of those treatments. Burlingame & Fuhriman's (1987) classification system of short-term treatments should be an aid to researchers in this area.

Two other interrelated areas were frequently and usefully addressed during the review period: client expectancies and help-seeking. A large number of studies focused on expectancies, both as independent and dependent variable. As but a few examples, client expectancies were studied in relation to gender (Yanico & Hardin 1985), help-seeking (Tinsley et al 1984), preferences (Tracey & Dundon 1988), fees (Subich & Hardin 1985), and individual vs group counseling (Subich & Coursol 1985). Many of these expectancy studies make use of the Expectancies About Counseling questionnaire (Tinsley et al 1980), a testimony to the utility of a thoughtfully developed and validated instrument. Tinsley et al (1988) have also provided a review of treatments aimed at manipulating clients' initial expectations for counseling, drawing conclusions that should be useful to practitioners and researchers alike. The more general area of expectancies has developed into a voluminous literature, and the time seems ripe for a large-scale review. Help-seeking tendencies also have been found to relate to a range of variables—e.g. social supports (Goodman et al 1984), type and perceived helpfulness of service (Puchkoff & Lewin 1987), prior help-seeking (Halgin et al 1987), depressed affect, and coping ability (Halgin et al 1987; Tracey et al 1984). The Tracey et al (1984) study is an excellent example of the complex interactions that may guide help-seeking, while Goodman et al (1984) demonstrates how this pragmatic research area may be profitably guided by theory.

We conclude this section with a brief discussion of group approaches to counseling. In a comprehensive and incisive review, Kaul & Bednar (1986) echo the criticisms leveled at other counseling research, taking group investigators to task for their narrow focus on outcome and calling for increased attention to unique group process variables as linked to outcome. During the period of this review, six outcome studies were located that explored the efficacy of a particular therapeutic approach (e.g. the utility of feminist therapy in groups for profoundly disturbed women; Alyn & Becker 1984), or a comparison of two or more treatments (e.g. cognitive vs interpersonal process groups in the treatment of depression; Hogg & Deffenbacher 1988). However, evidence that we are finally beginning to define and test the unique change mechanisms postulated to operate in groups is presented in three recent group-process studies. Morran et al (1985) analyzed interpersonal feedback in groups and offered clear support for the value of member feedback exchange as postulated by group theory. Two studies (Kivlighan et al 1984; McGuire et al 1986) examined the use and timing of structuring techniques. The Kivlighan et al study is particularly noted for its experimental rigor in manipulating content (anger or intimacy) and timing of structuring techniques in real client groups, and for its attempt to link unique theoretical assumptions regarding groups [stages and Yalom's (1986) oft-cited therapeutic factors] with client outcome. While the need for group process research is clear, it is also imperative to tie process investigations to group theory and to the specific change mechanisms postulated to operate in a group counseling format.

Career Behavior

Although recent studies (Fitzgerald & Osipow 1986; Pinkney & Jacobs 1985) imply diminished interest in vocational activities by counseling psychologists, vocational theory and research remain among the most empirically mature investigative efforts in counseling psychology (Borgen 1984a, Osipow 1987). Due to the enormity of the vocational literature and the recency of a comprehensive review (Osipow 1987), we offer only a broad overview here. For more thorough coverage, the reader is referred to the inclusive yearly reviews offered in *The Journal of Vocational Behavior (JVB)*, the handbooks of counseling psychology (Brown & Lent 1984) and vocational psychology (Walsh & Osipow 1983a,b), and the recent works cited herein.

One of the most useful recent developments in the vocational literature is the publication of comprehensive reviews and special journal issues addressing a particular vocational topic. Some of these have included self-efficacy theory (Lent & Hackett 1987), cognitive integration and differentiation (Neimeyer 1988), person-environment congruence (Spokane 1985), education and work (Fitzgerald 1986), dual-career families (Gilbert 1987), the "g" factor in employment (Gottfredson 1986), and person-environment fit (Spokane 1987). Additional reviews are found in highly important recently published books: *The Career Psychology of Women* (Betz & Fitzgerald 1987), which summarizes and analyzes the vast literature on women's career choice, implementation, and adjustment; and Walsh & Osipow's *Advances in Vocational Psychology* volumes on the assessment of interests (1986) and career decision-making (1989). Several observations can be made regarding the content of vocational research. Psychometric development and refinement continue to be the forte of this field, with continuing work in career maturity, interest measurement, occupational values, decision-making, work adjustment, and vocational stress and coping, to name but a few of the substantive areas of investigation. The importance of this research lies in its enormous influence on theory and practice, creating a productive cycle of conceptual, empirical, and practical work. Some of this research has led directly to increased attention to client diversity, particularly the vocational assessment and behavior of ethnic minorities. Through 1985, reviewers decried the lack of attention to cultural diversity (e.g. Greenhaus & Parasuraman 1986), while more recently we have witnessed the dramatic movement of ethnic minority vocational research into our core journals.

Research in women's career development continues to comprise some of the most vigorous and creative investigative work in vocational psychology (Slaney & Russell 1987). In fact, two salient new theoretical developments in vocational psychology during this decade [circumscription/compromise theory (Gottfredson 1981) and vocational self-efficacy theory (Betz & Hackett 1981; Hackett & Betz 1981)], grew out of the attempt to understand limitations in women's career choices. These theories (particularly self-efficacy) have immense heuristic value and contain significant implications for intervention, although empirical intervention studies are yet to be done (e.g. see Lent & Hackett 1987). An additional valuable contribution of the women's career development literature has been its effect on investigative efforts in men's career development; the literatures on occupational stress and strain (e.g. Osipow et al 1985) and dual-career families (Gilbert 1987) are excellent examples of our increasing interest in a broader gender perspective in vocational psychology (see Baruch et al 1987 for a valuable discussion of this phenomenon). Finally, research in women's vocational choice has generated extensive, integrative models of career development (e.g. Astin 1985; Eccles 1987; Farmer 1985), some of which have already been subjected to causal analysis (e.g. Betz & Fitzgerald 1987; Fassinger 1985) and offer promise for wide application of statistical modeling techniques in vocational psychology.

Vocational intervention studies suggest increased activity by counselors in career-planning assistance (e.g. Prediger & Sawyer 1986), and the empirical research finally appears to be addressing methodological concerns of earlier reviewers (see Myers's 1986 summary). Individual studies addressed parental assistance in career planning (Palmer & Cochran 1988), cognitive restructuring and decision-making training (Mitchell & Krumboltz 1987), social skills training (Mueser et al 1986), reentry women (Slaney & Lewis 1986), and attrition behavior (Robbins et al 1985). Clearly, the most important intervention study to emerge during this review period was the meta-analysis of Oliver & Spokane (1988), a thorough, well-executed exploration of 240 treatment control comparisons resulting from 58 vocational studies of 7311 subjects. Building on their earlier outcome work (Spokane & Oliver 1983), these investigators examined the relation between intervention characteristics and outcome, finding clear differences among treatment models; class interventions, for example, were most effective (but also costly in treatment hours), while individual counseling produced more client gain per hour than any other intervention mode. These integrative kinds of results have been sorely needed in vocational intervention research, and the Oliver & Spokane study should have extensive impact on future investigations.

Assessment

Recent surveys (Fitzgerald & Osipow 1986; Watkins et al 1988) indicate continued engagement by counseling psychologists in a wide range of assessment activities. This section focuses on the two major areas of assessment research during the review period: (a) clinical judgment and hypothesis testing, and (b) instrument development and refinement.

CLINICAL JUDGMENT   Two somewhat disturbing studies (Gelso et al 1985; Richardson 1984) suggested that topologies or subgroups of clients (e.g. personal vs vocational issues) were differentially treated by counselors in regard to quality of intake evaluation or interpersonal communication style. Several lines of research have sought to discover the cognitive processes and strategies that underlie counselors' hypotheses about clients. Hirsch & Stone (1983) attempted to determine whether "early convergence" to clinical judgment affected subsequent information-seeking by counselors. Others (Kurpius et al 1985; Morran 1986) have explored the relationship between counselors' internal dialogue and quality of clinical hypothesis formulation. In what is probably the most sustained effort in this area, Strohmer and colleagues have investigated the relationship between clinical hypothesis formation and such cognitive processes as confirmatory bias (Strohmer et al 1983; Strohmer & Newman 1983; Strohmer & Chiodo 1984) and the role of attributions in clinical judgment (Strohmer et al 1984; Haase et al 1983). Their most recent work uses student samples, extending their ideas from the domain of clinical judgment to personal (Strohmer et al 1988) and vocational (Blustein & Strohmer 1987) hypothesis testing. Overall, the research in clinical judgment represents sound integration of diverse psychological literatures, effective use of the experimental analogue, diversity and sophistication in statistical analyses, and much promise in stimulating future research efforts.

INSTRUMENT DEVELOPMENT   Most instrument development and validation reported in our core journals during the review period was undertaken using college students, reflecting not only the convenience of, but also our field's enduring interest in this population. Core psychometric concerns addressed in the work of this period were: (*a*) assessing the validity of a particular measurement approach to a psychological variable, usually irrational beliefs (Zurawski & Smith 1987), or other cognitive variables (e.g. self-efficacy expectations regarding assertiveness; Arisohn et al 1988); and (*b*) assessing the validity of different measurement approaches to the same variable (e.g. thought-listing vs structured questionnaires in assessing cognition; Myszka et al 1986; Tarico et al 1986). While the results of these studies are mixed, the oft-noted inconsistencies across assessment methods suggests the importance of multitrait-multimethod assessment both clinically and in research.

Other assessment research has explored college students' academic procrastination (Rothblum et al (1986), test anxiety (Bruch et al 1986), adjustment to college (Baker & Siryk 1984, 1986), psychological distress (Lustman et al 1984), and perceived social support (Brown et al 1987; Brown et al 1988). One of the most exciting lines of research to appear in recent years is that by Robbins & Patton and their colleagues, exploring the applicability of Kohut's self-psychology to personal and vocational assessment and intervention. Based on Kohut's central developmental constructs of grandiosity and idealization, Robbins & Patton (1985) developed Superiority and Goal Instability scales, which have subsequently been used in assessing adolescent pseudoautonomy and peer group dependence (Lapan & Patton 1986), predicting career decidedness following a career class intervention (Robbins & Patton 1985), assessing the differential effectiveness of self-directed vs interactional career groups (Robbins & Tucker 1986), and predicting adjustment among retirement-age adults (Smith & Robbins 1988). This, like most of the instrument development work reported here, is characterized by sustained effort, multiple validation studies including interventions, sophisticated and appropriate statistical techniques, sound theoretical foundations, strong heuristic value, and clear implications for intervention. In addition, the latter work extends its validation efforts to noncollege populations, a much-needed practice in all assessment research.

Counseling Diverse Populations

Although counseling psychology has not always lived up to its commitment to human diversity, there are two areas in which attention to diversity has burgeoned in recent years—those of gender issues and racial/ethnic minority research. The interest in gender stems from concern with the special needs of women, beginning in the early 1970s and increasing at a steady pace to the present, generating considerable empirical attention during that time (Atkinson & Hackett 1988; Richardson & Johnson 1984). The attention to racial/ethnic diversity, however, is an even more recent phenomenon. During the review period, for example, there was a remarkable increase in what has come to be termed "cross-cultural" scholarly literature. Important books (Atkinson et al 1983; Pederson 1985), chapters (Casas 1984), journal issues (Smith & Vasquez 1985), reviews (Atkinson 1983, 1985; Leong 1986; Ponterotto 1988), and original theories (Helms 1984; Smith 1985) were presented. Empirical research also appeared to accelerate during this period, especially regarding counseling by and with Black counselors and clients (e.g. Atkinson et al 1986; Pomales et al 1986; Ponterotto et al 1988; Watkins & Terrell 1988), but also regarding Asian-Americans (e.g. Tracey et al 1986), Hispanics (e.g. Taussig 1987), and Native Americans (e.g. Schinke et al 1988), as well as among different minority groups (e.g. Cook & Helms 1988; Folensbee et al 1986).

Despite these increases, criticisms of the usefulness and scientific quality of the research have been advanced (Atkinson 1983; Casas 1984, 1985). In a recent empirical analysis of studies appearing in *JCP* from 1976 through 1986, Ponterotto (1988) enumerated several strengths and weaknesses, three of which deserve particular attention. First, there is a great need for more field-based research, given the over-reliance on laboratory simulations in this area. Second, intracultural or within-group differences in racial/ethnic minority samples must be more intensively addressed so as to avert the infamous "uniformity myth" regarding these groups. Ponterotto points to studies by Parham & Helms (1985), Sanchez & Atkinson (1983), and Sue & Zane (1985) as good examples of studies incorporating individual-differences factors. Third, Ponterotto asserts that we must start letting our theoretical visions guide our research questions, since the lack of theory-guided research has resulted in much empirical fragmentation. Theories such as Helms's (1984) Black and White model of racial identity development as related to counseling is an example of what is needed at the theoretical level.

In addition to women and racial/ethnic groups, several other diverse client populations have begun to receive attention. For example, for the first time in *JCP*'s history, several papers pertinent to counseling religious clients appeared (Bergin et al 1987, 1988; Worthington 1988), and entire issues of journals were devoted to counseling victims of trauma and violence (Claiborn & Ibrahim 1987; Courtois & O'Neil 1988). Also appearing recently is a handbook for counseling non-ethnic minorities (Atkinson & Hackett 1988), which includes women, disabled, elderly, and gay and lesbian populations. However, particularly for the latter three groups, empirical research has lagged far behind theoretical and issue-oriented writing. For example, four analogue studies exploring counselor preferences with regard to physical disability (Freeman & Conoley 1986; Haley & Dowd 1988; Mallinckrodt & Helms 1986; Strohmer & Biggs 1983), as well as a study of barriers to service delivery to the disabled (Pelletier et al 1985), were located in our core journals, indicating some empirical work being done by counseling psychologists. However, a recent special issue of *TCP* (Ganikos & Blake 1984) devoted to counseling the aged made clear the paucity of intervention research with this population. Except for an attempt at instrument development (a geriatric scale of hopelessness; Fry 1984) and a study of peer counseling in a nursing home (Nagel et al 1988), empirical research on the elderly is absent from our core journals. Even more dramatic is the lack of attention to gay men and lesbians; except for one study early in the review period (Casas et al 1983), our journals were devoid of research on this population. Clearly, the specialty's commitment to human diversity needs to be better translated into empirical attention in the years ahead.

Supervision and Training

It would be difficult to locate a content area that has grown more or more effectively in recent years than that of counseling supervision. Not long ago, reviewers (Hansen et al 1976) underscored the small amount and narrow focus of research. Indeed, at the beginning of our review period Bartlett et al (1983), while noting improvement, lamented the lack of systematic, theory-guided research. Things have changed greatly.

The review period was ushered in by two important publications. An entire issue of *TCP* was devoted to counseling supervision (Bartlett et al 1983), and it contained discussions and integrations of different theoretical models. The second key publication was Russell et al's (1984) review, perhaps the most compelling analysis of the supervision literature to date. These two publications brought attention and coherence to supervision theory, and the latter even now serves as a wise guide to research issues and directions.

Virtually all currently popular supervision theory was presented shortly before or in the early part of the review period. Examples of influential theories are those in the special *TCP* issue edited by Bartlett et al (1983) as well as theoretical statements by Loganbill et al (1982), Bernard (1979), Littrell et al (1979), and Stoltenberg (1981). The present review period also witnessed vigorous efforts to test theories with overwhelming emphasis on developmental models of supervision. Regarding the theories that directed this research, Stoltenberg's (1981) counselor complexity model has been most fertile, underscoring how heuristic a cleanly stated and testable theory can be. Stoltenberg & Delworth's (1987) new integrated-developmental model, presented in book form, also has great promise.

The evidence supporting developmental models of supervision is striking (Heppner & Roehlke 1984; Rabinowitz et al 1986; Krause & Allen 1988; McNeill et al 1985; Worthington 1984; Wiley & Ray 1986), although Reising & Daniels (1983) remind us that counselor development does not progress uniformly in a stagewise way. Generally, however, the empirical evidence suggests that counselors progress cognitively and emotionally in a predictable manner as they receive training, and that training environments (e.g. supervisory behavior) are most effective when matching the developmental level of supervisee. Important findings also have accrued on the dimensions of supervision (Ellis et al 1988; Ellis & Dell 1986), verbal behavior in supervision (Holloway & Wampold 1983; Rickards 1984), supervisor experiences (Marikas et al 1985; Worthington & Stern 1985), and supervisor theoretical orientation (Goodyear et al 1984). Friedlander & Ward's (1984) careful, systematic development of the Supervisory Styles Inventory has resulted in an instrument that has great research promise. Finally, a major change in this area is that the attention of past years to skills training and supervisor technique (see Russell et al 1984; Marikis et al 1985) markedly declined. Useful studies could still be found (e.g. Thompson 1986), but attention seems to have shifted away from this line of work.

Prevention and Outreach

Historically, counseling psychology as a specialty has identified itself as working with normal populations in preventive (as well as remedial) interventions that extend beyond the counseling dyad to a variety of individual and group activities in the natural environment—in communities, schools, organizations, the workplace, and even globally (Ellis 1986; Rogers 1984). This section briefly reviews recent work in (*a*) consultation, (*b*) health counseling, and (*c*) self-help and computer-assisted interventions.

CONSULTATION   In general, the literature in regard to consultation is characterized by early-stage theoretical work. Furthermore, attention to practice far outstrips attention to scholarly matters—e.g. research and theory. A special issue of *TCP* (Gallesich 1985) offered useful conceptualizations of a meta-theory of consultation (Gallesich 1985), along with suggestions about service implementation (Kurpius 1985), counselor training (Brown 1985), and ethics (Robinson & Gross 1985). Another special issue of *TCP* (Binder & Binder 1983) focused on forensic interventions, outlining enormous potential for consultation and counseling activities. In terms of empirical work in forensic interventions and consultation, however, only two studies were found, one describing successful microtraining of empathic counseling skills in forensic psychiatric patients (Lomis & Baker 1985) and one addressing the effects of a moral discussion group on the development of delinquent boys (Niles 1986). Still sorely needed in the consultation area are testable theory (e.g. Gallesich 1985) and the development of a solid empirical base.

HEALTH COUNSELING   The review period highlighted counseling psychology's growing interest in matters of health. Major presentations were offered by Thoresen & Eagleston (1985) and Klippel & DeJoy (1984) in health psychology, and by Matheny et al (1986) in the companion area, stress and coping. Thoresen & Eagleston's (1985) discussion is a far-reaching one of health as life-style, research issues, and their own cognitive-social learning model of health. Matheny et al (1986) are exemplary in combining theories/ opinions with meta-analysis as a basis for their model of "stress coping." Empirical studies in health psychology and stress/coping focused on modification of Type A behavior (Kelly & Stone 1987; Prior et al 1983; Thurman 1985), anxiety in medical outpatients (Cragan & Deffenbacher 1984), nurses' stress in acute care settings (West et al 1984), path models of drug use (Newcomb et al 1988; Oetting & Beauvais 1987), the effects of exercise (Wilfley & Kunce 1986), and the etiology and treatment of eating disorders and body image problems (Dworkin & Kerr 1987; Johnson & Holloway 1988; Mintz & Betz 1988). The influence of behavioral and cognitive approaches to treatment is remarkable in the areas of health and stress. A special issue of the *American Psychologist* devoted to AIDS (Backer et al 1988) should also be noted here, since it includes intervention articles of value to counseling psychologists.

SELF-HELP AND COMPUTER-ASSISTED INTERVENTIONS   The period of this review witnessed growing concern with the proliferation of self-help materials, including computerized and computer-assisted interventions. Craighead et al's (1984) evaluation of written self-help materials concluded that a wider empirical base is needed for self-help to be a legitimate aspect of counseling psychology, citing problems such as diagnostic unreliability, inattention to treatment implementation considerations, lack of controlled research, ineffective programs, and the promotion of nonproblems. A crucial issue is the appropriateness of self-help approaches for particular clients, addressed in studies by Mahalik & Kivlighan (1988) investigating the extent to which client variables predicted the effectiveness of a self-help treatment for depression, and Kivlighan & Shapiro (1987) exploring the relation between Holland types and benefit from self-help career counseling. These studies underscore the importance of matching client attributes to treatments, and have strong implications for the development, marketing, and evaluation of self-help materials.

One area where self-help has become widespread is in computer applications, particularly career information and guidance systems. An early issue of *TCP* (Myers & Cairo 1983) sounded a note of promise in regard to computer-assisted counseling, but it has become increasingly apparent that potential for misuse necessitates much greater empirical scrutiny of these procedures than they have previously been given (Johnston et al 1988; Sampson 1986). The ease they offer makes these applications attractive for practice (e.g. computerized test interpretations), research (e.g. unobtrusive data collection during a decision-making process), and training (see Berven's 1985 use of standardized case simulations to evaluate clinical problem-solving skills). Concerns, however, have been raised in regard to excessive dependency on technology, possible misuse by nonprofessionals, and restriction of the counseling process to cognition, suggesting the need for more careful evaluation and use of these procedures. This important task becomes increasingly difficult as technological advances outstrip our sluggish empirical process.

TRENDS IN INTERVENTION THEORY AND RESEARCH

In this section, we examine what appear to be major trends in the scholarly literature. Most of the trends cut across the content areas just discussed and pertain to conceptual, methodological, and content developments in the field.

The Production of Integrative Reviews and Theoretical Formulations

Science advances through the interplay of theory, empircial research, and integrative reviews of knowledge. In surveying the counseling research scene in the not-so-distant past, the first author (Gelso 1979) noted the paucity of integrative, direction-pointing reviews as a serious deficiency, and suggested that the field had reached a level of maturity demanding such reviews in a wide range of specific areas. The lack of original intervention theory in the specialty has also been commented upon by observers, the typical lament being that we borrow our theory from other specialties such as clinical psychology.

Throughout the 1980s, and especially during the review period, major changes have occurred. There has been a virtual explosion of high-quality integrative reviews on specific topics, and many testable theoretical statements have been offered. In the early part of the review period, the tone was set with new handbooks of vocational (Walsh & Osipow 1983a,b) and counseling (Brown & Lent 1984) psychology, and many reviews (already cited) have been presented in book form, and in *JCP, TCP, JVB*, and other major outlets. In terms of theory development, many impressive efforts have been made. To name but a few, testable theoretical propositions have been developed by Helms (1984) regarding racial identity development and counseling, Howard et al (1986) on adaptive counseling, Stoltenberg & Delworth (1987) on supervision, Gelso & Carter (1985) on the counseling relationship, Hackett & Betz (1981) on self-efficacy theory and career development, Gladstein (1983) on empathy, Friedlander & Schwartz (1985) on self-presentation theory, Heppner & Krauskopf (1987) on problem-solving, and Matheny et al (1986) on stress coping. Although most of these theories draw from other areas of psychology (as integrative theories should), they are essentially counseling psychology theories developed by counseling psychologists. Whereas in the past observers frequently complained about the lack of theory and reviews to guide research, we suspect that the former (reviews and theory) may now have outstripped the latter (research). Numerous testable theoretical hypotheses reside in our literature and await empirical assault!

The Valuing of External Validity

What has been called the rigor-relevance controversy in counseling psychology research (Gelso 1979) appears to be part of the field's continuing search for the best ways to study our subject matter. The rigor side of the rigor-relevance continuum is reflected in an emphasis on experimental control and manipulation of independent variables, allowing for strong causal inferences with internal validity placed at a premium. The relevance side of the continuum, however, emphasizes clinical realism and research that is readily generalizable to actual counseling, with external validity placed at a premium.

During the review period, the pendulum of beliefs among counseling researchers has swung clearly and strongly to the relevance side of the rigor-relevance continuum, making external validity the rule of the day. In the literature we studied over the six-year review period, numerous calls across diverse literatures were seen for greater attention to external validity and, accordingly, for more field and less laboratory research. This trend toward external validity is a likely reaction to the steady diet of laboratory analogues we fed ourselves for many years (Gelso 1985; Highlen & Hill 1984). Some see a danger, though, that the movement toward external validity will become reflexive. Such worries are what prompted Stone (1984) to prepare a "defense of the artificial." Forsyth & Strong's (1986) thoughtful "unificationist" position on methodology may also be seen as an antidote to overemphasis on one side of the internal-external validity continuum. Finally, in pointing out how the pendulum of beliefs about methodological issues such as rigor vs relevance may swing back and forth, each as a reflexive response to the other, Highlen & Hill (1984) remind us that "Such unthinking reflex responses do little to further creative approaches to challenging problems. We therefore reaffirm our conviction that numerous methods can be useful in addressing complicated questions" (p. 383).

Openness to Alternative Methodologies

Occurring at the same time as the press for external validity, and perhaps stemming from similar motives and issues, has been a clear and strong trend toward research methods that are seen as alternatives to traditional approaches and the philosophies undergirding them (together called the "received view"). Receptivity to alternative methodologies is now at a high pitch, although many believe that current versions of the received view can accommodate our research needs effectively (e.g. Borgen 1984b; Dawis 1984). Borgen (1989) noted that the decade of the 1980s was ushered in by Gelso's (1979) call for methodological diversity. But the call came from within the received view (Polkinghorne 1984), and advocates of alternative methodologies believe it important to go beyond that view. Although it would be impossible to capture this trend with a word or two, examples of terms that seem to fit it are qualitative, molar, naturalistic, idiographic, field, subjective, holistic, and nondeterministic.

In terms of the major literature, a special subsection of *JCP* was devoted to the philosophical underpinnings of alternative approaches. Three major papers appeared in that section (Howard 1984; Patton 1984; Polkinghorne 1984), followed by reactions from six research leaders in the field. Howard (1985, 1986, 1989) has written prolifically on the active agent model and other alternative approaches, while feminist critiques of traditional psychological empiricism have also been highly influential (McHugh et al 1986; Unger 1983), particularly in debunking the myth of value-free science (Richardson & Johnson 1984). As the current paper is being written, a special issue of *TCP* devoted to alternative methodologies is just off the press, and the major treatise of that issue (Hoshmand 1989) is the first to address methods of training graduate students in alternate methodologies.

As is perhaps inevitable in movements of this sort, "straw persons" are often built up to fight against, leading to "arguments by shibboleth" (Borgen 1989). It sometimes appears, for example, that advocates of alternative methodologies attack a positivism that may no longer exist in psychology. But the trend toward alternative methods does appear to be going beyond exhortation and rhetoric. Research studies are slowly creeping into the literature (e.g. Heinemann & Shontz 1985; Hill et al 1983; Hill 1989; Lazarick et al 1988) and serving as models of alternative approaches in counseling research.

Increased Quantitative Sophistication

In contrast to the demand for alternative methodologies has been the perennial call for more sophisticated exploitation of research strategies already in use. Most often criticized are simplistic univariate design and analysis procedures, and the inability to extract causal explanations from correlational data. Whether or not nontraditional methodologies eventually offer us alternatives to these knotty problems, it is clear from the research reviewed here that we are experiencing a trend toward the use of more refined methodological strategies and, in particular, advanced statistical procedures. This trend toward greater quantitative sophistication is exemplified in a special issue of *JCP* (Wampold 1987) demonstrating the applicability of a variety of statistical techniques to counseling psychology research. Researchers are making increased use of such tools as cluster (Borgen & Barnett 1987) and factor analysis (Tinsley & Tinsley 1987), discriminant analysis (Betz 1987), and a range of multivariate procedures such as causal modeling (Fassinger 1987) that permit causal inferences from correlational data. Other promising techniques (e.g. multidimensional scaling; Fitzgerald & Hubert 1987) are just beginning to receive attention from counseling researchers.

Attention to Issues of Diversity

We have witnessed a powerful trend in concern with diverse populations. Ushering in this trend was attention to "women's" issues in the 1970s, initially focusing on sex bias in research, assessment, and treatment. Scrutiny of more recent empirical work finds us routinely testing for and reporting gender differences and similarities, incorporating gender considerations into our designs, and offering interventions based on the special needs of women. Moreover, there appears to be a shift to a broader psychology of gender where research on women has had a significant impact on the way we think about men (e.g. the recent *Handbook of Counseling and Psychotherapy with Men*, Scher et al 1987) and gender roles (see Cook's 1987 review of androgyny). It would appear that "women's" issues are finally in the mainstream of counseling psychology research.

A similar (if later) trend can be seen for research on racial/ethnic minorities, with a burgeoning of research and the beginnings of theoretical efforts in the latter part of this decade. Since racial/ethnic minority research and theory were discussed earlier, we here simply document an example of the increases. In Ponterotto's (1988) aforementioned review, it was noted that 5.7% of the articles in *JCP* from 1976 through 1986 had a racial/ethnic minority focus; in dividing this eleven-year period into 1976–1980 and 1981–1986, the percentages become 4.1 and 7.3, respectively. Our calculations for the period

1987–1988 indicate that 8.7% of *JCP*'s articles had a racial/ethnic minority focus, demonstrating dramatic increase overall. This high rate of publication appears to be reflected in other main counseling outlets as well (e.g. Pelsma & Cesari 1989).

There is no room for complacency here, since certain racial/ethnic minorities as well as other diverse populations continue to be seriously understudied. And there is immense need to study the applicability of much of our literature to groups diverse in age, gender, ethnicity, race, culture, sexual orientation, lifestyle, and (dis)ability. That notwithstanding, the trend in this direction is unmistakable.

A Full-Fledged Assault on the Counseling Process—Finally

A wise psychologist once commented that the only thing that could be said about counseling process researchers was that they had courage. How else could they dare to invest all the time and energy needed to unravel the awesome complexities of what goes on in counseling? In days of old it seemed that every few years a trend toward process was noted (at times referred to as a "flight"—e.g. from outcome), whereas the actual data did not indicate any such trend (Gelso 1979). We do not know if there was a quantitative increase in process research during the review period. But it does seem clear that, more than ever in counseling psychology, there is a sizeable coterie of dedicated researchers seeking to advance knowledge about the mysteries of counseling process. We have already noted the important programs by Hill, Tracey, Martin, Stiles, and Elliott. Several others could easily be added here, including some involved in group research, career research, and in social influence research that is process oriented.

An exciting element of the process research that has accumulated over the years is that we are now able to make some coherent, scientifically based generalizations about how process relates to outcome. Orlinsky & Howard's (1986) extensive review of the therapy literature is a major contribution in clarifying that process-outcome link. Virtually all counseling process research programs are now addressing the link.

The Search for Answers to Who, What, When, Where Questions

The question "Does counseling work?" absorbed the field for many years, and counseling and therapy researchers needed to continue that pursuit until the question was answered to everyone's satisfaction. It has been clearly answered in the affirmative now for several years. In the personal counseling or therapy area, the Lambert et al (1986) outcome review provides a decisive answer; in the career intervention area the verdict is also conclusive (Oliver & Spokane 1988).

During the review period, one could see a wholesale assault on the key question, framed many years ago by Krumboltz (1966): "[W]hich procedures and techniques, when used to accomplish what kinds of behavior change, are most effective with what kinds of clients when applied by what kinds of counselors?" (p. 22). Virtually all studies that looked at the effects of techniques or interventions incorporated counselor, client, or treatment factors into their designs. Simple experimental vs control group studies are now rare. Thus, as the progression of knowledge becomes apparent, equally evident is our pursuit of increasingly refined questions. Over a relatively long period (e.g. the 1960s and 1970s vs the 1980s), this research progression may represent the most powerful trend in all of counseling psychology.

POSTSCRIPT: INTEGRATION AND DIVERSITY

The French scientist Marie Curie once observed of her work: "One never notices what has been done; one can only see what remains to be done." Certainly, our empirical skepticism and restlessness provide energy for the process of scientific inquiry, but it is equally important to recognize what has been accomplished. During the period of this review, the counseling psychology literature manifested two overarching themes: integration and diversity. Integration can be seen in our attempts to consolidate the theoretical and empirical fragments or "nuggets of knowledge" (Krumboltz et al 1979) that have characterized our research in the past, while diversity is evident in our willingness to stretch the boundaries of our conceptualizations regarding appropriate content, methodologies, and client populations for our field. We are beginning to weave the inclusive, unifying "nomological nets" called for by Borgen (1984a). Unraveling the mysteries of what we discover in them will engage and inform counseling psychologists in the next decade.

ACKNOWLEDGMENTS

The authors thank Nancy E. Betz, Jean A. Carter, Bruce R. Fretz, and Clara E. Hill for their valuable critiques of an earlier version of this article.

Literature Cited

Alyn, J. H., Becker, L. A. 1984. Feminist therapy with chronically and profoundly disturbed women. *J. Couns. Psychol.* 31: 202–8

Arisohn, B., Bruch, M. A., Heimberg, R. G. 1988. Influence of assessment methods on self-efficacy and outcome expectancy ratings of assertive behavior. *J. Couns. Psychol.* 35:336–41

Astin, H. S. 1985. The meaning of work in women's lives: a sociopsychological model of career choice and work behavior. *Couns. Psychol.* 12:117–26

Atkinson, D. R. 1983. Ethnic similarity in counseling psychology: a review of research. *Couns. Psychol.* 11:79–92

Atkinson, D. R. 1985. A meta-review of research in cross-cultural counseling and psychotherapy. *J. Multicult. Couns.* 13:138–53

Atkinson, D. R., Schein, S. 1986. Similarity in counseling. *Couns. Psychol.* 14:319–54

Atkinson, D. R., Hackett, G., eds. 1988. *Counseling Non-Ethnic American Minorities.* Springfield, IL: Thomas

Atkinson, D. R., Furlong, M. J., Poston, W. C. 1986. Afro-American preference for counselor characteristics. *J. Couns. Psychol.* 33:326–30

Atkinson, D. R., Morten, G., Sue, D. W. 1983. *Counseling American Minorities: A Cross-Cultural Perspective.* Dubuque, Iowa: Brown

Auerbach, A. H., Johnson, M. 1977. Research on the therapist's level of experience. In *Effective Psychotherapy*, ed. A. S. Gurman, A. M. Razin, pp. 84–102. New York: Pergamon

Backer, T. E., Batchelor, W. F., Jones, J. M., Mays, V. M., eds. 1988. Psychology and AIDS. *Am. Psychol.* 43:835–937

Baker, R. W., Siryk, B. 1984. Measuring adjustment to college. *J. Couns. Psychol.* 31:179–89

Baker, R. W., Siryk, B. 1986. Exploratory intervention with a scale measuring adjustment to college. *J. Couns. Psychol.* 33:31–38

Barkham, M., Shapiro, D. A. 1986. Counselor verbal response modes and experienced empathy. *J. Couns. Psychol.* 33:3–10

Barrett-Lennard, G. T. 1986. The Relationship Inventory now: issues and advances in theory, method and use. In *The Psychotherapeutic Process*, ed. L. S. Greenberg, W. M. Pinsof, pp. 439–76. New York: Guilford

Bartlett, W. E., Goodyear, R. K., Bradley, F., eds. 1983. Supervision in counseling psychology II. *Couns. Psychol.* 11:9–79

Baruch, G. K., Biener, L., Barnett, R. C. 1987. Women and gender in research on work and family stress. *Am. Psychol.* 42:130–36

Bergin, A. E., Masters, K. S., Richards, P. S. 1987. Religiousness and mental health reconsidered. *J. Couns. Psychol.* 34:197–204

Bergin, A. E., Stinchfield, R. D., Gaskin, T. A., Masters, K. S., Sullivan, C. E. 1988. Religious life-styles and mental health: an exploratory study. *J. Couns. Psychol.* 35:91–98

Bernard, J. 1979. Supervision training: a discrimination model. *Couns. Educ. Superv.* 19:60–68

Berven, N. L. 1985. Reliability and validity of standardized case management simulations. *J. Couns. Psychol.* 32:397–409

Betz, N. E. 1987. Use of discriminant analysis in counseling psychology research. *J. Couns. Psychol.* 34:393–403

Betz, N. E., Fitzgerald, L. F. 1987. *The Career Psychology of Women.* Orlando, FL: Academic

Betz, N. E., Hackett, G. 1981. The relationship of career-related self-efficacy expectations to perceived career options in college women and men. *J. Couns. Psychol.* 28:399–410

Binder, A., Binder, V. L., eds. 1983. Special issue: counseling psychology in the justice system. *Couns. Psychol.* 11:3–99

Blustein, D. L., Strohmer, D. C. 1987. Vocational hypothesis testing in career decision-making. *J. Vocat. Behav.* 31:45–62

Bordin, E. S. 1987. Aim and trajectory. *Couns. Psychol.* 15:358–67

Borgen, F. H. 1984a. Counseling psychology. *Annu. Rev. Psychol.* 35:579–604

Borgen, F. H. 1984b. Are there necessary linkages between research practices and the philosophy of science? *J. Couns. Psychol.* 31:457–60

Borgen, F. H. 1989. Evaluation of eclectic epistemology. *Couns. Psychol.* 17:90–97

Borgen, F. H., Barnett, D. C. 1987. Applying cluster analysis in counseling psychology research. *J. Couns. Psychol.* 34:456–68

Brown, D. 1985. The preservice training and supervision of consultants. *Couns. Psychol.* 13:410–25

Brown, S. D., Alpert, D., Lent, R. W., Hunt, G., Brady, T. 1988. Perceived social support among college students: factor structure of the social support inventory. *J. Couns. Psychol.* 35:472–78

Brown, S. D., Brady, T., Lent, R. W., Wolfert, J., Hall, S. 1987. Perceived social support among college students: three studies of the psychometric characteristics and counseling uses of the social support inventory. *J. Couns. Psychol.* 34:337–54

Brown, S. D., Lent, R. W., eds. 1984. *Handbook of Counseling Psychology.* New York: Wiley

Brown, S. D., Reimer, D. A. 1984. Assessing attachment following divorce: development and psychometric evaluation of the Divorce Reaction Inventory. *J. Couns. Psychol.* 31: 520–31

Bruch, M. A., Pearl, L., Giordano, S. 1986. Differences in the cognitive processes of academically successful and unsuccessful test-anxious students. *J. Couns. Psychol.* 33:217–19

Bryant-Tuckett, R., Silverman, L. H. 1984. Effects of subliminal stimulation of symbiotic fantasies on the academic performance of emotionally handicapped students. *J. Couns. Psychol.* 31:295–305

Burlingame, G. M., Fuhriman, A. 1987. Conceptualizing short-term treatment: a comparative approach. *Couns. Psychol.* 15: 557–95

Casas, J. M. 1984. Policy, training, and research in counseling psychology: the racial/ethnic minority perspective. See Brown & Lent 1984, pp. 785–832

Casas, J. M. 1985. A reflection on the status of racial/ethnic minority research. *Couns. Psychol.* 13:581–99

Casas, J. M., Brady, S., Ponterotto, J. G.

1983. Sexual preference biases in counseling: an information processing approach. *J. Couns. Psychol.* 30:139–45

Claiborn, C. D. 1982. Interpretation and change in counseling. *J. Couns. Psychol.* 29:439–53

Claiborn, C. D., Dowd, E. T. 1985. Attributional interpretation in counseling: content versus discrepancy. *J. Couns. Psychol.* 32: 188–96

Claiborn, C. D., Ibrahim, F. A., eds. 1987. Counseling and violence. *J. Couns. Dev.* 65:338–90

Clarke, K. M., Greenberg, L. S. 1986. Differential effects of the Gestalt two-chair intervention and problem solving in resolving a decisional conflict. *J. Couns. Psychol.* 33:11–15

Conoley, C. W., Garber, R. A. 1985. Effects of reframing and self-control directives on loneliness, depression, and controliability. *J. Couns. Psychol.* 32:139–42

Cook, D. A., Helms, J. E. 1988. Visible racial/ethnic group supervisees' satisfaction with cross-cultural supervision as predicted by relationship characteristics. *J. Couns. Psychol.* 35:268–74

Cook, E. P. 1987. Psychological androgyny: a review of the research. *Couns. Psychol.* 15:471–513

Cooper, A., Stoltenberg, C. D. 1987. Comparison of a sexual enhancement and a communication training program on sexual and marital satisfaction. *J. Couns. Psychol.* 34: 309–14

Courtois, C. A., O'Neil, J. M., eds. 1988. Victimization. *Couns. Psychol.* 16:523–646

Cragan, M. K., Deffenbacher, J. L. 1984. Anxiety management training and relaxation as self-control in the treatment of general anxiety in medical outpatients. *J. Couns. Psychol.* 31:123–31

Craighead, L., McNamara, K., Horan, J. 1984. Perspectives on self-help and bibliotherapy: You are what you read. See Brown & Lent 1984, pp. 878–929

Crowley, C., Crowley, D., Clodfelter, C. 1986. Effects of a self-coping cognitive treatment for test anxiety. *J. Couns. Psychol.* 33:84–86

Dawis, R. V. 1984. Of old philosophies and new kids on the block. *J. Couns. Psychol.* 31:467–69

Deffenbacher, J. L., ed. 1988a. Cognitive-behavioral treatments of anxiety. *Couns. Psychol.* 16:3–10

Deffenbacher, J. L. 1988b. Cognitive-relaxation and social skills treatments of anger: a year later. *J. Couns. Psychol.* 35: 234–36

Deffenbacher, J. L. 1988c. Some recommendations and directions. *Couns. Psychol.* 16:91–95

Deffenbacher, J. L., Story, D. A., Stark, R. S., Hogg, J. A., Brandon, A. D. 1987. Cognitive-relaxation and social skills interventions in the treatment of general anger. *J. Couns. Psychol.* 34:171–76

Dendato, K. M., Diener, D. 1986. Effectiveness of cognitive/relaxation therapy and study-skills training in reducing self-reported anxiety and improving the academic performance of test-anxious students. *J. Couns. Psychol.* 33:131–35

Dill-Standiford, T. J., Stiles, W. B., Rorer, L. G. 1988. Counselor-client agreement on session impact. *J. Couns. Psychol.* 35:47–55

Dowd, E. T., Hughes, S. L., Brockbank, L., Halpain, D., Seibel, C., et al. 1988. Compliance-based and defiance-based intervention strategies. *J. Couns. Psychol.* 35:370–76

Dowd, E. T., Milne, C. R. 1986. Paradoxical interventions in counseling psychology. *Couns. Psychol.* 14:237–82

Dworkin, S. H., Kerr, B. A. 1987. Comparison of interventions for women experiencing body image problems. *J. Couns. Psychol.* 34:136–40

Eccles, J. 1987. Gender roles and women's achievement-related decisions. *Psychol. Women. Q.* 11:135–72

Elich, M., Thompson, R. W., Miller, L. 1985. Mental imagery as revealed by eye movements and spoken predicates: a test of neurolinguistic programming. *J. Couns. Psychol.* 32:622–25

Elliott, R. 1985. Helpful and nonhelpful events in brief counseling interviews: an empirical taxonomy. *J. Couns. Psychol.* 32:307–22

Ellis, A. 1986. Fanaticism that may lead to a nuclear holocaust: the contributions of scientific counseling and psychotherapy. *J. Couns. Dev.* 65:146–51

Ellis, M. V., Dell, D. M. 1986. Dimensionality of supervisor roles: supervisor's perception of supervision. *J. Couns. Psychol.* 33:282–91

Ellis, M. V., Dell, D. M., Good, G. E. 1988. Counselor trainees' perceptions of supervisory roles: two studies testing the dimensionality of supervision. *J. Couns. Psychol.* 35:315–24

Epperson, D. L., Bushway, D. J., Warman, R. E. 1983. Client self-termination after one counseling session: effects of problem recognition, counselor gender, and counselor experience. *J. Couns. Psychol.* 30:307–15

Farmer, H. S. 1985. Model of career and achievement motivation for women and men. *J. Couns. Psychol.* 32:363–90

Fassinger, R. E. 1985. A casual model of college women's career choice. *J. Vocat. Behav.* 27:123–53

Fassinger, R. E. 1987. Use of structural equation modeling in counseling psychology research. *J. Couns. Psychol.* 34:425–36

Fitzgerald, L. F. 1986. On the essential relations between education and work. *J. Vocat. Behav.* 28:254–84

Fitzgerald, L. F., Hubert, L. J. 1987. Multidimensional Scaling: some possibilities for counseling psychology. *J. Couns. Psychol.* 34:469–80

Fitzgerald, L. F., Osipow, S. H. 1986. An occupational analysis of counseling psychology: How special is the specialty? *Am. Psychol.* 41:535–44

Folensbee, R. W., Draguns, J. G., Danish, S. J. 1986. Impact of two types of counselor intervention on Black American, Puerto Rican, and Anglo-American clients. *J. Couns. Psychol.* 33:446–53

Foon, A. E. 1986. Effect of locus of control in counseling expectations of clients. *J. Couns. Psychol.* 33:462–64

Forsyth, D. R., Strong, S. R. 1986. The scientific study of counseling and psychotherapy: a unificationist view. *Am. Psychol.* 41:113–19

Freeman, S. T., Conoley, C. W. 1986. Training, experience, and similarity as factors of influence in preferences of deaf students for counselors. *J. Couns. Psychol.* 33:164–69

Friedlander, M. L., Highlen, P. S. 1984. A spatial view of the interpersonal structure of family interviews: similarities and differences across counselors. *J. Couns. Psychol.* 31:477–87

Friedlander, M. L., Highlen, P. S., Lassiter, W. L. 1985. Content analytic comparison of four expert counselors' approaches to family treatment: Ackerman, Bowen, Jackson, and Whitaker. *J. Couns. Psychol.* 32:171–80

Friedlander, M. L., Phillips, S. D. 1984. Stochastic process analysis of interactive discourse in early counseling interviews. *J. Couns. Psychol.* 31:139–48

Friedlander, M. L., Schwartz, G. S. 1985. Toward a theory of strategic self-presentation in counseling and psychotherapy. *J. Couns. Psychol.* 32:483–501

Friedlander, M. L., Ward, L. G. 1984. Developmental validation of the supervisory styles inventory. *J. Couns. Psychol.* 31:541–57

Fry, P. S. 1984. Development of a geriatric scale of hopelessness: implications for counseling and intervention with the depressed elderly. *J. Couns. Psychol.* 31:322–31

Gallesich, J. 1985. Toward a meta-theory of consultation. *Couns. Psychol.* 13:336–54

Ganikos, M., Blake, R., eds. 1984. Counseling psychology and aging. *Couns. Psychol.* 12:13–99

Garfield, S. L., Bergin, A. E., eds. 1986. *Handbook of Psychotherapy and Behavior Change.* New York: Wiley. 3rd ed.

Gazda, G. M., Rude, S. S., Weissberg, M., eds. 1988. The third national conference for counseling psychology: planning the future. *Coun. Psychol.* 16:323–439

Gelso, C. J. 1979. Research in counseling: methodological and professional issues. *Couns. Psychol.* 8:7–35

Gelso, C. J. 1985. Rigor, relevance, and counseling research: on the need to maintain our course between Scylla and Charybdis. *J. Couns. Dev.* 63:551–53

Gelso, C. J., Betz, N. E., Friedlander, M. L., Helms, J. E., Hill, C. E., et al. 1988. Research in counseling psychology: prospects and recommendations. *Couns. Psychol.* 16:385–406

Gelso, C. J., Carter, J. A. 1985. The relationship in counseling and psychotherapy: components, consequences, and theoretical antecedents. *Couns. Psychol.* 13:155–243

Gelso, C. J., Johnson, D. H. 1983. *Explorations in Time-Limited Counseling and Psychotherapy.* New York: Teachers College Press

Gelso, C. J., Prince, J., Cornfield, J. L., Payne, A. B., Royalty, G., et al. 1985. Quality of counselors intake evaluations for clients with problems that are primarily vocational versus personal. *J. Couns. Psychol.* 32:339–47

Gilbert, L. A., ed. 1987. Dual career families in perspective. *Couns. Psychol.* 15:3–145

Gladstein, G. A. 1983. Understanding empathy: integrating counseling, developmental and social psychology perspectives. *J. Couns. Psychol.* 30:467–82

Goodman, S. H., Sewell, D. R., Jampol, R. C. 1984. On going to the counselor: contributions of life stress and social supports to the decision to seek psychological counseling. *J. Couns. Psychol.* 31:306–13

Goodyear, R. K., Abadie, P. D., Efros, F. 1984. Supervisory theory into practice: differential perception of supervision by Ekstein, Ellis, Polster, and Rogers. *J. Couns. Psychol.* 31:228–37

Gottfredson, L. S. 1981. Circumscription and compromise: a developmental theory of occupational aspiration. *J. Couns. Psychol.* 28:545–79

Gottfredson, L. S., ed. 1986. The g factor in employment. *J. Vocat. Behav.* 29:293–513

Graunke, B., Roberts, T. K. 1985. Neurolinguistic programming: the impact of imagery tasks on sensory predicate usage: *J. Couns. Psychol.* 32:525–30

Greenhaus, J. H., Parasuraman, S. 1986. Vocational and organizational behavior, 1985: a review. *J. Vocat. Behav.* 29:115–76

Haase, R. F., Strohmer, D. C., Biggs, D. A., Keller, K. E. 1983. Mediational inferences in the process of counselor judgment. *J. Couns. Psychol.* 30:275–78

Hackett, G., Betz, N. E. 1981. A self-efficacy approach to the career development of women. *J. Vocat. Behav.* 18:326–39

Haley, T. J., Dowd, E. T. 1988. Responses of deaf adolescents to differences in counselor method of communication and disability status. *J. Couns. Psychol.* 35:258–62

Halgin, R. P., Weaver, D. D., Edell, W. S., Spencer, P. G. 1987. Relation of depression and help-seeking history to attitudes toward seeking psychological help. *J. Couns. Psychol.* 34:177–85

Hansen, J. C., Pound, R., Petro, C. 1976. Review of research on practicum supervision. *Couns. Educ. Superv.* 16:107–16

Harman, J. I. 1986. Relations among the components of the empathic process. *J. Couns. Psychol.* 33:371–76

Heatherington, L. 1988. Coding relational communication control in counseling: criterion validity. *J. Couns. Psychol.* 35:41–46

Heatherington, L., Allen, G. J. 1984. Sex and relational communication patterns in counseling. *J. Couns. Psychol.* 31:287–94

Heesacker, M. 1986a. Counseling pretreatment and the elaboration likelihood model of attitude change. *J. Couns. Psychol.* 33:107–14

Heesacker, M. 1986b. Extrapolating from the elaboration likelihood model of attitude change in counseling. In *Social Influence Processing In Counseling and Psychotherapy*, ed. F. J. Dorn, pp. 43–54. Springfield, IL: Thomas

Heinemann, A. W., Shontz, F. C. 1985. Methods of studying persons. *Couns. Psychol.* 13:111–25

Helms, J. E. 1984. Toward a theoretical explanation of the effects of race on counseling: a Black and White model. *Couns. Psychol.* 12:153–65

Heppner, P. P., Claiborn, C. D. 1989. Social influence research in counseling: a review and critique. *J. Couns. Psychol.* 36:365–87

Heppner, P. P., Krauskopf, C. J. 1987. An information-processing approach to personal problem solving. *Couns. Psychol.* 15:371–447

Heppner, P. P., Menne, M. M., Rosenberg, J. I. 1986. Some reflections on the social influence process in counseling. In *The Social Influence Process in Counseling and Psychotherapy*, ed. F. J. Dorn, pp. 137–43. Evanson, IL: Thomas

Heppner, P. P., Roehlke, H. J. 1984. Differences among supervisees at different levels of training: implications for a de-velopmental model of supervision. *J. Couns. Psychol.* 31:76–90

Highlen, P. S., Hill, C. E. 1984. Factors affecting client change in individual counseling: current status and theoretical speculations. See Brown & Lent 1984, pp. 334–96

Hill, C. E. 1989. *Therapist Techniques and Client Outcomes: Eight Cases of Brief Psychotherapy.* Newbury Park, CA: Sage

Hill, C. E., Carter, J. A., O'Farrell, M. K. 1983. A case study of the process and outcome of time-limited counseling. *J. Couns. Psychol.* 30:3–18

Hill, C. E., Helms, J. E., Spiegel, S. B., Tichenor, V. 1988a. Development of a system for categorizing client reactions to therapist interventions. *J. Couns. Psychol.* 35:27–36

Hill, C. E., Helms, J. E., Tichenor, V., Spiegel, S. B., O'Grady, K. E., et al. 1988b. Effects of therapist response modes in brief psychotherapy. *J. Couns. Psychol.* 35:222–33

Hill, C. E., O'Grady, K. E. 1985. List of therapist interventions illustrated in a case study and with therapists of varying orientations. *J. Couns. Psychol.* 32:3–22

Hirsch, P. A., Stone, G. L. 1983. Cognitive strategies and the client conceptualization process. *J. Couns. Psychol.* 30:566–72

Hoffman, J. A. 1984. Psychological separation of late adolescents from their parents. *J. Couns. Psychol.* 31:170–78

Hoffman, J. A., Weiss, B. 1987. Family dynamics and presenting problems in college students. *J. Couns. Psycho.* 34:157–6

Hogg, J. A., Deffenbacher, J. L. 1988. A comparison of cognitive and interpersonal-process group therapies in the treatment of depression among college students. *J. Couns. Psychol.* 35:304–10

Holloway, E. L., Wampold, B. E. 1983. Patterns of verbal behavior and judgments of satisfaction in the supervision interview. *J. Couns. Psychol.* 30:227–34

Hoshmand, L. L. S. T. 1989. Alternate research paradigms: a review and teaching proposal. *Couns. Psychol.* 17:3–80

Howard, G. S. 1984. A modest proposal for a revision of strategies for counseling research. *J. Couns. Psychol.* 31:430–42

Howard, G. S. 1985. Can research in the human sciences become more relevant to practice? *J. Couns. Dev.* 63:539–44

Howard, G. S. 1986. *Dare We Develop a Human Science.* Notre Dame, IN: Academic

Howard, G. S. 1989. *A Tale of Two Stories.* Notre Dame, IN: Academic

Howard, G. S., Nance, D. W., Myers, P. 1986. Adaptive counseling and therapy: an integrative, eclectic model. *Couns. Psychol.* 14:363–442

Johnson, M. 1986. From repugnance to cautious curiosity. *Couns. Psychol.* 14:297–302

Johnson, N. S., Holloway, E. L. 1988. Conceptual complexity and obsessionality in bulimic college women. *J. Couns. Psychol.* 32:251–57

Johnston, J. A., Buescher, K. L., Heppner, M. J. 1988. Computerized career information and guidance systems: caveat emptor. *J. Couns. Dev.* 67:39–41

Jones, A. S., Gelso, C. J. 1988. Differential effects of style of interpretation: another look. *J. Couns. Psychol.* 35:363–69

Kaul, T. J., Bednar, R. 1986. Experimental group research: results, questions and suggestions. See Garfield & Bergin 1986, pp. 671–714

Kelly, K. R., Stone, G. L. 1987. Effects of three psychological treatments and self-monitoring on the reduction of Type A behavior. *J. Couns. Psychol.* 34:46–54

Kiesler, D. J., Goldston, C. S. 1988. Client-therapist complementarity: an analysis of the Gloria films. *J. Couns. Psychol.* 35:127–33

Kivlighan, D. M., McGovern, T. V., Corazzini, J. G. 1984. Effects of content and timing of structuring interventions on group therapy process and outcome. *J. Couns. Psychol.* 31:363–70

Kivlighan, D. M., Shapiro, R. M. 1987. Holland type as a predictor of benefit from self-help career counseling. *J. Couns. Psychol.* 34:326–29

Klippel, J. A., DeJoy, D. M. 1984. Counseling psychology in behavioral medicine and health psychology. *J. Couns. Psychol.* 31:219–27

Kokotovic, A. M., Tracey, T. J. 1987. Premature termination at a university counseling center. *J. Couns. Psychol.* 34:80–82

Kraft, R. G., Claiborn, C. D., Dowd, E. T. 1985. Effects of positive reframing and paradoxical directives in counseling for negative emotions. *J. Couns. Psychol.* 32:617–21

Krause, A. K., Allen, G. J. 1988. Perceptions of counselor supervision: an examination of Stoltenberg's model from the perspectives of supervisor and supervisee. *J. Couns. Psychol.* 35:77–80

Krumboltz, J. D., ed. 1966. *Revolution in Counseling: Implications of Behavioral Science.* Boston, MA: Houghton-Mifflin

Krumboltz, J. D., Becker-Haven, J. F., Burnett, K. F. 1979. Counseling Psychology. *Annu. Rev. Psychol.* 30:555–602

Kunce, J. T., Priesmeyer, M. L. 1985.

Measuring family dynamics. *J. Couns. Psychol.* 32:40–46

Kurpius, D. J. 1985. Consultation interventions: successes, failures, and proposals. *Couns. Psychol.* 13:368–89

Kurpius, D. J., Benjamin, D., Morran, D. K. 1985. Effects of teaching a cognitive strategy on counselor trainee internal dialogue and clinical hypothesis formulation. *J. Couns. Psychol.* 32:263–71

Lambert, M. J., Shapiro, D. A., Bergin, A. E. 1986. The effectiveness of psychotherapy. See Garfield & Bergin 1986, pp. 157–212

Lapan, R., Patton, M. J. 1986. Self-psychology and the adolescent process: measures of pseudoautonomy and peer-group dependence. *J. Couns. Psychol.* 33:136–42

Larson, L. M., Heppner, P. P. 1985. The relationship of problem-solving appraisal to career decision and indecision. *J. Vocat. Behav.* 26:55–65

Lazarick, D. L., Fishbein, S. S., Loiello, M. A., Howard, G. S. 1988. Practical investigations of volition. *J. Couns. Psychol.* 35:15–26

Leong, F. T. L. 1986. Counseling and psychotherapy with Asian-Americans: review of literature. *J. Couns. Psychol.* 33:196–206

Levant, R. F., ed. 1983. Family counseling psychology. *Couns. Psychol.* 11:5–77

Lent, R. W., Hackett, G. 1987. Career self-efficacy: empirical status and future directions. *J. Vocat. Behav.* 30:347–82

Littrell, J. M., Lee-Borden, N., Lorenz, J. R. 1979. A developmental framework for counseling supervision. *Couns. Educ. Superv.* 19:129–36

Loganbill, C. R., Hardy, E. V., Delworth, V. 1982. Supervision: a conceptual model. *Couns. Psychol.* 10:3–42

Lomis, M. J., Baker, L. L. 1985. Microtraining of forensic psychiatric patients for empathic counseling skills. *J. Couns. Psychol.* 32:84–93

Lopez, F. G. 1987. The impact of parental divorce on college students development. *J. Couns. Dev.* 65:484–86

Lopez, F. G., Campbell, V. L., Watkins, C. E. 1986. Depression, psychological separation, and college adjustment: an investigation of sex differences. *J. Couns. Psychol.* 33:52–56

Lopez, F. G., Campbell, V. L., Watkins, C. E. 1988. Family structure, psychological separation, and college adjustment: a canonical analysis and cross-validation. *J. Couns. Psychol.* 35:402–9

Lustman, P. J., Sowa, C. J., O'Hara, D. J. 1984. Factors influencing college student health: development of the psychological distress inventory. *J. Couns. Psychol.* 31: 28–35

Magoon, T. M. 1989. *College and university counseling center data bank: analysis by enrollment.* College Park: Univ. Maryland. Mimeo

Mahalik, J. R., Kivlighan, D. M. 1988. Self-help treatment for depression: Who succeeds? *J. Couns. Psychol.* 35:237–42

Mahoney, M. J., Lyddon, W. J. 1988. Recent developments in cognitive approaches to counseling and psychotherapy. *Couns. Psychol.* 16:190–234

Mallinckrodt, B., Helms, J. E. 1986. Effect of disabled counselors' self-disclosures on client perceptions of the counselor. *J. Couns. Psychol.* 33:343–48

Marikas, D. A., Russell, R. K., Dell, D. M. 1985. Effects of supervisor experience level on planning and in-session supervisor verbal behavior. *J. Couns. Psychol.* 32:410–16

Martin, J. 1984. The cognitive mediational paradigm for research on counseling. *J. Couns. Psychol.* 31:558–71

Martin, J., Martin, W., Mechthild, M., Slemon, A. 1986. Empirical investigation of the cognitive mediational paradigm for research on counseling. *J. Couns. Psychol.* 33:115–23

Martin, J., Martin, W., Slemon, A. G. 1987. Cognitive mediation in person-centered and rational-emotive therapy. *J. Couns. Psychol.* 34:251–60

Martin, J., Stelmaczonek, K. 1988. Participants identification and recall of important events in counseling. *J. Couns. Psychol.* 35:385–90

Matheny, K. B., Aycock, D. W., Pugh, J. L., Curlette, W. L., Canella, K. A. S. 1986. Stress coping: qualitative and quantitative synthesis with implications for treatment. *Couns. Psychol.* 14:499–549

Maurer, R. E., Tindall, J. H. 1983. Effect of postural congruence on client's perception of counseling empathy. *J. Couns. Psychol.* 30:158–63

Marx, J. A., Gelso, C. J. 1987. Termination of individual counseling in a university counseling center. *J. Couns. Psychol.* 34:3–9

McGuire, J. M., Taylor, D. R., Broome, D. H., Blau, B. I., Abbott, D. W. 1986. Group structuring techniques and their influence on process involvement in a group counseling training group. *J. Couns. Psychol.* 33:270–75

McHugh, M. C., Koeske, R. D., Frieze, I. H. 1986. Issues to consider in conducting nonsexist psychological research: a guide for researchers. *Am. Psychol.* 41:879–90

McNamara, K., Horan, J. J. 1986. Experimental construct validity in the evalua-

tion of cognitive and behavioral treatments for depression. *J. Couns. Psychol.* 33:23–30

McNeill, B. W., May, R. J., Lee, V. E. 1987. Perception of counselor source characteristics by premature and successful terminators. *J. Couns. Psychol.* 34:86–89

McNeill, B. W., Stolenberg, C. D., Pierce, R. A. 1985. Supervisees' perceptions of their development: a test of the counselor complexity model. *J. Couns. Psychol.* 32:630–33

Mercier, M. A., Johnson, M. 1984. Representational system predicate use and convergence in counseling: Gloria revisited. *J. Couns. Psychol.* 31:161–69

Mintz, L. B., Betz, N. E. 1988. Prevalence and correlates of eating disordered behaviors among undergraduate women. *J. Couns. Psychol.* 35:463–71

Mitchell, L. K., Krumboltz, J. D. 1987. The effects of cognitive restructuring and decision-making training on career indecision. *J. Couns. Dev.* 66:171–74

Morran, D. K. 1986. Relationship of counselor self-talk and hypothesis formulation to performance level. *J. Couns. Psychol.* 33:395–400

Morran, D. K., Robison, F. F., Stockton, R. 1985. Feedback exchange in counseling groups: an analysis of message content and receiver acceptance as a function of leader versus member delivery, session, and valence. *J. Couns. Psychol.* 32:57–67

Mueser, K. T., Foy, D. W., Carter, M. J. 1986. Social skills training for job maintenance in a psychiatric patient. *J. Couns. Psychol.* 33:360–62

Myers, R. 1986. Research on educational and vocational counseling. See Garfield & Bergin 1986, pp. 715–38

Myers, R., Cairo, P. C., eds. 1983. Computer-assisted counseling. *Couns. Psychol.* 11:6–74

Myszka, M. T., Galassi, J. P., Ware, W. B. 1986. Comparison of cognitive assessment methods with heterosocially anxious college women. *J. Couns. Psychol.* 33:401–7

Nagel, J., Cimbolic, P., Newlin, M. 1988. Efficacy of elderly and adolescent volunteer counselors in a nursing home setting. *J. Couns. Psychol.* 35:81–86

Neal, G. W., Heppner, P. P. 1986. Problem-solving self-appraisal, awareness, and utilization of campus helping resources. *J. Couns. Psychol.* 33:39–44

Neimeyer, G. J. 1988. Cognitive integration and differentiation in vocational behavior. *Couns. Psychol.* 16:440–75

Newcomb, M. D., Chou, C.-P., Bentler, P. M., Huba, G. J. 1988. Cognitive motivations for drug use among adolescents: longitudinal tests of gender differences and predictors of change in drug use. *J. Couns. Psychol.* 35:426–38

Nezu, A. M., Ronan, G. F. 1988. Social problem solving as a moderator of stress-related depressive symptoms: a prospective analysis. *J. Couns. Psychol.* 35:134–38

Niles, W. J. 1986. Effects of a moral development discussion group on delinquent and predelinquent boys. *J. Couns. Psychol.* 33: 45–51

Oetting, E. R., Beauvais, F. 1987. Peer cluster theory, socialization characteristics, and adolescent drug use: a path analysis. *J. Couns. Psychol.* 34:205–13

O'Farrell, M., Hill, C. E., Patton, S. 1986. A comparison of two cases of counseling. *J. Couns. Dev.* 65:141–45

Oliver, L. W., Spokane, A. R. 1988. Career-intervention outcome: What contributes to client gain? *J. Couns. Psychol.* 35:447–62

Orlinsky, D. E., Howard, K. I. 1986. Process and outcome in psychotherapy. See Garfield & Bergin 1986, pp. 311–81

Osipow, S. H. 1987. Counseling psychology: theory, research, and practice in career counseling. *Annu. Rev. Psychol.* 38:257–78

Osipow, S. H., Doty, R. E., Spokane, A. R. 1985. Occupational stress, strain, and coping across the life span. *J. Vocat. Behav.* 27:98–108

Palmer, S., Cochran, L. 1988. Parents as agents of career development. *J. Couns. Psychol.* 35:71–76

Parham, T. A., Helms, J. E. 1985. Relation of racial identity attitudes to self-actualization and affective states of Black students. *J. Couns. Psychol.* 32:431–40

Parloff, M. B., Waskow, I. E., Wolfe, B. E. 1978. Research on therapist variables in relation to process and outcome. In *Handbook of Psychotherapy and Behavior Change*, ed. S. L. Garfield, A. E. Bergin, pp. 233–82. New York: Wiley. 2nd ed.

Patton, M. J. 1984. Managing social interaction in counseling: a contribution from the philosophy of science. *J. Couns. Psychol.* 31:442–56

Pederson, P. B., ed. 1985. *Handbook of Cross-Cultural Counseling and Therapy*. Westport, CT: Greenwood Press

Pekarik, G. 1988. Relation of counselor identification of client problem description to continuance in a behavioral weight loss program. *J. Couns. Psychol.* 35:66–70

Pelletier, J. R., Rogers, E. S., Dellario, D. J. 1985. Barriers to the provision of mental health services to individuals with severe physical disability. *J. Couns. Psychol.* 32: 422–30

Pelsma, D. M., Cesari, J. P. 1989. Content analysis of the *Journal of Counseling and*

Development: Vol. 48–66. *J. Couns. Dev.* 67:275–78

Perrin, D. K., Dowd, E. T. 1986. Effect of paradoxical and nonparadoxical self-disclosure on counselor social influence. *J. Couns. Psychol.* 33:207–10

Phillips, S. D., Pazienza, N. J., Ferrin, H. H. 1984. Decision-making styles and problem-solving appraisal. *J. Couns. Psychol.* 31: 497–502

Pinkney, J. W., Jacobs, D. 1985. New counselors and personal interest in the task of career counseling. *J. Couns. Psychol.* 32: 454–57

Polkinghorne, D. E. 1984. Further extensions of methodological diversity for counseling psychology. *J. Couns. Psychol.* 31:416–29

Pomales, J., Claiborn, C. D., LaFramboise, T. D. 1986. Effects of Black students' racial identity on perceptions of White counselors' varying in cultural sensitivity. *J. Couns. Psychol.* 33:57–61

Ponterotto, J. G. 1988. Racial/ethnic minority research in the *Journal of Counseling Psychology:* a content analysis and methodological critique. *J. Couns. Psychol.* 35: 410–18

Ponterotto, J. G., Alexander, C. M., Hinkston, J. A. 1988. Afro-American preferences for counselor characteristics: a replication and extension. *J. Couns. Psychol.* 35:175–82

Prediger, D. J., Sawyer, R. L. 1986. Ten years of career development: a nationwide study of high school students. *J. Couns. Dev.* 64:45–49

Prior, D. W., Goodyear, R. K., Holen, M. 1983. EMG biofeedback training of Type A and Type B behavior pattern subjects. *J. Couns. Psychol.* 30:316–22

Puchkoff, S. C., Levin, P. G. 1987. Student responsiveness to specialized college services: contribution of personality variables and perceptions of services. *J. Couns. Psychol.* 34:322–30

Rabinowitz, F. E., Heppner, P. P., Roehlke, H. J. 1986. Descriptive study of process and outcome variables of supervision over time. *J. Couns. Psychol.* 33:292–300

Rapaport, R. J., Rodolfa, E. R., Lee, V. E. 1985. Variables related to premature termination in a university counseling center: a reply to Saltzman's (1984) comment. *J. Couns. Psychol.* 32:469–71

Reising, G. N., Daniels, M. H. 1983. A study of Hogan's model of counselor supervision. *J. Couns. Psychol.* 31:235–44

Richardson, B. K. 1984. Empirically-derived client typologies—a missing link to the evaluation of the rehabilitation counseling process. *J. Couns. Psychol.* 31:132–38

Richardson, M. S., Johnson, M. 1984.

Counseling women. See Brown & Lent 1984, pp. 832–77

Rickards, L. D. 1984. Verbal interaction and supervisor perception in counselor supervision. *J. Couns. Psychol.* 31:262–65

Robbins, S. B., Jolkovski, M. P. 1987. Managing countertransference feelings: an interactional model using awareness of feeling and theoretical framework. *J. Couns. Psychol.* 34:276–82

Robbins, S. B., Mullison, D., Boggs, K., Riedesel, B., Jacobson, B. 1985. Attrition behavior before career development workshops. *J. Couns. Psychol.* 32:232–38

Robbins, S. B., Patton, M. J. 1985. Self-psychology and career development: construction of the superiority and goal instability scales. *J. Couns. Psychol.* 32:221–31

Robbins, S. B., Tucker, K. R. 1986. Relation of goal instability to self-directed and interactional career counseling workshops. *J. Couns. Psychol.* 33:418–24

Robinson, S. E., Gross, D. R. 1985. Ethics of consultation: the Canterville ghost. *Couns. Psychol.* 13:444–65

Rogers, C. R. 1984. One alternative to nuclear planetary suicide. *Couns. Psychol.* 12:3–12

Rothblum, E. D., Solomon, L. J., Murakami, J. 1986. Affective, cognitive and behavioral differences between high and low procrastinators. *J. Couns. Psychol.* 33:397–94

Russell, R. K., Crimmings, A. M., Lent, R. W. 1984. Counselor training and supervision: theory and research. See Brown & Lent 1984, pp. 625–81

Saltzman, C. 1984. Variables related to premature termination in a university counseling center: a comment on Rodolfa, Rapaport, and Lee. *J. Couns. Psychol.* 31:402–4

Sampson, J. P. 1986. Computer technology and counseling psychology: regression toward the machine? *Couns. Psychol.* 14:567–83

Sanchez, H. R., Atkinson, D. R. 1983. Mexican-American cultural commitment, preference for counselor ethnicity, and willingness to use counseling. *J. Couns. Psychol.* 30:215–20

Scher, M., Stevens, M., Good, G., Eichenfield, G. 1987. *Handbook of Counseling and Psychotherapy with Men.* Newbury Park, CA: Sage

Schinke, S. P., Orlani, M. A., Botvin, G. J., Gilchrist, L. D., Trimble, J. E., et al. 1988. Preventing substance abuse among American-Indian adolescents: a bicultural competence skills approach. *J. Couns. Psychol.* 35:87–90

Schwartz, G. S., Friedlander, M. L., Tedeschi, J. T. 1986. Effects of clients' attributional explanations and reasons for seeking help on counselors' impressions. *J. Couns. Psychol.* 33:90–93

Sharpley, C. F. 1984. Predicate matching in NLP: a review of research on the preferred representational system. *J. Couns. Psychol.* 31:238–48

Sharpley, C. 1987. Research findings on neurolinguistic programming: nonsupportive data or untestable theory? *J. Couns. Psychol.* 34:103–7

Shoham-Salomon, V., Jancourt, A. 1985. Differential effectiveness of paradoxical interventions for more versus less stress-prone individuals. *J. Couns. Psychol.* 32:449–53

Slaney, R. B., Lewis, E. T. 1985. Effects of career exploration on career undecided reentry women: an intervention and follow-up study. *J. Vocat. Behav.* 28:97–109

Slaney, R. B., Russell, J. E. A. 1987. Perspectives on vocational behavior, 1986: a review. *J. Vocat. Behav.* 31:111–73

Smith, E. J. 1985. Ethnic minorities: life stress, social support, and mental health issues. *Couns. Psychol.* 13:537–80

Smith, E. J., Vasquez, M. J., eds. 1985. Cross-cultural counseling. *Couns. Psychol.* 13:531–684

Smith, L. C., Robbins, S. B. 1988. Validity of the goal instability scale (modified) as a predictor of adjustment in retirement-age adults. *J. Couns. Psychol.* 35:325–29

Spiegel, S. B., Hill, C. E. 1989. Guidelines for research on therapist interpretation: toward greater methodological rigor and relevance to practice. *J. Couns. Psychol.* 36:121–29

Spokane, A. R. 1985. A review of research on person-environment congruence in Holland's theory of careers. *J. Vocat. Behav.* 26:306–43

Spokane, A. R. 1987. Conceptual and methodological issues in person-environmental fit research. *J. Vocat. Behav.* 31:217–361

Spokane, A. R., Oliver, L. W. 1983. The outcomes of vocational intervention. See Walsh & Osipow 1983a, pp. 99–136

Stiles, W. B., Shapiro, D. A., Firth-Cozens, J. A. 1988. Do sessions of different treatments have different impacts? *J. Couns. Psychol.* 35:391–96

Stiles, W. B., Snow, J. S. 1984. Counseling session impact as viewed by novice counselors and their clients. *J. Couns. Psychol.* 31:3–12

Stoltenberg, C. D. 1981. Approaching supervision from a developmental perspective: the counselor complexity model. *J. Couns. Psychol.* 28:59–65

Stoltenberg, C. D., Delworth, V. 1987. *Supervising Counselors and Therapists: A Developmental Approach.* San Francisco, CA: Jossey-Bass

Stone, G. L. 1984. Reaction: in defense of the "artifical." *J. Couns. Psychol.* 31:108–10

Strohmer, D. C., Biggs, D. A. 1983. Effects of counselor disability status on disabled subjects' perceptions of counselor attractiveness and expertness. *J. Couns. Psychol.* 30:202–8

Strohmer, D. C., Biggs, D. A., Haase, R. F., Keller, K. E. 1983. Hypothesis formation and testing in clinical judgment. *J. Couns. Psychol.* 30:607–10

Strohmer, D. C., Biggs, D. A., Keller, K. E., Thibodeau, J. R. 1984. Clinical judgment and affective disorders. *J. Couns. Psychol.* 31:99–103

Strohmer, D. C., Chiodo, A. L. 1984. Counselor hypothesis testing strategies: the role of initial impressions and self-schema *J. Couns. Psychol.* 31:510–19

Strohmer, D. C., Moilanen, D. L., Barry, L. J. 1988. Personal hypothesis testing: the role of consistency and self-schema. *J. Couns. Psychol.* 35:56–65

Strohmer, D. C., Newman, L. J. 1983. Counselor hypothesis-testing strategies. *J. Couns. Psychol.* 30:557–65

Strong, S. R. 1968. Counseling: an interpersonal influence process. *J. Couns. Psychol.* 15:215–24

Strong, S. R., Matross, R. P. 1973. Change processes in counseling and psychotherapy. *J. Couns. Psychol.* 20:25–37

Subich, L. M., Coursol, D. H. 1985. Counseling expectations of clients and nonclients for group and individual treatment modes. *J. Couns. Psychol.* 32:245–51

Subich, L. M., Hardin, S. I. 1985. Counseling expectations as a function of fee for service. *J. Couns. Psychol.* 32:323–28

Sue, S., Zane, N. W. S. 1985. Academic achievement and socioemotional adjustment among Chinese university students. *J. Couns. Psychol.* 32:570–79

Tarico, V. S., VanVelzen, D. R., Altmaier, E. M. 1986. Comparison of thought-listing rating methods. *J. Couns. Psychol.* 33:81–83

Taussig, I. M. 1987. Comparative responses of Mexican Americans and Anglo-Americans to early goal setting in a public mental health clinic. *J. Couns. Psychol.* 34:214–17

Thompson, A. P. 1986. Changes in counseling skills during graduate and undergraduate study. *J. Couns. Psychol.* 33:65–72

Thoresen, C. E., Eagleston, J. R. 1985. Counseling for health. *Couns. Psychol.* 13:15–88

Thurman, C. W. 1985. Effectiveness of cognitive-behavioral treatments in reducing Type A behavior among university faculty—one year later. *J. Couns. Psychol.* 32:445–48

Tinsley, H. E. A., Bowman, S. L., Ray, S. B. 1988. Manipulation of expectancies about counseling and psychotherapy: review and analysis of expectancy manipulation strategies and results. *J. Couns. Psychol.* 35:99–108

Tinsley, H. E. A., Brown, M. T., de St. Aubin, T. M., Lucek, J. 1984. Relation between expectancies for a helping relationship and tendency to seek help from a campus help provider. *J. Couns. Psychol.* 31:149–60

Tinsley, H. E. A., Tinsley, D. J. 1987. Uses of factor analysis in counseling psychology research. *J. Couns. Psychol.* 34:414–24

Tinsley, H. E. A., Workman, K. R., Kass, R. A. 1980. Factor analysis of the domain of client expectancies about counseling. *J. Couns. Psychol.* 27:561–70

Tolstedt, B. E., Stokes, J. P. 1983. Relation of verbal, affective, and physical intimacy to marital satisfaction. *J. Couns. Psychol.* 30:573–80

Tracey, T. J. 1985. Dominance and outcome: a sequential examination. *J. Couns. Psychol.* 32:119–22

Tracey, T. J. 1987. Stage differences in the dependencies of topic initiation and topic following behavior. *J. Couns. Psychol.* 34:123–31

Tracey, T. J., Dundon, M. 1988. Role anticipation and preference over the course of counseling. *J. Couns. Psychol.* 35:3–14

Tracey, T. J., Hays, K. A., Malone, J., Herman, B. 1988. Changes in counselor response as a function of experience. *J. Couns. Psychol.* 35:119–26

Tracey, T. J., Leong, F. T. L., Glidden, C. 1986. Help seeking and problem perception among Asian Americans. *J. Couns. Psychol.* 33:331–36

Tracey, T. J., Ray, P. B. 1984. Stages of successful time-limited counseling: an interactional examination. *J. Couns. Psychol.* 31:13–27

Tracey, T. J., Sherry, P., Bauer, G. P., Robbins, T. H., Todaro, T., et al. 1984. Help seeking as a function of student characteristics and program description: a logit-loglinear analysis. *J. Couns. Psychol.* 31:54–62

Unger, R. K. 1983. Through the looking glass: no wonderland yet! (the reciprocal relationship between methology and models of reality). *Psychol. Women Q.* 8:9–32

Walsh, W. B., Osipow, S. H., eds. 1983a. *Handbook of Vocational Psychology,* Vol. I: *Foundations.* Hillsdale, NJ: Erlbaum

Walsh, W. B., Osipow, S. H., eds. 1983b. *Handbook of Vocational Psychology,* Vol. II: *Applications.* Hillsdale, NJ: Erlbaum

Walsh, W. B., Osipow, S. H., eds. 1986. *Advances in Vocational Psychology*, Vol. 1: *The Assessment of Interests*. Hillsdale, NJ: Erlbaum

Walsh, W. B., Osipow, S. H., eds. 1989. *Advances in Vocational Psychology*, Vol. 2: *The Assessment of Career Decision-Making*. Hillsdale, NJ: Erlbaum

Wampold, B., ed. 1987. Quantitative foundations of counseling psychology research. *J. Couns. Psychol.* 34:363–489

Wampold, B. E., White, T. B. 1985. Research themes in counseling psychology: a cluster analysis of citations in the process and outcome section of the *Journal of Counseling Psychology. J. Couns. Psychol.* 32:123–26

Ward, L. G., Friedlander, M. L., Schoen, L. G., Klein, J. G. 1985. Strategic self-presentation in supervision. *J. Couns. Psychol.* 32:111–18

Watkins, C. E., Campbell, V. L., McGregor, P. 1988. Counseling psychologists' uses of and opinions about psychological tests: a contemporary perspective. *Couns. Psychol.* 16:476–86

Watkins, C. E., Terrell, F. 1988. Mistrust level and its effects on counseling expectations in Black client—White counselor relationships: an analogue study. *J. Couns. Psychol.* 35:194–97

West, D. J., Horan, J. J., Games, P. A. 1984. Component analysis of occupational stress inoculation applied to registered nurses in an acute care hospital setting. *J. Couns. Psychol.* 31:209–18

Westerman, M. A., Frankel, A. S., Tanaka, J. S., Kahn, J. 1987. Client cooperative interview behavior and outcome in paradoxical and behavioral brief treatment approaches. *J. Couns. Psychol.* 34:99–102

Wiley, M. D., Ray, P. B. 1986. Counseling supervision by developmental level. *J. Couns. Psychol.* 33:439–45

Wilfley, D., Kunce, J. 1986. Differential physical and psychological effects of exercise. *J. Couns. Psychol.* 33:337–42

Worthington, E. L. 1984. Empirical investigation of supervision of counselors as they gain experience. *J. Couns. Psychol.* 31:63–75

Worthington, E. L. 1988. Understanding the values of religious clients: a model and its application to counseling. *J. Couns. Psychol.* 35:166–74

Worthington, E. L., Stern, A. 1985. Effects of supervisor and supervisee degree level and gender on the supervisory relationship. *J. Couns. Psychol.* 32:252–62

Yalom, I. D. 1986. *Theory and Practice of Group Psychotherapy*. New York: Basic Books. 3rd ed.

Yanico, B. J., Hardin, S. I. 1985. Relation of type of problem and expectations of counselor knowledge and understanding to students' gender preferences for counselors. *J. Couns. Psychol.* 32:197–205

Zurawski, R. W., Smith, T. W. 1987. Assessing irrational beliefs and emotional distress: evidence and implications of limited discriminant validity. *J. Couns. Psychol.* 34:224–27

Annu. Rev. Psychol. 1990. 41:387–416

SOCIAL AND PERSONALITY DEVELOPMENT

W. Andrew Collins and Megan R. Gunnar

Institute of Child Development, University of Minnesota, Minneapolis, Minnesota 55455-0345

CONTENTS

INTRODUCTION

Social and personality development research is in the midst of one of the most expansionist periods in its history. In the five years since the last *Annual Review* chapter on the area (Parke & Asher 1983), the range of problems addressed has broadened, particularly in the areas of emotions, relationships, and contextual effects. Each of these areas is reviewed below.

Increasing attention is being paid to development after infancy. Adolescence and middle childhood (ages 6 to 12) have been the focus of considerable new conceptual and empirical work. This research addresses many

0066-4308/90/0201-0387$02.00

of the same core issues that have emerged in work on the early years of life: themes of biological-environmental interactions, the nature and role of contexts and their interrelations, and problems of assessing continuity and discontinuity (Collins 1984, 1988). At the same time research on infancy and early childhood has continued at a high rate. Within each section we indicate how current research is addressing development both in and after infancy.

Interest has also increased in basic constructs and processes of social and personality development in connection with naturally occurring stressors. Once strongly tied to the study of normative processes in the laboratory and special environments for children (e.g. nursery school classrooms and playgrounds), researchers in social and personality development are now addressing basic developmental processes across varied tasks and settings. We review recent findings on common perturbations in family life (such as divorce and remarriage) and on normative transitions, in connection with relevant broader research themes.

Our purview is the research literature since 1982. Space limitations have obliged us to distill, rather than to detail, the research and theory on the topics of the review. We have been highly selective in citing literature, often choosing one or very few citations as exemplars of research on problems to which a number of investigators are making important contributions. Where possible, we have cited recent review articles, so that interested readers can pursue topics in more detail. Of particular note is the recent compendium of reviews on topics in social and personality development included in the February 1989 special issue of the *The American Psychologist*. Finally, although problems of application and policy have provided an impetus for much current research on personality and social development, we have focused on the research literature itself. Examples of links between research and policy can be found in Stevenson & Siegel (1984).

EMOTIONS

After a long period of neglect, in the last decade emotions have regained a central role in theories of intrapersonal and interpersonal development (Campos et al 1983). This resurgence of interest can be traced to a rejecting of earlier views of emotions as disruptive of behavior and as primarily subjective, and an embracing of organizational approaches according to which emotions are meaningful, organized, and generally adaptive action systems (Fischer et al 1989). The adoption of this viewpoint has led to a striking increase in developmental theories of emotion. Whereas a little over a decade ago one was hard-pressed to identify any theory of emotion that dealt centrally with development, now there are at least five. These theories, despite their similarities, differ on three major characteristics: (*a*) the extent to which emotions are viewed as dimensional (e.g. the result of variations in hedonic tone and intensity) versus typological (e.g. discrete states with their own appearance, function, and phenomenology), (b) the extent to which they are seen as constructed versus biologically based, and (c) the extent to which the theory emphasizes individual differences versus normative development.

Of these differences, the constructivist versus nativist division drives the sharpest wedge between theories. In the most influential of the constructivist theories (Sroufe 1979), emotions are considered elements of the biological makeup of the human organism that do not exist in mature form at birth. Instead, there are thought to be precursor states during the first months that begin to differentiate around two to three months; these states become true emotions when the basic differentiation between self and surround has been made and when the infant can engage in cognitive appraisals of events during the latter part of the first year. Whereas Sroufe's theory emphasizes the importance of cognition in affective development, Lewis & Michaelson (1983) have advanced a much more extreme constructivist, cognitive-based theory in which learning is involved even in establishing the basic link between affects and facial expressions.

On the nativist side, the most dominant formulation is Izard's differential emotion theory (see review by Izard & Malatesta 1987), with the developmental elaborations contributed by and in collaboration with Malatesta (1989). Indeed, a good deal of the burgeoning of developmental research on emotion can be traced to the influence of this approach. Three ideas from the differential-emotion perspective have been especially influential: (a) There are a certain number of basic emotions that have distinct neural circuits, and many of these basic emotions are present very early in development. (b) There is an innate expression-feeling concordance that allows one to assess emotional state from facial expressions at least during infancy; over time this concordance becomes less reliable as the result of direct tuition in cultural display rules and other experiences. (c) Emotions organize behavior and shape personality through signalling the self and others and through regulating perceptions and cognitions. These ideas reflect the influence of ethological approaches to the study of human behavior. The third idea is also central to all organizational approaches to emotional development (Sroufe 1989).

Both constructivist and nativist perspectives take a componential approach to emotions, attempting to analyze the elicitation, signification, and reaction to emotions into discrete systems. In contrast, Campos et al (1989) have advanced a new working definition of emotion, heavily influenced by systems theory, in which emotion is considered to involve the indivisible contributions of the child's appreciation of the significance of an event, the feelings that are considered to be monitors of both the event's significance and the child's coping potential, and the action of the child in responding to the environment. The approach is characterized as a relational one, according to which emotions are processes of establishing, maintaining, and/or disrupting the relations between the individual and the internal or external environment. Campos et al have drawn heavily on research with infants and toddlers to support the perspective, but its developmental implications have not yet been elaborated.

These theories all emphasize the course of emotional development during infancy. In contrast, Fischer et al (1989) have recently advanced a theory that considers emotional development from infancy through the adult years. This theory is based on a "skill approach." Accordingly, emotions are seen as organized in a hierarchy of superordinate, basic, and subordinate categories that are defined in terms of prototypical event scripts. Emotion scripts develop through levels, each of which involves a series of steps with attendant skills and transformation rules that specify how skills can be coordinated and differentiated within levels. The levels reflect a basic developmental sequence (i.e. reflexes, sensorimotor actions, representations, abstractions); and skill levels are viewed as characteristics that vary with development, assessment condition, and emotional state.

While the above descriptions do not exhaust the list of recently proposed theories, they highlight three important areas of current research: (a) the importance of examining the infant's expression of and response to emotions; (b) the importance of understanding the post-socialization of emotions after infancy, as well as the child's developing understanding of emotions; and (c) the role of emotions in organizing behavior, cognitions, perceptions and, ultimately, personality.

Infancy Research

EMOTIONAL EXPRESSIONS   Attempts to document the reliability and validity of discrete emotion-coding systems (see review by Campos et al 1983) dominated research on infant emotional expressions during the early part of the decade. Evidence thus accumulated showing that at birth a number of the facial expressions associated with the primary emotions are observable and that by 7–9 months all the basic emotions can be detected (Izard & Malatesta 1987). Furthermore, these expressions are shown under appropriate incentive conditions (Rosenstein & Oster 1988), supporting an isomorphism between expression and feeling state during infancy.

More recent work has focused on what discrete emotion analyses can tell us about early socioemotional development. Several conclusions deserve special note. First, according to facial expressions, the predominant reaction to separation by the end of the first year is described as anger, not fear (Shiller et al 1986). Second, with regard to individual differences, there is striking stability over the first two years of life in the tendency of individuals to express emotions of anger and sadness (Izard et al 1987; Malatesta et al, unpublished). This finding supports the argument that the study of discrete emotion biases may prove an important contribution to our understanding of personality development. Interestingly, this stability has not been seen for the positive emotions, perhaps because the testing situations have included highly aversive elements (e.g. inoculations and separations). Finally, an often-noted limitation of the above work is the exclusive emphasis on facial expressions, despite a general agreement that emotions are also expressed in voice and gesture. With the exception of work on infant crying (see edited volume by Lester & Boukydis 1985), there continues to be little systematic work on the vocal or gestural development of emotion expression.

RESPONSES TO EMOTION   Infant perception of emotional expressions has become an active area of research during the last decade (see reviews by Nelson 1987; Oster et al 1989). As a result, a reasonable consensus has been achieved regarding when infants can discriminate various facial expressions of emotions. This ability appears to develop between 3 and 6 months, although there is still some disagreement over whether some capacity might be present at birth (Oster et al 1989). There is little agreement, however, about what characteristics infants use to make these discriminations, and whether or when infants begin to respond to these facial configurations as expressions of emotions per se. A reasonably conservative estimate is that the ability to perceive emotions in the faces of others is present in some degree by the last quarter of the first year. The best evidence for this comes from research on social referencing, an especially active area. Findings indicate that by 9–12 months babies look to others' faces when confronted with ambiguous events and use the affect displayed to guide their own behavioral reactions (see review by Klinnert et al 1983). By this age infants also have emotional reactions to others' emotional reactions, with joy stimulating infant joy and sadness disrupting infant play and stimulating both infant anger and sadness (Termine & Izard 1988).

Whether or not young infants can accurately perceive the emotional expressions of others, they are clearly affected, directly or indirectly, by the emotional states and expressions of their caregivers (e.g. Cohn & Tronick 1983; Radke-Yarrow et al 1985). Naturalistic studies have also documented how interested infants and toddlers are in the emotional interchanges taking place between the other people in their family (e.g. Dunn 1988). Indeed, one thrust of current research on toddlers and slightly older children is to demonstrate their apparent emotional precocity when dealing with the events of their day-to-day lives, as compared to their evident emotional immaturity when asked to respond to events in more controlled laboratory situations (Cummings et al 1984; Thompson 1987). This work may provide an important corrective to laboratory-based theories of the development of emotion cognition.

Socialization of Emotions

The study of emotion socialization is a new area that promises to increase in prominence. The theories outlined earlier predict that expressed and felt emotion diverge after infancy as the result of socialization pressures. Children must learn what emotions should be expressed in different situations (display rules), and to control both their expressed and felt emotions in emotionally charged situations (emotion regulation).

DISPLAY RULES   Research on the development of children's understanding and use of display rules has three foci. One is to determine children's understanding of the cognitive aspects of these social rules. For example, a recent emphasis has been on identifying when children understand the distinction between reality and appearance with regard to the emotional expressions of others. The answer appears to be between the ages of 4 and 6 years, or at about the same time as the distinction between reality and appearance emerges for physical objects (Harris & Gross 1988). A second focus, also social-cognitive in nature, is to understand how children make decisions about when and how to apply display rules. Here there is increasing evidence that sophisticated reasoning about display rules develops gradually throughout middle childhood and into the adolescent years (Saarni 1988).

A third focus is on when children begin to use display rules. The evidence is mixed. Saarni (1984), for example, has shown that even preadolescents are inept at using emotional expressions to hide their true feelings when confronted with an undesirable gift. In contrast, Lewis et al (1989) have reported that children as young as three appear somewhat adept at display rules. Specifically, they increase their smiling when lying about a transgression. Adults could not judge from a videotape which children were and were not telling the truth. Similarly, Cole (1986) has shown that three-year-old girls will smile when given an unattractive gift. These discrepancies in the ages reported for display-rule use may partly reflect differences between attempts and successes in posing emotions. Even adults are poor at accurately posing some emotions, and preschool children have been found to pose only a few emotions with accuracy (Lewis et al 1987). Thus, children may attempt to apply display rules long before their efforts are consistently successful. Future research is likely to address how children's attempts and successes map onto their social-cognitive understanding of display rules.

EMOTION REGULATION   How children regulate their felt and expressed emotions has emerged as a major domain of inquiry. The roots of this area are in psychoanalytic theorizing and in the early work by Murphy and others on coping. To a large extent, the empirical work on emotion regulation has been culled from other areas as researchers reframe work on topics such as attributions and self-control to highlight their implications for emotion regulation (see Dodge & Garber 1989). Recently both Kopp (1989) and Masters (1989) have offered hypothesis-generating models of emotion regulation. Masters's model emphasizes individual differences and focuses on the processes involved in emotion regulation after infancy, while considering their developmental antecedents. A unique aspect is the idea that, in addition to trying to modify unwanted emotions, children and adults also attempt to maintain and enhance desired emotional states. Masters specifies strategies and processes that might play a role in all three of these goals. In contrast, Kopp's model focuses on unpleasant emotions and assumes that individuals will be motivated to modify and/or escape those feelings. She has attempted to identify a developmental sequence to the ontogeny of emotion regulation in the first few years of life.

Emotions as Organizers of Behavior

The idea that emotions organize perceptions, actions, and ultimately personality is the central tenet of the organizational perspective (Sroufe 1983). With the exception of the research on quality of attachment, which we review below, this is also the least well documented aspect of the organizational approach, although the available data are encouraging. In addition to evidence accumulating on adults, studies now show that children's perceptions and cognitions are influenced by emotional states. Positive affect appears to enhance learning and reasoning, while negative affect, especially sadness, appears to disrupt cognition. Negative affect also may lead to a regression in children's ability to reason about emotions, perhaps helping to create situations where sadness fosters further sadness (Harris & Gross 1989).

The role of emotions in regulating prosocial and aggressive behavior has been frequently studied. Over the last decade, interest in the role of empathy as a facilitator of altruism and an inhibitor of aggression has continued to stimulate research (see reviews by Eisenberg & Miller 1987; Miller & Eisenberg 1988). Both linkages appear to exist; however, they account for relatively modest amounts of the variance, and the relations appear to be less consistent in early childhood than later in development. What is more profound, especially in early childhood, is the centrality of positive affect in the organization of prosocial behavior. A child who displays more positive affect is more likely both to elicit and to engage in prosocial behavior (Lennon &

Eisenberg 1987; Sroufe et al 1984). Similarly, the induction of positive affect enhances prosocial behavior among children, while the induction of sadness reduces it. Finally, evidence is also accumulating to show that positive affect may inoculate children, at least briefly, against some of the effects of negative affect (e.g. Carlson & Masters 1986). Such data continue to show the importance of emotions for the immediate regulation of behavior. A likely future direction is to link the development of emotion biases (Malatesta 1989) to characteristic modes of perception, attribution, and action.

Temperament

The last five years has seen a tremendous growth in research on temperament. This surge of research reflects both increased interest in genetic contributions to individual differences in behavior and a more sophisticated concept of temperament. Temperament is now conceived of as multidimensional and modifiable, and the emphasis is on developmental psychobiology and interactive social processes (Bates 1987; Goldsmith & Rieser-Danner 1989; Rothbart 1989). Although there is continued debate over the dimensions constituting the temperament construct, we have chosen to discuss temperament in this section to highlight its potential significance as the emotional substrate of later personality (Goldsmith & Campos 1982).

Space limitations preclude all but the most cursory discussion of this vast and rapidly growing area of research (see recent edited volumes by Lerner & Lerner 1986; Plomin & Dunn 1986). Five current foci of work are briefly mentioned. First, measurement issues continue to be of concern; however, the thrust of new instruments is towards more objective, often laboratory-based assessments and toward attempts to analyze emotional aspects of temperament into more discrete categories (e.g. Goldsmith & Rothbart 1988). Second, there is increased interest in identifying and understanding change as well as stability in temperament. There is evidence that some changes may be genetically influenced (Matheny 1989). Third, efforts continue to conceptualize the multidirectional flow of influence among temperament, relationship, and environment factors. Included in this focus are attempts to operationalize and examine processes like goodness-of-fit (Lerner et al 1986) and niche-picking (Scarr & McCartney 1983). Fourth, there is also continued emphasis on the physiological substrate of temperament (e.g. Kagan et al 1987; Gunnar et al 1989), with particular emphasis on behavior genetics. With regard to the latter, increasing sophistication of the statistical models relating genotypes to phenotypes (e.g. Goldsmith 1988) promises not only to enhance our understanding of temperament, but also to force consideration of the extent to which children reared in the same physical environment share the same psychological environment (Daniels & Plomin 1985; see critique by Goldsmith 1988, pp. 207–8). Finally, although infancy research remains prominent, the importance of temperament to later adjustment is increasingly the focus of empirical work (Lerner et al 1986).

RELATIONSHIPS

A second trend in the literature is toward the analysis of interpersonal relationships and their implications for social behavior and development. *Relationship* refers to the "content, patterning, and quality" of interaction, such that the unique conjoint patterns between individuals can be deduced (Hinde & Stevenson-Hinde 1987). In this section we review the conceptual and empirical bases for a focus on relationships as a significant unit of analysis in developmental research. In addition, we note specific implications of relationship approaches for studying families and peers and their functions in individual development.

The Relationships Perspective

Using relationships as one unit of analysis, rather than individual behavior or dyadic interactions, is a trend that derives from two partially overlapping bodies of work. Attachment theory (Bowlby 1973; Sroufe & Fleeson 1986; Waters et al 1986) emphasizes the *functions* of caregiver-child relationships in relation to concurrent felt security and later adaptation and coping. Attachment relationships are thought to constitute goal-corrected control systems that become internalized and are carried forward by the individual into subsequent interpersonal situations, thus conferring long-term significance upon the conjoint characteristics of parent-child dyads. A second direction, the microanalytic study of interactions (e.g. Hinde & Stevenson-Hinde 1987), underscores the importance of viewing children as embedded in a social network of multiple, interrelated dyads. Each dyad represents patterned interdependencies between two individuals and is engaged in patterned interdependencies with other dyads. Hinde's view is similar to that of Kelley et al (1983) and other theorists who study adult marital dyads and friendships. Although lacking the teleological predictions of attachment theory, these formulations emphasize relational rather than individual actions or measures of dyadic interaction alone.

Relationships in the Family

EARLY RELATIONSHIPS: ATTACHMENT   The study of attachment has dominated research on relationships for almost two decades. Several well-established phenomena have continued to be confirmed in recent studies (see review by Waters et al 1986). First, attachment classification, as assessed in the Strange Situation procedure, is generally stable, expect when notable changes or stresses occur. For example, whereas maltreated infants showed considerable instability in attachment classification assessed at 12, 18, and 24 months, a comparison group showed both more stable attachments and a higher proportion of infants classified as secure (Schneider-Rosen et al 1985). Second, secure attachment is associated concurrently with more freedom of exploration of the immediate environment and, in the longer term, with greater ego resiliency and curiosity, more adaptive problem-solving and quality of play, and greater competence when interacting with peers. Earlier findings have been elaborated by demonstrations that insecure attachment at 12 months predicts subsequent behavior problems in preschool, including excessive dependency for a sample of children from impoverished families (Erickson et al 1985; Renken et al 1989; Sroufe et al 1983), and psychopathology at age 6 (Lewis et al 1984). Third, individual differences in attachment may occur as a function of the relationship-relevant characteristics of members of the dyad. For example, insecure attachments are more likely among children of mothers with major depressions than children of mothers with minor depression or mothers who are not depressed (Radke-Yarrow et al 1985).

The maturing of this body of research has inevitably presented challenges to attachment theory, however, and these have stimulated considerable new theoretical writing and research. A particularly strong thrust comes from additional attention to the bases of attachment. Bowlby (1973) hypothesized that the history of a relationship is represented in an internal working model of self in relation to the other, which mediates the prediction and interpretation of behavior and one's own responses. New findings indicate that securely attached preschoolers and kindergartners display openness and fluency in interviews and projective assessments pertaining to attachment relationships, whereas insecurely attached individuals give more impoverished reports about and explanations of exchanges (Bretherton 1985, 1989; Kobak & Sceery 1988; Main et al 1985). These patterns parallel differences in observed caregiver-child interactions as a function of attachment classification. Waters (1989) has outlined a view in which processes of identification mediate the long-term manifestations of attachment relationships in individual development.

Methodological challenges have arisen from cross-cultural evidence. For example, the Strange Situation yields a variety of adaptational outcomes not predicted by the theory. Although secure attachments (B) are the modal classification across cultures, higher proportions of insecure avoidant (A) and resistant (C) attachment have been found among children from Israel (e.g. Sagi et al 1985), Japan (Miyake et al 1985; Takahashi 1986), and West Germany (e.g. Grossmann et al 1985). These findings indicate the need to validate the Strange Situation in any new cultural or subcultural application and have stimulated the development of new methods to assess attachment security outside the laboratory (e.g. Waters & Deane's 1985 Q-sort).

EXTENSION TO LATER DEVELOPMENTAL PERIODS   The growing interest in relationships across time has been accompanied by a shift from near-exclusive focus on infancy and the preschool period to a focus on middle childhood and adolescence (see Hartup & Rubin 1986). As a result of this shift, a variety of verbal and nonverbal measures have been developed for assessing relationships in older children, adolescents, and adults; these measures are conceptually parallel to measures of early attachment (e.g. Atkinson & Bell 1986; Frank et al 1988; Main et al 1985).

Descriptive research on parent-child interactions in middle childhood and adolescence has also increased (see reviews by Collins & Russell, unpublished; Maccoby 1984a; Montemayor 1983). Although not conceptualized within a relationships framework, these studies have indicated aspects of relationships that might be expected to change over time (e.g. mode and frequency of interactions) and those that are likely to remain relatively stable (e.g. indicators of positive affect, involvement in common activities). Descriptive studies have also been important in identifying links between interaction patterns and developmental outcomes. For example, indicators of individuation and connectedness in parent-adolescent problem-solving interactions are positively correlated with adolescents' ego identity status and role-taking skill (Grotevant & Cooper 1985; Hauser et al 1984). In general, relationship indicators of developmental significance are different in the studies of older individuals than in infancy, consistent with the different life circumstances and developmental tasks associated with later developmental periods.

ANALYSIS OF MULTIPLE RELATIONSHIPS   The study of relationships in the family extends beyond the mother-child dyad. Studies of both father-child and sibling dyads have increased, and the relational orientation of this research has intensified.

Mothers and fathers   A primary focus in the research on mother-child and father-child dyads has been the overlapping and complementary patterns of mothers' and fathers' capacities to care for and nurture their children, particularly during infancy (see Lamb et al 1987 for a review). Newer studies address the nature and functional significance of differences and similarities between mother-child and father-child interactions and relationships in both infancy (e.g. Bridges et al 1988) and middle childhood (see review by Collins & Russell, unpublished)

Continuities across age periods are apparent in four clusters of findings. First, although fathers are generally as significant and as competent in caregiving as mothers, differences consistently emerge in the amount and frequency of interaction and in the types of activities commonly shared by children with mothers and with fathers (e.g. Russell & Russell 1987; Youniss & Smollar 1985). Second, whereas the degree of positive and negative affect is generally similar, positive interactions with mothers are more likely to occur in connection with caretaking and those with fathers in connection with play (e.g. Bronstein 1984; Russell & Russell 1987; Youniss & Smollar 1985). Third, these differences appear to be linked to specific child behaviors. For example, infants' behaviors with their fathers are more predictive of behavior toward strangers than are behaviors toward mothers; and adolescents' communicativeness in family problem-solving tasks appears to be facilitated in typical exchanges with fathers but restricted by exchanges with mothers (e.g. Grotevant & Cooper 1985; Hauser et al 1984). Fourth, the degree of differentiation between mother-child and father-child dyads changes as a function of age. Compared to fathers, mothers are more likely to increase their involvement in both intimate and conflictual interactions with offspring in late childhood and adolescence (e.g. Steinberg 1987; Youniss & Smollar 1985). The latter is especially true during early adolescence as a function of pubertal maturation status (Hill 1988a; Steinberg 1987). Overall, however, adolescents continue to have warm engagement with both parents throughout the second decade (see review by Hill 1988b).

Siblings   The nature and functions of interactions between siblings are increasingly visible topics (see review by Dunn 1983). Recent studies emphasized more than earlier ones the varying qualities of sibling relationships (Furman & Buhrmester 1985; Vandell et al 1987) and their functional significance (e.g. Abramovitch et al 1986; Dunn & Munn 1985; Dunn 1988). Sibling relationships are multidimensional, incorporating warmth/closeness and companionship, relative status/power (include teaching/helping), conflict, and rivalry. The salience of the status/power dimension, however, appears to decrease with age (Furman & Buhrmester 1985; Vandell et al 1987). The importance of sibling conflict and negotiation in the emergence of social understanding and reciprocity at early ages has also been confirmed (see reviews by Dunn 1988; Shantz & Hobart 1989). Whether sibling relationships make a unique contribution to the development of social skills is still to be determined.

INTERRELATIONS AMONG RELATIONSHIPS   Relationships are dyadic, but dyadic interactions are affected by other relationships in which the dyad participates (see Parke & Tinsley 1987). Corroborating earlier findings, new evidence shows the systemic effects of the birth of a child on the marital dyad (Belsky 1989), and the change in parent-firstborn relations with the birth of a second child (e.g. Feiring et al 1983). The quality of relations in one dyad also affects the interactions occurring in other relationships (Sroufe & Fleeson 1988). For example, more positive mother-father relations predict more intense and positive father-child relationships both in infancy (Lamb & Elster 1985) and in middle childhood (Brody et al 1986). Interactions within dyads also appear to be influenced by the presence of other family members. Thus, mother-son dyads have been found to be more engaged, secure, and consistent with the father present, whereas fathers were more critical and less engaged and egalitarian toward sons when the mother was present (Gjerde 1986; see also Vuchinich et al 1988). Important questions to be addressed are why the configuration of interactors should make such a difference, and what these differences imply regarding the nature of relationships and the bases on which they are differentiated.

Relations among relationships are being examined in a life-course perspective. Some studies concern the association between the parent-grandparent relationship history and the parent-child relationships. As an instance, mothers' representations of their childhood family relationships have been found to correlate with both their behavior toward their preschool children and their children's behavior toward them in a laboratory problem-solving task (Crowell & Feldman 1988). Other studies focus on parent-child relationships in multi-generational families (e.g. Hagestad 1984; Parke 1988). For example, grandparents have been found to provide both support for their own children's child-rearing efforts and direct socialization of children via modelling and play interaction (see review by Tinsley & Parke 1987). These studies imply that relational antecedents in previous generations may indeed constrain the concurrent determinants of relationships.

STRESSORS IN FAMILY RELATIONSHIPS   Such perturbations in families as divorce (and, often remarriage), abuse, and/or neglect affect the quality of interpersonal relationships. (For an overview of psychosocial effects on children, see recent reviews on divorce and remarriage by Hetherington et al 1989 and Ihinger-Tallman 1988; and on family violence by Emery 1989; Youngblade & Belsky 1989).

Divorce   Divorce strains relationships between custodial mothers and both sons and daughters. Hetherington (1989) found that, among preschool-aged children, the first two years following a divorce was an intense period of disruption in family functioning and relationships. By the end of the second year, daughters of nonremarried divorced mothers typically had reestablished positive relations with their mothers, and this persisted through a follow-up assessment when the children were 10 years old. Disruption of mother-son relationships, however, continued as long as six years after divorce (i.e. negative, resistant behavior by the son; nagging, angry, and coercive behavior by mothers). When divorce occurs at or after preadolescence, cross-sectional studies indicate a high incidence of difficulties between mothers and both daughters and sons (Dornbusch et al 1987; Wallerstein et al 1988). As in intact families, such mother-daughter difficulties are more pronounced in cases of early pubertal maturation (Hetherington 1989).

Remarriage is an additional source of perturbation with different implications for parent-child relationships. In contrast to the aftermath of divorce, the introduction of a stepfather or a stepmother appears to be more difficult for daughters than sons (e.g. Clingempeel et al 1984; Peterson & Zill 1986). Indeed, when remarrige occurs before sons reach adolescence, mother-son relationships improve and are not different from those of sons in nondivorced comparison families. Stepfathers also report more positive relationships with boys than with girls. In general, early adolescents (roughly 9–15 years of age) whose parents remarry are less likely than younger children to adapt smoothly to having a stepparent (Hetherington 1989).

The reasons for these sex differences have not been examined directly. Except for studies of the aftermath of divorce, relatively few studies of relationships in single-parent households have been reported. Neither have relationships with noncustodial parents been extensively studied, although the few existing findings (Hetherington & Arasteh 1988) indicate highly varied patterns, depending on (a) the relationship continuing between the divorced parents and (b) the personality and adjustment of the noncustodial parent. Studies of relationships with custodial fathers and with noncustodial mothers are badly needed.

Abuse and neglect   The widespread incidence of child abuse and neglect is more extensively recognized than earlier. Its implications for a cluster of psychological difficulties in children have been well documented (see reviews cited above), and a number of these are pertinent to concurrent and later relationships. Consistent with earlier studies, abused children are frequently classified as insecurely attached (e.g. Lamb et al 1985; Lyons-Ruth et al 1987; Schneider-Rosen & Cicchetti 1984). Older maltreated children also experience more negative, punitive, and conflictual family environments overall (e.g. Patterson & Bank 1989; Trickett & Kuczynski 1986). Indeed, some of the psychosocial effects noted in the reviews cited earlier may reflect children's impaired competence in relationships (e.g. Main & George 1985).

One concern about abuse and neglect within families is intergenerational transmission of tendencies toward child maltreatment. Individuals with a history of maltreatment are more likely than others to maltreat their own offspring, although a substantial number do not (see reviews by Belsky & Pensky 1988; Kaufman & Zigler 1987). An important ameliorating factor in intergenerational transmission seems to be the individual's access to social support, both during childhood (by having one parent who was not maltreating) and later, when the individual becomes a parent (e.g. Egeland et al 1988). Factors that "break the cycle" of abuse are likely to be a major focus of research in the next five years.

Family relationships research thus addresses a broad range of issues. The literature is largely a North American one, and it has the further significant limitation of being almost exclusively focused on middle-class Caucasian families, many of them not representative of families in the United States. Greater attention to non-Caucasian families (see reviews by Harrison et al 1984; Scott-Jones & Nelson-LeGall 1986; Wilson 1989) is now providing a base for formulating more culturally sensitive research on relationships and their sequelae.

Relationships with Peers

Studies of close relationships between children concern almost exclusively individuals of the same age. Although a research area of long standing, the developmental course and functional significance of friendships have attracted increased attention in recent years (see edited volumes by Berndt & Ladd 1989 and Hartup & Rubin 1986). More recently, studies have been extended to include the second decade of life. Three especially active research areas have been (*a*) age-related patterns of friendship formation and change, (*b*) the nature and functions of conflict between friends, and (*c*) the interrelations of peer and family relationships.

AGE-RELATED PATTERNS   Friendships are marked by "reciprocity and commitment between individuals who see themselves as equals" (Hartup 1989:124). The preferences shown by young preschool children for certain other children as playmates constitute one early manifestation of friendship (e.g. Gottman 1983; Howes 1987; Parker & Gottman 1989). By age 4, children who are friends show evidence of mutuality and commitment, and these qualities of friendship become increasingly explicit in interview responses during middle childhood and adolescence (e.g. Berndt 1986; Furman & Bierman 1984; Youniss & Smollar 1985).

A series of behavioral differences between friends and nonfriends have been confirmed. Friends, compared with nonfriends, show greater sustained responsiveness to social overtures from each other (Howes 1983); higher levels of interaction, smiling and laughing, more frequent cooperation and collaboration in conversation (e.g. Parker & Gottman 1989); greater perceived social support (Berndt & Perry 1986); more readily resolved conflicts and continued interaction following conflict (Hartup et al 1988); and greater shared knowledge (Ladd & Emerson 1984). From middle childhood to early adolescence, intimacy becomes increasingly integral to friendship and friendship expectations (Buhrmester & Furman 1987; Diaz & Berndt 1982).

The implicit commitment between child friends is matched by longitudinal stability in their relationships. Howes (1987) reported that one- to six-year-olds tended to maintain their friendships, unless one member of the dyad was removed from the environment that the two shared (e.g. a day-care center). Similarly, the stability of school-age children's friendships increases between grades one and four but not between grades four and eight (Berndt et al 1986; Berndt & Hoyle 1985). Stability indexes are similar for boys and girls, although preadolescent and early adolescent girls report a smaller number of friendships than boys do, and girls' friendship groups are more likely than boys' to include new friends (Montemayor & van Komen 1985). Age-related changes in friendship stability are often attributed to the development of concepts of friendship as based in shared interests and mutual commitment, although little empirical attention has been given to this.

CONFLICT   Difficulty in peer relationships is common among troubled children, and rejection by peers is a correlate of adjustment problems in later life (see review by Parker & Asher 1987). Although studies presently do not differentiate between friendship experience and peer relations generally, it is likely that the deficits in question extend to close relationships between peers. Of special interest has been the significance of conflict and conflict management (see reviews by C. Shantz 1987; Shantz & Hobart 1989). Findings indicate that although friends are no less likely than acquaintances to engage in conflictual interactions, conflicts between friends are more skillfully managed than conflicts between nonfriends (Hartup et al 1988). The tendency to initiate conflicts and to manage them poorly may also be a significant determinant of social rejection (see review by Hartup 1989; D. Shantz 1986). Attributional biases may contribute to poor conflict-resolution skills (Dodge et al 1986), leading to a reputation for antisocial aggressiveness toward peers. Because appropriately regulated conflict, in the sense of the expression of differing perspectives, appears to be functional for development (see Berkowitz 1985), the place of conflict in peer-relationship differences is likely to receive further attention.

INTERRELATIONS AMONG RELATIONSHIPS: PARENTS AND PEERS   Peer relationships have only recently begun to be viewed in connection with social relationships in the family. Previous consideration of family and peers together focused mostly on incongruent influences in these two socialization arenas (see review by Hartup 1983). Attention is now being divided to the linkages between relationships with parents and the content and quality of peer relations (e.g. Jacobson & Wille 1986; Parke et al 1989).

Two somewhat different hypotheses have guided research in the area. One is that early attachment to a caregiver provides a prototype of, and support for, later relationships with peers (e.g. Elicker & Sroufe 1989). Several findings document that attachment security in early life is associated with good preschool peer relations (see review by Waters et al 1986 and a critique by Lamb & Nash 1989). An alternative view suggests that interactive skills generalize from parent to peer exchanges. For example, social competence among preschool children is associated with high levels of physical play with fathers and verbal exchanges that are initiated by mothers (MacDonald & Parke 1984; Parke et al 1989). Parental directiveness is associated generally with poor peer relations (e.g. Ladd & Golter 1988), although MacDonald & Parke (1984) found this not to be the case in father-daughter relations. The effects of parental directiveness may thus depend on the degree to which directive actions foster dependency and inhibition, rather than adaptive assertiveness.

Thus far, examination of the linkages between parent-child relations and peer relations have been global. We now need formulations that specify the aspects of interaction in one dyad that are likely to influence interactions in the other (Eckerman & Stein 1983; Lamb & Nash 1989; Parke et al 1989). These formulations should take account of bidirectional influence between cross-generational and same-generational dyads, as well as developmental changes in the nature and significance of interactions in one type of relationship for interactions in the other (Parke et al 1989). Several ongoing longitudinal studies (e.g. D. Baumrind, personal communication; Block 1987, L. A. Sroufe & B. Egeland, personal communication) address the long-term implications of differences in these relationships, both within and across families.

CONTEXTS

Despite early emphasis on ecological factors in behavior by Kurt Lewin and Roger Barker, the study of contexts has only recently become widely evident in research on social and personality development. A strong impetus in this direction came from Bronfenbrenner's (e.g. 1986) ecological analysis of the embeddedness of individuals and families in a layered array of social systems, both proximal (e.g. parents' workplaces) and more distal and molar (e.g. the social-structural and economic milieux). This model has much in common with general systems theory formulations (see Gunnar & Thelen 1989; Sameroff 1983).

Several current views elaborate these ecological models. Life-history research (e.g. Caspi 1987; Elder et al 1988) provides numerous examples of the ways individual development is affected by sociohistorical milieu as a function of the person's age, gender, and social strata. The life-span developmental perspective, with its strong emphasis on human plasticity (e.g. Baltes 1987; Lerner 1984; Thompson 1988b), also posits multiple interacting factors at different levels of ecological complexity and generality. Anthropologists (Super & Harkness 1986; Weisner 1984) interested in developmental processes use a related construct, the developmental niche—i.e. the general setting conditions, norms, and cultural forces that regulate the day-to-day physical and social characteristics that a child experiences. This concept is intended as a basis for examining the juncture of contextual forces and the development of the individual child. Magnusson (1985) and Valsiner & Benigni (1986) argue that this focus on child-environment transactions is the fundamental requirement for an ecological analysis of child behavior and development.

Social and Cultural Assumptions about Children and Development

Beliefs regarding children and development, especially among parents and teachers, are primary features of developmental niches, potentially influencing a wide range of feelings and behaviors pertinent to development (Goodnow 1988b; Sigel 1985; Super & Harkness 1986). The study of these adult cognitions and their implications has expanded greatly in the past five years. Particular attention has been given to parents' implicit beliefs about the ages at which a particular skill or quality would be expected to appear ("developmental timetables"). Mothers' beliefs about the age at which children should have a modicum of control over their emotions, comply with parents' demands, display verbal assertiveness, and show social skills in interaction with peers vary both between cultures (e.g. Japanese and US) and subcultures (e.g. Australian-born and Lebanese-born Australians) (Goodnow et al 1984). These differences may be linked to parent attributions about causes and responsibility for children's behavior. As children age (e.g. from 4 to 13), parents increasingly attribute misbehavior to the children's dispositions. Parents then become more upset and prefer relatively stringent punishment (Dix et al 1986).

Specific linkages between parental beliefs and specific actions and outcomes have been studied sporadically. Several recent proposals (Goodnow 1988b; Sigel 1985) indicate a need for conceptually guided mapping between parental cognition and behavior as well as for methods that tap the depth and rigidity of parental cognitions and sample the relevant topics and conditions for which linkages should be expected. In addition, greater attention is being given to the accuracy of parental cognitions (Miller 1988) and to the congruence between parental and child cognitions (Cashmore & Goodnow 1985) as a basis for linking cognition, affect, parent actions, and interpersonal variables.

Social Networks and Support

The study of social networks is closely tied to the ecological analysis of contexts. Work with mothers has provided considerable evidence showing that social support moderates the effects of stressful life circumstances. Social supports buffer the negative impact of infant irritability on maternal supportive caregiving (Crockenberg & McCluskey 1986) and are associated with attachment security among preschoolers (Crittenden 1985).

The social networks of children and adolescents are also receiving attention (e.g. Csikszentmihalyi & Larson 1984). Children's networks expand across ages, with same-sex contacts accounting for the most frequent and extensive child-child components (see review by Hartup 1983). The linkages between network changes and the significance of persons in children's development have not yet been addressed, other than to show that multiple interpersonal relations need to be considered as determinants of development. The evidence shows, however, that children's and adolescents' perceptions of the availability of social support are associated with positive psychosocial outcomes (e.g. enhanced self-esteem Hoffman et al 1988). Using a newly devised procedure called the Neighborhood Walk, Bryant (1985) interviewed 7- and 10-year-old children about the persons and situations whom they perceived to be relevant to social support and coping. Social support was positively related to prosocial behaviors and attitudes, such as empathy, tolerance of differences, and social perspective taking; effects were stronger for 10-year-olds than for 7-year-olds. The availability of support also protects against the stress of multiple changes during the transition to adolescence (Simmons & Blyth 1987); Simmons et al 1988).

Few studies have examined the implications of changes either in networks or in availability of support for concurrent functioning or for long-term sequelae in individual development (Blyth 1983; Ladd 1984). Additional efforts are also needed to explicate how social support operates to facilitate positive developmental outcomes.

Salient Contexts and Contextual Change

SCHOOLS AND SCHOOL TRANSITIONS   Schools have attracted increased attention because of the recognition that these institutions are major sources of socially imposed transitions (Higgins & Parsons 1983) as well as primary vehicles for the social and educational agenda (Entwisle & Stevenson 1987; see review by Minuchin & Shapiro 1983). Social relations in schools have received particular attention. Friend selection is affected by the structural and organizational characteristics of schools (Epstein 1989). Formation of cross-race friendships in integrated schools appears to be particularly dependent on classroom organization and "climate"; white students are more likely to form cross-race friendships when relative academic achievement is deemphasized and both races are assigned to ability groups for instruction (Hallinan & Teixeira 1987). Friendship choices, in turn, are associated with academic performance and aspirations to pursue higher education (see review by Epstein 1989). The causal status of this relation is unclear; both selective and socialization process probably occur. Finally, peers can and do, when teaching methods and classroom organization permit, significantly affect classroom learning (e.g. Damon & Phelps 1989; Slavin 1987).

Relations between family and school contexts have also begun to receive attention. School satisfaction has been shown to be a joint function of home-school authority congruence and individual variables, such as independence and internal locus of control (Epstein 1983). Generally, the greater parents' involvement with schools and children's school-related tasks, the higher the school performance of their offspring (Stevenson & Baker 1987). These findings are consistent with results of earlier evaluation research on Head Start and other early-childhood intervention programs (see review by Consortium for Longitudinal Studies 1983). The critical dimensions of congruency/incongruency between home and school are yet to be identified.

Transitions from one school setting to another are especially significant. To assess the effects of naturally occurring contextual changes in interaction with a variety of experiential and maturational variables, the transition to junior high school has been selected by several investigators (e.g. Hirsch & Rapkin 1987; Simmons & Blyth 1987). This transition is particularly disruptive to psychosocial functioning and school achievement for girls, who are especially likely to be undergoing rapid pubertal maturation and beginning to date.

WORK: EFFECTS ON FAMILIES AND CHILDREN   The role of work is also increasingly being studied (e.g. Gottfried & Gottfried 1988; Mortimer et al 1987; see review by Hoffman 1989). Earlier influential research by Kohn on variations in child-rearing values and goals as a function of occupation, and Bronfenbrenner's (1986) strong reminder that parents' work settings impinge on family relations and functioning have led to a number of large-scale longitudinal studies. Of particular interest are studies of family functioning and child outcomes in dual-career intact families, usually discussed in terms of maternal employment (see review by Spitze 1988). To date, little overall effect of maternal employment has been shown on security of attachment or children's adjustment. Variables such as the timing of returning to work after giving birth, maternal attitudes toward work and parent roles, status of the mother's paid position, and number of weekly work hours affect group differences among children of working mothers (Gottfried & Gottfried 1988). The generalizability of these findings, however, is limited because most samples have been relatively homogeneous, upper-middle-class, well-educated, and financially advantaged. Research is needed now to address such issues as how maternal employment might be linked to child outcome and how the linkage might change across development.

A contextual factor of considerable relevance to the effects of maternal employment is the use of alternative care arrangements. Nonparental child care remains a controversial topic (see review by Clarke-Stewart 1989), as it has been for more than 50 years. The crux of the controversy is how to interpret two common findings: (a) Infants of full-time working mothers are more likely to be classified as insecurely attached than infants of mothers who work only part-time or are at home full-time (e.g. Belsky & Rovine 1988; Chase-Lansdale & Owen 1987; Easterbrooks & Goldberg 1985); and (b) children who are in out-of-home child care as infants are subsequently less compliant to their parents and more aggressive toward their peers than comparison children (e.g. Haskins 1985; Vaughn et al 1985). Some reviewers (e.g. Belsky 1989) take these findings as indications that early out-of-home child care is developmentally disruptive. Others (e.g. Clarke-Stewart 1989; Phillips et al 1987; Thompson 1988a) question whether measures such as the Strange Situation can be interpreted in the same way for children in out-of-home care and whether compliance and higher aggressiveness may reflect independence and assertiveness rather than social maladjustment. Both sides agree, however, that the quality of infant day care and of parent-child interactions at home are variables of the greatest importance in determining outcome (e.g. Belsky 1989; Phillips et al 1987).

Children's and adolescents' own work experiences are associated with a mixture of positive and negative outcomes, depending on the type of work setting and ability of the adolescent to manage time and responsibilities effectively (e.g. Crouter 1984). Goodnow (1988a) has proposed that the study of household work is a particularly promising vehicle for analyzing the nature and influences of contextual variations in concepts of distributive justice and understanding of role-task correspondence.

FAMILY ECONOMIC CONDITIONS   The US economic recession of the early 1980s elicited several studies of the impact of sudden economic disadvantage (see review by McLoyd 1989). Retrospective research on the impact of the Great Depression (e.g. Elder et al 1988) directed the attention of investigators to short- and long-term social, emotional, and adaptational sequelae of sudden economic hardship in families, and to the mediating role of family relationships and child-rearing variables. Findings from economically depressed farming regions in the United States indicate both increased depression and loneliness as well as greater risk of adolescent drug use and delinquency when parental nurturance declines and discipline becomes more inconsistent and rejecting (Lempers et al 1989). Other evidence links unemployment and economic pressures to child abuse; recent research with urban families, however, indicates that, although unemployment has significant effects on fathers' self-esteem and family roles and relationships, negative effects on behavior toward children do not necessarily occur (e.g. Johnson & Abramovitch 1988; Ray & McLoyd 1986).

Prolonged economic disadvantage has not been studied extensively. Concern about this issue, prompted by the social problem of a growing underclass in the United States, is evident from a growing number of conferences and workshops on the topic. To date, no empirical research has been reported on the nature and degree of impact of current economic and living conditions on children and their development (A. C. Huston, personal communication).

Recent evidence thus adds substance to the claim that contextual factors play a significant moderating role in social behavior and psychosocial functioning. Nonetheless, empirical tests of this claim have been more opportunistic than theoretically driven. The frequently noted need for a conceptual framework for the analysis of contexts has only been partially addressed. New efforts are likely in research on the interaction of biologically based factors, such as temperament, maturational change (e.g. puberty), and gender, with specific contextual variations (see Calvert & Huston 1987; Maccoby 1988; Brooks-Gunn & Petersen 1983). Of particular interest are the implications of *niche-picking*—individual variation in responsiveness to, and selection of, specific aspects of the environment (e.g. Maccoby 1988; Plomin & Daniels 1987; Scarr & McCartney 1983). The hypothesis that niche-picking intensifies as a function of age (Scarr & McCartney 1983) points especially to the need for studies of developmental processes in conjunction with the opportunities, constraints, and demands of the salient contexts to which individuals must adapt.

CONCLUSION AND FUTURE DIRECTIONS

Research in social and personality development has increasingly moved toward an understanding of individual capacities in social and interpersonal contexts. Three elements have been highlighted in this distillation: emotional development, the nature and development of relationships involving children, and the moderating role of contexts as determinants of individual functioning. Future studies will undoubtedly explicate the processes involved in regulation of these multiple forces in child and adolescent development. In the case of emotional development, more studies will deal with regulation and modulation of felt and expressed emotion throughout the first two decades of life; in relationships, research will emphasize the collaborative and adaptational adjustments involved in the transformation of relationships from one period of life to another; and in contextual analyses, investigators will seek a better understanding of the transactional processes between individual differences and environmental potentialities.

These trends underscore the need for concerted attention to the interconnections between developmental processes and individual differences (Maccoby 1984b). Some recent work promises advances. For example, the study of the interplay between maturational changes and perturbations in relationships and contexts offers the potential for analyzing how individual trajectories might be altered in the course of major developmental transitions. The increasing attention to naturally occurring stressors will likely help us to address questions of this type.

A convergence can be noted, too, between the basic research and pressing social issues for children, families, and schools. Recent demographic trends and casualty statistics regarding adolescent pregnancy, the continuing problem of alcohol and drug use (exacerbated by the specter of AIDS), the incidence and sequelae of family violence, and a growing underclass indicate that the convergence is a timely one. The need to understand better the nature of these problems gives more urgency than ever before to research on the social capacities and predilections of children and adolescents.

ACKNOWLEDGMENTS

The authors acknowledge support from National Institutes of Health Grants No. MH 39267 (WAC) and HD 16494 (MRG). We are grateful for the comments of Willard W. Hartup and L. Alan Sroufe and the assistance of Pedra Meeks and Catherine O'Geay.

Literature Cited

Abramovitch, R., Corter, C., Pepler, D. J., Stanhope, L. 1986. Sibling and peer interaction: a final follow-up and a comparison. *Child Dev.* 57:217–29

Atkinson, B., Bell, N. 1986. *Attachment and autonomy in adolescence.* Presented at Bien. Meet. Soc. Res. Adol., 1st, Madison

Baltes, P. B. 1987. Theoretical propositions of life-span developmental psychology: on the dynamics between growth and decline. *Dev. Psychol.* 23:611–26

Bates, J. E. 1987. Temperament in infancy. See Osofsky 1987, pp. 1101–47

Belsky, J. 1989. Developmental risks associated with infant day care: attachment insecurity, noncompliance, and aggression. In *Balancing Working and Parenting: Psychological and Developmental Implications of Day Care,* ed. S. Chehrazi. New York: American Psychiatric Press. In press

Belsky, J., Pensky, E. 1988. Developmental history, personality, and family relationships: toward an emergent family system. In *Relationships within Families,* ed. R. Hinde, J. Stevenson-Hinde, pp. 193–217. Oxford: Oxford Univ. Press

Belsky, J., Rovine, M. J. 1988. Nonmaternal care in the first year of life and the security of infant-parent attachment. *Child Dev.* 59:157–67

Berkowitz, M. W., ed. 1985. *New Directions for Child Development. Ser. 29: Peer Conflict and Psychological Growth.* San Francisco: Jossey-Bass

Berndt, T. J. 1986. Children's comments about their friendships. In *Minnesota Symposia on Child Psychology: Cognitive Perspectives on Children's Social and Behavioral Development,* ed. M. Perlmutter, 18:189–212. Hillsdale, NJ: Erlbaum

Berndt, T. J., Hawkins, J. A., Hoyle, S. G. 1986. Changes in friendship during a school year: effects on children's and adolescents' impressions of friendship and sharing with friends. *Child Dev.* 57:1284–97

Berndt, T. J., Hoyle, S. G. 1985. Stability and change in childhood and adolescent friendships. *Dev. Psychol.* 21:1007–15

Berndt, T. J., Ladd, G. W., eds. 1989. *Peer Relationships in Child Development.* New York: Wiley

Berndt, T. J., Perry, T. B. 1986. Children's perceptions of friendships as supportive relationships. *Dev. Psychol.* 22:640–48

Block, J. 1987. *Longitudinal antecedents of ego-control and ego-resiliency in late adolescence.* Presented at Bien. Meet. Soc. Res. Child Dev., Baltimore

Blyth, D. A. 1983. Surviving and thriving in the social world: a commentary on six new studies of popular, rejected, and neglected children. *Merrill-Palmer Q.* 29:449–58

Bowlby, J. 1973. *Attachment and Loss.* Vol. 2: *Separation.* New York: Basic Books

Bretherton, I. 1985. Attachment theory: retrospect and prospect. See Bretherton & Waters 1985, pp. 3–35

Bretherton, I. 1989. Open communication and internal working models: their role in the development of attachment relationships. In *Nebraska Symposium on Motivation: Socioemotional Development*, ed. R. A. Thompson. Lincoln, NE: Univ. Nebr. Press. In press

Bretherton, I., Waters, E., eds. 1985. Growing points of attachment theory and research. *Monogr. Soc. Res. Child Dev.* 50:Serv. No. 209

Bridges, L. J., Connell, J. P., Belsky, J. 1988. Similarities and differences in infant-mother and infant-father interaction in the strange situation: a component process analysis. *Dev. Psychol.* 24:92–100

Brody, G., Pillegrini, A., Sigel, I. 1986. Marital quality and mother-child and father-child interactions with school-aged children. *Dev. Psychol.* 22:291–96

Bronfenbrenner, U. 1986. Ecology of the family as a context for human development: research perspectives. *Dev. Psychol.* 22:723–42

Bronstein, P. 1984. Differences in mothers' and fathers' behaviors toward children: a cross-cultural comparison. *Dev. Psychol.* 20:995–1003

Brooks-Gunn, J., Petersen, A. C., eds. 1983. *Girls at Puberty: Biological and Psychosocial Perspectives.* New York: Plenum

Bryant, B. 1985. The neighborhood walk: sources of support in middle childhood. *Monogr. Soc. Res. Child Dev.* 50:Ser. No. 210

Buhrmester, D., Furman, W. 1987. The development of companionship and intimacy. *Child Dev.* 58:1101–13

Calvert, S. L., Huston, A. C. 1987. Television and children's gender schemata. In *New Directions for Child Development: Children's Gender Schemata*, ed. L. S. Liben, M. L. Signorella, 38:75–88. San Francisco: Jossey-Bass

Campos, J. J., Barrett, K. C., Lamb, M. E., Goldsmith, H. H., Steinberg, C. 1983. Socioemotional development. In *Handbook of Child Psychology*, ed. M. M. Haith, J. J. Campos, 2:783–915. New York: Wiley

Campos, J. J., Campos, R. G., Barrett, K. C. 1989. Emergent themes in the study of emotional development and emotion regulation. *Dev. Psychol.* 25:394–402

Carlson, C. R., Masters, J. C. 1986. Inoculation by emotion: effects of positive emotional states on children's reactions to social comparison. *Dev. Psychol.* 22:760–65

Cashmore, J. A., Goodnow, J. J. 1985. Agreement between generations: a two-process approach. *Child Dev.* 56:493–501

Caspi, A. 1987. Personality in the life course. *J. Pers. Soc. Psychol.* 53:1203–13

Chase-Lansdale, P., Owen, M. T. 1987. Maternal employment in a family context: effects on infant-mother and infant-father attachments. *Child Dev.* 58:1505–12

Clarke-Stewart, K. A. 1989. Infant day care: maligned or malignant. *Am. Psychol.* 44:266–73

Clingempeel, W. G., Brand, C., Sevoli, R. 1984. Stepparent-stepchild relationships in stepmother and stepfather families: a multimethod study. *Fam. Relat.* 33:465–73

Cohn, J. F., Tronick, E. Z. 1983. Three-month-old infants' reaction to simulated maternal depression. *Child Dev.* 54:185–93

Cole, P. M. 1986. Children's spontaneous control of facial expression. *Child Dev.* 57:1309–21

Collins, W. A., ed. 1984. *Development during Middle Childhood: The Years from Six to Twelve.* Washington, DC: Natl. Acad. Press

Collins, W. A. 1984. The status of basic research on middle childhood. See Collins 1984, pp. 398–421

Collins, W. 1988. Research on the transition to adolescence: continuity in the study of developmental processes. See Gunnar & Collins 1988, pp. 1–15

Consortium for Longitudinal Studies. 1983. *As the Twig is Bent: Lasting Effects of Preschool Programs.* Hillsdale, NJ: Erlbaum

Crittenden, P. M. 1985. Social networks, quality of child rearing, and child development. *Child Dev.* 56:1299–1313

Crockenberg, S., McCluskey, K. 1986.

Change in maternal behavior during the baby's first year of life. *Child Dev.* 57:746–53

Crouter, A. C. 1984. Participative work as an influence on human development. *J. Appl. Dev. Psychol.* 5:71–90

Crowell, J. A., Feldman, S. S. 1988. Mothers' internal models of relationships and children's behavioral and developmental status: a study of mother-child interaction. *Child Dev.* 59:1273–85

Csikszentmihalyi, M., Larson, R. 1984. *Being Adolescent: Conflict and Growth in the Teenage Years.* New York: Basic Books

Cummings, E. M., Zahn-Waxler, C., Radke-Yarrow, M. 1984. Developmental changes in children's reactions to anger in the home. *J. Child Psychol. Psychiatr.* 25:63–74

Damon, W., Phelps, E. 1989. Strategic uses of peer learning in children's education. See Berndt & Ladd 1989, pp. 135–57

Daniels, D., Plomin, R. 1985. Differential experience of siblings in the same family. *Dev. Psychol.* 21:747–60

Diaz, R. M., Berndt, T. J. 1982. Children's knowledge of a best friend: fact or fancy? *Dev. Psychol.* 18:787–94

Dix, T., Ruble, D., Grusec, J., Nixon, S. 1986. Social cognition in parents: inferential and affective reactions to children of three age levels. *Child Dev.* 57:879–94

Dodge, K. A., Garber, J., eds. 1989. *The Development of Affect Regulation and Dysregulation.* New York: Cambridge Univ. Press. In press

Dodge, K. A., Pettit, G. S., McClaskey, C. L., Brown, M. M. 1986. Social competence in children. *Monogr. Soc. Res. Child Dev.* 51:Ser. No. 213

Dornbusch, S. M., Ritter, P. L., Leiderman, P. H., Roberts, D. F., Fraleigh, M. J. 1987. The relation of parenting style to adolescent school performance. *Child Dev.* 58:1244–57

Dunn, J. 1983. Sibling relationships in early childhood. *Child Dev.* 54:787–811

Dunn, J. 1988. *The Beginnings of Social Understanding.* Cambridge, MA: Harvard Univ. Press

Dunn, J., Munn, P. 1985. Becoming a family member: family conflict and the development of social understanding in the second year. *Child Dev.* 56:480–92

Easterbrooks, M. A., Goldberg, W. A. 1985. Effects of early maternal employment on toddlers, mothers and fathers. *Dev. Psychol.* 21:774–83

Eckerman, C. O., Stein, M. R. 1983. The toddler's emerging interactive skills. In *Peer Relationships and Social Skills in Childhood,* ed. K. Rubin, H. Ross, pp. 41–72. New York: Springer

Egeland, B., Jacobvitz, D., Sroufe, L. A. 1988. Breaking the cycle of abuse: relationship predictors. *Child Dev.* 59:1080–88

Eisenberg, N., Miller, P. A. 1987. The relation of empathy to prosocial and related behaviors. *Psychol. Bull.* 10:91–119

Elder, G. H. Jr., Caspi, A., Burton, L. M. 1988. Adolescent transition in developmental perspective: sociological and historical insights. See Gunnar & Collins 1988, pp. 151–80

Elicker, J., Sroufe, L. A. 1989. Predicting peer competence and peer relationships in childhood from early parent-child relationships. In *Family-Peer Relationships: Modes of Linkage,* ed. R. D. Parke, G. W. Ladd. Hillsdale, NJ: Erlbaum. In press

Emery, R. 1989. Family violence. *Am. Psychol.* 44:321–28

Entwisle, D. R., Stevenson, H. W. 1987. Schools and development. *Child Dev.* 58:1149–50

Epstein, J. L. 1983. Longitudinal effects of family-school-person interactions on student outcomes. In *Research in Sociology of Education and Socialization,* ed. A. Kerckhoff, 4:90–130. Greenwich, CT: JAI Press

Epstein, J. L. 1989. The selection of friends: changes across the grades and in different school environments. See Berndt & Ladd 1989, pp. 158–87

Erickson, M. F., Sroufe, L. A., Egeland, B. 1985. The relationship between quality of attachment and behavior problems in pre-school in a high-risk sample. See Bretherton & Waters 1985, pp. 147–66

Feiring, C., Lewis, M., Jaskir, J. 1983. Birth of a sibling: effect on mother-first born child interaction. *Dev. Behav. Pediatri.* 4:190–95

Fischer, K. W., Shaver, P., Carnodran, P. 1989. How emotions develop and how they organize development. *Cognit. Emot.* In press

Frank, S. J., Avery, C. B., Laman, M. S. 1988. Young adults' perceptions of their relationships with their parents: individual differences in connectedness, competence, and emotional autonomy. *Dev. Psychol.* 24:729–37

Furman, W., Bierman, K. L. 1984. Children's conceptions of friendship: a multimethod study of developmental changes. *Dev. Psychol.* 20:925–31

Furman, W., Buhrmester, D. 1985. Children's perceptions of the qualities of sibling relationships. *Child Dev.* 56:448–61

Gjerde, P. 1986. The interpersonal structure of family interaction settings: parent-adolescent relations in dyads and triads. *Dev. Psychol.* 22:297–304

Goldsmith, H. H. 1988. Human developmental behavioral genetics: mapping the effects of genes and environments. *Ann. Child Dev.* 5:187–227

Goldsmith, H. H., Campos, J. J. 1982. Towards a theory of infant temperament. In *The Development of Attachment and Affiliative Systems*, ed. R. N. Emde, R. J. Harmon, pp. 161–93. New York: Plenum

Goldsmith, H. H., Rieser-Danner, L. A. 1989. Assessing early temperament. In *Handbook of Psychological and Educational Assessment of Children*. Vol. 2: *Personality, Behavior, and Context*, ed. C. R. Reynolds, R. W. Kamphaus. New York: Guilford. In press

Goldsmith, H. H., Rothbart, M. K. 1988. *Oregon Center for the Study of Emotion Tech. Rep. 88-01.* Univ. Oregon, Eugene, OR

Goodnow, J. J. 1988a. Children's household work: its nature and functions. *Psychol. Bull.* 103:5–26

Goodnow, J. J. 1988b. Parents' ideas, actions, and feelings: models and methods from developmental and social psychology. *Child Dev.* 59:286–320

Goodnow, J. J., Cashmore, J., Cotton, S., Knight, R. 1984. Mothers' developmental timetables in two cultural groups. *Int. J. Psychol.* 19:193–205

Gottfried, A. E., Gottfried, A. W., eds. 1988. *Maternal Employment and Children's Development.* New York: Plenum

Gottman, J. M. 1983. How children become friends. *Monogr. Soc. Res. Child Dev.* 48: Ser. No. 201

Grossmann, K., Grossmann, K. E., Spangler, G., Suess, G., Unzner, L. 1985. Maternal sensitivity and newborns' orientation responses as related to quality of attachment in Northern Germany. See Bretherton & Waters 1985, pp. 233–56

Grotevant, H., Cooper, C. 1985. Patterns of interaction in family relationships and the development of identity exploration in adolescence. *Child Dev.* 56:415–28

Gunnar, M. R., Collins, W. A., eds. 1988. *The Minnesota Symposia on Child Psychology.* Vol. 21: *Development During the Transition to Adolescence.* Hillsdale, NJ: Erlbaum

Gunnar, M. R., Mangelsdorf, S., Larson, M., Hertsgaard, L. 1989. Attachment, temperament, and adrenocortical activity in infancy: a study of psychoendocrine regulation. *Dev. Psychol.* 25:355–63

Gunnar, M. R., Thelen, E., eds. 1989. *The Minnesota Symposia on Child Psychology.* Vol. 22: *Systems and Development.* Hillsdale, NJ: Erlbaum. In press

Hagestad, G. O. 1984. The continuous bond: a dynamic, multigenerational perspective on parent-child relations between adults. In

Parent-Child Interaction and Parent-Child Relations in Child Development, ed. M. Perlmutter, 17:129–58. Hillsdale, NJ: Erlbaum

Hallinan, M. T., Teixeira, R. A. 1987. Opportunities and constraints: black-white differences in the formation of interracial friendships. *Child Dev.* 58:1358–71

Harris, P. L., Gross, D. 1988. Children's understanding of real and apparent emotion. In *Developing Theories of Mind,* ed. J. W. Astington, P. L. Harris, D. R. Olson, pp. 295–314. New York: Cambridge Univ. Press

Harrison, A., Serafica, F., McAdoo, H. 1984. Ethnic families of color. In *The Family: Review of Child Development Research,* ed. R. D. Parke, 7:329–71. Chicago: Univ. Chicago Press

Hartup, W. W. 1983. Peer relations. See Hetherington 1983, pp. 103–96

Hartup, W. W. 1989. Social relationships and their developmental significance. *Am. Psychol.* 44:120–26

Hartup, W. W., Laursen, B., Stewart, M. I., Eastenson, A. 1988. Conflict and the friendship relations of young children. *Child Dev.* 59:1590–1600

Hartup, W. W., Rubin, Z., eds. 1986. *Relationships and Development.* Hillsdale, NJ: Erlbaum

Haskins, R. 1985. Public school aggression among children with varying day-care experience. *Child Dev.* 56:689–703

Hauser, S., Powers, S., Noam, G., Jacobson, A., Weiss, B., Follansbee, D. 1984. Familial contexts of adolescent ego development. *Child Dev.* 55:195–213

Hetherington, E. M., ed. 1983. *Handbook of Child Psychology.* Vol. 4: *Socialization, Personality, and Social Development.* New York: Wiley

Hetherington, E. M. 1989. Coping with family transitions: winners, losers, and survivors. *Child Dev.* 60:1–14

Hetherington, E. M., Arasteh, J. D., eds. 1988. *Impact of Divorce, Single Parenting, and Step-parenting on Children.* Hillsdale, NJ: Erlbaum

Hetherington, E. M., Stanley-Hagan, M., Anderson, E. R. 1989. Marital transitions: a child's perspective. *Am. Psychol.* 44:303–12

Higgins, E. T., Parsons, J. E. 1983. Social cognition and the social life of the child: stages as subcultures. In *Social Cognition and Social Development: A Sociocultural Perspective,* ed. E. T. Higgins, D. Ruble, W. Hartup, pp. 15–62. New York: Cambridge Univ. Press

Hill, J. P. 1988a. Adapting to menarche: familial control and conflict. See Gunnar & Collins 1988, pp. 43–78

Hill, J. P. 1988b. Research on adolescents and their families: past and prospect. In *New Directions for Child Development: Adolescent Social Behavior and Health*, ed. C. E. Irwin Jr., pp. 13–31. San Francisco: Jossey-Bass

Hinde, R., Stevenson-Hinde, J. 1987. Interpersonal relationships and child development. *Dev. Rev.* 7:1–21

Hirsch, B. J., Rapkin, B. D. 1987. The transition to junior high school: a longitudinal study of self-esteem, psychological symptomatology, school life, and social support. *Child Dev.* 58:1235–43

Hoffman, L. W. 1989. Effects of maternal employment in the two-parent family. *Am. Psychol.* 44:283–92

Hoffman, M. A., Ushpiz, V., Levy-Shiff, R. 1988. Social support and self-esteem in adolescence. *J. Youth Adolesc.* 17:307–16

Howes, C. 1983. Patterns of friendship. *Child Dev.* 54:1041–53

Howes, C. 1987. Peer interaction of young children. *Soc. Res. Child Dev. Monogr.* 53:Ser. No. 217

Ihinger-Tallman, M. 1988. Research on stepfamilies. *Annu. Rev. Sociol.* 14:25–48

Izard, C. E., Hembree, E. A., Huebner, R. R. 1987. Infants' emotion expressions to acute pain: developmental change and stability of individual differences. *Dev. Psychol.* 23:105–13

Izard, C. E., Malatesta, C. Z. 1987. Perspectives on emotional development I: differential emotions theory of early emotional development. See Osofsky 1987, pp. 494–554

Jacobson, J. L., Wille, D. E. 1986. The influence of attachment pattern on developmental changes in peer interaction from the toddler to the preschool period. *Child Dev.* 57:338–47

Johnson, L. C., Abramovitch, R. 1988. Paternal unemployment and family life. In *Ecological Research with Children and Families*, ed. A. R. Pence, pp. 49–75. New York: Teachers College Press

Kagan, J., Reznick, J. S., Snidman, N. 1987. The physiology and psychology of behavioral inhibition in children. *Child Dev.* 58:1459–73

Kaufman, J., Zigler, E. 1987. Do abused children become abusive parents? *Am. J. Orthopsychiatr.* 57:186–97

Kelley, H., Berscheid, E., Christensen, A., Harvey, J., Huston, T., et al. eds. 1983. *Close Relationships*. New York: Freeman

Klinnert, M. D., Campos, J. J., Sorce, J. F., Emde, R. N., Suejda, M. 1983. Emotions as behavior regulators: social referencing in infancy. In *Emotions in Early Development.* Vol. 2: *The Emotions*, ed. R. Plutchik, H.

Kellerman, pp. 57–86. New York: Academic

Kobak, R. R., Sceery, A. 1988. Attachment in late adolescence: working models, affect regulation, and representations of self and others. *Child Dev.* 59:135–46

Kopp, C. B. 1989. Regulation of distress and negative emotions: a developmental view. *Dev. Psychol.* 25:343–54

Ladd, G. W. 1984. Expanding our view of the child's social world: new territories, new maps, same directions? *Merrill-Palmer Q.* 30:317–20

Ladd, G. W., Emerson, E. S. 1984. Shared knowledge in children's friendships. *Dev. Psychol.* 20:932–40

Ladd, G., Golter, B. S. 1988. Parents' management of preschoolers' peer relations: is it related to children's social competence? *Dev. Psychol.* 24:109–17

Lamb, M. E., Elster, A. B. 1985. Adolescent mother-infant-father relationships. *Dev. Psychol.* 21:768–73

Lamb, M. E., Nash, A. 1989. Infant-mother attachment, sociability, and peer competence. See Berndt & Ladd 1989, pp. 219–45

Lamb, M., Pleck, J., Charnov, E., Levine, J. 1987. A biosocial perspective on paternal behavior and involvement. In *Parenting Across the Life Span: Biosocial Dimensions*, ed. J. Lancaster, J. Altmann, A. Rossi, L. Sherrod, pp. 111–42. New York: Aldine de Gruyter

Lamb, M. E., Pleck, J. H., Levine, J. A. 1985. The role of the father in child development: the effects of increased paternal involvement. In *Advances in Clinical Child Psychology*, ed. B. B. Lahey, A. E. Kazdin, 8:180–209. New York: Plenum

Lempers, J., Clark-Lempers, D., Simons, R. 1989. Economic hardship, parenting, and distress in adolescence. *Child Dev.* 60:25–39

Lennon, R., Eisenberg, N. 1987. Emotional displays associated with preschoolers' prosocial behavior. *Child Dev.* 58:992–1000

Lerner, J. V., Lerner, R. M., eds. 1986. *New Directions for Child Development*. Vol. 31: *Temperament and Social Interaction during Infancy and Childhood*. San Francisco: Jossey-Bass

Lerner, R. M. 1984. *On the Nature of Human Plasticity*. New York: Cambridge Univ. Press

Lerner, R. M., Lerner, J. V., Winelle, M., Hooker, K., Lenez, K., et al. 1986. Children and adolescents in their contexts: tests of the goodness of fit model. See Plomin & Dunn 1986, pp. 99–114

Lester, B. M., Boukydis, C. F. Z., eds. 1985.

Infant Crying: Theoretical and Research Perspectives. New York: Plenum

Lewis, M., Feiring, C., McGuffog, C., Jaskir, J. 1984. Predicting psychopathology in six-year-olds from early social relations. *Child Dev.* 55:123–36

Lewis, M., Michaelson, L. 1983. *Children's Emotions and Moods: Developmental Theory and Measurement.* New York: Plenum

Lewis, M., Stanger, C., Sullivan, M. W., Barone, P. 1989. Deception in three year olds. *Dev. Psychol.* 25:439–43

Lewis, M., Sullivan, M. W., Vasen, A. 1987. Making faces: age and emotion differences in the posing of emotional expressions. *Dev. Psychol.* 23:690–97

Lyons-Ruth, K., Connell, D. B., Zoll, D., Stahl, J. 1987. Infants at social risk: relations among infant maltreatment, maternal behavior, and infant attachment behavior. *Dev. Psychol.* 23:223–32

Maccoby, E. E. 1984a. Middle childhood in the context of the family. See Collins 1984, pp. 184–239

Maccoby, E. E. 1984b. Socialization and developmental change. *Child Dev.* 55:317–28

Maccoby, E. E. 1988. Gender as a social category. *Dev. Psychol.* 24:755–65

MacDonald, K., Parke, R. D. 1984. Bridging the gap: parent-child play interaction and peer interactive competence. *Child Dev.* 55:1265–77

Magnusson, D. 1985. Implications of an interactional paradigm for research on human development. *Int. J. Behav. Dev.* 8:115–37

Main, M., George, C. 1985. Responses of abused and disadvantaged toddlers to distress in agemates: a study in the day care setting. *Dev. Psychol.* 21:407–12

Main, M., Kaplan, K., Cassidy, J. 1985. Security in infancy, childhood, and adulthood: a move to the level of representation. See Bretherton & Waters 1985, pp. 66–104

Malatesta, C. Z. 1989. The role of emotions in the development and organization of personality. In *Nebraska Symposium on Motivation.* Vol. 36: *Socioemotional Development,* ed. R. A. Thompson. Lincoln: Univ. Nebr. Press. In press

Masters, J. C. 1989. Strategies and mechanisms for the personal and social control of emotion. See Dodge & Garber 1989. In press

Matheny, A. P. 1989. Children's behavioral inhibition over age and across situations: genetic similarity for a trait during change. *J. Pers.* In press

McLoyd, V. C. 1989. Socialization and development in a changing economy: the effects of paternal job and income loss on children. *Am. Psychol.* 44:293–302

Miller, P. A., Eisenberg, N. 1988. The relation of empathy to aggressive and externalizing/antisocial behavior. *Psychol. Bull.* 103:324–44

Miller, S. A. 1988. Parents' beliefs about children's cognitive development. *Child Dev.* 59:259–85

Minuchin, P., Shapiro, E. 1983. The school as a context for social development. See Hetherington 1983, pp. 197–294

Miyake, K., Chen, S., Campos, J. J. 1985. Infant temperament, mothers' mode of interaction, and attachment in Japan: an interim report. See Bretherton & Waters 1985, pp. 276–97

Montemayor, R. 1983. Parents and adolescents in conflict: all families some of the time and some families most of the time. *J. Early Adolesc.* 3:83–104

Montemayor, R., van Komen, R. 1985. The development of sex differences in friendship patterns and peer group structure during adolescence. *J. Early Adolesc.* 5:285–94

Mortimer, J., Lorence, J., Kumka, D. 1987. *Works, Family, and Personality: Transition to Adulthood.* Norwood, NJ: Ablex

Nelson, C. 1987. The recognition of facial expressions in the first two years of life: mechanisms of development. *Child Dev.* 58:889–909

Osofsky, J. D., ed. 1987. *Handbook of Infant Development.* New York: Wiley. 2nd ed.

Oster, H., Daily, L., Goldenthal, P. 1989. Processing facial affect. In *Handbook of Research on Face Processing,* ed. A. W. Young, H. D. Ellis, pp. 129–80. Amsterdam: North Holland

Parke, R. D. 1988. Families in life-span perspective: a multilevel developmental approach. In *Child Development in Life Span Perspective,* ed. E. M. Hetherington, R. M. Lerner, M. Perlmutter, pp. 159–90. Hillsdale, NJ: Erlbaum

Parke, R. D., Asher, S. R. 1983. Social and personality development. *Annu. Rev. Psychol.* 34:465–509

Parke, R. D., MacDonald, K. B., Burks, V. M., Carson, J., Bhavnagri, N., et al. 1989. Family and peer systems: in search of linkages. In *Family Systems of Life Span Development,* ed K. Kreppner, R. M. Lerner, pp. 65–92. Hillsdale, NJ: Erlbaum

Parke, R. D., Tinsley, B. J. 1987. Family interaction in infancy. In *Handbook of Infancy,* ed. J. Osofsky, pp. 579–641. New York: Wiley

Parker, J. G., Asher, S. R. 1987. Peer relations and later personal adjustment: Are low-accepted children at risk? *Psychol. Bull.* 102:357–89

Parker, J. G., Gottman, J. M. 1989. Social and emotional development in a relational context: friendship interaction from early childhood to adolescence. See Berndt & Ladd 1989, pp. 95–131

Patterson, G. R., Bank, L. 1989. Some amplifier and dampening mechanisms for pathologic processes in families. See Gunnar & Thelen 1989. In press

Peterson, J. L., Zill, N. 1986. Marital disruption, parent-child relationship, and behavior problems in children. *J. Marriage Fam.* 48: 295–307

Phillips, D., McCartney, K., Scarr, S. 1987. Child-care quality and children's social development. *Dev. Psychol.* 23:537–43

Plomin, R., Daniels, D. 1987. Why are children in the same family so different from one another? *Behav. Brain Sci.* 10:1–60

Plomin, R., Dunn, J., eds. 1986. *The Study of Temperament: Changes, Continuities and Challenges.* Hillsdale, NJ: Erlbaum

Radke-Yarrow, M., Cummings, E. M., Kuczynski, L., Chapman, M. 1985. Patterns of attachment in two- and three-year olds in normal families and families with parental depression. *Child Dev.* 56:884–93

Ray, S. A., McLoyd, V. C. 1986. Fathers in hard times: the impact of unemployment and poverty on paternal and marital relations. In *The Father's Role,* ed. M. E. Lamb, pp. 339–83. New York: Wiley

Renken, B., Egeland, B., Marvinney, D., Sroufe, L. A., Mangelsdorf, S. 1989. Early childhood antecedents of aggression and passive-withdrawal in early elementary school. *J. Pers.* In press

Rosenstein, D., Oster, H. 1988. Differential facial responses to four basic tastes in newborns. *Child Dev.* 59:1555–68

Rothbart, M. K. 1989. Biological processes in temperament. In *Temperament in Childhood,* ed. G. A. Kohnstamm, J. E. Bates, M. K. Rothbart. Sussex, Engl: Wiley

Russell, G., Russell, A. 1987. Mother-child and father-child relationships in middle childhood. *Child Dev.* 58:1573–85

Saarni, C. 1984. An observational study of children's attempts to monitor their expressive behavior. *Child Dev.* 55:1504–13

Saarni, C. 1988. Children's understanding of the interpersonal consequences of dissemblance of nonverbal emotion-expressive behavior. *J. Nonverbal Behav.* 12:273–92

Sagi, A., Lamb, M. E., Lewkowica, K. S., Shoham, R., Dvir, R., et al. 1985. Security of infant-mother, -father, and -metapelet attachments among kibbutz-reared Israeli children. See Bretherton & Waters 1985, pp. 257–75

Sameroff, A. 1983. Developmental systems: contexts and evolution. See Hetherington 1983, pp. 237–94

Scarr, S., McCartney, K. 1983. How people make their own environments: a theory of genotype → environment effects. *Child Dev.* 54:424–35

Schneider-Rosen, K., Braunwald, K. G., Carlson, V., Cicchetti, D. 1985. Current perspectives in attachment theory: illustration from the study of maltreated infants. See Bretherton & Waters 1985, pp. 194–210

Schneider-Rosen, K., Cicchetti, D. 1984. The relationship between affect and cognition in maltreated infants: quality of attachment and the development of visual self-recognition. *Child Dev.* 55:648–58

Scott-Jones, D., Nelson-LeGall, S. 1986. Defining black families: past and present. In *Redefining Social Problems,* ed. E. Seidman, J. Rappaport, pp. 83–100. New York: Plenum

Shantz, C. U. 1987. Conflicts between children. *Child Dev.* 58:283–305

Shantz, C. U., Hobart, C. J. 1989. Social conflict and development: peers and siblings. See Berndt & Ladd 1989, pp. 71–94

Shantz, D. W. 1986. Conflict, aggression, and peer status: an observational study. *Child Dev.* 57:1322–32

Shiller, V., Izard, C. E., Hembree, E. A. 1986. Patterns of emotion expression during separation in the Strange-Situation procedure. *Dev. Psychol.* 22:378–82

Sigel, I. E. 1985. A conceptual analysis of beliefs. In *Parental Belief Systems,* ed. L. Laosa, I. E. Sigel, pp. 345–72. Hillsdale, NJ: Erlbaum

Simmons, R. G., Blyth, D. A. 1987. *Moving into Adolescence: The Impact of Pubertal Change and School Context.* New York: Aldine de Gruyter

Simmons, R. G., Burgeson, R., Reef, M. J. 1988. Cumulative change at entry to adolescence. See Gunnar & Collins 1988, pp. 123–50

Slavin, R. E. 1987. Developmental and motivational perspectives on cooperative learning: a reconciliation. *Child Dev.* 58:1161–67

Spitze, G. 1988. Women's employment and family relations: a review. *J. Marriage Fam.* 50:595–618

Sroufe, L. A. 1979. Socioemotional development. In *Handbook of Infant Development,* ed. J. Osofsky, pp. 462–516. New York: Wiley. 1st ed.

Sroufe, L. A. 1983. Individual patterns of adaptation from infancy to preschool. In *Minnesota Symposia on Child Psychology: Development and Policy Concerning Children with Special Needs,* ed. M. Perlmutter, 16:41–81. Hillsdale, NJ: Erlbaum

Sroufe, L. A. 1989. The organization of emotional development. In *Approaches to Emotion,* ed. K. Scherer, P. Ekman, pp. 109–28. Hillsdale, NJ: Erlbaum

Sroufe, L. A., Fleeson, J. 1986. Attachment and the construction of relationships. See Hartup & Rubin 1986, pp. 51–71

Sroufe, L. A., Fleeson, J. 1988. The coherence of family relationships. In *Relationships Within Families: Mutual Influences*, ed. R. Hinde, J. Stevenson-Hinde, pp. 27–47. Oxford: Oxford Univ. Press

Sroufe, L. A., Fox, N. E., Pancake, V. R. 1983. Attachment and dependency in developmental perspective. *Child. Dev.* 54: 1615–27

Sroufe, L. A., Schork, E., Motti, F., Lawroski, N., LaFreniere, P. 1984. The role of affect in social competence. In *Emotion, Cognition and Behavior*, ed. C. Izard, J. Kagan, R. Zajonc, pp. 289–319. New York: Plenum

Steinberg, L. 1987. Impact of puberty on family relations: effects of pubertal status and pubertal timing. *Dev. Psychol.* 23:451–60

Stevenson, D. L., Baker, D. P. 1987. The family-school relation and the child's school performance. *Child Dev.* 58:1348–57

Stevenson, H. W., Siegel, A. E. 1984. *Child Development Research and Social Policy*. Chicago: Univ. Chicago Press

Super, C. Harkness, S. 1986. The developmental niche: a conceptualization at the interface of child and culture. *Int. J. Behav. Dev.* 9:545–69

Takahashi, K. 1986. Examining the Strange-Situation procedure with Japanese mothers and 12-month-old infants. *Dev. Psychol.* 22:265–70

Termine, N. T., Izard, C. E. 1988. Infants' responses to their mothers' expressions of joy and sadness. *Dev. Psychol.* 24:223–29

Thompson, R. A. 1987. Empathy and emotional understanding: the early development of empathy. In *Empathy and Its Development*, ed. N. Eisenberg, J. Strayer, pp. 119–45. Cambridge: Cambridge Univ. Press

Thompson, R. A. 1988a. The effects of infant day care through the prism of attachment theory: a critical appraisal. *Early Childhood Res. Q.* 3:273–82

Thompson, R. A. 1988b. Early development in life-span perspective. In *Life-Span Development and Behavior*, Vol. 9, ed. P. B. Baltes, D. L. Featherman, R. M. Lerner, pp. 129–72. Hillsdale, NJ: Erlbaum

Tinsley, B. J., Parke, R. D. 1987. Grandparents as interactive and social support agents for families with young infants. *Int. J. Aging Hum. Dev.* 25:259–77

Trickett, P., Kuczynski, L. 1986. Children's misbehaviors and parental discipline strategies in abusive and nonabusive families. *Dev. Psychol.* 22:115–23

Valsiner, J., Benigni, L. 1986. Naturalistic research and ecological thinking in the study of child development. *Dev. Rev.* 6:203–23

Vandell, D. L., Minnett, A. M., Santrock, J. W. 1987. Age differences in sibling relationships during middle childhood. *J. Appl. Dev. Psychol.* 8:247–57

Vaughn, B. E., Deane, K. E., Waters, E. 1985. The impact of out-of-home care on child-mother attachment quality: another look at some enduring questions. See Bretherton & Waters 1985, pp. 110–35

Vuchinich, S., Emery, R., Cassidy, J. 1988. Family members as third parties in dyadic family conflict: strategies, alliances, and outcomes. *Child Dev.* 59:1293–1302

Wallerstein, J., Corbin, S. B., Lewis, J. M. 1988. Children of divorce: a ten-year study. See Hetherington & Arasteh 1988, pp. 197–214

Waters, E. 1989. Attachment, identity, and identification: milestones and mechanisms. In *Minnesota Symposia on Child Psychology*. Vol. 23: *Self-Processes in Development*, ed. M. R. Gunnar, L. A. Sroufe. Hillsdale, NJ: Erlbaum. In press

Waters, E., Deane, K. E. 1985. Defining and assessing individual differences in attachment relationships: Q-methodology and the organization of behavior in infancy and early childhood. See Bretherton & Waters 1985, pp. 41–65

Waters, E., Hay, D., Richters, J. 1986. Infant-parent attachment and the origins of prosocial and antisocial behavior. In *Development of Antisocial and Prosocial Behavior: Research, Theories, and Issues*, ed. D. Olweus, J. Block, M. Radke-Yarrow, pp. 97–126. New York: Academic

Weisner, T. S. 1984. Ecocultural niches of middle childhood: a cross-cultural perspective. See Collins 1984, pp. 335–69

Wilson, M. 1989. Child development in the context of the black extended family. *Am. Psychol.* 44:380–85

Youngblade, L. M., Belsky, J. 1989. The social and emotional consequences of child maltreatment. In *Children at Risk: An Evaluation of Factors Contributing to Child Abuse and Neglect*. New York: Plenum. In press

Youniss, J., Smollar, J. 1985. *Adolescent Relations with Mothers, Fathers, and Friends*. Chicago: Univ. Chicago Press

Annu. Rev. Psychol. 1990. 41:417–40

PERSONALITY STRUCTURE: EMERGENCE OF THE FIVE-FACTOR MODEL

John M. Digman

Department of Psychology, University of Hawaii at Manoa, Honolulu, Hawaii 96822

CONTENTS

417

0066-4308/90/0201-0417$02.00

PROLOGUE

William McDougall (1932), writing in the first issue of *Character and Personality* (which later became the *Journal of Personality*), discussed at length the special meanings of "character" and "personality" for the two languages in which the new journal was to be published. Toward the end of his essay, he offered an interesting conjecture: "Personality may to advantage be broadly analyzed into five distinguishable but separable factors, namely, intellect, character, temperament, disposition, and temper. . . . each of these is highly complex [and] comprises many variables" (p. 15).

Although "factor," as McDougall used the term, is closer to "topic" than to contemporary usage of the term, the suggestion was an uncanny anticipation of the results of half a century of work to organize the language of personality into a coherent structure.

THE FIVE-FACTOR MODEL: A GRAND UNIFIED THEORY FOR PERSONALITY?

The past decade has witnessed a rapid convergence of views regarding the structure of the concepts of personality (i.e. the language of personality). It now appears quite likely that what Norman (1963) offered many years ago as an effort "toward an adequate taxonomy for personality attributes" has matured into a theoretical structure of surprising generality, with stimulating links to psycholinguistics and cross-cultural psychology, cognitive theory, and other areas of psychology. Further work will no doubt bring change, and clarification is needed at many points. Nonetheless, the hope that the method of factor analysis would bring a clarity to the domain of personality, a hope voiced years ago by Eriksen (1957) and Jensen (1958), seems close to realization.

HISTORICAL ROOTS OF THE FIVE ROBUST FACTORS OF PERSONALITY

As an excellent review by John et al (1988) points out, systematic efforts to organize the language of personality began shortly after McDougall's suggestion, although such efforts appear to be more surely linked to two German psychologists, Klages (1926) and Baumgarten (1933), than to McDougall. Klages suggested that a careful analysis of language would assist the understanding of personality, and this stimulated Baumgarten to examine personality terms commonly found in the German language.

As John et al note, the efforts of Baumgarten had little effect on the course of German psychology but did influence Allport & Odbert (1936) to undertake their own examination of language, and this was to have a direct effect on research efforts that followed, beginning with the systematic work of Cattell (1943, 1946, 1947, 1948).

Cattell's system, based on factor-analytic studies of peer ratings of college students, and later extended to both the questionnaire and objective-test realms, was welcomed in many quarters as a more objective approach to the organization of the thousands of terms in the English (or any) language used to describe individual differences. The system, however, was of daunting complexity, employing a minimum of 16 primary factors and 8 second-order factors (Cattell et al 1970). Even at the time of publication of the second rating study by Cattell (1948), Banks (1948) was highly critical of the analysis and offered an alternative and much simpler analysis of Cattell's correlations.

Efforts to replicate the early rating studies of Cattell began with the carefully crafted studies of Fiske (1949). Using 21 of Cattell's bipolar scales, Fiske was unable to find evidence for anything more complex than a five-factor solution. Dubious about the meaning of these factors, Fiske nonetheless provided interpretations that are not far off the mark of contemporary views. Fiske's work, although published in a journal frequently read by personality researchers, appears to have had little effect on the development of the three systems so commonly found in personality textbooks (e.g. Feshback & Weiner 1982; Maddi 1989): that is, the systems of Eysenck (1970), Guilford (1975), and Cattell (1965).

Toward the end of the 1950s an American Air Force attempt to predict officer effectiveness was undertaken by Tupes (1957). Subsequently, Tupes & Christal (1961) reported their factor analyses of the 30 Cattell bipolar scales they had used in the earlier study. Like Fiske before them, they were unable to find anything like the degree of complexity Cattell had reported but agreed with Fiske that five factors appeared to account for the observations remarkably well. Tupes & Christal went on to reanalyze Cattell's earlier work (based on the published correlations) and Fiske's correlations, finding all of them in rather good agreement in terms of five factors: *Surgency, Agreeableness, Dependability, Emotional Stability,* and *Culture.*

Unfortunately the Tupes & Christal study was published in an obscure Air Force technical report and remained unknown to virtually all personality researchers, while the publications of Cattell and Eysenck dominated the literature on personality structure as leading models obtained by factor analysis methods.

Norman (1963), however, knew of the report and replicated the five-factor structure, offering the trait dimensions as steps "toward an adequate taxonomy of personality attributes." Other studies corroborating the work of Fiske and Tupes & Christal were those of Borgatta (1964) and Smith (1967). Borgatta, aware of the report by Tupes & Christal, devised a set of behavior descriptors for peer ratings to reflect the five factors obtained by Tupes & Christal. Across five methods of data gathering in the course of a study of small group interaction, Borgatta found five stable factors. His interpretations have a current ring to them: *Assertiveness, Likeability, Emotionality, Intelligence,* and *Responsibility.* Smith (1967), using a set of bipolar scales from Cattell's studies for a study of peer ratings of college students, found evidence for only five factors.

Norman (1967) continued further, investigating various levels of abstraction, downward from the five-factor level, through an intermediate level, and eventually arriving at a three-tiered level of abstraction of personality descriptors. Since it is assumed by virtually all trait theorists (despite their critics) that personality traits, however assessed, have their links to behavior, a basic level is the specific response to a specific situation. Responses, if typically made to prototypic situations, are seen as habits, act frequencies, behavior aggregates, or specific items on inventories (e.g. "I seldom think about the future.") Figure 1 represents these four levels of abstraction. At the fourth level are the five broad constructs—the "Big Five"—generated by systematic trait research of the past 40 years.

The usefulness of one of these trait constructs was soon demonstrated by Smith (1967) and by N. Wiggins et al (1969). Using characteristics denoting the construct often referred to as Responsibility or Conscientiousness, these investigators noted the impressive predictions that could be made in the area of educational achievement for undergraduate and graduate students.

Thus, more than 20 years ago, the domain of personality attributes had been successfully analyzed, not just once, but by five competent, independent investigators, all of whom came to the same general conclusion: that the domain could be adequately described by five superordinate constructs. Then as now some difference of opinion existed about the interpretation of these constructs.

One might suppose, given the robustness of the studies conducted by independent investigators, that research would next have focused on these dimensions, clarifying them and seeking their antecedents and correlates as evidenced in personality development and important life events. However, the times were not right for these pursuits. First, many psychologists shifted their attention to issues that seemed to have greater social relevance for the late 1960s and 1970s. Second, a strong attack was launched upon the entire field of trait research by Mischel (1968), Peterson (1960), Ullmann & Krasner (1975), and other born-again fundamentalists, who excoriated trait theory as akin to scientific sin, while others (D'Andrade 1965; Shweder 1975; Wegner & Vallacher 1977) dismissed the study of personality traits as little more than illusions generated in the heads of personality researchers and their subjects alike. Third, the influence of radical behaviorism on a closely related field,

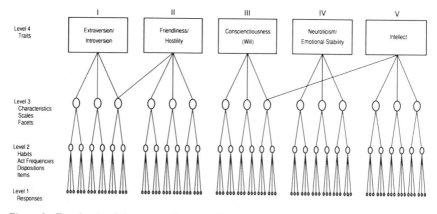

Figure 1   Four levels of abstraction, from specific behaviors to traits.

social psychology, led to a series of studies (e.g. Darley & Latane 1968; Milgram 1963) that seemed to demonstrate the overwhelming influence of the situation upon behavior. As an important paper by Funder & Ozer (1983) very neatly demonstrated, the enthusiasts for the situational view simply ignored much of the evidence, including the fact that situational variables usually failed to account for more than 15% of criterion variance, pushing instead an interpretation that happened to be in accord with the spirit of the times, both within psychology and in intellectual circles generally.

THE RECENT LITERATURE ON THE FIVE-FACTOR MODEL

Studies Based on Ratings

The past decade has seen a rapidly increasing interest in the five-factor model. As a result of his work on lexical analysis Goldberg (1981) noted the "robustness" of the model, stating that "it should be possible to argue the case that *any* model for structuring individual differences will have to encompass—at some level—something like these 'big five' dimensions" (p. 159).

Goldberg further suggested that the five major dimensions of the rating field could provide a framework for many theoretical organizations of personality concepts, including the views of Cattell (1957), Norman (1963), Eysenck (1970), Guilford (1975), Osgood et al (1975), and Wiggins (1980).

Digman & Takemoto-Chock (1981) reanalyzed six studies based on ratings, including the classic work of Cattell and Fiske, and reported the robustness of the five-factor solution of the rating domain, concluding that the five factors first identified by Fiske and by Tupes & Christal represented "an impressive theoretical structure. *Regardless of whether teachers rate children, officer candidates rate one another, college students rate one another, or clinical staff members rate graduate trainees, the results are pretty much the same"* (pp. 164–65).

Hogan (1983), reviewing many studies of trait organization, suggested that six major dimensions would probably encompass all the particulars of observation, as did Brand (1984). The principal difference between the six-factor and the five-factor model seems to involve a splitting of the usual Extraversion dimension into sociability and activity. [In the Hogan Personality Inventory (Hogan 1986) Extraversion is divided into Ambition (surgency or ascendancy) and Sociability.]

Recently, Goldberg (unpublished) has provided what he considers to be "standard markers of the Big Five," a set of 50 self-rating scales, 10 for each of the five trait dimensions. Reliability estimates for factor scores formed by unweighted summation of scale scores vary between .84 and .89. Goldberg also noted that the scores thus obtained correlated highly with the five trait scores of the Neuroticism, Extraversion, Openness Personality Inventory (NEO-PI) (Costa & McCrae 1985), an inventory specifically tailored along the lines of the Five-Factor Model.

McCrae & Costa (1985b) added 40 rating scales to a set of 40 developed previously by Goldberg (1983). Subjects from the Baltimore Longitudinal Study on Aging were rated by four or five peers who knew them well. Factor analysis of the 80 scales pointed to a familiar five-factor solution. Trait scores, obtained by unweighted summation of scale values, correlated generally in the high .40s with scores obtained by self-report, using a self-report version of the same instrument.

Interpretations of the Dimensions

While fairly good agreement appears to be developing concerning the *number* of necessary dimensions, there is less accord with respect to their meaning. Table 1 is based on the efforts of Goldberg (1981), Hogan (1983), Brand (1984), Digman (1988), and John (1989) to organize the various five-factor solutions that have been noted.

There is general agreement that Dimension I is Eysenck's (1947) Extraversion/Introversion and that IV represents the presence and effects of negative affect, or Tellegen's (1985) Negative Emotionality. To line up with the vast work of Eysenck over the years, Dimension IV is usually referred to as Neuroticism vs Emotional Stability. Here, then, are the original Eysenck "Big Two," first delineated over 40 years ago.

Dimension II has generally been interpreted as Agreeableness (Tupes & Christal 1961; Norman 1963; Goldberg 1981; Costa & McCrae 1985). Agreeableness, however, seems tepid for a dimension that appears to involve the more humane aspects of humanity—characteristics such as altruism, nur-

Table 1 The five robust dimensions of personality from Fiske (1949) to the present

Author	I	II	III	IV	V
Fiske (1949)	social adaptability	conformity	will to achieve[a]	emotional control	inquiring intellect
Eysenck (1970)	extraversion	——— P s y c h o t i c i s m ———		neuroticism	
Tupes & Christal (1961)	surgency	agreeableness	dependability	emotionality	culture
Norman (1963)	surgency	agreeableness	conscientiousness	emotional	culture
Borgatta (1964)	assertiveness	likeability	task interest	emotionality	intelligence
Cattell (1957)	exvia	cortertia	superego strength	anxiety	intelligence
Guilford (1975)	social activity	paranoid disposition	thinking introversion	emotional stability	
Digman (1988)	extraversion	friendly compliance	will to achieve	neuroticism	intellect
Hogan (1986)	sociability & ambition	likeability	prudence	adjustment	intellectance
Costa & McCrae (1985)	extraversion	agreeableness	conscientiousness	neuroticism	openness
Peabody & Goldberg (1989)	power	love	work	affect	intellect
Buss & Plomin (1984)	activity	sociability	impulsivity	emotionality	
Tellegen (1985)	positive emotionality		constraint	negative emotionality	
Lorr (1986)	interpersonal involve-ment	level of socialization	self-control	emotional stability	independent

[a] Not in the original analysis but noted in a re-analysis by Digman & Takemoto-Chock (1981).

turance, caring, and emotional support at the one end of the dimension, and hostility, indifference to others, self-centeredness, spitefulness, and jealousy at the other. Some years ago, Guilford & Zimmerman (1949) proposed Friendliness as a primary trait dimension. Fiske (1949) offered Conformity (to social norms). Reflecting both the agreeableness and docility inherent in the dimension Digman & Takemoto-Chock (1981) argued for Friendly Compliance versus Hostile Noncompliance as a more adequate interpretation.

The essence of Dimension III has proved no less difficult to capture. To many writers this has suggested Conscientiousness. However, as Digman & Inouye (1986) have pointed out, "conscientious," both as a scale in research and in its dictionary definition[1], is ambiguous, typically loading both factor dimensions II and III in studies. Noting several studies that have linked this dimension to educational achievement (Smith 1967; N. Wiggins et al 1969; Digman 1972b), Digman & Takemoto-Chock (1981) suggested either Will to Achieve or simply Will as the better term. The latter interpretation has a historical association with the early work of Webb (1915), who analyzed a set of 39 "character qualities," using Spearman's method of factoring, and noted, beyond the general intelligence factor, g, a second general factor of volition or will, w. "Conscientiousness," however, seems to have become the interpretation of general choice and will be employed here.

Dimension V has been variously interpreted as Intellect (Goldberg 1981; Hogan 1983; Digman & Inouye 1986), Intelligence (Borgatta 1964), and Openness (Costa & McCrae 1985). Quite likely it is all of these; that is, the factor dimension has pointed to a *domain* of trait characteristics that are more or less related. McCrae & Costa, their collection of scales emphasizing various characteristics of "openness" (e.g. openness to feelings and to new ideas, flexibility of thought, and readiness to indulgence in fantasy), find an Openness factor. Hogan (1986) has lumped cultural interests, educational aptitude, and creative interests under Intellectance. John (1989), reviewing the attempts of many researchers, noted that something like Intellect (e.g. Inquiring Intellect, Intelligence, Intellectance) had most frequently been employed.

As other literature on the five-factor model is reviewed below, the following trait names will be used: I: Extraversion/introversion (or Surgency); II: Friendliness/hostility (or Agreeableness); III: Conscientiousness (or Will); IV: Neuroticism/emotional stability (or Emotional Stability); and V: Intellect (or Openness).

---

[1]The *American Heritage Dictionary of the English Language* lists "1. Governed or accomplished according to conscience; scrupulous. 2. Thorough and painstaking; careful." The first definition applies to Dimension II, the second to III.

The Five-Factor Model as Represented in the Questionnaire Domain

Intimations that the Big Five might prove to be a model for the organization of traits as measured by questionnaires began to appear a decade ago. Digman (1979) analyzed the scale correlations of the High School Personality Questionnaire (HSPQ; Cattell & Cattell 1969) and found four second-order factors that gave some resemblance to rating factors I through IV. The various scales of the Personality Research Form (PRF; Jackson 1974) were then related to these four factors, producing substantial correlations that were in general as expected [e.g. .73 between n_{aff} (need for affiliation) and Factor II, Extraversion; $-.62$ between n_{imp} (need for Impulsiveness) and Factor III, Conscientiousness].

Goldberg (1981; 159), who may have been first to use the expression "Big Five," proposed that many well-known self-report inventories might reflect various aspects of the five-factor model.

An important study by Amelang & Borkenau (1982) not only supported the five-factor model; it also provided a fine response to Jensen's (1958) plea for the study that would answer questions concerning the relationships among the Cattell, Guilford, and Eysenck systems. The answer: They all fit into the five-factor model very nicely. Amelang & Borkenau apparently were unaware of the five-factor studies in the United States. Their study, therefore, provided a completely independent replication of the American studies.

More recent studies of the correlations of the scales of various inventories are in agreement with the Amelang-Borkenau conclusions. Birenbaum & Montag (1986), using an Israeli sample, factored the Sixteen Personality Factor Questionnaire (16PF) together with the Zuckerman Sensation Seeking Scales (Zuckerman et al 1964). They obtained a five-factor solution for the 16PF correlations that was subsequently replicated by Digman (1988). Like Amelang & Borkenau, Birenbaum & Montag appear to have been unaware of the five-factor model of the rating field.

In a series of studies Costa & McCrae have not only developed an inventory (Costa & McCrae 1985) to assess the five trait dimensions implied by the five robust factors of the rating domain, but have used the model and inventory in a series of studies that have demonstrated the ubiquity of the Big Five. The inventory began with an effort to move beyond the Eysenck "Big Two," Extraversion and Neuroticism. Analysis of the 16PF inventory (Costa & McCrae 1976) pointed to three meaningful clusters of scales, two of which mirrored the Eysenck Neuroticism and Extraversion dimensions, the third a set of scales suggesting "open vs closed to experience" (Costa & McCrae 1985; 26). Further development of the third dimension led to the creation of the NEO Personality Inventory (NEO-PI). The three original scales—N, E, and O—were subsequently joined by Scales A (Agreeableness, Dimension II of the five-factor model) and C (Conscientiousness, Dimension III). Using the NEO-PI as markers for the Big Five, Costa & McCrae have demonstrated the presence of the five-factor model in the Eysenck Personality Inventory (EPI; Eysenck & Eysenck 1964; McCrae & Costa 1985a), the Jackson Personality Research Form (PRF; Jackson 1974; Costa & McCrae 1988), the Myers-Briggs Type Indicator (MBTI; Myers & McCauley 1985; McCrae & Costa 1989), and the California Q-Set (Block 1961; McCrae et al 1986). Analysis of the Minnesota Multiphasic Personality Inventory (MMPI; Hathaway & McKinley 1951) by Costa et al (1986) in the context of the NEO-PI found four of the Big Five factors—Neuroticism, Extraversion, Agreeableness (Friendliness), and Openness (Intellect)—well represented. Conscientiousness, however, was conspicuous by its absence.

Borkenau & Ostendorf (in preparation) carried out an all too rare confirmatory factor analysis of the five-factor model. (Virtually all studies have employed the traditional exploratory model). Using a German language version of the NEO-PI, self-ratings and ratings by knowledgeable others for adults recruited by advertisement, they first reduced self-ratings and ratings by others to five factor scores, added the NEO-PI five scores, and employed LISREL (Joreskog & Sorbom 1984) to assess the adequacy of the five-factor model to account for the correlations involved among the 15 variables from the three data sources. The model that best fit the data was based on five oblique trait factors that mirrored the Big Five quite closely and three oblique method factors. A more extensive analysis of the complete data available, 60 basic scales in all, 20 for each method, could not support the five-factor model that was tested. The authors point out, however, that the model assumed simple structure, something that the five-factor model simply does not possess.

A variant of the five-factor model has been provided by Peabody (1967, 1984) and by Peabody & Goldberg (1989). Peabody, noting that evaluation is confounded with most of the characteristics employed in the rating field, has based his approach on attempts to remove this basic dimension from consideration of other dimensions. Analyzing seven data sets of characteristics of wide scope, Peabody & Goldberg recovered the usual five factors in both "internal" judgments (based on similarity ratings of characteristics by judges) and "external" judgments (the usual ratings of persons by observers). A smaller sixth factor, "Values," was noted in the analysis of "internal" judgments. Noting that factor loadings on the first three dimensions (Surgency, Agreeableness, and Conscientiousness) suggested a circular pattern, rather than one exhibiting a clear simple structure pattern, Peabody & Goldberg transformed the factor values on the three factor dimensions to a general

Evaluation dimension and two descriptive dimensions, Tight vs Loose and Assertive vs Unassertive.

The Peabody & Goldberg studies indicate one of the bemusing aspects of the technique of factor analysis: its well-known arbitrariness of solution. For the five-factor model one has at least two choices of model: one based on the usual solution that has dimensions reflecting a high degree of evaluation, or one that seeks to describe the dimensions in terms of a broad, general factor (such as the g factor of intelligence) and others that describe the residualized content of what remains after "partialling out" the general evaluative aspects of the dimensions.

The Five-Factor Model and Behavior

The five-factor model emerged from analyses of rating scales that required measured judgments of others; for example, to what degree is person X fearful, sympathetic, etc. Inventories typically ask for reports of behaviors ("I tend to avoid parties"). Buss and his associates (Buss & Craik 1980, 1985; Botwin & Buss 1989) have employed measures closer to actual behavior with what they have called the *act-frequency* approach, which involves reports of the frequencies with which specific acts (e.g. "She said I was irresponsible") are performed during a specified period of time. Although the frequency is as recalled, rather than as actually observed, analysis of 20 acts and their frequencies as reported provided strong support for the five-factor model. Borkenau (1988) had judges rate the prototypicality of 120 acts verbally described (in German for his German subjects), and patterned after the Big Five. Correlations were calculated for the characteristics (e.g. talkative) across the 120 acts. Factor analysis of these correlations produced the usual five factors, leading to the conclusion that "they may be identified as the five major dimensions of personality" (p. 350). An important methodological point to this study is that the correlations between pairs of characteristics (e.g. talkative and frank) were based on values obtained from different judges.

Block (1989), however, has taken strong exception to the act-frequency approach, noting that acts, as they are recalled from memory with respect to frequency of occurrence, are very similar to inventory items. Block also noted that the extreme specificity of some of the act statements employed by the method ("He turned his back to me") would probably lead to low levels of usefulness. Despite Block's criticism, the act-frequency approach may prove to be a useful research tool. What is apparent in the act-frequency approach is an effort to get closer to actual behavior, as opposed to opinions about persons (e.g. "X is reliable," in the case of ratings, or "I am careful about my appearance," in the case of an inventory). While such opinions (judgments, impressions) are presumably based on behavioral observation, they obviously may be distorted for many reasons.

Buss & Craik (1980), in presenting the act-frequency approach as an alternative procedure for data collection, also admitted that an "evident next step . . . calls for field studies . . . of acts observed in situ" (p. 390). As Block points out, this step has not been taken by the act-frequency approach enthusiasts, yet there is good evidence that judgments about persons, based upon recollections of their behavior, are rooted in actual behavior.

Such studies are not easily done on adults, unless the subjects are easily observed, as in institutions or laboratory situations. Years ago Borgatta (1964) demonstrated the linkage of peer ratings to laboratory behavior. More recently, Small et al (1983) reported a study of observed prosocial and dominance behaviors exhibited by a group of boys during a camping trip, using both peer ratings and frequency counts of actual behaviors. Correlations generally in the .70s and .80s were reported.

OTHER PERSONALITY SYSTEMS AND THE BIG FIVE

Cattell's System

As Goldberg (1981) has pointed out, Cattell's complex system has not been able to survive the test of independent replication. Beginning with Banks (1948) and Fiske (1949), no one (e.g. Howarth 1976; Digman & Takemoto-Chock 1981) has been able to find more than seven factors in the original correlations of the rating studies that were the basis of the system. However, the correlations of the 16PF scales, when factored, usually provide some indication of the Big Five (Birenbaum & Montag 1986; Noller et al 1987; Digman 1988). It is interesting that at one point Cattell (1956) himself was inclined to the view that the correlations of the 16PF scales would only support four factors. These four bear some resemblance to the Big Five.

Whatever the eventual fate of the Sixteen Personality Factor System, Cattell's contributions to the field, in the opinion of the writer (Digman 1972a) and of an earlier reviewer (Wiggins 1968), were important and essential for the development of a quantitative approach to personality assessment. The name of Lewis Thurstone will always be linked with a dimensional approach to ability. Raymond Cattell will be remembered as the pioneer geometer of the personality realm.

Eysenck's System

The "Big Two" initial dimensions of Eysenck, Neuroticism and Extraversion/Introversion, have appeared routinely in many factor studies of personality characteristics. To these two Eysenck subsequently added a Psychoticism dimension and set forth his view of the "three superfactors P, E, and N"

(Eysenck 1970). Like Guilford, Eysenck has considered intelligence (or intellect) to be something apart from temperament. Thus, the Big Five, if reduced to four superfactors, are almost in accord with the Eysenck three. It has been suggested (Zuckerman et al 1988; John 1989) that Eysenck's P factor is a blend of Dimensions II (Agreeableness) and III (Conscientiousness), and that *psychopathy* may be a better interpretation of the trait dimension.

Tellegen (1985), dissatisfied with the differences among traditional inventories, devised an 11-scale Multidimensional Personality Questionnaire (MPQ), which, when factored, provided three trait dimensions: Positive Emotionality, Negative Emotionality, and Constraint. He concluded that these three were very similar in content to Eysenck's Extraversion, Neuroticism, and Psychoticism dimensions. A three-factor solution of a variety of instruments by Zuckerman and his associates (1988) bears a striking similarity to the Tellegen model. Impulsive Unsocialized Sensation Seeking was offered as an alternative interpretation of Eysenck's Psychoticism factor.

Extraversion and Neuroticism, then, appear to be well established across many studies and across the rating and questionnaire domains. However, as Block (1977) has pointed out, Psychoticism as an interpretation of the third dimension is something else, and most critics of the Eysenck system believe that it was simply given an inappropriate label. The dimension appears to be an amalgam of Trait Dimensions II (Friendliness) and III (Conscientiousness or Will). Perhaps Eysenck, who enlarged his two-factor system with what seems great caution, may yet extend it to four and thus be in good agreement with the five-factor model.

Guilford's System

Noting that Guilford, like Eysenck, always viewed intellect as a domain separate from temperament, the four second-order factors suggested by Guilford (1975) appear to be supported by research (Amelang & Borkenau 1982) and to fit the four non-intellect factors of the five-factor model reasonably well. Based upon their study, however, Amelang & Borkenau suggested some reinterpretation of Guilford's primary scales and realignment of the primary scales to the higher level constructs.

Murray's Need System

Using Jackson's Personality Research Form (PRF; Jackson 1974) two independent studies (Borkenau & Ostendorf 1989; Costa & McCrae 1988) came to similar conclusions: The five broad dimensions of personality commonly noted in the rating field and increasingly noted in omnibus personality inventories subsume the many scales of the PRF. The Borkenau & Ostendorf study involved a factor analysis of German language versions of the NEO-PI, the EPI, the PRF, and the Freiberg Personality Inventory (FPI), a widely used personality inventory in Germany; the Costa & McCrae study used the PRF and the NEO-PI.

Most of the PRF scales correlated as one might expect with the various trait dimensions of the NEO-PI: e.g. n_{ach} with Conscientiousness, n_{aff} with Extraversion, n_{agg} (negatively) with Agreeableness, n_{def} with Neuroticism, and n_{und} with Openness. However, unlike many inventories, the PRF provided clear indicants of Dimension III (Conscientiousness or Will).

The Borkenau & Ostendorf study, like the earlier Amelang & Borkenau report, both based on a large number of different inventories, confirm what has been suspected (Goldberg 1981): the five-factor model is robust, not only across different studies and languages in the rating field, but across languages and different inventories, as well.

The Interpersonal Circle

Based on the theoretical views of Horney (1937) and Sullivan (1953), Leary (1957) proposed that interpersonal behaviors could meaningfully be organized in terms of a circular pattern around two main axes, Love-Hate and Power. Over the past two decades, two research groups, Lorr and his associates (Lorr & Youniss 1974; Lorr & Manning 1978; Lorr & Nerviano 1985; Lorr & Knight 1987) and J. Wiggins and his group (J. Wiggins 1980; J. Wiggins & Broughton 1985; J. Wiggins et al 1988, 1989) have investigated this domain extensively. Their work suggests that the Interpersonal Circle Model corresponds to Trait Dimensions I (Extraversion) and II (Friendliness). For Wiggins these dimensions are Power (Dominance vs Submissiveness) and Love (Love vs Hate).

Lorr's Interpersonal Style Inventory (ISI; Lorr 1986) contains five broad scales, three of which (Interpersonal Involvement, Socialization, and Autonomy) appear to reflect Dimensions I and II of the five-factor model. Two others, Self-Control and Stability are clearly related to Dimensions III (Conscientiousness) and IV (Neuroticism).

Wiggins and his associates (J. Wiggins et al 1988, 1989) have gone beyond simply relating interpersonal characteristics to two broad dimensions, mapping the interpersonal domain in terms of a geometric (circular) model, wherein the location of each characteristic, relative to others and to the two main dimensions, is determined.

Linguistic Analyses and the Five-Factor Model

Beginning with the work of Baumgarten (1933) and Allport & Odbert (1936), research related to the Big Five has had obvious links with language and the manner in which it is employed in describing persons. Goldberg (1981) provided an introduction to linguistic analysis for many personality researchers, and then showed the relevance of this for the realm of personality descriptors. As Goldberg noted, it was Osgood and his associates (1957) who conducted the best-known and most extensive investigation into the manner in which persons employ language as descriptors of objects, person objects included. It is widely known that Osgood's "Big Three" dimensions (Evaluation, Activity, and Potency) were obtained from factor analysis of scales across objects. What is not widely known, however, is that the initial analysis suggested more than three factors, or that a factor analysis conducted on a primitive computer in the middle 1950s, using the square root method of factoring, might produce a somewhat simplified analysis. Regardless, the cross-cultural stability of the system has been verified across many languages. Certain aspects of Peabody's (1967, 1984) system are related to the Osgood Evaluation, Activity, and Power dimensions. Since it has been noted that his system can be related to the five-factor model (Peabody & Goldberg 1989), one may surmise that the Big Five may possess as much cultural generality as does the Osgood system. Certainly, the work of Bond et al (1975), Amelang & Borkenau (1982), and Birenbaum & Montag (1986) suggests as much.

Hampson (1988) has reviewed the work of several investigators who adopted Rosch's model (Rosch et al 1976) of semantic categories for objects in the everyday world. Hampson noted that there is a "distinction between personality nouns and traits," and that "most personality theories have focused on trait-dimensions as opposed to personality types" (p. 202). Using the Rosch model, Hampson et al (1986) observed the manner in which subjects related personality characteristics at presumably different levels of *breadth* (abstractiveness). The results implied a three-tiered hierarchy of concepts for some (e.g. UNKIND/Selfish/stingy); a two-tiered hierarchy for others. Figure 1 is an example of such a hierarchy: The superordinate concepts at the top have the greatest breadth (and related "fuzziness"), while those at lower levels, although more precise (with related "fidelity"), may have less usefulness—at least to personality researchers—because of their narrow meaning. To a social psychologist the specific behavior of *stopping to help* may be the observation of basic meaning for a study of helping behavior; to the personality researcher, the observation of interest would be the less specific measure of *need for nurturance*.

Cantor & Mischel (1979) examined the manner in which subjects sorted person concepts into superordinate categories. It is interesting that the categories selected by these investigators were "the extraverted person," "the cultured person," "the person committed to a belief," and "the emotionally unstable person." The only personality type missing from this list to make it congruent with the Big Five is "the friendly person."

THEORETICAL CONJECTURES: WHY FIVE DIMENSIONS?

Revelle (1987: 487) felt that "the agreement among these descriptive dimensions is impressive . . . [but] there is a lack of theoretical explanation for the *how* and the *why* of these dimensions."

John (1989) has wondered, as have others (Goldberg 1983; Digman & Inouye 1986), why five? One possibility has been that the model, with its historic link to Cattell's original work, reflects the basic dimensionality of the scales originally chosen by Cattell (1943). That possibility seems to have been laid to rest by John's study. Using college students to rate their own personalities with terms chosen from the Adjective Check List (ACL; Gough & Heilbrun 1980), John found that the relationships among the 60 most commonly used terms gave the familiar five-factor solution. Factor V, a frequently debatable dimension, contained terms related to "culture" (artistic, sophisticated), "intelligence" (intelligent, complicated, sharp-witted), and "creativity" (imaginative, original, inventive).

Is the common finding of five—sometimes six, rarely more—factors underlying the manifest variation and covariation in a wide assortment of personality descriptors related to limitations on human information processing? There have been a few intimations of this (Goldberg 1983; Digman & Inouye 1986).

CORRELATES OF PERSONALITY DIMENSIONS

Heritability of Personality

Since the time of Cain and Abel parents and philosophers have wondered, as have Plomin & Daniels (1987), "Why are children in the same family so different from one another?" The genetic influence on personality was reviewed rather recently (Henderson 1982). Since that review the evidence for a strong hereditary effect on Positive Emotionality (Extraversion), Constraint (Conscientiousness), and Negative Emotionality (Neuroticism) has been strengthened by the first reports from the Minnesota Twin Study (Tellegen et al 1988). Agreeing with previous studies, the genetic contribution to the personality seems to be about 50%, with trivial amounts attributable to shared (e.g. family) environment. Rushton et al (1986) have reported similar results in a study of the heritabilities of altruism and aggression.

Direct Measures of Family Influence

The literature has long stressed the seeming importance of the family, particularly the behavior of parents toward children. Certainly, therapists would attest to a strong relationship here, based upon what their clients unfold to them about life in their families of origin. However, it is possible that parental practices are completely confounded with hereditary effects, as the studies reported above might suggest.

McCrae & Costa (1988) used the Parent-Child Relations Questionnaire (Siegelman & Roe, unpublished) in a retrospective study of parental practices, based on mature adults who were also given the NEO-PI inventory. Intraclass correlations based on siblings in the study were modest, between .27 and .37, except for the scale Casual-Demanding (r=.67). Correlations among the three parental practices scales and the five personality scales were also modest. Two correlations were as one would expect: the Loving-Rejecting scale correlated −.30 with Neuroticism and .23 with Agreeableness. These two relationships are similar to those found earlier by Digman & Digman (1980) in a study of the personality effects of environmental stressors, where the correlations between a measure of parent-child interaction and teacher ratings of Neuroticism and Hostility were typically in the .30's. In the former study, the ratings were retrospective and based on mature adults; in the latter, they were based on school children aged 12–14. It appears that the effect of parental rearing practices, although significant, is smaller than many of us have believed.

Cross-Cultural Comparisons

Bond et al (1975) translated Norman's 20 scales into Japanese and administered the scales to undergraduate students at a Japanese university. Factoring of the 20 scales led to a clear five-factor solution. These factors were quite comparable to those of the Norman (1963) factors, with coefficients of congruence generally in the high .80 to low .90 range. Factor V related less well (.72).

Bond et al also related their factors to those obtained by Guthrie & Bennett (1970) in a study of Philippine students. The first four factors were highly related to those obtained in the Guthrie-Bennett study. Factor V, however, related less clearly to the factor obtained in the Philippine study. (Factor V, it may be noted, has been the most debatable of the five dimensions; suggesting Culture to some researchers, Openness to others, and Intellect to yet another group.)

The German studies on the five-factor model have been noted above: a study by Amelang & Borkenau (1982) of various traditional inventories, and the analysis of a German version of the Jackson PRF by Borkenau & Ostendorf (1989). In Israel, Birenbaum & Montag's (1986) analysis of the 16PF was in terms of five factors that closely resembled an analysis of the inventory by Digman (1988).

The Big Five have appeared now in at least five languages, leading one to suspect that something quite fundamental is involved here. Is this the way people everywhere construe personality, regardless of language or culture?

Masculinity-Femininity and the Big Five

The feminist movement has stimulated studies that have examined traditional stereotypes and prototypes of masculinity and femininity, as well as providing contemporary scales for assessing these characteristics (Bem 1981; Farnill & Ball 1985). Some personality inventories (e.g. the CPI, the Comrey CPS, the GZTS) have always considered M/F an important aspect of personality.

An analysis of the Australian Sex Role Inventory was conducted by Farnill & Ball (1985). Factored together with the Personality Description Question-naire (PDQ), the Australian scale proved to be clearly multifactorial and related to three personality dimensions. One, which resembles a fusion of Big Five Dimensions I^+ and II^- (Extraverted and Hostile), was interpreted as prototypically undesirable masculinity. A second, an emotional factor and similar to Dimension IV (Neuroticism), was seen as undesirable femininity. Desirable femininity was suggested by the positive pole of a factor much like the positive pole of Dimension II (Friendliness). The analysis also noted a personality factor much like Dimension III (Conscientiousness). M/F appears to be a rather complex phenomenon, but at least partly related to the Big Five.

Personality Stability

As Costa & McCrae (1988) point out, most of the theories of the effects of aging on personality, while interesting, are not based on studies that have tracked persons over extended periods. An exception is Block's (1971) study, which presented evidence based on correlations of persons over time, the bulk of which were quite substantial. Conley (1984) did a follow-up on couples first assessed in the 1930s, using the Bernreuter Personality Inventory and the Bell Adjustment Inventory. Correlations with psychiatric symptoms in late adulthood in the .25 to .40 range were obtained.

A six-year longitudinal study of trait-stability was conducted by Costa & McCrae (1988), based on their Baltimore Longitudinal Study of Aging panel. Using their NEO-PI instrument, they noted retest correlations for Neuroti-cism, Extraversion, and Openness of .83, .82, and .83, respectively. These values approach the reliabilities of the scales themselves, leading to the conclusion most of us make with surprise upon seeing a good friend after many years of separation: He's just the same as he always was.

Costa & McCrae also noted very slight changes in mean levels over the six-year period. The effects were generally very slight (accounting for less than 1% of variance) across the 20 scales of the inventory. These persons maintained their own rank order, generally, over time with respect to these measures, and the group as a whole changed imperceptibly.

METHODOLOGICAL ISSUES

The Person-vs-Situation Debate

Carson (1989) feels that the debate may be over. Kendrick & Funder (1988) seem ready to move beyond the person-vs-situation controversy, finding some lessons to be derived from it. They examined many of the hypotheses that had been advanced by the situationists to account for whatever consistency had been reported and found that none of them (e.g. attribution, semantic illusions, stereotypes) held up under scrutiny. Agreeing with Mischel & Peake (1982) about the importance of behavioral relevance, Kendrick & Funder list other time-honored procedures for improving correlations based on ratings: the use of raters well acquainted with the ratees, the use of multiple behavioral observations and multiple observers, and the use of characteristics that are publicly observable.

Aggregation

The way out of the "personality correlation" bind of .30 or so, often mentioned as the most to be expected from personality measures, is a procedure that has been implicitly practiced almost since the dawn of scientific psychology. The procedure involves what in the past were known as "composite variables," what we now call "aggregation."

One recognizes the futility of trying to predict Johnny's answer to a single arithmetic question on a Friday afternoon test from an item on a quantitative aptitude test. Such correlations are likely to be very low for a variety of reasons treated in elementary statistics texts: dichotomous variables, unreliability of items, restriction of range, etc. What has been done in the field of educational assessment is to *aggregate* a set of, say, 80 items and to correlate the composite measure with an index of *general* achievement—the familiar grade average, a composite based not only on many measures of achievement, but on measures over time as well. Epstein (1986) has reminded those whose statistics lessons are not well remembered that aggregation is basically an application of the Spearman-Brown prophecy formula that predicts increases in reliability and related validity as a function of lengthened (i.e. increased) observation.

At this point I should like to take off my reviewer's hat and write as a researcher with experience directly related to the points raised by Kendrick & Funder. Some time ago I noted the benefits of the procedures recommended by Kendrick & Funder (Digman 1972b; Digman & Digman 1980). Aggregating teachers' ratings across several scales believed to be related to Trait Dimension III (which I now prefer to call Will, but at that time called the Monitor Factor) and across four teachers in four different elementary and intermediate school years, I obtained a robust (unit weighted) multiple correlation of .70 with subsequent high school grade average. Both independent and dependent variables, it should be noted, were composite variables, based upon a great deal of quantified observation over the years.

EPILOGUE

Hogan (R. Hogan, personal communication, September, 1985) may have expressed the greatest enthusiasm for the Big Five model:

> This is an area in which personality psychologists have a major scientific finding to report. We now can specify with some confidence the structure of the vocabulary that observers use to describe [persons]—put another way, we have a replicable model of the structure of personality from the viewpoint of an observer. . . . There is now considerable agreement that observers' impressions can be expressed in terms of about five dimensions.

John (1989) seems equally bullish, as do McCrae & Costa (1989). Others (Livneh & Livneh 1989; Waller & Ben-Porath 1987) have their reservations. There is probably no doubt in the reader's mind that I agree wholeheartedly with Hogan. At a minimum, research on the five-factor model has given us a useful set of very broad dimensions that characterize individual differences. These dimensions can be measured with high reliability and impressive validity. Taken together, they provide a good answer to the question of personality *structure*.

The *why* of personality is something else. If much of personality is genetically determined, if adult personality is quite stable, and if shared environment accounts for little variability in personality, what is responsible for the remaining variance? Perhaps it is here that the idiographic (i.e. idiosyncratic) study of the individual has its place. Or perhaps we shall have to study personality with far greater care and with much closer attention to the specifics of development and change than we have employed thus far.

Literature Cited

Allport, G. W., Odbert, H. S. 1936. Trait names: a psycho-lexical study. *Psychol. Monogr.* 47, No. 211

Amelang, M., Borkenau, P. 1982. Über die factorielle Struktur und externe Validität einiger Fragebogen-skälen zur Erfassung von Dimensionen der Extraversion und emotionalen Labilität. *Z. Diff. Diagnost. Psychol.* 3:119–46

Banks, C. 1948. Primary personality factors in women: a reanalysis, 1948. *Br. J. Psychol. Statist. Sect.* 1:204–18

Baumgarten, F. 1933. Die Charaktereigenshaften. *Beiträge zur Charakter- und Persönlichkeitsforschung: Monogr. 1.* Bern: A. Francke

Bem, S. L. 1981. *Bem Sex-Role Professional*

Manual. Palo Alto, CA: Consulting Psychologists Press

Birenbaum, M., Montag, I. 1986. On the location of the sensation seeking construct in the personality domain. *Mult. Behav. Res.* 21:357–73

Block, J. 1961. *The Q-Sort Method in Personality Assessment and Psychiatric Research.* Springfield, IL: Thomas

Block, J. 1971. *Lives Through Time.* Berkeley, CA: Bancroft Books

Block, J. 1977. The Eysencks and psychoticism. *J. Abnorm. Psychol.* 86:653–54

Block, J. 1989. Critique of the act frequency approach to personality. *J. Pers. Soc. Psychol.* 50:234–45

Bond, M. H., Nakazato, H. S., Shiraishi, D. 1975. Universality and distinctiveness in dimensions of Japanese person perception. *J. Cross-Cult. Psychol.* 6:346–55

Borgatta, E. F. 1964. The structure of personality characteristics. *Behav. Sci.* 12:8–17

Borkenau, P. 1988. The multiple classification of acts and the big five factors of personality. *J. Res. Pers.* 22:337–52

Borkenau, P., Ostendorf, F. 1989. A confirmatory factor analysis of the five-factor model of personality. *Mult. Behav. Res.* In press

Botwin, M. D., Buss, D. M. 1989. The structure of act report data: Is the five factor model of personality recaptured? *J. Pers. Soc. Psychol.* 56:988–1001

Brand, C. R. 1984. Personality dimensions: an overview of modern trait psychology. In *Psychology Survey 5*, ed. J. Nicholson, H. Beloff. Leicester, UK: Br. Psychol. Soc.

Buss, D. M., Craik, K. H. 1980. The frequency concept of disposition. *J. Pers.* 48:379–92

Buss, D. M., Craik, K. H. 1985. Why not measure that trait? Alternative criteria for identifying important dispositions. *J. Pers. Soc. Psychol.* 48:934–46

Cantor, N., Mischel, W. 1979. Prototypes in person perception. *Adv. Exp. Soc. Psychol.* 12:3–52

Carson, R. C. 1989. Personality. *Ann. Rev. Psychol.* 40:227–48

Cattell, R. B. 1943. The description of personality: basic traits resolved into clusters. *J. Abnorm. Soc. Psychol.* 38:476–506

Cattell, R. B. 1946. *The Description and Measurement of Personality.* Yonkers, NY: World Book

Cattell, R. B. 1947. Confirmation and clarification of primary personality factors. *Psychometrika* 12:197–220

Cattell, R. B. 1948. The primary personality factors in women compared with those in men. *Br. J. Psychol.* 1:114–30

Cattell, R. B. 1956. Second-order personality factors. *J. Consult. Psychol.* 20:411–18

Cattell, R. B. 1957. *Personality and Motivation Structure and Measurement.* New York: World Book

Cattell, R. B. 1965. *The Scientific Analysis of Personality.* London: Penguin

Cattell, R. B., Cattell, M. D. 1969. *The High School Personality Questionnaire.* Champaign, IL: Inst. Pers. Ability Testing

Cattell, R. B., Eber, H. W., Tatsuoka, M. M. 1970. *Handbook for the Sixteen Personality Factor Questionnaire.* Champaign, IL: Inst. Pers. Ability Testing

Conley, J. J. 1984. Longitudinal consistency of adult personality: Self-reported psychological characteristics across 45 years. *J. Pers. Soc. Psychol.* 37:1325–33

Costa, P. T. Jr., Busch, C. M., Zonderman, A. B., McCrae, R. R. 1986. Correlations of MMPI factor scales with measures of the Five-Factor Model of personality. *J. Pers. Assess.* 50:640–50

Costa, P. T. Jr., McCrae, R. R. 1976. Age differences in personality structure: a cluster analytic approach. *J. Gerontol.* 31:564–70

Costa, P. T. Jr., McCrae, R. R. 1985. *The NEO Personality Inventory.* Odessa, FL: Psychol. Assess. Resources

Costa, P. T. Jr., McCrae, R. R. 1988. Personality in adulthood: a six-year longitudinal study of self-reports and spouse ratings on the NEO Personality Inventory. *J. Pers. Soc. Psychol.* 54:853–63

Costa, P. T. Jr., McCrae, R. R. 1988. From catalog to classification: Murray's needs and the five factor model. *J. Pers. Soc. Psychol.* 55:258–65

D'Andrade, R. G. 1965. Trait psychology and componential analysis. *Am. Anthropol.* 67:215–28

Darley, J. M., Latane, B. 1968. Bystander intervention in emergencies: diffusion of responsibility. *J. Pers. Soc. Psychol.* 8:377–83

Digman, J. M. 1972a. The structure of child personality as seen in behavior ratings. In *Multivariate Personality Research*, ed. R. Dreger, pp. 587–611. Baton Rouge, LA: Claitor's Publishing

Digman, J. M. 1972b. *High school academic achievement as seen in the context of a longitudinal study of personality.* Presented at the Annu. Meet. Am. Psychol. Assoc., 80th, Honolulu

Digman, J. M. 1979. *The five major domains of personality variables: analysis of personality questionnaire data in the light of the five robust factors emerging from studies of rated characteristics.* Presented at Annu. Meet. Soc. Mult. Exp. Psychol., 19th, Los Angeles

Digman, J. M. 1988. *Classical theories of trait organization and the Big Five Factors of personality.* Presented at Annu. Meet. Am. Psychol. Assoc., Atlanta

Digman, J. M., Digman, K. C. 1980. Stress and competence in longitudinal perspective. In *Human Functioning in Longitudinal Perspective*, ed. S. Sells, R. Crandall, M. Roff, J. Strauss, W. Pollin. Baltimore: Williams & Wilkins

Digman, J. M., Inouye, J. 1986. Further specification of the five robust factors of personality. *J. Pers. Soc. Psychol.* 50:116–23

Digman, J. M., Takemoto-Chock, N. K. 1981. Factors in the natural language of personality: re-analysis, comparison and interpretation of six major studies. *Mult. Behav. Res.* 16:149–70

Epstein, S. 1986. Does aggregation produce

spuriously high estimates of behavior consistency? *J. Pers. Soc. Psychol.* 50:1199–1210

Eriksen, C. W. 1957. Personality. *Annu. Rev. Psychol.* 8:185–210

Eysenck, H. J. 1947. *Dimensions of Personality.* New York: Praeger

Eysenck, H. J. 1970. *The Structure of Human Personality.* London: Methuen. 3rd. ed.

Eysenck, H. J., Eysenck, S. B. G. 1964. *Manual of the Eysenck Personality Inventory.* London: University Press

Farnill, D., Ball, I. L. 1985. Male and female factor structures of the Australian Sex-Role Scale (Form A). *Aust. Psychol.* 20:205–14

Feshback, S., Weiner, B. 1982. *Personality.* Lexington, MA: Heath

Fiske, D. W. 1949. Consistency of the factorial structures of personality ratings from different sources. *J. Abnorm. Soc. Psychol.* 44:329–44

Funder, D. C., Ozer, D. J. 1983. Behavior as a function of the situation. *J. Pers. Soc. Psychol.* 44:107–12

Goldberg, L. R. 1981. Language and individual differences: the search for universals in personality lexicons. In *Review of Personality and Social Psychology,* ed. L. Wheeler, 2:141–65. Beverly Hills, CA: Sage

Goldberg, L. R. 1983. *The magical number five, plus or minus two: some conjectures on the dimensionality of personality descriptors.* Paper presented at a Res. Seminar, Gerontol. Res. Cent., Baltimore City Hospitals

Gough, H. G., Heilbrun, A. B. Jr. 1980. *The Adjective Check List Manual.* Palo Alto, CA: Consulting Psychologists Press. Rev. ed.

Guilford, J. P. 1975. Factors and factors of personality. *Psychol. Bull.* 82:802–14

Guilford, J. P., Zimmerman, W. S. 1949. *The Guilford-Zimmerman Temperament Survey.* Beverly Hills, CA: Sheridan Supply

Guthrie, G. M., Bennett, A. B. 1970. Cultural differences in implicit personality theory. *Int. J. Psychol.* 6:305–12

Hampson, S. E. 1988. *The Construction of Personality.* London: Routledge

Hampson, S. E., John, O. P., Goldberg, L. R. 1986. Category breadth and hierarchical structure in personality. *J. Pers. Soc. Psychol.* 51:37–54

Hathaway, S. R., McKinley, J. C. 1951. *The Minnesota Multiphasic Personality Inventory.* New York: Psychological Corporation. Rev. ed.

Henderson, N. D. 1982. Human behavior genetics. *Annu. Rev. Psychol.* 33:403–40

Hogan, R. 1983. Socioanalytic theory of personality. In *1982 Nebraska Symposium on Motivation: Personality—Current Theory and Research,* ed. M. M. Page, pp. 55–89. Lincoln, NE: Univ. Nebraska Press

Hogan, R. 1986. *Hogan Personality Inventory.* Minneapolis, MN: National Computer Systems

Horney, K. 1937. *The Neurotic Personality of Our Time.* New York: Norton

Howarth, E. 1976. Were Cattell's 'personality sphere' factors correctly identified in the first instance? *Br. J. Psychol.* 67:213–30

Jackson, D. N. 1974. *Personality Research Form Manual.* Port Huron: Research Psychologists Press. Rev. ed.

Jensen, A. R. 1958. Personality. *Annu. Rev. Psychol.* 9:295–322

John, O. P. 1989. Towards a taxonomy of personality descriptors. In *Personality Psychology: Recent Trends and Emerging Directions,* ed. D. Buss, N. Cantor. New York: Springer-Verlag

John, O. P., Angleitner, A., Ostendorf, F. 1988. The lexical approach to personality: a historical review of trait taxonomic research. *Eur. J. Pers.* 2:171–205

Joreskog, K. C., Sorbom, D. 1984. *LISREL VI.* Chicago: National Educational Resources

Kendrick, D. T., Funder, D. C. 1988. Profiting from controversy: lessons from the person-situation debate. *Am. Psychol.* 43:23–34

Klages, L. 1926. *The Science of Character.* (Transl. 1932). London: Allen & Unwin

Leary, T. 1957. *Interpersonal Diagnosis of Personality.* New York: Ronald Press

Livneh, H., Livneh, C. 1989. The five-factor model of personality: Is evidence for its cross-media premature? *Pers. Ind. Diff.* 10:75–80

Lorr, M. 1986. *Interpersonal Style Inventory: Manual.* Los Angeles: Western Psychological Services

Lorr, M., Knight, L. A. 1987. Higher-order factors assessed by the ISI and the PRF. *J. Clin. Psychol.* 43:96–99

Lorr, M., Manning, T. T. 1978. Higher order factors of the ISI. *Mult. Behav. Res.* 13:3–7

Lorr, M., Nerviano, V. J. 1985. Factors common to the ISI and the 16PF inventories. *J. Clin. Psychol.* 41:773–77

Lorr, M., Youniss, R. P. 1974. An inventory of interpersonal style. *J. Pers. Assess.* 37:165–73

Maddi, S. R. 1989. *Personality Theories: A Comparative Analysis.* Chicago, IL: Dorsey. 5th ed.

McCrae, R. R., Costa, P. T. Jr. 1985a. Comparison of EPI and psychoticism scales with measures of the five-factor theory of personality. *Pers. Ind. Diff.* 6:587–97

McCrae, R. R., Costa, P. T. Jr. 1985b. Updating Norman's "adequate taxonomy": intelligence and personality dimensions in natural languages and questionnaires. *J. Pers. Soc. Psychol.* 49:710–21

McCrae, R. R., Costa, P. T. Jr. 1988. Recalled parent-child relationships and adult personality. *J. Pers.* 56:417–34

McCrae, R. R., Costa, P. T. Jr. 1989. Reinterpreting the Myers-Briggs Type Indicator from the perspective of the five-factor model of personality. *J. Pers.* 57:17–40

McCrae, R. R., Costa, P. T. Jr., Busch, C. M. 1986. Evaluating comprehensiveness in personality systems: the California Q-Set and the five-factor model. *J. Pers.* 54:430–46

McDougall, W. 1932. Of the words character and personality. *Character Pers.* 1:3–16

Milgram, S. 1963. Behavioral study of obedience. *J. Abnorm. Soc. Psychol.* 67:371–78

Mischel, W. 1968. *Personality and Assessment.* New York: Wiley

Mischel, W., Peake, P. K. 1982. Beyond déjà vu in the search for cross-situational consistency. *Psychol. Rev.* 89:730–55

Myers, I. B., McCauley, M. H. 1985. *Manual: A Guide to the Development and Use of the Myers-Briggs Type Indicator.* Palo Alto, CA: Consulting Psychologists Press

Noller, P., Law, H., Comrey, A. 1987. Cattell, Comrey, and Eysenck personality factors: more evidence for the five robust factors? *J. Pers. Soc. Psychol.* 53:775–82

Norman, W. T. 1963. Toward an adequate taxonomy of personality attributes: replicated factor structure in peer nomination personality ratings. *J. Abnorm. Soc. Psychol.* 66:574–83

Norman, W. T. 1967. 2,800 personality trait descriptors: Normative operating characteristics for a university population. Res. Rept. 08310-1-T. Univ. Mich., Ann Arbor, MI

Osgood, C. E., May, W. H., Miron, M. S. 1975. *Cross-Cultural Universals of Affective Meaning.* Champaign, IL: Univ. Illinois

Osgood, C. E., Suci, G. J., Tannenbaum, P. H. 1957. *The Measurement of Meaning.* Urbana, IL: Univ. Illinois Press

Peabody, D. 1967. Trait inferences: evaluative and descriptive aspects. *J. Pers. Soc. Psychol. Monogr.* 7 (4, Whole No. 644)

Peabody, D. 1984. Personality dimensions through trait inferences. *J. Pers. Soc. Psychol.* 46:384–403

Peabody, D., Goldberg, L. R. 1989. Some determinants of factor representations of trait adjectives. *J. Pers. Soc. Psychol.* In press

Peterson, D. R. 1960. The age generality of personality factors derived from ratings. *Educ. Psychol. Meas.* 20:461–74

Plomin, R., Daniels, D. 1987. Why are children in the same family so different from one another? *Behav. Brain Sci.* 10:1–16

Revelle, W. 1987. Personality and motivation: sources of inefficiency in cognitive performance. *J. Res. Pers.* 21:436–52

Rosch, E., Mervis, C. B., Gray, W. D., Johnson, D., Boyes-Braem, P. 1976. Basic objects in natural categories. *Cogn. Psychol.* 8:382–439

Rushton, J. P., Fulker, D. W., Neale, M. C., Nias, D. K. B., Eysenck, H. J. 1986. Altruism and aggression: the heritability of individual differences. *J. Pers. Soc. Psychol.* 50:1192–98

Shweder, R. A. 1975. How relevant is an individual difference theory of personality? *J. Pers.* 43:455–84

Small, S. A., Zeldin, R. S., Savin-Williams, R. C. 1983. In search of personality traits: A multimethod analysis of naturally occurring prosocial and dominance behavior. *J. Pers.* 51:1–16

Smith, G. M. 1967. Usefulness of peer ratings of personality in educational research. *Educ. Psychol. Meas.* 27:967–84

Sullivan, H. S. 1953. *The Interpersonal Theory of Psychiatry.* New York: Norton

Tellegen, A. 1985. Structures of mood and personality and their relevance to assessing anxiety with an emphasis on self-report. In *Anxiety and the Anxiety Disorders,* ed. A. Tuma, J. Maser, pp. 681–706. Hillsdale, NJ: Erlbaum

Tellegen, A., Lykken, D. T., Bouchard, T. J., Wilcox, K. J., Segal, N. L., Rich, S. 1988. Personality similarity in twins reared apart and together. *J. Pers. Soc. Psychol.* 54: 1031–39

Tupes, E. C. 1957. Personality traits related to effectiveness of junior and senior Air Force officers. *USAF Personnel Training Res. Cent. Res. Rep. No.* 57-125

Tupes, E. C., Christal, R. E. 1961. Recurrent personality factors based on trait ratings. *USAF ASD Tech. Rep.* 61–97

Ullmann, L. P., Krasner, L. 1975. *A Psychological Approach to Abnormal Behavior.* Englewood Cliffs, NJ: Prentice-Hall. 2nd. ed.

Waller, N. G., Ben-Porath, Y. 1987. Is it time for clinical psychology to embrace the five-factor model of personality? *Am. Psychol.* 42:887–89

Webb, E. 1915. Character and intelligence. *Br. J. Psychol. Monogr. Ser.* 1(3)

Wegner, D. M., Vallacher, R. R. 1977. *Implicit Psychology: An Introduction to Social Cognition.* New York: Oxford

Wiggins, J. S. 1968. Personality structure. *Annu. Rev. Psychol.* 19:293–350

Wiggins, J. S. 1980. Circumplex models of

interpersonal behavior. In *Review of Personality and Social Psychology*, ed. L. Wheeler, 1:265–94. Beverly Hills, CA: Sage

Wiggins, J. S., Broughton, R. 1985. The Interpersonal Circle: a structural model for the integration of personality research. In *Perspectives in Personality*, ed. R. Hogan, W. H. Jones, 1:1–47. Greenwich, CT: JAI Press

Wiggins, J. S., Phillips, N., Trapnell, P. 1989. Circular reasoning about interpersonal behavior: evidence concerning some untested assumptions underlying diagnostic classification. *J. Pers. Soc. Psychol.* 52: 296–306

Wiggins, J. S., Trapnell, P., Phillips, N. 1988. Psychometric and geometric characteristics of the revised Interpersonal Adjective Scales (IAS-R). *Mult. Behav. Res.* 23:517–30

Wiggins, N., Blackburn, M., Hackman, J. R. 1969. The prediction of first-year success in psychology: peer ratings. *J. Educ. Res.* 63:81–85

Zuckerman, M., Kolln, E. A., Price, L., Zoob, I. 1964. Development of a sensation-seeking scale. *J. Consult. Clin. Psychol.* 32:420–26

Zuckerman, M., Kuhlman, D. M., Camac, C. 1988. What lies beyond E and N? Factor analyses of scales believed to measure basic dimensions of personality. *J. Pers. Soc. Psychol.* 54:96–107

Annu. Rev. Psychol. 1990. 41:441–77

ENVIRONMENTAL PSYCHOLOGY

Susan Saegert and Gary H. Winkel

Environmental Psychology Program, Graduate School, City University of New York, New York 10036

CONTENTS

INTRODUCTION

Important developments have occurred in the field of environmental psychology since work in the area was last summarized in this *Review* (Holahan 1986). In 1987, a two volume *Handbook of Environmental Psychology* was published (Stokols & Altman 1987): Part 1 (Volume 1) and Part 6 (Volume 2) contain papers in which various conceptual issues relevant to theory and methodology in environmental psychology are discussed; Parts 2 and 3

0066-4308/90/0201-0441$02.00

(Volume 1) deal with psychological processes (e.g. environmental cognition, personality and the environment, emotion and the environment) and with research conducted at different environmental scales (ranging from behavior–setting analysis to the interrelationships between community and environmental psychology); Part 4 (Volume 2) reviews work involving the applications of environmental psychology to community problems; and in Part 5 (Volume 2) authors from Europe, the Far East, Latin America, and the Soviet Union address environmental psychology.

During the same year (1987), a new series appeared called *Advances in Environment, Behavior, and Design* under the editorship of Ervin H. Zube and Gary T. Moore (Zube & Moore 1987, 1989). These volumes are organized around advances in theory, place research, user-group research, sociobehavioral research, research and design methods, and research utilization.

This period of extensive reflection on the accomplishments of the field has produced several distinct paradigms in specific research areas and at higher levels of theory. This contrasts with the situation identified by Holahan (1986) in which many of the substantive areas in environmental psychology have been hampered by the absence of a theoretical perspective on the person, the environment, and the person-in-the-environment. Yet the recent theoretical advances have not yet been fully reflected in current research. We therefore review these emerging paradigms here—their strengths, weaknesses, and directions for future research.

Examining specific bodies of substantive research and theory, we found differences in the general conception of person-environment relationships. At one level of analysis the relationship of person to environment is seen as essentially biologically adaptive. A second places this relationship at the scale of individual opportunity structures. A third incorporates both the form of the environment and the activities of individuals and groups into the sociocultural milieu. The limits of these perspectives give rise to various attempts at cross-paradigm synthesis. While in each conception the environment is seen as a vital contributor to person-environment relationships, the psychological heritage of most researchers leads to a focus on the characteristics and dynamics of persons; and although the field has always offered a contextual critique of psychology (Little 1987), the call for interdisciplinary, systems-oriented, and problem-centered research has not been easy to answer (Proshansky 1987). Here we examine critically the extent to which advances in environmental psychology confront the fact that many of our experiences in and uses of environments must be understood in the context of broader physical, economic, historical, and political forces. This review differs from earlier ones in its greater focus on the interdisciplinary nature of the field.

A second, related issue for the various paradigms concerns the relative contributions of the environment and the person to the state of person-environment relationships. While environmental psychologists often give too short shrift to context, scholars from other disciplines who work on an articulation between the individual and broader economic, social, and political structures often skip lightly over the acting, experiencing person.

Within each paradigm, various metatheoretical stances (Altman & Rogoff 1987) can be found. However, it is the increased attention to transactional approaches that primarily contributes to a need for cross-paradigm syntheses. The central qualities of the transactional approach are defined along five dimensions. The person-in-environment provides the unit of analysis. Both person and environment dynamically define and transform each other over time, as "aspects" of a unitary whole. Stability and change coexist continuously. The direction of change is emergent, not preestablished. If this is the case, it is important to look both for the sources of change within each paradigm and for the ways sources of change at one level affect other levels, creating new person-environment configurations.

The valid insights of transactionalism (Ittelson 1989) present problems for existing methodological approaches in each paradigm. Unlike other metatheoretical stances in psychology, transactionalists view the observer as a particular individual in a particular "location" with regard to a phenomenon. This perspective raises special problems for the empiricist tradition of research. One is the claim that new definitions of both person and environment may emerge in the course of transactions. While this possibility is accommodated in qualitative research, it can not be addressed when, as in quantitative studies, variables must retain an original definition. Additionally, transactionalists assume the embeddedness of the researcher in the situation studied. Such an assumption conflicts so strongly with empiricist traditions of social science that it has received scant attention. The recognition that researchers are particular people in particular times and places forces us to examine the intents of research, not just questions of research design and method (Saegert 1982). The specific and dynamic nature of transactional research has led to a debate about its generality. This debate focuses on the following issues: (a) the representativeness of situations and populations studied (Golledge 1988; R. Kaplan 1987); (b) the reliability and validity of measurement (R. Kaplan 1987; Winkel 1987); and (c) questions of transcontextual generality (Altman & Rogoff 1987; Golledge 1988; Saegert 1982, 1987). As we note in our final section, recognition of the historical and geographic specificity of research can help clarify the significant aspects of context to be addressed by research and the suitability of particular paradigms and methods.

SUBSTANTIVE PARADIGMS OF PERSON-ENVIRONMENT RELATIONSHIPS

The paradigms described in this section define the person, the environment, and person-environment transactions. Each amalgamates research from different disciplines. While these paradigms cut across research topics, most studies in particular areas fall within a central metaphor. For example, studies of environmental stress rely on the adaptation paradigm while recognizing context effects that may originate from person-environment transactions at other levels (cf Baum et al 1982). The chief characteristics of each paradigm are listed in Table 1.

Table 1 Paradigm characteristics

	Adaptation	Opportunity structures	Sociocultural forces	Historical synthesis
Definition of environment	physical qualities, interpersonal interactions, information	temporal and spatial structure of land uses, services, facilities	socially/culturally defined settings and systems	constraining/ enabling residue of human interactions with the other paradigms
Source of environmental change	natural and technological forces	planned or unplanned development	social, political and economic structure, culture	changes in all levels of environment and human action
Role of person	adapt to environment, manage stresses and hazards, interpret threats and resources, select adaptive responses on basis of personality and social context	maximize goals, meet needs, perform roles, find niche, accomplish personal projects	reproduce sociocultural system	interaction of development adaptation, pursuit of goals and performance of roles in relationship to preexisting and emerging environment
Source of person change	success or failure of adaptation, social support, interpretation of information	change in state of goals, needs, roles; personality or preference as determined by sociocultural system	temporal, age-linked or developmental fluctuation	conflicts of motives from the other paradigms; emergent groups, interpretations, actions

The paradigms can be understood as nested within each other. That is, sociocultural systems are expressed in time-geographic opportunity structures and the personal projects and plans individuals and groups attempt to carry out in them. At all levels of analysis, the adaptive requirements of person-environment relationships set limits both on viable activities of persons and groups and on habitable environmental forms. A need for a synthesis arises because processes described by each paradigm take place within historically developed places at particular points in time. Thus each level of analysis can affect the others.

The organization of this review around these different paradigms highlights relationships among different levels. The view we adopt of this interdependence draws on the work of Manicas & Secord (1983; Manicas 1986). Historically developed conditions (including ecological conditions) and the social structural forces of any particular period form the preconditions for individual and group action. Because they precede individual activity and are organized beyond the reach of most individual actions, they have greater weight in maintaining conditions and directing change. This position concurs with Gibson's (1979) definition of the relationship of the perceiving organism to the ecological environment but views the environment as socially constructed within the constraints of planetary evolution. However, individuals and groups can generate local effects and be significant factors in change in conjunction with the dynamics of historical change and social-structural dynamics. Wicker's (1987) reinterpretation of behavior-setting theory suggests some of the points at which individual- and group-initiated change might be most significant.

Environmental psychology has long been concerned with bringing about positive changes in person-environment relationships. Efforts to make practical improvements in these transactions provide another impetus for understanding the linkages among paradigms. For example, DiMento (1981) has attempted to identify ways that stress research could have an impact on public policy. Most such attempts require the researcher to place him/herself and the studied phenomenon in the context of broad social, political, and economic forces as well as in the context of historical changes. Efforts to bring about practical changes thus involve researchers in value judgments, communication, interpretation, critique, and participation in political processes (Albrecht & Lim 1986; Saegert 1987; Schneekloth 1987).

The adaptive paradigm lies most squarely within the psychological tradition and encompasses the largest body of work in environmental psychology. Environment-as-opportunity-structure also meshes well with the psychological emphasis on individual, cognitively mediated, goal-directed activity. The social-structural paradigm draws more extensively on interdisciplinary research and theory, as do efforts at cross-paradigm synthesis.

ADAPTATION PARADIGM

The most theoretically and methodologically mature areas in environmental psychology lie chiefly within the adaptive paradigm: environmental stressors, environmental perception and cognition, and environmental assessment. All derive their main theoretical constructs from an assumption that the goal of biological and psychological survival motivates behavior: The biological and psychological individual attempts to cope with threats, to meet basic biological needs, and to restore and expand capacities for coping and flourishing. Perception and cognition are regarded as geared to adaptational needs.

Knowing the Environment

All of the literature within the adaptive paradigm recognizes the adaptive significance of perceptual and cognitive processes. Research in environmental perception and cognition owe their general conceptual frameworks to theorists who view perception from an adaptive perspective (Brunswick 1956; Garling & Golledge 1989; Gibson 1979; Ittelson 1973; Neisser 1976; Piaget & Inhelder 1967). Gibson most clearly specifies the nature of the environment and its significance for perception, yet Gibson's emphasis on direct pick-up of information appears to undermine one of environmental psychology's main metaphors for environmental knowing, the cognitive map. Neisser's (1976) efforts to integrate Gibson's insights into a more cognitive and temporally extensive system through the use of the schema concept offers a promising approach for studies of environmental cognition. However, he fails to define salient characteristics and organization of the environment.

Definitions of the environment consistent with Neisser's model have been most influenced by Lynch's (1960) original specification of landmarks, nodes, paths, districts, and edges as salient landscape properties. His work has been replicated using more sophisticated methods (Aragones & Arrendondo 1985). Golledge's anchor-point theory (Garling & Golledge 1989) assumes that individuals hierarchically order places, paths, and areas in the environment, integrating new information through the addition of nodes and reorganization of networks. Both approaches have more in common with an opportunity-structure view of the environment than an adaptive one.

Stephen and Rachel Kaplan's (1973) model of environmental information processing based on an evolutionary perspective is less evident in recent work than the information-processing approaches rooted in a computer simulation metaphor (reviewed by Garling & Golledge 1989 and Golledge 1987). While this paradigm is important in psychology as a whole, information-processing models lack a conception of the environment and account for person-environment transactions primarily by referring to processes internal to the person. Such models give little attention to cognitive and perceptual processes as they occur in spatial behavior (Golledge 1987). A focus on representation articulates better with the emphasis on planning found in the opportunity-structure paradigm but is compatible with some adaptational theories (cf Wapner 1987). Integration of the two approaches might shift the adaptational paradigm away from its origins in nonhuman species and increase the focus on well-being and capacity development within the opportunity-structure paradigm. Passini & Proulx's (1988) comparison of blind and sighted people's processes of way-finding illustrates the continuity of conscious planning and perceptual information pick-up as well as their uses in compensating for visual impairment.

Heft & Wohlwill (1987) have provided a thoughtful critique of questions neglected because of the logical-geometric focus of most information-processing models. They have proposed the consideration of a model based on several distinguishable functions dependent on goals and environmental context such as learning the meaning of environments, way-finding, and geographical orientation. Studies of children reveal the interplay of spatial behavior and environmental knowledge and link these to differences in affective experiences and social development (reviewed in Heft & Wohlwill 1987). The significance of self-directed exploration has been particularly well documented (Acredolo et al 1984; Feldman & Acredolo 1979; Hazen 1982). Hart (1979, 1981) has most comprehensively placed exploration, learning of environmental meaning, and spatial representation in the context of the social and physical environment, thus suggesting relationships among the adaptive, opportunity-structure, and sociocultural paradigms.

As Golledge (1987) has noted, rarely are we completely lost. Even less often do we fail to survive because of inaccurate spatial information. However, such situations do exist—e.g. when we must find the right exit during a fire. Recently, arguments before the Nuclear Regulatory Commission concerning the opening of the Shoreham Nuclear Power Plant addressed, among other issues, the inefficiency of drivers in evacuating a familiar environment during a serious emergency. Researchers have failed to address perceptual and cognitive processes in such circumstances, despite their obvious importance. Evans and his colleagues (Evans et al 1984) and Saegert and her colleagues (Saegert et al 1975; Saegert 1981) have shown that environmental perception and cognition vary with exposure to environmental stressors. More theoretical and empirical work placing environmental perception and cognition in specific environmental contexts related to adaptive tasks would be useful.

Coping with Threat

Researchers have long attempted to extend findings and theoretical frameworks from biology to an analysis of human relations with the environment. Research on environmental stressors owes much to these attempts.

Environmental stress research explicitly focuses on the adaptive demands arising from physical characteristics of the environment. Evans & Cohen (1987) go beyond the frequently used classification of stressors into cataclysmic events, stressful life events, daily hassles, and ambient stressors (Baum et al 1982; Campbell 1983; Lazarus & Cohen 1977) to outline eight dimensions along which environmental stressors vary: perceptual salience; type of adjustment required; value or valence of the event; degree of controllability; predictability; necessity and importance; duration; and periodicity. They note that the physical nature of environmental stressors has been neglected in favor of psychological and sociological investigations of personal, organizational, and societal factors that influence stress and coping. The physical nature of human coping has been a more active area of study (Weiss & Baum 1987). Evans et al (1989) provide an important and unusual conceptual integration of environmental characteristics, pathological responses, growth promoting responses, and coping in their review of the role of the physical environment in child development. They identify six environmental characteristics affecting child development: pathogenic conditions (cf toxins); stimulation levels; functional complexity; control; structure and predictability; and exploration opportunities. Their suggestions about how these different conditions, children's responses to them, and their developmental consequences interact in later development especially warrant further investigation.

Despite the theoretical and methodological focus on individual adaptation to environmental threats, much of the stress research provides empirical links to other paradigms. The complexity of findings in these areas of research indicates that personal and social variables affect outcome measures (Evans et al 1988; Evans et al 1987). Behavioral responses to physical environmental conditions have also been shown to be mediated by sociocultural variables. Rotton's (1986) 48-nation investigation of the relationship between climate and homicide and suicide supported a mixed model of direct climatic effects, as well as cultural effects, on suicide. Gillis et al (1986) found differences in susceptibility to negative effects of high-density living among Canadian adolescents of Asian, Southern European, and British descent. Even such an apparently straightforward physiological variable as thermal comfort has been shown to depend on symbolic meanings and to vary with social and economic conditions (Heijs & Stringer 1988). Loo's (1986) study of Chinatown in San Francisco, while not explicitly addressing stress, explored the complex relationships among ethnicity, income, household composition, residential density, and land uses as they affected feelings of safety and residential satisfaction, placing the findings in the context of pro-growth pressures on urban development. Her analysis illustrates the historical and nested nature of adaptive, opportunity-structure, and sociocultural paradigms.

While these studies include socioeconomic and cultural factors as variables, they do not explain the processes by which the larger social context mediates perceptions of and reactions to environmental stressors. Nor do they portray the physical environment as shaped by socioeconomic and cultural forces. Evans et al (1988) address social processes by relating adverse mental health effects of residential crowding to withdrawal from social networks as a consequence of high home density. This study reveals some limitations of methodological individualism in the interactional tradition for actually describing social relationships. In practice, not only the target subject but also the people with whom he/she interacts are influenced by density conditions. The nature of their social relationships most likely emerges from their transactions with each other over time, as well as from individual and social interpretations given to these transactions. Further, even in a highly constrained housing market, the highest-density households, with the most deteriorated social relationships, may break down into smaller units.

The interactionist study of stress clarifies the adaptational capacities and limits of individuals but it muddies the ways individuals relate to each other to cope with and transform their environments and experiences. From a policy perspective, interactionist studies have the advantage of identifying quantitative and general responses to stressors. The transactionist emphasis on personal interpretation and emergence could lead policy makers to conclude that restrictions on, for example, noise levels or density in residential institutions would be unnecessary. Research on the effects of hospital environments on patients illustrates this conundrum. On the one hand, aspects of the physical environment can seriously affect patients' comfort and ability to recover (see Winkel & Holahan 1985). On the other, the organizational and economic structure of hospitals makes it likely that economic considerations as well as the needs and preferences of medical staff and administrators will be more significant determinants of hospital design decisions (Shumaker & Pequegnat 1989).

Recent work on child safety suggests promising ways to develop a more explicit model linking adaptive threats to social processes and environmental conditions (Garling & Valsiner 1985). Garling (1985) points out that an analysis of child safety must include not just children but also their parents and other caregivers who act in environments according to plans designed to prevent accidents. Using Valsiner's (1985) "individual-socioecological" framework, Valsiner & Mackie (1985) have studied the ways the home's physical characteristics and parent-child behaviors interact as toddlers learn to climb. Using interview and observational data, the investigators identified various sequence structures followed by children and parents during climbing episodes. One of the central elements in Valsiner & Mackie's analysis of toddler climbing involves parental estimates of children's capabilities to negotiate the environment. Not only do parents overestimate their children's abilities to negotiate the environment safely (Spencer & Blades 1985) but there are also discrepancies between parents' and children's assessments of the degree of danger associated with various hazards (Sheehy & Chapman 1985). Because parents overestimate the capacities of older children, they attribute more responsibility to them for certain types of accidents (Svensson-Garling et al 1985). Unfortunately, these studies have not covered the ways parent and child beliefs translate into action. However, Rothengatter (1981; cited in Sheehy & Chapman 1985) has reported that when children are aware of being observed, they act more safely than when observed unobtrusively. Taking positive actions to reduce accidents is the subject of research by Holden (1985). His approach involves understanding how parents can verbally structure the environment proactively both to divert attention from potentially dangerous problems and to direct the child toward activities that match their capabilities.

The literatures on stress and child safety portray the person as struggling against the environment to maintain health and well-being. Another approach to understanding adaptation might be to look for person-environment transactions that generate increased pleasure and well-being. In the following section we describe the work of environmental psychologists who link preference for and enjoyment of environments to the adaptive necessity of the restoration and expansion of human capacities.

Restoring and Expanding Human Capacities

S. Kaplan (1987) has offered a particularly clear statement linking environmental preferences to evolutionary demands. He points out that adaptation requires understanding and exploration as well as material resources that support life. Such an analysis seems to hold for auditory as well as visual environmental preferences (Porteous & Mastin 1985). However, Knopf (1987) has reviewed studies in which natural environments are studied within the opportunity-structure and sociocultural paradigms, some of which challenge an evolutionary interpretation. Rachel and Stephen Kaplan (1989) extend the concept of biological and psychological adaptation to include restorative and expansive experiences of environment. Their point of departure is not the survival-threatening stress state but the mental fatigue that accumulates in the process of pursuing goals. Their research shows how experiences of nature counteract depleted psychological resources. R. Kaplan (1985) has documented positive effects of "nearby nature" on housing and neighborhood satisfaction. Such nearby nature has been shown to meet a variety of needs ranging from territoriality, through recreation, to aesthetic appreciation (Clark & Manzo 1987; Talbot et al 1987). Studies of hospital patients indicate that views of natural environments facilitate physical recovery and satisfy psychological needs (Ulrich 1984; Verderber 1986; Verderber

& Reuman 1987). The Kaplans have found that an increased acceptance of limitations and of the ultimate impossibility of controlling the environment is associated with experiences of nature. This finding offers a perspective on human adaptive strategies that contrasts with the emphasis on control so prevalent in studies of stress and coping.

Like most research on stress, work on restorative and capacity-expanding involvement with the environment is frequently couched in terms of a transactional perspective (cf Reser & Scherl 1988). Methodologically, research on environmental preference in this tradition employs something closer to a trait perspective in which characteristics of the environment determine choice and preference. However, the Kaplans' (1989) longitudinal studies of the impact of wilderness experiences begins to look at how such experiences change the person. Some research (Kaplan & Kaplan 1989; Manzo & Weinstein 1987; Nohl 1987) discussing public participation in protecting and developing natural settings extends the transactional perspective to include transformations of the environment.

From a transactional perspective, temporal processes are neglected in this literature. Despite the longitudinal nature of the Kaplans' wilderness studies and the comparison of landscape preferences across age groups, temporal change is not directly addressed. Other researchers who focus on age-related changes in human capacities describe theoretically the processes of relating to the environment that are involved in the expansion and contraction of capacities (Lawton 1985a; Lawton & Nahemow 1973; Wapner 1987). Speculations about the positive outcomes of coping draw mainly on research on the impact of stress on young organisms to suggest ways the person may be changed at the physiological and psychological level so that future environmental transactions will be differently experienced (Aldwin & Stokols 1988). Wapner's (1987) model of development emphasizes goal orientation, planning, and multiple intentionality. Optimal development occurs when the person progressively differentiates personal capacities and environmental qualities that are then hierarchically integrated to improve the person's "capacity for flexibility, freedom, self-mastery and the capacity to shift from one mode of person-in-environment relationship to another as required by goals, by the demands of the situation, and by the instrumentalities available . . ." (p. 1444). Clearly, he also emphasizes organismic changes rather than changes the person makes in the environment.

In his large body of work on the person-environment transactions of older people, Lawton has moved from an interactionist perspective that predicted the well-being of older people on the basis of the match between their own competencies and the demands of the environment (Lawton & Nahemow 1973) to a transactional view in which the older person takes a proactive role in organizing the environment to increase density of control and interaction as some capacities diminish (Lawton 1985a). Other research (Leavitt & Saegert 1989; Saegert 1989), discussed in the final section below, extends the transactional analysis of increased capacity in older age, placing changes in the person, the environment, and their transaction in historical context.

Contributions and Weaknesses of the Adaptive Paradigm

The adaptive paradigm has the advantage of dealing with outcomes people care about: health, well-being, and capacities to accomplish goals. Since environmental psychology continues to seek improvement in the compatibility of the environment with people's needs, research in this tradition is essential. Yet studies of environmental cognition, environmental stressors, and other topics within the adaptive paradigm leave inexplicit the transactional nature of many of the processes and variables they employ (cf social relationships, interpretations). They also fail to place their data in the context of policy options, political influences, and economic and cultural factors.

The weakness of the paradigm lies in its treatment of the person as a biological and psychological individual and of the environment as naturally given. Despite the constant identification of real and perceived control as mechanisms for effective coping, the social, political, and economic processes that distribute control among people have been largely ignored. Even the Kaplans' more realistic recommendation for increased participation stops short of dealing with the social, economic, and political processes that shape participation and influence its efficacy.

The adaptive paradigm, with the exception of some of the work on perception and cognition, also fails to define systematically the environment experienced by the individual. Research tends to focus on processes internal to the individual and shortchanges more active interpretive and behavioral involvement with the environment. All too often, these tendencies result in a peculiarly contradictory view of the person as barely touched by the physical environment or inevitably determined by it. The opportunity-structure paradigm, discussed next, avoids some of these shortcomings.

THE ENVIRONMENT AS OPPORTUNITY STRUCTURE FOR GOAL-DIRECTED ACTION

The opportunity-structure paradigm is explicitly concerned with the relationship between the behavioral requirements of the active and goal-directed person and the qualities of the environment. Unlike the adaptive paradigm, work in this tradition presents environmental experiences primarily as a process of selecting the best options within a system of sociophysical constraints and opportunities. The rational planning aspect of human nature is emphasized rather than the biologically responsive aspects. By casting person-environment transactions in a goal-directed mode, personality- and role-related differences are predictable. The Swedish geographer Hagerstrand is most responsible for the development of the opportunity-structure approach. Useful expositions of this work can be found in Carlstein (1982), Thrift (1977), and Pred (1973, 1977, 1981).

Influenced in part by Lewin's Principles of Topological Psychology (Lewin 1936), Hagerstrand has attempted to understand the processes that characterize human behavior in the landscape, to create what he calls "time-geography." Human interaction is considered to be a path-allocation problem in space and time. Each individual is constrained in his or her actions by capability constraints (e.g. the person cannot be in two places at the same time), coupling constraints (requiring the person to allocate his/her paths so that they coincide with the paths of persons with whom he/she wishes to interact, and "steering constraints" (resulting from the normative and in-stitutional channelling and regulation of activities) (Carlstein 1982). It would be a mistake to assume, however, that time-geography is nothing but the study of constraints. Both voluntary and involuntary travels down various paths can enable as well as constrain. The project is a key concept in time-geographic analysis. It consists of "the entire series of tasks necessary to the completion of any goal-orientated [sic] behavior" (Pred 1981:236). Projects channel, and thus constrain, human actions in certain directions and hence require both time- and space-allocation decisions. Projects are also constrained and enabled by the environmental resources available for their completion. Hence, the environment can be represented as a texture of opportunity structures. The desirability of a rational fit between project and environment makes the paradigm's use in environmental planning un-derstandable (Hagerstrand 1983). Michelson (1985), for example, has used this approach in his study of the ways the community and its services (number of facilities, their location, opening and closing hours) constrain or enable the lives of parents who work. Michelson documents the stresses that working mothers, but not working fathers, encounter as a consequence of environ-ments and transport systems poorly organized to handle their needs. Women confront conflicts between their new roles as breadwinners and culturally embedded assumptions about gender that shape both the environment and parents' domestic roles.

Other authors working from a feminist perspective have provided extensive documentation of the social nature of projects and the extent to which most environments are more constraining than enabling for women (Peterson 1987; van Vliet 1988). Feminists have also sought ways of increasing the supportiveness of environments for women's projects. Wekerle (1988), for example, proposed neighborhood service centers, and Saegert (1988) sug-gested urban housing forms that support women in work and childrearing.

The time-geographic emphasis on problems of differential availability and access to community-level environmental options is also important to ecologically oriented developmental psychologists (Bronfenbrenner et al 1984). These authors point out that substantial variations in infant mortality can be accounted for by the varying availability and quality of prenatal care services. They also argue that major factors in the utilization of health, welfare, and social services are knowledge, accessibility, and adequate transport. Surprisingly, they were unable to locate any systematic research documenting the use of neighborhood-based delivery services and its relation to child health and well-being. Bronfenbrenner et al's paper deserves more attention from environmental psychologists. These authors review research designed to demonstrate community-level developmental effects on intellectual functioning, mental health, and child abuse that are germane to the opportunity-structure argument. They also develop a set of research criteria relevant to investigators attempting to document the importance of community-level effects in areas that traditionally have been viewed as issues in individual-level analysis.

Promises and Problems in the Opportunity-Structure Model

In contrast to the person-centered focus of much of the environmental research conducted within the adaptive paradigm, an opportunity-structure analysis underscores the importance of identifying how the structure of the environment may affect psychological functioning. For example, although not working within a time-geographic perspective, Carbonara-Moscati (1985) nicely identified sociophysical barriers to children's play in the urban environment. Bjorklid (1985) also demonstrated how children's play behavior is affected by the structure of their immediate living environment. This perspective fosters the use of methodologies that focus on how people actually organize their time and space. Both Michelson (1987) and Andorka (1987) review time-budget methods appropriate to work in this area. Finally, the approach encourages attempts to link psychological functioning (Michelson 1985) and social interactions (Pred 1985) to environmental structural arrangements.

Despite the central role that the project plays in time-geography, relatively little has been done with the concept empirically. We should note, however, that, apparently independently of Hagerstrand's work, Little (1983, 1987) has embarked on a research program investigating the concept of personal projects, including the development of a methodology for personal project analysis. Personal projects provide what Little calls "natural units of analysis" grounded in a temporal and spatial context. Palys & Little (1983) report a linkage between perceived life satisfaction and personal project systems.

The projects concept seems useful in a number of ways. It views the person as having not abstract goals but configurations of actions he/she hopes to accomplish. The project has a specific location in time and space. The formation, initiation, execution, and evaluation of projects are seen as socially rather than individually created. The utility of the personal projects notion could be extended if the following were identified: (*a*) behavior settings and environmental objects actually or potentially available in people's environments, (*b*) the sources and extent of environmental knowledge based on these settings and objects; (*c*) the range of people's understandings and beliefs about the facilitating and constraining components of the settings they use; (*d*) the valences associated with possible or actual uses of settings; and (*e*) the ways people structure time in relation to projects.

Despite the centrality of time use, time conflict, and the physical organization of the environment, little work, aside from that of Michelson (1985), has been directed toward these issues. Bond & Feather (1988) and Levine (1988) suggest that differences in this domain may be important both to psychological and physical health.

Wicker (1987) suggests ways that behavior settings integrate individual projects into group projects and connect both with necessary resources, as well as markets, client groups, or audiences. He views behavior settings as continually requiring human action to initiate and sustain them. At the same time settings stabilize and integrate individual behavior with group dynamics, resources, and routine goal achievement. His work could provide an avenue for linking opportunity structures more clearly to individual and group behavior. Time-geographic analysis augments behavior-setting theory by calling attention to the importance of the patterning of behavior settings for understanding behavior.

Two of the better illustrations of work relevant to desiderata *a* and *b*, above, can be found in Warren (1978) and Archea (1985). Through an analysis of 28 neighborhoods in Detroit, Warren was able to distinguish six neighborhood types and functions. He then linked these characteristics to use of neighborhood services and reliance on other neighbors. At the scale of single buildings, Archea (1985) suggests how the physical features of banks may affect opportunities for bank robbers. A similar analysis was made of videotapes of "sting" operations designed to catch people selling stolen goods. Taylor (1987) reviews much of the research bearing on criminal activities as a function of environmental opportunity structures.

With reference to point, *d*, above, Bronfenbrenner et al (1984) suggest that in order to use social services in our society, people must repeatedly demonstrate how socially, behaviorally, and economically inadequate they are (the "deficit model"). They hypothesize that the humiliations associated with these self and/or family characterizations may prevent the utilization of needed social and health services even if they are known and accessible. Bronfenbrenner et al's (1984) failure to find systematic research linking environmental opportunity structure to psychological processes developmentally illustrates one of the shortcomings of this paradigm. It does not in itself consider the consequences of person-environment transactions for health, well-being, and capacity development. One paper did, however, link person and environmental context to daily stress (Caspi et al 1987). Using time series analysis, these authors showed that what they called "chronic ecological stress" (occasioned by living in neighborhoods perceived as being unsafe, having few neighbors on which one could rely, and being an unsatisfactory place to live) resulted in consistently higher levels of daily stress over a 28-day period.

Critiques of the opportunity-structure paradigm have also been voiced by those working within the sociocultural framework. Among the most extensive (although sympathetic) of these come from geographers themselves. They place greater emphasis on the social context that gives rise to the built environment (Pred 1981, 1984; Thrift 1983). They recognize that while the individual may shape the society that structures the environment, society also shapes the individual. This relationship, however, is asymmetrical. Thrift (1983: 40) points out that environments "structure people's life paths in ways that are class specific." He also suggests that differences in class and other group memberships affect environmental knowledge which in turn influences the density, content, and scope of life paths. Environmental knowledge can be characterized by at least five types of environmental "unknowings" that can exist in a locale at any particular time: The environment can be (a) unknown; (b) not understood; (c) hidden from those in the setting; (d) undiscussed or taken for granted as "true" or "natural"; and (e) distorted. We find it fascinating that, despite Thrift's argument, two recent reviews of environmental cognition either do not mention social class differences (Heft & Wohlwill 1987) or only briefly note "ethnic and cultural" differences in environmental representation (Golledge 1987: 149). We believe that this situation exists largely because those working in this area are more interested in the processes or mechanisms of cognitive representation than in the content of representation implied by Thrift's analysis. Katz's (1989) work, described below, is an encouraging recent exception.

Attempts to provide both a class and social-structural cast to time-geography are no doubt linked to Marxist critiques of "behaviorist" efforts to account for the creation, maintenance, and destruction of the environments in which social groups operate (Harvey 1973, 1982, 1985). It is not necessary to be a Marxist, however, to appreciate the nature of the criticism since Hagerstrand does not really address the ways socioeconomic forces influence opportunity structures, nor does he direct much effort at understanding how meaning is both structured by and structures the environment. These issues are better addressed in the sociocultural paradigm.

SOCIOCULTURAL PARADIGMS

Although they are by no means central to the psychological project in the United States, arguments have been advanced regarding the importance of the multiple contexts within which psychological processes and contents are situated. Over 40 years ago, for example, Murphy (1947) discussed the need to consider the effects of historical and economic forces on personality development. During environmental psychology's formative period, some researchers were well aware of the extent to which environmental issues were a function of sociocultural and economic factors (Ittelson et al 1974). Only recently, however, have concerted efforts been made to develop theoretical and research perspectives linking macro-scale issues to social- and individual-level environmental concerns.

Bronfenbrenner (1977, 1979) has forcefully proposed a multi-scale "ecological" approach to human development that involves studies ranging from single settings to sociopolitical structures. He argues that a full understanding of human development requires the identification of the interdependencies existing between and among the different scales within which the person operates. To carry out his proposal, it would be necessary to attend to the processes considered central to the proponents of the sociocultural paradigm. Perhaps the most important of these is the emphasis on the person as a social agent rather than an autonomous individual having needs for survival or desires to carry out personal projects. The person as a social agent seeks and creates meaning in the environment. Since social interaction is a central feature of this paradigm, a second important process issue involves the understanding of interrelationships between the environment on the one hand and group formation and maintenance on the other. The emphasis on individual survival in the adaptive paradigm has its social counterpart in research documenting efforts to deal with environmental threats, not as an individual concern, but as a problem for the social structure within which the individual is embedded, whether it be family, neighborhood, nation, or even world society.

Environmental Meaning and Social Communication

Although psychologists discuss environmental meaning, they tend to characterize it primarily in terms of the categories that people use to organize mentally their physical worlds (Russell & Snodgrass, 1987). While concerned about categorization processes and their relationships to affective components of environmental evaluation, psychologists have neglected the sources of these category systems and the central problem of meaning generally (Harre & Secord 1973).

If psychologists have been remiss in this regard, those who are interested in the form and use of the built environment as a cultural process invoke meaning as a central element in their explanatory system (Rapoport, 1982). Although there are theoretical differences regarding the ontology of meanings, there is consensus that neither meanings nor actions are individual acts. Giddens (1984), for example, sees the constitution of meaning as related to rules and resources characteristic of social structure. Blumer (1969; 84) suggests that meanings are built up by people "through an interpretation of objects, situations, or the actions of others" in a social context. Another view of meaning derives from one of the definitions of culture provided by anthropologists—i.e. "culture as a symbolic process, in which one studies the constructed meaning system through participant observation" (Low 1986).

Meanings are not just constructed. They are also given by the culture and social structure within which the person operates. This distinction is important because in the literature reviewed below it will be seen that, with a few notable exceptions, most work in this area focuses on what has been given or can be read from the environment as a social/cultural product.

For Rapoport (1982), meaning stems from various levels of nonverbal communications from the environment to people. Environmental elements organized in space ranging from walls to people, become "indicators of social position, ways of establishing group or social identity, [and] ways of defining situations" within a specific culture which in turn lead to expected behaviors in the settings (Rapoport 1982: 181–82). The extent to which the environment works as a source of cues for appropriate behavior is culture specific and hence not necessarily cross-culturally transferable. Rapoport draws upon a wide range of anthropological, archaeological, and environmental research literature to illustrate his arguments.

The study of variations in environmental meanings can occur within a single culture if it is reasonably heterogeneous in social structure and subcultures. For example, Cherulnik & Wilderman (1986) demonstrated that by looking at photographs of homes built in 19th-century Boston, people could easily determine the occupational status and social class standing of their residents. Pavlides (1984: cited in Low 1987) showed how architectural details of Greek village houses communicated the resident's social status.

Reading the environment is not confined to the determination of social status, however. Low & Ryan (1985) found that the residents of a rural town in Pennsylvania consistently identified architectural elements of the area's stone farmhouses that gave the town its distinctive character. Brown's (1985) study, linking visual cues characteristic of homes to incidences of burglary, demonstrates the functional significance of meanings "read" from the environmment.

At the microsystem level, Sadalla et al (1987) describe a study in which upper middle-class homeowners were asked to rate themselves on various personality scales. The interiors and exteriors of their homes were also photographed. Raters shown the photographs were able to infer the homeowners' self concepts relatively accurately, with greatest accuracy achieved by those shown only the home interiors.

Rapoport's (1982) suggestion that environments communicate meanings that "trigger appropriate behaviors" is interesting particularly in the context of behavior-setting analysis (Wicker 1979). Barker's (1968) arguments regarding the power of settings to elicit appropriate behavior are well known. Not well understood in behavior-setting analysis are the social and environmental cues that people use to determine appropriate behavior. One promising study (Schutte et al 1985) examined the effects of situational prototypicality and constraints on both memory and predicted behavior within three settings (a job interview, a bar, and a park). Using work by Rapoport, these authors identified cues in the three settings that would be considered prototypical and nonprototypical. Their results indicated that the greater the prototypicality and the higher the level of situational constraint, the greater the consensus about the behaviors people would perform in the setting.

Despite the suggestiveness of these findings, Rapoport's arguments have several limitations. First, he includes little discussion of the degree to which patterns of settings communicate coherently (Conn & Saegert, unpublished). If messages from proximal settings conflict, what is "appropriate behavior"? Rapoport recognizes this problem but emphasizes the desirability of cue consistency (Rapoport 1982: 77–80). Second, his work includes little discussion of changes in meaning over time, although such changes are the rule rather than the exception (cf Saarinen 1988). Finally, most of the empirical evidence that Rapoport uses to support his thesis is inferential and rests on plausibility as a validity criterion. To illustrate the problematic nature of plausibility, consider a recent study on fear of crime as a function of environmental messages (Taylor et al 1985). The plausible hypothesis tested, that higher levels of physical deterioration would be associated with greater fear of crime, held only within moderate-income neighborhoods. This study suggests that the reading and/or interpretation of environmental messages may be considerably more complex in settings characterized by cultural and socioeconomic heterogeneity.

While important, the study of cultural meanings as a vehicle for communication does not exhaust the theoretical consequences of the meaning construct. Meaning and space are intimately tied to group formation and maintenance.

Group Formation and Maintenance

The formation, maintenance, and reproduction of social relationships generally occur in a spatial context. One of the most persistent issues in environmental social science has been the potential interpenetration of action and space for individual and social behavior. One approach to this subject has been taken by those working within the framework of territoriality. In her useful review of theoretical and empirical work on this concept, Brown (1987) acknowledges scholarly resistance to the incorporation of a construct drawn from animal ecology into theoretical systems relevant to human spatial activity. She points out, however, that claims regarding territorial behavior in animals have become considerably more flexible and contingent within the biological community. While covering studies of individual territorial activity that fit within the adaptive paradigm, Brown places greater emphasis on territoriality as both a regulator of social interaction and a medium (particularly through the use of territorial personalization) for the development and communication of personal and communal identity. These aspects of territoriality have been given greatest emphasis within the last ten years. For example, a number of workers have shown that holiday decorations on homes symbolize neighborhood group cohesiveness (Altman et al 1987; Brown & Werner 1985; Oxley et al 1986; Werner et al 1984).

The processes by which the built environment incorporates individuals into collectivist social systems is the subject of work by Duncan (1985a). Using anthropological data, he argues that myths link "the individual, the group, the home place, and the cosmos" (Duncan 1985b: 147). The central role that myth plays in the physical forms characteristic of traditional societies has also been documented by Hardie (1985), Saile (1985), and Werner et al (1985). The built form both articulates social categories and plays a powerful role in the reproduction of existing social relationships. In collectivist societies, the home is rarely seen as an expression of social status. People gain status from group membership. By contrast, people in individualistically oriented societies use physical objects to assert their individual identities and to display to others "who one is [and] what one's class, lifestyle, and tastes are . . ." (Duncan 1985b: 135).

Using data collected in Hyderabad, India, Duncan (1982) showed how the home and its uses had different within- and between-group meanings for traditional and new urban elites. Pratt (1982) reported that, compared to the upwardly mobile elites of one community, women who represented the more established elite were more likely to consider the interior design of their homes an expression of group membership and solidarity than an indicator of individual identity and taste.

In these studies, the environment is seen as a benign medium and resource for group development and maintenance. Group process, however, is equally important when the environment is a source and medium of threat.

Group Response to Threat

Given the spatially distributed and socially mediated nature of most environmental threats, a complete discussion of perceptions and of preventive or ameliorative action must place the individual in a social context. Two active areas of research address the interdependence of individual, group, community, and sometimes national or global responses to threat.

Studies of human responses to environmental hazards and resource shortages consider the ability of social systems to address problems such as the greenhouse effect, water pollution, toxic wastes, depletion of energy resources, and world hunger. For the most part, practical solutions to these problems have been approached as technological and engineering matters mired in political agendas. Of course these are also problems of human behavior at many levels (Stern & Oskamp 1987). In their effort to improve the preparedness of individuals, groups, and larger social units for hazards Cvetkovich & Earle (1985) have proposed classification of hazardous events according to their causes, their physical and psychosocial characteristics, and the responses to them of individuals and social aggregates.

Awareness of the interdependence of various levels of analysis pervades the research on hazards and resource management. For example, Palm (1986) examined the interrelationships among individual, business, and state actions (or inactions) both preventive and reparative as efforts are made to ameliorate the consequences of earthquakes. She found that the best-prepared individuals, aware of the community-level impacts of such a disaster, formed support groups to plan for the major earthquakes expected in California. However, as Cook (1983) points out in his study of efforts to prevent construction of a hazardous waste treatment plant, relatively few people participate in group efforts to prevent threat except when it is imminent.

That environmental concerns are socially embedded has repeatedly been demonstrated by findings that sociodemographic characteristics and political ideology best predict attitudes about the environment (Samdahl & Robertson 1989). Personal concerns, individual goals, and familiarity also affect beliefs and attitudes about environmental hazards and resources (De Young 1986; Levi & Holder 1986; Neuman 1986). However, these variables may not contribute significantly to the explanation of attitudes (van der Pligt et al 1986). Rather, personal determinants of attitudes seem to be related via belief systems to the social categories the individual occupies and to the effects of the resource or hazard in question on group and individual interests (Connerly 1986; de Haven-Smith 1988). A particularly interesting analysis of black Americans' environmental concerns (Taylor 1989) relates the ways they experience environmental deprivations to informational and resource limitations that in turn limit political participation on environmental issues.

Given their interrelatedness, greater attention should be paid to the processes characteristic of individual and group responses to threat. Edelstein's (1986) study provides an example of this approach. He documented the effects of toxic contamination of water in a residential community on the meaning of home. The interdependence of the nature of the physical threat, personal and household responses, and social group emergence illustrates the interplay of threat to physical health, psychological goals and meanings, cultural expectations, and economic constraints. His study also illustrated the issue theoretically identified by Cuthbertson & Nigg (1987): When technological disasters occur, ambiguity about their nature and consequences often leads to disagreements over who are the "true victims." Such conflict blocks the formation of therapeutic communities in response to natural disasters.

Studies of responses to technological hazards highlight the centrality of the social interpretation of environmental events. Pitt & Zube (1987) point out that resource managers and researchers hold contrasting views of the relationship between natural environments and adaptation. One group views survival as primarily a matter of meeting needs for shelter, food, and reproduction. For example, Buttel and his colleagues (1987) relate numerous rural-urban differences in attitudes toward environmental hazards and resource use to differences in the objective material conditions of survival for the two groups. In contrast, researchers concerned with cognitive and psychological experiences of the environment stress its aesthetic and recreational, or noncommodity, uses. These two views may shape each other over time. Saarinen (1988) documented a gradual convergence of (a) culturally based aesthetic judgments of landscapes with (b) the adaptive necessity of restricting water use in a desert environment in Tucson, Arizona. Others emphasize the difficulty of linking social processes of interpretation to successful adaptation (Stern & Oskamp 1987). Fischhoff et al (1987) detail the cognitive strategies people use to determine the risks associated with various hazards and how these influence adaptive responses. In many instances social, economic, and cultural differences among groups result in different, sometimes conflicting, interpretations of both threats and appropriate responses (Furby et al 1988; Svenson & Fischhoff 1985).

Models employed by some researchers studying environmental resources and human behavior have much in common with those relating environmental stressors to stress and coping. However, interpretation and action are both understood within a social, economic, and cultural framework. Taylor et al (1988) develop a predictive model of drought-related behaviors emphasizing—much as a typical model of responses to environmental stressors does—the role of interpretive processes based on prior experience. Sell et al (1988) have presented a model of perceptions of land use changes that identifies physical dimensions, temporal developments, and informational processes. The model resembles that of environmental stress described by Baum et al (1982). However, Sell et al also relate perceptions of change to more general cultural attitudes, whereas Baum et al do not. One might ask if culture plays a similar anchoring role in the perception of environmental stressors.

A second active area of research on group responses to threat involves crime—a spatially distributed and environmentally mediated social hazard. Both geographers and sociologists have focused on macro-level, spatially distributed predictors of deviant behavior such as percentage of home ownership, amount of overcrowded and substandard housing, degree of urbanization, and so on (Sampson & Groves 1989; Smith 1987; Taylor 1987). Sampson & Groves (1989) and Taylor (1987) agree that macro-level analyses are limited because in their reliance on aggregated statistical data they neglect community-level dynamics and do not provide a process-oriented explanation of criminal activity. One of the more significant community-level issues involves linking criminal activity to loss of social control. Sampson & Groves (1989) argue that both formal and informal social networks allow community residents to maintain effective social controls. They predict that communities that have few networks (i.e. are socially disorganized) will have problems controlling youth gangs, whose presence is associated with crime and delinquency rates. Using individual crime-survey data collected in England in 1982, they found support for their key hypothesis that social disorganization is intimately tied to various personal and property crimes. They cross-validated the findings using another national sample from 1984. This research is valuable because it moves directly to the community level.

How does social disorganization at the local level work? Taylor (1987) suggests that social control is a function of the degree of territorial control residents can exercise. He assumes that norms specify appropriate behavior for the street block. In blocks where residential and commercial buildings are mixed, residents encounter difficulties knowing who belongs on the street. It becomes difficult to establish norms of appropriate behavior in this kind of setting, thus reducing the territorial control exercised by residents.

Much research has been devoted to the social consequences of crime and fear of crime. Smith (1987) argues that the fear bred by crime reduces the quality of social life generally. Reports of restricted outdoor activity and avoidance of certain areas are frequent (Gates & Rohe 1987; Kail & Kleinman

1985). Smith cites a number of studies showing that high levels of fear inhibit collective efforts to control crime, but Gates & Rohe (1987) suggest that this may be true only for those who report less social control over their neighborhoods.

What factors lead to fear? First, while the experience of victimization is sufficient, it is not necessary (Gates & Rohe 1987; Kail & Kleinman 1985; Merry 1981; Rohe & Burby 1988; Smith 1987; Taylor 1987). A sense of personal vulnerability based on age and sex produces fear of crime (Gates & Rohe 1987; Kennedy & Silverman 1985; Smith 1987; Taylor 1987). Blacks are more fearful than whites (Smith 1987). Evidence that perceived social control reduces fear of crime is consistent (Rohe & Burby 1988), but the evidence that neighborhood social cohesion (which is a component of social control) does so is more problematic. Gates & Rohe (1987) report that those who neighbor more were more fearful, presumably because they discussed crime. Hunter & Baumer (1982) found that people who were more integrated into the community were less fearful. Rohe & Burby (1988) suggest that social integration may buffer the person, an effect that is dampened when criminal activity increases. However, these authors also found that social attachment to other residents reduced fear.

Since similarities in age, race, and ethnicity have been shown to influence patterns of social interaction, a number of authors have examined the role that social diversity plays in leading to fear of crime. In an interesting ethnographic study of an ethnically diverse (Chinese, blacks, and whites) neighborhood, Merry (1981) argues that fear is linked primarily to cultural misunderstandings that lead groups to fear one another's behaviors and intentions. Those from one cultural group who knew members of another group reported less fear. Fear of strangers has also been implicated in fear of crime (Hunter & Baumer 1982). Kennedy & Silverman (1985), however, found that perceived social diversity has less to do with fear than expected. Different age groups used different clues to diversity in relation to fear. Only the elderly consistently preferred social homogeneity.

Among environmental factors, deterioration has been linked to fear of crime. Taylor et al's (1985) work showed that perceived environmental deterioration was related to fear of crime for residents of moderate income neighborhoods only. Rohe & Burby (1988), however, found this link for residents of low-income housing projects.

Aside from this research on reading the potential for crime from disordered environments, relatively little recent work has focused on characteristics of the physical environment in relation to crime or fear of crime. Both density and crowding have been used to account in part for the presence of street corner gangs (Taylor 1987); but the correlation between two conceptually different constructs, density and urbanization, causes explanatory problems.

For example, Sampson & Groves (1989) found that degree of urbanization was related to various forms of criminal activity. Substitution of building density for urbanization yielded essentially the same findings. Oxley et al (1981) reported that greater urbanization is associated with increased social segmentation, which results in lower social participation and smaller social networks. Yet work on density has yielded similar findings (Baum & Paulus 1987). Gates & Rohe (1987) found that percentage of single family dwellings was linked to increased perceived social control, which lessened the fear of crime. They also reported that as the percentage of streets interior to the neighborhood having more than 10% commercial activities increased, perceived crime and fear decreased. [Contrast Taylor's (1987) arguments about the presence of nonresidential establishments in the environment.] Hassinger (1985) reports a relationship between the physical characteristics of areas traveled within a city and handgun ownership. Patterson (1985) implicates physical characteristics of transport systems in fear of crime among the elderly.

This evidence on group reactions to threat is intriguing, but the questions raised have not yet been answered.

Strengths and Weaknesses of the Paradigm

This paradigm explicitly recognizes that environmental meanings and actions are not solely individual constructions. The individual both defines and is defined by the groups in which he/she participates. The best literature in this area attempts to relate the individual, group, and social-structural characteristics of human responses to threat.

However, certain important elements are missing from the model. Proponents of the paradigm pay relatively little attention to the results of successful and unsuccessful group transactions regarding meaning. The social consequences of effective and ineffective group management of environmental threats are afforded better treatment, but effects at the individual level are largely ignored. The potential for a collaboration between those working in the adaptive and sociocultural paradigms seem obvious.

Much of the literature in this area focuses on the social use of the environment to incorporate individuals into groups. Most societies, however, contain multiple groups whose access to the economic and political power necessary to create meaning and define the use of space is unevenly distributed. One of the implications of this observation is that group affiliation, whether ascribed or achieved, does not guarantee access to the environmental resources necessary to meet individual or group needs. What is more, the environment can be instrumentally employed to achieve the goals of one group at the expense of others. Harvey (1973, 1982, 1985) forcefully argues that the economically dominant classes manipulate the environment to achieve their ends of capital accumulation. Using this framework, he attempts to account for phenomena like urban decay, regional development, and commercial relocation. Although not discussing the issue directly, he frequently refers to the social stresses that result from various forms of environmental manipulation. The problems considered by Harvey constitute an active area of research, not all of which stems from a Marxist perspective. A good introduction is provided by Gregory & Urry (1985).

Efforts to shape and control the environment by different groups also lead to the possibility of intergroup conflict, a neglected issue in much of the work reviewed here. However, Castells (1983) has recently focused his research on urban protest movements. Using both historical and contemporary studies of protest movements, he attempts to identify the factors that enable a movement to bring about environmental and social change.

This work has two important implications. First, the research findings are attributable neither to individual action alone nor solely to group action. Social meaning and the possibility or realization of social action frequently depend on the economic and political opportunities associated with the historical period within which the research is conducted. Second, without a consideration of economic forces, efforts to understand individual and group response to environmental change are often doomed (Molotch 1979). Given these criticisms (which can be applied to the adaptive and opportunities structure paradigms as well), we now consider research that aims toward a more synthetic approach to person-environment relationships.

TOWARD SYNTHESIS

The impetus for synthesis originates in certain practical and theoretical concerns. Practically, efforts to improve the relationship of people with their environment cut across the boundaries of these three paradigms. In studies of the workplace, for example, the need to accommodate employees' various work demands has led to consideration of factors associated with stress and adaptation, fit between the physical organization of the environment and task demands, small-group processes, and organizational dynamics (Sundstrom 1986, 1987). Wicker & King (1988) also relate the survival of small businesses to their cultural, economic, and historical context. While increased productivity and decreased costs usually motivate application of this research (Buffalo Organization for Social and Technological Innovation 1981; Stokols et al 1988), union representatives, too, have sought to use environment/ behavior research to improve working conditions during periods of economic retrenchment.

The more success environment/behavior researchers have had in applying their knowledge to real settings, the more synthetic are the bodies of knowledge that develop. Research on the relationship of the environment to the well-being of the elderly benefited from the combination of available federal funding, construction and rent subsidies for housing for the elderly, and to some extent, the activism of interest groups (Pynoos 1987). The body of work produced ranges from adaptive concerns through opportunity structure issues to social, cultural, and economic analysis, sometimes within the same studies (Carp 1987; Lawton 1985b; Rowles 1978; Windley & Scheidt 1982).

However useful a synthetic approach may promise to be, the ability of researchers and practitioners to deliver on the promise involves difficult decisions about the boundaries of the context and the relevant variables for attention (Wicker 1987; Stokols 1987). Transactionalism posits some issues that can inform decisions concerning problem definition and research processes. These include the following: the researchers' intentions, the specific historical and geographical nature of the problem or place in question, emergent person-environment relationships, and the research and action process.

Research Intentions

The practical intent of much work in environmental psychology has raised questions (usually ignored by the discipline) about the social and value bases of the choice of research problems and methods (Saegert 1982, 1986, 1987; Sime 1986; Stokols 1989). The aspect of transactionalism that places the researcher as an acting and knowing individual in the research context further requires acknowledgment of the researcher's interests. Saegert (1982, 1987) has identified three types of research intentions based on underlying assumptions about the relationship of research to social praxis: technological, interpretive, and transformative. Technological intentions assume that research findings will dictate the solution of problems. Consensus about goals and the use of resources to achieve them must include persons and institutions with sufficient authority and control of resources to support implementation. This consensus among researchers and actors must extend to the problem definition, methods, and results of the research to be applied. Interpretive research addresses issues that are not consensually defined. The goals include identification of divergent conceptions of people, environments, and their relationships. This approach emphasizes communication not just among researchers, or researchers and decision-makers, but rather among research participants, researchers, and other relevant social actors. Transformative intentions focus on the combination of interpretive and technological research to reconfigure the environment, the person, and the nature of their transactions. Stokols (1988) suggests several directions for the description and prediction of transformations in person-environment relationships, although his approach does not include discussion of transformation of the researcher and his/her relationship to the physical and social environment. The distinction between the intentions of positivistic research and those of phenomenological research (Franck 1987; Sime 1986) parallels that between technological and interpretive intentionality. The publically definable nature of positivist methods presumes agreement about language and problem definition. Phenomenologists (Seamon 1987) try by means of interpretation to identify the invariant structures of phenomena. However, their quest turns inward to reflection on experience and observation and outward to text. By taking interpretation of text as the model, the need to negotiate truth through dialog is avoided as it is by positivists. Thus, the many actors who must participate in a censensus directed toward change are ignored by both phenomenologists and positivists.

Historical and Geographic Specificity

The three paradigms described here aim to establish general relationships among the variables studied. The achievement of this goal, however, continues to elude researchers as findings either fail to be replicated or are found inapplicable to wider contexts. In an effort to overcome such problems, researchers often emphasize similarity of process despite differences in findings. Thus person–environment relationships become replicable forms with variable and uninteresting content. In contrast, researchers who view person-environment relationships as inherently specific to particular historical and geographic contexts tend to look for changes in person-environment relationship rather than trans-situational stability. Changes are seen as reflecting (a) historical and geographical configurations of person–environment relationships that are to some extent unique; (b) the emergence of new general constellations of social, cultural, and economic forces; and (c) the emergence of new human efforts to transform the conditions of life.

Several recent studies illustrate different weightings of the contribution of history, geography, and group and individual action. Katz's research (1988, 1989) on the acquisition and content of Sudanese children's environmental knowledge under conditions of socioeconomic transformation illustrates how historically grounded research can illuminate specific historical and geographic changes as they relate to social processes and psychological development. She traces changes from precapitalist to capitalist relationships of agricultural production as they ripple through the social and economic structure of village life into the socialization practices of families. Such changes affect children's knowledge and the activities of households as villagers seek both to adapt to new conditions and to conserve threatened modes of relationship to the environment. Rivlin & Wolfe (1985) analyze the effects of historical forces in the broader society upon child-environment transactions in a variety of institutions noting that children usually have little power to affect institutional environments. In contrast, Christensen (1988) focuses on the active striving of women who choose to work at home to cope with historically changing demographic and economic forces by redefining the nature of their relationships with their homes and work. Her findings reveal the efforts of women, caught in historic contradictions concerning gender, domesticity, and economic productivity, to negotiate new social contracts with their families and their employers or clients by transforming their uses of time and space. Her recognition that economic, social, and cultural factors frequently overwhelm such attempts at transformation led her to support legislation respectful of home-based work.

As the work of Katz and Christensen demonstrates, historically grounded research can reveal the emergence of new person–environment relationships. These investigators used a variety of methods to capture the emergent quality of the person–environment transactions, and both their writing and data-interpretation styles were important in conveying the substance and process of change.

Historical Emergence

The extent to which emergence is possible in a particular place and time depends on the nature of changes (at various scales) that affect the setting. Thus the choice of a problem, a location, a population, and a method affect the likelihood of discovering emergent transactions. These choices involve first a clarification of the researcher's intent. The researcher must determine his/her own relationship to the problem, location, and people to be studied. If it is the case that the researcher's reality determines the form of his/her research, then the authentic voices of researcher and research participants must be conveyed in the work so that the reader can understand the nature of the dialog (Saegert 1987; Riger 1988). Dialog that allows emerging redefinitions of self, other, and environment requires a freedom among participants to reveal interests and intents and the development of enough trust for such communication to proceed (Saegert 1989). Thus the researcher and research participants strive together to develop a definition of the situation and consensus about directions for change. If the direction is to be pursued in action, other relevant social actors must also be involved in the progress of conceptualization and consensus. Often, this process reveals real differences in interest that delineate points of conflict that should also be clarified. Both emerging consensus and conflict shape the course of feasible action.

Leavitt & Saegert's (1988, 1989) study of tenant's responses to landlord abandonment in Harlem grew out of the identification of the researchers' interest in the transformation of women's positions in society and the economy. Recognizing the significance of class and racial divisions among women, the researchers chose a situation that would create dialog between themselves and women more disadvantaged by their gender by virtue of their class and race. Landlord-abandoned housing provided a good site because most tenants would be low-income, minority women. Further, the housing environment has special significance because (a) housing is a basic need regardless of employment status or income; (b) research has shown that women of various classes and races are more involved in the making of homes and are more affected by their quality than are men (reviewed in Leavitt & Saegert 1989); and (c) since 1980, few if any federal or local housing policies have provided adequate housing for most women in this category. The researchers began by speaking with tenants who, in the wake of abandonment, had organized to save and then cooperatively own and manage their buildings. The situation appeared to be one where a more feminist housing alternative could emerge (Gilligan 1982; Hayden 1984; Leavitt & Saegert 1989; Saegert 1989). The research revealed the critical roles women and, unexpectedly, elderly people play in co-ops. It also clarified the importance of race and attachment to place in the specific responses of these Harlem residents to abandonment. Appropriate support from technical assistance groups, politicians, and governmental programs was also crucial. The configuration of these factors and the success or failure of tenant efforts were shaped by the dynamics of historical changes in social and political movements, the urban economy, the physical environment of New York, the ecology of community organizations, and governmental policies at all levels. The authors developed the Community Household Model to formalize their hypotheses about the conditions leading to empowerment of socially and economically disadvantaged women and to serve as a guideline for policymakers and advocates. This work led the authors to start action research programs. Saegert continued to work with co-ops and a technical assistance group in New York. Leavitt worked with public housing tenants in Los Angeles who were confronted with a decision about cooperatively buying their project.

Research and Action Process

Many environment/behavior researchers believe both the researcher and the research process can contribute to emergent relationships between people and their environments (Francis, et al 1987; Hardie 1989). Techniques for participatory research, planning, and design have led to some successes in changing environments and empowering people. For example, Chapin and his colleagues (Architecture Research Construction 1985) helped mentally retarded people first to understand the design and use of features they would like in their new shared home and then to construct them. As a result, residents showed improved functioning, greater satisfaction, and a more positive orientation toward the use of their neighborhoods. As both a therapeutic and design technique, Peled & Ayalon (1988) analyzed the differences between the meanings a husband and wife attached to their home. Hart (1987) described a wide range of planning and design projects in which children have contributed effectively while at the same time expanding their democratic participation skills. He and other experienced practitioners of participatory design also described the economic and social constraints operating on these processes and propose approaches that minimize their potential for cooptation and disempowerment (Hart 1987; Hester 1987; Ventriss 1987).

Here we have suggested the variety and accomplishment of interdisciplinary, transactional research within environmental psychology. The studies cited display a strong awareness of the effects of historical and local context on the nature and quality of person–environment relationships. We hope that the juxtaposition of the accomplishments and weaknesses of the various better-developed paradigms within the field will suggest fruitful approaches to the problems of identifying and bounding studies of person–environment transactions at all levels.

Literature Cited

Acredolo, L. P., Adams, A., Goodwyn, S. W. 1984. The role of self-produced movement and visual tracking in infant spatial orientation. *J. Exp. Child Psychol.* 38:312–27

Albrecht, J., Lim, G. C. 1986. A search for alternative planning theory: use of critical theory. *J. Arch. Plan. Res.* 3:117–32

Aldwin, C., Stokols, D. 1988. The effects of environmental change on individuals and groups: some neglected issues in stress research. *J. Environ. Psychol.* 8:57–75

Altman, I., Rogoff, B. 1987. World views in psychology: trait, interactional, organismic, and transactional perspectives. See Stokols & Altman 1987, 1:7–40

Altman, I., Werner, C. 1985. *Home Environments.* New York: Plenum. 339 pp.

Altman, I., Werner, C. M., Oxley, D., Haggard, L. M. 1987. Christmas Street as an example of transactionally oriented research. *Environ. Behav.* 19:501–24

Andorka, R. 1987. Time budgets and their uses. *Annu. Rev. Sociol.* 13:149–64

Aragones, J. I., Arrendondo, J. M. 1985. Structure of urban cognitive maps. *J. Environ. Psychol.* 5:197–212

Archea, J. C. 1985. The use of architectural props in the conduct of criminal acts. See Archea & Patterson 1985, pp. 245–60

Archea, J. C., Patterson, A. H., eds. 1985. Special issues: crime and the environment: new perspectives. *J. Arch. Plan. Res.* 2:4

Architecture Research Construction. 1985. *Community Group Homes: An Environmental Approach.* New York: Van Nostrand Reinhold. 208 pp.

Barker, R. 1968. *Ecological Psychology: Concepts and Methods for Studying the Environment of Human Behavior.* Stanford: Stanford Univ. Press. 242 pp.

Baum, A., Paulus, P. 1987. Crowding. See Stokols & Altman 1987, 1:533–70

Baum, A., Singer, J. E., Baum, C. 1982. Stress and the environment. In *Environmental Stress,* ed. G. W. Evans, pp. 15–44. New York: Cambridge Univ. Press. 400 pp.

Bjorklid, P. 1985. Children's outdoor environment from the perspectives of environmental and developmental psychology. See Garling & Valsiner 1985, pp. 91–106

Blumer, H. 1969. *Symbolic Interactionism: Perspective and Method.* Englewood Cliffs, NJ: Prentice-Hall. 208 pp.

Bond, M., Feather, N. 1988. Some correlates of structure and purpose in the use of time. *J. Pers. Soc. Psychol.* 55:321–29

Bronfenbrenner, U. 1979. *The Ecology of Human Development: Experiments by Nature and Design.* Cambridge, Mass: Harvard Univ. Press. 330 pp.

Bronfenbrenner, U. 1977. Toward an experimental ecology of human development. *Am. Psychol.* 32:513–31

Bronfenbrenner, U., Moen, P., Garbarino, J. 1984. Child, family, and community. In *Review of Child Development Research.* Vol. 7. *The Family,* ed. D. Parke, pp. 283–328. Chicago: Univ. Chicago Press

Brown, B. 1987. Territoriality. See Stokols & Altman 1987, 1:505–32

Brown, B. 1985. Residential territories: cues to burglary vulnerability. *J. Arch. Plan. Res.* 2:231–45

Brown, B., Werner, C. 1985. Social cohesiveness, territoriality, and holiday decorations. *Environ. Behav.* 17:539–65

Brunswick, E. 1956. *Perception and the Representative Design of Psychological Experiments.* Berkeley: Univ. Calif. Press

Buffalo Organization for Social and Technological Innovation. 1981. *The Impact of Office Environment on Productivity and Quality of Working Life: Comprehensive Findings.* Buffalo: BOSTI

Buttel, F. H., Murdock, S. H., Feistritz, F. L., Hamm, R. R. 1987. Rural environments. See Zube & Moore 1987, pp. 107–28

Campbell, J. 1983. Ambient stressors. *Environ. Behav.* 15:355–80

Carbonara-Moscati, V. 1985. Barriers to play activities in the city environment: a study of children's perceptions. See Garling & Valsiner 1985, pp. 119–26

Carlstein, T. 1982. *Time, Resources, Society, and Ecology: On the Capacity for Human Interaction in Space and Time: Preindustrial Societies.* London: Allen & Unwin. 437 pp.

Carp, F. 1987. Environment and aging. See Stokols & Altman 1987, 1:329–60

Caspi, A., Bolger, N., Eckenrode, J. 1987. Linking person and context in the daily stress process. *J. Pers. Soc. Psychol.* 52:184–95

Castells, M. 1983. *The City and the Grassroots,* Berkeley, CA: Univ. Calif. Press. 450 pp.

Cherulnik, P., Wilderman, S. 1986. Symbols of status in urban neighborhoods. *Environ. Behav.* 18:604–22

Christensen, K. 1988. *Women and Home-based Work: The Unspoken Contract.* New York: Henry Holt

Clark, H., Manzo, L. 1987. Community gardens: factors that influence participation. In *Proceedings of the 19th Annual Environmental Design Research Association Conference,* ed. D. Lawrence, R. Habe, A. Hacker, D. Sherrod, pp. 57–62. Washington, DC: Environ. Design Res. Assoc. 354 pp.

Connerly, C. E. 1986. Growth management concern: the impact of its definition on support for local growth controls. *Environ. Behav.* 18:707–32

Cook, J. 1983. Citizen response in a neighborhood under threat. *Am. J. Commun. Psychol.* 11:459–71

Cuthbertson, B. H., Nigg, J. M. 1987. Technological disaster and the nontherapeutic community: a question of true victimization. *Environ. Behav.* 19:452–83

Cvetkovich, G., Earle, T. C. 1985. Classifying hazardous events. *J. Environ. Psychol.* 5:5–35

de Haven-Smith, L. 1988. Environmental belief systems: public opinion on land use regulation in Florida. *Environ. Behav.* 20:176–99

De Young, R. 1986. Some psychological aspects of recycling: the structure of conservation satisfactions. *Environ. Behav.* 18:435–49

DiMento, J. F. 1981. Making usable information on environmental stressors: opportunities for the research and policy communities. *J. Soc. Issues* 37:172–202

Duncan, J. 1985a. Individual action and political power: a structuration perspective. In *The Future of Geography,* ed. R. Johnston. London: Methuen. 342 pp.

Duncan, J. 1985b. The house as symbol of social structure. See Altman & Werner 1985, pp. 133–51

Duncan, J. 1982. From container of women to status symbol: the impact of social structure on the meaning of the house. In *Housing and Identity: Cross Cultural Perspectives,* ed. J. Duncan, pp. 36–59. New York: Holmes & Meier. 250 pp.

Edelstein, M. R. 1986. Toxic exposure and the inversion of the home. *J. Arch. Plan. Res.* 3:237–51

Evans, G. W., Cohen, S. 1987. Environmental stress. See Stokols & Altman 1987, 1:571–610

Evans, G. W., Colume, S. D., Shearer, D. F. 1988. Psychological reactions to air pollution. *Environ. Res.* 45:1–15

Evans, G. W., Jacobs, S. V., Dooley, D., Catalano, R. 1987. The interaction of stressful life events and chronic strains on community mental health. *Am. J. Commun. Psychol.* 15:23–33

Evans, G. W., Kliewer, W., Martin, J. 1989. The role of the physical environment in the health and well being of children. In *New Directions in Health Psychology: Assessment,* ed. H. Schroeder. New York: Hemisphere Press. In press

Evans, G. W., Palsane, M. N., Lepore, S. J., Martin, J. 1988. Crowding and social support. In *Looking Back to the Future* (IAPS 10), ed. H. van Hoogdalem, N. L. Prak, T. J. M. van der Voordt, H. B. R. van Weger, pp. 125–31. The Netherlands: Delft Univ. Press

Evans, G. W., Skorpanich, M. A., Garling, T., Bryant, K. J., Bresolin, B. 1984. The effects of pathway configuration, landmarks, and stress on environmental cognition. *J. Environ. Psychol.* 4:323–35

Feldman, A., Acredolo, L. 1979. The effect

of active versus passive exploration on memory for spatial location in children. *Child Dev.* 50:698–704

Fischhoff, B., Svenson, O., Slovic, P. 1987. Active responses to environmental hazards: perceptions and decision making. See Stokols & Altman 1987, 2:1089–1133

Francis, M., Moore, R., Iacofano, D., Klein, S., Paxson, L. 1987. Special issue: design and democracy. *J. Arch. Plan. Res.* 4: Entire Issue

Franck, K. A. 1987. Phenomenology, positivism and empiricism as research strategies in environment-behavior research and in design. See Zube & Moore 1987, pp. 60–70

Furby, L., Slovic, P., Fischhoff, B., Gregory, R. 1988. Public perceptions of electric power transmission lines. *J. Environ. Psychol.* 8:19–43

Garling, T. 1985. Children's environments, accidents, and accident prevention: an introduction. See Garling & Valsiner 1985, pp. 3–12

Garling, T., Golledge, R. G. 1989. Environmental perception and cognition. See Zube & Moore 1989, pp. 203–38

Garling, T., Valsiner, J. 1985. *Children Within Environments: Toward a Psychology of Accident Prevention.* New York: Plenum. 249 pp.

Gates, L., Rohe, W. 1987. Fear and reactions to crime: a revised model. *Urban Aff. Q.* 22:425–53.

Gibson, J. J. 1979. *The Ecological Approach to Visual Perception.* Boston: Houghton-Mifflin. 336 pp.

Giddens, A. 1984. *The Constitution of Society.* Berkeley, CA: Univ. Calif. Press. 402 pp.

Gilligan, C. 1982. *In a Different Voice.* Cambridge, MA: Harvard Univ. Press. 184 pp.

Gillis, A. R., Richard, M. A., Hagan, J. 1986. Ethnic susceptibility to crowding: an empirical analysis. *Environ. Behav.* 18: 683–706

Golledge, R. 1987. Environmental cognition. See Stokols & Altman 1987, 1:131–74

Golledge, R. 1988. Comment on the *Handbook of Environmental Psychology. J. Env. Psychol.* 8:162–65

Gregory, D., Urry, J., eds. 1985. *Social Relations and Spatial Structure.* New York: St. Martin's Press. 440 pp.

Hagerstrand, T. 1983. In search for the sources of concepts. In *The Practice of Geography*, ed. A. Buttimer, pp. 238–56. London: Longman. 298 pp.

Hardie, G. 1985. Continuity and change in the Tswana's house and settlement form. See Altman & Werner 1985, pp. 213–36

Hardie, G. J. 1989. Environment and behavior research for developing countries. See Zube & Moore 1989, pp. 120–60

Harre, H., Secord, P. 1973. *The Explanation of Social Behavior.* Totowa, NJ: Littlefield, Adams. 327 pp.

Hart, R. 1981. Children's spatial representation of the landscape: lessons and questions from a field study. In *Spatial Representation and Behavior Across the Life Span*, ed. L. S. Liben, A. H. Patterson, N. Newcombe, pp. 195–233. New York: Aldine

Hart, R. 1979. *Children's Experience of Place.* New York: Irvington. 518 pp.

Hart, R. A. 1987. Children's participation in planning and design: theory, research, and practice. In *Spaces for Children*, ed. C. Weinstein, T. David, pp. 217–39. New York: Plenum. 318 pp.

Harvey, D. 1985. *Consciousness and the Urban Experience.* Baltimore, MD: The Johns Hopkins Press. 293 pp.

Harvey, D. 1982. *The Limits to Capital.* Oxford: Oxford Univ. Press. 478 pp.

Harvey, D. 1973. *Social Justice and the City.* London: Edward Arnold. 336 pp.

Hassinger, J. 1985. Fear of crime in public environments. See Archea & Patterson 1985, pp. 289–300

Hayden, D. 1984. *Redesigning the American Dream.* New York: Norton. 270 pp.

Hazen, N. L. 1982. Spatial exploration and spatial knowledge: individual and developmental differences in very young children. *Child Dev.* 53:826–33

Heft, H., Wohlwill, J. 1987. Environmental cognition in children. See Stokols & Altman 1987, 1:175–204

Heijs, W., Stringer, P. 1988. Research on residential thermal comfort: some contributions from environmental psychology. *J. Environ. Psychol.* 8:235–48

Hester, R. 1987. Participatory design and environmental justice: pas de deux or time to change partners? *J. Arch. Plan. Res.* 4:301–9

Holahan, C. 1986. Environmental psychology. *Annu. Rev. Psychol.* 37:381–407

Holden, G. 1985. How parents create a social environment via proactive behavior. See Garling & Valsiner 1985, pp. 193–216

Hunter, A., Baumer, T. 1982. Street traffic, social integration, and fear of crime. *Sociol. Inq.* 52:122–31

Ittelson, W. H. 1989. Notes on theory in environment and behavior research. See Zube & Moore 1989, pp. 71–83

Ittelson, W. H. 1973. Environment perception and contemporary perceptual theory. In *Environment and Cognition*, ed. W. H. Ittelson, pp. 2–20. New York: Seminar

Ittelson, W., Proshansky, H., Rivlin, L., Winkel, G. 1974. *An Introduction to Environmental Psychology.* New York: Holt, Rinehart, & Winston. 406 pp.

Kail,. B., Kleinman, P. 1985. Fear, crime, community organization, and limitations on daily routines. *Urban Aff. Q.* 20:400–8

Kaplan, R. 1987. Validity in environment/behavior research: some cross-paradigm concerns. *Environ. Behav.* 19:495–500

Kaplan, R. 1985. Nature at the doorstep: residential satisfaction and the nearby environment. *J. Arch. Plan. Res.* 2:115–28

Kaplan, R., Kaplan, S. 1989. *The Experience of Nature: A Psychological Perspective.* New York: Cambridge Univ. Press. In press

Kaplan, S. 1987. Aesthetics, affect, and cognition: environmental preference from an evolutionary perspective. *Environ. Behav.* 19:3–32

Kaplan, S., Kaplan, R. 1973. *Cognition and Environment.* New York: Praeger. 287 pp.

Katz, C. 1988. Children and the environment: work, play and learning in rural Sudan. *Child. Environ. Q.* 4:43–51

Katz, C. R. 1989. Apprehending the human environment: local knowledge under conditions of socioeconomic transformation in rural Sudan. *Ann. Assoc. Am. Geog.* In press

Kennedy, L., Silverman, R. 1985. Perceptions of social diversity and fear of crime. *Environ. Behav.* 17:275–95

Knopf, R. 1987. Human behavior, cognition, and affect in the natural environment. See Stokols & Altman 1987, 1:783–826

Lawton, M. P. 1985a. The elderly in context: perspectives from environmental psychology and gerontology. *Environ. Behav.* 17: 501–19

Lawton, M. P. 1985b. Housing and living environments of older people. In *Handbook of Aging and the Social Sciences,* ed. R. Binstock, E. Shanas, pp. 450–78. New York: Van Nostrand Reinhold. 809 pp.

Lawton, M. P., Nahemow, L. 1973. Ecology and the aging process. In *Psychology of Adult Development and Aging,* ed. C. Eisdorfer, M. P. Lawton, pp. 619–74. Washington, DC: Am. Psychol. Assoc.

Lazarus, R. S., Cohen, J. 1977. Environmental stress. In *Human Behavior and Environment,* ed. J. Wohlwill, I. Altman, pp. 90–127. New York: Plenum. 358 pp.

Leavitt, J., Saegert, S. 1989. *From Abandonment to Hope: Community Households in Harlem.* New York: Columbia Univ. Press. In press

Leavitt, J., Saegert, S. 1988. The community household: responding to housing abandonment in New York City. *Am. Plan. Assoc. J.* 54:489–500

Levi, D. J., Holder, E. E. 1986. Nuclear power: the dynamics of acceptability. *Environ. Behav.* 18:385–95

Levine, R. 1988. The pace of life across cultures. See McGrath 1988, pp. 39–62

Lewin, K. 1936. *Principles of Topological Psychology.* New York: McGraw-Hill. 231 pp.

Little, B. 1987. Personality and environment. See Stokols & Altman 1987, 1:205–44

Little, B. 1983. Personal projects: a rationale and method for investigation. *Environ. Behav.* 15:273–309

Loo, C. 1986. Neighborhood satisfaction and safety: a study of a low-income ethnic area. *Environ. Behav.* 18:109–31

Low, S. 1987. Qualitative methodology. See Zube & Moore 1987, pp. 279–303

Low, S. 1986. Teaching about culture and place: an anthropological perspective. In *Proceedings of the Built Form and Culture Conference,* ed. D. Saile. Lawrence, KA: Sch. Arch. Urban Design, Univ. Kansas

Low, S., Ryan, W. 1985. Noticing without looking: a methodology for the integration of architectural and local perceptions in Olney, Pennsylvania. *J. Arch. Plan. Res.* 2:3–22

Lynch, K. 1960. *The Image of the City.* Cambridge, MA: MIT Press. 194 pp.

Manicas, P. T. 1986. The concept of social structure. *J. Theory Soc. Behav.* 10:66–82

Manicas, P. T., Secord, P. F. 1983. Implications for psychology of the new philosophy of science. *Am. Psychol.* 38: 399–413

Manzo, L., Weinstein, N. D. 1987. Behavioral commitment to environmental protection: a study of active and nonactive members of the Sierra Club. *Environ. Behav.* 19:673–94

McGrath, J. 1988. *The Social Psychology of Time.* Newbury Park, CA: Sage. 183 pp.

Merry, S. 1981. *Urban Danger: Life in a Neighborhood of Strangers.* Philadelphia, PA: Temple Univ. Press. 278 pp.

Michelson, W. 1987. Measuring macroenvironment and behavior: the time budget and time geography. In *Methods in Environmental and Behavioral Research,* ed. R. Bechtel, R. Marans, W. Michelson, pp. 216–46. New York: Van Nostrand Reinhold. 415 pp.

Michelson, W. 1985. *From Sun to Sun: Daily Obligations and Community Structure in the Lives of Employed Women and Their Families.* Totowa, NJ: Rowman & Allanheld. 208 pp.

Molotch, H. 1979. Capital and neighborhood in the United States. *Urban Aff. Q.* 14:289–312

Murphy, G. 1947. *Personality: A Biosocial Approach to Origins and Structure.* New York: Harper

Neisser, U. 1976. *Cognition and Reality.* San Francisco: Freeman

Neuman, K. 1986. Personal values and commitment to energy conservation. *Environ. Behav.* 18:53–74

Nohl, W. 1987. The aesthetics of home separated gardens in Germany: traces of participatory aesthetics. *J. Arch. Plan. Res.* 4:212–27

Oxley, D., Barrera, M., Sadalla, E. 1981. Relationships among community size, mediators, and social support variables: a path analytic approach. *Am. J. Commun. Psychol.* 9:637–51

Oxley, D., Haggard, L., Werner, C., Altman, I. 1986. Transactional qualities of neighborhood social networks: a case study of "Christmas Street". *Environ. Behav.* 18:640–77

Palm, R. 1986. Coming home. *Ann. Am. Assoc. Geogr.* 76:469–79

Palys, T., Little, B. 1983. Perceived life satisfaction and the organization of personal project systems. *J. Pers. Soc. Psychol.* 44:1221–30

Passini, R., Proulx, G. 1988. Wayfinding without vision: an experiment with congenitally totally blind people. *Environ. Behav.* 20:227–52

Patterson, A. H. 1985. Fear of crime and other barriers to use of public transportation by the elderly. See Archea & Patterson 1985, pp. 277–88

Peled, A., Ayalon, O. 1988. The role of the spatial organization of the home in family therapy: a case study. *J. Environ. Psychol.* 8:87–106

Peterson, R. 1987. Gender issues in the home and urban environment. See Zube & Moore 1987, pp. 187–218

Piaget, J., Inhelder, B. 1967. *The Child's Conception of Space.* New York: Norton. 490 pp.

Pitt, D. G., Zube, E. H. 1987. Management of natural environments. See Stokols & Altman 1987, 2:1009–42

Porteous, D. J., Mastin, J. F. 1985. Soundscape. *J. Arch. Plan. Res.* 2:169–86

Pratt, G. 1982. The house as an expression of social worlds. See Duncan 1982, pp. 135–80

Pred, A. 1985. The social becomes the spatial, the spatial becomes the social: enclosures, social change and the becoming of places in the Swedish province of Skane. See Gregory & Urry 1985, pp. 337–65.

Pred, A. 1984. Place as historically contingent process: structuration and time geography of becoming places. *Ann. Am. Assoc. Geogr.* 74:279–97

Pred, A. 1981. Of paths and projects: individual behavior and its societal context. In *Behavioral Problems in Geography Revisited*, ed. K. Cox, R. Golledge, pp. 231–55. New York: Methuen

Pred, A. 1977. The choreography of existence: comments on Hagerstrand's time geography and it usefulness. *Econ. Geogr.* 53:207–21

Pred, A. 1973. Urbanization, domestic planning problems and Swedish geographical research. *Prog. Geogr.* 5:1–76

Proshansky, H. M. 1987. The field of environmental psychology: securing its future. See Stokols & Altman 1987, 2:1467–88

Pynoos, J. 1987. Housing the aged: public policy at the crossroads. In *Housing the Aged: Design Directives and Policy Considerations*, ed. V. Regnier, J. Pynoos, pp. 225–40. New York: Elsevier. 500 pp.

Rapoport, A. 1982. *The Meaning of the Built Environment.* Beverly Hills, CA: Sage.

Reser, J. P., Scherl, L. M. 1988. Clear and unambiguous feedback: a transactional and motivational analysis of environmental challenge and self-encounter. *J. Environ. Psychol.* 8:269–87

Riger, S. 1988. Ways of knowing and community-organizational research. Invited address, Conf. Res. Commun. Psychol.: Integrating Theories and Methodol., Chicago, Illinois, Sept.

Rivlin, L. G., Wolfe, M. 1985. *Institutional Settings in Children's Lives.* New York: Wiley & Sons. 250 pp.

Rohe, W. M., Burby, R. J. 1988. Fear of crime in public housing. *Environ. Behav.* 20:700–20

Rotton, J. 1986. Determinism redux: climate and cultural correlates of violence. *Environ. Behav.* 18:346–68

Rowles, G. D. 1978. *Prisoners of Space.* Boulder, CO: Westview. 216 pp.

Russell, J., Snodgrass, J. 1987. Emotion and the environment. See Stokols & Altman 1987, 1:245–80

Saarinen, T. F. 1988. Public perception of the desert in Tucson, Arizona. *J. Arch. Plan. Res.* 5:197–207

Sadalla, E., Vershure, B., Burroughs, J. 1987. Identity symbolism in housing. *Environ. Behav.* 19:569–87

Saegert, S. 1989. Unlikely leaders, extreme circumstances: older black women building community households. *Am. J. Commun. Psychol.* In press

Saegert, S. 1988. The androgynous city: from critique to practice. See van Vliet 1988, pp. 23–37

Saegert, S. 1987. Environmental psychology and social change. See Stokols & Altman 1987, 1:71–98

Saegert, S. 1986. Environmental psychology and the world beyond the mind. In *The G. Stanley Hall Lecture Series*, ed., V. P. Makosky, 6:129–64. Washington, DC: Am. Psychol. Assoc. 191 pp.

Saegert, S. 1982. Environment as material,

artifact, and matrix. New York: Cent. Hum. Environ. City Univ. New York Grad. Sch.

Saegert, S. 1981. Crowding and cognitive limits. In Cognition, Social Behavior, and the Environment, ed. J. Harvey, pp. 373–92. Hillsdale, NJ: Erlbaum. 605 pp.

Saegert, S., Mackintosh, E., West, S. 1975. Two studies of crowding in urban public spaces. Environ. Behav. 7:159–84

Saile, D. 1985. The ritual establishment of home. See Altman & Werner 1985, pp. 87–111

Samdahl, D. M., Robertson, R. 1989. Social determinants of environmental concern: specification and test of the model. Environ. Behav. 21:57–81

Sampson, R., Groves, W. 1989. Community structure and crime: testing social-disorganization theory. Am. J. Sociol. 94: 774–802

Schneekloth, L. H. 1987. Advances in practice in environment, behavior, and design. See Zube & Moore 1987, pp. 307–34

Schutte, N., Kenrick, D., Sadalla, E. 1985. The search for predictable settings: situational prototypes, constraint, and behavioral variation. J. Pers. Soc. Psychol. 49:121–28

Seamon, D. 1987. Phenomenology and environment-behavior research. See Zube & Moore 1987, pp. 4–28

Sell, J. L., Zube, E. H., Kennedy, C. L. 1988. Perception of land use change in a desert city. J. Arch. Plan. Res. 5:145–62

Sheehy, N., Chapman, A. 1985. Adults' and children's perceptions of hazard in familiar environments. See Garling & Valsiner 1985, pp. 51–64

Shumaker, S. A., Pequegnat, W. 1989. Hospital design, health providers, and the delivery of effective health care. See Zube & Moore 1989, pp. 161–202

Sime, J. D. 1986. Creating places or designing spaces? J. Environ. Psychol. 6:49–63

Smith, S. 1987. Fear of crime: beyond a geography of deviance. Prog. Hum. Geogr. 11: 1–23

Spencer, C., Blades, M. 1985. Children at risk: Are we underestimating their general environmental competence whilst overestimating their performance? See Garling & Valsiner 1985, pp. 39–50

Stern, P, C., Oskamp, S. 1987. Managing scarce environmental resources. See Stokols & Altman 1987, 2:1043–88

Stokols, D. 1989. Instrumental and spiritual views of people-environment relations. Am. Psychol. In press

Stokols, D. 1988. Transformational processes in people-environment relations. See McGrath 1988, pp. 233–54

Stokols, D. 1987. Conceptual strategies of environmental psychology. See Stokols & Altman 1:40–70

Stokols, D., Altman, I., eds. 1987. Handbook of Environmental Psychology, Vols. 1, 2. New York: Wiley. 887 pp., 1654 pp.

Stokols, D., Martin, J., Scharf, T., Churchman, A., Quinn, B., Wright, S., Seifert, M., McMahan, S., Sundstrom, E. 1988. Facilities design, employee productivity and organizational effectiveness. Int. Facil. Manage. Assoc. J. Winter:16–19

Sundstrom, E. 1987. Work environments: offices and factories. See Stokols & Altman 1987, 1:733–82

Sundstrom, E. 1986. Workplaces: The Psychology of the Physical Environment in Offices and Factories. New York: Cambridge Univ. Press. 461 pp.

Svenson, O., Fischhoff, B. 1985. Levels of environmental decisions. J. Environ. Psychol. 5:55–67

Svensson-Garling, A., Garling, T., Valsiner, J. 1985. Parents' knowledge of children's competence, perceptions of risk and causes of child accidents, and residential satisfaction. See Garling & Valsiner 1985, pp. 65–90

Talbot, J. F., Bardwell, L. V., Kaplan, R. 1987. The functions of urban nature: uses and values of different types of urban nature settings. J. Arch. Plan. Res. 4:47–63

Taylor, D. C. 1989. Blacks and the environment: toward an explanation of the concern and action gap between blacks and whites. Environ. Behav. 21:175–205

Taylor, J. G., Stewart, T. R., Downton, M. 1988. Perceptions of drought in the Ogallala Aquifer region. Environ. Behav. 20:150–75

Taylor, R. 1987. Toward an environmental psychology of disorder. See Stokols & Altman 1987, 1:951–86

Taylor, R., Shumaker, S., Gottfredson, S. 1985. Neighborhood-level links between physical features and local sentiments: deterioration, fear of crime, and confidence. J. Arch. Plan. Res. 2:261–75

Thrift, N. 1983. On the determination of social action in space and time. Environ. Plan.: Pt. D, Space Soc. 1:23–57

Thrift, N. 1977. Time and theory in human geography: part II. Prog. Hum. Geogr. 1:413–57

Ulrich, R. S. 1984. Views through a window may influence recovery from surgery. Science 224:420–21

Valsiner, J. 1985. Theoretical issues of child development and the problem of accident prevention. See Garling & Valsiner 1985, pp. 13–36

Valsiner, J., Mackie, C. 1985. Toddlers at home: canalization of climbing skills through culturally organized physical environments. See Garling & Valsiner 1985, pp. 165–92

van der Pligt, J., Eiser, J. R., Spears, R. 1986. Attitudes toward nuclear energy: familiarity and salience. *Environ. Behav.* 18:75–94

van Vliet, W., ed. 1988. *Women, Housing and Community.* Brookfield, VT: Avebury. 204 pp.

Ventriss, C. 1987. Critical issues of participatory decision making in the planning process: a reexamination. *J. Arch. Plan. Res.* 4:289–300

Verderber, S. 1986. Dimensions of person-window transactions in the hospital environment. *Environ. Behav.* 18:450–66

Verderber, S., Reuman, D. 1987. Windows, views, and health status in hospital therapeutic environments. *J. Arch. Plan. Res.* 4:120–33

Wapner, S. 1987. A holistic, developmental, systems-oriented environmental psychology: some beginnings. See Stokols and Altman 2:1433–66

Warren, D. 1978. Explorations in neighborhood differentiation. *Sociol. Q.* 19:310–31

Weiss, L., Baum, A. 1987. Physiological aspects of environment-behavior relationships. See Zube & Moore 1987, pp. 221–50

Wekerle, G. 1988. From refuge to service center: neighborhoods that support women. See van Vliet 1988, pp. 7–22

Werner, C., Altman, I., Oxley, D. 1985. Temporal aspects of homes: a transactional perspective. See Altman & Werner 1985, pp. 1–32

Werner, C., Brown, B., Peterson-Lewis, S. 1984. The individuality/community and accessibility/inaccessibility dialectics in Christmas decorations. Abstract in *Proceedings of the 15th Annual Environmental Design Research Association Conference,* ed. D. Duerk, D. Campbell, pp. 282. Washington, DC: Envir. Design Res. Assoc. 344 pp.

Wicker, A. 1987. Behavior settings reconsidered. See Stokols & Altman 1987, 1:613–54

Wicker, A. 1979. *An Introduction to Ecological Psychology.* Monterey, CA: Brooks/Cole. 228 pp.

Wicker, A. W., King, J. C. 1988. Life cycles of behavior settings. See McGrath 1988, pp. 182–200

Windley, P. G., Scheidt, R. J. 1982. An ecological model of mental health among small-town elderly. *J. Gerontol.* 37:235–42

Winkel, G. H. 1987. Implications of environmental context for validity assessments. See Stokols & Altman 1987, 1:71–98

Winkel, G. H., Holahan, C. J. 1985. The environmental psychology of the hospital: Is the cure worse than the illness? In *Beyond the Individual: Environmental Approaches and Prevention,* ed. A. Wandersman, R. Hess, pp. 11–34. New York: Haworth Press. 211 pp.

Zube, E., Moore, G. T., eds. 1987. *Advances in Environment, Behavior, and Design,* Vol. 1. New York: Plenum. 344 pp.

Zube, E. H., Moore, G. T., eds. 1989. *Advances in Environment, Behavior, and Design,* Vol. 2. New York: Plenum. 350 pp.

Annu. Rev. Psychol. 1990. 41:479–523

ATTITUDES AND ATTITUDE CHANGE

Abraham Tesser

Institute for Behavioral Research, University of Georgia, Athens GA 30602

David R. Shaffer

Department of Psychology, University of Georgia, Athens, GA 30602

CONTENTS

INTRODUCTION

According to McGuire (1986), the study of attitudes held hegemony in social psychology both in the 1920s and 1930s and in the 1950s and 1960s, has dominated the 1980s, and will continue to dominate social psychology into the 1990s. Previous eras of attitude research focused on measurement issues (e.g. Bogardus 1925; Thurstone & Chave 1929; Likert 1932) and attitude

479

0066-4308/90/0201-0479$02.00

change issues (e.g. Hovland et al 1953; Rosenberg et al 1960; Festinger 1957). According to McGuire, the recent thrust is concerned with attitude structure.

We reviewed the literature on attitudes and attitude change from January, 1986 through December, 1988 and were overwhelmed by the volume of relevant materials. In order to conserve time and space we were selective in the papers we cited and did not review research on the role of affect in attitude-change processes, an emerging part of the current zeitgeist. We found that McGuire (1986) was right: Attitude research is flourishing and attitude structure is an important topic. Attitude function and motivational themes have also become more important (Pratkanis et al 1989).

ATTITUDE STRUCTURE

Below we review what has become of the traditional definition of attitudes in terms of affect, cognition, and behavior. Although we later discuss the relationships among these aspects of functioning, we concentrate here on attitudes as if they were structures in memory. We examine the complexity and content of these structures and then look at values and the vertical structure of attitude.

Trashing the Tripartite Definition of Attitudes

McGuire (1969, 1985, 1989) has suggested that viewing behavior in terms of its cognitive, affective, and conative facets can be traced to antiquity. Contemporary attitude texts (e.g. Eiser 1986; Mueller 1986; Rajecki 1983) and researchers (e.g. Breckler 1984) have also used the tripartite division to characterize attitudes; and much contemporary attitude research activity concerns the relationships between thoughts and feelings (e.g. Millar & Tesser 1986a), between thoughts and behavior (e.g. Wilson & Dunn 1986), and between feelings and behavior (e.g. Isen 1987). There is also evidence for the convergent and discriminant validity of the tripartite model of attitudes (e.g. Breckler 1984).

Why, then, have a number of current workers (e.g. Cacioppo et al 1989; Eagly & Chaiken, in preparation; Fazio 1989; Greenwald 1989a; Zanna & Rempel 1988) raised questions about the tripartite definition? One reason is that researchers rarely if ever operationalize attitudes in terms of the tripartite definition or relate these multidimensional structures to something else, such as personality or developmental circumstances (e.g. Smith et al 1956). In most instances, the relationships among the three components are at stake, and investigators believe that the issues should be resolved empirically (or theoretically) rather than definitionally (Zanna & Rempel 1988). Moreover,

Cacioppo et al (1989) point out that support for the tripartite view (e.g. Breckler 1984) may depend upon mapping each of the components onto an evaluative dimension. Although it is unclear how else to go about this, it is clear that almost any attribute can be shown to have evaluative meaning. For example, Cacioppo, et al describe an unpublished study by T. Geen indicating that even dimensions not usually associated with the definition of attitudes (e.g. "activity" or "potency") can be shown to be related to evaluation when subjects are asked to scale the favorability of these dimensions for a particular object.

What are the alternatives to the tripartite definition? McGuire (1985, 1989) suggests that attitudes be defined as projection(s) on any dimension(s) of variability of interest to the investigator. However, the most popular alternative is an unidimensional definition of attitude in which an evaluation is central (e.g. Eagly & Chaiken, in preparation; Fazio 1989; Greenwald 1989b; Kruglanski 1989; Petty & Cacioppo 1986; Pratkanis 1989; Zanna & Rempel 1988). Fazio (1989), for example, argues that attitudes be defined as evaluative responses that serve a knowledge function. Zanna & Rempel (1988), in a most cogent discussion, suggest that attitudes are evaluations based on beliefs, feelings, and/or past behavior, implying that one may have different attitudes about (evaluations of) the same object at the same time (see also Millar & Tesser 1986b). If one's thoughts, feelings, or past behaviors are not evaluatively consistent and the basis for an attitude changes from one facet to another (or if one facet or another is made salient), then the evaluation of (attitude about) the object will change (Millar & Tesser 1989).

Zanna & Rempel (1988) distinguish between evaluation (the attitude) and affect. Unlike some workers (e.g. Ajzen 1985; Zajonc & Markus 1982), Zanna & Rempel restrict affect to experienced feelings or emotions, evaluation to pro-con cognitive categorization. When Breckler & Wiggins (1989a) examined the convergent and discriminant validity of a variety of self-report instruments measuring affect and evaluation they found a positive correlation among these indexes, the magnitude of which depended on the attitude domain. Controversial domains, for which the issues tend to be discussed and/or thought about more often (e.g. legalized abortion, nuclear weapons), are associated with stronger relationships between affect and evaluation than are less controversial domains (e.g. comprehensive exams). Although indexes of affect and evaluation were each positively related to a global measure of attitude (even when the other was statistically held constant), they were differentially related to behavior, thus showing their discriminant validity.

The distinction between affect and evaluation has implications for the measurement of attitudes. Most measures of attitude involve self-report. As long as affect and evaluation were seen as equivalent, self-report indexes seemed adequate. With the distinction between affect and evaluation has come greater sensitivity to the idea that all aspects of attitudes can be represented in a variety of ways, verbal/propositional representation being only one (Breckler & Wiggins 1989b). Many investigators believe that emotions have physiological components that may or may not be cognitively represented (e.g. Pennebaker 1982; Zajonc 1980) and easily or accurately available to self-report. At the same time, physiological measures are becoming more sophisticated and more informative regarding positive or negative affective tone than ever before (e.g. Cacioppo et al 1986b; Davidson 1984). Less apparent is the fact that cognitive and behavioral correlates of attitudes can also be represented physiologically and measured using physiological tools (e.g. Cacioppo et al 1989). For example, slight muscle movements around the mouth can reveal certain mental processes (e.g. Cacioppo et al 1984), and changes in pupil dilation can reveal attentional processes (e.g. Beatty 1986). Thus, physiologial measures of all attitudinal facets should become more important. Indeed, the National Science Foundation is currently funding a series of summer institutes to train senior researchers in pyschology in the use and interpretation of psychophysiological methods (Cacioppo 1987).

Attitudes as Associative Networks

A number of workers (e.g. Breckler & Wiggins 1989b; Fazio 1989; Pratkanis 1989; Judd & Krosnick 1989) have suggested that attitudes are representations in memory. This perspective, which draws heavily on recent advances in cognitive psychology, particularly the work on associative networks (e.g. Anderson 1983; Bower 1981), suggests that beliefs and feelings are associatively connected—both within attitudes and between attitudes. Through a process of "spreading activation," the activation of any element will "prime" or make it easier to elicit other elements (beliefs, feelings) to which it is connected.

In a creative and influential program of research, Fazio and his colleagues (see Fazio 1989) have shown how the strength of within-attitude association (i.e. between the attitude object and its evaluation) can be consequential. Attitude strength (measured by the speed with which a representation of the attitude object can elicit evaluation) is positively associated with both automaticity (e.g. Fazio et al 1986) and the predictability of behavior (e.g. Fazio 1986; Fazio & Williams 1986).

A nice illustration of the spreading activation approach in terms of between-attitude structures is presented by C. M. Judd, R. A. Drake, J. W. Downing, and J. A. Krosnick et al (1989 unpublished, Study 1). They predicted that responding to one attitude issue (e.g. a nuclear weapons freeze) should prime responses to a related issue (e.g. a nuclear test ban) more than to an unrelated issue (e.g. the right to an abortion). Indeed, response time to a second, related issue was faster than to an unrelated issue. This effect increased with the extremity of the initial attitude but not with the extremity of the primed (second) attitude. Also, consistent with the spreading activation hypothesis, Judd et al (unpublished, Studies 2 & 3) showed that asking questions (i.e. thought) about one issue tends to polarize attitudes (Tesser 1978) on a related issue but not on an unrelated issue. Finally, R. Tourangeau, K. Rasinski, and R. D'Andrade (unpublished) have looked at prime and target issues in terms of their similarity regarding topics and similarity regarding placement on a pro-con dimension. They found that spreading activation depends on "topical" similarity of the prime and the target (e.g. women's rights is closer to abortion than to welfare) rather than on the similarity of the prime and the target on a pro-con dimension.

Tourangeau & Rasinski (1988) further elaborated the implications of the associative network approach to context effects in attitude surveys. They suggested that attitudinal responses are the result of a four-stage process (see also Strack & Martin 1987), each stage of which can be affected by context: As in a conversation, context can affect *interpretation* regarding which attitude is relevant (Tourangeau et al 1989a), beliefs and feelings related to the context are more likely to be *retrieved* from memory (Tourangeau et al 1989b); attitude *judgments* may be assimilated or contrasted to the context (e.g. Martin 1986; Strack et al 1985); and the context may have an effect on the *response* selected.

Tourangeau & Rasinski's ideas (1988) suggest some interesting research. For example, if different contexts produce different attitudes solely by priming material already in memory, then persons without the appropriate material in memory will not show such effects. Also, if all the relevant material in memory is on one side of an issue different contexts will prime the same evaluation and again there will appear to be no effect. Together these implications lead to the prediction that persons for whom an area is important (so that they have the relevant beliefs in memory) and whose feelings are conflicted (so that both sides of the issue are represented) should show the largest context effects. In a telephone survey concerning a variety of current political issues, Tourangeau et al (1989a) confirmed this prediction.

STRUCTURAL PARAMETERS   A number of variables affect attitude structure, and structure in turn affects the way attitudes function. For example, attitudes about controversial issues (Pratkanis 1989) or attitudes held by persons who are activists (Eagly & Chaiken, in preparation) are more likely to have a bipolar than a unipolar representation. (A bipolar structure is one in which knowledge both for and against the individual's own position is represented, whereas only supporting knowledge is represented in a unipolar structure.)

Knowledge and the learning of attitude relevant material is more highly correlated with one's attitude for unipolar structures than bipolar structures (Pratkanis 1989).

The complexity of cognitive structures may affect attitude extremity. Broadly speaking, complexity has been measured in two ways: The Schroder et al school (e.g. Schroder et al 1967; Suedfeld & Tetlock 1977; Suedfeld & Bluck 1988) employs open-ended, subject-written statements, coding these for the presence and absence of cognitive differentiation and integration. The psychometric school (e.g. Judd & Lusk 1984; Linville 1982, 1985; Millar & Tesser 1986a) tends to use subject sorts and ratings as data, estimating integration (consistency) by means of intercorrelations among beliefs and estimating differentiation by means of information theory statistics (e.g. Scott 1969). The different approaches tend to yield different results. We focus first on the psychometric approach.

Greater complexity has sometimes been associated with more moderate attitudes (e.g. Linville 1982) and sometimes with more extreme attitudes (e.g. Chaiken & Yates 1985; Tesser & Leone 1977). Seeking to resolve the inconsistency, Judd & Lusk (1984) have provided evidence for the suggestion that the internal evaluative consistency of beliefs in a structure moderates the relationship between complexity (number of dimensions) and extremity: With high evaluative consistency greater complexity will lead to more extreme attitudes; with low evaluative consistency greater complexity will lead to more moderate attitudes.

In the political arena, experts tend to have well-developed (i.e. internally consistent) cognitive structures for thinking about the issues (e.g. Kinder & Sears 1985; Converse 1964, 1970). The usual measures of structure, however, are based on between-subject correlations, and such correlations need not reflect any particular individual's structure (Judd & Krosnick 1989). Recently, in a study of attitudes toward political candidates, Lusk & Judd (1988) examined the relationships among political expertise, structure measured on a within-subject basis, and attitude extremity. Consistent with the between-subject analyses, they found that experts had more knowledge of the candidates and that experts' knowledge was more evaluatively consistent. Moreover, experts evaluated the candidates more extremely than non-experts. The differences in extremity appeared to be at least partially mediated by the complexity of the representational cognitive structures. Using a sophisticated structural equation modeling approach, Sidanius (1988) examined the relationships among thought ("cognitive orientation"), complexity of cognitive structures ("political sophistication"), and attitude extremity ("political deviance"). His data was consistent with a model in which thought increased complexity (see also Milburn 1987; Millar & Tesser 1986a, Study 4), and complexity produced extreme attitudes. (He did not test the hypothesis that thought and complexity interact in producing extreme attitudes.)

Using different materials and an experimental design that varied subjects' opportunity for relevant thought, Millar & Tesser (1986a) also found that thought affected attitudes in a way consistent with the Judd & Lusk hypothesis. A couple of recent individual difference studies are also consistent. It could be argued that high dogmatic (Rokeach 1960) or low need-for-cognition individuals (Cacioppo & Petty 1984) have more evaluatively consistent structures than do low dogmatic or high need-for-cognition individuals. Thus, we would expect, and Leone has found, that thought results in greater polarization of attitudes for high than for low dogmatics (Leone & Ensley 1986) and for low than high need-for-cognition subjects (Leone 1989).

Millar & Tesser (1986a) reported evidence that motivation interacts with structure to affect polarization of attitudes. When the individual was committed to a particular attitude direction (e.g. pro vs con) then a complex structure with a large number of beliefs facilitated thought-related attitude polarization. On the other hand, when there was no motivational bias due to commitment, then the larger the set of beliefs the less the thought-related polarization.

The Schroder et al (1967) school predicts that moderate attitudes will be associated with more complex structures while extreme attitudes will correlate with less complex structures. For example, Tetlock (1984) found greater integrative complexity among moderate than among extreme socialists and conservatives, although the inflection point of maximum complexity tends to be slightly left of center. DeVries & Walker (1987) found greater complexity among persons with neutral attitudes about capital punishment than among persons who favored or opposed it.

To summarize, the psychometric school tends to find both positive and negative relationships between integrative complexity of structure and attitude extremity; the Schroder et al (1967) group tend to find a negative relationship between integrative complexity and extremity. Why? The explanation may lie in a difference between the kinds of issues the two groups study. According to Tetlock's (e.g. 1984, 1986, 1989) value pluralism model, different positions on an attitude continuum are likely to satisfy different important, terminal values (Rokeach 1973, 1979). Sometimes those values, for a particular issue, are in conflict (see also Billig et al 1988). For example, attitudes toward logging operations in a national forest may bring into conflict the values of wanting to protect the environment and wanting to maintain economic growth. Coming to grips with these conflicting values is reflected in a complex cognitive structure and a more moderate stance on the issue. On the other hand, there are some attitude issues for which conflicting values are not so clearly associated with particular positions—e.g. attitudes toward particular football plays (Tesser & Leone 1977) or attitudes toward the self (e.g. Linville 1985). Perhaps the Schroder group is more likely to study attitudes with conflicting values than the psychometric group the latter. Sidanius (1988) suggests that complexity may be negatively related to ego-defensiveness; ego-defensiveness is positively related to extremity on issues (such as racism) that serve an ego-defensive function. Perhaps, then, the Schroder group is more likely to study attitudes that serve an ego-defensive function.

Our own money is not on such issue-selection explanations of the difference in outcomes. Our guess is that the two approaches measure different phenomena. There may be relatively little correlation among various measures of cognitive complexity (e.g. Vannoy 1965). The psychometric group and the Schroder group seem to agree that greater complexity is associated with greater differentiation and greater integration. There also appears to be some agreement on differentiation—it is, roughly speaking, the number of relevant belief dimensions. The crucial difference is in what is meant by integration. For the psychometric group integration is some kind of consistency (usually evaluative), detected by the correlation among elements in the structure (e.g. Judd & Lusk 1984). For the Schroder group, integration is the extent to which an individual recognizes and incorporates the implications of evaluatively diverse elements in his/her view of the attitude object. Thus, a larger number of consistent elements (psychometric integration) will lead to a more extreme attitude while a larger number of incorporated but not necessarily evaluatively consistent elements (Schroder integration) will lead to a more moderate attitude.

IDEOLOGY: THE CONTENT OF BELIEF SYSTEMS   So far our discussion of the structure of attitudes has been abstract. We have dealt with how associative networks work without discussing their content. Belief systems are larger structures that link attitudes with one another. Although most contemporary American social psychologists focus on the individual (e.g. Dweck & Leggett 1988; Ross 1989), shared (or group) beliefs are also consequential (e.g. Bar-Tal 1986, 1989). A number of researchers, particularly Western Europeans (e.g. Emler 1987; Farr & Moscovici 1984; Furnham 1988; Jaspars 1983; Mugny & Catugati 1989), have begun to spell out the content of belief networks in a large number of knowledge domains.

Furnham (1988) provides a beautiful review of lay or implicit theories in the social sciences. These theories held by nonscientists about their social world tend to be content based and concrete. Most of us are familiar with implicit personality theories (e.g. Rosenberg & Sedlak 1972). Furnham reviews the content of theories that deal with human nature (e.g. Wrightsman

1974), psychology (e.g. Houston 1985; Sternberg 1985), psychiatry (e.g. Nunally 1961; Rippere 1981), medicine (Pendleton 1983), economics (e.g. Furnham & Lewis 1986), statistics (Kunda & Nisbett 1985), law (e.g. Hough & Mayhew 1985; Nicholson & Lucas 1984), and education (Emler et al 1987; Nicholls et al 1985). There is also work on persons as implicit physics theorists (e.g. Kaiser et al 1986). The studies of Davis (e.g. Davis & Todd 1982), the Hendricks (e.g. Hendrick & Hendrick 1987), Shaver (e.g. Hazan & Shaver 1987), and Sternberg (e.g. Sternberg & Grajek 1984) provide insights into implicit theories of love. Work continues on the content of beliefs about such social issues as abortion and welfare (e.g. Tourangeau et al 1989a,b).

In most cases, the mapping of a belief domain is a relatively straightforward task: One either asks respondents to indicate the extent to which they believe various assertions about the domain or analyzes the content of answers to open-ended questions about the domain. But not all domains are tractable. For example, such straightforward procedures make it appear that racial stereotypes are fading (e.g. Campbell 1971; Karlins et al 1969; Pettigrew 1988), while different approaches developed more recently are not quite so sanguine. According to Sears & Kinder (e.g. Kinder & Sears 1985; Sears & Kinder 1985), racial attitudes now manifest themselves not in traditional stereotypes but in symbolic racism, based on anti-black feeling coupled with traditional values such as individualism. Although the notion of symbolic racism is controversial (Eagley & Chaiken, in preparation), its manifest content includes "antagonism toward blacks' 'pushing too hard' and moving too fast . . . and resentment toward special favors for blacks, such as in 'reverse discrimination' . . . (Sears 1988:56).

The cognitive approach suggests, however, that even the more traditional stereotypes may still be present. In order to test hypotheses about how associative networks function (an unknown), investigators work with beliefs with a known (assumed) level of association (e.g. C. Judd, R. Drake, J. Downing, and J. Krosnick, unpublished). It is possible to turn this process on its head. We can assume that we know how the associative system works in order to test hypotheses about how closely beliefs are associated (e.g. how closely stereotypic beliefs are associated with racial categories). Using such a strategy in exciting research, Dovidio (e.g. Dovidio et al 1986; Dovidio & Gaertner 1986) and DeVine (1989a,b) have shown a lingering and automatic presence of racial stereotypes beyond what the checklist data suggest.

If racial stereotypes are less amenable to straightforward mapping than other beliefs, why is this the case? Perhaps it is because such stereotypes are socially undesirable (e.g. Sigall & Page 1971). Indeed, Katz (e.g. Katz et al 1986) has interpreted "amplification" of attitudes toward blacks as indicating ambivalence caused by harboring racist feelings while at the same time believing it is wrong to have such feelings. Others (e.g. Adorno et al 1950; Sidanius 1988) have suggested that racial beliefs are different from other beliefs because they serve an ego-defensive function. On the other hand, there is no evidence that other belief domains would not also produce discrepant results. They simply have not come under such close scrutiny.

Even beliefs about things or events that do not exist may affect attitudes. Recently, Kahneman & Miller (1986) have creatively and convincingly argued that subjunctive worlds—worlds that might have been, or what they call *counterfactuals*—can affect emotions and evaluations. (see also Markus & Nurius 1986). Imagined outcomes can affect emotional responses to events, compensation of victims in lawsuits (Miller & McFarland 1986), the locus of causality (Wells & Gavanski 1989), and even the ability to cope with an event (Taylor & Schneider 1989). The roles of normality-exceptionality (Gavanski & Wells 1989) and of attractiveness of victims (Gleicher et al 1989) in constructing counterfactuals are currently being investigated. Interest has increased in the determinants and content of ruminative processes (e.g. Martin & Tesser 1989; Klinger 1987), their temporal extent (e.g. Silver et al 1983), avoidance of them (Wegner et al 1987; Wenzlaff et al 1988), and their role in coping (e.g. Janoff-Bulman 1989; Thompson & Janigian 1988).

Values and the Vertical Structure of Attitudes

Values refer to preferred end states (e.g. terminal values such as freedom, equality) and preferred ways of doing things (i.e. instrumental values such as being honest or ambitious; e.g. Rokeach 1985). [Related concepts such as the imago (McAdams 1988), the life task (Cantor et al 1987), the personal project (Little 1987), the current concern (Klinger 1987), and the personal striving (Emmons 1989) are beginning to emerge and achieve some importance in personality theory.] One's commitment to values, particularly central values, seems to increase in the face of adversity (Lydon & Zanna 1988).

Because of the breadth of the value construct, attitudes and behavior are sometimes thought to be caused by them. Indeed, Rokeach has provided evidence in a variety of studies that the relative importance of the terminal value of equality (i.e. the value's rank among others for an individual) is related to racial attitudes and behavior (e.g. Rokeach 1985). A single television production based on this research, "The Great American Values Test," increased the relative importance of equality as a value. It also resulted in more positive attitudes toward and greater contributions of money to anti-racist and anti-sexist groups two to three months after the show among uninterrupted viewers (Ball-Rokeach et al 1984; Rokeach & Ball-Rokeach 1988). More recently, Prentice (1987) demonstrated that compared to persons with instrumental values (e.g. ambition), persons with symbolic values (e.g. a world at peace) were more likely to list favorite possessions that were symbolic (e.g. family heirlooms) rather than instrumental (e.g. computers) and to favor symbolic over instrumental attitude appeals. Using a structural equation modelling approach, Homer & Kahle (1988) found evidence consistent with the idea that values are antecedents of attitudes (and behaviors) toward natural foods.

Some of the more interesting work on values concerns the consequences of value conflict. As noted above, Tetlock (1986, 1989) suggests that when particular issues have contradictory implications for values the result is a more complex belief structure. Billig et al (1988) suggest that most everyday thinking is the result of ideological (value) dilemmas—e.g. for teachers and experts it is the dialectic between equality and authority. Katz & Haas (1988) suggest that the conflict between the values of communalism and individualism generates ambivalence in racial attitudes and can result in polarized attitudes.

ATTITUDES AS PREDICTORS OF BEHAVIOR

The Rational Actor

Fishbein & Ajzen's (1975; Ajzen & Fishbein 1980) theory of personal action continues to attract attention. This model assumes that the best predictor of behavior is intention. Behavioral intentions, in turn, are said to be a function of one's attitude toward the behavior and one's subjective norms. (A subjective norm is a cognitive representation of the extent to which significant others think one should enact the behavior.) Theoretically, behavioral intentions represent a weighted sum of these two predictors, although one or the other may be the more salient depending either on the situation (e.g. Budd 1986) or on dispositional variables such as self-monitoring (cf Miller & Grush 1986). Some have argued that interactive models predict behavior and behavioral intentions better than does Fishbein & Ajzen's summative model (e.g. Rabow et al 1987), but on the whole, the theory predicts behavior fairly well. In a meta-analytic review including 85 estimates, Sheppard et al (1988) calculated a mean R=.67, and successes with the model continue to appear in sizable numbers (e.g. Vinokur & Caplan 1987). (See Eagley & Chaiken, in preparation, for a wonderful description and review of the strengths and weaknesses of the Fishbein & Ajzen approach.)

The model has recently been expanded by Ajzen (1985; Ajzen & Madden 1986) to include perceived behavioral control, a variable similar to Bandura's notion of self-efficacy (e.g. Bandura 1986; Maddux & Stanley 1986). The control predictor has been added to broaden the scope of the theory beyond volitional acts and is hypothesized to affect behavior both directly and indirectly, through behavioral intentions. (The name of the model has been changed to the "theory of planned behavior" to register this addition.) In a preliminary study, Ajzen & Timko (1986) found that specific health behaviors correlated well with both specific attitudes and perceived control. Moreover, Ajzen & Madden (1986) found they could more accurately predict both (a) behavioral intentions concerning class attendance and "getting an A" and (b) the behavior "getting an A" by using the perceived behavioral control variable.

Adding variables similar to perceived control—e.g. locus of control, self-efficacy, or self-confidence—contributes to the accurate prediction of (a) behavioral intentions concerning dental hygiene (McCaul et al 1988) and (b) both intentions and behaviors concerning alcohol use (Schlegel et al 1987) and breast self-examination (Ronis & Kaiser 1989). Following up on Liska's (1984) objection to the restrictiveness of focusing only on volitional behaviors, Ritter (1988) found that a nonvolitional predictor, perceived availability of drugs (resources), was related to drug usage over a 10-year period. Coming from a background in "protection motivation" theory (e.g. Rogers 1983; Maddux & Rogers 1983), Maddux et al (1986) attempted to manipulate self-efficacy expectancy, outcome expectancy, and outcome value. Although there were some problems with the experimental manipulations, all three variables correlated significantly and about equally well with behavioral intentions. From a similar perspective, Wurtele (1988) found that health-related behavioral intentions were affected by manipulations of vulnerability and (with marginal significance) self-efficacy. Another variable that seems to operate the way perceived control does is commitment (e.g. Rusbult & Farrell 1983). Koslowsky et al (1988) have found that commitment to musical activities, by itself and in interaction with behavioral intentions, enhanced prediction of music-related behavior above what was obtained using behavioral intentions alone. Although not all attempts to use perceived control to predict behavior or behavioral intentions have met with success (e.g. Fishbein & Stasson 1989), it appears to have been a useful addition.

Fishbein & Ajzen (Ajzen & Fishbein 1980; see also, Abelson & Levi 1985; Jaccard & Becker 1985) suggest that prediction is best when one takes into account not only the target behavior (e.g. smoking) but the alternative as well (e.g. not smoking). Indeed, Kendzierski & Lamastro (1988) found that attitudes toward *not* lifting weights was a better predictor of number of days lifting weights than attitudes toward weight lifting. Jaccard et al (1989) found that neither attitudes toward diaphragm use nor attitudes toward getting pregnant predicted consistent diaphragm use. However, when the *difference* between these attitudes was used as a predictor, there did appear to be a threshold over which 90% of the women showed consistent diaphragm use. In the political realm, Fishbein et al (1989) were able to predict voting and candidate choice better from a relative measure of behavioral intentions—one that included both preferred candidate and intention *not* to vote—than from a single behavioral intention (although the significance of the difference was not reported).

The model is subject to the perennial methodological concerns about self-report (e.g. Warshaw et al 1986). Hessing et al (1988) found that attitudes and subjective norms correlated with self-reported tax evasion behavior but not with officially documented behavior. (Broad personality dispositions such as alienation and competitiveness correlated with the latter but not the former.) Feldman & Lynch (1988), arguing from a social cognition perspective, contend that measuring beliefs, attitudes, intentions, and behavior can (a) create these variables where they do not exist in long-term memory or (b) affect their intercorrelations where these variables do exist in long term memory. Some empirical evidence indicates the validity of such concerns. Persons appear to "know" the rules embedded in the theory of reasoned action, and such knowledge enables subjects to alter their responses to please the experimenter (Budd & Spencer 1986). Further, measures of the model's variables are usually juxtaposed, an order that makes the theoretical expectations of the model more visible than would a random order. Indeed, Budd (1987) found significantly better support for the reasoned action model with the usual contiguous order than with the random order.

The structure of the reasoned action model has also been examined. The beliefs (b_i) and evaluations (e_i) presumed to underlie attitudes (A_o) in the model typically use bipolar scaling, i.e. -3 to $+3$, and are combined multiplicatively. Hewstone & Young (1988) report that unipolar scaling (i.e. 1 to 7) and adding rather than multiplying beliefs and evaluations sometimes produces significantly better correlations with overall attitudes. Burnkrant & Page (1988) focused on the normative component of the model and found evidence that a multidimensional representation (in terms of referent other persons and the separation of normative rewards and punishments) provided a significantly better fit than the theory's unidimensional representation.

The Fishbein & Ajzen model has been extremely fruitful. We suspect that the theory will undergo even further refinement and will remain an influential approach for years to come.

The Nonrational Actor

Much recent research relating attitudes to behavior assumes that the actor does not rationally consider alternatives in order to decide on the best course of action. Instead people often behave on the basis of automatically activated attitudes or on the basis of how information is "framed." Indeed, when people are encouraged to think about their attitudes, the relationship between attitudes and behavior may diminish.

Ronis et al (1989) suggest that attitudes may sometimes be irrelevant in guiding behaviors. Working in the health area, they suggest that repeated behaviors such as smoking become habitual/automatic (see also Triandis 1980) and that such behaviors may become divorced from the attitudes to which they are logically related or which may have been important in their initiation (e.g. Dishman 1982). It is only when the individual encounters novelty or adversity in his behavior that he switches to a decision-making mode where attitudes (and self-efficacy) determine behavior. Mittal (1988) defines habit in terms of non-awareness and shows that both pro- and anti-intentional habits are significantly related to seat-belt use even after the effects of attitude are taken into account.

A nice set of studies by Fazio and associates (cf Fazio 1986, 1989) illustrates how attitudes may guide behavior, even when those attitudes are not thoughtfully applied. According to Fazio, highly accessible attitudes (i.e. those the respondent can provide with a short latency) are activated automatically (e.g. Shiffrin & Schneider 1977) in the presence of the attitude object (e.g. Fazio et al 1986). The affective responses associated with these highly accessible attitudes then color one's interpretation of the situation and the responses it calls for (e.g. Fazio & Williams 1986; Fazio & Houston, reported in Fazio 1989); hence, accessible attitudes do indeed guide behavior without the individual's intending them or being aware of their influence (Fazio, Powell & Williams, described in Fazio 1989; Fazio & Williams 1986; Kallgren & Wood 1986).

The way choices are framed can also be consequential for behavior. According to prospect theory (e.g. Kahneman & Tversky 1984), persons shun risk when considering possible gains and seek risk when dealing with possible losses. Thus, framing exactly the same risky behavioral choice in terms of a gain is less likely to elicit the behavior than is framing it in terms of a loss, even though the consequences are logically identical. For example, breast self-examination (BSE) is risky: One might detect cancer. Meyerowitz & Chaiken (1987) found a greater increase in positive BSE attitudes, intentions, and behaviors as a result of a negative appeal (you may lose if you neglect BSE) than as a result of a positive appeal (you may gain from BSE). Quattrone & Tversky (1988) found that similar differences in the framing of contests between political candidates and policy options led to similar lapses in rationality in voting behavior.

One of the most exciting research programs showing the "nonrational" connection between attitudes and behavior is Timothy Wilson's work on "reasons analysis." Wilson and his colleagues have shown in a variety of domains that having persons list their reasons for holding their attitudes actually reduces the correlation between attitudes and behaviors (e.g. Wilson et al 1984, 1989). This "reasons" effect is (a) not present if subjects focus on affect (Wilson & Dunn 1986); (b) more evident among low than among high self-monitors; and (c) more evident for low than for high knowledge domains (Wilson & Kraft 1989). Wilson suggests that persons often lack a well-developed set of conscious reasons for their attitudes. Therefore, when urged to provide reasons for their attitudes subjects generate material that does not represent the actual cognitive content of these attitudes. The immediate attitude measure thus captures this salient but unrepresentative cognitive material, which is not reflected in subsequent behavior. Hence, the correlation between attitudes and behavior is reduced.

Millar & Tesser (1986) build on this explanation by suggesting that self-reported attitudes are influenced by whatever information happens to be salient at the time of assessment. In Wilson's research, the instructions subjects received made cognitive aspects of attitude objects particularly salient. However, affective reactions to attitude objects could color self-reports just as easily if this information were more salient when attitudes are measured. Millar & Tesser recognize that a given behavior may have various functions: An act may serve primarily affective goals (i.e. may involve "consummatory" responses, such as playing with puzzles for entertainment) or primarily cognitive objectives (i.e. may involve "instrumental" responses, such as playing with puzzles to improve analytical ability). Thus, focus manipulation should attenuate the correlation between attitude and behavior only if there is a mismatch between what the focus manipulation makes salient (affect vs cognition) at attitude assessment and the objective of the behavior (consummatory vs instrumental) that one hopes to predict. If the affective and cognitive components of the attitude are consistent, then focusing on either component will yield the same behavior prediction and no difference between a match and a mismatch; therefore, (2) such mismatch effects should be more pronounced among subjects displaying less affective-cognitive consistency toward the attitude object. Both of these predictions have now received support (Millar & Tesser 1986a, 1989). To us this research suggests that behaviors may be no less differentiated than attitudes and that attention to what drives behavior may be just as important as which aspect of attitudes is being measured.

The Wilson-Millar/Tesser research indicates certain conditions under which forcing people to be analytical can uncouple attitudes and behavior. Obviously, this is not always the case. For example, values often guide behavior (Homer & Kahle 1988), and making one's own values salient and comparing them to the values of liked or disliked reference groups often results in lasting and desirable behavioral change (Rokeach 1973; Schwartz & Inbar-Saban 1988). Further, Langer (1989) suggests that although much behavior is mindless, mindfulness (i.e. conscious attention to one's actions) is *not* more effortful and may even enhance one's health; manipulations of mindfulness have been associated with increased longevity (Alexander et al

1989) and enhanced immune function (Jasnowski & Langer 1986, cited in Langer 1989).

Effects of Behavior on Attitudes

Understanding of induced-compliance effects (i.e. attitude change resulting from behaviors that individuals are persuaded or otherwise prevailed upon to enact) has steadily progressed over the past three years. Much of this progress stems, we believe, from more precise specifications of the personal/ situational moderators of three mechanisms presumed to underlie induced-compliance phenomena: self-perception processes (Bem 1972), dissonance reduction (Festinger 1957), and impression management/self-presentational concerns (e.g. Baumeister 1982; Schlenker 1987; Tedeschi 1981).

SELF-PERCEPTION PROCESSES   Additional support has emerged for the proposition (Fazio et al 1977) that self-perception processes mediate attitude change when behaviors fall within one's "latitude of acceptance," while dissonance reduction accounts for change induced by behaviors outside that latitude (Jones et al 1981; Rhodewalt & Agustsdottir 1986). However, the results of at least one recent study (B. R. Schlenker and J. V. Trudeau, unpublished) imply that this elegant resolution of the dissonance/self-perception controversy may apply only to individuals whose target beliefs are relatively strong. Participants with weak initial attitudes show induced-compliance effects more reflective of self-perception processes, regardless of where their behavior falls on the acceptance-rejection continuum. These findings pose no problem for either theory, however. They are congruent with assertions (e.g. Bem 1972; Fazio 1989) that self-perception processes will predominate when initial opinions are weak or otherwise inaccessible; they are also consistent with the fundamental proposition (Festinger 1957) that behavioral violations of unimportant attitudes create little if any dissonance. (See also Swann et al 1988 for another interesting demonstration that "belief certainty" interacts with the character of induced compliance to affect the extent of behaviorally induced attitude change.)

One noteworthy extension of self-perception theory is Crano's (e.g. Crano & Sivacek 1984; Crano et al 1988) "incentive-aroused ambivalence" interpretation of overjustification effects. According to Crano's model, overjustification of belief-consistent actions creates an ambivalence about these activities that is presumably necessary but not sufficient to promote attitude change (and/or decrements in intrinsic motivation). Recent research (i.e. Crano et al 1988) demonstrates the plausibility of this line of reasoning and points to an incentive-induced "attenuation of consensus" as the basis for one's readiness to change an overjustified initial attitude.

DISSONANCE AND SELF-PRESENTATION CONCERNS   The traditional view of dissonance as an unpleasant arousal that "drives" people to resolve the cognitive inconsistency that created it has come under increasingly intense scrutiny. What is now apparent is that people who freely choose to perform counterattitudinal acts that could have aversive consequences will, indeed, experience heightened physiological arousal (e.g. Croyle & Cooper 1983; Elkin & Leippe 1986). Yet the magnitude of this arousal often fails to forecast subjects' use of such dissonance-reduction strategies as attitude change, and there is some evidence that attitude change often fails to reduce and may even sustain or intensify existing arousal (Elkin & Leippe 1986; Gaes et al 1986). Thus, if dissonance is truly a drive-like state that demands reduction, it seems that reestablishment of cognitive consistency per se may not be the primary objective of those who experience it (cf Beckmann & Gollwitzer 1987; J. L. Cohen and D. L. Moore, unpublished; Dietrich & Berkowitz 1988).

What, then, might this objective be? Radical impression management theories (arguing that counterattitudinal advocates often feign new attitudes to avoid the embarrassment of appearing inconsistent to others: see Tedeschi 1981) have not fared well over the years (Chaiken & Stangor 1987; Rosenfeld et al 1986; Scher & Cooper 1989). However, revisions of dissonance theory that posit self-affirmational objectives (Greenwald & Ronis 1978; Steele & Liu 1983) and self-presentational concerns (Baumeister 1982; Schlenker 1987) as motives for genuine attitude change in induced-compliance settings are having an impact (see, for example, Dietrich & Berkowitz 1988; B. A. Elkin and M. R. Leippe, unpublished). Drawing from Tetlock's work on the psychological implications of accountability (e.g. Tetlock 1983, 1985; Tetlock & Kim 1987), Elkin & Leippe (unpublished) have recently demonstrated that the ways in which counterattitudinal advocates respond to their behaviorally induced arousal depends critically on whether the situation renders them accountable to themselves, to others, or to neither self nor others. Subjects made accountable only to themselves (by immediately responding to an anonymous postbehavioral questionnaire) quickly changed their attitudes as if to "explain" their counterattitudinal behavior and thereby reaffirm a positive (or consistent) self-image. Subjects made accountable to others also changed their attitudes, but only after thinking extensively about the target issue and formulating what appeared to be "publicly defensible" opinions. Finally, "no accountability" participants (who completed a postbehavioral questionnaire only after a lengthy delay) had thought little about the target issue and showed no attitude change. So it seems that dissonant acts induce cognitive change only when they in some way implicate the public or private aspects of self; in the absence of self-implication, passive forgetting of arousal (and the inconsistency that produced it) may be a relatively painless and efficient mode of dissonance reduction (see also Elkin & Leippe 1986).

Finally, compelling evidence has recently emerged against the notion that dissonance represents a master motive for consistency. Specifically, Scher & Cooper (1989) found that subjects who freely chose to perform acts that could produce aversive consequences subsequently experienced discomfort (dissonance) and changed their opinions, regardless of whether these actions were consistent (writing a proattitudinal essay) or inconsistent (writing a counterattitudinal essay) with their original beliefs. By contrast, neither proattitudinal nor counterattitudinal advocates experienced dissonance or changed their opinions if led to believe that their actions were unlikely to have aversive consequences. Not only do these findings challenge the assertion that one's behavior must be discrepant with initial attitudes to arouse dissonance, they also implicate felt responsibility for aversive outcomes as the motivational underpinning of this aversive state (see also Cooper & Fazio 1984).

SOCIAL/NORMATIVE INFLUENCES   Recent attempts to explore the impact of social/normative influences in induced-compliance settings have produced a most interesting outcome: Social support for freely enacted counterattitudinal behaviors attenuates attitude change (Stroebe & Diehl 1988; Zanna & Sande 1987). Zanna & Sande (1987) propose that individuals who have performed counterattitudinal acts alongside others (i.e. their "supporters") experience just as much dissonance as those acting alone. However, the collective nature of their actions permits the former subjects to diffuse responsibility for their conduct, thereby lessening the need for attitude change. By contrast, Stroebe & Diehl (1988) contend that social support merely functions as a consonant cognition (i.e. justification) for the counterattitudinal act, thereby attenuating attitude change by minimizing the amount of dissonance subjects experience. Though more research will be necessary to resolve this issue, preliminary data seems to favor the Stroebe & Diehl model. That is, the kinds of social support/nonsupport that Zanna & Sande think would minimize both diffusion of responsibility and attenuation of attitude change (i.e. co-action by similar/ likable others; noncompliance by dissimilar/unlikable others) are precisely those that seem to decrease subjects' uneasiness (dissonance?) over their counterattitudinal commitments while producing the largest attenuation effects (Stroebe & Diehl 1988).

Interestingly, when subjects have little choice about performing counterattitudinal acts, social support accentuates rather than inhibits attitude change (Kahle & Beatty 1987; Stroebe & Diehl 1988; Zanna & Sande 1987). Perhaps these "low-choice" subjects, who experience little if any dissonance over their induced compliance, simply treat social support as a consensus cue (cf Chaiken et al 1989) that prompts them to reconsider their own positions in the interest of being more accurate or in harmony with their peers. Indeed, the finding that such self-persuasion is more likely to occur when social support emanates from a similar (vs a dissimilar) other (Stroebe & Diehl 1988) is consistent with this line of reasoning.

ATTITUDE FUNCTIONS

As noted in Chaiken & Stangor's (1987) review in this series, the long-dormant functional theories of attitude are making a serious comeback. Although this "motivational" look at the attitude construct has yet to generate an impressive amount of empirical research (Greenwald 1989), the several articles (e.g. DeBono 1987; DeBono & Harnish 1988; Herek 1987a; Prentice 1987), chapters (e.g. Pratkanis & Greenwald 1989; Zanna & Rempel 1988), and the recent volume (Pratkanis et al 1989) that focus extensively on attitude functions clearly demonstrate the importance of this perspective to contemporary attitude theorists.

Conceptual Themes: What Functions Do Attitudes Serve?

Early functional theorists, e.g. Smith (1947), described seven broad and overlapping purposes that might be served by holding an attitude. The *object appraisal* function (Smith et al 1956) implies that attitudes are convenient guidelines for interpreting and categorizing environmental objects and events, and for deciding whether to approach or avoid these stimuli. This conception is a rough synthesis of what Katz (1960) called the *knowledge* and the *utilitarian* (or *instrumental* or *adjustive*) functions of attitudes. The two major functional theories also agreed that one might hold and express attitudes to cope with intrapsychic conflict (Katz's *ego-defensive* function; the *externalization* function of Smith et al 1956). However, the two camps differed about the part attitudes play in self-expression. Smith et al (1956) emphasized the *social adjustive* function, which refers to the role of attitudinal expression in the mediation of self-other relations. By contrast, Katz (1960) stressed a *value-expressive* function, proposing that attitudes are vehicles for expressing internalized values that are important to the self-concept.

Though there are undoubtedly several other purposes that attitudes could serve (cf R. Batra and O. T. Ahtola, unpublished; Shavitt 1989), an emerging consensus, stemming from recent conceptualizations of "attitude" as a symbolic representation of one's *evaluation* of an attitude object (e.g. Fazio 1986; Kruglanski 1989; Zanna & Rempel 1988), is that the primary purpose of holding an attitude is object appraisal (i.e. making evaluative judgments about an attitude object that will have clear behavioral implications; cf Fazio 1989; Greenwald 1989b). Greenwald (1989b) points out that even the so-called symbolic or self-expressive functions are easily interpreted in terms of object appraisal if we note that the attitude object one is appraising is the self, and that the underlying motive (or subfunction) for this appraisal is self-esteem maintenance. While we can accept this analysis as sensible and even appealing in the abstract, lumping all attitude functions (or subfunctions) under an object-appraisal umbrella does, in one sense, distract us from the conceptually intriguing and heuristically fruitful notion that different individuals might hold and express an attitude for very different purposes. Stated another way, the clearest and most readily falsifiable hypotheses to emerge from the functionalist perspective center on individual or situational variation in the functions that attitudes serve. Empirical support (or refutation) of these ideas must focus on such variation.

Operationalizing Attitude Functions

Early attempts to test functional hypotheses were plagued by a lack of unambiguous, objective procedures for assessing and operationalizing attitude functions (see Herek 1987a; Shavitt 1989; Snyder & DeBono 1989). Fortunately, recent adaptations of earlier methods and incorporation of new strategies from personality psychology and social cognition have brightened the measurement picture considerably.

PERSON VARIATIONS   Most recent functional research has continued to rely on the individual difference approach, assuming that variations in the motivational bases of attitudes might be measured directly, from subjects' commentary about their opinions, or indirectly, via personality measures. Two studies by Herek (1987a) illustrate the former strategy. Content analyses of subjects' essays on their views on homosexuality produced evidence for three primary functions that resembled Katz's instrumental, ego-defensive, and value-expressive goals and possessed a fair degree of construct and concurrent validity. Seeking a less cumbersome, more objective assessment device, Herek next constructed an Attitude Functions Inventory (AFI) by writing Likert-type items that represented the major functional themes in his subjects' essays. The instrument was then administered to a new sample to assess the functional bases of attitudes towards homosexuals and toward each of three stigmatizing illnesses (AIDS, cancer, and mental illness). Factor analyses of subjects' responses to the four versions of the AFI and converging personality data offered preliminary support for the existence of the four functions (i.e. instrumental, ego-defensive, value-expressive, and social-adjustive) the AFI purports to measure. Although tested and validated for only one attitudinal domain (stigmatized entities), we concur with Herek that the AFI could easily be reworded to assess the motivational underpinnings of almost any attitude.

Others (e.g. Herek 1987b; Jamieson & Zanna 1989; Prentice 1987; Snyder & DeBono 1989) propose that attitude functions can be operationalized indirectly via any number of personality dispositions (see Chaiken & Stangor 1987 and Shavitt 1989 for listings of such dispositions). Yet the functional significance of most dispositional variables remains unexplored. The notable exception is self-monitoring. Snyder & DeBono (1987, 1989) contend that attitudes of low self-monitors often serve a value-expressive function, whereas those of high self-monitors tend to be more social-adjustive in character. This assertion seems highly plausible from the results of Snyder & DeBono's research (described below), as well as from independent observations that low self-monitors are more likely than high self-monitors to appeal to values when justifying their attitudes (Kristiansen & Zanna 1988), to rely on personal evaluations and to downplay or ignore social-situational norms when making decisions (Jamieson & Zanna 1989), and to prefer attitude/value congruence to social/situational activity preferences when evaluating new acquaintances (Jamieson et al 1987). Yet, this "value-expressive" vs "social-adjustive" scheme may obscure other important differences in the attitude functions of high and low self-monitors, as there are circumstances under which the opinions of low self-monitors are more likely than those of their dimensional opposites to serve utilitarian (Shavitt & Fazio 1987, 1988; Shavitt et al 1988) and knowledge (Jamieson & Zanna 1989) goals as well. Thus, not only are the motivational underpinnings of low self-monitors' attitudes more variable than a value-expressive characterization would imply, but this variation further attests to the utility of the self-monitoring construct as a means of operationalizing attitude functions.

OBJECT VARIATIONS   Though functions served by objects and those served by attitudes toward those objects may not always coincide (cf Greenwald 1989b), both S. Shavitt's (unpublished, 1989) content analyses of subjects' object-relevant cognitive responses and Prentice's (1987; Abelson & Prentice 1989) multidimensional scaling procedures reveal that objects do reliably differ in the attitudinal functions they engage. Moreover, some objects typically serve a single function [e.g. air conditioners a utilitarian function, wedding rings a symbolic (or self-expressive) function], whereas others are more functionally diverse (e.g. automobiles various utilitarian, self-expressive, or social-adjustive functions). One simple strategy for operationalizing attitude functions employs two (or more) objects that serve single but contrasting objectives. By controlling the kinds of such single-function objects that subjects respond to, one can vary attitude functions (Shavitt 1989; see also Abelson & Prentice 1989 for a very different use of the object-variation theme to operationalize attitude functions).

SITUATIONAL VARIATIONS   Just as individuals may differ in the functions their attitudes serve, and attitude objects may be diverse in the functions they typically engage, so may situations vary in the objectives they are likely to evoke (Shavitt 1989; Snyder & DeBono 1989). For example, appeals for opinion accuracy under the cloak of anonymity may facilitate expression of value-based sentiments, whereas interactions with new acquaintances, public expressions of opinion, or the presence of reference group members should heighten social-adjustive concerns. Powerful failure manipulations or other threats to self-esteem should make ego-defensive considerations salient (Crocker et al 1987; Tesser 1988), while pressures for snap judgments or rapid decision-making should engage the knowledge function of attitudes (Jamieson & Zanna 1989). Even rather subtle priming manipulations (Higgins & Bargh 1987) have been shown to increase the salience of particular attitude functions (Schmitt 1988; Shavitt & Fazio 1987). Thus, by controlling the circumstances under which attitude objects or attitude-relevant data are encountered, one can manipulate the importance of various functional objectives.

Testing Functional Hypotheses

ATTITUDES AS FUNCTIONAL KNOWLEDGE STRUCTURES   A central premise of all functional theories is that attitudes enable individuals to appraise objects and situations and thereby impart structure or consistency to the social environment (Cacioppo et al 1989; Fazio 1989; Greenwald 1989b; Katz 1960; Pratkanis 1988, 1989; Smith et al 1956). Indeed, an impressive array of empirical research has been offered to demonstrate that attitudes (a) exert reliable effects on social information-processing (for recent reviews, see Chaiken & Stangor 1987; Pratkanis 1989; Pratkanis & Greenwald 1989), (b) influence social judgments and social decision-making (Bechtold et al 1986; Devine 1989a, b; R. H. Fazio and D. M. Driscoll, unpublished; R. H. Fazio and M. C. Powell, unpublished; Hamilton & Trolier 1986; Jamieson & Zanna 1989), and (c) guide behavioral responses toward attitude objects (Ajzen 1989; Chaiken & Stangor 1987, see below). From a functionalist perspective, however, a more critical issue is to specify the circumstances under which attitudes will operate as functional "knowledge" structures and have such effects.

Though almost everyone agrees that strong attitudes are more likely than weak ones to serve a knowledge or object-appraisal function, the many indicants of attitude strength (e.g. accessibility, centrality, certainty, extremity, importance, involvement, and relevance) are often intercorrelated (cf Abelson 1988; Fazio 1989; Krosnick 1988; Raden 1985; Swann et al 1988; van der Pligt et al 1986), thus making claims for one (or some combination) of them as the principal mediator of attitude functionality tenuous at best. Nevertheless, Fazio (1989, 1990) asserts that the strongest and most "functional" attitudes are those that are highly accessible. Fazio's empirical research has consistently demonstrated that highly accessible attitudes (as operationalized by quick reaction times to attitudinal inquiries or by having subjects repeatedly express their opinions) are more likely than less accessible attitudes (a) to be activated automatically in the presence of the attitude object (Fazio et al 1986; Sanbonmatsu & Fazio 1986; Sanbonmatsu et al 1986), (b) to bias information-processing in a direction implied by the valence of those attitudes (Fazio & Williams 1986; Houston & Fazio 1989; see also Lau 1989), (c) to ease the task of making expedient decisions (R. H. Fazio and D. M. Driscoll, unpublished; D. M. Sanbonmatsu and R. H. Fazio, unpublished), and (d) to predict subsequent behavior toward the attitude object (Fazio et al, unpublished, Fazio & Williams 1986). Though it remains to be established that all other strength-related attitudinal parameters are reflective of attitude accessibility, as has been suggested (Fazio 1986, 1989), it now seems apparent that readily accessible attitudes can promote the relatively effortless and expedient kind of environmental adaptations that Smith et al (1956) described when outlining their "object appraisal" function of attitude.

Drawing on Kruglanski's theory of lay epistemology (Kruglanski 1989; Kruglanski & Freund 1983), Zanna and his colleagues (Bechtold et al 1986; Jamieson 1987; Jamieson & Zanna 1985, 1986, 1989) have sought to demonstrate that attitudes are most likely to color our appraisals of objects and situations under circumstances that heighten the need for cognitive clarity or structure. Two experiments involving simulated court cases (Jamieson & Zanna 1985, 1989) nicely illustrate this approach. Subjects who had indicated their attitudes toward either affirmative action or capital punishment later served as jurors who were asked to render fair and impartial verdicts (a demand for objectivity) in either an affirmative action or a murder case. The evidence in each case was ambiguous. Prior to appraising the case-relevant information, subjects were told either that they had three minutes to reach a verdict (a high need for structure) or that no time constraints were imposed (a low need for structure). As predicted, jurors' verdicts were much less objective (i.e. more highly correlated with their preexisting attitudes) when rapid assessments of the evidence were required. Thus, as implied in the knowledge and object appraisal functions of earlier theories (Katz 1960; Smith et al 1956), attitudes strongly affected subjects' appraisals of ambiguous information and colored the decisions they reached when the need for structure was most readily apparent (see also Bechtold et al 1986; Jamieson & Zanna 1986).

FUNCTIONAL   MEDIATION   OF   ATTITUDE-BEHAVIOR   CONSISTENCY
Operating under the assumption that attitudes serve their underlying functions by guiding behaviors toward the attainment of these objectives, Shavitt (1989; Shavitt & Fazio 1987, 1988) proposes that attitude-behavior correlations will be highest when the function most salient when attitudes

are assessed matches the function most salient when behaviors are recorded. In the initial test of this hypothesis, Shavitt & Fazio (1987) manipulated the function salient at the time of attitude assessment via a questionnaire that required subjects to rate either 20 foods for taste (priming the utilitarian function) or 20 actions for the impressions they make on others (priming the social-adjustive function). This priming was followed by an assessment of subjects' attitudes toward two beverages, 7-Up and Perrier, the presumption being that subjects' attitudinal expressions would be heavily influenced by whichever attitude function had been made salient by the priming questionnaire. After a delay to permit the primed functions to dissipate, participants were asked to state their intentions to drink 7-Up (presumably a utilitarian commodity) and Perrier (presumably a social-adjustive commodity). Consistent with predictions, attitude-behavior correlations were substantially higher when the attitude function salient at the time of attitude assessment (i.e. the primed function) matched that salient at the time of behavioral assessment (i.e. the function normally engaged by the beverage). A follow-up study (Shavitt & Fazio 1988) produced the same pattern of results for high but not for low self-monitors, presumably because the clear and accessible attitudes of low self-monitoring individuals (cf Kardes et al 1986) are influenced less by ephemeral priming manipulations designed to vary the salience of attitude functions.

Though suggestive, the Shavitt & Fazio studies provide less than compelling evidence for their functional mediation hypothesis. This is because the functions presumed to be salient at the time of behavioral assessment were not necessarily purposes of the criterion behaviors (i.e. drinking) per se but rather, properties assumed to be inherent to the attitude objects in question. A clearer demonstration of the functional mediation of attitude-*behavior* consistency would require independent manipulations of both (*a*) the functions salient at the time of attitude assessment (which Shavitt & Fazio accomplished, we believe) and (*b*) the functional objectives of the behaviors one seeks to forecast (which is not as clear in Shavitt & Fazio's work). Though they did not couch it in terms of functional theory, Millar & Tesser (1986b) conducted such an experiment, finding significant attitude-behavior correlations only when the focus of subjects' thoughts at the time of attitude assessment matched the (manipulated) objectives of their subsequent behavior. So in a context where the functional goals of the criterion behaviors were made explicit, Millar & Tesser obtained results that support Shavitt & Fazio's functional analysis of attitude-behavior consistency.

FUNCTIONAL MEDIATION OF PERSUASION   Evidence is rapidly accumulating in support of a key proposition of all functional theories, namely that information directly relevant to the functions an attitude serves will be more persuasive than will data addressing function-irrelevant concerns. In three studies of advertising effectiveness, for example, Snyder & DeBono (1985, 1989) have shown that image-conscious high self-monitors, for whom attitudes often serve a social-adjustive function, form more positive attitudes toward consumer products if the ads appeal to social-adjustive considerations (i.e. images) than if they appeal to value-expressive ones (i.e. product quality), whereas just the reverse is true of low self-monitors, whose attitudes often serve a value-expressive function. Shavitt (1989) uses the object-variation methodology to produce similar outcomes: Attitudes formed toward utilitarian commodities (e.g. coffee, air conditioners) are more favorable if ads stress the products' utilitarian attributes rather than their implications for social identity, whereas favorable attitudes toward commodities serving a social-identity function (e.g. greeting cards, perfume) are more likely to result when ads highlight the products' relevance to one's identity rather than utilitarian considerations.

Even more impressive evidence for the functional mediation of persuasion is provided by DeBono's (1987) recent demonstrations that participants are more inclined to change existing attitudes when the message they receive explicitly undermines the functional utility of those attitudes while showing how the same goals might be achieved by adopting a new opinion. An equally important observation of this and related studies (i.e. DeBono & Harnish 1988; DeBono & Telesca 1988) was that subjects were more inclined to scrutinize, elaborate, and retain the message arguments when the content of the persuasive appeal and/or the attributes of its source made the functional underpinnings of their attitudes especially salient.

That subjects' message-processing strategies clearly depend on the functional relevance of the information they receive suggests that many of the situational variations in persuasion so elegantly described by cognitive response theorists (see below) might be explained in part by motivational variables heretofore ignored or underdescribed. At the very least, the clear demonstrations of functionally mediated social influence offered to date support an emerging consensus (e.g. DeBono 1987; Herek 1987a; Johnson & Eagly 1989; Shavitt 1989; Snyder & DeBono 1989) that a complete account of persuasion and other attitudinal phenomena must consider (or even assign prominence to) the motivational bases of individuals' attitudes and belief systems.

MESSAGE-BASED PERSUASION

Two very general accounts of how people influence each other's attitudes continue to dominate the theoretical picture in persuasion research: (a) The cognitive response approach is illustrated by Petty & Cacioppo's (1986) "central route to persuasion" and by Chaiken's (1987; Chaiken et al 1989) "systematic" processing. The central premise of these approaches is that recipients carefully process and elaborate the arguments of persuasive messages. (*b*) The "cognitive miser" perspective, as reflected in Petty & Cacioppo's (1986) "peripheral route to persuasion" and Chaiken's (1987; Chaiken et al 1989) "heuristic" processing, emphasizes factors other than argument-based thinking that may induce attitude change in persuasive contexts. Though not interchangeable (see Chaiken et al 1989), Chaiken's "cognitive heuristics" and the myriad of other peripheral factors that can induce attitude change in the absence of any systematic thinking about message content (e.g. affective mechanisms, perceptual-judgmental phenomena, consistency motives) tend to exert their maximal persuasive impact under roughly the same circumstances (see below). We therefore discuss these together in this review.

The Systematic or Central Route to Persuasion

Both Petty & Cacioppo's (1986) Elaboration Likelihood Model (ELM) and Chaiken's (1987; Chaiken et al 1989) Heuristic-Systematic Model (HSM) posit that careful consideration and elaboration of message arguments (i.e. systematic or central route processing) is likely to occur when recipients are both motivated and able to scrutinize the message. Research designed to test this proposition has assessed systematic processing through measures, for example, of reading time and argument recall (e.g. Mackie 1987; Mackie & Worth 1989), of number and/or valence of issue-relevant cognitions generated in thought-listing tasks (e.g. Harkins & Petty 1987; Wu & Shaffer 1987), and of recipients' ability to discriminate strong persuasive arguments from weak ones (e.g. Axsom et al 1987; Cacioppo et al 1986a). The latter two indexes are particularly useful because attitudes based on issue-relevant thinking are generally reflected in (or are predictable from) the extent and/or valence of recipients' listed thoughts; such attitudes are clearly influenced by the strength of message arguments (i.e. are more favorable to the message conclusion, given cogent rather than specious evidence; cf Chaiken et al 1989; Petty et al 1987a). By contrast, recipients who are unmotivated or unable to scrutinize message content will adopt opinions that are relatively insensitive to either the quality of message arguments or the character of any issue-relevant thinking reported on thought-listing measures.

The empirical quest continues to specify the variables that either motivate or enable recipients to process messages systematically. *Enabling* variables include repeated (vs single) exposures to persuasive argumentation (Cacioppo & Petty 1989; Lindskold et al 1986), absence (vs presence) of situational distractions (Moore et al 1986; Smith & Shaffer 1989a,b), an affectively neutral (vs happy) state of mind (Worth & Mackie 1987; Mackie & Worth 1989), extensive (vs little) prior knowledge about the message topic (Alba & Marmorstein 1987; Liberman et al 1988; Wood & Kallgren 1988), and direct (vs indirect) experience with the attitude object (Wu & Shaffer 1987). Variables that *motivate* issue-relevant thinking include dispositional factors such as high (vs low) self-acceptance (Chebat & Picard 1988), either high or low "certainty orientation" (depending on the personal relevance of the message topic; see Sorrentino et al 1988), and high (vs low) need for cognition (Axsom et al 1987; Chaiken et al 1989; Haugtvedt et al 1986, 1987). The motivational impetus of the latter variable is largely independent of enabling or "ability" factors, such as verbal intelligence (Cacioppo et al 1986a). Motivating situational variables include high (vs low) personal relevance of the message topic (e.g. Axsom et al 1987; Haugtvedt et al 1986; Howard-Pitney et al 1986; Leippe & Elkin 1987), high (vs low) match between the persuasive context and recipient's functional predispositions (DeBono 1987; DeBono & Harnish 1988), use of interrogative (vs assertive) formats to assess recipients' opinions (Petty et al 1987b), and delivery of independent arguments by multiple (vs single) spokespersons (Harkins & Petty 1987). Disagreement with the majority opinion of an important reference group induces issue-relevant thinking (Mackie 1987), even though consensus information from less important sources normally functions as a heuristic cue (i.e. "consensus implies correctness") to the validity of a message (cf Axsom et al 1987; Chaiken et al 1989; Haugtvedt et al 1986; Wiegman 1988).

MEDIATIONAL ISSUES   A central premise of most cognitive response theories (e.g. Greenwald 1968; Petty & Cacioppo 1981) is that recipients' attitudinal reactions to a persuasive communication will depend more on their cognitive appraisals of message content (elaborative processes) than on their learning and retention of the arguments themselves (reception processes). Indeed, empirical support for this contention can be found in several recent experiments (e.g. Cacioppo et al 1986a; Cacioppo & Petty 1989; DeBono & Harnish 1988; Harkins & Petty 1987; Leippe & Elkin 1987; Smith & Shaffer 1989a; Wood & Kallgren 1988), although measures of argument retention (recall) occasionally make meaningful and independent contributions to the prediction of postmessage attitudes (Chattopadhyay & Alba 1988; Mackie 1987, see below).

Recently, researchers have attempted to make more precise qualitative distinctions among the kinds of elaborations recipients generate and to determine whether some classes of elaborations are more powerful mediators of persuasion than are others. Shavitt & Brock (1986), for example, found that elaborations which in some way implicate the self are better predictors of postmessage attitudes than are either message elaborations that are not self-relevant or other cognitive responses pertaining to message execution. Chattopadhyay & Alba (1988) have reported that the number of abstract elaborations recipients generate (i.e. inferences stemming from the integration of two or more message arguments) is more closely linked to their attitudes than is a more traditional "net polarity" elaborative index. Abstract and self-relevant elaborations are also retained better over a week's time than are other kinds of message-based cognitions (Chattopadhyay & Alba 1988; S. Shavitt & T. C. Brock, unpublished), implying that people who reliably generate those "memorable" responses may tend to form postmessage attitudes that are relatively stable over time and resistant to counterattack (see Carnot et al 1985).

Given the above empirical record, one might be tempted to conclude that reception/retention processes play little if any part in inducing attitude change. Yet as Chaiken & Stangor (1987) have cogently argued, simple recall measures are (a) inherently insensitive assessments of other reception processes (i.e. attention, comprehension) thought to be implicated in persuasion, and (b) subject to range restrictions that may attenuate recall-attitude correlations. We add that, inasmuch as persuasive arguments may vary considerably in their evaluative implications, there is little reason to suppose that sheer quantity of recalled information should predict postmessage attitudes (see also Eagly & Chaiken 1984; Jepson & Chaiken 1989; McGuire 1972). Indeed, a recent study that assessed the evaluative implications (or perceived importance) of the arguments recipients recalled found that this "weighted" index was a strong predictor of attitudes; it predicted better than either the sheer number of arguments recalled or the number of favorable/unfavorable cognitive elaborations recipients generated (Chattopadhyay & Alba 1988). Thus more sensitive measures of argument retention might help to clarify the role of reception processes in message-based persuasion.

Methodological considerations aside, it has been argued (Asuncion & Mackie 1988; Chaiken & Stangor 1987) that a strong memory-attitude link should be most apparent for relatively unfamiliar or uninvolving issues presented in contexts where recipients either do not or cannot generate "on-line" integrations of message arguments to a meaningful attitudinal conclusion. Although observations from the impression-formation literature tend to support this model (cf Hastie & Park 1986), results of three relevant persuasion studies are mixed (Asuncion & Mackie 1988, Exp. 1 & 2; Chattopadhyay & Alba 1988). Chattopadhyay & Alba (1988) report strong memory-attitude relationships, even when attitudes had been formed "on-line". [See Mackie (1987) for evidence of recall-attitude linkages under circumstances that could have produced on-line assessments.]

Three of the four recent studies in which impressive recall-attitude relationships have emerged were out of the ordinary in that recipients displaying this memory-judgment link had been exposed to *two-sided* communications (i.e. majority vs minority arguments in Mackie 1987, Exp. 1 & 2; information about two competing consumer products in Chattopadhyay & Alba 1988). In the fourth study subjects evaluated a one-sided communication while knowing (from consensus information) that others like themselves disagreed with its conclusion (Mackie 1987, Exp. 3). Perhaps the need to decide the relative merits of two sides of an unfamiliar issue (a comparative processing goal) places a greater premium on message reception at the expense of elaboration, thus explaining the relatively strong memory-judgment links in the studies above. In the absence of such a comparative processing goal, recipients evaluating one-sided messages may be freer to devote more effort to elaborating the arguments they receive. Consistent with this logic, Chattopadhyay & Alba (1988) found both message recall and cognitive elaborations to be significant predictors of persuasion for recipients who had processed two sets of persuasive arguments, whereas only cognitive elaborations predicted the postmessage attitudes of recipients who had but one set of arguments to evaluate.

Except for continuing speculation about mechanisms underlying vividness effects (e.g. Meyerowitz & Chaiken 1987; Rippletoe & Rogers 1987; Rook 1987; Shedler & Manis 1986), and even suggestions that such effects may be illusory (Collins et al 1988), the recent literature has had little else to say about the role of reception processes in persuasion.

PERSISTENCE   In addition to clarifying the effects of certain message variables (e.g. Kaplowitz et al 1986; Meyerowitz & Chaiken 1987) and other contextual factors (e.g. Dew et al 1987; Lydon et al 1988; Miller 1988; Pratkanis et al 1988) presumed to influence attitudinal persistence, recent research has provided additional support for the contention (cf Petty & Cacioppo 1986) that attitudes based on issue-relevant thinking are stronger and more durable than those stemming from heuristic/peripheral mechanisms. Specifically, it has been shown that attitudes based on issue-relevant thinking are more temporally stable, at least over a 1–2 week period (Mackie 1987; Sorrentino et al 1988), are more resistant to counterattack (Wu & Shaffer 1987), and are more highly predictive of future behavior (Cacioppo et al 1986a; Leippe & Elkin 1987; see also Petty & Cacioppo 1986) than are peripherally mediated opinions. Moreover, the type of systematic processing in which recipients engage may be important, in that attitudes based on "self-relevant" message elaborations (see above) tend to be less susceptible to counterinfluence (Carnot et al 1985) and display greater attitude-behavior consistency (Shavitt & Brock 1986) than those based on other kinds of issue-relevant thinking. However, evidence regarding the resistance-to-persuasion effect is indirect and may hold only for counterattitudinal appeals (Wu & Shaffer 1987), and there are conceptual (cf Johnson & Eagly 1989; Kruglanski 1989) as well as methodological reasons (Chaiken et al 1989) for suspecting that past experimental operations may have conspired to make peripherally mediated attitudes induced in the laboratory a lot less persistent and robust than is typically the case outside the laboratory (cf Cacioppo et al 1986a; Dew et al 1987). Thus, it remains for future research to establish conclusively that attitudes based on systematic processing are inherently stronger or more durable than those induced via heuristic processes or other peripheral mechanisms.

MOTIVATIONAL BIASES   Cognitive response theorists have traditionally assumed that people strive to hold valid attitudes and, if motivated and able to process a message, will ordinarily elaborate message arguments in an objective and unbiased way. Yet biased processing (e.g. predominantly favorable elaborations of weak arguments or unfavorable reactions to strong ones) has been observed, particularly when the message conclusion is highly involving (Howard-Pitney et al 1986) and when recipients are knowledgeable about the message topic (Wood et al 1985), find themselves disagreeing with an important reference group (Mackie 1987), or have been forewarned of the content of the persuasive message and/or the speaker's persuasive intent (cf Petty & Cacioppo 1986).

That the above findings might be subsumed under the premise that systematic processing becomes biased at extreme levels of personal relevance or involvement (Petty & Cacioppo 1986), while appealing for its elegant simplicity, may be oversimplified. Johnson & Eagly (1989) have recently proposed that in social psychological usage the terms "relevance" or "involvement" refer to at least three qualitatively distinct motivational states, each of which activates a different aspect of the self-concept and has different effects on information processing and persuasion. *Value-relevant* involvement refers to the psychological state created by the activation of attitudes that are linked to important values—a state roughly synonymous with what social-judgment theorists call ego-involvement (Sherif & Sherif 1967) and functional theorists call value-expressive goals (Katz 1960). *Outcome-relevant* involvement, a term incorporating what cognitive response theorists call personal relevance or "issue involvement" (Leippe & Elkin 1987; Petty & Cacioppo 1986) and functional theorists call instrumental goals (Katz 1960), applies to contexts in which the message addresses utilitarian concerns and recipients are motivated to attain desirable outcomes or to avoid unpleasant ones. Finally, *impression-relevant* involvement, a motive viewed as synonymous with cognitive response theorists' "response involvement" (Leippe & Elkin 1987) and as similar to functional theorists' social-adjustive goals (Smith et al 1956), describes persuasive settings in which recipients' primary objective is to adopt opinions that will please or appease potential evaluators.

Johnson & Eagly's (1989) meta-analytic review of studies addressing the effects of "involvement" on persuasion revealed that increasing levels of value-relevant involvement inhibit attitude change, regardless of the quality of the message arguments. This observation suggests that value-relevant concerns may motivate recipients to defend their initial attitudes and underlying values, thereby biasing message elaborations in the direction of those attitudes. By contrast, recipients high in outcome-relevant involvement were persuaded more by strong arguments and somewhat less by weak ones than were their low-involvement counterparts—a pattern suggesting that outcome-relevant (instrumental) motives prompt a relatively objective assessment of message content. Finally, impression-relevant involvement has a small but reliable inhibiting influence on persuasion, regardless of the quality of the message arguments. The limited evidence available (Leippe & Elkin 1987; see also Tetlock 1983) suggests that any biased processing induced by impression-management concerns is directed toward the attainment of moderate or otherwise "defensible" attitudes.

This characterization of involvement as a family of qualitatively distinct motivational states implies that objective processing to achieve "valid" attitudes may occur far less frequently than is commonly assumed. In fact, such an "accuracy motive" may characterize only those message recipients faced with instrumentally relevant issues that are unfamiliar to them (Johnson & Eagly 1989). It is conceivable that the objective processing thought to underlie such "outcome-relevant" involvement effects would be overwhelmed by attitude-defensive, biased elaborations if subjects were more knowledgeable about the message topics (cf Wood et al 1985), or if the issues were linked more directly to recipients' most important interests, values, or reference groups (see Howard-Pitney et al 1986; Johnson & Eagly 1989; Mackie 1987). Of course, inferences drawn from correlational meta-analyses provide no direct evidence for the motivational influences on information processing that are presumed to underlie these "involvement" effects. Moreover, Petty & Cacioppo (1989), in a response to the Johnson & Eagly (1989) paper, suggest that the division of involvement into separate motivational systems may be premature.

Despite current interpretational ambiguities and empirical limitations, and despite the fact that other motives may also be implicated in coloring recipients' information processing (e.g. Kruglanski 1989), we view the rebirth of interest in motivational concerns as a promising framework for achieving a richer understanding of the processes and products of thought-induced persuasion (Millar & Tesser 1986a).

Heuristic Processing and Other Peripheral Modes

One assumption central to both Petty & Cacioppo's (1986) Elaboration Likelihood Model (ELM) and Chaiken's (1987; Chaiken et al 1989) Heuristic-Systematic Model (HSM) is that message recipients are "economy minded" souls who will expend only as much effort as is necessary to assess the validity of a persuasive communication or achieve other pertinent processing goals. Since processing of cognitive heuristics and other peripheral cues is presumed to be relatively effortless, message recipients who are otherwise unmotivated or unable to engage in more laborious forms of issue-relevant thinking should rely heavily on such "peripheral" information. Consistent with this logic are the results of several recent studies demonstrating that manipulations of superficial persuasion cues such as source attractiveness, likability, expertise, message length and/or number of arguments (irrespective of their strength), audience reactions, and consensus information often mediate persuasion when either the motivation or ability for issue-relevant thinking is low; these cues usually have less impact on attitudes when motivation and ability are high and the persuasive implications of such cues are attenuated by recipients' systematic processing (e.g. Alba & Marmorstein 1987; Axsom et al 1987, Chaiken 1987; DeBono & Harnish 1988; Haugtvedt et al 1986, 1987; Mackie 1987; Moore et al 1986; Wood & Kallgren 1988; Wu & Shaffer 1987).

Early descriptions of central and peripheral routes to persuasion as "qualitatively distinct" (e.g. Petty & Cacioppo 1981) have been interpreted by some (e.g. Stiff 1986) as implying that these two processes are mutually exclusive. Chaiken et al (1989) have challenged the latter view, arguing that heuristic (peripheral) and systematic (central) processing can co-occur and have additive or interactive effects on recipients' attitudinal judgments (see also Petty et al 1987a for another critique of the mutual exclusivity proposition). Perhaps because most previous tests of either the ELM or the HSM were designed as theoretical plausibility demonstrations (i.e. creating contexts in which one mode of processing or route to persuasion would predominate and influence attitudes more than the other), inferences about the possible interdependencies of the two processing modes are only now beginning to attract much attention. We focus here on some of these early returns, hoping to stimulate interest in this line of inquiry and thereby promote its continuance.

Logically, a cooccurrence assumption allows for the possibility that heuristic/peripheral and systematic/central influences might occur independently and produce additive effects on persuasion. Yet, even the hint of such additivity is rare in the literature, owing perhaps to strong methodological biases in existing studies against detecting such effects (see Chaiken et al 1989 for a discussion of this bias and suggestions for overcoming it). Thus, the final word on the additivity hypothesis remains to be written.

Several lines of evidence for the interdependence of the heuristic/peripheral and the systematic/central processing modes have recently emerged. For example, blatant incongruencies between the persuasive implications of a heuristic cue (e.g. consensus information) and message content (e.g. the conclusion drawn) can induce even low-involvement recipients to engage in extensive issue-relevant thinking and to form attitudes consistent with the thoughts thus generated (D. Maheswaran and S. Chaiken, unpublished). Thus people who are not ordinarily inclined to scrutinize message content may nevertheless do so when they don't trust their heuristic processing strategies.

As noted by Petty and associates (Petty & Cacioppo 1986; Petty et al 1987a), superficial persuasion cues might routinely affect the likelihood of systematic processing whenever recipients, being unclear about whether they can or should scrutinize a message (e.g. when their knowledge is only moderate or issue relevance is uncertain), look to the persuasive context to help them make that decision. Presumably, the presence of a strong or compelling cue (e.g. high source expertise) would render the message worthy of scrutiny, whereas a noncompelling cue (e.g. lack of expertise) might inhibit such effortful undertakings. Consistent with this notion are the results of several studies demonstrating that, when either the motivation or the ability for systematic processing is intermediate (or uncertain), recipients carefully scrutinize the message (and are persuaded more by strong arguments than by weak ones) *only* if the peripheral cues available to them (e.g. high source expertise) make it seem worthwhile to do so (cf Petty & Cacioppo 1986; Petty et al 1987a; Moore et al 1986).

In the research cited above, compelling peripheral cues produced a relatively unbiased assessment of message content—i.e. they enhanced the persuasive impact of strong arguments while noticeably undermining the effectiveness of weak ones. However, peripheral/heuristic input can induce biased systematic processing if recipients who lack knowledge about a message topic are nevertheless motivated to scrutinize arguments that prove to be ambiguous (Chaiken et al 1989). For example, heuristic processing of consensus information by motivated but otherwise unknowledgeable recipients leads to highly favorable elaborations of a majority (consensus) position but little or no systematic processing of minority views (Mackie 1987). Ambiguous (and even weak) legal evidence against a criminal defendant is elaborated and interpreted in overwhelmingly negative ways should a salient peripheral cue (e.g. the defendant's testimonial demeanor) suggest that he might be acting deceitfully (Hendry & Shaffer 1989; see Brekke & Borgida 1988; Leippe & Romancyzk 1987; and Shaffer 1985 for other instances in which peripheral cues may have induced biased processing of ambiguous legal evidence).

Finally, it seems that certain functional predispositions that transcend the persuasive context may determine whether a peripheral cue will act as a direct mediator of persuasion or as an impetus for systematic processing. DeBono & Harnish (1988) recently demonstrated that peripheral cues that can be linked to the functions that recipients' attitudes normally serve will induce issue-relevant thinking that, in turn, predicts recipients' postmessage opinions. By contrast, cues that are unrelated to the functional underpinnings of recipients' attitudes are processed heuristically and contribute to opinions that are not predictable from whatever cognitive responses recipients happen to generate.

CONCLUSIONS

Attitude research is flourishing. Although we see no fundamental paradigm shifts (Kuhn 1970), the work over the last three years involves solid advances in the normal science.

There has been an almost discipline-wide attempt to define attitudes formally to conform to typical usage by researchers—i.e. as an evaluative response toward an object. The application of ideas about associative memory networks has advanced our knowledge of how attitude structures work, and we are getting an incrementally better grasp on the role of complexity in these workings. At the same time we are learning more about the content of various belief domains.

The relationship between attitudes and behavior continues to occupy attention. While the theory of reasoned action remains the most popular single approach for predicting behavior from attitudes, work has been reported on nonrational factors such as habit, automaticity, and the sometimes disorienting effects of analyzing reasons for holding attitudes. Continued refinements in dissonance, self-perception, and self-presentation approaches have added to our understanding of the effects of behavior on attitudes.

Although cognitive approaches continue to be important, there is a definite upsurge in the use of motivational constructs in attitude research. Perhaps the most striking change over the period we reviewed was the renaissance of interest in the functional approach to attitudes. Empirical work is proceeding by looking at differences between people for whom attitudes about the same object serve different functions, differences between objects that generally serve different functions, and differences in situations that emphasize one function over another. These variations are helping us understand attitude-behavior consistency as well as attitude change.

The Petty & Cacioppo Elaboration Likelihood Model and the Chaiken Heuristic-Systematic Model continue as the dominant theoretical approaches to message-based persuasion. Work on the central/systematic route continues to deal with issues of message reception and elaboration, with reception (i.e. memory) playing an important role in persuasion, particularly for two-sided communications. There also appears to be evidence that motivational biases play a greater role in central processes than originally anticipated. Finally, there is evidence that central and peripheral processes are more interdependent than earlier work had implied.

Attitudes research maintains an important role in social psychology. The amount of it is prodigious, its content is varied, and its quality is often high. The enterprise appears vital, alive, productive and exciting.

ACKNOWLEDGMENTS

Though order of authorship was determined by prearrangement, both authors contributed equally to this chapter. We gratefully acknowledge the support of NIMH Grant No. 1R01MH41487-01 (A. Tesser, Pl) and No. 1R01MH43726-01 (D. Shaffer, Pl). John Achee helped organize some of the materials; and John Cacioppo, Shelley Chaiken, Alice Eagly, and Rich Petty made useful suggestions on a preliminary draft.

Literature Cited

Abelson, R. P. 1988. Conviction. *Am. Psychol.* 43:267–75
Abelson, R. P., Prentice, D. A. 1989. Beliefs as possessions—a functional perspective. See Pratkanis et al 1989, pp. 361–81
Ableson, R., Levi, A. 1985. Decision making and decision theory. In *The Handbook of Social Psychology*, ed. G. Lindzey, E. Aronson. Hillsdale, NJ: Erlbaum
Adorno, T. W., Frenkel-Brunswik, E., Levinson, D. J., Sanford, R. N. 1950. *The Authoritarian Personality*. New York: Harper & Row
Ajzen, I. 1985. From intentions to actions: a theory of planned behavior. In *Action-Control: From Cognition to Behavior*, ed. J. Kuhl, J. Beckman, pp. 11–39. Heidelberg: Springer
Ajzen, I. 1989. Attitude structure and behavior. See Pratkanis et al 1989, pp. 241–74
Ajzen, I., Fishbein, M. 1980. *Understanding Attitudes and Predicting Social Behavior*. Englewood-Cliffs, NJ: Prentice-Hall
Ajzen, I., Madden, J. T. 1986. Prediction of goal-directed behavior: attitudes, intentions and perceived behavioral control. *J. Exp. Soc. Psychol.* 22:453–74
Ajzen, I., Timko, C. 1986. Correspondence between health attitudes and behavior. *Basic Appl. Soc. Psychol.* 7:259–76
Alba, J. W., Marmorstein, H. 1987. The effects of frequency knowledge on consumer decision making. *J. Consum. Res.* 14:14–25
Aldrich, J. S., Sullivan, J. L., Borgida, E. 1989. *Foreign affairs and issue voting: Do presidential candidates waltz before a blind audience?* Am. Polit. Sci. Rev. 83:125–41
Alexander, C., Langer, E., Newman, R., Chandler, H., Davies, J. 1989. Aging, mindfulness, and transcendental meditation. *J. Pers. Soc. Psychol.* In press

Anderson, J. 1983. *The Architecture of Cognition*. Cambridge, MA: Harvard Univ. Press
Asuncion, A. G., Mackie, D. M. 1988. *Online and memory-based processing of attitude change*. Presented at Annu. Meet. Am. Psychol. Assoc., Atlanta
Axsom, D., Yates, S., Chaiken, S. 1987. Audience response as a heuristic cue in persuasion. *J. Pers. Soc. Psychol.* 53:30–40
Ball-Rokeach, S. J., Rokeach, M., Grube, J. W. 1984. *The Great American Values Test: Influencing Behavior and Belief Through Television*. New York: Free Press
Bandura, A. 1986. *Social Foundations of Thought and Action: A Social Cognitive Theory*. Englewood Cliffs, NJ: Prentice Hall
Bar-Tal, D. 1986. The Masada Syndrome: a case of central belief. In *Stress and Coping in Time of War*, ed. N. Milgram. New York: Brunner-Mazel
Bar-Tal, D. 1990. *Group Beliefs*. New York: Springer Verlag. In press
Baumeister, R. F. 1982. A self-presentational view of social phenomena. *Psychol. Bull.* 91:3–26
Beatty, J. 1986. The pupillary system. In *Psychophysiology: Systems, Processes, and Applications*, ed. M. G. H. Coles, E. Donchin, S. W. Porges, pp. 43–50. New York: Guilford Press
Bechtold, A., Narccarato, M. E., Zanna, M. P. 1986. *Need for structure and the prejudice-discrimination link*. Presented at Annu. Meet. Can. Psychol. Assoc., Toronto
Beckmann, J., Gollwitzer, P. M. 1987. Deliberative versus implementational states of mind: the issue of impartiality in predecisional and postdecisional information processing. *Soc. Cognit.* 5:259–79

Bem, D. J. 1972. Self-perception theory. *Adv. Exp. Soc. Psychol.* 6:1–62

Billig, M., Condor, S., Edwards, D., Gane, M., Middleton, D., Radley, A., eds. 1988. *Ideological Dilemmas: A Social Psychology of Everyday Thinking.* London: Sage

Bogardus, E. S. 1925. Measuring social distance. *J. Appl. Sociol.* 9:299–303

Bower, G. 1981. Mood and memory. *Am. Psychol.* 36:129–48

Breckler, S. J. 1984. Empirical validation of affect, behavior, and cognition as distinct attitude components. *J. Pers. Soc. Psychol.* 47:1191–1205

Breckler, S. J. 1989. Applications of covariance structure modeling in personality and social psychology: cause for concern? *Psychol. Bull.* In press

Breckler, S. J., Wiggins, E. C. 1989a. Affect versus evaluation in the structure of attitudes. *J. Exp. Soc. Psychol.* In press

Breckler, S. J., Wiggins, E. C. 1989b. On defining attitude theory: once more with feeling. See Pratkanis et al 1989, pp. 407–27

Brekke, N., Borgida, E. 1988. Expert psychological testimony in rape trials: a social-cognitive analysis. *J. Pers. Soc. Psychol.* 55:372–86

Budd, R. J. 1986. Predicting cigarette use: the need to incorporate measures of salience in the theory of reasoned action. *J. Appl. Soc. Psychol.* 16(8):663–85

Budd, R. J. 1987. Response bias and the theory of reasoned action. *Soc. Cogn.* 5(5):95–107

Budd, R. J., Spencer, C. P. 1986. Lay theories of behavioral intention: a source of response bias in the theory of reasoned action? *Br. J. Soc. Psychol.* 25:109–17

Burnkrant, R. E., Page, T. J. Jr. 1988. The structure and antecedents of the normative and attitudinal components of Fishbein's theory of reasoned action. *J. Exp. Soc. Psychol.* 24:66–87

Cacioppo, J. T., Petty, R. E. 1989. Effects of message repetition on argument processing, recall, and persuasion. *Basic Appl. Soc. Psychol.* 10:3–12

Cacioppo, J. T., Petty, R. E. 1984. The need for cognition: relationship to attitudinal processes. In *Social Perception in Clinical and Counseling Psychology,* ed. R. P. McGlynn, J. E. Maddux, C. D. Stoltenberg, J. Harvey, pp. 113–39. Lubbock, TX: Texas Tech. Univ. Press

Cacioppo, J. T., Petty, R. E., Geen, T. R. 1989. In *Attitude Structure and Function: From the Tripartite to the Homeostasis Model of Attitudes,* ed. A. R. Pratkanis, S. J., Breckler, A. G. Greenwald, pp. 275–309. Hillsdale, NJ: Erlbaum

Cacioppo, J. T., Petty, R. E., Kao, C. F., Rodriguez, R. 1986a. Central and peripheral routes to persuasion: an individual difference perspective. *J. Pers. Soc. Psychol.* 51:1032–43

Cacioppo, J. T., Petty, R. E., Losch, M. E., Kim, H. S. 1986b. Electromyographic activity over facial muscle regions can differentiate the valence and intensity of affective reactions. *J. Pers. Soc. Psychol.* 50:260–68

Cacioppo, J. T., Petty, R. E., Marshall-Goodell, B. 1984. Electromyographic specificity during simple physical and attitudinal tasks: location and topographical features of integrated EMG responses. *Biol. Psychol.* 18:85–121

Campbell, A., ed. 1971. *White Attitudes toward Black People.* Ann Arbor, MI: Inst. Soc. Res.

Cantor, N., Brower, A., Niedenthal, P., Langston, C., Brower, A. 1987. Life tasks, self-concept ideals, and cognitive strategies in a life transition. *J. Pers. Soc. Psychol.* 53:1178–91

Carnot, C., Shavitt, S., Brock, T. C. 1985. *Manipulating beliefs about beliefs: perceived self-relevance of thought lends to persistent persuasion.* Presented at Annu. Meet. Midwest. Psychol. Assoc., Chicago

Chaiken, S. 1987. The heuristic model of persuasion. In *Social Influence: The Ontario Symposium,* ed. M. P. Zanna, J. M. Olson, C. P. Herman, 5:3–39. Hillsdale, NJ: Erlbaum

Chaiken, S., Liberman, A., Eagly, A. H. 1989. Heuristic and systematic information processing within and beyond the persuasion context. In *Unintended Thought: Limits of Awareness, Intention, and Control,* ed. J. S. Uleman, J. A. Bargh, pp. 212–52. New York: Guilford. In press

Chaiken, S., Stangor, C. 1987. Attitudes and attitude change. *Annu. Rev. Psychol.* 38:575–630

Chaiken, S., Yates, S. 1985. Affective-cognitive consistency and thought induced attitude polarization. *J. Pers. Soc. Psychol.* 49:1470–81

Chattopadhyay, A., Alba, J. W. 1988. The situational importance of recall and inference in consumer decision making. *J. Consum. Res.* 15:1–12

Chebat, J., Picard, J. 1988. Receivers' self-acceptance and the effectiveness of two-sided messages. *J. Soc. Psychol.* 128:253–62

Collins, R. L., Taylor, S. E., Wood, J. V., Thompson, S. C. 1988. The vividness effect: elusive or illusory? *J. Exp. Soc. Psychol.* 24:1–18

Converse, P. E. 1964. The nature of belief

systems in the mass public. In *Ideology and Discontent*, ed. D. E. Apter. New York: Free Press

Converse, P. E. 1970. Attitudes and non-attitudes: continuation of a dialog. In *The Quantitative Analysis of Social Problems*, ed. E. R. Tufte. Reading, MA: Addison-Wesley

Cooper, J., Fazio, R. H. 1984. A new look at dissonance theory. *Adv. Exp. Soc. Psychol.* 17:229–66

Crano, W. D., Gorenflo, D. W., Shakelford, S. L. 1988. Overjustification, assumed consensus, and attitude change: further investigation of the incentive-arousal hypothesis. *J. Pers. Soc. Psychol.* 55:12–22

Crano, W. D., Sivacek, J. 1984. The influence of incentive-arousal ambivalence on overjustification effects in attitude change. *J. Pers. Soc. Psychol.* 20:137–58

Crocker, J., Thompson, L. L., McGraw, K. M., Ingerman, C. 1987. Downward comparison, prejudice, and evaluations of others: effects on self-esteem and threat. *J. Pers. Soc. Psychol.* 52:907–16

Croyle, R. T., Cooper, J. 1983. Dissonance arousal: physiological evidence. *J. Pers. Soc. Psychol.* 45:782–91

Davidson, R. J. 1984. Affect, cognition and hemispheric specialization. In *Emotion, Cognition and Behavior*, ed. C. E. Isard, J. Kagan, R. Zajonc. New York & London: Cambridge Univ. Press

Davis, K. E., Todd, M. 1982. Friendship and love relationships. *Adv. Descr. Psychol.* 2:79–122

DeBono, K. G. 1987. Investigating the social-adjustive and value-expressive functions of attitudes: implications for persuasion processes. *J. Pers. Soc. Psychol.* 52:279–87

DeBono, K. G., Harnish, R. J. 1988. Source expertise, source attractiveness, and the processing of persuasive information: a functional approach. *J. Pers. Soc. Psychol.* 55:541–46

DeBono, K. G., Telesca, C. 1988. *The role of source physical attractiveness in the persuasion process: a functional perspective.* Presented at Annu. Meet. East. Psychol. Assoc., Buffalo

DeVine, P. G. 1989a. Automatic and controlled processes in prejudice: the role of stereotypes and personal beliefs. See Pratkanis et al 1989, pp. 181–212

Devine, P. G. 1989b. Stereotypes and prejudice: their automatic and controlled components. *J. Pers. Soc. Psychol.* 56:5–18

deVries, B., Walker, L. J. 1987. Conceptual/integrative complexity and attitudes toward capital punishment. *Pers. Soc. Psychol. Bull.* 13:448–57

Dew, M. A., Bromet, E. J., Schulberg, N. C. 1987. Application of a temporal persistence model to community residents' long-term beliefs about the Three Mile Island nuclear accident. *J. Appl. Soc. Psychol.* 17:1071–91

Dietrich, D. M., Berkowitz, L. 1988. *Motivation for dissonance reduction: negative state relief or self-esteem restoration?* Presented at Annu. Meet. Am. Psychol. Assoc., Atlanta

Dishman, R. K. 1982. Compliance/adherence in health-related exercise. *Health Psychol.* 3:237–67

Dovidio, J. F., Evans, N., Tyker, R. B. 1986. Racial stereotypes: the contents of their cognitive representations. *J. Exp. Soc. Psychol.* 22:22–37

Dovidio, J. F., Gaertner, S. L. 1986. Prejudice, discrimination, and racism: historical trends and contemporary approaches. In *Prejudice, Discrimination, and Racism: Theory and Research*, ed. J. F. Dovidio, S. L. Gaertner. New York/Orlando, FL: Academic

Dweck, C. S., Leggett, E. L. 1988. A social cognitive approach to motivation and personality. *Psychol. Rev.* 95:256–73

Eagly, A. H., Chaiken, S. 1984. Cognitive theories of persuasion. *Adv. Exp. Soc. Psychol.* 17:267–359

Eiser, J. R., ed. 1986. *Social Psychology: Attitudes, Cognition, and Social Behavior.* Cambridge: Cambridge Univ. Press

Elkin, R. A., Leippe, M. R. 1986. Physiological arousal, dissonance, and attitude change: evidence for a dissonance-arousal link and a "don't remind me" effect. *J. Pers. Soc. Psychol.* 51:55–65

Emler, N. 1987. Socio-moral development from the perspective of social representations. *J. Theory Soc. Behav.* 17:371–88

Emler, N., Ohana, J., Moscovici, S. 1987. Children's beliefs about institutional roles: a cross national study of representations of the teacher's role. *Br. J. Psychol.* 57:26–37

Emmons, R. A. 1989. The personal striving approach to personality. In *Goal Concepts in Personality and Social Psychology*, ed. L. A. Pervin, pp. 87–126. Hillsdale, NJ: Erlbaum

Farr, R., Moscovici, S., eds. 1984. *Social Representations.* Cambridge: Cambridge Univ. Press

Fazio, R. H. 1986. How do attitudes guide behavior? In *The Handbook of Motivation and Cognition: Foundations of Social Behavior*, ed. R. M. Sorrentino, E. T. Higgins, pp. 204–43. New York: Guilford Press

Fazio, R. H. 1989. On the power and functionality of attitudes: the role of attitude accessibility. See Pratkanis et al 1989, pp. 153-79

Fazio, R. H. 1990. Multiple processes by which attitudes guide behavior: the MODE model as an integrative framework. *Adv. Exp. Soc. Psychol.* In press

Fazio, R. H., Sanbonmatsu, D. M., Powell, M. C. 1986. On the automatic activation of attitudes. *J. Pers. Soc. Psychol.* 50:229-38

Fazio, R. H., Williams, C. J. 1986. Attitude accessibility as a moderator of the attitude-perception and attitude-behavior relations: an investigation of the 1984 presidential election. *J. Pers. Soc. Psychol.* 51:505-14

Fazio, R. H., Zanna, M. P., Cooper, J. 1977. Dissonance and self-perception: an integrative view of each theory's proper domain of application. *J. Exp. Soc. Psychol.* 13:464-79

Feldman, J. M., Lynch, J. G. Jr. 1988. Self-generated validity and other effects of measurement on belief, attitude, intention and behavior. *J. Appl. Psychol.* 73:421-35

Festinger, L. 1957. *A Theory of Cognitive Dissonance.* Stanford: Stanford Univ. Press

Fishbein, M., Ajzen, I. 1975. *Belief, Attitude, Intention, and Behavior: An Introduction to Theory and Research.* Reading, MA: Addison-Wesley

Fishbein, M., Middlestadt, S. E. 1987. Using the theory of reasoned action to develop educational interventions: applications to illicit drug use. *Health Educ. Res.* 2(4): 361-71

Fishbein, M., Middlestadt, S. E., Chung, J. K. 1989. Predicting participation and choice: First-time voters in U.S. partisan elections. In *Mass Media and Political Thought: An Information Processing Approach,* ed. S. Kraus, R. Perloff, pp. 65-82. New York: Sage

Fishbein, M., Stasson, M. 1989. The role of desires, self-predictions, and perceived control in the prediction of training session attendance. *J. Appl. Soc. Psychol.* In press

Fraser, R. T., Trejo, W. R., Fishbein, M., Middlestadt, S. 1987. Influences on joining behavior for epilepsy-affiliated groups. *Adv. Epileptol.* 16:661-63

Furnham, A. F. 1988. *Lay Theories: Everyday Understanding of Problems in the Social Sciences.* New York: Pergamon

Furnham, A., Lewis, A. 1986. *The Economic Mind.* Brighton: Wheatsheaf

Gaes, G. G., Melburg, V., Tedeschi, J. T. 1986. A study examining the arousal properties of the forced-compliance situation. *J. Exp. Soc. Psychol.* 22:36-47

Gavanski, I., Wells, G. L. 1989. Counterfactual processing of normal and exceptional events. *J. Exp. Soc. Psychol.* 25:314-25

Gleicher, F. H., Kost, A., Baker, S. M.,

Stratham, A., Richman, S. A., Sherman, S. J. 1989. The role of counterfactual thinking in judgements of affect. *Pers. Soc. Psychol. Bull.* In press

Greenwald, A. G. 1989a. Why are attitudes important? See Pratkanis et al 1989, pp. 1-10

Greenwald, A. G. 1989b. Why attitudes are important: Defining attitude and attitude theory 20 years later. See Pratkanis et al 1989b, pp. 429-40

Greenwald, A. G. 1968. Cognitive learning, cognitive response to persuasion and attitude change. In *The Psychological Foundations of Attitudes,* ed. A. G. Greenwald, T. C. Brock, T. M. Ostrom, pp. 147-70. New York: Academic

Greenwald, A. G., Ronis, D. L. 1978. Twenty years of cognitive dissonance: case study of the evolution of a theory. *Psychol. Rev.* 85:53-57

Hamilton, D. L., Trolier, T. K. 1986. Stereotypes and stereotyping: an overview of the cognitive approach. In *Prejudice, Discrimination, and Racism,* ed. J. F. Dovidio, S. L. Gaertner, pp. 127-63. Orlando, FL: Academic

Harkins, S. G., Petty, R. E. 1987. Information utility and the multiple source effect. *J. Pers. Soc. Psychol.* 52:260-68

Hastie, R., Park, B. 1986. The relationship between memory and judgment depends on whether the judgment task is memory-based or on-line. *Psychol. Rev.* 93:258-68

Haugtvedt, C. P., Petty, R. E., Cacioppo, J. T. 1986. *Need for cognition and use of peripheral cues.* Presented at Annu. Meet. Midwest. Psychol. Assoc., Chicago

Haugtvedt, C. P., Petty, R. E., Cacioppo, J. T., Steidler, T. 1987. Personality and ad effectiveness: exploring the utility of need for cognition. *Adv. Consum. Res.* 15:209-12

Hazan, C., Shaver, P. 1987. Romantic love conceptualized as an attachment process. *J. Pers. Soc. Psychol.* 52(3):511-24

Hendrick, S. S., Hendrick, C. 1987. Love and sex attitudes: a close relationship. *Adv. Pers. Relat.* 1:141-69

Hendry, S. H., Shaffer, D. R. 1989. On testifying in one's own behalf: interactive effects of evidential strength and defendant's testimonial demeanor on jurors' decisions. *J. Appl. Psychol.* In press

Herek, G. M. 1987a. Can functions be measured? A new perspective on the functional approach to attitudes. *Soc. Psychol. Q.* 50:285-303

Herek, G. M. 1987b. Religious orientation and prejudice: a comparison of racial and sexual attitudes. *Pers. Soc. Psychol. Bull.* 13:34-44

Hessing, D. J., Elffers, H., Weigel, R. H. 1988. Exploring the limits of self-reports and reasoned action: an investigation of the psychology of tax evasion behavior. *J. Pers. Soc. Psychol.* 54(3):405–13

Hewstone, M., Young, L. 1988. Expectancy-value models of attitude: measurement and combination of evaluations and beliefs. *J. Appl. Soc. Psychol.* 18(11):958–71

Higgins, E. T., Bargh, J. A. 1987. Social cognition and social perception. *Annu. Rev. Psychol.* 38:369–425

Homer, P. M., Kahle, L. R. 1988. A structural equation test of the value-attitude-behavior hierarchy. *J. Pers. Soc. Psychol.* 54(4):638–46

Hough, M., Mayhew, P. 1985. *Taking Account of Crime*. London: HMSO

Houston, D. A., Fazio, R. H. 1989. Biased processing as a function of attitude accessibility: making objective judgments subjectively. *Soc. Cogn.* 7:51–66

Houston, J. 1985. Untutored lay knowledge of the principles of psychology: Do we know anything they don't? *Psychol. Rep.* 57:567–70

Hovland, C. I., Janis, I. L., Kelley, H. H., eds. 1953. *Communication and Persuasion*. New Haven: Yale Univ. Press

Howard-Pitney, B., Borgida, E., Omoto, A. M. 1986. Personal involvement: an examination of processing differences. *Soc. Cogn.* 4:39–57

Isen, A. M. 1987. Positive affect, cognitive processes, and social behavior. *Adv. Exp. Soc. Psychol.* 20:203–53

Jaccard, J. J., Becker, M. 1985. Attitudes and behavior: an information integration perspective. *J. Exp. Soc. Psychol.* 18:222–45

Jaccard, J., Helbig, D. W., Wan, C. K., Gutman, M. A., Kritz-Silverstein, D. C. 1989. Individual differences in attitude-behavior consistency: the prediction of contraceptive behavior. *J. Appl. Soc. Psychol.* In press

Jamieson, D. W. 1987. Going with gut feelings: the impact of arousal and self-monitoring on attitude utilization and formation. *Diss. Abstr.* 47:3161B–62B

Jamieson, D. W., Lydon, J. E., Zanna, M. P. 1987. Attitude and activity preference similarity: differential bases of attraction for low and high self-monitors. *J. Pers. Soc. Psychol.* 53:1052–60

Jamieson, D. W., Zanna, M. P. 1985. *Moderating the attitude-behavior relation: the joint effects of arousal and self-monitoring*. Presented at Annu. Meet. Can. Psychol. Assoc., Halifax

Jamieson, D. W., Zanna, M. P. 1986. *Attitude formation: dispositional and situational determinants of affect strength and complexity*. Presented at Annu. Meet. Can. Psychol. Assoc., Toronto

Jamieson, D. W., Zanna, M. P. 1989. Need for structure in attitude formation and expression. See Pratkanis et al 1989, pp. 383–406

Janoff-Bulman, R. 1989. Assumptive worlds and the stress of traumatic events: applications of the schema construct. *Soc. Cogn.* 7:113–36

Jaspars, J. M. 1983. The process of causal attribution in common sense. In *Attribution Theory: Social and Functional Extensions*, ed. M. Hewstone. Oxford: Blackwell

Jepson, C., Chaiken, S. 1989. Chronic issue-specific fear inhibits systematic processing of persuasive communications. *J. Soc. Behav. Pers.* In press

Johnson, B. T., Eagly, A. H. 1989. The effects of involvement on persuasion. *Psychol. Bull.* In press

Jones, E. E., Rhodewalt, F., Berglas, S., Skelton, J. A. 1981. Efforts of strategic self-presentation on subsequent self-esteem. *J. Pers. Soc. Psychol.* 41:407–21

Judd, C. M., Krosnick, J. A. 1989. The structural bases of consistency among political attitudes: effects of political expertise and attitude importance. See Pratkanis et al 1989, pp. 99–128

Judd, C. M., Lusk, C. M. 1984. Knowledge structures and evaluative judgments: effects of structural variables on judgment extremity. *J. Pers. Soc. Psychol.* 46:1193–207

Kahle, L. R., Beatty, S. E. 1987. Cognitive consequences of legislating postpurchase behavior: growing up with the bottle bill. *J. Appl. Soc. Psychol.* 17:828–43

Kahneman, D., Miller, A. 1986. Norm theory: comparing reality to its alternatives. *Psychol. Rev.* 93:136–53

Kahneman, D., Tversky, A. 1984. Choices, values and frames. *Am. Psychol.* 39:341–50

Kaiser, M. K., Jonides, J., Alexander, J. 1986. Intuitive reasoning about abstract and familiar physics problems. *Mem. Cogn.* 14:308–12

Kallgren, C. A., Wood, W. 1986. Access to attitude-relevant information in memory as a determinant of attitude-behavior consistency. *J. Exp. Soc. Psychol.* 22:328–38

Kaplowitz, S. A., Fink, E. L., Armstrong, G. B., Bauer, C. L. 1986. Message discrepancy and the persistence of attitude change: implications of an information integration model. *J. Exp. Soc. Psychol.* 22:507–30

Kardes, F. R., Sanbonmatsu, D. M., Voss, R. T., Fazio, R. H. 1986. Self-monitoring and attitude accessibility. *Pers. Soc. Psychol. Bull.* 12:468–74

Karlins, M., Coffman, T. L., Walters, G. 1969. On the fading of social stereotypes. *J. Pers. Soc. Psychol.* 13:1–16

Katz, D. 1960. The functional approach to the study of attitudes. *Public Opin. Q.* 24:163–204

Katz, I., Hass, R. G., Wachenhut, J. 1986. Racial ambivalence, value duality, and behavior. In *Prejudice, Discrimination, and Racism: Theory and Research*, ed. J. F. Dovidio, S. L. Gaertner. New York/Orlando, FL: Academic

Katz, I., Hass, R. G. 1988. Racial ambivalence and American value conflict: correlational and priming studies of dual cognitive structures. *J. Pers. Soc. Psychol.* 55:893–907

Kendzierski, D., Lamastro, V. D. 1988. Reconsidering the role of attitudes in exercise behavior: a decision theoretic approach. *J. Appl. Soc. Psychol.* 18:737–59

Kinder, D. R., Sears, D. O. 1985. Public opinion and political action. In *Handbook of Social Psychology*, ed. G. Lindzey, E. Aronson. New York: Random House. 3rd ed.

Kline, S. L. 1987. Self-monitoring and attitude-behavior correspondence in cable television subscription. *J. Soc. Psychol.* 127(6):605–9

Klinger, E. 1987. The interview questionnaire technique: reliability and validity of a mixed idiographic-nomothetic measure of motivation. In *Advances in Personality Assessment*, ed. J. N. Butcher, C. D. Spielberger, 6:31–48. Hillsdale, NJ: Erlbaum

Koslowsky, M., Kluger, A. N., Yinon, Y. 1988. Predicting behavior: combining intention with investment. *J. Appl. Psychol.* 73:102–6

Kristiansen, C. M., Zanna, M. P. 1988. Justifying attitudes by appealing to values: a functional perspective. *Br. J. Soc. Psychol.* 27:247–56

Krosnick, J. A. 1988. Attitude importance and attitude change. *J. Exp. Soc. Psychol.* 24:240–55

Kruglanski, A. W. 1989. *The Cognitive-Motivational Bases of Human Knowledge: A Theory of Lay Epistemics.* New York: Plenum. In press

Kruglanski, A. W., Freund, T. 1983. The freezing and unfreezing of lay inferences: effects on impressional primary, ethnic stereotyping, and numerical anchoring. *J. Exp. Soc. Psychol.* 19:448–68

Kunda, Z., Nisbett, R. 1985. *The psychometrics of everyday life.* Paper presented at the Annu. BPS Conf., Wales

Kuhn, T. 1970. *The Structure of Scientific Revolutions.* Chicago: Univ. Chicago Press. 2nd enl. ed.

Langer, E. J. 1989. Minding matters the consequences of mindlessness/mindfulness. *Adv. Exp. Soc. Psychol.* In press

Lau, R. R. 1989. Construct accessibility and electoral choice. *Polit. Behav.* 11:5–32

Leippe, M. R., Elkin, R. A. 1987. When motives clash: issue involvement and response involvement as determinants of persuasion. *J. Pers. Soc. Psychol.* 52:269–78

Leippe, M. R., Romanczyk, A. 1987. Children on the witness stand: a communication/persuasion analysis of jurors' reactions to child witnesses. In *Children's Eyewitness Memory*, ed. S. J. Ceci, M. P. Toglia, D. F. Ross, pp. 155–77. New York: Springer-Verlag

Leone, C. 1989. Self-generated attitude change: Some effects of thought and dogmatism on attitude polarization. *Pers. Indiv. Diff.* In press

Leone, C., Ensley, E. 1986. Self-generated attitude change: a person by situation analysis of attitude polarization and attenuation. *J. Res. Pers.* 20:434–46

Liberman, A., de la Hoz, V., Chaiken, S. 1988. *Prior attitudes as heuristic information.* Presented at Annu. Meet. West. Psychol. Assoc., Burlingame, CA

Likert, R. 1932. A technique for the measurement of attitudes. *Arch. Psychol.* 140

Lindskold, S., Han, G., Betz, B. 1986. Repeated persuasion in interpersonal conflict. *J. Pers. Soc. Psychol.* 51:1183–88

Linville, P. W. 1982. The complexity extremity effect and age based stereotyping. *J. Pers. Soc. Psychol.* 42:193–210

Linville, P. W. 1985. Self-complexity and affective extremity: Don't put all of your eggs in one basket. *Soc. Cogn.* 3:94–120

Liska, A. E. 1984. A critical examination of the causal structure of the Fishbein/Ajzen attitude-behavior model. *Soc. Psychol. Q.* 47:61–74

Little, B. 1987. Personal projects and fuzzy selves: aspects of self-identity in adolescence. In *Self and Identity: Perspectives Across the Life Span*, ed. T. Honess, K. Yardley, pp. 230–45. New York: Routledge & Kegan Paul

Lusk, C. M., Judd, C. M. 1988. Political expertise and the structural mediators of candidate evaluations. *J. Exp. Soc. Psychol.* 24:105–26

Lydon, J. E., Zanna, M. P. 1988. *Commitment in the face of adversity: a value affirmation approach.* Presented at Annu. Meet. Am. Psychol. Assoc., Atlanta

Lydon, J., Zanna, M. P., Ross, M. 1988. Bolstering attitudes by autobiographical recall: attitude persistence and selective memory. *Pers. Soc. Psychol. Bull.* 14:78–86

Mackie, D. M. 1987. Systematic and nonsystematic processing of majority and minority persuasive communications. *J. Pers. Soc. Psychol.* 53:41–52

Mackie, D. M., Worth, L. T. 1989. Processing deficits and the mediation of positive affect in persuasion. *J. Pers. Soc. Psychol.* 57:27–40

Maddux, J. E., Norton, L. W., Stoltenberg, C. D. 1986. Self-efficacy expectancy, outcome expectancy, and outcome value: relative effects on behavioral intentions. *J. Pers. Soc. Psychol.* 4:783–89

Maddux, J. E., Rogers, R. W. 1983. Protection motivation and self efficacy: a revised theory of fear appeals and attitude change. *J. Exp. Soc. Psychol.* 19:469–79

Maddux, J. E., Stanley, M. A. 1986. Self-efficacy theory in contemporary psychology: an overview. *J. Soc. Clin. Psychol.* 4(3):249–55

Markus, H., Nurius, P. 1986. Possible selves. *Am. Psychol.* 41:954–69

Martin, L. 1986. Set/reset: use and disuse of concepts in impression formation. *J. Pers. Soc. Psychol.* 51:493–504

Martin, L., Tesser, A. 1989. Toward a motivational and structural model of ruminative thought. In *The Direction of Thought: The Limits of Awareness, Intention, and Control,* ed. J. S. Uleman, J. A. Bargh, pp. 306–26. New York: Guilford. In press

McAdams, D. P. 1988. Biography, narratives, and lives: an introduction. *J. Pers.* 56:1–18

McCaul, K. D., O'Neill, H. K., Glasgow, R. E. 1988. Predicting the performance of dental hygiene behaviors: an examination of the Fishbein and Ajzen model and self-efficacy expectations. *J. Appl. Soc. Psychol.* 18(2):114–28

McGuire, W. J. 1969. The nature of attitudes and attitude change. In *The Handbook of Social Psychology,* ed. G. Lindzey, E. Aronson, 3:136–314. Reading, MA: Addison-Wesley

McGuire, W. J. 1972. Attitude change: the information-processing paradigm. In *Experimental Social Psychology,* ed. C. G. McClintock, pp. 108–141. New York: Holt, Rinehart & Winston

McGuire, W. J. 1984. Public communication as a strategy for inducing health-promoting behavioral change. *Prevent. Med.* 13:299–319

McGuire, W. J. 1985. Attitudes and attitude change. In *Handbook of Social Psychology,* ed. G. Lindzey, E. Aronson, 2:233–346. New York: Random House

McGuire, W. J. 1986. The vicissitudes of attitudes and similar representational constructs in twentieth century psychology. *Eur. J. Soc. Psychol.* 16:89–130

McGuire, W. J. 1989. The structure of individual attitudes and of attitude systems. See Pratkanis et al 1989, pp. 37–69

Meyerowitz, B. E., Chaiken, S. 1987. The effects of message framing on breast self-examination attitudes, intentions, and behavior. *J. Pers. Soc. Psychol.* 52(3):500–10

Milburn, M. A. 1987. Ideological self-schemata and schematically induced attitude consistency. *J. Exp. Soc. Psychol.* 23:383–98

Millar, M. G., Tesser, A. 1986a. Thought-induced attitude change: the effects of schema structure and commitment. *J. Pers. Soc. Psychol.* 51:259–69

Millar, M. G., Tesser, A. 1986b. Effects of affective and cognitive focus on the attitude-behavior relationship. *J. Pers. Soc. Psychol.* 51:270–76

Millar, M. G., Tesser, A. 1989. The effects of affective-cognitive consistency and thought on attitude behavior relations. *J. Exp. Soc. Psychol.* 25:189–202

Miller, D. T., McFarland, C. 1986. Counterfactual thinking and victim compensation: a test of norm theory. *Pers. Soc. Psychol. Bull.* 12:513–19

Miller, L. E., Grush, J. E. 1986. Individual differences in attitudinal versus normative determination of behavior. *J. Exp. Soc. Psychol.* 22:190–202

Miller, R. L. 1988. *Attitude change: consensus versus significant others as effective attributional sources.* Presented at Annu. Meet. Am. Psychol. Assoc., Atlanta

Mittal, B. 1988. Achieving higher seat belt usage: the role of habit in bridging the attitude-behavior gap. *J. Appl. Soc. Psychol.* 18(12):993–1016

Moore, D. L., Hausknecht, D., Thamodaran, K. 1986. Time compression, response opportunity, and persuasion. *J. Consum. Res.* 13:85–99

Mueller, D. J. 1986. *Measuring Social Attitudes: A Handbook for Researchers and Practitioners.* New York: Teachers College Press

Mugny, G., Catugati, F. 1989. *The Social Representation of Intelligence.* Cambridge: Cambridge Univ. Press. In press

Nicholls, J., Patashnick, M., Nolen, S. 1985. Adolescents' theories of education. *J. Educ. Psychol.* 77:683–92

Nicholson, J., Lucas, M., eds. 1984. *All in the Mind: Psychology in Action.* London: Methuen

Nunnally, J. 1961. *Popular Conceptions of Mental Health.* New York: Holt, Rinehart & Winston

Pendleton, D. 1983. Doctor-patient communication: a review. In *Doctor-Patient*

Communication, ed. D. Pendleton, J. Halser, pp. 5–53. London: Academic

Pennebaker, J. W. 1982. *The Psychology of Physical Symptoms.* New York: Springer-Verlag

Pettigrew, T. F. 1988. *The nature of modern racism.* Presented at Meet. Soc. Exp. Soc. Psychol., Madison

Petty, R. E., Cacioppo, J. T. 1981. *Attitudes and Persuasion: Classic and Contemporary Approaches.* Dubuque, IA: Brown. 314 pp.

Petty, R. E., Cacioppo, J. T. 1986. The elaboration likelihood model of persuasion. *Adv. Exp. Soc. Psychol.* 19:123–205

Petty, R. E., Cacioppo, J. T. 1989. Involvement and persuasion: tradition versus integration. *Psychol. Bull.* In press

Petty, R. E., Kasmer, J. A., Haugtvedt, C. P., Cacioppo, J. T. 1987a. Source and message factors in persuasion: a reply to Stiff's critique of the elaboration likelihood model. *Commun. Monogr.* 54:233–49

Petty, R. E., Rennier, G. A., Cacioppo, J. T. 1987b. Assertion versus interrogation format in opinion surveys: questions enhance thoughtful responding. *Public Opin. Q.* 51:481–94

Pratkanis, A. R. 1988. The attitude heuristic and selective fact identification. *Br. J. Soc. Psychol.* 27:257–63

Pratkanis, A. R. 1989. The cognitive representation of attitudes. See Pratkanis et al 1989, pp. 71–93

Pratkanis, A. R., Breckler, S. J., Greenwald, A. G., eds. 1989. *Attitude Structure and Function.* Hillsdale, NJ: Erlbaum

Pratkanis, A. R., Greenwald, A. G. 1989. A socio-cognitive model of attitude structure and function. *Adv. Exp. Soc. Psychol.* 22:245–85

Pratkanis, A. R., Greenwald, A. G., Leippe, M. R., Baumgardner, M. H. 1988. In search of reliable persuasion effects: III. The sleeper effect is dead. Long live the sleeper effect. *J. Pers. Soc. Psychol.* 54:203–18

Prentice, D. A. 1987. Psychological correspondence of possessions, attitudes, and values. *J. Pers. Soc. Psychol.* 53:993–1003

Quattrone, G. A., Tversky, A. 1988. Contrasting rational and psychological analyses of political choice. *Am. Polit. Sci. Rev.* 82(3):719–36

Rabow, J., Neuman, C. A., Hernandez, A. C. R. 1987. Contingent consistency in attitudes, social support and the consumption of alcohol: additive and interactive effects. *Soc. Psychol. Q.* 50(1):56–63

Raden, D. 1985. Strength-related attitude dimensions. *Soc. Psychol. Q.* 48:312–30

Rajecki, D. W. 1983. *Attitudes: Themes and*

Advances. Sunderland, MA: Sinauer Associates

Rhodewalt, F., Agustsdottir, S. 1986. Effects of self-presentation on the phenomenal self. *J. Pers. Soc. Psychol.* 50:47–55

Rippere, V. 1981. How depressing: another cognitive dimension of commonsense knowledge. *Behav. Res. Ther.* 19:169–81

Rippletoe, P. A., Rogers, R. W. 1987. Effects of components of protection-motivation theory on adaptive and maladaptive coping with a health threat. *J. Pers. Soc. Psychol.* 52:596–604

Ritter, C. 1988. Resources, behavior intentions, and drug use: a ten-year national panel analysis. *Soc. Psychol. Q.* 51(3):250–64

Rogers, R. W. 1983. Cognitive and psychological processes in fear appeals and attitude change: a revised theory of protection motivation. In *Social Psychophysiology: A Sourcebook,* ed. J. T. Cacioppo, R. E. Petty, pp. 153–76. New York: Guilford Press

Rokeach, M. 1960. *The Open and Closed Mind.* New York: Basic Books

Rokeach, M. 1973. *The Nature of Human Values.* New York: Free Press

Rokeach, M. 1979. *Understanding Human Values: Individual and Social.* New York: Free Press

Rokeach, M. 1985. Inducing change and stability in belief systems and personality structures. *J. Soc. Issues* 41:153–71

Rokeach, M., Ball-Rokeach, S. J. 1988. *Stability and change in American values priorities, 1968–1981.* Presented at the Meet Am. Assoc. Public Opin. Res. Toronto

Ronis, D. L., Kaiser, M. K. 1989. Correlates of breast self-examination in a sample of college women: analyses of linear structural relations. *J. Appl. Soc. Psychol.* In press

Ronis, D. L., Yates, J. F., Kirscht, J. P. 1989. Attitudes, decisions, and habits as determinants of repeated behavior. See Pratkanis et al 1989, pp. 213–39

Rook, K. S. 1987. Effects of case history versus abstract information on health attitudes and behaviors. *J. Appl. Soc. Psychol.* 17:533–53

Rosenberg, M. J., Hovland, C. I. 1960. Cognitive, affective, and behavioral components of attitude. See Rosenberg et al 1960

Rosenberg, M. J., Hovland, C. I., McGuire, W. J., Abelson, R. P., Brehm, J. W., eds. 1960. *Attitude Organization and Change: An Analysis of Consistency among Attitude Components,* pp. 1–14. New Haven, CT: Yale Univ. Press

Rosenberg, S., Sedlak, A. 1972. Structural

representations of implicit personality theories. *Adv. Exp. Soc. Psychol.* 6:235–97

Rosenfeld, P., Kennedy, J. G., Giacalone, R. A. 1986. Decision making: a demonstration of the post decision dissonance effect. *J. Soc. Psychol.* 126:663–65

Ross, M. 1989. The relation of implicit theories to the construction of personal histories. *Psychol. Rev.* 96(2):341–57

Rusbult, C. E., Farrell, D. 1983. A longitudinal test of the investment model: the impact on job satisfaction, job commitment, and turnover of variation in rewards, costs, alternatives, and investment. *J. Appl. Psychol.* 68(3):429–38

Sanbonmatsu, D. M., Fazio, R. H. 1986. *The automatic activation of attitudes toward products.* Presented at Annu. Meet. Assoc. Consum. Res., Toronto

Sanbonmatsu, D. M., Osborne, R. E., Fazio, R. H. 1986. The measurement of automatic attitude activation. Presented at Annu. Meet. Midwest Psychol. Assoc., Chicago

Schlegel, R. P., d'Avernas, J. R., Zanna, M., DiTecco, D., Manske, S. R. 1987. Predicting alcohol use in young adult males: a comparison of the Fishbein-Ajzen Model and Jessors' Problem Behavior Theory. *Drugs Soc.: J. Contemp. Issues* 1:7–24

Schlenker, B. R. 1987. Threats to identity: self-identification and social stress. In *Coping with Negative Life Events: Clinical and Social Psychological Perspectives,* ed. C. R. Snyder, C. E. Ford, pp. 273–321. New York: Plenum

Scher, S. J., Cooper, J. 1989. The motivational basis of dissonance: the singular role of behavioral consequences. *J. Pers. Soc. Psychol.* 56:899–906

Schmitt, B. H. 1988. *Situational determinants of attitude functions: effects on the perception and evaluation of advertisements.* Presented at Meet. Assoc. Consum. Res., Honolulu

Schroder, H. M., Driver, M. J., Streufert, S. 1967. *Human Information Processing.* New York: Holt Rinehart & Winston

Schwartz, S. H., Inbar-Saban, N. 1988. Value self-confrontation as a method to aid in weight loss. *J. Pers. Soc. Psychol.* 54(3):396–404

Scott, W. A. 1969. Structure of natural cognitions. *J. Pers. Soc. Psychol.* 12:261–78

Sears, D. O. 1988. Symbolic racism. In *Eliminating Racism: Profiles in Controversy,* ed. P. A. Katz, D. A. Taylor. New York: Plenum

Sears, D. O., Kinder, D. R. 1985. Whites' opposition to busing: on conceptualizing and operationalizing group conflict. *J. Pers. Soc. Psychol.* 38:1141–47

Shaffer, D. R. 1985. The defendant's testimony. In *The Psychology of Evidence and Trial Procedure,* ed. S. Kassin, L. S. Wrightsman, pp. 124–49. Beverly Hills, CA: Sage

Shavitt, S. 1989. Operationalizing functional theories of attitude. See Pratkanis et al 1989, pp. 311–37

Shavitt, S., Brock, T. C. 1986. Self-relevant responses in commercial persuasion: field and experimental tests. In *Advertising and Consumer Psychology,* ed. J. Olson, K. Sentis, 3: 149–71. New York: Praeger

Shavitt, S., Fazio, R. H. 1987. *Attitude functions in the attitude-behavior relationship.* Presented at Annu. Meet. Midwest, Psychol. Assoc., Chicago

Shavitt, S., Fazio, R. H. 1988. *Attitude functions and self-monitoring in the attitude-behavior relation.* Presented at Annu. Meet. Midwest. Psychol. Assoc., Chicago

Shavitt, S., Han, S., Kim, Y. C., Tillman, C. 1988. *Attitude objects and self-monitoring interactively affect attitude functions.* Presented at Annu. Meet. Midwest Psychol. Assoc., Chicago

Shedler, J., Manis, M. 1986. Can the availability heuristic explain vividness effects? *J. Pers. Soc. Psychol.* 51:26–36

Sheppard, B. H., Hartwick, J., Warshaw, P. R. 1988. A theory of reasoned action: a meta-analysis of past research with recommendations for modifications and future research. *J. Cons. Res.* 15:325–43

Sherif, M., Sherif, C. W. 1967. Attitude as the individual's own categories: the social judgment-involvement approach to attitude and attitude change. In *Attitude, Ego-Involvement, and Change,* ed. C. W. Sherif, M. Sherif, pp. 105–89. New York: Wiley

Shiffrin, R. M., Schneider, W. 1977. Controlled and automatic human information processing: II. Perceptual learning, automatic attending and a general theory. *Psychol. Rev.* 84:127–90

Sidanius, J. 1988. Political sophistication and political deviance: a structural equation examination of context theory. *J. Pers. Soc. Psychol.* 55:37–51

Sigall, H., Page, R. 1971. Current stereotypes: a little fading, a little faking. *J. Pers. Soc. Psychol.* 18:247–55

Silver, R. L., Boon, C., Stones, M. H. 1983. Searching for meaning in misfortune: making sense of incest. *J. Soc. Issues* 39:81–102

Smith, M. B. 1947. The personal setting of public opinions: a study of attitudes toward Russia. *Public Opin. Q.* 11:507–23

Smith, M. B., Bruner, J. S., White, R. W. 1956. *Opinions and Personality.* New York: Wiley

Smith, S. M., Shaffer, D. R. 1989a. *Speech rate, message valence, and persuasion*. Presented at Annu. Meet. Southeast. Psychol. Assoc., Washington, DC

Smith, S. M., Shaffer, D. R. 1989b. *Speech rate, message quality, message relevance, and attitude change*. Presented at Annu. Meet. Am. Psychol. Assoc., New Orleans

Snyder, M., DeBono, K. G. 1985. Appeals to image and claims about quality: understanding the psychology of advertising. *J. Pers. Soc. Psychol.* 49:586–97

Snyder, M., DeBono, K. G. 1987. A functional approach to attitudes and persuasion. In *Social Influence: The Ontario Symposium*, ed. M. P. Zanna, J. M. Olson, C. P. Herman, 5:107–25. Hillsdale, NJ: Erlbaum

Snyder, M., DeBono, K. G. 1989. Understanding the functions of attitudes: lessons from personality and social behavior. See Pratkanis et al 1989, pp. 339–59

Sorrentino, R. M., Bobocel, D. R., Gitta, M. Z., Olson, J. M., Hewitt, E. C. 1988. Uncertainty orientation and persuasion: individual differences in the effects of personal relevance on social judgments. *J. Pers. Soc. Psychol.* 55:357–71

Steele, C., Liu, T. 1983. Dissonance processes as self-affirmation. *J. Pers. Soc. Psychol.* 45:5–19

Sternberg, R. 1985. Implicit theories of intelligence, creativity and wisdom. *J. Pers. Soc. Psychol.* 49:607–27

Sternberg, R. J., Grajek, S. 1984. The nature of love. *J. Pers. Soc. Psychol.* 47:312–29

Stiff, J. B. 1986. Cognitive processing of persuasive message cues: a meta-analytic review of the effects of supporting information on attitudes. *Commun. Monogr.* 53:75–89

Strack, F., Martin, L. 1987. Thinking, judging and communicating: a Process account of context effects in attitude surveys. In *Social Information Processing and Survey Methodology*, ed. H. Hippler, N. Schwarz, S. Sudman, pp. 123–48. New York: Springer-Verlag

Strack, F., Schwarz, N., Gschneidinger, E. 1985. Happiness and reminiscing: the role of time perspective, affect, and mode of thinking. *J. Pers. Soc. Psychol.* 47:1460–69

Stroebe, W., Diehl, M. 1988. When social support fails: supporter characteristics in compliance-induced attitude change. *Pers. Soc. Psychol. Bull.* 14:136–44

Suedfeld, P., Bluck, S. 1988. Changes in integrative complexity prior to surprise attacks. *J. Conflict Resolut.* 32(4):626–35

Suedfeld, P., Tetlock, P. 1977. Integrative complexity of communication in in-

ternational crises. *J. Conflict Resolut.* 21:169–84

Swann, W. B. Jr., Pelham, B. W., Chidester, T. R. 1988. Change through paradox: using self-verification to alter beliefs. *J. Pers. Soc. Psychol.* 54:268–73

Taylor, S. E., Schneider, S. K. 1989. Coping and the simulation of events. *Soc. Cognit.* 7:176–96

Tedeschi, J. T. 1981. *Impression Management Theory and Social Psychological Research.* New York: Academic

Tesser, A. 1978. Self-generated attitude change. *Adv. Exp. Soc. Psychol.* 11:181–227

Tesser, A. 1988. Toward a self-evaluation maintenance model of social behavior. *Adv. Exp. Soc. Psychol.* 21:181–227

Tesser, A., Leone, C. 1977. Cognitive schemas and thought as determinants of attitude change. *J. Exp. Soc. Psychol.* 13:340–56

Tetlock, P. E. 1983. Accountability and complexity of thought. *J. Pers. Soc. Psychol.* 45:74–83

Tetlock, P. E. 1984. Cognitive style and political belief systems in the British House of Commons. *J. Pers. Soc. Psychol.* 46:365–75

Tetlock, P. E. 1985. Accountability: a social check on the fundamental attribution error. *Soc. Psychol. Q.* 48:227–36

Tetlock, P. E. 1986. A value pluralism model of ideological reasoning. *J. Pers. Soc. Psychol.* 50:819–27

Tetlock, P. E. 1989. Structure and function in political belief systems. See Pratkanis et al 1989, pp. 129–51

Tetlock, P. E., Kim, J. I. 1987. Accountability and judgment processes in a personality prediction task. *J. Pers. Soc. Psychol.* 52:700–9

Thompson, S. C., Janigian, A. S. 1988. Life schemes: a framework for understanding the search for meaning. *J. Soc. Clin. Psychol.* 7:260–80

Thurstone, L. L., Chave, E. J. 1929. *The Measurement of Attitude.* Chicago: Univ. Chicago Press

Toneatto, T., Binik, Y. 1987. The role of intentions, social norms, and attitudes in the performance of dental flossing: a test of the theory of reasoned action. *J. Appl. Soc. Psychol.* 17(6):593–603

Tourangeau, R., Rasinski, K. A. 1988. Cognitive processes underlying context effects in attitude measurement. *Psychol. Bull.* 103:299–314

Tourangeau, R., Rasinski, K. A., Bradburn, N., D'Andrade, R. 1989a. Carryover effects in attitude surveys. *Pub. Opin. Q.* In press

Tourangeau, R., Rasinski, K. A., Bradburn, N., D'Andrade. R. 1989b. Belief accessibility and context effects in attitude measurement. *J. Exp. Soc. Psychol.* In press

Triandis, H. C. 1980. Values, attitudes, and interpersonal behavior. In *Nebraska Symposium on Motivation, 1979*, ed. M. M. Page, pp. 195–259. Lincoln: Univ. Nebraska Press

van der Pligt, J. Eiser, J. R., Spears, R. 1986. Construction of a nuclear power station in one's locality: attitudes and salience. *Basic Appl. Soc. Psychol.* 7:1–15

Vannoy, J. S. 1965. Generality of cognitive complexity-simplicity as a personality construct. *J. Pers. Soc. Psychol.* 2:385–96

Vinokur, A., Caplan, R. D. 1987. Attitudes and social support: determinants of jobseeking behavior and well-being among the unemployed. *J. Appl. Soc. Psychol.* 17(12):1007–24

Warsaw, P. R., Calantone, R., Joyce, M. 1986. A field application of the Fishbein and Ajzen intention model. *J. Soc. Psychol.* 126(1):135–36

Wegner, D. M., Schneider, D. J., Carter S. R., White, T. L. 1987. Paradoxical effects of thought suppression. *J. Pers. Soc. Psychol.* 47:237–52

Wells, G. L., Gavanski, I. 1989. Mental simulation of causality. *J. Pers. Soc. Psychol.* 56:161–69

Wentzlaff, R., Wegner, D. M., Roper, D. W. 1988. Depression and mental control: the resurgence of unwanted negative thoughts. *J. Pers. Soc. Psychol.*:882–92

Wiegman, O. 1987. Attitude change in a realistic experiment: the effect of party membership and audience reaction during an interview with a Dutch politician. *J. Appl. Soc. Psychol.* 17:37–49

Wilson, T. D., Dunn, D. S. 1986. Effects of introspection on attitude-behavior consistency: analyzing reasons versus focusing on feelings. *J. Exp. Soc. Psychol.* 22:249–63

Wilson, T. D., Dunn, D. S., Bybee, J. A., Hyman, D. B., Rotondo, J. A. 1984. Effects of analyzing reasons on attitude-behavior consistency. *J. Pers. Soc. Psychol.* 47:5–16

Wilson, T. D., Dunn, D. S., Kraft, D., Lisle, D. J. 1989. Introspection, attitude change, and attitude-behavior consistency: the disruptive effects of explaining why we feel the way we do. *Adv. Exp. Soc. Psychol.* 22:287–343

Wilson, T. D., Kraft, D. 1989. The disruptive effects of explaining attitudes: the moderating effects of knowledge about the attitude object. *J. Exp. Soc. Psychol.* In press

Wood, W., Kallgren, C. A. 1988. Communicator attributes and persuasion: recipients' access to attitude-relevant information in memory. *Pers. Soc. Psychol. Bull.* 14:172–82

Wood, W., Kallgren, C. A., Priester, R. M. 1985. Access to attitude-relevant information in memory as a determinant of persuasion: the role of message attributes. *J. Exp. Soc. Psychol.* 21:73–85

Worth, I. T., Mackie, D. M. 1987. Cognitive mediation of positive affect in persuasion. *Soc. Cogn.* 5:76–94

Wrightsman, L. 1974. *Assumptions About Human Nature: A Social-Psychological Approach.* Monterey, CA: Brooks/Cole

Wu, C., Shaffer, D. R. 1987. Susceptibility to persuasive appeals as a function of source credibility and prior experience with the attitude object. *J. Pers. Soc. Psychol.* 52:677–88

Wurtele, S. K. 1988. Increasing women's calcium intake: the role of health beliefs, intentions, and health value. *J. Appl. Soc. Psychol.* 18(8):627–39

Young, J., Borgida, E., Sullivan, J., Aldrich, J. 1987. Personal agendas and the relationship between self-interest and voting behavior. *Soc. Psychol. Q.* 50:64–71

Zajonc, R. B. 1980. Feeling and thinking: preferences need no inferences. *Am. Psychol.* 25:151–75

Zajonc, R. B., Markus, H. 1982. Affective and cognitive factors in preferences. *J. Consum. Res.* 9:123–31

Zanna, M. P., Rempel, J. K. 1988. Attitudes: a new look at an old concept. In *The Social Psychology of Knowledge,* ed. D. Bar-Tal, A. Kruglanski. New York: Cambridge Univ. Press

Zanna, M. P., Sande, G. N. 1987. The effects of collective action on the attitudes of individual group members: a dissonance analysis. In *Social Influence: The Ontario Symposium,* ed. M. P. Zanna, J. M. Olson, C. P. Herman, 5:151–63. Hillsdale, NJ: Erlbaum

Annu. Rev. Psychol. 1990. 41:525–56

MORAL RULES: THEIR CONTENT AND ACQUISITION

John M. Darley

Department of Psychology, Princeton University, Princeton, New Jersey 08540

Thomas R. Shultz

Department of Psychology, McGill University, Montreal, Quebec, Canada, H3A 1B1

CONTENTS

INTRODUCTION

This is the first time that a chapter on the moral judgments of children has appeared in the *Annual Review of Psychology*. To limit our coverage of what is now a vast literature, we focus on newer information-processing approaches to moral judgments. Other perspectives have been the subject of

525

0066-4308/90/0201-0525$02.00

other reviews: The latest version of *The Handbook of Child Development* (Mussen 1984) has several relevant chapters. The moral development chapter by Rest covers many of the issues in moral development from a Kohlbergian but empirically rigorous perspective. Segments of the moral judgment literature are reviewed by DePalma & Foley (1975) and Likona (1976). Rushton (1980) and Staub (1984) examine altruism. Kagan & Lamb (1987) have recently edited a book on the emergence of morality in young children. All of these provide more detail on many of the topics on which we touch, and consider topics that we do not discuss.

History of The Field

PIAGET   The major impetus for the empirical study of moral judgments was provided by Piaget's (1932) *The Moral Judgment of the Child,* which stimulated in American centers of developmental research an explosion of increasingly sophisticated experimental studies on "the intention-consequence relationship." Piaget was taken to have concluded that children in the egocentric stage of development did not use intention information in morally judging the perpetrator of a harmful act, but instead based their judgments only on the degree of damage done by the act. (We discuss the empirical standing of the intention-consequence relationship below. Here, we seek to characterize the historical trends Piaget set in motion.) Because Piaget's experimental designs were flawed, many researchers set out to do more careful studies. In addition, certain aspects of Piaget's assertions struck angry sparks from an American tradition that was behavioristic, focussed on individual differences, psychometrically rigorous, and meliorist. Piaget was read as asserting that younger children *could not* make intention-based moral judgments and that all children made the transition to a post-operationalist stage at about the same age and thus should suddenly develop an intention-based morality in chronological lockstep. In response to this reading Americans working on what we might call the "Piagetian contention" produced studies more precise in design and more concerned with proper scaling of the children's answers. They tested larger samples of children, in order to establish the range of variation expected from the prevailing individual-difference perspective. Consistent with American optimism, such designs sought to demonstrate that at least some younger children could make intention-based judgments.

Although these studies, too, were flawed, they were important in the history of psychology. They established a tradition of the empirical study of human judgments, as opposed to behaviors. Thus developmental psychology came to the study of cognition far earlier than did many other fields of psychology.

KOHLBERG   The second landmark in the field is the work of Lawrence Kohlberg (1969, 1981; see Rest 1984 and Kurtines & Gewirtz 1989 for recent presentations). Influenced both by the stage theory of Piaget and by certain moral philosophers, Kohlberg and his associates have added several metatheoretical postulates to the theory of developmental stages.

Kohlberg held that moral judgments progress through an unvarying series of stages. Although interactions with peers provide its impetus, the progression is irreversible; and not all people reach the highest stages of moral development. Kohlberg assessed moral development by having trained coders examine a person's justifications for his/her decisions on a series of morally tough calls. Should Heinz break into a drugstore to obtain expensive medicine that would ameliorate his wife's illness? By evaluating not the decision itself but the justifications behind it,[1] Kohlbergians have seemed to assume that all moral decisions are equally amenable to justification. (More likely they have taken the methodological stance that one most clearly reveals a moral rationale by presenting a person with a decision among morally equivalent outcomes.)

The Kohlbergian enterprise is now a large one. A number of psychologists are committed to the validity and utility of the theory. Various training programs are now in effect to improve people's moral reasoning, and Kohlbergians speculate on how society might be reorganized to improve the general quality of moral reasoning. The enterprise is also highly controversial and subject to many philosophical and psychological criticisms.

Our review, guided by current information-processing perspectives, focuses on the specific principles individuals use to make specific moral judgments (e.g. responsibility, blame, and punishment for moral transgressions) and on rules for the distribution of rewards. Eventually we contrast our approach and the differently aimed Kohlbergian research program.

NEO-KOHLBERGIANS AND CRITICS   Several researchers who began working within the Kohlberg tradition have significantly emended his views. For example, Kohlberg suggested that children began by regarding moral rules as rules about social conventions and only at later stages recognized their different status. Turiel (1983) and others (Nucci & Nucci 1982; Smetana 1983) have demonstrated that children understand this distinction early. Children experience moral rules as obligatory, universal, and unalterable; conventional rules as based on society consensus are alterable. Children develop parallel and independent perspectives on the two sorts of rules. Still, Turiel discriminates attitudes toward conventions into stages, and takes a

---

[1]Rest (1975) has worked out a more objectively scorable test to measure Kohlberg's stages and subjected it to extensive and careful psychometric explorations (Rest et al 1978).

structural developmental perspective on what drives children through stages. More recently, Shweder (Shweder et al 1987) has suggested that the relationships between "morality" and "convention" differ sharply between cultures, and that the Western concept of morality as a matter of contractual relationships between autonomous individuals pursuing their own self-interest causes our separation of the two. Based on his research among Brahman and Untouchable families in India, he shows that the social practices of a culture can be regarded as moral imperatives.

This raises the question of the cultural universality of moral principles (see Shweder et al 1987 for an illuminating discussion of this point). Kohlberg claimed a cross-cultural universality for his stages, but Gilligan's findings (1982) challenge the claim. Like an anthropologist reporting on the moral principles of another culture, Gilligan has argued that the higher morality of women differs from that of men. It is based on attachment to others and therefore on both the minimization of harm and the importance of care and attention in sustaining the networks of human relationship. She also suggests that Kohlberg's stages inappropriately enshrine our Western liberal capitalistic view of autonomous individuality. Gilligan has identified a legitimate domain of moral concern, but it is likely that both women and men understand the moral relevance of harm-doing and of positive obligation.

The Influence of the Early Research Traditions on the Field

Several themes are characteristic of the early work. First is the view that moral judgments are made according to one's stage of moral development. This notion implies that moral judgments across different moral domains will show an underlying stage-based unity. Relevant to evaluating this view are various current inquiries (e.g. Gelman & Baillergeon 1983; Shantz 1984) into the generality of the development of judgment.

Second is the tendency to think of moral development as dependent on cognitive development, and of changes in moral judgment as evidence of changes in cognitive development. In Piaget's notion of "structural parallelism," sophistication of moral judgment was a function of cognitive developmental stage. Many recent studies have maintained this orientation, first correlating Piagetian stage with moral judgment; more recently (and more successfully), studies have postulated the dependence of certain sophisticated moral capacities (e.g. to use a proportional equity distribution rule) on certain underlying cognitive capacities.

Later theorists saw a more complex set of forces driving moral development. Kohlberg's theory emphasized the role of peer interaction (see Walker 1980 for a good discussion). Selman (1971) further specified the relationships between cognitive development and peer interaction, and argued for the centrality of the child's developing capacities for perspective-taking.

Certain cognitive developments are necessary for attaining certain of Selman's (1971) perspective-taking stages, which in turn are necessary for attaining certain moral judgmental stages. However, cognitive development alone is insufficient to bring a child to make judgments at a particular level of moral development; peer interactional influences are likewise necessary to actualize the potential changes in moral perspective.

Among psychologists the study of moral judgments was one of the first examples of a sustained concern for cognition. Not surprisingly, researchers found many questions to explore about judgments; it must have seemed premature to them to relate cognitions to behaviors in the field of morality. Thus initially it was left to the behaviorists to study moral behavior (e.g. Hartshorne & May 1928; Aronfreed 1968), creating a disconnection that can be observed to this day: The categories into which research on children's moral judgments can be coded differ greatly from those used by students of moral behavior.

The study of moral judgments emerged as cognitive in orientation, and its strengths and weaknesses followed more or less directly from this fact: a well-developed concern for the structure of moral reasoning, and for the relationships between moral and other cognitions; a postponement of inquiry into the relationship between moral behavior and moral judgments, and into the social-interactional context for the learning of moral judgments. The Kohlbergian tradition presents dilemmas in which both judgment options contain roughly balanced elements of rightness and wrongness, and then looks at the rationalizations for whichever judgment option is chosen. This practice obscures the fact that there are cases in which almost any individual judging the case would find one action option clearly morally preferable to another. In this review we attempt to elucidate the rules that lead to the moral judgments in these cases, and to assess the ways children learn those rules.

The Domains of Moral Judgment

Acts are judged morally right or wrong depending on whether they obey or violate some *moral rule*. A rule is a moral one if adherence to it is experienced as obligatory, if it applies to all people regardless of their attitude toward it, and if its force is impersonal and external (Shweder et al 1981). Because the sphere of morality is culturally defined, we make a consequential and value-laden judgment in choosing the domains to cover in this review. Likewise the literature we review here suggests our culture's moral emphases. The bulk of the experimental literature involves the elements of retributive justice—guilt and innocence, punishment and responsibility. A second topic, heavily studied at the adult level and now being rapidly adopted in the developmental literature, is the fair distribution of rewards. Less frequently studied, although certainly within the sphere of morality, are prosocial behaviors. Finally, there is a growing recognition of the importance of empirically analyzing "procedural justice," those rules by means of which rewards and punishments are allocated. We consider each of these areas in turn, giving by far the most attention to retributive justice.

RETRIBUTIVE JUSTICE

Whenever someone has been harmed, a number of issues arise. If the harm was caused by someone else's action, is the agent morally responsible for the harm? Is the agent blameworthy? How much should a blameworthy agent be punished? Because the perpetrators of harm may be punished, the term *retributive* justice is appropriate.

Review of the Literature

What reasoning principles do ordinary people use in evaluating the infliction of harm, and how do they learn them? Let's begin with the literature on adults' judgment about harm-doing.

ADULT RULES   A number of contemporary investigators of the psychology of retributive justice (Darley & Zanna 1982; Jaspars et al 1983; Shaver 1985; Shultz & Schleifer 1983) have found theoretical inspiration in philosophical analyses of morality or law (Austin 1956; Feinberg 1968; Harper & James 1956; Hart 1968; Hart & Honoré 1959). These philosophical treatments tend to be conceptually rigorous, logically consistent, and of fairly broad scope. In general, psychological studies inspired by these philosophical analyses have focused on determining the information and inference rules ordinary people use in their judgments of harm-doing. Thus, it is appropriate to call these *information-processing* theories. In contrast to Kohlberg's concentration on rationalization of past moral decisions, the emphasis here is on the use of rules of reasoning to process case information. Such information processing is thought to generate moral decisions themselves, quite apart from its effect on how these decisions might be justified later.

One such philosophically inspired pyschological theory was developed by Shultz and Schleifer (Shultz & Schleifer 1983; Shultz et al 1981), and others have developed ideas parallel to their model. Shaver (1985) has reviewed and summarized much of the relevant philosophical and psychological work and has proposed a psychological theory that overlaps the Shultz-Schleifer model in a number of respects. Darley & Zanna (1982) have conducted psychological experiments on the moral acceptability of certain defenses drawn from legal philosophy. Jaspars and Fincham (Fincham & Jaspars 1980; Jaspars et al

1983) have reviewed and contributed to much of this law-inspired psychological literature, and Lloyd-Bostock (1983) has provided an extended rationale for drawing on common legal principles. Here we draw most heavily on the Shultz-Schleifer model, involving the other contributors when appropriate.

The theory focuses on cases in which a person may have done something to harm someone else. It specifies that major decisions in such cases focus on whether that person is the cause of the harm, is morally responsible for the harm, and is deserving of blame; a final decision concerns how much, if any, punishment should be administered. Each major decision after the first makes use of information processed during previous major decisions. The relations among the major decisions can be described in terms of presupposition. Figure 1 illustrates the major concepts in the model.

As indicated, judgments of moral responsibility presuppose those of causation. If the protagonist is judged not to have caused the harm, then there is no need to consider whether he is morally responsible for it. Similarly, judgments of blame presuppose those of moral responsibility. And finally, decisions about punishment presuppose judgments of blame. A person is morally responsible for harm that he caused if the harm cannot be excused. Blame results from a decision that a person is at fault, given that he has caused and is responsible for the harm. Without moral responsibility, there is no need to consider blame. The decision to punish involves assigning the consequences that should befall the blameworthy person. If the person is not blameworthy, then no decision needs to be taken about punishment.

According to this model the first major judgment to be made concerns the causation of the harm. Causation is determined by a combination of generative and conditional information. The generative view of causation (Shultz & Kestenbaum 1985) holds that an effect is generated or produced by transmission from the cause. Supplementing this generative approach is the *not but for* (or *sine qua non*) test, which is widely used in jurisprudence (Harper & James 1956). The *not but for* rule holds that a person's behavior is a cause of harm if and only if the harm would not have occurred without it. The test thus focuses on the necessary conditions of responsibility. Shultz et al (1981) found strong evidence that adults use necessary conditions in judging the causation of harm. Other researchers (Hart & Honoré 1959; Hilton & Slugoski 1986; Gorovitz 1965; Kahneman & Miller 1986) have argued that people use sufficient conditions, asking whether the protagonist's action distinguishes the current harm-producing situation from some appropriate standard in which harm did not result. Psychological evidence on the use of sufficient conditions has been inconclusive, with some research supporting this principle (Hilton & Slugoski 1986) and other research indicating it does not figure importantly in causal judgments (Shultz et al 1981).

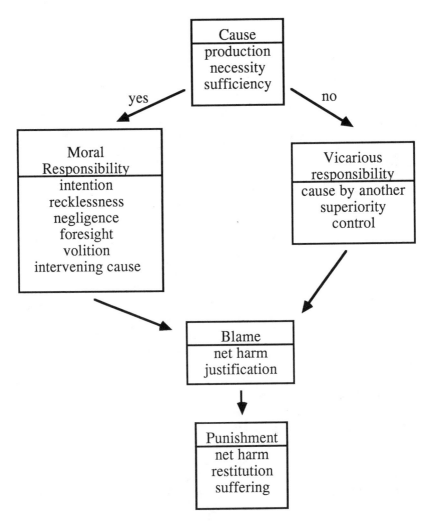

Figure 1   Overview of the Shultz-Schleifer model.

The next major judgment in the model, that regarding moral responsibility, is made by a joint consideration of causation and excuses. A person is not held morally responsible for harm he/she caused accidentally (i.e. without intention, recklessness, or negligence), involuntarily (i.e. under pressure or duress), or without foresight of the resulting harm (Shultz et al 1981; Shultz & Wright 1985; Shultz et al 1986). Nor is the agent judged responsible if the causal chain leading from the action to the harm is broken by some unforeseen event that exacerbated the harm (Fincham & Shultz 1981).

In judging intention, the so-called matching rule is preferred and is used whenever the protagonist's plan is known (Shultz & Wells 1985). If that plan is known and the harm is included in the plan, then it is concluded that the harm was intended unless the harm was not caused as planned (Shultz 1988). If the actor's plan is not known, then judges fall back on various objective heuristics such as valence, monitoring, and discounting (Shultz & Wells 1985): Did the harmful outcome have positive valence for the actor, did the actor monitor the relation between action and outcome, and is it possible to discount intention because of alternate external causes?

If intention is not attributed to the harm-causer, then the harm is said to be "done by accident" and other decisions about the act must be made. Briefly (see Karlovac & Darley 1989 for a more extended discussion), if the harm could have been foreseen by a prudent individual, then the actor can be punished if he/she failed to take available precautions. Accidental harms may be divided into three categories: (*a*) In cases of unforeseeable accident, the perpetrator of harm is normally not blamed. (*b*) An individual is negligent (D'Arcy 1963) if he or she acts without due care when harms are foreseeable. (*c*) An individual who flagrantly fails to take precautions, even when the risks of his or her actions are both foreseeable and high, may be judged recklessly or criminally negligent. Those who do negligent harm are judged less responsible than those who do intentional harm, more responsible than those who do accidental harm (Karlovac & Darley 1989; Shultz & Wright 1985).

In negligence cases ordinary people find principles of liability or restitution more appropriate than those of retribution. Perpetrators of criminal recklessness, however, are judged not only to be liable for the damage, but also to deserve retributive punishment for immoral action. It is unclear whether this fact contradicts Shaver's (1985) contention that moral blame requires the assessment of intent. An individual judged reckless may be perceived to have committed his/her act intentionally.

In cases where it is judged that the harm was done intentionally, blame is a joint function of moral responsibility, the presence of net harm, and justification for the harm. If the protagonist is morally responsible for the harm and there is some net harm (i.e. more harm than benefit to the victim), then the protagonist is blameworthy unless the harm is justified. The distinction between excuses and justifications is a subtle one (Austin 1956). Excuses are offered when one admits to having caused harm, but does not accept responsibility for it. The bank manager who admits to letting burglars into the bank vault but who did so because the burglars held his family hostage is pleading the excuse of duress. If such an excuse is accepted, the act was not immoral and the question of blame does not arise. A justification comes into play, on the other hand, when the actor accepts moral responsibility for the harm but denies that it was a bad thing to do, thereby avoiding blame (perhaps even earning credit). The soldier who shoots the enemy or the executioner who hangs the convicted murderer acts under the justification of "public duty." Self-defense is often claimed to justify what would otherwise be punishable harm-doing. The general notion behind justification is this: If society agrees that the act did more good than harm, then the harm was justified—unless there was a less harmful way of achieving the same good.

A weaker class of defenses exists, generally called mitigating circumstances. Such a circumstance (e.g. a reported provocation) generally reduces but does not eliminate blameworthiness.

If the protagonist is blameworthy, then punishment can be assigned (Harper & James 1956; Hart & Honoré 1959). Following the retribution theory of punishment (Hart 1968), we suggest that punishment is directly proportional to the net amount of harm, scaled down by restitution the perpetrator has made and the degree to which the perpetrator has suffered as a result of having caused the harm. Many psychological experiments have found that a major determinant of the amount of punishment is the severity of the harm (e.g. DeJong et al 1976; Shaw & Reitan 1969).

The discussion so far has focused on holding someone blameworthy for harm that he/she has directly caused. However, blame can be assigned in the absence of direct causation. A parent, for example, may be held liable for harm caused by his/her child. This is accomplished through the mechanism of vicarious responsibility. Ordinary subjects hold someone vicariously responsible only when that person is in a superior position to the perpetrator and should have prevented the perpetrator from causing harm (Shultz et al 1987). The concept of vicarious responsibility provides an interesting perspective on the famous Milgram experiments. Had harm actually been done by the electric shocks, the experimenter who commanded the teacher to continue giving the shocks would be judged morally more responsible and more blameworthy than the teacher.

CHILDRENS' RULES   A number of developmental studies have touched on issues related to the information-processing theory of adult judgments sketched above. Owing to Piaget's influence, vast numbers of experiments in the literature treat issues of harmful intent and the severity of harm. Such experiments usually test Piaget's prediction of an age-related shift from a focus on consequences to a consideration of intention. Children use these two concepts in the way specified by the model. For example, children as young as 6 or 7 years view intentional harm as more blameworthy (e.g. Berndt & Berndt 1975; Ferguson & Rule 1983) and more punishable (e.g. Miller & McCann 1979) than accidental harm (cf reviews by Karniol 1978; Keasey 1978).

Darley & Zanna (1982) found that 7-year-olds (but not 6-year-olds) punished intentional harm more than unintentional-but-foreseeable harm and the latter more than accidental harm. Evidence for the use of the various heuristics for judging intentionality (matching, valence, monitoring, and discounting) has been found in children as young as 3–4 years (Shultz 1980; Shultz & Wells 1985). Foreseeable harm is judged to be worse than un-foreseen harm by 3–4-year-olds (Nelson-LeGall 1985) and by 7-year-olds (Darley & Zanna 1982).

Evidence for the mitigation of punishment based on various justifications (necessity, public duty, and provocation) was found by Darley et al (1978) for children of 6 years and older (see also Berndt 1977). Hommers & Anderson (1985) reported strong effects of restitution on the punishment responses of children 4–5 years old and older. Apologies effectively mitigate punishment by children as young as 6–7 years (Leon 1982; Darby & Schlenker 1982).

Research designed to test the Shultz-Schleifer model developmentally provided support for the view that children reasoned according to some aspects of the model, particularly in their use of necessity information to determine causation and volition information to determine moral responsibility (Schleifer et al 1983). The most direct test of the model utilized a simplified interview procedure devised to bring the task within the conceptual grasp of young children (Shultz et al 1986). The results indicated a fairly sophisticated use of a variety of the moral concepts by children from 5 years of age. Children revealed evidence of knowing that judgments of punishment presupposed judgments of moral responsibility and that moral responsibility judgments presuppose causal judgments. They also used information on intention and negligence to assign moral responsibility and information on restitution to assign punishment. Developmental trends in this experiment included an increasing sensitivity to these concepts, greater tolerance for harm-doing, and more emphasis on restitution rather than punishment with increasing age.

Zanna (1988) reported on cross-sectional and short-term longitudinal studies of the development of concepts of intention, foreseeability, and justification. His findings suggest that between the ages of 4 and 6 years children come to distinguish between intentional and unintentional harm and then to distinguish simultaneously between foreseeable and unforeseeable harm, on the one hand, and justified and unjustified harm on the other.

Does the model apply outside the lab? Observations by Walton and Sedlak (Walton 1985; Walton & Sedlak 1982) suggest that the way children deal with transgressions in an open classroom setting is closely related to the rules of the information-processing model. Children 5–10 years old reacted to confrontations over their possible transgressions by: (a) denying that they caused the alleged harm [called "denial" by Walton (1985)], (b) making excuses for the harm they caused, (*c*) justifying their harm-producing actions, or (*d*) validating the accusation [called "compliance" by Walton (1985)]. These reaction categories are virtually identical to the Shultz-Schleifer model's main issues of causation, responsibility, blame, and punishment, respectively. An interesting observation is that the excuse types spontaneously used by children corresponded to the subcategories of foreseeability [called "deny knowledge" by Walton (1985)], voluntariness [called "deny control" by Walton (1985)], and intention, all of which also appear in the proposed model. From the examples provided, admission of guilt seems often to be accompanied by some sort of restitution or apology, as one would expect. Thus, both experimental and naturalistic investigations have been converging on the sort of rule-based model of retributive justice outlined above. The literature further suggests that children's and adults' retributive judgments follow much the same rules. Sedlak (1979) presents evidence, however, that children and adults sometimes use different inferential patterns to provide information missing in the scenarios they are presented with. The two groups therefore sometimes arrive at different judgments of blameworthiness and punishment.

Contrasts between the Information-Processing and Rationalization Approaches

There are major differences between our information-processing approach and a Kohlbergian or other rationalization approach to moral reasoning. Kohlberg's primary interest was in a subject's rationalization for a prior moral judgment. In contrast, information-processing researchers attempt to assess the rules used to make moral judgments. As stimulus input to the decision maker, Kohlberg uses moral dilemmas, difficult questions without clear-cut moral answers. Information-processing researchers, on the other hand, use simpler, clearer cases (similar to those used in Piaget's 1932 research) to aid in the diagnosis of reasoning rules. In the information-processing approach, use of a particular rule of reasoning is identified by finding that differences in judgment are produced by manipulated differences in rule-relevant information presented to the subjects. Thus, while the rationalization approach requires the subject to have direct conscious access to the rule he or she uses, the information-processing approach does not.

These differences have some interesting implications for developmental findings. Rationalization researchers generally find fairly slow moral development, with the transition from conventional to principled reasoning, for example, occurring only in middle adolescence, if it occurs at all. We suggest that this apparent slowness can be traced to the use of difficult, complicated cases, and to the requirement that respondents, who may to begin with have poor access to the rules they use in making moral decisions, produce complex verbal responses for the researcher. Difficult cases are, of course, hard to present except as long verbal narratives, which are likely to be difficult for children to comprehend. Even adults have poor conscious access to rules that govern their reasoning (Nisbett & Wilson 1977), and this may be true of children's access to their own moral reasoning. Cognitive developmental research (Brainerd 1973) has shown that young children's verbal responses lag significantly behind their capacity for correct judgments.

Thus rationalization studies may dramatically underestimate children's moral reasoning abilities. This suspicion seems confirmed by the information-processing studies, the naturalistic setting research (e.g. Turiel 1983), and the naturalistic observational studies, all of which find evidence for sophisticated moral reasoning in remarkably young children.

An additional methodological question concerns the precise relation between the reasons children make particular moral judgments and the reasons they give an interrogator for making these judgments. Reasons given after the fact may bear little systematic relation to the reasons the decision was actually taken. If this could be demonstrated, the implications for the vast rationalization literature would be serious. [See Shweder & Much (1989) for a discussion of the potential for multiple and contradictory codings of moral justifications.]

Computational Modeling of Moral Reasoning

The possible advantages of computational modeling of psychological processes are well known. They include the requirement for the rigorous specification of psychological theories and the assessment of the computational sufficiency of these theories.

RULE-BASED MODELING   Shultz (1986, 1987) has been developing a computer program to simulate how the ordinary person (down to about 5 years old) reasons about harm-doing. The program is called MR, for Moral Reasoner. MR provides a convenient way of rigorously specifying the aspects of our information-processing approach that were taken from the Shultz-Schleifer theory and a technique for getting the theory to generate conclusions that can be compared to those produced by human subjects.

MR has been implemented as a production system. Production systems typically contain three main components: a set of production rules, a working memory buffer, and an interpreter. Production rules are written in if-then or condition-action form.

The interpreter drives the system. As shown in Figure 2, the interpreter acts in a three-phase cycle of matching, selecting, and acting. In the matching phase, the contents of the working memory buffer (WM) are matched against the conditions of the production rules. Those rules whose conditions are satisfied are indexed for possible firing. In the selection phase, conflict

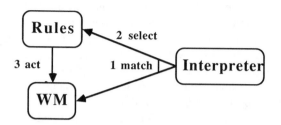

Figure 2 Production system architecture. WM = working memory.

resolution strategies are employed to select one rule from this set for firing. In the action phase, that rule is actually fired, carrying out a sequence of actions many of which update the contents of working memory. This restarts the three-phase cycle, and the cycling continues until no more rules can be fired.

A pseudo-English version of a production rule in the MR program may be given as an example: If the protagonist produced the harm and the protagonist's action was not accidental and the protagonist's action was voluntary and the harm was a foreseeable consequence of the protagonist's action and there was no intervening cause of the harm, then the protagonist is morally responsible for the harm.

This rule and 38 others implement the theory. MR accepts a case described in terms of categorical values on a number of features (e.g. high foreseeability of the harm) and produces a series of conclusions on other concepts in the model such as responsibility, blame, and punishment. Simulation of many cases from Anglo-American law and from traditional, nonliterate cultures produced high rates of agreement with actual outcomes, suggesting that the theory is computationally sufficient to qualitatively match human reasoning about blame in cases of harm-doing. Despite these global agreements on blame, additional research is needed to provide a more refined and more complete test of MR by examining the intermediate decisions of ordinary subjects. Additional rules may be needed to deal with the ways defenses modify judgments about blameworthiness and punishment.

From the standpoint of developmental psychology, it is of interest whether and how production systems can acquire and modify their own rule-bases. Artificial Intelligence (AI) researchers are expending considerable effort in this direction, resulting in a variety of proposals for learning techniques (Klahr et al 1987). So far, no results have been reported in the realm of constructing a rule-base for moral reasoning.

An AI sub-area called "legal reasoning" is beginning to attract attention (Gardner 1987). "Legal AI" is oriented towards devising programs that reason about the law, but such models may also help to explain common-sense moral reasoning.

An issue fundamental for psychological theories of moral reasoning has been raised in legal AI research. It concerns whether legal reasoning (Gardner 1987; Rissland 1985) proceeds by retrieval from memory of (*a*) similar cases, which are then instantiated and tweaked to fit the present case, or (*b*) rules of reasoning. Storage and subsequent refinement of a few general and powerful rules might be more efficient than maintenance of a large database of potentially relevant cases, but the construction of such rules would require a sophisticated technique for abstracting and generalizing from cases as they are processed. A case-based technique, on the other hand, would require sophisticated techniques for retrieving and modifying relevant cases. Moral reasoners may use some combination of these techniques—e.g. using moral rules for most reasoning while retaining exceptions to these rules as cases. Ascertaining the memory representational system for the retention of moral rules is crucial for future psychological research.

CONNECTIONIST MODELING   Both the case-based and rule-based computational modeling techniques discussed above operate at the symbolic level: Each of the manipulated data structures refers to some concept. Connectionist models embody an entirely different computational architecture. A typical connectionist model consists of a network that learns connection strengths among its nodes. As activation spreads across the network, it produces a kind of reasoning by pattern completion (Rumelhart & McClelland 1986a,b). Although connectionist models have so far been applied mainly to low-level perceptual processes, they may also be useful in elucidating higher-level reasoning and problem solving (McClelland 1988).

A pioneering attempt to apply a connectionist computational model to legal cases was presented by Thagard (1989). He applied his model to two "who-done-it?" cases in which the prosecution and the defense advocated incompatible ways of explaining the evidence. The model was named ECHO (Explanatory Coherence by Harmony Optimization), as it sought to find the most coherent explanation for a set of facts. Pennington & Hastie (1981, 1986, 1988) have investigated the decision process in simulations of trials by jury. Their theory emphasizes how the juror organizes not the rules used to make judgments but the complex information emerging during the trial. Their emphasis on the seminal role of a coherent causal explanation is consistent with the information-processing model of retributive justice presented above and with the connectionist approach.

Given a network of coherence and incoherence relations among propositions describing the evidence and competing claims of the case, ECHO spreads activation in such a way as to maximize the coherence of the network, sometimes favoring one explanation over another. Like the rule-based MR model, ECHO is a performance model that does not yet simulate learning of the ability to solve cases. Unlike MR, ECHO does not deal with a full range of moral concepts, but rather focuses on the issue of how the harm was caused. ECHO's preliminary success suggests that connectionist models may apply to a more complete range of moral reasoning issues.

A connectionist approach to an MR sort of model might offer two advantages. One is that the constraints in a connectionist program are inherently soft, thus naturally allowing for exceptions to rules. The other is that such a network would likely produce "conceptual leakage." This is the tendency, observed in some human subjects, to let concepts influence each other that should not in a rule-based account. An example is when variables that should directly influence only responsibility (e.g. voluntariness) also affect ratings of causation (Shultz et al 1981).

Learning Principles of Moral Judgment

We treat here the social contexts in which principles of moral judgment are acquired during development. Two points must be made. First, we include our discussion of learning under the retributive justice heading because most of the empirical work we cite concerned this topic. Second, although we term the content of moral learning "rules," it remains possible that moral reasoning proceeds from sets of cases retained in memory.

There are both experimental and observational studies about how children learn moral rules. We point out the limits of what can be inferred from each kind of study, and note that the two research methods, together, often surpass these limits. Experimental studies generally employ an intervention to produce learning of a moral rule—e.g. a respected other such as Superman or a Sesame Street character explicity articulates a moral rule. The experiment can show conclusively that learning of a moral rule can result from such an intervention. Experimentalists often forget, however, that this does not demonstrate that real children in the real world learn moral rules in this way. Observational studies that determine the frequency with which authoritative others actually do transmit explicit moral rules to children give us a sense of how important this cause of moral learning actually is. On the other hand, once it is established that this sort of intervention occurs frequently and is followed by changes in children's moral judgments, experiments can assure us that it is this intervention that causes the learning—a conclusion difficult to draw from observational studies alone.

THE SOCIAL CONTEXTS FOR THE LEARNING OF MORAL RULES   Several observational projects provide insights into children's moral learning. Walton & Sedlak (1982) have observed peer interactions and peer-teacher interactions within a day-care setting. Dunn and her colleagues (Dunn & Dale 1984; Dunn & Munn 1986, 1987) have observed sibling and parent-child interactions in homes of two-child families. Edwards (1980, 1987) has contrasted data sets from Kenya and the United States. Three related conclusions arise from their observations: (*a*) Learning morality is a matter of learning rules. These rules are transmitted at specified times and by individuals licensed by the culture to do so. The adults or older sibs who take on the rule teaching role only occasionally state the rules as they invoke them. (*b*) Rules tend to be somewhat open to exceptions[2] ("Three strikes and you're out"—unless the catcher drops the third strike. "Hitting others is wrong"—unless the other is a bully. In addition, there is room for interpretation during instantiation of the rules. "I didn't really hit you, it was just a tap.") (*c*) Moral rules are learned in the same context as various other restrictions, and the language of instruction often fails to discriminate among different kinds of prohibitions. "Don't do that" or "That's dangerous" may be said when a child is poking a fork into an electrical outlet, playing too near a precious vase, hitting a younger sibling, or doing something aesthetically repellent. Children, particularly younger ones, may thus confuse moral rules and rules that govern conduct in other situations.

This conflation may explain Piaget's observation that children sometimes seem to expect punishment for a moral transgression to arise from the physical world (see Karniol 1980 for a review of the literature on "immanent justice"). Of course if a child pushes a fork into the electrical outlet, a punishment *will* immediately be inflicted by the physical world. If the child has not yet differentiated moral prohibitions from warnings about physical danger, confusion of the two kinds of punishment is not surprising. Nor would it be surprising if the child were to misinterpret prohibition of a fork probing episode as a moral reproof.

WHEN DO MORAL QUESTIONS ARISE IN INTERACTIONS?   Observational studies frequently support a *social constructionist* account of the learning of morality. In the course of such studies moral questions often arise not because an immoral act has been committed but because one interactant signals disapproval of another's conduct (Dunn & Munn 1987; Edwards 1980, 1987; Much & Shweder 1978; Walton & Sedlak 1982). The challenged interactant deals with the challenge, prompting (in Goffman's useful phrase) a "remedial exchange." During this interaction the "accused" child can employ several strategies. The child can, in the terminology of the rapidly growing literature on excuses or accounts (Austin 1956; Goffman 1971; Semin & Manstead

---

[2]From a computational standpoint, this may mean only that rules have multiple conditions—e.g. **unless**-conditions, or negated **if**-conditions. (A negated **if**-condition would occur if no element is contained in working memory that says the catcher dropped the ball.) A less benign possibility is that some rules are so soft they are not rules at all, but merely tendencies, whose contradictions must be worked out, perhaps by constraint satisfaction.

1983; Scott & Lyman 1968), *justify* his/her actions ("I got off my cot at naptime because I thought there was a fire, so I came to find the teacher"), *excuse* the action, *mitigate* its seriousness, or *deny* that it breaks the rule.

Experimental research (Darley et al 1978; Rule et al 1974, 1975) demonstrates that children as young as 6 years recognize excuses and take them into account in assigning punishments for moral transgressions. Dunn's (1987) observational data show that 30–36-month-old children can be remarkably adroit at manipulating moral rules to support their own interests in family disputes.

Walton & Sedlak (1982) examined remedial exchanges taking place in kindergarten through 5th-grade elementary school open classrooms. They emphasized the role of the interaction between the "perpetrator" and the "accuser" in determining the meaning of a morally dubious act. In their social constructionist ("symbolic interactionist") account, the interpretation of the situation, and therefore the assignment of responsibilities within it, was negotiated via dialog between the participants. Such dialog followed a set sequence. It generally began with a direct or indirect challenge from the accuser, which could be met with either defiance, a counterchallenge, an offer of remedy for the injury, or an ambiguous response.

As the social constructionist perspective suggests, the relative power of the interactants was important in determining whose construction would prevail. The form and outcome of the exchange differed depending on whether it took place between children or between children and supervising adults. Adults were more likely than children to lead off with a direct challenge to a child. When challenged by an adult rather than a child, a child was more likely to give a remedial response indicating general acceptance of the validity of the challenge. A challenge from teachers was likely to cause children to make belated compliant moves or to give excuses that denied knowledge of the rule ("I wasn't there when you told us"). When challenged by another child, and not in the presence of a teacher, a child was likely to respond defiantly or with a counterchallenge (Walton 1985), to deny being the cause of the effect, and to deny the validity of the broken rule.

Walton & Sedlak's work suggests two conclusions. First, and somewhat contrary to other theorists' emphasis on the role of peer interaction, the adult plays a continuing and critical role in forming moral judgment rules. The teacher or other adult in the interaction often plays the role of accuser (although another child can also play this role), and always plays the role of judge—by keeping the "trial" on track, by judging the validity of the accused child's defensive responses, and by assigning punishment. (Dunn's observational data on parents tends to confirm the adult's role as judge.) Other children usually figure as victims, sometimes as accusers, and occasionally (particularly if they are older) as surrogates for the adult judges. This adult-driven enquiry is one major interaction setting in which the child first learns moral rules.

In the social constructionist account a child learns that a moral challenge is an occasion for negotiation about the meaning of an incident—negotiation carried out through specific claims based upon general rules. However, the social construction process is subject to three sets of constraints. First, authorities are sometimes involved in the construction processes; their constructions are authoritative not simply because of their power, but also because of the legitimacy the culture grants them. The other two constraints concern excuses, which must be both appropriately scaled and factual.

Denials, excuses, and justifications must have the appropriate scale or scope. ("I forgot and let the bathwater run" may mitigate the punishment for flooding the bathroom, but it won't do so for drowning a sibling.) To be effective they had also better be factual. (Judges check against fabrication.) A transcript published by Walton (1985) shows a teacher ruthlessly pressing a line of questioning that makes clear to a child that the original excuse of "I wasn't there" (when directions were given) is untenable, and concludes with the teacher assigning punishment to the then-miserable child. The moral negotiation process is thus constrained for all participants by the recognition that many of its terms refer to accepted rules and matters of verifiable fact. In learning moral rules a child has considerable leeway to construe the meanings of the complex and ambiguous sanctions he or she observes, but cognitive and cultural constraints operate as well.

ALTERNATE CONTEXTS FOR THE LEARNING OF MORAL RULES   Adult-driven inquisitions are usually painful for children, a fact likely to motivate the child to discover the rules by paying careful attention in settings where the rules can be learned without risk of punishment. In a day-care or kindergarten classroom, for example, a child can observe rule-relevant exchanges between supervising adults and other children, his or her peers. In many cultures, television provides another, often potent opportunity for the observational learning of morality. Studies showing relationships between frequency of TV watching and subsequent aggressive behaviors hint at TV-influenced alterations of underlying moral judgmental patterns, but this complex topic we leave to other reviews.

During moral rule learning, children must come to tentative understanding of rules, and it would be extremely useful if there were contexts in which they could test those understandings without risking punishment if their understandings are wrong. Dunn's observational research discovers and documents two such "protected" contexts. The first is "pretend play." Beginning at about 18 months, children who have a close and affectionate relationship with an older sibling are drawn into "let's pretend we are. . . ." play by the older sibling (Dunn & Dale 1984; Dunn & Munn 1986). In these settings, moral incidents of considerable complexity are often represented. In them, younger and older children often take on various social roles, and the older child often responds to moves by the younger with expressions of pleasure and pain, often announcing punishments for the "transgressions" of the younger child. The younger child can here observe the effects of his or her "transgressions" both in the emotions realistically enacted by the older child and in the enacted versions of the punishments they would provoke.

Mothers in Dunn's sample provided a second protected context for the learning of moral rules, meeting the child's threatened (and occasionally actual) transgressions with joking threats of punishment. Further, when parents playfully threaten or commit domestic transgressions, 2–3-year-olds often announce their punishments. The parents' responses to these imagined punishments, and the ways they plead for mitigation, can instruct the child about moral rules.

INDIVIDUAL DIFFERENCES IN MORAL RULE SETS   Children are disposed to extract rules from the observation of concrete instances. In the domain of moral reasoning they are abetted in this endeavor when adults explicitly extract the general rule for the child. ("Well then, since you did it by accident, I won't punish you.") Observational evidence suggests that adults perform this service infrequently; children must often infer the general rule that lies behind their seniors' specific prohibitions. In the process, different children can come to construe general cultural rules in significantly different ways.

Although different children may extract very different rules from their moral learning experiences, the versions children learn tend to correlate positively with their parents' versions (e.g. Dunn & Munn 1987; Zanna 1988). After demonstrating that adults differ in how they integrate the intent of a harm-doer with the degree of harm caused to arrive at a punishment, Leon (1984) showed that in a majority of cases children's integration schemes matched those of their mothers.

How do individuals come to learn variant moral rules? First, children learn morality from parents or guardians, so a child who lives with morally deviant parents is likely to learn a deviant system of morality. The deviance is likely to be greater where the parents belong to a subgroup in which other adults practice the same deviant system of morality.

Second, some children, unable to make sense of their parents' rule systems, may learn only that they will be punished regardless of the validity of their defenses. Such children may cling to whatever fragments of a general code seem occasionally to render their parental environment predictable. Others, whose parents do not examine the factual correctness of their claims or do not punish fabrications, may learn that "morality" is a process of defensive rationalization untethered by fact. (Such a child may show psychopathic tendencies.)

OTHER DOMAINS OF MORAL JUDGMENTS

Distributive Justice

ADULT RULES   People contribute differentially to the production of an entity with value. In psychology, "equity theorists" (Adams 1965; Homans 1961; Leventhal 1976, 1980; Leventhal et al 1973; Walster et al 1973) study the equitable distribution of rewards among producers of value—i.e. "distributive justice" (Cohen & Greenberg 1982). Given the philosophical complexity of the issue and the difficulty of establishing standards of fairness (Rawls 1971) it is not surprising that no single set of rules satisfies all mature adults, even in a single culture. Within a culture, allocation rules depend on the class of resources being allocated. Within our culture, for instance, we judge it fair when votes are allocated equally to all individuals, grades are allocated according to ability, and medical care is allocated according to need.

Researchers studying the reward-allocating behaviors of adult individuals would probably assent to the following generalizations: First, while there is no agreement among individuals on a single distribution function that is exactly fair, there is wide agreement that some distributions (e.g. those that assign no compensation to an individual who contributed significant inputs) are unfair. Second, as the inputs move away from the simple and often identical-in-kind inputs arranged in the classical brief laboratory experiment, to the more complex mixes of resource, intellectual, and labor inputs required to make more complex products, the distributive issues get more complex, and the range of solutions regarded as fair becomes correspondingly broader. Third, individuals tend to adopt distribution schemes that benefit themselves, or those with whom they identify (Damon 1981).

CHILDREN'S ALLOCATION RULES   The empirical literature on distributive justice in children suffers from the absence of a model of adult distributive practices to which children's judgments might be compared. Nonetheless, elegant and sophisticated studies of children's distributive practices have been reported (Damon 1981). Hook and Cook review what we might call "standard paradigm studies" in which a child, told about the different work inputs of himself and other children, is asked to apportion the reward for the joint product (Hook 1978; Hook & Cook 1979). Children below age 5 seem to use an "equality rule" of allocation. They split rewards equally, regardless of differences in inputs. Some studies show evidence of self-interest in this age group—the children allocating to themselves rewards higher than they would deserve by other standards. From ages 6–13 children distribute reward according to an approximate or "ordinal equity" rule in which the person who did more of the work gets more of the reward. Only older children use a proportional equity rule in which the rewards are distributed in a reasonably exact ratio to the inputs. Even adults sometimes use an ordinal rather than a proportional equity pattern.

Reviewing the development of various logical-mathematical problem-solving skills, Hook concludes that children younger than 13 probably fail to use proportional equity allocations because they do not yet know how to calculate the relevant ratios. Gunzburger et al (1977) found that some teenagers used sophisticated strategies in allocating payments, including one that they called "social responsibility." In this strategy the allocator deviated from a proportional equity allocation, decreasing allocations to the group in order to increase the allocation to an individual who would have made higher inputs had external factors not prevented him from doing so.

Damon (1975) has suggested a Kohlbergian developmental pattern in the concept of distributive fairness. At first a child tends to distribute goods according to who most wants them; at the next stage distributions seem fair to a child if they correspond to some external characteristic of the recipient such as age, size, or prestige. Next develops a reliance upon what we have called an equality rule, in which all receive equally regardless of contribution, followed by use of the proportional equity rule. Finally, a distributive morality emerges, in which distributions are considered fair if they correlate with recipients' assessed needs. Using a scale based on Damon's categories, Enright and his associates (Enright et al 1980a,b) have shown that lower-socioeconomic-status (SES) children entering kindergarten lag behind their middle-SES peers in distributive justice development, a lag still evident in the third grade. The allocations of low-SES children may be more deprivation-driven than those of higher-SES peers. Low-SES children may also get less practice than higher-SES peers at holding roles in which allocation decisions are made.

IS THERE A GENERAL DEVELOPMENTAL SEQUENCE? If a needy person neglected out of laziness to contribute to a joint product, a need-based reward allocation would seem unfair. If, on the other hand (as often happens in the standard research paradigm), children discovered that there was to be a reward for the joint product only after the product was completed, an equality-based distribution of the reward would seem both fair and a wise protection of group solidarity (Damon 1981). The fairness of allocation rules is a function of social situation (Lerner 1974). A recognition of this fact requires a shift away from a research strategy predicated on the assumption that children pass through an invariant set of "stages of distributive justice," each described by the adoption of a different allocation rule.

Adults often attempt explicitly to work out the allocation rules in advance of contribution; they seek a distributive contract. How would children set up such allocation contracts in advance? What fairness rules would they propose, or how would they react to the experimenter's proposals? Fruitful research lies in this direction.

Prosocial Behavior and Thought

In a series of small but perceptible steps the "distributive justice case" turns into the "prosocial case." Questions about the share of reward due to various individuals shade into questions about allocation of one's own resources to help people in need or distress. The "prosocial" case differs from the standard punishment-oriented case in that the actor must choose between satisfying his or her own needs and wants and satisfying the needs and wants of another "in contexts in which laws, punishments, authorities, formal obligations, and other external criteria are irrelevant" (Eisenberg-Berg 1979:128). In research on distributive justice, the focus of experimentation is on the actor's choice among a culturally standard set of alternative distribution rules. No such easily applicable rules are apparent for the prosocial case, so one of the first tasks of researchers is to suggest them.

ADULT RULES   Batson (1987; Batson & Coke 1981) maintains that prosocial behaviors sometimes arise from altruistic motives, while Cialdini (Cialdini et al 1981) suggests that prosocial behaviors may still be motivated by general self-interest. Hoffman (1975, 1981), tending to agree with Batson, suggests that an empathic response has evolved in humans that, independent of egoistic motivation but in interaction with cognitive development, predisposes people to help others in distress.

DETERMINANTS OF CHILDREN'S PROSOCIAL BEHAVIORS   Bryan (1972) and Radke-Yarrow et al (1984) have reviewed developmental trends in prosocial behaviors. Bar-Tal (1982) has suggested a set of cognitive prerequisites for helping behavior. Tests of these suggestions have produced mixed results (Bar-Tal et al 1985). Rushton's (1976) review of altruistic behavior of children finds (a) characteristic correlations of around .30 between altruistic behaviors across situations, (b) complex and frequently equivocal relationships between cognitive-developmental variables and altruistic behavior, and (c) some support for the role of variables suggested by a social learning theory in increasing altruistic behavior.

In a series of studies, Eisenberg-Berg (Eisenberg-Berg & Mussen 1978; Eisenberg-Berg & Hand 1979; Eisenberg et al 1984) presented children with prosocial dilemmas and asked them what they would do and why. Children's reasoning and actions were then coded as hedonistic, pragmatic, concerned for others' needs, empathic, and sympathetic. It was not always easy to categorize the reasoning patterns of those who decided to help. A child's decision to help may be governed by different impulses in different cases (e.g. now by empathy with a distressed friend, now by a more reasoned concern for the needs of a stranger), and these subjects may not have good cognitive access to the determinants of their judgments and behaviors. Nevertheless, Eisenberg-Berg (1979:135) reports that "elementary school children's reasoning tends to be hedonistic, stereotyped approval and interpersonally oriented, and/or involved the labeling of others' needs. High school students verbalized many of the same types of reasoning . . . but also used . . . reasoning which reflected strongly empathic and more abstract and/or internalized moral concerns." Children who decided not to help characteristically supported their choice by producing hedonistic reasons—that they would have to miss the birthday party or give away treasured possessions to help.

In dealing with prosocial choices children rarely refer to "authority- and punishment-oriented moral reasoning" (Eisenberg-Berg 1979:136). This suggests that the determinants of prosocial thought and action are not described or driven by the reasoning coded in Kohlbergian stages. Instead, the thought structures for the various domains of moral thought and action are apparently quite different, and broadly independent.

Procedural Justice

In an impressive series of experiments, Thibaut & Walker (1975) drew the attention of the experimental community to issues of "procedural justice." Scholars of procedural justice point out that ordinary people have standards for the "fair" resolution of moral questions.

ADULT PROCEDURAL JUSTICE RULES   Procedural justice, unlike retributive or distributive justice, is not an area of substantive rules. Instead, among psychologists it is generally understood to refer to the fairness of the practices and procedures by means of which other moral questions are decided, and also to the unbiasedness of the deciders. Thus Tyler (1988) draws on the theories of Thibaut & Walker (1975) and Leventhal (1976) to formulate various criteria for procedural fairness, and shows that citizens involved in the court system judge whether that system acted fairly in terms of seven criteria: the degree to which the authorities appeared motivated to act fairly, judgments of their honesty, the degree to which they followed ethical principles of conduct, the extent to which opportunities for participants to present their points of view were provided, the quality of the decisions made, the opportunities for error correction, and whether the authorities behaved in a biased fashion. Self-interest obviously affects these criteria of procedural fairness: Judgments in my favor I am likely to deem fair. Still, the list provides a reasonable set of possibilities to explore with children.

PROCEDURAL JUSTICE IN CHILDREN   Not a great deal of work has been done exploring children's notions of procedural justice, although many of the observations made by those who create distributive or retributive dilemmas for children touch on procedural considerations.

One developmental scenario envisions the following: Younger children judge fairness largely on judgment outcome. At some subsequent age, children become procedural fanatics, who judge an outcome's fairness largely in terms of whether it was arrived at via correct procedures. Finally, a more complex schema arises, in which youngsters form their own judgments about the just outcome, based on whatever they know about the case. If the case decision is in accord with their perception of the just outcome, they judge the procedure fair. If they judge the outcome unjust, they then will see the procedures that reached it as unjust. If they are uncertain about the just outcome, their perceptions that the procedures were fair will make them more likely to judge the arrived-at outcome as fair. Our intuition is that the third model would hold at all ages, suggesting that concern for procedural justice emerges secondary to the other moral judgment processes.

The procedures by means of which resources are allocated and blame and punishment are assigned in a group are culturally constructed and transmitted. In a culture such as ours, with its emphasis on rational choice, the social contract and market relationships—procedures agreed on between parties in advance—are "fair by mutual agreement."

PROCEDURAL JUSTICE COMPONENTS IN OTHER DOMAINS   In the case of distributive justice, we have already noted the importance of procedural and contractual considerations. Lerner (1974) alluded to specific distribution rules, agreed on in advance or culturally accepted, the application of which would be judged fair by the participants in ensuing transactions. Among adults, a person who wishes an unusual distribution arrangement to prevail in a future interaction is obliged to get the other interactants' assent to that wish before each expends effort. It would be possible to analyze the emergence of such negotiations in the transcripts of various observational studies of children. Because they are based on recognition of the conventional, generally unspoken, exchange rules in various settings, negotiation skills may emerge relatively late in development.

Mills & Clark (1982) have shown that adults expect strikingly different kinds of exchange relationships to prevail in two classes of relationships. In "exchange relationships," if one participant benefits the other then a rapid reciprocation of the benefit in kind is normatively preferable. In "intimate relationships," on the contrary, such reciprocation is considered gross and insulting. Partners in an intimate relationship are expected to sense and respond to each other's needs, without calculating a tit-for-tat exchange. The intimate relationship may first be experienced in the close, same-sex friendships formed during childhood. The capacity to participate in intimate relationships in adulthood may depend on having experienced and rehearsed such relationships as a child. Infant-parent relationships provide another source of learning about intimate relationships.

In the domain of retributive judgments, procedural requirements for the determination of guilt and the assignment of penalties are likely given considerable weight. (No well-worked-out adult model integrates the existing research with our observations that people are impatient with procedural fairness considerations when they fear victimization or identify with victims.) Children recognize procedural concerns at an earlier age than is suggested by cognitively driven accounts. They raise procedural justice considerations with considerable sophistication when it serves their self-interest to do so. "You're not my mother"—the young child's retort when accused by a non-parental adult of a transgression—is at heart a procedural claim. In one of the few experiments on children's recognition of procedural justice considerations Gold et al (1984) showed that first-graders consistently recognized fairness-relevant variations in procedures. Children were told a story in which a parent inferred a perpetrator's guilt from circumstantial evidence. Children thought that parental punishment inflicted on the accused perpetrator was unfair if another explanation for the harm was possible, and if the parent failed to obtain potentially relevant information by questioning a witness. This kind of an assessment suggests that these children apply moral judgment rules such as "Someone must cause harm in order to be held responsible for it." Assessment differences found between first- and fifth-graders were likely due to differences in the way the first-graders comprehended the story, rather than to differences in how they processed the information after comprehending it.

Procedural concerns do not seem to arise in the prosocial domain of moral obligation.

CONCLUSIONS

The prototypical study of the moral judgments of children demonstrates that there are various levels of moral judgment and that each level will be attained only when a child either (a) achieves certain cognitive capacities on which these judgments depend (a generally Piagetian approach) or (b) reaches a particular stage of moral development (a Kohlbergian approach). While this approach has led to some important discoveries, we question its continuing utility. Developmental psychologists now focus less upon the putative cognitive stages of reasoning and more upon the mental representations of the elements of a knowledge domain and the rules the reasoner develops for manipulating them. Such now seems the appropriate approach to the investigation of moral judgments. For instance, Eisenberg-Berg's study of how people reason about prosocial actions, and of the relationships between reasoning and action, genuinely illuminates that domain of moral judgment. Similar analyses of other moral domains would be useful.

We no longer expect the connections between moral reasoning and general cognitive processes to be as simple as Piaget supposed. The learning of moral judgment begins early in life and is of great consequence to the child. Given this early appearance and importance, we doubt that the understanding of the moral and intentional world depends on the comprehension of many aspects of the physical world. Of course, moral reasoning requires a grasp of causation; but as we read the evidence, children make good, early progress in understanding both the moral and physical domains and do not often (as many have suggested) confuse the two.

Several areas of moral concern would profit from empirical attention. Reduction of procedural justice conflicts by means of agreements made in advance about distribution of rewards for joint endeavors deserves investigation. Given children's intense interest in what is and isn't "fair," the development of procedural justice concerns would seem a profitable area of study. Research is also needed on the obligation of obedience to authority.

Social and cognitive psychology have let developmental psychology down. Research on the moral judgments of children suffers from the absence of models of adult moral reasoning. (We have now proposed such a model in the domain of retributive justice.) This has particularly harmed theories of the learning of moral judgments. Uncertainty about what principles adults seek to transmit complicates the study of how these principles are transmitted in their various culturally complex and indirect contexts. In the hope of advancing research, we have suggested a set of social contexts critical to the learning of the principles of retributive justice.

Both of us are experimentalists by training and inclination, so we are surprised by how much of value to the study of moral judgments has arisen from the observational studies we reviewed. Because observational studies assess children in settings familiar to them, they tell us at what ages and in what sequences various moral capabilities appear.[3] Such studies also reveal the contexts in which children actually learn moral rules.

---

[3]It could be argued that observational studies suggest but that only experiments can prove what capabilities the child possesses. However, we think the observational transcripts of Dunn, of Sedlak & Walton, and of Shweder convincingly demonstrate children's capacities. Observational studies will at least help experimentalists to determine the transgressions and distributive problems that children commonly face. Experimental scenarios can then present children with problems in forms familiar to them.

Because observational studies are labor intensive we are pleased to see that experimental research in moral judgment has greatly improved, both in analytic sophistication and in providing vivid stimuli that capture and hold the child's attention. Many studies can now determine whether the different moral response patterns of younger children spring from different rules for the processing of information, different inferences about absent information, or differences in initial comprehension of the information.

Converging evidence shows that children are capable of making moral judgments at a much earlier age than previously thought. According to the recent literature, moral capacity is well developed although by no means completely developed in the third year of life (Kagan 1987).

Both experimental and observational research is hindered by reliance on language as the central means of communicating with children about moral judgment. We must learn to find evidence of moral reaction in nonverbal behavior. Happily, other areas of developmental psychology have pioneered the use of such techniques, so the resources for this sort of research are considerable.

Finally, studies, whether observational or experimental, of the moral judgmental systems of other cultures are important. They remind us that our own society uses only one of many definitions of morality. While cross-cultural observations challenge us to specify the universals of morality, they also teach us how extraordinarily difficult it is to do so.

Literature Cited

Adams, J. S. 1965. Inequity in social exchange. In *Advances in Experimental Social Psychology*, Vol. 2, ed. L. Berkowitz. New York: Academic

Aronfreed, J. 1968. *Conduct and Conscience.* New York: Academic

Austin, J. L. 1956. A plea for excuses. *Proc. Aristotelian Soc.* 57:1–30

Bar-Tal, D. 1982. Sequential development of helping behavior: a cognitive-learning model. *Dev. Rev.* 2:101–24

Bar-Tal, D., Korenfeld, D., Raviv, A. 1985. Relationships between the development of helping behavior and the development of cognition, social perspective, and moral judgment. *Genet. Soc. Gen. Psychol. Monogr.* 111:23–40

Batson, C. D. 1987. Pro-social motivation: Is it ever truly altruistic? *Adv. Exp. Soc. Psychol.* 20:65–122

Batson, C. D., Coke, J. S. 1981. Empathy: a source of altruistic motivation for helping? In *Altruism and Helping Behavior: Social, Personality, and Developmental Perspectives,* ed. J. P. Rushton, R. M. Sorrentino, pp. 167–87. Hillsdale, NJ: Erlbaum Assoc.

Berndt, T. J. 1977. The effect of reciprocity norms on moral judgment and causal attribution. *Child Dev.* 48:1322–30

Berndt, T. J., Berndt, E. G. 1975. Children's use of motives and intentionality in person perception and moral judgment. *Child Dev.* 46:904–12

Brainerd, C. J. 1973. Judgments and explanations as criteria for the presence of cognitive structures. *Psychol. Bull.* 79:172–79

Bryan, J. 1972. Why children help. *J. Soc. Issues* 28:87–101

Cialdini, R. B., Baumann, D. J., Ienrick, D. T. 1981. Insights from sadness: a three-step model of the development of altruism as hedonism. *Dev. Rev.* 1:207–23

Cohen, R. L., Greenberg, J. 1982. The justice concept in social psychology. In *Equity and Justice in Social Behavior,* ed. J. Greenberg, R. L. Cohen, pp. 1–41. New York: Academic

Damon, W. 1975. Early conceptions of positive justice as related to the development of logical operations. *Child Dev.* 46:301–12

Damon, W. 1981. The development of justice and self-interest change in childhood. In *The Justice Motives in Social Behavior*, ed. M. J. Lerner, S. Lerner, pp. 57–72. New York: Plenum

Darby, B. W., Schlenker, B. R. 1982. Children's reactions to apologies. *J. Pers. Soc. Psychol.* 43:742–53

D'Arcy, E. 1963. *Human Acts: An Essay in Their Moral Evaluation.* Oxford: Clarendon

Darley, J. M., Klosson, E. C., Zanna, M. P. 1978. Intentions and their contexts in the moral judgments of children and adults. *Child Dev.* 49:66–74

Darley, J. M., Zanna, M. P. 1982. Making moral judgments. *Am. Sci.* 70:515–21

DeJong, W., Morris, W. N., Hastorf, A. H. 1976. Effect of an escaped accomplice on the punishment assigned to a criminal defendant. *J. Pers. Soc. Psychol.* 33:192–98

DePalma, D. J., Foley, J. M. 1975. *Moral Development: Current Theory and Research.* Hillsdale, NJ: Erlbaum Assoc.

Dunn, J. 1987. The beginnings of moral understanding: development in the second year. See Kagan & Lamb 1987, pp. 91–112

Dunn, J., Dale, N. 1984. I a Daddy: 2-year-olds' collaboration in joint pretend with sibling and with mother. In *Symbolic Play: The Development of Social Understanding*, ed. I. Bretherton, pp. 131–58. New York: Academic

Dunn, J., Munn, P. 1987. Development of justification in disputes with mother and sibling. *Dev. Psychol.* 23:791–98

Dunn, J., Munn, P. 1986. Sibling quarrels and maternal intervention: individual differences in understanding and aggression. *J. Child Psychol. Psychiatry Allied Discip.* 27:583–95

Edwards, C. P. 1980. The development of moral reasoning in cross-cultural perspective. In *Handbook of Cross-Cultural Human Development*, ed. R. H. Munroe, R. L. Munroe, B. B. Whiting. New York: Garland Press

Edwards, C. P. 1987. Culture and the construction of moral values. A comparative ethnography of moral encounters in two cultural settings. See Kagan & Lamb 1987, pp. 123–51

Eisenberg, N., Pasternak, J. F., Cameron, E., Tryon, K. 1984. The relation of quantity and mode of prosocial behavior to moral cognitions and social style. *Child Dev.* 55:1479–85

Eisenberg-Berg, N. 1979. Development of children's pro-social moral judgment. *Dev. Psychol.* 15:128–37

Eisenberg-Berg, N., Hand, M. 1979. The relationship of preschoolers' reasoning about pro-social moral conflicts to prosocial behavior. *Child Dev.* 50:356–63

Eisenberg-Berg, N., Mussen, P. 1978. Empathy and moral development in adolescence. *Dev. Psychol.* 14:185–86

Enright, R. D., Enright, W. F., Manheim, L. A., Harris, B. E. 1980a. Distributive justice development and social class. *Dev. Psychol.* 6:555–63

Enright, R. D., Franklin, C. C., Manheim, L. A. 1980b. Children's distributive justice reasoning: a standardized and objective scale. *Dev. Psychol.* 16:193–202

Feinberg, J. 1968. Action and responsibility. In *The Philosophy of Action*, ed. A. R. White, pp. 95–119. Oxford: Oxford Univ. Press

Ferguson, T. J., Rule, B. G. 1983. An attributional perspective on anger and aggression. In *Aggression: Theoretical and Empirical Reviews*, ed. R. G. Geen, E. I. Donnerstein, 1:41–74. New York: Academic

Fincham, F. D., Jaspars, J. M. 1980. Attribution of responsibility: from man the scientist to man as lawyer. *Adv. Exp. Soc. Psychol.* 13:81–138

Fincham, F. D., Shultz, T. R. 1981. Intervening causation and the mitigation of responsibility for harm. *Br. J. Soc. Psychol.* 20:113–20

Gardner, A. 1987. *An Artificial Intelligence Approach to Legal Reasoning.* Cambridge, MA: MIT Press

Gelman, R., Baillargeon, R. 1983. A review of some Piagetian concepts. In *Manual of Child Psychology*, Vol. 3, *Cognitive Development*, ed. J. H. Flavell, E. M. Markma. New York: Wiley

Gilligan, C. 1982. *In a Different Voice: Psychological Theory and Women's Development.* Cambridge, MA: Harvard Univ. Press

Goffman, E. 1971. *Relations in Public.* New York: Harper & Row

Gold, L. J., Darley, J. M., Hilton, J. L., Zanna, M. P. 1984. Children's perceptions of procedural justice. *Child Dev.* 55:1752–59

Gorovitz, S. 1965. Causal judgment and causal explanation. *J. Philos.* 62:695–711

Gunzburger, D. W., Wegner, D. M., Anooshian, L. 1977. *Hum. Dev.* 20:160–70

Harper, F. V., James, F. 1956. *The Law of Torts*, Vol. 2. Boston: Little, Brown

Hart, H. L. A. 1968. *Punishment and Responsibility: Essays in the Philosophy of Law.* Oxford: Clarendon Press

Hart, H. L. A., Honoré, A. M. 1959. *Causation in the Law.* Oxford: Clarendon Press

Hartshorne, H., May, M. A. 1928. *Studies in the Nature of Character: Studies in Deceit.* New York: Macmillan

Hilton, D. J., Slugoski, B. R. 1986. Knowledge-based causal attribution: the abnormal conditions focus model. *Psychol. Rev.* 93: 75–88

Hoffman, M. L. 1975. Developmental synthesis of affect and cognition and its implications for altruistic motivation. *Dev. Psychol.* 11:607–22

Hoffman, M. L. 1981. Is altruism part of human nature? *J. Pers. Soc. Psychol.* 40:121–37

Homans, G. C. 1961. *Social Behavior: Its Elementary Forms.* New York: Harcourt, Brace & World

Hommers, W., Anderson, N. H. 1985. Recompense as a factor in assigned punishment. *Br. J. Dev. Psychol.* 3:75–86

Hook, J. G. 1978. The development of equity and logicomathematical thinking. *Child Dev.* 49:1035–44

Hook, J. G., Cook, T. D. 1979. Equity theory and the cognitive ability of children. *Psychol. Bull.* 86:429–45

Jaspars, J., Fincham, F. D., Hewstone, M., eds. 1983. *Attribution Theory and Research: Conceptual, Developmental and Social Dimensions.* London: Academic

Kagan, J. 1987. Introduction. See Kagan & Lamb 1987, pp.

Kagan, J., Lamb, S., eds. 1987. *The Emergence of Morality in Young Children.* Chicago: Univ. Chicago Press

Kahneman, D., Miller, D. T. 1986. Norm theory: comparing reality to its alternatives. *Psychol. Rev.* 93:136–53

Karlovac, M., Darley, J. M. 1989. Attribution of responsibility for accidents: a negligence law analogy. *Soc. Cogn.* 4:287–318

Karniol, R. 1978. Children's use of intention cues in evaluating behavior. *Psychol. Bull.* 85:76–85

Karniol, R. 1980. A conceptual analysis of immanent justice responses in children. *Child Dev.* 51:118–30

Keasey, C. B. 1978. Children's developing awareness of intentionality and motives. In *Nebraska Symposium on Motivation,* ed. C. B. Keasey, pp. 219–60. Lincoln: Univ. Nebraska Press

Klahr, D., Langley, P., Neches, R., eds. 1987. *Production System Models of Learning and Development.* Cambridge, MA: MIT Press

Kohlberg, L. 1969. Stage and sequence: the cognitive-developmental approach to socialization. In *Handbook of Socialization Theory and Research,* ed. D. A. Goslin. New York: Rand McNally

Kohlberg, L. 1981. *Essays on Moral Development.* Vol. 1. *The Philosophy of Moral Development: Moral Stages and the Idea of Justice.* San Francisco: Harper & Row

Kurtines, W., Gewirtz, J., eds. 1989. *Moral Development Through Social Interaction.* New York: Wiley

Leon, M. 1982. Rules in children's moral judgments: integration of intent, damage, and rationale information. *Dev. Psychol.* 18:835–42

Leon, M. 1984. Rules mothers and sons use to integrate intent and damage information in their moral judgments. *Child Dev.* 55:2106–13

Lerner, M. 1974. The justice motive: "equity" and "parity" among children. *J. Pers. Soc. Psychol.* 29:539–50

Leventhal, G., Popp, A., Sawyer, L. 1973. Equity or equality in children's allocation of reward to other persons? *Child Dev.* 44: 753–63

Leventhal, G. S. 1976. The distribution of reward and resources in groups and organizations. *Adv. Exp. Soc. Psychol.* 9:91–131

Leventhal, G. S. 1980. "What should be done with equity theory?" In *Social Exchange: Advances in Theory and Research,* ed. K. J. Gergen, M. S. Greenberg, R. H. Weiss. New York: Plenum

Likona, T. 1976. *Moral Development and Behaviour. Theory Research and Social Issues.* New York: Holt

Lloyd-Bostock, S. 1983. Attributions of cause and responsibility as social phenomena. In *Attribution Theory and Research: Conceptual, Developmental and Social Dimensions,* ed. J. Jaspars, F. D. Fincham, M. Hewstone. New York: Academic

McClelland, J. L. 1988. *Parallel distributed processing: implications for cognition and development.* Tech. Rep. AIP-47, Dept. Psychol., Carnegie-Mellon Univ.

Miller, D. T., McCann, C. D. 1979. Children's reactions to the perpetrators and victims of injustices. *Child Dev.* 50:861–68

Mills, J., Clark, M. 1982. Exchange in communal relationship. In *Review of Personality and Social Psychology,* ed. L. Wheeler, pp. 121–44. Beverly Hills: Sage

Much, N., Shweder, R. A. 1978. Speaking of rules: the analysis of culture in breach. In *New Directions in Child Development.* Vol. 2. *Moral Development,* ed. W. Damon. San Francisco: Jossey-Bass

Mussen, P. H., ed. 1984. *Handbook of Child Psychology,* Vols. 3, 4. New York: Wiley

Nelson-LeGall, S. A. 1985. Motive-outcome matching and outcome foreseeability: effects on attribution of intentionality and moral judgments. *Dev. Psychol.* 21:332–37

Nisbett, R. E., Wilson, T. D. 1977. Telling more than we know: verbal reports on mental processes. *Psychol. Rev.* 84:231–59

Nucci, L., Nucci, M. 1981. Children's social interactions in the context of moral and conventional transgressions. *Child Dev.* 53: 403–12

Pennington, N., Hastie, R. 1981. Juror decision making models: the generalization gap. *Psychol. Bull.* 89:246–87

Pennington, N., Hastie, R. 1986. Evidence evaluation in complex decision making. *J. Pers. Soc. Psychol.* 51:242–58

Pennington, N., Hastie, R. 1988. Explanation-based decision making: effects of memory structure on judgment. *J. Exp. Psychol.: Learn. Mem. Cogn.* 14:521–33

Piaget, J. (1932) 1965. *The Moral Judgment of the Child.* New York: Free Press

Radke-Yarrow, M., Zahn-Waxler, C., Chapman, M. 1984. Children's pro-social dispositions and behavior. See Mussen 1984, 3:469–546

Rawls, J. 1971. *A Theory of Justice.* Cambridge, MA: Harvard Univ. Press

Rest, J. R. 1984. Morality. See Mussen 1984, 3:556–629

Rest, J. R., Davison, M. L., Robbins, S. 1978. Age trends in judging moral issues: a review of cross-sectional, longitudinal, and sequential studies of the defining issues test. *Child Dev.* 49:263–79

Rissland, E. L. 1985. AI and legal reasoning. *Proc. Int. Joint Conf. Artif. Intell.* 1254–60

Rule, B. G., Dyck, R., McAra, M. J., Nesdale, A. J. 1975. Judgments of aggression serving personal versus pro-social purposes. *Soc. Behav. Pers.* 3:55–63

Rule, B. G., Nesdale, A. R., McAra, M. J. 1974. Children's reactions to information about the intentions underlying an aggressive act. *Child Dev.* 45:795–98

Rumelhart, D. E., McClelland, J. L., eds. 1986a. *Parallel Distributed Processing: Explorations in the Microstructure of Cognition.* Vol. 1: *Foundations.* Cambridge, MA: MIT Press

Rumelhart, D. E., McClelland, J. L., eds. 1986b. *Parallel Distributed Processing: Explorations in the Microstructure of Cognition.* Vol. 2: *Psychological and Biological Models.* Cambridge, MA: MIT Press

Rushton, J. P. 1976. Socialization and the altruistic behavior of children. *Psychol. Bull.* 83:898–913

Rushton, J. P. 1980. *Altruism, Socialization and Society.* Englewood Cliffs, NJ: Prentice Hall

Schleifer, M., Shultz, T. R., Lefebvre-Pinard, M. 1983. Children's judgments of causality, responsibility and punishment in cases of harm due to omission. *Br. J. Dev. Psychol.* 1:87–97

Scott, M. B., Lyman, S. M. 1968. Accounts. *Am. Sociol. Rev.* 23:46–62

Sedlak, A. 1979. Developmental differences in understanding plans and evaluating actors. *Child Dev.* 50:536–60

Selman, R. L. 1971. The relation of role taking to the development of moral judgment in children. *Child Dev.* 42:79–91

Semin, G. R., Manstead, A. S. R. 1983. *The Accountability of Conduct: A Social Psychological Analysis, European Monographs in Social Psychology,* ed. H. Tajfel. New York: Academic

Shantz, C. U. 1984. Social cognition. See Mussen 1984, 3:495–555

Shaver, K. 1985. *The Attribution of Blame.* New York: Springer-Verlag

Shaw, M. E., Reitan, H. T. 1969. Attribution of responsibility as a basis for sanctioning behavior. *Br. J. Soc. Clin. Psychol.* 8:217–26

Shultz, T. R. 1980. Development of the concept of intention. *Minn. Symp. Child Psychol.* 13:131–64

Shultz, T. R. 1986. *A computational model of blaming.* Presented at the Ann. Meet. Soc. Exp. Soc. Psychol., Phoenix

Shultz, T. R. 1987. *A computational model of causation, responsibility, blame, and punishment.* Presented at the Meet. Soc. Res. Child Dev., Baltimore

Shultz, T. R. 1988. Assessing intention: a computational model. In *Developing Theories of Mind,* ed. J. Astington, P. Harris, D. Olson, pp. 341–67. Cambridge: Cambridge Univ. Press

Shultz, T. R., Jaggi, C., Schleifer, M. 1987. Assigning vicarious responsibility. *Eur. J. Soc. Psychol.* 17:377–80

Shultz, T. R., Kestenbaum, N. R. 1985. Causal reasoning in children. In *Annals of Child Development,* ed. G. J. Whitehurst, 2:195–249. Greenwich, CT: JAI Press

Shultz, T. R., Schleifer, M. 1983. Towards a refinement of attribution concepts. In *Attribution Theory and Research: Conceptual, Developmental and Social Dimensions,* ed. J. Jaspars, F. D. Fincham, M. Hewstone, pp. 37–62. London: Academic

Shultz, T. R., Schleifer, M., Altman, I. 1981. Judgments of causation, responsibility, and punishment in cases of harm-doing. *Can. J. Behav. Sci.* 13:238–53

Shultz, T. R., Wells, D. 1985. Judging the intentionality of action-outcomes. *Dev. Psychol.* 21:83–89

Shultz, T. R., Wright, K. 1985. Concepts of negligence and intention in the assignment of moral responsibility. *Can. J. Behav. Sci.* 17:97–108

Shultz, T. R., Wright, K., Schleifer, M. 1986. Assignment of moral responsibility and punishment. *Child Dev.* 57:177–84

Shweder, R. A., Mahapatra, M., Miller, J. G. 1987. Culture and moral development. See Kagan & Lamb 1987, pp. 1–90

Shweder, R. A., Much, N. C. 1989. Determinations of meaning, discourse, and moral socialization. In *Moral Development Through Social Interaction*, ed. W. Kartines, J. Gewirtz. New York: Wiley

Shweder, R. A., Turiel, E., Much, N. C. 1981. The moral intuitions of the child. In *Social Cognitive Development: Frontiers and Possible Futures*, ed. J. H. Flavell, L. Ross. New York: Cambridge Univ. Press

Smetana, J. G. 1983. Social cognitive development: domain distinctions and coordinations. *Dev. Rev.* 3(2):131–47

Staub, E., ed. 1984. *The Development and Maintainance of Prosocial Behavior: International Perspectives on Positive Morality.* New York: Plenum

Thagard, P. 1989. Explanatory coherence. *Behav. Brain Sci.* 12:435–67

Thibaut, J., Walker, L. 1975. *Procedural Justice: A Psychological Analysis.* Hillsdale, NJ: Erlbaum

Turiel, E. 1983. *The Development of Social Knowledge: Morality and Convention.* New York: Cambridge Univ. Press

Tyler, T. 1988. What is procedural justice: criteria used by citizens to assess the fairness of legal procedures. *Law Soc. Rev.* 22:103–35

Walker, L. J. 1980. Cognitive and perspective-taking prerequisites for moral development. *Child Dev.* 51:131–39

Walster, E., Berscheid, E., Walster, W. 1973. New directions in equity research. *J. Pers. Soc. Psychol.* 25:151–96

Walton, M. D. 1985. Negotiation of responsibility: judgments of blameworthiness in a natural setting. *Dev. Psychol.* 21: 725–36

Walton, M. D., Sedlak, A. J. 1982. Making amends: a grammar-based analysis of children's social interaction. *Merrill-Palmer Q.* 28:389–412

Zanna, M. P. 1988. *The development of judgments of responsibility of foreseeable and unforeseeable accidents and intentional harms.* Presented at the Meet. Univ. Waterloo Conf. on Child Dev.

Annu. Rev. Psychol. 1990. 41:557–84

THE ATONIA AND MYOCLONIA OF ACTIVE (REM) SLEEP

Michael H. Chase and Francisco R. Morales

Department of Physiology, Department of Anatomy and Cell Biology, and the Brain Research Institute, University of California, Los Angeles, California 90024

CONTENTS

0066-4308/90/0201-0557$02.00
557

INTRODUCTION

The cessation of gross body movements and relaxation of the peripheral musculature are obvious, externally observable components of active (REM)[1] sleep; less obvious are the dynamic patterns of motor control that are actively promulgated during this state. During active sleep, inhibitory and excitatory motor commands descend from brainstem structures to project upon motoneurons (for reviews, see Pompeiano 1967; Chase 1983). The dynamism of these influences becomes evident when they cease to function properly. For example, some humans, when they enter REM sleep, thrash violently about, leap out of bed, and may even attack their bedpartners; they are not paralyzed during REM sleep as most people are. This recently recognized syndrome is called REM Behavior Disorder (Mahowald & Schenck 1989). Long before this syndrome was recognized in humans, it was found that cats sustaining brainstem lesions thrash violently about and often appear to attack nonexistent prey when they enter active sleep: They are not paralyzed during active sleep as are normally functioning mammals (Jouvet & Delorme 1965; Henley & Morrison 1974). This pattern of behavior is called REM Sleep Without Atonia. It is hypothesized that REM Behavior Disorder in humans is comparable to REM Sleep Without Atonia.

Motor commands that emanate from or are relayed through the brainstem to suppress or initiate movements are eventually directed to somatic motoneurons.[2] Motoneurons are defined unambiguously; they are nerve cells with axons terminating on skeletal muscle fibers. Their significance resides in the fact that they are the principal access of the central nervous system to the peripheral somatic musculature. Sherrington stressed this point by referring to motoneurons as the "final common pathway" (Sherrington 1906). Each motoneuron and the muscle fibers that it innervates form a *motor unit*. It is truly a functional unit because all of the muscle fibers supplied by a single motoneuron contract synchronously. When the muscle units innervated by a motoneuron are monitored, a perfect correlation is observed between the discharge of the motoneuron and the action potentials of individual muscle fibers. Most of our muscles are constantly active (i.e. contracting) when we are awake, especially when we maintain a specific posture or perform a specific movement. Thus, even when muscles are not contracting in response to specific descending commands from a forebrain area, an asynchronous, sustained firing of motoneurons maintains low levels of muscle contraction, or muscle tone. When motoneurons cease discharging, as they do during

---

[1]Rapid eye movement (REM) sleep; also known as paradoxical sleep.
[2]Unless otherwise specified, all references to motoneurons will be to alpha, rather than gamma or beta motoneurons.

almost the entire period of active sleep, *atonia* results. The discharge of motoneurons during active sleep involves the synchronous activation of groups of motor units. The resulting myoclonic activity is evidenced behaviorally as brief, rapid, jerky muscle contractions.

The processes of excitation and inhibition of motoneurons can be monitored by recording, with a microelectrode placed within the motoneuron, the changes in electrical potential across the motoneuron membrane. By this means we can differentiate between processes that cannot be directly resolved using extracellular recording methodologies. For example, intracellular recording can tell us whether a reduction in motoneuron excitability is due to direct inhibition or to disfacilitation (i.e. the withdrawal of facilitatory drives). Additionally, we can distinguish the presence of facilitatory drives from disinhibition (i.e. the simple withdrawal of inhibition). A detailed analysis of individual excitatory or inhibitory postsynaptic potentials can also be obtained by recording intracellularly. Information of this nature is unavailable when recordings are performed with an extracellularly located recording electrode.

In order to examine the modulation of membrane potential and synaptic activity during the behaviors of sleep and wakefulness, we developed experimental techniques for recording intracellularly from identified motoneurons in the brainstem and lumbar spinal cord of the cat (Chase et al 1980; Morales et al 1981). These intracellular techniques were necessary because the activities of motor as well as sensory and integrative systems are differentially modulated during sleep and wakefulness. In fact, numerous phenomena and physiological processes are present during only one state of sleep or wakefulness and absent during another (Chase 1980; Steriade & Hobson 1976). The techniques for chronic intracellular recording in the intact, unanesthetized, undrugged, normally respiring cat were described in Morales et al 1981. These techniques have also been employed for recording intracellularly from brainstem reticular neurons (Chase et al 1981; Ito & McCarley 1984).

One of the primary objectives of this chapter is to review data describing the neural mechanisms, circuitry, and pharmacological basis for atonia during active sleep. These data have been derived from intracellular recording and microiontophoretic experiments conducted during the last 15 years (for a review of previous related literature, see Pompeiano 1967). We also survey recently developed data that are beginning to provide a comprehensive description of the neural bases for the paradoxical presence of muscle twitches and jerks that occur during the rapid eye movement periods of active sleep. In addition, we briefly survey a number of hypotheses that purport to describe the brainstem circuitry that controls motor inhibition during active sleep, placing their evolution in historical perspective. Unless otherwise specified, the data presented in this chapter were obtained from the brainstem and spinal cord motoneurons of chronic cats. (These data are presented in greater detail in Chase 1980, 1983; Chase & Morales 1982, 1983; Morales et al 1987a,b; see also Glenn & Dement 1981.)

BASIC PATTERNS OF MUSCLE ACTIVITY DURING SLEEP

In humans, the passage from wakefulness to sleep is accompanied by a decrease in muscle tone (Kleitman 1963; Pompeiano 1967). One of the first investigators to describe this phenomenon was Pakhomov (1947), who measured the tonus of the flexors of the fingers with a complex hydrodynamic system of tubes. Atonia (the complete lack of tone of somatic muscles) was subsequently found to occur in humans during the state of active sleep (Kleitman 1963). In 1959, Jouvet and coworkers observed atonia of the neck muscles of the cat during active sleep (Jouvet et al 1959). Thus, in humans and cats, as well as in many other species (Chase 1980; Kleitman 1963), it is well established that there is a cessation of muscle tone during active sleep. However, muscle atonia during active sleep is not the sole reflection of active sleep-specific patterns of motor control, for there are also episodes of myoclonic activity during this state.

In 1932, Lisi described muscular twitches and jerks during sleep in humans and in a variety of domestic animals. These muscle contractions were more evident in flexor than in extensor muscles and were more frequently observed in the distal than in the proximal musculature (Pompeiano 1978). The episodes of muscular activation are of short duration and are most intense during the periods of rapid eye movements (REM) of active sleep. In fact, the rapid eye movements themselves can be viewed as myoclonic activity. Other muscles, such as the middle ear muscles, exhibit phasically occurring short-duration periods of activation (Baust et al 1964).

Although active sleep may appear to involve only minor, sporadic, and insignificant movements of isolated muscles, the underlying motor control landscape is actually ravished by storms of inhibition and brief whirlwinds of excitation directed toward "the final common pathway," the somatic motoneuron. Thus, from the perspective of somatic motoneurons and other neurons throughout the nervous system, active sleep is an exceptionally "active" state.

MOTONEURON MEMBRANE POTENTIAL DURING ACTIVE SLEEP

The membrane potential of a motoneuron is determined by unequal concentrations of ions inside and outside the cell and the differential permeability of the membrane to diverse ions. Experimentally, an initial membrane potential is recorded when a cell is first penetrated with a microelectrode. A final determination of the resting membrane potential is obtained by taking, as a reference, the voltage recorded by the microelectrode when it is immediately withdrawn from the cell and is located juxtacellularly. Generally, when a neuron is hyperpolarized, it is less excitable; when it depolarizes, it is more excitable. Along with membrane potential levels, variations in action potential activity, rheobase, and input resistance can be assessed to determine changes in excitability as well as to provide clues about the processes that underlie changes in excitability.

Motoneuron Membrane Potential during the Transition from Quiet Sleep to Active Sleep[3]

Motoneurons are hyperpolarized during active sleep as compared with quiet (NREM) sleep (Figure 1). The degree of hyperpolarization varies from 2 to 10 mV; its development parallels the various ways in which active sleep emerges from quiet sleep. For example, although the onset of active sleep is demarcated by neocortical electroencephalographic desynchronization and a reduction in muscle tone, these indexes are not always present at the same time, and either may precede the other as the animal enters the active sleep state. When bursts of rapid eye movements (REMs) occur during active sleep, the membrane potential is hyperpolarized to an even greater extent—except for brief periods of depolarization that often culminate in the development of action potentials (see below).

Motoneuron Membrane Potential during the Transition from Active Sleep to Wakefulness

In the transition from active sleep to wakefulness, the membrane potential rapidly depolarizes (Figure 1). The degree of depolarization is equal to or exceeds the level maintained during the preceding episode of quiet (NREM) sleep.

In summary, somatic motoneurons are hyperpolarized during active sleep as compared with quiet sleep (and wakefulness).

Motoneuron Action Potentials

Motoneuron action potentials arise as the result of a summation of ionic currents generated at synapses on their soma and/or dendrites. These ionic currents converge in the region of the axon's initial segment, which is the most excitable portion of the motoneuron. If the voltage change produced by synaptic currents is above a certain threshold, an action potential is triggered, first in the initial segment, then in the soma, and possibly in the proximal

---

[3]Unless otherwise specified, active sleep data will represent those obtained during the non-rapid-eye-movement periods of active sleep.

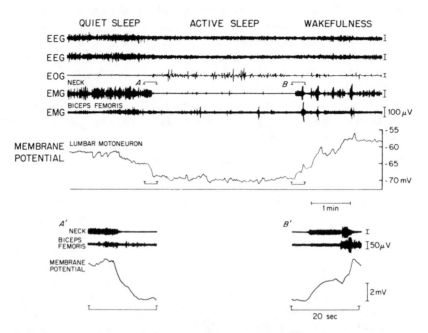

Figure 1 Intracellular record from a lumbar motoneuron during sleep and wakefulness: correlation of membrane potential and behavioral state. This figure highlights membrane hyperpolarization that accompanies active sleep. Hyperpolarization commenced prior to the cessation of muscle tone, which was accompanied by a further and rather sharp increase in membrane polarization (*A*, and shown oscilloscopically at higher gain and expanded time-base in *A'*). At the termination of active sleep, the membrane depolarized coincident with the resumption of muscle tone and behavioral awakening (*B, B'*). Note the brief periods of depolarization during active sleep and wakefulness, which were accompanied by phasic increases in muscle activity (i.e. muscular twitches during active sleep and leg movements during wakefulness). Spike potentials often occurred during these periods of depolarization but are not evident in this figure because the DC record was passed through a 0.2-cps high-frequency polygraphic filter. This motoneuron was recorded for 28 min; the traces shown were obtained 12 min after the cell was impaled. The first and second polygraph traces are those of EEG activity recorded from left and right frontal-parietal cortex, respectively. Reprinted from *Exp. Neurol.* 62:821–27, 1978 [Figure 2] by permission from Academic Press, Inc.

dendrites. Consequently, motoneuron action potentials exhibit two basic deflections or spikes, the initial segment (IS) and soma-dendritic (SD) spikes, which reflect activity in the most excitable regions of the cell (Burke & Rudomín 1977).

The interval between the IS and SD spikes, referred to as the IS-SD delay, is lengthened when the animal enters active sleep, indicating that the motoneuron soma is inhibited during this state. During bursts of REMS, the IS-SD delay is further prolonged and/or the SD spike is blocked. These variations in IS and SD spikes are indirect evidence of an increase in conductance of the soma membrane, which is the basis for postsynaptic inhibition (Brock et al 1953; Llinás & Terzuolo 1964).

Motoneuron Rheobase

Rheobase is defined operationally as the minimal amplitude of an electrical current of sufficient duration ($\approx$20 ms) that, when injected into a cell, will elicit an action potential.

Rheobase during quiet sleep is comparable to that present during wakefulness, whereas it is significantly greater in active sleep than in quiet sleep. The increase in rheobasic current during active sleep is illustrated in Figure 2. These data indicate a dramatic decrease in cellular excitability during active

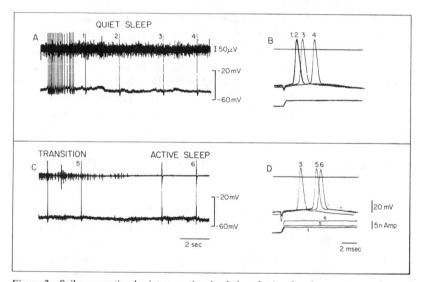

Figure 2 Spike generation by intrasomatic stimulation. In A, after the spontaneous burst of spike activity in the initial portion of the record had receded, four consecutive threshold determinations were performed during quiet sleep utilizing currents of 4 nA and 20-msec duration. Note that membrane potential fluctuations present during quiet sleep were only accompanied by changes in the latency of the direct spikes (B). Shown in C and D is an increase in threshold that commenced in the transition period (5) after quiet sleep and was most pronounced during active sleep (6). In D the increase is shown for spikes obtained during quiet sleep (3), the transition period (5), and active sleep (6). During active sleep a threshold increase of 110% was observed. Note that both the overshoot and absolute amplitude of the direct spike were smaller during active sleep than during quiet sleep. These reductions in spike size commenced during the transition period. The lower traces in B and D reflect the intrasomatic depolarizing current. The heavy line crossing the spike tips represents zero voltage obtained when the electrode was withdrawn from the motoneuron. Upper traces in A and C are the EMG recordings. Reprinted from *Brain Res.* 225:179–295, 1981 [Figure 4] by permission from Elsevier/North-Holland Biomedical Press.

sleep. Although hyperpolarization is always accompanied by an elevated rheobase, hyperpolarization alone cannot completely account for the increase in rheobase current. An analysis of the data from rheobasic determinations and input resistance (see below) indicates that motoneuron membrane current flow is "shunted" by an increase in the membrane conductance during active sleep; thus, both hyperpolarization and increased conductance appear to contribute to the observed increase in motoneuron rheobase during active sleep.

Motoneuron Input Resistance

The way a motoneuron responds to injected electrical or synaptic currents is related to its input resistance. This basic property of motor cells depends principally upon the specific resistivity of the cell membrane, its area, and the geometric characteristics of its dendritic tree (Burke & Rudomín 1977). During active sleep, compared with quiet sleep, there is a striking (44%) decrease in input resistance (Morales & Chase 1981). When REMs occur during active sleep, there are frequent phasic decreases in the voltage drop produced by the same current, indicating a continuously fluctuating motoneuron input resistance. These changes in input resistance, along with the other determinations presented above, provide convincing evidence that motoneurons are postsynaptically inhibited during active sleep.

POSTSYNAPTIC CONTROL OF MOTONEURONS DURING ACTIVE SLEEP

In the preceding section, we presented evidence that motoneurons are subjected to postsynaptic inhibition during active sleep. Because the synapse is the point of contact and site of communication for postsynaptic inhibition (as well as for postsynaptic excitation), knowledge of the active sleep-dependent patterns of synaptic transmission is critical to understanding active sleep-dependent patterns of motor control.

Inhibitory Control of Motoneurons

In an effort to elucidate further the bases for motoneuron inhibition during active sleep, high-gain intracellular recordings were obtained from motoneurons during active sleep (as well as during quiet sleep and wakefulness). Spontaneous inhibitory postsynaptic potential (IPSP) activity was found to dominate these intracellularly derived records, as described below (Morales et al 1987b).

During wakefulness and quiet sleep, intracellular records of motoneurons reveal relatively few spontaneous IPSPs. During active sleep, the number of IPSPs greatly increases (Figure 3). Even more manifest is the development of

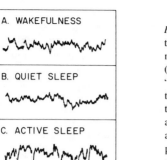

A. WAKEFULNESS

B. QUIET SLEEP

C. ACTIVE SLEEP

1 2 |2mV
    50ms

1
2 |1mV
    2ms

Figure 3 High-gain intracellular recording of the membrane potential activity of a tibial motoneuron during wakefulness (A), quiet sleep (B), and active sleep (C). Note the appearance, "de novo" during AS, of large-amplitude, repetitively occurring inhibition postsynaptic potentials. Two representative potentials, which were aligned by their origins, are shown at higher gain and at an expanded time base (C1, 2). These potentials were photographed from the screen of a digital oscilloscope. The analog-to-digital conversion rate was 50 μs/bin. During these recordings the membrane potential during active sleep was -67.0 mV; the antidromic action potential was 78.5 mV. Reprinted from *Exp. Neurol.* 98:418–35, 1987 [Figure 1] by permission from Academic Press, Inc.

large-amplitude active sleep-specific IPSPs; that is, IPSPs unique to this particular behavioral state. The amplitude and time course of these active sleep-specific IPSPs differentiate them both from the smaller potentials impinging on motoneurons during quiet sleep and from other small-amplitude IPSPs that also appear during active sleep. In addition, the large-amplitude active sleep-specific IPSPs are more readily reversed by the iontophoretic injection of chloride ions than are the smaller potentials, a finding that indicates that the synapses responsible for the large amplitude IPSPs are situated closer to the soma region; they are, therefore, strategically located to enforce the suppression of motoneuron activity.

The frequency of occurrence of motoneuron IPSPs during behavioral states was examined by determining the interpotential intervals of IPSPs during quiet sleep, the initial period of active sleep, and the NREM periods of active sleep. Interpotential intervals are significantly shorter during both the initial period of active sleep and throughout active sleep than during quiet sleep.

There is little doubt that there is (*a*) a unique set of inhibitory synapses that generate these active sleep-specific IPSPs, because these IPSPs occur only during active sleep, and/or (*b*) a unique pattern of activation of inhibitory interneurons during active sleep, which implies the existence of inhibitory interneurons driven to discharge, selectively, during active sleep. The responsible interneurons may be situated in the spinal cord close to their target pools of motoneurons (Morales et al 1982; Takakusaki et al 1989). Alternatively, the active sleep inhibitory interneurons may be located not in the spinal cord, but in the brainstem; they would then be expected to have long projection axons that end directly on spinal motoneurons (see Chase & Morales 1989 and Morales et al 1988 for a discussion of the possible location of the inhibitory interneurons). For brainstem motoneurons, the inhibitory interneurons that generate active sleep-specific IPSPs are, without doubt, located in the brainstem (see the section below on brainstem control of motoneurons during active sleep). Irrespective of the location of the interneurons that give rise to the active sleep-specific IPSPs, we suggest that these IPSPs represent the final synaptic expression of an inhibitory system responsible for promoting the suppression of motoneuron activity during active sleep and for the development of muscle atonia.

Excitatory Control of Motoneurons during Active Sleep

As described above, postsynaptic inhibition is one of the principal synaptic processes affecting motoneurons during the non-REM periods of active sleep. In fact, the inhibitory phenomena described in the previous section are not only present, they are enhanced during the REM periods of active sleep. How could there then be twitches and jerks of the eyes and limbs during REM periods? The answer is simple, for most REM periods are accompanied not only by increased motoneuron inhibition, but also by the onslaught of potent motor excitatory drives (Figure 4).

The excitatory drives directed to motoneurons during the REM periods of active sleep result in the generation of depolarizing and spike potentials. In contrast to the gradual depolarization that always precedes neuronal discharge during wakefulness (Figure 4), in most instances during active sleep there is an initial hyperpolarization followed immediately by a depolarization shift and action potential generation. These depolarization shifts in membrane potential appear to be the result of cumulative EPSP activity, for the following reasons. First, examination of high-gain, high-speed records reveals that each depolarization consists of the summation of wavelets that are comparable in form to previously described EPSPs (Burke 1967). Second, the depolarizing potentials remain even after the intracellular injection of chloride ions and after the juxtacellular microiontophoretic application of strychnine.

Thus, from time to time for reasons as yet unknown, during the REM periods of active sleep excitatory drives overpower the omnipresent inhibitory drives; motoneurons discharge and the muscle fibers that they innervate contract. At these times, even though the excitatory drives are actually accompanied by an increase in inhibitory drives, the excitatory drives predominate and motoneurons discharge. But when motoneurons do discharge during the REM periods of active sleep, the resultant contraction of the muscles they innervate is unlike that which occurs during any other state. Movements are twitchy and apparently without purpose.

The co-activation of opposing synaptic drives may appear, from a functional perspective, to be paradoxical. However, some sense may be made of these

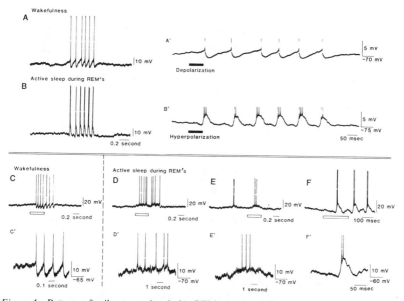

Figure 4   Patterns of spike generation during REM periods of active sleep. (A) During wakefulness, depolarization (bar in A') was the initial membrane potential event. (B) During REM periods, each depolarization shift was preceded by hyperpolarization (bar in B') (see also F and F'). Full-sized spikes developed in both examples; in B doublets, triplets, and quadruplets accompanied each depolarizing shift. The open bars indicate the period of the traces shown in C'–F'. (C) Spike generation during wakefulness. (D) An irregular pattern of spike activity. (E) Intermittent bursts and (F) spike doublets during REM periods. An increase in hyperpolarizing subthreshold synaptic activity during interspike intervals is present in D' and E'. A and B are records from a single tibial motoneuron and C through E from a single peroneal motoneuron; F is from another peroneal cell. Reprinted from *Science* 221:1195–98, 1983 [Figure 1] by permission from the American Association for the Advancement of Science.

processes when they are examined individually. For example, the inhibitory input present during active sleep may, by suppressing contraction of the somatic musculature, protect the organism at a time when it is blind and unconscious. Although we do not understand the function of the REM periods of active sleep, we do know that during these periods most populations of cortical and subcortical cells discharge at rates that often exceed those characteristic of wakefulness (Steriade & Hobson 1976). In fact, activity along practically all motor pathways is greatly enhanced in an apparently random manner during active sleep and especially during the REM periods of active sleep (Evarts 1964; Marchiafava & Pompeiano 1964; Steriade & Hobson 1976). Episodes of motoneuron spike potentials that result in myoclonic activity during REM periods may have no specific functional significance; they may simply reflect the status of a highly activated nervous system whose motor facilitatory pathways are discharging at extremely high rates. It is also possible that myoclonic activity represents brief episodes of an otherwise integrated behavior that is suppressed by the presence of motor inhibition. Clearly, without a compensatory increase in motor inhibition during all REM periods, movement (integrated or random) would disrupt the functional integrity of this behavioral state.

NEUROTRANSMITTER CONTROL OF MOTONEURONS DURING ACTIVE SLEEP

In this section we focus on the neurotransmitters that mediate the unique inhibitory postsynaptic potentials that occur during active sleep. Also examined are the neurotransmitters that mediate the excitatory potentials responsible for the phasic discharge of motoneurons during the REM periods of active sleep.

Inhibitory Neurotransmitters

Studies conducted in acute and/or anesthetized and/or decerebrate cats have convincingly demonstrated that strychnine antagonizes the postsynaptic inhibitory actions of alpha- and beta-amino acids such as glycine and beta-alanine. Based upon these studies, it is generally accepted that glycine is a major inhibitory transmitter for motoneurons of the spinal cord (Curtis & Johnston 1974; Davidoff & Hackman 1985; Young & McDonald 1983). In similar preparations, picrotoxin and bicuculline have been shown to be effective antagonists for the postsynaptic inhibitory actions of gamma-amino acids (e.g. gamma-aminobutyric acid, or GABA) (Curtis et al 1968; Davidoff & Hackman 1985; Krnjevic et al 1976; Nistri 1983).

Our experimental approach was to examine the effect of the antagonists of glycine (i.e. strychnine) and GABA (i.e. picrotoxin and bicuculline) on the frequency of occurrence and waveform parameters of the IPSPs that occur during the non-REM periods of active sleep. The convulsant properties of strychnine, picrotoxin, and bicuculline, and their effects on numerous physiological systems and cell groups (Curtis 1969), precluded their usefulness when systemically or intrathecally injected. To circumvent these problems and to localize their site of action, we administered these inhibitory neurotransmitter antagonists juxtacellularly, by microiontophoresis, onto the surface of motoneurons that were being recorded intracellularly during naturally occurring episodes of quiet and active sleep.

As previously described, the membrane potential of lumbar motoneurons during the atonia of active sleep is dominated by a barrage of IPSPs, including the large-amplitude AS (active sleep) -IPSPs unique to this state (Morales &

A. Active Sleep, Control

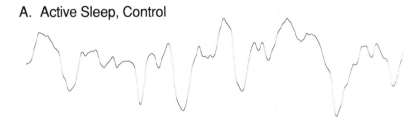

B. Active Sleep, Strychnine

0.5 mV

10 ms

Figure 5   Effect of microiontophoretically ejected strychnine on the membrane potential activity of a sciatic motoneuron recorded during the atonia of active sleep. Each trace is a high-gain record of membrane activity before (A) and after (B) strychnine ejection. Note that the control membrane potential activity during the atonia of active sleep was characterized predominantly by large-amplitude spontaneously occurring IPSPs (A), which were completely abolished (B) following the ejection of strychnine (15 nM, 225 nA, 1.5 min). The tip of the recording micropipette extended 60 μm beyond the ejection micropipette, thus allowing strychnine to be ejected adjacent to the somatic portion of the motoneuron. Antidromic spike amplitude, 66 mV. Reprinted from *J. Neurosci.* 9(3):743–51, 1989 [Figure 2] by permission from the Society for Neuroscience.

Chase 1982; Morales et al 1987b). In certain motoneurons, strychnine blocked completely all IPSPs. Figure 5 is a high-gain intracellular recording of membrane activity from such a lumbar motoneuron during the atonia of active sleep. This cell was impaled during the preceding episode of quiet sleep; its membrane activity was monitored throughout the transition and then during the entire ensuing episode of active sleep. A sample record of high-gain membrane activity in the same cell following the juxtacellular ejection of strychnine indicates that IPSP activity was completely suppressed and remained so throughout the period of active sleep. In some motoneurons, however, some residual IPSP activity followed strychnine application, all of small amplitude.

The AS-IPSPs are either diminished in amplitude or completely abolished following the microiontophoretic application of strychnine. It is well established that strychnine markedly reduces or abolishes Ia and recurrent inhibition as well as the postsynaptic inhibition induced by stimulation of the brainstem reticular formation (Cullheim & Kellerth 1981; Curtis 1962, 1969; Curtis et al 1968; Kawai & Sasaki 1964; Larson 1969; Llinás 1964). These and the other studies mentioned previously indicate that glycine (or a structurally related compound) is probably released from the terminals of segmental inhibitory interneurons that impinge on alpha-motoneurons (Curtis et al 1968; Werman et al 1968; see also reviews by Curtis 1969; Davidoff & Hackman 1983; Young & McDonald 1983). Our finding that AS-IPSPs are abolished by microiontophoretic strychnine strongly suggests, on the basis of this compound's documented actions, that these inhibitory potentials are mediated by glycine or glycine-like substances. [We have also recently demonstrated that strychnine suppresses the IPSPs induced in lumbar motoneurons during the atonia of active sleep following stimulation of the medullary nucleus reticularis gigantocellularis (Soja et al 1987).]

The AS-IPSPs are likely generated by local spinal cord inhibitory interneurons because we have no evidence of a long monosynaptic inhibitory projection to lumbar motoneurons from brainstem sites (Baldissera et al 1981; Jankowska et al 1968). Spinal cord Ia inhibitory interneurons may be a candidate source; their inhibitory actions on spinal motoneurons are reduced or abolished by strychnine (Curtis 1962, 1969; Curtis et al 1976; Larson 1969; Cullheim & Kellerth 1981). In addition, the inhibitory interneurons recently described by Hongo et al (1983) or those described by Mori et al (1986) and Takakusaki et al (1989) may be involved in generating these IPSPs. At the present time only Renshaw cells can be excluded as being responsible for generating the AS-IPSPs of lumbar motoneurons during the atonia of active sleep (Morales et al 1988).

The population of IPSPs that remained following the microiontophoresis of strychnine resembled, in terms of their amplitude distribution and the relationship between their amplitude and rise-time, the small amplitude IPSPs that inhibit motoneurons during active sleep (as well as during quiet sleep and wakefulness; cf Morales et al 1987b). We cannot be certain whether the IPSPs that remained in some cells after strychnine application are the small-amplitude IPSPs of active sleep, or are AS-IPSPs whose amplitudes have been partially suppressed by strychnine. However, these results indicate that both groups of potentials may be mediated by glycine because, in several of the motoneurons examined, all inhibitory synaptic potentials were abolished by strychnine administration.

One explanation for the finding that repeated microiontophoretic applications of strychnine did not block all IPSP activity in some cells pertains to certain problems associated with microiontophoretic experiments (see review by Stone 1985). For example, if a drug is ejected onto or near the soma of the cell that is being recorded, synapses located on the dendritic tree may be less affected because of a diminished concentration of the ejected drug. Thus, strychnine-sensitive IPSPs generated at more distal dendritic sites may be only partially blocked, or even unaffected, by somatic drug applications. Indeed, the small-amplitude IPSPs of active sleep appear to originate from synapses located more distally than those of the AS-IPSPs (Morales & Chase 1982; Engelhardt et al 1985). Thus, by virtue of their synaptic location alone, the small-amplitude IPSPs may be less susceptible to juxtasomatically applied strychnine. Therefore, the residual potentials may simply reflect incomplete coverage of the synaptic loci by strychnine.

Neither picrotoxin nor bicuculline, when released microiontophoretically near the somata of individual motoneurons, suppressed the large-amplitude AS-IPSPs or the small-amplitude IPSPs of active sleep. Thus, glycine, but not GABA, appears to be the principal postsynaptic inhibitory neurotransmitter responsible for muscle atonia during active sleep.

Excitatory Neurotransmitters

The membrane potential activity of lumbar motoneurons during REM periods of active sleep is characterized by glycinergic inhibitory processes, as described above, as well as by brief periods of strychnine-sensitive hyperpolarization; but there are also complex patterns of paroxysmal depolarizing shifts that lead to full-size or partial amplitude action potentials (Chase & Morales 1982, 1983). The neurotransmitter(s) responsible for these state-dependent excitatory processes, which can eventuate in myoclonic activity, had not been investigated prior to our recent studies of the effects of excitatory amino acid antagonists on the phasic depolarizing events that occur during REM periods of active sleep (Soja et al 1988).

In a recent set of studies, the excitatory amino acid antagonist kynurenic acid was iontophoretically released next to intracellularly recorded motoneurons during wakefulness, quiet sleep, and the transition into and throughout active sleep. Intracellularly recorded compound mono- and polysynaptic EPSPs, evoked by low-intensity sciatic nerve stimulation during wakefulness and quiet sleep, were utilized as controls for the actions of kynurenic acid, which markedly suppressed or abolished these EPSPs. On the other hand, short-latency IPSPs of peripheral origin were not blocked. These data indicate that the drug was adequately released and was capable of specifically blocking excitatory neurotransmission.

During REM periods of active sleep, kynurenic acid suppressed the naturally occurring phasic depolarizing membrane shifts and action potentials. Membrane potential activity during REM periods following kynurenic acid application was characterized only by marked recurrent hyperpolarizations. On the other hand, microiontophoresis of the selective N-methyl-D-aspartate

(NMDA) antagonist 2-amino-5-phosphonovaleric acid (APV) suppressed polysynaptic EPSPs evoked by sciatic nerve stimulation and motoneuronal depolarizations induced by juxtacellularly applied NMDA; it failed to block the naturally occurring phasic depolarizing membrane shifts during the REM periods of active sleep.

On the basis of the documented selectivity of kynurenic acid and APV in antagonizing the postsynaptic actions of NMDA versus non-NMDA-like excitatory amino acids, the present results suggest that the postsynaptic excitatory drives that impinge on lumbar motoneurons during the REM periods of active sleep are mediated primarily by a non-NMDA neurotransmitter.

These pharmacological data indicate that glycine (or a glycinergic substance) is the inhibitory neurotransmitter that mediates these active sleep-specific IPSPs, and that a non-NMDA neurotransmitter mediates the depolarizations that evoke action potential activity during the REM periods of active sleep.

BRAINSTEM CONTROL OF MOTONEURONS DURING ACTIVE SLEEP

Induction of Atonia by Carbachol Microinjection Into the Pons

Numerous articles in recent years describe the induction of active sleep—or components of active sleep—following the injection of small amounts of carbachol, a cholinergic agent, into the pontine area of the brainstem (George et al 1964; Baxter 1969; Mitler & Dement 1974; Baghdoyan et al 1984; Katayama et al 1984; Shiromani et al 1986; Morales et al 1987a). The general region for the cholinoceptive induction of active sleep—or components of active sleep—lies in the rostrodorsal pontine tegmentum (Baghdoyan et al 1987).

Although there are slight differences and minor disagreements about the specific sites optimal for the induction of active sleep, or any of its components, investigators agree that a common, and even defining characteristic of the "carbachol" effect is the reduction of muscle tone that can occur in isolation but is often accompanied by other physiological changes that are more (EEG) or less (eye movements) similar to those that take place during naturally occurring active sleep (Morales et al 1987a).

In an effort to determine whether, in fact, the mechanisms responsible for the reduction of motor activity following intrapontine carbachol administration are similar to those that control the reduction in motor activity under normal physiological conditions during active sleep, an intracellular analysis was undertaken of lumbar motoneuron membrane potential activity and of the synaptic control of these motoneurons before and after the intrapontine microinjection of carbachol (Morales et al 1987a). This study was accomplished by measuring ventral root activity, the amplitude of the Ia-monosynaptic reflex, and the basic electrophysiological properties of lumbar motoneurons in conjunction with the administration of carbachol into the pontine tegmentum.

Under control conditions (i.e. pre-carbachol administration) in the decerebrate cat, ventral root activity consists of a steady background of tonically discharging small units and phasic bursts of large units (Figure 6, A and B). The background small-unit activity is most likely the result of the discharge of small alpha- and gamma-motoneurons, because these motoneurons discharge tonically in this preparation; the bursts of large units presumably reflect the phasic activity of large alpha-motoneurons (Granit 1955; Matthews 1972). The initial effect of carbachol microinjection into the pontine reticular formation consists of the abolition of phasic ventral root discharge; shortly thereafter, tonic discharge also disappears, resulting in a complete suppression of ventral root activity (Figure 6). The suppression of ventral root activity following the injection of carbachol is accompanied by a sustained reduction in the amplitude of the Ia-monosynaptic reflex (Morales et al 1987a).

A profound reduction in the excitability of motoneurons also occurs during motor suppression induced by carbachol, even though the average motoneuron membrane potential values are not significantly different. Rheobasic currents increase 88% after carbachol administration. The cellular basis for this change in excitability was examined by measuring the input resistance of motoneurons and by determining the critical threshold voltage for the generation of an action potential, as presented below.

There is a 47% decrease in mean input resistance after carbachol microinjection (Figure 7). Examples of the voltage response to the injection of a 1-nA depolarizing current pulse in two representative motoneurons, one recorded before and the other during carbachol-induced motor suppression, are shown in Figure 7, C and D, respectively. This change in input resistance most likely reflects increased membrane conductance, as has been postulated for a number of different inhibitory processes (Carlen & Durand 1981; Carlen et al 1980; Coombs et al 1955; Llinás & Terzuolo 1964; Morales & Chase 1981; Smith et al 1967). It follows that because of the "shunting" effect produced when there is an increase in membrane conductance, additional depolarizing current would have to be injected in order to elicit a direct action potential, given that the firing threshold voltage remains constant. The identical values for threshold voltage indicate that the increase in rheobase is not due to a modification of the threshold voltage induced by carbachol but, rather, that it can be explained on the basis of an increase in conductance. Confirmation of a conductance change was obtained by an analysis of the

A Tonic Activity

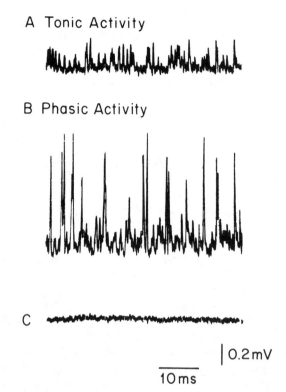

B Phasic Activity

C

$|0.2\,mV$

$\overline{10\,ms}$

Figure 6   Examples of ventral root recordings and the suppression of activity after pontine carbachol microinjection. These recordings were obtained from a thin filament that was dissected from the L_7 ventral root as indicated on the *left side* of the diagram of the experimental paradigm illustrated in Figure 3A. The predominant pattern of activity consisted of a continuous discharge of relatively small units, as illustrated in A. Sporadic bursts of large units, shown in B, were also present. The discharge of the tonically active small units and the phasic larger units ceased after carbachol administration (C). Reprinted from *J. Neurophysiol.* 57(4):1118–29, 1987 [Figure 2] by permission from the American Physiological Society.

shortening of the membrane time constant induced by pontine carbachol microinjection. Overall, across motoneurons, there is a 41% decrease in the mean membrane time constant after carbachol administration.

During active sleep, as described above, large spontaneous inhibitory synaptic potentials bombard lumbar motoneurons in conjunction with somatomotor atonia (Morales & Chase 1982). Consequently, high-gain membrane potential recordings were examined in order to determine whether inhibitory synaptic potentials could also be detected during carbachol-induced motor suppression. Figure 8 illustrates intracellular records from the same motoneuron before and after carbachol was injected into the pontine reticular formation. There is a striking similarity between the potentials presented in this figure and those recorded during naturally occurring active sleep, as

A ·EXPERIMENTAL PARADIGM   B AVERAGE INPUT RESISTANCE

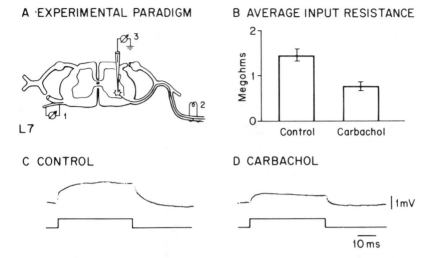

C CONTROL   D CARBACHOL

Figure 7   Decrease of motoneuron input resistance during carbachol-induced motor suppression. (A) Diagram of the experimental paradigm. On one side of the cord, the dorsal roots (L_6 to S_2) were cut and the peripheral nerves were placed on bipolar stimulating electrodes [only one nerve and one electrode (2) are shown for illustration purposes]; motoneurons were penetrated with glass microelectrodes (3) and identified by antidromic stimulation. On the contralateral side a rootlet was separated from L_7 ventral root and placed on a bipolar recording electrode (1) in order to monitor motor activity. (B) Each bar represents the mean motoneuron input resistance obtained across motoneurons during control conditions and after carbachol administration. The brackets indicate the standard error of the mean of each population. There was a significant decrease in input resistance (47%) during carbachol-induced motor suppression. (C, D: *upper traces*) Computer-averaged responses to 50-ms current pulses of 1 nA *(lower traces)* in two different motoneurons, one recorded during control conditions (C) and the other after pontine carbachol administration (D). Reprinted from *J. Neurophysiol.* 57(4):1118–29, 1987 [Figure 4] by permission from the American Physiological Society.

shown in Figure 3. Overall, there was a statistically significant increase in the median inhibitory postsynaptic potential frequency after carbachol microinjection.

   The changes in the electrophysiological properties of motoneurons and the presence of IPSPs indicate that they are postsynaptically inhibited after carbachol is microinjected into the pontine reticular formation. Similar changes in the electrophysiological properties of motoneurons and the development of a barrage of IPSPs arise during naturally occurring active sleep.

   On the basis of these data we suggest that the postsynaptic inhibition of motoneurons following carbachol administration is due to the activation of a cholinoceptive brainstem-spinal cord inhibitory system that is also responsible for motoneuron inhibition and generalized atonia in the chronic animal during active sleep.

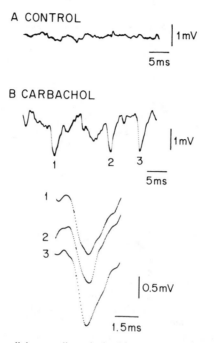

A CONTROL

1mV

5ms

B CARBACHOL

1mV

1   2 3

5ms

1

2

3

0.5mV

1.5ms

Figure 8 High-gain intracellular recordings obtained from a single hindlimb motoneuron during precarbachol control conditions (A) and 26 min after carbachol microinjection into the pontine reticular formation (B). Following carbachol microinjection, hyperpolarizing potentials were easily distinguishable. Potentials labeled 1–3 are shown in an expanded format. These recordings were obtained by employing a KCl-filled microelectrode. A 5-nA depolarizing current was injected to displace the membrane potential away from the equilibrium potential; this procedure facilitated the observation of these potentials and, in addition, avoided shifting the equilibrium potential to a depolarized value by the retention of Cl ions. The waveforms of these potentials were remarkably similar to those that appear exclusively during active sleep in intact animals under natural conditions [compare, for example, the potentials illustrated in this figure with those of Figure 2A in Morales & Chase 1982]. Reprinted from *J. Neurophysiol.* 57(4):1118–29, 1987 [Figure 6] by permission from the American Physiological Society.

Elimination of Atonia by Brainstem Lesions

Motor atonia can be induced by cholinergic stimulation of the pontine brainstem; it can be eliminated by destroying certain pontine sites. As with chemical stimulation, lesions can block active sleep—or components of active sleep. It is also possible, by reducing the size of the lesion, to eliminate selectively the suppression of motor activity that normally accompanies active sleep but leave operative the other physiological patterns of activity normally present during this state. When this occurs a syndrome develops that is called REM Sleep Without Atonia—REM sleep in the presence of muscle tone. The resultant patterns of motor activity depend upon the exact size and placement of the lesion. One may observe either very moderate behaviors, such as the slight lifting of the head or isolated limb movements, or integrated patterns of exploratory, aggressive, or other behaviors. For a survey of the effects of brain lesions on motor behavior, see Siegel (1989).

NEURONAL SYSTEMS RESPONSIBLE FOR MOTONEURON CONTROL DURING ACTIVE SLEEP

The existence of active sleep-specific IPSPs reflects the activity of supraspinal centers that, directly or indirectly, activate inhibitory interneurons that discharge during active sleep. We know the key neuronal centers that control motor inhibition during active sleep are situated caudal to the anterior border of the mesencephalon because a midbrain transection does not eliminate intermittent periods of motor suppression and correlated epiphenomena during this state. On the other hand, following a transection caudal to the medulla, facial muscles continue to be subjected to inhibition during active sleep, while limb and trunk muscles are unaffected by changes in the animal's state. Thus, a critical neuronal population responsible for somatomotor inhibition during active sleep must be located within the confines of the lower brainstem. These neurons may project directly to motoneurons or may exert their effects indirectly by activating segmental circuitry.

Numerous hypotheses have been advanced to account for the manner in which pontomedullary mechanisms promote the inhibition of motoneurons during active sleep. The antecedent hypotheses for those proposed below were summarized by Pompeiano (1967), who stated that it is generally assumed that both the tonic and phasic manifestations of desynchronized sleep result from the activity of brainstem structures, which are mainly localized in the nucleus reticularis pontis caudalis and oralis. In recent years these early concepts have been elaborated by the following individuals and their coworkers: Chase, Mori, Morrison, Sakai, and Siegel. Here we summarize each school of thought, in part by quoting directly from published reports.

Chase (1976) proposed that atonia during active sleep results from a cascade of neuronal activity beginning with the discharge of cells in the pontine tegmentum. The discharge of these cells, in or in the vicinity of the nucleus pontis oralis, results in the activation of cells in the medullary tegmentum. These medullary cells, located in or in the vicinity of the nucleus reticularis gigantocellularis, directly, or through an inhibitory interneuron, provide a postsynaptic drive that inhibits motoneurons during active sleep.

The bases for this hypothesis originated in a series of experiments dealing with the effects of electrical stimulation of the orbital cortex and nucleus pontis oralis on motor activity during states of sleep and wakefulness (Chase 1983). These stimulation experiments were founded on the supposition that if a given neural area participates in a key fashion in the normal pattern of motor control that occurs during a given state, it would then, when stimulated during that state, induce a pattern of somatomotor modulation consonant with what occurs spontaneously. On the other hand, and even more definitively, the induction of a different pattern of motor control would indicate that the area under investigation was not a participant in the natural, spontaneously occurring state-dependent pattern of motor control.

Following this line of reasoning, and for reasons detailed by Chase (1976, 1983), the motor response to electrical stimulation of the orbital cortex and sites within the mesencephalon, pons, and medulla were examined. The orbital cortical control of motor (reflex) activity was unidimensional and consisted of decreasing effectiveness for motor suppression in the continuum of wakefulness to quiet sleep to active sleep. It was concluded that the orbital cortical potential for motor suppression was "turned on" during wakefulness but was "turned off" during active sleep. Examination of brainstem sites revealed a far different picture, for an area was found at the ponto-mesencephalic border that was not only "turned on" during wakefulness but was also "turned on" during active sleep; however, the directions of its motor effect during these states were diametrically opposite. For each state the response was in a direction and to an extent generally comparable to what occurs during the normal state-dependent modulation of motor activity.

The key site at the pontomesencephalic border is located in or in the immediate vicinity of the nucleus pontis oralis. [Incidentally, the region of the nucleus pontis oralis is the same as that found by cholinergic activation to produce motor inhibition and whose destruction results in the absence of motor suppression during active sleep (see the section above on brainstem control of motoneurons during active sleep).] In the initial stimulation experiments, during wakefulness (and quiet sleep) excitation of the nucleus pontis oralis was found to be accompanied by somatic reflex facilitation. As soon as the animal entered into active sleep, the identical stimulus produced reflex suppression. This phenomenon, which was termed "reticular response-reversal," is most dramatically evident when one is observing a freely moving cat. During wakefulness and quiet sleep, reflex activity is greatly augmented by reticular stimulation. At the very moment that the animal enters into active sleep, the reflex becomes strongly suppresssed or eliminated, and all without the intervention of the investigator or any change in stimulating or recording parameters. Should the animal then awaken, the reflex is immediately again facilitated by pontis oralis stimulation. *It is the animal's state alone that "determines" whether the response is one of motor suppression or facilitation.*

Based upon this apparent functional reorganization of the processes of motor control within the region of the pontis oralis, we directed our efforts toward elucidating the mechanisms that underlie the phenomenon of pontomesencephalic reticular response-reversal by determining the basis for the paradoxical finding that brainstem sites apparently can change their motor signature from facilitation to suppression, or from suppression to facilitation, in a manner bound exclusively to the animal's state. The synaptic basis for the phenomenon of response-reversal was explored by recording intracellularly from masseter motoneurons in conjunction with stimulation of the nucleus pontis oralis. We found that a prominent depolarizing potential (i.e. EPSP activity) is induced in these motoneurons during wakefulness and quiet sleep (Chandler et al 1980). The reflex facilitatory response recorded electromyographically during these states can thus be accounted for by the induction of depolarizing potentials. On the other hand, during active sleep, a synaptic drive is generated that produces a prominent hyperpolarizing potential (i.e. IPSP activity), which accounts for the electromyographically recorded reflex suppression observed during this state. It is clear that this pattern of membrane potential modulation represents the basis for the paradoxical phenomenon of reticular response-reversal.

These data resulted in the presentation of a more complete description of the 1976 model of motor control, as follows (Chase 1983):

> We have previously proposed a model of state-dependent motor control wherein there is excitatory input to the NGC [nucleus reticularis gigantocellularis] during active sleep that originates from cells within or in the vicinity of the nucleus pontis oralis (i.e. the pontomesencephalic reticular formation) (Chase 1976, 1980; Chase et al 1981). We suggest that during active sleep, tonic somatomotor inhibition is mediated either directly or indirectly by the medullary reticular formation which has been selectively activated by pontomesencephalic neurons (e.g. the nucleus pontis oralis) during this state. An as yet unidentified gating mechanism, or perhaps reciprocal feedback circuitry, operating selectively during AS, would then be responsible for the establishment of a link from the rostral reticular site to the caudal reticular site. During wakefulness and quiet sleep the link is not expected to be functional; the pontomesencephalic reticular formation would then be able to exert its well-documented motor facilitatory effects [reviewed by Chase (1980)].

A number of other hypotheses have been advanced regarding the pontomedullary control of somatomotor inhibition during active sleep. The concepts of Sakai et al (1981) are as follows:

> Evidence is presented for the existence of two supraspinal centers responsible for atonia during PS: the peri-locus coeruleus (LCα) and medial part of the LCα in the pons, and the n. reticularis magnocellularis (Mc) in the medulla oblongata. It is concluded that during PS, the peri-LCα and LCα cells exert an excitatory influence on the Mc neurons, which in turn exert a generalized inhibition on spinal motoneurons.

The peri-LCα (peri-locus coeruleus alpha) is coextensive with or immediately adjacent to the nucleus pontis oralis, depending on the stereotaxic
atlas employed and the nomenclature chosen. The nucleus reticularis mag-
nocellularis is different from the nucleus reticularis gigantocellularis, but they
are adjacent nuclei whose boundaries are indistinct and whose neuronal
populations overlap. Thus, we conclude that the hypothesis of Sakai, in its
essential characteristics, is similar to that proposed by Chase and coworkers.

Mori and coworkers have published numerous studies dealing with
motoneuron inhibition during active sleep, although their principal interests
lie in postural control mechanisms. In a recent review Mori et al (1986)
summarized their motor control hypothesis as follows:

> [A]ctivation of neural pathways originating from the cells in the nucleus PoO [nucleus
> pontis oralis] to the spinal cord by way of the cells in the nucleus Gc [reticularis
> gigantocellularis] result in the suppression of postural tonus in the reflex standing, de-
> cerebrate cat, and possibly also in a freely moving, awake cat.

They extend this concept to account for the suppression of motor activity
during active sleep in the intact cat. This hypothesis is remarkably similar to
those presented by Chase and Sakai. Recently, Siegel explored the pons and
medulla and hypothesized that "the pontine triggering of atonia is mediated by
medullary mechanisms consisting of glutamate- and ACh-sensitive neurons
localized in NMC [nucleus magnocellularis] and NPM [nucleus para-
medianus], respectively" (Lai & Siegel 1988).

As noted previously, the sites of lesions that eliminate the motor atonia
during active sleep are roughly equivalent to those that (a) promote atonia
following carbachol administration and (b) promote inhibition during active
sleep by electrical stimulation (reticular response-reversal). Morrison (1988),
in describing REM sleep without atonia, has hypothesized that lesions block
an inhibitory influence normally acting on a brainstem locomotor system that
provides a tonic drive to a spinal locomotor generator and an excitatory effect
on the medullary area that inhibits spinal motor neurons. Although the pontine
and medullary sites are unspecified, an analysis of the data reveals that the
lesions are in, or in the vicinity of, the nucleus reticularis pontis oralis and
nucleus reticularis gigantocellularis, respectively.

Thus, the model of motor inhibitory control during active sleep that we put
forth in 1976 (Chase 1976) remains strong. However, it must be emphasized
that it is still a model, and that its circuitry and mechanisms must be validated
by direct means, and validation must be replicated. Even though we and
others have worked on the problem of motor control during active sleep for
many years and have accumulated solid data regarding the inhibition and
excitation of motoneurons during this state, the controlling neuronal processes
remain terra incognita.

Summary

Postsynaptic inhibition is a principal process responsible not only for the atonia of the somatic musculature during active sleep but also for the phasic episodes of decreased motoneuron excitability that accompany bursts of REMs during this state. These postsynaptic processes are dependent upon the presence of active sleep-specific IPSPs, which are apparently mediated by glycine. The phasic excitation of motoneurons during REM periods is due to excitatory postsynaptic potentials that, when present, encounter a motoneuron already subjected to enhanced postsynaptic inhibition. These EPSPs are mediated by a non-NMDA neurotransmitter.

Thus, from the perspective of motoneurons, active sleep can be characterized as a state abundant in the availability of strikingly potent patterns of postsynaptic inhibition and, during REM periods, not only by enhanced postsynaptic excitation, but also by enhanced postsynaptic inhibition. The site of origin of these inhibitory and excitatory drives is, at present, less clearly defined. There is a consensus that the structure(s) from which the inhibitory drives emanate are located in the lower brainstem, with a cholinoceptive trigger zone situated in the dorsolateral pontine tegmentum in or in the vicinity of the nucleus pontis oralis. We have suggested that from this cholinoceptive trigger zone there emanates an excitatory drive that directly, or through interneurons, excites a medullary area in or in the vicinity of the nucleus reticularis gigantocellularis. Thus, a cascade of cholinoceptively activated excitatory activity proceeds to eventually activate inhibitory interneurons whose activation results in motoneuron inhibition and muscle atonia during active sleep. Resolution of the precise location and mechanisms of interaction of the supraspinal inhibitory and excitatory motoneuron control mechanism constitutes a major goal of future experiments and the next major challenge for researchers in this field.

Literature Cited

Baghdoyan, H. A., Rodrigo-Angulo, M. L., McCarley, R. W., Hobson, J. A. 1984. Site-specific enhancement and suppression of desynchronized sleep signs following cholinergic stimulation of three brainstem regions. *Brain Res.* 306:39–52

Baghdoyan, H. A., Rodrigo-Angulo, M. L., McCarley, R. W., Hobson, J. A. 1987. A neuroanatomical gradient in the pontine tegmentum for the cholinoceptive induction of desynchronized sleep signs. *Brain Res.* 414:245–61

Baldissera, F., Rodrigo-Angulo, H., Illert, M. 1981. Integration in spinal neuronal systems. In *Handbook of Physiology*, Vol. 2, *The Nervous System, Part 1, Motor Control*, pp. 509–96. Bethesda, MD: Am. Physiol. Assoc.

Baust, W., Berlucchi, G., Moruzzi, G. 1964. *Arch. Ital. Biol.* 102:657–74

Baxter, B. L. 1969. Induction of both emotional behavior and a novel form of REM sleep by chemical stimulation applied to cat mesencephalon. *Exp. Neurol.* 23:220–29

Brock, L. G., Coombs, J. S., Eccles, J. C. 1953. Intracellular recording from antidromically activated motoneurons. *J. Physiol.* 122:429–61

Burke, R. E. 1967. Composite nature of the monosynaptic excitatory potential. *J. Neurophysiol.* 30:1114–36

Burke, R. E., Rudomín, P. 1977. Spinal neurons and synapses. In *Handbook of Physiology, The Nervous System,* pp. 877–944. Bethesda, MD: Am. Physiol. Soc.

Carlen, P. L., Durand, D. 1981. Modelling the postsynaptic location and magnitude of tonic conductance changes resulting from neurotransmitters or drugs. *Neuroscience* 6:839–46

Carlen, P. L., Werman, R., Yaari, Y. 1980. Postsynaptic conductance increase associated with presynaptic inhibition in cat lumbar motoneurones. *J. Physiol.* 298:539–56

Chandler, S. H., Nakamura, Y., Chase, M. H. 1980. Intracellular analysis of synaptic potentials induced in trigeminal jaw-closer motoneurons by pontomesencephalic reticular stimulation during sleep and wakefulness. *J. Neurophysiol.* 44:372–82

Chase, M. H. 1976. A model of central neural processes controlling motor behavior during active sleep and wakefulness. In *Mechanisms in Transmission for Signals for Conscious Behavior,* ed. T. Desiraju, pp. 99–121. Amsterdam: Elsevier

Chase, M. H. 1980. The motor functions of the reticular formation are multifaceted and state-determined. In *Reticular Formation Revisited,* ed. J. M. Hobson, M. A. B. Brazier, pp. 449–72. New York: Raven Press

Chase, M. H. 1983. Synaptic mechanisms and circuitry involved in motoneuron control during sleep. *Int. Rev. Neurobiol.* 24:213–58

Chase, M. H., Chandler, S. H., Nakamura, Y. 1980. Intracellular determination of the membrane potential of trigeminal motoneurons during sleep and wakefulness. *J. Neurophysiol.* 44:349–58

Chase, M. H., Enomoto, S., Murakami, T. 1981. Intracellular potential of medullary reticular neurons during sleep and wakefulness. *Exp. Neurol.* 71:226–33

Chase, M. H., Morales, F. R. 1982. Phasic changes in motoneuron membrane potential during REM periods of active sleep. *Neurosci. Lett.* 34:177–82

Chase, M. H., Morales, F. R. 1983. Subthreshold excitatory activity and motoneuron discharge during REM periods of active sleep. *Science* 221:1195–98

Chase, M. H., Morales, F. R. 1989. The control of motoneurons during sleep. In *Principles and Practice of Sleep Medicine,* ed. M. H. Kryger, T. Roth, W. C. Dement, pp. 75–85. Philadelphia: Saunders

Coombs, J. S., Eccles, J. C., Fatt, P. 1955. The specific ionic conductance and the ionic movement across the motoneuronal membrane that produce the inhibitory synaptic potential. *J. Physiol.* 130:326–73

Cullheim, S., Kellerth, J. O. 1981. Two kinds of recurrent inhibition of cat spinal alphamotoneurones as differentiated pharmacologically. *J. Physiol.* 312:209–24

Curtis, D. R. 1962. The depression of spinal inhibition by electrophoretically administered strychnine. *Int. J. Neuropharmacol.* 1:239–50

Curtis, D. R. 1969. The pharmacology of spinal postsynaptic inhibition. *Prog. Brain Res.* 31:171–89

Curtis, D. R., Johnston, G. A. R. 1974. Amino acid transmitters in the mammalian central nervous system. *Ergeb. Physiol.* 69:97–188

Curtis, D. R., Game, C. J. A., Lodge, D., McCullough, R. M. 1976. A pharmacological study of Renshaw cell inhibition. *J. Physiol.* 258:227–42

Curtis, D. R., Hosli, L., Johnston, G. A. R., Johnston, I. H. 1968. The hyperpolarization of spinal motoneurones by glycine and related amino acids. *Exp. Brain Res.* 5:235–58

Davidoff, R. A., Hackman, J. C. 1983. Spinal inhibition. In *Handbook of the Spinal Cord, Vols. 2, 3: Anatomy and Physiology,* ed. R. A. Davidoff. New York: Dekker

Davidoff, R. A., Hackman, J. C. 1985. GABA: presynaptic actions. In *Neurotransmitter Actions in the Vertebrate Nervous System,* ed. M. A. Rogawski, L. L. Barker, pp. 3–32. New York: Plenum

Engelhardt, J. K., Morales, F. R., Soja, P. J., Chase, M. H. 1985. Location on alpha motoneurons of synapses responsible for spontaneous IPSPs occurring during active sleep or carbachol-induced atonia. *Biophys. J.* 47:51a (Abstr.)

Evarts, E. V. 1964. Temporal patterns of discharge of pyramidal tract neurons during sleep and waking in the monkey. *J. Neurophysiol.* 27:152–71

George, R., Haslett, W. L., Jenden, D. J. 1964. A cholinergic mechanism in the brainstem reticular formation: induction of paradoxical sleep. *Int. J. Neuropharmacol.* 3:541–52

Glenn, L. L., Dement, W. C. 1981. Membrane potential, synaptic activity, and excitability of hindlimb motoneurons during wakefulness and sleep. *J. Neurophysiol.* 46:839–54

Granit, R. 1955. *Receptors and Sensory Perception.* New Haven, CT: Yale Univ. Press

Henley, K., Morrison, A. R. 1974. A reevaluation of the effects of lesions of the positive tegmentum and locus coeruleus on phenomena of paradoxical sleep in the cat. *Acta Neurobiol. Exp.* 34:215–32

Hongo, T., Jankowska, E., Ohno, T., Sasaki, S., Yamashita, M., Yoshida, K. 1983. The same interneurones mediate inhibition of dorsal spinocerebellar tract cells and lumbar motoneurones in cat. *J. Physiol.* 342:161–80

Ito, K., McCarley, R. W. 1984. Alterations in membrane potential and excitability of cat medial pontine reticular formation neurons during changes in naturally occuring sleep-wake states. *Brain Res.* 292:16–75

Jankowska, E., Lund, S., Lundberg, A., Pompeiano, O. 1968. Inhibitory effects evoked through ventral reticulospinal pathways. *Arch. Ital. Biol.* 106:124–40

Jouvet, M., Delorme, F. 1965. Locus coeruleus et sommeil paradoxal. *C. R. Soc. Biol.* 159:895–99

Jouvet, M., Michel, F., Courjon, J. 1959. Sur en stade d'activité éléctric cerébrale rapid ou cours du sommeil physiologique. *C. R. Soc. Biol.* 153:1024–28

Katayama, Y., DeWitt, D. S., Becker, D. P., Hayes, R. L. 1984. Behavioral evidence for cholinoceptive pontine inhibitory area: descending control of spinal motor output and sensory input. *Brain Res.* 296:241–62

Kawai, I., Sasaki, L. 1964. Effects of strychnine upon supraspinal inhibition. *Jpn. J. Physiol.* 14:309–17

Kleitman, N. 1963. *Sleep and Wakefulness.* Chicago: Univ. Chicago Press. 552 pp.

Krnjevic, K., Puil, E., Werman, R. 1976. GABA and glycine actions in spinal motoneurons. *Can. J. Physiol. Pharmacol.* 55:658–69

Lai, Y. Y., Siegel, J. M. 1988. Medullary regions mediating atonia. *J. Neurosci.* 8(12):4790–96

Larson, M. D. 1969. An analysis of the action of strychnine on the recurrent IPSP and amino acid induced inhibition in the cat spinal cord. *Brain Res.* 15;185–200

Lisi, L. de. 1932. Su di un fenomeno motorio constante del sonno normale: le mioclonie ipniche fisiologiche. I. Descrizione. *Riv. Patol. Nerv. Ment.* 39:481–96

Llinás, R. 1964. Mechanisms of supraspinal actions upon spinal cord activities. Pharmacological studies on reticular inhibition of alpha extensor motoneurons. *J. Neurophysiol.* 27:1127–37

Llinás, R., Terzuolo, C. A. 1964. Mechanisms of supraspinal actions upon spinal cord activities. Reticular inhibitory mechanisms on alpha-extensor motoneurons. *J. Neurophysiol.* 27:579–91

Mahowald, M. W., Schenck, C. H. 1989. REM sleep behavior disorder. In *Principles and Practice of Sleep Medicine*, ed. M. H. Kryger, T. Roth, W. C. Dement, pp. 389–401. Philadelphia: Saunders

Marchiafava, P. L., Pompeiano, O. 1964. Pyramidal influences on spinal cord during desynchronized sleep. *Arch. Ital. Biol.* 102:500–29

Matthews, P. B. C. 1972. *Mammalian Muscle Receptors and Their Central Actions.* London: Arnold

Mitler, M. M., Dement, W. C. 1974. Cataleptic-like behavior in cats after microinjection of carbachol in the pontine reticular formation. *Brain Res.* 68:335–43

Morales, F., Chase, M. H. 1981. Postsynaptic control of lumbar motoneuron excitability during active sleep in the chronic cat. *Brain Res.* 225:279–95

Morales, F. R., Chase, M. H. 1982. Repetitive synaptic potentials responsible for inhibition of spinal cord motoneurons during active sleep. *Exp. Neurol.* 78:471–76

Morales, F. R., Schadt, J., Chase, M. H. 1981. Intracellular recording from spinal cord motoneurons in the chronic cat. *Physiol. Behav.* 27:355–62

Morales, F. R., Fung, S. J., Boxer, P. A., Chase, M. H. 1982. Interneuron activity in the lumbar spinal cord during active sleep. *Sleep Res.* 11:26 (Abstr.)

Morales, F. R., Englehardt, J. K., Soja, P. J., Pereda, A. E., Chase, M. H. 1987a. Motoneuron properties during motor inhibition produced by microinjection of carbachol into the pontine reticular formation of the decerebrate cat. *J. Neurophysiol.* 57(4):1118–29

Morales, F. R., Boxer, P., Chase, M. H. 1987b. Behavioral state-specific inhibitory postsynaptic potentials impinge on cat lumbar motoneurons during active sleep. *Exp. Neurol.* 98:418–35

Morales, F. R., Engelhardt, J. K., Pereda, A. E., Yamuy, J., Chase, M. H. 1988. Renshaw cells are inactive during motor inhibition elicited by the pontine microinjection of carbachol. *Neurosci. Lett.* 86:289–95

Mori, S., Ohta, Y., Takakusaki, K., Matsuyama, K., Sugaya, K. 1986. Pontomedullary and spinal mechanisms of postural suppression in a decerebrate, reflex standing cat. *Satellite Symp. 30th Int. Congr. Physiol. Sci., Novel Approaches to the Study of Motor Systems*, Banff, Alberta, Canada, 10–13 July

Morrison, A. R. 1988. Paradoxical sleep with atonia. *Arch. Ital. Biol.* 126:275–89

Nistri, A. 1983. Spinal cord pharmacology of GABA and chemically related amino acids. In *Handbook of the Spinal Cord*, Vol. 1: *Pharmacology*, ed. R. A. Davidoff, pp. 45–104. New York: Marcel Dekker

Pakhomov, A. N. 1947. A new method of measuring and recording muscle tonus, and its application to the study of the physiology of sleep in man. *Fiziol. Zh. SSSR* 33:245–54

Pompeiano, O. 1967. The neurophysiological mechanisms of the postural and motor events during desynchronized sleep. *Res. Publ. Assoc. Res. Nerv. Ment. Dis.* 45:351–423

Pompeiano, O. 1978. The generation of rhythmic discharges during bursts of REM. In *Abnormal Neuronal Discharges*, ed. N. Chalazonitis, M. Boisson. New York: Raven

Sakai, K., Sastre, J.-P., Kanamori, N., Jouvet, M. 1981. State-specific neurons in the ponto-medullary reticular formation with special reference to the postural atonia during paradoxical sleep in the cat. In *Brain Mechanisms and Perceptual Awareness*, ed. O. Pompeiano, C. Ajmone Marsan. New York: Raven

Sherrington, C. S. 1906. *The Integrative Action of the Nervous System*. New Haven, CT: Yale Univ. Press

Shiromani, P. J., Siegel, J. M., Tomaszewski, K. S., McGinty, D. J. 1986. Alterations in blood pressure and REM sleep after pontine carbachol microinfusion. *Exp. Neurol.* 91:285–92

Siegel, J. M. 1989. Brainstem mechanisms generating REM sleep. In *Principles and Practice of Sleep Medicine*, ed. M. H. Kryger, T. Roth, W. C. Dement, pp. 104–20. Philadelphia: Saunders

Smith, T. G., Wuerker, R. B., Frank, K. 1967. Membrane impedance changes during synaptic transmission in cat spinal motoneurons. *J. Neurophysiol.* 30:1072–96

Soja, P. J., López, F., Morales, F. R., Chase, M. H. 1988. Depolarizing synaptic events influencing cat lumbar motoneurons during rapid eye movement episodes of active sleep are blocked by kynurenic acid. *Soc. Neurosci.* 14(2):941

Soja, P. J., Morales, F. R., Baranyi, A., Chase, M. H. 1987. Effect of inhibitory amino acid antagonists on IPSPs induced in lumbar motoneurons upon stimulation of the nucleus reticularis gigantocellularis during active sleep. *Brain Res.* 423:353–58

Steriade, M., Hobson, J. A. 1976. Neuronal activity during the sleep-waking cycle. *Prog. Neurobiol.* 6:155–376

Stone, T. W. 1985. *Microiontophoresis and Pressure Ejection*. Chichester, NY: Wiley

Takakusaki, K., Ohta, Y., Mori, S. 1989. Single medullary reticulospinal neurons exert postsynaptic inhibitory effects via inhibitory interneurons upon alpha-motoneurons innervating cat hindlimb muscles. *Exp. Brain Res.* 74:11–23

Werman, R., Davidoff, R. A., Aprison, M. H. 1968. Inhibitory action of glycine on spinal neurons in the cat. *J. Neurophysiol.* 31:81–95

Young, A. B., MacDonald, R. L. 1983. Glycine as a spinal cord neurotransmitter. In *Handbook of the Spinal Cord*, Vol. 1: *Pharmacology*, ed. R. A. Davidoff, pp. 1–44. New York: Dekker

Annu. Rev. Psychol. 1990. 41:585–634

PROGRESS IN SMALL GROUP RESEARCH

John M. Levine and Richard L. Moreland

Department of Psychology, University of Pittsburgh, Pittsburgh, Pennsylvania 15260

CONTENTS

INTRODUCTION

Research on small groups (1977–1980) was reviewed for this series by McGrath & Kravitz (1982). Here, we review work done since then. Rather than selecting a limited set of issues for detailed analysis, we decided to write a more general overview. This decision reflected our view that the field, though quite vigorous, is badly fragmented, as evidenced by the failure of researchers working on related problems to acknowledge one another's work. Ironically, this unfortunate situation is due to one of the strengths of the field, namely its multidisciplinary nature. People who study small groups tend to publish in (and read) different journals, depending on their disciplines. Much of the vitality of the field is thus invisible to those within it, not to mention those outside it.

Because research on intergroup relations has recently been reviewed (Messick & Mackie 1989), we focus on processes that occur within groups. We also exclude such large-group phenomena as organizational behavior, social movements, school desegregation, mob behavior, and community social change. Work on special kinds of small groups (e.g. therapy groups, families, children's groups) is typically excluded because of its limited generalizability. Finally, we do not cover dyadic relationships. Research on such relationships has been reviewed recently by Clark & Reis (1988), and we believe that dyads are very different from larger groups.

We organized relevant work published between 1980 and early 1989 in terms of five basic aspects of small groups–their ecology, composition, structure, internal conflicts, and performance. In the following sections, we review and evaluate this work and offer suggestions for future research. Because of space limits, our citations are representative rather than exhaustive; many relevant studies could not be included.[1]

THE ECOLOGY OF SMALL GROUPS

Every group occupies some setting, and every setting affects its occupants in some way. As a result, no group can be fully understood unless its setting is analyzed. Analyses of settings reveal a variety of environmental factors, ranging from the physical to the social to the temporal. Most researchers study the physical environments of groups, but some research on their social and temporal environments can also be found. And though most researchers study the effects of environmental factors on groups, attempts by groups to control those factors are sometimes studied as well.

Physical Environments

The physical environments of small groups evoke a great deal of research interest. One popular research area is crowding (see reviews by Baum & Paulus 1987; Paulus & Nagar 1989). The effects of crowding are studied in residential areas, college dormitories, and prisons, as well as laboratory

---

[1]A longer version of this chapter is available from the authors.

settings. As people feel more crowded, they exhibit greater stress, worse performance (especially on complex tasks), and more negative social relations. These effects are thought to be mediated by several factors, including loss of control, cognitive overload, and behavioral constraints. Research on crowding always involves groups of subjects, yet the effects of crowding are usually measured at the individual level. Some exceptions to this trend can be found in studies of groups that form as an adaptive response to crowding (e.g. Gormley & Aiello 1982; Webb et al 1986). Apparently some groups can protect their members from the effects of crowding by minimizing any loss of control, cognitive overload, or behavioral constraints.

A related area of research involves small groups that work in such "exotic" environments as outer space, underground or underwater, and combat (see Harrison & Connors 1984 for a review). These environments are generally dangerous, impoverished, and confining. Most researchers study how individuals respond to such environments, but some studies of group responses are done as well. These studies show that stronger leadership, increased cohesiveness, and greater conformity pressures are all common among these groups. Groups that work in such environments apparently try to eliminate or control any internal problems so that their external problems can be dealt with more effectively.

Research on exotic environments is often atheoretical, but an influential paper by Staw et al (1981) may help to guide future studies. Staw and his colleagues argue that individuals, groups, and organizations all respond to threat by becoming more "rigid." This rigidity involves a restriction in information processing (e.g. narrower attention, reduced communication), as well as a constriction in control (e.g. reliance on tradition, centralized power). Only a few researchers (e.g. Argote et al 1988; Gladstein & Reilly 1985) have tested these ideas, but their results are promising.

Another area of research on physical environments involves small groups that work in factories or offices (see Sundstrom 1986 for a review). Researchers who study these groups assume that working conditions affect job satisfaction, which in turn affects worker productivity. Such aspects of factories and offices as temperature, lighting, floor space, and noise indeed seem to affect workers (e.g. Oldham & Rotchford 1983). Most researchers focus on individual rather than group reactions to working conditions, despite the fact that work is often performed in small groups. Perhaps judgments about working conditions are made collectively rather than individually. Several theorists (e.g. Salancik & Pfeffer 1978) have argued that social comparison processes influence workers' opinions about whether their jobs are interesting, their salaries are adequate, and so on. It would not be surprising if judgments about the work environment were affected by social comparison processes as well.

The computerization of offices is leading researchers to study the impact of technology on work groups (see reviews by DeSanctis & Gallupe 1987; Kiesler et al 1984). A variety of computer systems are studied, including (a) simple word-processing or accounting programs, (b) complex collaborative writing/editing programs, (c) electronic mail, bulletin boards, or meeting rooms, and (d) group decision support systems. The clearest evidence involves electronic communication, which seems to affect work groups by reducing overall communication, equalizing participation levels, weakening status systems, emphasizing informational rather than normative influence, and encouraging certain forms of deviance (Hiltz et al 1986; McGuire et al 1987; Siegel et al 1986). There is little evidence that electronic communication improves group productivity.

The research discussed thus far focuses on how the physical environment affects small groups. There are also several ways in which a group might control its environment. Many groups, for example, are mobile enough to seek out pleasant environments and avoid unpleasant ones. Some groups can alter their environments to make them more pleasant. Finally, all groups can interpret their environments in ways that make them seem more or less pleasant.

Few researchers study how small groups move into and out of environments, though several observers (e.g. Paulus & Nagar 1989) acknowledge the importance of such behavior. A more popular research area is how small groups try to change their environments. Most of this research involves territoriality (see Taylor 1988 for a review). Research on group territories can be divided into two general categories. Many groups, such as neighborhood groups (Greenbaum & Greenbaum 1981), youth gangs, recreational groups (Smith 1981), and sports teams (Varca 1980), establish territories and then defend them against outsiders. Groups that are more homogeneous, stable, and cohesive, and whose sense of social identity is stronger, are more likely to be territorial. Some groups also apportion their territory among members, usually on the basis of status. Territoriality of this sort can be observed within families (Sebba & Churchman 1983), work groups (Konar et al 1982), and even college classes (Haber 1982).

Territoriality is alleged to serve many purposes for small groups. When a group establishes a territory and then defends it against outsiders, the group can (a) protect valuable resources, (b) improve living/working conditions, (c) gain a sense of privacy, (d) control social interactions, (e) become more cohesive, and (f) express its social identity. When certain members take or are given special areas of a group's territory for their own, they can enjoy some of these same benefits at a more personal level. However, there is no clear evidence that territoriality actually produces any of these benefits for either groups or their members.

Several theorists (e.g. Stokols 1981; Stokols & Shumaker 1981) are beginning to analyze how small groups interpret various aspects of their physical environments. Stokols argues that when a group occupies a place for a long time and conducts many activities there, that place acquires special meanings that are shared among group members. These meanings may be functional, motivational, or evaluative in nature, and can produce "place dependence" and other important consequences. These ideas are intriguing, but largely untested as yet.

Social Environments

Fewer researchers study the social environments of small groups. The most popular research area is clearly intergroup relations. We do not discuss this area in detail, but it is worth noting that research on intergroup relations often reflects two simplistic assumptions. First, many researchers seem to assume that groups relate to one another in a social vacuum. Most studies focus on just two groups, each completely separate from the other. Yet nearly all groups are bound together in some way, because they share members, have developed "weak ties" (cf Granovetter 1973), or are embedded within the same social network. Also, other groups or individuals often intervene in intergroup relations when they believe that their own outcomes can be affected. As a result, intergroup relations are complex, involving many actors related to one another in a variety of ways.

Many researchers also seem to assume that intergroup relations are always competitive, yet there is considerable evidence of cooperation among small groups. Sometimes this cooperation is indirect, as when one group imitates others by importing their procedures (cf Feldman 1984), or uses other groups for the purpose of social comparison (e.g. Levine & Moreland 1987). More direct forms of cooperation are also possible, as when groups exchange valuable resources, form alliances to attain common goals, or merge to form new groups. These and other noncompetitive relations among small groups deserve more research attention.

Another area of research on social environments involves small groups embedded within large organizations. Most of this research focuses on work groups in business corporations (e.g. Alderfer & Smith 1982; Ancona 1987), but some studies on local chapters of social movements can also be found (e.g. Fine & Stoecker 1985; Lofland & Jamison 1984). Organizations provide a setting within which informal groups can grow (e.g. Fontana 1985; Tichy 1981), and the health of a small group often depends on the success of the organization in which it is embedded (Greenhalgh 1983; Krantz 1985); but even a small group embedded within a large organization can try to control its environment. Ancona argues that work groups adapt to corporate settings through such activities as negotiation (bargaining for resources), scanning (acquiring information), profile management (impressing others), and buffering (defense). She finds that special roles (e.g. ambassador, scout, guard) associated with these activities develop within work groups and that groups performing these activities more effectively are more successful (Ancona & Caldwell 1988).

All groups are embedded within a culture. Some of the variability among groups may thus reflect cultural differences, and some of the changes that groups undergo may reflect cultural trends. Evidence regarding these matters is available (e.g. Mann 1980; Nagao & Davis 1980), but too little is yet known to reach any firm conclusions. Cultural influences on small groups clearly deserve more research attention.

A third area of research on social environments involves small groups that share one or more members. A single person can belong to many different groups. This produces interdependence among those groups, because experiences in one group can affect that person's behavior in all the others. Many examples of this phenomenon can be found in families. Bronfenbrenner (1986) notes that child development, which seems to occur primarily within the family, can also be affected by other groups to which children and their parents belong. Sometimes two groups overlap so much that they are almost inseparable. Family businesses, for example, are both strengthened and weakened by the merging of family and business affairs. As a result, they must evolve special procedures for regulating the boundary between those two worlds (Davis & Stern 1980).

Finally, small groups are often influenced by people who are not actually group members, such as prospective and ex-members (Levine & Moreland 1985), friends and relatives (Stark & Bainbridge 1980), customers or clients (Greer 1983; Jorgensen & Jorgensen 1982), and enemies (Erickson 1981; Reitzes & Diver 1982). The mere presence of such persons can influence a group, as when group members close ranks to confront an enemy. More direct forms of influence are also possible, as when people are recruited into groups by their friends.

Temporal Environments

Research on the temporal environments of small groups is more common, though by no means abundant. The most popular research area is group development. Because most relevant studies focus on therapy, training, or self-analytic groups, we will not discuss them here (for reviews see Lacoursiere 1980 or Moreland & Levine 1988). We believe, however, that several points regarding such research are worth making. First, many studies are difficult to evaluate because they involve qualitative analyses of a few groups (often only one) in which the researcher was an active participant. As a result, their internal validity can be questioned. Second, the theories that these studies test are not always clear about such issues as the number of stages through which groups develop, the behaviors exhibited by group members during those stages, the rate at which group development occurs, and so on. Even when quantitative data are collected, such theories may be difficult to confirm or disconfirm (cf Cissna 1984), because they can account for almost any pattern of results. Finally, most theorists argue that group development is a recapitulation of the childhood experiences of individual group members. Other factors that might affect group development, such as (a) the beliefs and expectations that current members share about their group (Long 1984), (b) the arrival of new group members or the departure of old ones (Moreland & Levine 1988), and (c) changes in the group's physical or social environment (Gersick 1988), are rarely acknowledged.

One promising trend in research on group development is a recent focus on task-oriented groups (e.g. Gersick 1988; Insko et al 1980, 1982, 1983; Katz 1982). Insko and his colleagues, for example, created small work groups and then changed their composition by periodically replacing "oldtimers" with "newcomers." The groups exhibited marked increases in productivity over time, reflecting the acquisition and transmission by group members of knowledge about the task (cf Argote et al 1990). As time passed, leaders were more likely to emerge in the groups as well, usually because of seniority. Gersick observed a peculiar pattern of development in natural work groups. When given a job to do within specified time limits, group members started to work immediately, without much strategic analysis. But after about half of their allotted time was gone, they paused to make strategic changes and then worked hard to finish the job on time. Finally, Katz found that as work groups grew "older," they often refused or neglected to consult key information sources both inside and outside their organizations. This insularity limited their performance, especially on more complex tasks.

The goal of most research on group development is to learn why and how small groups change over time. It is important to remember, however, that every group operates at some developmental level and that its level of development can affect many other aspects of the group. Moreland & Levine (1988), for example, describe several ways in which the socialization of new members and the resocialization of marginal members might vary among groups at different developmental levels. And several studies (e.g. Greene & Schriesheim 1980) show that the effectiveness of a leader's style depends on a group's developmental level. All of this suggests that researchers should be cautious about interpreting their findings without considering the developmental levels of the groups they are studying.

Another area of research on temporal environments involves group formation and termination. Several studies of group formation can be found (cf Farrell 1982; Hogg 1987; Wicker & King 1988). In a review and analysis of this area, Moreland (1987) argues that group formation should be viewed as a process of social integration. Several forms of social integration (environmental, behavioral, affective, cognitive) seem to produce small groups; the challenge is to discover how these processes work together to create a particular group. Research on group termination is less common, though several studies can be found (e.g. Greenhalgh 1983; Krantz 1985; Wicker & King 1988). Many of these focus on the emotional consequences of group termination. Sutton & Zald (1985), however, take a somewhat broader approach, arguing that the demise of social systems (e.g. couples, organizations, communities) involves (a) attributional negotiations regarding who is to blame, (b) "disbanding" activities aimed at ending old relationships with fellow group members, and (c) "reconnecting" activities aimed at beginning new relationships with members of the group and/or outsiders. Insofar as these activities proceed smoothly, distress over the termination of a group can be minimized.

A rather new area of research on temporal environments involves the effects of time limits or deadlines on work groups (e.g. Isenberg 1981; Kelly & McGrath 1985; McGrath et al 1984). One particularly interesting phenomenon, discovered by McGrath and his colleagues, is "behavioral entrainment." When a work group is given a specific amount of time to do a job, its members initially adjust their behavior to "fit" whatever time is available to them. If time is scarce, for example, then group members work harder, worry less about the quality of their output (on maximizing tasks), and focus on task rather than social or emotional issues. If more time becomes available, then those workers ought to relax, but in fact they continue to work as though time were still scarce. The practial implications of this phenomenon are considerable and worthy of further investigation.

Although the passage of time affects small groups in many ways, groups are not helpless time travelers. There is some evidence that they try instead to control the passage of time. For example, McGrath & Rotchford (1983) argue that organizations (and presumably the work groups embedded within them) face three general temporal problems: uncertainty, conflicts of interest, and scarcity. They solve these problems through scheduling, synchronization, and allocation (respectively). Subtler approaches to temporal issues can be found in other kinds of groups. Stokols & Jacobi (1984), for example, believe that social groups vary in their "temporal orientations" (traditional, present-focused, futuristic, coordinated) and that the behavior of group members often depends on these orientations. Several researchers (e.g. Jacobi & Stokols 1983) are studying the role that traditions and periodic rituals can play in strengthening small groups.

THE COMPOSITION OF SMALL GROUPS

Because the members of a small group are its most important resource and events within a group often reflect the people who belong to it, many researchers study the composition of small groups. Some researchers regard group composition as a causal factor, whereas others regard it as a contextual factor or as a consequence. Some researchers focus on the size of a group, whereas others focus on the demographic characteristics, abilities, opinions, or personalities of its members. Finally, researchers measure group composition in several ways. Some prefer measures of central tendency, whereas others prefer measures of variability or study special configurations of group members.

Composition as a Cause

Most researchers regard group composition as a causal factor that can affect many other aspects of group life. One area of relevant research involves the effects of group size. As a group grows larger, it also changes in other ways, generally for the worse. People who belong to larger groups are less satisfied with group membership, participate less often in group activities, and are less likely to cooperate with one another (e.g. Kerr 1989a; Markham et al 1982; Pinto & Crow 1982). There is also more misbehavior in larger groups, perhaps because group members feel more anonymous or are less self-aware (e.g. Latane 1981; Prentice-Dunn & Rogers 1989). Finally, although larger groups are potentially more productive, coordination problems and motivation losses often prevent them from achieving that potential (e.g. Albanese & Van Fleet 1985; Gooding & Wagner 1985; Harkins & Szymanski 1987).

Another area of research involves the demographic characteristics of group members, such as age and sex. Pfeffer (1983), for example, argues that variability in age can create conflict within work groups, because differences in training and experience lead workers of different ages to disagree with one another about their jobs. Turnover is indeed greater in work groups whose members vary more widely in age (e.g. Wagner et al 1984). Reviewing the results of many studies comparing the performance of male and female groups, Wood (1985) found that male groups generally perform better than female groups. She claimed, however, that a group's success really depends on how well the interaction style of its members fits the requirements of their task. Male groups should thus do better when agentic activities (e.g. giving opinions and suggestions) are required, whereas female groups should do better when communal activities (e.g. being friendly and agreeing with others) are required (cf Wood et al 1985).

The abilities of group members are the focus of many studies on the effects of group composition (e.g. Bantel & Jackson 1989; Tziner & Eden 1985).

Most of these studies reflect a pragmatic desire to create successful groups by selecting people who can work together productively (cf Foushee 1984; Harrison & Connors 1984). Tziner & Eden, for example, studied the effects of soldiers' ability levels on their performance in tank crews. Every crew contained three soldiers, who were either high or low in general ability. The results revealed that the more high-ability soldiers a crew contained, the better it performed. There were some interesting interactive effects of ability on performance as well. For example, crews whose members were all high in ability performed better than expected, whereas crews whose members were all low in ability performed worse than expected.

Research on the effects of group composition also focuses on the opinions of group members. There is considerable evidence, for example, that the distribution of opinions among group members can influence their decision-making, especially when certain social decision schemes are used (see Stasser et al 1989a for a review). There is also some recent interest in "scientific jury selection," a procedure that lawyers can use to saturate juries with people who favor their positions. Although this procedure raises some controversial legal and ethical issues, only a few studies of scientific jury selection can be found (e.g. Patterson 1986), and their results suggest that its impact on jury decision-making may be weak.

Finally, some research on the effects of group composition involves the personalities of group members (e.g. DeBiasio 1986; Driskell et al 1987). Research of this sort is especially popular among clinical psychologists, who want to create more effective therapy groups by selecting clients with particular disorders (cf Erickson, 1986). Some therapists favor homogeneous therapy groups, which engender feelings of warmth and acceptance that many clients need. Other therapists favor heterogeneous groups, which engender conflicts that (though painful) often produce personal growth in clients. Unfortunately, the available research evidence does not reveal which kinds of therapy groups are best.

Research on the effects of group composition is often atheoretical, but some theoretical development is under way. Mullen (1983, 1987), for example, argues that the proportion of group members who possess a particular characteristic (of any sort) is a key factor in producing many compositional effects. As that proportion grows smaller, each person who possesses the characteristic becomes increasingly self-aware. That awareness leads the person to compare his or her current behavior with salient behavioral standards. If the results of those comparisons are negative (as they often are), then the prospects for significant self-improvement are assessed. When those prospects seem good, the person tries harder to match the behavioral standards, but when those prospects seem poor, the person withdraws from the situation. Mullen and his colleagues use this theory to reanalyze the results of previous research on many topics, such as productivity in work groups (Mullen & Baumeister 1987).

Composition as a Context

Some researchers regard the composition of a small group as a social context within which other psychological phenomena unfold. Group composition moderates those phenomena, rather than causing them directly. Schrager (1986) studied the effects of academic ability on the college grades of freshmen living in various group settings (e.g. fraternity houses, residence halls). Although these effects were generally positive, their strength varied with the social climates of the groups. The more emphasis a group placed on traditional academic values, the more impact a student's academic ability had on his or her college grades. Wright et al (1986) studied the behavioral determinants of popularity in children's peer groups. They found that popularity often depends on the match between a child's own behavior and the behavior of his or her peers. Aggressive children, for instance, were very unpopular in groups where aggression was rare, but not in groups where aggression was common. Finally, several studies show that the effectiveness of various leadership styles depends on the characteristics of followers (e.g. Schriesheim 1980). And Simonton (1985) offers some intriguing analyses of how the relative intelligence of leaders (compared to their followers) can affect the amount and type of influence they exert.

Contextual effects may play an important role in the behavior of males and females in mixed-sex groups. Several reviews of this area are available (e.g. Anderson & Blanchard 1982; Dion 1985; Eagly 1987; Martin & Shanahan 1983). The sex differences observed in such groups are generally weak (e.g. Mabry 1985), can be eliminated or even reversed by situational factors (e.g. Wood & Karten 1986), and may have more to do with gender than with sex (e.g. Porter et al 1985). Nevertheless, the available evidence suggests that in mixed-sex groups, males are (*a*) more active and influential than females, (*b*) more likely than females to engage in agentic activities, but less likely to engage in communal activities, and (*c*) more concerned than females about resolving issues of status, power, and wealth.

It may seem odd to claim that sexual heterogeneity in small groups is a contextual rather than a causal factor in social behavior. Yet most researchers believe that membership in a mixed-sex group simply reminds people of their conventional sex roles, which in turn leads them to adopt those roles, either through personal choice or through processes of behavior confirmation. As the proportions of males and females in a group diverge, sex roles should become even more salient, thereby strengthening sex differences in social behavior (cf. Mullen 1983). Many researchers, intrigued by the work of Kanter (1977), study groups containing a single "token" member. Kanter claimed that token females experience a variety of problems in work groups, ranging from social isolation to role entrapment to powerlessness. Several studies seem to support her claims (e.g. Izraeli 1983; Lord & Saenz 1985; South et al 1982), but the level of support is sometimes weak. A few studies indicate that token males do not experience the same problems as token females (e.g. Craig & Sherif 1986; Crocker & McGraw 1984). Also, token females who have higher status in the group (e.g. Fairhurst & Snavely 1983), or who adopt certain behavioral styles toward males (e.g. Ridgeway 1982), are less likely to experience the problems that Kanter described.

For some psychologists, the contextual effects of group composition are a potentially confounding factor that must be eliminated or controlled by procedural or analytical means. These attitudes are changing, however, as papers appear describing how studies of small groups can be designed to allow contextual effects to emerge (e.g. Rousseau 1985) and how the results of those studies can be analyzed to reveal the nature and extent of those effects (e.g. Blalock 1984; Kenny 1985). As research on group composition becomes more sophisticated, contextual effects are likely to be more appreciated.

Composition as a Consequence

A few researchers regard the composition of a small group as the product of other factors. Their work focuses, of course, on natural groups, whose composition can vary more or less freely. Studies on the sizes of natural groups suggest that people strongly prefer smaller groups. Burgess (1984), for example, observed casual groups of people at shopping malls, airports, amusement parks, and so on. No groups containing more than seven persons were observed, and about 90% of the groups were either dyads or triads. McPherson (1983) surveyed people about the voluntary associations to which they belonged. Groups of this sort were much larger, some containing several hundred members, but about 70% of the groups contained fewer than ten members, and less formal groups tended to be smaller. Why people prefer smaller groups is unclear. Burgess suggests that small groups maximize the advantages of group membership for inclusive fitness, whereas McPherson suggests that competition among groups for members of different types constrains how large those groups can become. As we noted earlier, larger groups also suffer from many problems that might lead people to avoid them.

Natural groups can also vary in the characteristics of their members. Many studies show that people who belong to the same group generally resemble one another (e.g. Magaro & Ashbrook 1985; McPherson & Smith-Lovin 1986). This homogeneity, which may involve any characteristic, can be attributed in part to the process of group formation. Groups usually form among similar people (e.g. Feld 1982; Fontana 1985), but other processes can contribute to homogeneity among group members as well. These processes include the entry and subsequent socialization of new group members and the resocialization and subsequent exit of marginal group members.

Entry into most small groups depends on the motivation of the person and the group. People are often drawn to groups whose members seem similar to themselves (e.g. Royal & Golden 1981), and groups are often drawn to people who seem similar to their members. In fact, many groups recruit new members primarily through social networks of friends and relatives (e.g. Stark & Bainbridge 1980). The level of homogeneity within a group clearly increases when entry decisions (by either party) are based on interpersonal similarities. Once someone enters a group, the process of socialization begins (e.g. Cushman 1986; Vaught & Smith 1980). Attempts are made by newcomers and oldtimers to alter one another in ways that make them more compatible. Successful socialization often increases homogeneity within the group even further.

Although group members may be similar in many ways, their relationships can become strained. When conflicts arise and cannot be easily resolved, the process of resocialization begins (e.g. Levine 1989). Full and marginal members of the group attempt to alter one another in ways that will restore their compatibility. Successful resocialization helps to preserve group homogeneity, but if resocialization fails, then marginal members leave the group. Exit from most small groups depends on a person's motivation to quit the group and the group's motivation to eject him or her. People are often repelled by groups whose members seem different from themselves (e.g. Bouma 1980), and groups are often repelled by people who seem different from other members (e.g. Brinkerhoff & Burke 1980). Once again, the level of homogeneity within a group increases when exit decisions (by either party) are based on interpersonal differences.

Researchers who study such processes as entry, socialization, resocialization, and exit in small groups often work in isolation from one another. However, a general model of group socialization proposed recently by Moreland & Levine (1982, 1984, 1989) may help to integrate their work. The model explains temporal changes in individual-group relations in terms of three basic processes—evaluation, commitment, and role transition. According to the model, the group and each of its members engage in an ongoing evaluation of the rewardingness of their own and alternative relationships. On the basis of these evaluations, feelings of mutual commitment arise. These feelings change in systematic ways over time, rising or falling to previously established decision criteria. When a decision criterion is crossed, a role transition takes place, the person enters a new phase of group membership, and the relationship between the group and the person changes. Evaluation proceeds, along different dimensions, producing further changes in commitment and other role transitions. Moreland & Levine use their model to explore several aspects of small groups, including group development (Moreland & Levine 1988) and innovation (Levine & Moreland 1985). There have been few empirical tests of the model as yet, but the results so far (e.g. Moreland 1985; Pavelchak et al 1986) seem promising.

THE STRUCTURE OF SMALL GROUPS

In order to achieve their common goals, the members of a small group must establish and maintain productive interpersonal relationships. The structure of a group is the pattern of relationships that emerges among its members. Many aspects of group structure can be studied, but most researchers focus on status systems, norms, roles, or cohesion. Although researchers who study different aspects of group structure seldom collaborate, they often struggle with the same issues, such as (a) the proper conceptualization and/or measurement of group structure, (b) the psychological processes that produce group structure, and (c) the effects of structure on a group and its members.

Status Systems

Status systems reflect the general pattern of social influence among group members. Several methods for measuring status are available. Some researchers observe the nonverbal behavior of group members (e.g. Harper 1985). People with higher status are more likely than others to stand up straight, maintain eye contact, speak in a firm voice with few hesitations, and be physically intrusive. Other researchers record group members' verbal behavior (e.g. Skvoretz 1988; Weisfeld & Weisfeld 1984). People with higher status speak more often than others, are more likely to criticize, command, or interrupt others, and are spoken to more often than others. Status is sometimes measured by asking group members who is more popular, seems more capable, or has more influence on the group (e.g. Ridgeway 1981; Strodtbeck & Lipinski 1985). Finally, a few researchers assess how much influence group members actually exert on one another (e.g. Bottger 1984; Ridgeway 1987). As most of these methods suggest, status is generally treated as an individual rather than a group characteristic.

A major issue is how status systems are produced within small groups. Status was once viewed as a reward that people earned by helping a group to achieve its goals, making personal sacrifices on behalf of the group, or conforming to group norms. These behaviors are indeed important sources of status (e.g. Bottger 1984; Insko et al 1982; Weisfeld & Weisfeld 1984), but there is also some evidence that status systems develop very quickly, perhaps within minutes after most groups are formed (e.g. Barchas & Fisek 1984). It seems unlikely that people could earn status (by whatever means) in so little time, so other psychological processes must be capable of producing status systems. Apparently, these alternative processes require little or no interaction among group members.

There are two major theoretical explanations for the rapid development of status systems within small groups. The "expectation states" theorists (e.g. Berger et al 1980) argue that group members, soon after meeting one another, form expectations about each person's probable contributions to the achievement of group goals. These expectations are based on personal characteristics that people purposely reveal to one another (e.g. intelligence, training) or that are readily apparent (e.g. sex, age). Personal characteristics more relevant to the achievement of group goals have more impact on expectations, but even irrelevant ones are evaluated. People who possess more valuable characteristics evoke more positive expectations and are thus assigned higher status in the group. Initial status assignments can be modified as actual contributions to the achievement of group goals are observed and evaluated, but people whose initial status assignments are unfairly low often have trouble proving their worth to other group members later on (e.g. Ridgeway 1982).

A second explanation for the rapid development of status systems within small groups is offered by "ethological" theorists (e.g. Mazur 1985) who argue that group members, soon after meeting one another, assess the strength of each person by evaluating his or her appearance and demeanor. These evaluations are based on a variety of personal characteristics, including size, musculature, and facial expression. People who seem especially weak or strong are assigned low or high status (respectively) at once; everyone else engages in brief dominance "contests." These contests, which are often quite subtle (e.g. staring at someone until he or she looks away), produce "winners" and "losers" who are assigned status accordingly. Again, initial status assignments can be modified as time passes and further information about group members becomes available.

The views of both expectation-states theorists (Berger & Zelditch 1985) and of ethological theorists (Dovidio & Ellyson 1985; Keating 1985) have received empirical support. Which group of theorists, then, offers the "best" explanation for the development of status systems? An initial study by Lee & Ofshe (1981) claimed a victory for the ethological theorists, but that claim evoked considerable controversy and led other researchers to perform similar studies (e.g. Mohr 1986; Tuzlak & Moore 1984). Most of these researchers claimed victories for the expectation-states theorists. The whole debate is far from settled, though a recent attempt by Ridgeway (1984) to integrate the two theoretical perspectives seems promising and has some empirical support (Ridgeway 1987).

Many researchers who study status systems are intrigued by their possible effects. For example, a person's status often affects his or her relations with other group members. People with higher status have more opportunities to exert social influence, try to influence other group members more often, and are indeed more influential than people with lower status (e.g. Gray et al 1982; Skvoretz 1988; Weisfeld & Weisfeld 1984). A person's status can also affect how he or she is evaluated by others. Even when they behave in similar ways, people with higher status are often evaluated more positively than people with lower status (e.g. Humphrey 1985; Sande et al 1986). Finally, a person's status can affect his or her self-evaluations. People with higher status often have more self-esteem than people with lower status (e.g. Moore 1985; Sande et al 1986). It is noteworthy that the effects of status systems are usually studied at the individual rather than the group level, even though such systems are supposedly adaptive for small groups.

Norms

Norms are shared expectations about how the members of a group ought to behave. A group's norms can be measured in a variety of ways. By simply observing the behavior of group members, researchers can often make inferences about that group's norms (e.g. Graves et al 1982; Watson 1982). Behavioral regularities are interpreted as conformity to group norms, whereas behavioral irregularities (especially when they evoke strong reactions) are interpreted as deviance from those norms. Another, more popular method is to ask a group's members to describe its norms (e.g. Argote 1989; Henderson & Argyle 1986). Although people may disagree about group norms, recent analyses (e.g. Jacobsen & Van der Voordt 1980; Rossi & Berk 1985) suggest that the patterns of consensus and dissensus among group members can be meaningful. Finally, the most common method is to ask each member of a group about his or her personal expectations for the behavior of others (e.g. McKirnan 1984; O'Reilly & Caldwell 1985). These responses are then aggregated, using procedures developed by Jackson (1965), McKirnan (1980), and others, to produce statistical indices that capture many important aspects of the group's norms. As most of these methods suggest, norms are generally treated as group rather than individual characteristics.

Research on group norms often takes place in laboratory settings. Some researchers who study laboratory groups are interested in allocation norms (see Komorita 1984b for a review). Several norms of this sort (e.g. equity, equality, needs) can be identified, and much is known about both their causes and effects. Other laboratory researchers are interested in decision-making norms (see Miller 1989 for a review). Several norms of this sort (e.g. unanimity, majority rules) can be identified as well, and though their causes are not yet clear, much is known about their effects. Researchers who study groups in natural settings find a wide variety of norms there, some of which emerge in nearly every group. These generic norms involve (*a*) sharing the rewards or costs of group membership, (*b*) preventing conflicts among group members, (*c*) regulating contacts with outsiders, and (*d*) expressing a group's core values.

How are norms produced within small groups? Several theoretical perspectives regarding this issue can be found (e.g. Bettenhausen & Murnighan 1985; Feldman 1984; Opp 1982). Feldman, for example, argues that the initial patterns of behavior in a group often solidify into norms. Norms can also be imported from the surrounding social environment, mandated by a group's leader, or created in response to critical events in a group's history. Opp argues that norms can arise through institutional, voluntary, or evolutionary processes. Institutional norms are mandated by a group's leader or by external authorities. Voluntary norms are negotiated among group members, often in order to resolve conflict. Evolutionary norms arise when behaviors that satisfy one person are learned by others, causing them to spread throughout a group. The resulting pattern of behavior generates expectations, at first about how people are likely to behave and then later about how people ought to behave. Finally, Bettenhausen & Murnighan argue that norms arise through cognitive processes. People bring to a group scripts that specify proper behavior in various situations. These scripts are activated whenever someone classifies a new situation as similar to others that he or she has already encountered. The speed with which norms develop and the amount of negotiation they require depend on the extent to which group members share scripts and classify situations in the same way.

Studies of the effects of norms on groups and their members usually focus on conformity and deviance (see below), but there is also some research on how norms affect group performance. Obviously, performance is enhanced when the norms within a group regarding effort, efficiency, quality control, and so on are positive rather than negative, but even positive work norms are not enough to guarantee success. Several studies suggest that the intensity of those norms, the level of normative consensus among group members, and the group's cohesion may all be important factors as well (e.g. Argote 1989; O'Reilly & Caldwell 1985).

Roles

Roles are shared expectations about how a particular person in a group ought to behave. There are several ways in which roles can be measured. Some researchers study formal roles (e.g. therapist, foreman, team captain) or informal roles with objective referents (e.g. newcomer, parent). Measurement issues scarcely arise in these studies. Most researchers, however, study informal roles that are more subjective. One method for measuring these roles is to observe group members, searching for people who exhibit idiosyncratic patterns of behavior (e.g. Eagle & Newton 1981). Zurcher (1983) offers some excellent suggestions for field studies of roles, and the development of SYMLOG (cf Isenberg & Ennis 1981) allows observers to measure the roles of any group on the same general dimensions (friendly/unfriendly, dominant/ submissive, instrumental/expressive). Another method is to ask people to describe the roles in their group and to identify who plays them (e.g. Ancona & Caldwell 1988; Rees & Segal 1984). Often special informants (leaders) are used for this purpose, thereby avoiding problems posed by disagreements among group members about their roles. Finally, the most common method is to ask each group member to describe the role(s) he or she plays (e.g. Jackson & Schuler 1985). These descriptions are usually taken at face value; corroboration from other group members is seldom obtained. As most of these methods suggest, roles are generally treated as individual rather than group characteristics.

A few roles can be found in nearly all groups, and these are especially interesting to researchers. One common role is that of leader. We will discuss leadership in more detail below, but it is worth noting here that group members often share prototypes of the ideal leader, and their evaluations of a leader can depend on the prototypicality of his or her behavior (Lord 1985). Another role that can be found in most groups, at one time or another, is that of newcomer. Moreland & Levine (1989) argue that newcomers are expected to be anxious, passive, dependent, and conforming, and that those who play this role more effectively are more likely to be accepted by oldtimers. Several researchers are interested in how newcomers cope with their difficult situation (see Moreland & Levine 1989 for a review). A final example of a common role is that of scapegoat. Socioanalytic theorists (e.g. Wells 1980) argue that group members are often unable to integrate their positive and negative qualities into coherent and/or acceptable self-images. To resolve these internal conflicts, they project their negative qualities onto a scapegoat. The scapegoat thus provides a valuable service for the group—a service that no one in the group may fully understand.

Much research on roles involves the special conflicts they can create for groups and their members. Some of these conflicts arise from the process of role assignment, when decisions are made about who should play which roles. Moreland & Levine (1982) describe some of the tactics that group members use to maneuver themselves and one another into (or out of) various roles. Once someone begins to play a role, other conflicts can arise. A person may lack the knowledge, ability, or motivation to play a role effectively, or discover that it is inconsistent with roles he or she already plays. Group members may also disagree about how a role should be played or who should play it. Studies of role conflicts in work groups (see Jackson & Schuler 1985 for a recent review) reveal increased tension and decreased productivity within such groups whenever role conflicts arise. Role conflicts can some-times be resolved by changing a role in suitable ways. Such role innovation depends on several factors, including the self-confidence of the person play-ing the role, the level of consensus among other group members about how the role should be played, and the importance of the role for the group (cf Brett 1984; Nicholson 1984). Finally, role transitions are often a source of conflict for groups and their members. Moreland & Levine (1984) describe and suggest solutions to some of the problems that arise as people move from one role to another. And there are many studies of job changes, which involve role transitions within the same work group or between work groups of the same sort (cf Brett, 1984).

Little is known about the psychological processes that produce roles within small groups, although some speculation can be found (e.g. Diamond & Allcorn 1986). Researchers are more interested in the effects of roles, but most of their work involves the impact of role-playing on mental health and the incorporation of roles into the self-concepts of those who play them. Few researchers study the effects of roles on a group, though there is some evidence that role differentiation is associated with improved group perform-ance (e.g. Roger & Reid 1982).

Cohesion

Finally, many researchers who study the structure of small groups focus on cohesion. Most of their work involves military units, sports teams, or therapy groups, and is aimed at making those groups more successful by strengthen-ing their cohesion. The main issue for these researchers is how the cohesion of a group should be conceptualized and/or measured. Unfortunately, there is much confusion regarding that issue (cf Drescher et al 1985; Evans & Jarvis 1980). Some of this confusion arises from the fact that cohesion is studied under different guises, including "solidarity," "morale," "climate," and "sense of community." Another source of confusion is that cohesion itself appears to be a complex construct. Several factor analyses of cohesion measures can be found (e.g. Carron et al 1985; Gal & Manning 1987; Stokes 1983). The results of these analyses vary considerably from one study to another but generally reveal a variety of factors. Finally, confusion about cohesion often arises because the same phenomenon (e.g. self-disclosure) can be regarded as a cause for, an effect of, or a measure of cohesion.

Researchers use many different methods for measuring cohesion. A few try to measure cohesion by observing the nonverbal behavior of group members (e.g. Piper et al 1983; Tickle-Degen & Rosenthal 1987). Members of cohe-sive groups are more likely than others to stand or sit close together, focus their attention on one another, show signs of mutual affection, and display coordinated patterns of behavior. Some researchers also record the verbal behavior of group members (e.g. Eder 1988; Owen 1985). Members of cohesive groups are more likely than others to participate actively in conversations, engage in self-disclosure or collaborative narration, and develop a special argot. A more common (and traditional) method for measuring cohesion is to ask people to evaluate one another and/or their group. Their responses are then aggregated to produce a single index of cohesion (e.g. Keller 1986; Manning & Fullerton 1988). A final method is to transform cohesion into a kind of commitment. Several researchers (e.g. Carron et al 1985) now measure cohesion by asking people to describe their personal feelings about a group and its members. Their responses are not aggregated, but are simply used as predictors of personal behavior. This method clearly differs from the others by leading researchers to treat cohesion as an individual rather than a group characteristic.

How is cohesion produced in small groups? Several factors may be important. First, simply assembling people into a group is enough to produce some cohesion (Hogg 1987), and the more time people spend together, the stronger their cohesion becomes (e.g. Manning & Fullerton 1988). Second, cohesion is stronger in groups whose members like one another (e.g. Piper et al 1983; Stokes 1983). Anything that produces such liking (e.g. propinquity, competence, real or perceived similarity) can thus strengthen group cohesion. Third, groups that people find more rewarding tend to have stronger cohesion (e.g. Ruder & Gill 1982; Stokes 1983). A group can be rewarding because people enjoy its activities, approve of its goals, or believe that membership will be useful to them in other contexts. Groups are naturally more rewarding when they succeed rather than fail, though some groups can preserve (if not strengthen) their cohesion even when they fail (e.g. Brawley et al 1987). Finally, leaders can often strengthen group cohesion by encouraging feelings of warmth and acceptance among followers, or simply by serving as targets for projective identification (e.g. Piper et al 1983; Smith 1983).

Cohesion can have many effects on a group and its members. One helpful effect of cohesion is that a group becomes easier to maintain—members of cohesive groups are more likely than others to participate in group activities, stay in the group themselves and convince others to join, and resist attempts to disrupt the group (e.g. Brawley et al 1988; Carron et al 1988). Cohesion also increases conformity to group norms (e.g. O'Reilly & Caldwell 1985; Rutkowski et al 1983). This effect can be helpful when deviance endangers the group, or harmful when innovation is required. Janis (1982), for example, claims that "groupthink" often arises when highly cohesive groups place too much emphasis on conformity. Although the evidence supporting this claim is weak (cf McCauley 1989), it is clear that conformity pressures within cohesive groups could become harmful.

Many studies suggest that cohesion affects group performance (e.g. Keller

1986; Miesing & Preble 1985). However, most of these studies involve correlational rather than experimental designs, making it difficult to ascertain whether (*a*) cohesion improves performance, (*b*) successful performance strengthens cohesion, or (*c*) both effects occur. A few studies involving causal modeling of the relationship between cohesion and performance are available (e.g. Landers et al 1982; Williams & Hacker 1982), but their results are inconclusive. When cohesion is manipulated experimentally, its effects on performance can be interpreted more clearly. These effects are complex; they depend on such factors as the abilities of group members (Tziner & Vardi 1983), the leader's style (Tziner & Vardi 1982), the type of task the group is performing (e.g. Carron & Chelladurai 1981; Zaccaro & McCoy 1988), or which aspect of group cohesion is assessed.

CONFLICTS WITHIN SMALL GROUPS

Conflict arises when group members believe that their goals cannot be achieved simultaneously (Pruitt & Rubin 1986). Conflict can involve many issues, including the distribution of physical resources, access to information, and the power to make decisions. Although conflict sometimes fosters innovation and thereby enhances individual and group welfare (Levine & Moreland 1985; Nemeth & Staw 1989), it often has serious negative consequences, including interpersonal hostility, reduced performance, and even group dissolution. Group members thus devote considerable time and energy to controlling whatever conflict occurs.

Social Dilemmas

An important form of conflict occurs when individual group members engage in behavior that would have negative consequences if everyone engaged in it. These social dilemmas can be either "collective traps" or "collective fences." In traps, behaviors that are rewarding to individuals yield negative outcomes when exhibited by enough people. In fences, behaviors that are costly to individuals yield negative outcomes when avoided by enough people. Both collective traps and fences may involve temporal delay between positive and negative consequences. Several paradigms are used to investigate behavior in social dilemmas. Four of the most important are N-person prisoner's dilemma (NPD) games, replenishable resource traps, public goods provisions, and delay fences, in which the group's goal is to maintain, rather than provide, a public good (Messick & Brewer 1983).

Research on social dilemmas is done by investigators from several disciplines, including social psychology, political science, sociology, and economics. Several reviews of the psychological research can be found (e.g. Messick & Brewer 1983; Orbell & Dawes 1981). Two classes of solutions to social dilemmas are commonly distinguished. Individual solutions involve changing the behaviors of individual group members, whereas structural solutions involve removing the dilemma through group action. Although this distinction is useful, it is not always clear why a particular variable (e.g. opportunity for communication) belongs in one category (individual) rather than the other (structural).

Research on individual solutions suggests that group members' social values and motives influence their behavior in dilemma situations (e.g. Liebrand 1986). Rapoport's work on the provision of step-level public goods also treats altruism and other social values as potentially important determinants of behavior (e.g. Rapoport 1987). The effects of culture and gender on dilemma behavior are investigated by some researchers as well (e.g. Stockard et al 1988; Yamagishi 1988).

Communication among group members can increase cooperation in social dilemmas (e.g. Orbell et al 1988). Dawes and his colleagues believe that discussion facilitates cooperation by promoting group identity and/or providing an opportunity for members to make promises that they will cooperate (though these promises are only binding if everyone makes them). Caporael et al (1989) bolster their group identity explanation of dilemma behavior by citing evidence against egoistic incentive explanations. The notion that group identity can facilitate cooperation in dilemmas is consistent with work by other investigators (e.g. Kramer & Brewer 1986).

Finally, in a series of studies using resource dilemmas, Messick and his colleagues identified three factors that affect group members' harvest decisions, which represent an individual-level solution to a dilemma. These factors are a desire to accumulate the resource (i.e. self-interest), a desire to use the resource responsibly, and a desire to conform to an implicit group norm (e.g. Samuelson & Messick 1986; Samuelson et al 1986).

Research on structural solutions to dilemmas focuses on the impact of such variables as the payoff system (e.g. Dawes et al 1986), how cooperative and competitive decisions are framed (e.g. Rutte et al 1987), group size (e.g. Kerr 1989a), and social norms (e.g. Kerr 1989b). In his social-dilemma analysis of motivational losses in work groups, Kerr suggests several structural solutions to this type of social fence (Kerr 1986).

When will group members give up individual control over resources in favor of structural solutions involving collective action (e.g. privatization of resources, election of a powerful leader, development of a punishment system)? Messick and his colleagues find that structural solutions are preferred when the group is inefficient in dealing with the common resource and free access to the resource produces large inequities in members' outcomes (e.g. Samuelson & Messick 1986; Samuelson et al 1986). Yamagishi (1986) offers a "structural goal/expectation" theory, which assumes that structural solutions to dilemmas are adopted when group members develop the goal of mutual cooperation, understand the effectiveness of structural solutions, and realize the difficulty of attaining this goal through elementary cooperation alone (e.g. Yamagishi 1988).

Social-dilemma studies, which ostensibly pit self-interest against group interest, generally involve rather pallid groups. For example, group members are strangers, role and status structures are not allowed to develop, the group is expected to exist for only a short period, and all members have equal wealth and power. Although shortcomings of the typical social-dilemma paradigm are recognized (e.g. Messick & Brewer 1983; Yamagishi 1986), investigators rarely make serious efforts to eliminate them. The failure to devote more attention to power differences among group members is particularly interesting, since a common structural solution to dilemmas is the appointment of a powerful leader who makes allocation decisions for the group.

Power

Power involves the ability to influence or control other people. The possession of power clearly allows people to resolve conflicts to their own advantage, but it can have other effects as well. According to Shaw (1981), compared to low-power group members, those with high power exert more control over group activities, are better liked, receive more deferential behavior, and are more attracted to the group. The exercise of power can also affect a member's tension level (e.g. Fodor 1985) as well as his or her self-evaluations and evaluations of others (Kipnis 1984).

Several studies focus on the tactics that group members use in attempting to influence one another. In some studies, the behavior of group members is observed during interaction (or simulated interaction) with subordinates, peers, and/or superiors (e.g. Instone et al 1983; Steckler & Rosenthal 1985). In other studies, group members are asked to describe the influence tactics they employ (e.g. Kipnis & Schmidt 1983). The relative status of group members affects the influence tactics they use as well as their overall motivation to exert control (e.g. Ford & Zelditch 1988). Finally, some studies focus on how group members respond to others' exercise of power (e.g. Podsakoff & Schriesheim 1985).

Various theoretical perspectives on the distribution of power are available (e.g. Cobb 1984). Those based on Emerson's power-dependence theory are the most prevalent (Cook 1987). The basic idea of Emerson's theory is that the power of A over B is equal to B's dependence upon A, which varies positively with the value of the resource that A provides for B and negatively with the availability of this resource outside the A-B relationship. The theory also asserts that power imbalance produces asymmetrical exchange between actors, which moves toward an equilibrium. One set of studies focuses on power use in dyads (e.g. Molm 1987), while another involves larger exchange networks, which are viewed as sets of linked dyadic relationships (e.g. Cook et al 1983). The power-dependence perspective helps us to understand several aspects of group process, including bargaining (e.g. Bacharach & Lawler 1981; Hegtvedt & Cook 1987) and coalition formation (e.g. Cook & Gillmore 1984).

Bargaining

Bargaining situations run the gamut from simple to complex. In the simplest case, two persons are not allowed to communicate with one another and receive payoffs based on their independent choices to cooperate or defect. In the most complex case, several persons are allowed to communicate freely and receive payoffs based on their joint agreements. We do not review research on two-person bargaining unless the impact of the larger social environment is explicit. Several excellent discussions of "pure" two-party bargaining are available (e.g. McClintock et al 1983; Pruitt 1981; Pruitt & Rubin 1986).

Two areas of research on dyadic bargaining involve the effects of third parties on participants' behavior. One research area concerns representative bargaining, in which each bargainer represents the interests of constituents. McGrath (1984) provides a typology of different relationships between representatives and their constituents, noting, for example, that a representative may or may not be a member of his or her own constituency. Carnevale (1985), who studies representatives belonging to their constituent groups, distinguishes between feeling responsible for representing the constituency, feeling accountable for the outcome of representation, and feeling under surveillance for both the process and outcome of representation. He finds that surveillance and accountability produce different effects and that the impact of accountability is mediated by such factors as the competitive/noncompetitive definition of the situation and the representative's relationship with his or her constituency (e.g. Ben Yoav & Pruitt 1984). Recent research by Insko and his colleagues on individual versus group competition is also relevant to representative bargaining (Insko et al 1987). A second research area concerns the role of outsiders (e.g. mediators, arbitrators, fact finders) who try to reduce conflict between bargainers. Studies on this topic investigate third-party intervention in diverse contexts, ranging from disagreements between college students in the laboratory to disputes between heads of state (e.g. Rubin 1981; Welton & Pruitt 1987).

Several useful analyses of third-party intervention are available (e.g. Carnevale 1986). The work of Rubin & Pruitt (Pruitt & Rubin 1986; Rubin 1981) is particularly helpful. They differentiate third-party roles on several dimensions (e.g. formal vs informal, invited vs noninvited, impartial vs partial) and discuss three tactics that third parties can use to intervene successfully: modifying the physical and social structure of the conflict, changing the issue structure, and increasing the motivation of bargainers to reach agreement. Finally, Rubin & Pruitt emphasize that third parties do not always facilitate conflict resolution and sometimes unintentionally exacerbate conflict (e.g. by forming a coalition with one of the bargainers or suggesting inadequate solutions). Third parties also occasionally seek to create conflict they assume might be useful (e.g. van de Vliert 1985).

Research on bargaining is sometimes done in group (as opposed to strictly dyadic) settings. Some of this research concerns organizations, where the larger social context influences what happens between the bargainers (e.g. Lewicki et al 1986). An important issue in organizational (as well as other) settings is the impact of bargainers' concerns about justice and fairness on their use of power and reactions to various allocation schemes (e.g. Hegtvedt & Cook 1987). Other research deals with "group negotiation," which occurs when three or more people (representing their own interests) seek to resolve conflicting preferences (e.g. Bazerman et al 1989). Bazerman and his colleagues claim that integrative agreements are harder to achieve in larger groups than in dyads because larger groups impose greater information-processing demands on their members, have more complex interpersonal dynamics, and often use negotiation management techniques that have negative consequences. Research on the effects of such variables as agendas and decision rules provides some support for these claims (e.g. Thompson et al 1988).

Coalition Formation

Group conflicts can sometimes be resolved through coalition formation, when two or more members agree to cooperate in order to obtain a mutually desired outcome. Both coalition formation and two-party bargaining are studied extensively; but whereas research on two-party bargaining is often criticized as atheoretical, research on coalition formation is positively theory ridden. Experiments often attempt to test hypotheses derived from competing theories, and reviews of coalition formation research are typically organized around theoretical controversies.

Coalition formation is studied by researchers from several disciplines using a variety of methodologies. We focus on social pyschological research, which tests descriptive theories that predict which coalitions will form and how coalition members will divide rewards. All of these theories assume that group members seek to maximize a divisible reward (e.g. money, points). Summaries of this work can be found in Komorita (1984a). Those interested in game theoretic models should consult reviews by Kahan & Rapoport (1984) and Wilke (1985).

Five theories (minimum resource, minimum power, weighted probability, bargaining, equal excess) are relevant to *simple* games, where all coalitions are defined as either "winning" or "losing." These games can be studied with and without the assignment of resource weights to group members. Such weights are important because they influence both the number and sizes of minimal winning coalitions (strategic function) and the division of reward within coalitions (normative function). Research on simple games provides more support for weighted-probability, bargaining, and equal-excess theories than for minimum-resource and minimum-power theories. However, the relative accuracy of the former three theories is not yet clear (e.g. Komorita & Nagao 1983; Kravitz 1987; Nail & Cole 1985). These three theories all involve comparisons between alternatives, but they differ in other ways (e.g. emphasis on strategic versus normative function of resources, static versus dynamic predictions).

Some theories (bargaining, equal excess, Shapley-*w*) are relevant to *multivalued* games, where winning and losing coalitions are not defined and the values of various possible coalitions may differ. With a few exceptions, such games are studied without the assignment of resource weights to group members. Research on multivalued games provides a murky theoretical picture (e.g. Komorita & Miller 1986; Miller & Komorita 1986a; Miller & Wong 1986). Although equal-excess theory seemed ascendant a few years ago (Komorita 1984a), the situation today is less clear. Perhaps new work on process theories will be helpful in revealing the mechanisms underlying coalition formation in multivalued games (cf Komorita & Ellis 1988).

Most research on coalition formation is experimental and involves highly contrived, artificial settings. When more naturalistic studies are conducted, a number of interesting issues emerge that coalition researchers often neglect in their quest for elegant mathematical models. Some studies are done, for example, on how leader behavior affects the formation of "revolutionary coalitions" among subordinates (Lawler 1983), how family coalitions maintain existing status relationships between parents and children (Bonacich et al 1985), and how the presence of agendas and decision rules affects coalition behavior in negotiating groups (Thompson et al 1988).

Several commentators note weaknesses in social psychological and game theoretic analyses of coalition formation and suggest new directions for theory and research. For example, Cook & Gillmore (1984) criticize social psychological theories on several grounds, including the assumption that actors have full knowledge of the objective characteristics of the game, the emphasis on intra-coalition dynamics to the exclusion of the larger social context, and the failure to consider past and future relations between actors. They advocate a power-dependence approach to explain the emergence of coalitions in ongoing social exchange networks and to clarify links between coalition mobilization and the distribution of power in these networks. Researchers interested in coalitions within organizational contexts (e.g. Murnighan 1986) offer several other good suggestions. Miller & Komorita (1986b), for example, describe many aspects of organizations that are not considered in most laboratory research on coalitions. These include the presence of earned (as opposed to assigned) resources, restrictions on information and communication, the ideological nature of coalition payoffs, the probabilistic nature of coalition success, and the fact that coalitions are not always necessary for winning. They conclude that coalition formation research would benefit from less emphasis on theory testing. We believe that the problem is not theory testing per se, but rather the narrow scope of the theories that are being tested.

Majority and Minority Influence

In some groups, people begin their relationship on an agreeable basis but later split into coalitions, or factions, to secure access to valued resources. In other groups, people begin their relationship as members of factions that disagree about some issue; groups often contain two such factions differing in size (i.e. a majority and a minority). These factions attempt to influence one another in a variety of ways. Majority and minority influence are the focus of much theoretical and empirical work, several reviews of which are available (e.g. Levine 1989; Levine & Russo 1987).

Majority and minority influence are relevant to conflict for two reasons. First, group members are usually not seeking to reach a joint decision that is binding on everyone, as in the decision-making research discussed below. Second, research on majorities and minorities is heavily influenced by Moscovici's (1985) position that conflict and behavioral style, rather than dependence and uncertainty reduction, are the critical determinants of social influence. In particular, Moscovici has focused attention on social change (innovation), which he believes often occurs when a minority creates conflict with a majority.

Much of the research on majority and minority influence reflects a controversy about whether the two kinds of influence are mediated by a single psychological process (e.g. Doms & Van Avermaet 1985; Latane & Wolf 1981; Tanford & Penrod 1984) or by two different processes (e.g. Maass et al 1987; Moscovici 1985; Mugny 1982; Nemeth 1986). Unfortunately, relatively few studies actually explore the impact of majority and minority pressure on psychological processes, and the results of these studies are mixed (e.g. Mackie 1987; Nemeth & Kwan 1985). Recently, two thoughtful analyses indicate that the "either-or" character of the one-process versus two-process debate is deceptive and that the truth may be more complex (and more interesting) than either position implies. Chaiken & Stangor (1987) argue that multiple cognitive processes (e.g. heuristic processing, message- and issue-relevant thinking) may underlie both majority and minority influence, and that the motives operating in a social-influence setting constrain the cognitive process(es) that occur there. Kruglanski & Mackie (1989) describe several criteria for assessing the validity of one-process versus two-process explanations, review research using these criteria, and find support for a weak version of the two-process position. They suggest that researchers abandon the debate and concentrate on identifying which differences between majorities and minorities affect their ability to exert influence.

Although Moscovici's position has been dominant during the last few years, other theoretical approaches shed important light on majority and minority influence (e.g. Kaplan 1987; Stasser et al 1989a; Turner et al 1987). Research indicates that a number of situational variables affect majority and minority influence. Majority influence is affected by such factors as the majority's size (e.g. Insko et al 1985), the extremity of the majority's position (e.g. Campbell et al 1986), the majority's perceived competence (e.g. Mugny 1985), and exposure to dissenters from the majority position (e.g. Kerr et al 1987). Minority influence is affected by such factors as the extremity and consistency of the minority's position (e.g. Levine & Ruback 1980; Nemeth & Brilmayer 1987), the level of social support for the majority's position (e.g. Doms & Van Avermaet 1985), the minority's "idiosyncrasy credits" (e.g. Lortie-Lussier 1987), and the social categorization of the majority and minority (e.g. Clark & Maass 1988).

As all of this indicates, a good deal of theoretical and empirical attention is devoted to majority and minority influence in laboratory groups. Several theorists are now beginning to consider innovation outside the laboratory. Gerard (1985) discusses the factors that lead dissident minorities in real-world settings to adopt consistent behavioral styles. Levine & Moreland (1985) use their group-socialization model to explain innovation on the part of prospective, new, full, marginal, and ex-members of groups. And Nemeth & Staw (1989) discuss the trade-offs between social control and innovation in small groups and organizations.

THE PERFORMANCE OF SMALL GROUPS

Although conflicts in small groups are important, there is also considerable cooperation among members who have common motives and interests, work together to produce a group product, and share the resulting rewards. Group performance is the process and outcome of members' joint efforts to achieve a collective goal. Research on group performance can be divided into three general topics: leadership, productivity, and decision-making.

Leadership

Leadership is a universal aspect of human groups (Hollander 1985), perhaps because group performance is facilitated by the exercise of organizational, directive, and motivational functions. Leadership is studied by researchers from many fields (e.g. Graumann & Moscovici 1986; Hunt et al 1988). Research on leadership can be organized in terms of three major theoretical orientations (Chemers 1987): leader-oriented approaches, transactional and exchange approaches, and cognitive approaches.

Some leader-oriented approaches focus on the relationship between a leaders' personality or behavior and various situational factors. The best known example is Fiedler's (1978) contingency theory. Reviews of relevant research yield some support for Fiedler's position (e.g. Chemers 1987; Peters et al 1985), and contingency theory continues to generate new work (e.g. Chemers & Ayman 1985; Rice et al 1982). Of particular interest is research by Fiedler and his colleagues on the role of stress and intelligence in leadership (e.g. Chemers et al 1985; Fiedler & Garcia 1987). Two additional contingency theories are House's (1971) path-goal theory and Vroom & Yetton's (1973) normative decision theory. Neither of these theories is studied as often as Fiedler's theory, but both provide useful perspectives on leadership (e.g. Field 1982; Fry et al 1986; Schriesheim & DeNisi 1981).

In addition to research on these three contingency theories, a substantial amount of work focuses on aspects of leader behavior. Researchers explore how the performance of followers is affected by a leader's rewards and punishments (e.g. Podsakoff & Todor 1985), role clarification and discipline (e.g. Yukl & Van Fleet 1982), and democratic decision-making (e.g. Weiss & Friedrichs 1986). Related work on the impact of leaders' personality characteristics is also being done (e.g. Strube et al 1989). Several theoretical papers analyze leader behavior and follower performance. Some of these analyses involve particular kinds of groups, such as business organizations (e.g. Hackman & Walton 1986) and military units (e.g. Henderson 1985). Other analyses are more general (e.g. Griffin 1987). Of particular interest is recent work on transformational, or charismatic, leadership (e.g. Conger & Kanungo 1988).

Transactional and exchange theories of leadership emphasize the development and maintenance of leader-member relations through the exchange of valued resources (Hollander 1985). Leader legitimacy is important, because it is the basis for leaders' authority over their followers. Leaders often obtain legitimacy through appointment or election. Legitimacy gained in these two ways has different effects on leader-follower relations (e.g. Ben-Yoav et al 1983). Legitimacy can also be obtained by exhibiting commitment to group goals and competence on group tasks (e.g. Price & Garland 1981); leaders often use impression-management techniques to convince followers of their commitment and competence (cf Leary et al 1986).

Not all leaders are appointed or elected; some "emerge" during the course of group interaction (Schneier & Goktepe 1983). Research on emergent leadership suggests that several factors can affect a member's perceived right to exert influence. These include individual-difference factors, such as personality traits (e.g. Kenny & Zaccaro 1983) and sex (e.g. Geis et al 1985). Other determinants of emergent leadership are verbal participation rate (e.g. Stein & Heller 1983) and seniority (e.g. Insko et al 1982). Related to leadership emergence is leader succession; several useful analyses of succession in organizational contexts are available (e.g. Hall 1986).

Perhaps the best-known exchange perspective on leadership is the vertical dyad linkage (VDL) theory proposed by Graen and his colleagues (e.g. Dansereau et al 1975). They assert that leaders develop different exchange relationships with different followers and hence treat them in different ways. Although some aspects of the theory are controversial (e.g. Vecchio & Gobdel 1984), dyadic leader-follower relations are clearly an important component of leadership (e.g. Crouch & Yetton 1988; Dienesch & Liden 1986). Other work also supports the importance of reciprocal relations between leaders and their followers (e.g. Griffin et al 1987).

Cognitive theories of leadership focus on followers' and leaders' thoughts and feelings about one another. We have already described some work on followers' cognitions in our discussion of emergent leaders. Other research deals with elected or appointed leaders. Evidence suggests that reactions to such leaders (by followers or even outsiders) are influenced by a variety of factors, including the leader's style (e.g. Tjosvold et al 1983) and the group's level of success (e.g. Larson et al 1984). Work by Lord and his colleagues on implicit leadership theories, which are relevant to emergent as well as to appointed and elected leaders, is especially interesting. People apparently possess shared beliefs about leaders' behaviors and traits, which affect how they encode leader information, form perceptions of leaders, and recall relevant information (e.g. Lord 1985; see also Rush & Russell 1988). Finally, leaders' thoughts and feelings about followers are also studied extensively. Much of this work was stimulated by Green & Mitchell's (1979) argument that information about followers' behavior triggers attributional responses from leaders, which in turn affect how they evaluate their followers. Although not without its critics, the leader-attribution perspective has a good deal of empirical support (e.g. Ashkanasy 1989; Gioia & Sims 1986).

Although some argue that the concept of leadership has been romaticized and overemphasized (e.g. Meindl et al 1985), interest in the topic remains high. The vitality of the field contradicts the disenchantment that afflicts some observers, and we agree with Chemers (1987) that "leadership research can drive toward a bright future, if only the perennial mourners would move the hearse out of the road" (p. 272).

Productivity

By group productivity we mean tangible outcomes of group members' activities that can be evaluated in terms of quality. We do not discuss work on how the mere presence of others affects individual performance. Readers interested in this topic can consult one of several reviews dealing with social facilitation (e.g. Geen 1989).

Theoretical analyses of group productivity focus on work groups in organizational settings. This is not surprising, given current interest in organizations and the widely held assumption that work groups are a major determinant of organizational effectiveness. Several interesting analyses of group productivity in organizations are available (e.g. Gladstein 1984; Hackman 1987), but Goodman and his colleagues (Goodman et al 1986, 1987) criticize current models of group productivity for being too general and difficult to test. They urge theorists to develop more specific models, to define group effectiveness more carefully, and to consider new ways in which effectiveness is influenced by a group's task and technology, cohesiveness, and norms. Research indicates that these and other factors can indeed affect group productivity. As we mentioned earlier, group performance depends, at least in part, on the abilities and personalities of group members and the size and cohesiveness of the group. The group's task, technology, and reward structure are also important, as are the quantity and quality of intermember communication and the behavior of the group leader.

A good deal of research on group productivity has sought to clarify "social loafing"—the tendency of group members to expend less effort when working together than when working alone. Social loafing is a robust phenomenon that occurs on both physical tasks, such as shouting (Williams et al 1981), and cognitive tasks, such as brainstorming (Harkins & Petty 1982). Although easy to produce in the laboratory, social loafing is not inevitable when people work together. Loafing can be reduced or eliminated by increasing the identifiability and uniqueness of members' contributions to a task (e.g. Harkins & Petty 1982; Kerr & Bruun 1981), the ease with which those contributions can be evaluated (e.g. Harkins & Szymanski 1987), members' involvement in the task and accountability for their work (e.g. Brickner et al 1986; Weldon & Gargano 1988), and task attractiveness (e.g. Zaccaro 1984). Finally "free-rider" and "sucker" effects are other possible explanations for reduced motivation in groups (e.g. Kerr 1983; Kerr & Bruun 1983).

Because motivation and coordination losses often inhibit group productivity, various strategies have been suggested for helping groups to function more effectively. Besides some general techniques applicable to a wide range of groups and settings (e.g. Hackman 1987), several specific techniques have been suggested. Although none of these is a panacea, each appears to be useful in some situations. Three techniques involve substantial changes in how work groups function. Team development encompasses a range of activities (e.g. problem identification, sensitivity training, role analysis) designed to increase group members' interpersonal and task skills (e.g. Buller

1986). Quality circles, popularized by the Japanese, involve regular meetings in which group members discuss production problems and solutions to these problems (e.g. Marks et al 1986). Autonomous work groups allow members who work on interdependent tasks to control the management and execution of these tasks (e.g. Goodman et al 1988). Autonomous work groups are compatibile with sociotechnical systems theory, which holds that group self-regulation improves both morale and productivity (e.g. Guzzo et al 1985). A closely related perspective, contingency theory, claims that performance can be improved by tailoring group structure and process to the demands the group faces (e.g. Schoonhoven 1981).

Two other techniques involve attempts to increase the effort group members devote to a task. In participative goal setting, members decide together on their production goals (e.g. Pearson 1987). Interest in this technique stems from the team development and autonomous work group approaches and from research on the relationship between goals and individual performance (see Locke et al 1981). Other work suggests that agreement between members' individual and collective goals may facilitate group performance (Mackie & Goethals 1987). Task design can also make groups more productive. Tasks were once assumed to have objective attributes (e.g. autonomy, feedback, variety) that affected group members' motivation directly. Group productivity could thus be enhanced by appropriate changes in critical task attributes. This approach is now being challenged, and to a large extent replaced, by Salancik & Pfeffer's (1978) social information processing (SIP) model, which emphasizes task perceptions based on information obtained from other people (e.g. Griffin 1987). According to the SIP model, methods designed to enhance productivity must influence group members' *perceptions* of their task, rather than (or in addition to) its objective characteristics.

Of course, groups do not typically cease to exist once they create a product. Instead, members often reflect on the quality of the product and the process by which it was created, and these reflections affect their feelings and behaviors. Many studies focus on the attributions that members make for a group's success or failure. These attributions often reflect two forms of bias (Leary & Forsyth 1987). Egocentric, or self-serving, bias occurs when members attribute group success to their own contributions but attribute failure to other causes (e.g. Miller & Schlenker 1985). Sociocentric, or group-serving, bias occurs when members attribute group success to the contributions of the entire membership, but attribute failure to other causes (e.g. Adams et al 1985). Several explanations for egocentric and sociocentric biases have been offered (e.g. information processing, self-esteem, self-presentation), and all appear to have some validity. A more complex typology of possible attributions for group performance is offered by Zaccaro et al 1987. Finally, it is important to note Wicklund's (1989) work on the appropriation of ideas, which sheds light on responsibility attribution for "intellectual" products.

As Leary & Forsyth (1987) point out, outcome attributions can have important implications for group processes. One such process is the allocation of rewards and costs among group members. These allocations can be made by group members themselves or by outsiders. Research on the allocation process indicates that the use of particular allocation rules (e.g. equity, equality, need) is determined by group factors, such as success and morale (e.g. Elliott & Meeker 1986); recipient factors, such as performance and need (e.g. Tindale & Davis 1985); and allocator factors, such as motives and values (e.g. Stake 1983). As noted earlier, allocations of rewards and costs can often affect status, conflict, and leadership in groups.

Several theoretical analyses of the causes and consequences of allocation decisions in groups can be found (e.g. Komorita 1984b). All are based, at least in part, on comparisons between the outcomes of different group members. In an effort to provide an integrated perspective on outcome comparisons in group contexts, Levine & Moreland (e.g. 1987) offer a model based on the identities of the source and target of comparison (self/self, self/other, group/group), their group identifications (intragroup, intergroup), and the time period(s) during which the outcomes under consideration occur (intratemporal, intertemporal). Using that model, they offer predictions about when different comparisons are made, how the results of multiple comparisons are integrated, and what consequences different comparisons can have.

Decision-Making

An important aspect of group performance is decision-making. Groups frequently struggle for consensus on issues that affect the welfare of their members and/or outsiders. Both the process and outcome of decision-making are influenced by the kind of task the group is working on. These tasks include generating plans, generating ideas, solving problems with a correct answer, deciding issues with no correct answer, and resolving conflicts of viewpoint (McGrath 1984). General reviews of research on group decision-making are available (e.g. Brandstatter et al 1982), as are reviews dealing with specific kinds of groups, such as juries (e.g. Stasser et al 1982) and organizations (e.g. Guzzo 1982).

Many investigators attempt to describe the process of group decision-making. Some of these descriptions are qualitative, whereas others are quantitative. In the former category, efforts are often made to assess the accuracy of Bales & Strodtbeck's (1951) three-stage model of group decision-making (orientation, evaluation, control). Research provides little support for that model (e.g. Hirokawa 1983). Other qualitative models are also available, including Poole's structurational model (e.g. Poole et al 1985) and Burnstein & Berbaum's (1983) model of decision-making by high-level governmental groups. The latter is particularly interesting because it deals with groups that exist for relatively long periods and make life-or-death decisions.

Three of the most important quantitative theories of group decision-making are the social decision scheme (SDS) model, the social transition scheme (STS) model, and the social interaction sequence (SIS) model (see Stasser et al 1989a). These models differ in important ways. For example, SDS focuses on a group's final decision, STS focuses on transitions from one configuration of member preferences to another, and SIS focuses on changes in members' preferences and subjective certainty levels. Nevertheless, all three models combine individual preferences or dispositions to yield group outcomes. These models are useful in analyzing several aspects of group decision-making, including majority influence (e.g. Davis et al 1988) and the role of individual differences (e.g. Kirchler & Davis 1986). Laughlin and his colleagues also use the SDS and STS models to clarify group decision-making on intellective tasks (e.g. Laughlin & Futoran 1985).

Computer simulation represents an important trend in quantitative models of group decision-making. The SIS model uses computer simulation, as do such models as JUS (Hastie et al 1983) and DISCUSS (Stasser 1988). Simulations are useful for two reasons: They can account for a large amount of existing data on group decision-making, and they raise interesting issues for future research. Stasser (1988), for example, suggests that minorities facilitate group performance by helping to uncover "hidden" information.

The quality of group decision-making is an issue that intrigues many researchers. Some of their work involves comparisons between individual and group performance (see Hill 1982). For example, Laughlin and his colleagues demonstrate that groups are superior to individuals on induction tasks, because groups are able to recognize correct hypotheses once they are proposed (e.g. Laughlin & McGlynn 1986). Their work on collective induction also clarifies majority and minority influence on tasks that have intellective characteristics. More attention is also being paid to differences between group and individual memory (e.g. Clark & Stephenson 1989; Wegner et al 1985).

Other research on the quality of group decision-making focuses less on individual-group comparisons and more on factors that affect the process and outcome of group discussion. One such factor is the decision rule that a group adopts for combining members' individual preferences. Several studies show that groups implicitly use different decision rules on different types of tasks (Laughlin & Ellis 1986). Other studies show that explicitly adopted decision rules have important effects on both the process and outcome of decision-making (see Miller 1989). A second factor is the bias introduced into group decisions by members' failure to exchange unshared information. The exchange of such information is generally associated with better group decisions (e.g. Vinokur et al 1985). However, Stasser and his colleagues (e.g. Stasser et al 1989b) find that group discussion is often ineffective for disseminating unshared information. Instead, discussion is dominated by information that members share and that supports their existing preferences.

The failure of group members to exchange information is a major component of "groupthink," defined as extreme concurrence-seeking that produces poor group decisions. According to Janis (1982), several factors (e.g. high group cohesiveness, directive leadership, external threats) lead to symptoms of groupthink (e.g. illusions of invulnerability, pressure on dissenters), which in turn harm decision-making (e.g. by restricting the consideration of alternatives). The groupthink notion is intuitively appealing, and Janis offers many insights into the operation of some historically important policy groups. Unfortunately, the theory has certain conceptual limitations and (as we noted earlier) weak research support.

One alleged outcome of groupthink is the propensity to make risky decisions. For many years, this propensity was termed the "risky shift." But current research focuses on group polarization (the tendency of individuals' opinions to be more extreme after discussion than before) and group choice shifts (the tendency of group decisions to be more extreme than the average of members' initial opinions). Although polarization and choice shifts may be mediated by somewhat different mechanisms (Hinsz & Davis 1984; McGrath 1984), most reviewers treat them together. The available evidence suggests that persuasive argumentation and social comparison are the best general explanations for polarization and choice shifts (Isenberg 1986). These effects can also be analyzed by means of social combination models (e.g. Crott et al 1986), variable perspective theory (Ono & Davis 1988), and social identification theory (e.g. Mackie 1986).

Because so many problems can plague group decision-making, several techniques have been developed to help groups make better decisions. Some of these are simply computational schemes for combining members' preferences in ways that enhance group accuracy (e.g. Shapley & Grofman 1984). Other techniques involve some form of intervention in the group's activities. Perhaps the best-known intervention is brainstorming, in which group members are encouraged to suggest new ideas in a criticism-free environment. Unfortunately, brainstorming seems to be ineffective—nominal groups generally perform better than real groups (Diehl & Stroebe 1987). Recent research suggests that productivity loss in brainstorming groups is due to production blocking rather than "free riding" or evaluation apprehension (Diehl & Stroebe 1987) and that systematic relationships exist between vocal parameters of group discussion and the production of ideas (Ruback et al

1984). Research is being done on several other intervention techniques, including the Nominal Group Technique (Bartunek & Murnighan 1984), the Delphi process (e.g. Erffmeyer & Lane 1984), and applications of Social Judgment Theory (e.g. Cook & Hammond 1982). All of these techniques have strong advocates, but the boundary conditions for their effectiveness have not been established.

Participation in decision-making can affect how group members think and behave afterwards. Several studies show, for example, that initial group decisions influence subsequent decisions and that experienced decisionmakers behave differently from inexperienced ones (e.g. Davis 1984). Research also indicates that participation in group decision-making affects members' subsequent opinions about the discussion topic (e.g. Isenberg 1986; Sande & Zanna 1987). A few studies suggest that group members (and outsiders) often assume a close correspondence between a group's decision and the preferences of its members. Because of this "group attribution error," perceptions of opinions within a group are sometimes distorted (e.g. Allison & Messick 1987).

CONCLUSION

Having surveyed nearly a decade's worth of research on small groups, we conclude with two general observations that summarize our beliefs about the current state of the field and our expectations for its future.

Groups Are Alive and Well, but Living Elsewhere

Fifteen years ago, the social psychologist Ivan Steiner (1974) wrote an optimistic analysis of the future of group dynamics, arguing that the zeitgeist was favorable for a resurgence of interest in this important but neglected topic. Steiner (1986) recently concluded that his analysis was wrong. With the benefit of hindsight, he argued that social psychology is wedded to theories and research methods inimical to the study of small groups. Steiner also warned that "the group is too important to an understanding of human behavior and the workings of society to be forever neglected. If social psychologists do not research the group, someone else surely will" (p. 283).

In our opinion, Steiner's warning comes too late. Despite all the excellent research on small groups within social psychology, that discipline has already lost its dominance in this field. The torch has been passed to (or, more accurately, picked up by) colleagues in other disciplines, particularly organizational psychology. They have no doubts about the importance of small groups and are often in the forefront of group research. So, rather than lamenting the decline of interest in groups, we should all be celebrating its resurgence, albeit in a different locale.

There is Nothing So Good as a Practical Theory

Current research on small groups is based largely on practical concerns with improving their performance (cf Zander, 1982). Much of the world's work is done by small groups (e.g. juries, work units, army squads, athletic teams), so many people care deeply about this issue. A practical orientation to small groups should be welcomed, because it encourages researchers to tackle more complex and interesting problems than they might otherwise attempt. That orientation also has important (and largely positive) implications for theory, methodology, and funding.

Far from being atheoretical, most research on small groups is strongly tied to theory and meant to promote theoretical development. The main difference between current and older work is that more researchers are seeking to develop theories that can account for complex behavior in natural groups, rather than simple behavior in laboratory groups. A wide range of social psychological theories are applicable to small groups (e.g. Mullen & Goethals 1987), and alongside the traditional theoretical approaches, psychoanalytic, evolutionary, and systems theories are now becoming more popular (e.g. Barchas 1986; Smith & Berg 1987; Von Cranach et al 1986).

From a methodological viewpoint, a practical orientation to small groups is weakening the reliance of many researchers on laboratory experimentation and fostering the use of field research, observational techniques, and archival analyses. This trend seems likely to continue, as does the increasing use of computer simulations (e.g. Stasser 1988), thought experiments (e.g. Davis & Kerr 1986), and social network analyses (e.g. Willer & Anderson 1981). Researchers are also likely to make use of new methods for assessing and analyzing group process (e.g. Dabbs & Ruback 1987; Futoran et al 1989).

Because the effectiveness of work groups is so important to business and military organizations a practical orientation to small groups may improve prospects for research funding. This happy state of affairs, however, depends on two factors. The first, which researchers neither welcome nor control, is continued evidence that work groups performing critical tasks often fail tragically (cf Foushee, 1984). The second, which researchers both welcome and control, is evidence that we can make useful suggestions for improving group performance and preventing such tragedies.

ACKNOWLEDGMENTS

Preparation of this chapter was supported by OERI Contract N00014-85-K-0337 from the Office of Educational Research and Improvement, Department of Education, to the Learning Research and Development Center, University of Pittsburgh. Our thanks are extended to Deborah Connell and Dan Grech for their valuable assistance.

Literature Cited

Adams, J. B., Adams, J., Rice, R. W., Instone, D. 1985. Effects of perceived group effectiveness and group role on attributions of group performance. *J. Appl. Soc. Psychol.* 15:387–98

Albanese, R., Van Fleet, D. D. 1985. Rational behavior in groups: The free-riding tendency. *Acad. Mange. Rev.* 10:244–55

Alderfer, C. P., Smith, K. K. 1982. Studying intergroup relations embedded in organizations. *Adm. Sci. Q.* 27:35–65

Allison, S. T., Messick, D. M. 1987. From individual inputs to group outputs, and back again: Group processes and inferences about members. See Hendrick 1987, 8:111–43

Ancona, D. G. 1987. Groups in organizations: Extending laboratory models. See Hendrick 1987, 9:207–30

Ancona, D. G., Caldwell, D. F. 1988. Beyond task and maintenance: Defining external functions in groups. *Group Organ. Stud.* 13:468–94

Anderson, L. R., Blanchard, P. N. 1982. Sex differences in task and social-emotional behavior. *Basic Appl. Soc. Psychol.* 3:109–39

Argote, L. 1989. Agreement about norms and work unit effectiveness: Evidence from the field. *Basic Appl. Soc. Psychol.* 10:131–40

Argote, L., Beckman, S. L., Epple, D. 1990. The persistence and transfer of learning in organizational settings. *Manage. Sci.* In press

Argote, L., Turner, M. E., Fichman, M. 1988. To centralize or not to centralize: The effects of uncertainty and threat on group structure and performance. *Organ. Behav.* 42:1–17

Ashkanasy, N. M. 1989. Causal attribution and supervisors' response to subordinate performance: The Green and Mitchell model revisited. *J. Appl. Soc. Psychol.* 19:309–30

Bacharach, S. B., Lawler, E. J. 1981. *Bargaining: Power, Tactics, and Outcomes*. San Francisco: Jossey-Bass

Bales, R. F., Strodtbeck, F. L. 1951. Phases in group problem solving. *J. Abnorm. Soc. Psychol.* 46:485–95

Bantel, K. A., Jackson, S. E. 1989. Top management and innovations in banking: Does the composition of the top team make a difference? *Strat. Mange. J.* In press

Barchas, P. R. 1986. A sociophysiological orientation to small groups. See Lawler 1986, pp. 209–45

Barchas, P. R., Fisek, M. H. 1984. Hierarchical differentiation in newly formed groups of rhesus and humans. In *Essays Toward A Sociophysiological Perspective*, ed. P. R. Barchas, pp. 23–33. Westport: Greenwood Press

Bartunek, J. M., Murnighan, J. K. 1984. The nominal group technique: Expanding the basic procedure and underlying assumptions. *Group Organ. Stud.* 9:417–32

Baum, A., Paulus, P. B. 1987. Crowding. In *Handbook of Environmental Psychology*, ed. D. Stokols, I. Altman, pp. 533–70. New York: Wiley

Bazerman, M. H., Mannix, E., Sondak, H., Thompson, L. 1989. Negotiator behavior and decision processes in dyads, groups, and markets. In *Advances in Applied Social Psychology*, ed. J. S. Carroll, Vol. 4. Beverly Hills: Sage. In press

Ben-Yoav, O., Hollander, E. P., Carnevale, P. J. D. 1983. Leader legitimacy, leader-follower interaction, and followers' ratings of the leader. *J. Soc. Psychol.* 121:111–15

Ben-Yoav, O., Pruitt, D. G. 1984. Accountability to constituents: A two-edged sword. *Organ. Behav.* 34:283–95

Berger, J., Rosenholtz, S. J., Zelditch, M. 1980. Status organizing processes. *Annu. Rev. Sociol.* 6:479–508

Berger, J., Zelditch, M., eds. 1985. *Status, Rewards, and Influence*. San Francisco: Jossey-Bass

Berkowitz, L., ed. 1984. *Advances in Experimental Social Psychology*, Vol. 18. Orlando: Academic

Bettenhausen, K., Murnighan, J. K. 1985. The emergence of norms in competitive decision-making groups. *Adm. Sci. Q.* 30: 350–72

Blalock, H. M. 1984. Contextual-effects models: Theoretical and methodological issues. *Annu. Rev. Sociol.* 10:353–72

Blumberg, H. H., Hare, A. P., Kent, V., Davies, M. F., eds. 1983. *Small Groups and Social Interaction*, Vol. 1. Chichester: Wiley

Bonacich, P., Grusky, O., Peyrot, M. 1985. Family coalitions: A new approach and method. *Soc. Psychol. Q.* 48:42–50

Bottger, P. C. 1984. Expertise and air time as bases of actual and perceived influence in problem-solving groups. *J. Appl. Psychol.* 69:214–21

Bouma, G. D. 1980. Keeping the faithful: Patterns of membership retention in the Christian Reformed Church. *Sociol. Anal.* 41:259–64

Brandstatter, H., Davis, J. H., Stocker-Kreichgauer, G., eds. 1982. *Group Decision Making*. London: Academic

Brawley, L. R., Carron, A. V., Widmeyer, W. N. 1987. Assessing the cohesion of teams: Validity of the Group Environment Questionnaire. *J. Sport Psychol.* 9:275–94

Brawley, L. R., Carron, A. V., Widmeyer, W. N. 1988. Exploring the relationship between cohesion and group resistance to disruption. *J. Sport Exerc. Psychol.* 10:199–213

Brett, J. M. 1984. Job transitions and personal and role development. In *Research in Personnel and Human Resources Management,* ed. K. M. Rowland, G. R. Ferris, 2:155–85. Greenwich: JAI Press

Brickner, M. A., Harkins, S. G., Ostrom, T. M. 1986. Effects of personal involvement: Thought-provoking implications for social loafing. *J. Pers. Soc. Psychol.* 51:763–69

Brinkerhoff, M. B., Burke, K. L. 1980. Disaffiliation: Some notes on "falling from the faith." *Sociol. Anal.* 41:41–54

Bronfenbrenner, U. 1986. Ecology of the family as a context for human development: Research perspectives. *Dev. Psychol.* 22:737–42

Brown, B. B., Werner, C. M. 1985. Social cohesiveness, territoriality, and holiday decorations: The influence of cul-de-sacs. *Environ. Behav.* 17:539–65

Buller, P. F. 1986. The team building-task performance relation: Some conceptual and methodological refinements. *Group Organ. Stud.* 11:147–68

Burgess, J. W. 1984. Do humans show a "species-typical" group size? Age, sex, and environmental differences in the size and composition of naturally-occurring causal groups. *Ethol. Sociobiol.* 5:51–57

Burnstein, E., Berbaum, M. L. 1983. Stages in group decision making: The decomposition of historical narratives. *Polit. Psychol.* 4:531–61

Campbell, J. D., Tesser, A., Fairey, P. J. 1986. Conformity and attention to the stimulus: Some temporal and contextual dynamics. *J. Pers. Soc. Psychol.* 51:315–24

Caporael, L. R., Dawes, R. M., Orbell, J. M., van de Kragt, A. J. C. 1989. Selfishness examined: Cooperation in the absence of egoistic incentives. *Behav. Brain Sci.* In press

Carnevale, P. J. D. 1985. Accountability of group representatives and intergroup relations. See Lawler 1985, pp. 227–48

Carnevale, P. J. D. 1986. Mediating disputes and decisions in organizations. See Lewicki et al 1986, pp. 251–69

Carron, A. V., Chelladurai, P. 1981. The dynamics of group cohesion in sport. *J. Sport Psychol.* 3:123–39

Carron, A. V., Widmeyer, W. N., Brawley, L. R. 1985. The development of an instrument to assess cohesion in sports teams: The Group Environment Questionnaire. *J. Sport Psychol.* 7:244–67

Carron, A. V., Widmeyer, W. N., Brawley, L. R. 1988. Group cohesion and individual adherence to physical activity. *J. Sport Exerc. Psychol.* 10:127–38

Chaiken, S., Stangor, S. 1987. Attitudes and attitude change. *Annu. Rev. Psychol.* 38:575–630

Chemers, M. M. 1987. Leadership processes: Intrapersonal, interpersonal, and societal influences. See Hendrick 1987, 8:252–77

Chemers, M. M., Ayman, R. 1985. Leadership orientation as a moderator of the relationship between job performance and job satisfaction of Mexican managers. *Pers. Soc. Psychol. Bull.* 11:359–67

Chemers, M. M., Hays, R. B., Rhodewalt, F., Wysocki, J. 1985. A person-environment analysis of job stress: A contingency model explanation. *J. Pers. Soc. Psychol.* 49:628–35

Cissna, K. N. 1984. Phases in group development: The negative evidence. *Small Group Behav.* 15:3–32

Clark, M. S., Reis, H. T. 1988. Interpersonal processes in close relationships. *Annu. Rev. Psychol.* 39:609–72

Clark, N. K., Stephenson, G. M. 1989. Group remembering. See Paulus 1989, pp. 357–91

Clark, R. D. III, Maass, A. 1988. Social categorization in minority influence: The case of homosexuality. *Eur. J. Soc. Psychol.* 18:347–64

Cobb, A. T. 1984. An episodic model of power: Toward an integration of theory and research. *Acad. Manage. Rev.* 9:482–93

Conger, J. A., Kanungo, R. N., eds. 1988. *Charismatic Leadership: The Elusive Factor in Organizational Effectiveness.* San Francisco: Jossey-Bass

Cook, K. S., ed. 1987. *Social Exchange Theory.* Newbury Park: Sage

Cook, K. S., Emerson, R. M., Gillmore, M. R., Yamagishi, T. 1983. The distribution of power in exchange networks: Theory and experimental results. *Am. J. Sociol.* 89:275–305

Cook, K. S., Gillmore, M. R. 1984. Power, dependence, and coalitions. See Lawler 1984, pp. 27–58

Cook, R. L., Hammond, K. R. 1982. Interpersonal learning and interpersonal conflict reduction in decision-making groups. See Guzzo 1982, pp. 13–40

Craig, J. M., Sherif, C. W. 1986. The effectiveness of men and women in problem-solving groups as a function of group gender composition. *Sex Roles* 14:453–66

Crocker, J., McGraw, K. M. 1984. What's good for the goose is not good for the gander: Solo status as an obstacle to occupational achievement for males and females. *Am. Behav. Sci.* 27:357–69

Crott, H. W., Zuber, J. A., Schermer, T. 1986. Social decision schemes and choice shift: An analysis of group decisions among bets. *J. Exp. Soc. Psychol.* 22:1–21

Crouch, A., Yetton, P. 1988. Manager-subordinate dyads: Relationships among task and social contact, manager friendliness and subordinate performance in management groups. *Organ. Behav.* 41:65–82

Cummings, L. L., Staw, B. M., eds. 1983. *Research in Organizational Behavior*, Vol. 5. Greenwich: JAI Press

Cummings, L. L., Staw, B. M., eds. 1985. *Research in Organizational Behavior*, Vol. 7. Greenwich: JAI Press

Cummings, L. L., Staw, B. M., eds. 1987. *Research in Organizational Behavior*, Vol. 9. Greenwich: JAI Press

Cushman, P. 1986. The self besieged: Recruitment-indoctrination processes in restrictive groups. *J. Theor. Soc. Behav.* 16:1–32

Dabbs, J. M., Ruback, R. B. 1987. Dimensions of group process: Amount and structure of vocal interaction. *Adv. Exp. Soc. Psychol.* 20:123–69

Dansereau, F., Graen, G., Haga, W. J. 1975. A vertical dyad linkage approach to leadership within formal organizations: A longitudinal investigation of the role making process. *Organ. Behav.* 13:46–78

Davis, J. H. 1984. Order in the courtroom. In *Psychology and Law: Topics From an International Conference*, ed. D. J. Muller, D. E. Blackman, A. J. Chapman, pp. 251–65. New York: Wiley

Davis, J. H., Kerr, N. L. 1986. Thought experiments and the problem of sparse data in small-group performance research. See Goodman 1986, pp. 305–49

Davis, J. H., Stasson, M., Ono, K., Zimmerman, S. 1988. Effects of straw polls on group decision making: Sequential voting pattern, timing, and local majorities. *J. Pers. Soc. Psychol.* 55:918–26

Davis, P., Stern, D. 1980. Adaptation, survival, and the growth of the family business: An integrated systems perspective. *Hum. Relat.* 34:207–24

Dawes, R. M., Orbell, J. M., Simmons, R. T., van de Kragt, A. J. C. 1986. Organizing groups for collective action. *Am. Polit. Sci. Rev.* 80:1171–85

DeBiasio, A. R. 1986. Problem solving in triads composed of varying numbers of field-dependent and field-independent subjects. *J. Pers. Soc. Psychol.* 51:749–54

DeSanctis, G., Gallupe, B. 1987. A foundation for the study of group decision support systems. *Mange. Sci.* 33:589–609

Diamond, M. A., Allcorn, S. 1986. Role formation as defensive activity in bureaucratic organizations. *Polit. Psychol.* 7:709–32

Diehl, M., Stroebe, W. 1987. Productivity loss in brainstorming groups: Toward the solution of a riddle. *J. Pers. Soc. Psychol.* 53:497–509

Dienesch, R. M., Liden, R. C. 1986. Leader-member exchange model of leadership: A critique and further development. *Acad. Manage. Rev.* 11:618–34

Dion, K. L. 1985. Sex, gender, and groups: Selected issues. In *Women, Gender, and Social Psychology*, ed. V. E. O'Leary, R. K. Unger, B. S. Wallston, pp. 293–347. Hillsdale: Erlbaum

Doms, M., Van Avermaet, E. 1985. Social support and minority influence: The innovation effect reconsidered. See Moscovici et al 1985, pp. 53–74

Dovidio, J. F., Ellyson, S. L. 1985. Patterns of visual dominance behavior in humans. See Ellyson & Dovidio 1985, pp. 129–49

Drescher, S., Burlingame, G., Fuhriman, A. 1985. Cohesion: An odyssey in empirical understanding. *Small Group Behav.* 16:3–30

Driskell, J. E., Hogan, R., Salas, E. 1987. Personality and group performance. See Hendrick 1987, 9:91–112

Eagle, J., Newton, P. M. 1981. Scapegoating in small groups: An organizational approach. *Hum. Relat.* 34:283–301

Eagly, A. H. 1987. *Sex Differences in Social Behavior: A Social-Role Interpretation*. Hillsdale: Erlbaum

Eder, D. 1988. Building cohesion through collaborative narration. *Soc. Psychol. Q.* 51:225–35

Elliott, G. C., Meeker, B. F. 1986. Achieving fairness in the face of competing concerns: The different effects of individual and group characteristics. *J. Pers. Soc. Psychol.* 50:754–60

Ellyson, S. L., Dovidio, J. F., eds. 1985. *Power, Dominance, and Nonverbal Behavior*. New York: Springer-Verlag

Erffmeyer, R. C., Lane, I. M. 1984. Quality and acceptance of an evaluative task: The effects of four group decision-making formats. *Group Organ. Stud.* 9:509–29

Erickson, B. H. 1981. Secret societies and social structure. *Soc. Forces* 60:188–210

Erickson, R. C. 1986. Heterogeneous groups: A legitimate alternative. *Group* 10:21–26

Evans, N. J., Jarvis, P. A. 1980. Group cohesion: A review and re-evaluation. *Small Group Behav.* 11:359–70

Fairhurst, G., Snavely, B. K. 1983. Majority and token minority group relationships: Power acquisition and communication. *Acad. Mange. Rev.* 8:292–300

Farrell, M. P. 1982. Artists' circles and the development of artists. *Small Group Behav.* 13:452–74

Feld, S. L. 1982. Structural determinants of similarity among associates. *Am. Sociol. Rev.* 47:797–801

Feldman, D. C. 1984. The development and

enforcement of group norms. *Acad. Mange. Rev.* 9:47–53

Fiedler, F. 1978. The contingency model and the dynamics of the leadership process. *Adv. Exp. Soc. Psychol.* 11:59–112

Fiedler, F. E., Garcia, E. 1987. *New Approaches to Effective Leadership: Cognitive Resources and Organizational Performance.* New York: Wiley

Field, R. G. 1982. A test of the Vroom-Yetton normative model of leadership. *J. Appl. Psychol.* 67:523–32

Fine, G. A., Stoecker, R. 1985. Can the circle be unbroken? Small groups and social movements. See Lawler 1985, pp. 1–28

Fodor, E. M. 1985. The power motive, group conflict, and physiological arousal. *J. Pers. Soc. Psychol.* 49:1408–15

Fontana, L. 1985. Clique formation in a regional health planning agency. *Hum. Relat.* 38:895–910

Ford, J. B., Zelditch, M. Jr. 1988. A test of the law of anticipated reactions. *Soc. Psychol. Q.* 51:164–71

Foushee, H. C. 1984. Dyads and triads at 35,000 feet: Factors affecting group process and aircrew performance. *Am. Psychol.* 39:885–93

Fry, L. W., Kerr, S., Lee, C. 1986. Effects of different leader behaviors under different levels of task interdependence. *Hum. Relat.* 39:1067–82

Futoran, G. C., Kelly, J. R., McGrath, J. E. 1989. TEMPO: A time-based system for analysis of group interaction process. *Basic Appl. Soc. Psychol.* 10:In press

Gal, R., Manning, F. J. 1987. Morale and its components: A cross-national comparison. *J. Appl. Soc. Psychol.* 17:369–91

Geen, R. G. 1989. Alternative conceptions of social facilitation. See Paulus 1989, pp. 15–51

Geis, F. L., Boston, M. B., Hoffman, N. 1985. Sex of authority role models and achievement by men and women: Leadership performance and recognition. *J. Pers. Soc. Psychol.* 49:636–53

Gerard, H. B. 1985. When and how the minority prevails. See Moscovici et al 1985, pp. 171–86

Gersick, C. J. G. 1988. Time and transition in work teams: Toward a new model of group development. *Acad. Manage. J.* 31:9–41

Gioia, D. A., Sims, H. P. Jr. 1986. Cognition-behavior connections: Attribution and verbal behavior in leader-subordinate interactions. *Organ. Behav.* 37:197–229

Gladstein, D. L. 1984. Groups in context: A model of task group effectiveness. *Adm. Sci. Q.* 29:499–517

Gladstein, D. L., Reilly, N. P. 1985. Group decision making under threat: The tycoon game. *Acad. Manage. J.* 28:613–27

Gooding, R. Z., Wagner, J. A. 1985. A meta-analytic review of the relationship between size and performance: The productivity and efficiency of organizations and their sub-units. *Adm. Sci. Q.* 30:462–81

Goodman, P. S., ed. 1986. *Designing Effective Work Groups.* San Francisco: Jossey-Bass

Goodman, P. S., Devadas, R., Hughson, T. L. G. 1988. Groups and productivity: An analysis of self-managing teams. In *Productivity in Organizations,* ed. J. P. Campbell, pp. 295–327. San Francisco: Jossey-Bass

Goodman, P. S., Ravlin, E. C., Argote, L. 1986. Current thinking about groups: Setting the stage for new ideas. See Goodman 1986, pp. 1–33

Goodman, P. S., Ravlin, E., Schminke, M. 1987. Understanding groups in organizations. See Cummings & Staw 1987, pp. 121–73

Gormley, F. P., Aiello, J. R. 1982. Social density, interpersonal relationships, and residential crowding stress. *J. Appl. Soc. Psychol.* 12:222–36

Granovetter, M. S. 1973. The strength of weak ties. *Am. J. Sociol.* 78:1360–80

Graumann, C. F., Moscovici, S., eds. 1986. *Changing Conceptions of Leadership.* New York: Springer-Verlag

Graves, T. D., Graves, N. B., Semu, V. N., Sam, I. A. 1982. Patterns of public drinking in a multiethnic society: A systematic observational study. *J. Stud. Alcohol* 43:990–1009

Gray, L. N., Griffith, W. I., von Broembsen, M. H., Sullivan, M. J. 1982. Group differentiation: Temporal effects of reinforcement. *Soc. Psychol. Q.* 45:44–49

Green, S. G., Mitchell, T. R. 1979. Attributional processes of leaders in leader-member interactions. *Organ. Behav.* 23:429–58

Greenbaum, P. E., Greenbaum, S. D. 1981. Territorial personalization: Group identity and social interaction in a Slavic-American neighborhood. *Environ. Behav.* 13:574–89

Greene, C. N., Schriesheim, C. A. 1980. Leader-group interactions: A longitudinal field investigation. *J. Appl. Psychol.* 65:50–59

Greenhalgh, L. 1983. Organizational decline. In *Research in the Sociology of Orgnaizations,* ed. S. B. Bacharach, 2:231–76. Greenwich: JAI Press

Greer, D. L. 1983. Spectator booing and the home advantage: A study of social influence in the basketball arena. *Soc. Psychol. Q.* 46:252–61

Griffin, R. W. 1987. Toward an integrated theory of task design. See Cummings & Staw 1987, pp. 79–120

Griffin, R. W., Skivington, K. D., Moorhead,

G. 1987. Symbolic and international perspectives on leadership: An integrative framework. *Hum. Relat.* 40:199–218

Guzzo, R. A., ed. 1982. *Improving Group Decision Making in Organizations.* New York: Academic

Guzzo, R. A., Jette, R. D., Katzell, R. A. 1985. The effects of psychologically based intervention programs on worker productivity: A meta-analysis. *Personnel Psychol.* 38:275–91

Haber, G. M. 1982. Spatial relations between dominants and marginals. *Soc. Psychol. Q.* 45:219–28

Hackman, J. R. 1987. The design of work teams. In *Handbook of Organizational Behavior,* ed. J. Lorsch, pp. 315–42. Englewood Cliffs: Prentice-Hall

Hackman, J. R., Walton, R. E. 1986. Leading groups in organizations. See Goodman 1986, pp. 72–119

Hall, D. T. 1986. Dilemmas in linking succession planning to individual executive learning. *Hum. Resour. Manage.* 25:235–65

Hare, A. P. 1981. Group size. *Am. Behav. Sci.* 24:695–708

Harkins, S. G., Petty, R. E. 1982. Effects of task difficulty and task uniqueness on social loafing. *J. Pers. Soc. Psychol.* 43:1214–29

Harkins, S. G., Szymanski, K. 1987. Social loafing and social facilitation: New wine in old bottles. See Hendrick 1987, 9:167–88

Harper, R. G. 1985. Power, dominance, and nonverbal behavior: An overview. See Ellyson & Dovidio 1985, pp. 29–48

Harrison, A. A., Connors, M. M. 1984. Groups in exotic environments. See Berkowitz 1984, pp. 49–87

Hastie, R., Penrod, S. D., Pennington, N. 1983. *Inside the Jury.* Cambridge: Harvard Univ. Press

Hegtvedt, K. A., Cook, K. S. 1987. The role of justice in conflict situations. See Lawler & Markovsky 1987, pp. 109–36

Henderson, M., Argyle, M. 1986. The informal rules of working relationships. *J. Occup. Behav.* 7:259–75

Henderson, W. D. 1985. *Cohesion: The Human Element in Combat.* Washington: National Defense Univ. Press

Hendrick, C., ed. 1987. *Review of Personality and Social Psychology.* Vols. 8, 9. Newbury Park: Sage

Hill, G. W. 1982. Group versus individual performance: Are $N + 1$ heads better than one? *Psychol. Bull.* 91:517–39

Hiltz, S. R., Johnson, K., Turoff, M. 1986. Experiments in group decision making: Communication process and outcome in face-to-face versus computerized conferences. *Hum. Commun. Res.* 13:225–52

Hinsz, V. B., Davis, J. H. 1984. Persuasive arguments theory, group polarization, and choice shifts. *Pers. Soc. Psychol. Bull.* 10:260–68

Hirokawa, R. Y. 1983. Group communication and problem-solving effectiveness: An investigation of group phases. *Hum. Commun. Res.* 9:291–305

Hogg, M. 1987. Social identity and group cohesiveness. In *Rediscovering the Social Group: A Self-Categorization Theory,* ed. J. C. Turner, pp. 89–116. Oxford: Basil Blackwell

Hollander, E. P. 1985. Leadership and power. See Lindzey & Aronson 1985, pp. 485–537

House, R. J. 1971. A path-goal theory of leader effectiveness. *Adm. Sci. Q.* 16:321–38

Humphrey, R. 1985. How work roles influence perception: Structural-cognitive processes and organizational behavior. *Am. Sociol. Rev.* 50:242–52

Hunt, J. G., Baliga, B. R., Dachler, H. P., Schriesheim, C. A., eds. 1988. *Emerging Leadership Vistas.* Lexington: D.C. Heath

Insko, C. A., Gilmore, R., Drenana, S., Lipsitz, A., Moehle, D., et al. 1983. Trade versus expropriation in open groups: A comparison of two types of social power. *J. Pers. Soc. Psychol.* 44:977–99

Insko, C. A., Gilmore, R., Moehle, D., Lipsitz, A., Drenan, S., et al. 1982. Seniority in the generational transition of laboratory groups: The effects of social familiarity and task experience. *J. Exp. Soc. Psychol.* 18:557–80

Insko, C. A., Pinkley, R. L., Hoyle, R. H., Dalton, B., Hong, G., et al. 1987. Individual versus group discontinuity: The role of intergroup contact. *J. Exp. Soc. Psychol.* 23:250–67

Insko, C. A., Smith, R. H., Alicke, M. D., Wade, J., Taylor, S. 1985. Conformity and group size: The concern with being right and the concern with being liked. *Pers. Soc. Psychol. Bull.* 11:41–50

Insko, C. A., Thibaut, J. W., Moehle, D., Wilson, M., Diamond, W. D., et al. 1980. Social evolution and the emergence of leadership. *J. Pers. Soc. Psychol.* 39:431–48

Instone, D., Major, B., Bunker, B. B. 1983. Gender, self confidence, and social influence strategies: An organizational simulation. *J. Pers. Soc. Psychol.* 44:322–33

Isenberg, D. J. 1981. Some effects of time-pressure on vertical structure and decision-making accuracy in small groups. *Organ. Behav. Hum. Perform.* 27:119–34

Isenberg, D. J. 1986. Group polarization: A critical review and meta-analysis. *J. Pers. Soc. Psychol.* 50:1141–51

Isenberg, D. J., Ennis, J. B. 1981. Perceiving group members: A comparison of derived and imposed dimensions. *J. Pers. Soc. Psychol.* 41:293–305

Izraeli, D. N. 1983. Sex effects or structural effects? An empirical test of Kanter's theory of proportions. *Soc. Forces* 62:153–65

Jackson, J. M. 1965. Structural characteristics of norms. In *Current Studies in Social Psychology*, ed. I. D. Steiner, M. Fishbein, pp. 301–9. New York: Holt, Rinehart, & Winston

Jackson, S. E., Schuler, R. S. 1985. A meta-analysis and conceptual critique of research on role ambiguity and role conflict in work settings. *Organ. Behav.* 36:16–78

Jacobi, M., Stokols, D. 1983. The role of tradition in group-environment relations. In *Environmental Psychology: Directions and Perspectives*, ed. N. R. Feimer, E. S. Geller, pp. 157–79. New York: Praeger

Jacobsen, C., Van der Voordt, T. J. M. 1980. Interpreting modal frequencies to measure social norms. *Sociol. Methods Res.* 8:470–86

Janis, I. L. 1982. *Groupthink*. Boston: Houghton Mifflin. 2nd ed.

Jorgensen, D. L., Jorgensen, L. 1982. Social meanings of the occult. *Sociol. Q.* 23:373–89

Kahan, J. P., Rapoport, A. 1984. *Theories of Coalition Formation*. Hillsdale: Erlbaum

Kanter, R. M. 1977. Some effects of proportions on group life: Skewed sex ratios and responses to token women. *Am. J. Sociol.* 82:965–90

Kaplan, M. F. 1987. The influencing process in group decision making. See Hendrick 1987, 8:189–212

Katz, R. 1982. The effects of group longevity on project communication and performance. *Adm. Sci. Q.* 27:81–104

Keating, C. F. 1985. Human dominance signals: The primate in us. See Ellyson & Dovidio 1985, pp. 89–108

Keller, R. T. 1986. Predictors of the performance of project groups in R & D organizations. *Acad. Manage. J.* 29:715–26

Kelly, J., McGrath, J. E. 1985. Effects of time limits and task types on task performance and interaction of four-person groups. *J. Pers. Soc. Psychol.* 49:395–407

Kenny, D. A. 1985. The generalized group effect model. In *Individual Development and Social Change: Exploratory Analysis*, ed. J. Nesselroade, A. von Eye, pp. 343–57. Orlando: Academic

Kenny, D. A., Zaccaro, S. J. 1983. An estimate of variance due to traits in leadership. *J. Appl. Psychol.* 68:678–85

Kerr, N. L. 1983. Motivation losses in task-performing groups: A social dilemma analysis. *J. Pers. Soc. Psychol.* 45:819–28

Kerr, N. L. 1986. Motivational choices in task groups: A paradigm for social dilemma research. See Wilke et al 1986, pp. 1–27

Kerr, N. L. 1989a. Illusions of efficacy: The effects of group size on perceived efficacy in social dilemmas. *J. Exp. Soc. Psychol.* 25:287–313

Kerr, N. L. 1989b. Norms in social dilemmas. In *Social Dilemmas: Social Psychological Perspectives*, ed. D. Schroeder. New York: Praeger. In press

Kerr, N. L., Bruun, S. E. 1981. Ringelmann revisited: Alternative explanations for the social loafing effect. *Pers. Soc. Psychol. Bull.* 7:224–31

Kerr, N. L., Bruun, S. E. 1983. Dispensability of member effort and group motivation losses: Free-rider effects. *J. Pers. Soc. Psychol.* 44:78–94

Kerr, N. L., MacCoun, R. J., Hansen, C. H., Hymes, J. A. 1987. Gaining and losing social support: Momentum in decision-making groups. *J. Exp. Soc. Psychol.* 23:119–45

Kiesler, S., Siegel, J., McGuire, T. W. 1984. Social psychological aspects of computer-mediated communication. *Am. Psychol.* 39:1123–34

Kipnis, D. 1984. The use of power in organizations and in interpersonal settings. See Oskamp 1984, pp. 179–210

Kipnis, D., Schmidt, S. 1983. An influence perspective on bargaining within organizations. In *Negotiating in Organizations*, ed. M. H. Bazerman, R. J. Lewicki, pp. 303–19. Beverly Hills: Sage

Kirchler, E., Davis, J. H. 1986. The influence of member status differences and task type on group consensus and member position change. *J. Pers. Soc. Psychol.* 51:83–91

Komorita, S. S. 1984a. Coalition bargaining. See Berkowitz 1984, pp. 183–245

Komorita, S. S. 1984b. The role of justice and power in reward allocation. In *Progress in Applied Social Psychology*, ed. G. M. Stephenson, J. H. Davis, 2:185–206. Chichester: Wiley

Komorita, S. S., Ellis, A. L. 1988. Level of aspiration in coalition bargaining. *J. Pers. Soc. Psychol.* 54:421–31

Komorita, S. S., Miller, C. E. 1986. Bargaining strength as a function of coalition alternatives. *J. Pers. Soc. Psychol.* 51:325–32

Komorita, S. S., Nagao, D. 1983. The functions of resources in coalition bargaining. *J. Pers. Soc. Psychol.* 44:95–106

Konar, E., Sundstrom, E., Brady, K., Mandel, D., Rice, R. 1982. Status demarcation in the office. *Environ. Behav.* 14:561–80

Kramer, R. M., Brewer, M. B. 1986. Social group identity and the emergence of cooperation in resource conservation dilemmas. See Wilke et al 1986, pp. 205–34

Krantz, J. 1985. Group process under conditions of organizational decline. *J. Appl. Behav. Sci.* 21:1–17

Kravitz, D. A. 1987. Size of smallest coalition

as a source of power in coalition bargaining. *Eur. J. Soc. Psychol.* 17:1–21

Kruglanski, A., Mackie, D. M. 1989. Majority and minority influence: A judgmental process analysis. In *Advances in European Social Psychology*, ed. W. Stroebe, M. Hewstone. London: Wiley. In press

Lacoursiere, R. B. 1980. *The Life Cycle of Groups: Group Developmental Stage Theory*. New York: Human Sci. Press

Landers, D. M., Wilkinson, M. O., Hatfield, B. D., Barber, H. 1982. Causality and the cohesion-performance relationship. *J. Sport Psychol.* 4:170–83

Larson, J. R. Jr., Lingle, J. H., Scerbo, M. M. 1984. The impact of performance cues on leader-behavior ratings: The role of selective information availability and probabilistic response bias. *Organ. Behav.* 33:323–49

Latane, B. 1981. The psychology of social impact. *Am. Psychol.* 36:343–56

Latane, B., Wolf, S. 1981. The social impact of majorities and minorities. *Psychol. Rev.* 88:438–53

Laughlin, P. R., Ellis, A. L. 1986. Demonstrability and social combination processes on mathematical intellective tasks. *J. Exp. Soc. Psychol.* 22:177–89

Laughlin, P. R., Futoran, G. C. 1985. Collective induction: Social combination and sequential transition. *J. Pers. Soc. Psychol.* 48:608–13

Laughlin, P. R., McGlynn, R. P. 1986. Collective induction: Mutual group and individual influence by exchange of hypotheses and evidence. *J. Exp. Soc. Psychol.* 22:567–89

Lawler, E. J. 1983. Cooptation and threats as "divide and rule" tactics. *Soc. Psychol. Q.* 46:89–98

Lawler, E. J., ed. 1984. *Advances in Group Processes*, Vol. 1. Greenwich: JAI Press

Lawler, E. J., ed. 1985. *Advances in Group Processes*, Vol. 2. Greenwich: JAI Press

Lawler, E. J., ed. 1986. *Advances in Group Processes*, Vol. 3. Greenwich: JAI Press

Lawler, E. J., Markovsky, B., eds. 1987. *Advances in Group Processes*, Vol. 4. Greenwich: JAI Press

Leary, M. R., Forsyth, D. R. 1987. Attributions of responsibility for collective endeavors. See Hendrick 1987, 8:167–88

Leary, M. R., Robertson, R. B., Barnes, B. D., Miller, R. S. 1986. Self-presentations of small group leaders: Effects of role requirements and leadership orientation. *J. Pers. Soc. Psychol.* 51:742–48

Lee, M. T., Ofshe, R. 1981. The impact of behavioral style and status characteristics on social influence: A test of two competing theories. *Soc. Psychol. Q.* 44:73–82

Levine, J. M. 1989. Reaction to opinion deviance in small groups. See Paulus 1989, pp. 187–231

Levine, J. M., Moreland, R. L. 1985. Innovation and socialization in small groups. See Moscovici et al 1985, pp. 143–69

Levine, J. M., Moreland, R. L. 1987. Social comparison and outcome evaluation in group contexts. In *Social Comparison, Social Justice, and Relative Deprivation: Theoretical, Empirical, and Policy Perspectives*, ed. J. C. Masters, W. P. Smith, pp. 105–27. Hillsdale: Erlbaum

Levine, J. M., Ruback, R. B. 1980. Reaction to opinion deviance: Impact of a fence straddler's rationale on majority evaluation. *Soc. Psychol. Q.* 43:73–81

Levine, J. M., Russo, E. M. 1987. Majority and minority influence. See Hendrick 1987, 8:13–54

Lewicki, R. J., Sheppard, B. H., Bazerman, M. H., eds. 1986. *Research on Negotiation in Organizations*, Vol. 1. Greenwich: JAI Press

Liebrand, W. B. G. 1986. The ubiquity of social values in social dilemmas. See Wilke et al 1986, pp. 113–33

Lindzey, G., Aronson, E., eds. 1985. *The Handbook of Social Psychology*, Vol. 2. New York: Random House. 3rd ed.

Locke, E. A., Shaw, K. N., Saari, L. M., Latham, G. P. 1981. Goal setting and task performance: 1969–1980. *Psychol. Bull.* 90:125–52

Lofland, J., Jamison, M. 1984. Social movement locals: Modal member structures. *Sociol. Anal.* 45:115–29

Long, S. 1984. Early integration in groups: "A group to join and a group to create." *Hum. Relat.* 37:311–32

Lord, R. G. 1985. An information processing approach to social perceptions, leadership and behavioral measurement in organizations. See Cummings & Staw 1985, pp. 87–128

Lord, R. G., Saenz, D. S. 1985. Memory deficits and memory surfeits: Differential cognitive consequences of tokenism for tokens and observers. *J. Pers. Soc. Psychol.* 49:918–26

Lortie-Lussier, M. 1987. Minority influence and idiosyncrasy credit: A new comparison of the Moscovici and Hollander theories of innovation. *Eur. J. Soc. Psychol.* 17:431–46

Maass, A., West, S. G., Cialdini, R. B. 1987. Minority influence and conversion. See Hendrick 1987, 8:55–79

Mabry, E. 1985. The effects of gender composition and task structure on small group interaction. *Small Group Behav.* 16:75–96

Mackie, D. M. 1986. Social identification effects in group polarization. *J. Pers. Soc. Psychol.* 50:720–28

Mackie, D. M. 1987. Systematic and nonsystematic processing of majority and minority persuasive communications. *J. Pers. Soc. Psychol.* 53:41–52

Mackie, D. M., Goethals, G. R. 1987. Individual and groups goals. See Hendrick 1987, 8:144–66

Magaro, P. A., Ashbrook, R. M. 1985. The personality of societal groups. *J. Pers. Soc. Psychol.* 48:1479–89

Mann, L. 1980. Cross-cultural studies of small groups. In *Handbook of Cross-Cultural Psychology,* ed. H. C. Triandis, R. W. Brislin, 5:155–209. Boston: Allyn & Bacon

Manning, F. J., Fullerton, T. D. 1988. Health and well-being in highly cohesive units of the U. S. Army. *J. Appl. Social. Psychol.* 18:503–19

Markham, S. E., Dansereau, F., Alutto, J. A. 1982. Group size and absenteeism rates: A longitudinal analysis. *Acad. Manage. J.* 25:921–27

Marks, M. L., Mirvis, P. H., Hackett, E. J., Grady, J. F. 1986. Employee participation in a Quality Circle program: Impact on quality of work life, productivity, and absenteeism. *J. Appl. Psychol.* 71:61–69

Martin, P. Y., Shanahan, K. A. 1983. Transcending the effects of sex composition in small groups. *Social Work Groups* 6:19–32

Mazur, A. 1985. A biosocial model of status in face-to-face groups. *Soc. Forces* 64:377–402

McCauley, C. 1989. The nature of social influence in groupthink: Compliance and internalization. *J. Pers. Soc. Psychol.* 57: 250–60

McClintock, C. G., Stech, F. J., Keil, L. J. 1983. The influence of communication on bargaining. In *Basic Group Processes,* ed. P. B. Paulus, pp. 205–33. New York: Springer-Verlag

McGrath, J. E. 1984. *Groups: Interaction and Performance.* Englewood Cliffs: Prentice-Hall. 302 pp.

McGrath, J. E., ed. 1988. *The Social Psychology of Time: New Perspectives.* Newbury Park: Sage

McGrath, J. E., Kelley, J. R., Machatka, D. E. 1984. The social psychology of time: Entrainment of behavior in social and organizational settings. See Oskamp 1984, pp. 21–44

McGrath, J. E., Kravitz, D. A. 1982. Group research. *Annu. Rev. Psychol.* 33:195–230

McGrath, J. E., Rotchford, N. 1983. Time and behavior in organizations. See Cummings & Staw 1983, pp. 57–101

McGuire, T. W., Kiesler, S., Siegel, J. 1987. Group and computer-mediated discussion effects on risk decision making. *J. Pers. Soc. Psychol.* 52:917–30

McKirnan, D. J. 1980. The identification of

deviance: A conceptualization and initial test of a model of social norms. *Eur. J. Soc. Psychol.* 10:75–93

McKirnan, D. J. 1984. The identification of alcohol problems: Socioeconomic status differences in social norms and causal attributions. *Am. J. Commun. Psychol.* 12:465–84

McPherson, J. M. 1983. The size of voluntary associations. *Soc. Forces* 61:1044–64

McPherson, J. M., Smith-Lovin, L. 1986. Sex segregation in voluntary associations. *Am. Sociol. Rev.* 51:61–79

Meindl, J. R., Ehrlich, S. B., Dukerich, J. M. 1985. The romance of leadership. *Adm. Sci. Q.* 30:78–102

Messick, D. M., Brewer, M. B. 1983. Solving social dilemmas: A review. In *Review of Personality and Social Psychology,* ed. L. Wheeler, P. Shaver, 4:11–44. Beverly Hills: Sage

Messick, D. M., Mackie, D. M. 1989. Intergroup relations. *Annu. Rev. Psychol.* 40:45–81

Miesing, P., Preble, J. F. 1985. Group processes and performance in a complex business simulation. *Small Group Behav.* 16: 325–38

Miller, C. E. 1989. The social psychological effects of group decision rules. See Paulus 1989, pp. 327–55

Miller, C. E., Komorita, S. S. 1986a. Changes in outcomes in coalition bargaining. *J. Pers. Soc. Psychol.* 51:721–29

Miller, C. E., Komorita, S. S. 1986b. Coalition formation in organizations: What laboratory studies do and do not tell us. See Lewicki et al 1986, pp. 117–37

Miller, C. E., Wong, J. 1986. Coalition behavior: Effects of earned versus unearned resources. *Organ. Behav.* 38:257–77

Miller, R. S., Schlenker, B. R. 1985. Egotism in group members: Public and private attributions of responsibility for group performance. *Soc. Psychol. Q.* 48:85–89

Mohr, P. 1986. Demeanor, status cue, or performance? *Soc. Psychol. Q.* 49:228–36

Molm, L. D., 1987. Power-dependence theory: Power processes and negative outcomes. See Lawler & Markovsky 1987, pp. 171–98

Moore, J. C. 1985. Role enactment and self identity. See Berger & Zelditch 1985, pp. 262–316

Moreland, R. L. 1985. Social categorization and the assimilation of "new" group members. *J. Pers. Soc. Psychol.* 48:1173–90

Moreland, R. L. 1987. The formation of small groups. See Hendrick 1987, 8:80–109

Moreland, R. L., Levine, J. M. 1982. Socialization in small groups: Temporal changes in individual-group relations. *Adv. Exp. Soc. Psychol.* 15:137–92

Moreland, R. L., Levine, J. M. 1984. Role

transitions in small groups. In *Role Transitions: Explorations and Explanations,* ed. V. L. Allen, E. van de Vliert, pp. 181–95. New York: Plenum

Moreland, R. L., Levine, J. M. 1988. Group dynamics over time: Development and socialization in small groups. See McGrath 1988, pp. 151–81

Moreland, R. L., Levine, J. M. 1989. Newcomers and oldtimers in small groups. See Paulus 1989, pp. 143–86

Moscovici, S. 1985. Social influence and conformity. See Lindzey & Aronson 1985, pp. 347–412

Moscovici, S., Mugny, G., Van Avermaet, E., eds. 1985. *Perspectives on Minority Influence.* Cambridge: Cambridge Univ. Press

Mugny, G. 1982. *The Power of Minorities.* New York: Academic

Mugny, G. 1985. Direct and indirect influence in the Asch paradigm: Effects of "valid" or "denied" information. *Eur. J. Soc. Psychol.* 15:457–61

Mullen, B. 1983. Operationalizing the effect of the group on the individual: A self-attention perspective. *J. Exp. Soc. Psychol.* 19:295–322

Mullen, B. 1987. Self-attention theory: The effects of group composition on the individual. See Mullen & Goethals 1987, pp. 125–46

Mullen, B., Baumeister, R. F. 1987. Group effects on self-attention and performance: Social loafing, social facilitation, and social impairment. See Hendrick 1987, 9:189–206

Mullen, B., Goethals, G. R., eds. 1987. *Theories of Group Behavior.* New York: Springer-Verlag

Murnighan, J. K. 1986. Organizational coalitions: Structural contingencies and the formation process. See Lewicki et al 1986, pp. 155–73

Nagao, D. H., Davis, J. H. 1980. Some implications of temporal drift in small parameters. *J. Exp. Soc. Psychol.* 16:479–96

Nail, P. R., Cole, S. G. 1985. A critical comparison of bargaining theory and the weighted probability model of coalition behaviour. *Br. J. Soc. Psychol.* 24:259–66

Nemeth, C. 1986. Differential contributions of majority and minority influence. *Psychol. Rev.* 93:23–32

Nemeth, C., Brilmayer, A. G. 1987. Negotiation versus influence. *Eur. J. Soc. Psychol.* 17:45–56

Nemeth, C., Kwan, J. L. 1985. Originality of word associations as a function of majority vs. minority influence. *Soc. Psychol. Q.* 48:277–82

Nemeth, C. J., Staw, B. M. 1989. The tradeoffs of social control and innovation in

groups and organizations. *Adv. Exp. Soc. Psychol.* 22:175–210

Nicholson, N. 1984. A theory of work role transitions. *Adm. Sci. Q.* 29:172–91

Oldham, G., Rotchford, N. L. 1983. Relationships between office characteristics and employee reactions: A study of the physical environment. *Adm. Sci. Q.* 28:542–56

Ono, K., Davis, J. H. 1988. Individual judgment and group interaction: A variable perspective approach. *Organ. Behav.* 41:211–32

Opp, K. D. 1982. The evolutionary emergence of norms. *Br. J. Soc. Psychol.* 21:139–49

Orbell, J., Dawes, R. 1981. Social dilemmas. In *Progress in Applied Social Psychology,* ed. G. M. Stephenson, J. H. Davis, 1:37–65. Chichester: Wiley

Orbell, J. M., van de Kragt, A. J. C., Dawes, R. M. 1988. Explaining discussion-induced cooperation. *J. Pers. Soc. Psychol.* 54:811–19

O'Reilly, C. A., Caldwell, D. F. 1985. The impact of normative social influence and cohesiveness on task perceptions and attitudes: A social-information processing approach. *J. Occup. Psychol.* 58:193–206

Oskamp, S., ed. 1984. *Applied Social Psychology Annual,* Vol. 5. Beverly Hills: Sage

Owen, W. F. 1985. Metaphor analysis of cohesiveness in small discussion groups. *Small Group Behav.* 16:415–24

Patterson, A. H. 1986. Scientific jury selection: The need for a case specific approach. *Soc. Action Law* 11:105–9

Paulus, P. B., ed. 1989. *Psychology of Group Influence.* Hillsdale: Erlbaum. 2nd ed.

Paulus, P. B., Nagar, D. 1989. Environmental influences on groups. See Paulus 1989, pp. 111–42

Pavelchak, M. A., Moreland, R. L., Levine, J. M. 1986. Effects of prior group memberships on subsequent reconnaissance activities. *J. Pers. Soc. Psychol.* 50:56–66

Pearson, C. A. L. 1987. Participative goal setting as a strategy for improving performance and job satisfaction: A longitudinal evaluation with railway track maintenance gangs. *Hum. Relat.* 40:473–88

Peters, L. H., Hartke, D. D., Pohlmann, J. T. 1985. Fiedler's contingency theory of leadership: An application of the meta-analysis procedures of Schmidt and Hunter. *Psychol. Bull.* 97:274–85

Pfeffer, J. 1983. Organizational demography. See Cummings & Staw 1983, pp. 299–357

Pinto, L. J., Crow, K. E. 1982. The effect of size on other structural attributes of congregations within the same denomination. *J. Sci. Study Relig.* 21:304–16

Piper, W. E., Marrache, M., LaCroix, R., Richardsen, A. M., Jones, B. D. 1983.

Cohesion as a basic bond in groups. *Hum. Relat.* 36:93–108

Podsakoff, P. M., Schriesheim, C. A. 1985. Field studies of French and Raven's bases of power: Critique, reanalysis, and suggestions for future research. *Psychol. Bull.* 97:387–411

Podsakoff, P. M., Todor, W. D. 1985. Relationships between leader reward and punishment behavior and group processes and productivity. *J. Manage.* 11:55–73

Poole, M. S., Seibold, D. R., McPhee, R. D. 1985. Group decision-making as a structurational process. *Q. J. Speech* 71:74–102

Porter, N., Geis, F. L., Cooper, E., Newman, E. 1985. Androgyny and leadership in mixed-sex groups. *J. Pers. Soc. Psychol.* 49:808–23

Prentice-Dunn, S., Rogers, R. W. 1989. Deindividuation and the self-regulation of behavior. See Paulus 1989, pp. 87–109

Price, K. H., Garland, H. 1981. Influence mode and competence: Compliance with leader suggestions. *Pers. Soc. Psychol. Bull.* 7:117–122

Pruitt, D. G. 1981. *Negotiation Behavior.* New York: Academic

Pruitt, D. G., Rubin, J. Z. 1986. *Social Conflict: Escalation, Stalemate, and Settlement.* New York: Random House

Rapoport, A. 1987. Research paradigms and expected utility models for the provision of step-level public goods. *Psychol. Rev.* 94:74–83

Rees, C. R., Segal, M. W. 1984. Role differentiation in groups: The relationship between instrumental and expressive leadership. *Small Group Behav.* 15:109–23

Reitzes, D. C., Diver, J. K. 1982. Gay bars as deviant community organizations: The management of interactions with outsiders. *Deviant Behav.* 4:1–18

Rice, R. W., Marwick, N. J., Chemers, M. M., Bentley, J. C. 1982. Task performance and satisfaction: Least preferred coworker (LPC) as a moderator. *Pers. Soc. Psychol. Bull.* 8:534–41

Ridgeway, C. L. 1981. Nonconformity, competence, and influence in groups: A test of two theories. *Am. Sociol. Rev.* 46:333–47

Ridgeway, C. L. 1982. Status in groups: The importance of motivation. *Am. Sociol. Rev.* 47:76–88

Ridgeway, C. L. 1984. Dominance, performance, and status in groups. See Lawler 1984, pp. 59–93

Ridgeway, C. L. 1987. Nonverbal behavior, dominance, and the basis of status in task groups. *Am. Sociol. Rev.* 52:683–94

Roger, D. B., Reid, R. L. 1982. Role differentiation and seating arrangements: A further study. *Br. J. Soc. Psychol.* 21:23–29

Rossi, P. H., Berk, R. A. 1985. Varieties of normative consensus. *Am. Sociol. Rev.* 50:333–47

Rousseau, D. M. 1985. Issues of level in organizational research: Multi-level and cross-level perspectives. See Cummings & Staw 1985, pp. 1–37

Royal, E. G., Golden, S. B. 1981. Attitude similarity and attraction to an employee group. *Psychol. Rep.* 48:251–54

Ruback, R. B., Dabbs, J. M., Hopper, C. H. 1984. The process of brainstorming: An analysis with individual and group vocal parameters. *J. Pers. Soc. Psychol.* 47:558–67

Rubin, J. Z., ed. 1981. *Dynamics of Third Party Intervention: Kissinger in the Middle East.* New York: Praeger

Ruder, M. K., Gill, D. L. 1982. Immediate effects of win-loss on perceptions of cohesion in intramural and intercollegiate volleyball teams. *J. Sport Psychol.* 4:227–34

Rush, M. C., Russell, J. E. A. 1988. Leader prototypes and prototype-contingent consensus in leader behavior descriptions. *J. Exp. Soc. Psychol.* 24:88–104

Rutkowski, G. K., Gruder, C. L., Romer, D. 1983. Group cohesiveness, social norms, and bystander intervention. *J. Pers. Soc. Psychol.* 44:545–52

Rutte, C. G., Wilke, H. A. M., Messick, D. M. 1987. The effects of framing social dilemmas as give-some or take-some games. *Br. J. Soc. Psychol.* 26:103–8

Salancik, G., Pfeffer, J. 1978. A social information processing approach to job attitudes and task design. *Adm. Sci. Q.* 23:224–53

Samuelson, C. D., Messick, D. M. 1986. Inequities in access to and use of share resources in social dilemmas. *J. Pers. Soc. Psychol.* 51:960–67

Samuelson, C. D., Messick, D. M., Rutte, C. G., Wilke, H. 1984. Individual and structural solutions to resource dilemmas in two cultures. *J. Pers. Soc. Psychol.* 47:94–104

Samuelson, C. D., Messick, D. M., Wilke, H. A. M., Rutte, C. G. 1986. Individual restraint and structural change as solutions to social dilemmas. See Wilke et al 1986, pp. 29–53

Sande, G. N., Ellard, J. W., Ross, M. 1986. Effect of arbitrarily assigned status labels on self-perceptions and social perceptions: The mere position effect. *J. Pers. Soc. Psychol.* 50:684–89

Sande, G. N., Zanna, M. P. 1987. Cognitive dissonance theory: Collective actions and individual reactions. See Mullen & Goethals 1987, pp. 49–69

Schneier, C. E., Goktepe, J. R. 1983. Issues in emergent leadership: The contingency model of leadership, leader sex, and leader behavior. See Blumberg et al 1983, pp. 413–21

Schoonhoven, C. B. 1981. Problems with contingency theory: Testing assumptions hidden within the language of contingency "theory." *Adm. Sci. Q.* 26:349–77

Schrager, R. H. 1986. The impact of living group social climate on student academic performance. *Res. Higher Ed.* 25:265–76

Schriesheim, C. A., DeNisi, A. S. 1981. Task dimensions as moderators of the effects of instrumental leadership: A two-sample replicated test of path-goal leadership theory. *J. Appl. Psychol.* 66:589–97

Schriesheim, J. F. 1980. The social context of leader-subordinate relationships: An investigation of the effects of group cohesiveness. *J. Appl. Psychol.* 65:183–94

Sebba, R., Churchman, A. 1983. Territories and territoriality in the home. *Environ. Behav.* 15:191–210

Shapley, L., Grofman, B. 1984. Optimizing group judgmental accuracy in the presence of interdependencies. *Public Choice* 43:329–43

Shaw, M. E. 1981. *Group Dynamics: The Psychology of Small Group Behavior.* New York: McGraw-Hill. 3rd ed.

Siegel, J., Dubrovsky, V., Kiesler, S., McGuire, T. 1986. Group processes in computer-mediated communication. *Organ. Behav.* 37:157–87

Simonton, D. K. 1985. Intelligence and personal influence in groups: Four nonlinear models. *Psychol. Rev.* 92:532–47

Skvoretz, J. 1988. Models of participation in status-differentiated groups. *Soc. Psychol. Q.* 51:43–57

Smith, H. W. 1981. Territorial spacing on a beach revisited: A cross-national exploration. *Soc. Psychol. Q.* 44:132–37

Smith, K. K., Berg, D. N. 1987. *Paradoxes of Group Life: Understanding Conflict, Paralysis, and Movement in Group Dynamics.* San Francisco: Jossey-Bass

Smith, R. B. 1983. Why soldiers fight. Part I. Leadership, cohesion, and fighter spirit. *Qual. Quant.* 18:1–32

South, S. J., Bonjean, C. M., Markham, W. T., Corder, J. 1982. Social structure and intergroup interaction: Men and women of the federal bureaucracy. *Am. Sociol. Rev.* 47:587–99

Stake, J. E. 1983. Factors in reward distribution: Allocator motive, gender, and Protestant ethic endorsement. *J. Pers. Soc. Psychol.* 44:410–18

Stark, R., Bainbridge, W. S. 1980. Networks of faith: Interpersonal bonds and recruitment to cults and sects. *Am. J. Sociol.* 85:1376–95

Stasser, G. 1988. Computer simulation as a research tool: The DISCUSS model of group decision making. *J. Exp. Soc. Psychol.* 24:393–422

Stasser, G., Kerr, N. L., Bray, R. M. 1982. The social psychology of jury deliberations: Structure, process, and product. In *The Psychology of the Courtroom*, ed. N. L. Kerr, R. M. Bray, pp. 221–56. New York: Academic

Stasser, G., Kerr, N. L., Davis, J. H. 1989a. Influence processes and consensus models in decision-making groups. See Paulus 1989, pp. 279–326

Stasser, G., Taylor, L. A., Hanna, C. 1989b. Information sampling in structured and unstructured discussions of three- and six-person groups. *J. Pers. Soc. Psychol.* 57:67–78

Staw, B. M., Sandelands, L. E., Dutton, J. E. 1981. Threat-rigidity effects in organizational behavior: A multi-level analysis. *Adm. Sci. Q.* 26:501–24

Steckler, N. A., Rosenthal, R. 1985. Sex differences in nonverbal and verbal communication with bosses, peers, and subordinates. *J. Appl. Psychol.* 70:157–63

Stein, R. T., Heller, T. 1983. The relationship of participation rates to leadership status: A meta-analysis. See Blumberg et al 1983, pp. 401–6

Steiner, I. D. 1974. Whatever happened to the group in social psychology? *J. Exp. Soc. Psychol.* 10:94–108

Steiner, I. D. 1986. Paradigms and groups. *Adv. Exp. Soc. Psychol.* 19:251–89

Stockard, J., van de Kragt, A. J. C., Dodge, P. J. 1988. Gender roles and behavior in social dilemmas: Are there sex differences in cooperation and in its justification? *Soc. Psychol. Q.* 51:154–63

Stokes, J. P. 1983. Components of group cohesion: Intermember attraction, instrumental value, and risk taking. *Small Group Behav.* 14:163–73

Stokols, D. 1981. Group x place interactions: Some neglected issues in psychological research on settings. In *Toward a Psychology of Situations: An Interactional Perspective*, ed. D. Magnusson, pp. 393–415. Hillsdale: Erlbaum

Stokols, D., Jacobi, M. 1984. Traditional, present-oriented, and futuristic modes of group-environment relations. In *Historical Social Psychology*, ed. K. Gergen, M. Gergen, pp. 303–34. Hillsdale: Erlbaum

Stokols, D., Shumaker, S. A. 1981. People in places: A transactional view of settings. In *Cognition, Social Behavior, and the Environment*, ed. J. H. Harvey, pp. 441–88. Hillsdale: Erlbaum

Strodtbeck, F. L., Lipinski, R. M. 1985. Becoming first among equals: Moral considerations in jury foreman selection. *J. Pers. Soc. Psychol.* 49:927–36

Strube, M. J., Keller, N. R., Oxenberg, J., Lapidot, D. 1989. Actual and perceived group performance as a function of group composition: The moderating role of the Type A and B behavior patterns. *J. Appl. Soc. Psychol.* 19:140–58

Sundstrom, E. 1986. *Workplaces: The Psychology of the Physical Environment in Offices and Factories.* Cambridge: Cambridge Univ. Press

Sutton, R. I., Zald, M. N. 1985. *Social system demise: The disbanding and reconstruction of couples, organizations, communities, and regimes.* Presented at Ann. Meet. Am. Sociol. Assoc., Washington, DC

Tanford, S., Penrod, S. 1984. Social influence model: A formal integration of research on majority and minority influence processes. *Psychol. Bull.* 95:189–225

Taylor, R. B. 1988. *Human Territorial Functioning: An Empirical, Evolutionary Perspective on Individual and Small Group Territorial Cognitions, Behaviors, and Consequences.* Cambridge: Cambridge Univ. Press

Thompson, L. L., Mannix, E. A., Bazerman, M. H. 1988. Group negotiation: Effects of decision rule, agenda, and aspiration. *J. Pers. Soc. Psychol.* 54:86–95

Tichy, N. M. 1981. Networks in organizations. In *Handbook of Organizational Design*, ed. P. C. Nystrom, W. H. Starbuck, 2:225–49. New York: Oxford Univ. Press

Tickle-Degen, L., Rosenthal, R. 1987. Group rapport and nonverbal behavior. See Hendrick 1987, 9:113–36

Tindale, R. S., Davis, J. H. 1985. Individual and group reward allocation decisions in two situational contexts: Effects of relative need and performance. *J. Pers. Soc. Psychol.* 48:1148–61

Tjosvold, D., Andrews, R., Jones, H. 1983. Cooperative and competitive relationships between leaders and subordinates. *Hum. Relat.* 36:1111–24

Turner, J. C., Hogg, M. A., Oakes, P. J., Reicher, S. D., Wetherell, M. S. 1987. *Rediscovering the Social Group: A Self-Categorization Theory.* Oxford: Basil Blackwell

Tuzlak, A., Moore, J. C. 1984. Status, demeanor, and influence: An empirical reassessment. *Soc. Psychol. Q.* 47:178–83

Tziner, A., Eden, D. 1985. Effects of crew composition on crew performance: Does the whole equal the sum of its parts? *J. Appl. Psychol.* 70:85–93

Tziner, A., Vardi, Y. 1982. Effects of command style and group cohesiveness on the performance of self-selected tank crews. *J. Appl. Psychol.* 67:769–75

Tziner, A., Vardi, Y. 1983. Ability as a moderator between cohesiveness and tank

crews' performance. *J. Occup. Behav.* 4: 137–43

van de Vliert, E. 1985. Escalative intervention in small-group conflicts. *J. Appl. Behav. Sci.* 1:19–36

Varca, P. E. 1980. An analysis of home and away game performance of male college basketball teams. *J. Sport Psychol.* 2:245–57

Vaught, C., Smith, D. L. 1980. Incorporation and mechanical solidarity in an underground coal mine. *Sociol. Work Occup.* 7:159–87

Vecchio, R. P., Gobdel, B. C. 1984. The vertical dyad linkage model of leadership: Problems and prospects. *Organ. Behav.* 34:5–20

Vinokur, A., Burnstein, E., Sechrest, L., Wortman, P. M . 1985. Group decision making by experts: Field study of panels evaluating medical technologies. *J. Pers. Soc. Psychol.* 49:70–84

Von Cranach, M., Ochsenbein, G., Valach, L. 1986. The group as a self-active system: Outline of a theory of group action. *Eur. J. Soc. Psychol.* 16:193–229

Vroom, V. H., Yetton, P. W. 1973. *Leadership and Decision-Making.* Pittsburgh: Univ. Pittsburgh Press

Wagner, W. G., Pfeffer, J., O'Reilly, C. C. 1984. Organizational demography and turnover in top management groups. *Adm. Sci. Q.* 29:74–92

Watson, J. M. 1982. Righteousness on two wheels: Bikers as a secular sect. *Sociol. Spectr.* 2:333–49

Webb, B., Worchel, S., Reichers, L., Wayne, W. 1986. The influence of categorization on perceptions of crowding. *Pers. Soc. Psychol. Bull.* 12:539–46

Wegner, D. M., Giuliano, T., Hertel, P. 1985. Cognitive interdependence in close relationships. In *Compatible and incompatible relationships*, ed. W. J. Ickes, pp. 253–76. New York: Springer-Verlag

Weisfeld, G. E., Weisfeld, C. C. 1984. An observational study of social evaluation: An application of the dominance hierarchy model. *J. Genet. Psychol.* 145:89–99

Weiss, M. R., Friedrichs, W. D. 1986. The influence of leader behaviors, coach attributes, and institutional variables on performance and satisfaction of collegiate basketball teams. *J. Sport Psychol.* 8:332–46

Weldon, E., Gargano, G. M. 1988. Cognitive loafing: The effects of accountability and shared responsibility on cognitive effort. *Pers. Soc. Psychol. Bull.* 14:159–71

Wells, L. 1980. The group-as-a-whole: A systematic socio-analytic perspective on interpersonal and group relations. In *Advances in Experimental Social Processes*, ed. C. P. Alderfer, C. L. Cooper, 2:165–99. Chichester: Wiley

Welton, G. L., Pruitt, D. G. 1987. The mediation process: The effects of mediator bias and disputant power. *Pers. Soc. Psychol. Bull.* 13:123–33

Wicker, A. W., King, J. C. 1988. Life cycles of behavior settings. See McGrath 1988, pp. 182–200

Wicklund, R. A. 1989. The appropriation of ideas. See Paulus 1989, pp. 393–423

Wilke, H. A. M., ed. 1985. *Coalition Formation.* Amsterdam: Elsevier

Wilke, H. A. M., Messick, D. M. Rutte, C. G., eds. 1986. *Experimental Social Dilemmas.* Frankfurt am Main: Verlag Peter Lang

Willer, D., Anderson, B., eds. 1981. *Networks, Exchange and Coercion: The Elementary Theory and its Applications.* New York: Elsevier

Williams, J. M., Hacker, C. M. 1982. Causal relationships among cohesion, satisfaction, and performance in women's intercollegiate field hockey teams. *J. Sport Psychol.* 4: 324–37

Williams, K., Harkins, S., Latane, B. 1981. Identifiability as a deterrent to social loafing: Two cheering experiments. *J. Pers. Soc. Psychol.* 40:303–11

Wood, W. 1985. Meta-analytic review of sex differences in group performance. *Psychol. Bull.* 102:53–71

Wood, W., Karten, S. J. 1986. Sex differences in interaction style as a product of perceived sex differences in competence. *J. Pers. Soc. Psychol.* 50:341–47

Wood, W., Polek, D., Aiken, C. 1985. Sex differences in group task performance. *J. Pers. Soc. Psychol.* 48:63–71

Wright, J. C., Giammarino, M., Parad, H. W. 1986. Social status in small groups: Individual-group similarity and the social "misfit." *J. Pers. Soc. Psychol.* 50:523–36

Yamagishi, T. 1986. The structural goal/expectation theory of cooperation in social dilemmas. See Lawler 1986, pp. 51–87

Yamagishi, T. 1988. The provision of a sanctioning system in the United States and Japan. *Soc. Psychol. Q.* 51:265–71

Yukl, G. A., Van Fleet, D. D. 1982. Cross-situational, multimethod research on military leader effectiveness. *Organ. Behav.* 30:87–108

Zaccaro, S. J. 1984. Social loafing: The role of task attractiveness. *Pers. Soc. Psychol. Bull.* 10:99–106

Zaccaro, S. J., McCoy, M. C. 1988. The effects of task and interpersonal cohesiveness on performance of a disjunctive group task. *J. Appl. Soc. Psychol.* 18:837–51

Zaccaro, S. J., Peterson, C., Walker, S. 1987. Self-serving attributions for individual and group performance. *Soc. Psychol. Q.* 50:257–63

Zander, A. 1982. *Making Groups Effective.* San Francisco: Jossey-Bass

Zurcher, L. A. 1983. *Social Roles: Conformity, Conflict, and Creativity.* Beverly Hills: Sage

Annu. Rev. Psychol. 1990. 41:635–58

VISUAL SENSITIVITY AND PARALLEL RETINOCORTICAL CHANNELS

Robert Shapley

Center for Neural Science, Departments of Psychology and Biology, New York University, New York NY 10003

CONTENTS

Visual Sensitivity and Neural Mechanisms

There has been some excitement lately in relating psychophysical properties of visual sensitivity to neural mechanisms in the retina and in cerebral cortex. Parallel processing of visual information by the P and M retinocortical pathways has been a major focus of this interest. Visual psychophysicists and neuroscientists have devoted enthusiastic attention to each other's results. In this review I summarize the major psychophysical and neurophysiological findings on the role of P and M pathways that may allow a unified explanation for visual sensitivity, and also analyze several proposed hypotheses.

0066-4308/90/0201-0635$02.00

The focus of interest is the degree to which color vision and achromatic vision may be thought of as parallel and independent sensory analyses of the visual scene. Theories of color vision have traditionally considered responses to black and white as the result of a neural mechanism different from those (the color-opponent neurons) that can discriminate among wavelengths or wavelength distributions (see, for example, Hurvich & Jameson 1957). This dualistic approach was reinforced by the neurophysiological work of De Valois and of Gouras and their colleagues in an earlier era of visual neurophysiology (reviewed in De Valois & De Valois 1975; and in Gouras 1984). The idea arose of a separate set of color-blind retinal ganglion cells that were "broad band" (i.e. sensitive to a broad band of the visible spectrum) and responsible for the visibility of black and white patterns. The numerous color-opponent ganglion cells were supposed to be the sole means by which signals about color traveled from eye to brain. Then opinion's pendulum swung the other way and hypotheses were formulated about how all of vision, both achromatic and chromatic, could be derived from the response characteristics of the color-opponent type of neuron (see e.g. DeValois & DeValois 1975; Ingling & Martinez-Uriegas 1983; Kelly 1983; Derrington et al 1984; Rohaly & Buchsbaum 1988, 1989). More recently, some neurophysiologists have returned to the dual-channel point of view (Shapley & Perry 1986; Livingstone & Hubel 1987, 1988; Lee et al 1988; Kaplan et al 1990).

As an advocate for a version of chromatic/achromatic dualism and parallelism, I here review the evidence for both sides in this ongoing debate. However, while trying to do justice to the single achromatic/chromatic channel hypothesis, I show why the idea of separate parallel neural channels is more appealing. The channels probably do not correspond exactly with the achromatic and chromatic channels of psychophysics, and they probably interact more than some theories predict. Nevertheless, there is good reason to believe there are two separate pathways carrying different kinds of signals about the appearance of the outside world. Much of the evidence is neurophysiological, but there are also compelling results from studies of motion, contour perception, and the visual consequences of diseases of the retina and optic nerve. For a somewhat different point of view, the reader should consult the chapter by Lennie et al (1989).

In the literature discussed in this review, authors frequently apply a neurophysiological result from the study of monkeys to human perception, and vice versa. This requires the strong assumption that the visual pathways in humans and monkeys function in a very similar way. Support for this assumption comes mainly from the work of R. L. DeValois and his colleagues (DeValois et al 1974a,b). They showed that for Old-World monkeys, such as the rhesus or cynomolgus monkeys generally used in neurophysiological experiments on vision, detailed behavioral measurements of the spectral sensitivity function, wavelength discrimination function, and contrast sensitivity function resemble those in humans. The neuroanatomy of the human retinocortical pathway is similar to that of Old-World monkeys. More recent evidence on similarities in detailed structure and layout of the retina in human and macaque monkeys strengthens the argument for functional similarity (Rodieck 1988). Moreover, while cone photoreceptors are only the beginning of the pathway, evidence on the detailed quantitative similiarity of the spectral sensitivity curves of these receptors in humans and macaque monkeys (Baylor et al 1987; Schnapf et al 1987) reinforces the idea of cross-species similarities in visual function. The evidence for similarity of visual function concerns Old-World monkeys (e.g. the different macaque species) and does not apply to New World monkeys (e.g. squirrel monkeys). The direct relevance of the elegant work on the neuroanatomy and neurophysiology of the squirrel monkey visual system to human vision is at present problematical.

P (Parvocellular) and M (Magnocellular) Pathways

The story about parallel channels for color and brightness really begins in the layering of the lateral geniculate nucleus (LGN). For many years there was a mystery about the multilayered structure of the LGN of Old World primates, including humans (Walls 1942). In the main body of the Old World primate's LGN there are six clearly segregated layers of cells. The four more dorsal layers are composed of small cells and are named the parvocellular layers. The two more ventral layers, composed of larger neurons, are called magnocellular layers. Recent work on functional connectivity and the visual function of single neurons has revealed that the different types of cell layers in the LGN receive afferent input from different types of retinal ganglion cells. The evidence on functional connectivity of retina to LGN comes from Leventhal et al (1981) and Perry et al (1984), who labeled axon terminals in specific LGN layers of the macaque monkey with horseradish peroxidase (HRP) and looked back in the retina to see which ganglion cells were labeled retrogradely. Direct electrophysiological evidence about retina-to-LGN connectivity comes from Kaplan & Shapley (1986), who recorded excitatory synaptic potentials (from retinal ganglion cells) extracellularly in different LGN layers and found that different types of retinal ganglion cell drove different LGN layers. For example, LGN cells that are excited by deep blue (short-wavelength) light are only found in the parvocellular layers. These "blue-excitatory" LGN cells receive excitatory synaptic input from "blue-excitatory" ganglion cells; "blue-excitatory" ganglion cells provide direct excitatory input only to parvocellular LGN neurons of the "blue-excitatory" type. The specificity of ganglion cell types exactly matches that of their LGN targets. Our direct evidence about this issue confirmed the earlier correlative results of DeValois et al (1966) and Wiesel & Hubel (1966) in the LGN, and Gouras (1968), DeMonasterio & Gouras (1975), and Schiller & Malpeli (1977) on retinal ganglion cells.

As discussed below in more detail, parvocellular neurons are color opponent. This means that their responses, to stimuli that fill their entire receptive fields, change sign from excitatory to inhibitory contingent on the wavelength of the stimulating light (DeValois et al 1966). The property of color-opponency is conferred on them by their ganglion cell inputs (Gouras 1968; Schiller & Malpeli 1977; Kaplan & Shapley 1986), from the class of ganglion cells called P cells by Shapley & Perry (1986). From the neuroanatomical work, one may infer that P cells are very numerous and densely packed, with small cell bodies and dendritic trees.

Magnocellular neurons are generally thought to give the same sign of response to all wavelengths of light; this property is referred to as broad-band spectral sensitivity (Gouras 1968; Schiller & Malpeli 1977). However, only some (about half) of the magnocellular cells are truly broad band; the other magnocellular neurons are color opponent by the above definition. These are the cells Wiesel & Hubel (1966) called Type IV. They have an excitatory receptive-field center mechanism that is broad band, and an antagonistic inhibitory surround mechanism that is selectively sensitive to long-wavelength red light. The properties of the magnocellular neurons, both broad-band and Type IV, are determined almost completely by their retinal ganglion cell inputs (Kaplan & Shapley 1986). The HRP experiments of Leventhal et al (1981) and Perry et al (1984) showed that magnocellular cells receive input from a class of retinal ganglion cells somewhat larger in cell body size and dendritic extent than P cells. This group of ganglion cells was labeled M cells by Shapley & Perry (1986).

Contrast Gain in M and P Pathways

Besides their spectral sensitivities, the other property that distinguishes parvocellular from magnocellular neurons is contrast gain. In vision research contrast denotes the variation in the amount of light in a stimulus, normalized by the mean amount of light. For example, in a periodic grating pattern in which the peak amount of light is P and the least amount of light is T (for trough), then contrast is defined as, $C = (P - T)/(P + T)$. This definition goes back to Rayleigh (1889) and Michelson (1927). Contrast is the stimulus variable that the retina responds to under photopic conditions (Robson 1975; and many others reviewed in Shapley & Enroth-Cugell 1984). It is thought that such response-dependence on contrast evolved because the contrasts of reflecting objects are invariant with changes in illumination occasioned by shadows, weather, or the passage of the sun. The retina thus sends signals to the brain that are more closely linked to surface properties of reflecting objects than to variations in illumination.

Contrast gain is defined as the change in response of the neuron per unit change in contrast, in the limit as the contrast goes to zero. Contrast gain is thus the differential responsiveness of the neuron to contrast around the operating point of the mean illumination. The different contrast gains of parvocellular and magnocellular LGN neurons are illustrated in Figure 1 (Shapley & Kaplan, unpublished; compare with retinal ganglion cells in Kaplan & Shapley 1986). As can be seen from the figure, the response as a function of contrast grows much more steeply for the magnocellular neuron than for the parvocellular, especially at low contrast near the behavioral detection threshold. This is a general finding. The ratio of the average contrast gains of the population of magnocellular neurons to the population average of parvocellular neurons is approximately eight under mid-photopic conditions (Kaplan & Shapley 1982; Hicks et al 1983; Derrington & Lennie 1984). Subsequently, Ehud Kaplan and I showed that this contrast gain difference in LGN neurons is already set up in the retina. The retinal ganglion cells that innervated magnocellular neurons had eight times the contrast gain of ganglion cells that provided the excitatory drive for parvocellular LGN neurons (Kaplan & Shapley 1986).

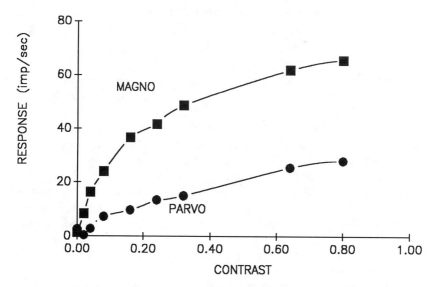

Figure 1 Responses of macaque LGN neurons as a function of contrast. One on-center magnocellular neuron and one off-center (+g−r) parvocellular neuron are shown. Mean luminance was 60 cd/m². Responses were calculated as the best-fitting Fourier component at 4 Hz, the temporal frequency of the drift.

We still do not know the mechanistic reason for the substantial differences in contrast gain for cells in the two pathways. Various factors may contribute. The receptive field centers of P cells are smaller than those of M cells, and if the local contrast gains from points in each field are equal, then the larger summing area of the M cells would lead to a higher contrast gain for an optimal sine grating pattern (see Enroth-Cugell & Robson 1966). Though this factor must contribute something, it does not seem to account for all the differences between M and P. In P cells, but not M cells, antagonistic interactions may occur between cone types within the receptive field center. Though this may be the case in many neurons, it is possible to find P cells in which the center is driven predominantly by one cone type only. Both these hypotheses are considered in the review by Kaplan et al (1990). Neither is sufficient to account for all the difference between M and P contrast gains. This is a problem that needs more research. Whatever the complete explanation is, it must involve retinal mechanisms, since the M and P differences in contrast gain begin in the retina.

Next, we must consider in more detail the responses of P and M neurons to chromatic stimuli. This discussion requires a prior analysis of the three cone photoreceptors in the Old World primate retina, and the effect of the properties of the cones on chromatic responses.

Three Photoreceptors and Spectral Sensitivity

Discussion of the spectral sensitivities of the photoreceptors must precede consideration of the chromatic properties of P and M pathways and the chromatic sensitivity of the human observer.

There are three cone photoreceptor types in human and macaque retinas. The spectral sensitivities of these photoreceptors have been determined for macaque retina by Baylor et al (1987) and for human retina by Schnapf et al (1987), using suction electrodes to measure cone photocurrent directly. These direct measurements of photoreceptor spectral sensitivities are in generally good agreement with microspectrophotometric measurements of cone absorption spectra (Bowmaker & Dartnall 1980; Bowmaker et al 1980). The photocurrent measurements agree even more closely with estimates of cone spectral sensitivity based on human psychophysics (Smith & Pokorny 1975). The Smith & Pokorny fundamentals (estimated cone spectral sensitivities as measured at the retina after the light has been prefiltered by the lens) are three smooth functions of wavelength peaking at 440 nm (b cones), 530 nm (g cones), and 560 nm (r cones).

The human sensitivity to light across the visible spectrum under photopic, daylight conditions is called the *photopic luminosity function*, denoted V_λ. It might be thought that the easiest, and certainly the most straightforward, way to determine V_λ would be to measure psychophysically the sensitivity for increments of light of different wavelength on a photopic background. However, the photopic luminosity function is not measured in this way, mainly because such measurements are variable between and within observers because of the complexity of the visual system (Sperling & Harwerth 1971; King-Smith & Carden 1976). Rather, the procedure known as heterochromatic flicker photometry has been employed. Monochromatic light of a given wavelength is flickered against a white light at a frequency of 20 Hz or above, and the radiance of the monochromatic light is adjusted until the perception of flicker disappears or is minimized (Coblentz & Emerson 1917). This technique exploits the fact that neural mechanisms that can respond to the color of the monochromatic light are not able to follow fast flicker. The photopic luminosity function has been measured more recently using contour distinctness (Wagner & Boynton 1972) and minimal motion (Cavanagh et al 1987) as response criteria. These measurements agree remarkably well with the luminosity function determined by flicker in the same subjects.

The *luminance* of a light source is its effectiveness in stimulating the visual neural mechanism that has as its spectral sensitivity the photopic luminosity function. Thus, the luminance of any light may be computed by multiplying its spectral radiance distribution, wavelength by wavelength, by the photopic luminosity function, and summing the products.

The spectral sensitivities of the r and g cones and the photopic luminosity function are graphed in Figure 2. The purpose of this graph is to show the degree of overlap of the two longer-wavelength cones with the photopic

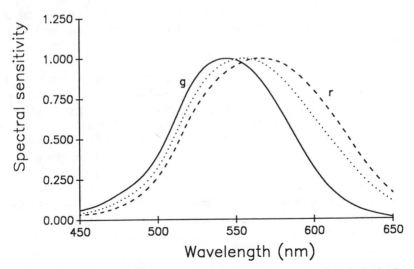

Figure 2   Spectral sensitivity functions of the r and g cones, and the photopic luminosity function (dotted line). Data are redrawn from Smith & Pokorny (1975).

luminosity function, and also to demonstrate the closeness of the luminosity function to the r cone sensitivity especially at longer wavelengths. This becomes significant in the consideration of cone contrasts in chromatic, isoluminant stimuli. The photopic luminosity curve graphed in Figure 2 is an average of curves from many subjects. There is substantial variation in the normal population in the peak wavelength and particularly in the long-wavelength limb of the V_λ curve (Coblentz & Emerson 1917; Crone 1959). For example, some people who have normal color vision can have half a log unit less relative sensitivity to 620 nm light than the average observer (Coblentz & Emerson 1917). There is variance also in the reported spectral sensitivity of cones (Baylor et al 1987) and in the pigments' spectral absorption (Bowmaker et al 1980).

Color Exchange and Isoluminance

Color exchange, or silent substitution (Estevez & Spekreijse (1974, 1982), is a technique for identifying contributions from particular photoreceptors or spectral response mechanisms. For any spectral sensitivity function, and any two lights with different spectral distributions within the band of the sensitivity function, one can perform a color-exchange experiment that will provide a characteristic color balance for that particular spectral sensitivity. For example, if one chooses two monochromatic lights with wavelengths such that they are equally effective at stimulating the r cone, then temporal alternation between these two lights at equal quantum flux should cause no variation in the response of the r cone. The same argument works for the photopic luminosity function which presumably is the spectral sensitivity of a neural mechanism that receives additive inputs from r and g cones. Two lights that, when exchanged, produce no response from the luminance mechanism are called *isoluminant*.

The results of a simulated color-exchange experiment on cones and a broad-band cell with a V_λ spectral sensitivity are illustrated in Figure 3. The calculations are based on the spectral sensitivities of the r and g cones and the photopic luminosity function as graphed in Figure 2. The spectral distributions of the light sources were those of the red and green phosphors on standard color television sets, designated P22 phosphors. The red phosphor is narrow-band centered around 630 nm. The green phosphor is more broad band centered around 530 nm. Such colored lights have been used in many of the experiments reviewed here (Derrington et al 1984; DeValois & Switkes 1983; Kaplan et al 1988; Livingstone & Hubel 1987; Tootell et al 1988b). The experiment simulated is color exchange between the red (R) and green (G) phosphors. The G/R ratio is the ratio of the luminances of the green and red phosphors. In this simulated experiment, the luminance of the red phosphor (R) was held fixed and the luminance of G was varied. When the luminance of

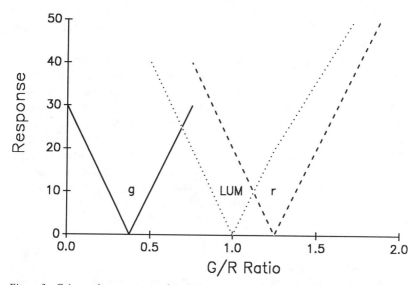

Figure 3   Color exchange response functions for r and g cones and luminance. The predicted response of the cones to different G/R ratios was calculated from the cross-product of the G and R phosphors with the spectral sensitivities of the g and r cones from Figure 2. In the calculation, contrast of the R phosphor was fixed at 0.8. Contrast of the G phosphor varied so as to change the G/R ratio.

the green phosphor is approximately 0.4 that of the red (G/R ratio 0.4), the response of the g cones is nulled. When the G/R ratio is about 1.2, the r cone response is nulled.

Notice that the shape of the response of each of these spectral mechanisms is similar; near the null the response vs G/R ratio forms a V. This is based on the assumption of small signal linearity, a good assumption in the case of macaque P and M pathways (Kaplan & Shapley 1982; Derrington et al 1984; Blakemore & Vital-Durand 1986). A spectral mechanism that sums the responses of g and r cones will have a null in a color exchange experiment at a G/R ratio between the nulls of the two cones. If the spectral sensitivity of the summing mechanism is Kr + g, where K is a number between zero and infinity, then when K approaches zero, the color-exchange null approaches the g cone from above. When K goes to infinity, the color-exchange null approaches the r cone null, from below. The null of the luminosity curve between the cone nulls in Figure 3 is a case in point. For that curve K is approximately 2. One must qualify the assertion to include the condition that the photoreceptor signals have the same time course, and that in the process of summation their time courses are unaffected. The existence of sharp Vs in color exchange experiments on M ganglion cells and magnocellular cells is reasonably good evidence that r and g cones have similar time courses under the conditions of those experiments (Lee et al 1988; Kaplan et al 1988; Shapley & Kaplan 1989).

Next, we consider what happens in a color-exchange experiment on a color-opponent neuron. In such a cell, r and g cone signals are not summed but subtracted. The results of Figure 4 would ensue. The luminosity color-exchange results are included for comparison with three different possible color-opponent cells: one in which the strength of r and g signals is equal but the sign is opposite (g − r); one in which signals from g cones are twice as strong as those from r cones (2g − r); and one in which signals from r cones are twice as strong as those from g cones (2r − g). The curves would be unaffected if the signs of the cone inputs were reversed since only magnitude of response is plotted. What is striking about these simple calculations is that opponent neurons have no null response between the cone nulls along the G/R axis. The g − r response is perfectly constant. The 2g − r and 2r − g cells show response variation but no null. This result is general for any neural mechanism with a spectral sensitivity Kr − g, where K is a number greater than zero and less than infinity. As K goes to zero the null of the mechanism approaches the g cone null from below; as K goes to infinity, the null of the mechanism approaches the r cone null from above. As before, all these

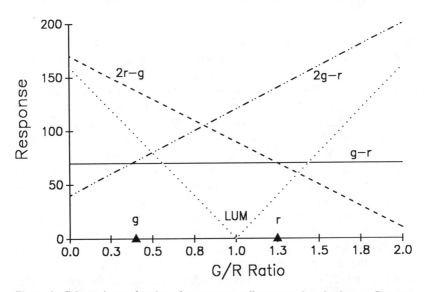

Figure 4   Color-exchange functions for opponent cells compared to luminance. Response magnitude as a function of G/R ratio is plotted for three different opponent neurons, with cone balances as labeled. The color-exchange response function for luminance is again shown (labeled LUM). As in Figure 3, calculations were done with fixed contrast on the R phosphor and varying contrast on the G phosphor.

statements hinge on small-signal linearity and identity of temporal response properties for g and r cones. Similarity of response time courses in r and g cones was found in parvocellular color-opponent neurons by Gielen et al (1982), who used color-exchange to isolate responses of the different cones. There have been several demonstrations of small-signal linearity in P and parvocellular neurons (Shapley et al 1981; Kaplan & Shapley 1982; Derrington & Lennie 1984; Derrington et al 1984).

Responses of M and P Neurons to Isoluminant Stimuli

One particular color-exchange experiment has become crucial, namely measuring responses of P and M neurons to isoluminant color exchange. In their large paper on perceptual effects of parallel processing in the visual cortex, Livingstone & Hubel (1987) assumed that because magnocellular cells were broad band, their responses would be nulled at isoluminance. As the above discussion demonstrates, this is a non sequitur. To repeat, there could be a whole family of broad-band neurons in the visual pathway that summed signals from r and g cones with different weighting factors K_i, such that spectral sensitivity of the i-th mechanism was $K_i r + g$. Each mechanism would have a null at a different point on the G/R axis. The striking thing about M cells and magnocellular neurons is that, for stimuli that produce responses from the receptive-field center mechanism, the position of the null on the color-exchange axis is close to that predicted from the human photopic luminosity function, V_λ (Lee et al 1988; Shapley & Kaplan 1989; Kaplan et al 1990). There is no more variability in the position of the color-exchange null in the neurophysiological data than there is in psychophysical experiments on the luminosity function in humans (Crone 1959) or in behavioral experiments on macaques (DeValois et al 1974a). A crucial experiment would be to measure the variability of the isoluminant point within a large population of M cells from the same individual monkey, but this is so difficult it has not yet been done.

There are other experiments that indicate that, under stimulus conditions where the center of the receptive field is not the only response mechanism contributing to the response, M and magnocellular neurons do not have a color-exchange null at isoluminance. Lee et al (1988) reported that large disks that stimulate center and surround have nulls away from isoluminance. Shapley & Kaplan (1989) used heterochromatic sine gratings to study chromatic properties of receptive field mechanisms. Heterochromatic sine gratings are formed by producing a sine grating on, say, the red phosphor of a color monitor, and producing an identical sine grating on the green phosphor except for an exact 180° phase shift. Thus where the red phosphor has a bright red bar the green phosphor has a dark green bar, and vice versa. The sum of these two grating patterns in antiphase yields as a spatial pattern a red-green, ergo heterochromatic, grating. Shapley & Kaplan (1989) reported that heterochromatic sine gratings of low spatial frequency may produce no color null in magnocellular neurons. Derrington et al (1984), using the technique of modulation in color space (discussed below), found that many magnocellular units exhibited properties expected of color-opponent cells. Undoubtedly, all these results are related to the earlier work of Wiesel & Hubel (1966), who found that many magnocellular neurons had a receptive-field surround that was more red sensitive than the receptive-field center. Such neurons could behave as color-opponent cells to stimulate that covered both center and surround if the spectral sensitivities of center and surround were different enough. Similar M ganglion cells were reported by DeMonasterio & Schein (1980). Thus, in psychophysical experiments, if the stimulus is designed to tap the receptive-field center of cells in the M pathway, it will elicit a spectral sensitivity function like V_λ. Such a stimulus will be nulled in a color-exchange experiment at isoluminance. However, should other stimuli be detected by the M-magnocellular pathway but not isolate the central receptive-field mechanism, one might discover a color-opponent mechanism driven by M cells.

There is another result that indicates a failure of nulling at isoluminance in magnocellular neurons. This is the second-harmonic distortion discovered by Schiller & Colby (1983). In color exchange experiments with large-area stimuli, these investigators often found strong frequency-doubled responses. Such results were not reported by Derrington et al (1984), who found frequency doubling rarely (20% of the time) in their experiments. Shapley & Kaplan (1989) reported that frequency doubling was dependent on spatial frequency of the pattern used for color exchange. Center-isolating stimuli elicited no frequency doubling; but it could be observed when spatial frequency was so low, less than 0.5 c/deg, that the receptive-field surround could contribute to the M cell's response. This also could contribute to failure to achieve sharp psychophysical isoluminance with stimuli of large area or low spatial frequency, even with stimuli that isolated a perceptual mechanism driven only by the M pathway.

Chromatic Opponency in P and M Cells

The basis for wavelength selectivity in the visual pathway is antagonistic (excitatory vs inhibitory) interactions between signals from different cone types. The simplest type of antagonism is subtraction. There is good evidence for subtractive interactions between r and g cones on P ganglion cells (DeMonasterio & Gouras 1975; Zrenner & Gouras 1983) and parvocellular neurons (DeValois et al 1966; Wiesel & Hubel 1966; Derrington et al 1984). The classical evidence is a change in sign of response with wavelength

(DeValois et al 1966). For example, many P cells that receive opponent inputs from r and g cones have a sign change at a wavelength near 570 nm. The "blue-excitatory" cells referred to above often have a change from excitation at short wavelengths to inhibition at long wavelengths at around 490 nm. These cells receive excitatory input from b cones and inhibitory input from some combination of r and g cones.

The precise mapping of cone types to receptive-field mechanisms is a problem not yet solved. Wiesel & Hubel (1966) postulated that color-opponent cells received excitatory (or inhibitory) input from one cone type in the receptive-field center and antagonistic inputs from a complementary cone type in the receptive-field surround. However, the detailed quantitative evidence that would be needed to support or to reject this hypothesis was not available then, and it is still not in hand today. One problem is spatially isolating center from surround: Receptive fields in the monkey's retina, and presumably in the human's too, are quite small. Though Wiesel & Hubel's (1966) proposal may be correct, there are a number of other possibilities. One alternative hypothesis is that there is mixed receptor input to the receptive-field surround, and only or predominantly one cone input to the center of the receptive field (see Kaplan et al 1990).

Some fascinating facts are known about the proportions of color-opponent P and parvocellular cells that have r cone centers and g cone centers. DeMonasterio & Gouras (1975) found that the majority of P ganglion cells in the central 5° of the visual field had g cone centers. The g cone input might be excitatory or inhibitory. The proportion of P cells with r cone centers increased with retinal eccentricity, as later confirmed by Zrenner & Gouras (1983). A similar finding about the high proportion of g cone centers among central parvocellular neurons in LGN was reported by DeValois et al (1977). This is worth dwelling on for a moment, especially because the finding of DeValois et al (1977) was apparently later misinterpreted by Ingling & Tsou (1988). DeValois et al (1977) stated that $+g-r$ opponent cells had excitatory centers; thus the excitatory g cone input was to the center. They also wrote that $+r-g$ neurons had inhibitory centers. This means again that the g cone input went to the center of the receptive field, as inhibition. Ingling & Tsou (1988) seemed to take this to mean that the neurons with r cone input to the center had inhibitory centers, a misinterpretation of the data. The three studies cited all concur that in central vision there is a preponderance of P cells, and parvocellular neurons, with g cone input to the center of their receptive fields. Ingling & Martinez-Uriegas (1983) had earlier used this fact to explain the hue shift towards green of a flickering yellow light.

The reason that the proportion of P cells driven by g cones is significant is that the M cell centers are dominated by r cones, and the difference in cone connectivity to the different pathways may illuminate functional specialization. Referring back to Figures 2 and 3, we see that the V_λ function lies closer to the r cone spectral sensitivity. The V_λ isoluminant point is at a relative cone weight of 2 : 1 for r to g cones. From color-exchange experiments on macaque M cells we can infer that the cone weighting is about 2r for every g cone signal for the M cell center. This bias in favor of the r cones in the M pathway seems to be the opposite of the g cone bias in the centrally located P cells.

The diminution in relative numbers of those P cells with g cone receptive-field centers at increasing retinal eccentricity is associated with a decline in perceived saturation of colors of stimuli presented to the periphery of the visual field (Gordon & Abramov 1977). There is evidence against the idea that this shift to the r cones in P cells occurs because of an increasing proportion of r cone photoreceptors with eccentricity (reviewed in Shapley & Perry 1986). Rather, the r shift appears to be a result of eccentricity-dependent shifts in cone-to-P cell connectivity.

Modulation in Color Space

Chromatic opponency of LGN cells has been investigated using a technique very similar to color exchange, namely modulation in color space around a white point. This technique grew out of psychophysical investigations of chromatic opponent mechanisms.

The color space that is used is a re-mapping of cone excitation space. Any spectral distribution over the visible spectrum can be represented as a three-dimensional vector of cone excitations. The three coordinate axes in this vector space are b, r, and g cone excitation by the light. Based on earlier work of MacLeod & Boynton (1979), Krauskopf et al (1982) proposed a (linear) mapping of this space into another color space in which the axes were luminance modulation, b excitation (Constant R and G), and r and g modulation such that b cone excitation was constant (Constant B axis). The Constant B and Constant R and G axes formed a plane, the Isoluminant Plane. These axes would be preferred modulation directions for color-opponent mechanisms: Lights along the Constant B axis would stimulate cells that received $+r-g$ or $+g-r$ input, while the Constant R and G axis would isolate those lights that only excited cells that received excitation (or inhibition) from b cones. Krauskopf et al (1982) demonstrated that these three axes were preferred axes for habituation of the response to chromatic flicker. Krauskopf et al (1982) named these axes "cardinal directions of color space." It is important to note that the transformation from r,g,b space to cardinal direction (CD) space is a linear transformation but angles are not preserved. Thus, the cone vectors which are all orthogonal in r,g,b space are no longer orthogonal in CD space. The vectors for r and g cones are about 45 deg from the b cone vector in CD space (Derrington et al 1984). In CD space, the r and g cone vectors are only 10–20° apart and are mapped close to the luminance axis (Derrington et al 1984)—i.e. almost orthogonal to the isoluminant plane.

Derrington et al (1984) used stimuli modulated along different vectors in this CD space to characterize macaque LGN neurons. Modulation in the isoluminant plane should have been ineffective in stimulating neurons with a spectral sensitivity like V_λ, the photopic luminosity function. Each neuron should have a null plane, like the isoluminant plane for luminance units, within which color modulation should be ineffective. The elevation of this null plane with respect to the isoluminant plane is a measure of the degree to which the neuron's response is determined by opponent mechanisms. The closer to zero the elevation, the more nearly the neuron's response is completely determined by luminance. Since the cone vectors are pointing so close to the luminance direction in CD space, neurons that are being driven by either the r or the g cone will have a null plane near the isoluminant plane, with a low elevation. Derrington et al (1984) used the position of the null planes in CD space for each neuron to calculate cone weighting factors for each neuron studied. They also measured the effects of spatial and temporal frequency on these derived cone weights. They found that virtually every parvocellular neuron was color opponent in that at least two cone weights were of opposite sign; that temporal frequency up to 16 Hz had little effect on the position of null planes and thus cone weights; that increasing spatial frequency had a marked effect in lowering elevation of null planes, thus reducing the strength of the cone weight from the receptive field surround; and that magnocellular responses to large-area stimuli were often color opponent, but their null planes were pushed down towards zero elevation by grating stimuli, as the V_λ spectral sensitivity of the receptive-field center was revealed.

Comparison of Achromatic and Chromatic Contrast Sensitivity

The spatial characteristics of vision have been studied for many years by measuring the contrast sensitivity function for sinusoidal gratings (e.g. Campbell & Robson 1968; DeValois et al 1974b, among many others). These have traditionally been achromatic measurements, and the contrast sensitivity has been taken to be the reciprocal of the luminance contrast at psychophysical threshold. More recently, luminance contrast sensitivity has been compared with the spatial frequency dependence of chromatic contrast sensitivity as measured with isoluminant heterochromatic grating patterns (van der Horst et al 1967; Kelly 1983; Mullen 1985). An example of the kind of results obtained is shown in Figure 5 from Mullen's (1985) paper. The luminance contrast sensitivity function is band-pass while the chromatic contrast sensitivity is low pass and cuts off at a fairly low spatial frequency compared with

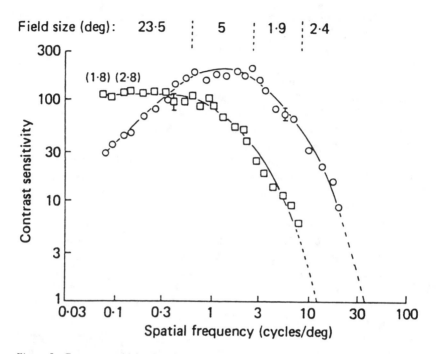

Figure 5 Contrast sensitivity functions for luminance and isoluminant color gratings. The luminance data are drawn as empty circles; the red-green grating data are drawn as empty squares. The luminance data were taken with a cathode ray tube (CRT) display filtered through a 526 nm narrow-band filter, while the red-green data are for an isoluminant sine grating where the red member of the antiphase pair was produced by a CRT filtered through a 602 nm narrow-band filter, while the green grating was filtered through the same 526 nm filter as for the luminance grating. The field size at the top of the graph indicates the size af the stimulus screen, in degrees of visual angle, for the various measurements. Reproduced with permission from Mullen (1985).

luminance. Thus, at this mean luminance, the subject could resolve 30 c/deg with the luminance system but only about 10 c/deg with the chromatic system. Parvocellular neurons respond much better to isoluminant heterochromatic gratings of low spatial frequency because, under those conditions, the antagonistic center and surround become synergistic (DeValois & DeValois 1975). However, Type IV M cells also become more sensitive at low spatial frequencies of heterochromatic gratings because of their color opponency.

The responses to middle and high spatial frequencies are better when luminance than when isoluminant gratings are used as stimuli as in Figure 5. Thus, if the data were plotted as response vs G/R ratio, one should expect a dip in response near isoluminance. Such results were reported by Mullen (1985). It would be important to measure the isoluminant G/R ratio on the same subject with heterochromatic flicker photometry or minimal motion or minimally distinct border to see whether the same or different spectral mechanisms are at work in detecting the heterochromatic gratings.

K. K. DeValois & Switkes (1983) and Switkes et al (1988) have demonstrated that heterochromatic grating patterns are detected by spatial frequency channels like those involved in achromatic grating detection (Campbell & Robson 1968; Graham 1980). Thus, elevation of threshold for detecting an isoluminant grating is produced by preexposure to an isoluminant grating of the same spatial frequency, and less elevation of threshold is produced by more distant spatial frequencies. Moreover, color gratings mask and adapt color and luminance gratings but, as discussed below, luminance gratings may facilitate detection of color gratings.

The work on spatial frequency channels in color throws a new light on receptive-field models that have sought to explain chromatic and luminance spatial contrast sensitivity functions in terms of single channel receptive field models (Kelly 1983; Rohaly & Buchsbaum 1988, 1989). The chromatic contrast sensitivity function is an envelope of chromatic spatial frequency channels, just as the luminance contrast sensitivity function is thought to be an envelope of the well-studied achromatic spatial frequency channels. Single-channel models, though they may be of heuristic value in summarizing a body of data, must be only a first approximation to a true mechanistic model of these multichannel systems.

One recent paper about the spatial properties of chromatic spatial channels may advance our understanding of the peculiar contribution of color to spatial vision (Troscianko & Harris 1988). These authors estimated the spatial phase sensitivity in compound sine gratings that were the sum of a fundamental component and its third harmonic, both set at twice detection threshold. Phase discrimination at isoluminance was worse than for all other color balances tested. The authors hypothesize that color information comes into the cortex with a great amount of positional uncertaintly and that this leads to losses in phase discrimination when only color is available as a stimulus.

Possible Neural Substrates for Contrast Sensitivity

The M and P pathways must be the conduits for signals about detection of contrast. The high-gain M system is well suited to handle detection of grating patterns with low to medium spatial frequencies (Shapley & Perry 1986; Kaplan et al 1990). The numerous P cells may be required to represent veridically the spatial waveform for grating patterns near the acuity limit (Lennie et al 1989).

Recent neurophysiological results by Purpura et al (1988) indicate that the P cells become visually unresponsive to grating patterns when the mean luminance drops below 0.1 cd/m^2, at the rod/cone break. M cells become less sensitive progressively as mean luminance is reduced, but they remain responsive into the scotopic range. We suggested that these results might mean that spatial vision under scotopic conditions would be dependent on M cell signals. Wiesel & Hubel (1966) and Gielen et al (1982) reported rod-driven responses in parvocellular LGN cells under scotopic adapting conditions, an apparent contradiction to the results of Purpura et al (1988). However, both these sets of authors reported that a rod-driven parvocellular neuron was rarely encountered; moreover, they did not test for spatial vision under scotopic conditions. In the Purpura et al study, we did observe rod-driven responses in P cells but only with very low spatial frequency gratings or diffuse light as spatial stimuli.

Cortical Target Areas For P and M Signals

V1   There is indirect evidence that magnocellular and parvocellular signals are kept somewhat segregated within striate cortex, V1. Hawken & Parker (1984) and Hawken et al (1988) have shown that cortical neurons with high contrast gain, like magnocellular neurons, can be found in layer IVc α of V1. Color-opponent neurons are located in layer IVc β, and these are presumably the targets of the LGN afferents from parvocellular cells.

There are subdivisions within the upper layers of the cortex, layers II and III, that may be preferentially influenced by magnocellular signals. All of layers II and III receive inputs from layer IVc β, so, presumably receive parvocellular signals filtered through the cortical network. However, from experiments of labeling of active cells with 2-deoxyglucose, Tootell et al (1988a) found that there was weak but significant labeling of the cytochrome oxidase blobs in layers II and III of V1 cortex when low-contrast stimuli were used. The cytochrome oxidase blobs were shown by Livingstone & Hubel (1984) to contain cortical neurons broadly tuned for orientation. Tootell et al's (1988a) finding may mean that magnocellular and parvocellular signals converge onto blob neurons.

The cytochrome oxidase blobs have been found to form a network throughout macaque V1 (Horton 1984; Livingstone & Hubel 1984), and it has been hypothesized that they form a separate system for the analysis of color (Livingstone & Hubel 1984, 1987). Many of the cells in the blobs are color selective. The real test of this idea is whether cells in the inter-blob regions of layers II and III of V1 are not color selective or are substantially less color selective than blob neurons. There are recent single-unit data on this question from Lennie et al (1989b), and the results indicate that color selectivity in blob cells is not different from that in inter-blob cells. Furthermore, Tootell et al (1988b) used isoluminant color gratings to label layer II-III cells with 2-deoxyglucose; labeled cells were found throughout the upper layers, though there was stronger labeling of the blobs with diffuse color patterns. These data are essentially consistent with the findings of Lennie et al (1989b).

V2 Using cytochrome oxidase as a marker, Tootell et al (1983) demonstrated stripe-like structures in secondary visual cortex V2 in macaque monkeys. Subsequently, Shipp & Zeki (1985) and DeYoe & Van Essen (1985) have shown that distinct anatomical regions within primary visual cortex make characteristic connections with regions in macaque V2. Neurons in the blobs of V1 are connected to one of the sets of darker stripes in V2; neurons in the inter-blob regions of layers II and III are connected to stripe-like regions of low cytochrome-oxidase staining in V2. Livingstone & Hubel (1987), from their measurements in squirrel monkeys, also propose that layer IVb, which receives magnocellular signals from layer IVc alpha, projects to the alternating dark cytochrome stripes in macaque V2. The functional consequence of this complex sequence of connection is that parallel functional pathways proceed from V1 to V2. Livingstone & Hubel (1987; 1988) have made a detailed psychophysical linking proposition based on this anatomy and the receptive-field properties of neurons in V2. They propose that blob cells, connecting to one set of V2 stripes, constitute a system for color vision. The putative magnocellular pathway from layer IVc α through layer IVb to the other set of dark V2 stripes is supposed to be important for responding to objects in depth. The interblob neurons in V1, connected to pale stripes in V2, are supposed to be important for form vision, mainly because neurons located in pale stripes in V2 were found to be end stopped—i.e. more strongly responsive to corners and the ends of lines than to long contours (Hubel & Livingstone 1987).

Among the psychophysical proposals discussed by Livingstone & Hubel (1987), one particularly attractive idea is that magnocellular signals form the basic excitatory drive of the motion pathway.

Motion

Motion perception is greatly disturbed at isoluminance. Heterochromatic color gratings appear to move more slowly (Cavanagh et al 1984; Livingstone & Hubel 1987). Apparent motion is greatly reduced or abolished (Ramachandran & Gregory 1978; Livingstone & Hubel 1987). However, Livingstone & Hubel (1987) state that they observed reduction in apparent motion at a G/R ratio that was 20% less than the G/R ratio for isoluminance determined with flicker photometry. This is significant because it may indicate that contrast in a cone mechanism, or some other neural mechanism than the specific V_λ mechanism, is being selected in these experiments. Many experiments on isoluminant vision have been designed with random dot kinematograms (Ramachandran & Gregory 1978) or random dot stereograms (Livingstone & Hubel 1987). These may all be subject to artifacts as a result of chromatic aberration (Flitcroft 1989). Chromatic aberration may affect spatial frequencies as low as 4 c/deg; it certainly may affect experiments with random dot patterns, which will be broad band in spatial frequency.

Cavanagh et al (1987) used a minimum-motion technique to estimate the cone inputs to the motion mechanism as well as to determine spatial and temporal tuning of the motion pathway. One of their chief findings was that b cones provide little input to the motion pathway. Furthermore, minimum motion and flicker photometry give virtually the same isoluminant point for a given pair of colored lights. This is strong evidence for a single pathway with a single spectral tuning curve, as would be the case if M signals were the front end for the motion signal. However, there is a motion response to isoluminant stimuli; the motion system just signifies a lower velocity. Furthermore, evidence from motion aftereffects (Cavanagh & Favreau 1985; Mullen & Baker 1985) also indicates there may be some, albeit weaker, inputs from color-opponent signals to the motion pathway. There are many sites along the visual pathway at which interactions may occur (see below) and where a magnocellular signal might be modulated by parvocellular signals before it reached the site of motion perception. The evidence for parvocellular inputs involves suprathreshold motion. I have some preliminary evidence that, at motion threshold, isoluminant stimuli are particularly ineffective.

Interactions between M and P Pathways

The evidence reviewed so far has shown the remarkable independence of P and M pathways as they travel in parallel to cortex from the retina, and through visual cortex. However, several psychophysical experiments on facilitation of detection and on suppression of detection indicate substantial coupling between chromatic and achromatic signals. First, there are the results of Switkes et al (1988) on masking and facilitation of color by luminance, and luminance by color. To me the most interesting of many interesting results in this paper is the facilitation of detection of isoluminant color patterns by luminance patterns even if the latter are substantially suprathreshold. This suggests to me that one of the functions of the magnocellular pathway might be to gate parvocellular signals into the cortex. This concept would also make sense of Kelly's finding that isoluminant chromatic patterns suffer great losses in contrast sensitivity when stabilized on the retina (Kelly 1983). It is well known that parvocellular signals are sustained in time when the stimulus is a colored pattern (e.g. Schiller & Malpeli 1978). Yet, an image defined solely by color fades faster and more completely than a luminance pattern.

Other studies that suggest a role for luminance signals in facilitating or gating chromatic signals are the investigations of the gap effect by Boynton et al (1977) and by Eskew (1989). These studies show that luminance steps near the border of a colored test object may facilitate chromatic discrimination. The effect is significant only for colored stimuli that are defined by b cone modulation. Yet the effect does indicate the possibility for interaction between M and P pathways.

While luminance facilitates color, color stimuli suppress the response to luminance variations. This is seen in the masking data of K. DeValois & Switkes (1983) and Switkes et al (1988). Such an effect is also evident in the chromatic suppression of flicker detection described by Stromeyer et al (1987). Another kind of evidence comes from the flash-on-flash paradigm of Finkelstein & Hood (1982), who showed that detection of a brief flash, while mediated by a V_λ mechanism, could be suppressed by superimposition of a flashed background. The spectral sensitivity of the flashed background was broad, like those seen by Sperling & Harwerth (1971) and King-Smith & Carden (1976), indicating suppression from opponent mechanisms. All of these phenomena, while elicited with different stimuli, have the common theme of color suppressing luminance.

Conclusions

In order to make some sense of the implications of possible roles of P and M pathways in visual processing, we had to consider optics, photoreceptors, the retina, the LGN, areas V1 and V2 in visual cortex, and psychophysics. Much was omitted. But I have attempted to examine the critical evidence on the roles these cell types might play in vision. It seems to me the weight of the evidence is that M cells are the luminance pathway, though they do not control the finest achromatic acuity. P cells must provide color signals, but it seems they may need cooperation from the M pathway for that signal to be interpreted by the brain. Cooperative and suppressive interactions, revealed mainly so far by psychophysical experiments, demonstrate that these pathways may start out in parallel but they converge.

ACKNOWLEDGMENTS

The ideas presented were refined in consultation with many people. Foremost I would like to thank my colleague Ehud Kaplan. Then let me also thank Jim Gordon, Keith Purpura, Norman Milkman, Clay Reid, and Michael Hawken. Preparation of this article was partly supported by NIH grant EY 01472, and NSF grant BNS 870606, and by a grant from the Sloan Foundation.

Literature Cited

Baylor, D. A., Nunn, B. J., Schnapf, J. L. 1987. Spectral sensitivity of cones of the monkey *Macaca fascicularis*. *J. Physiol.* 390:145–60

Blakemore, C. B., Vital-Durand, F. 1986. Organization and post-natal development of the monkey's lateral geniculate nucleus. *J. Physiol.* 380:453–91

Bowmaker, J. K., Dartnall, H. J. A. 1980. Visual pigments of rods and cones in a human retina. *J. Physiol.* 298:501–11

Bowmaker, J. K., Dartnall, H. J. A., Mollon, J. D. 1980. Microspectrophotometric demonstrations of four classes of photoreceptor in an Old World primate, *Macaca fascicularis*. *J. Physiol.* 298:131–43

Boynton, R. M., Hayhoe, M. M., MacLeod, D. I. A. 1977. The gap effect: chromatic and achromatic visual discrimination as affected by field separation. *Optica Acta* 24:159–77

Campbell, F. W., Robson, J. G. 1968. Application of Fourier analysis to the visibility of gratings. *J. Physiol.* 197:551–66

Cavanagh, P., Anstis, S. M., MacLeod, D. I. A. 1987. Equiluminance: spatial and temporal factors and the contribution of blue-sensitive cones. *J. Opt. Soc. Am.* A4:1428–38

Cavanagh, P., Favreau, O. E. 1985. Color and luminance share a common motion pathway. *Vis. Res.* 25:1595–1601

Cavanagh, P., Tyler, C. W., Favreau, O. E. 1984. Perceived velocity of moving chromatic gratings. *J. Opt. Soc. Am.* A1:893–99

Coblentz, W. W., Emerson, W. B. 1917. Relative sensibility of the average eye to light of different colors and some practical applications to radiation problems. *Bull. Bur. Stand.* 14:167–236

Crone, R. 1959. Spectral sensitivity in color defective subjects and heterozygous carriers. *Am. J. Ophthalmol.* 48:231–35

DeMonasterio, F. M., Gouras, P. 1975. Functional properties of ganglion cells in the rhesus monkey retina. *J. Physiol.* 251:167–95

DeMonasterio, F. M., Schein, S. J. 1980. Protan-like spectral sensitivity of foveal Y ganglion cells of the retina of macaque monkeys. *J. Physiol.* 299:385–96

Derrington, A. M., Krauskopf, J., Lennie, P. 1984. Chromatic mechanisms in lateral geniculate nucleus of macaque. *J. Physiol.* 357:241–65

Derrington, A. M., Lennie, P. 1984. Spatial and temporal contrast sensitivities of neurones in the lateral geniculate nucleus of macaque. *J. Physiol.* 357:219–40

De Valois, K. K., Switkes, E. 1983. Simultaneous masking interactions between chromatic and luminance gratings. *J. Opt. Soc. Am.* 73:11–18

De Valois, R. L., Abramov, I., Jacobs, G. H. 1966. Analysis of response patterns of LGN cells. *J. Opt. Soc. Am.* 56:966–77

De Valois, R. L., De Valois, K. K. 1985. Neural coding of color. In *Handbook of Perception: Seeing*, ed. E. C. Carterette, M. P. Friedman, 5:117–66. New York: Academic

De Valois, R. L., Morgan, H. C., Polson, M. C., Mead, W. R., Hull, E. M. 1974a. Psychophysical studies of monkey vision. I. Macaque luminosity and color vision tests. *Vis. Res.* 14:53–67

De Valois, R. L., Morgan, H. C., Snodderly, D. M. 1974b. Psychophysical studies of monkey vision. III. Spatial luminance contrast sensitivity tests of macaque and human observers. *Vis. Res.* 14:75–81

De Valois, R. L., Snodderly, D. M., Yund, E. W., Hepler, N. K. 1977. Responses of macaque lateral geniculate cells to luminance and color figures. *Sens. Process.* 1:244–59

DeYoe, E. A., Van Essen, D. C. 1985. Segregation of efferent connections and receptive field properties in visual area V2 of macaque. *Nature* 317:58–59

Enroth-Cugell, C., Robson, J. G. 1966. The contrast sensitivity of retinal ganglion cells of the cat. *J. Physiol.* 187:517–52

Eskew, R. T. 1989. The gap effect revisited: slow changes in chromatic sensitivity as affected by luminance and chromatic borders. *Vis. Res.* 29:717–29

Estevez, O., Spekreijse, H. 1974. A spectral compensation method for determining the flicker characteristics of the human colour mechanism. *Vis. Res.* 14:823–30

Estevez, O., Spekreijse, H. 1982. The "Silent Substitution" method in visual research. *Vis. Res.* 22:681–91

Finkelstein, M. A., Hood, D. C. 1982. Opponent-color cells can influence detection of small, brief lights. *Vis. Res.* 22:89–95

Flitcroft, D. I. 1989. The interactions between chromatic aberration, defocus, and stimulus chromaticity: implications for visual physiology and colorimetry. *Vis. Res.* 29:349–60

Gielen, C. C. A. M., van Gisbergen, J. A. M., Vendrik, A. J. H. 1982. Reconstruction of cone system contributions to responses of colour-opponent neurones in monkey lateral geniculate. *Biol. Cybern.* 44:211–21

Gordon, J., Abramov, I. 1977. Color vision in the peripheral retina. II. Hue and saturation. *J. Opt. Soc. Am.* 67:202–7

Gouras, P. 1968. Identification of cone mechanisms in monkey retinal ganglion cells. *J. Physiol.* 199:533–47

Gouras, P. 1984. Color vision. In *Progress in Retinal Research,* ed. N. Osborne, G. Chader, 3:227–62. Oxford: Pergamon

Graham, N. 1980. Spatial-frequency channels in human vision: detecting edges without edge detectors. In *Visual Coding and Adaptability,* ed. C. S. Harris. Hillsdale, NJ: Erlbaum

Gregory, R. 1977. Vision with isoluminant colour contrast. 1. A projection technique and observations. *Perception* 6:113–19

Hawken, M. J., Parker, A. J. 1984. Contrast sensitivity and orientation selectivity in lamina IV of the striate cortex of Old World monkeys. *Exp. Brain Res.* 54:367–72

Hawken, M. J., Parker, A. J., Lund, J. S. 1988. Laminar organization and contrast sensitivity of direction-selective cells in the striate cortex of the Old-World monkey. *J. Neurosci.* 8:3541–48

Hicks, T. P., Lee, B. B., Vidyasagar, T. R. 1983. The responses of cells in macaque lateral geniculate nucleus to sinusoidal gratings. *J. Physiol.* 337:183–200

Horton, J. C. 1984. Cytochrome oxidase patterns: a new cytoarchitectonic feature of monkey striate. *Philos. Trans. R. Soc. London Ser.* B 304:199–253

Hubel, D. H., Livingstone, M. S. 1987. Segregation of form, color, and stereopsis in primate area 18. *J. Neurosci.* 7:3378–3415

Hurvich, L., Jameson, D. 1957. An opponent process theory of color vision. *Psychol. Rev.* 64:384–404

Ingling, C. R., Martinez-Uriegas, E. 1983. Simple opponent receptive fields are asymmetrical: G-cone centers predominate. *J. Opt. Soc. Am.* 73:1527–32

Ingling, C. R., Tsou, B. H. P. 1988. Spectral sensitivity for flicker and acuity criteria. *J. Opt. Soc. Am.* A8:1374–78

Kaplan, E., Lee, B. B., Shapley, R. 1990. New views of primate retinal function. In *Progress in Retinal Research,* ed. N. Osborne, G. Chader, Vol. 9. Oxford: Pergamon. In press

Kaplan, E., Shapley, R. 1982. X and Y cells in the lateral geniculate nucleus of macaque monkeys. *J. Physiol.* 330:125–43

Kaplan, E., Shapley, R. 1986. The primate retina contains two types of ganglion cells, with high and low contrast sensitivity. *Proc. Natl. Acad. Sci. USA* 83:2755–57

Kaplan, E., Shapley, R., Purpura, K. 1988. Color and luminance contrast as tools for probing the organization of the primate retina. *Neurosci. Res. (Suppl.)* 2:s151–66

Kelly, D. 1983. Spatiotemporal variation of

chromatic and achromatic contrast thresholds. *J. Opt. Soc. Am.* 73:742–50

King-Smith, P. E., Carden, D. 1976. Luminance and opponent-color contributions to visual detection and adaptation and to temporal and spatial integration. *J. Opt. Soc. Am.* 66:709–17

Krauskopf, J., Williams, D. R., Heeley, D. W. 1982. Cardinal directions of color space. *Vis. Res.* 22:1123–31

Lee, B. B., Martin, P. R., Valberg, A. 1988. The physiological basis of heterochromatic flicker photometry demonstrated in the ganglion cells of the macaque retina. *J. Physiol.* 404:323–47

Lennie, P., Trevarthen, C., Waessle, H., Van Essen, D. 1989. Parallel processing of visual information. In *Visual Perception: The Neurophysiological Foundations,* ed. L. Spillman, J. Werner, Ch. 6. New York: Academic

Lennie, P., Krauskopf, J., Sclar, G. 1989b. Chromatic mechanisms in striate cortex of macaque. *J. Neuroscience.* Submitted

Leventhal, A. G., Rodieck, R. W., Dreher, B. 1981. Retinal ganglion cell classes in the old-world monkey: morphology and central projections. *Science* 213:1139–42

Livingstone, M. S., Hubel, D. H. 1984. Anatomy and physiology of a color system in the primate visual cortex. *J. Neurosci.* 4:309–56

Livingstone, M. S., Hubel, D. H. 1987. Psychophysical evidence for separate channels for the perception of form, color, motion, and depth. *J. Neurosci.* 7:3416–68

Livingstone, M. S., Hubel, D. H. 1988. Segregation of form, color, movement, and depth: anatomy, physiology, and perception. *Science* 240:740–49

MacLeod, D. I. A., Boynton, R. M. 1979. Chromaticity diagram showing cone excitation by stimuli of equal luminance. *J. Opt. Soc. Am.* 69:1183–86

Michelson, A. A. 1927. *Studies in Optics.* Chicago: Univ. Chicago Press. p. 31

Mullen, K. 1985. The contrast sensitivity of human colour vision to red-green and blue-yellow chromatic gratings. *J. Physiol.* 359:381–400

Mullen, K. T., Baker, C. L. 1985. A motion aftereffect from an isoluminant stimulus. *Vis. Res.* 25:685–88

Perry, V. H., Oehler, R., Cowey, A. 1984. Retinal ganglion cells that project to the dorsal lateral geniculate nucleus in the macaque monkey. *Neuroscience* 12:1101–23

Purpura, K., Kaplan, E., Shapley, R. M. 1988. Background light and the contrast gain of primate P and M retinal ganglion cells. *Proc. Natl. Acad. Sci. USA* 85:4534–37

Ramachandran, V. S., Gregory, R. 1978. Does colour provide an input to human motion perception? *Nature* 275:55–56

Rayleigh, J. W. S. 1989. On the limit to interference when light is radiated from moving molecules. *Philos. Mag.* 27:298–304

Robson, J. G. 1975. Receptive fields: neural representation of the spatial and intensive attributes of the visual image. In *Handbook of Perception: Seeing,* ed. E. C. Carterette, M. P. Friedman, 5:81–116. New York: Academic

Rodieck, R. W. 1988. The primate retina. *Comp. Primate Biol.* 4:203–78

Rohaly, A. M., Buchsbaum, G. 1988. Inference of global spatiochromatic mechanisms from contrast sensitivity functions. *J. Opt. Soc. Am.* A5:572–76

Rohaly, A. M., Buchsbaum, G. 1989. Global spatiochromatic mechanism accounting for luminance variations in contrast sensitivity functions. *J. Opt. Soc. Am.* A6:312–17

Schiller, P. H., Colby, C. L. 1983. The responses of single cells in the lateral geniculate nucleus of the rhesus monkey to color and luminance contrast. *Vis. Res.* 23:1631–41

Schiller, P. H., Malpeli, J. G. 1977. Properties and tectal projections of monkey ganglion cells. *J. Neurophysiol.* 40:428–45

Schiller, P. H., Malpeli, J. G. 1978. Functional specificity of lateral geniculate laminae in the rhesus monkey. *J. Neurophysiol.* 41:788–97

Schnapf, J. L., Kraft, T. W., Baylor, D. A. 1987. Spectral sensitivity of human cone photoreceptors. *Nature* 325:439–41

Shapley, R., Enroth-Cugell, C. 1984. Visual adaptation and retinal gain controls. In *Progress in Retinal Research,* ed. N. Osborne, G. Chader, 3:263–346. Oxford: Pergamon

Shapley, R., Kaplan, E. 1989. Responses of magnocellular LGN neurons and M retinal ganglion cells to drifting heterochromatic gratings. *Inv. Ophthalmol. Vis. Sci. Suppl.* 30:323

Shapley, R., Kaplan, E., Soodak, R. 1981. Spatial summation and contrast sensitivity of X and Y cells in the lateral geniculate nucleus of the macaque. *Nature* 292:543–45

Shapley, R., Perry, V. H. 1986. Cat and monkey retinal ganglion cells and their visual functional roles. *Trends Neurosci.* 9:229–35

Shipp, S., Zeki, S. 1985. Segregation of pathways leading from area V2 to areas V4 and

V5 of macaque visual cortex. *Nature* 315:322–25

Smith, V. C., Pokorny, J. 1975. Spectral sensitivity of the foveal cone photopigments between 400 and 500 nm. *Vis. Res.* 15:161–72

Sperling, H. G., Harwerth, R. S. 1971. Red-green cone interactions in the increment-threshold spectral sensitivity of primates. *Science* 172:180–84

Stromeyer, C. F., Cole, G. R., Kronauer, R. E. 1987. Chromatic suppression of cone inputs to the luminance flicker mechanism. *Vis. Res.* 27:1113–37

Switkes, E., Bradley, A., DeValois, K. K. 1988. Contrast dependence and mechanisms of masking interactions among chromatic and luminance gratings. *J. Opt. Soc. Am.* A7:1149–62

Tootell, R. B. H., Hamilton, S. L., Switkes, E. 1988a. Functional anatomy of macaque striate cortex. IV. Contrast and magno-parvo streams. *J. Neurosci.* 8:1594–1609

Tootell, R. B. H., Silverman, M. S., DeValois, R. L., Jacobs, G. H. 1983. Functional organization of the second visual cortical area in primates. *Science* 220:737–39

Tootell, R. B. H., Silverman, M. S., Hamilton, S. L., DeValois, R. L., Switkes, E. 1988b. Functional anatomy of macaque striate cortex. III. Color. *J. Neurosci.* 8:1569–93

Troscianko, T., Harris, J. 1988. Phase discrimination in chromatic compound gratings. *Vis. Res.* 28:1041–49

van der Horst, G. J. C., de Weert, C. M. M, Bouman, M. A. 1967. Transfer of spatial chromaticity contrast at threshold in the human eye. *J. Opt. Soc. Am.* 57:126–66

Wagner, G., Boynton, R. M. 1972. Comparison of four methods of heterochromatic photometry. *J. Opt. Soc. Am.* 62:1508–15

Walls, G. L. 1942. *The Vertebrate Eye and Its Adaptive Radiation.* Michigan: Cranbrook Press

Wiesel, T. N., Hubel, D. H. 1966. Spatial and chromatic interactions in the lateral geniculate body of the rhesus monkey. *J. Neurophysiol.* 29:1115–56

Zrenner, E., Gouras, P. 1983. Cone opponency in tonic ganglion cells and its variation with eccentricity in rhesus monkey retina. In *Colour Vision,* ed. J. D. Mollon, L. T. Sharpe, pp. 211–24. London: Academic

Annu. Rev. Psychol. 1990. 41:659–88

INDIVIDUAL PSYCHOTHERAPY:
Process and Outcome

Marvin R. Goldfried

Department of Psychology, State University of New York at Stony Brook, Stony Brook, New York 11794

Leslie S. Greenberg

Department of Psychology, York University, North York, Ontario, Canada M3J 1P3

Charles Marmar

Department of Psychiatry, University of California, San Francisco, California 94143

CONTENTS

659

GENERAL INTRODUCTION[1]

The days have long since gone when it was possible to review the progress of psychotherapy in a single chapter as Snyder (1950) did in the first *Annual Review of Psychology (ARP)* chapter on the topic written some 40 years ago. Even the efficacy of psychotherapy is too global an issue, as psychosocial interventions have operated from within different theoretical conceptualizations, been applied to various disorders, and taken the form of differing modalities. In an attempt to deal with this diversity, and in the spirit of the trend toward the integration of the psychotherapies, this chapter was written by three therapy researchers and practicing clinicians familiar with different clinical problems and identifying with the field's three primary conceptual orientations—behaviorial, experiential, and psychodynamic. Even so, the review was a major undertaking, reflecting the clear signs of progress, if not rapidly growing maturity, in the field.

In their *ARP* chapter Parloff et al (1986) reviewed meta-analyses concerned with the effectiveness of psychotherapy. Consistent with the trend toward the evaluation of the effectiveness of psychosocial interventions for particular disorders, the importance of such general meta-analyses has recently declined. In addition to moving toward the question of therapeutic efficacy for specific disorders, there is also a growing trend toward grappling with the question of how therapeutic change takes place when it does. This concern for studying the process of change, which we believe to be crucial in enhancing the efficacy of our procedures, is a dominant theme of the present review.

Much of what has been happening in the field of psychotherapy is highlighted in volumes such as the third edition of Garfield & Bergin's (1986) *Handbook of Psychotherapy and Behavior Change* and Huber's (1987) *Progress in Psychotherapy Research*. A notable addition to the most recent *Handbook* is a chapter by Klerman (1986) on drugs and psychotherapy, reflecting the movement in recent years toward the use of pharmacotherapy together with—or instead of—psychosocial interventions in the treatment of various disorders.

Since the last *ARP* review, the National Institute of Mental Health (NIMH) has undergone a reorganization. Programs are now clustered according to diagnostic categories. The Psychosocial Treatment Research Branch has been eliminated, and applications involving psychosocial interventions are included within programs dealing with specific disorders. Although there is much to be said for the focus on the effectiveness of treatment for specific clinical problems grouped according to *Diagnostic and Statistical Manual* (DSM III-R) categories, the change raises the question of whether support can

---

[1]The chapter focuses specifically on individual psychotherapy with adults, and includes work appearing between 1985 and 1988.

be available for clinically relevant problems that do not necessarily have a DSM label—e.g. anger (Deffenbacher et al 1987). In an attempt to recapture the psychosocial intervention thread that runs through the varying NIMH programs, a Psychotherapy Consortium is being developed within NIMH that will attempt to identify existing gaps in psychotherapy research.

TRENDS AND ISSUES

Clinical Trials

Randomized clinical trials—comparisons among contrasting treatments or between treatment and control groups—remain a major focus of activity in psychotherapy reasearch. This paradigm, however, continues to stir up controversy, in part because different treatments have tended to yield roughly comparable outcomes, but also because studies are complex, time consuming, and expensive; methodological issues limit the validity and generalizability of the findings; and even the best-financed investigators have difficulty mounting a coherent program of sequential trials (Kazdin 1986).

For the most part, randomized trials have focused on DSM Axis I disorders, a strategy that ignores important heterogeneity with respect to "interpersonal" problems. The latter, reflected in recurrent maladaptive interpersonal relationship patterns, may interact in complex and often unknown ways with treatment approaches. Greater attention to locating subjects with Axis II diagnoses, together with the use of such evaluation procedures as the Structural Analysis of Social Behavior (Benjamin et al 1986), the Core Conflictual Relationship Theme coding (Luborsky et al 1988), and the Inventory of Interpersonal Problems (Horowitz et al 1988), may lead to advances in the understanding of differential treatment efficacy.

Kazdin (1986) and Strupp (1986) have advocated the study of process in comparative outcome trials, a strategy that has proved useful in a recent study of the relationship of the therapeutic alliance to outcome in behavioral, cognitive, and brief dynamic therapy for late-life depression (Marmar et al 1990).

Methodological Developments

The development of methods for demonstrating clinical (in addition to statistical) significance has been one of the major advances in outcome research (Jacobson 1988). Power considerations in design have also become a topic of major interest, with concern being expressed about the possibility of ever attaining adequate power in differential treatment designs (Kazdin 1986).

Criteria of adequate design for outcome studies now seem well established (Shapiro 1989; Kazdin 1986). The generalizability of findings from studies using solicited clients has been questioned (Krupnick et al 1986); and interesting conceptual and methodological issues have been raised in comparative studies of psychotherapy and pharmacotherapy regarding the differences in their active ingredients, expected treatment effects, time course of treatments, and potential sources of bias (Elkin et al 1988). As noted above, the ferment around meta-analysis has died down; no panacea, this procedure is now seen as fruitful when used appropriately (Bowers & Clum 1988). The role and utility of placebo controls continue to be discussed. Horvath (1988) argues that placebo treatments, as used to date, are not composed of common factors; Parloff (1986) asserts that placebo controls cannot serve as a primary test of the efficacy of psychosocial therapies but can properly address questions about how a treatment works.

In process research, sequential analytic methods have been developed and applied to the testing of hypotheses. Methodological shortcomings in population/treatment interaction research designs have been noted, and the use of regression techniques rather than analysis of variance (ANOVA) is strongly recommended for identifying treatment-relevant patient attributes. Weaknesses in individualized measures of change have been discussed (Beutler & Hamblin 1986) and it has been suggested that rather than identifying individual targets of change, it is better to select a sample on the basis of preexisting similarity on a dimension that is then used as the index of change for all patients.

Hayes and colleagues (1987) have made the important suggestion that the treatment utility of assessment should be given greater consideration, and have described methods of studying the contribution of assessment to treatment. A final methodological innovation comes in the form of an interesting study of the dose-effect relationship in psychotherapy (Howard et al 1986), in which probit analysis was applied to over 2400 patients. By the 8th session, approximately 50% of patients were measurably improved, with approximately 75% improved after 26 sessions.

Training, Utilization of Research Findings, and Therapy Manuals

Resulting in part from the growing popularity of therapy manuals, the field of psychotherapy has experienced a renewed interest in training issues. Indeed, the Special Series in the October 1988 issue of the *Journal of Consulting and Clinical Psychology* is devoted specifically to this topic.

The predominant model for training psychotherapists continues to involve individual supervision. Based on their own findings and those of others, Guest & Beutler (1988) emphasize that trainees depend on support from their supervisors at first and only later benefit from specific technical skills. In evaluating the effectiveness of the training process, Newman and colleagues (1988) suggest the use of a constant-stimulus model, whereby trainees' clinical formulations and recommendations with a standard set of clinical material can be compared with those of more seasoned clinicians.

Another approach to assessing the effectiveness of training has involved the use of therapist competency scales. Shaw & Dobson (1988) recommended the use of such scales in clinical training, provided they are obtained across a wide range of cases that vary in level of difficulty. It has been demonstrated that such competency measures can be reliably obtained (Vallis et al 1986; Rounsaville et al 1986). Their use is particularly important inasmuch as Butler & Strupp (1990) have observed that even with careful training in time-limited dynamic psychotherapy, experienced therapists continue to have difficulty in following the therapeutic guidelines. This essentially confirms what we all know from clinical experience, namely that some therapists are better than others—regardless of training.

To what extent do practicing therapists actually draw on psychotherapy research findings? Morrow-Bradley & Elliott (1986) report that research utilization depended on theoretical orientation. Specifically, behavior therapists found research findings more useful than did psychodynamic therapists. The most typical criticism by all therapists was that the research tended to be oversimplified and irrelevant to their actual clinical work. These findings also suggest that the process-outcome model of research, especially one that focuses on significant change events (Rice & Greenberg 1984; Strupp 1986), and a data base that reflects the compilation of results across practicing therapists (McCullough et al 1986), are more likely than are standard clinical trials to have implications for the practicing clinician.

For years, psychotherapy researchers have wondered how best to transmit research findings to the practicing therapist. At a Society for Psychotherapy Research Roundtable discussion on this topic participants expressed their dismay that the practicing clinician was not a "good consumer." Had the Roundtable been a corporate board, however, the focus would no doubt have been on the limits of the marketing approach, not the inadequacy of the consumer.

Practicing clinicians have long lamented that psychotherapy researchers often write for other psychotherapy researchers and are only secondarily concerned with the utility of their findings for therapists. This was confirmed in a study by Cohen and his associates (1986), who found that clinicians reported that the methodological emphasis in written reports—though clearly crucial in drawing appropriate conclusions regarding the research findings—did not provide them with the information needed to carry out the intervention in question.

In marked contrast to the utilization of research findings, interest in therapy manuals has grown rapidly. This increase in the popularity of treatment manuals is due no doubt to their use in training therapists as part of the NIMH

Treatment of Depression Collaborative Research Program (Elkin et al 1985). In the September 1988 issue of *The American Psychologist,* the American Psychological Association solicited manuscripts for 100- to 125-page "How-to-do-it" volumes. Lambert & Ogles (1988) reviewed the literature on therapy manuals. Those available cover a broad spectrum, including generic guidelines organized according to phases of treatment (Kanfer & Schefft 1988) and the therapeutic use of interpersonal communication between patient and therapist (Kiesler 1988). More typically, however, manuals deal with specific disorders, ranging from panic and obsessive-compulsive disorders to problems such as bulimia (Barlow & Cerny 1988; Turner & Beidel 1988; Weiss et al 1985).

We also note an irony regarding the utility of therapy manuals for the training of therapists. The availability of such manuals has been the by-product of an NIMH requirement that such guidelines be included in all funded research. The requirement aimed at assuring treatment integrity, enabling readers to identify more readily the nature of the intervention being studied. Thus, even though the original intent was otherwise, therapy manuals may have served indirectly to transmit the innovative and effective interventions of researchers to the practicing clinician.

Trends in Psychodynamic, Behavioral, and Experiential Therapies

We have organized this chapter according to issues and clinical problems, rather than therapeutic orientations. Several interesting trends within the psychodynamic, behavioral, and experiential orientations are nonetheless worth noting briefly.

PSYCHODYNAMIC THERAPY   A major thrust of research activities in the area of psychodynamic therapy has been in the evaluation of the efficacy of brief dynamic psychotherapy (Koss et al 1986), and several important efforts have been made to use manual-based brief dynamic psychotherapy interventions (Strupp & Binder 1984; Luborsky 1984). Brief dynamic therapy has been shown to be effective for the treatment of stress and bereavement disorders (Marmar & Horowitz 1988); late life depression (Thompson et al 1987); adjustment, affective, and personality disorders (Marziali 1984); and various other disorders.

Recent studies have also attempted to elucidate the active ingredients in brief dynamic psychotherapies. Convergent findings from different groups of investigators have supported the role of the therapeutic or working alliance as a predictor of outcome (Frieswyk et al 1986). For motivated, psychologically minded, and higher functioning patients, greater frequency of transference interpretations is associated with better outcome (Marziali 1984). With less motivated and more disturbed patients, however, greater emphasis on transference interpretations is associated with poorer therapeutic alliance (Marmar et al 1989) and poorer outcome (Horowitz et al 1984). Therapists who pass key transference tests by intervening in a way that allows patients to control and master their unconscious wishes both facilitate the emergence of therapeutically important material and achieve better outcomes (Sampson & Weiss 1986).

Empirical studies of longer-term dynamic psychotherapies and formal psychoanalysis have, for logistic reasons, been more limited in scope. A notable exception has been a series of studies by the Mount Zion psychotherapy research group, summarized by Sampson & Weiss (1986). This group has identified the therapeutic conditions associated with the emergence of anxiety-producing content and provided evidence for both the therapeutic value of patient efforts to disconfirm pathogenic transferential beliefs and the tendency of patients to relinquish defenses and bring forward painful mental contents under conditions of safety (i.e. when they believe they will not endanger the therapist or themselves in this process).

BEHAVIOR THERAPY   As behavior therapy has developed and matured, the cognitive influence that began in the 1970s has become part of the mainstream. Books describing cognitive-behavioral methods continue to be written (Beck & Emery 1985; Dobson 1988; Dryden & Golden 1986; Guidano 1987; Mahoney & Freeman 1985), and Dobson (1988) estimates that no fewer than 22 variations of cognitive-behavior therapy now exist.

A cognitive-behavioral intervention procedure that has been gaining in popularity consists of training in problem solving. Based on the assumption that problematic human behavior often results from ineffective responses to difficult life circumstances, such training provides individuals with a generalized skill for coping with social and interpersonal problems. Close to 20 years after it was introduced into the behavioral literature (D'Zurilla & Goldfried 1971), problem solving has been found useful in dealing with a variety of clinical problems, including stress, depression, suicidal behavior, agoraphobia, alcoholism, drug addiction, marital and family conflict, psychiatric disorders, antisocial child behavior, mental retardation, and primary prevention (Castles & Glass 1986; D'Zurilla 1986; Kazdin et al 1987; Nezu et al 1989; Platt et al 1988).

Wachtel's (1982) edited volume on resistance, containing four behavioral and four psychodynamic chapters, apparently provided the impetus for behavior therapists to attend to the issue of treatment adherence, and specific guidelines have been developed for dealing with such issues (Meichenbaum & Turk 1987). A particularly interesting study by Patterson & Forgatch (1985) has pinpointed the types of therapist behavior that lead to client noncompliance (e.g. confrontation) or adherence (e.g. support).

Very much a reflection of the coping-skills model that now characterizes behavior therapy, pioneering work on relapse prevention in the treatment of such addictive behaviors as alcoholism, smoking, and overeating has been given increasing recognition (Brownell et al 1986; Marlatt & Gordon 1985). The important distinction is made between a "lapse" and a "relapse" so that slips during the course of and following therapy are construed as temporary setbacks rather than as failures of intervention. Clients are taught to identify the situations that may result in such lapses and are provided with anxiety-reduction and interpersonal skills to deal more effectively with events that might otherwise contribute to a relapse.

EXPERIENTIAL THERAPY   With the exception of work on focused expressive psychotherapy for constricted affect (Daldrup et al 1988) and emotionally focused therapy (Greenberg & Johnson 1988), little evaluation research has been done in experiential therapy over the review period. The experiential tradition is either in danger of becoming extinct, or can perhaps more positively be seen as being absorbed by other approaches and as evolving into an integrative/eclectic approach.

Mahrer (1986) has been the most prolific writer and researcher on experiential therapy, emphasizing the importance of experiencing and "good moments" (i.e. significant episodes) in therapy (Mahrer & Nadler 1986). A number of European researchers are generating interesting new research programs on the immediate impacts of intervention (Bastine et al 1989; Saachse 1989). Greenberg & Safran (1987), drawing on developments in experimental and theoretical psychology, have laid out an integrative model of emotional processing. They suggest that emotion provides the organism with biologically adaptive feedback about its responses to situations. They distinguish among four classes of emotion—primary, secondary, instrumental and maladaptive—adding that only primary emotion provides adaptive information. They define a set of principles for working with emotion in therapy and a set of therapeutic cognitive/affective processing tasks in which emotion plays an important role. This view offers a new theoretical framework for understanding experiential therapy and has provided a perspective on the process of psychotherapy in the treatment of depression, anxiety, and marital conflict (Greenberg & Johnson 1988; Safran & Greenberg 1988). This focus on emotion in therapy and dysfunction helps to add to behavioral and cognitive views, resulting in a more complete view of human functioning. Clarke & Greenberg (1986) have also demonstrated the superiority of an emotionally focused intervention—the gestalt two-chair dialog—over problem solving for resolving decisional conflict.

Training in the experiential tradition has been reviewed and a number of manual-based forms of this therapy are emerging (Greenberg & Goldman

1988). A new compendium of papers on client-centered and experiential therapy (Lietar et al 1989), drawn from the first international conference on this topic, attempts to set the direction for this approach in the post-Rogers era.

Individual Psychotherapy and the Social System

Among the many difficulties in writing a chapter that reviews the work on individual psychotherapy is the fact that such interventions often focus on the patients'/clients' larger social systems as well. Wachtel & Wachtel (1986) provide a theoretical perspective and therapeutic guidelines according to which psychodynamic therapy and family interventions may be integrated. In justifying the relevance of working with the family of a patient being seen in individual therapy, they refer to the construct of "cyclical psychodynamics," whereby a patient's anticipation of another individual's reaction may result in the self-fulfilling prophecy. Although it may be possible to produce changes by working with the individual, the Wachtels suggest that therapeutic change may be facilitated by reworking these distorted perceptions and interactions in the presence of the very individuals with whom the problematic interpersonal relationships are likely to occur.

A fair amount of research has been conducted on the interaction between schizophrenic patients and their families, particularly on the role "expressed emotion"—family members' tendency toward criticism and emotional over-involvement—plays in predicting relapse (Falloon 1988; Hooley 1985). The vulnerable individual lives in a social system in which chronic interpersonal stressors are present, typically in the form of highly controlling relatives. When combined with neuroleptic medication, family therapy improves patient functioning and decreases relapse (Falloon et al 1985). The importance of working with families and spouses has extended to other disorders as well, including agoraphobia, depression, and alcoholism (Cerney et al 1987, Chambless et al 1986; Jacobson et al 1989). Preliminary studies by Beach & O'Leary (1986) of the role dysfunctional marital relationships may play in depression have found symptom reduction resulting from successful marital intervention.

Cognitive Science and Therapeutic Change

Because various theoretical approaches to therapy hold that cognitive distortions are central to psychopathology, it is not surprising that the language, concepts, and findings from the cognitive sciences—cognitive psychology and social cognition—have begun to occupy a salient place in the psychotherapy literature. An increasing number of authors specifically apply social information processing to clinical psychology and psychotherapy intervention (Abramson 1988; Ingram 1986; Turk & Salovey 1988). The concept of "schema" has been found particularly useful in understanding the cognitive biases that stem from a client's past experiences.

Literature from the cognitive sciences has helped us to understand anxiety (Ingram & Kendall 1987), depression (Segal 1988), worry (Borkovec et al 1987), and personality disorders (Murray 1988). Concepts from cognitive psychology and social cognition have also been used to elucidate how therapeutic change occurs (Greenberg & Safran 1987; Mahoney 1988; Winfrey & Goldfried 1986). In writing about the behavioral approach to fear reduction, Foa & Kozak (1986) have made use of an information-processing model to explain the effectiveness of exposure methods, suggesting that memory and meaning structures underlying emotional reactions are changed during the therapeutic intervention. Forsterling (1986) has offered therapeutic guidelines that emphasize change in unrealistic beliefs by the alteration of faulty attributions. Constructs from the cognitive sciences have also been used in the attempt to reconceptualize psychodynamic therapy (Horowitz 1988). Singer (1985) and Westen (1988) have provided an intriguing conceptualization of transference as involving an interpersonal script, reflecting the cognitive, emotional, and behavioral rules for dealing with certain prototypic interpersonal situations.

Constructs from the cognitive sciences may provide therapists and psychotherapy researchers with both a common basis for discourse across their various orientations and a vehicle for retrieving basic research findings in the area of cognitive functioning that may have important implications for better understanding the therapeutic change process.

The Process of Change

A new generation of process research has emerged over this period (Greenberg & Pinsof 1986; Dahl et al 1988). Special sections on process research have appeared in the 1989 issues of the *Journal of Consulting and Clinical Psychology* and the *Zeitschrift für klinische Psychologie*. Research has moved from a study of single, in-therapy interactions and association between variables to more complex functional study of change processes (Stiles et al 1986). In this new approach, investigators analyze in-therapy change performances in detail in an attempt to determine the therapeutic action of the treatment (Rice & Greenberg 1984; Safran et al 1988; Mahrer 1985; Weiss & Sampson 1986). Important to this approach has been the specification of intermediate-level psychological determinants of problems that mediate between diagnostic grouping and type of intervention. This level of specification provides for more refined differential intervention possibilities. With specification of the more intermediate psychological determinants of problems—e.g. pathogenic beliefs (Weiss & Sampson 1986) and the plans to overcome these beliefs (Curtis et al 1988), core conflictual relationship themes (Luborsky et al 1988), conflict splits (Rice & Greenberg 1984), problematic reactions (Rice & Greenberg 1984), negative interpersonal cycles (Strupp & Binder 1984), and unfinished business (Daldrup et al 1988; Greenberg & Safran 1987)—it becomes possible to determine the interventions most appropriate at specific points in therapy, the type of in-therapy occurrence to which interventions are applicable, and the types of intermediate change that are expected (Safran et al 1986; Silberschatz et al 1990). Thus interpretations of core conflictual relationship themes affect self-understanding more than do interpretations of other themes (Luborsky et al 1988). Studying the effects of specific therapist actions in psychoanalysis, the Mount Zion group (Weiss & Sampson 1986) has shown that interpretations judged to be plan compatible lead to improved functioning on a number of process measures (Silberschatz et al 1986).

The study of significant events in psychotherapy (Bastine et al 1989; Elliott et al 1985) in a variety of ways (Mahrer & Nadler 1986) has given process research a new sense of vigor. Studies of the effects of specific types of interpretations in psychodynamic therapy (Dahl et al 1988), of gestalt two-chair dialog for resolving conflict (Clarke & Greenberg 1986), and of systematic evocative responding for resolving problematic reactions in client-centered therapy (Rice & Saperia 1984) have been reported. The investigation of significant events, such as therapy episodes in which relationships are discussed, has begun to reveal the mechanisms of the change process. Among the mechanisms studied have been the role of the wish and the expected response of self and others in conflictual relationships (Luborsky et al 1988) and the role of the softening of introjected self-criticism in resolving intrapersonal conflict (Rice & Greenberg 1984). Analyses of significant events have demonstrated the importance of the disconfirmation of pathogenic beliefs in the therapeutic relationship and the value of vivid reprocessing of one's construals of a problematic situation so as to gain a new view of one's self-in-the-world functioning (Rice & Greenberg 1984).

The current generation of process research promises to forge a new link between assessment and intervention. Patients diagnosed as depressed or as having a generalized anxiety disorder may be suffering from the disorder for a variety of reasons. Thus, a depression may be due to loss and unresolved grief, loss of self-esteem, interpersonal problems, marital conflict, lack of interpersonal skills, the inability to express emotion, or to a combination of these. This calls for an understanding both of the determinants of any client's disorder and the mechanisms of change, and of the interventions needed to produce change for these determinants. Research must aim to demonstrate that for *this* determinant, *this* intervention produces *this* type of change process, resulting in *this* type of outcome. As suggested by Arkowitz (1989), knowledge of psychopathology provides information about *what* to change, whereas our understanding of psychotherapy process tells us *how* change may be brought about.

Another major trend evident in the process literature is toward the description and measurement of the therapeutic working alliance (Bordin 1979) as the overarching general process variable that relates to outcome (Alexander & Luborsky 1986; Hartley 1985; Marmar et al 1986; Horvath & Greenberg 1986). Although much of the theoretical and empirical work on the alliance has come from the psychodynamic and client-centered traditions, the role of the alliance has recently been recognized in cognitive and behavioral psychotherapy (Deffenbacher 1985; Gelso & Carter 1985; Rush 1985), as well as in pharmacotherapy (Docherty & Feister 1985). These developments have contributed to a view that the alliance is central to the change process and to the prediction of outcome in a variety of treatments proposing various mechanisms of action. Interest is also growing in the identification of the dimensions of this complex construct. For example, Marmar and colleagues (1990) reported five dimensions based upon a principal-component factor analysis of a 31-item measure: patient commitment, patient working capacity, therapist understanding and involvement, therapist negative contribution, and disagreement on goals and strategies. Horvath & Greenberg (1986), building on Bordin's (1979) model, assessed three dimensions—personal bond, agreement on goals, and agreement on tasks—and reported encouraging preliminary findings on the predictive utility of the measure.

The field has witnessed the construction and application of a variety of other process instruments (Greenberg & Pinsof 1986) measuring such aspects of the therapeutic process as interpersonal interaction (Benjamin et al 1986; Henry et al 1986), client perceptual processing (Toukmanian 1986), negative indicators (Suh et al 1986; Rosser 1988), and a variety of aspects of language in psychotherapy (Russell 1987). Therapist verbal response modes (Elliott et al 1987) continue to be studied and are being supplemented by interesting new measures of therapist's and client's intentions (Hill et al 1988; Hill & O'Grady 1985) and client's subjective recall of impacts using interpersonal process recall (Elliott 1986). A psychotherapy process Q-sort (Jones et al 1988) and a system for coding the therapeutic focus (Goldfried & Newman 1986a) have been devised in an attempt to provide a standard language for the description and classification of therapy process. These have been used to demonstrate the importance of both common and specific factors. Glass & Arnkoff (1988) found that both common and specific factors played a role in change, although Butler & Strupp (1986) have questioned the usefulness of the dichotomy.

Patient involvement and the therapeutic relationship have been related to outcome in a group of adult outpatients in brief psychodynamic therapy (Windholz & Silberschatz 1988). Research reviews have also shown that therapists account more for outcome variance than does type of treatment (Luborsky et al 1986a) and that those therapist variables that best relate to outcome involve the therapy experiences of the participants (e.g. empathy) rather than extratherapy traits (e.g. emotional adjustment) (Lafferty et al 1989). Process variables rather than patient/client preexisting traits have also been shown to be the best predictors of outcome, as have therapists' ratings of patient's/client's involvement (Kolb et al 1985). Matching of therapist internal-external focus with patient/client defensive style has been shown to be a significant predictor of outcome (Calvert et al 1988). The SASB—Structural Analysis of Social Behavior—developed by Benjamin and her associates (Benjamin et al 1986) has been found to be a particularly valuable instrument in categorizing helpful and harmful therapeutic interactions (Henry et al 1986).

There have been impressive attempts to develop a computer-based content analysis system for therapy text (Kaechele 1988; Mergenthaler & Kaechele 1985), and Dahl (1988) has sought to analyze patient verbal productions in therapy to discover repetitive structures or frames of mind.

Review chapters have appeared on therapist variables (Beutler et al 1986), client variables (Garfield 1986), and process variables related to outcome (Orlinksy & Howard 1986). Based on their comprehensive review, Orlinsky & Howard (1986) have provided a generic model of psychotherapy that contains five conceptual elements—the therapeutic contract, interventions, bonds, patient self-relatedness, and therapeutic realizations. They suggest that the therapeutic bond (preparing the patient for participation and collaborative sharing of responsibility for problem solving) plus skillful interventions focused on feeling are therapeutically effective; within limits, the amount of therapy is positively correlated with effectiveness.

The investigation of complex change processes rather than a search for simple associations between variables promises to help us unravel how therapy works and thus to improve both therapy and the research that informs practice (Thompson 1987). Methodological developments and the construction of new in-session and post-session measures to capture change process are needed. Finally, Stiles (1988) cogently argues that process-outcome correlations may be inherently misleading, in that process components may have more to say about specific patient requirements than they do about outcome. These assertions should be heeded as the field begins seriously to attempt to relate process to outcome.

PROCESS AND OUTCOME FOR SPECIFIC DISORDERS

The efficacy of psychotherapy can only be evaluated meaningfully within the context of specific clinical problems. Here we highlight progress made for anxiety disorders, depression, and selected other clinical problems.

Anxiety Disorders

Research on the clinical efficacy of psychosocial interventions for anxiety disorders has proceeded at a rapid pace, a number of important books having been published in this area (Barlow 1988; Beck & Emery 1985; Last & Hersen 1988; Marks 1987; Mavissakalian et al 1985; Michelson & Ascher 1987; Shaw et al 1986).

Exposure to the object of fear continues to be the treatment of choice for simple phobia. Indeed, Ghosch and co-workers (1988) have demonstrated that self-treatment for this disorder can be clinically effective. While patients found that a live therapist added tolerance and understanding to the treatment, use of either a self-help book or a set of computer-assisted instructions was comparably effective.

Although Barlow & Wolfe's (1981) report of the NIMH-SUNY Albany Research Conference recommended that process research be conducted with simple phobias, little has been done to date. Marshall (1985) found that with height phobics, duration of exposure is positively related to outcome. He also found that cognitive coping procedures significantly added to the effectiveness of exposure at follow-up.

Treatment development and research on agoraphobia and panic disorders have made particularly important strides over the past several years. Self-paced exposure helps agoraphobics as much as therapist accompaniment does (Ghosch & Marks 1987; Michelson et al 1986). With the exception of the extent of "fear of fear," no clear-cut predictors of successful outcome following exposure treatment have been identified (Chambless & Gracely 1988). Although marital adjustment does not predict outcome (Arrindell et al 1986), the involvement of one's spouse in the intervention enhances the effectiveness of exposure (Cerney et al 1987).

A well-controlled study by Telch et al (1985) investigated the relative contributions of exposure and imipramine in the reduction of avoidance and panic. A combination of exposure and imipramine was more effective than either alone. Imipramine, when combined with instructions to avoid exposure to fearful situations, was *not* clinically effective in reducing panic attacks, raising questions about the mechanisms associated with the pharmacological intervention.

Along with the reorganization of DSM III-R that made panic disorders a primary diagnosis, with the secondary emphasis on varying degress of agoraphobic avoidance, there has been a marked shift toward the direct treatment of panic. Ley (1985) has suggested that panic attacks are antecedent to behavioral avoidance and result from the experience of symptoms associated with hyperventilation, such as palpitations and dyspnea. The role of cognitive distortion has also been added to this conceptualization, maintaining that the somatic sensations associated with hyperventilation and anxiety are misinterpreted, resulting in a further increase in anxiety and panic. Thus, a treatment package for panic disorders with agoraphobia has been developed combining relaxation, breathing retraining, cognitive restructuring, simulation of the sensations of panic attacks within the session for practice in coping, and exposure. This treatment appears to eliminate panic attacks (Barlow 1988; Beck 1988; Clark et al 1985; Shear et al 1987). If these preliminary findings hold up under further test, we may have witnessed a major breakthrough in the psychosocial treatment of anxiety disorders.

A treatment procedure for general anxiety disorders has been developed by Butler and associates (1987) involving coping relaxation, cognitive restructuring, and graded exposure. This anxiety-management procedure proved more effective than a waiting-list control. A 6-month follow-up on the treatment group indicated that, based on Hamilton Anxiety Scores, patients' anxiety had been reduced by an average of 69%, surpassing the 62% reduction obtained in previous research using drugs (Barlow 1988). A study by Borkovec and co-workers (1987) demonstrated that a relaxation and cognitive-behavior therapy intervention package was more effective than relaxation combined with nondirective therapy. Ongoing research by Borkovec and associates (Borkovec et al 1986) on the characteristics of, and interventions with, worriers may have important implications for the treatment of this disorder as well.

As estimated by Foa and her colleagues (1985), controlled outcome studies on obsessive-compulsive disorders using exposure and response prevention indicate that approximately 51% of the patients treated were symptom free at termination; an additional 39% were moderately improved. Although this intervention procedure has typically been administered in a hospital setting, it can be applied effectively on an out-patient basis as well (Emmelkamp 1987).

Process research on the treatment of obsessive-compulsive disorders has yielded interesting findings. For example, Kozak et al (1988) found that fear activation during exposure sessions was positively related to successful outcome. It has also been found that overvalued ideation (strongly held and emotionally laden beliefs) and depression interfered with successful treatment; relapse was more likely when only moderate improvement had occurred at termination than when much improvement had occurred (Steketee & Foa 1985). Severity of rituals, social disability, overvalued ideation, but not depression predicted improvement (Basoglu et al 1988).

Preliminary clinical observations by Turner et al (1990) suggest that exposure and response prevention, when following by a trial of fluoxetine, may provide dramatic reductions in both obsessional ideation and ritualistic behavior. Other research, on the other hand, has found that clomipramine plus exposure was no more effective than placebo plus exposure, and that anti-exposure instructions with clomipramine were not as effective as was clomi-pramine administered with exposure (Marks et al 1988).

Exposure procedures do not enjoy the same clear-cut success with social phobics as they do with patients having anxiety disorders. Thus, Emmelkamp and his colleagues (1985) found that both cognitive restructuring and self-instructional training were as effective as exposure in treating social phobics. When cognitive restructuring is combined with exposure, its effectiveness is apparently enhanced (Mattick & Peters 1988). One of the difficulties in evaluating the effectiveness of treatment with this disorder is the heterogene-ity of the category (Heimberg et al 1987). Quite often the literature refers to "social anxiety," leaving it unclear whether "social phobia," "avoidant per-sonality disorder," or a combination of the two has been investigated. Also, the situations in which the anxiety appears can vary, including same-sex interactions, opposite-sex relations, public speaking, and fear of scrutiny by others. To complicate matters still further, individuals may or may not show phobic avoidance in any of these situations. Depending upon the specific problem, the effectiveness of any given intervention is likely to vary, and work on individual differences in this area is just beginning (Arnkoff et al 1987).

Depression

The collaborative depression study, the first multi-site coordinated psy-chotherapy study by the NIMH (Elkin et al 1985), compared two forms of psychotherapy—cognitive-behavioral and interpersonal—with imipramine and pill placebo, each also involving supportive clinical management. According to the initial findings of this study (Elkin et al 1990) there is little evidence that either psychotherapy is more effective than the other, or that the psychotherapies are significantly less effective than the standard reference drug treatment. In fact, all four treatment conditions, including placebo, evidence significant change from pre- to post-treatment. Comparing each of the psychotherapies with the placebo condition, there was limited evidence for the superior effectiveness of interpersonal psychotherapy in reducing depressive symptomatology, and none for the specific effectiveness of cogni-tive-behavior therapy (Elkin et al 1990).

To evaluate the effects of these treatments fully we must await the impor-tant follow-up data on maintenance of improvement and prevention of re-lapse. It should be noted, however, that when patients in this study were dichotomized on initial level of severity and impairment, some differences between treatments did emerge. For the more severely depressed and func-tionally impaired, the imipramine treatment fared best, with it and in-terpersonal therapy resulting in higher rates of recovery than the placebo plus clinical management condition, which did poorly with this group. For the less severe patients, there was no evidence for the specific effectiveness of any of the treatments over the placebo plus clinical management condition.

With the failure to demonstrate the clear superiority of any treatment in the collaborative depression study, we are left posing the obvious question: What are the curative elements in the treatments? We hope the field will be pushed to specify more precisely the change processes that may be involved in these treatments, such as the helping alliance and support that may operate across treatments, including placebo, and the more specific processes that may be operating differentially in each treatment.

Some comparisons of psychotherapy and drug treatment have suggested that combined treatment may present definite advantages over either treatment alone (Frank & Kupfer 1987; Weissman et al 1987; Hollon et al 1988), others have shown no differences between psychotherapy and psychotherapy plus medication at termination (Beck et al 1985), and still others have shown advantages at follow-up for patients who received cognitive-behavior therapy (Simons et al 1986). In the comparison of a cognitive-behavioral (prescriptive) therapy and a dynamic-experiential (exploratory) treatment of depression and anxiety, Shapiro & Firth (1987) found a slight advantage for the prescriptive approach, especially on symptom reduction.

Other approaches to the treatment of depression continue to be developed. Behavioral and problem-solving approaches have been shown to be effective (Brown & Lewinsohn 1984; Hoberman & Lewinsohn 1985; Nezu et al 1989; Rehm et al 1987) in both individual and group treatment (Teri & Lewinsohn 1986). A move to more integrative conceptualizations of the determinants and the treatment of depression is also evident (Lewinsohn et al 1985; Nezu et al 1989). As has been done in the case of anxiety disorders, the field needs to move beyond differential treatment research toward an even more specific understanding of how the variables associated with depression vary among populations. This in turn will lead to differential interventions based on an assessment of the specific determinants and an understanding of the mechanism required for changing them.

Research and discussion on a variety of determinants and mechanisms of change have already begun. Thus, logical analysis and hypothesis testing have been proposed as carrying some of the action in cognitive-behavior therapy (Jarrett & Nelson 1987), as have explanatory style (Seligman et al 1988), learned resourcefulness (Simons et al 1985), and attributional style (DeRubeis et al 1988). The role of cognition in terms of self-schemata (Segal 1988) and thinking patterns (Rush & Weissenburger 1986) has been both strongly asserted (Hollon et al 1987; Segal & Shaw 1986) and strongly critiqued (Coyne & Gotlib 1986) as an important mediating factor in depression. Social problem solving (Nezu et al 1989), inability to express intense affect (Beutler et al 1986), and marital distress (Beach & O'Leary 1986;

Jacobson et al 1987) have also been suggested as mediating variables. Relapse in depression (Kupfer & Frank 1987) and its determinants (Gonzales et al 1985) have been investigated, as have predictors of depression (Lewinsohn et al 1988; Essex et al 1985). In addition to the above variables, a number of personality features of depression and its treatment have been studied (Frank et al 1987; Pilkonis & Frank 1988; Shea et al 1987). This finer analysis of the disorder in terms of both personality and mediating mechanisms points the way to a future in which specific interventions can be prescribed based on functional assessments of the specific determinants of the disorder in a particular patient.

Other Disorders

Space limitations allow us to touch only a few other clinical problems, such as personality disorders, schizophrenia, and bulimia. Reviews of current work on other disorders, such as addictions (Marlatt et al 1988) and the general topic of behavioral medicine (Holroyd & Creer 1986), are available elsewhere.

In contrast to the paucity of controlled research on individual therapy with *personality disorders*, a growing clinical research literature indicates the value of group treatment with this population. The rationale for group therapy includes more manageable regression, dilution of transference reactions, opportunity to use group relationships to address fundamental interpersonal deficits, and cost offset for medical utilization. Preliminary empirical data (e.g. Budman & Gurman 1988; Kretsch et al 1987; Linehan 1987; Marziali & Munroe-Blum 1987) support the value of group therapy alone and in combination with individual supportive-expressive psychotherapy for severe disorders.

Because of the high relapse rate of successfully treated *schizophrenic* inpatients after their return to the community—even when they are compliant with outpatient long-term maintenance chemotherapy—psychosocial treatments continue to be a focus of research and development for this disorder. Both American and British studies have demonstrated that schizophrenic patients who live in families characterized by high "expressed emotion" (criticism, hostility, and emotional overinvolvement) are at greater risk. Family treatments aimed at reduction of negative expressed emotion have had demonstrable beneficial effects on the course of the illness (Falloon et al 1985). The seminal work of Goldstein (1984) on the effect of such negative interactional patterns in the families of schizophrenic patients continues to motivate interest in this area, with a number of clinical trials of family therapy presently in progress.

Wallace & Liberman (1985) have reported that male schizophrenic inpatients from families having high levels of expressed emotion who received social-skills training in addition to chemotherapy, milieu therapy, and multi-family group therapy, did better at two-year follow-up in terms of social functioning, symptomatic relapses, and rehospitalization than did a group that additionally received holistic health treatment. In a randomized trial, Hogarty & Anderson (1986) have similarly demonstrated the additive effects of combining social skills training and family education approaches in reducing relapse rates in both male and female schizophrenic patients recruited from families having high levels of expressed emotion.

Adaptations of cognitive-behavior therapy to address the cognitive deficits specific to schizophrenia, including attentional, perceptual, and thought-organization deficits, have shown initial promise. In 1973, Meichenbaum & Cameron described a self-instructional program in which chronic schizophrenic patients were trained to cue themselves internally to improve task-appropriate cognition, increase resistance to distraction, and sustain a longer attentional focus. In a review of the efficacy of this approach, Bentall and colleagues (1987) concluded that greater success is achieved when self-instructions are tailored to an individual patient's deficits and are made more specifically task relevant. Generic instructions, on the other hand, have led to negative reactions.

Brenner and associates (1987) have reported on work at the University of Bern on the development of a cognitive-behavior therapy approach for schizophrenics, integrating group skills training with a laboratory task format. Kraemer and co-workers (1988) have combined the Bern approach with self-instructional training and demonstrated that this combination of cognitive approaches was helpful in the management of schizophrenia. Studies are ongoing to determine the optimal utilization of less costly generic approaches versus more individually tailored cognitive treatments targeted to the cognitive deficits specific to the schizophrenic spectrum disorders.

There has been a sharp increase in research on the treatment of eating disorders, especially *bulimia nervosa*. Fairburn (1985) reported the development of a cognitive-behavior therapy program for normal-weight bulimics that attempts to normalize eating habits and revise maladaptive beliefs and attitudes concerning body image and weight. Fairburn and his associates (1986) found that an 18-week program of cognitive-behavior therapy and short-term focal psychotherapy both yielded significant improvements that were maintained over a 1-year period, with patients in the cognitive-behavioral condition showing greater reduction in general psychopathology and improvement in social adjustment. Garner and co-workers (1987), in a review of the cognitive-behavior therapy literature, indicated that the median percentage reduction in binge frequency is 79%. Moreover, in eight of the nine studies in the review, further improvement in binge behavior followed treatment termination.

Wilson and his colleagues (1986) conducted a controlled evaluation of cognitive-behavioral treatment of bulimia, in which the additive effect of exposure plus response prevention was investigated. In the exposure plus response prevention approach, clients are exposed to "forbidden" foods and prevented from vomiting once they have consumed these foods. At termination, 71% of the subjects who received combined cognitive-behavior therapy and exposure plus response prevention sessions had stopped binge eating and vomiting, compared to 33% of the subjects who had received cognitive restructuring therapy alone. Leitenberg and associates (1990), however, reported that exposure plus response prevention was only slightly more effective in reducing vomiting and in normalizing eating patterns than the cognitive-behavioral program of Fairburn; all active treatment conditions were more effective than a waiting-list control.

PSYCHOTHERAPY INTEGRATION

Although psychotherapy integration aroused interest as early as the 1930s (Goldfried & Newman 1986b), it has in recent years moved from being a latent issue to a significant theme, reaching international (e.g. Bastine 1986) and psychiatric audiences (Babcock 1988; Beitman et al 1989). In addition to the marked increase in the number of articles and chapters on this topic, the number of books devoted to this topic continues to increase (Beitman 1987; Lecomte & Castonguay 1987; London 1986; Norcross 1986, 1987; Perry et al 1985; Wachtel 1987).

Within cognitive-behavior therapy, there is an increased recognition that what people "tell themselves" may actually be a reflection of a deeper cognitive structure (Biran 1988; Mahoney 1988; Neimeyer 1986). The "schema" construct has begun to play a particularly salient role in cognitive-behavior therapy (Guidano 1987; Mahoney 1988; Young 1990), referring to those cognitive representations stemming from past experience that are used to make sense out of—but also at times to distort—current life events. In work reminiscent of Kelly's (1955) earlier theorizing on the subject, Safran and associates (1986) differentiate between core and peripheral cognitive processes, which are believed to be arranged in hierarchical order on the basis of their generality. The most superordinate structures refer to the core processes, which are perhaps roughly analogous to the "underlying" dynamics within a psychodynamic model.

The interpersonal determinants of clinical problems have been more openly acknowledged by behavior therapists, where it has been found that the treatment of marital problems is just as effective as cognitive-behavior therapy in the treatment of depression (Beach & O'Leary 1986; Jacobson et al 1987). Thus, even when operating from a cognitive-behavioral vantage point, one needs to acknowledge the potential interpersonal determinants of depression. In this regard, Anchin (1987) has described the way that interpersonal theory may assist behavior therapists in conducting a functional analytic approach to clinical assessment.

Another integrative trend involves the attention paid to personality disorders by behavior therapists. This is in marked contrast to the early work done within behavior therapy, which was reluctant to acknowledge the construct of personality, let alone personality disorders. Personality disorders have been used to predict success in the treatment of Axis I disorders (Turner 1987) and have also been targets for intervention in and of themselves (Linehan 1987; Young 1990). In the treatment of borderline personality disorders, Linehan (1987) has outlined what she calls "dialectical behavior therapy," which addresses itself to the client's sensitivity to criticism, on the one hand, and the need to learn better ways to cope, on the other. In a clinical tour de force, Linehan has developed an intervention that underscores the acceptance, understanding, and validation of clients just as they are, and at the same time makes available to them interventions that can assist them in better coping with life events. Outcome research to demonstrate the efficacy of this approach is currently under way.

Messer (1986) has offered suggestions for how psychodynamic and behavioral therapists may each incorporate contributions from the other's orientations, and Goldfried & Wachtel (1987) have discussed the issues involved in psychotherapy integration as viewed from behavioral and psychodynamic orientations. Points of similarity and dissimilarity between the two orientations are illustrated in a dialog between Lazarus and Messer (1988) over an actual case.

Although sympathetic to the integration movement, Goldfried & Safran (1986) have expressed concern that in the absence both of comparative process research on different therapy orientations and of studies that demonstrate the enhanced effectiveness of an integrated approach to therapy, the movement may inadvertently foster the development of competing integrating systems. An NIMH conference on research directions for psychotherapy integration has acknowledged that the area is currently characterized more by dialog than by research (Wolfe & Goldfried 1988). Referring to the observation by Lief (1985) that the field is more in need of "desegregation" than "integration," the conference recommended that research begin on a comparison of the change process as it occurs within the differing orientations. The language barrier was noted as an obstacle to be overcome, which in itself provided the topic of a Special Section in the 1987 issue of the *Journal of Integrative & Eclectic Psychotherapy*. It was suggested that in addition to our usual theoretical jargon, the vernacular be used initially to communicate among the different orientations, and that a common operationally defined research language be developed for purposes of comparative empirical analyses. Finally, it was recommended that psychotherapeutic concepts be translated into a basic research language (e.g. that of cognitive psychology) so that experimental and social psychology research findings can be tied to the psychotherapy literature.

In light of the fact that 30–40% of the therapists in the United States identify themselves as eclectic (Norcross 1986), and because no orientation has consistently been found superior to any other (Stiles et al 1986), integrative themes will likely continue to characterize future work in psychotherapy.

CLOSING COMMENTS

In December 1985, the Evolution of Psychotherapy Conference was held in Phoenix (Zeig 1987). Billed as the Woodstock of psychotherapy, with some 7,000 professionals in attendance, it was organized in the hope that by bringing together the major proponents of different schools of therapy, the diversity that characterizes the field would somehow be sorted out.

Just as our clients are unlikely to change as the result of a single experience, the differences among various schools of psychotherapy could not be reconciled by a large-scale "happening." Rather, for the field of psychotherapy to develop a more unified paradigm, the mechanisms common to effective procedures must be empirically established. Moreover, we must determine in what cases psychosocial interventions can be viable alternatives to pharmacotherapy—an issue of growing concern to the field. A consensus about what constitutes a clinically meaningful and empirically grounded psychotherapeutic intervention is likely to result from research efforts that focus on specific problems, where the goal is not only to determine what procedures work, but also to understand better the processes associated with their effectiveness.

ACKNOWLEDGMENTS

We extend our gratitude to Cecily Osley for her invaluable assistance in the preparation of this chapter, which was supported in part by NIMH Grant No. 40196 awarded to the first author.

Literature Cited

Abramson, L. Y., ed. 1988. *Social Cognition and Clinical Psychology.* New York: Guilford

Alexander, L. B., Luborsky, L. 1986. The Penn Helping Alliances Scales. See Greenberg & Pinsof 1986

Anchin, J. C. 1987. Functional analysis and the social-interactional perspective: toward an integration in the behavior change enterprise. *J. Integr. Eclect. Psychother.* 6:387–99

Arkowitz, H. 1990. The role of theory in psychotherapy integration. *J. Integr. Eclect. Psychother.* In press

Arnkoff, D. B., Glass, C. R., Shea, C. A., McKain, T. L., Sydnor-Greenberg, J. M. 1987. Client predispositions toward cognitive and social skills treatments for shyness. *J. Integr. Eclect. Psychother.* 6:154–64

Arrindell, W. A., Emmelkamp, P. M. G., Sanderman, R. 1986. Marital quality and general life adjustment in relation to treatment outcome in agoraphobia. *Adv. Behav. Res. Ther.* 8:139–85

Babcock, H. H., ed. 1988. Integrative psychotherapy: collaborative aspects of behavioral and psychodynamic therapies. *Psychiatr. Ann.* 18:271–72

Barlow, D. H. 1988. *Anxiety and Its Disorders.* New York: Guilford

Barlow, D. H., Cerny, J. A. 1988. *Psychological Treatment of Panic.* New York: Guilford

Barlow, D. H., Wolfe, B. E. 1981. Behavioral approaches to anxiety disorders: a report on the NIMH-SUNY Albany research conference. *J. Consult. Clin. Psychol.* 49:448–54

Basoglu, M., Lax, T., Kasvikis, Y., Marks, I. M. 1988. Predictors of improvement in obsessive-compulsive disorder. *J. Anxiety Disord.* 2:299–317

Bastine, R. 1986. Psychotherapie-Integration: Entwicklung und Stand. In *Psychology Mitte der 80-er Jahre,* ed. A. Schorr, 3:234–44. Bonn: Deutscher Psychol. Verlag

Bastine, R., Fiedler, P., Kommer, D. 1989. What is therapeutic in psychotherapy? Status and systematizing of psychotherapeutic process research. *Z. Klin. Psychol.* 18:In press

Beach, S. R. H., O'Leary, K. D. 1986. The treatment of depression occurring in the context of marital discord. *Behav. Ther.* 17:43–49

Beck, A. T. 1988. Cognitive approaches to panic disorder: theory and therapy. In *Panic: Psychological Perspectives,* ed. S. Rachman, J. D. Maser. Hillsdale, NJ: Erlbaum

Beck, A. T., Emery, G. 1985. *Anxiety Disorders and Phobias: A Cognitive Perspective.* New York: Basic Books

Beck, A. T., Hollon, S. D., Young, J. E., Bedrosian, R. C., Budenz, D. 1985. Treatment of depression with cognitive therapy and amitriptyline. *Arch. Gen. Psychiatry* 42:142–48

Beitman, B. D. 1987. *The Structure of Individual Psychotherapy.* New York: Guilford

Beitman, B. D., Goldfried, M. R., Norcross, J. C. 1989. The movement toward integrating the psychotherapies: an overview. *Am. J. Psychiatry* 146:138–47

Benjamin, L. S., Foster, S. W., Roberto, L. G., Estroff, S. E. 1986. Breaking the family code: analysis of tapes of family interactions by structural Analysis of Social Behavior (SASB). See Greenberg & Pinsof 1986, pp. 391–438

Bentall, R., Higson, P., Lowe, C. 1987. Teaching self-instructions to chronic schizophrenic patients: efficacy and generalization. *Behav. Psychother.* 15:58–76

Beutler, L. E., Crago, M., Arizmendi, T. G. 1986. Therapist variables in psychotherapy process and outcome. See Garfield & Bergin 1986, pp. 257–310

Beutler, L. E., Engle, D., Oro-Beutler, M., Daldrup, R. 1986. Inability to express intense affect: a common link between depression and pain. *J. Consult. Clin. Psychol.* 54:752–59

Beutler, L., Hamblin, D. 1986. Individualized outcome measures of internal change: Methodological considerations. *J. Consult. Clin. Psychol.* 54:48–53

Biran, M. 1988. Cognitive and exposure treatment for agoraphobia: reexamination of the outcome research. *J. Cognit. Psychother: Int. Q.* 2:165–78

Bordin, E. S. 1979. The generalizability of the psychoanalytic concept of the working alliance. *Psychotherapy* 16:252–60

Borkovec, T. D., Mathews, A. M., Chambers, A., Ebrahimi, S., Lytle, R., et al. 1987. The effects of relaxation training with cognitive or nondirective therapy and the role of relaxation-induced anxiety in the treatment of generalized anxiety. *J. Consult. Clin. Psychol.* 55:883–88

Borkovec, T. D., Metzger, R. L., Pruzinsky, T. 1986. Anxiety, worry, and the self. In *Perception of Self in Emotional Disorder and Psychotherapy,* ed. L. M. Hartman, K. R. Blankstein, pp. 219–60. New York: Plenum

Bowers, T., Clum, G. 1988. Relative contributions of specific and nonspecific treatment effects: Meta analysis of placebo-controlled behavior therapy research. *Psychol. Bull.* 103:315–23

Brenner, H., Bodel, B., Kube, G., Roder, V. 1987. Kognitive Therapie bei Schizophren: Problemanalyse und empirische Ergebnisse. *Nervenarzt* 58:72–83

Brown, R. A., Lewinsohn, P. M. 1984. A psychoeducational approach to the treatment of depression: comparison of group, individual and minimal contact procedures. *J. Consult. Clin. Psychol.* 52:774–83

Brownell, K. D., Marlatt, G. A., Lichtenstein, E., Wilson, G. T. 1986. Understanding and preventing relapse. *Am. Psychol.* 41:765–82

Budman, S. H., Gurman, A. S. 1988. *The Theory and Practice of Group Therapy.* New York: Guilford

Butler, G., Cullington, A., Hibbert, G., Klimes, I., Gelder, M. 1987. Anxiety management for persistent generalized anxiety. *Br. J. Psychiatry* 151:535–42

Butler, S. F., Strupp, H. H. 1986. Specific and nonspecific factors in psychotherapy. A problematic paradigm for psychotherapy research. *Psychotherapy* 23:30–40

Butler, S. F., Strupp, H. H. 1990. The effects of training psychoanalytically oriented therapists to use a manual. In *Psychodynamic*

Treatment Research, ed. N. E. Miller, J. Docherty, L. Luborsky. New York: Basic Books. In press

Calvert, S., Beutler, L., Grago, M. 1988. Psychotherapy outcome as a function of therapist patient matching on selected variables. *J. Soc. Clin. Psychol.* 6:104–17

Castles, E. E., Glass, C. R. 1986. Training in social and interpersonal problem-solving skills for mildly and moderately mentally retarded adults. *Am. J. Ment. Defic.* 91:35–42

Cerney, J. A., Barlow, D. H., Craske, M. G., Himadi, W. G. 1987. Couples treatment of agoraphobia: a two-year follow-up. *Behav. Ther.* 18:401–15

Chambless, D. L., Goldstein, A. J., Gallagher, R., Bright, P. 1986. Integrating behavior therapy and psychotherapy in the treatment of agoraphobia. *Psychotherapy* 23:150–59

Chambless, D. L., Gracely, E. J. 1988. Prediction of outcome following in vivo exposure treatments of agoraphobia. In *Panic and Phobias II: Treatments and Variables Affecting Outcome,* ed. I. Hand, H. U. Wittchen, pp. 209–20. Berlin: Springer-Verlag

Clark, D. M., Salkovskis, P. M., Chalkley, A. J. 1985. Respiratory control as a treatment for panic attacks. *J. Behav. Ther. Exp. Psychiatry* 16:23–30

Clarke, K., Greenberg, L. 1986. Differential effects of the gestalt two chair intervention and problem solving in resolving decisional conflict. *J. Couns. Psychol.* 33:48–53

Cohen, L. H., Sargent, M. M., Sechrest, L. B. 1986. Use of psychotherapy research by professional psychologists. *Am. Psychol.* 41:198–206

Coyne, J. C., Gotlib, I. 1986. Studying the role of cognition in depression: well-trodden paths and cul-de-sacs. *Cogn. Ther. Res.* 10:695–705

Curtis, J., Silberschatz, G., Sampson, H., Weiss, J., Rosenberg, S. 1988. Developing reliable psychodynamic case formulations: an illustration of the plan diagnosis method. *Psychotherapy* 25:256–65

Dahl, H. 1988. Frames of mind. See Dahl et al 1988

Dahl, H., Kachele, H., Thoma, H., eds. 1988. *Psychoanalytic Process Research Strategies.* Heidelberg: Springer-Verlag

Daldrup, R., Beutler, L., Engle, D., Greenberg, L. 1988. *Focused Expressive Psychotherapy.* New York: Guilford Press

Dance, K., Neufeld, R. 1988. Aptitude treatment interaction research in the clinical setting: a review of attempts to dispel the "Patient Uniformity" myth. *Psychol. Bull.* 104:192–213

Deffenbacher, J. L., Story, D. A., Stack, R.

S., Hogg, J. A., Brandon, A. D. 1987. Cognitive-relaxation and social skills interventions in the treatment of general anger. *J. Couns. Psychol.* 34:171–76

DeRubeis, R. J., Evans, M. D., Hollon, S. D., Garvey, M. J., Grove, W. M. 1988. *Active components and mediating mechanisms in cognitive therapy, pharmacotherapy, and combined cognitive-pharmacotherapy for depression. III. Processes of change in the CPT project.* Presented at 141st Annu. Meet. Am. Psychiatr. Assoc., Montreal

Dobson, K. S., ed. 1988. *Handbook of Cognitive-Behavioral Therapies.* New York: Guilford

Docherty, J., Feister, S. 1985. The therapeutic alliance in pharmacotherapy. In *Psychiatry Update,* Vol. 4, ed. A. Francis. Washington, DC: Am. Psychiatr. Assoc. Press

Dryden, W., Golden, W. L., eds. 1986. *Cognitive Behavioral Approaches to Psychotherapy.* London: Harper & Row

D'Zurilla, T. J. 1986. *Problem-Solving Therapy.* New York: Springer

D'Zurilla, T. J., Goldfried, M. R. 1971. Problem solving and behavior modification. *J. Abnorm. Psychol.* 78:107–26

Elkin, I., Parloff, M. B., Hadley, S. W., Autry, J. H. 1985. NIMH treatment of depression collaborative research program: background and research plan. *Arch. Gen. Psychiatry* 42:305–16

Elkin, I., Pilkonis, P., Docherty, J., Sotsky, S. 1988. Conceptual and methodological issues in comparative studies for psychotherapy and pharmacotherapy, I. *Am. J. Psychiatry* 145:909–17

Elkin, I., Shea, M. T., Watkins, J. T., Imber, S. D., Sotsky, S. M., et al. 1990. NIMH treatment of depression collaborative research program: general effectiveness of treatments. *Arch. Gen. Psychiatry.* In press

Elliott, R. 1986. Interpersonal process recall (IPR) as a psychotherapy process research method. See Greenwood & Pinsof 1986

Elliott, R., Hill, C., Stiles, W. B., Friedlander, M., Mahrer, A., et al. 1987. Primary therapist response modes: comparison of six rating systems. *J. Couns. Psychol.* 55:218–23

Elliott, R., James, E., Reimschuessel, C., Cislo, D., Sack, N. 1985. Significant events and the analysis of immediate therapeutic impacts. *Psychotherapy* 22:620–30

Emmelkamp, P. M. G. 1987. Obsessive-compulsive disorders. See Michelson & Ascher 1987, pp. 310–31

Emmelkamp, P. M. G., Mersch, P. P., Vissia, E., van der Helm, M. 1985. Social phobia: a comparative evaluation of cognitive and behavioral interventions. *Behav. Res. Ther.* 23:365–69

Essex, M. J., Klein, M. H., Lohr, M. J., Benjamin, L. S. 1985. Intimacy and depression in older women. *Psychiatry*, 48:159–78

Fairburn, C. G. 1985. A cognitive-behavioral treatment of bulimia. In *Handbook of Psychotherapy for Anorexia Nervosa and Bulimia*, ed. D. M. Gardner, P. E. Garfinkle, pp. 160–92. New York: Guilford

Fairburn, C. G., Kirk, J., O'Connor, M., Cooper, P. J. 1986. A comparison of two psychological treatments for bulimia. *Behav. Res. Ther.* 24:629–43

Falloon, I. R. H. 1988. Expressed emotion: current status. *Psychol. Med.* 18:269–74

Falloon, I. R. H., Boyd, J. L., McGill, C. W., Williamson, M., Razani, J., et al. 1985. Family management in the prevention of morbidity of schizophrenia. *Arch. Gen. Psychiatry* 42:887–95

Foa, E. B., Kozak, M. J. 1986. Emotional processing of fear: exposure to corrective information. *Psychol. Bull.* 99:20–35

Foa, E. B., Steketee, G. S., Ozarow, B. J. 1985. Behavior therapy with obsessive-compulsives: from theory to treatment. See Mavissakalian et al 1985

Forsterling, F. 1986. Attributional conceptions in clinical psychology. *Am. Psychol.* 41:275–85

Frank, E., Kupfer, D. J. 1987. Efficacy of combined imipramine and interpersonal psychotherapy. *Psychopharm. Bull.* 23:4–7

Frank, E., Kupfer, D. J., Jacob, M., Jarrett, D. 1987. Personality features and response to acute treatment in recurrent depression. *J. Pers. Disord.* 1:14–26

Frieswyk, S. H., Allen, J. G., Colson, D. B., Coyne, L., Gabbard, G. O., et al. 1986. Therapeutic alliance: its place as a process and outcome variable in dynamic psychotherapy research. *J. Consult. Clin. Psychol.* 54:32–38

Garfield, S. L. 1986. Research on client variables in psychotherapy. See Garfield & Bergin 1986, pp. 213–56

Garfield, S. L., Bergin, A. E., eds. 1986. *Handbook of Psychotherapy and Behavior Change.* New York: Wiley. 3rd ed.

Garner, D. M., Fairburn, C. G., Davis, R. 1987. Cognitive-behavioral treatment of bulimia nervosa. *Behav. Modif.* 11:398–431

Gelso, C. J., Carter, J. A. 1985. The relationship in counseling and psychotherapy: components, consequences, and theoretical antecedents. *Counsel. Psychol.* 113:155–244

Ghosch, A., Marks, I. M. 1987. Self-treatment of agoraphobia by exposure. *Behav. Ther.* 18:3–16

Ghosch, A., Marks, I. M., Carr, A. C. 1988. Therapist contact and outcome of self-exposure treatment for phobias. *Br. J. Psychiatry* 152:234–38

Glass, C., Arnkoff, D. 1988. Common and specific factors in client descriptions of and explanations for change. *J. Integr. Eclect. Psychother.* 7:427–40

Goldfried, M. R., Newman, C. 1986a. Psychotherapy integration: a look at what therapists actually do. Presented at Meet. Am. Psychol. Assoc., Washington DC

Goldfried, M. R., Newman, C. 1986b. Psychotherapy integration: an historical perspective. See Norcross 1986, pp. 25–61

Goldfried, M. R., Safran, J. D. 1986. Future directions in psychotherapy integration. See Norcross 1986, pp. 463–83

Goldfried, M. R., Wachtel, P. L. 1987. Clinical and conceptual issues in psychotherapy integration: a dialogue. *J. Integr. Eclect. Psychother.* 6:131–44

Goldstein, M. J. 1984. Family intervention programs. In *Schizophrenia: Treatment, Management, and Rehabilitation*, ed. A. S. Bellak. Orlando, Fla: Grune & Stratton

Gonzales, L. R., Lewinsohn, P. M., Clarke, G. N. 1985. Longitudinal follow-up of unipolar depressives: an investigation of predictors of relapse. *J. Consult. Clin. Psychol.* 4:461–69

Greenberg, L. S., Goldman, R. 1988. Training in experiential therapy. *J. Consult. Clin. Psychol.* 56:696–702

Greenberg, L. S., Johnson, S. 1988. *Emotionally Focused Therapy For Couples.* New York: Guilford

Greenberg, L. S., Pinsof, W. M., eds. 1986. *The Psychotherapeutic Process: A Research Handbook.* New York: Guilford

Greenberg, L. S., Safran, J. D. 1987. *Emotion in Psychotherapy.* New York: Guilford

Guest, P. D., Beutler, L. E. 1988. Impact of psychotherapy supervision on therapist orientation and values. *J. Consult. Clin. Psychol.* 56:653–58

Guidano, V. F. 1987. *Complexity of the Self.* New York: Guilford

Hartley, D. 1985. Research on the therapeutic alliance in psychotherapy. In *Psychiatry Update*, Vol. 4, ed. A. Francis. Washington, DC: Am. Psychiatr. Assoc. Press

Hayes, S., Nelson, R., Jarrett, R. 1987. The treatment utility of assessment. *Am. Psychol.* 42:963–74

Heimberg, R. G., Dodge, C. S., Becker, R. E. 1987. Social phobia. See Michelson & Ascher 1987, pp. 280–309

Henry, W., Schacht, T., Strupp, H. 1986. Structural analysis of social behavior: application to a study of interpersonal process in differential psychotherapeutic outcome. *J. Consult. Clin. Psychol.* 54:27–31

Hill, C., Helms, J., Spiegel, S., Tichenor, V. 1988. Development of a system for categorizing client reactions to therapist interventions. *J. Couns. Psychol.* 35:27–36

Hill, C., O'Grady, K. 1985. List of therapist intentions illustrated in a single case and with therapists of varying theoretical orientations. *J. Couns. Psychol.* 32:3–22

Hoberman, H. M., Lewinsohn, P. M. 1985. The behavioral treatment of depression. In *Handbook of Depression: Treatment, Assessment and Research*, ed. E. Beckham, W. Leber, pp. 39–81. Homewood, Ill: Dorsey Press

Hogarty, G. E., Anderson, C. M. 1986. Family psychoeducation, social skills training, and maintenance chemotherapy in the aftercare treatment of schizophrenia. *Arch. Gen. Psychiatry* 43:633–42

Hollon, S. D., DeRubeis, R. J., Evans, M. D., Wiemer, M. M., Garvey, M. J. 1988. *Cognitive therapy, pharmacotherapy, and combined cognitive-pharmacotherapy in the treatment of depression. I. Differential outcome in the CPT project.* Presented at 141st Annu. Meet. Am. Psychiatr. Assoc., Montreal

Hollon, S. D., Evans, M. D., DeRubeis, R. J. 1987. Causal mediation of change in treatment for depression: discriminating between nonspecificity and noncausality. *Psychol. Bull.* 102:139–49

Holroyd, K. A., Creer, T. L., eds. 1986. *Self-Management of Chronic Disease.* New York: Academic

Hooley, J. M. 1985. Expressed emotion: a review of the critical literature. *Clin. Psychol. Rev.* 5:119–39

Horowitz, M. J. 1988. *Introduction to Psychodynamics.* New York: Basic Books

Horowitz, M. J., Marmar, C. R., Weiss, D. S., DeWitt, K. N., Rosenbaum, R. 1984. Brief psychotherapy of bereavement reactions: the relationship of process to outcome. *Arch. Gen. Psychiatry* 41:438–48

Horowitz, L. M., Rosenberg, S. E., Baer, B. A., Ureno, G., Villasenor, V. S. 1988. Inventory of interpersonal problems: psychometric properties and clinical applications. *J. Consult. Clin. Psychol.* 56:885–92

Horvath, A., Greenberg, L. S. 1986. The development of the Working Alliance Inventory. See Greenberg & Pinsof 1986

Horvath, P. 1988. Placebos and common factors in two decades of psychotherapy research. *Psychol. Bull.* 104:214–25

Howard, K. I., Kopta, S. M., Krause, M. S., Orlinsky, D. E. 1986. The dose-effect relationship in psychotherapy. *Am. Psychol.* 41:159–64

Huber, W., ed. 1987. *Progress in Psychotherapy Research.* Louvain-la-Neuve: Presses Univ. de Louvain

Ingram, R. E., ed. 1986. *Information Processing Approaches to Clinical Psychology.* New York: Academic

Ingram, R. E., Kendall, P. C. 1987. The cognitive side of anxiety. *Cogn. Ther. Res.* 11:523–36

Jacobson, N. S. 1988. Defining clinically significant change: an introduction. *Behav. Assess.* 10:131–32

Jacobson, N. S., Holtzworth-Munroe, A., Schmaling, K. B. 1989. Marital therapy and spouse involvement in the treatment of depression, agoraphobia, and alcoholism. *J. Consult. Clin. Psychol.* 57:5–10

Jacobson, N. S., Schmaling, K. B., Salusky, S., Follette, V., Dobson, K. 1987. *Marital therapy as an adjunct treatment for depression.* Presented at Annu. Meet. Assoc. Adv. Behav. Ther., Boston

Jarrett, R. B., Nelson, R. O. 1987. Mechanisms of change in cognitive therapy of depression. *Behav. Ther.* 18:227–41

Jones, E. E., Cumming, D., Horowitz, M. J. 1988. Another look at the nonspecific hypothesis of therapeutic effectiveness. *J. Consult. Clin. Psychol.* 56:48–55

Kächele, H. 1986. *Maschinelle Inhaltsanalyse in der Psychoanalytischen Prozessforschung.* Ulm: Psz Verlag

Kächele, H. 1988. Cinical and scientific aspects of the Ulm process model of psychoanalysis. *Int. J. Psycho-Anal.* 69:65–73

Kanfer, F. H., Schefft, B. K. 1988. *Guiding the Process of Therapeutic Change.* Champaign, Ill: Research Press

Kazdin, A. 1986. Comparative outcome studies of psychotherapy: methodological issues and strategies. *J. Consult. Clin. Psychol.* 54:95–105

Kazdin, A. E., Esveldt-Dawson, K., French, N. H., Unis, A. S. 1987. Problem-solving skills training and relationship therapy in the treatment of antisocial child behavior. *J. Consult. Clin. Psychol.* 55:76–85

Kelly, G. A. 1955. *The Psychology of Personal Constructs.* New York: Norton

Kiesler, D. J. 1988. *Therapeutic Metacommunication: Therapist Impact Disclosure as Feedback in Psychotherapy.* Palo Alto: Consulting Psychologists Press. 64 pp.

Klerman, G. L. 1986. Drugs and psychotherapy. See Garfield & Bergin 1986, pp. 777–818

Kolb, D., Davis, C., Beutler, L. 1985. Patient and therapy process variables relating to dropout and change in psychotherapy. *Psychotherapy* 22:702–10

Koss, M. P., Strupp, H. H., Butcher, J. N. 1986. Brief psychotherapy methods in clinical research. *J. Consult. Clin. Psychol.* 54:60–67

Kozak, M. J., Foa, E. B., Steketee, G. 1988. Process and outcome of exposure treatment with obsessive-compulsives: Psychophysiological indicators of emotional processing. *Behav. Ther.* 19:157–69

Kraemer, S., Zinner, H., Moller, H. 1988. *Cognitive therapy and social skills training in chronic schizophrenic patients: preliminary results of differential effects.* Presented at World Congr. Behav. Ther., Edinburgh, UK

Kretsch, R., Goren, Y., Wasserman, A. 1987. Change patterns of borderline patients in individual and group therapy. *Int. J. Group Psychother.* 37:95–112

Krupnick, J., Shea, T., Elkin, I. 1986. Generalizability of treatment studies utilizing solicited patients. *J. Consult. Clin. Psychol.* 53:68–78

Kupfer, D. J., Frank, E. 1987. Relapse in recurrent unipolar depression. *Am. J. Psychiatry* 144:86–88

Lafferty, P., Beutler, L., Crago, M. 1989. Differences between more and less effective psychotherapists: a study of select therapist variables. *J. Consult. Clin. Psychol.* 57:76–80

Lambert, M. J., Ogles, B. M. 1988. Treatment manuals: problems and promise. *J. Integr. Eclect. Psychother.* 7:187–204

Last, C. G., Hersen, M., eds. 1988. *Handbook of Anxiety Disorders.* New York: Pergamon

Lazarus, A. A., Messer, S. B., 1988. Clinical choice points: behavioral versus psychoanalytic interventions. *Psychotherapy* 25:59–70

Lecomte, C., Castonguay, L. G., eds. 1987. *Rapprochement et Integration en Psychotherapie.* Montreal: Gaetan Morin Editeur

Leitenberg, H., Rosen, J. C., Gross, J., Nudelman, S., Vera, L. 1990. Exposure plus response prevention treatment of bulimia nervosa. *J. Consult. Clin. Psychol.* In press

Lewinsohn, P. M., Hoberman, H. M., Rosenbaum, M. 1988. A prospective study of risk factors for unipolar depression. *J. Abnorm. Psychol.* 97:251–64

Lewinsohn, P. M., Hoberman, H. M., Teri, L., Hautzinger, M. 1985. An integrative theory of depression. In *Theoretical Issues in Behavior Therapy,* ed. S. Reiss, R. R. Bootzin, pp. 331–59. New York: Academic

Ley, R. 1985. Blood, breath, and fears: a hyperventilation theory of panic attacks and agoraphobia. *Clin. Psychol. Rev.* 5:271–85

Lief, H. I. 1985. *Psychotherapy: integration or segregation?* Presented at 1st Annu. Conf. Soc. Explor. Psychother. Integr., Annapolis

Lietar, G., Rombauts, J., Van Balen, R. 1989. *Client Centered and Experiential Psychotherapy: Toward the Nineties.* Leuven, Belgium: Univ. Leuven Press

Linehan, M. M. 1987. Dialectical behavioral therapy: A cognitive behavioral approach to parasuicide. *J. Pers. Disord.* 1:328–33

London, P. 1986. *The Modes and Morals of Psychotherapy.* New York: Hemisphere Publishing Corp. 2nd ed.

Luborsky, L. 1984. *Principles of Psychoanalytic Psychotherapy: A Manual for Supportive-Expressive (SE) Treatment.* New York: Basic Books

Luborsky, L., Crits-Christoph, P., McLellan, A., Woody, G., Piper, W., et al. 1986a. Do therapists vary much in their success? *Am. J. Orthopsychiatry* 56:501–12

Luborsky, L., Crits-Christoph, P., Melon, J. 1986b. Objective measures of the transference concept. *J. Consult. Clin Psychol.* 54:39–47

Luborsky, L., Crits-Christoph, P., Mintz, J., Auerbach, A. 1988. *Who Will Benefit From Psychotherapy: Predicting Therapeutic Outcomes.* New York: Basic Books

Mahoney, M. J. 1988. *Emotional processes in human psychological change.* Presented at Am. Assoc. Adv. Sci., Boston

Mahoney, M. J., Freeman, A., eds. 1985. *Cognition and Psychotherapy.* New York: Plenum

Mahrer, A. 1985. *Psychotherapeutic Change: An Alternative Approach to Meaning and Measurement.* New York: Norton

Mahrer, A. 1986. *Therapeutic Experiencing: The Process of Change.* New York: Norton

Mahrer, A., Nadler, W. 1986. Good moments in psychotherapy. A preliminary review, a test and some promising research avenues. *J. Consult. Clin. Psychol.* 54:10–15

Marks, I. M. 1987. *Fears, Phobias, and Rituals.* New York: Oxford Univ. Press

Marks, I. M., Lelliott, P., Basoglu, M., Noshirvani, H., Monteiro, W., et al. 1988. Clomipramine, self-exposure and therapist-aided exposure for obsessive-compulsive rituals. *Br. J. Psychiatry* 152:522–34

Marlatt, G. A., Baer, J. S., Donovan, D. M., Kivlahan, D. R. 1988. Addictive behaviors: etiology and treatment. *Annu. Rev. Psychol.* 1988:223–52

Marlatt, G. A., Gordon, J. R., eds. 1985. *Relapse Prevention.* New York: Guilford

Marmar, C. R., Gaston, L., Gallagher, D., Thompson, L. W. 1990. Alliance and outcome in late-life depression. *J. Nerv. Ment. Dis.* In Press

Marmar, C. R., Horowitz, M. J. 1988. Diagnosis and phase-oriented treatment of post-traumatic stress disorder. In *Human Adaptation to Extreme Stress,* ed. J. P. Wilson, Z. Harel, B. Kahana, pp. 81–103

Marmar, C. R., Marziali, E., Horowitz, M. J., Weiss, D. S. 1986. The development of the Therapeutic Alliance Rating System. In *The Psychotherapeutic Process: A Research Handbook.* New York: Guilford

Marmar, C. R., Weiss, D. W., Gaston, L. 1989. Toward the validation of the California Therapeutic Alliance Rating System. *Psychol. Assess.: J. Consult. Clin. Psychol.* 1:46–52

Marshall, W. L. 1985. The effects of variable exposure in flooding therapy. *Behav. Ther.* 16:117–35

Marziali, E. 1984. Prediction of outcome of brief psychotherapy from therapist interpretive interventions. *Arch. Gen. Psychiatry* 41:301–4

Marziali, E., Munroe-Blum, H. 1987. A group approach: the management of projective identification in group treatment of self-destructive borderline patients. *J. Pers. Disord.* 1:340–43

Mattick, R. P., Peters, L. 1988. Treatment of severe social phobia: effects of guided exposure with and without cognitive restructuring. *J. Consult. Clin. Psychol.* 56:251–60

Mavissakalian, M., Turner, S. M., Michelson, L., eds. 1985. *Obsessive-Compulsive Disorders: Psychological and Pharmacological Treatment.* New York: Plenum

McCullough, L., Farrell, A. D., Longabaugh, R. 1986. The development of microcomputer-based mental health information system: a potential tool for bridging the scientist-practitioner gap. *Am. Psychol.* 41:207–14

Meichenbaum, D., Cameron, R. 1973. Training schizophrenics to talk to themselves: a means of development of self-controls. *Behav. Ther.* 4:515–25

Meichenbaum, D., Turk, D. C. 1987. *Facilitating Treatment Adherence: A Practitioner's Guidebook.* New York: Plenum

Mergenthaler, E., Kaechele, H. 1985. Changes of latent meaning structures in psychoanalysis. *Sprache und Datenverarbeitung* 9:21–28

Messer, S. B. 1986. Behavior and psychoanalytic perspectives at therapeutic choice points. *Am. Psychol.* 41:1261–72

Michelson, L., Ascher, L. M., eds. 1987. *Anxiety and Stress Disorders.* New York: Guilford

Michelson, L., Mavissakalian, M., Marchione, K., Dancu, C., Greenwald, M. 1986. The role of self-directed in vivo exposure in cognitive, behavioral, and psychophysiological treatments of agoraphobia. *Behav. Ther.* 17:91–108

Morrow-Bradley, C., Elliott, R. 1986. Utilization of psychotherapy research by practicing psychotherapists. *Am. Psychol.* 41:188–97

Murray, E. J. 1988. Personality disorders: a cognitive view. *J. Pers. Disord.* 2:37–43

Neimeyer, R. A. 1986. Personal construct therapy. In *Cognitive Behavioral Approaches to Psychotherapy,* ed. W.

Dryden, W. L. Golden, pp. 225–60. London: Harper & Row

Newman, F. L., Kopta, S. M., McGovern, M. P., Howard, K. I., McNeilly, C. L. 1988. Evaluating trainees relative to their supervisors during the psychology internships. *J. Consult. Clin. Psychol.* 56:659–65

Nezu, A. M., Nezu, C. M., Perri, M. G. 1989. *Problem-Solving Therapy for Depression: Theory, Research, and Clinical Guidelines.* New York: Wiley & Sons

Norcross, J. C., ed. 1986. *Handbook of Eclectic Psychotherapy.* New York: Brunner/Mazel

Norcross, J. C., ed. 1987. *Casebook of Eclectic Psychotherapy.* New York: Brunner/Mazel

Orlinsky, D. E., Howard, K. I. 1986. Process and outcome in psychotherapy. See Garfield & Bergin 1986, pp. 311–81

Parloff, M. 1986. Placebo controls in psychotherapy: a sine qua non or a placebo for research problems? *J. Consult. Clin. Psychol.* 54:79–87

Parloff, M. B., London, P., Wolfe, B. 1986. Individual psychotherapy and behavior change. *Annu. Rev. Psychol.* 37:321–49

Patterson, G. R., Forgatch, M. S. 1985. Therapist behavior as a determinant for client noncompliance: a paradox for the behavior modifier. *J. Consult. Clin. Psychol.* 53:846–51

Perry, S., Frances, A., Clarkin, J. 1985. *A DSM-III Casebook of Differential Therapeutics.* New York: Brunner/Mazel

Pilkonis, P. A., Frank, E. 1988. Personality pathology in recurrent depression: nature, prevalence, and relationship to treatment response. *Am. J. Psychiatry* 145:435–41

Platt, J. J., Taube, D. O., Metzger, D. S., Duome, M. J. 1988. Training in interpersonal problem solving (TIPS). *J. Cogn. Psychother.: Int. Q.* 2:5–34

Rehm, L. P., Kaslow, N. J., Rabin, A. S. 1987. Cognitive and behavioral targets in a self-control therapy program for depression. *J. Consult. Clin. Psychol.* 55:60–67

Rice, L., Greenberg, L. S. 1984. *Patterns of Change.* New York: Guilford

Rice, L., Saperia, E. 1984. Task analysis of the resolution of problematic reactions. In *Patterns of change: Intensive Analysis of Psychotherapy Press,* ed. L. N. Rice, L. S. Greenberg. New York: Guilford

Rosser, C. 1988. *Negative effects in psychotherapy: studies utilizing the Vanderbilt Negative Indicators Scale in the Vanderbilt II Project.* Presented at Soc. Psychother. Res. Meet., Santa Fe

Rounsaville, B. J., Chevron, E. S., Weissman, M. M., Prusoff, B. A., Frank, E. 1986. Training therapists to perform interpersonal psychotherapy in clinical trials. *Compar. Psychiatry.* 27:364–71

Rush, A. J. 1985. The therapeutic alliance in short-term directive psychotherapies. In *Psychiatry Update,* Vol. 4, ed. A. Francis. Washington, DC: Am. Psychiatr. Assoc. Press

Rush, A. J., Weissenburger, J. 1986. Do thinking patterns predict depressive symptoms? *Cogn. Ther. Res.* 10:225–36

Russell, R. 1987. *Language in Psychotherapy.* New York: Plenum

Saachse, R. 1989. Concrete interventions are crucial. In *Client Centered and Experiential Psychotherapy: Toward the Nineties,* ed. G. Lietar, J. Rombauts, R. van Balen. Leuven, Belgium: Univ. Leuven Press

Safran, J. D., Greenberg, L. S. 1988. The treatment of anxiety and depression: the process of affective change. In *Anxiety and Depression: Distinctive and Overlapping Features,* ed. P. Kendall, D. Watson. Orlando: Academic

Safran, J. D., Greenberg, L. S., Rice, L. 1988. Integrating psychotherapy research and practice modeling the change process. *Psychotherapy* 25:1–17

Safran, J. D., Vallis, T. M., Segal, Z. V., Shaw, B. F. 1986. Assessment of core cognitive processes in cognitive therapy. *Cogn. Ther. Res.* 10:509–26

Sampson, H., Weiss, J. 1986. Testing hypotheses: the approach of the Mount Zion Psychotherapy Research Group. See Greenberg & Pinsof 1986, pp. 591–613

Segal, Z. V. 1988. Appraisal of the self-schema construct in cognitive models of depression. *Psychol. Bull.* 103:147–62

Segal, Z. V., Shaw, B. F. 1986. Cognition in depression: a reappraisal of Coyne and Gotlib's critique. *Cogn. Ther. Res.* 10:671–93

Seligman, M. P., Castellon, C., Cacciola, J., Schulman, P., Luborsky, L., et al. 1988. Explanatory style change during cognitive therapy for unipolar depression. *J. Abnorm. Psychol.* 97:13–18

Shapiro, D. 1988. Outcome research. In *Skills and Methods in Mental Health Research,* ed. G. Parry, F. Watts. New York: Erlbaum

Shapiro, D., Firth, J. 1987. Prescriptive v. exploratory psychotherapy: outcomes of the Sheffield psychotherapy project. *Br. J. Psychiatry* 151:790–99

Shaw, B. F., Dobson, K. S. 1988. Competency judgments in the training and evaluation of psychotherapies. *J. Consult. Clin. Psychol.* 56:666–72

Shaw, B. F., Segal, Z. V., Vallis, T. M., Cashman, F. E., eds. 1986. *Anxiety Disorders.* New York: Plenum

Shea, M. T., Glass, D. R., Pilkonis, P. A., Watkins, J., Docherty, J. P. 1987. Frequency and implications of personality disorders in a sample of depressed outpatients. *J. Pers. Disord.* 1:27–42

Shear, M. K., Ball, G., Josephson, S. 1987. An empirically developed cognitive-behavioral treatment of panic. *J. Integr. Eclect. Psychother.* 6:421–33

Silberschatz, G., Curtis, J., Nathans, S. 1990. Using the patient's plan to assess progress in psychotherapy. *Psychotherapy* In press

Silberschatz, G., Fretter, P., Curtis, J. 1986. How do interpretations influence the process of psychotherapy? *J. Consult. Clin. Psychol.* 54:646–52

Simons, A. D., Lustman, P. J., Wetzel, R. D., Murphy, G. E. 1985. Predicting response to cognitive therapy of depression: the role of learned resourcefulness. *Cogn. Ther. Res.* 9:79–89

Simons, A. D., Murphy, G. E., Levine, J. L., Wetzel, R. D. 1986. Cognitive therapy and pharmacotherapy for depression. *Arch. Gen. Psychiatry* 43:43–48

Singer, J. L. 1985. Transference and the human condition: a cognitive-affective perspective. *Psychoanal. Psychol.* 2:189–219

Snyder, W. U. 1950. Clinical methods: psychotherapy. *Annu. Rev. Psychol.* 1:221–34

Steketee, G., Foa, E. B. 1985. Obsessive-compulsive disorder. In *Clinical Handbook of Psychological Disorders,* ed. D. H. Barlow, pp. 69–144. New York: Guilford

Stiles, W. B. 1988. Psychotherapy process-outcome correlations may be misleading. *Psychotherapy* 25:27–35

Stiles, W. B., Shapiro, D. A., Elliott, R. 1986. "Are all psychotherapies equivalent?" *Am. Psychol.* 42:165–80

Strupp, H. H. 1986. Psychotherapy: research, practice, and public policy (how to avoid dead ends). *Am. Psychol.* 41:120–30

Strupp, H., Binder, J. 1984. *Psychotherapy in a New Key.* New York: Basic Books

Suh, C. S., Strupp, H. H., Samples O'Malley, S. 1986. The Vanderbilt process measures: the psychotherapy process scale (VPPS) and the negative indicators scale (VNIS). See Greenberg & Pinsof 1986, pp. 285–323

Telch, M. J., Agras, W. S., Barr Taylor, C., Roth, W. T., Gallen, C. C. 1985. Combined pharmacological and behavioral treatment for agoraphobia. *Behav. Res. Ther.* 23:325–35

Teri, L., Lewinsohn, P. M. 1986. Individual and group treatment of unipolar depression: comparison of treatment outcome and identification of predictors of successful treatment outcome. *Behav. Ther.* 17:215–28

Thompson, J. 1987. *The Processes of Psychotherapy.* Lanham, Md: University Press of America

Thompson, L. W., Gallagher, D., Breckenridge, J. S. 1987. Comparative effectiveness of psychotherapies for depressed elders. *J. Consul. Clin. Psychol.* 55:385–90

Toukmanian, S. G. 1986. A measure of client perceptual processing. See Greenberg & Pinsof 1986

Turk, D. C., Salovey, P., eds. 1988. *Reasoning, Inference, and Judgment in Clinical Psychology.* New York: The Free Press

Turner, S. M. 1987. The effects of personality disorder diagnosis on the outcome of social anxiety symptom reduction. *J. Pers. Disord.* 1:136–43

Turner, S. M., Beidel, D. C. 1988. *Treating Obsessive-Compulsive Disorder.* New York: Pergamon

Turner, S. M., Beidel, D. C., Stanley, M. A., Jacob, R. G. 1990. A comparison of fluoxetine and flooding and response prevention in the treatment of obsessive-compulsive disorder. *J. Anxiety Disord.* In press

Vallis, T. M., Shaw, B. F., Dobson, K. S. 1986. The cognitive therapy scale: psychometric properties. *J. Consult. Clin. Psychol.* 54:381–85

Wachtel, E. F., Wachtel, P. L. 1986. *Family Dynamics in Individual Psychotherapy.* New York: Guilford

Wachtel, P. L., ed. 1982. *Resistance.* New York: Plenum

Wachtel, P. L. 1987. *Action and Insight.* New York: Guilford

Wallace, C. J., Liberman, R. P. 1985. Social skills training for patients with schizophrenia: a controlled clinical trial. *Psychiatr. Res.* 15:239–47

Weiss, J., Sampson, H. 1986. *The Psychoanalytic Process.* New York: Guilford

Weiss, L., Katzman, M., Wolchik, S. 1985. *Treating Bulimia: A Psychoeducational Approach.* Elsmford, NY: Pergamon

Weissman, M. M., Jarrett, R. B., Rush, J. A. 1987. Psychotherapy and its relevance to the pharmacotherapy of major depression: a decade later (1967–1985). In *Psychopharmacology: The Third Generation of Progress,* ed. H. Meltzer, pp. 1059–69. New York: Raven

Westen, D. 1988. Transference and information processing. *Clin. Psychol. Rev.* 8:161–79

Wilson, G. T., Rossiter, E., Kleinfield, E. I., Lindholm, L. 1986. Cognitive-behavioral treatment of bulimia nervosa: a controlled evaluation. *Behav. Res. Ther.* 24:277–88

Windholz, M. J., Silberschatz, G. 1988. Vanderbilt psychotherapy Process Scale: a replication with adult outpatients. *J. Consult. Clin. Psychol.* 56:56–60

Winfrey, L. P., Goldfried, M. R. 1986. Human change processes examined from an information processing perspective. In *Information Processing Approaches to Psychopathology and Clinical Psychology,* ed. R. E. Ingram. New York: Academic

Wolfe, B. E., Goldfried, M. R. 1988. Research on psychotherapy integration: recommendations and conclusions from an NIMH workshop. *J. Consult. Clin. Psychol.* 56:448–51

Young, J. E. 1990. *Schema-Focused Cognitive Therapy for Personality Disorders and Difficult Patients.* Sarasota, Fla: Professional Resource Exchange

Zeig, J. K., ed. 1987. *The Evolution of Psychotherapy.* New York: Brunner/Mazel

AUTHOR INDEX

Bruch, M. A., 366
Brucks, M., 245, 254, 266, 267
Bruner, J. S., 480, 497, 500, 501, 508
Brunstetter, R. W., 42
Brunswick, E., 446
Bruun, S. E., 615
Bruzzone, D. E., 275
Bryan, J., 547
Bryan, R. G., 192, 195
Bryant, B., 405
Bryant, K. J., 447
Bryant, W. K., 273
Bryant-Tuckett, R., 358
Bryden, M. P., 57, 64, 67, 72
Buchsbaum, G., 636, 651
Budd, R. J., 489, 491
Budenz, D., 675
Budman, S. H., 676
Buescher, K. L., 371
Buhrmester, D., 398, 402
Bull, D., 341
Bullemer, P., 130
Buller, P. F., 295, 616
Bunker, B. B., 607
Bunnell-McKenzie, J., 182
Burby, R. J., 464
Burch, P. R., 37, 299
Burgeson, R., 405
Burgess, J. W., 596
Burke, K. L., 597
Burke, M. C., 261, 262
Burke, M. J., 291, 292, 302, 306, 308, 309
Burke, R. E., 562, 564, 566
Burke, R. R., 257
Burks, V. M., 403
Burlingame, G. M., 362, 603
Burnett, K. F., 376
Burnkrant, R. E., 491
Burns, T. F., 142
Burnstein, E., 618, 619
Burroughs, J., 459
Burroughs, W. J., 257
Burton, L. A., 58, 71, 72, 74
Burton, L. M., 404, 407
Burton, S., 249, 268
Busch, C. M., 426
Busch, P. S., 273
Bushway, D. J., 361
Buss, D. M., 427, 428
Buss, W. C., 273
Butcher, J. N., 664
Butler, G., 673
Butler, S. F., 663, 670
Butler, S. K., 291
Buttel, F. H., 462
Butters, N., 131
Buyukkurt, B. K., 259
Bybee, J. A., 492
Bycio, P., 297
Byrne, R. M. J., 330

C

Cacciola, J., 675
Cachiero, H., 179, 180
Cacioppo, J. T., 255, 256, 480, 482, 485, 500, 503-5, 507-11
Cadotte, E. R., 269
Cairo, P. C., 371
Calantone, R., 491
Calder, B. J., 276
Caldwell, D. F., 590, 600-2, 604
Caldwell, G. S., 90
Caldwell, R. A., 156
Calvert, S. L., 408, 671
Calvin, P., 257
Camac, C., 429
Camacho, T., 144
Camacho, T. C., 151
Camargo, E. G., 277
Cameron, E., 547
Cameron, R., 677
Camp, B. W., 37, 38
Campbell, A., 487
Campbell, B. A., 173, 197, 198, 200, 201
Campbell, C. S., 84, 86
Campbell, D. J., 295, 299
Campbell, D. T., 157
Campbell, F. W., 649, 651
Campbell, J., 448
Campbell, J. D., 612
Campbell, V. L., 362, 365
Campion, M. A., 294
Campos, J. J., 388-91, 394, 396
Campos, R. G., 389
Canella, K. A. S., 370, 372
Canino, G., 39
Canino, I. A., 40
Cantor, N., 431, 488
Cantwell, D. P., 42
Caplan, R. B., 142
Caplan, R. D., 152, 489
Caplinger, T. E., 32, 34, 45
Caporael, L. R., 606
Carbonara-Moscati, V., 454
Carden, D., 641, 655
Cardy, R. L., 292, 293
Carew, T. J., 172
Carey, S., 343
Carlen, P. L., 573
Carlson, C. R., 394
Carlson, L., 272
Carlson, V., 396
Carlstein, T., 453
Carnevale, P. J. D., 608, 613
Carnodran, P., 388, 390
Carnot, C., 96, 507
Carp, F.,
Carpenter, B. N., 300
Carpenter, G. S., 258

Carr, A. C., 672
Carroll, J. B., 15
Carron, A. V., 603-5
Carson, J., 403
Carson, R. C., 435
Carter, D. S., 96, 97, 102
Carter, J. A., 359, 360, 362, 372, 374, 670
Carter, M. J., 365
Carter, R. C., 291
Carter, S. R., 488
Cartwright, D., 228
Casas, J. M., 367, 368
Cascio, W. F., 290, 291, 308, 310
Casey, R. J., 25, 27, 28, 35, 38, 39, 48
Cashman, F. E., 672
Cashmore, J. A., 404, 405
Caspi, A., 404, 407, 456
Cassidy, J., 396, 397, 399
Castellon, C., 675
Castells, M., 466
Castles, E. E., 665
Castonguay, L. G., 678
Castro, C. A., 201
Catalano, R., 145, 448
Cattell, M. D., 425
Cattell, R. B., 419, 421, 423, 425, 428, 432
Catterson, D., 180
Catugati, F., 486
Cauce, A. M., 148
Cavanagh, P., 641, 653, 654
Cave, C. B., 62
Cellar, D. F., 294
Celsi, R. L., 259
Cermak, S., 131
Cerny, J. A., 36, 664, 667, 672
Cesari, J. P., 375
Chaiken, S., 484, 492, 495-97, 499, 500, 503-7, 509, 510, 611
CHAKRAVARTI, D., 243-88; 246, 247, 258
Chalkley, A. J., 673
Challis, B. H., 122, 127
Chamberlain, P., 36
Chamberlin, R., 153
Chambers, A., 668, 673
Chambless, D. L., 667, 672
Champion, C. H., 294
Chan, W. S., 272
Chandler, H., 494
Chandler, S. H., 559, 579
Chapman, A., 450
Chapman, J. P., 346
Chapman, L. J., 346
Chapman, M., 391, 396, 547
Chappell, E. T., 192
Charnov, E., 397
Charns, M. P., 302

SUBJECT INDEX

CUMULATIVE INDEXES

CONTRIBUTING AUTHORS, VOLUMES 35–41

CHAPTER TITLES, VOLUMES 35–41

731